Collins
ESSENTIAL ROAD ATLAS
BRITAIN

Contents

Route planning

Route planning maps	ii-vii
Restricted motorway junctions	viii-ix
Motorway services information	x-xi
Orbital motorway maps - M25 & Birmingham	xii-xiii
Risk rating of Britain's motorways and A roads	xiv-xv
Distance chart	xvi

Urban approach maps (1 mile to 1 inch)   1-32

Symbols used on maps / Locator map	1
Plymouth	2
Bournemouth	3
Southampton & Portsmouth	4-5
Swansea	6
Cardiff & Newport	7
Bristol	8
Milton Keynes	9
London	10-13
West Midlands	14-15
Coventry	16
Leicester	17
Derby & Nottingham	18-19
Stoke-on-Trent	20
Sheffield	21
Merseyside	22-23
Greater Manchester	24-25
Leeds & Bradford	26-27
Newcastle upon Tyne & Sunderland	28
Middlesbrough	29
Glasgow	30-31
Edinburgh	32

Street maps   33-91

Symbols used on maps / Locator map	33	Hastings	75
Birmingham	34-35	Hereford	75
Edinburgh	36-37	Hull	76
Glasgow	38-39	Inverness	76
Leeds	40-41	Leicester	77
Liverpool	42-43	Lincoln	77
London	44-45	Middlesbrough	78
Manchester	46-47	Milton Keynes	78
Birmingham index	48	Newcastle upon Tyne	79
Edinburgh index	49	Norwich	79
Glasgow index	51	Nottingham	80
Leeds index	52	Oxford	80
Liverpool index	54	Perth	81
London index	56	Plymouth	81
Manchester index	60	Portsmouth	82
Aberdeen	63	Reading	82
Bath	63	Salisbury	83
Blackpool	64	Scarborough	83
Bournemouth	64	Sheffield	84
Bradford	65	Southampton	84
Brighton	65	Stoke-on-Trent	85
Bristol	66	Stratford-upon-Avon	85
Cambridge	66	Sunderland	86
Canterbury	67	Swansea	86
Cardiff	67	Swindon	87
Carlisle	68	Torquay	87
Cheltenham	68	Watford	88
Chester	69	Weston-super-Mare	88
Coventry	69	Winchester	89
Derby	70	Windsor	89
Dover	70	Worcester	90
Dundee	71	York	90
Durham	71		
Eastbourne	72	**Airport plans**	
Exeter	72	Birmingham International	91
Folkestone	73	Gatwick	91
Gloucester	73	Glasgow	91
Guildford	74	Heathrow	91
Harrogate	74	Manchester	91
		Stansted	91

Road maps   92-279

Symbols used on maps & key to map pages	92-93
England, Wales & Southern Scotland (3.2 miles to 1 inch)	94-253
Northern Scotland (4.2 miles to 1 inch)	254-279

Index   280-318

Collins

Published by Collins
An imprint of HarperCollins Publishers
Westerhill Road, Bishopbriggs, Glasgow G64 2QT

www.harpercollins.co.uk

Copyright © HarperCollins Publishers Ltd 2013

Collins® is a registered trademark of HarperCollins Publishers Limited

Mapping generated from CollinsBartholomew digital databases

Contains Ordnance Survey data © Crown copyright and database right (2013)

The grid on this map is the National Grid taken from the Ordnance Survey map with the permission of the Controller of Her Majesty's Stationery Office.

Please note that roads and other facilities which are under construction at the time of going to press, and are due to open before the end of 2013, are shown in this atlas as open. Roads due to open during 2014 or begin construction before the end of June 2014 are shown as 'proposed or under construction'.

Printed in China

ISBN 978 0 00 749709 6   Imp 001

e-mail: roadcheck@harpercollins.co.uk    Follow us @collinsmaps

Information for the alignment of the Wales Coast Path provided by © Natural Resources Wales. All rights reserved. Contains Ordnance Survey Data. Ordnance Survey Licence number 100019741. Crown Copyright and Database Right (2013).

Information on fixed speed camera locations provided by PocketGPSWorld.com

With thanks to the Wine Guild of the United Kingdom for help with researching vineyards.

Information regarding blue flag beach awards is current as of summer 2009. For latest information please visit www.blueflag.org.uk

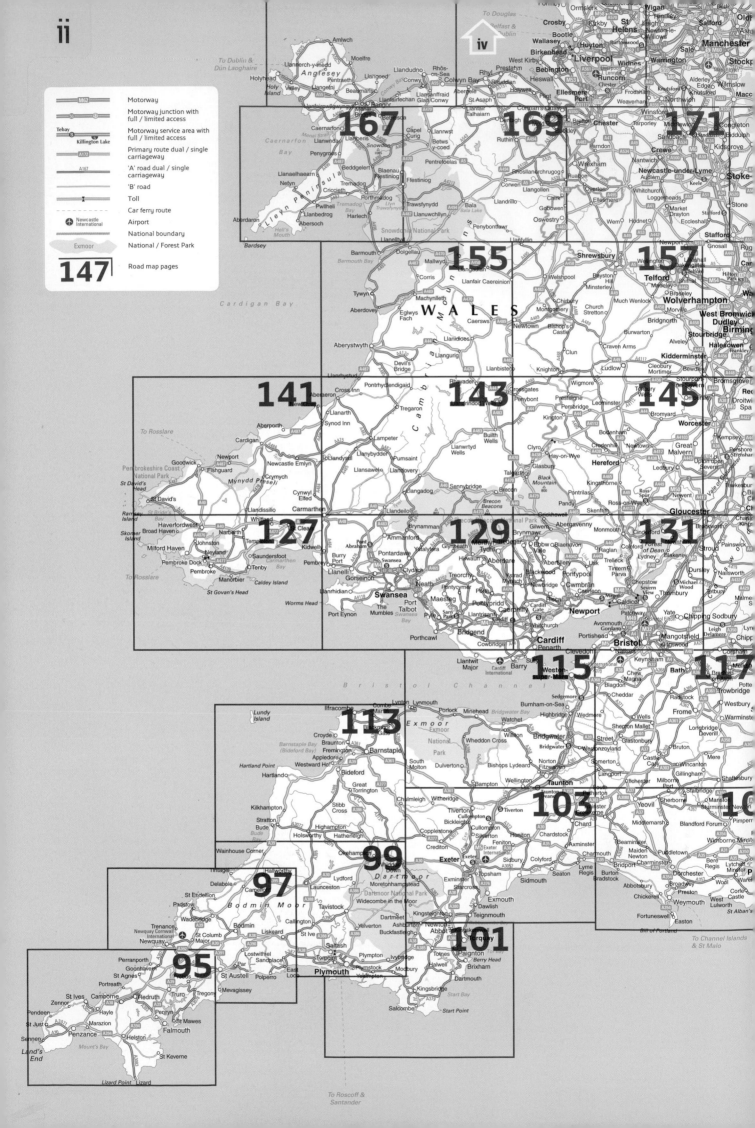

ii

Legend

Symbol	Description
M62	Motorway
S	Motorway junction with full / limited access
Tebay / Killington Lake	Motorway service area with full / limited access
A172	Primary route dual / single carriageway
A167	'A' road dual / single carriageway
	'B' road
T	Toll
	Car ferry route
Newcastle International	Airport
	National boundary
Exmoor	National / Forest Park
147	Road map pages

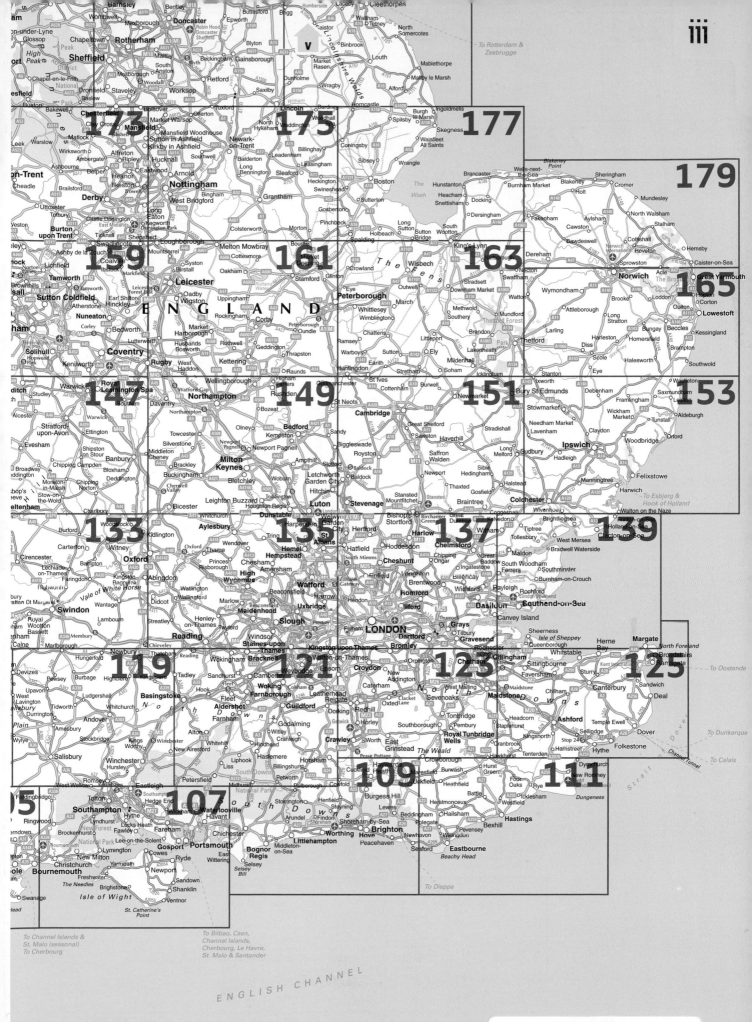

SCALE 1:1,408,450

| 0 | 10 | 20 | 30 | 40 miles |

| 0 | 10 | 20 | 30 | 40 | 50 | 60 kilometres |

22 miles to 1 inch / 14 km to 1 cm

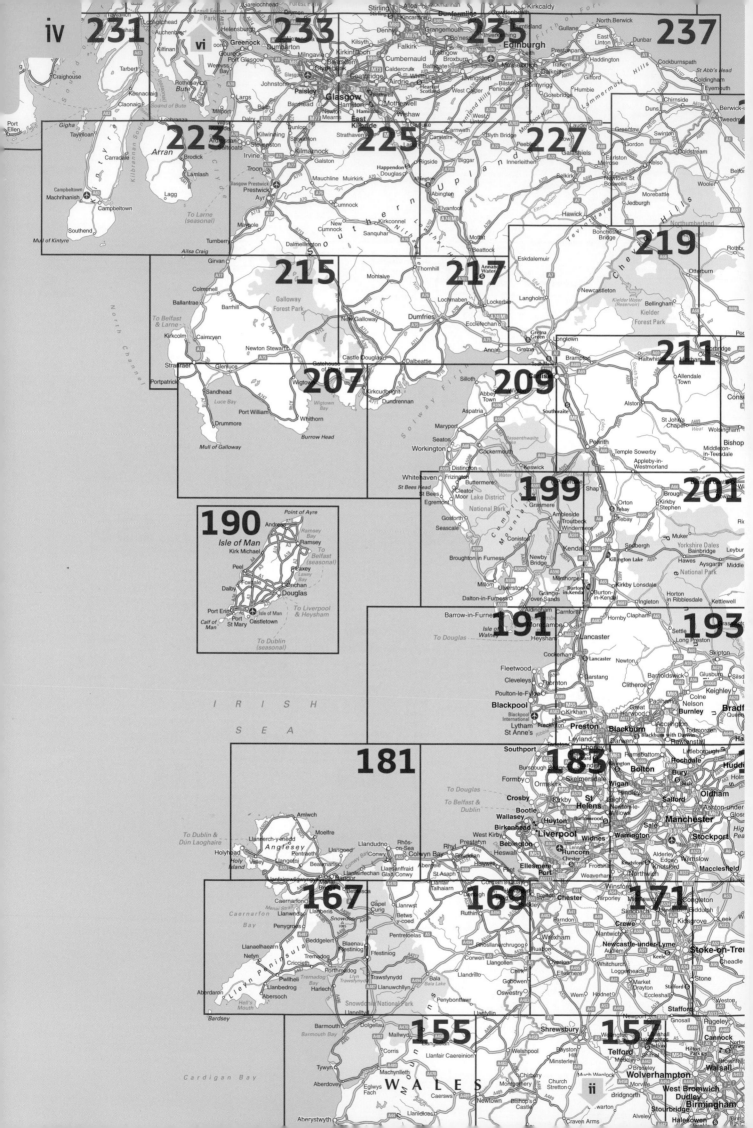

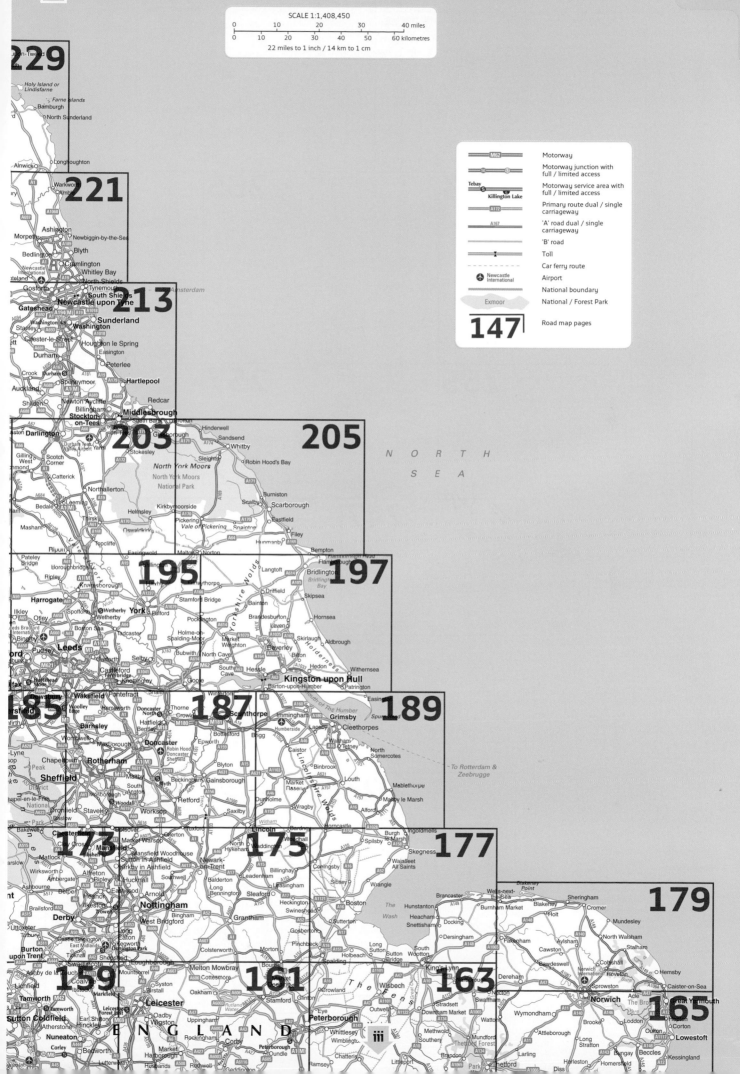

SCALE 1:1,408,450

| 0 | 10 | 20 | 30 | 40 miles |
| 0 | 10 | 20 | 30 | 40 | 50 | 60 kilometres |

22 miles to 1 inch / 14 km to 1 cm

Motorway	M62
Motorway junction with full / limited access	
Motorway service area with full / limited access	Tebay / Killington Lake
Primary route dual / single carriageway	A172
'A' road dual / single carriageway	A167
'B' road	
Toll	
Car ferry route	
Airport	Newcastle International
National boundary	
National / Forest Park	Exmoor
Road map pages	147

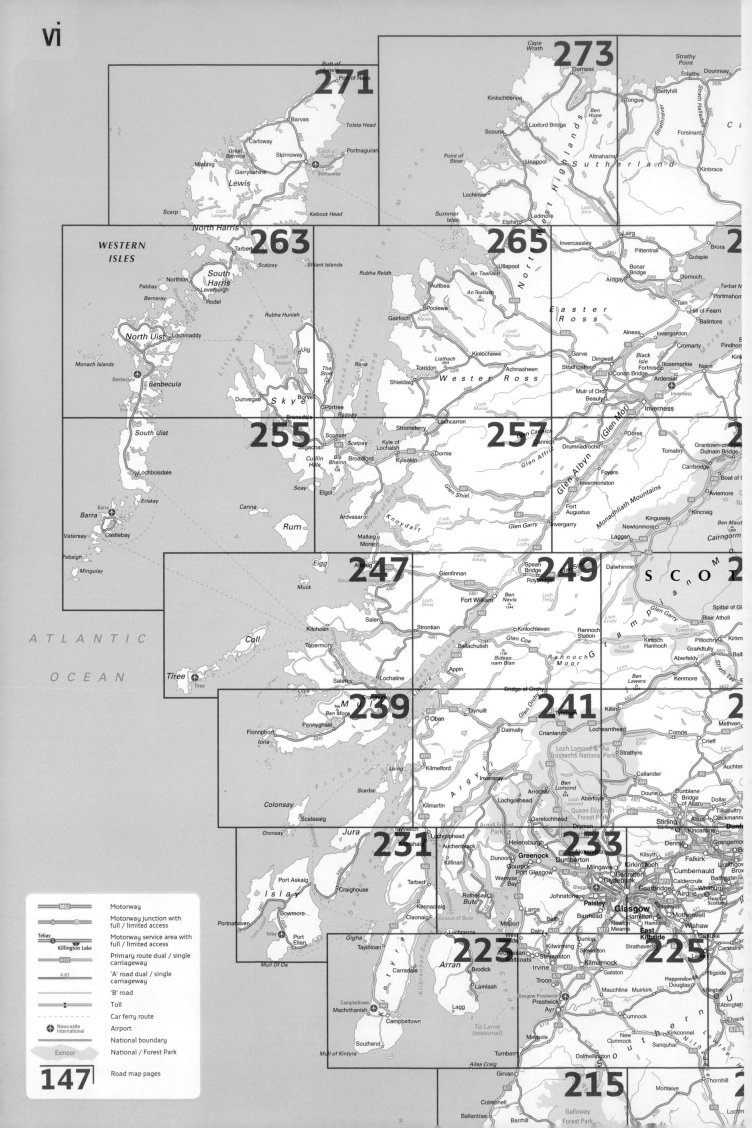

271
273
263
265
255
257
247
249
239
241
231
233
223
225
215

WESTERN
ISLES

North Harris

South
Harris

North Uist

Benbecula

South Uist

Barra

ATLANTIC

OCEAN

Lewis

Skye

Rum

Coll

Tiree

Mull

Islay

Jura

Colonsay

Arran

Kintyre

Glasgow

Inverness

Fort William

Oban

Sutherland

North West Highlands

Wester Ross

Easter Ross

	Motorway
	Motorway junction with full / limited access
	Motorway service area with full / limited access
	Primary route dual / single carriageway
	'A' road dual / single carriageway
	'B' road
	Toll
	Car ferry route
	Airport
	National boundary
	National / Forest Park
147	Road map pages

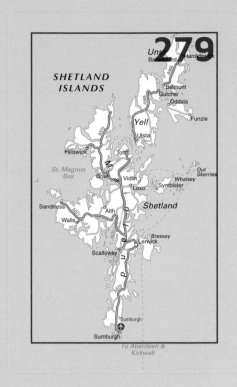

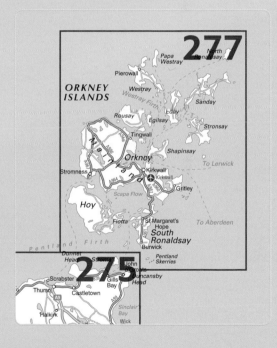

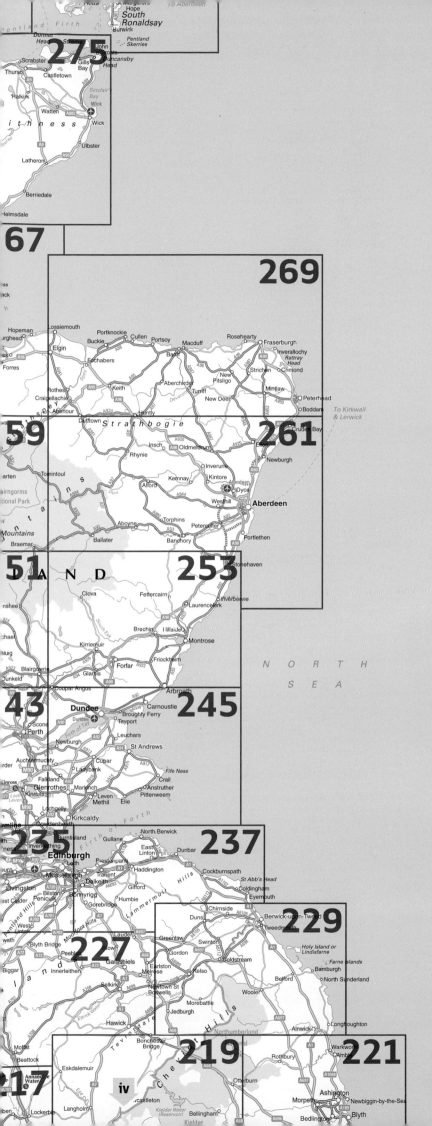

SCALE 1:1,408,450

| 0 | 10 | 20 | 30 | 40 miles |

| 0 | 10 | 20 | 30 | 40 | 50 | 60 kilometres |

22 miles to 1 inch / 14 km to 1 cm

Restricted motorway junctions

A1(M) LONDON TO NEWCASTLE

(2)
Northbound : No access
Southbound : No exit
(3)
Southbound : No access
(5)
Northbound : No exit
Southbound : No access
: No exit
(41)
Northbound : No exit to M62 Eastbound
(43)
Northbound : No exit to M1 Westbound
Dishforth
Southbound : No access from A168 Eastbound
(57)
Northbound : No access
: Exit only to A66(M) Northbound
Southbound : Access only from A66(M) Southbound
: No exit
(65)
Northbound : No access from A1
Southbound : No exit to A1

A3(M) PORTSMOUTH

(1)
Northbound : No exit
Southbound : No access
(4)
Northbound : No access
Southbound : No exit

A38(M) BIRMINGHAM

Victoria Road
Northbound : No exit
Southbound : No access

A48(M) CARDIFF

Junction with M4
Westbound : No access from M4 (29) Eastbound
Eastbound : No exit to M4 (29) Westbound
(29A)
Westbound : No exit to A48 Eastbound
Eastbound : No access from A48 Westbound

A57(M) MANCHESTER

Brook Street
Westbound : No exit
Eastbound : No access

A58(M) LEEDS

Westgate
Southbound : No access
Woodhouse Lane
Westbound : No exit

A64(M) LEEDS

Claypit Lane
Eastbound : No access

A66(M) DARLINGTON

Junction with A1(M)
Northbound : No access from A1(M) Southbound
: No exit
Southbound : No access
: No exit to A1(M) Northbound

A74(M) LOCKERBIE

(18)
Northbound : No access
Southbound : No exit

A167(M) NEWCASTLE

Campden Street
Northbound : No exit
Southbound : No access
: No exit

M1 LONDON TO LEEDS

(2)
Northbound : No exit
Southbound : No access
(4)
Northbound : No exit
Southbound : No access
(6A)
Northbound : Access only from M25 (21)
: No exit
Southbound : No access
: Exit only to M25 (21)
(7)
Northbound : Access only from A414
: No exit
Southbound : No access
: Exit only to A414

M1 LONDON TO LEEDS (continued)

(17)
Northbound : No access
: Exit only to M45
Southbound : Access only from M45
: No exit
(19)
Northbound : Exit only to M6
Southbound : Access only from M6
(21A)
Northbound : No access
Southbound : No exit
(23A)
Northbound : No access from A453
Southbound : No exit to A453
(24A)
Northbound : No exit
Southbound : No access
(35A)
Northbound : No access
Southbound : No exit
(43)
Northbound : No access
: Exit only to M621
Southbound : No exit
: Access only from M621
(48)
Northbound : No exit to A1(M) Southbound
: Access only from A1(M) Northbound
Southbound : Exit only to A1(M) Southbound
: No access

M2 ROCHESTER TO CANTERBURY

(1)
Westbound : No exit to A2 Eastbound
Eastbound : No access from A2 Westbound

M3 LONDON TO WINCHESTER

(8)
Westbound : No access
Eastbound : No exit
(10)
Northbound : No access
Southbound : No exit
(13)
Southbound : No exit to A335 Eastbound
: No access
(14)
Westbound : No access
Eastbound : No exit

M4 LONDON TO SWANSEA

(1)
Westbound : No access from A4 Eastbound
Eastbound : No exit to A4 Westbound
(2)
Westbound : No access from A4 Eastbound
: No exit to A4 Eastbound
Eastbound : No access from A4 Westbound
: No exit to A4 Westbound
(21)
Westbound : No access from M48 Eastbound
Eastbound : No exit to M48 Westbound
(23)
Westbound : No exit to M48 Eastbound
Eastbound : No access from M48 Westbound
(25)
Westbound : No access
Eastbound : No exit
(25A)
Westbound : No access
Eastbound : No exit
(29)
Westbound : No access
: Exit only to A48(M)
Eastbound : Access only from A48(M) Eastbound
: No exit
(38)
Westbound : No access
(39)
Westbound : No exit
Eastbound : No access
: No exit
(41)
Westbound : No exit
Eastbound : No access
(42)
Westbound : No exit to A48
Eastbound : No access from A48

M5 BIRMINGHAM TO EXETER

(10)
Northbound : No exit
Southbound : No access
(11A)
Northbound : No access from A417 Eastbound
Southbound : No exit to A417 Westbound

M6 COVENTRY TO CARLISLE

Junction with M1
Northbound : No access from M1 (19) Southbound
Southbound : No exit to M1 (19) Northbound
(3A)
Northbound : No access from M6 Toll
Southbound : No exit to M6 Toll
(4)
Northbound : No exit to M42 Northbound
: No access from M42 Southbound
Southbound : No exit to M42
: No access from M42 Southbound
(4A)
Northbound : No access from M42 (8)
Northbound
: No exit
Southbound : No access
: Exit only to M42 (8)
(5)
Northbound : No access
Southbound : No exit
(10A)
Northbound : No access
: Exit only to M54
Southbound : Access only from M54
: No exit
(11A)
Northbound : No exit to M6 Toll
Southbound : No access from M6 Toll
(24)
Northbound : No exit
Southbound : No access
(25)
Northbound : No access
Southbound : No exit
(30)
Northbound : Access only from M61 Northbound
: No exit
Southbound : No access
: Exit only to M61 Southbound
(31A)
Northbound : No access
Southbound : No exit

M6 Toll BIRMINGHAM

(T1)
Northbound : Exit only to M42
: Access only from A4097
Southbound : No exit
: Access only from M42 Southbound
(T2)
Northbound : No exit
: No access
Southbound : No access
(T5)
Northbound : No exit
Southbound : No access
(T7)
Northbound : No access
Southbound : No exit
(T8)
Northbound : No access
Southbound : No exit

M8 EDINBURGH TO GLASGOW

(8)
Westbound : No access from M73 (2)
Southbound
: No access from A8 Eastbound
: No access from A89 Eastbound
Eastbound : No access from A89 Westbound
: No exit to M73 (2) Northbound
(9)
Westbound : No exit
Eastbound : No access
(13)
Westbound : Access only from M80
Eastbound : Exit only to M80
(14)
Westbound : No exit
Eastbound : No access
(16)
Westbound : No access
Eastbound : No exit
(17)
Eastbound : Access only from A82,
not central Glasgow
: Exit only to A82,
not central Glasgow
(18)
Westbound : No access
Eastbound : No access
(19)
Westbound : Access only from A814 Eastbound
Eastbound : Exit only to A814 Westbound,
not central Glasgow

M8 EDINBURGH TO GLASGOW (cont)

(20)
Westbound : No access
Eastbound : No exit
(21)
Westbound : No exit
Eastbound : No access
(22)
Westbound : No access
: Exit only to M77 Southbound
Eastbound : Access only from M77 Northbound
: No exit
(23)
Westbound : No access
Eastbound : No exit
(25A)
Eastbound : No exit
Westbound : No access
(28)
Westbound : No access
Eastbound : No exit
(28A)
Westbound : No access
Eastbound : No exit

M9 EDINBURGH TO STIRLING

(2)
Westbound : No exit
Eastbound : No access
(3)
Westbound : No access
Eastbound : No exit
(6)
Westbound : No exit
Eastbound : No access
(8)
Westbound : No exit
Eastbound : No access

M11 LONDON TO CAMBRIDGE

(4)
Northbound : No access from A1400 Westbound
: No exit
Southbound : No access
: No exit to A1400 Eastbound
(5)
Northbound : No access
Southbound : No exit
(8A)
Northbound : No access
Southbound : No exit
(9)
Northbound : No access
Southbound : No exit
(13)
Northbound : No access
Southbound : No exit
(14)
Northbound : No access from A428 Eastbound
: No exit to A428 Westbound
: No exit to A1307
Southbound : No access from A428 Eastbound
: No access from A1307
: No exit

M20 LONDON TO FOLKESTONE

(2)
Westbound : No exit
Eastbound : No access
(3)
Westbound : No access
: Exit only to M26 Westbound
Eastbound : Access only from M26 Eastbound
: No exit
(11A)
Westbound : No exit
Eastbound : No access

M23 LONDON TO CRAWLEY

(7)
Northbound : No exit to A23 Southbound
Southbound : No access from A23 Northbound
(10A)
Southbound : No access from B2036
Northbound : No exit to B2036

Restricted motorway junctions are shown on the maps as:

M25 LONDON ORBITAL MOTORWAY

(1B)
Clockwise : No access
Anticlockwise : No exit

(5)
Clockwise : No exit to M26 Eastbound
Anticlockwise : No access from M26 Westbound

Spur of M25 (5)
Clockwise : No access from M26 Westbound
Anticlockwise : No exit to M26 Eastbound

(19)
Clockwise : No access
Anticlockwise : No exit

(21)
Clockwise : No access from M1 (6A) Northbound
: No exit to M1 (6A) Southbound
Anticlockwise : No access from M1 (6A) Northbound
: No exit to M1 (6A) Southbound

(31)
Clockwise : No exit
Anticlockwise : No access

M26 SEVENOAKS

Junction with M25 (5)
Westbound : No exit to M25 Anticlockwise
: No exit to M25 spur
Eastbound : No access from M25 Clockwise
: No access from M25 spur

Junction with M20
Westbound : No access from M20 (3) Eastbound
Eastbound : No exit to M20 (3) Westbound

M27 SOUTHAMPTON TO PORTSMOUTH

(4) West
Westbound : No exit
Eastbound : No access

(4) East
Westbound : No access
Eastbound : No exit

(10)
Westbound : No access
Eastbound : No exit

(12) West
Westbound : No exit
Eastbound : No access

(12) East
Westbound : No access from A3
Eastbound : No exit

M40 LONDON TO BIRMINGHAM

(3)
Westbound : No access
Eastbound : No exit

(7)
Eastbound : No exit

(8)
Northbound : No access
Southbound : No exit

(13)
Northbound : No access
Southbound : No exit

(14)
Northbound : No exit
Southbound : No access

(16)
Northbound : No exit
Southbound : No access

M42 BIRMINGHAM

(1)
Northbound : No exit
Southbound : No access

(7)
Northbound : No access
: Exit only to M6 Northbound
Southbound : Access only from M6 Northbound
: No exit

(7A)
Northbound : No access
: Exit only to M6 Eastbound
Southbound : No access
: No exit

(8)
Northbound : Access only from M6 Southbound
: No exit
Southbound : Access only from M6 Southbound
: Exit only to M6 Northbound

M45 COVENTRY

Junction with M1
Westbound : No access from M1 (17) Southbound
Eastbound : No exit to M1 (17) Northbound

Junction with A45
Westbound : No exit
Eastbound : No access

M48 CHEPSTOW

M4
Westbound : No exit to M4 Eastbound
Eastbound : No access from M4 Westbound

M49 BRISTOL

(18A)
Northbound : No access from M5 Southbound
Southbound : No access from M5 Northbound

M53 BIRKENHEAD TO CHESTER

(11)
Northbound : No access from M56 (15) Eastbound
: No exit to M56 (15) Westbound
Southbound : No access from M56 (15) Eastbound
: No exit to M56 (15) Westbound

M54 WOLVERHAMPTON TO TELFORD

Junction with M6
Westbound : No access from M6 (10A) Southbound
Eastbound : No exit to M6 (10A) Northbound

M56 STOCKPORT TO CHESTER

(1)
Westbound : No access from M60 Eastbound
: No access from A34 Northbound
Eastbound : No exit to M60 Westbound
: No exit to A34 Southbound

(2)
Westbound : No access
Eastbound : No exit

(3)
Westbound : No exit
Eastbound : No access

(4)
Westbound : No access
Eastbound : No exit

(7)
Westbound : No access
Eastbound : No exit

(8)
Westbound : No exit
Eastbound : No access

(9)
Westbound : No exit to M6 Southbound
Eastbound : No access from M6 Northbound

(15)
Westbound : No access
: No access from M53 (11)
Eastbound : No exit
: No exit to M53 (11)

M57 LIVERPOOL

(3)
Northbound : No exit
Southbound : No access

(5)
Northbound : Access only from A580 Westbound
: No exit
Southbound : No access
: Exit only to A580 Eastbound

M58 LIVERPOOL TO WIGAN

(1)
Westbound : No access
Eastbound : No exit

M60 MANCHESTER

(2)
Westbound : No exit
Eastbound : No access

(3)
Westbound : No access from M56 (1)
: No access from A34 Southbound
: No exit to A34 Northbound
Eastbound : No access from A34 Southbound
: No exit to M56 (1)
: No exit to A34 Northbound

(4)
Westbound : No access
Eastbound : No exit to M56

M60 MANCHESTER *(continued)*

(5)
Westbound : No access from A5103 Southbound
: No exit to A5103 Southbound
Eastbound : No access from A5103 Northbound
: No exit to A5103 Northbound

(14)
Westbound : No access from A580
: No exit to A580 Northbound
Eastbound : No access from A580 Westbound
: No exit to A580

(16)
Westbound : No access
Eastbound : No exit

(20)
Westbound : No access
Eastbound : No exit

(22)
Westbound : No access

(25)
Westbound : No access

(26)
Eastbound : No access
: No exit

(27)
Westbound : No exit
Eastbound : No access

M61 MANCHESTER TO PRESTON

(2)
Northbound : No access from A580 Eastbound
: No access from A666
Southbound : No exit to A580 Westbound

(3)
Northbound : No access from A580 Eastbound
: No access from A666
Southbound : No exit to A580 Westbound

Junction with M6
Northbound : No access from M6 (30) Southbound
Southbound : No access from M6 (30) Northbound

M62 LIVERPOOL TO HULL

(23)
Westbound : No exit
Eastbound : No access

(32A)
Westbound : No exit to A1(M) Southbound

M65 BURNLEY

(9)
Westbound : No exit
Eastbound : No access

(11)
Westbound : No access
Eastbound : No exit

M66 MANCHESTER TO EDENFIELD

(1)
Northbound : No access
Southbound : No exit

Junction with A56
Northbound : Exit only to A56 Northbound
Southbound : Access only from A56 Southbound

M67 MANCHESTER

(1)
Westbound : No exit
Eastbound : No access

(2)
Westbound : No access
Eastbound : No exit

M69 COVENTRY TO LEICESTER

(2)
Northbound : No exit
Southbound : No access

M73 GLASGOW

(1)
Northbound : No access from A721 Eastbound
Southbound : No exit to A721 Eastbound

(2)
Northbound : No access from M8 (8) Eastbound
Southbound : No exit to M8 (8) Westbound

M74 GLASGOW

(1A)
Westbound : No exit to M8 Kingston Bridge
Eastbound : No access from M8 Kingston Bridge

(3)
Westbound : No access
Eastbound : No exit

(3A)
Westbound : No exit
Eastbound : No access

M74 GLASGOW *(continued)*

(7)
Northbound : No exit
Southbound : No access

(9)
Northbound : No access
: No exit
Southbound : No access

(10)
Southbound : No exit

(11)
Northbound : No access
Southbound : No access

(12)
Northbound : Access only from A70 Northbound
Southbound : Exit only to A70 Southbound

M77 GLASGOW

Junction with M8
Northbound : No exit to M8 (22) Westbound
Southbound : No access from M8 (22) Eastbound

(4)
Northbound : No exit
Southbound : No access

(6)
Northbound : No exit to A77
Southbound : No access from A77

(7)
Northbound : No access
: No exit

(8)
Northbound : No access
Southbound : No access

M80 STIRLING

(4A)
Northbound : No exit
Southbound : No exit

(6A)
Northbound : No exit
Southbound : No exit

(8)
Northbound : No access from M876
Southbound : No exit to M876

M90 EDINBURGH TO PERTH

(2A)
Northbound : No access
Southbound : No exit

(7)
Northbound : No exit
Southbound : No access

(8)
Northbound : No access
Southbound : No exit

(10)
Northbound : No access from A912
: No exit to A912 Southbound
Southbound : No access from A912 Northbound
: No exit to A912

M180 SCUNTHORPE

(1)
Westbound : No exit
Eastbound : No access

M606 BRADFORD

Straithgate Lane
Northbound : No access

M621 LEEDS

(2A)
Northbound : No exit
Southbound : No access

(5)
Northbound : No access
Southbound : No exit

(6)
Northbound : No exit
Southbound : No access

M876 FALKIRK

Junction with M80
Westbound : No exit to M80 (8) Northbound
Eastbound : No access from M80 (8) Southbound

Junction with M9
Westbound : No access
Eastbound : No exit

Motorway services information

All motorway service areas have fuel, food, toilets, disabled facilities and free short-term parking

For further information on motorway services providers:
Moto www.moto-way.com
Euro Garages www.eurogarages.com
RoadChef www.roadchef.com
Extra www.extraservices.co.uk
Welcome Break www.welcomebreak.co.uk
Westmorland www.westmorland.com

Motorway	Junction	Service provider	Service name	Fuel supplier	Information	Accommodation	Conference facilities	Showers	M&S Simply Food	Costa Coffee	Starbucks	Burger King	KFC	McDonalds	Wimpy
A1(M)	1	Welcome Break	South Mimms	BP	●	●	●	●		●	●	●	●		
	10	Extra	Baldock	Shell	●	●		●	●			●	●		
	17	Extra	Peterborough	Shell	●	●		●	●				●	●	
	34	Moto	Blyth	Esso	●	●		●	●	●		●			
	46	Moto	Wetherby	BP	●	●		●	●	●		●			
	61	RoadChef	Durham	Total	●	●	●		●				●		
	64	Moto	Washington	BP	●	●		●		●		●			
A74(M)	16	RoadChef	Annandale Water	BP	●	●			●						
	22	Welcome Break	Gretna Green	BP	●	●		●		●	●	●			
M1	2-4	Welcome Break	London Gateway	Shell	●	●	●	●		●					
	11-12	Moto	Toddington	BP	●			●	●	●	●	●			
	14-15	Welcome Break	Newport Pagnell	Shell	●	●				●	●	●			
	15A	RoadChef	Northampton	BP	●	●							●		
	16-17	RoadChef	Watford Gap	BP	●	●							●		
	21-21A	Welcome Break	Leicester Forest East	BP	●	●	●	●		●		●			
	22	Euro Garages	Markfield	BP	●	●		●		●		●			
	23A	Moto	Donington Park	BP	●	●	●	●	●	●		●			
	25-26	Moto	Trowell	BP	●	●		●	●	●	●	●			
	28-29	RoadChef	Tibshelf	Shell	●	●	●			●			●		
	30-31	Welcome Break	Woodall	Shell	●	●				●	●	●			
	38-39	Moto	Woolley Edge	BP	●	●		●	●	●		●			
M2	4-5	Moto	Medway	BP	●		●		●		●				
M3	4A-5	Welcome Break	Fleet	Shell	●	●	●	●		●	●	●			
	8-9	Moto	Winchester	Shell	●	●		●		●		●			
M4	3	Moto	Heston	BP	●	●	●	●	●	●		●			
	11-12	Moto	Reading	BP	●	●	●	●	●	●		●			
	13	Moto	Chieveley	BP	●				●	●		●			
	14-15	Welcome Break	Membury	BP	●	●		●		●		●			
	17-18	Moto	Leigh Delamere	BP	●	●	●	●	●	●		●			
	23A	RoadChef	Magor	Esso	●	●		●					●		
	30	Welcome Break	Cardiff Gate	Total	●	●		●		●	●				
	33	Moto	Cardiff West	Esso	●	●		●		●		●			
	36	Welcome Break	Sarn Park	Shell	●	●		●		●	●				
	47	Moto	Swansea	BP	●	●				●		●			
	49	RoadChef	Pont Abraham	Texaco	●					●					
M5	3-4	Moto	Frankley	BP	●		●		●		●				
	8	RoadChef	Strensham (South)	BP	●				●				●		
	8	RoadChef	Strensham (North)	Texaco	●	●	●						●		
	13-14	Welcome Break	Michaelwood	BP	●	●				●	●	●			
	19	Welcome Break	Gordano	Shell	●	●		●		●	●	●			
	21-22	RoadChef	Sedgemoor (South)	Total	●	●				●			●		
	21-22	Welcome Break	Sedgemoor (North)	Shell	●	●	●	●		●	●	●			
	24	Moto	Bridgwater	BP	●		●		●		●				
	25-26	RoadChef	Taunton Deane	Shell	●	●	●			●			●		
	27	Moto	Tiverton	Shell	●		●		●		●				
	28	Extra	Cullompton	Shell				●		●		●			
	29-30	Moto	Exeter	BP	●	●		●	●	●		●			

Motorway	Junction	Service provider	Service name	Fuel supplier	Information	Accommodation	Conference facilities	Showers	M&S Simply Food	Costa Coffee	Starbucks	Burger King	KFC	McDonalds	Wimpy
M6	3-4	Welcome Break	Corley	Shell	●	●				●	●	●			
	10-11	Moto	Hilton Park	BP	●	●		●	●	●		●			
	14-15	RoadChef	Stafford (South)	Esso	●	●	●	●		●				●	
	14-15	Moto	Stafford (North)	BP	●	●		●		●		●			
	15-16	Welcome Break	Keele	Shell	●			●		●	●	●			
	16-17	RoadChef	Sandbach	Esso		●				●				●	
	18-19	Moto	Knutsford	BP	●	●		●	●	●		●			
	27-28	Welcome Break	Charnock Richard	Shell	●	●				●		●			
	32-33	Moto	Lancaster	BP	●	●		●		●		●			
	35A-36	Moto	Burton-in-Kendal (N)	BP					●		●				
	36-37	RoadChef	Killington Lake (S)	BP	●	●				●					
	38-39	Westmorland	Tebay	Total	●	●	●								
	41-42	Moto	Southwaite	BP	●	●		●	●	●		●			
	44-45	Moto	Todhills	BP/Shell	●	●				●					
M6 Toll	T6-T7	RoadChef	Norton Canes	BP	●	●									
M8	4-5	BP	Heart of Scotland	BP				●	●	●					
M9	9	Moto	Stirling	BP	●	●			●		●	●			
M11	8	Welcome Break	Birchanger Green	Shell	●	●	●	●		●	●	●			
M18	5	Moto	Doncaster North	BP	●	●		●		●		●			
M20	8	RoadChef	Maidstone	Esso	●	●		●					●		
	11	Stop 24	Stop 24	Shell	●			●	●	●					
M23	11	Moto	Pease Pottage	BP	●			●	●	●		●			
M25	5-6	RoadChef	Clacket Lane	Total	●	●				●				●	
	9-10	Extra	Cobham	Shell	●	●		●	●				●		
	23	Welcome Break	South Mimms	BP	●	●		●		●	●				
	30	Moto	Thurrock	Esso	●	●		●	●	●		●			
M27	3-4	RoadChef	Rownhams	Esso	●	●				●			●		
M40	2	Extra	Beaconsfield	Shell	●		●		●		●		●		
	8	Welcome Break	Oxford	BP	●			●		●	●	●			
	10	Moto	Cherwell Valley	Esso	●	●	●	●	●	●		●			
	12-13	Welcome Break	Warwick	BP	●	●	●	●		●	●	●			
M42	2	Welcome Break	Hopwood Park	Shell	●			●		●	●	●			
	10	Moto	Tamworth	Esso	●	●	●	●	●	●		●			
M48	1	Moto	Severn View	BP	●	●		●		●		●			
M54	4	Welcome Break	Telford	Shell	●	●		●		●		●			
M56	14	RoadChef	Chester	Shell	●	●				●			●		
M61	6-7	Euro Garages	Rivington	BP	●			●		●		●			
M62	7-9	Welcome Break	Burtonwood	Shell	●			●		●	●	●			
	18-19	Moto	Birch	BP	●	●		●		●		●			
	25-26	Welcome Break	Hartshead Moor	Shell	●	●		●		●	●	●			
	33	Moto	Ferrybridge	Esso	●	●		●		●		●			
M65	4	Extra	Blackburn with Darwen	Shell	●	●		●	●				●		
M74	4-5	RoadChef	Bothwell (South)	BP	●	●		●		●			●		
	5-6	RoadChef	Hamilton (North)	BP	●	●		●		●			●		
	11-12	Cairn Lodge	Happendon	Shell	●	●			●	●					
	12-13	Welcome Break	Abington	Shell	●	●	●	●		●					
M90	6	Moto	Kinross	BP	●	●		●		●	●				

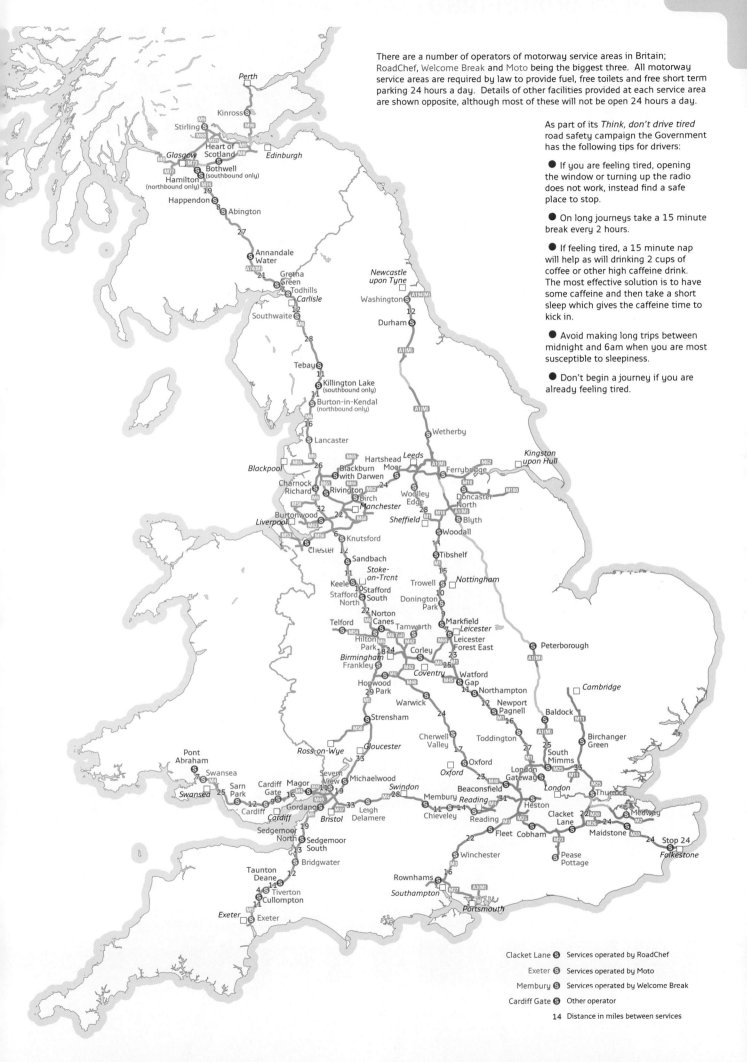

There are a number of operators of motorway service areas in Britain; RoadChef, Welcome Break and Moto being the biggest three. All motorway service areas are required by law to provide fuel, free toilets and free short term parking 24 hours a day. Details of other facilities provided at each service area are shown opposite, although most of these will not be open 24 hours a day.

As part of its *Think, don't drive tired* road safety campaign the Government has the following tips for drivers:

● If you are feeling tired, opening the window or turning up the radio does not work, instead find a safe place to stop.

● On long journeys take a 15 minute break every 2 hours.

● If feeling tired, a 15 minute nap will help as will drinking 2 cups of coffee or other high caffeine drink. The most effective solution is to have some caffeine and then take a short sleep which gives the caffeine time to kick in.

● Avoid making long trips between midnight and 6am when you are most susceptible to sleepiness.

● Don't begin a journey if you are already feeling tired.

Clacket Lane Ⓢ Services operated by RoadChef
Exeter Ⓢ Services operated by Moto
Membury Ⓢ Services operated by Welcome Break
Cardiff Gate Ⓢ Other operator
14 Distance in miles between services

M25 orbital map

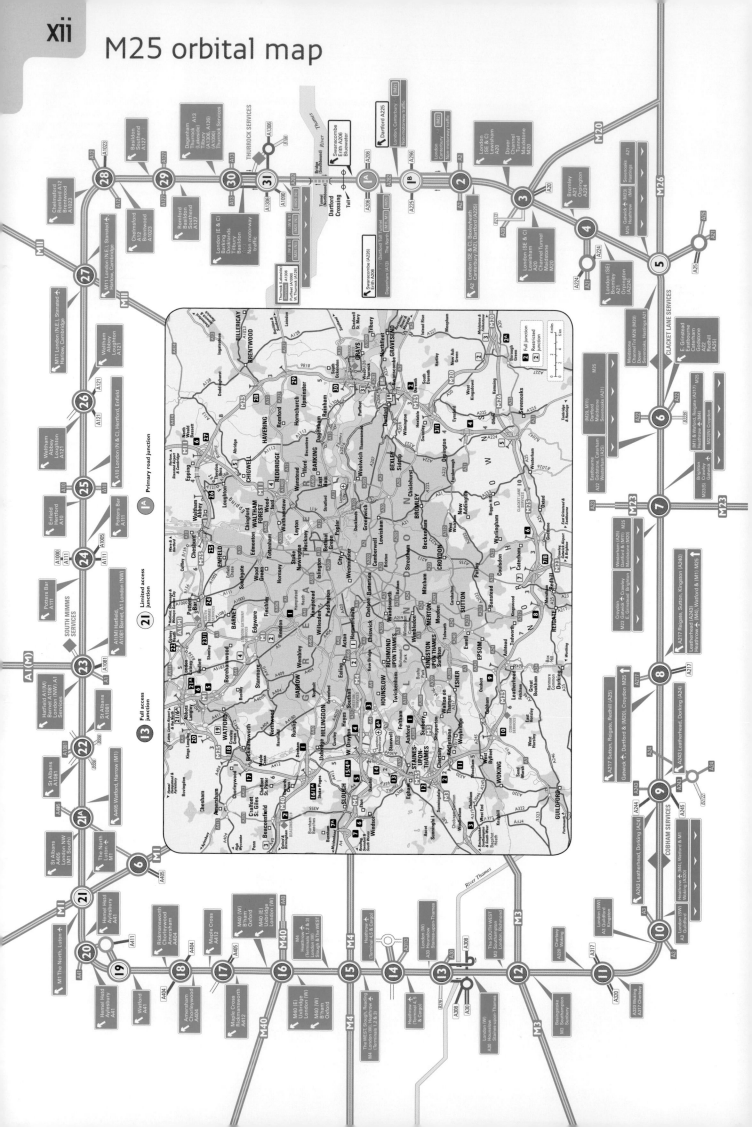

M6

M6 The SOUTH, B'ham
The S. WEST (M5)

The SOUTH M6 Toll

A4601

A460

11ᴬ

T8 M6 Toll

A460

A34 A460

A5

T7

Toll

A5195 Brownhills, Burntwood
The SOUTH, Lichfield M6 Toll

T6 Toll

NORTON CANES SERVICES

A5195

A5148 Lichfield, (A38) Burton
The SOUTH, Tamworth M6 Toll

A5 A5148

T5 Toll

A5

A5 Tamworth (M42 North)
The SOUTH, Birmingham
Sutton Coldfield M6 Toll

A5 A38

A5

T4 Toll

A5

A38

A460 (M6 south) Wolverhampton

A460 The NORTH WEST (M6, North) Stafford, telford M6 Toll

A34 A5

A34 A460 Walsall, Cannock Rugeley TOLLS

A5195 Brownhills, Burntwood
The NORTH WEST (M6 North), Cannock M6 Toll

A5127

A38 Burton, Lichfield A5 Tamworth

A38 The NORTH WEST (M6 North), Cannock M6 Toll

Toll

A38 Birmingham Sutton Coldfield

M6 Toll London, Coventry, (M6, M42)

A38

M6

11

A460

A460 Wolverhampton Cannock

A460 Cannock

HILTON PARK SERVICES

M54

M54 NORTH (& MID) WALES Wolverhampton & Telford

The NORTH WEST & Stafford M6

10ᴬ

T3 Tolls

A446 (M42 North) Coleshill

A38 Sutton Coldfield

The NORTH WEST Cannock, Lichfield M6 Toll

M6 Toll London, Coventry, (M6, M42(S))

A446

10 A454

A454 Walsall

A461 Wednesbury

The SOUTH & Birmingham M6

A454

A454 Walsall, W'hampton (Cent. & East)

The North West, Telford (M54), W'hampton (N) M6

A461

A446

T2 A4091

A446

9 A4148

A461 Wednesbury

The NORTH WEST, Walsall & W'hampton M6

M6

London (M1 & M40) Birmingham (N. E. & Cen.) N.E.C. & ✈

The SOUTH WEST Birmingham (W & S) West Bromwich

M5 M6 M6

8

A34 Birmingham (N)

London (M1 & M40) Birmingham (S & Cen.) N.E.C. & ✈ M6

A34

8 M6 **7**

A34

T1 A446

A4097

9 M42

A446

M42

A38(M) & A38 B'ham (E, Cen, & NE) & Lichfield

London (M1 & M40) N.E.C. & B'ham M6

A5127

A38

6 A38

A452

A4097 A446 M42 The N. EAST (M1), Tamworth

The NORTH WEST Cannock, Lichfield M6 Toll

M6 Toll

A446

M42(N) Birmingham (Cen, E. N. & W)

M42 The SOUTH WEST (M5) (M6, South M40) Birmingham (S), N.E.C. & ✈ London, Coventry

8

8

M6 London (M1 & M40) Birmingham (N & E)

The NORTH WEST Walsall Wolverhampton M6

The SOUTH WEST M5 Birmingham (W & S) West Bromwich

The NORTH WEST & Wolverhampton M6

A34 Birmingham (N) & Walsall

The NORTH WEST The SOUTH WEST B'ham (W & S) (M5) M6

6

5 M6 **4ᴬ**

M42 & M6

M42 M6 LONDON (M1) Coventry N.E.C.

M42 The NORTH (M1) The SOUTH (M6) & ✈

A38(M)

1

A41

A41

A41 West Bromwich, Sandwell & B'ham (N & W)

The SOUTH WEST & Birmingham (W & S) M5

A454 A38(M)

Stay in lane through ◆ markings

B4147 A452

A452 B'ham (E) & Sutton Coldfield

M6 & A38(M), A38 B'ham (Cen & NE) ➡ M6 M6

A446

M42 The SOUTH WEST (M5) B'ham (S), N.E.C. & ✈ London, (S & W), (M40) Coventry (S & W)

M42 London (N & E) (M1) Coventry (N & E)

7ᴬ

7 **4** M6 **3ᴬ**

M6 London (M1), Coventry

The N. WEST (M6Toll) The N. EAST (M1), Tamworth M42

A38 A4540

A4540

A38

A41 West Bromwich & B'ham (NW)

The NORTH (M1 & M6), Birmingham (N), N.E.C. ✈ M5

M5

M6 The NORTH WEST, B'ham
The NORTH WEST (M6Toll) The NORTH EAST (M1) M6

A45 B'ham (S.E.) 🚉 N.E.C. Coventry

The SOUTH WEST (M5), LONDON (M40), Birmingham (SE), Solihull M42

2 A4123

A4123 Birmingham (W) & Dudley

The SOUTH WEST & Birmingham (S) M5

A45

A45 B'ham (S.E.) 🚉 N.E.C., Coventry (S & W)

The NORTH, B'ham (E, N & Cen), Coventry (N & E) M42

6 A45

A4123 Dudley, W'hampton & Sandwell

The NORTH (M1 & M6), Birmingham (N) M5

A456 Kidderminster

The SOUTH WEST & Birmingham (S) M5

A41 Solihull

A41 Solihull

5 A4141

3 A456

A456 Birmingham (W & Cen)

FRANKLEY SERVICES

A3400 Henley-in-Arden

A34

4 A3400

A38 B'ham (SW) Bromsgrove

A491 A38

A38

A34 Shirley

M42

4

A38 Birmingham (SW), A491 Stourbridge

M42 (M40) N.E.C. & ✈

M42 & M5

M5 The SOUTH WEST Worcester

M5

M40 London, Warwick, Stratford The SOUTH WEST (M5), Birmingham (S & W)

3ᴬ M42

M40

The NORTH M42 Solihull, B'ham (E) N.E.C. ✈

M42 London Warwick Stratford M40

4ᴬ M42

M42 The NORTH EAST (M1), London (M40) N.E.C. & ✈

M42 & M5

M5 The NORTH WEST (M6) B'ham (W, N & Cen)

A38

A441 Birmingham (S)

HOPWOOD PARK SERVICES

A435 B'ham (S), Redditch Evesham

A435

1 M42 **2** M42 **3** M42

A441

A38

A38 Bromsgrove

A38 The NORTH WEST B'ham (W.N &Cen) Stourbridge (M6)

M5 The SOUTH WEST Worcester

M5

A441

A441 Birmingham (S)

A435

A435 B'ham (S), Redditch Evesham

M40

Map labels (inset top): Norton Canes, Burntwood, LICHFIELD, Great Wyrley, Cheslyn Hay, Brownhills, Hammerwich, Shenstone, Fazeley, Cannock, Essington, Hilton Park, WALSALL, Aldridge, SUTTON COLDFIELD, Curdworth, Water Orton, Coleshill, DUDLEY, WEST BROMWICH, BIRMINGHAM, HALESOWEN, BIRMINGHAM INTERNATIONAL

Map labels (inset bottom): SUTTON COLDFIELD, Curdworth, Water Orton, Coleshill, DUDLEY, WEST BROMWICH, BIRMINGHAM, HALESOWEN, BIRMINGHAM INTERNATIONAL, Bickenhill, SOLIHULL, Knowle, Hampton in Arden, Wythall, Hopwood, Alvechurch, Romsley, Catshill, Marlbrook, Cofton Hackett, Barnt Green

Scale: 0 1 2 miles

🔵 Full junction 🔵 Restricted junction

3 Full access junction **4ᴬ** Limited access junction **T4** Full access junction M6 Toll **T1** Limited access junction M6 Toll

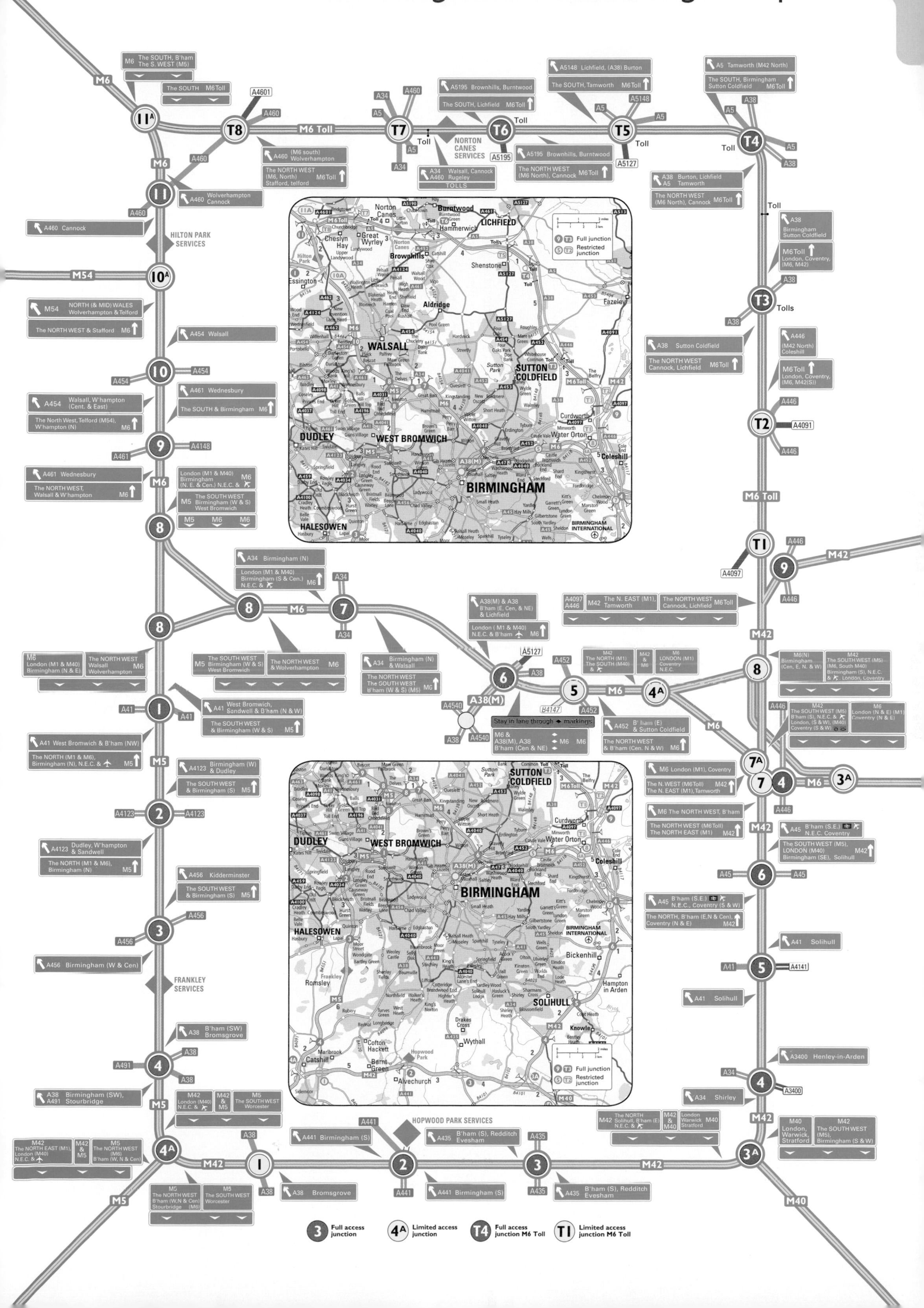

Risk rating of Britain's motorways and A roads

EuroRAP

This map shows the statistical risk of death or serious injury occurring on Britain's motorway and A road network for 2006-2010. Covering 45,000km in total, these roads represent just 11% of Britain's road length but carry 56% of the traffic. Half of Britain's fatal crashes occur on these roads.

The risk is calculated by comparing the frequency of road crashes resulting in death and serious injury on every stretch of road with how much traffic each road is carrying. For example, if there are 20 collisions on a road carrying 10,000 vehicles a day, the risk is 10 times higher than if the road has the same number of collisions but carries 100,000 vehicles.

Some of the roads shown have had improvements made to them recently, but during the survey period the risk of a fatal or serious injury collision on the black road sections was 27 times higher than on the safest (green) roads.

For more information on the Road Safety Foundation go to **www.roadsafetyfoundation.org.**

For more information on the statistical background to this research, visit the EuroRAP website at **www.eurorap.org.**

Road Assessment Programme Risk Rating

Low risk (safest) roads
Low-medium risk roads
Medium risk roads
Medium-high risk roads
High risk roads

Motorway
Single and dual carriageway
Linking roads

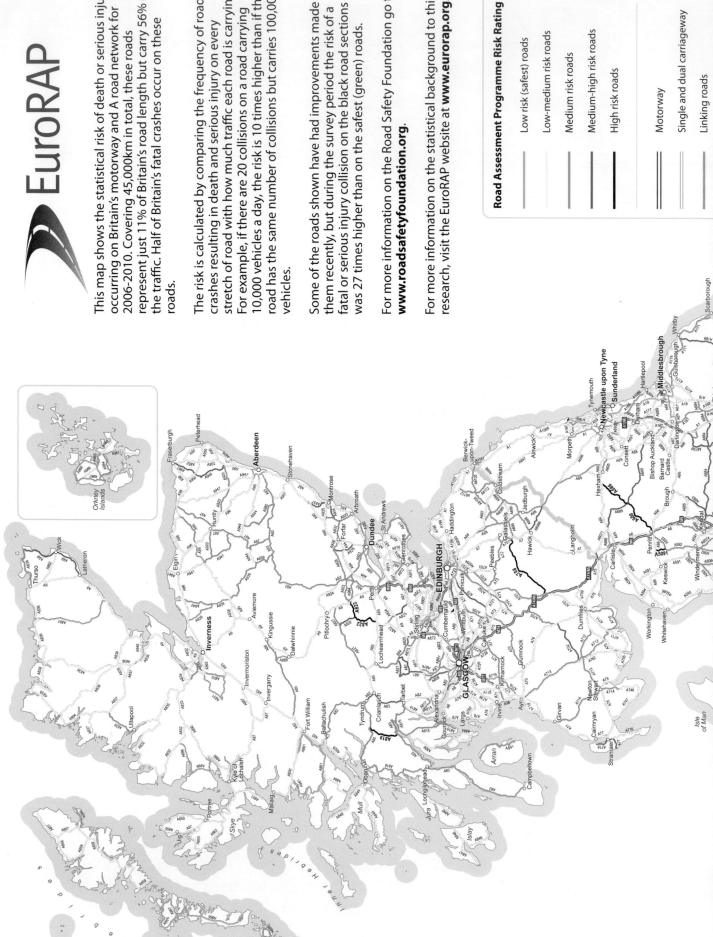

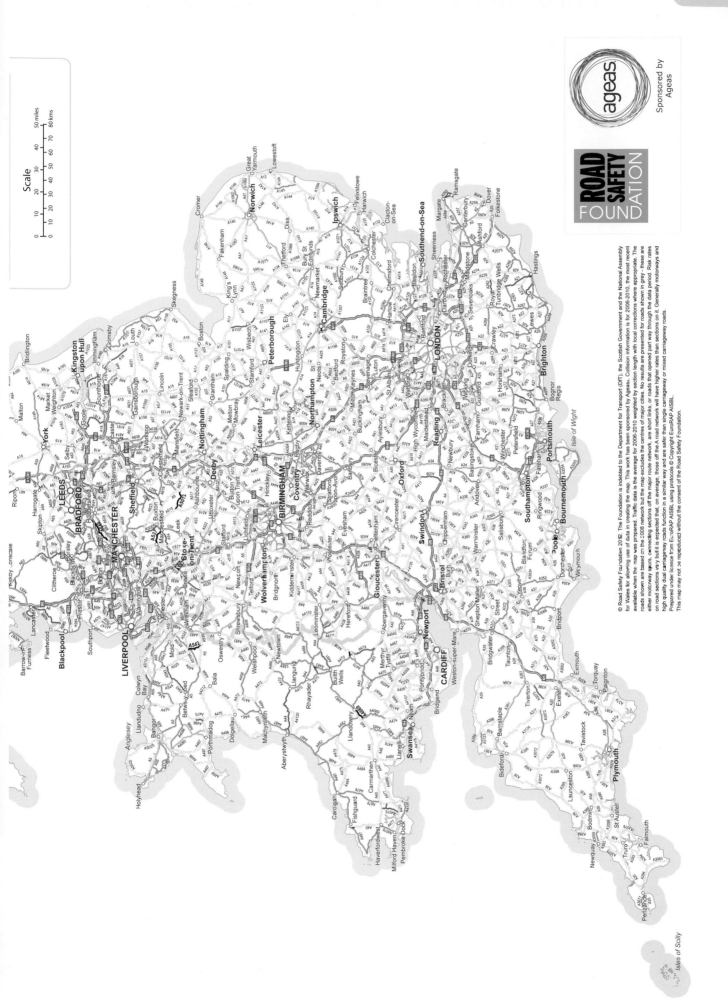

Distance chart

Distances between two selected towns in this table are shown in miles and kilometres. In general, distances are based on the shortest routes by classified roads.

Distance in kilometres

Distance in miles

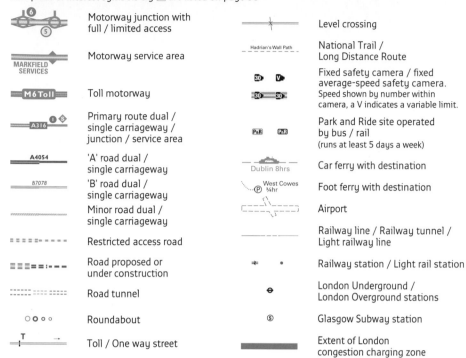

Symbols used on the map

Blue place of interest symbols e.g ★ are listed on page 93

Symbol	Description
	Motorway junction with full / limited access
MARKFIELD SERVICES	Motorway service area
M6Toll	Toll motorway
A316	Primary route dual / single carriageway / junction / service area
A4054	'A' road dual / single carriageway
B7078	'B' road dual / single carriageway
	Minor road dual / single carriageway
	Restricted access road
	Road proposed or under construction
	Road tunnel
○○●○○	Roundabout
T	Toll / One way street

Symbol	Description
	Level crossing
Hadrian's Wall Path	National Trail / Long Distance Route
30 V	Fixed safety camera / fixed average-speed safety camera. Speed shown by number within camera, a V indicates a variable limit.
P&R P&R	Park and Ride site operated by bus / rail (runs at least 5 days a week)
Dublin 8hrs	Car ferry with destination
West Cowes ¾hr	Foot ferry with destination
	Airport
	Railway line / Railway tunnel / Light railway line
⇄ •	Railway station / Light rail station
⊖	London Underground / London Overground stations
Ⓢ	Glasgow Subway station
	Extent of London congestion charging zone

Symbol	Description
	Notable building
H	Hospital
362 ▲	Spot height (in metres) / Lighthouse
	Built up area
	Woodland / Park
	National Park
	Heritage Coast
BRISTOL	County / Unitary Authority boundary and name
SEE PAGE 68	Area covered by street map

Locator map

Urban approach maps	
Birmingham	14-15
Bournemouth	3
Bradford	26-27
Bristol	8
Cardiff	7
Coventry	16
Derby	18-19
Edinburgh	32
Glasgow	30-31
Greater Manchester	24-25
Leeds	26-27
Leicester	17
Liverpool	22-23
London	10-13
Manchester	24-25
Merseyside	22-23
Middlesbrough	29
Milton Keynes	9
Newcastle upon Tyne	28-29
Newport	7
Nottingham	18-19
Plymouth	2
Portsmouth	4-5
Sheffield	21
Southampton	4-5
Stoke-on-Trent	20
Sunderland	28-29
Swansea	6
West Midlands	14-15

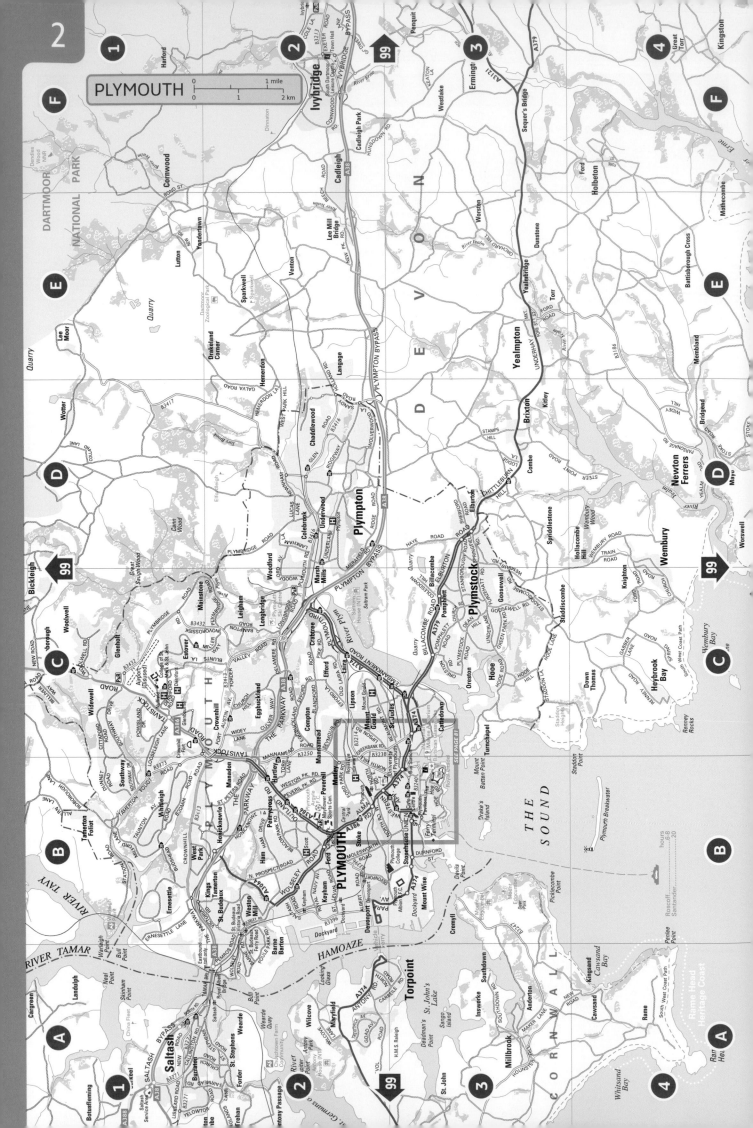

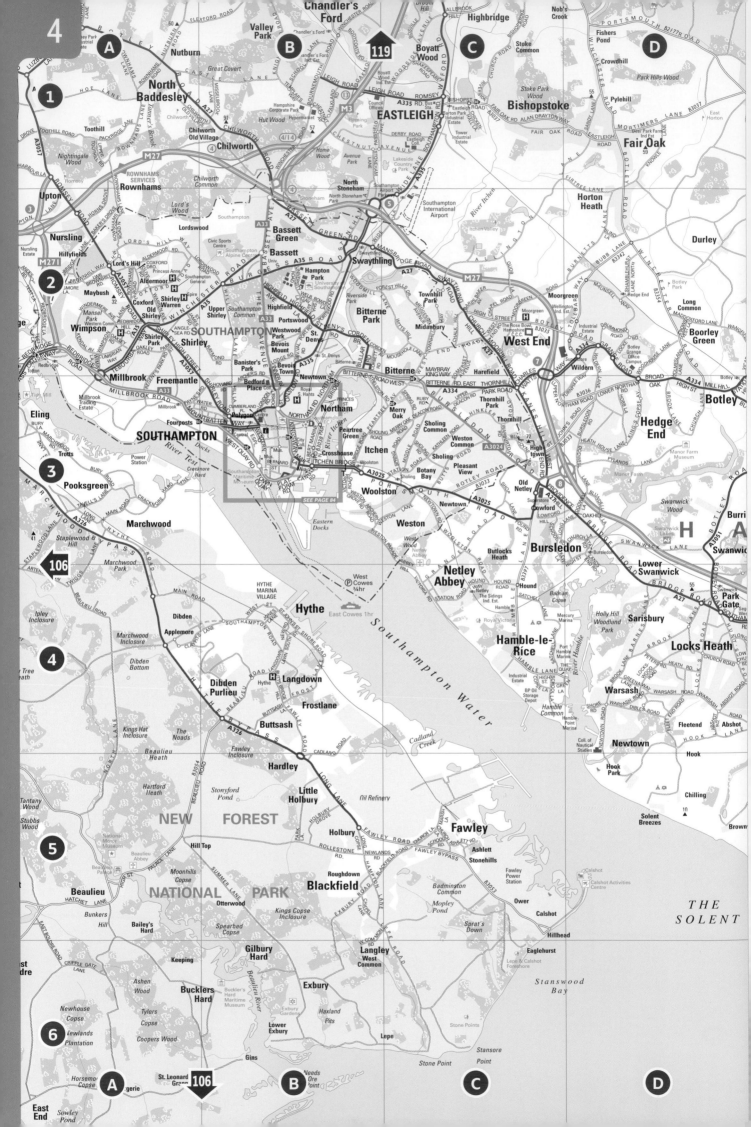

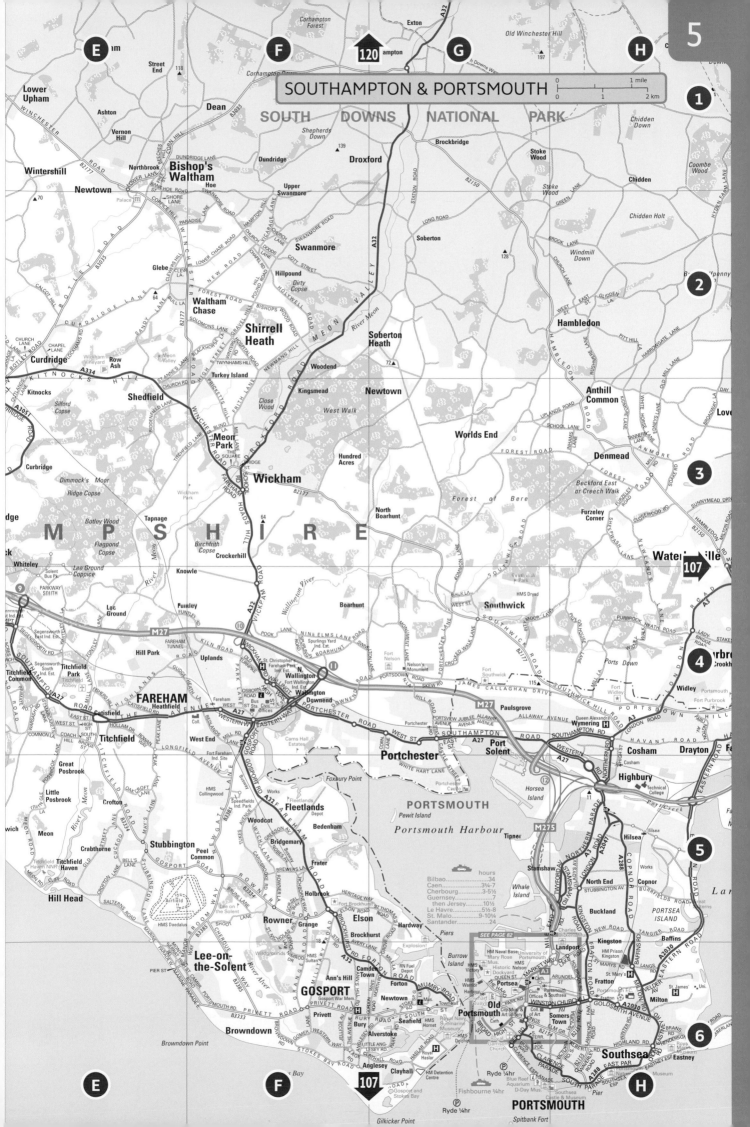

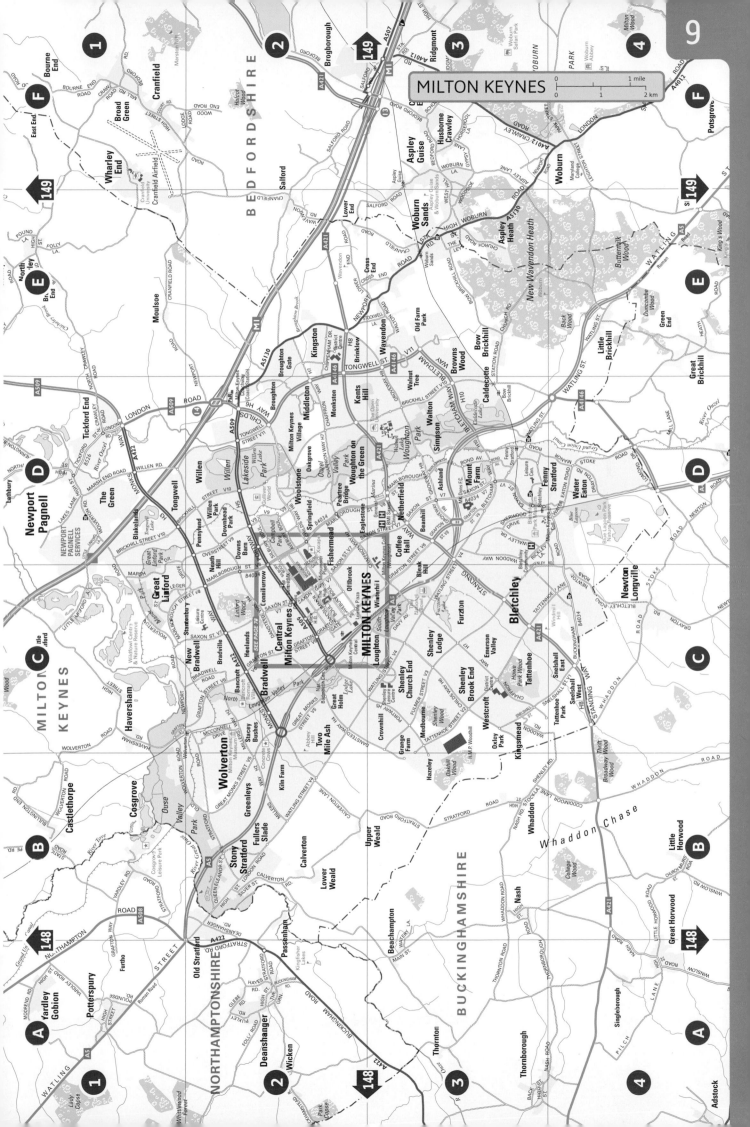

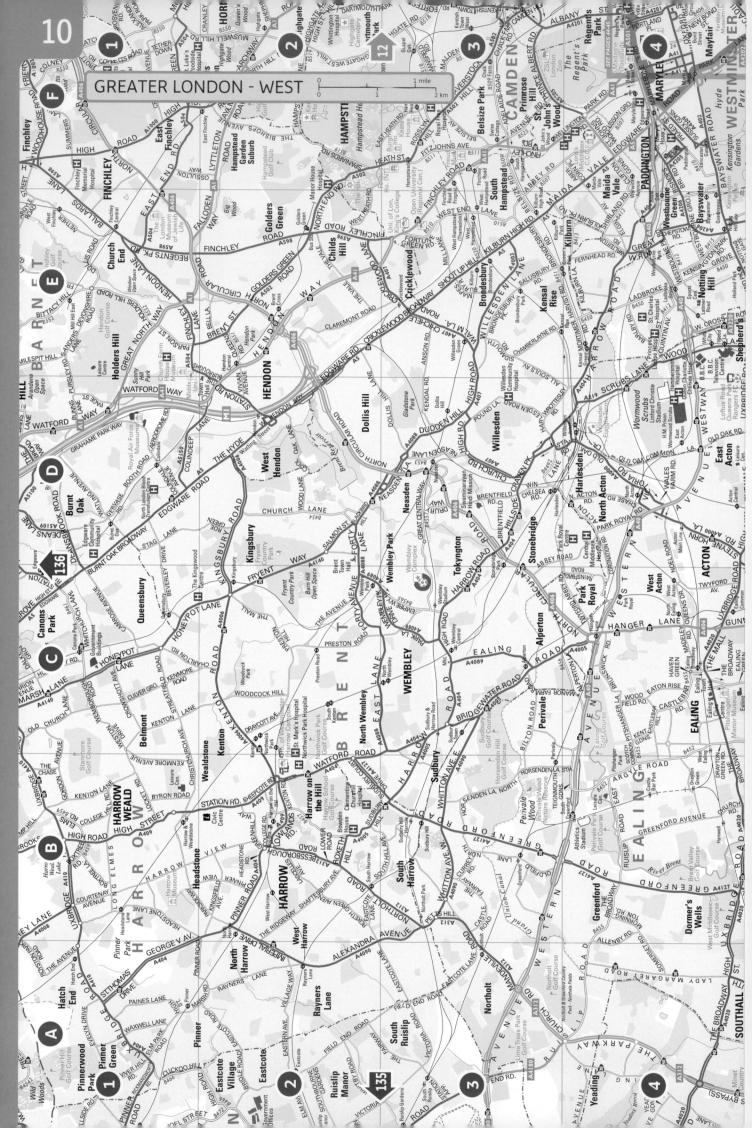

GREATER LONDON - EAST

SEE PAGES 44-45

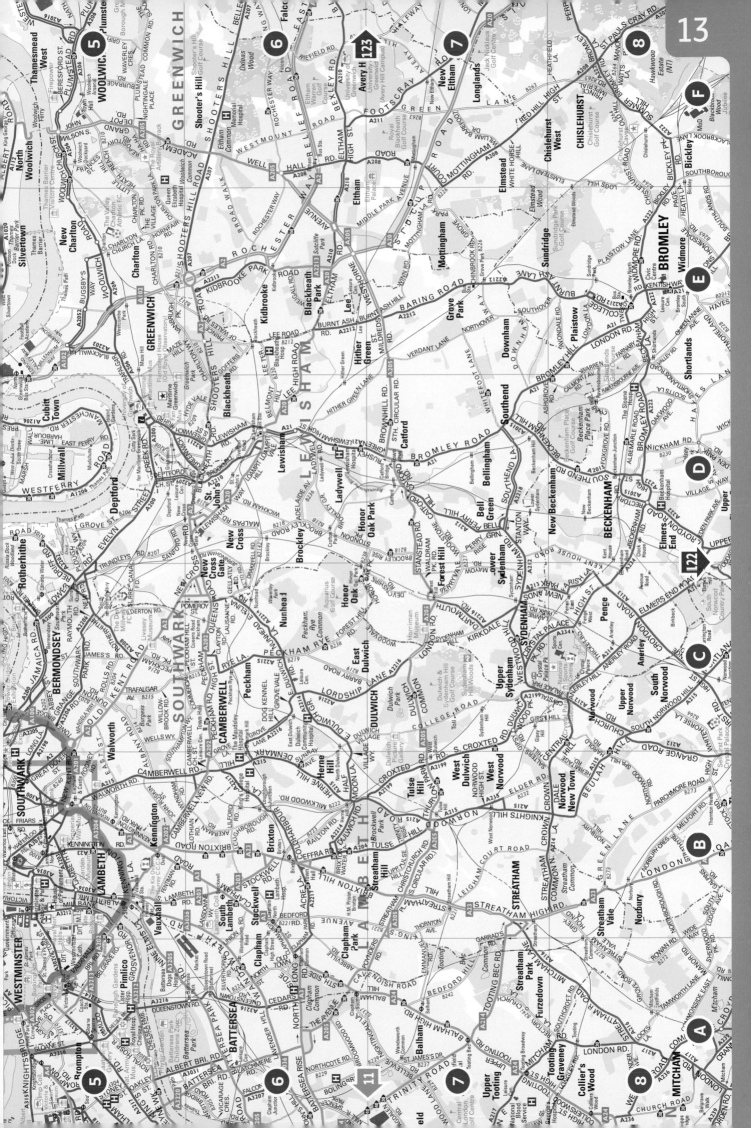

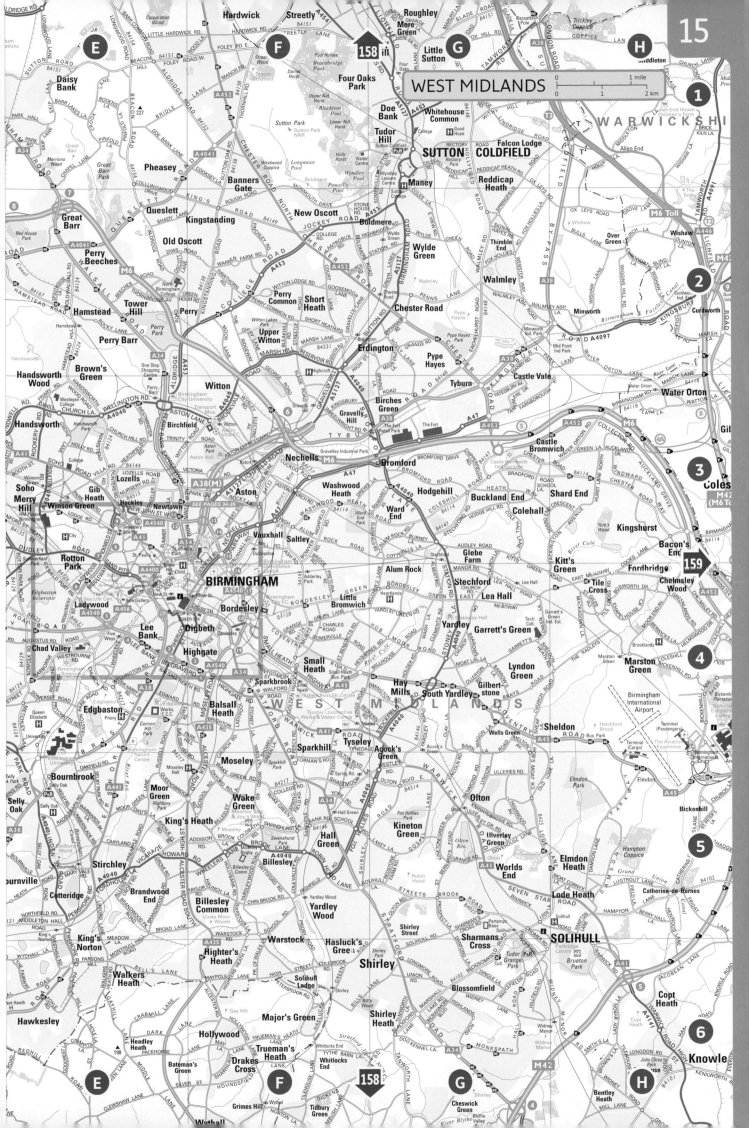

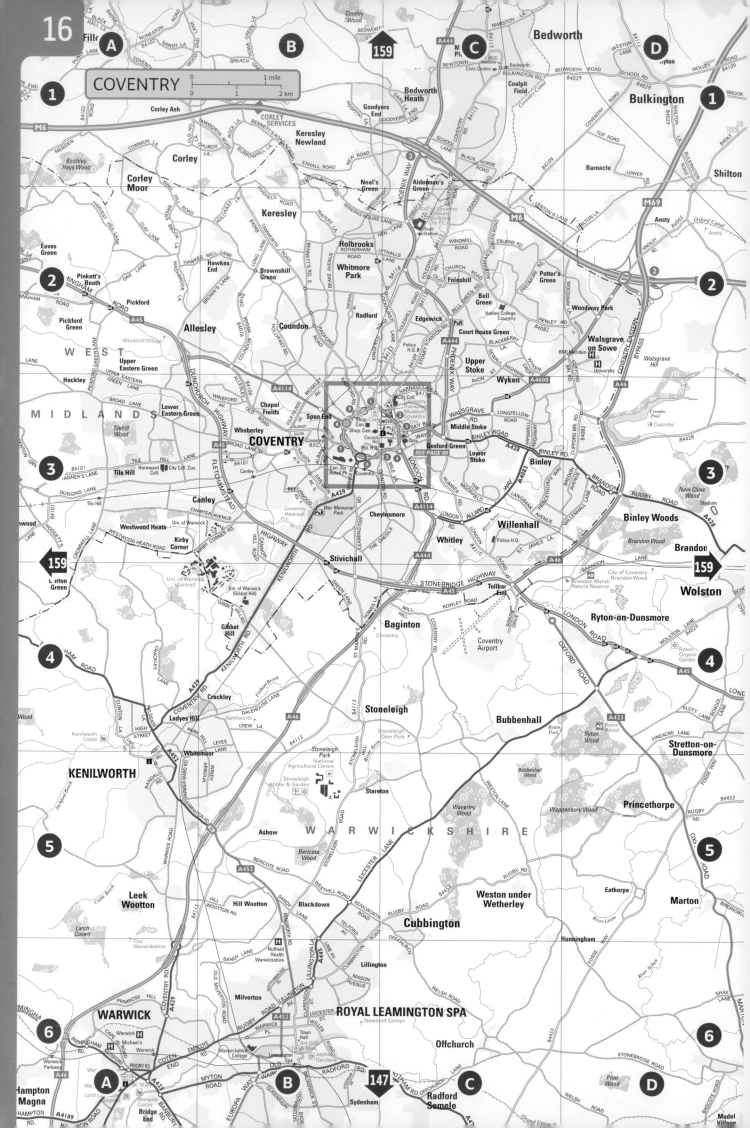

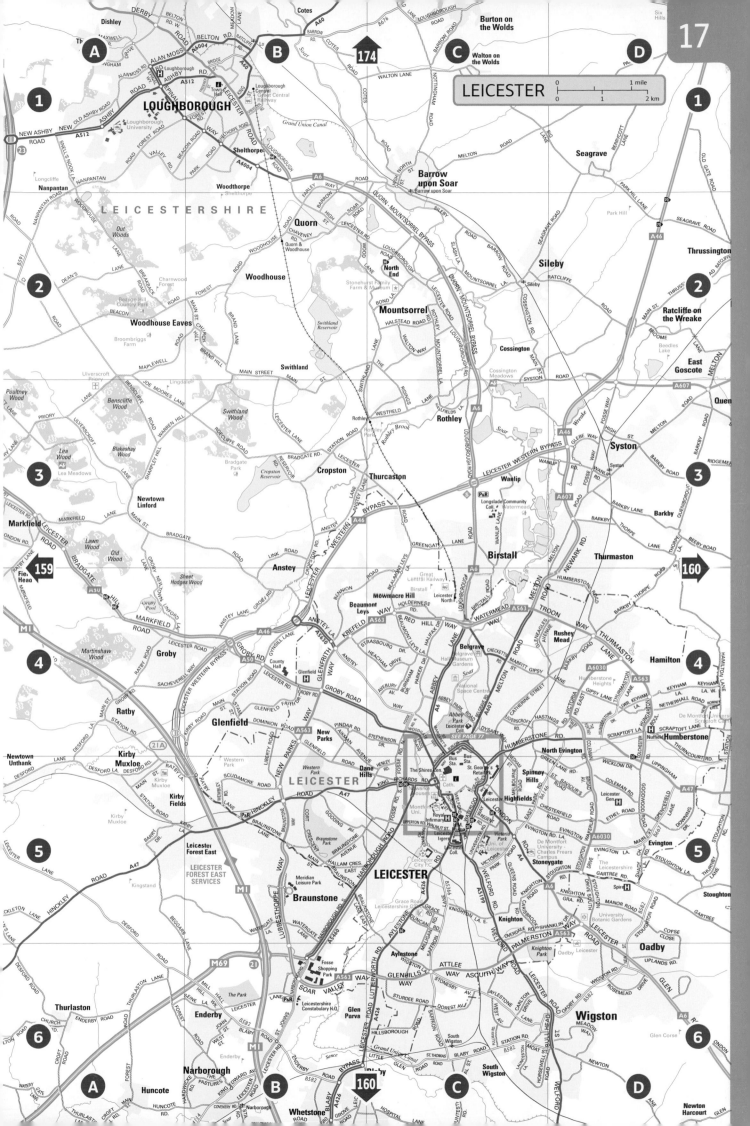

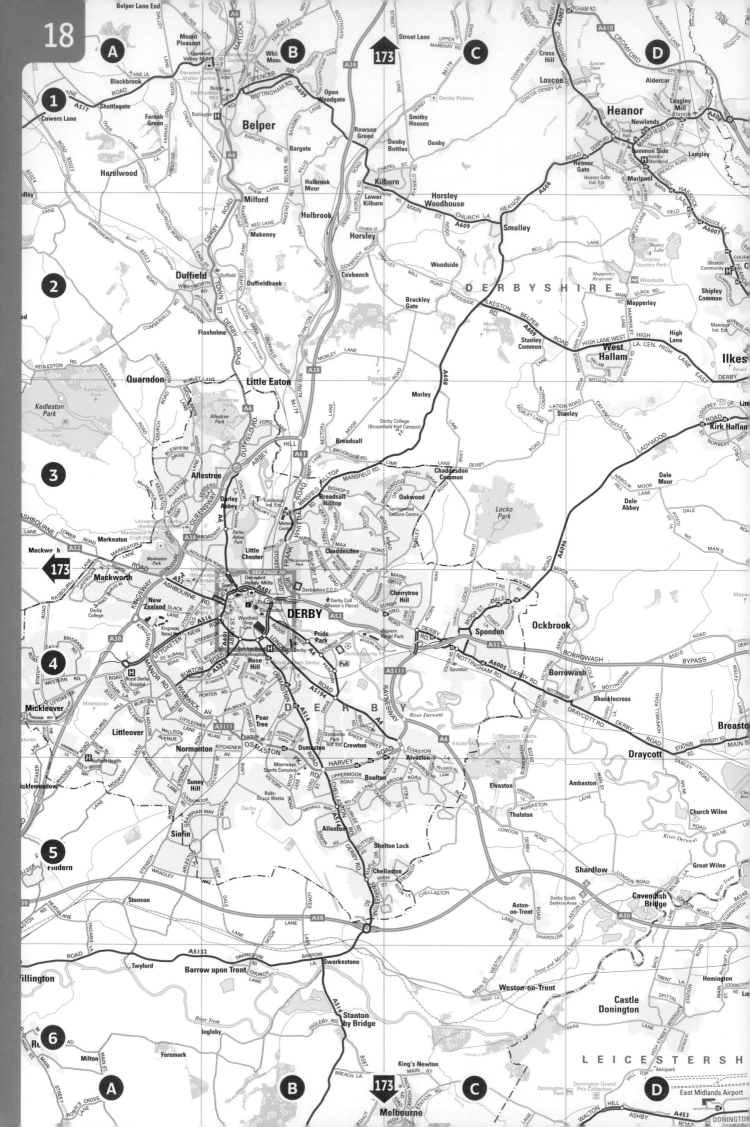

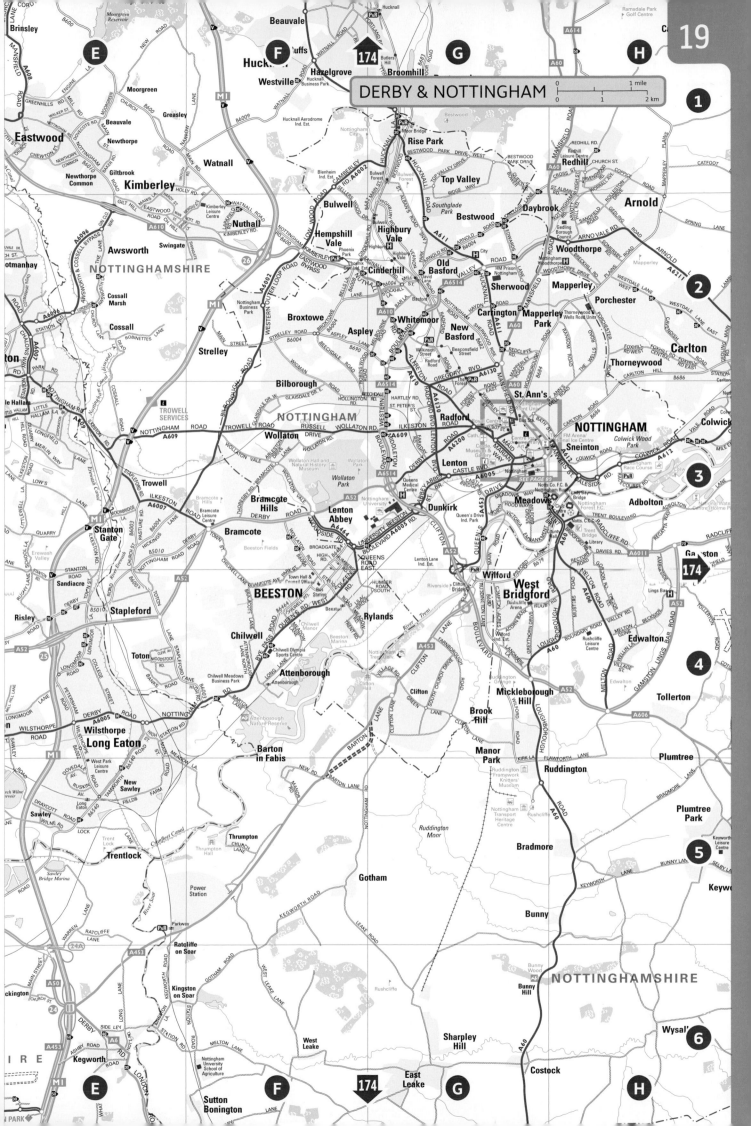

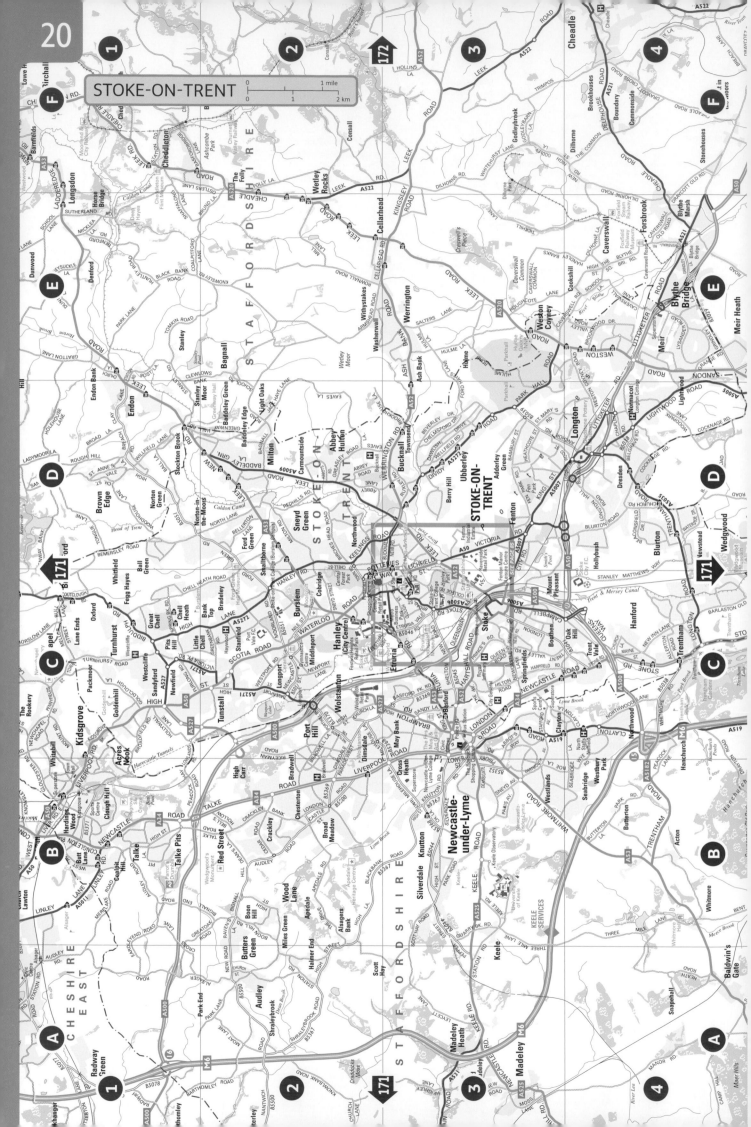

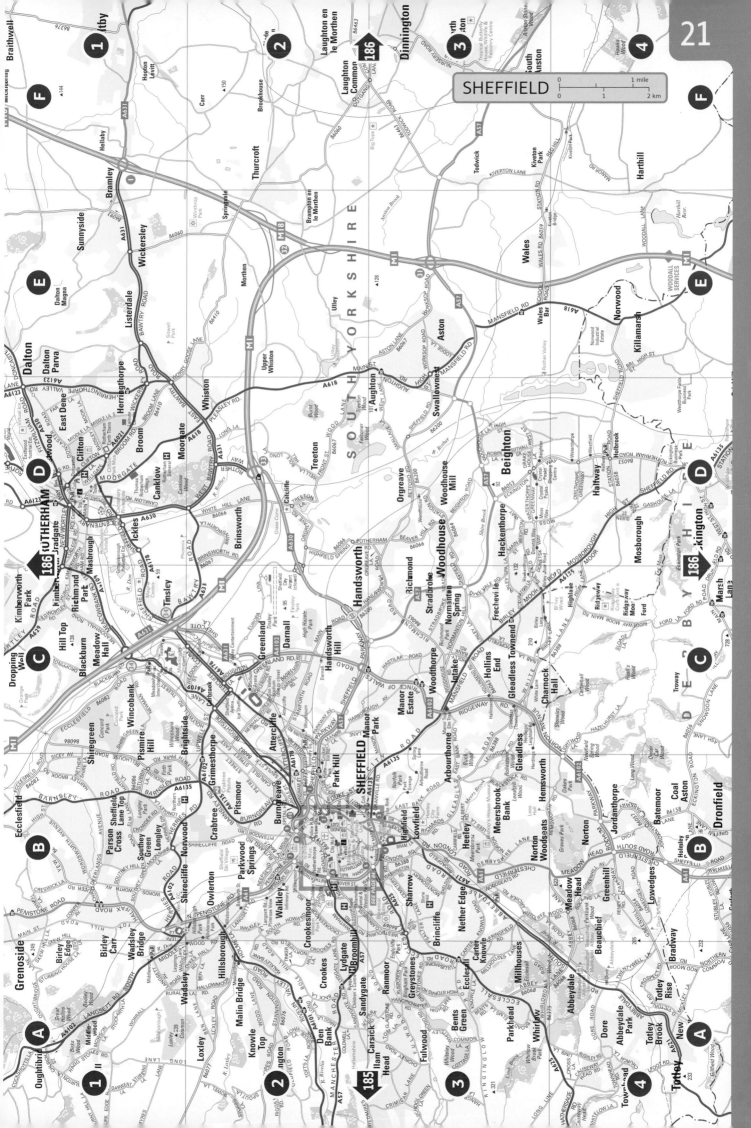

SHEFFIELD

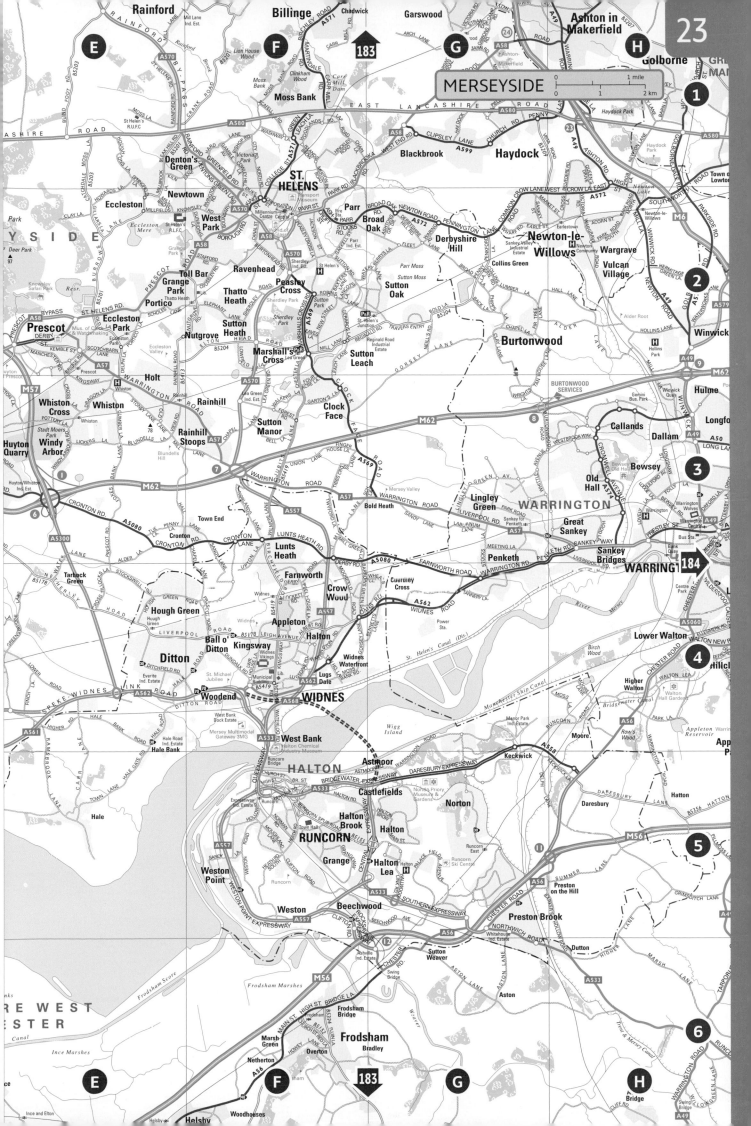

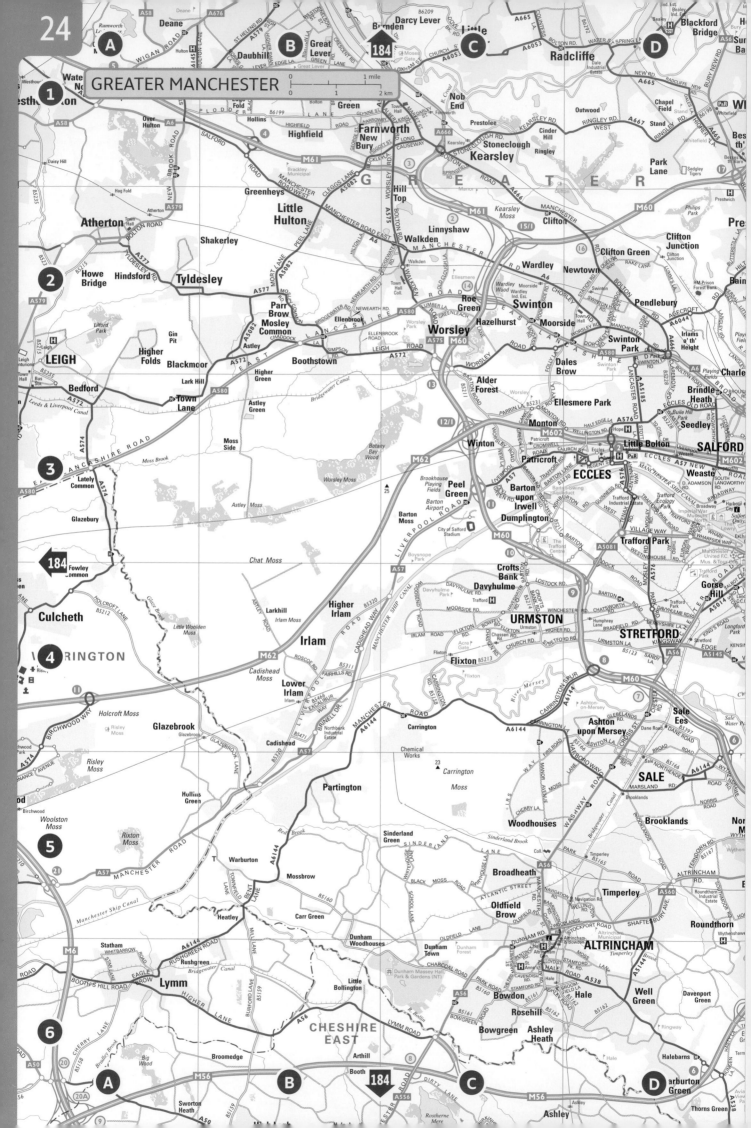

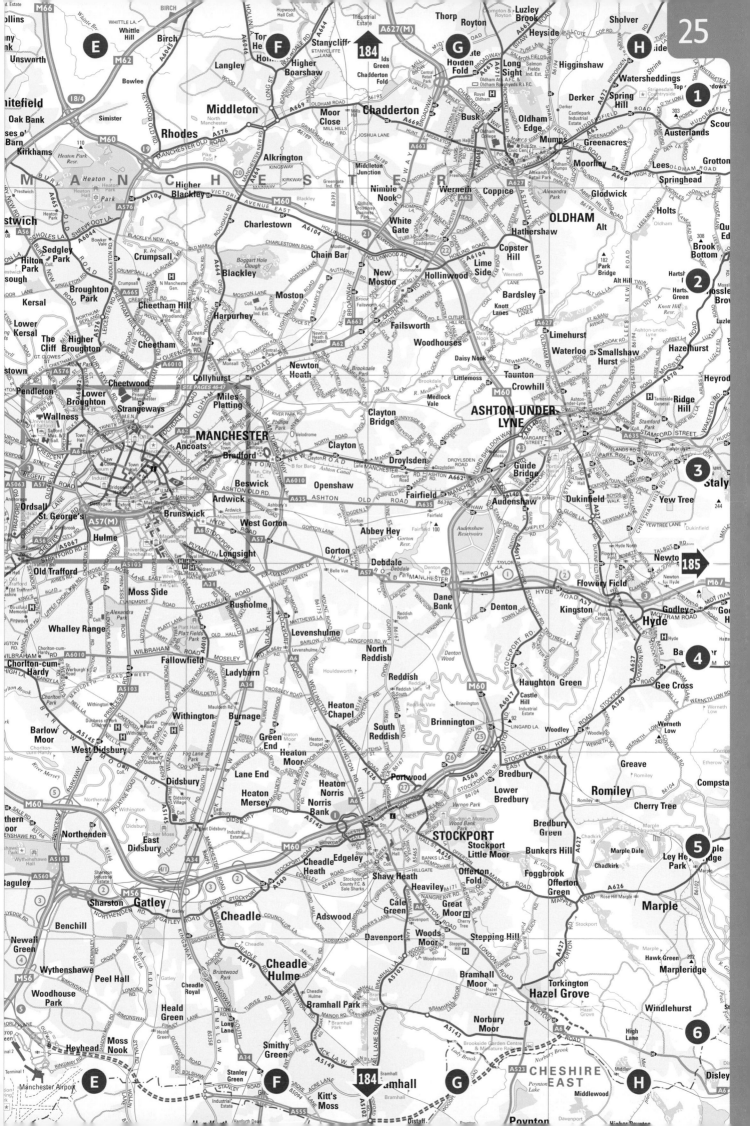

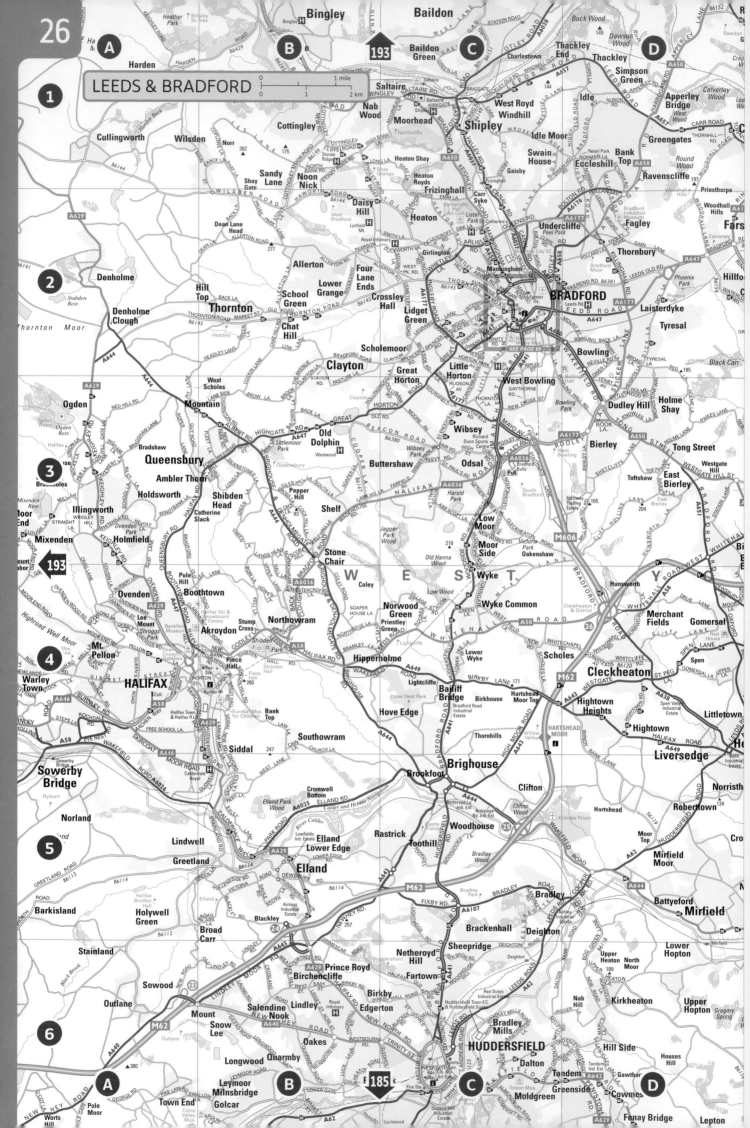

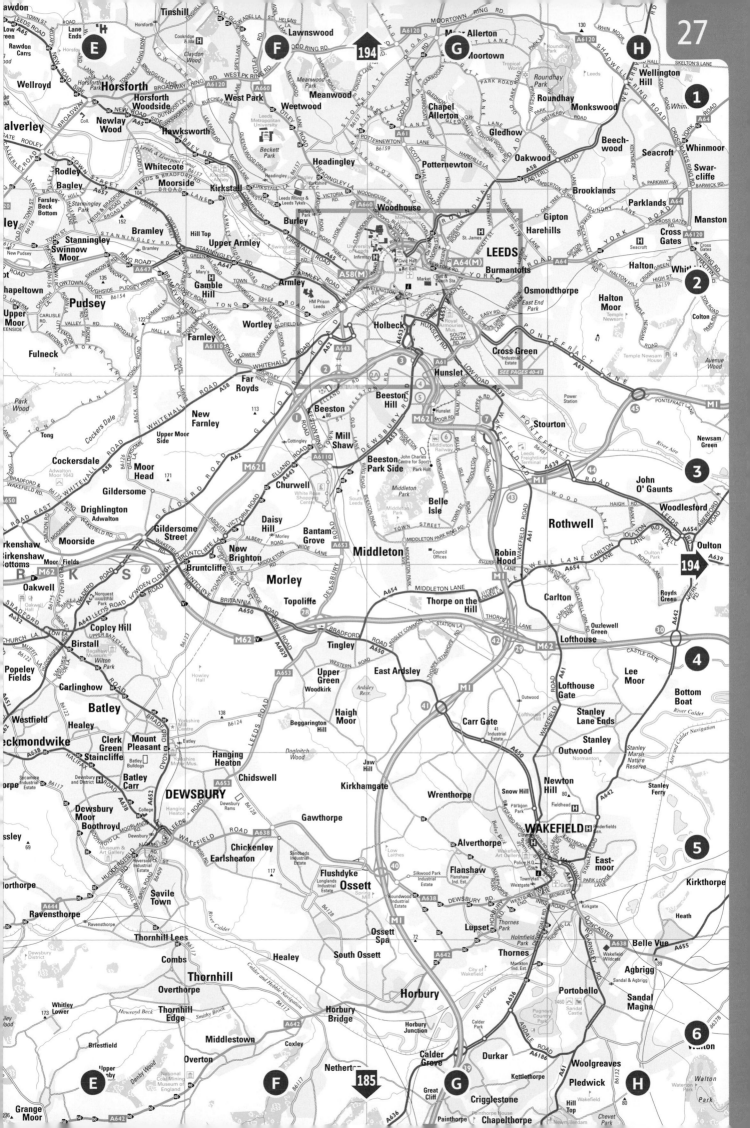

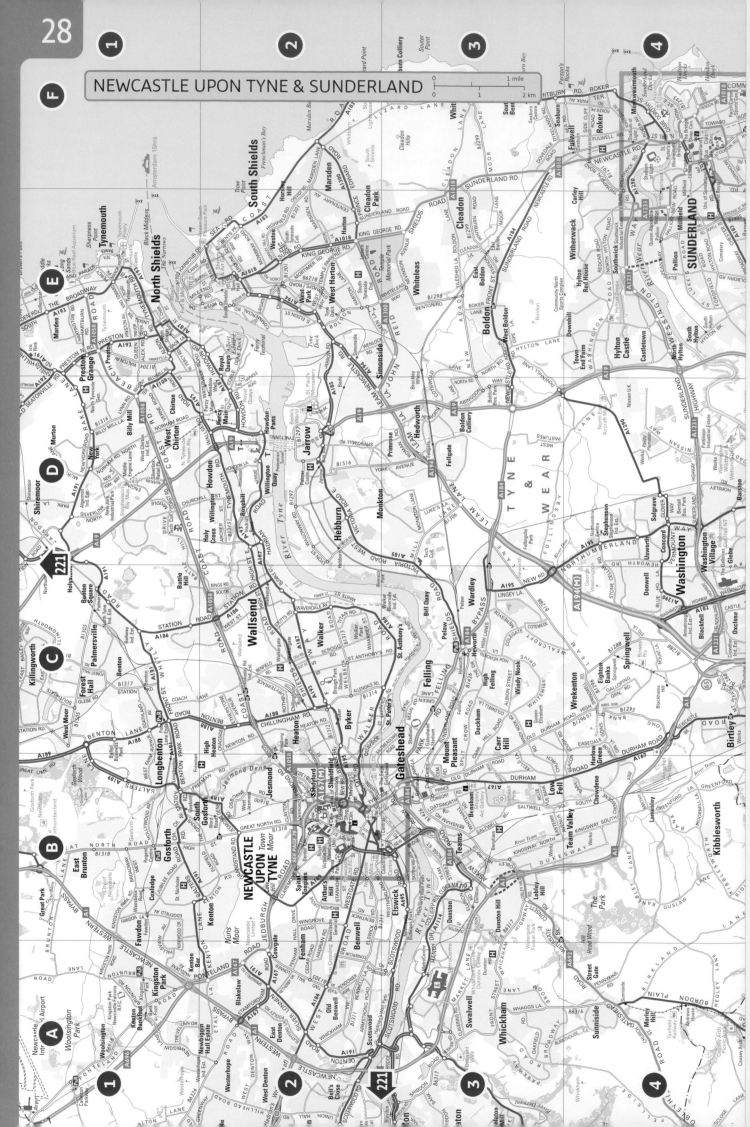

NEWCASTLE UPON TYNE & SUNDERLAND

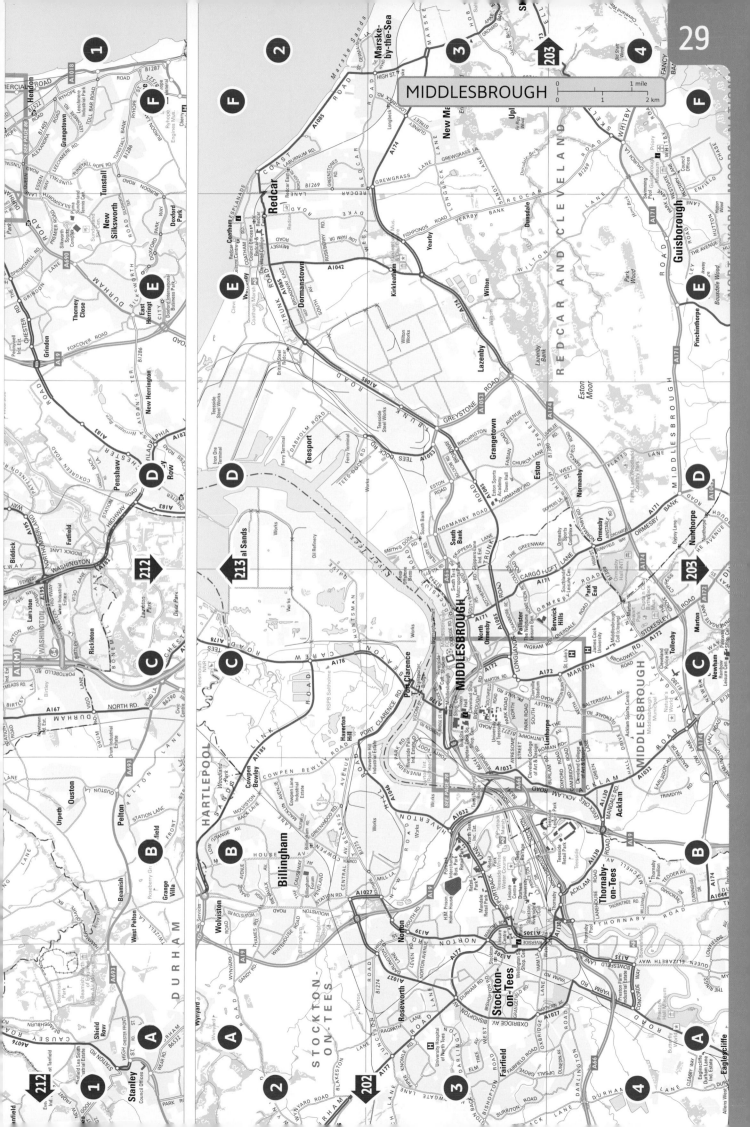

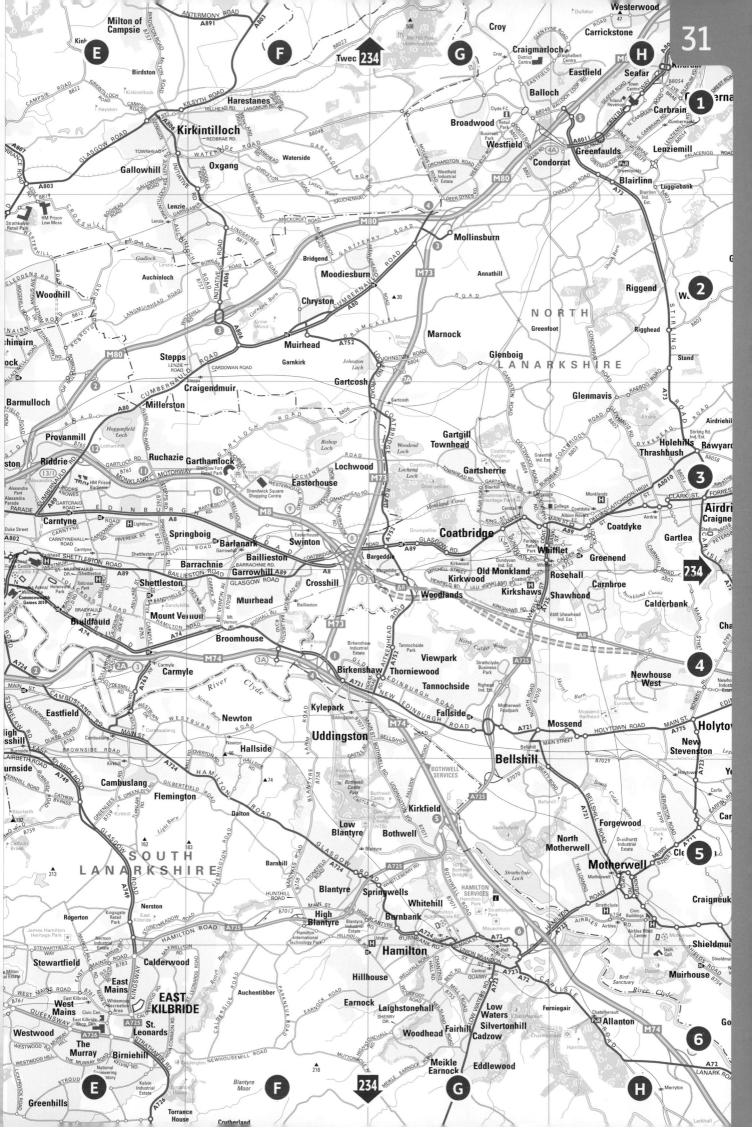

Symbols used on the map

M8	Motorway	Bus / Coach station		Embassy	
A4 ①	Primary route dual / single carriageway / Junction	P&R	Park and Ride site - rail operated (runs at least 5 days a week)	Cinema	
A40	'A' road dual / single carriageway		Extent of London congestion charging zone	Cathedral / Church	
B507	'B' road dual / single carriageway	Dublin 8hrs	Vehicle / Pedestrian ferry	Mosque / Synagogue / Other place of worship	
Toll	Other road dual / single carriageway / Toll	P P	Car park	Leisure & tourism	
7	One way street / Orbital route		Theatre	Shopping	
	Access restriction		Major hotel	Administration & law	
	Pedestrian street		Public House	Health & welfare	
	Street market	Pol	Police station	Education	
	Minor road / Track	Lib	Library	Industry / Office	
FB	Footpath / Footbridge	PO	Post Office	Other notable building	
	Road under construction		Visitor information centre (open all year / seasonally)	Park / Garden / Sports ground	
	Main / other National Rail station		Toilet	Cemetery	
	London Underground / Overground station				
	Light Rail / Station				

Locator map

Street maps

Aberdeen	63	Leeds index	52
Bath	63	Leicester	77
Birmingham	34-35	Lincoln	77
Birmingham index	48	Liverpool	42-43
Blackpool	64	Liverpool index	54
Bournemouth	64	London	44-45
Bradford	65	London index	56
Brighton	65	Manchester	46-47
Bristol	66	Manchester index	60
Cambridge	66	Middlesbrough	78
Canterbury	67	Milton Keynes	78
Cardiff	67	Newcastle upon Tyne	79
Carlisle	68	Norwich	79
Cheltenham	68	Nottingham	80
Chester	69	Oxford	80
Coventry	69	Perth	81
Derby	70	Plymouth	81
Dover	70	Portsmouth	82
Dundee	71	Reading	82
Durham	71	Salisbury	83
Eastbourne	72	Scarborough	83
Edinburgh	36-37	Sheffield	84
Edinburgh index	49	Southampton	84
Exeter	72	Stoke-on-Trent	85
Folkestone	73	Stratford-upon-Avon	85
Glasgow	38-39	Sunderland	86
Glasgow index	51	Swansea	86
Gloucester	73	Swindon	87
Guildford	74	Torquay	87
Harrogate	74	Watford	88
Hastings	75	Weston-super-Mare	88
Hereford	75	Winchester	89
Hull (Kingston upon Hull)	76	Windsor	89
Inverness	76	Worcester	90
Leeds	40-41	York	90

Airport plans

Birmingham International	91
Gatwick	91
Glasgow	91
Heathrow	91
Manchester	91
Stansted	91

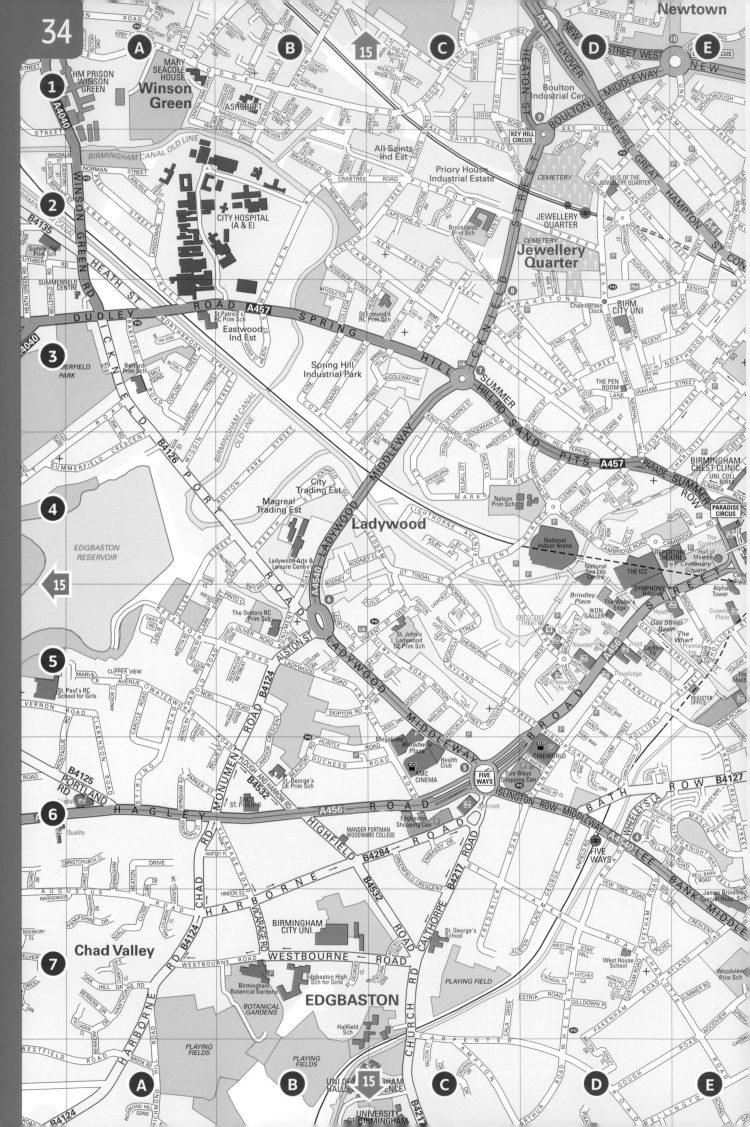

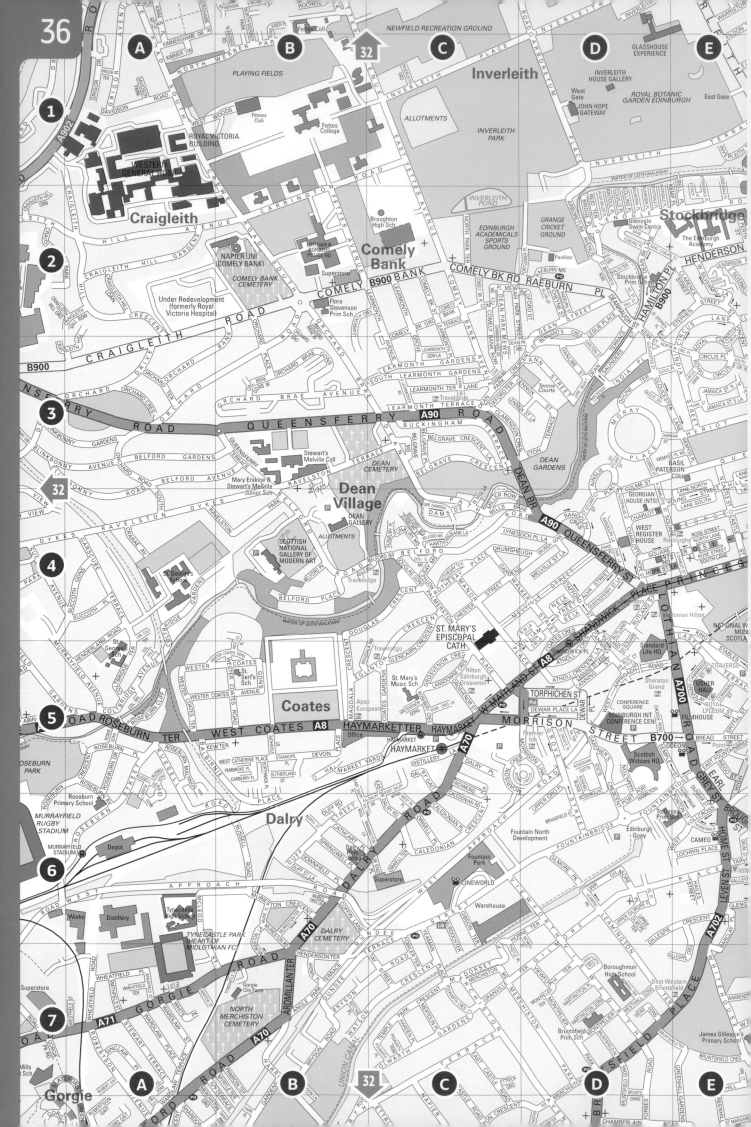

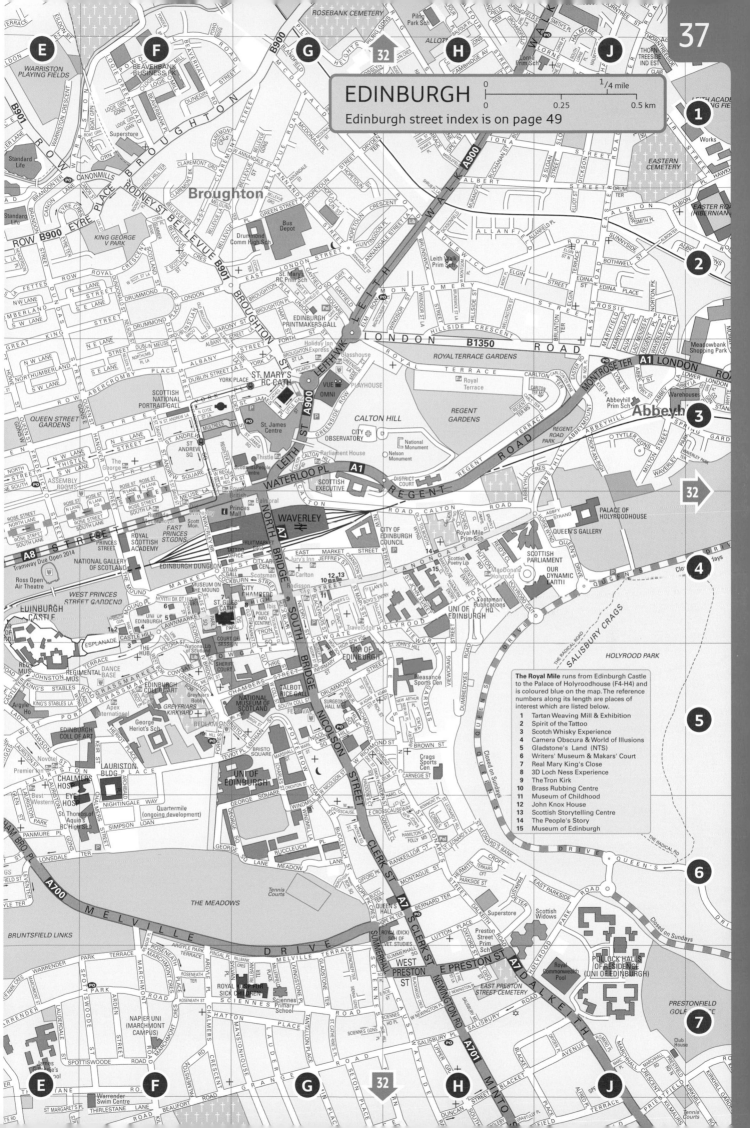

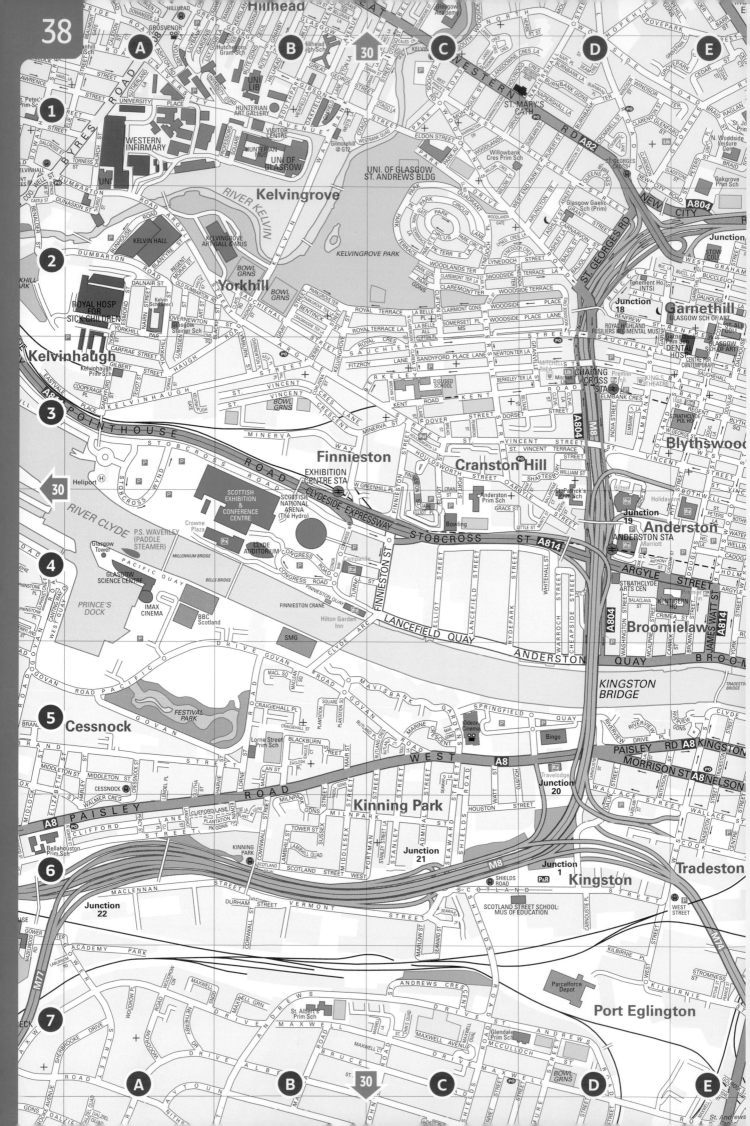

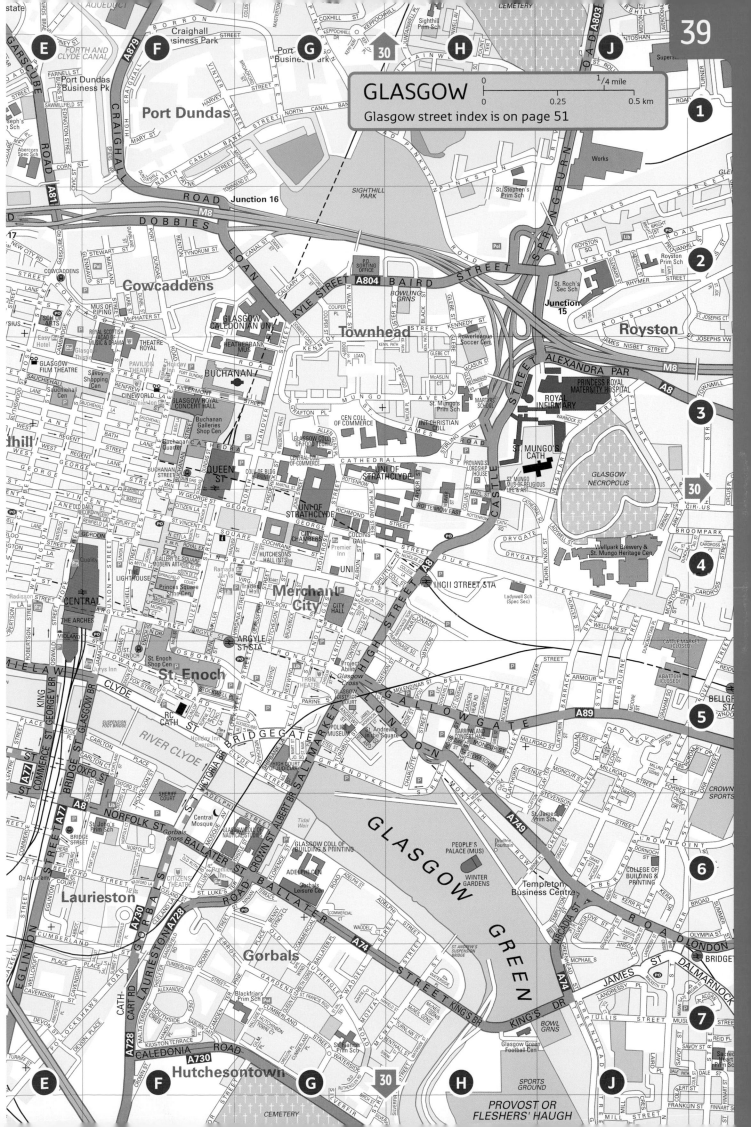

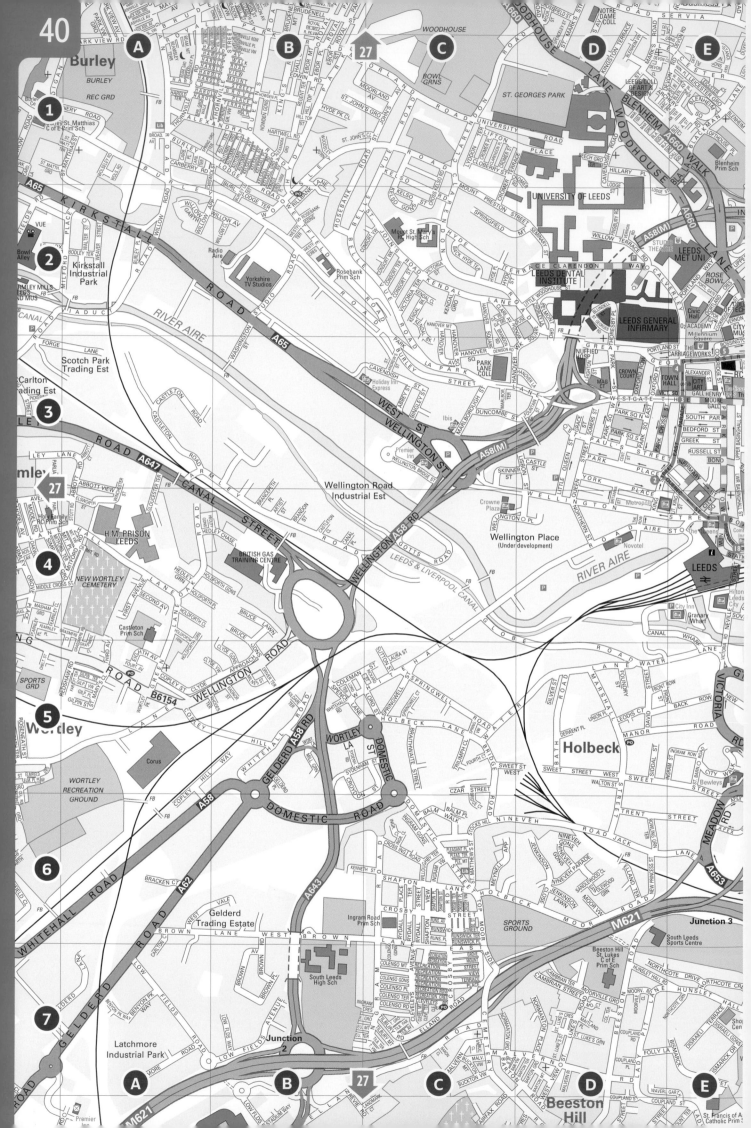

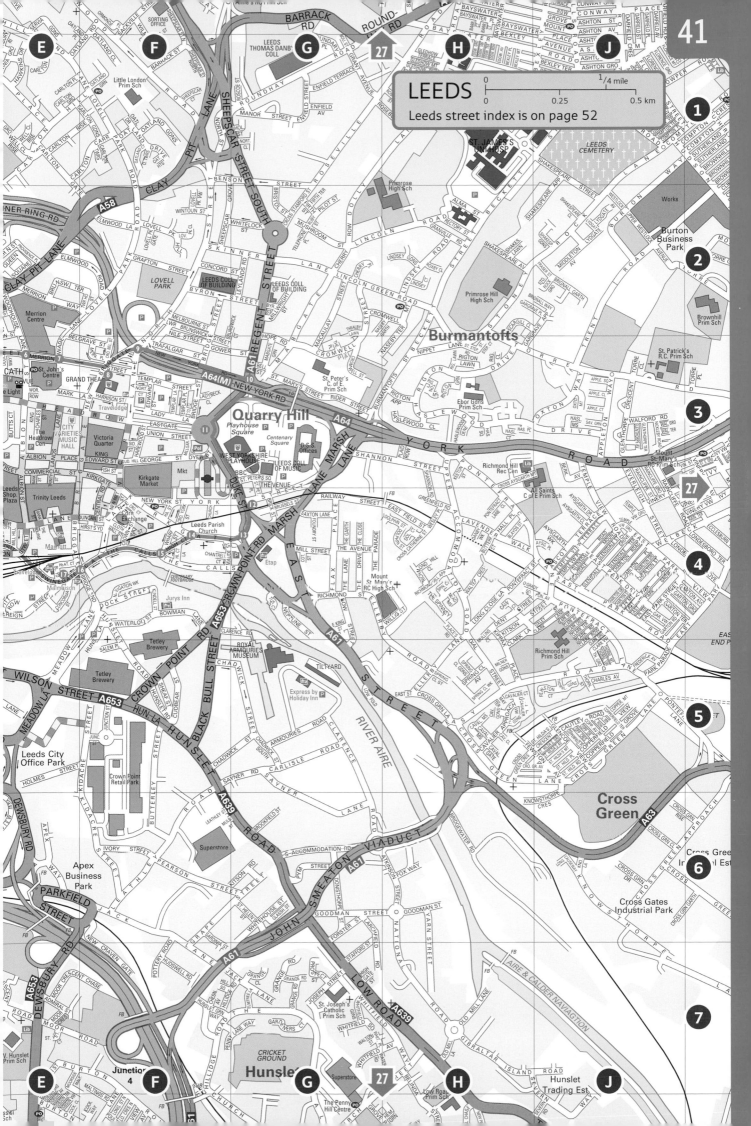

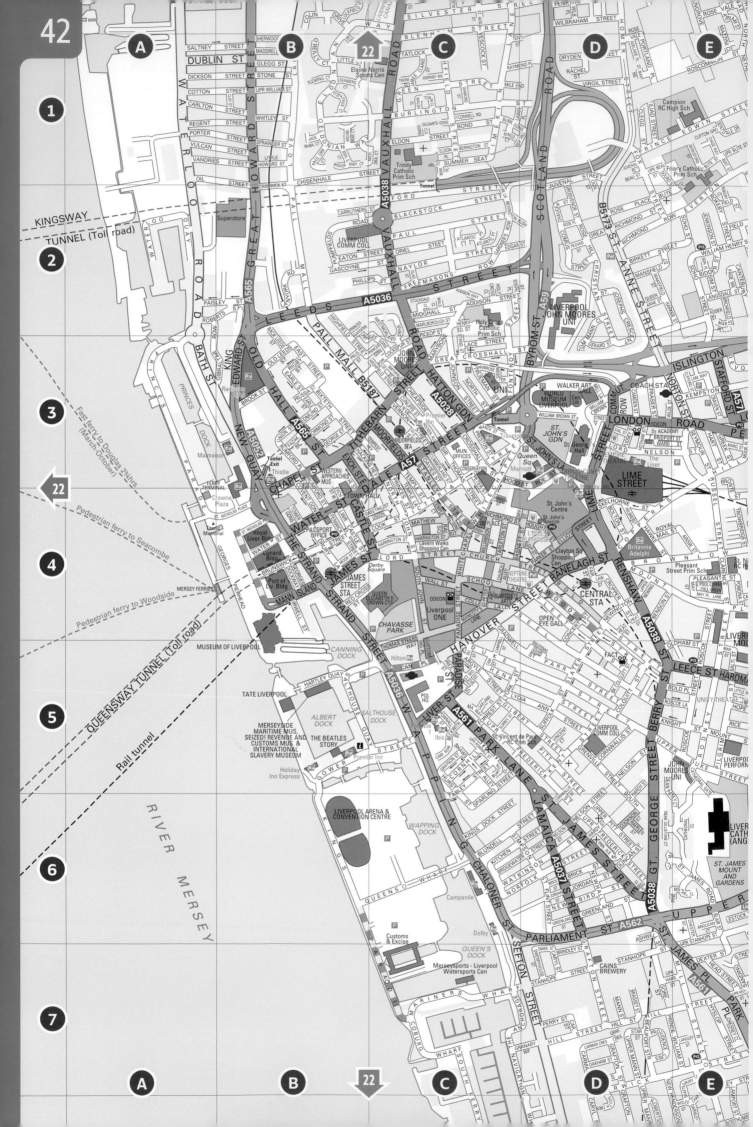

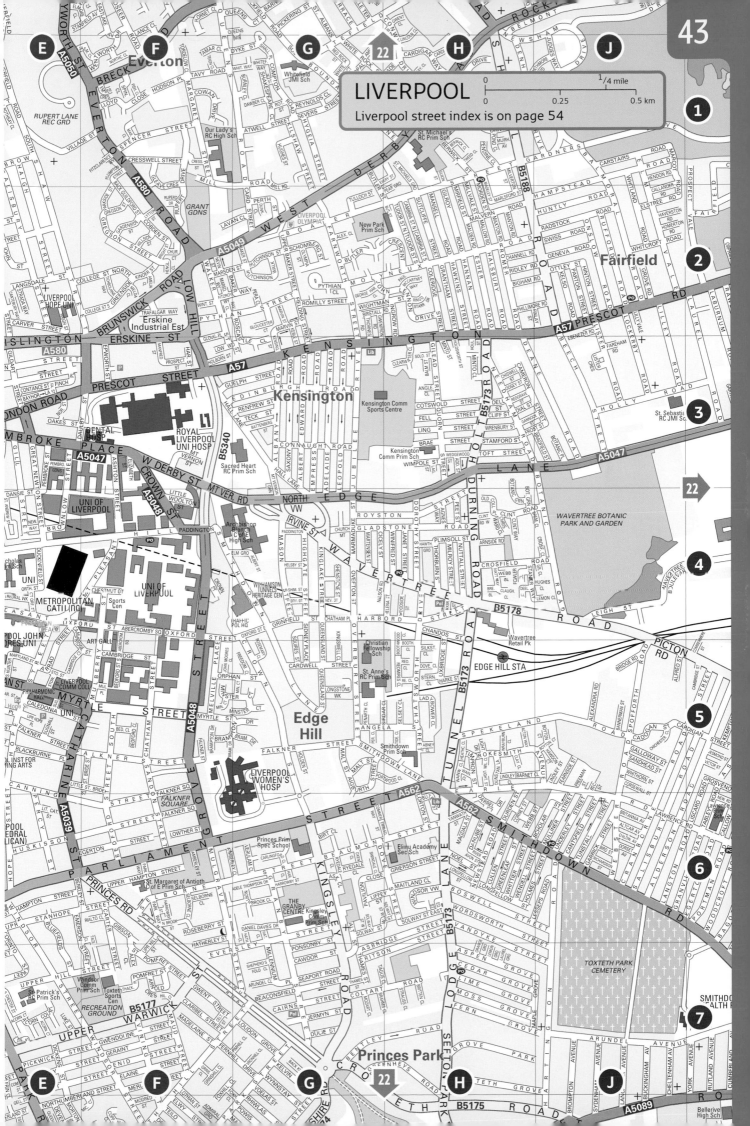

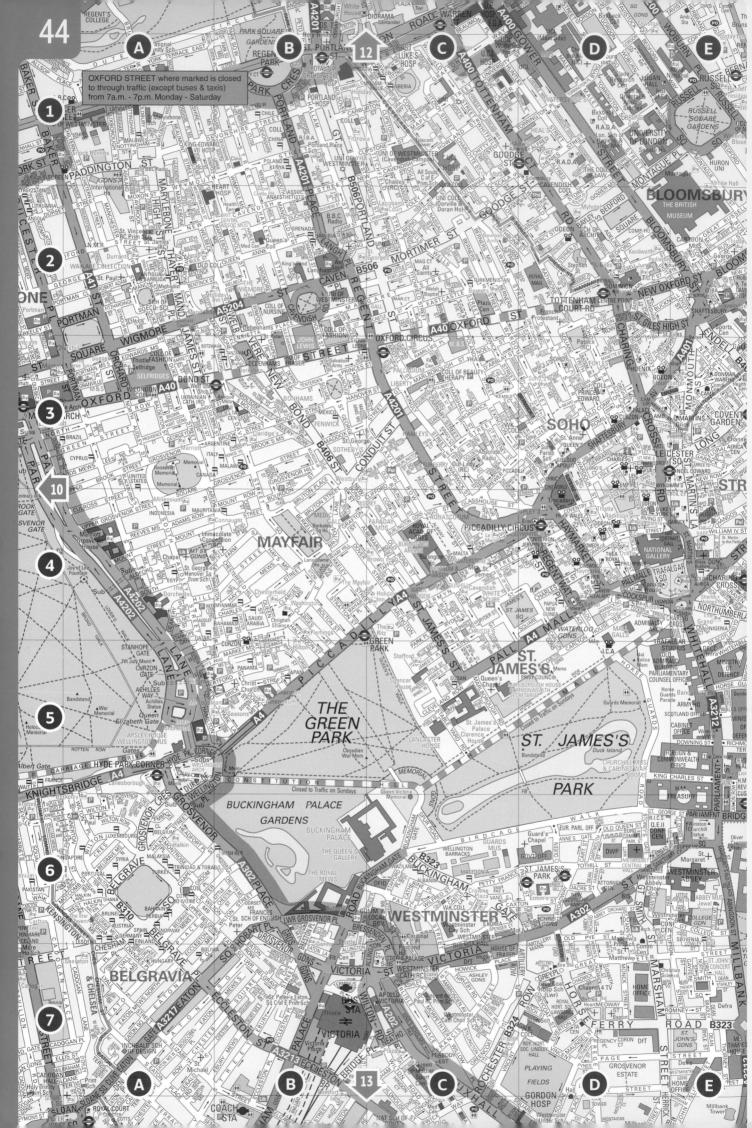

OXFORD STREET where marked is closed to through traffic (except buses & taxis) from 7a.m. - 7p.m. Monday - Saturday

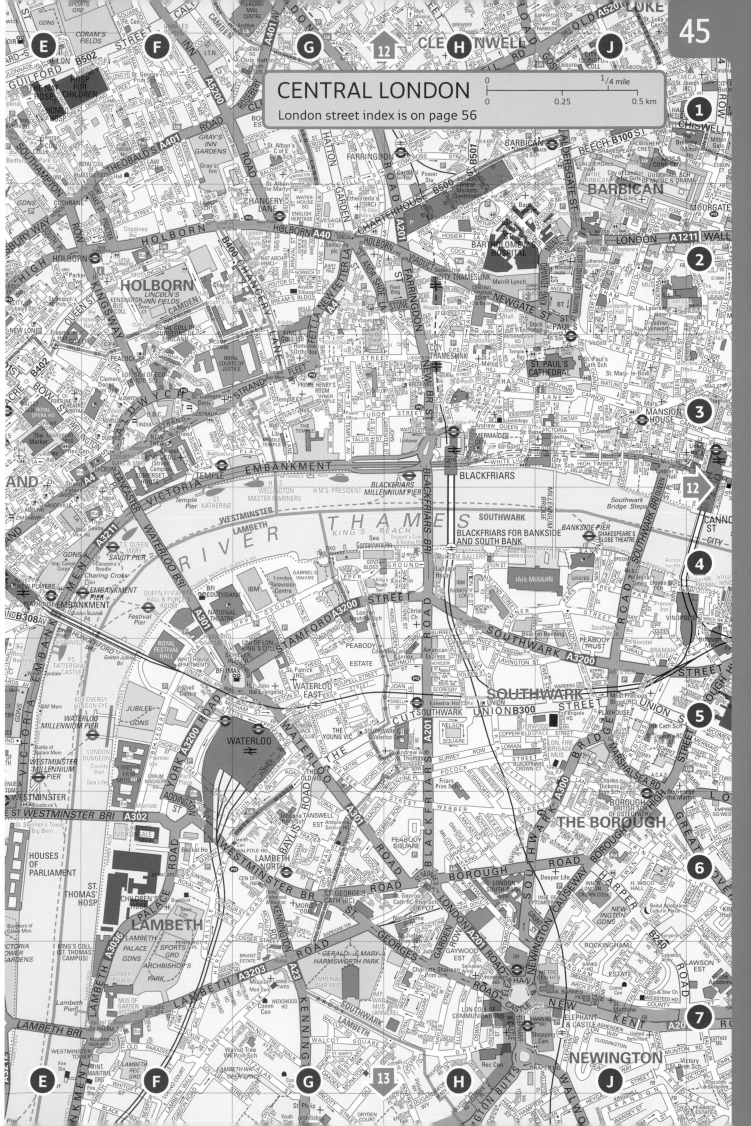

CENTRAL LONDON

London street index is on page 56

1/4 mile

0   0.25   0.5 km

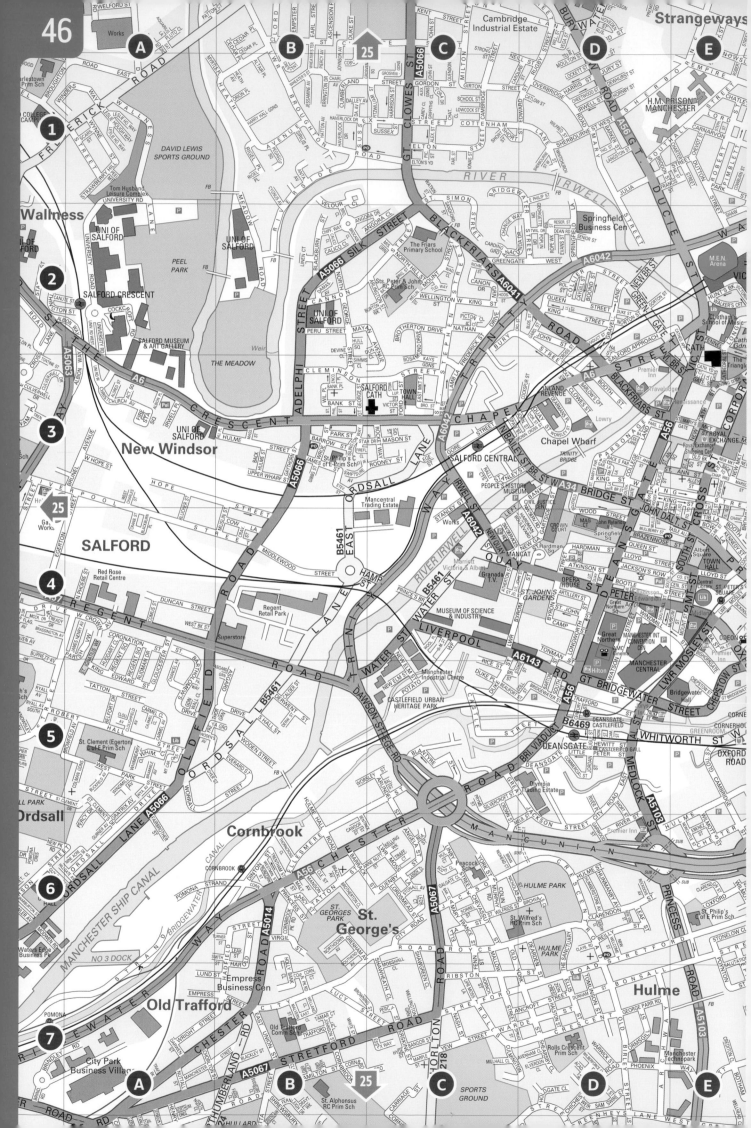

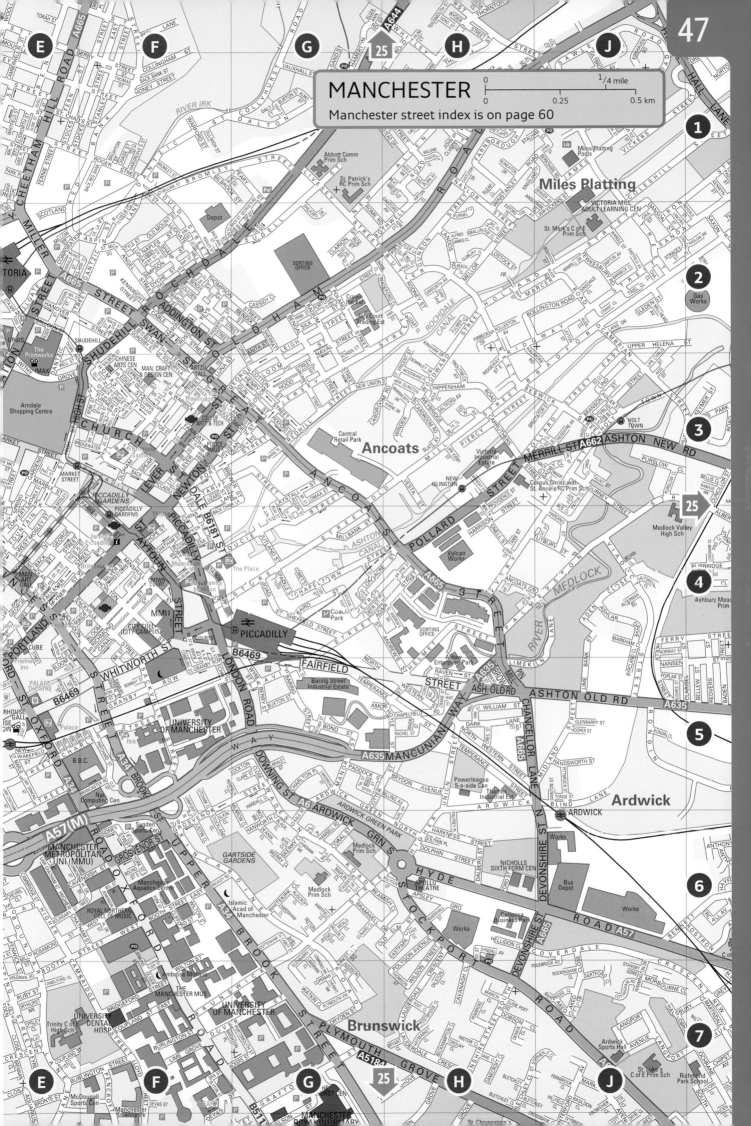

Indexes to street maps

General abbreviations

All	Alley
App	Approach
Arc	Arcade
Av/Ave	Avenue
Bdy	Broadway
Bldgs	Buildings
Br/Bri	Bridge
Cen	Central, Centre
Ch	Church
Chyd	Churchyard
Circ	Circus
Clo	Close
Cor	Corner
Cres	Crescent
Ct	Court
Ctyd	Courtyard
Dr	Drive
E	East
Embk	Embankment
Est	Estate
Flds	Fields
Gdn	Garden
Gdns	Gardens
Grd	Ground
Grn	Green
Gro	Grove
Ho	House
La	Lane
Lo	Lodge
Mans	Mansions
Mkt/Mkts	Market/Markets
Ms	Mews
N	North
Par	Parade
Pas	Passage
Pk	Park
Pl	Place
Rd	Road
Ri	Rise
S	South
Sq	Square
St	Street
St.	Saint
Ter	Terrace
Twr	Tower
W	West
Wf	Wharf
Wk	Walk
Yd	Yard

Place names are shown in bold type

Birmingham street index

A
Abbey St 34 C1
Abbey St N 34 C1
Aberdeen St 34 A2
Acorn Gro 34 C4
Adams St 35 H2
Adderley St 35 H5
Adelaide St 35 G6
Albert St 35 G4
Albion St 34 D3
Alcester St 35 G7
Aldgate Gro 35 E2
Alfred Knight Way 34 E6
Allcock St 35 H5
Allesley St 35 G1
Allison St 35 G5
All Saints Rd 34 C1
All Saints St 34 C2
Alston St 34 B5
Anchor Cl 34 A5
Anchor Cres 34 B1
Anderton St 34 C4
Angelina St 35 G7
Ansbro Cl 34 A2
Arden Gro 34 C5
Arthur Pl 34 D4
Ascot Cl 34 A5
Ashted Lock 35 H3
Ashted Wk 35 J2
Ashton Cft 34 C5
Aston 35 H1
Aston Br 35 G1
Aston Brook St 35 G1
Aston Brook St E 35 H1
Aston Expressway 35 G2
Aston Rd 35 H1
Aston St 35 G3
Attenborough Cl 35 F1
Auckland Rd 35 J7
Augusta St 34 D2
Augustine Gro 34 B1
Austen Pl 34 C7
Autumn Gro 34 E1
Avenue Cl 35 J1
Avenue Rd 35 H1

B
Bacchus Rd 34 A1
Bagot St 35 G2
Balcaskie Cl 34 A7
Banbury St 35 G4
Barford Rd 34 A3
Barford St 35 G6
Barn St 35 H5
Barrack St 35 J3
Barrow Wk 35 F7
Barr St 34 D1
Bartholomew Row 35 G4
Bartholomew St 35 G4
Barwick St 35 F4
Bath Pas 35 F5
Bath Row 34 D6
Bath St 35 F3
Beak St 35 F5
Beaufort Gdns 34 A1
Beaufort Rd 34 B6
Bedford Rd 35 J6
Beeches, The 34 D7
Belgrave Middleway 35 F7
Bell Barn Rd 34 D6
Bellcroft 34 C5
Bellevue 35 F7
Bellis St 34 A6
Belmont Pas 35 J4
Belmont Row 35 H3
Benacre Dr 35 H4
Bennett's Hill 35 F4
Benson Rd 34 A1
Berkley St 34 D5
Berrington Wk 35 G7
Birchall St 35 G6
Bishopsgate St 34 D5
Bishop St 35 G7
Bissell St 35 G7
Blews St 35 G2
Bloomsbury St 35 J2
Blucher St 35 E5
Blyton Cl 34 A3
Boar Hound Cl 34 C3
Bodmin Gro 35 J1
Bolton St 35 J5
Bond Sq 34 C3
Bond St 35 E3
Bordesley 35 J5
Bordesley Circ 35 J6
Bordesley Middleway 35 J7
Bordesley Pk Rd 35 J6
Bordesley St 35 G4
Boulton Middleway 34 D1
Bow St 35 F6
Bowyer St 35 J6
Bracebridge St 35 G1
Bradburn Way 35 J2
Bradford St 35 G5
Branston St 34 D2
Brearley Cl 35 F2
Brearley St 35 F2
Bredon Cft 34 B1
Brewery St 35 G2
Bridge St 34 E5
Bridge St W 35 E1
Brindley Dr 34 D4
Brindley Pl 34 D5
Bristol St 35 F7
Broad St 34 D6
Broadway Plaza 34 C6
Bromley St 35 H5
Bromsgrove St 35 F6
Brookfield Rd 34 B2
Brook St 34 E3
Brook Vw Cl 34 E1
Broom St 35 H6
Brough Cl 35 J1
Browning St 34 C5
Brownsea Dr 35 E5
Brunel St 35 E5
Brunswick St 34 D5
Buckingham St 35 E2
Bullock St 35 H2
Bull St 35 F4

C
Cala Dr 34 C7
Calthorpe Rd 34 C7
Cambridge Rd 34 D4
Camden Dr 34 D3
Camden Gro 34 D3
Camden St 34 B2
Camp Hill 35 J7
Camp Hill Middleway 35 H7
Cannon St 35 F4
Capstone Av 34 C2
Cardigan St 35 H3
Carlisle St 34 A2
Carlyle Rd 34 A5
Caroline St 34 E3
Carpenter Rd 34 C7
Carrs La 35 G4
Carver St 34 C3
Cawdor Cres 34 B6
Cecil St 35 F2
Cemetery La 34 D2
Centenary Sq 34 E4
Central Pk Dr 34 A1
Central Sq 34 E5
Chad Rd 34 A7
Chadsmoor Ter 35 J1
Chad Valley 34 A7
Chamberlain Sq 35 E4
Chancellor's Cl 34 A7
Chandlers Cl 34 B1
Chapel Ho St 35 H5
Chapmans Pas 35 E5
Charles Henry St 35 G7
Charlotte Rd 34 D7
Charlotte St 34 E4
Chatsworth Way 34 E6
Cheapside 35 G6
Cherry St 35 F4
Chester St 35 H1
Chilwell Cft 35 F1
Christchurch Cl 34 A6
Church Rd 34 C7
Church St 35 F3
Civic Cl 34 D4
Clare Dr 34 A7
Clarendon Rd 34 A5
Clark St 34 A5
Claybrook St 35 F6
Clement St 34 D4
Clipper Vw 34 A5
Clissold Cl 35 G7
Clissold St 34 B2
Cliveland St 35 F3
Clyde St 35 H6
Colbrand Gro 35 E7
Coleshill St 35 G4
College St 34 B3
Colmore Circ 35 F3
Colmore Row 35 F4
Commercial St 34 E5
Communication Row 34 D6
Constitution Hill 34 E2
Conybere St 35 G7
Cope St 34 B3
Coplow St 34 A3
Cornwall St 35 E4
Corporation St 35 F4
Coveley Gro 34 B1
Coventry Rd 35 J6
Coventry St 35 G5
Cox St 35 E3
Coxwell Gdns 34 B5
Crabtree Rd 34 B2
Cregoe St 34 E6
Crescent, The 34 C1
Crescent Av 34 C1
Cromwell St 35 J1
Crondal Pl 34 D7
Crosby Cl 34 C4
Cumberland St 34 D5
Curzon Circ 35 H3
Curzon St 35 H4

D
Daisy Rd 34 A5
Dale End 35 G4
Daley Cl 34 C4
Dalton St 35 G4
Darnley Rd 34 B5
Dartmouth Circ 35 G1
Dartmouth Middleway 35 G2
Dart St 35 J6
Darwin St 35 G6
Dean St 35 G5
Deeley Cl 34 D7
Denby Cl 35 J2
Derby St 35 J4
Devonshire Av 34 B1
Devonshire St 34 B1
Digbeth 35 G6
Digbeth 35 G5
Dollman St 35 J3
Dover St 34 B1
Duchess Rd 34 B6
Duddeston Manor Rd 35 J2
Dudley St 35 F5
Dymoke Cl 35 G7

E
Edgbaston 34 B7
Edgbaston St 35 F5
Edmund St 35 E4
Edward St 34 D4
Eldon Rd 34 A5
Elkington St 35 G1
Ellen St 34 C3
Ellis St 35 E5
Elvetham Rd 34 D7
Embassy Dr 34 C6
Emily Gdns 34 A3
Emily St 35 G7
Enfield Rd 34 D6
Enterprise Way 35 G2
Ernest St 35 E6
Erskine St 35 J3
Essex St 35 F6
Essington St 34 D5
Estria Rd 34 C7
Ethel St 35 F4
Exeter Pas 35 F6
Exeter St 35 F6
Eyre St 34 B3
Eyton Cft 35 H7

F
Farmacre 35 J5
Farm Cft 34 D1
Farm St 34 D1
Fawdry St 35 J4
Fazeley St 35 G4
Felsted Way 35 J3
Ferndale Cres 35 H7
Finstall Cl 35 J3
Five Ways 34 C6
Fleet St 34 E4
Floodgate St 35 H5
Florence St 35 E6
Ford St 34 C1
Fore St 35 F4
Forster St 35 H3
Foster Gdns 34 B1
Fox St 35 G4
Francis Rd 34 B5
Francis St 35 J3
Frankfort St 35 F1
Frederick Rd 34 C7
Frederick St 34 D3
Freeman St 35 G4
Freeth St 34 B4
Friston Av 34 C6
Fulmer Wk 34 C4

G
Garrison Circ 35 J4
Garrison La 35 J4
Garrison St 35 J4
Gas St 34 D5
Gas St Basin 34 E5
Geach St 35 F1
Gee St 35 F1
George Rd 34 D7
George St 34 D4
George St W 34 C3
Gibb St 35 H5
Gilby Rd 34 C5
Gilldown Pl 34 D7
Glebeland Cl 34 C5
Gloucester St 35 F5
Glover St 35 J5
Gooch St 35 F7
Gooch St N 35 F6
Goode Av 34 C1
Goodman St 34 C4
Gopsal St 35 H3
Gough St 35 E5
Grafton Rd 35 J7
Graham St 34 D3
Grant St 35 E6
Granville St 34 D5
Graston Cl 34 C5
Great Barr St 35 H5
Great Brook St 35 H3
Great Charles St Queensway 35 E4
Great Colmore St 34 E6
Great Hampton Row 34 E2
Great Hampton St 34 D2
Great King St 34 D1
Great King St N 34 E1
Great Lister St 35 H2
Great Tindal St 34 C4
Greenfield Cres 34 C6
Green St 35 H6
Grenfell Dr 34 A7
Grosvenor St 35 G4
Grosvenor St W 34 C5
Guest Gro 34 D1
Guild Cl 34 B5
Guild Cft 35 F1
Guthrie Cl 35 E1

H
Hack St 35 H5
Hadfield Cft 34 E2
Hagley Rd 34 A6
Hall St 34 E3
Hampshire Dr 34 A7
Hampton St 35 E2
Hanley St 35 F2
Hanwood Cl 35 G7
Harborne Rd 34 A7
Harford St 34 E2
Harmer St 34 C2
Harold Rd 34 A5
Hartley Pl 34 A6
Hatchett St 35 F1
Hawthorn Cl 35 J5
Hawthorne Rd 34 A7
Heath Mill La 35 H5
Heath St S 34 B3
Heaton Dr 34 A7
Heaton St 34 D1
Helena St 34 D4
Heneage St 35 H2
Heneage St W 35 H3
Henley St 35 J7
Henrietta St 35 F3
Henstead St 35 F6
Herne Cl 34 C3
Hickman Gdns 34 B5
Highfield Rd 34 B6
Highgate 35 H7
Highgate St 35 G7
High St 35 G4
Hilden Rd 35 J3
Hill St 35 E4
Hinckley St 35 F5
Hindlow Cl 35 J3
Hindon Sq 34 B7
Hingeston St 34 C2
Hitches La 34 D7
Hobart Cft 35 J2
Hobson Cl 34 B1
Hockley Brook Cl 34 B1
Hockley Cl 35 F1
Hockley Hill 34 D1
Hockley St 34 D2
Holland St 34 D4
Holliday Pas 34 E5
Holliday St 34 E5
Holloway Circ 35 F5
Holloway Head 35 E6
Holt St 35 G2
Holywell Cl 34 B5
Hooper St 34 B3
Hope St 35 F7
Hospital St 35 F1
Howard St 35 E2
Howe St 35 H3
Howford Gro 35 J2
Hubert St 35 H1
Hunter's Vale 34 D1
Huntly Rd 34 B6
Hurdlow Av 34 C2
Hurst St 35 F5
Hylton St 34 D2
Hyssop Cl 35 J2

I
Icknield Port Rd 34 A3
Icknield Sq 34 B4
Icknield St 34 C3
Inge St 35 F6
Inkerman St 35 J3
Irving St 35 E6
Islington Row Middleway 34 C6
Ivy La 35 J4

J
Jackson Cl 35 J7
James St 34 E3
James Watt Queensway 35 G3
Jennens Rd 35 G4
Jewellery Quarter 34 D2
Jinnah Cl 35 G7
John Bright St 35 F5
John Kempe Way 35 H7

K
Keeley St 35 J5
Keepers Cl 34 B1
Kellett Rd 35 H2
Kelsall Cft 34 C4
Kelsey Cl 35 J2
Kemble Cft 35 F7
Kendal Rd 35 J7
Kenilworth Ct 34 A6
Kent St 35 F6
Kent St N 34 B1
Kenyon St 34 E3
Ketley Cft 35 G7
Key Hill 34 D2
Key Hill Dr 34 D2
Kilby Av 34 C4
King Edwards Rd 34 D4
Kingston Rd 35 J5
Kingston Row 34 D4
Kirby Rd 34 A1
Knightstone Av 34 C2
Kyotts Lake Rd 35 J7

L
Ladycroft 34 C5
Ladywell Wk 35 F5
Ladywood 34 C4
Ladywood Middleway 34 B5
Ladywood Rd 34 B5
Lancaster Circ 35 G3
Landor St 35 J4
Langdon St 35 J4
Lansdowne St 34 A2
Latimer Gdns 35 E7
Lawden Rd 35 J6
Lawford Cl 35 J3
Lawford Gro 35 G7
Lawley Middleway 35 H3
Ledbury Cl 34 B5
Ledsam St 34 C4
Lee Bk 35 E7
Lee Bk Middleway 34 D6
Lee Cres 34 D7
Lee Mt 34 D7
Lees St 34 B1
Legge La 34 D3
Legge St 35 G2
Lennox St 35 E1
Leopold St 35 G7
Leslie Rd 34 A5
Leyburn Rd 34 C5
Lighthorne Av 34 C4
Link Rd 34 A3
Lionel St 34 E4
Lister St 35 G3
Little Ann St 35 H5
Little Barr St 35 J4
Little Broom St 35 H6
Little Edward St 35 J5
Little Francis Grn 35 J2
Little Shadwell St 35 F3
Liverpool St 35 H5
Livery St 35 F3
Locke Pl 35 J4
Lodge Rd 34 A1
Lombard St 35 G6
Longleat Way 34 D6
Lord St 35 H2
Louisa St 34 D4
Loveday St 35 F3
Love La 35 G2
Lower Dartmouth St 35 J4
Lower Essex St 35 F6
Lower Loveday St 35 F2
Lower Severn St 35 F5
Lower Temple St 35 F4

Lower Twr St 35 F2
Lower Trinity St 35 H5
Lowe St 35 J6
Ludgate Hill 35 E3
Lytham Cft 35 E6

M
Macdonald St 35 G6
Malcolmson Cl 34 A7
Manchester St 35 F2
Margaret St 35 E4
Mariner Av 34 A5
Marroway St 34 A3
Marshall St 35 E5
Mary Ann St 35 E3
Mary St 34 E3
Mason Way 34 E6
Masshouse La 35 G4
Mearse Cl 34 C2
Melton Dr 34 D7
Meredith Pool Cl 34 A1
Meriden St 35 G5
Merryhill Dr 34 A1
Meyrick Wk 34 A6
Middleway Vw 34 C3
Midford Grn 34 E6
Milford Cft 35 E2
Milk St 35 H5
Miller St 35 F1
Mill La 35 G5
Mill St 35 G2
Milton St 35 F1
Moat La 35 G5
Moland St 35 G2
Montague St 35 J4
Monument Rd 34 B6
Moore's Row 35 H5
Moorings, The 34 B1
Moorsom St 35 F1
Moor St Queensway 35 G4
Moreton St 34 C3
Morville St 34 C5
Mosborough Cres 34 E1
Mosedale Way 35 E6
Moseley Rd 35 H6
Moseley St 35 G6
Moss Ho Cl 34 D6
Mostyn Rd 34 A5
Mott St 34 E2
Mowbray St 35 F7
Murrell Cl 35 F7
Musgrave Rd 34 A1
Myddleton St 34 B3

N
Navigation St 35 E5
Navigation Way 34 B1
Nechells Parkway 35 H3
Needless All 35 F4
Nelson St 34 D4
New Bartholomew St 35 G4
Newbold Cft 35 J1
New Bond St 35 J5

New Canal St 35 G4
Newhall Hill 34 D3
Newhall St 34 E3
Newhope Cl 35 F7
New John St 35 G2
New John St W 34 E1
New Mkt St 35 E4
New Moseley Rd 35 H7
New Spring St 34 C2
New Spring St N 34 B2
New St 35 F4
New Summer St 35 F2
Newton St 35 G4
Newtown 34 E1
Newtown Dr 34 D1
Newtown Middleway 35 F1
New Town Row 35 F1
Niall Cl 34 A7
Noel Rd 34 A5
Norman St 34 A2
Northampton St 34 D2
Northbrook St 34 A3
Northumberland St 35 J3
Northwood St 34 D3
Norton St 34 B1
Nova Scotia St 35 G4
Nursery Rd 34 D1

O
Oak Hill Dr 34 A7
Old Br St 34 D1
Old Camp Hill 35 J6
Old Smithy Pl 34 C1
Old Snow Hill 35 F3
Old Sq 35 F4
Oliver Rd 34 B5
Oliver St 35 J1
Oozells St 34 D5
Orchid Dr 35 E1
Orwell Pas 35 G5
Osler St 34 A5
Oxford St 35 G5

P
Paddocks Grn 34 B2
Pakenham Rd 34 D7
Palmer St 35 J5
Palomino Pl 34 B4
Pannel Cft 35 F1
Parade 34 D4
Paradise Circ 34 E4
Paradise St 35 E4
Parker St 34 A6
Parkfield Cl 34 D7
Park Rd 34 C1
Park Rd S 34 C1
Park St 35 G5
Paxton Rd 34 C2
Peel St 34 A2
Pemberton St 34 D2
Penn St 35 H3
Pershore St 35 F5
Pickford St 35 H5

Pinfold St 35 E4
Pinto Cl 34 B5
Pitsford St 34 C2
Pitt St 35 H3
Plough & Harrow Rd 34 B6
Pool St 35 G1
Pope St 34 C3
Port Hope Rd 35 J7
Powell St 34 D3
Power Cres 34 C5
Price St 35 F3
Princip St 35 F3
Printing Ho St 35 F3
Priory
   Queensway, The 35 G4
Pritchett St 35 F2
Proctor St 35 H2

Q
Quayside 34 B1
Queens Hosp Cl 34 D6
Quigley Av 35 J5

R
Radnor St 34 B1
Radshaw Cl 34 D6
Rake Way 34 D5
Rann Cl 34 C5
Ravenhurst St 35 H6
Rawlins St 34 C5
Rea St 35 G6
Rea St S 35 G6
Rea Ter 35 H5
Rectory Gro 34 A1
Regent Par 34 D3
Regent Pl 34 D3
Regent St 34 D3
Reservoir Retreat 34 B5
Reservoir Rd 34 A5
Richard St 35 H2
Rickman Dr 35 E7
Ridley St 34 E6
River St 35 H5
Rocky La 35 J1
Rodney Cl 34 B4
Rosebery St 34 B2
Roseland Way 34 D6
Rotton Pk St 34 B4
Rupert St 35 H2
Ruston St 34 C5
Ryland Rd 34 D7
Ryland St 34 C5

S
Sadlers Wk 34 B5
St. Andrew's Rd 35 J4
St. Chad's Queensway 35 F3
St. Georges Cl 34 B7
St. Georges St 35 E2
St. Helen's Pas 34 D3
St. James Pl 35 J3
St. James Rd 34 C6
St. Jude's Pas 35 F5

St. Lukes Rd 35 F7
St. Marks Cres 34 C4
St. Marks St 34 C3
St. Martin's Circ
   Queensway 35 F5
St. Martin's Sq 35 G5
St. Martin's St 34 D6
St. Mary's Row 35 F3
St. Paul's Sq 34 E3
St. Phillips Pl 34 C4
St. Stephen's St 35 F1
St. Vincent St 34 C4
St. Vincent St W 34 B5
Salop St 35 H7
Sampson Rd 35 J7
Sampson Rd N 35 J6
Sand Pits 34 C3
Sandy Way 34 D5
Scotland St 34 D4
Sefton Rd 34 A5
Severn St 35 E5
Shadwell St 35 F3
Shawbury Gro 35 H7
Shaw's Pas 35 G4
Sheepcote St 34 C4
Shefford Rd 35 G1
Shepherds Gdns 34 D6
Sherborne Gro 34 C4
Sherborne St 34 C5
Sheringham 34 A6
Sherlock St 35 F7
Shetland Cl 34 B5
Shillcock Gro 35 F2
Shire Cl 34 A4
Shyltons Cft 34 C5
Skinner La 35 G6
Skipton Rd 34 B5
Sloane St 34 D4
Smallbrook
   Queensway 35 F5
Smith St 34 E1
Snow Hill Queensway 35 F3
Soho Pool Way 34 B1
Southacre Av 35 F7
South Rd 35 J7
Spencer St 34 D2
Spooner Cft 35 F7
Springbank Rd 34 E7
Springfield St 34 B4
Spring Gro Gdns 34 A1
Spring Hill 34 B3
Spring Hill Pas 34 C3
Spring St 35 E7
Stainsby Av 34 D1
Stanhope Rd 35 G7
Staniforth St 35 G2
Star Hill 34 D7
Station St 35 F5
Steelhouse La 35 F3
Stephenson Pl 35 F5
Stephenson St 35 F4
Steward St 34 B3
Stirling Rd 34 A6

Stoke Way 34 D5
Stone Rd 35 E7
Stone Yd 35 H5
Stour St 34 B3
Stratford Pl 35 H7
Stratford Rd 35 J7
Stratford St N 35 J7
Suffolk St
   Queensway 35 E5
Sugden Gro 35 F6
Summer Cft 35 F1
Summerfield Rd 34 A3
Summer Hill Rd 34 C3
Summer Hill St 34 D4
Summer Hill Ter 34 D3
Summer La 35 F3
Summer Rd 34 E7
Summer Row 34 E4
Sutton St 35 E6
Swallow St 35 E5

T
Talbot St 34 A1
Temple Pas 35 F4
Temple Row 35 F4
Temple Row W 35 F4
Temple St 35 F4
Tenby St 34 D3
Tenby St N 34 D3
Tennant St 34 D6
Theatre App 35 F5
Theresa Rd 35 J7
Thomas St 35 G1
Thorp St 35 F6
Tower St 35 F2
Townsend Way 34 D4
Trent St 35 H5
Trinity Ter 35 J6

U
Unett St 34 E1
Union Pas 35 F4
Union St 35 F4
Upper Dean St 35 F5
Upper Gough St 35 E6
Upper Marshall St 35 E5
Upper Trinity St 35 H5
Uxbridge St 35 E1

V
Vaughton St 35 G7
Vaughton St S 35 G7
Vauxhall Gro 35 J3
Vauxhall Rd 35 J3
Venture Way 35 H2
Verbena Gdns 35 J2
Vere St 35 F7
Vernolds Cft 35 F6
Vesey St 35 F3
Viaduct St 35 J4
Vicarage Rd 34 B6
Victoria Sq 35 E4
Victor Rd 34 A1

Vittoria St 34 D3
Vyse St 34 D3

W
Walter St 35 J1
Wardlow Rd 35 J2
Ward St 35 F2
Warner St 35 H6
Warstone La 34 C3
Warstone Par E 34 D2
Warwick Pas 35 F4
Warwick St 35 H6
Washington St 34 E5
Waterloo St 35 E4
Waterside Dr 34 A1
Waterside Vw 34 B2
Water St 35 E3
Waterworks Rd 34 A5
Watery La Middleway 35 J4
Weaman St 35 F3
Well La 35 G5
Well St 34 D2
Westbourne Cres 34 C7
Westbourne Gdns 34 B7
Westbourne Rd 34 A7
Western Rd 34 B3
West Grn Cl 34 D7
Westhorpe Gro 34 E1
Westley St 35 J5
Wharf, The 34 E5
Wharf La 34 C1
Wharfside St 35 E5
Wharf St 34 B1
Wheeler St 35 E1
Wheeley's La 34 D6
Whitehouse St 35 H1
Whitmore St 34 C1
Whittall St 35 F3
Wiggin St 34 A4
William Booth La 35 F3
William Henry St 35 J1
William St 34 D6
William St N 35 F2
Willow Gdns 34 A3
Windmill St 35 F6
Windrush Way 35 E7
Windsor St 35 H2
Windsor St S 35 H3
Winson Grn 34 A1
Witton St 35 J4
Woodcock St 35 G3
Woodcote Way 34 B2
Woodview Dr 34 E7
Wrentham St 35 F6
Wrottesley St 35 F5
Wyndham Rd 34 A6
Wynn St 35 E6

Y
Yew Tree Rd 34 D6

Edinburgh street index

A
Abbeyhill 37 J3
Abbeyhill 37 J3
Abbeyhill Cres 37 H4
Abbey La 37 J3
Abbeymount 37 J3
Abbey Strand 37 J4
Abbey St 37 J3
Abercromby Pl 37 F3
Admiral Ter 36 D7
Ainslie Pl 36 D3
Albany La 37 F2
Albany St 37 F3
Albany St La 37 F3
Albert St 37 H1
Albion Gdns 37 J2
Albion Pl 37 J2
Albion Rd 37 J2
Albion Ter 37 J2
Alfred Pl 37 J7
Allanfield 37 H2
Allanfield Pl 37 H2
Allan St 36 D2
Alva Pl 37 J3
Alva St 36 D4
Angle Pk Ter 36 B7
Annandale St 37 G1
Annandale St La 37 G2
Ann St 36 D3
Arboretum Av 36 D2
Arboretum Pl 36 D1

Archibald Pl 37 F6
Arden St 37 F7
Ardmillan Pl 36 B7
Ardmillan Ter 36 B7
Argyle Pk Ter 37 F7
Argyle Pl 37 F7
Arthur St 37 H1
Arthur St La 37 H1
Atholl Cres 36 D5
Atholl Cres La 36 D5
Avondale Pl 36 D1

B
Back Dean 36 B4
Bakehouse Cl 37 H4
Balbirnie Pl 36 A5
Balmoral Pl 36 D2
Bank St 37 F4
Barclay Pl 36 E7
Barony St 37 F2
Beaverbank Pl 37 F1
Beaverhall Rd 37 F1
Bedford St 36 D2
Belford Av 36 A3
Belford Br 36 C4
Belford Gdns 36 A3
Belford Ms 36 C4
Belford Pk 36 B4
Belford Pl 36 B4
Belford Rd 36 C4
Belgrave Cres 36 C3

Belgrave Cres La 36 C3
Belgrave Ms 36 C3
Belgrave Pl 36 C3
Bellevue 37 F2
Bellevue Cres 37 F2
Bellevue Gdns 37 G1
Bellevue Gro 37 G2
Bellevue La 37 F2
Bellevue Pl 37 F2
Bellevue Rd 37 G2
Bellevue St 37 G2
Bellevue Ter 37 F2
Bell Pl 36 E1
Bells Brae 36 C4
Bell's Mills 36 B4
Bernard Ter 37 H6
Blacket Av 37 H7
Blacket Pl 37 H7
Blackfriars St 37 G4
Blackwood Cres 37 H7
Blair St 37 G4
Blandfield 37 G1
Boat Grn 37 F1
Borthwick Pl 36 B5
Bothwell St 37 J2
Bowmont Pl 37 H6
Boyd's Entry 37 G4
Brandfield St 36 D6
Brandon St 37 E2

Brandon Ter 37 E2
Bread St 36 E5
Bridge Pl 36 D2
Briery Bauks 37 H5
Brighton St 37 G5
Bristo Pl 37 F5
Bristo Port 37 F5
Brougham Pl 37 E6
Brougham St 36 E6
Broughton 37 F1
Broughton Mkt 37 F3
Broughton Pl 37 G2
Broughton Pl La 37 G2
Broughton Rd 37 F1
Broughton St 37 G2
Broughton St La 37 G3
Brown's Cl 37 H4
Brown St 37 H5
Brunswick Rd 37 H2
Brunswick St 37 H2
Brunswick St La 37 H2
Brunton Ter 37 J3
Bruntsfield Av 36 D7
Bruntsfield Cres 36 E7
Bruntsfield Gdns 36 D7
Bruntsfield Ter 36 D7
Bryson Rd 36 B7
Buccleuch Pl 37 G6
Buccleuch St 37 G6
Buccleuch Ter 37 G6
Buchanan St 37 H1

Buckingham Ter 36 C3

C
Caledonian Cres 36 C6
Caledonian Pl 36 C6
Caledonian Rd 36 C6
Calton Hill 37 G3
Calton Rd 37 G3
Cambridge Av 37 H1
Cambridge Gdns 37 H1
Cambridge St 36 E5
Campbell's Cl 37 H4
Candlemaker Row 37 F5
Canning St 36 D5
Canning St La 36 D5
Canongate 37 G4
Canon La 37 E2
Canonmills 37 E1
Canon St 37 E1
Carberry Pl 36 B5
Carlton St 36 D3
Carlton Ter 37 H3
Carlton Ter Brae 37 J3
Carlton Ter La 37 H3
Carlton Ter Ms 37 H3
Carlton Wynd 37 H4
Carlyle Pl 37 J3
Carnegie St 37 H5
Carrington Rd 36 B2
Castle Hill 37 F4
Castle St 36 E4

Castle Ter 36 E4
Cathcart Pl 36 B6
Cathedral La 37 G3
Causewayside 37 H7
Chalmers Cres 37 F7
Chalmers St 37 F5
Chambers St 37 F5
Chapel St 37 G5
Charles St 37 G5
Charlotte La 36 D4
Charlotte Sq 36 D4
Chester St 36 C4
Cheyne St 36 D2
Chuckie Pend 36 D5
Circus Gdns 36 E3
Circus La 36 E3
Circus Pl 36 E3
Claremont Bk 37 F2
Claremont Cres 37 F1
Claremont Gro 37 F1
Clarence St 36 E2
Clarendon Cres 36 C3
Clerk St 37 G6
Coates 36 B5
Coates Cres 36 D5
Coates Gdns 36 C5
Cochran Ter 37 F2
Cockburn St 37 F4
Coffin La 36 B6
Collins Pl 36 D2
Coltbridge Av 36 A5

Coltbridge Gdns	36 A5	Dunedin St	37 F1	Green St	37 G2	King's Stables La	37 E5
Coltbridge Millside	36 A5	Dunrobin Pl	36 D2	Greyfriars Pl	37 F5	King's Stables Rd	36 E4
Coltbridge Ter	36 A5			Grigor Av	36 A1	Kirkhill Rd	37 J7
Coltbridge Vale	36 A5	**E**		Grigor Dr	36 A1	Kyle Pl	37 J3
Colville Pl	36 D2	Earl Grey St	36 E5	Grigor Gdns	36 A1		
Comely Bk	36 C2	East Adam St	37 G5	Grigor Ter	36 A1	**L**	
Comely Bk	36 B2	East Castle Rd	36 C7	Grindlay St	36 E5	Lady Lawson St	37 E5
Comely Bk Av	36 C2	East Claremont St	37 F2	Grosvenor Cres	36 C5	Lady Menzies Pl	37 J3
Comely Bk Gro	36 C3	East		Grosvenor Gdns	36 C5	Lady Wynd	37 F5
Comely Bk Pl	36 C2	Crosscauseway	37 G6	Grosvenor St	36 C5	Lamb's Cl	37 H6
Comely Bk Pl Ms	36 C2	Easter Dalry Dr	36 B6	Grove St	36 D5	Lansdowne Cres	36 C5
Comely Bk Rd	36 C2	Easter Dalry Pl	36 B5	Gullan's Cl	37 G4	Lauderdale St	37 E7
Comely Bk Row	36 C2	Easter Dalry Rigg	36 B6	Guthrie St	37 G5	Lauder Rd	37 G7
Comely Bk St	36 C2	Easter Dalry Rd	36 C5			Lauriston Gdns	37 E5
Comely Bk Ter	36 C2	Easter Dalry Wynd	36 C6	**H**		Lauriston Pk	37 E5
Conference Sq	36 D5	Easter Rd	37 J3	Haddon's Ct	37 G5	Lauriston Pl	37 E6
Cornwallis Pl	37 F2	East Fettes Av	36 C1	Hailes St	36 E6	Lauriston St	37 E5
Cornwall St	36 E5	East		Halmyre St	37 J1	Lawnmarket	37 F4
Cowan's Cl	37 G6	Fountainbridge	36 E5	Hamilton Pl	36 D2	Leamington Rd	36 D6
Cowgate	37 F5	East London St	37 G2	Hamilton's Folly Ms	37 H6	Leamington Ter	36 D6
Cowgatehead	37 F5	East Mkt St	37 G4	Hammermen's Entry	37 H4	Learmonth Av	36 B2
Craigleith	36 A2	East Montgomery Pl	37 H2	Hanover St	37 F3	Learmonth Cres	36 B3
Craigleith Hill		East Newington Pl	37 H7	Harden Pl	36 C7	Learmonth Gdn La	36 C3
Cres	36 A2	East Parkside	37 H6	Hardwell Cl	37 H6	Learmonth Gdns	36 C3
Craigleith Hill		East Preston St	37 H7	Harrismith Pl	37 J2	Learmonth Gdns Ms	36 C3
Gdns	36 A2	East Preston St La	37 H7	Harrison La	36 B7	Learmonth Gro	36 C3
Craigleith Hill Ln	36 A2	East Sciennes St	37 G7	Harrison Rd	36 B7	Learmonth Pl	36 C2
Craigleith Hill		East Scotland St La	37 F2	Hartington Gdns	36 D7	Learmonth Ter	36 C3
Row	36 A2	East Silvermills La	36 E2	Hartington Pl	36 D7	Learmonth Ter La	36 C3
Cranston St	37 G4	Edina Pl	37 J2	Hart St	37 G2	Learmonth Vw	36 C3
Crarae Av	36 A4	Edina St	37 J2	Hatton Pl	37 F7	Leith St	37 G3
Crewe Rd S	36 A1	Edinburgh Quay	36 D6	Haugh St	36 D2	Leith Wk	37 G3
Crichton St	37 G5	Eglinton Cres	36 B5	Hawthornbank La	36 C4	Lennox St	36 C3
Croft-an-Righ	37 J3	Eildon St	36 E1	Hawthornden Pl	37 H1	Lennox St La	36 C3
Cumberland St	36 E2	Eildon Ter	36 E1	Haymarket	36 C5	Leslie Pl	36 D3
Cumberland St		Elder St	37 F3	Haymarket Ter	36 B5	Leven St	36 E6
N E La	37 E2	Elgin St	37 H2	Haymarket Yards	36 B5	Leven Ter	37 E6
Cumberland St		Elgin St N	37 J2	Henderland Rd	36 A5	Liddesdale Pl	36 E1
N W La	37 E2	Elgin Ter	37 J2	Henderson Pl	37 E2	Little King St	37 G3
Cumberland St		Elliot St	37 J2	Henderson Pl La	37 E2	Livingstone Pl	37 G7
S E La	37 E2	Elm Row	37 G2	Henderson Row	36 E2	Lochend Cl	37 H4
Cumberland St		Eton Ter	36 D3	Henderson Ter	36 B7	Lochrin Pl	36 E6
S W La	37 E2	Ettrickdale Pl	36 E1	Heriot Br	37 F5	Logan St	37 F2
Cumin Pl	37 G7	Ettrick Gro	36 C7	Heriot Hill Ter	37 F2	Logie Grn Gdns	37 F1
		Eyre Cres	37 E2	Heriot Pl	37 F5	Logie Grn Ln	37 F1
D		Eyre Pl	37 E2	Heriot Row	36 E3	Logie Grn Rd	37 F1
Dalkeith Rd	37 H6	Eyre Ter	37 E2	Hermits Cft	37 H6	Logie Mill	37 F1
Dalmeny St	37 H1			High Riggs	36 E5	London Rd	37 J3
Dalry	36 B6	**F**		High Sch Wynd	37 G4	London St	37 F2
Dalry Gait	36 C5	Fettes Av	36 B2	High Sch Yards	37 G5	Lonsdale Ter	37 E6
Dalry Pl	36 C5	Fettes Row	37 E2	High St	37 F4	Lorne Pl	37 J1
Dalry Rd	36 B7	Findhorn Pl	37 G7	Hill Pl	37 G5	Lorne Sq	37 J1
Damside	36 C4	Fingal Pl	37 F7	Hillside Cres	37 H2	Lorne St	37 J1
Danube St	36 D3	Forbes St	37 H6	Hillside St	37 H2	Lothian Rd	36 D4
Darnaway St	36 D3	Forres St	36 D3	Hill Sq	37 G5	Lothian St	37 G5
Davidson Pk	36 A1	Forrest Hill	37 F5	Hill St	36 E3	Lower Gilmore Pl	36 D6
Davidson Rd	36 A1	Forrest Rd	37 F5	Hill St La N	36 E3	Lower London Rd	37 J3
Davie St	37 G5	Forth St	37 G3	Hill St La S	36 E4	Lutton Pl	37 H6
Dean Bk La	36 D2	Fountainbridge	36 D6	Holyrood Gait	37 H4	Lynedoch Pl La	36 C4
Dean Br	36 C3	Fowler Ter	36 C6	Holyrood Pk Rd	37 H7	Lyne St	37 J3
Deanhaugh St	36 D2	Frederick St	37 E3	Holyrood Rd	37 G4		
Dean Pk Cres	36 C3			Home St	36 E6	**M**	
Dean Pk Ms	36 C2	**G**		Hope Pk Cres	37 G6	McDonald Pl	37 G1
Dean Pk St	36 C2	Gardner's Cres	36 D5	Hope Pk Ter	37 G6	McDonald Rd	37 G1
Dean Path	36 C3	Garscube Ter	36 A4	Hope St	36 D4	McDonald St	37 G1
Dean St	36 D3	Gayfield La	37 G2	Hope St La	36 D4	Mackenzie Pl	36 D3
Dean Ter	36 D3	Gayfield Pl La	37 G2	Hopetoun Cres	37 G2	McLeod St	36 A6
Dean Village	36 B4	Gayfield Sq	37 G2	Hopetoun St	37 G2	McNeill St	36 D6
Devon Pl	36 B5	Gayfield St	37 G2	Horne Ter	36 C6	Magdala Cres	36 B5
Dewar Pl	36 D5	Gayfield St La	37 G2	Horse Wynd	37 J4	Magdala Ms	36 B5
Dewar Pl La	36 D5	Gentle's Entry	37 H4	Howden St	37 G5	Malta Grn	36 D2
Dicksonfield	37 H2	George IV Br	37 F4	Howe St	37 E3	Malta Ter	36 D2
Dickson St	37 J1	George Sq	37 F6	Hugh Miller Pl	36 D2	Manor Pl	36 C4
Distillery La	36 C5	George Sq La	37 F6	Hunter Sq	37 G4	Mansionhouse Rd	37 G7
Dorset Pl	36 C7	George St	36 E4	Huntingdon Pl	37 G2	Marchhall Cres	37 J7
Douglas Cres	36 B4	Gibson Ter	36 C6	Hutton Rd	37 H4	Marchhall Pl	37 J7
Douglas Gdns	36 C4	Gifford Pk	37 G6			Marchhall Rd	37 J7
Douglas Gdns Ms	36 C4	Gillespie Cres	36 D6	**I**		Marchmont Cres	37 F7
Doune Ter	36 D3	Gillespie St	36 D6	India Pl	36 D3	Marchmont Rd	37 F6
Downfield Pl	36 B6	Gilmore Pk	36 D6	India St	36 E3	Marchmont St	37 E7
Drumdryan St	36 E6	Gilmore Pl	36 D7	Infirmary St	37 G5	Market St	37 F4
Drummond Pl	37 F2	Gilmour St	37 G5	**Inverleith**	36 C1	Marshall's Ct	37 G3
Drummond St	37 G5	Gladstone Ter	37 G7	Inverleith Gro	36 C1	Marshall St	37 G5
Drumsheugh		Glencairn Cres	36 C5	Inverleith Pl	36 C1	Maryfield	37 J3
Gdns	36 C4	Glenfinlas St	36 D4	Inverleith Ter	36 D1	Maryfield Pl	37 J3
Drum Ter	37 J2	Glengyle Ter	36 E6	Inverleith Ter La	36 E1	Meadow La	37 G6
Dryden Gait	37 G1	Glenogle Rd	36 D2	Iona St	37 H1	Meadow Pl	37 F7
Dryden Gdns	37 G1	Glen St	37 E5	Ivy Ter	36 A7	Melgund Ter	37 E6
Dryden Pl	37 J7	Gloucester La	36 D3			Melville Dr	37 E6
Dryden St	37 G1	Gloucester Pl	36 D3	**J**		Melville Pl	36 C4
Dryden Ter	37 G1	Gloucester Sq	36 D3	Jamaica St	36 E3	Melville St	36 C4
Dublin Meuse	37 F3	Gloucester St	36 D3	Jamaica St N La	36 E3	Melville St La	36 D4
Dublin St	37 F2	Gorgie Rd	36 A7	Jamaica St S La	36 E3	Melville Ter	37 G7
Dublin St La N	37 F2	Grange Rd	37 F7	Jameson Pl	37 H1	Merchant St	37 F5
Dublin St La S	37 F3	Granville Ter	36 C7	Jeffrey St	37 G4	Merchiston Av	36 C7
Duff Rd	36 B6	Grassmarket	37 F5	Johnston Ter	37 E5	Merchiston Gro	36 A7
Duff St	36 B6	Great King St	37 E3			Merchiston Ms	36 C7
Duff St La	36 B6	Great Stuart St	36 D4	**K**		Merchiston Pk	36 C7
Dumbiedykes Rd	37 H5	Greenhill Ct	36 E7	Keir St	37 F5	Mertoun Pl	36 C7
Dunbar St	36 E5	Greenhill Gdns	36 E7	Kemp Pl	36 D1	Meuse La	37 F4
Dundas St	37 E2	Greenhill Pl	36 E7	Kerr St	36 D2	Middlefield	37 H1
Dundee St	36 B7	Greenhill Ter	36 E7	Kew Ter	36 A5	Millerfield Pl	37 G7
Dundee Ter	36 B7	Greenside La	37 G3	Kimmerghame Dr	36 A1	Miller Row	36 C4
Dundonald St	37 F2	Greenside Row	37 G3	Kimmerghame Vw	36 A1	Milton St	37 J3
						Minto St	37 H7

Moncrieff Ter	37 G7	Polwarth Cres	36 C7				
Montague St	37 H6	Polwarth Gdns	36 C7				
Montgomery St	37 G2	Polwarth Pk	36 C7				
Montgomery St La	37 G2	Polwarth Pl	36 C7				
Montpelier	36 D7	Ponton St	36 D6				
Montpelier Pk	36 D7	Portgower Pl	36 D2				
Montpelier Ter	36 D7	Port Hamilton	36 D6				
Montrose Ter	37 J3	Potterrow	37 G5				
Moray Pl	36 D3	Powderhall Rd	37 F1				
Morrison Circ	36 C5	Priestfield Rd N	37 J7				
Morrison Cres	36 D5	Primrose Ter	36 B7				
Morrison Link	36 D5	Princes St	36 D4				
Morrison St	36 C5						
Mound, The	37 F4	**Q**					
Mound Pl	37 F4	Queen's Dr	37 H5				
Multrees Wk	37 F3	Queensferry Rd	36 B3				
Murano Pl	37 H2	Queensferry St	36 D4				
Murdoch Ter	36 C6	Queensferry St La	36 D4				
Murieston Cres	36 B6	Queensferry Ter	36 B5				
Murieston Cres La	36 B6	Queen St	36 E3				
Murieston La	36 B7	Queen St Gdns E	37 F3				
Murieston Pl	36 B6	Queen St Gdns W	37 E3				
Murieston Rd	36 B6						
Murieston Ter	36 B6	**R**					
Myrtle Ter	36 B7	Raeburn Ms	36 D2				
		Raeburn Pl	36 D2				
N		Raeburn St	36 D2				
Napier Rd	36 C7	Ramsay Gdn	37 F4				
Nelson St	37 F2	Ramsay La	37 F4				
New Arthur Pl	37 H5	Randolph Cres	36 D4				
Newington Rd	37 H7	Randolph La	36 D4				
New John's Pl	37 H6	Randolph Pl	36 D4				
New Skinner's Cl	37 G4	Rankeillor St	37 H6				
New St	37 G4	Ravelston Dykes	36 A4				
Newton St	36 A7	Ravelston Pk	36 A4				
Nicolson Sq	37 G5	Ravelston Ter	36 B4				
Nicolson St	37 G5	Regent Pl	37 J3				
Niddry St	37 G4	Regent Rd	37 G3				
Niddry St S	37 G5	Regent Ter	37 H3				
Nightingale Way	37 F6	Regent Ter Ms	37 H3				
North Bk St	37 F4	Register Pl	37 F3				
North Br	37 G4	Reid's Cl	37 H4				
North Castle St	36 E3	Reid Ter	36 D2				
North Charlotte St	36 D3	Richmond La	37 G5				
North Clyde St La	37 F3	Richmond Pl	37 G5				
Northcote St	36 B6	Richmond Ter	36 C5				
North E Circ Pl	36 E3	Riego St	36 E5				
North Pk Ter	36 C2	Rillbank Cres	37 G7				
North Richmond St	37 G5	Rillbank Ter	37 G7				
North St. Andrew La	37 F3	Rintoul Pl	36 D2				
North St. Andrew St	37 F3	Ritchie Pl	36 B7				
North St. David St	37 F3	Robertson Av	36 A7				
Northumberland		Robertson Gait	36 A7				
Pl La	37 F3	Robertson's Cl	37 G5				
Northumberland St	37 E3	Rodney Pl	37 F2				
Northumberland		Rodney St	37 F1				
St N E La	37 F3	Romero Pl	37 J7				
Northumberland		Rosebank Cotts	36 D5				
St N W La	37 E3	Rosebery Cres	36 C5				
Northumberland		Rosebery Cres La	36 C5				
St S E La	37 F3	Roseburn Av	36 A5				
Northumberland		Roseburn Cliff	36 A5				
St S W La	37 E3	Roseburn Dr	36 A5				
North Werber Pk	36 A1	Roseburn Gdns	36 A5				
North Werber Pl	36 B1	Roseburn Maltings	36 A5				
North W Circ Pl	36 D3	Roseburn Pl	36 A5				
Norton Pk	37 J2	Roseburn Ter	36 A5				
		Rosemount Bldgs	36 D6				
O		Roseneath Pl	37 F7				
Old Broughton	37 F2	Roseneath St	37 F7				
Old Fishmarket Cl	37 G4	Roseneath Ter	37 F7				
Old Tolbooth Wynd	37 H4	Rose St	36 E4				
Orchard Bk	36 A3	Rose St N La	36 E4				
Orchard Brae	36 B2	Rose St S La	36 E4				
Orchard Brae Av	36 B3	Rossie Pl	37 J2				
Orchard Brae Gdns	36 B3	Rosslyn Cres	37 G1				
Orchard Brae		Rosslyn Ter	37 H1				
Gdns W	36 B3	Rothesay Ms	36 C4				
Orchard Brae W	36 B2	Rothesay Pl	36 C4				
Orchard Cres	36 A3	Rothesay Ter	36 C4				
Orchard Dr	36 A3	Roxburgh Pl	37 G5				
Orchard Gro	36 B2	Roxburgh St	37 G5				
Orchard Pl	36 B2	Royal Circ	36 E3				
Orchard Rd	36 A3	Royal Cres	37 F2				
Orchard Rd S	36 A3	Royal Ter	37 G3				
Orchard Ter	36 A3	Russell Gdns	36 A5				
Orwell Pl	36 C6	Russell Rd	36 A5				
Orwell Ter	36 C6	Rutland Ct La	36 D5				
Oxford St	37 H6	Rutland Sq	36 D4				
Oxford Ter	36 C3	Rutland St	36 D4				
P		**S**					
Palmerston Pl	36 C4	St. Andrew Sq	37 F3				
Panmure Pl	37 E6	St. Bernard's Cres	36 D3				
Papermill Wynd	37 G1	St. Bernard's Row	36 D2				
Parkside St	37 H6	St. Catherine's Pl	37 J7				
Parkside Ter	37 H6	St. Clair Av	37 J1				
Parliament Sq	37 F4	St. Clair Pl	37 J1				
Pembroke Pl	36 B5	St. Clair Rd	37 J1				
Perth St	36 E2	St. Clair St	37 J1				
Picardy Pl	37 G3	St. Colme St	36 D4				
Pilrig Gdns	37 G1	St. David's Pl	36 D5				
Pilrig Glebe	37 H1	St. David's Ter	36 D5				
Pleasance	37 G5	St. Giles St	37 F4				

St. James Pl 37 G3
St. James Sq 37 G3
St. John's Hill 37 H5
St. John St 37 H4
St. Leonard's Bk 37 H6
St. Leonard's Hill 37 H6
St. Leonard's La 37 H6
St. Leonard's St 37 H6
St. Mary's St 37 G4
St. Patrick Sq 37 G6
St. Stephen Pl 36 D2
St. Stephen St 36 D3
St. Vincent St 36 E2
Salisbury Ms 37 H7
Salisbury Pl 37 H7
Salisbury Rd 37 H7
Saunders St 36 D3
Saxe Coburg Pl 36 D2
Saxe Coburg St 36 D2
Sciennes 37 G7
Sciennes Gdns 37 G7
Sciennes Hill Pl 37 G7
Sciennes Ho Pl 37 G7
Sciennes Pl 37 G7
Sciennes Rd 37 F7
Scotland St 37 F2
Semple St 36 D5
Seton Pl 37 G7
Shandwick Pl 36 D5
Shaw's Pl 37 H1
Shaw's St 37 H1
Shaw's Ter 37 H1
Shrub Pl La 37 H1
Sienna Gdns 37 G7

Silvermills 36 E2
Simon Sq 37 G5
Simpson Loan 37 F6
Sinclair Cl 36 A7
Sinclair Gdns 36 A7
Sinclair Pl 36 A7
Sloan St 37 J1
Smithfield St 36 A7
South Br 37 G4
South Charlotte St 36 E4
South Clerk St 37 H6
South Coll St 37 G5
South E Circ Pl 36 E3
South Gray's Cl 37 G4
South Learmonth Av 36 C3
South Learmonth Gdns 36 C3
South Lorne Pl 37 J1
South Oxford St 37 H7
South St. Andrew St 37 F3
South St. David St 37 F3
South Sloan St 37 J1
Spence St 37 J7
Spey St 37 H1
Spey St La 37 H1
Spey Ter 37 H1
Spittal St 36 E5
Spottiswoode Rd 37 E7
Spottiswoode St 37 F7
Spring Gdns 37 J3
Springwell Pl 36 B6
Stafford St 36 D4
Stanhope Pl 36 B5
Stanhope St 36 B5

Stevenlaw's Cl 37 G4
Stewart Ter 36 A7
Stockbridge 36 E2
Succoth Gdns 36 A4
Succoth Pl 36 A4
Summer Bk 37 F2
Summerhall 37 G6
Summerhall Sq 37 H7
Sunbury Ms 36 C4
Sunbury Pl 36 C4
Sunbury St 36 C4
Sunnyside 37 J2
Sutherland St 36 B5
Sylvan Pl 37 G7

T
Tantallon Pl 37 G7
Tarvit St 36 E6
Tay St 36 C7
Temple Pk Cres 36 C7
Terrars Cft 37 H6
Teviotdale Pl 36 D1
Teviot Pl 37 F5
Thirlestane Rd 37 E7
Thistle Pl 36 C7
Thistle St 37 E3
Thistle St N E La 37 F3
Thistle St N W La 37 E3
Thistle St S W La 37 E3
Thornybauk 36 E6
Torphichen St 36 D5
Tron Sq 37 G4
Tynecastle La 36 B7
Tynecastle Ter 36 A7

Tytler Gdns 37 J3

U
Union St 37 G2
Upper Bow 37 F4
Upper Coltbridge Ter 36 A4
Upper Damside 36 C4
Upper Dean Ter 36 D3
Upper Gilmore Pl 36 D6
Upper Gilmore Ter 36 D6
Upper Gray St 37 H7
Upper Gro Pl 36 D6

V
Valleyfield St 36 E6
Veitch's Sq 36 D2
Victoria St 37 F5
Viewcraig Gdns 37 H4
Viewcraig St 37 H5
Viewforth 36 C6
Viewforth Gdns 36 D7
Viewforth Sq 36 D7
Viewforth Ter 36 D7

W
Walker St 36 C4
Wardlaw Pl 36 A7
Wardlaw St 36 A7
Warrender Pk Cres 36 E7
Warrender Pk Rd 36 E7
Warrender Pk Ter 37 E7
Warriston Cres 37 E1
Warriston Rd 37 E1
Washington La 36 B6

Waterloo Pl 37 G3
Watson Cres 36 B7
Waverley Br 37 F4
Waverley Pk 37 J3
Waverley Pk Ter 37 J3
Waverley Pl 37 J3
Wellington St 37 H2
Wemyss Pl 36 E3
Wemyss Pl Ms 36 D3
West Adam St 37 G5
West Annandale St 37 F1
West App Rd 36 D5
West Bow
West Bryson Rd 36 B7
West Castle Rd 36 C7
West Catherine Pl 36 B5
West Coates 36 A5
West Coll St 37 G5
West Crosscauseway 37 G6
West End Pl 36 C6
Wester Coates Av 36 A5
Wester Coates Gdns 36 A5
Wester Coates Pl 36 B5
Wester Coates Rd 36 B5
Wester Coates Ter 36 A5
Westfield St 36 A7
Westhall Gdns 36 D7
West Maitland St 36 C5
West Mill La 36 C4
West Montgomery Pl 37 H2
West Newington Pl 37 H7
West Nicolson St 37 G5
West Norton Pl 37 J3
West Pk Pl 36 C6

West Port 37 E5
West Preston St 37 H7
West Register St 37 F3
West Register St La 37 F3
West Richmond St 37 G5
West Scotland St La 37 F2
West Silvermills La 36 E2
West Tollcross 36 E6
West Wds 36 A1
Wheatfield Pl 36 A7
Wheatfield Rd 36 A7
Wheatfield St 36 A7
Wheatfield Ter 36 A7
Whitehouse Ln 36 E7
White Pk 36 A7
William St 36 D4
William St N E La 36 D4
William St N W La 36 D4
William St S E La 36 D4
William St S W La 36 D5
Windmill La 37 G6
Windmill St 37 G6
Windsor St 37 H2
Windsor St La 37 H2

Y
Yeaman Pl 36 C6
York La 37 G3
York Pl 37 F3
Young St 36 D4
Young St La N 36 E4
Young St La S 36 E4

Glasgow street index

A
Abbotsford Pl 39 E7
Abercromby Dr 39 J5
Abercromby Sq 39 J5
Abercromby St 39 J6
Academy Pk 38 A7
Adams Ct La 39 F5
Adelphi St 39 F6
Admiral St 38 C6
Aird's La 39 G5
Albert Br 39 G6
Albert Dr 38 B7
Albion Gate 39 G4
Albion St 39 G5
Alexander Cres 39 F7
Alexandra Par 39 J3
Allen Glen Pl 39 G3
Anchor La 39 F4
Anderston 38 E4
Anderston Quay 38 C5
Anson St 39 J7
Anthony St 38 D4
Arcadia Pl 39 J6
Arcadia St 39 J6
Argyle St 39 F4
Argyll Arc 39 F4
Ark La 39 J4
Arlington St 38 D2
Armour St 39 J5
Arthur St 38 A2
Ashley La 38 D2
Ashley St 38 D2
Ashton La 38 A1
Ashton Rd 38 A1
Auchentoshan Ter 39 J1

B
Bain St 39 H5
Baird St 39 H2
Balaclava St 38 D4
Baliol La 38 D2
Baliol St 38 D2
Ballantrae Ct 38 D4
Ballater Pl 39 G7
Ballater St 39 F6
Bank St 38 B1
Barrack St 39 J5
Barrington Dr 38 C1
Bath La 38 D3
Bath St 38 D3
Beaumont Gate 38 A1
Bedford La 39 F6
Bedford St 39 E6
Bell St 39 G4
Beltane St 38 D3
Benny Lynch Ct 39 G6
Benthall St 39 G7
Bentinck St 38 B2
Berkeley St 38 C3
Berkeley Ter La 38 C3

Binnie Pl 39 H6
Bishop St 38 D4
Blackburn St 38 B5
Blackfriars St 39 G4
Blackie St 38 B3
Black St 39 H2
Blantyre St 38 A2
Blythswoodhill 38 E3
Blythswood Sq 38 E3
Blythswood St 38 E4
Bothwell La 38 E4
Bothwell La (Hillhead) 38 C1
Bothwell St 38 E4
Braid Sq 38 E1
Braid St 38 E1
Breadalbane St 38 C3
Brechin St 38 C3
Bridgegate 39 F5
Bridge St 39 E6
Bridgeton Cross 39 J6
Bright St 39 J2
Broadford St 39 G1
Broomielaw 38 E5
Broompark Dr 39 J4
Brown St 38 E5
Bruce Rd 38 B7
Brunswick St 39 G4
Buccleuch La 38 E2
Buccleuch St 38 D2
Buchanan St 39 F4
Bunhouse Rd 38 A2
Burnbank Gdns 38 D1
Burnbank La 38 D1
Burnbank Pl 38 D1
Burnbank Ter 38 D1
Burns St 39 E1
Bute Gdns 38 B1
Bute La 38 B1

C
Cadogan St 38 E4
Cadzow St 38 D4
Caledonian Cres 38 C1
Caledonia Rd 39 F7
Caledon La 38 A1
Caledon St 38 A1
Calgary St 39 G2
Cambridge St 39 E3
Camden Ter 39 F7
Canal St 39 G2
Candleriggs 39 G5
Cardwell St 38 E7
Carfrae St 38 A3
Carlton Ct 39 E5
Carlton Pl 39 F5
Carnarvon St 38 D2
Carnoustie Pl 38 D6
Carnoustie St 38 D6
Carrick St 38 E5
Carrington St 38 D1

Castle St 39 H4
Cathcart Rd 39 F7
Cathedral Sq 39 H4
Cathedral St 39 F3
Cavendish Pl 39 E7
Cavendish St 39 E7
Cecil St 38 B1
Cedar Ct 38 E1
Cedar St 38 E1
Centre St 38 E6
Cessnock 38 A5
Chalmers St 39 J5
Charles St 39 J2
Charlotte St 39 H5
Cheapside St 38 D5
Chisolm St 39 G5
Church St 38 A2
Circus Dr 39 J4
Citizen La 39 F4
Civic St 39 E2
Clairmont Gdns 38 C2
Claremont Pl 38 C2
Claremont St 38 C3
Claremont Ter 38 C2
Claremont Ter La 38 C2
Clarendon Pl 38 D1
Clarendon St 38 D1
Clayslaps Rd 38 B2
Claythorn Av 39 H6
Claythorn Circ 39 H5
Claythorn Pk 39 H6
Claythorn St 39 J5
Claythorn Ter 39 J5
Cleland La 39 F6
Cleland St 39 F6
Cleveland La 38 D3
Cleveland St 38 D3
Clifford La 38 A6
Clifford Pl 38 A6
Clifford St 38 A6
Cliff Rd 38 C1
Clifton Pl 38 C3
Clifton St 38 C2
Clutha St 38 A6
Clyde Arc 38 B5
Clyde Pl 38 E5
Clydeside Expressway 38 B4
Clyde St 39 F5
Cobden Rd 39 J1
Coburg St 39 E6
Cochrane St 39 G4
College La 39 H4
College St 39 G4
Collins St 39 H4
Commerce St 39 E5
Commercial Ct 39 G6
Commercial Rd 39 G7
Congress Rd 38 B4
Congress Way 38 B4
Cook St 38 E6

Cooperage Pl 38 A3
Corn St 39 E1
Cornwall St S 38 B7
Corunna St 38 B3
Couper Pl 39 G2
Couper St 39 G2
Cowan La 38 C1
Cowan St 38 D1
Cowcaddens 39 F2
Cowcaddens Rd 39 E2
Cownall St 38 A5
Cragmaddie Ter La 38 B2
Craighall Rd 39 F1
Craigiehall Pl 38 B5
Craigiehall St 38 B5
Cranston Hill 38 C3
Cranston St 38 C4
Cressnock St 38 A5
Crimea St 38 D4
Cromwell La 38 D1
Cromwell St 38 D1
Crownpoint Rd 39 J6
Crown St 39 F7
Cumberland Pl 39 G7
Cumberland St 39 E6

D
Dale Path 39 J7
Dalhouse St 38 E3
Dalhousie La 38 E2
Dalintober St 38 D6
Dalmarnock Rd 39 J7
Dalnair St 38 A2
Derby St 38 B3
Devon Pl 39 E7
Devon St 39 E7
Dixon St 39 F5
Dobbies Ln 39 F2
Dobbie's Ln Pl 39 G3
Dornoch St 39 J6
Dorset St 38 C3
Douglas La 38 E3
Douglas St 38 E4
Dover St 38 C3
Drake St 39 J6
Drury St 39 F4
Drygate 39 H4
Duke St 39 H4
Dunblane St 39 F2
Dunchattan Pl 39 J5
Dunchattan St 39 J4
Dundashill 39 F1
Dundas La 39 F3
Dundas St 39 F3
Dunearn St 38 D1
Dunlop St 39 F5
Durham St 38 B6

E
Eaglesham Ct 38 B5

Eaglesham Pl 38 B5
Eagle St 39 F1
Earlston Av 39 J2
Earlston Pl 39 J2
East Bath La 39 F3
East Campbell St 39 H5
Edington St 39 E1
Edwin St 38 B6
Eglinton Ct 39 E6
Elcho St 39 J5
Elderslie St 38 C2
Eldon St 38 C1
Elie St 38 A1
Elliot Pl 38 C4
Elliot St 38 C4
Elmbank Cres 38 D3
Elmbank St 38 D3
Elmbank St La 38 D3
Errol Gdns 39 F6
Esmond St 38 A2
Eton La 38 B1
Exchange Pl 39 F4

F
Falfield St 38 E7
Farnell St 39 E1
Finnieston 38 B3
Finnieston Quay 38 B4
Finnieston Sq 38 C3
Finnieston St 38 C4
Firpark St 39 J3
Firpark Ter 39 J4
Fitzroy La 38 B3
Florence St 39 G6
Forbes Dr 39 J6
Forbes St 39 J5
Fountainwell Av 39 H1
Fountainwell Dr 39 H1
Fountainwell Pl 39 H1
Fountainwell Rd 39 H1
Fountainwell Sq 39 H1
Fountainwell Ter 39 H1
Fox St 39 F5
Francis St 38 E7

G
Gadshill St 39 J2
Gallowgate 39 H5
Garnethill 38 E2
Garnethill St 38 E2
Garnet St 38 D3
Garscube Rd 39 E2
Garth St 39 G4
George Sq 39 F4
George St 39 G4
Gibson St 39 H5
Gibson St (Hillhead) 38 B1
Gilbert St 38 A3
Gilmour Pl 39 G7
Gladstone St 38 D1

Glasgow Br 39 F5
Glassford St 39 G4
Glebe Ct 39 H3
Glebe St 39 H2
Glenbarr St 39 J2
Glenfarg St 38 D1
Glenmavis St 39 F2
Gloucester St 38 D6
Goosedubbs 39 G5
Gorbals 39 G7
Gorbals St 39 F7
Gordon La 39 F4
Gordon St 39 F4
Gourock St 38 E7
Govan Rd 38 A5
Grace St 38 C4
Grafton Pl 39 G3
Graham Sq 39 J5
Graignestock St 39 J6
Granby La 38 B1
Grant St 38 D2
Granville St 38 D3
Gray St 38 B3
Great Dovehill 39 H5
Great George St 38 B1
Green, The 39 J7
Greendyke St 39 G5
Greenhead St 39 J6
Green St 39 J6
Grovepark Ct 38 D1
Grovepark Gdns 38 D1

H
Hallside Pl 39 G7
Handel Pl 39 F7
Hanover St 39 F4
Harley St 38 A6
Harvey St 39 F1
Harvie St 38 B5
Hastie St 38 A2
Haugh Rd 38 A3
Hayfield Ct 39 G7
Hayfield St 39 G7
Herbertson St 39 E6
High Craighall Rd 39 F1
High St 39 G5
Hillhead St 38 B1
Hill St 38 D2
Holland St 38 D3
Holm St 38 E4
Holyrood Cres 38 C1
Holyrood Quad 38 D1
Hopehill Rd 38 D1
Hope St 39 E4
Houldsworth La 38 C3
Houldsworth St 38 C3
Houston Pl 38 C5
Houston St 38 C6
Howard St 39 F5
Hunter St 39 H5

Huntingdon Rd 39 H1
Huntingdon Sq 39 H1
Hutcheson St 39 G5
Hutchesontown 39 G7
Hutchinson Town Ct 39 G7
Hydepark St 38 C5

I
India St 38 D3
Ingram St 39 G4

J
Jamaica St 39 F5
James Morrison St 39 G5
James Nisbet St 39 J3
James St 39 J7
James Watt St 38 E5
Jocelyn Sq 39 G5
John Knox St 39 J4
John St 39 G4

K
Kelvingrove 38 B2
Kelvingrove St 38 B3
Kelvinhaugh 38 A3
Kelvinhaugh Gate 38 A3
Kelvinhaugh Pl 38 B3
Kelvinhaugh St 38 A3
Kelvin Way 38 B2
Kennedy Path 39 G3
Kennedy St 39 G3
Kent Rd 38 C3
Kent St 39 H5
Keppochhill Pl 39 G1
Keppochhill Way 39 G1
Kerr Dr 39 J6
Kerr Pl 39 J6
Kerr St 39 J6
Kidston Pl 39 F7
Kidston Ter 39 F7
Kilbarchan St 39 E6
Kilbirnie Pl 38 D7
Kilbirnie St 38 D7
Killermont St 39 F3
King George V Br 39 E5
King's Br 39 H7
King's Dr 39 H7
Kingston 38 D6
Kingston St 38 E5
King St 39 G5
Kinning Pk 38 B6
Kinning St 38 D6
Kyle St 39 G2

L
La Belle Allee 38 C2
La Belle Pl 38 C2
Ladywell St 39 J4
Laidlaw St 38 D6
Laird Pl 39 J7
Lambhill Quad 38 B6
Lambhill St 38 B6
Lanark St 39 H5
Lancefield Quay 38 C4
Lancefield St 38 C4
Landressy Pl 39 J7
Landressy St 39 J7
Langshot St 38 A6
Lansdowne Cres 38 C1
Lansdowne Cres La 38 C1
Larbert St 39 F2
Laurieston 39 F6
Laurieston Rd 39 F7
Lendel Pl 38 A6
Lilybank Gdns 38 A1
Lilybank Gdns La 38 A1
Lilybank Ter 38 B1
Lister St 39 H2
Little Dovehill 39 H5
Little St 38 C4
London Rd 39 G5
Lorne St 38 B5
Lumsden St 38 A3
Lymburn St 38 B2
Lynedoch Cres 38 C2
Lynedoch Cres La 38 C2

Lynedoch Pl 38 C2
Lynedoch St 38 C2
Lynedoch Ter 38 D2

M
Mcalpine St 38 D5
McAslin Ct 39 H3
Mcaslin St 39 H3
McCulloch St 38 C7
Mcfarlane St 39 H5
McIntosh Ct 39 J4
McIntosh St 39 J4
Mcintyre St 38 D4
MacKeith St 39 J7
MacKinlay St 39 E7
Maclean Sq 38 B5
Maclean St 38 B5
Maclennan St 38 A6
Macleod St 39 H4
McNeil Gdns 39 H7
McNeil St 39 G7
McPhail St 39 J7
McPhater St 39 F2
Mair St 38 B5
Maitland St 39 F2
Malta Ter 39 F7
Manresa Pl 39 E1
Marine Cres 38 C5
Marine Gdns 38 C5
Marlow St 38 C7
Martha St 39 G3
Mart St 39 G5
Mary St 39 F1
Mauchline St 38 E7
Mavisbank Gdns 38 B5
Maxwell Av 38 C7
Maxwell Dr 38 B7
Maxwell Gdns 38 B7
Maxwell Grn 38 B7
Maxwell La 38 C7
Maxwell Oval 38 C7
Maxwell Rd 38 C7
Maxwell St 39 F5
Megan Gate 39 J7
Megan St 39 J7
Melbourne St 39 J5
Melrose St 38 D1
Merchant City 39 G4
Merchant La 39 G5
Metropole La 39 F5
Middlesex Gdns 38 B6
Middlesex St 38 B6
Middleton St 38 A5
Midland St 39 E4
Midwharf St 39 F1
Miller St 39 F4
Millroad Dr 39 J5
Millroad Gdns 39 J5
Millroad St 39 H5
Milnpark Gdns 38 B6
Milnpark St 38 B6
Milton St 39 F2
Minerva St 38 B3
Minerva Way 38 B3
Mitchell La 39 F4
Mitchell St 39 F4
Moffat St 39 G7
Moir St 39 H5
Molendinar St 39 H5
Moncur St 39 H5
Montague St 38 C1
Monteith Pl 39 H6
Monteith Row 39 H5
Montrose St 39 G4
Moore St 39 J5
Morrison Ct 38 D5
Morrison St 38 D5
Mosque Av 39 F6
Muslin St 39 J7

N
Naburn Gate 39 F7
Nairn St 38 A2
Napiershall La 38 D1
Napiershall Pl 38 D1

Napiershall St 38 D1
Nelson Mandela Pl 39 F4
Nelson St 38 E5
Netherby Dr 38 A7
New City Rd 38 D2
Newton St 38 D2
Newton Ter La 38 C3
New Wynd 39 G5
Nicholas St 39 H4
Nicholson St 39 F6
Norfolk Ct 39 F6
Norfolk St 39 F6
North Canal Bk 39 G1
North Canal Bk St 39 F1
North Claremount St 38 C2
North Ct 39 F4
North Ct La 39 F4
North Dr 39 F4
North Frederick Path 39 G3
North Frederick St 39 G4
North Gower St 38 A6
North Hanover St 39 G4
North Portland St 39 G4
North St 38 D2
North Wallace St 39 G2

O
Oakfield Av 38 B1
Oakfield La 38 B1
Oak St 38 D4
Old Dumbarton Rd 38 A2
Old Rutherglen Rd 39 G5
Old Wynd 39 G5
Oregon Pl 39 G7
Orr St 39 J6
Osborne St 39 F5
Oswald St 39 E5
Otago La 38 C1
Otago La N 38 C1
Otago St 38 B1
Overnewton Pl 38 B3
Overnewton Sq 38 A3
Overnewton St 38 A2
Oxford La 39 F6
Oxford St 39 E5

P
Pacific Dr 38 A5
Pacific Quay 38 A4
Paisley Rd 38 D5
Paisley Rd W 38 C5
Palmerston Pl 38 B3
Parine St 39 G5
Park Av 38 C1
Park Circ 38 C2
Park Circ La 38 C2
Park Circ Pl 38 C2
Park Dr 38 C1
Park Gdns 38 C2
Park Gdns La 38 C2
Park Gate 38 C2
Parkgrove Ter 38 B2
Parkgrove Ter La 38 B2
Park Quad 38 C2
Park Rd 38 C1
Park St S 38 C2
Park Ter 38 C2
Park Ter E La 38 C2
Park Terrrace La 38 C2
Parsonage Row 39 H4
Parsonage Sq 39 H4
Parson St 39 H3
Paterson St 38 D6
Payne St 39 F1
Pembroke St 38 C3
Percy St 38 A6
Perth St 38 D4
Piccadilly St 38 D4
Pine Pl 39 G7
Pinkston Dr 39 H2
Pinkston Rd 39 H1
Pitt St 38 E4
Plantation Pk Gdns 38 A6
Plantation Sq 38 B5
Port Dundas 39 F1
Port Dundas La 39 F3

Port Dundas Rd 39 F2
Port Eglington 38 D7
Portman St 38 C6
Port St 38 C3
Portugal St 39 F6
Possil Rd 39 E1
Professors Sq 38 B1
Provanhill St 39 J2

Q
Queen Elizabeth Gdns 39 G7
Queens Cres 38 D1
Queen St 39 F4

R
Radnor St 38 B2
Raglan St 38 E1
Regent Moray St 38 A2
Renfield La 38 E4
Renfield St 39 F4
Renfrew Ct 39 F3
Renfrew La 39 F3
Renfrew St 38 D2
Renton St 39 F2
Rhymer St 39 J2
Richmond St 39 G4
Ritchie St 38 E7
Riverview Dr 38 D5
Riverview Gdns 38 E5
Riverview Pl 38 D5
Robertson La 38 E4
Robertson St 39 E5
Rodney St 39 E1
Ropework La 39 F5
Rose St 39 E3
Ross St 39 H5
Rottenrow 39 G3
Rottenrow E 39 H4
Royal Bk Pl 39 F4
Royal Cres 38 B3
Royal Ex Ct 39 F4
Royal Ex Sq 39 F4
Royal Ter 38 B2
Royal Ter La 38 B2
Royston 39 J2
Roystonhill 39 J2
Royston Rd 39 J2
Royston Sq 39 J2
Rupert St 38 D1
Rutland Ct 38 C5
Rutland Cres 38 C5
Rutland Pl 38 B5

S
St. Andrews Cres 38 C7
St. Andrew's La 39 G5
St. Andrews Rd 38 C7
St. Andrews Sq 39 G5
St. Andrews St 39 G5
St. Clair St 38 D1
St. Enoch 39 F5
St. Enoch Sq 39 F4
St. Francis Rigg 39 G7
St. Georges Rd 38 B2
St. Georges Rd 38 D2
St. James Rd 39 G3
St. John's Ct 38 B7
St. John's Quad 38 C7
St. Josephs Vw 39 J2
St. Luke's Pl 39 F6
St. Luke's Ter 39 F6
St. Margaret's Pl 39 G5
St. Marys La 39 F4
St. Mungo Av 39 G3
St. Mungo Pl 39 H3
St. Ninian Ter 39 F6
St. Peters La 38 E4
St. Peters St 38 E2
St. Rollox Brae 39 J1
St. Valentine Ter 39 G7
St. Vincent Cres 38 B3
St. Vincent Cres La 38 B3
St. Vincent La 38 E3
St. Vincent Pl 39 F4
St. Vincent St 38 C3
St. Vincent Ter 38 C3

Salisbury La 39 F7
Salisbury St 39 F7
Salkeld St 38 E7
Saltmarket 39 G5
Sandiefield Rd 39 F7
Sandyford Pl La 38 C3
Sandyford St 38 A3
Saracen Head Rd 39 H5
Sauchiehall La 38 E3
Sauchiehall St 38 B2
Savoy St 39 J7
Sawmillfield St 39 E1
Scotland St 38 C6
Scotland St W 38 B6
Scott St 38 E3
Seamore St 38 D1
Seaward La 38 C5
Seaward Pl 38 C6
Seaward St 38 C6
Shaftesbury St 38 D3
Shamrock St 38 E2
Shields Rd 38 C6
Shipbank La 39 G5
Shuttle St 39 G4
Sighthill 39 H1
Silverfir St 39 G7
Silvergrove St 39 J6
Snowdon St 39 G7
Somerset Pl Ms 38 C2
South Ex Ct 39 F4
South Frederick St 39 G4
Southpark Av 38 B1
Southpark La 38 B1
South Portland St 39 F5
Southside Cres 39 F7
South Woodside Rd 38 C1
Spiers Wf 39 F1
Spoutmouth 39 H5
Springburn Rd 39 J2
Springfield Ct 39 F4
Springfield Quay 38 C5
Spring Wynd 39 G7
Stafford St 39 G2
Stanley St 38 C6
Stanley St La 38 C6
Steel St 39 G5
Stevenson St 39 J6
Stewart St 39 F2
Stirlingfauld Pl 39 F7
Stirling Rd 39 H3
Stobcross Rd 38 A3
Stobcross St 38 C4
Stobcross Wynd 38 A3
Stockwell Pl 39 F5
Stockwell St 39 F5
Stromness St 38 E7
Suffolk St 39 H5
Surrey St 39 F7
Sussex St 38 B6
Sutherland La 38 A1
Swan St 39 G2
Sydney St 39 J5

T
Taylor Pl 39 H3
Taylor St 39 H4
Templeton St 39 J6
Teviot St 38 A3
Thistle St 39 G6
Thistle Ter 39 F7
Thornbank St 38 A3
Thurso St 38 A2
Tobago Pl 39 J5
Tobago St 39 J6
Toll La 38 C5
Tontine La 39 G5
Torness St 38 A1
Tower St 38 B6
Townhead 39 G2
Townsend St 39 F2
Tradeston 38 E6
Tradeston St 38 E6
Trongate 39 G5
Tullis Ct 39 J7
Tullis St 39 J7
Tunnel St 38 B4

Tureen St 39 J5
Turnbull St 39 G5
Turnlaw St 39 H7
Turriff St 39 E7
Tyndrum St 39 F2

U
Union Pl 39 F4
Union St 39 F4
Unity Pl 38 E1
University Av 38 A1
University Gdns 38 A1
University Pl 38 A1

V
Vermont St 38 B6
Victoria Br 39 F5
Viewfield La 38 B1
Vinter St 39 F1
Virginia Pl 39 G4
Virginia St 39 G4

W
Waddell Ct 39 G6
Waddell St 39 G7
Wallace St 38 D5
Walls St 39 G4
Walmer Cres 38 A6
Warnock St 39 J3
Warroch St 38 D5
Washington St 38 D5
Waterloo La 39 E4
Waterloo St 38 E4
Waterside Pl 39 H7
Waterside St 39 G7
Watson St 39 G5
Watt St 38 C6
Weaver St 39 H4
Wellcroft Pl 39 E7
Wellington La 38 E4
Wellington St 39 E4
Wellpark St 39 J4
Westbank La 38 B1
Westbank Quad 38 B1
West Campbell St 38 E4
West End Pk St 38 C2
West George La 38 E3
West George St 39 E3
West Graham St 38 D2
West Greenhill Pl 38 B3
West Nile St 39 F4
West Prince's La 38 C1
West Princes St 38 C1
West Regent La 39 E3
West Regent St 39 E3
West St 38 D7
Whitehall St 38 D4
William St 38 D3
Willowbank Cres 38 C1
Willowbank St 38 C1
Wilson St 39 G4
Windsor St 38 D1
Windsor Ter 38 D1
Wishart St 39 J4
Woodlands Dr 38 C1
Woodlands Gate 38 C2
Woodlands Rd 38 C1
Woodlands Ter 38 C2
Woodrow Circ 38 A7
Woodrow Pl 38 A7
Woodrow Rd 38 A7
Woodside Cres 38 D2
Woodside Pl 38 C2
Woodside Pl La 38 C2
Woodside Ter 38 C2
Woodside Ter La 38 C2

Y
Yorkhill 38 B2
Yorkhill Par 38 A2
Yorkhill St 38 A3
York St 38 E5

Leeds street index

A
Abbey St 40 C3
Abbott Ct 40 A3
Abbott Rd 40 A4
Abbott Vw 40 A3
Admiral St 41 E7
Aire St 40 D4
Albion Pl 41 E3

Albion St 41 E3
Alexander St 40 E3
Alexandra Gro 40 B1
Alexandra Rd 40 A1
Alma St 41 H2
Anderson Av 41 H1
Anderson Mt 41 H1
Apex Vw 40 E6

Apex Way 41 E6
Appleton Cl 41 J3
Appleton Ct 41 J3
Appleton Sq 41 J3
Appleton Way 41 J3
Archery Pl 40 D1
Archery Rd 40 D1
Archery St 40 E1

Archery Ter 40 E1
Armley Rd 40 A3
Armouries Rd 41 G5
Artist St 40 B4
Ascot Ter 41 J4
Ashley Av 41 J1
Ashley Rd 41 J1
Ashley Ter 41 J1

Ashton Av 41 J1
Ashton Gro 41 J1
Ashton Mt 41 J1
Ashton Pl 41 J1
Ashton Ter 41 J1
Ashton Vw 41 J1
Ashville Vw 40 A1
Assembly St 41 F4

Atkinson St 41 G6
Autumn Av 40 B1
Autumn Gro 40 B1
Autumn Pl 40 B1
Autumn St 40 B1
Autumn Ter 40 B1
Avenue, The 41 G4
Aysgarth Cl 41 J4

Aysgarth Dr	41 J4			
Aysgarth Pl	41 J4			
Aysgarth Wk	41 J4			

B

Back Ashville Av	40 A1
Back Hyde Ter	40 C2
Back Row	40 E5
Balm Pl	40 C6
Balm Wk	40 C6
Bank St	41 E4
Baron Cl	40 C7
Barrack St	41 F1
Barran Ct	41 H1
Barton Gro	40 D7
Barton Mt	40 D7
Barton Pl	40 C7
Barton Rd	40 C7
Barton Ter	40 D7
Barton Vw	40 C7
Bath Rd	40 D5
Bayswater Vw	41 H1
Beamsley Gro	40 A1
Beamsley Mt	40 A1
Beamsley Pl	40 A1
Beamsley Ter	40 A1
Beckett St	41 H3
Bedford St	40 E3
Beech Gro Ter	40 D1
Belgrave St	41 E3
Belinda St	41 H7
Belle Vue Rd	40 B2
Bell St	41 G3
Belmont Gro	40 D2
Benson St	41 F1
Benyon Pk Way	40 A7
Berking Av	41 J3
Bertrand St	40 C6
Bexley Av	41 H1
Bexley Gro	41 J1
Bexley Mt	41 H1
Bexley Pl	41 H1
Bexley Rd	41 J1
Bexley Ter	41 J1
Bingley St	40 C3
Bishopgate St	40 E4
Bismarck Dr	40 E7
Bismarck St	40 E7
Black Bull St	41 F5
Blackman La	40 E1
Blandford Gdns	40 D1
Blandford Gro	40 D1
Blayds St	41 H4
Blayd's Yd	41 E4
Blenheim Av	40 E1
Blenheim Ct	40 E1
Blenheim Cres	40 E1
Blenheim Gro	40 E1
Blenheim Sq	40 E1
Blenheim Vw	40 D1
Blenheim Wk	40 D1
Blundell St	40 D2
Boar La	40 E4
Bodley Ter	40 A2
Bond St	40 E3
Boundary Pl	41 G1
Boundary St	41 G1
Bourse, The	41 E4
Bowling Grn Ter	40 D6
Bowman La	41 F4
Bow St	41 G4
Bracken Ct	40 A6
Braithwaite St	40 C5
Brancepeth Pl	40 B4
Brandon Rd	40 C2
Brandon St	40 B4
Branksome Pl	40 B1
Brick St	41 G4
Bridge Ct	40 C5
Bridge End	41 E4
Bridge Rd	40 C5
Bridge St	41 F3
Bridgewater Rd	41 H6
Briggate	41 E4
Brignall Garth	41 J2
Brignall Way	41 H2
Bristol St	41 G2
Britannia St	40 D4
Broadway Av	40 A1
Brookfield St	41 G6
Brown Av	40 B7
Brown La E	40 B6
Brown La W	40 A6
Brown Pl	40 B7
Brown Rd	40 B7
Bruce Gdns	40 B4
Bruce Lawn	40 B4
Brunswick Ct	41 F3
Brunswick Ter	41 E2
Brussels St	41 G4
Buckton Cl	40 C7
Buckton Mt	40 C7
Buckton Vw	40 C7
Burley	40 A1
Burley Lo Pl	40 B2
Burley Lo Rd	40 A1
Burley Lo St	40 B2
Burley Lo Ter	40 B1
Burley Pl	40 A2
Burley Rd	40 A1
Burley St	40 C3
Burmantofts	
Burmantofts St	41 H3
Burton Row	41 G3
Burton St	41 E7
Burton Way	41 J2
Butterfield St	41 H4
Butterley St	41 F6
Butts Ct	41 E3
Byron St	41 F2

C

Cain Cl	41 H4
Call La	41 F4
Calls, The	41 F4
Calverley St	40 D2
Cambrian St	40 D7
Cambrian Ter	40 D7
Canal Pl	40 B4
Canal St	40 A3
Canal Wf	40 D4
Carberry Pl	40 A1
Carberry Rd	40 A1
Carberry Ter	40 A1
Carlisle Rd	41 G5
Carlton Carr	41 E1
Carlton Ct	40 A7
Carlton Gdns	41 E1
Carlton Gate	41 E1
Carlton Gro	41 E1
Carlton Hill	41 E1
Carlton Pl	41 E1
Carlton Ri	41 E1
Carlton Twrs	41 F1
Carlton Vw	41 E1
Castle St	40 D3
Castleton Cl	40 B4
Castleton Rd	40 A3
Cautley Rd	41 J5
Cavalier App	41 H5
Cavalier Cl	41 H5
Cavalier Ct	41 H5
Cavalier Gdns	41 H5
Cavalier Gate	41 H5
Cavalier Ms	41 H5
Cavalier Vw	41 H5
Cavendish Rd	40 D1
Cavendish St	40 C3
Cemetery Rd	40 C7
Central Rd	41 F4
Central St	40 D3
Chadwick St	41 F5
Chadwick St S	41 G5
Chantrell Ct	41 F4
Charles Av	41 J5
Charlton Gro	41 J4
Charlton Pl	41 J4
Charlton Rd	41 J4
Charlton St	41 J4
Cherry Pl	41 G2
Cherry Row	41 G2
Chesney Av	41 F7
Chiswick St	40 A2
Chorley La	40 D2
Churchill Gdns	40 E1
Church La	41 F4
City Sq	40 E4
City Wk	40 E5
Claremont Av	40 C2
Claremont Gro	40 C2
Claremont Vw	40 C2
Clarence Rd	41 G5
Clarendon Pl	40 C1
Clarendon Rd	40 C1
Clarendon Way	40 D2
Clark Av	41 J4
Clark Cres	41 J4
Clark Gro	41 J5
Clark La	41 H5
Clark Mt	41 J4
Clark Rd	41 J5
Clark Row	41 J5
Clark Ter	41 J4
Clark Vw	41 J5
Clay Pit La	41 E2
Cleveleys Av	40 C7
Cleveleys Mt	40 C7
Cleveleys Rd	40 C7
Cleveleys St	40 C7
Cleveleys Ter	40 C7
Cloberry St	40 C1
Close, The	41 G4
Cloth Hall St	41 F4
Clyde App	40 A5
Clyde Gdns	40 B5
Clyde Vw	40 A5
Coleman St	40 B5
Colenso Gdns	40 C7
Colenso Mt	40 C7
Colenso Pl	40 C7
Colenso Rd	40 C7
Colenso Ter	40 C7
Colville Ter	40 D7
Commercial St	41 E3
Compton Av	41 J1
Compton Cres	41 J1
Compton Gro	41 J1
Compton Mt	41 J1
Compton Pl	41 J1
Compton Rd	41 J1
Compton St	41 J1
Compton Ter	41 J1
Compton Vw	41 J1
Concordia St	41 E4
Concord St	41 F2
Consort St	40 C2
Consort Ter	40 C2
Consort Vw	40 B2
Consort Wk	40 C2
Constance Gdns	40 E1
Constance Way	40 E1
Cookridge St	40 E3
Copley Hill	40 A5
Copley Hill Way	40 A6
Copley St	40 A5
Copperfield Av	41 J5
Copperfield Cres	41 J5
Copperfield Gro	41 J5
Copperfield Mt	41 J5
Copperfield Pl	41 J5
Copperfield Row	41 J5
Copperfield Ter	41 J5
Copperfield Vw	41 J5
Copperfield Wk	41 J5
Copperfiield Dr	41 J5
Cotton St	41 G4
Coupland Pl	40 D7
Coupland Rd	40 D7
Cowper Av	41 J1
Cowper Cres	41 J1
Cowper Rd	41 J1
Cromer Pl	40 C1
Cromer Rd	40 C1
Cromer St	40 C1
Cromer Ter	40 C2
Cromwell Mt	41 G2
Cromwell St	41 G3
Crosby Pl	40 C6
Crosby Rd	40 C7
Crosby St	40 C6
Crosby Ter	40 C6
Crosby Vw	40 C6
Cross Aysgarth Mt	41 H4
Cross Belgrave St	41 F3
Cross Catherine St	41 H4
Cross Grn	
Cross Grn App	41 J6
Cross Grn Av	41 H5
Cross Grn Cl	41 J6
Cross Grn Cres	41 H5
Cross Grn Dr	41 J6
Cross Grn Garth	41 J6
Cross Grn La	41 H5
Cross Grn Ri	41 J6
Cross Grn Way	41 J6
Cross Ingram Rd	40 C6
Cross Kelso Rd	40 C2
Cross Mitford Rd	40 A4
Cross Stamford St	41 G2
Cross York St	41 F4
Crown Ct	41 F4
Crown Pt Rd	41 F5
Crown St	41 F4
Croydon St	40 B5
Cudbear St	41 F5
Czar St	40 C5

D

Danby Wk	41 H4
David St	40 D5
Dene Ho Ct	40 E1
Denison Rd	40 C3
Dent St	41 H4
Derwent Pl	40 D5
Devon Cl	40 D1
Devon Rd	40 D1
Dewsbury Rd	40 E6
Dial St	41 H5
Disraeli Gdns	40 E7
Disraeli Ter	40 E7
Dock St	41 F4
Dolly La	41 G2
Dolphin Ct	41 H4
Dolphin St	41 H4
Domestic Rd	40 B6
Domestic St	40 C5
Donisthorpe St	41 G6
Drive, The	41 G4
Driver Ter	40 B5
Dudley Way	41 E3
Duke St	41 F3
Duncan St	41 E4
Duncombe St	40 C3
Duxbury Ri	40 E1
Dyer St	41 F3

E

East Fld St	41 H4
Eastgate	41 F3
East King St	41 G4
East Par	40 E3
East Pk Dr	41 J4
East Pk Gro	41 J4
East Pk Mt	41 J4
East Pk Par	41 J4
East Pk Pl	41 J4
East Pk Rd	41 J4
East Pk St	41 J4
East Pk Ter	41 J4
East Pk Vw	41 J4
East St	41 G4
Easy Rd	41 H5
Ebor Mt	40 B1
Ebor Pl	40 B1
Ebor St	40 B1
Edgware Av	41 H1
Edgware Gro	41 H1
Edgware Mt	41 H1
Edgware Pl	41 H1
Edgware Row	41 H1
Edgware St	41 H1
Edgware Ter	41 H1
Edgware Vw	41 H1
Edward St	41 F3
Edwin Rd	40 B1
Eighth Av	40 A5
Elland Rd	40 C7
Elland Ter	40 D6
Ellerby La	41 H5
Ellerby Rd	41 G4
Elmtree La	41 G7
Elmwood La	41 F2
Elmwood Rd	41 E2
Elsworth St	40 A4
Enfield Av	41 G1
Enfield St	41 G1
Enfield Ter	41 G1
Euston Gro	40 B7
Euston Mt	40 B7
Euston Ter	40 B7
Everleigh St	41 J3

F

Far Cft Ter	40 A5
Fewston Av	41 H5
Fewston Ct	41 J5
Finsbury Rd	40 D2
First Av	40 A4
Firth St	41 G2
Firth Ter	41 G2
Fish St	41 F3
Flax Pl	41 G4
Florence Av	41 J1
Florence Gro	41 J1
Florence Mt	41 J1
Florence Pl	41 J1
Florence St	41 J1
Folly La	40 D7
Forster St	41 G6
Foundry St (Holbeck)	40 C6
Foundry St (Quarry Hill)	41 G4
Fountain St	40 D3
Fourteenth Av	40 A5
Fourth Ct	40 C5
Fox Way	41 H6
Fraser St	41 J2
Frederick Av	41 J5
Front Row	40 D5
Front St	40 D5

G

Gardeners Ct	41 G7
Gargrave App	41 H3
Gargrave Pl	41 H2
Garth, The	41 G4
Garton Av	41 J4
Garton Gro	41 J4
Garton Rd	41 J4
Garton Ter	41 J4
Garton Vw	41 J4
Gelderd Pl	40 B5
Gelderd Rd	40 A7
George St	41 F3
Gibraltar Island Rd	41 H7
Gilpin Pl	40 A5
Gilpin St	40 A5
Gilpin Ter	40 A5
Gilpin Vw	40 A5
Glasshouse St	41 G6
Gledhow Mt	41 H1
Gledhow Pl	41 H1
Gledhow Rd	41 H1
Gledhow Ter	41 H1
Glencoe Vw	41 J5
Glensdale Gro	41 J4
Glensdale Mt	41 J4
Glensdale Rd	41 J4
Glensdale St	41 J4
Glensdale Ter	41 J4
Glenthorpe Av	41 J3
Glenthorpe Cres	41 J3
Glenthorpe Ter	41 J3
Globe Rd	40 D3
Gloucester Ter	40 A4
Goodman St	41 G6
Gotts Rd	40 C4
Gower St	41 F3
Grace St	40 D3
Grafton St	41 F2
Grange Cl	41 G7
Grange Rd	41 G7
Grant Av	41 G1
Granville Rd	41 H2
Grape St	41 F7
Grasmere Cl	40 A5
Grassmere Rd	40 A5
Great George St	40 D3
Great Wilson St	40 E5
Greek St	40 E3
Greenfield Rd	41 H4
Green La	40 A5
Grosvenor Hill	41 E1

H

Hall Gro	40 B1
Hall La	40 A4
Hall Pl	41 H4
Hanover Av	40 C2
Hanover La	40 D3
Hanover Mt	40 C2
Hanover Sq	40 C2
Hanover Wk	40 C3
Harewood St	41 F3
Harold Av	40 A1
Harold Gro	40 A1
Harold Mt	40 A1
Harold Pl	40 A1
Harold Rd	40 A1
Harold St	40 A1
Harold Ter	40 A1
Harold Vw	40 A1
Harold Wk	40 A1
Harper St	41 F4
Harrison St	41 F3
Hartwell Rd	40 B1
Haslewood Cl	41 H3
Haslewood Ct	41 H3
Haslewood Dene	41 H3
Haslewood Dr	41 H3
Haslewood Ms	41 J3
Haslewood Pl	41 H3
Haslewood Sq	41 H3
Hawkins Dr	41 E1
Headrow, The	40 D3
Heaton's Ct	41 E4
Hedley Chase	40 A4
Hedley Gdns	40 A4
Hedley Grn	40 A4
High	41 G7
High Ct	41 F4
High Ct La	41 F4
Hillary Pl	40 D1
Hillidge Rd	41 F7
Hillidge Sq	41 F7
Hill Top Pl	40 B1
Hill Top St	40 B1
Hirst's Yd	41 F4
Holbeck	40 D5
Holbeck La	40 C5
Holbeck Moor Rd	40 C6
Holdforth Cl	40 A4
Holdforth Gdns	40 A4
Holdforth Grn	40 A4
Holdforth Pl	40 A4
Holmes St	41 E5
Holroyd St	41 G1
Hope Rd	41 G3
Howden Gdns	40 B1
Howden Pl	40 B1
Hudson Rd	41 J1
Hudswell Rd	41 F7
Hunslet	41 G7
Hunslet Grn Way	41 F7
Hunslet Hall Rd	40 E7
Hunslet La	41 F5
Hunslet Rd	41 F4
Hyde Pk Cl	40 B1
Hyde Pk Rd	40 B1
Hyde Pl	40 C2
Hyde St	40 C2
Hyde Ter	40 C2

I

Infirmary St	40 E3
Ingram Cl	40 C6
Ingram Cres	40 B7
Ingram Gdns	40 C6
Ingram Rd	40 C7
Ingram Row	40 E5
Ingram St	40 E5
Ingram Vw	40 C6
Inner Ring Rd	40 E2
Ivory St	41 F6

J

Jack La	40 D6
Jenkinson Cl	40 D6
Jenkinson Lawn	40 D6
John Smeaton Viaduct	41 G6
Joseph St	41 G7
Junction St	41 F5

K

Keeton St	41 H3
Kelsall Av	40 B1
Kelsall Gro	40 B2
Kelsall Pl	40 B1
Kelsall Rd	40 B1
Kelsall Ter	40 B1
Kelso Gdns	40 C1
Kelso Rd	40 C1
Kelso St	40 C2
Kendal Bk	40 C2
Kendal Cl	40 C2
Kendal Gro	40 C2
Kendal La	40 C2
Kendell St	41 F4
Kenneth St	40 B6
Kepler Gro	41 H1
Kepler Mt	41 H1
Kepler Ter	41 H1
Kidacre St	41 F5
Kildare Ter	40 B5
King Charles St	41 E3
King Edward St	41 F3
Kings Av	40 B2
King's Rd	40 B1
Kingston Ter	40 D1
King St	40 D4
Kippax Pl	41 H4
Kirkgate	41 F4
Kirkstall Rd	40 A2
Kitson Rd	41 G6
Kitson St	41 H4
Knowsthorpe Cres	41 H5
Knowsthorpe La	41 J6

L

Ladybeck Cl	41 F3
Lady La	41 F3
Lady Pit La	40 D7
Lands La	41 E3
Lane, The	41 G4
Larchfield Rd	41 G6
Latchmore Rd	40 A7
Laura St	40 C5
Lavender Wk	41 H4
Leathley La	41 F6
Leathley Rd	41 F6
Leathley St	41 F6
Leicester Cl	40 E1
Leicester Gro	40 E1
Leicester Pl	40 D1
Leighton St	40 D3
Leodis Ct	40 D5
Leylands Rd	41 G2
Lifton Pl	40 C1
Lincoln Grn Rd	41 G2
Lincoln Rd	41 G2
Lindsey Ct	41 H2
Lindsey Gdns	41 H2
Lindsey Rd	41 H2
Lisbon St	40 D3
Little King St	40 E4
Little Queen St	40 D4
Little Woodhouse St	40 D2
Livinia Gro	40 E1
Lodge St	40 D1
Lofthouse Pl	40 E1
Londesboro Gro	41 J4
Long Causeway	41 H6
Long Cl La	41 H4
Lord St	40 C5
Lord Ter	40 B5
Lovell Pk Cl	41 F2
Lovell Pk Gate	41 F2
Lovell Pk Hill	41 F2
Lovell Pk Rd	41 F2
Lovell Pk Vw	41 F2
Lower Basinghall St	40 E3
Lower Brunswick St	41 F2
Low Flds Av	40 B7
Low Flds Rd	40 A7
Low Flds Way	40 B7
Low Fold	41 G5
Low Rd	41 G7
Low Whitehouse Row	41 G6
Ludgate Hill	41 F3
Lyddon Ter	40 C1
Lydgate	41 J2

Street	Ref	Street	Ref
Lydia St	41 F3	Nile St	41 F3
M		Nineveh Gdns	40 D6
Mabgate	41 G3	Nineveh Par	40 D6
Mabgate Grn	41 G3	Nineveh Rd	40 C6
Macaulay St	41 G3	Nippet La	41 H3
Maitland Pl	40 D7	Normanton Gro	40 C7
Maltings Rd	41 F7	Normanton Pl	40 D7
Malvern Gro	40 D7	Nortech Cl	41 G1
Malvern Ri	40 D7	Northcote Cres	40 E7
Malvern Rd	40 C7	Northcote Dr	40 D7
Malvern St	40 C7	Northcote Grn	40 D7
Malvern Vw	40 C7	North Ct	41 F3
Manor Rd	40 D5	Northern St	40 D4
Manor St	41 G1	North St	41 F3
Mark La	41 E3	**O**	
Marlborough Gdns	40 D1	Oak Rd	40 A4
Marlborough Gro	40 D1	Oatland Cl	41 F1
Marlborough St	40 C3	Oatland Ct	41 F1
Marlborough Twrs	40 C3	Oatland Dr	41 F1
Marshall St	40 D5	Oatland Gdns	41 F1
Marsh La	41 G4	Oatland Grn	41 F1
Maude St	41 F4	Oatland Hts	41 F1
May Ter	41 H5	Oatland La	41 E1
Meadowcroft Ms	41 H4	Oatland Rd	41 E1
Meadow La	41 E5	Oatland Twrs	41 F1
Meadow Rd	40 E6	O'Grady Sq	41 H4
Melbourne St	41 F2	Old Mill La	41 H7
Merrion Pl	41 F3	Oval, The	41 G7
Merrion St	41 E3	Oxford Pl	40 D3
Merrion Way	41 E2	Oxford Row	40 D3
Meynell App	40 C6	Oxley St	41 J4
Middleton Av	41 J2	Oxton Mt	41 J3
Milford Pl	40 A2	Oxton Way	41 J3
Millgarth St	41 F3	**P**	
Mill Grn	40 B5	Parade, The	41 G4
Mill Hill	41 E4	Park Cross St	40 D3
Mill St	41 G4	Parkfield St	41 E6
Millwright St	41 G2	Park La	40 C3
Milner Gdns	41 H5	Park Par	41 J5
Milnes St	40 B5	Park Pl	40 D3
Mitford Rd	40 A4	Park Row	40 E3
Mitford Vw	40 A4	Park Sq E	40 D3
Moor Cres	41 E7	Park Sq N	40 D3
Moor Cres Chase	41 E7	Park Sq S	40 D3
Moorland Av	40 B1	Park Sq W	40 D3
Moorland Rd	40 B1	Park St	40 D3
Moor Rd	41 E7	Park Vw Rd	40 A1
Moorside Maltings	41 E7	Pearson St	41 F6
Moor Vw	40 D6	Penny La Way	41 F7
Moorvile Cl	40 D7	Pilot St	41 G2
Moorville Ct	40 D7	Pitt Row	41 E4
Moorville Gro	40 D7	Place's Rd	41 H4
Moorville Rd	40 D7	Plaid Row	41 H3
Mount Preston St	40 C2	Playhouse Sq	41 G3
Mulberry St	41 F6	Pleasant Mt	40 C6
Mullins Ct	41 H5	Pleasant Pl	40 C6
Mushroom St	41 G2	Pleasant Ter	40 C6
N		Pontefract Av	41 J4
Naseby Garth	41 G2	Pontefract La	41 H3
Naseby Ter	41 H3	Pontefract La Cl	41 H4
National Rd	41 H6	Pontefract St	41 H4
Navigation Wk	41 F4	Portland Cres	40 E2
Neptune St	41 G4	Portland Gate	40 E2
Neville St	40 E4	Portland St	40 D3
New Briggate	41 F3	Portland Way	40 E2
New Craven Gate	41 F6	Pottery Rd	41 F7
New La	40 E5	Prosper St	41 G7
New Mkt St	41 F4	Providence Pl	41 E2
New Princess St	40 D6	Pym St	41 G6
New Sta St	40 E4	**Q**	
New York Rd	41 G3	**Quarry Hill**	41 G3
New York St	41 F4	Quebec St	40 D3
Nickleby Rd	41 J3		

Street	Ref	Street	Ref
Queen Sq	41 E2	St. Luke's Cres	40 D7
Queens Rd	40 B1	St. Luke's Grn	40 D7
Queen St	40 D4	St. Luke's Rd	40 D7
R		St. Luke's St	40 D7
Radnor St	40 B5	St. Mark's Av	40 D1
Railway St	41 G4	St. Mark's Rd	40 D1
Raincliffe Gro	41 J3	St. Mark's St	40 D1
Raincliffe Rd	41 J3	St. Mary's Cl	40 A5
Raincliffe St	41 J3	St. Mary's St	41 G3
Recreation Cres	40 C7	St. Matthew's St	40 C6
Recreation Gro	40 C7	St. Matthias St	40 A1
Recreation Mt	40 C7	St. Matthias Ter	40 A1
Recreation Pl	40 C7	St. Paul's St	40 D3
Recreation Row	40 C7	St. Peter's Ct	41 E7
Recreation St	40 C7	St. Peter's Pl	41 G3
Recreation Ter	40 C7	St. Peter's Sq	41 G3
Recreation Vw	40 C7	St. Stephen's Ct	41 H3
Rectory St	41 H2	St. Stephen's Rd	41 H3
Redshaw Rd	40 A5	Salem Pl	41 F5
Regent St	41 G3	Sandlewood Cl	40 D6
Regent Ter	40 B1	Sandlewood Grn	40 D6
Rhodes Ter	40 A5	Sardinia St	41 F6
Richmond Hill App	41 H4	Saville Grn	41 J3
Richmond Hill Cl	41 H4	Saxton La	41 G4
Richmond St	41 G4	Sayner La	41 G5
Rickard St	40 C5	Sayner Rd	41 F5
Rider St	41 G3	Scargill Cl	41 H2
Rigton App	41 H3	Scarth Av	41 J1
Rigton Cl	41 H3	Second Av	40 A4
Rigton Dr	41 H3	Seminary St	40 D2
Rigton Grn	41 H3	Severn Way	41 H7
Rigton Lawn	41 H3	Shafton La	40 C6
Rigton Ms	41 H3	Shafton Pl	40 C6
Rillbank La	40 B2	Shafton St	40 C6
Roscoe St	41 G1	Shafton Vw	40 C6
Rosebank Gdns	40 B2	Shakespeare App	41 H2
Rosebank Rd	40 B2	Shakespeare Av	41 H2
Rosebud Wk	41 G1	Shakespeare Cl	41 J2
Roseville Rd	41 G1	Shakespeare Gdns	41 J2
Roseville St	41 H1	Shakespeare Lawn	41 H2
Rossington St	40 E3	Shakespeare St	41 J1
Roundhay Rd	41 G1	Shannon Rd	41 H3
Roxby Cl	41 H2	Shannon St	41 G3
Royal Pk Av	40 B1	Sheaf St	41 F5
Royal Pk Gro	40 B1	Sheepscar Ct	41 F1
Royal Pk Rd	40 A1	Sheepscar Gro	41 F2
Royal Pk Ter	40 B1	Sheepscar St N	41 F1
Ruby St	41 G2	Sheepscar St S	41 F1
Runswick Av	40 C6	Siddal St	40 D5
Runswick Pl	40 C6	Sidney St	41 F3
Runswick St	40 C6	Silver St	40 D5
Runswick Ter	40 C6	Skinner La	41 F2
Russell St	40 E3	Skinner St	40 C3
Rydall Pl	40 C6	Somers St	40 D3
Rydall St	40 C6	South Accommodation Rd	41 G6
Rydall Ter	40 C6	South Par	40 E3
S		Sovereign St	40 E4
Sackville St	41 F1	Spence La	40 B5
St. Andrew's St	40 C3	Spenceley St	40 D1
St. Barnabas Rd	40 E5	Spinney, The	41 H4
St. Georges Rd	40 D2	Spinneyfield Ct	41 H4
St. Helen's St	41 G6	Spring Cl Av	41 H5
St. Hilda's Av	41 J5	Spring Cl Gdns	41 H5
St. Hilda's Cres	41 H5	Spring Cl St	41 H5
St. Hilda's Gro	41 J5	Spring Cl Wk	41 H5
St. Hilda's Mt	41 J5	Springfield Mt	40 C2
St. Hilda's Pl	41 J5	Spring Gro Ter	40 A1
St. Hilda's Rd	41 J5	Spring Gro Vw	40 B1
St. John's Av	40 C1	Spring Gro Wk	40 A1
St. John's Cl	40 B1	Springwell Ct	40 C5
St. John's Gro	40 B1	Springwell Rd	40 C5
St. John's Rd	40 B2	Springwell St	40 C5
St. Luke's Cescent	40 D7	Springwell Vw	40 C5
		Stafford St	41 G7

Street	Ref	Street	Ref
Stanley Av	41 J1	Victoria Rd	40 E5
Stanley Pl	41 J1	Victoria Sq	40 D3
Stanley Rd	41 J1	Victoria St	40 C2
Stanley Ter	41 J1	Victoria Ter	40 C2
Stocks Hill	40 C6	Village Ter	40 A1
Stoney Rock Gro	41 J2	Vinery Mt	41 J4
Stoney Rock La	41 H2	Vinery Pl	41 J4
Stott Rd	40 A4	Vinery St	41 J3
Studio Rd	40 B2	Vinery Ter	41 J4
Sutton St	40 C5	**W**	
Sweet St	40 D5	Wade La	41 E3
Sweet St W	40 C5	Walford Gro	41 J3
Sydenham Rd	40 B5	Walford Rd	41 J3
Sydenham St	40 B5	Walford Ter	41 J3
T		Walter Cres	41 H4
Telephone Pl	41 G2	Walter St	40 A2
Templar La	41 F3	Walton St	40 D5
Templar Pl	41 F3	Washington St	40 B3
Templar St	41 F3	Water La	40 C5
Temple Vw Gro	41 J4	Waterloo Rd	41 G7
Temple Vw Pl	41 J4	Waterloo St	41 F4
Temple Vw Rd	41 J3	Waverley Garth	40 D7
Temple Vw Ter	41 J4	Weaver St	40 A2
Thealby Cl	41 G3	Welbeck Rd	41 J4
Thealby Lawn	41 G2	Well Cl Ri	40 E1
Thealby Pl	41 G3	Wellington Br St	40 C5
Third Av	40 A5	Wellington Pl	40 C4
Thirsk Row	40 D4	Wellington Rd	40 B4
Thoresby Pl	40 D3	Wellington St	40 D4
Thornleigh Gdns	41 J5	Wesley Pl	41 H4
Thornleigh Gro	41 J5	Westfield Cres	40 B2
Thornleigh Mt	41 J5	Westfield Rd	40 B2
Thornleigh St	41 J5	Westfield Ter	40 B2
Thornleigh Vw	41 J5	Westgate	40 D3
Thornville Pl	40 B1	Westlock Av	41 J2
Thornville Rd	40 A1	West St	40 C3
Thornville Row	40 B1	West Vale	40 A6
Thornville St	40 B1	Wharf St	41 F4
Thornville Vw	40 B1	Whitehall Rd	40 B5
Tilbury Av	40 C7	Whitehouse St	41 G7
Tilbury Gro	40 C7	Whitelock St	41 F2
Tilbury Mt	40 C7	Whitfield Av	41 G7
Tilbury Par	40 C7	Whitfield Gdns	41 G7
Tilbury Rd	40 C7	Whitfield Pl	41 G7
Tilbury Ter	40 C7	Whitfield Sq	41 G7
Tilbury Vw	40 C7	Whitfield Way	41 G7
Tong Rd	40 A5	Willis St	41 H4
Top Moor Side	40 C6	Willoughby Ter	40 C6
Torre Cl	41 J3	Willow App	40 A2
Torre Dr	41 J2	Willow Av	40 A2
Torre Rd	41 H3	Willow Cl	40 B2
Tower Ho St	41 F2	Willow Garth	40 A2
Trafalgar St	41 F3	Willow Rd	40 A2
Trent Rd	41 J3	Willow Ter Rd	40 D2
Trent St	40 D6	Wilmington St	41 F1
Trinity St	41 E3	Winchester St	40 A4
Triumph Cl	40 C5	Winfield Gro	40 E1
Turlow Ct	41 G4	Winfield Pl	40 E1
U		Winfield Ter	40 E1
Union Pl	40 D5	Wintoun St	41 F2
Union St	41 F3	Wolseley Rd	40 A1
University Rd	40 C1	Woodhouse La	40 D1
Upper Accommodation Rd	41 H3	Woodhouse Sq	40 D3
Upper Basinghall St	40 E3	Woodsley Grn	40 B1
Upper N St	40 E2	Woodsley Rd	40 B2
Upper Westlock Av	41 J2	Wormald Row	41 E3
V		Wortley La	40 B5
Vernon Rd	40 D2	Wortley Pk	40 A5
Vernon St	40 E2	**Y**	
Vicar La	41 F3	Yarn St	41 H6
		York Pl	40 D3
		York Rd	41 H3
		York St	41 F4

Liverpool street index

Street	Ref	Street	Ref
A		Alexandra Rd	43 J5
Abercromby Sq	43 F4	Alex Cl	43 F7
Abney Cl	43 H5	Alfred Ms	42 D6
Acorn Ct	43 E7	Alfred St	43 J5
Acton Way	43 H5	Altcar Av	43 J6
Adderley St	43 H3	Alt St	43 G6
Addison St	42 C2	Amberley St	43 F6
Addison Way	42 C2	Amelia Cl	43 F2
Adelaide Pl	42 D1	Amethyst Cl	43 G1
Adelaide Rd	43 G4	Anchorage, The	42 C7
Adele Thompson Dr	43 F6	Angela St	43 G5
Agnes Way	43 H4	Anglezark Cl	43 H3
Aigburth St	43 G5	Anglican Ct	42 E6
Ainsworth St	42 E4	Archbishop Warlock Ct	42 B1
Albany Rd	43 G3	Argyle St	42 C5
Albert Edward Rd	43 G3	Arley St	42 C1
Albert St	43 G4	Arnold Cres	43 F7
Alderson Rd	43 J6	Arnside Rd	43 H4
Alexandra Cl	43 G2		

Street	Ref	Street	Ref
Arrad St	43 E5	Balm St	43 H3
Arundel Av	43 J7	Baltimore St	42 E5
Arundel Cl	43 G7	Bannerman St	43 J5
Asbridge St	43 G7	Barnet Cl	43 H5
Ashton St	43 F3	Basnett St	42 C4
Ashwell St	42 D6	Bath St	42 A3
Askham Cl	43 G6	Battenberg St	43 G3
Aspen Gro	43 H7	Bayhorse La	43 E3
Atlantic Pt	42 C2	Beaconsfield St	43 G7
Atwell St	43 G1	Beaufort St	43 D7
B		Beaumont St	43 G6
Back Colquitt St	42 D5	Beau St	42 D1
Back Guildford St	43 F1	Beckwith St	42 C5
Back Kelvin Gro	43 G7	Bective St	43 J5
Back Leeds St	42 B2	Bedford Cl	43 F5
Baker St	43 G2	Bedford St S	43 F6
Baker Way	43 F2	Beech St	43 J3
Balmoral Rd	43 J1	Benson St	42 D4
		Bentley Rd	43 G7

Street	Ref	Street	Ref
Beresford St	42 E1	Blackstock St	42 C2
Berington St	42 C1	Blair St	42 E6
Berkley St	43 E6	Blenheim St	42 C1
Berry St	42 D5	Bluefields St	43 E6
Berwick Cl	43 H1	Blundell St	42 C6
Berwick St	43 H1	Boaler St	43 G2
Bevington Bush	42 C2	Bold Pl	42 D5
Bevington Hill	42 C1	Bold St	42 D4
Bidder St	42 E2	Bolton St	42 D4
Bigham Rd	43 H2	Bond St	42 C1
Birchfield St	42 E2	Boothwood Cl	43 H5
Bird St	43 J6	Boswell St	43 H6
Birkett St	42 D2	Botanic Grn	43 H3
Birstall Rd	43 G2	Botanic Pl	43 J3
Birt Cl	43 G6	Botanic Rd	43 J3
Bishop Sheppard Ct	42 B1	Boundary La	43 G1
Bixteth St	42 B3	Boyton Ct	43 J5
Blackburne Pl	43 E5	Bradfield St	43 H3
		Brae St	43 H3

Brahms Cl 43 G7
Brampton Dr 43 F5
Brassey St 42 D7
Breames Cl 43 H4
Breck Rd 43 F1
Bremner Cl 43 H4
Brick St 42 D6
Bridge Rd 43 J5
Bridgewater St 42 C6
Bridport St 42 D3
Bright St 43 F2
Brindley St 42 D7
Britannia Av 43 J6
Britten Cl 43 H7
Bronte St 42 E3
Brook St 42 B3
Brownlow Hill 42 D4
Brownlow St 43 E4
Brow Side 43 E1
Brunswick Rd 43 F3
Brunswick St 42 B4
Bryges St 43 G4
Brythen St 42 C4
Burlington St 42 C1
Burnley Cl 43 G1
Burroughs Gdns 42 C1
Burrows Ct 42 B1
Burton Cl 42 C5
Bute St 42 D2
Bute St (Edge Hill) 43 H6
Butler Cres 43 G2
Butler St 43 G1
Button St 42 C4
Byrom St 42 D3

C
Cadogan St 43 J5
Caird St 43 G2
Cairns St 43 G7
Caledonia St 43 E5
Callander Rd 43 J2
Cambria St N 43 H2
Cambria St S 43 H2
Cambridge Ct 43 E5
Cambridge St 43 E4
Camden St 42 D3
Cameo Cl 43 G1
Cameron St 43 H3
Campbell St 42 C5
Canada Boul 42 B4
Canning Pl 42 C4
Canning St 43 E5
Canterbury St 42 E2
Canterbury Way 43 E2
Cantsfield St 43 J6
Cardigan St 43 J5
Cardigan Way 43 H1
Cardwell St 43 G5
Carlingford Cl 43 G6
Carlton St 42 A1
Carmarthen Cres 42 D7
Carpenters Row 42 C5
Carruthers St 42 B2
Carstairs Rd 43 J1
Carter St 43 F6
Carver St 43 E2
Caryl St 42 D7
Castle St 42 B4
Catharine St 43 F5
Cathedral Cl 42 E6
Cathedral Gate 42 E5
Cathedral Wk 42 E4
Cawdor St 43 G7
Cazneau St 42 D1
Cedar Gro 43 H7
Celtic St 43 F7
Chadwick St 42 B2
Chaloner St 42 C6
Chandos St 43 H4
Channell Rd 43 H2
Chapel St 42 B4
Chase Way 42 E1
Chatham Pl 43 G4
Chatham St 43 F5
Chatsworth Dr 43 H5
Chaucer St 42 D2
Cheapside 42 C3
Chesney Cl 42 E7
Chesterfield St 42 E6
Chester St 42 E7
Chestnut St 43 F4
Chichester Cl 43 J5
Childwall Av 43 J6
Chisenhale St 42 B1
Chiswell St 43 H3
Christian St 42 D2
Chris Ward Cl 43 H4
Church All 42 C4
Church Mt 43 G4
Church St 42 C4
Churton Ct 43 F2
Cicely St 43 G4
Clarence St 42 E4
Claribel St 43 F7

Claughton Cl 43 H4
Claypole Cl 43 H5
Clay St 42 B1
Clearwater Cl 43 H3
Clegg St 42 D1
Clement Gdns 42 C1
Cleveland Sq 42 C5
Clifford St 42 E3
Cliff St 43 H3
Clifton Gro 43 E1
Clint Rd 43 H4
Clint Rd W 43 H4
Clint Way 43 H4
Coal St 42 D3
Cobden St 43 F2
Coburg Wf 42 C7
Cockspur St 42 C3
Coleridge St 43 H2
College La 42 C4
College St N 43 E2
College St S 43 F2
Colquitt St 42 D5
Coltart Rd 43 G7
Comberme St 43 E7
Commerce
  Way 43 G6
Commutation
  Row 42 D3
Compton Rd 43 G1
Comus St 42 D2
Concert St 42 D5
Connaught Rd 43 G3
Contance St 43 E3
Cookson St 42 D6
Cook St 42 C4
Copperas Hill 42 D4
Corinto St 42 E6
Corney St 43 H6
Cornhill 42 C5
Cornwallis St 42 D5
Corsewall St 43 J5
Cotswold St 43 H3
Cotton St 42 A1
Covent Gdn 42 B3
Cowan Dr 43 F1
Cranborne Rd 43 J6
Craven St 42 E3
Cresswell St 43 F1
Cropper St 42 D4
Crosfield Cl 43 J4
Crosfield Rd 43 H4
Crosshall St 42 C3
Crown St 43 F3
Croxteth Gro 43 H7
Croxteth Rd 43 G7
Crump St 42 D6
Cullen St 43 H6
Cumberland St 42 C3
Cunliffe St 42 C3
Custom Ho Pl 42 C5

D
Dale St 42 B4
Daniel Davies Dr 43 G6
Dansie St 43 E4
Danube St 43 H6
Darrel Dr 43 H6
Daulby St 43 F3
Davies St 42 C3
Dawber Cl 43 G1
Dawson St 42 C4
Dean Dillistone Ct 42 D6
Deane Rd 43 H3
Dean Patey Ct 42 D5
Deeley Cl 43 H4
Dell St 43 H3
Denham Dr 43 H1
Denham Way 43 H1
Dentdale Dr 43 E1
Devon St 42 E3
Dexter St 42 E7
Dial St 43 H3
Diamond St 42 C1
Dickens St 43 E7
Dickson St 42 A1
Dombey St 43 E7
Dorothy St 43 H4
Dorrit St 43 E7
Dorset Av 43 J6
Douro St 42 D1
Dovestone Cl 43 H5
Dove St 43 G6
Drury La 42 B4
Dryden St 42 D1
Dublin St 42 A1
Ducie St 43 G7
Duckinfield St 43 E4
Duke St 42 C5
Duncan St 42 D6
Dunkeld Cl 43 G2
Dunstan La 43 H5
Durden St 43 H6
Durning Rd 43 H3

Dwerryhouse St 42 D7
Dyke St 43 F1

E
Earle Rd 43 H6
Earle St 42 B3
East St 42 B3
Eaton St 42 B2
Ebenezer Rd 43 J3
Eden St 43 H6
Edgar St 42 C2
Edge Hill 43 G5
Edge La 43 G4
Edinburgh Rd 43 G3
Edmund St 42 B3
Egerton St 43 E6
Elaine St 43 F7
Eldonian Way 42 B1
Eldon Pl 42 C1
Eldon St 42 C1
Elizabeth St 43 F3
Elliot St 42 D4
Elm Gro 43 F4
Elm Vale 43 J1
Elstree Rd 43 J2
Ember Cres 43 F1
Embledon St 43 G6
Emerson St 43 E6
Empress Rd 43 G4
Enid St 43 F7
Epworth St 43 F3
Erin Cl 43 E7
Erskine St 43 F3
Esher Rd 43 H2
Eversley St 43 F7
Everton Brow 42 E2
Everton Rd 43 F1
Every St 43 G1
Exchange St E 42 B3
Exchange St W 42 B3

F
Fairclough St 42 D4
Fairfield 43 J2
Falkland St 43 E3
Falkner Sq 43 F6
Falkner St 43 E5
Fareham Rd 43 J3
Farnworth St 43 G2
Fazakerley St 42 B3
Fearnside St 43 J5
Fell St 43 H3
Fenwick St 42 B4
Fern Gro 43 H7
Fernhill Dr 43 F7
Fielding St 43 G2
Field St 42 E2
Finch Pl 43 E3
Finlay St 43 H2
Fishguard Cl 43 F1
Fitzclarence Way 43 F1
Fitzpatrick Ct 42 B1
Fitzroy Way 43 F2
Fleet St 42 D4
Fleming Ct 42 B1
Flint St 42 D6
Fontenoy St 42 C3
Ford St 42 C2
Forrest St 42 C5
Fowler Cl 43 H4
Foxhill Cl 43 F7
Fox St 42 D1
Fraser St 42 D3
Freedom Cl 43 G5
Freeman St 43 J5
Freemasons' Row 42 C2
Frost St 43 H3

G
Galloway St 43 J5
Gannock St 43 H3
Gardenside St 43 F2
Gardners Dr 43 H1
Gardner's Row 42 C2
Garrick St 43 J6
Gascoyne St 42 B2
Geneva Rd 43 J2
George Harrison Cl 43 G2
Georges Dockway 42 B3
George St 42 B3
Geraint St 43 F7
Gerard St 42 D3
Gibraltar Row 42 B3
Gibson St 43 F6
Gilbert St 42 C5
Gildarts Gdns 42 C1
Gildart St 43 E3
Gilead St 43 H3
Gill St 43 E3
Gilroy Rd 43 H2
Gladstone Rd 43 G4
Gladstone St 43 H5
Gleave Cres 43 F1
Glegg St 42 B1

Gloucester Ct 43 G2
Gloucester Pl 43 F3
Gore St 42 D7
Gower St 42 B5
Gradwell St 43 C4
Grafton Cres 42 D7
Grafton St 42 D6
Granary Wf 42 C7
Granby St 43 G6
Grantham St 43 H2
Granville Rd 43 J6
Grayson St 42 C5
Great Crosshall St 42 C3
Great George Pl 42 D6
Great George St 42 D6
Great Howard St 42 B2
Great Nelson St 42 D1
Great Newton St 43 E3
Great Orford St 43 E4
Great Richmond St 42 D2
Greek St 42 E3
Greenheys Rd 43 G7
Greenland St 42 D6
Green La 42 E4
Greenleaf St 43 H6
Greenside 43 F2
Green St 42 C1
Gregson St 43 F2
Grenville St S 42 D5
Gresley Cl 43 J4
Grierson St 43 H6
Grinfield St 43 G4
Grinshill Cl 43 F7
Grosvenor St 42 D1
Grove Pk 43 H7
Grove Rd 43 J2
Grove St 43 F6
Guelph St 43 F3
Guion St 43 H1
Gwendoline St 43 F7
Gwenfron Rd 43 G2
Gwent St 43 F7

H
Hackins Hey 42 B3
Haigh St 42 E1
Hale St 42 C3
Hall La 43 F3
Halsbury Rd 43 H2
Hampstead Rd 43 J2
Hampton St 43 E6
Hannan Rd 43 H2
Hanover St 42 C5
Harbord St 43 H7
Hardman St 42 E5
Hardy St 42 D6
Harewood St 43 G1
Harker St 42 D2
Harke St 43 H5
Harper St 43 F3
Harrington St 42 C4
Harrowby Cl 43 G6
Harrowby St 43 F6
Hartley Quay 42 B5
Hart St 42 E3
Hatherley Cl 43 G6
Hatherley St 43 F7
Hatton Gdn 42 C3
Haverston Rd 43 J2
Hawdon Ct 43 J5
Hawke St 42 D4
Hawkins St 43 H2
Hawthorn Gro 43 H4
Head St 42 E7
Heathcote Cl 43 H5
Heathfield St 42 D4
Helena St 43 H4
Helsby St 43 G4
Hendon Rd 43 J1
Henglers Cl 43 F2
Henry Edward St 42 C2
Henry St 42 C5
Hewitts Pl 42 C3
Highfield St 42 B2
Highgate St 43 G4
High St 42 B3
Hilbre St 42 D4
Hillaby Cl 43 F7
Hillside St 43 F2
Hill St 42 D7
Hinton St 43 J2
Hockenhall All 42 C3
Hodson Pl 43 F1
Holborn St 43 F3
Holden St 43 G5
Holdsworth St 43 H3
Holly Rd 43 J3
Holmes St 43 H6
Holt Rd 43 H3
Holy Cross Cl 42 C2
Homerton Rd 43 J2
Hood St 42 C3
Hope Pl 43 E5
Hope St 43 E6

Hornby Wk 42 C1
Hotham St 42 D3
Houghton St 42 D4
Houlton St 43 H3
Hughes Cl 43 J4
Hughes St 43 G1
Huntly Rd 43 J2
Hurst St 42 C5
Huskisson St 43 E6
Hutchinson St 43 G2
Hutchinson Wk 43 G2
Hygeia St 43 G1
Hyslop St 42 E7

I
Iliad St 42 D1
Ingrow Rd 43 H2
Irvine St 43 E3
Irwell St 42 B4
Islington 42 E3
Ivatt Way 43 H4

J
Jack McBain Ct 42 B1
Jade Rd 43 H1
Jamaica St 42 D6
James Clarke St 42 C1
James St 42 B4
Janet St 43 H4
Jasmine Cl 43 E1
Jenkinson St 42 E2
Jermyn St 43 G7
Jet Cl 43 H1
John Lennon Dr 43 G2
John Moores Cl 43 F5
Johnson St 42 C3
John St 42 E2
Jordan St 42 D6
Jubilee Dr 43 G3
Judges St 43 J1
Judges Way 43 J1
Juvenal Pl 42 D1
Juvenal St 42 D2

K
Keble St 43 G2
Kelso Rd 43 J2
Kelvin Gro 43 G7
Kempston St 43 E3
Kenley Cl 43 H1
Kensington 43 G3
Kensington 43 G3
Kensington St 43 G2
Kent St 42 D5
Kilshaw St 43 G1
Kimberley Cl 43 F6
Kinder St 43 F2
King Edward St 42 B3
Kingsley Rd 43 G6
Kings Dock St 42 C6
Kingsley Rd 43 G6
Kings Par 42 B5
Kingsway Ct 42 C1
Kingswell Cl 43 G4
Kitchen St 42 C6
Knight St 42 D5

L
Lace St 42 C3
Ladybower Cl 43 H5
Laggan St 43 H3
Lairds Pl 42 C1
Lakeland Cl 42 C5
Lambert Way 42 E3
Lamport St 42 E7
Lance Cl 43 F1
Langley St 42 E7
Langsdale St 42 E2
Langton Rd 43 J1
Lanyork Rd 42 B2
Laurel Gro 43 H7
Lavan Cl 42 C2
Lawrence Rd 43 J6
Lawton St 42 D4
Laxey St 42 E7
Leece St 42 E5
Leeds St 42 B2
Leigh St 42 C4
Leigh St (Edge Hill) 43 J4
Lemon Cl 43 J4
Lemon Gro 43 H7
Leopold Rd 43 G4
Lesseps Rd 43 H6
Lestock St 42 E6
Liffey St 43 G6
Lightwood Dr 43 H5
Lightwood St 43 H5
Lilley Rd 43 J2
Lilly Vale 43 J2
Lime Gro 43 F4
Limekiln La 42 C1
Lincoln Cl 43 H1
Lindley Cl 43 H5

Lindley St 43 J5
Ling St 43 H3
Lister Cres 43 J3
Lister Rd 43 J2
Little Catherine St 43 E6
Little Ct 42 B1
Little Hardman St 42 E5
Little Howard St 42 B1
Little St. Bride St 43 E5
Little Woolton St 43 F4
Liver St 42 C5
Lloyd Cl 43 F1
Lockerby Rd 43 J2
Lodge La 43 H7
London Rd 42 D3
Longfellow St 43 H6
Longstone Wk 43 G5
Lord Nelson St 42 D3
Lord St 42 C4
Lorton St 43 H6
Lothian St 43 F7
Loudon Gro 43 G7
Love La 42 B1
Lower Castle St 42 B4
Low Hill 43 F2
Lowther St 43 F6
Low Wd St 43 F3
Luke St 43 E7
Lyceum Pl 42 D4
Lydia Ann St 42 C5
Lytton St 43 F2

M
Maddrell St 42 B1
Madelaine St 43 F7
Madeley St 43 H1
Magdala St 43 H6
Maitland Cl 43 H6
Malden Rd 43 H2
Mallow Rd 43 H2
Malt St 43 G5
Malvern Rd 43 H2
Manchester St 42 C3
Manesty's La 42 C4
Manfred St 43 F3
Mann Island 42 B4
Mann St 42 D7
Mansell Rd 43 H2
Mansfield St 42 D2
Manton Rd 43 H2
Maple Gro 43 H7
Marathon Cl 43 F1
Marcot Rd 43 J1
Margaret St 43 F1
Mariners Wf 42 C7
Maritime Pl 42 E2
Maritime Way 42 C5
Marlborough St 42 C2
Marlsford St 43 H2
Marmaduke St 43 G4
Marquis St 42 E3
Marsden St 43 F2
Marsden Way 43 F2
Marshall Pl 42 C1
Martensen St 43 G4
Marvin St 43 G2
Marybone 42 C3
Maryland St 43 E5
Mason St 43 G4
Mathew St 42 C4
Maud St 43 F7
Maxton Rd 43 H2
Mayfair Cl 43 H1
May Pl 42 E4
May St 42 E4
Melda Cl 43 F2
Melville Pl 43 F5
Merlin St 43 F7
Michael
  Dragonette Ct 42 C1
Midghall St 42 C2
Mile End 42 C1
Millennium Pl 43 G7
Mill La 42 D3
Mill Rd 43 F1
Mill St 42 E7
Millvale St 43 H1
Milroy St 43 H4
Milverton St 43 H1
Minshull St 43 F4
Minster Ct 43 F5
Minto Cl 43 H3
Minto St 43 H3
Mirfield St 43 H2
Molyneux Rd 43 G2
Montgomery
  Way 43 H1
Moorfields 42 C3
Moor Pl 42 E3
Moor St 42 B4
Morden St 43 H1
Moss Gro 43 H7
Mount Pleasant 42 D4
Mount St 42 E5

Mount Vernon Grn 43 G3
Mount Vernon Rd 43 F4
Mount Vernon St 43 F3
Mozart Cl 43 G7
Muirhead Av 43 H1
Mulberry Pl 43 F5
Mulberry St 43 F5
Mulgrave St 43 F6
Mulliner St 43 J6
Myrtle St 43 E5

N
Navigation Wf 42 C7
Naylor St 42 C2
Needham Rd 43 H3
Nelson Rd 43 G4
Nelson St 42 D6
Netherfield Rd S 42 E1
Nevin St 43 F2
Nevison St 43 G4
New Bird St 42 D6
New Grey Rock Cl 43 G1
Newhall St 42 D6
New Henderson St 42 D7
Newington 42 D4
New Quay 42 B3
New Red Rock Vw 43 G1
Newsham Dr 43 H1
Newstead Rd 43 H6
Newton Way 43 E4
Noel St 43 H6
Norfolk St 42 C6
Norman St 43 E3
Northbrook Cl 43 G6
North Brook St 43 F6
Northcote Cl 43 F1
North John St 42 C3
North St 42 C3
North Vw 43 G4
Norton St 42 D3
Norwood Gro 43 H1
Nuttall St 43 H4

O
Oakes St 43 E3
Oakham St 42 D7
O'Connell Rd 42 C1
Odsey St 43 H3
Oil St 42 A1
Old Coll Pl 43 H4
Old Hall St 42 B3
Oldham St 42 D5
Old Leeds St 42 B3
Olympia St 43 G2
Onslow Rd 43 J2
Opal Cl 43 G1
Orange Gro 43 H7
O'Reilly Ct 42 B1
Oriel Steet 42 C2
Ormond St 42 B3
Orphan St 43 F5
Orthes St 43 E4
Ottley St 43 J2
Overbury St 43 G4
Overton St 43 G4
Oxendale Cl 43 G6
Oxford St 43 E4
Oxford St E 43 G4

P
Paddington 43 F4
Page Wk 42 E2
Paisley St 42 A2
Pall Mall 42 B2
Paradise St 42 C5

Parker St 42 D4
Park La 42 C5
Park Pl 42 E7
Park Rd 43 E7
Parkside St 43 F2
Park Way 43 F6
Parliament Cl 42 E6
Parliament St 42 D6
Parr St 42 D5
Parton St 43 J2
Paul McCartney Way 43 H2
Paul Orr Ct 42 B1
Paul St 42 C2
Pavilion Cl 43 G6
Pear Gro 43 H2
Pearl Way 43 G1
Peet St 43 H4
Pembroke Gdns 43 E3
Pembroke Pl 42 E3
Pembroke St 43 E4
Penarth Cl 43 G5
Pendine Cl 43 H1
Penlinken Dr 43 H1
Penvalley Cres 43 H1
Peover St 42 D2
Pera Cl 43 G2
Percy St 43 E6
Perrygate Cl 43 G5
Perry St 42 D7
Perth St 43 G2
Peter's Arcade 42 C4
Peter St 42 C3
Phillimore Rd 43 H2
Pickop St 42 C3
Pickwick St 43 E7
Picton Rd 43 J5
Pilgrim St 42 E5
Pimhill Cl 43 G7
Pine Ms 42 E6
Pinetop Cl 43 H1
Pitt St 42 D5
Pleasant St 42 E4
Plimsoll St 43 H4
Plumpton St 43 F1
Pomfret St 43 F7
Pomona St 42 E4
Pond Cl 43 H1
Ponsonby St 43 G7
Porter St 42 A1
Portland Pl 42 D1
Portwood Cl 43 G5
Pownall Sq 42 C3
Pownall St 42 C5
Prescot Rd 43 J2
Prescot St 43 F3
Preston St 42 C3
Price St 42 C5
Primrose Hill 42 C3
Prince Albert Ms 42 D6
Prince Edwin St 42 D1
Princes Av 43 F6
Princes Gdns 42 B2
Princes Par 42 A3
Princes Pk 43 G7
Princes Rd 43 F6
Princes St 42 C3
Prince William St 42 D7
Prospect St 43 F3
Providence Cres 42 D7
Prussia St 42 B3
Pudsey St 42 D3
Pumpfields Rd 42 B2
Pythian Cl 43 G2
Pythian St 43 F2

Q
Queen Anne St 42 D2
Queensland St 43 G4
Queens Sq 42 D3
Queens Wf 42 B6
Quorn St 43 H3

R
Rachel St 42 D1
Radstock Rd 43 J2
Raffles St 42 D6
Rainford Gdns 42 C4
Rainford Sq 42 C4
Ranelagh St 42 D4
Raven Cl 43 F2
Raymond Pl 42 C1
Red Cross St 42 B4
Redgrave St 43 H3
Redmires Cl 43 H5
Red Rock St 43 G1
Regent St 42 A1
Renfrew St 43 G3
Renshaw St 42 D4
Reservoir St 43 F1
Reynolds Cl 43 G1
Rialto Cl 43 F6
Rice St 42 E5
Richardson St 43 J6
Richmond Row 42 D2
Richmond St 42 C4
Ridley Rd 43 H2
Rigby St 42 B3
Ringo Starr Dr 43 H2
Ritson St 43 G7
River Avon St 43 H6
Roberts St 42 A2
Roderick St 42 E2
Rodney St 42 E5
Roe St 42 D3
Rokeby Cl 42 E2
Rokeby St 42 E2
Rokesmith Av 43 H5
Romer Rd 43 H2
Romilly St 43 G2
Roscastle Cl 43 G2
Roscoe La 42 D5
Roscoe St 42 E5
Roscommon St 42 D1
Roseberry St 43 F6
Rose Hill 42 D2
Rosemary Cl 43 G4
Rose Pl 42 D2
Rothsay Cl 42 E1
Rothwell St 43 G1
Royal Mail St 42 D4
Royston St 43 G4
Rufford Rd 43 J2
Rumford Pl 42 B3
Rumford St 42 B3
Rupert Dr 43 F2
Russel St 42 E3
Ryedale Cl 43 G6

S
St. Andrew St 42 E4
St. Anne St 42 D2
St. Bride St 43 F5
St. James Pl 42 D6
St. James Rd 42 E6
St. James St 42 D6
St. John's La 42 C3
St. Josephs Cres 42 D2
St. Martins Ms 42 D1
St. Michaels Gro 43 H1
St. Nicholas Pl 42 A4

St. Stephen's Pl 42 C2
Salisbury Rd 43 J6
Salisbury St 42 E1
Salthouse Quay 42 B5
Saltney St 42 A1
Sandhead St 43 J5
Sandino St 42 E7
Sandon St 43 F5
Saxon Cl 43 G1
Saxony Rd 43 G3
Scholar St 43 J6
Schomberg St 43 G2
School La 42 C4
Scotland Rd 42 D2
Seaport Rd 43 G4
Seddon St 42 C5
Seel St 42 C4
Sefton Pk Rd 43 H7
Sefton St 42 C6
Selborne Cl 43 F6
Selborne St 43 F6
Selsey Cl 43 H5
Severs St 43 G1
Seymour St 42 E3
Shakespeare Cl 43 G1
Shallcross Pl 43 G1
Shaws All 42 C5
Shaw St 43 E1
Sheil Rd 43 H1
Shenstone St 43 G4
Shepherd's Fold Cl 43 G7
Sherwood St 42 B1
Shimmin St 43 G4
Sidney Pl 43 G4
Silkstone Cl 43 H5
Simpson St 42 C6
Sim St 42 E2
Sirdar Cl 43 H5
Sir Thomas St 42 C3
Skelhorne St 42 D4
Slater St 42 D5
Smithdown La 43 F4
Smithdown Rd 43 H6
Smithfield St 42 C3
Soho Pl 42 E2
Soho St 42 E2
Solomon St 43 H3
Solway St E 43 H6
Solway St W 43 G6
South Chester St 42 E7
Southern Cres 42 D7
South Ferry Quay 42 C7
South Hunter St 43 E5
South John St 42 C4
Sparling St 42 C6
Spekeland Rd 43 H5
Spencer St 43 F1
Spindle Cl 43 F1
Spofforth Rd 43 J5
Sprainger St 42 B1
Springfield 42 D2
Squires St 43 G4
Stafford St 42 E3
Stamford St 43 H3
Standish St 42 C3
Stanhope St 42 D7
Stanier Way 43 H4
Stanley St 42 C3
Star St 42 D7
Steinberg Ct 42 B1
Sterndale Cl 43 H5
Stockdale Cl 42 C2
Stone St 42 B1
Stowell St 43 E5
Strada Way 43 E2
Strand, The 42 B4

Strand St 42 B4
Strathmore Rd 43 H1
Strauss Cl 43 H7
Suffolk St 42 D5
Sugnall St 43 E5
Summer Seat 42 C1
Surrey St 42 C5
Sutcliffe St 43 H2
Sweeting St 42 B4
Swindale Cl 43 G6
Swiss Rd 43 J2

T
Tabley St 42 C6
Tace Cl 43 F6
Tagus Cl 43 G7
Tamar Cl 43 F1
Tarleton St 42 C4
Tatlock St 42 C1
Tavy Rd 43 F1
Teck St 43 G3
Teign Cl 43 F1
Tempest Hey 42 B3
Temple Ct 42 C4
Temple La 42 C3
Temple 42 C3
Tenterden St 42 C1
Thackeray Pl 43 F7
Thames St 42 G7
Thomas St Way 42 C5
Thorburn St 43 H4
Thornes Rd 43 G2
Tichbourne Way 43 F2
Tideswell Cl 43 H5
Timpron St 43 H5
Titchfield St 42 C1
Tithebarn St 42 B3
Tobin Cl 42 C1
Toft St 43 H3
Tom Mann Cl 42 D3
Tordelow Cl 43 F1
Tower Gdns 42 B4
Trafalgar Way 43 F2
Trowbridge St 42 E4
Trueman St 42 C3
Tudor St N 43 H2
Tudor St S 43 H2
Tulloch St 43 G2
Tunnel Rd 43 H5
Tunstall St 43 J6
Tweed Cl 43 H1
Twomey Cl 42 C1

U
Underley St 43 J6
Union Ct 42 C4
Union St 42 B3
Upper Baker St 43 G2
Upper Beau St 42 D1
Upper Bute St 42 E1
Upper Duke St 42 D5
Upper Frederick St 42 C5
Upper Hampton St 43 F6
Upper Harrington St 42 D7
Upper Hill St 43 E7
Upper Hope Pl 43 E5
Upper Mann St 42 D7
Upper Mason St 43 G4
Upper Newington 42 D4
Upper Parliament St 42 D6
Upper Pitt St 42 D6
Upper Pownall St 42 C5
Upper Stanhope St 43 E6
Upper Warwick St 43 E7
Upper William St 42 B1
Uxbridge St 43 H5

V
Vandries St 42 A1
Vandyke St 43 H6
Vauxhall Rd 42 C2
Vernon St 42 C3
Verulam Cl 43 G6
Victoria St 42 C4
Village St 43 E1
Vincent Ct 42 D5
Vining St 43 F7
Virgil St 42 D1
Voelas St 43 G7
Vronhill St 43 G7
Vulcan St 42 A1

W
Wainwright Cl 43 H5
Wakefield St 42 D2
Waldron Cl 42 C2
Walker St 43 F2
Wall St 42 C4
Walsh Cl 42 C1
Wapping 42 C5
Ward St 42 D3
Warwick St 42 E7
Waterloo Quay 42 A2
Water St 42 B4
Watkinson St 42 C6
Watmough St 42 E1
Wavertree Boul 43 J4
Wavertree Rd 43 G4
Webb Cl 43 H4
Webb St 43 H6
Webster Rd 43 J6
Webster St 42 C3
Wedgewood St 43 H3
Wendell St 43 H6
Wentworth Dr 43 F1
West Derby Rd 43 G2
West Derby St 43 F3
Westmorland Dr 42 C2
Whitcroft Rd 43 J2
Whitechapel 42 C4
Whitefield Rd 43 G1
Whitefield Way 43 G1
White Rock Ct 43 G1
White Rock St 43 G1
Whithorn St 43 J5
Whitland Rd 43 J1
Whitley St 42 B1
Whittier St 43 H6
Wightman St 43 G2
Wilde St 42 D3
Wilfer Cl 43 H5
William Brown St 42 D3
William Henry St 42 E2
Williamson St 42 C4
Wimpole St 43 H3
Windsor St 43 E6
Windsor Vw 43 H6
Winifred St 43 H4
Winter St 43 F2
Wolstenholme Sq 42 D5
Woodside St 43 H4
Wood St 42 D4
Wordsworth St 43 H6
Wrayburn Cl 43 H5
Wrenbury St 43 H3
Wynnstay St 43 G7

Y
Yanwath St 43 H6
York St 42 C5

London street index

A
Abbey Orchard St SW1 44 D6
Abingdon St SW1 44 E6
Achilles Way W1 44 A5
Adam & Eve Ct W1 44 C2
Adams Row W1 44 A4
Adam St WC2 45 E4
Addington St SE1 45 F6
Addle Hill EC4 45 H3
Adelaide St WC2 44 E4
Adeline Pl WC1 44 D2
Adelphi Ter WC2 45 E4
Agar St WC2 44 E4
Air St W1 44 C4
Alaska St SE1 45 G5
Albany W1 44 C4
Albany Ctyd W1 44 C4

Albemarle St W1 44 B4
Albemarle Way EC1 45 H1
Albert Barnes Ho SE1 45 J7
Albion Pl EC1 45 H1
Albion Way EC1 45 H1
Aldburgh Ms W1 44 A2
Aldermanbury EC2 45 J2
Aldermanbury Sq EC2 45 J2
Aldersgate St EC1 45 J2
Aldford St W1 44 A4
Aldwych WC2 45 F3
Alfred Ms W1 44 D1
Alfred Pl WC1 44 D1
Allington St SW1 44 C7
All Souls Pl W1 44 B2
Ambassador's Ct SW1 44 C5
Ambrosden Av SW1 44 C7
Amen Cor EC4 45 H3

Amen Ct EC4 45 H2
America St SE1 45 J5
Andrew Borde St WC2 44 D2
Andrewes Ho EC2 45 J2
Andrews Crosse WC2 45 G3
Angel Ct SW1 44 C5
Angel St EC1 45 J2
Apothecary St EC4 45 H3
Apple Tree Yd SW1 44 C4
Apsley Way W1 44 A5
Aquinas St SE1 45 G4
Archer St W1 44 D3
Arches, The WC2 45 E4
Archibald Ms W1 44 A4
Arch St SE1 45 J7
Argyll St W1 44 C3
Aria Ho WC2 45 E2
Arlington St SW1 44 C4

Arne St WC2 45 E3
Arneway St SW1 44 D7
Arrol Ho SE1 45 J7
Artillery Mans SW1 44 D6
Artillery Pl SW1 44 D7
Artillery Row SW1 44 D7
Arundel Gt Ct WC2 45 F3
Arundel St WC2 45 F3
Ashenden SE17 45 J7
Ashentree Ct EC4 45 G3
Ashland Pl W1 44 A1
Ashley Gdns SW1 44 C7
Ashley Pl SW1 44 C7
Astbury Ho SE11 45 G7
Audley Sq W1 44 A4
Austral St SE11 45 H7
Ave Maria La EC4 45 H3
Avery Row W1 44 B3

Avonmouth St SE1 45 J6
Avon Pl SE1 45 J6
Aybrook St W1 44 A2
Aylesbury St EC1 45 H1
Ayres St SE1 45 J5

B
Babmaes St SW1 44 D4
Back Hill EC1 45 G1
Bainbridge St WC1 44 D2
Baker's Ms W1 44 A2
Baker's Row EC1 45 G1
Baker's Yd EC1 45 G1
Balderton St W1 44 A3
Baldwin's Gdns EC1 45 G1
Balfour Ms W1 44 A4
Balfour Pl W1 44 A4
Baltic St E EC1 45 J1

Baltic St W EC1 45 J1
Banbury Ct WC2 44 E3
Bank End SE1 45 J4
Banks Ho SE1 45 J7
Bankside SE1 45 J4
Bankside Lofts SE1 45 H4
Banner St EC1 45 J1
Barbican EC2 45 J2
Barbican, The EC2 45 J1
Barbon Cl WC1 45 E1
Barge Ho St SE1 45 G4
Barkham Ter SE1 45 G6
Barley Mow Pas EC1 45 H2
Barlow Pl W1 44 B4
Barnard's Inn EC1 45 G2
Barons Pl SE1 45 G6
Barrett St W1 44 A3
Barter St WC1 45 E2

Entry	Ref
Bartholomew Cl EC1	45 J2
Bartholomew Pl EC1	45 J2
Bartlett Ct EC4	45 G2
Bartletts Pas EC4	45 G2
Barton St SW1	44 E6
Bastion Highwalk EC2	45 J2
Bateman's Bldgs W1	44 D3
Bateman St W1	44 D3
Bath Ct EC1	45 G1
Bath Ter SE1	45 J7
Bayley St WC1	44 D3
Baylis Rd SE1	45 G6
Beak St W1	44 C3
Bear All EC4	45 H2
Bear Gdns SE1	45 J4
Bear La SE1	45 H4
Bear St WC2	44 D3
Beauchamp St EC1	45 G2
Beaumont Ms W1	44 A1
Beaumont St W1	44 A1
Bedford Av WC1	44 D2
Bedfordbury WC2	44 E3
Bedford Ct WC2	44 E4
Bedford Pl WC1	44 E1
Bedford Row WC1	45 F1
Bedford Sq WC1	44 D2
Bedford St WC2	44 E3
Bedford Way WC1	44 D1
Bedlam Ms SE11	45 G7
Beech St EC2	45 J1
Beeston Pl SW1	44 B7
Belgrave Ms N SW1	44 A6
Belgrave Ms S SW1	44 A6
Belgrave Ms W SW1	44 A6
Belgrave Pl SW1	44 A6
Belgrave Sq SW1	44 A6
Belgrave Yd SW1	44 B7
Belgravia SW1	44 A7
Bell Wf La EC4	45 J4
Bell Yd WC2	45 G2
Belvedere Bldgs SE1	45 H6
Belvedere Pl SE1	45 H6
Belvedere Rd SE1	45 F5
Benjamin St EC1	45 H1
Bennet's Hill EC4	45 H3
Bennet St SW1	44 C4
Bennetts Yd SW1	44 D7
Bentinck Ms W1	44 A2
Bentinck St W1	44 A2
Berkeley Sq W1	44 B4
Berkeley St W1	44 B4
Bernard St WC1	44 E1
Berners Ms W1	44 C2
Berners Pl W1	44 C2
Berners St W1	44 C2
Berwick St W1	44 D3
Betterton St WC2	44 E3
Bingham Pl W1	44 A1
Binney St W1	44 A3
Birdcage Wk SW1	44 C6
Bird St W1	44 A3
Bishop's Ct EC4	45 H2
Bishop's Ct WC2	45 G2
Bishops Ter SE11	45 G7
Bittern St SE1	45 J6
Blackburne's Ms W1	44 A3
Blackfriars Br EC4	45 H3
Blackfriars Br SE1	45 H3
Blackfriars Ct EC4	45 H3
Black Friars La EC4	45 H3
Blackfriars Pas EC4	45 H3
Blackfriars Rd SE1	45 H6
Bleeding Heart Yd EC1	45 G2
Blenheim St W1	44 B3
Bloomfield Pl W1	44 B3
Bloomsbury WC1	44 D2
Bloomsbury Ct WC1	45 E2
Bloomsbury Pl WC1	45 E1
Bloomsbury Sq WC1	45 E2
Bloomsbury St WC1	44 D2
Bloomsbury Way WC1	44 E2
Blore Ct W1	44 D3
Blue Ball Yd SW1	44 C5
Bolsover St W1	44 B1
Bolt Ct EC4	45 G3
Bolton St W1	44 B4
Book Ms WC2	44 D3
Booth La EC4	45 J3
Booth's Pl W1	44 C2
Borough, The SE1	45 J6
Borough High St SE1	45 J6
Borough Rd SE1	45 H6
Borough Sq SE1	45 J6
Boscobel Pl SW1	44 A7
Boswell Ct WC1	45 E1
Boswell St WC1	45 E1
Boundary Row SE1	45 H5
Bourchier St W1	44 D3
Bourdon Pl W1	44 B3
Bourdon St W1	44 B3
Bourlet Cl W1	44 C2
Bourne Est EC1	45 G1
Bouverie St EC4	45 G3
Bow Chyd EC4	45 J3
Bow La EC4	45 J3
Bow St WC2	45 E3
Boyce St SE1	45 F5
Boyfield St SE1	45 H6
Boyle St W1	44 C3
Brackley St EC1	45 J1
Brad St SE1	45 G5
Bread St EC4	45 J3
Bream's Bldgs EC4	45 G2
Bressenden Pl SW1	44 B6
Brewer's Grn SW1	44 D6
Brewers Hall Gdns EC2	45 J2
Brewer St W1	44 C3
Briant Est SE1	45 G7
Briant Ho SE1	45 F7
Brick Ct EC4	45 G3
Brick St W1	44 B5
Bride Ct EC4	45 H3
Bride La EC4	45 H3
Bridewell Pl EC4	45 H3
Bridford Ms W1	44 B1
Bridge Pl SW1	44 B7
Bridge St SW1	44 E6
Bridgewater Sq EC2	45 J1
Bridgewater St EC2	45 J1
Bridle La W1	44 C3
Brinton Wk SE1	45 H5
Briset St EC1	45 H1
Britton St EC1	45 H1
Broadbent St W1	44 B3
Broad Ct WC2	45 E3
Broad Sanctuary SW1	44 D6
Broadstone Pl W1	44 A2
Broad Wk W1	44 A4
Broadwall SE1	45 G4
Broadway SW1	44 D6
Broadwick St W1	44 C3
Broad Yd EC1	45 H1
Brockham St SE1	45 J6
Broken Wf EC4	45 J3
Bromley Pl W1	44 C1
Brook Dr SE11	45 G7
Brooke's Ct EC1	45 G1
Brookes Mkt EC1	45 G1
Brook's Ms W1	44 B3
Brook St EC1	45 G1
Brook St W1	44 A3
Brown Hart Gdns W1	44 A3
Browning Ms W1	44 B2
Brownlow Ms WC1	45 F1
Brownlow St WC1	45 F2
Brunswick Sq WC1	45 E1
Bruton La W1	44 B4
Bruton Pl W1	44 B4
Bruton St W1	44 B4
Brydges Pl WC2	44 E4
Buckingham Arc WC2	45 E4
Buckingham Gate SW1	44 C6
Buckingham Ms SW1	44 C6
Buckingham Pl SW1	44 C6
Buckingham St WC2	45 E4
Buckley St SE1	45 G5
Bucknall St WC2	44 D2
Bull Inn Ct WC2	45 E4
Bulstrode Pl W1	44 A2
Bulstrode St W1	44 A2
Burdett St SE1	45 G6
Burgon St EC4	45 H3
Burleigh St WC2	45 F3
Burlington Arc W1	44 C4
Burlington Gdns W1	44 C4
Burrell St SE1	45 H4
Burrows Ms SE1	45 H5
Bury Pl WC1	44 E2
Bury St WC1	44 E2
Butler Pl SW1	44 D6
Byng Pl WC1	44 D1
Bywell Pl W1	44 C2

C

Entry	Ref
Cadogan La SW1	44 A7
Cahill St EC1	45 J1
Caleb St SE1	45 J5
Cambridge Circ WC2	44 D3
Candover St W1	44 C2
Cannon St EC4	45 J3
Canon Row SW1	44 E6
Canterbury Ho SE1	45 F6
Canvey St SE1	45 H4
Capener's Cl SW1	44 A6
Capper St WC1	44 C1
Carburton St W1	44 B1
Carey La EC2	45 J2
Carey St WC2	45 F3
Carlisle La SE1	45 F7
Carlisle Pl SW1	44 C7
Carlisle St W1	44 D3
Carlos Pl W1	44 A4
Carlton Gdns SW1	44 D5
Carlton Ho Ter SW1	44 D5
Carlton St SW1	44 D4
Carmelite St EC4	45 G3
Carnaby St W1	44 C3
Carpenter St W1	44 B4
Carrington St W1	44 B5
Carteret St SW1	44 D6
Carter La EC4	45 H3
Carthusian St EC1	45 J1
Carting La WC2	45 E4
Castle Baynard St EC4	45 H3
Castlebrook Cl SE11	45 H7
Castle La SW1	44 C6
Castle Yd SE1	45 H4
Cathedral Piazza SW1	44 C7
Cathedral Wk SW1	44 C6
Catherine Pl SW1	44 C6
Catherine St WC2	45 F3
Catherine Wheel Yd SW1	44 C5
Catton St WC1	45 F2
Cavendish Ms N W1	44 B1
Cavendish Ms S W1	44 B2
Cavendish Pl W1	44 B2
Cavendish Sq W1	44 B2
Caxton St SW1	44 C6
Cecil Ct WC2	44 D4
Centaur St SE1	45 F6
Centrepoint WC1	44 D2
Chadwick St SW1	44 D7
Chancel St SE1	45 H4
Chancery La WC2	45 G2
Chandos Pl WC2	44 E4
Chandos St W1	44 B2
Chapel Pl W1	44 B3
Chapel St SW1	44 A6
Chaplin Cl SE1	45 G5
Chapone Pl W1	44 D3
Chapter Ho Ct EC4	45 J3
Charing Cross SW1	44 D4
Charing Cross Rd WC2	44 D2
Charles II St SW1	44 D4
Charles St W1	44 B4
Charlotte Ms W1	44 C1
Charlotte Pl W1	44 C2
Charlotte St W1	44 C1
Charterhouse, The EC1	45 H1
Charterhouse Bldgs EC1	45 H1
Charterhouse Ms EC1	45 H1
Charterhouse Sq EC1	45 H1
Charterhouse St EC1	45 H1
Cheapside EC2	45 J3
Chenies Ms WC1	44 D1
Chenies St WC1	44 D1
Chequer St EC1	45 J1
Cherry Tree Wk EC1	45 J1
Chesham Cl SW1	44 A7
Chesham Ms SW1	44 A6
Chesham Pl SW1	44 A7
Chesham St SW1	44 A7
Cheshire Ct EC4	45 G3
Chester Cl SW1	44 A6
Chesterfield Gdns W1	44 B4
Chesterfield Hill W1	44 B4
Chesterfield St W1	44 B4
Chester Ms SW1	44 B6
Chester Sq SW1	44 B7
Chester Sq Ms SW1	44 B7
Chester St SW1	44 A6
Chicheley St SE1	45 F5
Chichester Rents WC2	45 G2
Chiltern St W1	44 A1
Ching Ct WC2	44 E3
Chiswell St EC1	45 J1
Chitty St W1	44 C1
Christ Ch Pas EC1	45 H2
Church Entry EC4	45 H3
Church Pl SW1	44 C4
Churchyard Row SE11	45 H7
Clare Mkt WC2	45 F3
Clarges Ms W1	44 B4
Clarges St W1	44 B4
Clarke's Ms W1	44 A1
Clement's Inn WC2	45 F3
Clement's Inn Pas WC2	45 F3
Clennam St SE1	45 J5
Clerkenwell EC1	45 H1
Clerkenwell Grn EC1	45 G1
Clerkenwell Rd EC1	45 G1
Cleveland Ms W1	44 C1
Cleveland Pl SW1	44 C4
Cleveland Row SW1	44 C5
Cleveland St W1	44 C1
Clifford's Inn Pas EC4	45 G3
Clifford St W1	44 C4
Clink St SE1	45 J4
Clipstone Ms W1	44 C1
Clipstone St W1	44 B1
Cliveden Pl SW1	44 A7
Cloak La EC4	45 J3
Cloth Ct EC1	45 H2
Cloth Fair EC1	45 H2
Cloth St EC1	45 J1
Coach & Horses Yd W1	44 B3
Coburg Cl SW1	44 C7
Cock La EC1	45 H2
Cockpit Steps SW1	44 D6
Cockpit Yd WC1	45 F1
Cockspur Ct SW1	44 D4
Cockspur St SW1	44 D4
Coin St SE1	45 G4
Cole St SE1	45 J6
Coley St WC1	45 F1
College Hill EC4	45 J3
College Ms SW1	44 E6
College St EC4	45 J3
Collinson St SE1	45 J6
Collinson Wk SE1	45 J6
Colnbrook St SE1	45 H7
Colombo St SE1	45 H5
Colonnade WC1	44 E1
Colville Pl W1	44 C2
Computer Pass EC2	45 J2
Concert Hall App SE1	45 F5
Conduit Ct WC2	44 E3
Conduit St W1	44 B3
Cons St SE1	45 G5
Constitution Hill SW1	44 B5
Conway Ms W1	44 C1
Conway St W1	44 C1
Cooper Cl SE1	45 G6
Copeland Ho SE11	45 F7
Copperfield St SE1	45 H5
Coptic St WC1	44 E2
Coral St SE1	45 G6
Coram St WC1	44 E1
Cork St W1	44 C4
Cork St Ms W1	44 C4
Corner Ho St WC2	44 E4
Cornwall Rd SE1	45 G4
Cosmo Pl WC1	45 E1
Cosser St SE1	45 G6
Cottesloe Ms SE1	45 G6
County St SE1	45 J7
Covent Gdn WC2	45 E3
Covent Gdn Mkt WC2	45 E3
Coventry St W1	44 D4
Cowcross St EC1	45 H1
Cowley St SW1	44 E6
Craig's Ct SW1	44 E4
Cramer St W1	44 A2
Cranbourn St WC2	44 D3
Crane Ct EC4	45 G3
Cranfield Row SE1	45 G6
Craven Pas WC2	44 E4
Craven St WC2	44 E4
Crawford Pas EC1	45 G1
Creed La EC4	45 H3
Crescent Row EC1	45 J1
Cripplegate St EC2	45 J1
Cromwell Twr EC2	45 J1
Cross Keys Cl W1	44 A2
Cross Keys Sq EC1	45 J2
Crown Ct EC2	45 J3
Crown Ct WC2	45 E3
Crown Office Row EC4	45 G3
Crown Pas SW1	44 C5
Cubitts Yd WC2	45 E3
Cuddington SE17	45 J7
Culross St W1	44 A4
Cursitor St EC4	45 G2
Curzon Gate W1	44 A5
Curzon Sq W1	44 A5
Curzon St W1	44 A5
Cut, The SE1	45 G5
Cypress Pl W1	44 C1

D

Entry	Ref
Dacre St SW1	44 D6
Dane St WC1	45 F2
Dansey Pl W1	44 D3
Dante Pl SE11	45 H7
Dante Rd SE11	45 H7
D'Arblay St W1	44 C3
Dartmouth St SW1	44 D6
Davidge St SE1	45 H6
Davies Ms W1	44 B3
Davies St W1	44 B3
Deacon Way SE17	45 J7
Dean Bradley St SW1	44 E7
Dean Farrar St SW1	44 D6
Dean Ryle St SW1	44 E7
Deans Ct EC4	45 H3
Deans Ms W1	44 B2
Dean Stanley St SW1	44 E7
Dean St W1	44 D3
Dean's Yd SW1	44 D6
Dean Trench St SW1	44 E7
Denman St W1	44 D4
Denmark Pl WC2	44 D2
Denmark St WC2	44 D3
Derby Gate SW1	44 E5
Derby St W1	44 A5
Dering St W1	44 B3
Devereux Ct WC2	45 G3
Devonshire Cl W1	44 B1
Devonshire Ms N W1	44 B1
Devonshire Ms S W1	44 B1
Devonshire Ms W W1	44 B1
Devonshire Pl W1	44 A1
Devonshire Pl Ms W1	44 A1
Devonshire Row Ms W1	44 B1
Devonshire St W1	44 B1
De Walden St W1	44 A2
Dickens Ms EC1	45 H1
Dickens Sq SE1	45 J6
Disney Pl SE1	45 J5
Disney St SE1	45 J5
Distaff La EC4	45 J3
Doby Ct EC4	45 J3
Dodson St SE1	45 G6
Dolben St SE1	45 H5
Dombey St WC1	45 F1
Doon St SE1	45 G5
Dorrington St EC1	45 G1
Dorrit St SE1	45 J5
Dorset Bldgs EC4	45 H3
Dorset Ms SW1	44 B6
Dorset Ri EC4	45 H3
Doughty Ms WC1	45 F1
Dover St W1	44 B4
Dover Yd W1	44 B4
Downing St SW1	44 E5
Down St W1	44 B5
Down St Ms W1	44 B5
Doyce St SE1	45 J5
D'Oyley St SW1	44 A7
Drake St WC1	45 F2
Draper Ho SE1	45 H7
Drury La WC2	45 E3
Dryden St WC2	45 E3
Duchess Ms W1	44 B2
Duchess St W1	44 B2
Duchy Pl SE1	45 G4
Duchy St SE1	45 G4
Duck La W1	44 D3
Dufferin St EC1	45 J1
Dufour's Pl W1	44 C3
Dugard Way SE11	45 H7
Duke of Wellington Pl SW1	44 A5
Duke of York St SW1	44 C4
Duke's Ms W1	44 A2
Duke St SW1	44 C4
Duke St W1	44 A2
Duke's Yd W1	44 A3
Duncannon St WC2	44 E4
Dunns Pas WC1	45 E2
Dunstable Ms W1	44 A1
Durham Ho St WC2	45 E4
Dyer's Bldgs EC1	45 G2
Dyott St WC1	44 E2

E

Entry	Ref
Eagle Ct EC1	45 H1
Eagle Pl SW1	44 C4
Eagle St WC1	45 F2
Earlham St WC2	44 D3
Earnshaw St WC2	44 D2
Easley's Ms W1	44 A2
Eastcastle St W1	44 C2
East Harding St EC4	45 G2
East Pas EC1	45 H1
East Poultry Av EC1	45 H2
Eaton Gate SW1	44 A7
Eaton La SW1	44 B7
Eaton Ms N SW1	44 A7
Eaton Ms S SW1	44 A7
Eaton Ms W SW1	44 A7
Eaton Pl SW1	44 A7
Eaton Row SW1	44 B6
Eaton Sq SW1	44 B6
Eaton Ter SW1	44 A7
Eaton Ter Ms SW1	44 A7
Ebury Ms SW1	44 B7
Ebury Ms E SW1	44 B7
Ebury St SW1	44 B7
Eccleston Br SW1	44 B7
Eccleston Ms SW1	44 A7
Eccleston Pl SW1	44 B7
Eccleston St SW1	44 B7
Edwards Ms W1	44 A3
Elba Pl SE17	45 J7
Elephant & Castle SE1	45 H7
Elephant Rd SE17	45 J7
Elizabeth Ct SW1	44 D7
Elizabeth St SW1	44 A7
Ellington Ho SE1	45 J6
Elliotts Row SE11	45 H7
Elm Ct EC4	45 G3
Elm St WC1	45 F1
Elverton St SW1	44 D7
Ely Ct EC1	45 G2
Ely Pl EC1	45 G2
Embankment Pier WC2	45 F4
Embankment Pl WC2	45 E4
Emerald St WC1	45 F1
Emerson St SE1	45 J4
Emery Hill St SW1	44 C7
Emery St SE1	45 G6
Endell St WC2	44 E2
Errol St EC1	45 J1
Essex Ct EC4	45 G3
Essex St WC2	45 G3
Euston Rd NW1	44 B1
Evelyn Yd W1	44 D2
Ewer St SE1	45 J5
Excel Ct WC2	44 D4
Exchange Ct WC2	45 E4
Exeter St WC2	45 E3
Exton St SE1	45 G5
Eyre St Hill EC1	45 G1

F

Entry	Ref
Falconberg Ct W1	44 D2
Falconberg Ms W1	44 D2
Falcon Ct EC4	45 G3
Falmouth Rd SE1	45 J6
Fann St EC1	45 J1
Fann St EC2	45 J1
Fareham St W1	44 D2
Farm St W1	44 B4
Farnham Pl SE1	45 H5
Farringdon La EC1	45 G1
Farringdon St EC4	45 H2
Faulkner's All EC1	45 H1
Ferrybridge Ho SE11	45 F7
Fetter La EC4	45 G3
Field Ct WC1	45 F2
Fisher St WC1	45 E2
Fitzalan St SE11	45 G7
Fitzhardinge St W1	44 A2
Fitzmaurice Pl W1	44 B4
Fitzroy Ct W1	44 C1
Fitzroy Ms W1	44 C1
Fitzroy Sq W1	44 C1
Fitzroy St W1	44 C1
Fives Ct SE11	45 H7
Flaxman Ct W1	44 D3
Fleet St EC4	45 G3
Flitcroft St WC2	44 D2
Floral St WC2	44 E3
Florin Ct EC1	45 J1
Foley St W1	44 C2
Fore St EC2	45 J2
Fortune St EC1	45 J1
Forum Magnum Sq SE1	45 F5
Foster La EC2	45 J2
Foubert's Pl W1	44 C3
Fountain Ct EC4	45 G3
Fountain Sq SW1	44 B7
Fox & Knot St EC1	45 H1
Francis St SW1	44 C7
Frazier St SE1	45 G6
Friars St EC4	45 H5
Friar St EC4	45 H3
Friary Ct SW1	44 C5
Friday St EC4	45 J3
Frith St W1	44 D3
Fulwood Pl WC1	45 F2
Furnival St EC4	45 G2
Fynes St SW1	44 D7

G

Entry	Ref
Gabriel's Wf SE1	45 G4
Gage St WC1	45 E1
Galen Pl WC1	45 E2
Gambia St SE1	45 H5
Ganton St W1	44 C3
Garbutt Pl W1	44 A1
Garden Row SE1	45 H7
Gardners La EC4	45 J3
Garlick Hill EC4	45 J3
Garrick St WC2	44 E3
Garrick Yd WC2	44 E3
Gate Ho Sq SE1	45 J4
Gate St WC2	45 F2
Gaunt St SE1	45 H6
Gayfere St SW1	44 E7
Gaywood Est SE1	45 H7
Gaywood St SE1	45 H7
Gees Ct W1	44 A3
George Ct WC2	45 E4
George Mathers Rd SE11	45 H7
George Yd W1	44 A3
Geraldine St SE11	45 H7
Gerald Ms SW1	44 A7
Gerald Rd SW1	44 A7
Gerrard Pl W1	44 D3

Gerrard St W1	**44** D3	Grosvenor Gdns Ms N SW1	**44** B7
Gerridge St SE1	**45** G6	Grosvenor Gdns Ms S SW1	**44** B7
Gilbert Pl WC1	**44** E2	Grosvenor Hill W1	**44** B3
Gilbert St W1	**44** A3	Grosvenor Pl SW1	**44** A6
Gildea St W1	**44** B2	Grosvenor Sq W1	**44** A3
Gillingham Row SW1	**44** C7	Grosvenor St W1	**44** B3
Gillingham St SW1	**44** C7	Grotto Pas W1	**44** A1
Giltspur St EC1	**45** H2	Groveland Ct EC4	**45** J3
Gladstone St SE1	**45** H6	Guildhall Yd EC2	**45** J2
Glasshill St SE1	**45** H5	Guildhouse St SW1	**44** C7
Glasshouse St W1	**44** C4	Guilford Pl WC1	**45** F1
Glasshouse Yd EC1	**45** J1	Guilford St WC1	**45** E1
Globe St SE1	**45** J6	Gunpowder Sq EC4	**45** G2
Globe Yd W1	**44** B3	Gutter La EC2	**45** J2

H

Half Moon Ct EC1 **45** J2
Half Moon St W1 **44** B4
Halkin Arc SW1 **44** A6
Halkin Ms SW1 **44** A6
Halkin Pl SW1 **44** A6
Halkin St SW1 **44** A6
Hallam Ms W1 **44** B1
Hallam St W1 **44** B1
Hamilton Ms W1 **44** B5
Hamilton Pl W1 **44** A5
Ham Yd W1 **44** D3
Hand Ct WC1 **45** F2
Hanging Sword All EC4 **45** G3
Hanover Pl WC2 **45** E3
Hanover Sq W1 **44** B3
Hanover St W1 **44** B3
Hanson St W1 **44** C1
Hanway Pl W1 **44** D2
Hanway St W1 **44** D2
Hare Ct EC4 **45** G3
Hare Pl EC4 **45** G3
Harewood Pl W1 **44** B3
Harley Pl W1 **44** B2
Harley St W1 **44** B2
Harmsworth Ms SE11 **45** H7
Harp All EC4 **45** H2
Harpur Ms WC1 **45** F1
Harpur St WC1 **45** F1
Hat & Mitre Ct EC1 **45** H1
Hatfields SE1 **45** G4
Hatton Gdn EC1 **45** G1
Hatton Pl EC1 **45** G1
Hatton Wall EC1 **45** G1
Haunch of Venison Yd W1 **44** B3
Hay Hill W1 **44** B4
Hayles St SE11 **45** H7
Haymarket SW1 **44** D4
Haymarket Arc SW1 **44** D4
Hayne St EC1 **45** H1
Hay's Ms W1 **44** B4
Hayward's Pl EC1 **45** H1
Headfort Pl SW1 **44** A6
Heddon St W1 **44** C3
Hedger St SE11 **45** H7
Hen & Chicken Ct EC4 **45** G3
Henrietta Pl W1 **44** B3
Henrietta St WC2 **45** E3
Herald's Pl SE11 **45** H7
Herbal Hill EC1 **45** G1
Hercules Rd SE1 **45** F7
Herrick St SW1 **44** D7
Hertford St W1 **44** B4
High Holborn WC1 **45** E2
High Timber St EC4 **45** J3
Hills Pl W1 **44** C3
Hill St W1 **44** A4
Hind Ct EC4 **45** G3
Hinde St W1 **44** A2
Hindon Ct SW1 **44** C7
Hobart Pl SW1 **44** B6
Holborn EC1 **45** G2
Holborn WC2 **45** F2
Holborn Circ EC1 **45** G2
Holborn Pl WC1 **45** F2
Holborn Viaduct EC1 **45** G2
Holland St SE1 **45** H4
Hollen St W1 **44** C2
Holles St W1 **44** B2
Holmes Ter SE1 **45** G5
Holsworthy Sq WC1 **45** F1
Holyoak Rd SE11 **45** H7
Honey La EC2 **45** J3
Hood Ct EC4 **45** G3
Hop Gdns WC2 **44** E4
Hopkins St W1 **44** C3
Hopton's Gdns SE1 **45** H4
Hopton St SE1 **45** H4
Hornbeam Cl SE11 **45** G7
Horse & Dolphin Yd W1 **44** D3
Horseferry Rd SW1 **44** D7
Horse Guards Av SW1 **44** E5

Horse Guards Rd SW1 **44** D5
Horsemongers Ms SE1 **45** J6
Horse Ride SW1 **44** D5
Hosier La EC1 **45** H2
Houghton St WC2 **45** F3
Howick Pl SW1 **44** C7
Howland Ms E W1 **44** C1
Howland St W1 **44** C1
Hudson's Pl SW1 **44** B7
Huggin Ct EC4 **45** J3
Huggin Hill EC4 **45** J3
Hulme Pl SE1 **45** J6
Hungerford Br SE1 **45** E4
Hungerford Br WC2 **45** E4
Hungerford La WC2 **44** E4
Huntley St WC1 **44** C1
Hunt's Ct WC2 **44** D4
Hutton St EC4 **45** G3
Hyde Pk Cor W1 **44** A5

I

India Pl WC2 **45** F3
Ingestre Pl W1 **44** C3
Ingram Cl SE11 **45** F7
Inigo Pl WC2 **44** E3
Inner Temple La EC4 **45** G3
Invicta Plaza SE1 **45** H4
Ireland Yd EC4 **45** H3
Irving St WC2 **44** D4
Isaac Way SE1 **45** J5
Isabella St SE1 **45** H5
Ivybridge La WC2 **45** E4

J

Jacob's Well Ms W1 **44** A2
James St W1 **44** A2
James St WC2 **45** E3
Jermyn St SW1 **44** C4
Jerusalem Pas EC1 **45** H1
Jervis Ct W1 **44** B3
Joan St SE1 **45** H5
Jockey's Flds WC1 **45** F1
Johanna St SE1 **45** G6
John Adam St WC2 **45** E4
John Carpenter St EC4 **45** H3
John Milton Pass EC2 **45** J3
John Princes St W1 **44** B2
John's Ms WC1 **45** F1
John St WC1 **45** F1
Jones St W1 **44** B4
Jubilee Mkt Hall WC2 **45** E3
Juxon St SE11 **45** F7

K

Kean St WC2 **45** F3
Keeley St WC2 **45** F3
Kell St SE1 **45** H6
Kemble St WC2 **45** F3
Kemp's Ct W1 **44** C3
Kendall Pl W1 **44** A2
Kennet Wf La EC4 **45** J3
Kennington Rd SE1 **45** G6
Kennington Rd SE11 **45** G7
Kenrick Pl W1 **44** A1
Keppel Row SE1 **45** J5
Keppel St WC1 **44** D1
Keyworth Pl SE1 **45** H6
Keyworth St SE1 **45** H6
King Charles St SW1 **44** D5
King Edward St EC1 **45** J2
King Edward Wk SE1 **45** G6
Kinghorn St EC1 **45** J2
King James Ct SE1 **45** H6
King James St SE1 **45** H6
Kingly Ct W1 **44** C3
Kingly St W1 **44** C3
Kings Bench St SE1 **45** H5
Kings Bench Wk EC4 **45** G3
Kingscote St EC4 **45** H3
King's Ms WC1 **45** F1
Kings Pl SE1 **45** J6
King's Reach Twr SE1 **45** G4
King's Scholars' Pas SW1 **44** C7
King St EC2 **45** J3
King St SW1 **44** C5
King St WC2 **44** E3
Kingsway WC2 **45** F2
Kinnerton St SW1 **44** A6
Kirby St EC1 **45** G1
Kirkman Pl W1 **44** D2
Kirk St WC1 **45** F1
Knightrider St EC4 **45** J3

L

Lambeth SE1 **45** F7
Lambeth Br SE1 **45** E7
Lambeth Br SW1 **45** E7
Lambeth Hill EC4 **45** J3
Lambeth Palace Rd SE1 **45** F7
Lambeth Pier SE1 **45** E7

Lambeth Rd SE1 **45** F7
Lambeth Rd SE11 **45** F7
Lambeth Twrs SE11 **45** G7
Lambeth Wk SE11 **45** F7
Lambs Conduit Pas WC1 **45** F1
Lamb's Conduit St WC1 **45** F1
Lamlash St SE11 **45** H7
Lamp Office Ct WC1 **45** F1
Lancashire Ct W1 **44** B3
Lancaster Pl WC2 **45** F3
Lancaster St SE1 **45** H6
Lanesborough Pl SW1 **44** A5
Langham Pl W1 **44** B2
Langham St W1 **44** B2
Langley Ct WC2 **44** E3
Langley St WC2 **44** E3
Lansdowne Row W1 **44** B4
Lansdowne Ter WC1 **45** E1
Lant St SE1 **45** J5
Lauderdale Twr EC2 **45** J1
Launcelot St SE1 **45** G6
Lavington St SE1 **45** H5
Lawrence La EC2 **45** J3
Laystall St EC1 **45** G1
Laytons Bldgs SE1 **45** J5
Lazenby Ct WC2 **44** E3
Leake St SE1 **45** F5
Leather La EC1 **45** G2
Lees Pl W1 **44** A3
Leicester Ct WC2 **44** D3
Leicester Pl WC2 **44** D3
Leicester Sq WC2 **44** D4
Leicester St WC2 **44** D3
Leigh Hunt St SE1 **45** J5
Leigh Pl EC1 **45** G1
Leopards Ct EC1 **45** G1
Leo Yd EC1 **45** H1
Lewisham St SW1 **44** D6
Lexington St W1 **44** C3
Library St SE1 **45** H6
Lily Pl EC1 **45** G1
Limeburner La EC4 **45** H3
Lincoln's Inn WC2 **45** F2
Lincoln's Inn Flds WC2 **45** F2
Lindsey St EC1 **45** H1
Lisle St WC2 **44** D3
Litchfield St WC2 **44** D3
Little Argyll St W1 **44** C3
Little Britain EC1 **45** J2
Little Chester St SW1 **44** A6
Little Coll St SW1 **44** E6
Little Dean's Yd SW1 **44** E6
Little Dorrit Ct SE1 **45** J5
Little Essex St WC2 **45** G3
Little George St SW1 **44** E6
Little Newport St WC2 **44** D3
Little New St EC4 **45** G2
Little Portland St W1 **44** C2
Little Russell St WC1 **44** E2
Little St. James's St SW1 **44** C5
Little Sanctuary SW1 **44** D6
Little Smith St SW1 **44** D6
Little Titchfield St W1 **44** C2
Little Trinity La EC4 **45** J3
Little Turnstile WC1 **45** F2
Livonia St W1 **44** C3
Lollard St SE11 **45** F7
Loman St SE1 **45** H5
Lombard La EC4 **45** G3
London Cen Mkts EC1 **45** H1
London Rd SE1 **45** H6
London Silver Vaults WC2 **45** G2
London Trocadero, The W1 **44** D4
London Wall EC2 **45** J2
Long Acre WC2 **44** E3
Long La EC1 **45** H1
Longridge Ho SE1 **45** J7
Long's Ct WC2 **44** D3
Longstone Ct SE1 **45** J6
Longville Rd SE11 **45** H7
Long Yd WC1 **45** F1
Lord N St SW1 **44** E7
Love La EC2 **45** J2
Lover's Wk W1 **44** A4
Lower Belgrave St SW1 **44** B7
Lower Grosvenor Pl SW1 **44** B6
Lower James St W1 **44** C3
Lower John St W1 **44** C3
Lower Marsh SE1 **45** G6
Lower Rd SE1 **45** G5
Lowndes Cl SW1 **44** A7
Lowndes Ct W1 **44** C3
Lowndes Pl SW1 **44** A7

Ludgate Bdy EC4 **45** H3
Ludgate Circ EC4 **45** H3
Ludgate Hill EC4 **45** H3
Ludgate Sq EC4 **45** H3
Lumley Ct WC2 **45** E4
Lumley St W1 **44** A3
Luxborough St W1 **44** A1
Lyall Ms SW1 **44** A7
Lyall Ms W SW1 **44** A7
Lyall St SW1 **44** A7
Lygon Pl SW1 **44** B7

M

McAuley Cl SE1 **45** G6
Macclesfield St W1 **44** D3
McCoid Way SE1 **45** J6
Macfarren Pl NW1 **44** A1
Macklin St WC2 **45** E2
Mac's Pl EC4 **45** G2
Maddox St W1 **44** B3
Magpie All EC4 **45** G3
Maiden La SE1 **45** J4
Maiden La WC2 **45** E4
Maidstone Bldgs Ms SE1 **45** J5
Malet Pl WC1 **44** D1
Malet St WC1 **44** D1
Mall, The SW1 **44** C5
Maltravers St WC2 **45** F3
Manchester Ms W1 **44** A2
Manchester Sq W1 **44** A2
Manchester St W1 **44** A2
Mandeville Pl W1 **44** A2
Manette St W1 **44** D3
Mansfield Ms W1 **44** B2
Mansfield St W1 **44** B2
Maple Pl W1 **44** C1
Maple St W1 **44** C1
Margaret Ct W1 **44** C2
Margaret St W1 **44** B2
Marigold All SE1 **45** H4
Market Ct W1 **44** C2
Market Ms W1 **44** B5
Market Pl W1 **44** C2
Marlborough Ct W1 **44** C3
Marlborough Rd SW1 **44** C5
Marshall St W1 **44** C3
Marshalsea Rd SE1 **45** J5
Marsham St SW1 **44** D7
Martin Ho SE1 **45** J7
Martlett Ct WC2 **45** E3
Marylebone High St W1 **44** A1
Marylebone La W1 **44** B3
Marylebone Ms W1 **44** B2
Marylebone Pas W1 **44** C2
Marylebone St W1 **44** A2
Masons Arms Ms W1 **44** B3
Mason's Yd SW1 **44** C4
Matthew Parker St SW1 **44** D6
Matthews Yd WC2 **44** E3
Maunsel St SW1 **44** D7
Mayfair W1 **44** B4
Mayfair Pl W1 **44** B4
Mays Ct WC2 **44** E4
Meadow Row SE1 **45** J7
Mead Row SE1 **45** G6
Meard St W1 **44** D3
Medway St SW1 **44** D7
Melbourne Pl WC2 **45** F3
Memel Ct EC1 **45** J1
Memel St EC1 **45** J1
Mepham St SE1 **45** F5
Mercer St WC2 **44** E3
Merrick Sq SE1 **45** J6
Metro Cen Hts SE1 **45** J7
Meymott St SE1 **45** H5
Middlesex Pas EC1 **45** H2
Middle St EC1 **45** J1
Middle Temple EC4 **45** G3
Middle Temple La EC4 **45** G3
Middleton Pl W1 **44** C2
Midford Pl W1 **44** C1
Milcote St SE1 **45** H6
Milford La WC2 **45** F3
Milk St EC2 **45** J3
Millbank SW1 **44** E7
Millbank Ct SW1 **44** E7
Millennium Br EC4 **45** J3
Millennium Br SE1 **45** J3
Miller Wk SE1 **45** G5
Millman Ms WC1 **45** F1
Millman St WC1 **45** F1
Mill St W1 **44** B3
Milroy Wk SE1 **45** H4
Minera Ms SW1 **44** A7
Mint St SE1 **45** J5
Mitre Ct EC2 **45** J2
Mitre Rd SE1 **45** G5
Monck St SW1 **44** D7
Monkton St SE11 **45** G7
Monkwell Sq EC2 **45** J2

Monmouth St WC2 **44** E3
Montague Pl WC1 **44** D1
Montague St EC1 **45** J2
Montague St WC1 **44** E1
Montreal Pl WC2 **45** F3
Montrose Pl SW1 **44** A6
Moor St W1 **44** D3
Morley St SE1 **45** G6
Morpeth Ter SW1 **44** C7
Mortimer Mkt WC1 **44** C1
Mortimer St W1 **44** C2
Morton Pl SE1 **45** G7
Morwell St WC1 **44** D2
Mount Pleasant WC1 **45** F1
Mount Row W1 **44** B4
Mount St W1 **44** A4
Mount St Ms W1 **44** B4
Moxon St W1 **44** A2
Munton Rd SE17 **45** J7
Murphy St SE1 **45** G6
Museum St WC1 **44** E2

N

Nag's Head Ct EC1 **45** J1
Nassau St W1 **44** C2
Neal St WC2 **44** E3
Neal's Yd WC2 **44** E3
Neathouse Pl SW1 **44** C7
Nelson Sq SE1 **45** H5
Newall Ho SE1 **45** J6
New Bond St W1 **44** B3
New Br St EC4 **45** H3
Newburgh St W1 **44** C3
New Burlington Ms W1 **44** C3
New Burlington Pl W1 **44** C3
New Burlington St W1 **44** C3
Newbury St EC1 **45** J2
Newcastle Cl EC4 **45** H2
New Cavendish St W1 **44** B1
New Change EC4 **45** J3
New Compton St WC2 **44** D3
New Fetter La EC4 **45** G2
Newgate St EC1 **45** H2
New Globe Wk SE1 **45** J4
Newington SE1 **45** J7
Newington Causeway SE1 **45** H7
New Inn Pas WC2 **45** F3
New Kent Rd SE1 **45** J7
Newman Pas W1 **44** C2
Newman's Row WC2 **45** F2
Newman St W1 **44** C2
Newman Yd W1 **44** C2
Newnham Ter SE1 **45** G6
New N St WC1 **45** F1
New Oxford St WC1 **44** D2
Newport Ct WC2 **44** D3
Newport Pl WC2 **44** D3
New Row WC2 **44** E3
New Sq WC2 **45** F2
New St Sq EC4 **45** G2
Newton St WC2 **45** E2
New Turnstile WC1 **45** F2
Nicholson St SE1 **45** H5
Nightingale Ms SE11 **45** H7
Noble St EC2 **45** J2
Noel St W1 **44** C3
Norfolk Row SE1 **45** F7
Norris St SW1 **44** D4
North Audley St W1 **44** A3
North Cres WC1 **44** D1
Northington St WC1 **45** F1
North Ms WC1 **45** F1
Northumberland Av WC2 **44** E4
Northumberland St WC2 **44** E4
Norwich St EC4 **45** G2
Nottingham Ct WC2 **44** E3
Nottingham Pl W1 **44** A1
Nottingham St W1 **44** A1
Nottingham Ter NW1 **44** A1

O

Oakden St SE11 **45** G7
Oakey La SE1 **45** G6
Oat La EC2 **45** J2
Odhams Wk WC2 **45** E3
Ogle St W1 **44** C1
Old Bailey EC4 **45** H3
Old Barrack Yd SW1 **44** A5
Old Bond St W1 **44** C4
Old Brewers Yd WC2 **44** E3
Old Bldgs WC2 **45** G2
Old Burlington St W1 **44** C3
Oldbury Pl W1 **44** A1
Old Cavendish St W1 **44** B2
Old Compton St W1 **44** D3
Old Fish St Hill EC4 **45** J3
Old Fleet La EC4 **45** H2

Old Gloucester St WC1 45 E1
Old Mitre Ct EC4 45 G3
Old N St WC1 45 F1
Old Palace Yd SW1 44 E6
Old Paradise St SE11 45 F7
Old Pk La W1 44 A5
Old Pye St SW1 44 D6
Old Queen St SW1 44 D6
Old Seacoal La EC4 45 H2
Old Sq WC2 45 F2
O'Meara St SE1 45 J5
Onslow St EC1 45 G1
Ontario St SE1 45 H7
Orange St WC2 44 D4
Orange Yd W1 44 D3
Orchard St W1 44 A3
Orde Hall St WC1 45 F1
Orient St SE11 45 H7
Ormond Cl WC1 45 E1
Ormond Ms WC1 45 E1
Ormond Yd SW1 44 C4
Osnaburgh St NW1 44 B1
Ossington Bldgs W1 44 A1
Oswin St SE11 45 H7
Outer Circle NW1 44 A1
Oxendon St SW1 44 D4
Oxford Circ Av W1 44 C3
Oxford St W1 44 C2
Oxo Twr Wf SE1 45 G4

P
Paddington St W1 44 A1
Pageantmaster Ct EC4 45 H3
Page St SW1 44 D7
Palace Pl SW1 44 C6
Palace St SW1 44 C6
Pall Mall SW1 44 C5
Pall Mall E SW1 44 D4
Palmer St SW1 44 D6
Pancras La EC4 45 J3
Panton St SW1 44 D4
Panyer All EC4 45 J3
Paris Gdn SE1 45 H4
Park Cres W1 44 B1
Park Cres Ms E W1 44 B1
Park Cres Ms W W1 44 B1
Parker Ms WC2 45 E2
Parker St WC2 45 E2
Park La W1 44 A5
Park Pl SW1 44 C5
Park Sq Ms NW1 44 B1
Park St SE1 45 J4
Park St W1 44 A3
Parliament Sq SW1 44 E6
Parliament St SW1 44 E6
Parliament Vw Apts SE1 45 F7
Passing All EC1 45 H1
Pastor St SE11 45 H7
Paternoster Row EC4 45 J3
Paternoster Sq EC4 45 H3
Paul's Wk EC4 45 H3
Peabody Est EC1 45 J1
Peabody Est SE1 45 G5
Peabody Est SW1 44 C7
Peabody Sq SE1 45 H6
Peabody Trust SE1 45 J5
Pearman St SE1 45 G6
Pear Pl SE1 45 G5
Pear Tree Ct EC1 45 G1
Pemberton Row EC4 45 G2
Pembroke Cl SW1 44 A6
Penhurst Pl SE1 45 F7
Pepper St SE1 45 J5
Percy Ms W1 44 D2
Percy Pas W1 44 C2
Percy St W1 44 D2
Perkin's Rents SW1 44 D6
Perkins Sq SE1 45 J4
Perrys Pl W1 44 D2
Peters Hill EC4 45 J3
Peter's La EC1 45 H1
Peter St W1 44 C3
Petty France SW1 44 C6
Phipp's Ms SW1 44 B7
Phoenix St WC2 44 D3
Piccadilly W1 44 B5
Piccadilly Arc SW1 44 C4
Piccadilly Circ W1 44 D4
Piccadilly Pl W1 44 C4
Pickering Pl SW1 44 C5
Pickwick St SE1 45 J6
Picton Pl W1 44 A3
Pilgrim St EC4 45 H3
Pineapple Ct SW1 44 C6
Pitt's Head Ms W1 44 A5
Playhouse Yd EC4 45 H3
Plaza Shop Cen, The W1 44 C2
Pleydell Ct EC4 45 G3
Pleydell St EC4 45 G3
Plough Pl EC4 45 G2

Plumtree Ct EC4 45 G2
Pocock St SE1 45 H5
Poland St W1 44 C3
Pollen St W1 44 B3
Polperro Ms SE11 45 G7
Pontypool Pl SE1 45 H5
Pooles Bldgs EC1 45 G1
Poppins Ct EC4 45 H3
Porter St SE1 45 J4
Portland Ms W1 44 C3
Portland Pl W1 44 B1
Portman Ms S W1 44 A3
Portman St W1 44 A3
Portpool La EC1 45 G1
Portsmouth St WC2 45 F3
Portugal St WC2 45 F3
Powis Pl WC1 45 E1
Pratt Wk SE11 45 F7
Price's St SE1 45 H5
Priest Ct EC2 45 J2
Primrose Hill EC4 45 G3
Prince's Arc SW1 44 C4
Princes Pl SW1 44 C4
Princess St SE1 45 H7
Princes St W1 44 B3
Princeton St WC1 45 F1
Printers Inn Ct EC4 45 G2
Printer St EC4 45 G2
Procter St WC1 45 F1
Providence Ct W1 44 A3
Prudent Pas EC2 45 J2
Puddle Dock EC4 45 H3

Q
Quadrant Arc W1 44 C4
Quality Ct WC2 45 G2
Queen Anne Ms W1 44 B2
Queen Anne's Gate SW1 44 D6
Queen Anne St W1 44 B2
Queenhithe EC4 45 J3
Queen's Head Pas EC4 45 J2
Queen Sq WC1 45 E1
Queen Sq WC1 45 E1
Queen St EC4 45 J3
Queen St W1 44 B4
Queen St Pl EC4 45 J4
Queens Yd WC1 44 C1
Queen Victoria St EC4 45 H3
Quilp St SE1 45 J5

R
Ramillies Pl W1 44 C3
Ramillies St W1 44 C3
Rathbone Pl W1 44 D2
Rathbone St W1 44 C2
Raymond Bldgs WC1 45 F1
Ray St EC1 45 G1
Ray St Br EC1 45 G1
Redcross Way SE1 45 J5
Red Lion Ct EC4 45 G2
Red Lion Sq WC1 45 F2
Red Lion St WC1 45 F1
Red Lion Yd W1 44 A4
Red Pl W1 44 A3
Reeves Ms W1 44 A4
Regency Pl SW1 44 D7
Regency St SW1 44 D7
Regent Pl W1 44 C3
Regent St SW1 44 D4
Regent St W1 44 B2
Remnant St WC2 45 F2
Renfrew Rd SE11 45 H7
Rennie St SE1 45 H4
Rex Pl W1 44 A4
Richardson's Ms W1 44 C1
Richbell Pl WC1 45 F1
Richmond Bldgs W1 44 D3
Richmond Ms W1 44 D3
Richmond Ter SW1 44 E5
Ridgmount Gdns WC1 44 D1
Ridgmount Pl WC1 44 D1
Ridgmount St WC1 44 D1
Riding Ho St W1 44 C2
Risborough St SE1 45 H5
Rising Sun Ct EC1 45 H2
River Ct SE1 45 H4
Robert Adam St W1 44 A2
Roberts Ms SW1 44 A7
Robert St WC2 45 E4
Rochester Row SW1 44 D7
Rochester St SW1 44 D7
Rockingham Est SE1 45 J7
Rockingham St SE1 45 J7
Rodney Pl SE17 45 J7
Rodney Rd SE17 45 J7
Roger St WC1 45 F1
Rolls Bldgs EC4 45 G2
Rolls Pas EC4 45 G2
Romilly St W1 44 D3

Romney Ms W1 44 A1
Romney St SW1 44 D7
Roscoe St EC1 45 J1
Rose All SE1 45 J4
Rose & Crown Ct EC2 45 J2
Rose & Crown Yd SW1 44 C4
Rosebery Av EC1 45 G1
Rosebery Sq EC1 45 G1
Rose St EC4 45 H2
Rose St WC2 44 E3
Rotary St SE1 45 H6
Rotherham Wk SE1 45 H5
Rotten Row SW1 44 A5
Roupell St SE1 45 G5
Royal Arc W1 44 C4
Royal Ms, The SW1 44 B6
Royal Opera Arc SW1 44 D4
Royal St SE1 45 F6
Royalty Ms W1 44 D3
Rugby St WC1 45 F1
Rupert Ct W1 44 D3
Rupert St W1 44 D3
Rushworth St SE1 45 H5
Russell Ct SW1 44 C5
Russell Sq WC1 44 E1
Russell St WC2 45 E3
Russia Row EC2 45 J3
Rutherford St SW1 44 D7
Rutland Pl EC1 45 J1
Ryder Ct SW1 44 C4
Ryder St SW1 44 C4
Ryder Yd SW1 44 C4

S
Sackville St W1 44 C4
Saddle Yd W1 44 B4
Saffron Hill EC1 45 G1
Saffron St EC1 45 G1
Sail St SE11 45 F7
St. Albans Ct EC2 45 J2
St. Albans St W1 44 D4
St. Alphage Gdns EC2 45 J2
St. Andrew's Hill EC4 45 H3
St. Andrew St EC4 45 G2
St. Anne's Ct W1 44 D3
St. Ann's La SW1 44 D6
St. Ann's St SW1 44 D6
St. Anselm's Pl W1 44 B3
St. Brides Av EC4 45 H3
St. Bride St EC4 45 H2
St. Christopher's Pl W1 44 A2
St. Clement's La WC2 45 F3
St. Cross St EC1 45 G1
St. Ermin's Hill SW1 44 D6
St. Georges Circ SE1 45 H6
St. Georges Ct EC4 45 H2
St. Georges Ms SE1 45 G6
St. Georges Rd SE1 45 G6
St. George St W1 44 B3
St. Giles High St WC2 44 D2
St. Giles Pas WC2 44 D3
St. James's SW1 44 D5
St. James's Ct SW1 44 C6
St. James's Mkt SW1 44 D4
St. James's Palace SW1 44 C5
St. James's Pk SW1 44 D5
St. James's Pl SW1 44 C5
St. James's Sq SW1 44 C4
St. James's St SW1 44 C4
St. John's La EC1 45 H1
St. John's Path EC1 45 H1
St. John's Pl EC1 45 H1
St. John's Sq EC1 45 H1
St. John St EC1 45 H1
St. Margaret's Ct SE1 45 J5
St. Margaret's St SW1 44 E6
St. Martin's La WC2 44 E3
St. Martin's-le-Grand EC1 45 J2
St. Martin's Ms WC2 45 E4
St. Martin's Pl WC2 44 E4
St. Martin's St WC2 44 D4
St. Mary's Gdns SE11 45 G7
St. Mary's Wk SE11 45 G7
St. Matthew St SW1 44 D7
St. Olaves Gdns SE11 45 G7
St. Paul's Chyd EC4 45 H3
St. Vincent St W1 44 A2
Salisbury Ct EC4 45 H3
Salisbury Sq EC4 45 G2
Sanctuary, The SW1 44 D6
Sanctuary St SE1 45 J6
Sandell St SE1 45 G5
Sandland St WC1 45 F2
Saperton Wk SE11 45 F7
Sardinia St WC2 45 F2
Savile Row W1 44 C3
Savoy Bldgs WC2 45 E4
Savoy Ct WC2 45 E4
Savoy Hill WC2 45 E4
Savoy Pl WC2 45 E4

Savoy Row WC2 45 F3
Savoy St WC2 45 F3
Savoy Way WC2 45 F4
Sawyer St SE1 45 J5
Scala St W1 44 C1
Scoresby St SE1 45 H5
Scotland Pl SW1 44 E4
Scovell Cres SE1 45 J6
Scovell Rd SE1 45 J6
Secker St SE1 45 G5
Sedding St SW1 44 A7
Sedley Pl W1 44 B3
Sekforde St EC1 45 H1
Serjeants Inn EC4 45 G3
Serle St WC2 45 F2
Sermon La EC4 45 J3
Seymour Ms W1 44 A2
Shaftesbury Av W1 44 D3
Shaftesbury Av WC2 44 D3
Shakespeare Twr EC2 45 J1
Shavers Pl SW1 44 D4
Sheffield St WC2 45 F3
Shelton St WC2 45 E3
Shepherd Mkt W1 44 B4
Shepherd's Pl W1 44 A3
Shepherd St W1 44 B5
Sheraton St W1 44 D3
Sherlock Ms W1 44 A1
Sherwood St W1 44 C3
Shoe La EC4 45 G2
Shorts Gdns WC2 44 E3
Short St SE1 45 G5
Shropshire Pl WC1 44 C1
Sicilian Av WC1 45 E2
Sidford St SE1 45 F7
Silex St SE1 45 H6
Silk St EC2 45 J1
Silver Pl W1 44 C3
Silvester St SE1 45 J6
Skinners La EC4 45 J3
Slingsby Pl WC2 44 E3
Smart's Pl WC2 45 E2
Smeaton Ct SE1 45 J7
Smithfield St EC1 45 H2
Smith's Ct W1 44 C3
Smith Sq SW1 44 E7
Smokehouse Yd EC1 45 H1
Snow Hill EC1 45 H2
Snow Hill Ct EC1 45 H2
Soho W1 44 C3
Soho Sq W1 44 D2
Soho St W1 44 D2
Southampton Bldgs WC2 45 G2
Southampton Pl WC1 45 E2
Southampton Row WC1 45 E1
Southampton St WC2 45 E3
South Audley St W1 44 A4
South Cres WC1 44 D2
South Eaton Pl SW1 44 A7
South Molton La W1 44 B3
South Molton St W1 44 B3
South Sq WC1 45 G2
South St W1 44 A4
Southwark SE1 45 H5
Southwark Br EC4 45 J4
Southwark Br SE1 45 J4
Southwark Br Rd SE1 45 H6
Southwark St SE1 45 H4
Spanish Pl W1 44 A2
Spenser St SW1 44 C6
Spring Gdns SW1 44 D4
Spur Rd SE1 45 G5
Spur Rd SW1 44 C6
Stable Yd SW1 44 C5
Stable Yd Rd SW1 44 C5
Stacey St WC2 44 D3
Stafford Pl SW1 44 C6
Stafford St W1 44 C4
Staining La EC2 45 J2
Stamford St SE1 45 G5
Stangate SE1 45 F6
Stanhope Gate W1 44 A4
Stanhope Row W1 44 B5
Staple Inn WC1 45 G2
Staple Inn Bldgs WC1 45 G2
Star Yd WC2 45 G2
Station App SE1 45 F5
Stedham Pl WC1 44 E2
Stephen Ms W1 44 D2
Stephen St W1 44 D2
Stew La EC4 45 J3
Stillington St SW1 44 C7
Stone Bldgs WC2 45 F2
Stonecutter St EC4 45 H2
Stones End St SE1 45 J6
Store St WC1 44 D2
Storey's Gate SW1 44 D6
Strand WC2 44 E4
Strand La WC2 45 F3
Stratford Pl W1 44 B3

Stratton St W1 44 B4
Streatham St WC1 44 D2
Strutton Grd SW1 44 D6
Stukeley St WC1 45 E2
Stukeley St WC2 45 E2
Sturge St SE1 45 J5
Sudrey St SE1 45 J6
Suffolk Pl SW1 44 D4
Suffolk St SW1 44 D4
Sullivan Rd SE11 45 G7
Summers St EC1 45 G1
Sumner St SE1 45 H4
Surrey Row SE1 45 H5
Surrey St WC2 45 F3
Sutton La EC1 45 H1
Sutton Row W1 44 D2
Sutton's Way EC1 45 J1
Sutton Wk SE1 45 F5
Swallow Pl W1 44 B3
Swallow St W1 44 C4
Swan St SE1 45 J6
Swiss Ct W1 44 D4
Sycamore St EC1 45 J1

T
Tachbrook Ms SW1 44 C7
Tallis St EC4 45 G3
Tanswell Est SE1 45 G6
Tanswell St SE1 45 G6
Tarn St SE1 45 J7
Tavistock St WC2 45 E3
Telford Ho SE1 45 J7
Temple Av EC4 45 G3
Temple La EC4 45 G3
Temple Pl WC2 45 F3
Temple W Ms SE11 45 H7
Tenison Ct W1 44 C3
Tenison Way SE1 45 G5
Tenterden St W1 44 B3
Terminus Pl SW1 44 B7
Thavies Inn EC1 45 G2
Thayer St W1 44 A2
Theed St SE1 45 G5
Theobald's Rd WC1 45 F1
Thirleby Rd SW1 44 C7
Thomas Doyle St SE1 45 H6
Thorney St SW1 44 E7
Thornhaugh Ms WC1 44 D1
Thornhaugh St WC1 44 D1
Thrale St SE1 45 J5
Three Barrels Wk EC4 45 J4
Three Cups Yd WC1 45 F1
Three Kings Yd W1 44 B3
Tilney St W1 44 A4
Tiverton St SE1 45 J7
Took's Ct EC4 45 G2
Torrington Pl WC1 44 C1
Torrington Sq WC1 44 D1
Tothill St SW1 44 D6
Tottenham Ct Rd W1 44 C1
Tottenham Ms W1 44 C1
Tottenham St W1 44 C2
Toulmin St SE1 45 J6
Tower Ct WC2 44 E3
Tower Royal EC4 45 J3
Tower St WC2 44 D3
Trafalgar Sq SW1 44 D4
Trafalgar Sq WC2 44 D4
Trebeck St W1 44 B4
Treveris St SE1 45 H5
Trig La EC4 45 J3
Trinity Ch Sq SE1 45 J6
Trinity St SE1 45 J6
Trio Pl SE1 45 J6
Trump St EC2 45 J3
Trundle St SE1 45 J5
Tudor St EC4 45 G3
Tufton St SW1 44 D6
Turk's Head Yd EC1 45 H1
Turnagain La EC4 45 H2
Turnmill St EC1 45 G1
Tweezer's All WC2 45 G3
Twyford Pl WC2 45 F2
Tyler's Ct W1 44 D3

U
Ufford St SE1 45 G5
Ulster Pl NW1 44 B1
Ulster Ter NW1 44 B1
Union Jack Club SE1 45 G5
Union St SE1 45 H5
University St WC1 44 C1
Upper Belgrave St SW1 44 A6
Upper Brook St W1 44 A4
Upper Grosvenor St W1 44 A4
Upper Grd SE1 45 G4
Upper James St W1 44 C3
Upper John St W1 44 C3
Upper Marsh SE1 45 F6
Upper St. Martin's La WC2 44 E3

Upper Tachbrook St SW1 44 C7
Upper Thames St EC4 45 H3
Upper Wimpole St W1 44 B1

V
Valentine Pl SE1 45 H5
Valentine Row SE1 45 H6
Vandon Pas SW1 44 C6
Vandon St SW1 44 C6
Vane St SW1 44 C7
Vauxhall Br Rd SW1 44 C7
Vere St W1 44 B3
Vernon Pl WC1 45 E2
Verulam Bldgs WC1 45 F1
Verulam St WC1 45 G1
Vesage Ct EC1 45 G2
Victoria Embk EC4 45 F4
Victoria Embk SW1 45 E5
Victoria Embk WC2 45 F4
Victoria Pl SW1 44 B7
Victoria Sq SW1 44 B6
Victoria Sta SW1 44 B7
Victoria St SW1 44 C7
Vigo St W1 44 C4
Villiers St WC2 44 E4
Vincent Sq SW1 44 C7
Vincent St SW1 44 D7
Vine Hill EC1 45 G1
Vine St W1 44 C4
Vine St Br EC1 45 G1
Vine Yd SE1 45 J5
Vintners Ct EC4 45 J3
Virgil St SE1 45 F6
Viscount St EC1 45 J1

W
Waithman St EC4 45 H3
Walcot Sq SE11 45 G7
Walcott St SW1 44 C7
Walkers Ct W1 44 D3
Wallis All SE1 45 J5
Wallside EC2 45 J2
Walnut Tree Wk SE11 45 G7
Walworth Rd SE1 45 J7
Walworth Rd SE17 45 J7
Wardens Gro SE1 45 J5
Wardour Ms W1 44 C3
Wardour St W1 44 D3
Wardrobe Ter EC4 45 H3
Warner St EC1 45 G1
Warner Yd EC1 45 G1
Warren Ms W1 44 C1
Warren St W1 44 B1
Warwick Ct WC1 45 F2
Warwick Ho St SW1 44 D4
Warwick La EC4 45 H3
Warwick Pas EC4 45 H2
Warwick Row SW1 44 B6
Warwick Sq EC4 45 H2
Warwick St W1 44 C3
Warwick Yd EC1 45 J1
Watergate EC4 45 H3
Watergate Wk WC2 45 E4
Waterhouse Sq EC1 45 G2
Waterloo Br SE1 45 F4
Waterloo Br WC2 45 F4
Waterloo Pl SW1 44 D4
Waterloo Rd SE1 45 G5
Waterloo Sta SE1 45 G5
Water St WC2 45 F3
Watling Ct EC4 45 J3
Watling St EC4 45 J3
Waverton St W1 44 A4
Webber Row SE1 45 G6
Webber St SE1 45 G5
Wedgwood Ho SE11 45 G7
Wedgwood Ms W1 44 D3
Weighhouse St W1 44 A3
Welbeck St W1 44 B2
Welbeck Way W1 44 B2
Well Ct EC4 45 J3
Weller St SE1 45 J5
Wellington St WC2 45 E3
Wells Ms W1 44 C2
Wells St W1 44 C2
Wesley St W1 44 A2
West Cen St WC1 44 E2
West Eaton Pl SW1 44 A7
West Eaton Pl Ms SW1 44 A7
West Halkin St SW1 44 A7
West Harding St EC4 45 G2
Westminster SW1 44 C6
Westminster Br SE1 44 E6
Westminster Br SW1 44 E6
Westminster Br Rd SE1 45 F6
Westminster Gdns SW1 44 E7
Westmoreland St W1 44 A2

West One Shop Cen W1
West Poultry Av EC1 **45 H2**
West Smithfield EC1 **45 H2**
West Sq SE11 **45 H7**
West St WC2 **44 D3**
Weymouth Ms W1 **44 B1**
Weymouth St W1 **44 A2**
Wheatley St W1 **44 A2**
Whetstone Pk WC2 **45 F2**
Whichcote St SE1 **45 G5**
Whitcomb St WC2 **44 D4**
Whitefriars St EC4 **45 G3**

Whitehall SW1 **44 E4**
Whitehall Ct SW1 **44 E5**
Whitehall Gdns SW1 **44 E5**
Whitehall Pl SW1 **44 E5**
White Hart St EC4 **45 H2**
White Horse All EC1 **45 H1**
White Horse Ms SE1 **45 G6**
White Horse St W1 **44 B5**
White Lion Hill EC4 **45 H3**
White Lyon Ct EC2 **45 J1**
Whitfield Pl W1 **44 C1**
Whitfield St W1 **44 D2**
Whitgift St SE11 **45 F7**

Whittlesey St SE1 **45 G5**
Whitworth Ho SE1 **45 J7**
Wicksteed Ho SE1 **45 J7**
Wigmore Pl W1 **44 B2**
Wigmore St W1 **44 A3**
Wilcox Pl SW1 **44 C7**
Wild Ct WC2 **45 F2**
Wild St WC2 **45 E3**
William IV St WC2 **44 E4**
Willoughby St WC1 **44 E2**
Willow Pl SW1 **44 C7**
Wilton Cres SW1 **44 A6**

Wilton Ms SW1 **44 A6**
Wilton Pl SW1 **44 A6**
Wilton Rd SW1 **44 B7**
Wilton Row SW1 **44 A6**
Wilton St SW1 **44 B6**
Wilton Ter SW1 **44 A6**
Wimpole Ms W1 **44 B1**
Wimpole St W1 **44 B2**
Wincott St SE11 **45 G7**
Windmill St W1 **44 D2**
Windmill Wk SE1 **45 G5**
Windsor Pl SW1 **44 C7**
Wine Office Ct EC4 **45 G2**

Winnett St W1 **44 D3**
Winsley St W1 **44 C2**
Woburn Sq WC1 **44 D1**
Wollaston Cl SE1 **45 J7**
Woodstock Ms W1 **44 A2**
Woodstock St W1 **44 B3**
Wood St EC2 **45 J3**
Wootton St SE1 **45 G5**

Y
Yarmouth Pl W1 **44 B5**
York Bldgs WC2 **45 E4**
York Gate NW1 **44 A1**

York Pl WC2 **45 E4**
York Rd SE1 **45 F5**
Yorkshire Grey Yd WC1 **45 F2**
York Ter E NW1 **44 A1**
York Ter W NW1 **44 A1**

Z
Zoar St SE1 **45 J4**

Manchester street index

A
Abingdon St **47 E4**
Academy Wk **46 D7**
Ackers St **47 F7**
Acton Sq **46 A3**
Adair St **47 G4**
Addington St **47 F2**
Addison Cl **47 G7**
Adelphi St **46 B3**
Aden Cl **47 J4**
Adlington St **47 H5**
Adstone Cl **47 J3**
Adswood St **47 J3**
Airton Cl **47 H1**
Aked Cl **47 J7**
Albion Pl **46 A3**
Albion St **46 D5**
Albion Way **46 A3**
Alderman Sq **47 J4**
Aldred St **46 A3**
Alexander Gdns **46 C1**
Alexandra St **46 C1**
Alfred James Cl **47 H2**
Alker Rd **47 J2**
Alley St **46 E3**
Almond St **47 G1**
Altair Pl **46 B1**
Amory St **47 G5**
Anaconda Dr **46 C2**
Ancoats **47 G3**
Ancoats Gro **47 H4**
Ancroft St **46 C7**
Angela St **46 C6**
Angel St **47 F2**
Angora Cl **46 B2**
Angora Dr **46 B2**
Anita St **47 G3**
Anne Nuttall St **46 B6**
Anscombe Cl **47 H1**
Antares Av **46 B1**
Apsley Gro **47 H6**
Aquarius St **47 E7**
Archway **46 D7**
Ardwick **47 J5**
Ardwick Grn N **47 G5**
Ardwick Grn S **47 G5**
Arlington St **46 C2**
Arnott Cres **46 E7**
Artillery St **46 D4**
Arundel St **46 C5**
Asgard Dr **46 B5**
Asgard Grn **46 B5**
Ashlar Dr **47 J4**
Ashley St **47 F2**
Ashton New Rd **47 J3**
Ashton Old Rd **47 H5**
Aspin La **47 F2**
Atherton St **46 C4**
Atkinson St **46 D4**
Atwood St **47 E5**
Auburn St **47 F4**
Audlem Cl **47 J2**
Augustus St **47 E1**
Avenham Cl **46 D7**
Aytoun St **47 F4**

B
Back Acton St **47 F4**
Back Ashley St **47 F2**
Back Bk St **47 F1**
Back Br St **46 D3**
Back China La **47 F4**
Back Coll Land **46 D3**
Back George St **47 E4**
Back Hampson St **47 H1**
Back Hulme St **46 B3**
Back Junct St **47 G4**
Back Piccadilly **47 F3**
Back Pool Fold **46 E3**
Back Red Bk **47 F1**
Back St. George's Rd **47 G2**
Back's Par **46 D3**
Back Thomas St **47 F3**

Back Turner St **47 F3**
Badby Cl **47 J3**
Bainbridge Cl **47 J7**
Baird St **47 G4**
Bale St **46 E4**
Balloon St **47 E2**
Balmforth St **46 C5**
Balsam Cl **47 G6**
Bangor St **46 C7**
Bankmill Cl **47 G6**
Bank Pl **46 B3**
Bank St **46 B3**
Baptist St **47 F2**
Barbeck Cl **47 J2**
Baring St **47 G5**
Barker St **46 D1**
Barlow Pl **47 G6**
Barlow's Cft **46 D3**
Barnett Dr **46 C2**
Barrack St **46 B6**
Barrhill Cl **46 C6**
Barrow St **46 B3**
Barton St **46 D5**
Basildon Cl **47 J7**
Beamish Cl **47 G6**
Beattock St **46 C6**
Beaufort St **46 C5**
Beaver St **47 E5**
Beckhampton Cl **47 H7**
Bednal Av **47 J1**
Beechcroft Cl **47 H2**
Belfort Dr **46 A5**
Bendix St **47 F2**
Bengal St **47 G2**
Bennett St **47 J6**
Bentinck St **46 B6**
Bent St **47 E1**
Berkshire Rd **47 J1**
Berry St **47 G5**
Beswick Row **47 E2**
Beswick St **47 H3**
Betley St **47 G4**
Bevan Cl **47 J4**
Bilbrook St **47 F1**
Billing Av **47 G5**
Binns Pl **47 G3**
Birchin La **47 F3**
Birchvale Cl **46 D6**
Birt St **47 H1**
Bishopsgate **46 E4**
Blackburn Pl **46 A4**
Blackburn St **46 B2**
Blackfriars Rd **46 C2**
Blackfriars St **46 D3**
Blackhill Cl **47 G6**
Blackley St **46 B7**
Blacklock St **46 E1**
Blantyre St **46 C5**
Bletchley Cl **47 H7**
Blind La **47 J5**
Blisworth Cl **47 J3**
Bloom St **47 F4**
Blossom St **46 D2**
Blossom St (Ancoats) **47 G3**
Blucher St **46 A4**
Blyton St **47 F7**
Boad St **47 G4**
Bollington Rd **47 H2**
Bombay St **47 F5**
Bond St **47 G5**
Bonsall St **46 D7**
Boond St **46 D2**
Booth St **46 E4**
Booth St (Salford) **46 D3**
Booth St E **47 F6**
Booth St W **47 E7**
Bootle St **46 D4**
Botham Cl **46 E7**
Bothwell Rd **47 G2**
Boundary La **47 E6**
Boundary St E **47 F6**
Boundary St W **47 E6**
Bourdon St **47 J2**

Bow La **46 E4**
Bow St **46 D4**
Brackley Av **46 B6**
Bradford Rd **47 H3**
Bradleys Ct **47 F3**
Braley St **47 G5**
Bramble Av **46 A5**
Bramwell Dr **47 G6**
Brancaster Rd **47 F5**
Branson St **47 J3**
Brazennose St **46 D4**
Brazil St **47 F5**
Brennan Cl **47 E7**
Brewer St **47 F3**
Brian Redhead Ct **46 C6**
Brickley St **47 E1**
Brick St **47 F3**
Briddon St **46 D1**
Bridgeford St **47 F7**
Bridge St **46 D3**
Bridge St W **46 D3**
Bridgewater Pl **47 E3**
Bridgewater St **46 D5**
Bridgewater St (Salford) **46 C1**
Bridgewater Viaduct **46 D5**
Briggs St **46 C2**
Brighton Pl **47 F7**
Brighton St **47 F1**
Brindle Pl **47 E7**
Brocade Cl **46 B2**
Brock St **47 G3**
Bromley St **47 F1**
Bronte St **47 E7**
Brook St **47 F5**
Brotherton Cl **46 B6**
Brotherton Dr **46 C2**
Browfield Av **46 A5**
Brown Cross St **46 C3**
Browning St **46 B7**
Browning St (Salford) **46 C3**
Brown St **46 E4**
Brunel Av **46 A3**
Brunswick **47 G7**
Brunswick St **47 F7**
Bryant Cl **47 H7**
Brydon Av **47 H5**
Buckfield Av **46 A5**
Bugle St **46 D5**
Bunsen St **47 F3**
Burlington St **47 E7**
Burnell Cl **47 H2**
Burstock St **47 F1**
Burton St **47 G1**
Burton Wk **46 B2**
Bury St **46 C2**
Butler La **47 H2**
Butler St **47 H2**
Butter La **46 D3**
Buxton St **47 G5**
Byrcland Cl **47 J5**
Byron St **47 F4**

C
Cable St **47 F2**
Cabot St **47 G6**
Cakebread St **47 G5**
Calder St **46 B5**
Calico Cl **46 B2**
Camberwell St **47 E1**
Cambrian St **47 J2**
Cambridge St **46 E5**
Cambridge St (Salford) **46 C1**
Camelford Cl **47 E7**
Cameron St **46 D5**
Canal St **47 F4**
Cannon St **46 B2**
Canon Ct **46 E3**
Canon Grn Dr **46 C2**
Carding Gro **46 C2**
Cardroom Rd **47 G3**
Carey Cl **47 C1**

Carib St **46 D7**
Carmel Av **46 A5**
Carmel Cl **46 A5**
Carnarvon St **46 E1**
Caroline St **46 C1**
Carpenters La **47 F3**
Carriage St **46 C7**
Carruthers St **47 H3**
Cassidy Cl **47 G2**
Castle St **46 C5**
Caterham St **47 J4**
Cathedral App **46 E2**
Cathedral Gates **46 E3**
Cathedral St **46 E3**
Cathedral Yd **46 E3**
Catlow La **47 F3**
Catlow St **46 D1**
Cavalier St **47 J3**
Cavanagh Cl **47 H7**
Cavell St **47 F3**
Cavendish St **46 E6**
Cawdor St **46 B6**
Caxton St **46 D3**
Caygill St **46 D2**
Cedar Pl **46 B1**
Central St **46 E4**
Century St **46 D5**
Chadderton St **47 F2**
Chain St **47 F4**
Chancel Av **46 A5**
Chancellor La **47 H5**
Chancery La **46 E4**
Change Way **46 C2**
Chapelfield Rd **47 H5**
Chapel St **46 C3**
Chapeltown St **47 G4**
Chapel Walks **46 E3**
Charles St **47 E5**
Charley Av **46 B1**
Charlotte St **47 E4**
Charlton Pl **47 G5**
Charnley Cl **47 J2**
Charter St **46 D1**
Chase St **47 F1**
Chatford Cl **46 C1**
Chatham St **47 F4**
Chatley St **46 E1**
Cheapside **46 E4**
Cheetham Hill Rd **47 E2**
Cheetwood St **46 D1**
Chepstow St **46 E5**
Cherryton Wk **47 G7**
Chesshyre Av **47 J3**
Chester Rd **46 B6**
Chester St **46 E6**
Chevassut St **46 C6**
Cheviot St **46 E1**
Chevril Cl **47 E6**
Chichester Rd **46 D7**
Chiffon Way **46 B2**
China La **47 F4**
Chippenham Rd **47 H3**
Chorlton Rd **46 C7**
Chorlton St **46 E5**
Chorlton St (Old Trafford) **46 A7**
Christchurch Av **46 A3**
Churchgate Bldgs **47 G4**
Church St **47 F3**
Cinder St **47 G2**
Cipher St **47 G2**
City Rd **46 B7**
City Rd E **46 D6**
Clarence St **46 E4**
Clarendon St **46 D6**
Clare St **47 G5**
Clarion St **47 G2**
Clayburn Rd **46 D6**
Cleminson St **46 B3**
Cleworth St **46 B6**
Clifford St **47 F6**
Clifton Gro **46 B7**
Clifton St **46 B7**

Clive St **47 F2**
Cloak St **47 F5**
Cloughfield Av **46 A5**
Clowes St **46 D3**
Cobourg St **47 F4**
Coburg Av **46 B1**
Cockcroft Rd **46 A2**
Cockspur St **46 D3**
Coleshill St **47 J1**
Colin Murphy Rd **46 C6**
College Land **46 D3**
Collier St **46 D5**
Collier St (Salford) **46 D2**
Collingham St **47 F1**
Collyhurst Rd **47 G1**
Colman Gdns **46 A5**
Comet St **47 G4**
Commercial St **46 D5**
Comus St **46 A4**
Concert La **47 E4**
Congou St **47 G4**
Cooper St **46 E4**
Coop St **47 F3**
Copeman Cl **47 G7**
Copperas St **47 F3**
Coral St **47 G6**
Cork St **47 J4**
Cornbrook **46 B6**
Cornbrook Ct **46 B7**
Cornbrook Gro **46 B7**
Cornbrook Pk Rd **46 B6**
Cornbrook St **46 B7**
Cornell St **47 G2**
Coronation Sq **47 H5**
Coronation St **46 A4**
Corporation St **46 E3**
Cottenham La **46 C1**
Cottenham St **47 G6**
Cotter St **47 G5**
Cottingham Rd **47 J7**
Cotton St **47 G3**
County St **46 E4**
Coupland St **47 E7**
Coupland St E **47 F7**
Coverdale Cres **47 H6**
Cowan St **47 J3**
Cowburn St **46 E1**
Cow La **46 B4**
Crabbe St **47 F1**
Cranbourne St **46 A4**
Crane St **47 H5**
Cranfield Cl **47 J2**
Craven St **46 B4**
Crediton Cl **46 E7**
Cresbury St **47 H5**
Crescent, The **46 A2**
Cross Keys St **47 F2**
Crossley Ct **47 J3**
Cross St **46 E4**
Cross St (Salford) **46 D3**
Crown La **47 F2**
Crown St **46 C5**
Crown St (Salford) **46 C2**
Culmington Cl **46 C7**
Cumberland St **46 B1**
Cumbrian Cl **47 G6**
Cunard Cl **47 G6**
Cygnus Av **46 B1**
Cyrus St **47 J3**

D
Dainton St **47 J5**
Daintry Cl **46 D6**
Dalberg St **47 H6**
Dale St **47 F3**
Dalley Av **46 B1**
Dalton Ct **47 G1**
Dalton St **47 G1**
Damask Av **46 B2**
Danebank Wk **47 G6**
Danecroft Cl **47 H7**
Danson St **47 J2**

Dantzic St **47 E3**
Dark La **47 H5**
Dartford Cl **47 J7**
Darton Av **47 J2**
Darwen St **46 A7**
Davy St **47 G1**
Dawson St **46 B5**
Dean Rd **46 D2**
Deansgate **46 D4**
Dean St **47 F3**
Deanwater Cl **47 G6**
Dearden St **46 D6**
Dearmans Pl **46 D3**
Deer St **47 G4**
Denewell Cl **47 H7**
Denver Av **47 J1**
Derby St **47 E1**
Derwent St **46 B5**
Devas St **47 F7**
Devine Cl **46 B2**
Devonshire St **47 H7**
Devonshire St N **47 J6**
Devonshire St S **47 H7**
Dewhurst St **46 D1**
Dickinson St **46 E4**
Dilston Cl **47 H7**
Dinsdale Cl **47 J2**
Dinton St **46 B6**
Dobson St **47 H7**
Dolefield **46 D3**
Dolphin Pl **47 H6**
Dolphin St **47 H6**
Donald St **47 F5**
Dorsey St **47 F3**
Dover St **47 F7**
Downing St **47 G5**
Downley Dr **47 H3**
Drayton Wk **46 B7**
Droitwich Rd **47 H1**
Dryden St **47 G7**
Dryhurst Wk **47 E7**
Ducie St **47 F4**
Duke Pl **46 C5**
Duke St **46 C5**
Duke St (Salford) **46 D2**
Dulwich St **47 F1**
Duncan St **46 A4**
Dun Cl **46 B3**
Dunham St **46 D7**
Dunlop St **46 D3**
Durant St **47 F2**
Durling Av **47 H6**
Dutton St **46 E1**
Dyche St **47 F2**
Dyer St **46 A5**

E
Eagle St **47 F2**
Eastburn Av **47 H1**
Eastfield Av **47 J2**
Eastleigh Dr **47 H1**
East Mkt St **46 C3**
East Newton St **47 H2**
Eastnor Cl **46 B7**
East Ordsall La **46 B4**
Eastpark Cl **47 H6**
East Philip St **46 D1**
East Union St **46 B7**
Ebden St **47 F4**
Ebenezer St **46 E6**
Echo St **47 F5**
Eden Cl **46 E7**
Edgehill St **47 F3**
Edge St **47 F3**
Edward St **46 D1**
Egerton Rd **46 C5**
Egerton St **46 C3**
Elbe St **47 H5**
Eliza St **46 C6**
Ellesmere St **46 B6**
Ellis St **46 D7**
Elsworth St **47 E1**
Elton St **46 C1**

Elton's Yd 46 C1
Elverdon Cl 46 D7
Empire St 46 E1
Empress St 46 A7
Encombe Pl 46 B3
Epping St 46 E6
Epsley Cl 47 E7
Epworth St 47 H4
Errington Dr 46 B1
Erskine St 46 C7
Essex St 46 E4
Essex Way 46 C7
Etruria Cl 47 J7
Evans St 46 D2
Everard St 46 B5
Every St 47 H4
Exford Cl 47 H2
Eyre St 47 E7

F

Fairbrother St 46 A6
Fairfield St 47 G5
Fair St 47 G4
Falkland Av 47 J1
Faraday St 47 F3
Farnborough Rd 47 H1
Farrell St 46 C1
Farwood Cl 46 B7
Faulkner St 47 E4
Federation St 47 E2
Fennel St 46 E2
Fenn St 46 C7
Fenwick St 47 E6
Ferdinan St 47 H1
Fernbrook Cl 47 J7
Fernie St 47 E1
Fernleigh Dr 46 B7
Fern St 47 E1
Ferry St 47 J4
Filby Wk 47 J1
Firbeck Dr 47 H2
Firefly Cl 46 B3
Fire Sta Sq 46 A3
Fir St 47 H1
Fitzwilliam St 46 C1
Flatley Cl 47 E7
Flora Dr 46 C1
Ford St 47 H6
Ford St (Salford) 46 C3
Foundry La 47 F3
Fountain St 47 E4
Four Yards 46 E4
Frances St 47 G6
Francis St 46 D1
Frederick St 46 C3
Freeman Sq 47 F7
Freya Gro 46 A5
Frobisher Cl 47 J7
Frost St 47 J3
Fulmer Dr 47 H2

G

Gaitskell Cl 47 J4
Galgate Cl 46 C6
Garden La 46 D3
Garden St 46 D2
Garden Wall Cl 46 A5
Garforth Av 47 H2
Gartside St 46 D4
Garwood St 46 D6
Gateaton St 46 E3
Gaythorn St 46 B3
George Leigh St 47 F3
George Parr Rd 46 D7
George St 47 E4
Georgette Dr 46 D2
Gibbs St 46 B3
Gibson Pl 47 E1
Girton St 46 C1
Glasshouse St 47 G2
Gleden St 47 J2
Glenbarry Cl 47 G7
Glenbarry St 47 J5
Gloucester St 46 E5
Gloucester St (Salford) 46 A5
Goadsby St 47 F2
Gold St 47 F4
Gordon St 46 C1
Gore St 47 F4
Gore St (Salford) 46 C3
Gorton St 46 D2
Goulden St 47 F2
Gould St 47 F1
Grafton St 47 G7
Granby Row 47 F5
Granshaw St 47 J2
Gratrix Av 46 A6
Gravell La 46 D2
Grear Ducie St 46 E2
Great Ancoats St 47 F3
Great Bridgewater St 46 D5
Great Clowes St 46 C1
Great Ducie St 46 D1
Great George St 46 B3
Great Jackson St 46 C5
Great John St 46 C4
Great Marlborough St 47 E5
Greek St 47 F6
Green Gate 46 D2
Greengate W 46 C2
Grenham Av 46 B6
Griffiths Cl 46 C1
Groom St 47 F6
Grosvenor Gdns 46 C1
Grosvenor Sq 46 C1
Grosvenor St 47 F6
Guide Post Sq 47 H7
Gunson St 47 H2
Gun St 47 G3
Gurner Av 46 A6
Gurney St 47 J3

H

Hackleton Cl 47 J3
Hadfield St 46 B7
Half St 46 D2
Hall St 46 E4
Halmore Rd 47 H2
Halsbury Cl 47 J7
Halston St 46 D7
Hamerton Rd 47 G1
Hamilton Gro 46 B7
Hamilton St 46 B7
Hampson St 47 H1
Hamsell Rd 47 G6
Handsworth St 47 J5
Hanging Ditch 46 E3
Hanover St 47 E2
Hanworth Cl 47 G6
Harding St 47 J4
Harding St (Salford) 46 D2
Hardman Sq 46 D4
Hardman St 46 D4
Hardshaw Cl 47 G6
Harehill Cl 47 G5
Hare St 47 F3
Hargreave's St 47 F1
Harkness St 47 H6
Harold St 46 B7
Harriett St 47 H2
Harrison St 47 H4
Harrison St (Salford) 46 C1
Harris St 46 D1
Harry Hall Gdns 46 B1
Harter St 47 E4
Hartfield Cl 47 G6
Hart St 47 F4
Hatter St 47 F2
Hatton Av 46 B1
Haverlock Dr 46 B1
Haymarket Cl 47 H7
Heath Av 46 B1
Helga St 47 H1
Hellidon Cl 47 H6
Helmet St 47 H5
Henry St 47 G3
Henry St (Old Trafford) 46 A7
Hewitt St 46 D5
Heyrod St 47 G4
Higher Ardwick 47 H6
Higher Cambridge St 47 E6
Higher Chatham St 47 E6
Higher Ormond St 47 F6
Higher Oswald St 47 F2
Higher York St 47 F6
High St 47 E3
Hillcourt St 47 F6
Hillfield Cl 47 J7
Hillkirk St 47 J3
Hilton St 47 F3
Hinton St 47 G2
Hodson St 46 C2
Holdgate Cl 46 D7
Holkham Cl 47 H3
Holland St 47 H2
Holly Bk Cl 46 B6
Holly St 47 J4
Holt Town 47 J3
Honey St 47 F1
Hood St 47 G3
Hooper St 47 J5
Hope St 47 F4
Hope St (Salford) 46 A3
Hornby St 46 D1
Hornchurch St 46 C7
Horne Dr 47 H3
Houldsworth St 47 F3
Hoyle St 47 H5
Huddart Cl 46 A5
Hughes St 47 J5
Hull Sq 46 B2
Hulme 46 D7
Hulme Ct 46 C6
Hulme Hall Rd 46 B5
Hulme Pl 46 B3
Hulme St 46 D6
Hulme St (Salford) 46 B3
Humberstone Av 46 D6
Hunmanby Av 46 D6
Hunt's Bk 46 E2
Hyde Gro 47 G7
Hyde Pl 47 H7
Hyde Rd 47 H6
Hyde St 46 C7

I

Inchley Rd 47 F6
Instow Cl 47 H7
Ionas St 46 C1
Irk St 47 F1
Iron St 47 J2
Irwell Pl 46 A3
Irwell St 46 D1
Irwell St (Salford) 46 C3
Islington Way 46 B3

J

Jackson Cres 46 C6
Jackson's Row 46 D4
James Henry Av 46 A4
James St 47 J1
James St (Salford) 46 B3
Jenkinson St 47 F6
Jersey St 47 G3
Jerusalem Pl 46 D4
Jessamine Av 46 B1
Jessel Cl 47 G6
Joddrell St 46 D4
John Clynes Av 47 H1
John Dalton St 46 D3
Johnson Sq 47 H1
Johnson St 46 B7
Johnson St (Salford) 46 C3
John St 47 F3
John St (Lower Broughton) 46 C1
John St (Salford) 46 D2
Joiner St 47 F3
Jordan St 46 D5
Joynson Av 46 B1
Julia St 46 D1
Jury St 46 D1
Justin Cl 47 F6
Jutland St 47 G4

K

Kale St 47 G6
Kays Gdns 46 C3
Keele Wk 47 H1
Kelling Wk 46 C6
Kelvin St 47 F3
Kennedy St 46 E4
Kenwright St 47 F2
Kincardine Rd 47 F6
King Edward St 46 A5
Kingham Dr 47 H2
Kingsfold Av 47 H1
Kingsland Cl 47 H1
King St 46 D3
King St (Salford) 46 D2
King St W 46 D3
Kirkgate Cl 47 H2
Kirkhaven Sq 47 J1
Kirkstall Sq 47 G7
Kirkwood Dr 47 H1

L

Lackford Dr 47 H1
Lamb La 46 C3
Lamport Cl 47 F5
Lanchester St 47 J2
Landos Rd 47 H2
Langholme Cl 46 C6
Langport Av 47 J7
Langston St 46 D1
Lanstead Dr 47 J2
Lauderdale Cres 47 H7
Laystall St 47 G3
Layton St 47 J2
Leaf St 46 D6
Leak St 46 B6
Ledburn Ct 46 C6
Left Bk 46 C4
Lena St 47 F4
Leslie Hough Way 46 A1
Lever St 47 E3
Lewis St 47 J1
Leycroft St 47 G4
Lidbrook Wk 47 J7
Lime Bk St 47 J5
Lime Gro 47 F7
Limekiln La 47 H5
Linby St 46 C6
Lind St 47 J3
Linen Ct 46 B2
Linsley St 46 D2
Linton Cl 47 H4
Litcham Cl 47 F5
Little Ancoats St 47 F3
Little Holme St 47 J3
Little John St 46 C4
Little Lever St 47 F3
Little Nelson St 47 F2
Little Peter St 46 D5
Little Pit St 47 G3
Little Quay St 46 D4
Liverpool Rd 46 C4
Livesey St 47 G1
Lizard St 47 F3
Lloyd St 46 D4
Lloyd St N 47 F7
Lockett St 46 D1
Lockton Cl 47 G5
Lomax St 47 G3
London Rd 47 F4
Longacre St 47 G4
Long Millgate 46 E2
Longworth St 46 D4
Loom St 47 G3
Lordsmead St 46 C6
Lord St 46 E1
Lostock St 47 H2
Lowcock St 46 C1
Lower Byrom St 46 C4
Lower Chatham St 47 E6
Lower Mosley St 46 D5
Lower Moss La 46 C6
Lower Ormond St 47 E5
Lower Vickers St 47 J2
Lowndes Wk 47 G6
Loxford St 46 E6
Lucy St 46 B7
Ludgate Hill 47 F2
Ludgate St 47 F2
Luna street 47 F3
Lund St 46 A7
Lupton St 46 C3
Lyceum Pl 47 E6

M

Maidford Cl 47 J3
Major St 47 E4
Makin St 47 E5
Mallard St 47 E5
Mallow St 46 C6
Malta St 47 H3
Malt St 46 B6
Malvern St 46 B7
Manchester St 46 A7
Mancunian Way 46 C6
Mangle St Street 47 F3
Manor St 47 G5
Manson Av 46 B6
Maplin Cl 47 G6
Marble St 47 E3
Marcer Rd 47 H2
Marchmont Cl 47 H7
Market St 46 E3
Markfield Av 47 J7
Markham Cl 47 J4
Marple St 46 C7
Marsden St 46 E3
Marshall St 47 F2
Marshall St (Ardwick) 47 H6
Marsworth Dr 47 H3
Mary France St 46 C6
Mary St 46 D1
Mason St 47 F2
Mason St (Salford) 46 C3
Massey St 46 B3
Mayan Av 46 B2
Mayes St 47 E2
Mayo St 47 H5
Mays St 47 F2
Meadow Rd 46 B1
Medlock St 46 D5
Melbourne St 46 C6
Mellor St 47 H2
Melville St 46 C3
Merrill St 47 H3
Middlewood St 46 B4
Midland St 47 J5
Miles Platting 47 J1
Milk St 47 E3
Millbank St 47 G4
Millbeck St 47 E6
Miller St 47 E2
Mill Grn St 47 H5
Millhall Cl 46 C7
Millhead Av 47 J2
Millow St 47 E2
Milnrow Cl 47 F5
Milton St 46 C1
Mincing St 47 F2
Minshull St 47 F4
Minshull St S 47 F4
Mistletoe Grn 46 C2
Moorhead St 47 G2
Morbourne Cl 47 J7
Mosley St 47 E4
Mosscott Wk 47 G5
Mosshall Cl 46 C7
Moulton St 46 D1
Mouncey St 47 E5
Mount Carmel Cres 46 A5
Mount St 46 E4
Mount St (Salford) 46 C2
Mozart Cl 47 H2
Mullberry St 46 D4
Munday St 47 H3
Munster St 47 E2
Murrey St 47 G3
Museum St 46 E4
Muslin St 46 B4
Myrtle Pl 46 A1

N

Nancy St 46 B6
Nansen St 47 J5
Naples St 47 F2
Nash St 46 C7
Nathan Dr 46 C2
Naval St 47 G3
Naylor St 47 H1
Neild St 47 G5
Neill St 46 C1
Nelson St 47 J1
Nether St 47 G5
New Allen St 47 G2
Newbeck St 47 F2
New Br St 46 D2
Newcastle St 46 E6
New Cath St 46 E3
Newcombe St 46 E1
New Elm St 46 C4
New Gartside St 46 D4
New Islington 47 H3
New Mkt 46 E3
New Mkt St 46 E3
New Mt St 47 F2
New Quay St 46 C4
Newton St 47 F3
New Union St 47 G3
New Vine St 46 D6
New Wakefield St 47 E5
New Welcome St 46 D6
New Windsor 46 A3
Nicholas St 47 E4
Nine Acre Dr 46 A6
Niven St 47 G5
North Bailey St 46 C3
Northdown Av 46 B6
North George St 46 B2
North Hill St 46 C2
North Phoebe St 46 A4
North Star Dr 46 B3
Northumberland Cl 46 A7
Northumberland Cres 46 A7
North Western St 47 G5
North W Services Rd 46 D3
Norton St 46 D2
Norway St 47 J4
Nuneaton Dr 47 H1
Nuttall St 46 A7

O

Oakford Av 47 G1
Oak St 47 F3
Old Bk St 46 E3
Old Birley St 46 D7
Oldbury Cl 47 H2
Old Elm St 47 G6
Oldfield Rd 46 A5
Oldham Rd 47 F3
Oldham St 47 F3
Old Medlock St 46 C4
Old Mill St 47 G3
Old Mt St 47 F2
Old Trafford 46 A7
Old York St 46 C6
Oliver St 47 F7
Ordsall Dr 46 A6
Ordsall La 46 A5
Oregon Cl 47 G6
Orion Pl 46 B1
Ormsgill St 46 D7
Orsett Cl 47 H1
Osborne St 47 G1
Oswald St 47 E2
Oswald St (Ancoats) 47 H4
Overbridge Rd 46 D1
Oxford Rd 47 E5
Oxford St 46 E4

P

Paddock St 47 G5
Palfrey Pl 47 H6
Pall Mall 46 E4
Palmerston St 47 H4
Parish Vw 46 A4
Parker St 47 F3
Park Pl 47 E1
Park St 46 E1
Park St (Salford) 46 B3
Parsonage 46 D3
Parsonage La 46 D3
Parsonage Way 46 A5
Paton St 47 F4
Pattishall Cl 47 J4
Peak St 47 G3
Peary St 47 G1
Peel Mt 46 A1
Pegasus Sq 46 B1
Pembroke Cl 47 H7
Pencroft Way 47 F7
Penfield Cl 47 F5
Percy Dr 46 A6
Percy St 46 C7
Peru St 46 B2
Peter St 46 D4
Phoenix St 47 E3
Phoenix Way 46 D7
Piccadilly 47 F3
Pickford St 47 G3
Picton Cl 46 C2
Picton St 46 C1
Piercy Av 46 B1
Piercy St 47 H3
Pigeon St 47 G3
Pimblett St 46 E1
Pine St 47 E4
Pin Mill Brow 47 H5
Pittbrook St 47 J5
Plymouth Gro 47 G7
Plymouth Vw 47 G7
Pochin St 47 J1
Poland St 47 G2
Polebrook Av 47 H7
Police St 46 D3
Pollard St 47 H4
Pollard St E 47 H3
Polygon Av 47 H7
Polygon St 47 G6
Pomona Strand 46 A6
Poplar St 47 J5
Poplin Dr 46 D2
Portland St 47 E5
Portsmouth St 47 G7
Port St 47 F3
Portugal St 47 G2
Portugal St E 47 G4
Postal St 47 G3
Postbridge Cl 47 H7
Potato Wf 46 C5
Poynton St 46 E6
Price St 47 J3
Primrose St 47 G2
Prince's Br 46 C1
Princess Rd 46 D6
Princess St 46 E4
Princess St (Cornbrook) 46 B6
Pritchard St 47 F5
Providence St 47 H4
Pryme St 46 C5
Purslow Cl 47 J3

Q

Quay St 46 C4
Quay St (Salford) 46 D3
Queen St 46 D4
Queen St (Salford) 46 D2
Quenby St 46 C6
Quendon Av 46 C1

R

Rachel St 47 H5
Radium St 47 G2
Ralli Cts 46 C3
Randerson St 47 G5
Rankin Cl 46 D7
Raven St 47 H5
Reather Wk 47 H1
Red Bk 47 E2
Redfern St 47 E2
Redhill St 47 G3
Red Lion St 47 F3
Regent Sq 46 A5
Reilly St 46 D6
Reservoir St 46 D2
Reyner St 47 E4
Rial Pl 47 E7
Ribston St 46 C7
Rice St 46 C5
Richmond St 47 F4
Richmond St (Salford) 46 C2
Ridgefield 46 D3
Ridgeway St E 47 H3
Ridgway St 47 H3
Riga St 47 F2
Rigel Pl 46 B1
Rigel St 47 H2
Rimworth Dr 47 H1
Ringstead Dr 47 G1
Ripley Cl 47 H4
River Pl 46 D5
Riverside 46 B2
River St 46 D6
River St (Ardwick) 47 H5
Robert St 46 E1

Roby St 47 F4
Rochdale Rd 47 F2
Rockdove Av 46 D6
Rocket Way 46 C3
Rockingham Cl 47 J7
Rodney St 47 H2
Rodney St (Salford) 46 C3
Roe St 47 G2
Roger St 47 F1
Rolla St 46 D2
Rolleston Av 47 H2
Rolls Cres 46 C7
Roman St 47 F3
Rome Rd 47 G2
Rondin Cl 47 J5
Rondin Rd 47 J5
Rope Wk 46 D2
Rosamond Dr 46 C3
Rosamond St W 47 E6
Rosewell Cl 47 J1
Rostron Av 47 J6
Rowendale St 46 D5
Royce Rd 46 C6
Roydale St 47 J2
Royds Cl 47 J7
Ruby St 47 E7
Rudcroft Cl 47 G6
Rudman Dr 46 A5
Rugby St 46 D1
Runcorn St 46 B6

S

Sackville St 47 E4
Sagar St 46 D1
St. Andrew's Sq 47 H4
St. Andrew's St 47 G4
St. Ann's Sq 46 D3
St. Ann St 46 D3
St. Bartholomew's Dr 46 A4
St. Chad's St 47 E1
St. Clement's Dr 46 A5
St. George's 46 B6
St. Ignatius Wk 46 A5
St. James's Sq 46 E4
St. James St 47 E4
St. John St 46 D4
St. Mary's Gate 46 E3
St. Mary's
Parsonage 46 D3
St. Mary's St 46 C3
St. Michael's Sq 47 F2
St. Nicholas Rd 46 C6
St. Philip's St 46 B3
St. Simon St 46 C1
St. Stephen's Cl 47 H7
St. Stephen St 46 C3
St. Thomas St 47 F1
St. Vincent St 47 H3
St. Wilfrids St 46 C6
Salford 46 A4
Salford App 46 D3
Salmon St 47 F3
Saltford Av 47 H3
Salutation St 46 E7
Samouth Cl 47 H2
Sam Swire St 46 D7
Samuel Ogden St 47 F5
Sanctuary, The 46 D7
Sandal St 47 J2
Sandford St 46 C1
Sand St 47 G1
Sawley Rd 47 J1
Scarsdale St 46 A1
School Ct 47 G3
School St 47 F2
School St (Salford) 46 C1
Scotland 47 E2
Scotporth Cl 46 C6
Sefton Cl 47 G6
Senior St 46 D2
Seymour Cl 46 A7
Sharp St 47 F2
Shaw Cres 46 E2
Shawgreen Cl 46 C6
Shawheath Cl 46 C6
Shearsby Cl 46 D7
Sheffield St 47 G4
Sherborne St 46 D1
Sherbourne St W 46 D1
Sherratt St 47 G2
Shetland Rd 47 H1
Shilford Dr 47 G2
Shortcroft St 46 D5
Short St 47 F3
Short St (Salford) 46 C1
Shrewsbury St 46 B7
Shudehill 47 F3
Sidney St 47 F6
Sidney St (Salford) 46 C3
Silkin Cl 47 F6
Silk St 47 G2
Silk St (Salford) 46 B2
Silvercroft St 46 C5
Silver St 47 F4

Simeon St 47 F2
Simms Cl 46 B3
Simpson St 47 F2
Sirius Pl 46 B1
Skerry Cl 47 G6
Skip Pl 47 E1
Slate Av 47 H3
Sleaford Cl 47 H1
Smallridge Cl 47 H2
Smith St 46 A6
Smithy La 46 D3
Snell St 47 H4
Soar St 47 F3
Sorrel St 46 C6
Southall St 46 D4
Southall St
(Strangeways) 46 D1
Southend Av 46 B7
Southern St 46 D5
Southgate 46 D3
South Hall St 46 B5
South King St 46 D3
Southmill St 46 E4
South Pump St 47 F4
South W Services Rd 46 C4
Sparkle St 47 G4
Spa St 47 F7
Spaw St 46 C3
Spear St 47 F3
Spectator St 47 H3
Springfield La 46 D2
Springfield Sq 46 D4
Spring Gdns 47 E4
Spruce St 46 C7
Stalham Cl 47 H1
Stanley Rd 46 B7
Stanley St 47 F1
Stanley St (Salford) 46 C4
Stansby Gdns 47 J7
Station App (for
Oxford Road
Station) 47 E5
Station App (for
Piccadilly Station) 47 F4
Staverton Cl 47 G6
Stephen St 46 E1
Stevenson Pl 47 F3
Stevenson Sq 47 F3
Stevenson St 46 B3
Stockland Cl 47 F6
Stockport Rd 47 H6
Stocks St 47 E1
Stocks St E 47 E1
Stonall Av 46 C6
Stonelow Cl 46 E6
Stone St 46 C5
Store St 47 F4
Stracey St 47 J2
Strawberry Hill 46 A1
Stretford Rd 46 B7
Style St 47 F2
Sudbury Cl 46 B7
Sudell St 47 G2
Sussex St 46 B1
Swan St 47 F2
Swiftsure Av 46 B3
Syndall Av 47 H6
Syndall St 47 H6

T

Talgarth Rd 47 G1
Tamar Ct 46 B7
Tame St 47 H4
Tariff St 47 F3
Tasle All 46 D4
Tatton St 46 B6
Tatton St (Salford) 46 A5
Taunton St 47 J3
Tavery Cl 47 H3
Tebutt St 47 G2
Teer St 47 J3
Temperance St 47 G5
Tewkesbury Rd 47 J2
Thirsk St 47 G5
Thomas St 47 F3
Thompson St 47 F2
Thompson St
(Strangeways) 46 D1
Thomson St 47 H7
Thor Grn 46 B5
Thornage Dr 47 H1
Thorncross Cl 46 B6
Thornden Rd 47 J1
Thornley Brow 47 E2
Thornton St 47 H1
Tib La 46 E4
Tib St 47 F3
Tideswell Av 47 H2
Tidworth Av 47 H3
Tinsley Cl 47 J2
Tivoli St 46 D4
Todd St 47 E2
Tomlinson St 46 D7
Tonge St 47 J5

Tonman St 46 D4
Torquay Cl 47 H7
Towcester Cl 47 J3
Town Hall La 46 E3
Trafford Bk Rd 46 A7
Trafford Ct 46 C6
Trafford Pl 46 B7
Trafford St 46 D5
Travis St 47 G5
Trentham St 46 B6
Trinity Way 46 B5
Tristam Cl 47 G6
Troutbeck Av 47 H3
Trumpet St 46 D5
Tudbury Way 46 C2
Tuer St 47 F7
Turner St 47 F3
Turner St
(Old Trafford) 46 A6
Tutbury St 47 H4
Twillbrook Dr 46 D2

U

Union St 47 F3
Union St (Ardwick) 47 H5
University Rd 46 A2
University Rd W 46 A2
Upper Brook St 47 F6
Upper Cyrus St 47 J3
Upper Helena St 47 J2
Upper Kirby St 47 H3
Upper Moss La 46 C7
Upper Wf St 46 B3

V

Varley St 47 J1
Vauxhall St 47 G1
Velour Cl 46 B1
Vesta St 47 H3
Viaduct St 47 J4
Viaduct St (Salford) 46 D2
Vickers St 47 J1
Victoria Br St 46 D3
Victoria Sta App 46 E2
Victoria St 46 E3
Victor St 47 G1
Victor St (Salford) 46 C3
Virgil St 46 B6

W

Wadeford Cl 47 G2
Wadeson Rd 47 G5
Wadlow Cl 46 C2
Walker's Cft 46 E2
Wallness 46 A1
Wallness La 46 A1
Warde St 46 C7
Wardle St 47 J2
Warford St 47 F1
Warmington Dr 47 J7
Warwick St 47 F3
Warwick St (Hulme) 46 D7
Waterloo St 47 E4
Water St 46 B5
Water St (Ardwick) 47 H5
Watkin Cl 47 G7
Watkin St 46 C1
Watson St 46 D5
Weald Cl 47 G6
Weir St 46 D7
Welland Cl 46 B7
Wellhead Cl 46 E7
Wellington Grn 46 C7
Wellington St 46 C2
Well St 47 E3
West Bk St 46 A4
West Charles St 46 A3
West Crown Av 46 A4
West Hope St 46 A3
West King St 46 C2
Westminster St 46 B6
West Mosley St 47 E4
Weston St 47 J3
West Pk St 46 A5
Weybridge Rd 47 H3
Whalley St 47 H2
Wheater's Cres 46 B1
Wheater's St 46 B1
Wheater's Ter 46 B1
Whimberry Cl 46 A5
Whitchurch St 46 D1
Whitekirk Cl 47 G6
White St 46 B7
Whitfield St 47 E1
Whittle's Cft 47 G4
Whittle St 47 F3
Whitworth St 47 F5
Whitworth St W 46 D5
Wilberforce Cl 46 D7
Wilfred St 46 D1
William Chadwick Cl 47 H1
Williamson St 47 F1
William St 47 H5
Wilmott St 46 E6

Wilson St 47 H7
Wilton Pl 46 B3
Wilton St 47 F6
Winder Dr 47 H3
Windmill Av 46 A5
Windmill St 46 D4
Winfell Dr 47 J2
Winscombe Dr 47 H1
Winser St 47 E5
Winstanley Rd 47 H2
Withy Gro 47 E3
Woden's Av 46 A5
Woden St 46 B5
Woodlark Cl 46 B3
Wood St 46 D4
Woodward Pl 47 H3
Woodward St 47 H3
Woollam Pl 46 C4
Worrall St 46 A5
Worsley St 46 B5
Worsley St (Salford) 46 D3
Wright St 46 A7
Wroe St 46 B3
Wyatt Av 46 A5
Wynne St 46 A1
Wyre St 47 G5

Y

Yew St 46 C7
Yorkshire St 46 D3
York St 47 E3
York St (Hulme) 46 C6
York St (off Charles
Street) 47 E5
York St E 47 F6

Z

Zion Cres 46 D7

Tourist Information Centre: 23 Union Street
Tel: 01224 288828

Albert Quay	C3	Hutcheon Street	B2
Albert Street	B2	Justice Mill Lane	B3
Albury Road	B3	King's Crescent	C1
Albyn Place	A3	King Street	C1
Argyll Place	A2	Langstane Place	B3
Ashgrove Road	A1	Leadside Road	B2
Ashgrove Road West	A1	Leslie Terrace	B1
Ash-hill Drive	A1	Links Road	C2
Ashley Road	A3	Linksfield Road	C1
Back Hilton Road	A1	Loch Street	B2
Baker Street	B2	Maberly Street	B2
Beach Boulevard	C2	Market Street	C3
Bedford Place	B1	Menzies Road	C3
Bedford Road	B1	Merkland Road East	C1
Beechgrove Terrace	A2	Mid Stocket Road	A2
Belgrave Terrace	A2	Mile-end Avenue	A2
Berryden Road	B1	Miller Street	C2
Blaikie's Quay	C3	Mount Street	B2
Bon-Accord Street	B3	Nelson Street	C2
Bonnymuir Place	A2	North Esplanade East	C3
Bridge Street	B2	North Esplanade West	C3
Brighton Place	A3	Orchard Street	C1
Cairncry Road	A1	Osborne Place	A3
Canal Road	B1	Palmerston Road	C3
Carden Place	A3	Park Road	C1
Carlton Place	A3	Park Street	C2
Cattofield Place	A1	Pittodrie Place	C1
Causewayend	B1	Pittodrie Street	C1
Chapel Street	B2	Powis Place	B1
Claremont Street	A3	Powis Terrace	B1
Clifton Road	A1	Queens Road	A3
College Bounds	B1	Queens Terrace	A3
College Street	C3	Regent Quay	C2
Commerce Street	C2	Rosehill Crescent	A1
Commercial Quay	C3	Rosehill Drive	A1
Constitution Street	C2	Rosemount Place	A1
Cornhill Drive	A1	Rose Street	B2
Cornhill Road	A1	Rubislaw Terrace	B3
Cornhill Terrace	A1	St. Swithin Street	A3
Cotton Street	C2	Schoolhill	B2
Cromwell Road	A3	Seaforth Road	C1
Desswood Place	A3	Sinclair Road	C3
Devonshire Road	A3	Skene Square	B2
Elmbank Terrace	B1	Skene Street	B2
Esslemont Avenue	B2	South Crown Street	B3
Ferryhill Road	B3	South Esplanade West	C3
Fonthill Road	B3	Spital	C1
Forest Road	A3	Springbank Terrace	B3
Forest Avenue	A3	Spring Gardens	B2
Fountainhall Road	A2	Stanley Street	A3
Froghall Terrace	B1	Sunnybank Road	B1
Gallowgate	C2	Sunnyside Road	B1
George Street	B1	Union Glen	B3
Gillespie Crescent	A1	Union Grove	A3
Gladstone Place	A3	Union Street	B3
Golf Road	C1	Urquhart Road	C2
Gordondale Road	A2	Victoria Bridge	C3
Great Southern Road	B3	Victoria Road	C3
Great Western Road	A3	Walker Road	C3
Guild Street	C3	Waterloo Quay	C2
Hamilton Place	A2	Waverley Place	B3
Hardgate	B3	Well Street	C3
Hilton Drive	A1	Westburn Drive	A1
Hilton Place	A1	Westburn Road	A2
Hilton Street	A1	West North Street	C2
Holburn Road	B3	Whitehall Place	A2
Holburn Street	B3	Whitehall Road	A2
Holland Street	B1	Willowbank Road	B3

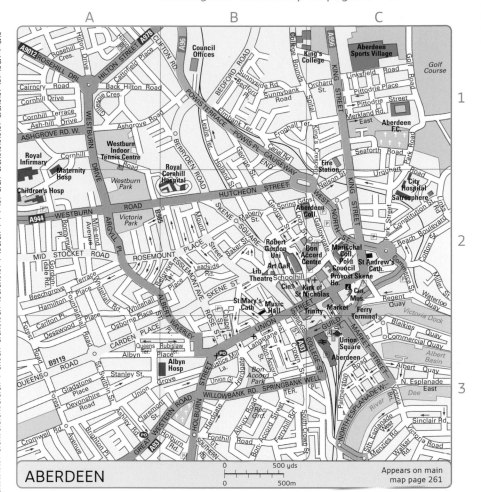

ABERDEEN

Appears on main map page 261

Tourist Information Centre: Abbey Chambers, Abbey Churchyard
Tel: 0906 711 2000

Ambury	A3	Pierrepont Street	B3
Archway Street	C3	Pulteney Gardens	C3
Argyle Street	B2	Pulteney Mews	C1
Avon Street	A2	Pulteney Road	C2
Barton Street	A2	Queen Street	A2
Bath Street	B2	Quiet Street	A1
Bathwick Hill	C1	Rossiter Road	B3
Beau Street	B2	Royal Crescent	A1
Bennett Street	A1	St. James's Parade	A2
Bridge Street	B2	St. John's Road	B1
Broad Quay	B3	St. Marks Road	B3
Broad Street	B1	Sawclose	A2
Broadway	C3	Southgate Street	B3
Brock Street	A1	Spring Crescent	C3
Chapel Row	A2	Stall Street	B2
Charles Street	A2	Sutton Street	C1
Charlotte Street	A1	Sydney Place	C1
Cheap Street	B2	The Circus	A1
Claverton Street	B3	Union Street	B2
Corn Street	A3	Upper Borough Walls	A2
Daniel Street	C1	Walcot Street	B1
Darlington Street	C1	Wells Road	A3
Dorchester Street	B3	Westgate Buildings	A2
Edward Street	C1	Westgate Street	A2
Excelsior Street	C3	Wood Street	A1
Ferry Lane	C2	York Street	B2
Gay Street	A1		
George Street	A1		
Grand Parade	B2		
Great Pulteney Street	C1		
Green Park Road	A2		
Green Street	B1		
Grove Street	B1		
Henrietta Gardens	C1		
Henrietta Mews	C1		
Henrietta Road	B1		
Henrietta Street	B1		
Henry Street	B2		
High Street	B2		
Holloway	A3		
James Street West	A2		
John Street	A1		
Kingsmead East	A2		
Kingsmead Square	A2		
Lansdown Road	B1		
Laura Place	B1		
Lime Grove	C2		
Lime Grove Gardens	C2		
Lower Borough Walls	B2		
Lower Bristol Road	A3		
Magdalen Avenue	A3		
Manvers Street	B3		
Milk Street	A2		
Milsom Street	B1		
Monmouth Place	A1		
Monmouth Street	A2		
Newark Street	B3		
New Bond Street	B2		
New King Street	A2		
New Orchard Street	B2		
New Street	A2		
North Parade	B2		
North Parade Road	C2		
Old King Street	A1		
Orange Grove	B2		
Paragon	B1		

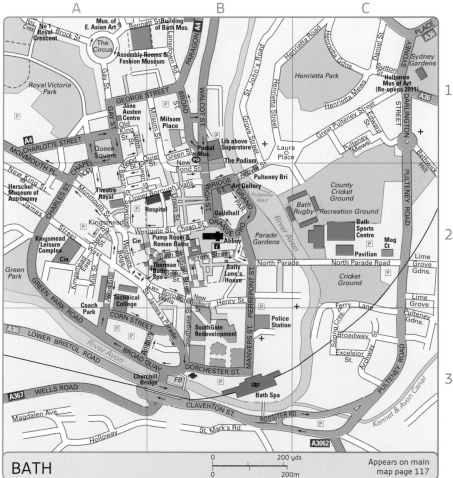

BATH

Appears on main map page 117

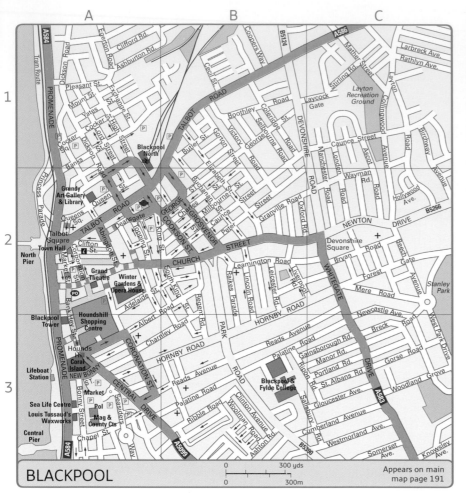

BLACKPOOL

Scale: 0 — 300 yds / 0 — 300m

Appears on main map page 191

Tourist Information Centre: 1 Clifton Street
Tel: 01253 478222

Abingdon Street	A2
Adelaide Street	A2
Albert Road	A3
Ascot Road	C1
Ashburton Road	A1
Ashton Road	B3
Bank Hey Street	A2
Banks Street	A1
Beech Avenue	C2
Birchway Avenue	C1
Bonny Street	A3
Boothley Road	B1
Breck Road	C3
Bryan Road	C2
Buchanan Street	B2
Butler Street	B1
Caunce Street	B2/C1
Cecil Street	B1
Central Drive	A3
Chapel Street	A3
Charles Street	B2
Charnley Road	A3
Church Street	B2
Clifford Road	A1
Clifton Street	A2
Clinton Avenue	B3
Cocker Square	A1
Cocker Street	A1
Coleridge Road	B1
Collingwood Avenue	C1
Cookson Street	B2
Coopers Way	B1
Coronation Street	A3
Corporation Street	A2
Cumberland Avenue	C3
Deansgate	A2
Devonshire Road	B1
Devonshire Square	C2
Dickson Road	A1
Egerton Road	A1
Elizabeth Street	B1
Exchange Street	A1
Forest Gate	B3
Gainsborough Road	C3
George Street	B2/B1
Gloucester Avenue	C3
Gorse Road	C3
Gorton Street	B1
Granville Road	B2
Grosvenor Street	B2
High Street	A1
Hollywood Avenue	C2
Hornby Road	A3
Hounds Hill	A3
King Street	A2
Knowsley Avenue	C3
Larbreck Avenue	C1
Laycock Gate	C1
Layton Road	C1
Leamington Road	B2
Leicester Road	B2
Lincoln Road	B2
Liverpool Road	B2
London Road	C1
Lord Street	A1
Manchester Road	C1
Manor Road	C3
Market Street	A2
Mather Street	C1
Mere Road	C2
Milbourne Street	B2
Mount Street	A1
New Bonny Street	A3
Newcastle Avenue	C2
Newton Drive	C2
Oxford Road	B2
Palatine Road	B3
Park Road	B3
Peter Street	B2
Pleasant Street	A1
Portland Road	C3
Princess Parade	A2
Promenade	A1
Queens Square	A2
Queen Street	A2
Rathlyn Avenue	C1
Reads Avenue	B3
Regent Road	B2
Ribble Road	B3
Ripon Road	B3
St. Albans Road	C3
Salisbury Road	C3
Seasiders Way	A3
Selbourne Road	B1
Somerset Avenue	C3
South King Street	B2
Stirling Road	C1
Talbot Road	A2/B1
Talbot Square	A2
Topping Street	A2
Victory Road	B1
Wayman Road	C2
Westmorland Avenue	C3
West Park Drive	C2
Whitegate Drive	C2/C3
Woodland Grove	C3
Woolman Road	B3
Yates Street	A1

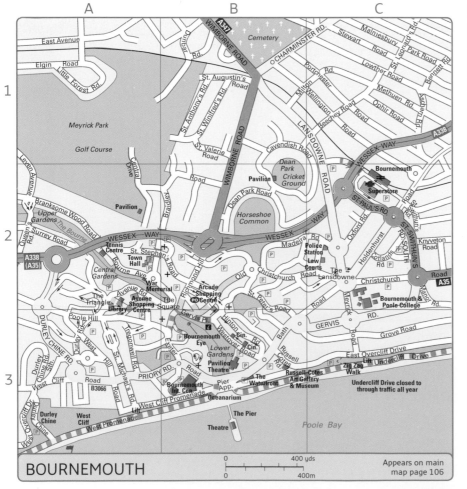

BOURNEMOUTH

Scale: 0 — 400 yds / 0 — 400m

Appears on main map page 106

Tourist Information Centre: Westover Road
Tel: 0845 05 11 700

Ascham Road	C1
Avenue Road	A2
Bath Road	B3
Beechey Road	C1
Bennett Road	C1
Bourne Avenue	A2
Braidley Road	B2
Branksome Wood Road	A2
Cavendish Road	B1
Central Drive	A1
Charminster Road	B1
Christchurch Road	C2
Cotlands	C2
Dean Park Road	B2
Dunbar Road	B1
Durley Chine	A3
Durley Chine Road	A3
Durley Chine Road South	A3
Durley Road	A3
East Avenue	A1
East Overcliff Drive	C3
Elgin Road	A1
Exeter Road	B3
Gervis Place	B3
Gervis Road	C3
Grove Road	C3
Hinton Road	B3
Holdenhurst Road	C2
Knyveton Road	C2
Lansdowne Road	B1
Leven Avenue	A1
Little Forest Road	C1
Lowther Road	C1
Madeira Road	B2
Malmesbury Park Road	C1
Manor Road	C2
Methuen Road	C2
Meyrick Road	C2
Milton Road	B1
Old Christchurch Road	B2
Ophir Road	C1
Oxford Road	C2
Pier Approach	B3
Poole Hill	A3
Portchester Road	C1
Priory Road	A3
Queen's Road	A2
Richmond Hill	B2
Russell Cotes Road	B3
St. Augustin's Road	B1
St. Anthony's Road	B1
St. Leonard's Road	C1
St. Michael's Road	A3
St. Pauls' Road	C2
St. Peter's Road	B2
St. Stephen's Road	A2
St. Swithun's Road	C2
St. Swithun's Road South	C2
St. Valerie Road	B1
St. Winifred's Road	B1
Stewart Road	C1
Surrey Road	A2
The Lansdowne	C2
The Square	B2
The Triangle	A2
Tregonwell Road	A3
Undercliff Drive	C3
Wellington Road	C1
Wessex Way	A2/C1
West Cliff Promenade	A3
West Cliff Road	A3
West Hill Road	A3
West Overcliff Drive	A3
West Promenade	A3
Westover Road	B3
Wimborne Road	B2

Tourist Information Centre: City Hall, Centenary Square
Tel: 01274 433678

Street	Grid	Street	Grid
Akam Road	A1	John Street	A2
Ann Place	A3	Kirkgate	B2
Ashgrove	A3	Leeds Road	C2
Balme Street	B1	Little Horton Lane	A3
Bank Street	B2	Lower Kirkgate	B2
Baptist Place	A1	Lumb Lane	A1
Barkerend Road	C1	Manchester Road	B3
Barry Street	A2	Manningham Lane	A1
Bolling Road	C3	Mannville Terrace	A3
Bolton Road	C1	Manor Row	B1
Brearton Street	A1	Melbourne Place	A3
Bridge Street	B2	Midland Road	B1
Britannia Street	B3	Moody Street	C3
Broadway	B2	Morley Street	A3
Burnett Street	C2	Neal Street	A3
Caledonia Street	B3	Nelson Street	B3
Canal Road	B1	North Parade	B1
Captain Street	C1	North Street	C1
Carlton Street	A2	North Wing	C1
Carter Street	C3	Nuttall Road	C1
Centenary Square	B2	Otley Road	C1
Chain Street	A1	Paradise Street	A1
Channing Way	B2	Park Road	B3
Chapel Street	C2	Peckover Street	C2
Charles Street	B2	Prince's Way	B2
Cheapside	B2	Prospect Street	C3
Chester Street	A3	Radwell Drive	A3
Churchbank	C2	Rawson Place	B1
Claremont	C1	Rawson Road	A1
Croft Street	B3	Rebecca Street	A1
Darfield Street	A1	Rouse Fold	C3
Darley Street	B1	Russell Street	A3
Drake Street	B2	Salem Street	B1
Drewton Road	A1	Sawrey Place	A3
Dryden Street	C3	Sedgwick Close	A1
Duke Street	B1	Sharpe Street	B3
Dyson Street	A1	Shipley Airedale Road	C1
East Parade	C2	Simes Street	A1
Edmund Street	A3	Snowden Street	A1
Edward Street	C3	Sunbridge Road	A1
Eldon Place	A1	Sylhet Close	A1
Fairfax Street	C3	Ternhill Grove	B3
Filey Street	C2	Tetley Street	A2
Fitzwilliam Street	C3	The Tyrls	B2
Fountain Street	A1	Thornton Road	A2
George Street	C2	Trafalgar Street	A1
Godwin Street	B2	Trinity Road	A3
Gracechurch Street	A1	Tumbling Hill Street	A2
Grafton Street	A3	Valley Road	B1
Grattan Road	A2	Vaughan Street	A1
Great Horton Road	A3	Vicar Lane	C2
Grove Terrace	A3	Vincent Street	A2
Guy Street	C3	Wakefield Road	C3
Hall Ings	B2	Wapping Road	C1
Hall Lane	C3	Water Lane	A2
Hallfield Road	A1	Westgate	A1
Hamm Strasse	B1	Wigan Street	A2
Hammerton Street	C2		
Hanover Square	A1		
Harris Street	C2		
Heap Lane	C1		
Houghton Place	A1		
Howard Street	A3		
Hustlergate	B2		
Ivegate	B2		
James Street	B2		

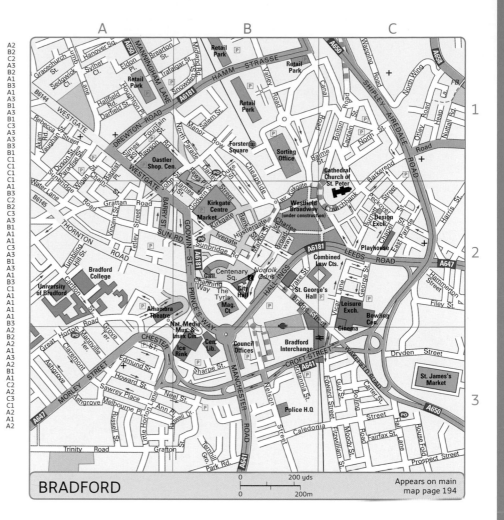

BRADFORD

| 0 | 200 yds |
| 0 | 200m |

Appears on main map page 194

Tourist Information Centre: Royal Pavilion Shop,
4-5 Pavilion Buildings Tel: 0300 3000088

Street	Grid	Street	Grid
Addison Road	A1	Southover Street	C2
Albion Hill	C2	Springfield Road	B1
Beaconsfield Road	B1	Stafford Road	A1
Brunswick Square	A2	Stanford Road	B1
Buckingham Place	B2	Sussex Street	C2
Buckingham Road	B2	Terminus Road	B2
Carlton Hill	C2	The Lanes	B3
Cheapside	B2	The Upper Drive	A1
Church Street	B2	Trafalgar Street	B2
Churchill Square	B3	Union Road	C1
Clifton Hill	A2	Upper Lewes Road	C1
Clyde Road	B1	Upper North Street	A2
Davigdor Road	A1	Upper Rock Gardens	C3
Ditchling Rise	B1	Viaduct Road	B1
Ditchling Road	C1	Victoria Road	A2
Dyke Road	B2	Waterloo Street	A2
Dyke Road Drive	B1	Wellington Road	C1
Eastern Road	C3	West Drive	C2
Edward Street	C3	West Street	B3
Elm Grove	C1	Western Road	A2
Fleet Street	B2	Wilbury Crescent	A1
Florence Road	B1	York Avenue	A2
Freshfield Road	C3	York Place	C2
Furze Hill	A2		
Gloucester Road	B2		
Grand Junction Road	B3		
Hamilton Road	B1		
Hanover Street	C2		
Highdown Road	A1		
Holland Road	A2		
Hollingdean Road	C1		
Howard Place	B1		
Islingword Road	C1		
John Street	C2		
King's Road	A3		
Lansdowne Road	A2		
Lewes Road	C1		
London Road	B1		
Lyndhurst Road	A1		
Madeira Drive	C3		
Marine Parade	C3		
Montefiore Road	A1		
Montpelier Road	A2		
New England Road	B1		
New England Street	B1		
Nizells Avenue	A1		
Norfolk Terrace	A2		
North Road	B2		
North Street	B2		
Old Shoreham Road	A1		
Old Steine	C3		
Park Crescent Terrace	C1		
Park Street	C2		
Port Hall Road	A1		
Preston Circus	B1		
Preston Road	B1		
Preston Street	A3		
Prince's Crescent	C1		
Queen's Park Road	C2		
Queen's Road	B2		
Richmond Place	C2		
Richmond Road	C1		
Richmond Street	C2		
Richmond Terrace	C2		
St. James's Street	C3		
Somerhill Road	A2		

BRIGHTON

| 0 | 200 yds |
| 0 | 200m |

Appears on main map page 109

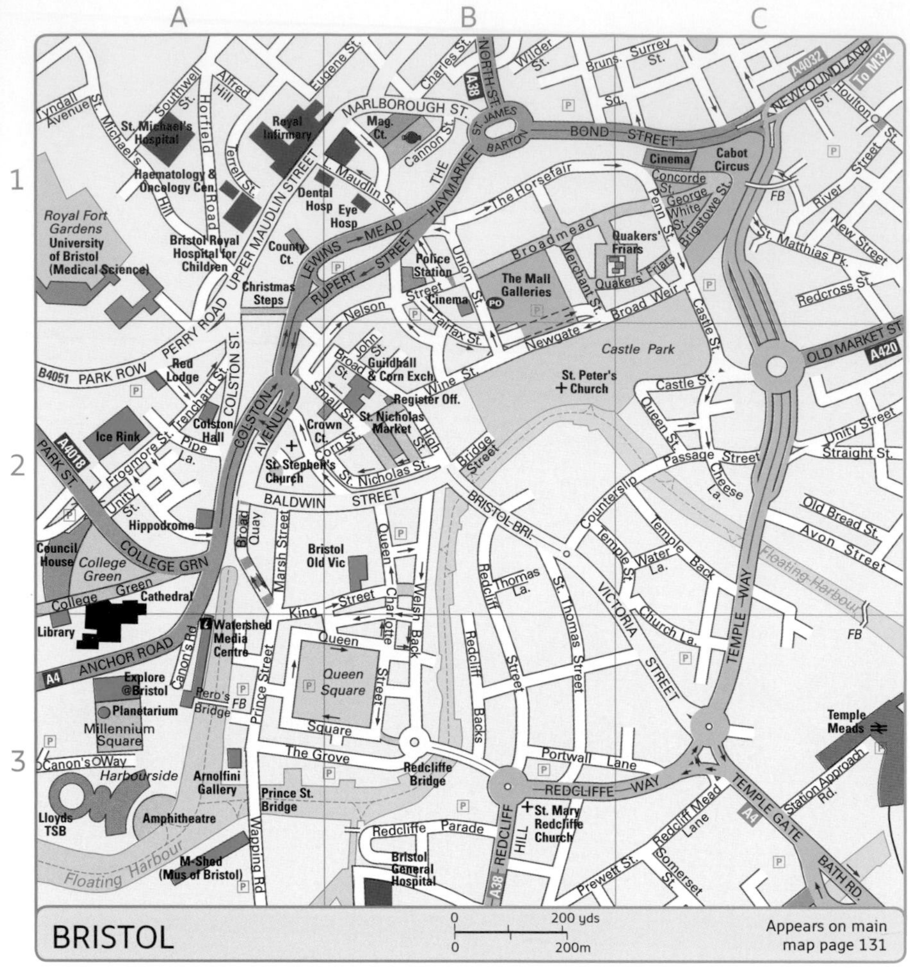

BRISTOL

Tourist Information Centre: E Shed 1, Canons Road
Tel: 0906 711 2191

Appears on main map page 131

CAMBRIDGE

Tourist Information Centre: Wheeler Street
Tel: 0871 226 8006

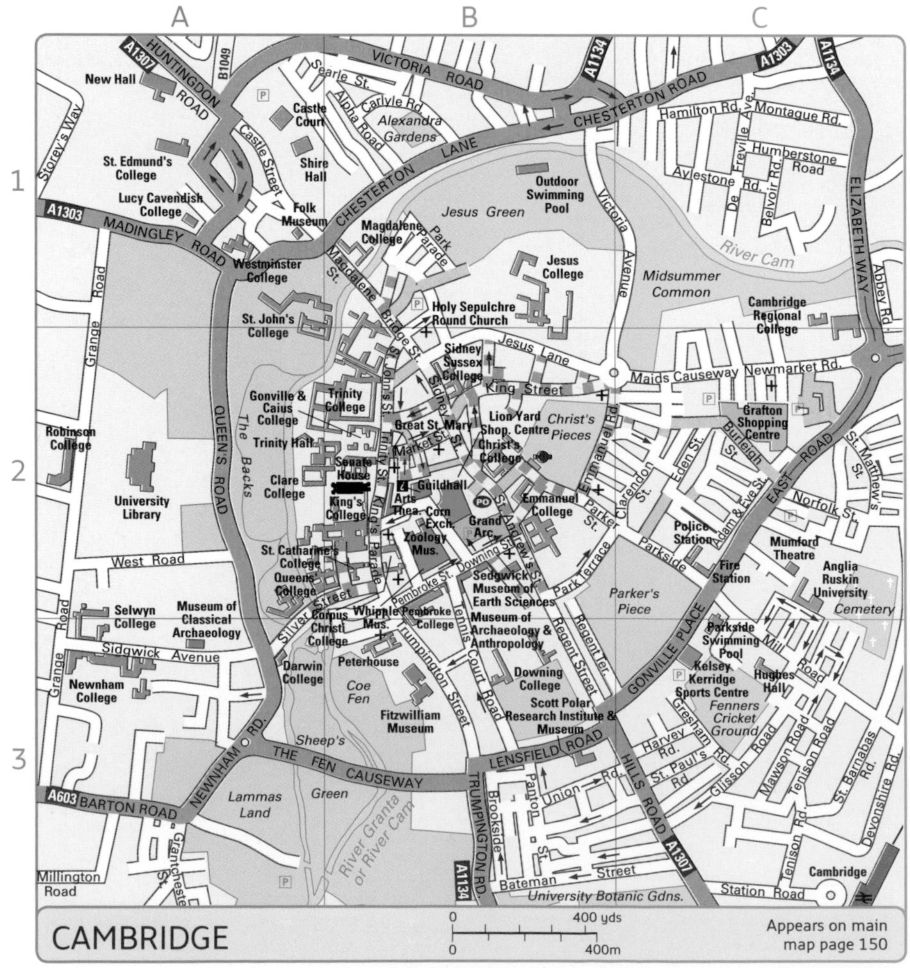

Appears on main map page 150

Canterbury

Tourist Information Centre: 12-13 Sun Street, The Buttermarket
Tel: 01227 378100

Best Lane	B2	Watling Street	B2
Borough Northgate	B1	Whitehall Gardens	A2
Broad Street	C1	Whitehall Road	A2
Burgate	B2	Wincheap	A3
Castle Row	A3	York Road	A3
Castle Street	A3		
College Road	C1		
Cossington Road	C3		
Craddock Road	C1		
Dover Street	C2		
Edgar Road	C1		
Ersham Road	C3		
Forty Acres Road	A1		
Gordon Road	A3		
Havelock Street	C1		
Hawk's Lane	B2		
High Street	B2		
Ivy Lane	C2		
King Street	B1		
Kirby's Lane	A1		
Lansdown Road	B3		
Longport	C2		
Lower Bridge Street	C2		
Lower Chantry Lane	C2		
Marlowe Avenue	B3		
Martyrs' Field Road	A3		
Mead Way	A2		
Military Road	C1		
Monastery Street	C2		
New Dover Road	C3		
North Holmes Road	C1		
North Lane	A1		
Nunnery Fields	C3		
Oaten Hill	C3		
Old Dover Road	C3		
Orchard Street	A1		
Oxford Road	B3		
Palace Street	B2		
Pin Hill	A3		
Pound Lane	A1		
Puckle Lane	C3		
Rheims Way	A2		
Rhodaus Town	B3		
Roper Road	A1		
Rose Lane	B2		
St. Dunstan's Street	A1		
St. George's Lane	B2		
St. George's Place	C2		
St. George's Street	B2		
St. Gregory's Road	C1		
St. Margarets Street	B2		
St. Peter's Lane	B1		
St. Peter's Place	A2		
St. Peter's Street	A1		
St. Radigund's Street	B1		
St. Stephen's Road	B1		
Simmonds Road	A3		
Station Road East	A3		
Station Road West	A1		
Stour Street	A2		
The Causeway	B1		
The Friar's	B2		
Tourtel Road	C1		
Tudor Road	A3		
Union Street	C1		
Upper Bridge Street	B3		

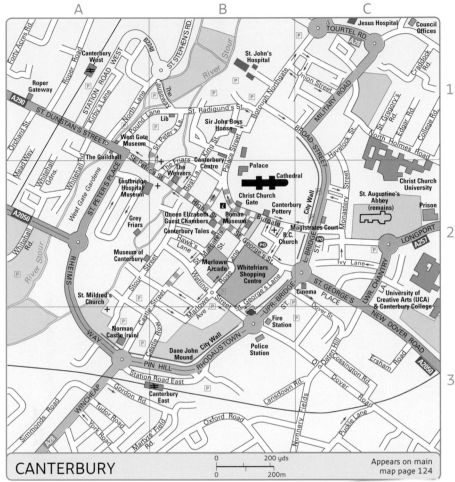

CANTERBURY

200 yds / 200m

Appears on main map page 124

Cardiff

Tourist Information Centre: The Old Library, Trinity Street
Tel: 029 2087 3573

Adam Street	C3	Moira Terrace	C2
Albany Road	C1	Moy Road	C1
Allerton Street	A3	Museum Avenue	B1
Arran Place	C1	Neville Street	A2
Arran Street	C1	Newport Road	C2
Basil Place	B1	Newport Road Lane	C2
Bedford Street	C1	Ninian Park Road	A3
Boulevard de Nantes	B2	North Road	A1
Bridge Street	B3	Oxford Lane	C2
Brook Street	A3	Park Grove	B2
Bute Street	B3	Park Place	B1
Bute Terrace	B3	Park Street	B3
Castle Street	A2	Partridge Road	C1
Cathays Terrace	B1	Penarth Road	B3
Cathedral Road	A2	Pendyris Street	A3
Celerity Drive	C3	Pitman Street	A2
Central Link	C3	Planet Street	C2
Charles Street	B2	Queen Street	B2
Churchill Way	C2	Rhymney Street	B1
City Road	C1	Richard Street	B1
Clare Road	A3	Richmond Road	C1
Clare Street	A2	Ryder Street	A2
Claude Road	C1	St. Mary Street	B3
Coburn Street	B1	St. Peters Street	C2
College Road	B2	Salisbury Road	B1
Colum Road	A1	Schooner Way	C3
Corbett Road	B1	Senghennydd Road	B1
Cornwall Street	A3	Stafford Road	A3
Cottrell Road	C1	Strathnairn Street	C1
Cowbridge Road East	A2	Stuttgarter Strasse	B2
Craddock Street	A3	Taffs Mead Embankment	B3
Craiglee Drive	C3	Talbot Street	A2
Croft Street	C1	Thesiger Street	B1
Crwys Road	B1	The Parade	C2
Cyfartha Street	C1	The Walk	C1
De Burgh Street	A2	Tudor Street	A3
Despenser Street	A3	Tyndall Street	C3
Duke Street	B2	Wedmore Road	A3
Dumfries Place	C2	Wells Street	A3
Ellen Street	C3	West Grove	C2
Elm Street	C1	Westgate Street	B2
Fanny Street	B1	Windsor Place	B2
Fitzhamon Embankment	A3	Windsor Road	C2
Flora Street	B1	Wood Street	B3
Glossop Road	C2	Woodville Road	B1
Gordon Road	C1	Wordsworth Avenue	C2
Greyfriars Road	B2	Working Street	B2
Hamilton Street	A2	Wyeverne Road	B1
Harriet Street	B1		
Herbert Street	C3		
High Street	B2		
Hirwain Street	B1		
Keppoch Street	C1		
Kingsway	B2		
Lewis Street	A2		
Longcross Street	C2		
Maindy Road	A1		
Mardy Street	A3		
Mark Street	A2		
Merches Gardens	A3		
Merthyr Street	B1		
Meteor Street	C2		
Mill Lane	B3		
Minny Street	B1		
Miskin Street	B1		
Moira Place	C2		

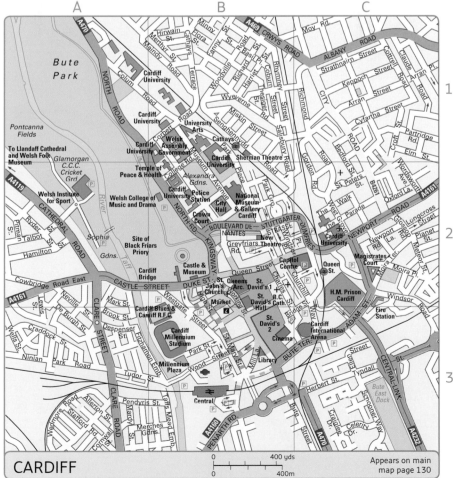

CARDIFF

400 yds / 400m

Appears on main map page 130

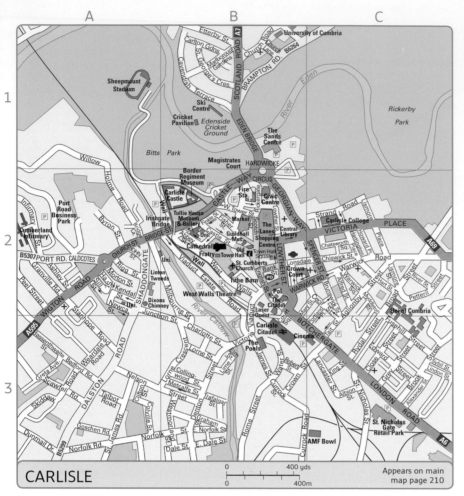

CARLISLE

Appears on main map page 210

Tourist Information Centre: Old Town Hall, Green Market
Tel: 01228 625600

Abbey Street	B2	Lancaster Street	C3
Aglionby Street	C2	Lime Street	B3
Albion Street	C3	Lindon Street	C3
Alexander Street	C3	Lismore Place	C2
Alfred Street	C2	Lismore Street	C2
Ashley Street	A2	London Road	C3
Bank Street	B2	Lonsdale	B2
Bassenthwaite Street	A3	Lorne Crescent	B3
Bedford Road	A3	Lorne Street	B3
Botchergate	B3	Lowther Street	B2
Brampton Road	B1	Marlborough Gardens	B1
Bridge Lane	A2	Mary Street	A2
Bridge Street	A2	Metcalfe Street	C3
Broad Street	C2	Milbourne Street	A2
Brook Street	C3	Morton Street	A2
Brunswick Street	C2	Myddleton Street	C2
Byron Street	A2	Nelson Street	A3
Caldcotes	A2	Newcastle Street	A2
Carlton Gardens	B1	Norfolk Road	A3
Castle Street	B2	Norfolk Street	A3
Castle Way	B2	Peel Street	A2
Cavendish Terrace	B1	Petteril Street	C2
Cecil Street	C2	Port Road	A2
Charlotte Street	B3	Portland Place	C3
Chatsworth Square	C2	Rickergate	B2
Chiswick Street	C2	Rigg Street	A2
Church Lane	B1	River Street	C2
Church Road	B1	Robert Street	B3
Church Street	C2	Rome Street	B3
Clifton Street	A3	Rydal Street	C3
Close Street	C3	St. George's Crescent	B1
Collingwood Street	B3	St. James Road	A3
Colville Street	A3	St. Nicholas Street	C3
Crown Street	B3	Scawfell Road	A3
Currock Road	B3	Scotch Street	B2
Currock Street	B3	Scotland Road	B1
Dale Street	B3	Shaddongate	A2
Denton Street	B3	Silloth Street	A2
Dunmail Drive	A3	Skiddaw Road	A3
East Dale Street	B3	Spencer Street	C2
East Norfolk Street	B3	Stanhope Road	A2
Eden Bridge	B1	Strand Road	C2
Edward Street	C3	Sybil Street	C3
Elm Street	B3	Tait Street	C3
English Street	B2	Talbot Road	A3
Etterby Street	B1	Trafalgar Street	B3
Finkle Street	B2	Viaduct Estate Road	B2
Fisher Street	B2	Victoria Place	C2
Fusehill Street	C3	Victoria Viaduct	B3
Georgian Way	B2	Warwick Road	B2
Goschen Road	A3	Warwick Square	C2
Graham Street	B3	Water Street	B3
Granville Road	A2	Weardale Road	A3
Greta Avenue	A3	West Tower Street	B2
Grey Street	C3	West Walls	B2
Hardwicke Circus	B1	Westmorland Street	B3
Hart Street	C2	Wigton Road	A2
Hartington Place	C2	Willow Holme Road	A1
Hawick Street	A2		
Howard Place	C2		
Infirmary Street	A2		
James Street	B3		
John Street	A2		
Junction Street	A2		
Kendal Street	A2		
King Street	C3		

CHELTENHAM

Appears on main map page 146

Tourist Information Centre: 77 Promenade
Tel: 01242 522878

Albany Road	A3	Portland Street	B2
Albert Road	C1	Prestbury Road	C1
Albion Street	B2	Princes Road	A3
All Saints Road	C2	Priory Street	C3
Andover Road	A3	Promenade	B2
Arle Avenue	A1	Rodney Road	B2
Ashford Road	A3	Rosehill Street	C3
Bath Parade	B2	Royal Well Road	B2
Bath Road	B3	St. George's Place	B2
Bayshill Road	A2	St. George's Road	A2
Berkeley Street	B2	St. James Street	B2
Brunswick Street	B1	St. Johns Avenue	B2
Carlton Street	C2	St. Margaret's Road	B1
Central Cross Drive	C1	St. Paul's Road	B1
Christchurch Road	A2	St. Paul's Street North	B1
Churchill Drive	C3	St. Paul's Street South	B1
Clarence Road	B1	St. Stephen's Road	A3
College Lawn	B3	Sandford Mill Road	C3
College Road	B3	Sandford Road	B3
Cranham Road	C3	Sherborne Street	C2
Douro Road	A2	Southgate Drive	B3
Dunalley Street	B1	Strickland Road	C3
Eldon Road	C2	Suffolk Road	A3
Evesham Road	C1	Suffolk Square	A3
Fairview Road	B2	Sun Street	A1
Folly Lane	B1	Swindon Road	A1
Gloucester Road	A2	Sydenham Road	B3
Grafton Road	A3	Sydenham Villas Road	C3
Hales Road	C3	Tewkesbury Road	A1
Hanover Street	B1	Thirlestaine Road	B3
Hayward's Road	C3	Tivoli Road	A3
Henrietta Street	B2	Townsend Street	A1
Hewlett Road	C2	Vittoria Walk	B3
High Street	B1	Wellington Road	C1
Honeybourne Way	A1	West Drive	B1
Hudson Street	B1	Western Road	A2
Imperial Square	B2	Whaddon Road	C1
Keynsham Road	B3	Winchcombe Street	B2
King Alfred Way	C3	Windsor Street	C1
King's Road	C2		
Lansdown Crescent	A3		
Lansdown Road	A3		
London Road	C3		
Lupiatt Road	A3		
Malvern Road	A2		
Market Street	A1		
Marle Hill Parade	B1		
Marle Hill Road	B1		
Millbrook Street	A1		
Montpellier Spa Road	B3		
Montpellier Street	A3		
Montpellier Terrace	A3		
Montpellier Walk	A3		
New Street	B2		
North Place	B2		
North Street	B2		
Old Bath Road	C3		
Oriel Road	B2		
Overton Road	A2		
Painswick Road	A3		
Parabola Road	A2		
Park Place	A2		
Park Street	A1		
Pittville Circus	C1		
Pittville Circus Road	C2		
Pittville Lawn	C1		

Chester

Tourist Information Centre: Town Hall, Northgate Street
Tel: 01244 402111

Bath Street	C2	Queen's Park Road	B3
Bedward Row	A2	Queen's Road	C1
Black Diamond Street	B1	Queen Street	B2
Black Friars	A3	Raymond Street	A1
Bold Square	B2	Russel Street	C2
Boughton	C2	St. Anne Street	B1
Bouverie Street	A1	St. George's Crescent	C3
Bridge Street	B2	St. John's Road	C3
Brook Street	B1	St. John Street	B2
Canal Street	A1	St. Martins Way	A1
Castle Drive	A3	St. Oswalds Way	A1
Charles Street	B1	St. Werburgh Street	B2
Cheyney Road	A1	Seller Street	C2
Chichester Street	A1	Sibell Street	C1
City Road	C2	Souter's Lane	B3
City Walls Road	A2	Stanley Street	A2
Commonhall Street	A2	Station Road	C1
Cornwall Street	B1	Steam Mill Street	C2
Crewe Street	C1	Talbot Street	B1
Cuppin Street	A3	The Bars	C2
Dee Hills Park	C2	The Groves	B3
Dee Lane	C2	Trafford Street	B1
Deva Terrace	C2	Union Street	B2
Duke Street	B3	Upper Northgate Street	A1
Eastgate Street	B2	Vicar's Lane	B2
Edinburgh Way	C3	Victoria Crescent	C3
Egerton Street	B1	Victoria Place	B2
Elizabeth Crescent	C3	Victoria Road	A1
Foregate Street	B2	Walker Street	C1
Forest Street	B2	Walpole Street	A1
Francis Street	C1	Walter Street	B1
Frodsham Street	B2	Watergate Street	A2
Garden Lane	A1	Water Tower Street	A2
George Street	B1	Weaver Street	A2
Gloucester Street	B1	White Friars	A3
Grey Friars	A3	York Street	B2
Grosvenor Park Terrace	C2		
Grosvenor Road	A3		
Grosvenor Street	A3		
Handbridge	B3		
Hoole Road	B1		
Hoole Way	B1		
Hunter Street	A2		
King Street	A2		
Leadworks Lane	C2		
Lightfoot Street	C1		
Louise Street	A1		
Love Street	B2		
Lower Bridge Street	B3		
Lower Park Road	C3		
Mill Street	C2		
Milton Street	B1		
Newgate Street	B2		
Nicholas Street	A2		
Nicholas Street Mews	A2		
Northern Pathway	C3		
Northgate Avenue	B1		
Northgate Street	A2		
Nun's Road	A3		
Old Dee Bridge	B3		
Pepper Street	B3		
Phillip Street	C1		
Prince's Avenue	C1		
Princess Street	A2		
Queen's Avenue	C1		
Queen's Drive	C3		

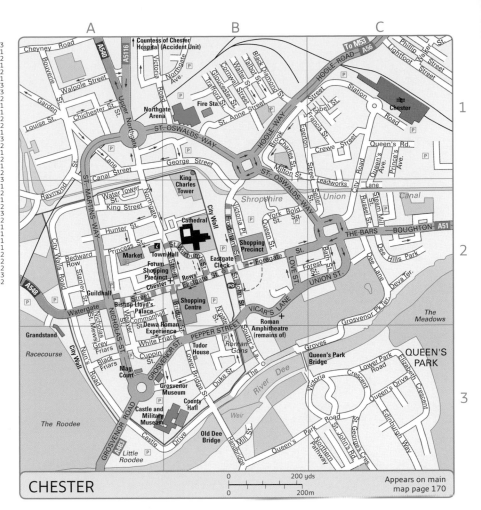

CHESTER

Appears on main map page 170

Coventry

Tourist Information Centre: St. Michael's Tower, Coventry Cathedral   Tel: 024 7622 5616

Abbott's Lane	A1	New Union Street	B2
Acacia Avenue	C3	Norfolk Street	A2
Albany Road	A3	Oxford Street	C2
Alma Street	C2	Park Road	B3
Asthill Grove	B3	Parkside	B3
Barker's Butts Lane	A1	Primrose Hill Street	C1
Barras Lane	A2	Priory Street	B2
Berry Street	C1	Puma Way	B3
Bishop Street	B1	Quarryfield Lane	C3
Blythe Road	C1	Queen's Road	A3
Bond Street	A2	Queen Street	C1
Bramble Street	C2	Queen Victoria Road	A2
Bretts Close	C1	Quinton Road	B3
Broadway	A3	Radford Road	A1
Burges	B2	Raglan Street	C2
Butts Road	A2	Regent Street	A3
Cambridge Street	C1	Ringway Hill Cross	A2
Canterbury Street	C1	Ringway Queens	A2
Clifton Street	C1	Ringway Rudge	A2
Colchester Street	C1	A2	
Cornwall Road	C3	Ringway St. Johns	B3
Corporation Street	B2	Ringway St. Nicholas	B1
Coundon Road	A1	Ringway St. Patricks	B3
Coundon Street	A2	Ringway Swanswell	
Cox Street	C2	B2	
Croft Road	A2	Ringway Whitefriars	C2
Drapers Fields	B1	St. Nicholas Street	B1
Earl Street	B2	Sandy Lane	B1
East Street	C2	Seagrave Road	C3
Eaton Road	B3	Silver Street	B1
Fairfax Street	D2	Sky Blue Way	C2
Far Gosford Street	C2	South Street	C2
Foleshill Road	B1	Spencer Avenue	A3
Fowler Road	A1	Spon Street	A2
Gordon Street	A3	Srathmore Avenue	C3
Gosford Street	C2	Stoney Road	B3
Greyfriars Road	A2	Stoney Stanton Road	B1
Gulson Road	C2	Swanswell Street	B1
Hales Street	B2	The Precinct	B2
Harnall Lane East	C1	Tomson Avenue	A1
Harnall Lane West	B1	Trinity Street	B2
Harper Road	C2	Upper Hill Street	A2
Harper Street	B2	Upper Well Street	B2
Hertford Street	B2	Vauxhall Street	C2
Hewitt Avenue	A1	Vecqueray Street	C2
High Street	B2	Victoria Street	C1
Hill Street	A2	Vine Street	C1
Holyhead Road	A2	Warwick Road	A3
Hood Street	C2	Waveley Road	A2
Howard Street	B1	Westminster Road	A3
Jordan Well	C2	White Street	B1
King William Street	C1	Windsor Street	A2
Lamb Street	B2	Wright Street	C1
Leicester Row	B1		
Leigh Street	C1		
Little Park Street	B3		
London Road	C3		
Lower Ford Street	C2		
Market Way	B2		
Meadow Street	A2		
Michaelmas Road	A3		
Middleborough Road	A1		
Mile Lane	B3		
Mill Street	A1		
Minster Road	A2		
Much Park Street	B2		

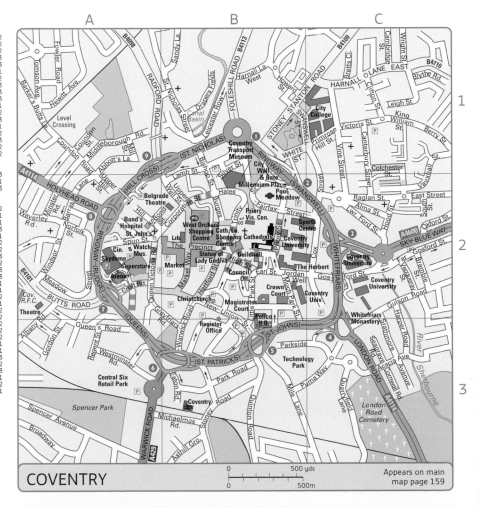

COVENTRY

Appears on main map page 159

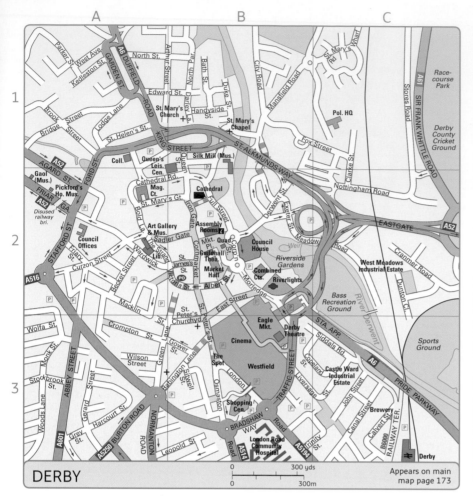

DERBY

Tourist Information Centre: Assembly Rooms, Market Place
Tel: 01332 255802

Abbey Street	A3	Railway Terrace	C3
Agard Street	A1	Sadler Gate	B2
Albert Street	B2	St. Alkmunds Way	B1
Arthur Street	A1	St. Helen's Street	A1
Babington Lane	A3	St. James Street	B2
Bath Street	B1	St. Mary's Gate	A2
Becket Street	A2	St. Mary's Wharf Road	C1
Bold Lane	A2	St. Peter's Churchyard	B3
Bradshaw Way	B3	St. Peter's Street	B2
Bridge Street	A1	Siddals Road	C3
Brook Street	A1	Sir Frank Whittle Road	C1
Burton Road	A3	Sitwell Street	B3
Calvert Street	C3	Stafford Street	A2
Canal Street	C3	Station Approach	C2
Cathedral Road	A2	Stockbrook Street	A3
City Road	B1	Stores Road	C1
Clarke Street	C2	The Strand	A2
Copeland Street	B3	Traffic Street	B3
Cornmarket	B2	Trinity Street	B3
Corporation Street	B2	Victoria Street	A2
Cranmer Road	C2	Wardwick	A2
Crompton Street	A3	West Avenue	A1
Curzon Street	A2	Wilson Street	A3
Darley Lane	B1	Wolfa Street	A3
Derwent Street	B2	Woods Lane	A3
Duffield Road	A1		
Duke Street	B1		
Dunton Close	C2		
Eastgate	C2		
East Street	B2		
Edward Street	A1		
Exeter Street	B2		
Ford Street	A2		
Fox Street	B1		
Friar Gate	A2		
Friary Street	A2		
Full Street	B2		
Garden Street	A1		
Gerard Street	A3		
Gower Street	B3		
Green Lane	A3		
Grey Street	A3		
Handyside Street	B1		
Harcourt Street	A3		
Iron Gate	B2		
John Street	C3		
Kedleston Street	A1		
King Street	A1		
Leopold Street	A3		
Liversage Street	B3		
Lodge Lane	A1		
London Road	B3		
Macklin Street	A2		
Mansfield Road	B1		
Market Place	B2		
Meadow Road	B2		
Monk Street	A3		
Morledge	B2		
Normanton Road	A3		
North Parade	B1		
North Street	A1		
Nottingham Road	C2		
Osmaston Road	B3		
Parker Street	A1		
Pride Parkway	C3		
Queen Street	B1		

Appears on main map page 173

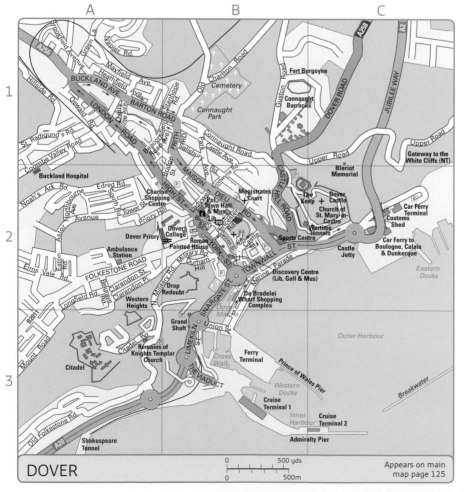

DOVER

Tourist Information Centre: Old Town Gaol, Biggin Street
Tel: 01304 205108

Astor Avenue	A2
Barton Road	A1
Beaconsfield Avenue	A1
Beaconsfield Road	A1
Belgrave Road	A2
Biggin Street	B2
Bridge Street	B2
Brookfield Avenue	A1
Buckland Avenue	A1
Cannon Street	B2
Canons Gate Road	B2
Castle Avenue	B1
Castle Hill Road	B2
Castle Street	B2
Cherry Tree Avenue	A1
Citadel Road	A3
Clarendon Place	A2
Clarendon Street	A2
Connaught Road	B1
Coombe Valley Road	A2
Dover Road	C1
Durham Hill	B2
Eaton Road	A2
Edred Road	A2
Elms Vale Road	A2
Folkestone Road	A2
Frith Road	B1
Godwyne Road	B2
Green Lane	A1
Guston Road	B1
Heathfield Avenue	A1
High Street	B2
Hillside Road	A1
Jubilee Way	C1
Ladywell	B2
Limekiln Street	B3
London Road	A1
Longfield Road	A2
Maison Dieu Road	B2
Marine Parade	B2
Mayfield Avenue	A1
Military Road	B2
Mount Road	A3
Napier Road	A1
Noah's Ark Road	A2
Northbourne Avenue	A2
North Military Road	A2
Old Charlton Road	B1
Old Folkestone Road	A3
Oswald Road	A1
Park Avenue	B1
Pencester Road	B2
Priory Hill	A2
St. Radigund's Road	A1
Salisbury Road	B1
Snargate Street	B3
South Road	A2
Stanhope Road	B1
The Viaduct	B3
Tower Road	A2
Townwall Street	B2
Union Street	B3
Upper Road	C1
York Street	B2

Appears on main map page 125

Tourist Information Centre: Discovery Point, Discovery Quay
Tel: 01382 527527

Adelaide Place	A1	South Marketgait	B3
Albany Terrace	A1	South Tay Street	A3
Albert Street	C2	Strathmartine Road	B1
Alexander Street	B1	Tannadice Street	B1
Ann Street	B1	Tay Road Bridge	B3
Arbroath Road	C2	Trades Lane	B2
Arklay Road	C1	Upper Constitution Street	A1
Arklay Terrace	C1	Victoria Road	B2
Arthurstone Terrace	C2	Victoria Street	C2
Barrack Road	A2	Ward Road	A2
Blackness Road	A2	West Marketgait	A2
Blinshall Street	A2	West Port	A2
Brewery Lane	A2	William Street	C2
Brook Street	A2		
Broughty Ferry Road	C2		
Brown Street	A2		
Bruce Street	A1		
Byron Street	A1		
Canning Street	B1		
City Square	B3		
Clepington Road	C1		
Constitution Road	B2		
Constitution Street	B1		
Court Street	C1		
Cowgate Street	B2		
Dens Road	B1		
Douglas Street	A2		
Dudhope Street	A1		
Dudhope Terrace	C1		
Dundonald Street	C1		
Dura Street	C2		
East Dock Street	C2		
East Marketgait	B2		
Fairbairn Street	B1		
Greenmarket	B3		
Guthrie Street	A2		
Hawkhill	A2		
High Street	B3		
Hill Street	B1		
Hilltown	B1		
Kenmore Terrace	A1		
Killin Avenue	A1		
Kinghorne Road	A1		
King Street	B2		
Larch Street	A2		
Law Crescent	A1		
Lawside Avenue	A1		
Law Street	A1		
Leng Street	A1		
Lochee Road	A2		
Lower Princes Street	C2		
Mains Road	B1		
Main Street	B1		
Meadowside	B2		
Morgan Street	C2		
Murraygate	B2		
Nelson Street	B2		
Nethergate	A3		
North Marketgait	A2		
Perth Road	A3		
Polepark Road	A2		
Princes Street	C2		
Riverside Drive	A3		
Roseangle	A3		
Rosebank Road	B2		
Seagate	B2		

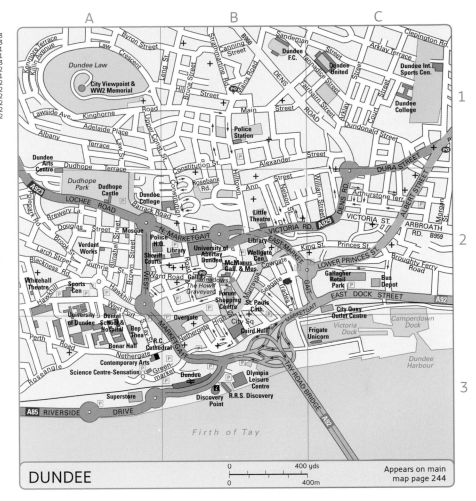

Tourist Information Centre: 2 Millennium Place
Tel: 0191 384 3720

Aykley Heads	A1
Church Street	B3
Clay Lane	A3
Claypath	B2
Crossgate	B2
Crossgate Peth	A3
Darlington Road	A3
Dryburn Road	A1
Durham Road	A1
Fieldhouse Lane	A1
Framwelgate	B2
Framwelgate Peth	B1
Framwelgate Waterside	B2
Gilesgate	C2
Great North Road	A1
Green Lane	C2
Grove Street	B3
Hallgarth Street	C3
Hawthorn Terrace	A2
Leazes Road	B2
Margery Lane	B3
Market Place	B2
Millburngate Bridge	B2
Newcastle Road	A1
New Elvet	B2
North Bailey	B2
North End	A1
North Road	B2
Old Elvet	C2
Pity Me Bypass	A1
Potters Bank	A3
Quarryheads Lane	D3
Providence Row	B2
Redhills Lane	A2
St. Monica Grove	A2
Sidegate	B2
Silver Street	B2
South Bailey	B3
South Road	B3
South Street	B3
Southfield Way	A1
Stockton Road	B3
Sutton Street	B2
The Avenue	A3
Toll House Road	A2
Western Hill	A2
Whinney Hill	C3
Whitesmocks	A1

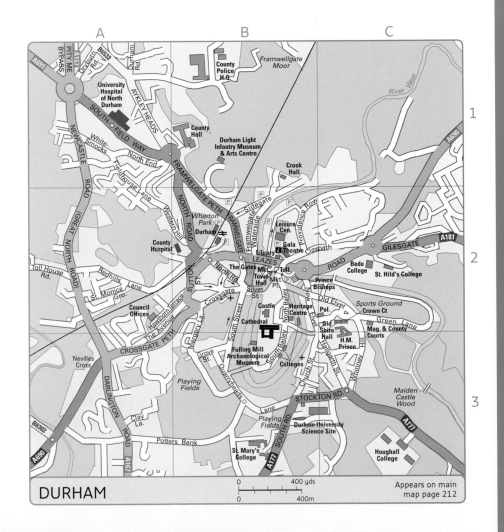

Eastbourne Exeter

Edinburgh street map on pages 36-37

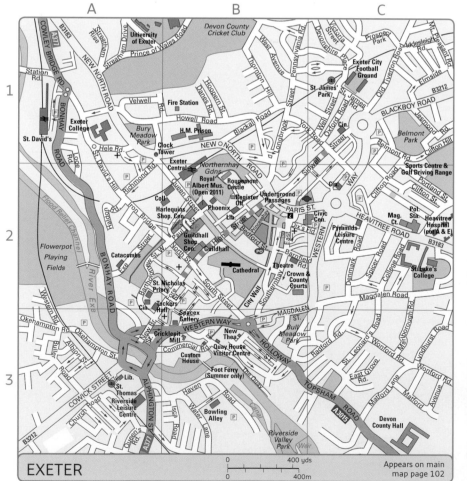

EASTBOURNE

Tourist Information Centre: 3 Cornfield Road			
Tel: 0871 663 0031			

Arlington Road	A2	The Avenue	B2
Arundel Road	B1	The Goffs	A1
Ashford Road	B2/C2	Trinity Trees	C2
Avondale Road	C1	Upper Avenue	B1
Bedfordwell Road	B1	Upperton Lane	B2
Belmore Road	C1	Upperton Road	A1
Blackwater Road	B3	Watts Lane	A1
Borough Lane	A1	Whitley Road	A1
Bourne Street	B1	Willingdon Road	A1
Carew Road	A1/B1	Winchcombe Road	C1
Carlisle Road	A3		
Cavendish Avenue	C1		
Cavendish Place	C2		
College Road	B3		
Commercial Road	B2		
Compton Place Road	A2		
Compton Street	B3		
Cornfield Terrace	B2		
Denton Road	A3		
Devonshire Place	B2		
Dittons Road	A2		
Dursley Road	C2		
Enys Road	B1		
Eversfield Road	B1		
Fairfield Road	A3		
Firle Road	C1		
Furness Road	B3		
Gaudick Road	A3		
Gilbert Road	C1		
Gildredge Road	B2		
Gorringe Road	B1		
Grand Parade	C3		
Grange Road	B3		
Grassington Road	B3		
Grove Road	B2		
Hartfield Road	B1		
Hartington Place	C2		
High Street	A1		
Hyde Gardens	B2		
King Edward's Parade	B3		
Langney Road	C2		
Lewes Road	B1		
Marine Parade	C2		
Mark Lane	B2		
Meads Road	A3		
Melbourne Road	C1		
Mill Gap Road	A1		
Mill Road	A1		
Moat Croft Road	A1		
Moy Avenue	C1		
Ratton Road	A1		
Royal Parade	C2		
Saffrons Park	A3		
Saffrons Road	A2		
St. Anne's Road	A1		
St. Leonard's Road	B2		
Seaside	C2		
Seaside Road	C2		
Selwyn Road	A1		
Silverdale Road	B3		
South Street	B2		
Southfields Road	A2		
Station Parade	B2		
Susan's Road	C2		
Sydney Road	C2		
Terminus Road	B2		

Appears on main map page 110

EXETER

Tourist Information Centre: Dix's Field			
Tel: 01392 665700			

Albion Street	A3	St. James' Road	C1
Alphington Street	A3	St. Leonard's Road	C3
Barnfield Road	B2	Sidwell Street	B2
Bartholomew Street West	A2	Southernhay East	B2
Bedford Street	B2	South Street	B2
Belmont Road	C1	Spicer Road	C2
Blackboy Road	C1	Station Road	A1
Blackall Road	B1	Streatham Drive	A1
Bonhay Road	A2	Streatham Rise	A1
Buller Road	A3	The Quay	B3
Church Road	A3	Thornton Hill	B1
Clifton Hill	C1	Topsham Road	B3
Clifton Road	C2	Velwell Road	A1
Clifton Street	C2	Victoria Street	C1
College Road	C2	Water Lane	B3
Commercial Road	B3	Well Street	C1
Cowick Street	A3	West Avenue	B1
Cowley Bridge Road	A1	Western Road	A2
Danes Road	B1	Western Way	C2
Denmark Road	C2	Wonford Road	C3
Devonshire Place	C1	York Road	B1
Dix's Field	B2		
East Grove Road	C3		
Elmside	C1		
Exe Street	A2		
Fore Street	B2		
Haldon Road	A2		
Haven Road	B3		
Heavitree Road	C2		
Hele Road	A1		
High Street	B2		
Holloway Street	B3		
Hoopern Street	B1		
Howell Road	B1		
Iddesleigh Road	C1		
Iron Bridge	A2		
Isca Road	B3		
Jesmond Road	C1		
Longbrook Street	B1		
Looe Road	A1		
Lyndhurst Road	C3		
Magdalen Road	C2		
Magdalen Street	B3		
Marlborough Road	C3		
Matford Avenue	C3		
Matford Lane	C3		
Mount Pleasant Road	A3		
New Bridge Street	A3		
New North Road	A1/B1		
North Street	B2		
Okehampton Road	A3		
Okehampton Street	A3		
Old Tiverton Road	C1		
Oxford Road	C1		
Paris Street	B2		
Paul Street	B2		
Pennsylvania Road	B1		
Portland Street	C2		
Prince of Wales Road	A1		
Princesshay	B2		
Prospect Park	C1		
Queen's Road	A3		
Queen Street	B2		
Radford Road	C3		
Richmond Road	A2		
St. David's Hill	A1		

Appears on main map page 102

Tourist Information Centre: Discover Folkestone,
20 Bouverie Place. Tel: 01303 258594

Alder Road	B2	Westbourne Gardens	A3
Archer Road	C2	Wingate Road	B1
Bathurst Road	A2	Wood Avenue	C1
Beatty Road	C1	Wilton Road	A2
Black Bull Road	B2		
Bournemouth Road	B2		
Bouverie Road West	A3		
Bradstone Road	B2		
Broadfield Road	A2		
Broadmead Road	B2		
Brockman Road	B2		
Canterbury Road	C1		
Castle Hill Avenue	B3		
Cheriton Gardens	B3		
Cheriton Road	A2/B2		
Cherry Garden Avenue	A1		
Christ Church Road	B3		
Churchill Avenue	B1		
Clifton Crescent	A3		
Coniston Road	A1		
Coolinge Road	B2		
Cornwallis Avenue	A2		
Dawson Road	B2		
Dixwell Road	A3		
Dolphins Road	B1		
Dover Hill	C1		
Dover Road	C1		
Downs Road	B1		
Earles Avenue	A3		
Foord Road	B2		
Godwyn Road	A3		
Grimston Avenue	A3		
Grimston Gardens	A3		
Guildhall Street	B2		
Guildhall Street North	B2		
Harbour Way	C2		
Hill Road	C1		
Ivy Way	C1		
Joyes Road	C1		
Linden Crescent	B2		
Links Way	A1		
Lower Sandgate Road	A3		
Lucy Avenue	A1		
Manor Road	B3		
Marine Parade	B3		
Marshall Street	C1		
Mead Road	B2		
Old High Street	C3		
Park Farm Road	B1		
Pavilion Road	B2		
Radnor Bridge Road	C2		
Radnor Park Avenue	A2		
Radnor Park Road	B2		
Radnor Park West	A2		
Sandgate Hill	A3		
Sandgate Road	B3		
Shorncliffe Road	A2		
Sidney Street	C2		
The Leas	B3		
The Stade	C3		
The Tram Road	C2		
Tontine Street	C2		
Turketel Road	A3		
Tyson Road	C1		
Wear Bay Crescent	C2		
Wear Bay Road	C1		

FOLKESTONE

0	200 yds
0	200m

Appears on main
map page 125

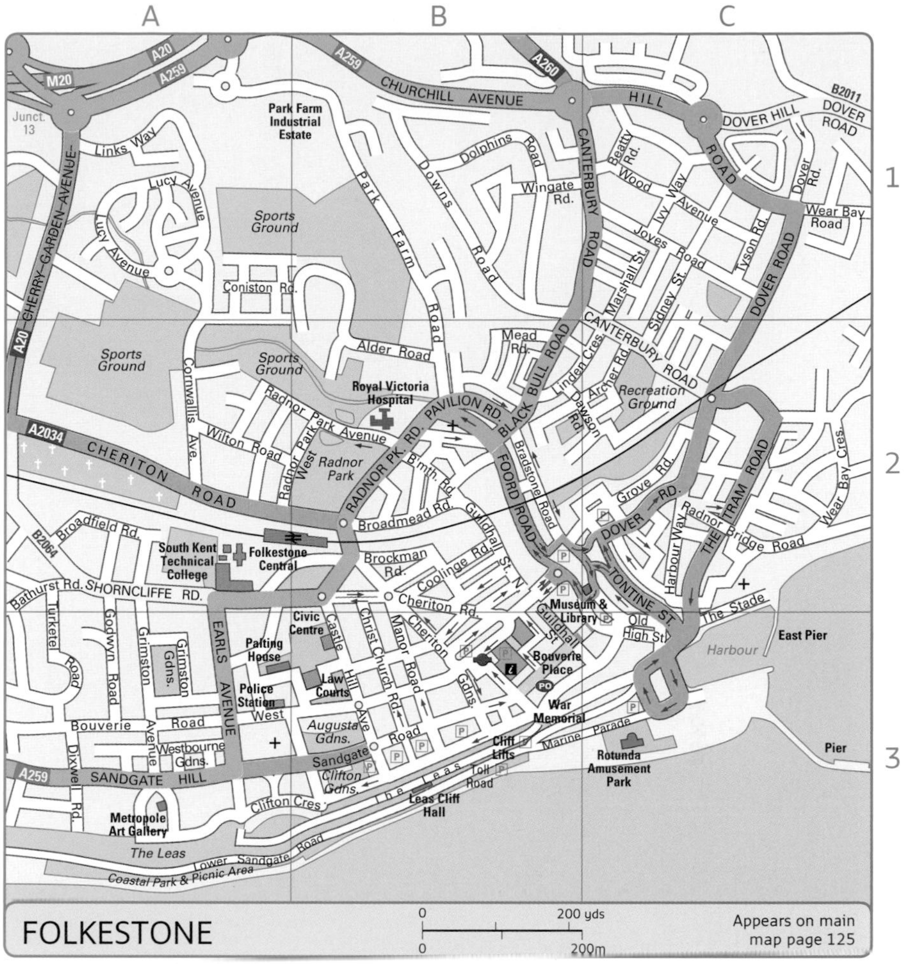

Tourist Information Centre: 28 Southgate Street
Tel: 01452 396572

Adelaide Street	B3	St. Oswald's Road	A1
Alexandra Road	B1	Secunda Way	A3
Alfred Street	C2	Severn Road	A2
Alma Place	A3	Seymour Road	A3
Alvin Street	B1	Southgate Street	A2
Archdeacon Street	A1	Spa Road	A2
Argyll Road	C1	Stanley Road	B3
Askwith Road	C3	Station Road	B2
Barnwood Road	C1	Stroud Road	A3
Barton Street	B2	The Quay	A2
Black Dog Way	B1	Tredworth Road	B3
Bristol Road	A3	Trier Way	A3
Brunswick Road	B2	Upton Street	B3
Bruton Way	B2	Vicarage Road	C3
Calton Road	B3	Victoria Street	B2
Castle Meads Way	A1	Wellington Street	B2
Cecil Road	A3	Westgate Street	A1
Cheltenham Road	C1	Weston Road	A3
Churchill Road	A3	Wheatstone Road	B3
Clifton Road	A3	Willow Avenue	C3
Conduit Street	B3	Worcester Street	B1
Coney Hill Road	C3		
Dean's Way	B1		
Denmark Road	B1		
Derby Road	B2		
Estcourt Road	B1		
Eastern Avenue	C3		
Eastgate Street	B2		
Frampton Road	A3		
Gouda Way	A1		
Great Western Road	B2		
Greyfriars	B2		
Hatherley Road	B3		
Heathville Road	B1		
Hempsted Lane	A2		
Henry Road	B1		
High Street	B3		
Hopewell Street	B3		
Horton Road	C2		
Howard Street	B3		
India Road	C2		
King Edward's Avenue	B3		
Kingsholm Road	B1		
Lansdown Road	B1		
Linden Road	A3		
Llanthony Road	A2		
London Road	B1		
Lower Westgate Street	A1		
Marlborough Road	C3		
Merevale Road	C1		
Metz Way	B2		
Midland Road	B3		
Millbrook Street	B2		
Myers Road	C2		
Northgate Street	B2		
Oxford Road	B3		
Oxstalls Lane	C1		
Painswick Road	C3		
Park Road	B2		
Parkend Road	B3		
Pitt Street	B1		
Quay Street	A2		
Regent Street	B3		
Robinson Road	A3		
Ryecroft Street	B3		
St. Ann Way	A3		

GLOUCESTER

0	500 yds
0	500m

Appears on main
map page 132

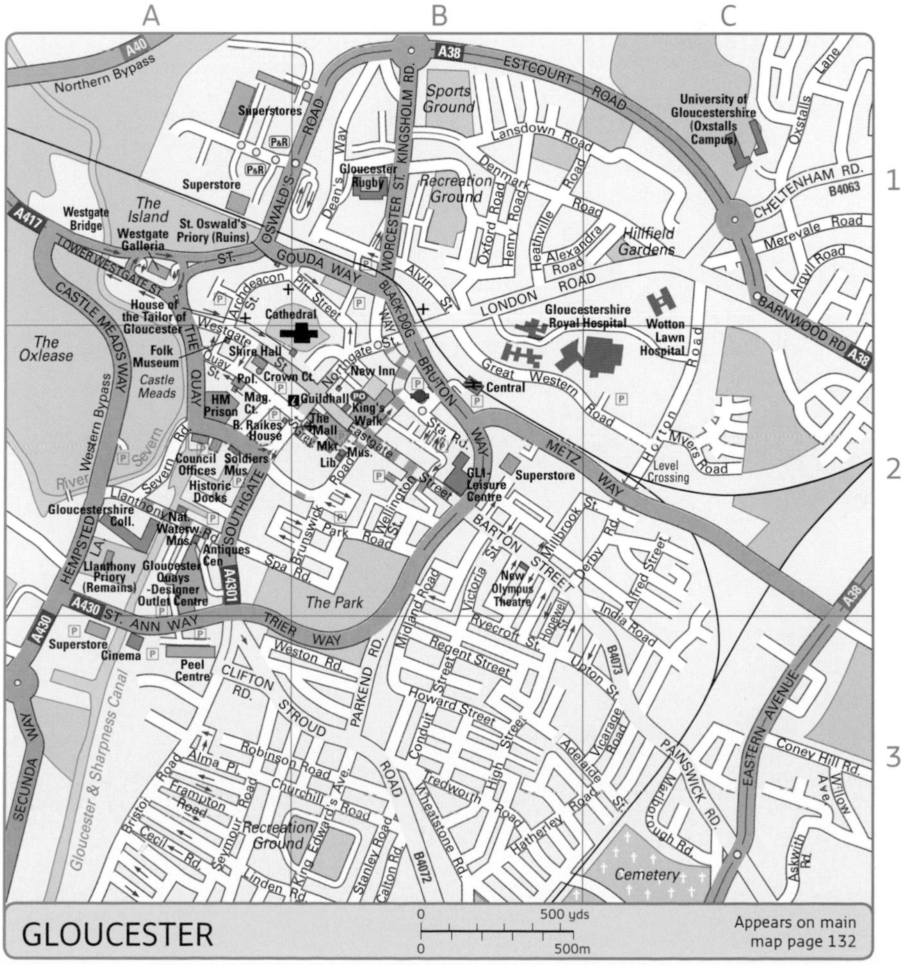

GUILDFORD

Tourist Information Centre: 14 Tunsgate
Tel: 01483 444333

Abbot Road	C3	Portsmouth Road	B3
Artillery Road	B1	Poyle Road	C3
Artillery Terrace	B1	Quarry Street	B2
Bedford Road	B1	Queens Road	C1
Bridge Street	B2	Rookwood Court	A3
Bright Hill	C2	Rupert Road	A2
Brodie Road	C2	Sand Terrace	B1
Bury Fields	B3	Semaphore Road	C3
Bury Street	B3	South Hill	C2
Castle Hill	C3	Springfield Road	A1
Castle Square	C2	Station Approach	C1
Castle Street	B2	Station View	A1
Chessey Street	C1	Stoke Road	C1
Cheselden Road	C2	Swan Lane	B2
Commercial Road	B1	Sydenham Road	C2
Dapdune Court	B1	Testard Road	A2
Dapdune Road	B1	The Bars	B2
Dapdune Wharf	B1	The Mount	A3
Dene Road	C1	Tunsgate	C2
Denmark Road	C1	Upperton Road	A2
Denzil Road	A2	Victoria Road	C1
Drummond Road	B1	Walnut Tree Close	A1
Eagle Road	C1	Warwicks	C3
Eastgate Gardens	C1	Wharf Road	B1
Falcon Road	C1	Wherwell Road	A2
Farnham Road	A2	William Road	B1
Flower Walk	B3	Wodeland Avenue	A3
Fort Road	C3	Woodbridge Road	B1
Foxenden Road	C1	York Road	B1
Friary Bridge	B2		
Friary Street	B2		
Genyn Road	A2		
George Road	B1		
Great Quarry	C3		
Guildford Park Avenue	A1		
Guildford Park Road	A2		
Harvey Road	C2		
Haydon Place	B1		
High Pewley	C3		
High Street	B2/C2		
Laundry Road	B1		
Lawn Road	B3		
Leap Lane	B2		
Leas Road	B1		
Ludlow Road	A2		
Mareschal Road	A3		
Margaret Road	B1		
Market Street	B2		
Martyr Road	B2		
Mary Road	B1		
Millbrook	B3		
Millmead	B2		
Millmead Terrace	B3		
Mount Pleasant	A3		
Mountside	A3		
Nether Mount	A3		
Nightingale Road	C1		
North Place	B1		
North Street	B2		
Onslow Road	C1		
Onslow Street	B2		
Oxford Road	C2		
Pannells Court	C2		
Park Road	B1		
Park Street	B2		
Pewley Hill	C2		

Appears on main map page 121

HARROGATE

Tourist Information Centre: Royal Baths, Crescent Road
Tel: 01423 537300

Ainsty Road	C1	Regent Grove	C1
Albert Street	B2	Regent Parade	C1
Alexandra Road	B1	Regent Street	C1
Arthington Avenue	B2	Regent Terrace	C1
Beech Grove	A3	Ripon Road	A1
Belford Road	B2	Robert Street	B3
Bower Road	B1	St. James Drive	C3
Bower Street	B2	St. Mary's Walk	A3
Cambridge Street	B2	Skipton Road	C1
Cavendish Avenue	C3	South Park Road	B3
Chelmsford Road	B2	Springfield Avenue	A1
Cheltenham Mount	B1	Spring Grove	A1
Chudleigh Road	C1	Spring Mount	A1
Clarence Drive	A2	Station Avenue	B2
Claro Road	C1	Station Parade	B2
Cold Bath Road	A3	Stray Rein	B3
Commercial Street	B1	Stray Walk	C3
Coppice Drive	A1	Studley Road	B1
Cornwall Road	A2	Swan Road	A2
Crescent Gardens	A2	The Grove	C1
Dragon Avenue	B1	Tower Street	B3
Dragon Parade	B1	Trinity Road	B3
Dragon Road	B1	Valley Drive	A2
Duchy Road	A1	Victoria Avenue	B2
East Parade	B2	Victoria Road	A3
East Park Road	B2	West End Avenue	A3
Franklin Mount	B1	West Park	B2
Franklin Road	B1	Woodside	B2
Gascoigne Crescent	C1	York Place	B3
Glebe Avenue	A2	York Road	A2
Glebe Road	A3		
Grove Park Terrace	C1		
Grove Road	B1		
Harcourt Drive	C2		
Harcourt Road	C1		
Heywood Road	A3		
Hollins Road	A1		
Homestead Road	B2		
James Street	B2		
Kent Road	A1		
King's Road	A2		
Knaresborough Road	C2		
Lancaster Road	A3		
Leeds Road	B3		
Lime Grove	C1		
Lime Street	C1		
Mayfield Grove	B1		
Montpellier Hill	A2		
Montpellier Street	A2		
Mowbray Square	C1		
North Park Road	C2		
Oatlands Drive	C3		
Otley Road	A3		
Oxford Street	B2		
Park Chase	C1		
Park Drive	B3		
Park Parade	C2		
Park Road	A3		
Park View	B2		
Parliament Street	A2		
Princes Villa Road	B2		
Providence Terrace	B1		
Queen Parade	C2		
Queen's Road	A3		
Raglan Street	B2		
Regent Avenue	C1		

Appears on main map page 194

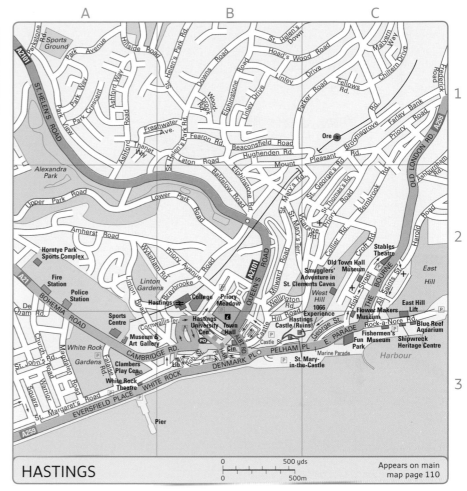

Tourist Information Centre: Queens Square, Priory Meadow
Tel: 0845 274 1001

Albert Road	B3	St. Margaret's Road	A3
All Saints Street	C2	St. Mary's Road	B2
Amherst Road	A2	St. Mary's Terrace	B2
Ashburnham Road	C2	St. Thomas's Road	C2
Ashford Road	A1	Thanet Way	A1
Ashford Way	A1	The Bourne	C2
Baldslow Road	B2	Upper Park Road	A2
Beaconsfield Road	B1	Vicarage Road	B2
Bembrook Road	C2	Warrior Square	A3
Bohemia Road	A2	Wellington Road	B2
Braybrooke Road	B2	White Rock	A3
Broomsgrove Road	C1	Woodbrook Road	B1
Cambridge Road	A3	Wykeham Road	A2
Castle Hill Road	B2		
Castle Street	B3		
Chiltern Drive	C1		
Church Road	A3		
Collier Road	C2		
Cornwallis Terrace	A3		
Croft Road	C2		
De Cham Road	A3		
Denmark Place	B3		
Downs Road	B1		
East Parade	C3		
Elphinstone Road	B1		
Eversfield Place	A3		
Falaise Road	A3		
Farley Bank	C1		
Fearon Road	B1		
Fellows Road	C1		
Frederick Road	C1		
Freshwater Avenue	A1		
George Street	C3		
Harold Place	B3		
Harold Road	C2		
High Street	C2		
Hillside Road	A1		
Hoad's Wood Road	B1		
Hughenden Road	B1		
Laton Road	B1		
Linley Drive	B1		
Linton Road	A2		
Lower Park Road	A2		
Magdalen Road	A3		
Malvern Way	C1		
Marine Parade	C3		
Milward Road	B2		
Mount Pleasant Road	B1		
Old London Road	C2		
Park Avenue	A1		
Park Crescent	A1		
Park View	A1		
Park Way	A1		
Parker Road	B1		
Parkstone Road	A1		
Pelham Place	B3		
Priory Avenue	B2		
Priory Road	C2		
Queen's Road	B2		
Robertson Street	B3		
Rock-a-Nore Road	C3		
St. George's Road	C2		
St. Helen's Down	B1		
St. Helen's Park Road	B2		
St. Helen's Road	A1		
St. John's Road	A3		

HASTINGS

0   500 yds
0   500m

Appears on main
map page 110

Tourist Information Centre: 1 King Street
Tel: 01432 268430

Aubrey Street	B2	Vaughan Street	C2
Barrs Court Road	C1	Victoria Street	A2
Barton Road	A2	West Street	B2
Barton Yard	A2	Widemarsh Street	B2
Bath Street	C2	Wye Street	B3
Belmont Avenue	A3		
Berrington Street	B2		
Bewell Street	B2		
Blackfriars Street	B1		
Blueschool Street	B1		
Brewers Passage	B2		
Bridge Street	B2		
Broad Street	B2		
Canonmoor Street	A1		
Cantilupe Street	C2		
Castle Street	B2		
Catherine Street	B1		
Central Avenue	C2		
Church Street	B2		
Commercial Road	C1		
Commercial Street	B2		
Coningsby Street	B1		
East Street	B2		
Edgar Street	B1		
Eign Gate	B2		
Eign Street	A2		
Ferrers Street	A2		
Friars Street	A2		
Gaol Street	C2		
Green Street	C3		
Grenfell Road	C3		
Greyfriars Avenue	A3		
Greyfriars Bridge	B2		
Grove Road	C3		
Harold Street	C3		
High Street	B2		
High Town	B2		
King Street	B2		
Kyrle Street	C2		
Maylord Street	B2		
Mill Street	C3		
Monkmoor Street	C1		
Moorfield Street	A1		
Moor Street	B1		
Mostyn Street	A1		
Nelson Street	C3		
Newmarket Street	B1		
Park Street	C3		
Penhaligon Way	A1		
Plough Lane	A1		
Portland Street	A1		
Quay Street	B2		
Ryeland Street	A2		
St. Guthlac Street	C2		
St. James Road	C3		
St. Martin's Avenue	B3		
St. Martin's Street	B3		
St. Owen Street	B2		
Station Approach	C1		
Station Road	A2		
Stonebow Road	C1		
Symonds Street	C2		
The Atrium	B1		
Turner Street	C3		
Union Street	B2		
Union Walk	C1		

HEREFORD

0   250 yds
0   250m

Appears on main
map page 145

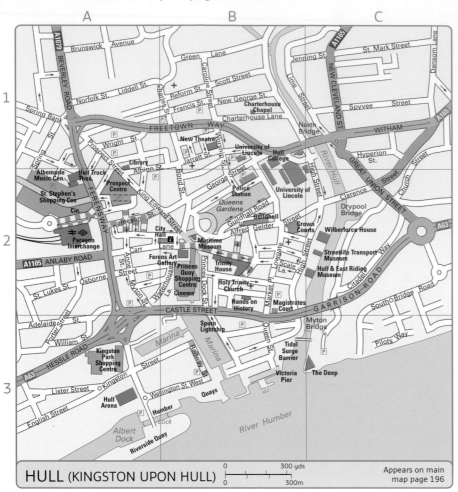

HULL (KINGSTON UPON HULL)

0	300 yds
0	300m

Appears on main map page 196

Tourist Information Centre: 1 Paragon Street
Tel: 0844 811 2070

Adelaide Street	A3
Albion Street	A2
Alfred Gelder Street	B2
Anlaby Road	A2
Anne Street	A2
Beverley Road	A1
Bond Street	B2
Brunswick Avenue	A1
Caroline Street	B1
Carr Lane	A2
Castle Street	B2
Charles Street	B1
Charterhouse Lane	B1
Church Street	C2
Citadel Way	C2
Clarence Street	B1
Cleveland Street	C1
Dansom Lane	C1
English Street	A3
Ferensway	A2
Francis Street	B1
Freetown Way	A1
Garrison Road	C2
George Street	B2
Great Union Street	C1
Green Lane	B1
Guildhall Road	B2
Hessle Road	A3
High Street	C1
Hyperion Street	C1
Jameson Street	A2
Jarratt Street	B1
Jenning Street	B1
King Edward Street	A2
Kingston Street	A3
Liddell Street	A1
Lime Street	B1
Lister Street	A3
Lowgate	B2
Market Place	B2
Myton Street	A2
New Cleveland Street	C1
New George Street	B1
Norfolk Street	A1
North Bridge	B1
Osborne Street	A2
Pilots Way	C3
Porter Street	A3
Princes Dock Street	B2
Prospect Street	A1
Queen Street	B3
Reform Street	B1
St. Lukes Street	A2
St. Mark Street	C1
Scale Lane	B2
Scott Street	B1
Scott Street Bridge	B1
South Bridge Road	C2
Spring Bank	A1
Spring Street	A2
Spyvee Street	C1
Waterhouse Lane	A2
Wellington Street West	A3
William Street	A3
Witham	C1
Worship Street	B1
Wright Street	A1

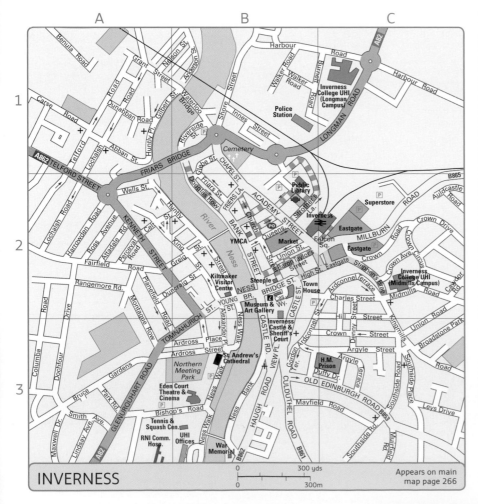

INVERNESS

0	300 yds
0	300m

Appears on main map page 266

Tourist Information Centre: Castle Wynd
Tel: 01463 252401

Abban Street	A1
Academy Street	B2
Alexander Place	B2
Anderson Street	B1
Ardconnel Street	B3
Ardconnel Terrace	C2
Ardross Place	B3
Ardross Street	B3
Argyle Street	C3
Argyle Terrace	C3
Attadale Road	A2
Auldcastle Road	C2
Bank Street	B2
Baron Taylor's Street	B2
Benula Road	A1
Bishop's Road	A3
Bridge Street	B2
Broadstone Park	C3
Bruce Gardens	A3
Burnett Road	C1
Carse Road	A1
Castle Road	B2
Castle Street	B2
Castle Wynd	B2
Cawdor Road	C2
Celt Street	A2
Chapel Street	B1
Charles Street	C2
Church Street	B2
Columba Road	A3
Crown Avenue	C2
Crown Circus	C2
Crown Drive	C2
Crown Road	C2
Crown Street	C3
Culduthel Road	B3
Denny Street	C3
Dochfour Drive	A3
Douglas Row	B1
Duffy Drive	B3
Duncraig Street	A2
Eastgate	C2
Fairfield Road	A2
Falcon Square	B2
Friars Bridge	A1
Friars Lane	B2
Friars Street	B2
Gilbert Street	A1
Glebe Street	B1
Glen Urquhart Road	A3
Gordon Terrace	B3
Grant Street	A1
Greig Street	A2
Harbour Road	B1
Harrowden Road	A2
Haugh Road	B3
High Street	B2
Hill Street	C2
Hontly Place	A1
Huntly Street	A2
Innes Street	B1
Kenneth Street	A2
Kingsmills Road	C2
King Street	A2
Leys Drive	C3
Lindsay Avenue	A3
Lochalsh Road	A1
Longman Road	C1
Maxwell Drive	A3
Mayfield Road	B3
Midmills Road	C2
Millburn Road	C2
Montague Row	A2
Muirfield Road	C3
Nelson Street	A1
Ness Bank	B3
Ness Bridge	B2
Ness Walk	B3
Old Edinburgh Road	B3
Park Road	A3
Perceval Road	A2
Planefield Road	A2
Queensgate	B2
Rangemore Road	A2
Riverside Street	B1
Ross Avenue	A2
Shore Street	B1
Smith Avenue	A3
Southside Place	C3
Southside Road	C3
Stephen's Brae	C2
Strother's Lane	B2
Telford Road	A1
Telford Street	A1
Tomnahurich Street	A3
Union Road	C3
Union Street	B2
View Place	B3
Walker Road	B1
Waterloo Bridge	B1
Wells Street	A2
Young Street	B2

LEICESTER

Tourist Information Centre: 7-9 Every Street, Town Hall Square
Tel: 0844 888 5181

Street	Grid	Street	Grid
Abbey Street	B1	Market Place South	B2
Albion Street	B2	Market Street	B2
All Saints Road	A2	Mill Lane	A3
Aylestone Road	B3	Millstone Lane	B2
Bassett Street	A1	Montreal Road	C1
Bath Lane	A2	Morledge Street	C2
Bedford Street North	C1	Narborough Road	A3
Belgrave Gate	B1	Narborough Road North	A2
Bell Lane	C1	Nelson Street	C3
Belvoir Street	B2	Newarke Close	A3
Braunstone Gate	A2	Newarke Street	B2
Burgess Street	B1	Northgate Street	A1
Burleys Way	B1	Ottawa Road	C1
Byron Street	B1	Oxford Street	B2
Cank Street	B2	Pasture Lane	A1
Castle Street	A2	Peacock Lane	B2
Charles Street	C2	Pocklingtons Walk	B2
Christow Street	C1	Prebend Street	C3
Church Gate	B1	Princess Road East	C3
Clarence Street	B1	Pringle Street	A1
Clyde Street	C1	Queen Street	C2
College Street	C2	Regent Road	B3
Colton Street	C2	Regent Street	C3
Conduit Street	C2	Repton Street	A1
Crafton Street East	C1	Rutland Street	C2
Cravan Street	A1	Samuel Street	C2
De Montfort Street	C3	Sanvey Gare	A1
Deacon Street	B3	Saxby Street	C3
Dryden Street	B1	Slater Street	A1
Duns Lane	A2	Soar Lane	A1
Dunton Street	A1	South Albion Street	C2
Eastern Boulevard	A3	Southampton Street	C2
Friar Lane	B2	Sparkenhoe Street	C2
Friday Street	B1	St. George Street	C2
Frog Island	A1	St. George's Way	C2
Gallowtree Gate	B2	St. John's Street	B1
Gaul Street	A3	St. Margaret's Way	A1
Glebe Street	C2	St. Matthew's Way	C1
Gotham Street	C3	St. Nicholas Circle	A2
Granby Street	B2	Swain Street	C2
Grange Lane	B3	Swan Street	A1
Grasmere Street	A3	Taylor Road	C1
Great Central Street	A1	Thames Street	B1
Halford Street	B2	The Gateway	A3
Havelock Street	B3	The Newarke	A2
Haymarket	B1	Tigers Way	B3
High Street	B2	Tower Street	B3
Highcross Street	A1	Tudor Road	A1
Hobart Street	C2	Ullswater Street	A3
Horsfair Street	B2	University Road	C3
Humberstone Gate	B2	Upperton Road	A3
Humberstone Road	C1	Vaughan Way	A1
Infirmary Road	B3	Vestry Street	C2
Jarrom Street	A3	Walnut Street	A3
Jarvis Street	A2	Waterloo Way	C3
Kamloops Crescent	C1	Welford Road	B2
Kent Street	C1	Wellington Street	B2
King Richard's Road	A2	West Street	B3
King Street	B2	Western Boulevard	A3
Lancaster Road	B3	Western Road	A3
Lee Street	B1	Wharf Street North	C1
Lincoln Street	C2	Wharf Street South	C1
London Road	C3	Wilberforce Road	A3
Loseby Lane	B2	Windermere Street	A3
Lower Brown Street	B2	Woodboy Street	C1
Manitoba Road	C1	Yeoman Street	B2
Mansfield Street	B1	York Road	B2

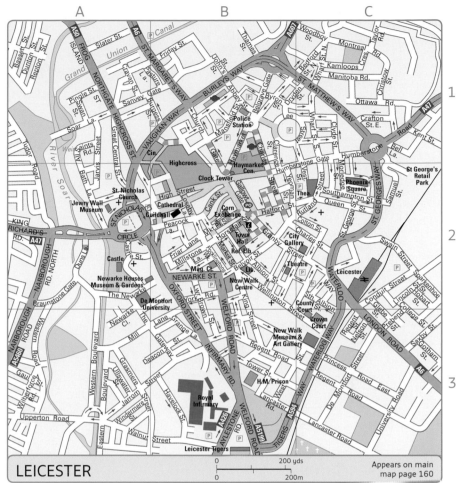

LEICESTER

0 — 200 yds
0 — 200m

Appears on main
map page 160

LINCOLN

Tourist Information Centre: 9 Castle Hill
Tel: 01522 873000

Street	Grid	Street	Grid
Alexandra Terrace	A2	Spa Road	C3
Baggholme Road	C2	St. Anne's Road	C3
Bailgate	B1	St. Giles Avenue	C1
Beaumont Fee	B2	St. Mark Street	B3
Beevor Street	A3	St. Mary's Street	B3
Brayford Way	A3	St. Rumbold Street	B2
Brayford Wharf North	A2	Stamp End	C3
Broadgate	B2	Steep Hill	B2
Broadway	B1	The Avenue	A2
Bruce Road	C1	Tritton Road	A3
Burton Road	A1	Union Row	B2
Canwick Road	B3	Upper Lindum Street	C2
Carholme Road	A2	Upper Long Leys Road	A1
Carline Road	A1	Vere Street	B1
Carr Street	A2	Vine Street	C2
Cheviot Street	C2	Waterside North	B3
Church Lane	B1	Waterside South	B3
Clasketgate	B2	West Parade	A2
Croft Street	B2	Westgate	B1
Cross Street	B3	Wigford Way	B2
Curle Avenue	C1	Wilson Street	A1
Drury Lane	B2	Winn Street	C2
East Gate	B2	Wragby Road	C2
Firth Road	A3	Yarborough Road	A1
George Street	C3		
Great Northern Terrace	B3		
Greetwell Close	C1		
Greetwell Road	C2		
Gresham Street	A2		
Hampton Street	A2		
Harvey Street	A2		
High Street	B3		
John Street	C2		
Langworthgate	B1		
Lee Road	C1		
Lindum Road	B2		
Lindum Terrace	C2		
Long Leys Road	A1		
Mainwaring Road	C1		
Mill Road	A1		
Milman Road	C2		
Monks Road	C2		
Monson Street	B3		
Moor Street	A2		
Mount Street	A1		
Nettleham Road	B1		
Newland	A2		
Newland Street West	A2		
Newport	B1		
Northgate	B1		
Orchard Street	A2		
Pelham Bridge	B3		
Portland Street	B3		
Portland Street	B3		
Pottergate	B2		
Queensway	C1		
Rasen Lane	B1		
Richmond Road	A2		
Ripon Street	B3		
Rope Walk	A3		
Rosemary Lane	B2		
Ruskin Avenue	C1		
Saltergate	B2		
Sewell Road	C2		
Silver Street	B2		
Sincil Bank	B3		

LINCOLN

0 — 200 yds
0 — 200m

Appears on main
map page 187

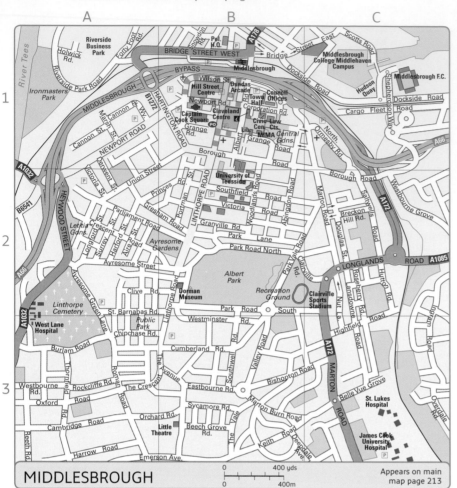

MIDDLESBROUGH

Appears on main map page 213

Tourist Information Centre: Town Hall, Albert Road
Tel: 01642 729700

Abingdon Road	B2	Roman Road	A3
Aire Street	A2	Roseberry Road	C2
Albert Road	B1	Saltwells Road	C2
Ayresome Green Lane	A2	Scotts Road	C1
Ayresome Street	A2	Sheperdson Way	C1
Beech Grove Road	B3	Snowdon Road	B1
Belle Vue Grove	C3	Southfield Road	B2
Bishopton Road	B3	Southwell Road	B3
Borough Road	B1/C3	St. Barnabas Road	A2
Breckon Hill Road	C2	Surrey Street	A2
Bridge Street East	B1	Sycamore Road	B3
Bridge Street West	B1	The Avenue	B3
Burlam Road	A3	The Crescent	A3
Cambridge Road	A3	The Vale	B3
Cannon Park Way	A1	Thornfield Road	A3
Cannon Street	A1	Union Street	A2
Cargo Fleet Road	C1	Valley Road	B3
Chipchase Road	A3	Victoria Road	B2
Clairville Road	B2	Victoria Street	A1
Clive Road	A2	Westbourne Grove	C2
Corporation Road	B1	Westbourne Road	A3
Crescent Road	A2	Westminster Road	B3
Cumberland Road	B3	Wilson Street	B1
Deepdale Avenue	B3	Woodlands Road	B2
Derwent Street	A1		
Dockside Road	B1/C1		
Douglas Street	C2		
Eastbourne Road	B3		
Emerson Avenue	B3		
Forty Foot Road	A1		
Grange Road	B1		
Granville Road	B2		
Gresham Road	A2		
Harford Street	A2		
Harrow Road	A3		
Hartington Road	A1		
Heywood Street	A2		
Highfield Road	C3		
Holwick Road	A1		
Hudson Quay	C1		
Hutton Road	C2		
Ingram Road	C2		
Keith Road	B3		
Lansdowne Road	C2		
Linthorpe Road	B3		
Longford Street	A2		
Longlands Road	C2		
Marsh Street	A1		
Marton Burn Road	B3		
Marton Road	C2/C3		
Newport Road	A1/B1		
North Ormesby Road	C1		
Nut Lane	C2		
Orchard Road	A3		
Overdale Road	C3		
Oxford Road	A3		
Park Lane	B2		
Park Road North	B2		
Park Road South	B2		
Park Vale Road	B2		
Parliament Road	A2		
Portman Street	B2		
Princes Road	A2		
Reeth Road	A3		
Riverside Park Road	A1		
Rockcliffe Road	A3		

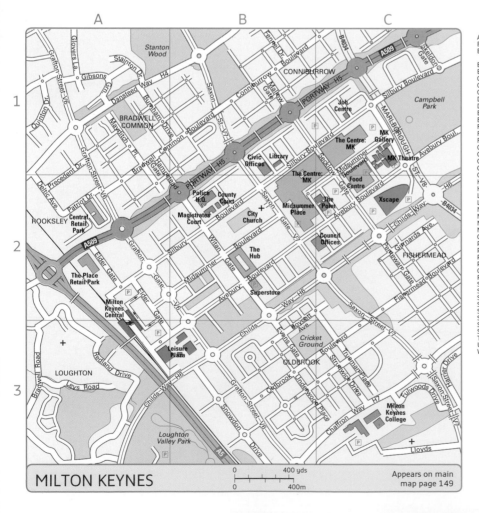

MILTON KEYNES

Appears on main map page 149

Avebury Boulevard	B2/C1		
Boycott Avenue	B3		
Bradwell Common Boulevard	A1		
Bradwell Road	A3		
Burnham Drive	A1		
Chaffron Way	C3		
Childs Way	A3/C2		
Conniburrow Boulevard	B1		
Dansteed Way	A1		
Deltic Avenue	A2		
Elder Gate	A2		
Evans Gate	B3		
Fennel Drive	B1		
Fishermead Boulevard	C2		
Fulwoods Drive	C3		
Gibsons Green	A1		
Glovers Lane	A1		
Grafton Gate	A2		
Grafton Street	A1/B3		
Gurnards Avenue	C2		
Hampstead Gate	A1		
Harrier Drive	C3		
Leys Road	A3		
Lloyds	C3		
Mallow Gate	B1		
Marlborough Street	C1		
Mayditch Place	A1		
Midsummer Boulevard	B2/C1		
Oldbrook Boulevard	B3		
Patriot Drive	A2		
Pentewan Gate	C2		
Portway	B2/C1		
Precedent Drive	A2		
Quinton Drive	A1		
Redland Drive	A3		
Saxon Gate	B2		
Saxon Street	B1/C3		
Secklow Gate	C1		
Silbury Boulevard	B2/C1		
Skeldon Gate	C1		
Snowdon Drive	B3		
Stainton Drive	A1		
Strudwick Drive	C3		
Trueman Place	C3		
Underwood Place	B3		
Witan Gate	B2		

Newcastle upon Tyne

Tourist Information Centre: 8-9 Central Arcade
Tel: 0191 277 8000

Street	Grid	Street	Grid
Albert Street	C2	Pitt Street	A2
Ancrum Street	A1	Portland Road	C1
Argyle Street	C2	Portland Terrace	A1
Askew Road	C3	Pottery Lane	A3
Barrack Road	A1	Quarryfield Road	C3
Barras Bridge	B1	Quayside	C3
Bath Lane	A2	Queen Victoria Road	B1
Bigg Market	B2	Railway Street	A3
Blackett Street	B2	Redheugh Bridge	A3
Byron Street	C1	Richardson Road	A1
Chester Street	C1	Rye Hill	A3
City Road	C2	St. James Boulevard	A3
Claremont Road	B1	St. Mary's Place	B1
Clarence Street	C2	St. Thomas Street	B1
Clayton Street	B2	Sandyford Road	B1/C1
Clayton Street West	A3	Scotswood Road	A3
Corporation Street	A2	Skinnerburn Road	B3
Coulthards Lane	C3	South Shore Road	C3
Crawhall Road	C2	Stanhope Street	A2
Dean Street	B2	Starbeck Avenue	C1
Diana Street	A2	Stodart Street	C1
Elswick East Terrace	A3	Stowell Street	A2
Eskdale Terrace	C1	Strawberry Place	A2
Essex Close	A3	Summerhill Grove	A2
Falconar Street	C1	Swing Bridge	B3
Forth Banks	B3	The Close	B3
Forth Street	A3	Tyne Bridge	C3
Gallowgate	A2	Union Street	C2
Gateshead Highway	C3	Warwick Street	C1
George Street	A3	Wellington Street	A2
Gibson Street	C2	West Street	C3
Grainger Street	B2	Westgate Road	A2
Grantham Road	C1	Westmorland Road	A3
Grey Street	B2	Windsor Terrace	B1
Hanover Street	B3	York Street	A2
Hawks Road	C3		
Helmsley Road	C1		
High Street	C3		
Hillgate	C3		
Howard Street	C2		
Hunters Road	A1		
Ivy Close	A3		
Jesmond Road	C1		
Jesmond Road West	B1		
John Dobson Street	B2		
Kelvin Grove	C1		
Kyle Close	A3		
Lambton Street	C3		
Mansfield Street	A2		
Maple Street	A3		
Maple Terrace	A3		
Market Street	B2		
Melbourne Street	C2		
Mill Road	C3		
Neville Street	A3		
New Bridge Street	C2		
Newgate Street	B2		
Northumberland Road	B2		
Northumberland Street	B1		
Oakwellgate	C3		
Orchard Street	B3		
Oxnam Crescent	A1		
Park Terrace	B1		
Percy Street	B2		
Pilgrim Street	B2		
Pipewellgate	B3		

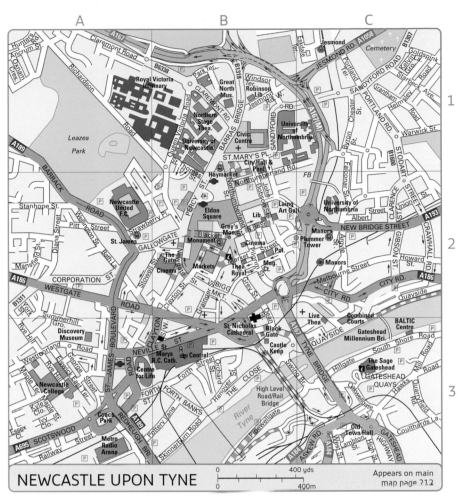

NEWCASTLE UPON TYNE

0 — 400 yds
0 — 400m

Appears on main map page 212

Norwich

Tourist Information Centre: The Forum, Millennium Plain
Tel: 01603 213999

Street	Grid	Street	Grid
Albion Way	C3	Queens Road	B3
All Saints Green	B3	Rampant Horse Street	B2
Ashby Street	B3	Recorder Road	C2
Bakers Road	A1	Red Lion Street	B2
Bank Plain	B2	Riverside	C3
Barker Street	A1	Riverside Road	C2
Barn Road	A2	Rosary Road	C2
Barrack Street	B1	Rose Lane	B2
Bedford Street	B2	Rouen Road	B3
Ber Street	B3	Rupert Street	A3
Bethel Street	A2	Russell Street	A1
Bishopbridge Road	C2	St. Andrew's Street	B2
Bishopgate	C2	St. Augustine's Street	A1
Botolph Street	B1	St. Benedict's Street	A2
Brazen Gate	B3	St. Crispin's Road	A1
Britannia Road	C1	St. Faiths Lane	B2
Brunswick Road	A3	St. George's Street	B1
Bullclose Road	B1	St. Giles Street	A2
Canary Way	C3	St. James Close	C1
Carrow Hill	C3	St. Leonards Road	C2
Carrow Road	C3	St. Martin's Road	A1
Castle Meadow	B2	St. Stephen's Road	A3
Chapel Field Road	A2	St. Stephen's Street	B3
Chapelfield North	A2	Silver Road	B1
City Road	B3	Silver Street	B1
Clarence Road	C3	Southwell Road	B3
Colegate	B1	Surrey Street	B3
Coslany Street	A2	Sussex Street	A1
Cowgate	B1	Theatre Street	A2
Dereham Road	A2	Thorn Lane	B3
Duke Street	B1	Thorpe Road	C2
Earlham Road	A2	Tombland	B2
Edward Street	B1	Trinity Street	A3
Elm Hill	B2	Trory Street	A2
Fishergate	B1	Union Street	A3
Gas Hill	C1	Unthank Road	A3
Grapes Hill	A2	Vauxhall Street	A3
Grove Avenue	A3	Victoria Street	A3
Grove Road	A3	Wensum Street	B1
Grove Walk	A3	Wessex Street	A3
Gurney Road	C1	Westwick Street	A1
Hall Road	B3	Wherry Road	C3
Hardy Road	C3	Whitefriars	B1
Heathgate	C1	Wodehouse Street	B1
Heigham Street	A1	York Street	A3
Horns Lane	B3		
Ipswich Road	A3		
Ketts Hill	C1		
King Street	B3		
Koblenz Avenue	C3		
Lothian Street	A1		
Lower Clarence Road	C2		
Magdalen Street	B1		
Magpie Road	B1		
Market Avenue	B2		
Marlborough Road	B1		
Mountergate	B2		
Mousehold Street	C1		
Newmarket Road	A3		
Newmarket Street	A3		
Oak Street	A1		
Orchard Street	A1		
Palace Street	B2		
Pitt Street	B1		
Pottergate	A2		
Prince of Wales Road	B2		

NORWICH

0 — 400 yds
0 — 400m

Appears on main map page 178

NOTTINGHAM

Tourist Information Centre: 1-4 Smithy Row
Tel: 08444 77 56 78

Abbotsford Drive	B1	Maid Marian Way	A2
Albert Street	B2	Mansfield Road	B1
Angel Row	A2	Manvers Street	C2
Barker Gate	C2	Market Street	B2
Bath Street	C1	Middle Pavement	B2
Beacon Hill Rise	C1	Milton Street	B1
Bellar Gate	C2	Mount Street	A2
Belward Street	C2	North Church Street	B1
Bridlesmith Gate	B2	North Sherwood Street	B1
Broad Street	B2	Park Row	A2
Brook Street	C1	Park Terrace	A2
Burton Street	A1	Park Valley	A2
Canal Street	B3	Peel Street	A1
Carlton Street	B2	Pelham Street	B2
Carrington Street	B3	Pennyfoot Street	C2
Castle Boulevard	A3	Peveril Drive	A3
Castle Gate	B2	Pilcher Gate	B2
Castle Meadow Road	A3	Plantagenet Street	C1
Castle Road	A3	Popham Street	B3
Chapel Bar	A2	Poplar Street	C2
Chaucer Street	A1	Queens Road	B3
Cheapside	B2	Queen Street	B2
City Link	C3	Regent Street	A2
Clarendon Street	A1	Robin Hood Street	C1
Cliff Road	B3	Roden Street	C1
Clumber Street	B2	St. Ann's Well Road	C1
College Street	A2	St. James Street	A2
Collin Street	B3	St. Mary's Gate	B2
Cranbrook Street	C2	St. Peter's Gate	B2
Cromwell Street	A1	Shakespeare Street	A1
Curzon Street	B1	Shelton Street	B1
Derby Road	A2	Sneinton Road	C2
Dryden Street	A1	South Parade	B2
Fisher Gate	C2	South Sherwood Street	B1
Fishpond Drive	A3	Southwell Road	C2
Fletcher Gate	B2	Station Street	B3
Forman Street	B2	Stoney Street	C2
Friar Lane	A2	Talbot Street	A1
Gedling Street	C2	The Great Northern Close	C3
George Street	B2	The Rope Walk	A2
Gill Street	A1	Union Road	B1
Glasshouse Street	B1	Upper Parliament Street	A2
Goldsmith Street	A1	Victoria Street	B2
Goose Gate	C2	Warser Gate	B2
Hamilton Drive	A3	Waverley Street	A1
Hampden Street	A1	Wheeler Gate	B2
Handel Street	C2	Wilford Street	A3
Heathcote Street	B2	Wollaton Street	A2
High Pavement	B2	Woolpack Lane	C2
Hockley	C2		
Hollowstone	C2		
Hope Drive	A3		
Huntingdon Drive	A2		
Huntingdon Street	B1		
Instow Rise	C1		
Kent Street	B1		
King Edward Street	B2		
King Street	B2		
Lamartine Street	C1		
Lenton Road	A3		
Lincoln Street	B2		
Lister Gate	B3		
London Road	C3		
Long Row	B2		
Low Pavement	B2		
Lower Parliament Street	B2		

Appears on main map page 173

OXFORD

Tourist Information Centre: 15-16 Broad Street
Tel: 01865 252200

Albert Street	A1
Banbury Road	B1
Beaumont Street	A2
Becket Street	A2
Blackhall Road	B1
Botley Road	A2
Broad Street	B2
Canal Street	A1
Cattle Street	B2
Cornmarket	B2
Cowley Place	C3
Folly Bridge	B3
George Street	A2
Great Clarendon Street	A1
Hart Street	A1
High Street	B2
Hollybush Row	A2
Holywell Street	B2
Hythe Bridge Street	A2
Iffley Road	C3
Juxon Street	A1
Keble Road	B1
Kingston Road	A1
Littlegate Street	B3
Longwall Street	C2
Magdalen Bridge	C2
Manor Road	C2
Mansfield Road	C1
Marlborough Road	B3
Merton Street	B3
Mill Street	A2
Museum Road	B1
Nelson Street	A2
New Road	A2
Norham Gardens	B1
Observatory Street	A1
Oxpens Road	A3
Paradise Street	A2
Park End Street	A2
Parks Road	B1
Plantation Road	A1
Queen Street	B2
Rewley Road	A2
Richmond Road	A1
Rose Place	B3
St. Aldate's	B3
St. Bernards Road	A1
St. Cross Road	C1
St. Ebbe's Street	B3
St. Giles	B1
St. Thomas' Street	A2
South Parks Road	B1
Speedwell Street	B3
Thames Street	B3
Trinity Street	A3
Turl Street	B2
Walton Crescent	A1
Walton Street	A1
Walton Well Road	A1
Woodstock Road	A1

Appears on main map page 134

PERTH

Tourist Information Centre: Lower City Mills, West Mill Street
Tel: 01738 450600

Abbot Crescent	A3	Shore Road	C3
Abbot Street	A3	South Methven Street	B2
Albany Terrace	A1	South Street	B2
Atholl Street	B1	Strathmore Street	C1
Balhousie Street	B1	Stuart Avenue	A3
Barossa Place	B1	Tay Street	C2
Barossa Street	B1	Victoria Street	B2
Barrack Street	B1	Watergate	C2
Bowerswell Road	C2	Whitefriars Crescent	A2
Caledonian Road	B2	Whitefriars Street	A2
Canal Street	B2	William Street	B2
Cavendish Avenue	A3	Wilson Street	A3
Charlotte Street	B1	Young Street	A3
Clyde Place	A3	York Place	A2
Darnhall Drive	A3		
Dundee Road	C2		
Dunkeld Road	A1		
Edinburgh Road	B3		
Feus Road	A1		
Friar Street	A3		
George Street	C2		
Glasgow Road	A2		
Glover Street	A2		
Gowrie Street	C1		
Gray Street	A2		
Graybank Road	A2		
Hay Street	B1		
High Street	B2		
Isla Road	C1		
Jeanfield Road	A2		
King's Place	B3		
King James Place	B3		
King Street	B2		
Kinnoull Street	B1		
Kinnoull Terrace	C2		
Knowelea Place	A3		
Leonard Street	B2		
Lochie Brae	C1		
Long Causeway	A1		
Main Street	C1		
Manse Road	C2		
Marshall Place	B3		
Melville Street	B1		
Mill Street	B2		
Milne Street	B2		
Murray Crescent	A3		
Needless Road	A3		
New Row	B2		
North Methven Street	B1		
Park Place	A3		
Perth Bridge	C1		
Pickletullum Road	A2		
Pitcullen Terrace	C1		
Pitheavlis Crescent	A3		
Princes Street	C3		
Priory Place	B3		
Queen Street	A3		
Queens Bridge	C2		
Raeburn Park	A3		
Riggs Road	A2		
Rose Crescent	A2		
Rose Terrace	B1		
St. Catherines Road	A1		
St. John Street	C2		
St. Leonard's Bank	B3		
Scott Street	B2		

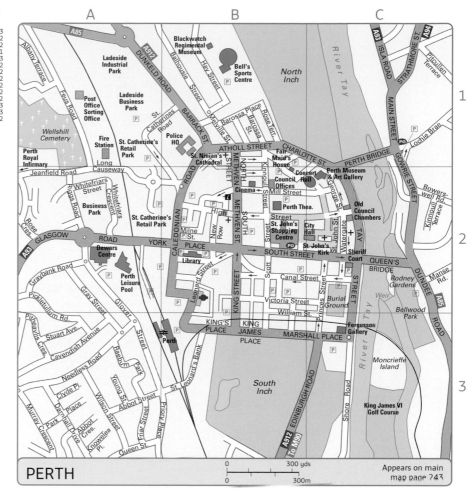

PERTH

0 — 300 yds
0 — 300m

Appears on main map page 243

PLYMOUTH

Tourist Information Centre: Plymouth Mayflower Centre,
3-5 The Barbican Tel: 01752 306330

Alexandra Road	C1	North Street	B2
Alma Road	A1	Notte Street	B3
Armada Street	B2	Oxford Street	A2
Armada Way	B2	Pentillie Road	B1
Ashford Road	C1	Ponsonby Road	A1
Barbican Approach	C3	Princess Street	B3
Beaumont Road	C2	Queen's Road	C1
Beechwood Avenue	B1	Royal Parade	B2
Belgrave Road	C1	Salisbury Road	C2
Bretonside	B2	Saltash Road	A1
Buckwell Street	B3	Seaton Avenue	B1
Camden Street	B2	Seymour Avenue	C2
Cattledown Road	C3	Southside Street	B3
Cecil Street	A2	Stoke Road	A2
Central Park Avenue	A1	Stuart Road	A1
Charles Street	B2	Sutton Road	C2
Citadel Road	A3	Sydney Street	A1
Clarence Place	A2	Teats Hill Road	C3
Cliff Road	A3	The Crescent	A3
Clifton Place	B1	Tothill Avenue	C2
Clovelly Road	C3	Tothill Road	C2
Cobourg Street	B2	Union Street	A2
Coleridge Road	C1	Vauxhall Street	B3
Connaught Avenue	C1	West Hoe Road	A3
Cornwall Street	B2	Western Approach	A2
Dale Road	B1	Whittington Street	A1
De-La-Hay Avenue	A1	Wilton Street	A2
Desborough Road	C2	Wyndham Street	A2
Drake Circus	B2		
East Street	A3		
Ebrington Street	B2		
Elliot Street	A3		
Embankment Road	C2		
Exeter Street	B2		
Ford Park Road	B1		
Furzehill Road	C1		
Gdynia Way	C3		
Glen Park Avenue	B1		
Grand Parade	A3		
Greenbank Avenue	C2		
Greenbank Road	C1		
Grenville Road	C2		
Harwell Street	A2		
Hill Park Crescent	B1		
Hoe Road	B3		
Houndiscombe Road	B1		
James Street	B2		
King Street	A2		
Knighton Road	C2		
Lipson Hill	C1		
Lipson Road	C2		
Lisson Grove	C1		
Lockyer Street	B3		
Looe Street	B2		
Madeira Road	B3		
Manor Road	A2		
Martin Street	A3		
Mayflower Street	B2		
Millbay Road	A3		
Mount Gould Road	C1		
Mutley Plain	B1		
New George Street	A2		
North Cross	B2		
North Hill	B2		
North Road East	B2		
North Road West	A2		

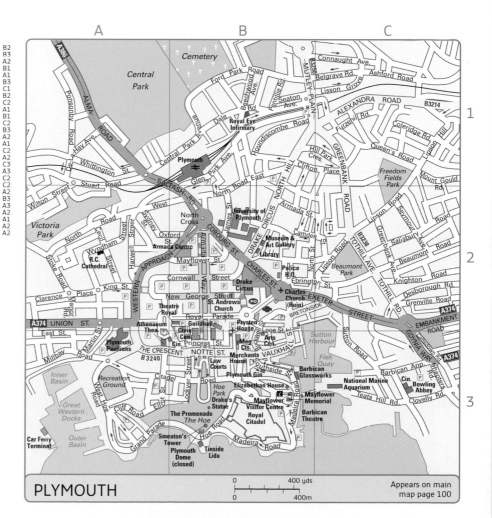

PLYMOUTH

0 — 400 yds
0 — 400m

Appears on main map page 100

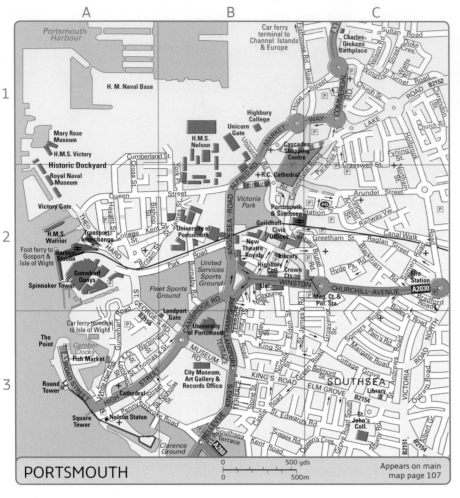

PORTSMOUTH

Albany Road	C3	Penny Street	A3
Albert Grove	C3	Queen's Crescent	C3
Alfred Road	B2	Queen Street	A2
Anglesea Road	B2	Raglan Street	C2
Arundel Street	C2	Railway View	C2
Astley Street	B3	St. Andrews Road	C3
Bailey's Road	C2	St. Edward's Road	B3
Bellevue Terrace	B3	St. George's Road	A2
Belmont Street	C3	St. James Road	B3
Bishop Street	A1	St. James Street	B2
Blackfriars Road	C2	St. Paul's Road	B3
Bradford Road	C2	St. Thomas's Street	A3
Britain Street	A1	Somers Road	C2
Broad Street	A3	Southsea Terrace	B3
Burnaby Road	B2	Station Street	C2
Cambridge Road	B3	Stone Street	B3
Canal Walk	C2	Sultan Road	C1
Castle Road	B3	Sussex Street	B3
Church Road	C1	The Hard	A2
Church Street	C1	Turner Road	C1
Clarendon Street	C1	Unicorn Road	B1
College Street	A2	Upper Arundel Street	C2
Commercial Road	B2	Victoria Road North	C3
Cottage Grove	C3	Warblington Street	A3
Crasswell Street	C1	Watts Road	C1
Cross Street	A1	White Hart Road	A3
Cumberland Street	A1	Wingfield Street	C1
Duke Crescent	C1	Winston Churchill Avenue	B2
Edinburgh Road	B2	York Place	B2
Eldon Street	B3		
Elm Grove	C3		
Flathouse Road	C1		
Fyning Street	C1		
Green Road	B3		
Greetham Street	C2		
Grosvenor Street	C3		
Grove Road South	C3		
Gunwharf Road	A3		
Hampshire Terrace	B3		
Havant Street	A2		
High Street	A3		
Holbrook Road	C1		
Hope Street	B1		
Hyde Park Road	C2		
Isambard Brunel Road	B2		
Kent Road	B3		
Kent Street	A1		
King Charles Street	A3		
King's Road	B3		
King's Terrace	B3		
King Street	B3		
Lake Road	C1		
Landport Terrace	B3		
Lombard Street	B3		
Margate Road	C3		
Market Way	B1		
Melbourne Place	B2		
Museum Road	B3		
Nelson Road	C1		
Norfolk Street	B3		
Northam Street	C2		
Outram Road	C3		
Pain's Road	C3		
Paradise Street	C1		
Park Road	B2		
Pembroke Road	A3		

Appears on main map page 107

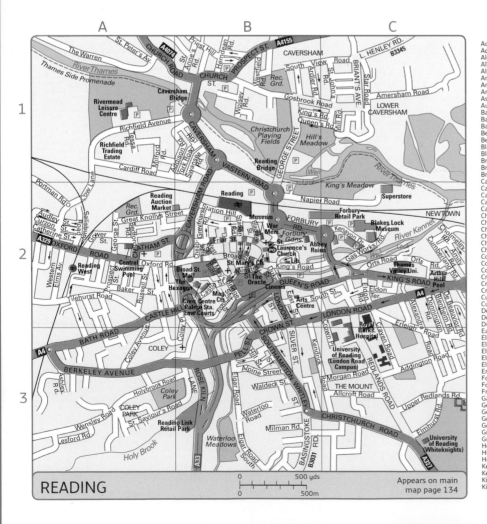

READING

Addington Road	C3	Lesford Road	A3
Addison Road	A1	London Road	C2
Alexandra Road	C2	London Street	B2
Allcroft Road	C3	Lower Henley Road	C1
Alpine Street	B3	Mill Road	C1
Amersham Road	C1	Milford Road	A1
Amity Road	A2	Milman Road	B3
Ardler Road	B1	Minster Street	B2
Ashley Road	A3	Morgan Road	C3
Audley Street	A2	Napier Road	B2
Baker Street	A2	Orts Road	C2
Basingstoke Road	B3	Oxford Road	A2
Bath Road	A3	Pell Street	B3
Bedford Road	A2	Portman Road	A1
Berkeley Avenue	A3	Priest Hill	B1
Blagrave Street	B2	Prospect Street Caversham	B1
Blenheim Road	C2	Prospect Street Reading	A2
Briant's Avenue	C1	Queen's Road Caversham	B1
Bridge Street	B2	Queen's Road Reading	B2
Broad Street	B2	Richfield Avenue	A1
Cardiff Road	A2	Rose Kiln Lane	B3
Castle Hill	A2	Russell Street	A2
Castle Street	B2	St. Anne's Road	B1
Catherine Street	A2	St. John's Road	C1
Caversham Road	B2	St. Mary's Butts	B2
Chatham Street	A2	St. Peters Avenue	A1
Cheapside	B2	St. Saviours Road	A3
Cholmeley Road	C2	Silver Street	B3
Christchurch Road	C3	South Street	B2
Church Road	A1	Southampton Street	B3
Church Street	B1	South View Road	B1
Coley Avenue	A3	Star Road	C1
Coley Place	A2	Station Hill	B2
Cow Lane	A2	Station Road	B2
Craven Road	C3	Swansea Road	B1
Crown Place	C2	Tessa Road	A1
Crown Street	B3	The Warren	A1
Cumberland Road	C2	Tilehurst Road	A2
Curzon Street	A2	Upper Redlands Road	C3
De Beauvoir Road	C2	Vastern Road	B1
Donnington Road	C2	Waldeck Street	B3
Duke Street	B2	Waterloo Road	B3
East Street	B2	Wensley Road	A3
Eldon Road	C2	Western Elms Avenue	A2
Eldon Terrace	C2	Westfield Road	B1
Elgar Road	B3	West Street	B2
Elgar Road South	B3	Whitley Street	B3
Elmhurst Road	C3	Wolsey Road	B1
Erleigh Road	C2	York Road	B1
Fobney Street	B2		
Forbury Road	B2		
Friar Street	B2		
Gas Work Road	C2		
George Street Caversham	B1		
George Street Reading	A2		
Gosbrook Road	B1		
Gower Street	A2		
Great Knollys Street	A2		
Greyfriars Road	B2		
Hemdean Road	B1		
Hill Street	B3		
Holybrook Road	A3		
Kenavon Drive	C2		
Kendrick Road	B3		
King's Road Caversham	B1		
King's Road Reading	B2		

Appears on main map page 134

Salisbury

Tourist Information Centre: Fish Row
Tel: 01722 334956

Albany Road	B1	Salt Lane	B2
Ashley Road	A1	Scots Lane	B2
Avon Terrace	A1	Silver Street	B2
Barnard Street	C2	Southampton Road	C3
Bedwin Street	B1	Swaynes Close	B1
Belle Vue Road	B1	Swaynes Close	B1
Bishops Walk	B3	Trinity Street	C2
Blackfriars Way	C3	Wain-a-long Road	C1
Blue Boar Row	B2	West Walk	B3
Bourne Avenue	C1	Wilton Road	A1
Bourne Hill	C1	Winchester Street	B2
Bridge Street	B2	Windsor Road	A2
Brown Street	B2	Wyndham Road	B1
Butcher Row	B2	York Road	A1
Carmelite Way	B3		
Castle Street	B1		
Catherine Street	B2		
Chipper Lane	B2		
Churchfields Road	A2		
Churchill Way East	C2		
Churchill Way North	B1		
Churchill Way South	C3		
Churchill Way West	A1		
Clifton Road	A1		
College Street	C1		
Crane Bridge Road	A2		
Crane Street	B2		
De Vaux Place	B3		
Devizes Road	A1		
Elm Grove Road	C2		
Endless Street	B1		
Estcourt Road	C1		
Exeter Street	B3		
Fairview Road	C1		
Fisherton Street	A2		
Fowlers Hill	C2		
Fowlers Road	C2		
Friary Lane	C3		
Gas Lane	A1		
Gigant Street	C2		
Greencroft Street	C1		
Hamilton Road	B1		
High Street	B2		
Ivy Street	B2		
Kelsey Road	C1		
Laverstock Road	C2		
Manor Road	C1		
Marsh Lane	A1		
Meadow Road	A1		
Milford Hill	C2		
Milford Street	B2		
Mill Road	A2		
Millstream Approach	B1		
Minster Street	B2		
New Canal	B2		
New Street	B2		
North Walk	B3		
Park Street	C1		
Pennyfarthing Street	B2		
Queens Road	B1		
Rampart Road	C2		
Rollestone Street	B1		
St. Ann Street	C3		
St. John's Street	B2		
St. Marks Road	C1		
St. Paul's Road	A1		

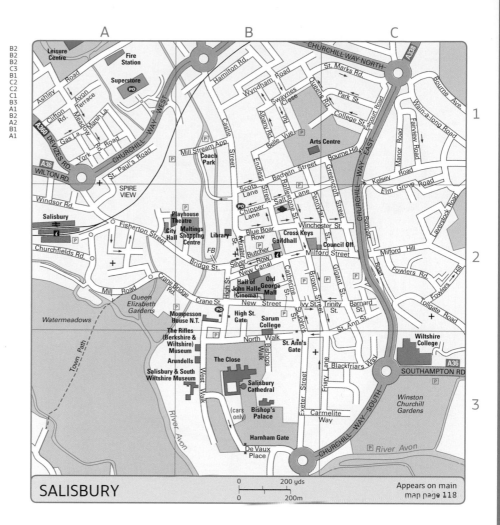

SALISBURY

0   200 yds
0   200m

Appears on main
map page 118

Scarborough

Tourist Information Centre: Brunswick Shopping Centre,
Unit 15a, Westborough   Tel: 01723 383636

Aberdeen Walk	B2	Valley Bridge Road	B2
Albion Road	B3	Valley Road	A3
Ashville Avenue	A2	Vernon Road	B2
Avenue Road	A3	Victoria Park Mount	A1
Belmont Road	B3	Victoria Road	A3
Candler Street	A2	Victoria Street	B2
Castle Road	B2	West Street	B3
Chatsworth Gardens	A1	Westborough	A3
Columbus Ravine	A2	Westbourne Grove	B3
Commercial Street	A3	Westover Road	B3
Cross Street	B2	Westwood	B3
Dean Road	A2	Westwood Road	A3
Eastborough	B2	Weydale Avenue	A1
Esplanade	B3	Wykeham Street	A3
Falconers Rd	B2		
Falsgrave Road	A3		
Foreshore Road	B2		
Franklin Street	A2		
Friargate	B2		
Friarsway	B2		
Garfield Road	A2		
Gladstone Road	A2		
Gladstone Street	A2		
Gordon Street	A2		
Grosvenor Road	B3		
Highfield	A3		
Hoxton Road	A2		
Longwestgate	C2		
Manor Road	A2		
Marine Drive	C1		
Mayville Avenue	A2		
Moorland Road	A1		
New Queen Street	B1		
Newborough	B2		
North Marine Road	B1		
North Street	B2		
Northstead Manor Drive	A1		
Northway	A2		
Norwood Street	A2		
Oak Road	A3		
Peasholm Crescent	A1		
Peasholm Drive	A1		
Peasholm Road	A1		
Prince Of Wales Terrace	B3		
Princess Street	C2		
Prospect Road	A2		
Queen Street	B2		
Queen's Parade	B1		
Raleigh Street	A2		
Ramshill Road	B3		
Roscoe Street	A3		
Rothbury Street	A2		
Royal Albert Drive	B1		
Royal Avenue	B3		
Sandside	C2		
Seamer Road	A3		
St. James Road	A3		
St. John's Avenue	A3		
St. John's Road	A3		
St. Thomas Street	B2		
Tollergate	B1		
Trafalgar Road	A1		
Trafalgar Square	B1		
Trafalgar Street West	A2		
Trinity Road	A3		
Valley Bridge Parade	B3		

SCARBOROUGH

0   400 yds
0   400m

Appears on main
map page 204

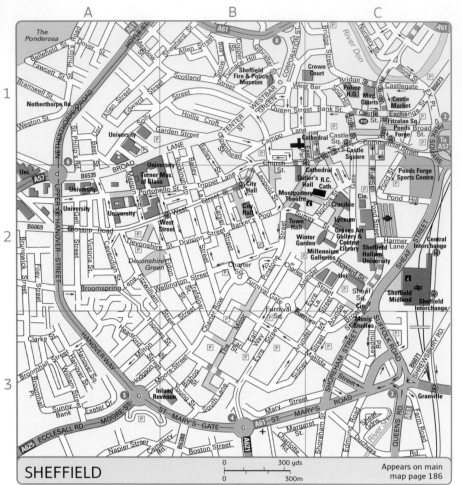

SHEFFIELD

Appears on main map page 186

Tourist Information Centre: 14 Norfolk Row
Tel: 0114 221 1900

Allen Street	B1	Hanover Square	A3
Angel Street	C1	Hanover Street	A3
Arundel Gate	B2	Hanover Way	A3
Arundel Lane	C3	Harmer Lane	C2
Arundel Street	B3	Haymarket	C1
Bailey Lane	B1	Headford Street	A3
Bailey Street	B1	High Street	C1
Bank Street	C1	Hodgson Street	A3
Barker's Pool	B2	Hollis Croft	B1
Beet Street	A1	Howard Street	C2
Bellefield Street	A1	Hoyle Street	A1
Bishop Street	B3	Leadmill Road	C3
Blonk Street	C1	Leopold Street	B2
Boston Street	B3	Mappin Street	A2
Bower Street	B1	Margaret Street	B3
Bramwell Street	A1	Mary Street	B3
Bridge Street	C1	Matilda Street	C3
Broad Lane	A2	Meadow Street	A1
Broad Street	C1	Milton Street	A3
Broomhall Street	A3	Moore Street	A3
Broomhall Place	A3	Napier Street	A3
Broomspring Lane	A2	Netherthorpe Road	A1
Brown Street	C3	Norfolk Street	C2
Brunswick Street	A2	Nursery Street	C1
Campo Lane	B1	Pinstone Street	B2
Carver Street	B2	Pond Hill	C2
Castle Square	C1	Pond Hill	C2
Castle Street	C1	Pond Street	C2
Castlegate	C1	Portobello Street	A2
Cavendish Street	A2	Queen Street	B1
Cemetery Road	A3	Queens Road	C3
Charles Street	B2/C2	Rockingham Street	B2
Charlotte Road	B3	St. Mary's Gate	B3
Charter Row	B3	St. Mary's Road	B3
Charter Square	B2	St. Philip's Road	A1
Church Street	B1	Scotland Street	B1
Clarke Street	A3	Sheaf Gardens	C3
Commercial Street	C1	Sheaf Square	C2
Copper Street	B1	Sheaf Street	C2
Corporation Street	B1	Shepherd Street	B1
Devonshire Street	A2	Shoreham Street	C3
Division Street	B2	Shrewsbury Road	C3
Dover Street	A1	Sidney Street	B3
Duchess Road	C3	Snig Hill	C1
Earl Street	B3	Snow Lane	B1
Earl Way	B3	Solly Street	A1
East Parade	C1	South Lane	B3
Ecclesall Road	A3	Spring Street	B1
Edmund Road	C3	Suffolk Road	C3
Edward Street	A1	Sunny Bank	A3
Eldon Street	B2	Surrey Street	B2
Exchange Street	C1	Tenter Street	B1
Exeter Drive	A3	The Moor	B3
Eyre Lane	C2	Thomas Street	A3
Eyre Street	B3	Townhead Street	B1
Farm Road	C3	Trafalgar Street	B2
Fawcett Street	A1	Trippet Lane	B2
Filey Street	A2	Upper Allen Street	A1
Fitzwilliam Street	A2	Upper Hanover Street	A2
Flat Street	C1	Victoria Street	A2
Furnace Hill	B1	Waingate	C1
Furnival Gate	B2	Wellington Street	B2
Furnival Square	B2	West Bar	B2
Furnival Street	B2	West Street	B2
Garden Street	A1	Westbar Green	B1
Gell Street	A2	Weston Street	A1
Gibraltar Street	B1	William Street	A3
Glossop Road	A2	Young Street	B3

SOUTHAMPTON

Appears on main map page 106

Tourist Information Centre: 9 Civic Centre Road
Tel: 023 8083 3333

Above Bar Street	B2	Queensway	B3
Albert Road North	C3	Radcliffe Road	C1
Argyle Road	B1	Roberts Road	A1
Bedford Place	A1	St. Andrews Road	B1
Belvidere Road	C2	St. Mary's Road	B1
Bernard Street	B3	St. Mary Street	B2
Brintons Road	B1	Shirley Road	A1
Britannia Road	C1	Solent Road	A2
Briton Street	B3	Southern Road	A2
Burlington Road	A1	South Front	B2
Canute Road	B3	Terminus Terrace	B3
Castle Way	B2	Town Quay	A3
Central Bridge	B3	Trafalgar Road	B3
Central Road	B3	West Quay Road	A2
Chapel Road	B2	West Road	B3
Civic Centre Road	A2	Western Esplanade	A2
Clovelly Road	B1	Wilton Avenue	A1
Commercial Road	A1		
Cranbury Avenue	B1		
Cumberland Place	A1		
Denzil Avenue	B1		
Derby Road	C1		
Devonshire Road	A1		
Dorset Street	B1		
East Park Terrace	B1		
East Street	B2		
Endle Street	C2		
European Way	B3		
Golden Grove	B2		
Graham Road	B1		
Harbour Parade	A2		
Hartington Road	C1		
Henstead Road	A1		
Herbert Walker Avenue	A2		
High Street	B2		
Hill Lane	A1		
Howard Road	A1		
James Street	B2		
Kent Street	C1		
Kingsway	B2		
Landguard Road	A1		
London Road	B1		
Lyon Street	B1		
Marine Parade	C2		
Marsh Lane	B2		
Melbourne Street	C2		
Millbank Street	C1		
Milton Road	A1		
Morris Road	A1		
Mount Pleasant Road	B1		
Newcombe Road	A1		
New Road	B2		
Northam Road	C1		
North Front	B2		
Northumberland Road	C1		
Ocean Way	B3		
Onslow Road	B1		
Orchard Lane	B2		
Oxford Avenue	B1		
Oxford Street	B3		
Palmerston Road	B1		
Peel Street	C1		
Platform Road	B3		
Portland Terrace	A2		
Pound Tree Road	B2		
Princes Street	C1		

Tourist Information Centre: Victoria Hall, Bagnall Street, Hanley Tel: 01782 236000

Albion Street	B1	Snow Hill	B2
Ashford Street	B2	Stafford Street	B1
Avenue Road	B2	Station Road	B3
Aynsley Road	B2	Stoke	B3
Bedford Road	B2	Stoke Road	B3
Bedford Street	A2	Stone Street	A3
Belmont Road	A1	Stuart Road	C2
Beresford Street	B2	Sun Street	B1
Berry Hill Road	C2	The Parkway	B2
Boon Avenue	A3	Trentmill Road	C2
Botteslow Street	C1	Victoria Road	C2
Boughey Road	B3	Warner Street	B1
Broad Street	B1	Waterloo Road	C1
Bucknall New Road	C1	Wellesley Street	B2
Bucknall Old Road	C1	Wellington Road	C1
Cauldon Road	B2	West Avenue	A3
Cemetery Road	A2	Westland Street	A3
Church Street	B3	Yoxall Avenue	A3
Clough Street	A1		
College Road	B2		
Commercial Road	C1		
Copeland Street	B3		
Dewsbury Road	C3		
Eagle Street	C1		
Eastwood Road	C1		
Elenora Street	B3		
Etruria Road	A1		
Etruria Vale Road	A1		
Etruscan Street	A2		
Festival Way	A1		
Forge Lane	A1		
Garner Street	A2		
Glebe Street	B3		
Greatbatch Avenue	A3		
Hanley	B1		
Hartshill Road	A3		
Hill Street	A3		
Honeywall	A3		
Howard Place	B2		
Ivy House Road	C1		
Leek Road	B3		
Lichfield Street	C1		
Liverpool Road	B3		
Lordship Lane	B3		
Lytton Street	B3		
Manor Street	C3		
Marsh Street	B1		
Newlands Street	B2		
North Street	A2		
Old Hall Street	B1		
Oxford Street	A3		
Parliament Row	B1		
Potteries Way	B1		
Potters Way	C1		
Prince's Road	A3		
Quarry Avenue	A3		
Quarry Road	A3		
Queen's Road	A3		
Queensway	A2		
Rectory Road	B2		
Regent Road	B2		
Richmond Street	A3		
Ridgway Road	B2		
Seaford Street	B2		
Shelton New Road	A2		
Shelton Old Road	A3		

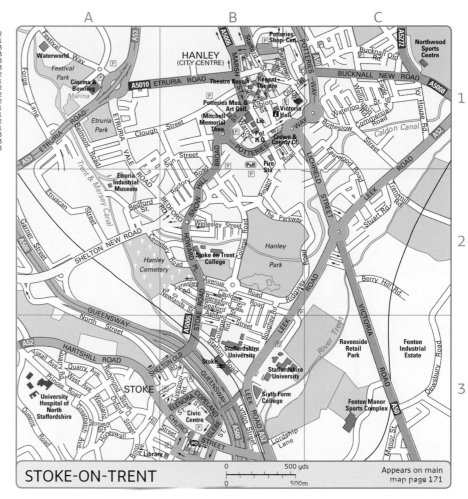

STOKE-ON-TRENT

0 — 500 yds
0 — 500m

Appears on main map page 171

Tourist Information Centre: Bridgefoot Tel: 01789 264293

Albany Road	A2	Swan's Nest Lane	C2
Alcester Road	A1	The Waterways	A1
Arden Street	A1	Tiddington Road	C2
Avonside	B3	Trinity Street	B3
Banbury Road	C2	Tyler Street	B1
Bancroft Place	C2	Union Street	B2
Birmingham Road	A1	Warwick Court	B1
Brewery Street	B1	Warwick Crescent	C1
Bridgefoot	C2	Warwick Road	C1
Bridge Street	B2	Waterside	B2
Bridgeway	C2	Welcombe Road	C1
Bridgetown Road	C3	Westbourne Grove	A2
Broad Street	A3	Western Road	A1
Broad Walk	A3	West Street	A3
Bull Street	A3	Wharf Road	A1
Chapel Lane	B2	Windsor Street	B2
Chapel Street	B2	Wood Street	B2
Cherry Orchard	A3		
Chestnut Walk	A2		
Church Street	B2		
Clopton Bridge	C2		
Clopton Road	B1		
College Lane	B3		
College Street	B3		
Ely Street	B2		
Evesham Place	A3		
Evesham Road	A3		
Great William Street	B1		
Greenhill Street	A2		
Grove Road	A2		
Guild Street	D1		
Henley Street	B1		
High Street	B2		
Holtom Street	A3		
John Street	B1		
Kendall Avenue	B1		
Maidenhead Road	B1		
Mansell Street	A1		
Meer Street	B2		
Mill Lane	B3		
Mulberry Street	B1		
Narrow Lane	A3		
New Street	B3		
Old Town	B3		
Old Town Square	A3		
Old Tramway Walk	C3		
Orchard Way	A3		
Payton Street	B1		
Red Lion Court	B2		
Rother Street	A2		
Ryland Street	B3		
St. Andrews Crescent	A2		
St. Gregory's Road	B1		
Sanctus Drive	A3		
Sanctus Road	A3		
Sanctus Street	A3		
Sandfield Road	A3		
Scholar's Lane	A3		
Seven Meadow Road	A3		
Shakespeare Street	B1		
Sheep Street	B2		
Shipston Road	C3		
Shottery Road	A2		
Shrieve's Walk	B2		
Southern Lane	B3		
Station Road	A1		

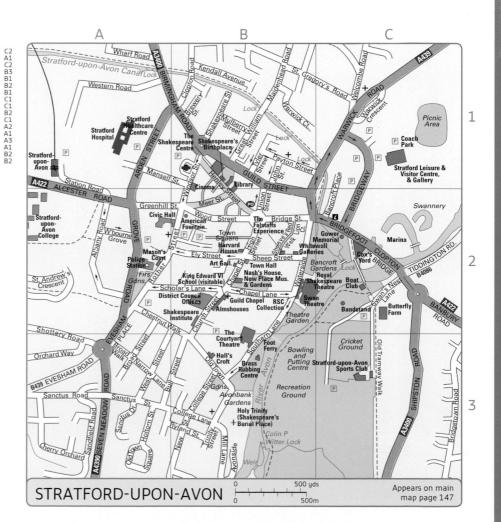

STRATFORD-UPON-AVON

0 — 500 yds
0 — 500m

Appears on main map page 147

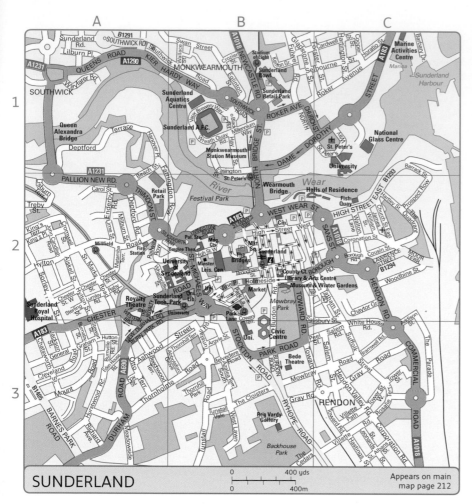

SUNDERLAND

0	400 yds		
0	400m		

Appears on main
map page 212

Tourist Information Centre: 50 Fawcett Street
Tel: 0191 553 2000

Abbotsford Grove	B3	Lime Street	A2
Addison Street	C3	Livingstone Road	B2
Aiskell Street	A2	Lumley Road	A2
Argyle Street	B3	Matamba Terrace	A2
Ashwood Street	A3	Milburn Street	A2
Azalea Terace South	B3	Millennium Way	B1
Barnes Park Road	A3	Moor Terrace	C2
Barrack Street	C1	Mount Road	A3
Beach Street	A2	Mowbray Road	B3
Beechwood Terrace	A3	New Durham Road	A3
Belvedere Road	B3	Newcastle Road	B1
Black Road	B1	North Bridge Street	B2
Borough Road	B2/C2	Otto Terrace	A3
Bramwell Road	C3	Pallion New Road	A2
Brougham Street	B2	Park Lane	B2
Burdon Road	B3	Park Road	B3
Burn Park Road	A3	Peel Street	B3
Burnaby Street	A3	Prospect Row	C2
Burnville Road	A3	Queens Road	A1
Carol Street	A2	Raby Road	A2
Chatsworth Street	A3	Railway Row	A2
Chaytor Grove	C2	Roker Avenue	B1/C1
Chester Road	A2	Rosalie Terrace	C3
Chester Street	A2	Ryhope Road	B3
Church Street East	C2	St. Albans Street	C3
Church Street North	B1	St. Leonards Street	C3
Cleveland Road	A3	St. Marks Road	A2
Commercial Road	C3	St. Mary's Way	B2
Cooper Street	C1	St. Michaels Way	B2
Coronation Street	C2	St. Peter's Way	C1
Corporation Road	C3	Salem Road	C3
Cousin Street	C2	Salem Street	C3
Cromwell Street	A2	Salisbury Street	B2
Crozier Street	B1	Sans Street	C2
Dame Dorothy Street	B1	Selbourne Street	B1
Deptford Road	A2	Silksworth Row	A2
Deptford Terrace	A1	Sorley Street	A2
Durham Road	A3	Southwick Road	A1
Easington Street	B1	Southwick Road	B1
Eden House Road	A3	Stewart Street	A3
Eglinton Street	B1	Stockton Road	B3
Enderby Road	A2	Suffolk Street	C3
Farringdon Row	A1	Sunderland Road	A1
Forster Street	C1	Swan Street	B1
Fox Street	A3	Tatham Street	C2
Fulwell Road	B1	The Cedars	B3
General Graham Street	A3	The Cloisters	B3
Gladstone Street	B1	The Parade	C3
Gray Road	B3/C3	The Quadrant	C2
Hanover Place	A1	The Royalty	A2
Hartington Street	C1	Thornhill Park	B3
Hartley Street	C2	Thornhill Terrace	B3
Hastings Street	C3	Thornholme Road	A3
Hay Street	B1	Toward Road	B2/C3
Hendon Road	C2	Tower Street	C3
Hendon Valley Road	C3	Tower Street West	C3
High Street East	C2	Trimdon Street	A2
High Street West	B2	Tunstall Road	B3
Holmeside	B2	Tunstall Vale	B3
Horatio Street	C1	Vaux Brewery Way	B1
Hurstwood Road	A3	Villette Road	C3
Hutton Street	A3	Vine Place	B2
Hylton Road	A2	Wallace Street	B3
Hylton Road	A2	West Lawn	B3
Jackson Street	A3	West Wear Street	B2
James William Street	C2	Western Hill	A2
Kenton Grove	B1	Wharncliffe Street	A2
Kier Hardy Way	A1	White House Road	C3
King's Place	A2	Woodbine Street	C2
Lawrence Street	C2	Wreath Quay Road	B1

SWANSEA

0	500 yds		
0	500m		

Appears on main
map page 128

Tourist Information Centre: Plymouth Street
Tel: 01792 468321

Aberdyberthi Street	C1	Mount Pleasant	B2
Albert Row	B3	Mumbles Road	A3
Alexandra Road	B2	Neath Road	C1
Argyle Street	A3	Nelson Street	B3
Baptist Well Place	B1	New Cut Road	C2
Baptist Well Street	B1	New Orchard Street	B1
Beach Street	A3	Nicander Parade	A2
Belgrave Lane	A3	Norfolk Street	A3
Belle Vue Way	B2	North Hill Road	B1
Berw Road	A1	Orchard Street	B2
Berwick Terrace	B1	Oxford Street	A3
Bond Street	A3	Oystermouth Road	A3
Brooklands Terrace	A2	Page Street	B2
Brunswick Street	A3	Pant-y-Celyn Road	A3
Brynmor Crescent	A3	Park Terrace	B1
Brynymor Road	A3	Pedrog Terrace	A1
Burrows Place	C3	Penlan Crescent	A2
Cambrian Place	C3	Pentre Guinea Road	C1
Carig Crescent	A1	Pen-y-Craig Road	A1
Carlton Terrace	B2	Picton Terrace	A2
Carmarthen Road	B1	Powys Avenue	A1
Castle Street	B2	Princess Way	B2
Clarence Terrace	B3	Quay Parade	C2
Colbourne Terrace	B1	Rhondda Street	A2
Constitution Hill	A2	Rose Hill	A2
Creidiol Road	A1	St. Elmo Avenue	C1
Cromwell Street	A2	St. Helen's Avenue	A3
Cwm Road	C1	St. Helen's Road	A3
De La Beche Street	B2	St. Mary Street	B2
Delhi Street	C2	Singleton Street	B3
Dillwyn Street	B3	Somerset Place	C3
Dyfatty Street	B1	South Guildhall Road	B2
Dyfed Avenue	A2	Strand	C2
Earl Street	C1	Taliesyn Road	A2
East Burrows Road	C3	Tan-y-Marian Road	A2
Eigen Crescent	A1	Tegid Road	A1
Emlyn Road	A1	Teilo Crescent	A1
Fabian Way	C2	Terrace Road	A2
Fairfield Terrace	A2	The Kingsway	B2
Ffynone Drive	A2	Townhill Road	A1
Ffynone Road	A2	Trawler Road	B3
Foxhole Road	C1	Villiers Street	C1
Glamorgan Street	B3	Vincent Street	A3
Gors Avenue	A1	Walter Road	A3
Granagwen Road	B1	Watkin Street	B1
Grove Place	B2	Waun-Wen Road	B1
Gwent Road	A1	Wellington Street	B3
Gwili Terrace	A1	West Way	B3
Hanover Street	A2	Westbury Street	A3
Heathfield	B2	Western Street	A3
Hewson Street	A2	William Street	C1
High Street	B2	Windmill Terrace	C3
High View	B1	York Street	C3
Islwyn Road	A1		
Kilvey Road	C1		
Kilvey Terrace	C2		
King Edward's Road	A3		
King's Road	C2		
Llangyfelach Road	B1		
Long Ridge	B1		
Mackworth Street	C2		
Maesteg Street	C1		
Mansel Street	A2		
Mayhill Road	A1		
Milton Terrace	B2		
Morris Lane	C2		

Tourist Information Centre: 37 Regent Street
Tel: 01793 530328

Albion Street	A3
Bath Road	B3
Beatrice Street	B1
Beckhampton Street	C2
Birch Street	A2
Bridge Street	B2
Broad Street	C1
Canal Walk	B2
Caulfield Road	C1
Church Place	A2
Cirencester Way	C1
Clifton Street	B3
Commercial Road	B2
County Road	C1
Cricklade Street	C3
Curtis Street	B2
Dean Street	A2
Drove Road	C3
Eastcott Hill	B3
Edmund Street	B2
Elmina Road	C1
Euclid Street	C2
Faringdon Road	A2
Farnsby Street	B2
Fleet Street	B2
Fleming Way	B2
Gladstone Street	C1
Goddard Avenue	B3
Great Western Way	A1
Grosvenor Road	A3
Groundwell Road	C2
Hawksworth Way	A1
High Street	C3
Holbrook Way	B2
Hythe Road	B3
Islington Street	B2
Jennings Street	A2
Kemble Drive	A1
Kent Road	B3
Kingshill Street	A3
Lansdown Road	B3
Manchester Road	B1
Market Street	B2
Milford Street	B2
Milton Road	B2
Morris Street	A1
Newburn Crescent	A2
Newcombe Drive	A1
North Star Avenue	B1
Ocotal Way	C1
Okus Road	A3
Park Lane	A2
Penzance Drive	A2
Plymouth Street	C2
Princes Street	C2
Queen Street	B2
Radnor Street	A3
Redcliffe Street	A2
Regent Street	B2
Rodbourne Road	A1
Rosebery Street	C1
Spring Gardens	C2
Stafford Street	B3
Station Road	B1
Swindon Road	B3
The Parade	B2

Upham Road	C3
Victoria Road	C2
Westcott Place	A3
Western Street	C3
William Street	A3
York Road	C2

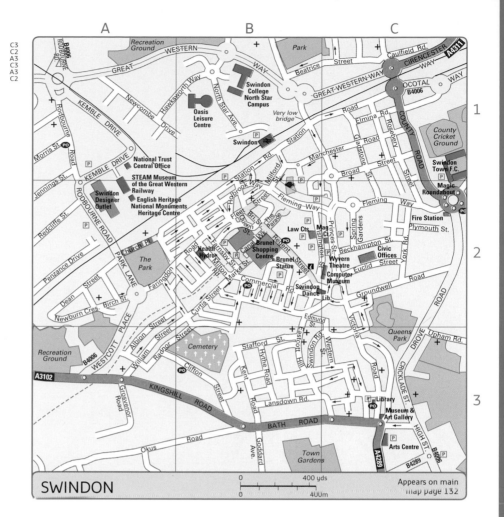

Tourist Information Centre: Vaughan Parade
Tel: 01803 211211

Abbey Road	B2
Ash Hill Road	B1
Avenue Road	A2
Bampfylde Road	A2
Barton Road	A1
Belgrave Road	A2
Belmont Road	C1
Braddons Hill Road East	C2
Bridge Road	A2
Bronshill Road	B1
Brunswick Square	B1
Carlton Road	C1
Cary Parade	C3
Cedars Road	C2
Chestnut Avenue	A2
Cockington Lane	A3
Croft Road	B2
Crownhill Park	A1
Dunmere Road	C1
East Street	A1
Ellacombe Church Road	C1
Ellacombe Road	B1
Falkland Road	A2
Falkland Road	A2
Fleet Street	B2
Forest Road	B1
Goshen Road	A2
Hatfield Road	B1
Hennapyn Road	A3
Higher Warbrry Road	C2
Hillesdon Road	C2
Kenwyn Road	C1
Lower Warberry Road	C2
Lucius Street	A2
Lymington Road	B1
Mallock Road	A2
Market Street	B2
Marnham Road	C1
Meadfoot Lane	C3
Meadfoot Road	C3
Middle Warberry Road	C2
Mill Lane	A2
Newton Road	A1
Old Mill Road	A2
Old Mill Road	A3
Parkfield Road	B1
Parkhill Road	C3
Prince's Road	C2
Princes Road East	C2
Quinta Road	C1
Rathmore Road	A3
Reddenhill Road	C1
Rosehill Road	C2
Sanford Road	A2
Seaway Lane	A3
Shedden Hill	B2
Sherwell Lane	A2
Solsbro Road	A3
South Street	A2
St. Lukes Road	B2
St. Marychurch Road	B2
St. Michael's Road	A1
Stitchill Road	C2
Strand	C3
Teignmouth Road	A1
The King's Drive	A2

Thurlow Road	B1
Tor Hill Road	B2
Torbay Road	A3
Torwood Gardens Road	C3
Torwood Street	C3
Union Street	B2
Upton Hill	B1
Upton Road	A1
Vanehill Road	C3
Victoria Parade	C3
Walnut Road	A3
Warbro Road	C1
Warren Road	B2
Windsor Road	C1

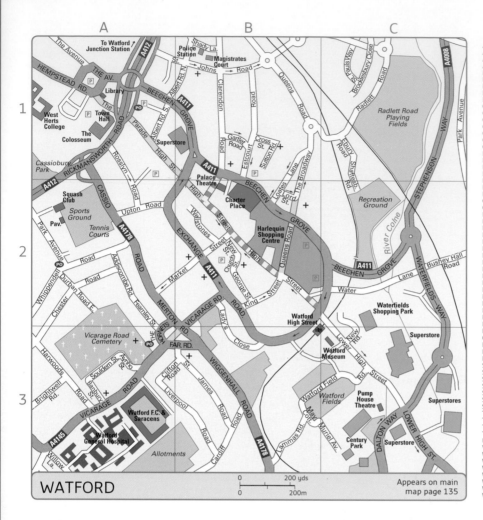

WATFORD

Street	Grid
Addiscombe Road	A2
Albert Road North	A1
Albert Road South	A1
Aynho Street	A3
Banbury Street	A3
Beechen Grove	A1/C2
Brightwell Road	A3
Brocklesbury Close	C1
Bushey Hall Road	C2
Cardiff Road	B3
Cassio Road	A2
Chester Road	A2
Church Street	B2
Clarendon Road	B1
Clifton Road	A3
Cross Street	B1
Dalton Way	C3
Durban Road East	A2
Ebury Road	C1
Estcourt Road	B1
Exchange Road	A2
Farraline Road	A3
Fearnley Street	A2
Garlet Road	B1
George Street	B2
Harwoods Road	A3
Hempsted Road	A1
High Street	A1/B2
King Street	B2
Lady's Close	B2
Lammas Road	B3
Liverpool Road	A3
Loates Lane	B2
Lord Street	B2
Lower High Street	C3
Market Street	A2
May Cottages	B3
Merton Road	A2
Muriel Avenue	B3
New Road	C3
New Street	B2
Park Avenue	C1
Park Avenue	A2
Queens Road	B1/B2
Radlett Road	C1
Rickmansworth Road	A2
Rosslyn Road	A1
Shaftesbury Road	C1
Souldern Street	A3
St. James Road	B3
St. Johns Road	A1
St. Pauls Way	C1
Stephenson Way	C2
Sutton Road	B1
The Avenue	A1
The Broadway	B2
The Hornets	A3
The Parade	A1
Upton Road	A2
Vicarage Road	A3/B2
Water Lane	C2
Waterfields Way	C2
Watford Field Road	B3
Wellstones	B2
Whippendell Road	A2
Wiggenhall Road	B3
Willow Lane	A3

Appears on main map page 135

WESTON-SUPER-MARE

Tourist Information Centre: Winter Gardens, Royal Parade
Tel: 01934 417117

Street	Grid	Street	Grid
Addicott Road	B3	Stafford Road	C2
Albert Avenue	B3	Station Road	B2
Alexandra Parade	B2	Sunnyside Road	B3
Alfred Street	B2	Swiss Road	C2
All Saints Road	B1	The Centre	B2
Amberey Road	C3	Trewartha Park	C1
Arundell Road	B1	Upper Church Road	A1
Ashcombe Gardens	C1	Walliscote Road	B3
Ashcombe Road	C2	Waterloo Street	B2
Atlantic Road	A1	Whitecross Road	B3
Baker Street	B2	Winterstoke Road	C3
Beach Road	B3		
Beaconsfield Road	B2		
Birnbeck Road	A1		
Boulevard	B2		
Brendon Avenue	C1		
Bridge Road	C2		
Brighton Road	B3		
Bristol Road	B1		
Carlton Street	B2		
Cecil Road	B1		
Clarence Road North	B3		
Clarendon Road	C2		
Clevedon Road	B3		
Clifton Road	B3		
Drove Road	C3		
Earlham Grove	C2		
Ellenborough Park North	B3		
Ellenborough Park South	B3		
Exeter Road	B3		
George Street	B2		
Gerard Road	B1		
Grove Park Road	B1		
High Street	B2		
Highbury Road	A1		
Hildesheim Bridge	B2		
Hill Road	C1		
Jubilee Road	B2		
Kenn Close	C3		
Kensington Road	C3		
Knightstone Road	A1		
Langford Road	C3		
Lewisham Grove	C2		
Locking Road	C2		
Lower Bristol Road	C1		
Lower Church Road	A1		
Manor Road	C1		
Marchfields Way	C3		
Marine Parade	B3		
Meadow Street	B2		
Milton Road	C2		
Montpelier	B1		
Neva Road	B2		
Norfolk Road	C3		
Oxford Street	B2		
Queen's Road	B1		
Rectors Way	C3		
Regent Street	B2		
Ridgeway Avenue	B3		
Royal Crescent	A1		
St. Paul's Road	B3		
Sandford Road	C2		
Severn Road	B3		
Shrubbery Road	A1		
South Road	A1		
Southside	B1		

Appears on main map page 115

Tourist Information Centre: Guildhall, High Street
Tel: 01962 840500

Alison Way	A1
Andover Road	A1
Archery Lane	A2
Bar End Road	C3
Barfield Close	C3
Beaufort Road	A3
Beggar's Lane	C2
Blue Ball Hill	C2
Bridge Stret	C2
Broadway	B2
Canon Street	B3
Chesil Street	C3
Christchurch Road	A3
City Road	A1
Clifton Hill	A2
Clifton Road	A1
Clifton Terrace	A2
Colebrook Street	B2
College Street	B3
College Walk	B3
Compton Road	A3
Cranworth Road	A1
Culver Road	B3
Domum Road	C3
Durngate	C2
East Hill	C3
Eastgate Street	C2
Easton Lane	C1
Ebden Road	C1
Edgar Road	A3
Elm Road	A1
Fairfield Road	A1
Friarsgate	B2
Gordon Road	B1
Great Minster Street	B2
Hatherley Road	A1
High Street	B2
Hyde Abbey Road	B1
Hyde Close	B1
Hyde Street	B1
Jewry Street	B2
King Alfred Place	B1
Kingsgate Street	B3
Little Minster Street	B2
Lower Brook Street	B2
Magdalen Hill	C2
Market Lane	B2
Middle Brook Street	B2
Middle Road	A2
Milland Road	C3
North Walls	A1
Parchment Street	B2
Park Avenue	B1
Peninsula Square	A2
Portal Road	C3
Quarry Road	C3
Romans' Road	A3
Romsey Road	A2
St. Catherine's Road	C3
St. Cross Road	A3
St. George's Street	B2
St. James Lane	A2
St. James Villas	A3
St. John's Street	C2
St. Michael's Road	A3
St. Paul's Hill	A1
St. Peter Street	B2
St. Swithun Street	B3
St. Thomas Street	B3
Saxon Road	B1
Silver Hill	B2
Southgate Street	A3
Staple Gardens	B2
Station Road	A1
Step Terrace	A2
Stockbridge Road	A1
Sussex Street	A2
Swan Lane	B1
Symond's Street	B3
Tanner Street	B2
The Square	B2
Tower Street	A2
Union Street	C2
Upper Brook Street	B2
Upper High Street	A2
Wales Street	C2
Water Lane	C2
Wharf Hill	C3
Worthy Lane	A1

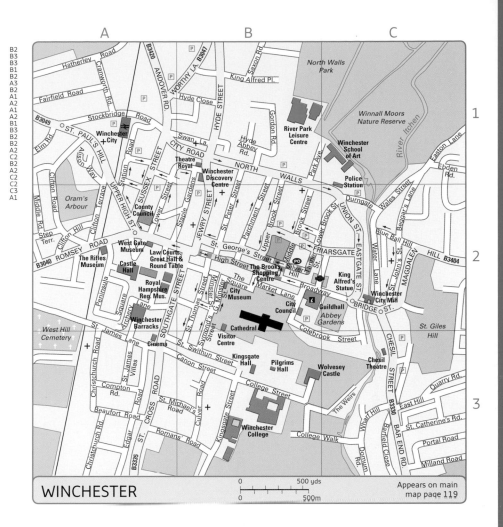

WINCHESTER

Appears on main map page 119

Tourist Information Centre: Old Booking Hall, Central Station
Tel: 01753 743900

Adelaide Square	C3
Albert Street	A2
Alexandra Road	B3
Alma Road	B2/B3
Arthur Road	B2
Barry Avenue	B1
Bexley Street	B2
Bolton Avenue	B3
Bolton Crescent	B3
Bolton Road	B3
Bulkeley Avenue	A3
Castle Hill	C2
Charles Street	B2
Clarence Crescent	B2
Clarence Road	A2
College Crescent	A3
Dagmar Road	B2
Datchet Road	C1
Frances Road	B3
Goslar Way	A2
Goswell Road	B2
Green Lane	A2
Grove Road	B2
Helston Lane	A2
High Street (Eton)	B1
High Street (Windsor)	C2
Imperial Road	A3
King Edward VII Avenue	C1
Kings Road	C3
Meadow Lane	B1
Mill Lane	A1
Osborne Road	B3
Oxford Road	B2
Park Street	C2
Parsonage Lane	A2
Peascod Street	B2
Peel Close	A3
Princess Avenue	A3
Romney Lock Road	C1
St. Leonards Road	B3
St. Marks Road	B2
Sheet Street	C2
South Meadow Lane	B1
Springfield Road	A3
Stovell Road	A1
Thames Street	C1
The Long Walk	C3
Upcroft	A3
Vansittart Road	B2
Victoria Street	B2
Victor Road	B3
Westmead	A3
Windsor & Eton Relief Road	A2
York Avenue	A3
York Road	A3

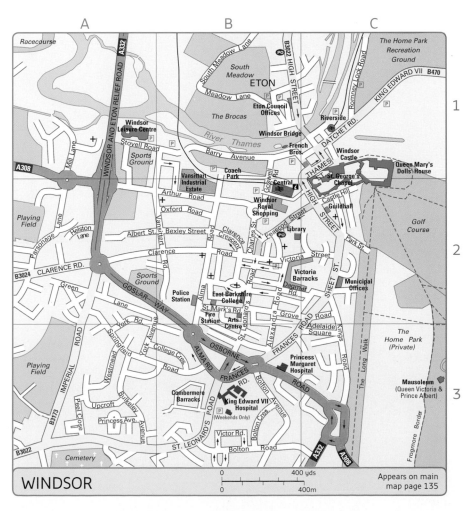

WINDSOR

Appears on main map page 135

WORCESTER

Tourist Information Centre: The Guildhall, High Street
Tel: 01905 726311

Street	Grid		Street	Grid
Albany Terrace	A1		Sherriff Street	C1
Albert Road	C3		Shrub Hill	C2
Angel Place	A2		Shrub Hill Road	C2
Angel Street	B2		Sidbury	B3
Arboretum Road	B1		Southfield Street	B1
Back Lane South	A1		Spring Hill	C2
Bath Road	B3		Stanley Road	C3
Bridge Street	A2		Tallow Hill	C2
Britannia Road	A1		Tennis Walk	A1
Britannia Square	A1		The Butts	A2
Broad Street	A2		The Cross	B2
Carden Street	B3		The Moors	A1
Castle Street	A2		The Shambles	B2
Charles Street	B3		The Tything	A1
Chestnut Street	B1		Tolladine Road	C1
Chestnut Walk	B1		Trinity Street	B2
City Walls Road	B2		Upper Tything	A1
Cole Hill	C3		Vincent Road	C3
College Street	B3		Washington Street	B1
Compton Road	C3		Westbury Street	B1
Copenhagen Street	A3		Wyld's Lane	C3
Croft Road	A2			
Deansway	A2			
Dent Close	C3			
Dolday	A2			
Farrier Street	A2			
Foregate Street	B2			
Fort Royal Hill	C3			
Foundry Street	B3			
Friar Street	B3			
George Street	C2			
Grand Stand Road	A2			
High Street	B2			
Hill Street	C2			
Hylton Road	A2			
Infirmary Walk	A2			
Kleve Walk	B3			
Lansdowne Crescent	B1			
Lansdowne Walk	C1			
London Road	B3			
Loves Grove	A1			
Lowesmoor	B2			
Lowesmoor Place	B2			
Midland Road	C3			
Moor Street	A1			
Newport Street	A2			
New Road	A3			
New Street	B2			
Northfield Street	B1			
North Quay	A2			
Padmore Street	B2			
Park Street	B3			
Park Street	C3			
Pheasant Street	B2			
Pump Street	B3			
Rainbow Hill	B1			
Richmond Hill	C3			
St. Martin's Gate	B2			
St. Mary's Street	A1			
St. Oswalds Road	A1			
St. Paul's Street	B2			
Sansome Street	B2			
Sansome Walk	B1			
Severn Street	B3			
Severn Terrace	A1			
Shaw Street	A2			

Appears on main map page 146

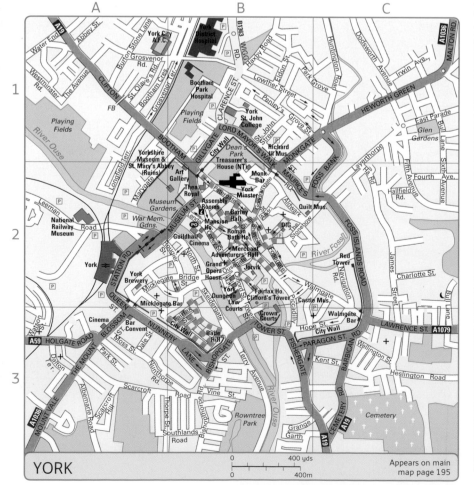

YORK

Tourist Information Centre: 1 Museum Street
Tel: 01904 550099

Street	Grid		Street	Grid
Abbey Street	A1		Paragon Street	B3
Albemarle Road	A3		Park Grove	B1
Aldwark	B2		Park Street	A3
Barbican Road	C3		Penley's Grove Street	B1
Bishopthorpe Road	B3		Petergate	B2
Bishopgate Street	B3		Piccadilly	B2
Blossom Street	A3		Queen Street	A2
Bootham	A1		Rougier Street	B2
Bootham Crescent	A1		St. Andrewgate	B2
Bridge Street	B2		St. John Street	B1
Bull Lane	C1/C2		St. Maurice's Road	B2
Burton Stone Lane	A1		St. Olave's Road	A1
Cemetery Road	C3		Scarcroft Hill	A3
Charlotte Street	C2		Scarcroft Road	A3
Church Street	B2		Shambles	B2
Clarence Street	B1		Sixth Avenue	C1
Clifford Street	B2		Skeldergate	B2
Clifton	A1		Southlands Road	A3
Coney Street	B2		Station Road	A2
Dale Street	A3		Terry Avenue	B3
Dalton Terrace	A3		The Avenue	A1
Dodsworth Avenue	C1		The Mount	A3
East Parade	C1		The Stonebow	B2
Eldon Street	B1		Thorpe Street	A3
Fairfax Street	B3		Tower Street	B2
Fifth Avenue	C1		Vine Street	B3
Fishergate	B3		Walmgate	B2
Foss Bank	C2		Water End	A1
Fossgate	B2		Watson Street	A3
Foss Islands Road	C2		Wellington Street	C3
Fourth Avenue	C2		Westminster Road	A1
Gillygate	B1		Wigginton Road	B1
Goodramgate	B2			
Grange Garth	B3			
Grosvenor Road	A1			
Grosvenor Terrace	A1			
Hallfield Road	C2			
Haxby Road	B1			
Heslington Road	C3			
Heworth Green	C1			
Holgate Road	A3			
Hope Street	B3			
Huntington Road	C1			
Irwin Avenue	C1			
James Street	B2			
Kent Street	C3			
Lawrence Street	C3			
Layerthorpe	C2			
Leeman Road	A2			
Lendal	B2			
Longfield Terrace	A2			
Lord Mayor's Walk	B1			
Lowther Street	B1			
Malton Road	C1			
Marygate	A2			
Maurices Road	B2			
Micklegate	A2			
Monkgate	B1			
Moss Street	A3			
Mount Vale	A3			
Museum Street	B2			
Navigation Road	C2			
North Street	B2			
Nunnery Lane	A3			
Nunthorpe Road	A3			
Ousegate	B2			

Appears on main map page 195

Key to map symbols

🅿 Short stay car park 🅿 Mid stay car park 🅿 Long stay car park 🅿 Other car park ▮ Airport terminal building

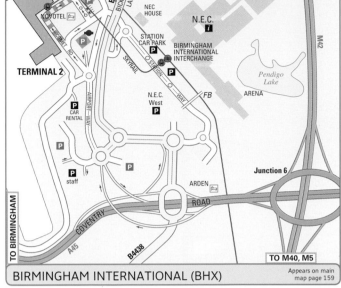

BIRMINGHAM INTERNATIONAL (BHX)

Appears on main map page 159

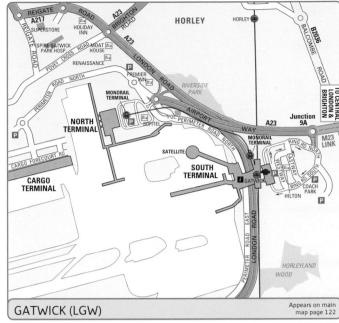

GATWICK (LGW)

Appears on main map page 122

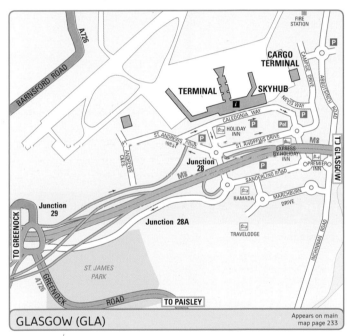

GLASGOW (GLA)

Appears on main map page 233

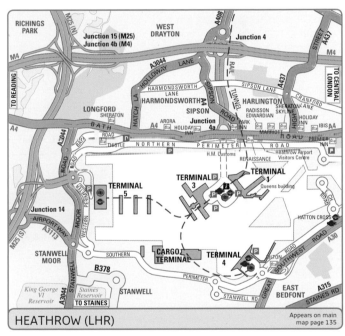

HEATHROW (LHR)

Appears on main map page 135

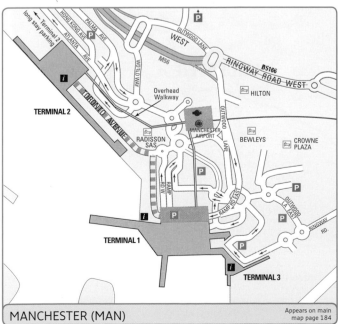

MANCHESTER (MAN)

Appears on main map page 184

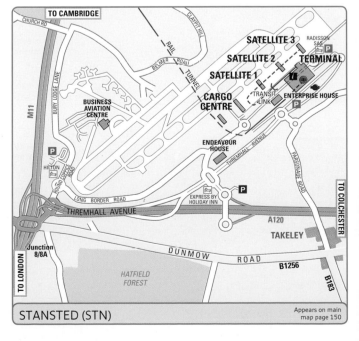

STANSTED (STN)

Appears on main map page 150

Symbols used on the map

M5 Motorway

M6 Toll Toll motorway

8 / **9** Motorway junction with full / limited access
(in congested areas there is just a numbered symbol)

Maidstone
Birch
Sarn
Motorway service area with off road / full / limited access

A556 Primary route dual / single carriageway

S 24 hour service area on primary route

Peterhead Primary route destination
Primary route destinations are places of major traffic importance linked by the primary route network. They are shown on a green background on direction signs.

A30 'A' road dual / single carriageway

B1403 'B' road dual / single carriageway

Minor road

Road with restricted access

Roads with passing places

Road proposed or under construction

33 Multi-level junction with full / limited access
(with junction number)

Roundabout

4 Road distance in miles between markers

Road tunnel

Steep hill
(arrows point downhill)

Toll Level crossing /Toll

St. Malo 8hrs Car ferry route with journey times

Railway line /station / tunnel

Wales Coast Path National Trail / Long Distance Route

---

30 **V** Fixed safety camera
Speed limit shown by a number within the camera, a V indicates a variable limit.

30 **30** Fixed average-speed safety camera
Speed limit shown by a number within the camera.

✈ ✈ Airport with / without scheduled services

(H) Heliport

P&R **P&R** Park and Ride site operated by bus / rail
(runs at least 5 days a week)

Built up area

□ □ ▫ Town / Village / Other settlement

Hythe Seaside destination

—·—·— National boundary

KENT County / Unitary Authority boundary and name

0	150	300	500	700	900	metres
water 0	490	985	1640	2295	2950	feet

Land height reference bar

Heritage Coast

National Park

Regional / Forest Park boundary

Woodland

Danger Zone Military range

·468 ▲941 Spot / Summit height
(in metres)

Lake / Dam / River / Waterfall

Canal / Dry canal / Canal tunnel

Beach / Lighthouse

SEE PAGE 3 Area covered by urban area map

Reading our maps

Park & Ride
Sites are shown that operate at least 5 days a week. Bus operated sites have a yellow symbol and rail operated sites a pink symbol.

Distances
Blue numbers give distances in miles between junctions shown with a blue marker

Multi-level junctions
Non-motorway junctions where slip roads are used to access the main roads

Motorway service area

World Heritage site
Places of interest defined by UNESCO as special on a world scale.

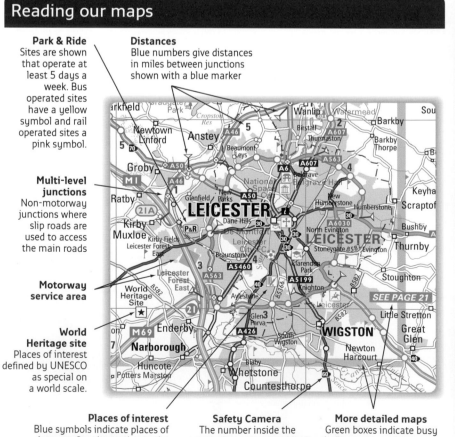

Places of interest
Blue symbols indicate places of interest. See the section to the right for the different types of feature represented on the map.

Safety Camera
The number inside the camera shows the speed limit at the camera location.

More detailed maps
Green boxes indicate busy built-up-areas where more detailed mapping is available.

Places of interest

A selection of tourist detail is shown on the mapping. It is advisable to check with the local tourist information centre regarding opening times and facilities available.

Any of the following symbols may appear on the map in maroon  which indicates that the site has World Heritage status.

i	Tourist information centre (open all year)
i	Tourist information centre (open seasonally)
𝕞	Ancient monument
🐠	Aquarium
🏛	Aqueduct / Viaduct
🌳	Arboretum
⚔ 1643	Battlefield
⚑	Blue flag beach
▲ 🚐	Camp site / Caravan site
🏰	Castle
🕳	Cave
🌲	Country park
🏏	County cricket ground
🥃	Distillery
✝	Ecclesiastical feature
🎪	Event venue
🐾	Farm park
🌸	Garden
⛳	Golf course
🏠	Historic house
⛵	Historic ship
⚽	Major football club
£	Major shopping centre / Outlet village
🏟	Major sports venue
🏁	Motor racing circuit
🚲	Mountain bike trail
🏛	Museum / Art gallery
🦉	Nature reserve (NNR indicates a National Nature Reserve)
🐎	Racecourse
🚂	Rail Freight Terminal
⛷ 🎿	Ski slope (artificial / natural)
🦅	Spotlight nature reserve (Best sites for access to nature)
🚂	Steam railway centre / preserved railway
🏄	Surfing beach
🎡	Theme park
🎓	University
🍇	Vineyard
🐘	Wildlife park / Zoo
🦋	Wildlife Trust nature reserve
★	Other interesting feature
(NT) (NTS)	National Trust / National Trust for Scotland property

Map scale

A scale bar appears at the bottom of every page to help with distances.

0   2   4   6 miles
0   2   4   6   8   10 km

England, Wales & Southern Scotland are at a scale of 1:200,000 or 3.2 miles to 1 inch
Northern Scotland is at a scale of 1:263,158 or 4.2 miles to 1 inch.

Map pages

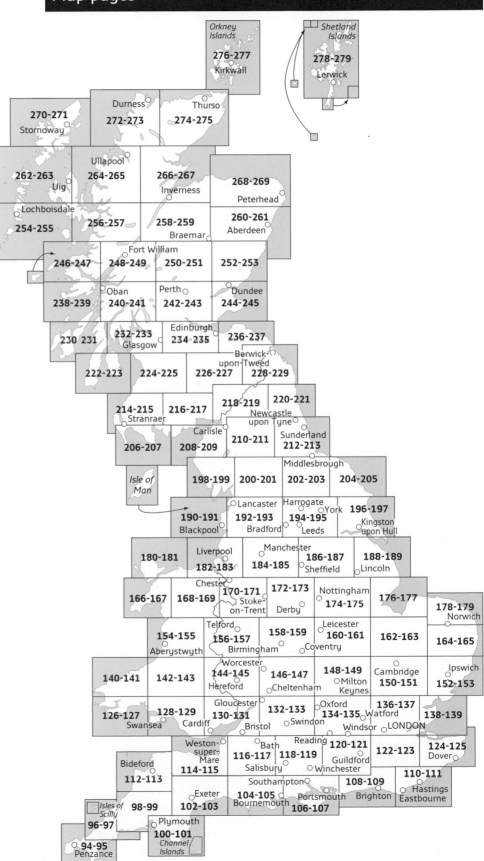

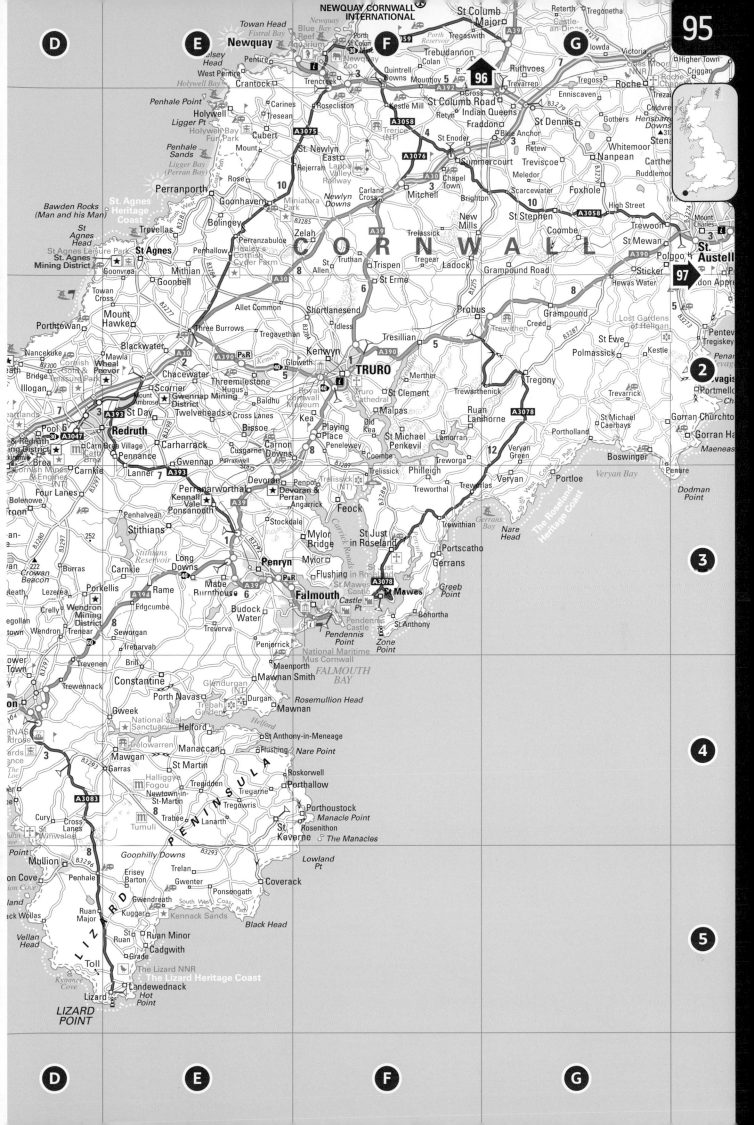

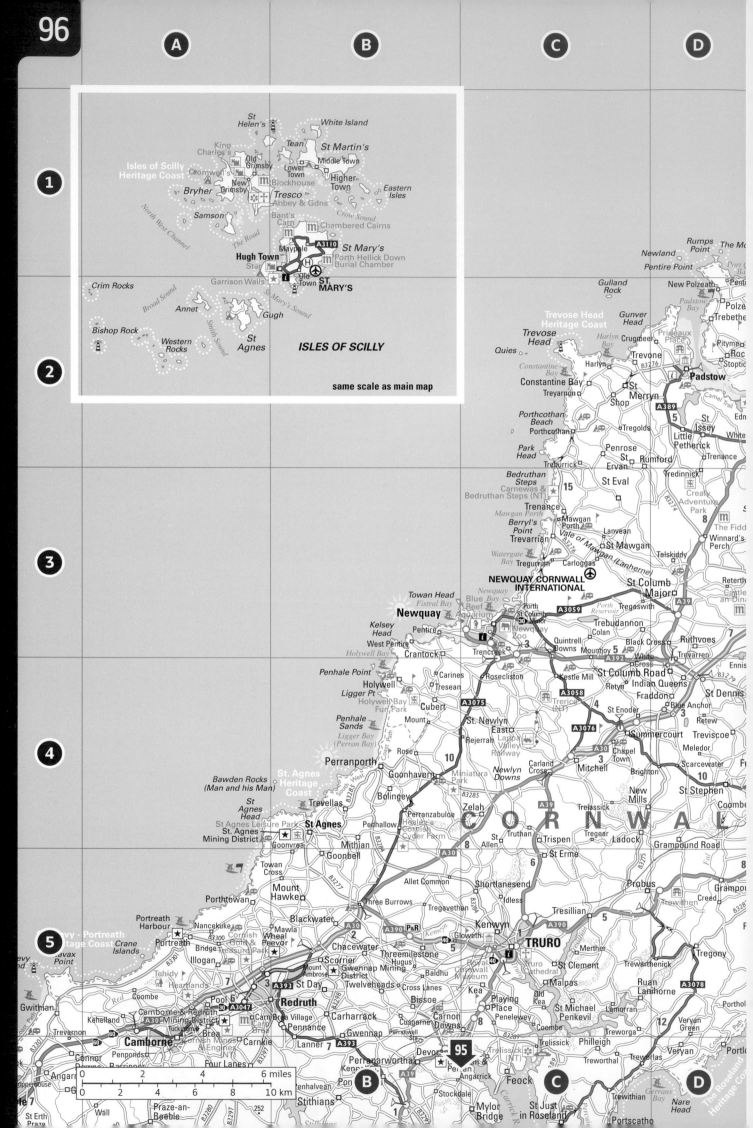

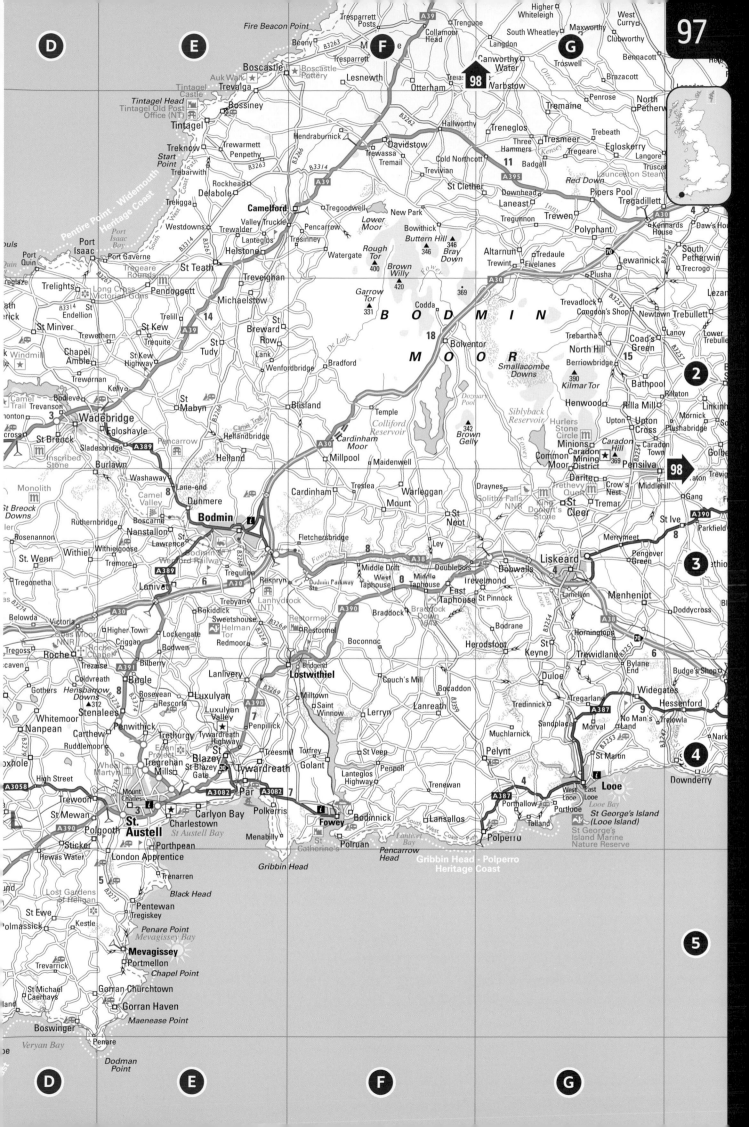

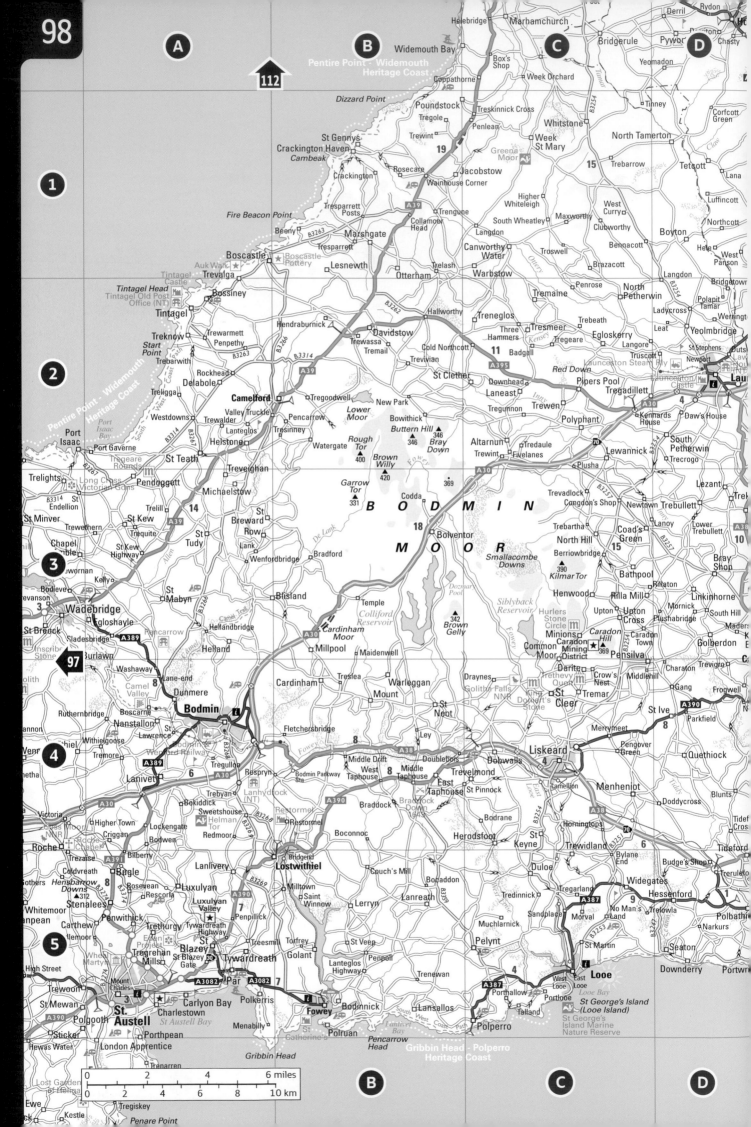

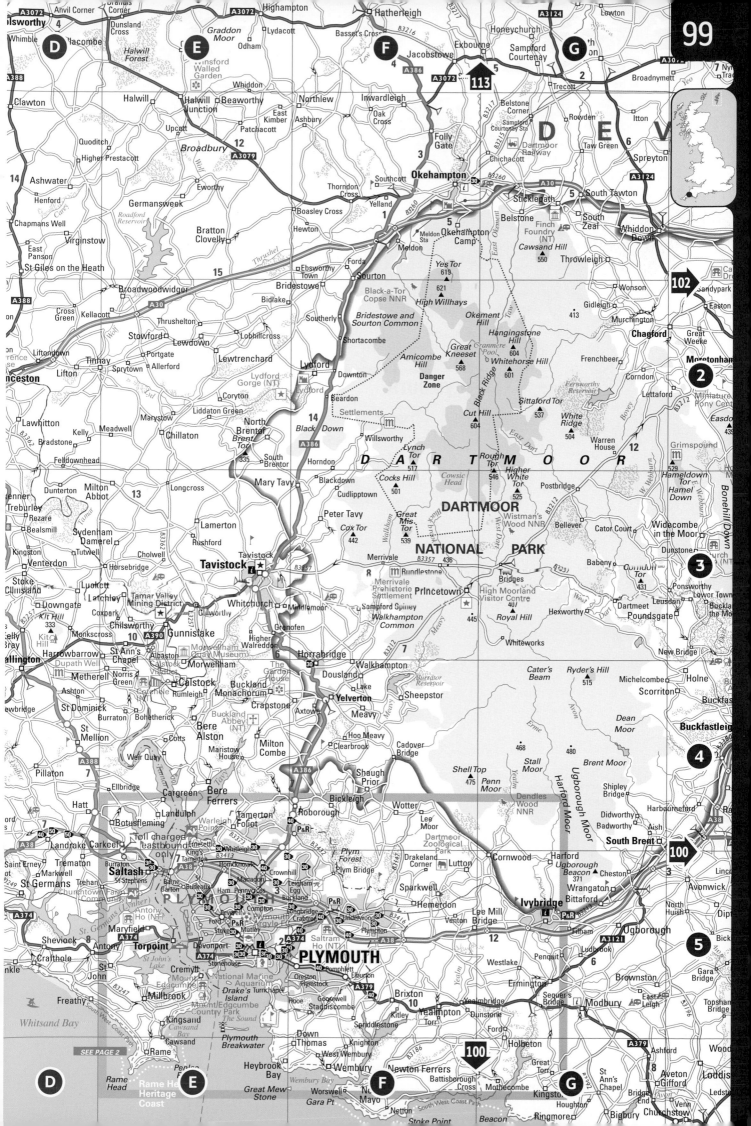

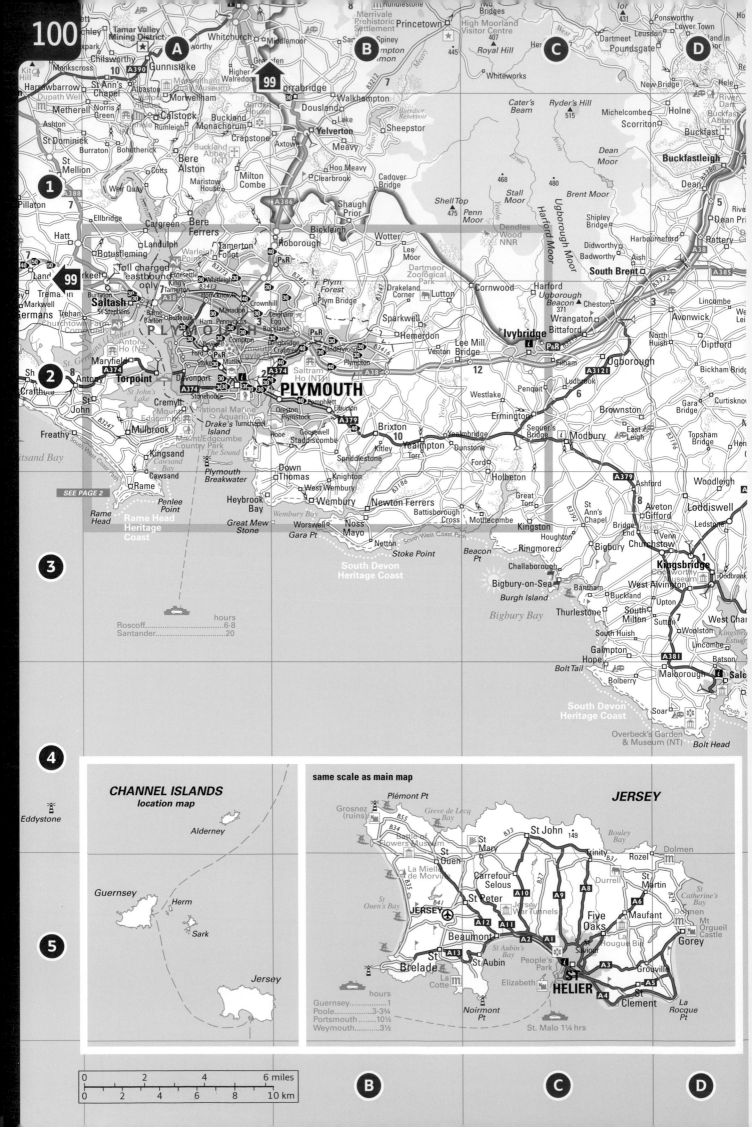

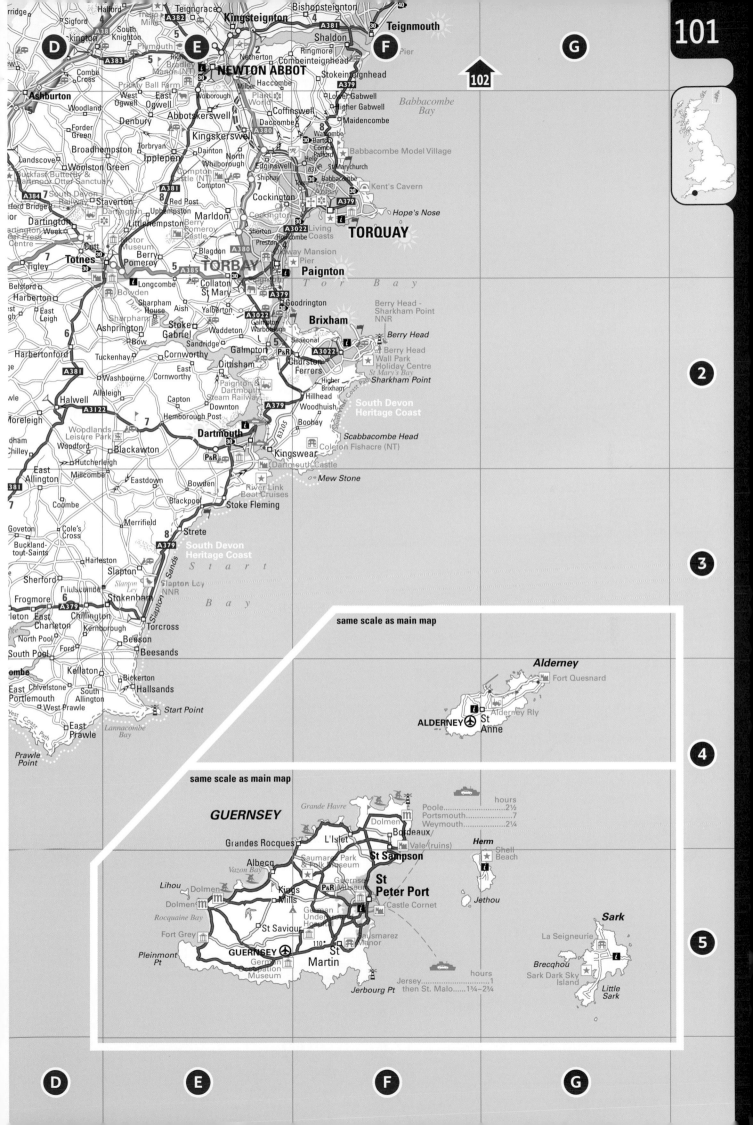

102

D **E** **F** **G**

Halford
Sigford
Teigngrace
Kingsteignton
Bishopsteignton
Teignmouth
A382
A381
A381
A30

South
Knighton
Netherton
Combeinteignhead
Shaldon
Pier
Plymouth
Bradley
Manor (NT)
NEWTON ABBOT
Ringmore
Combeinteignhead
Stokeinteignhead

Combe
Cross
Haccombe
Lower Gabwell
Higher Gabwell
Babbacombe Bay

Ashburton
Woodland
West
Ogwell
East
Ogwell
Volborough
Prickly Ball Farm
Plant World
Milber
Coffinswell
Daccombe
Maidencombe

Forder
Green
Denbury
Abbotskerswell
A380
Watcombe
Babbacombe Model Village

Broadhempston
Torbryan
Kingskerswell
Dainton
North
Whilborough
Edginswell
Combe
Pafford
St Marychurch
Kent's Cavern

Landscove
Woolston Green
Ipplepen
Compton
Castle (NT)
Compton
Shiphay
Babbacombe
Torre
Abbey

Buckfast Butterfly &
Dartmoor Otter Sanctuary
A381
Red Post
Upham
Marldon
Berry
Pomeroy
Castle
Preston
Cockington
TORQUAY
Hope's Nose

A384
South Devon
Railway
Staverton
Littlehempston
A380
Living
Coasts
A3022

Dartington
Week
Dartington
Press
Centre
Cott
Motor
Museum
Berry
Pomeroy
Blagdon
Shorton
Holcombe
Preston
A3022
Pier
Paignton

Totnes
Tigley
Longcombe
Collaton
St Mary
T o r *B a y*

Belsford
Bowden
Sharpham
House
Aish
Yalberton
Goodrington

Harberton
East
Leigh
Sharpham
Ashprington
Stoke
Gabriel
Waddeton
Galmpton
Warborough
A379
Berry Head –
Sharkham Point
NNR

A381
Bow
Sandridge
Brixham
Berry Head

Harbertonford
Tuckenhay
Cornworthy
East
Cornworthy
A3022
Berry Head
Wall Park
Holiday Centre
St Mary's Bay

Halwell
Washbourne
Allaleigh
Capton
Paignton &
Dartmouth
Steam Railway
Higher
Brixham
Hillhead
Sharkham Point

A3122
Hemborough Post
Downton
Woodhuish
Boohay
**South Devon
Heritage Coast**

Moreleigh
Woodford
Blackawton
Dartmouth
Scabbacombe Head

East
Allington
Millcombe
Eastdown
Bowden
Kingswear
Coleton Fishacre (NT)
Dartmouth Castle

A381
Coombe
Blackpool
Stoke Fleming
River Link
Boat Cruises
Mew Stone

Goveton
Cole's
Cross
Merrifield
Strete
A379
**South Devon
Heritage Coast**

Buckland-
tout-Saints
Harleston
Slapton
S t a r t

Sherford
Frogmore
Chillington
Kernborough
Slapton Ley
NNR
Slapton
Sands
B a y

East
Charleton
A379
Stokenham
Torcross

North Pool
Ford
Beeson
Beesands

South Pool
Kellaton
Bickerton
Hallsands

East
Portlemouth
Chivelstone
South
Allington
Start Point

West Prawle
East
Prawle
*Lannacombe
Bay*

Prawle
Point

---

same scale as main map

Alderney
Fort Quesnard

ALDERNEY
St
Anne
Alderney Rly

---

same scale as main map

Grande Havre
	hours
Poole	2½
Portsmouth	7
Weymouth	2¼

GUERNSEY
Dolmen
L'Islet
Bordeaux
Herm

Grandes Rocques
Saumarez Park
& Folk Museum
Vale (ruins)
Shell
Beach

Albecq
Vazon Bay
St Sampson

Lihou
Dolmen
Kings
Mills
Guernsey
Museum
**St
Peter Port**
Jethou

Dolmen
P&R
German
Underground
Hospital
Castle Cornet

Rocquaine Bay
St Saviour

Fort Grey
Sausmarez
Manor
Sark
La Seigneurie

Pleinmont
Pt
GUERNSEY
110
**St
Martin**
Brecqhou
Sark Dark Sky
Island

German
Occupation
Museum
	hours
Jersey	1
then St. Malo	1¾–2¾

Jerbourg Pt
*Little
Sark*

D **E** **F** **G**

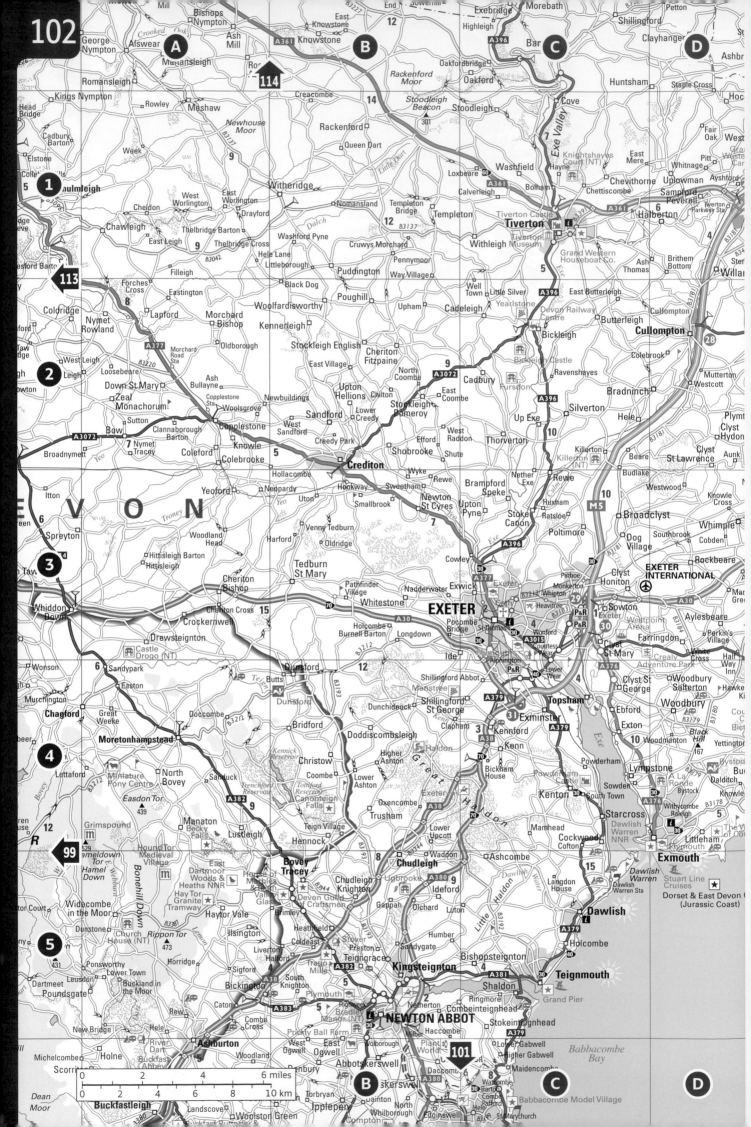

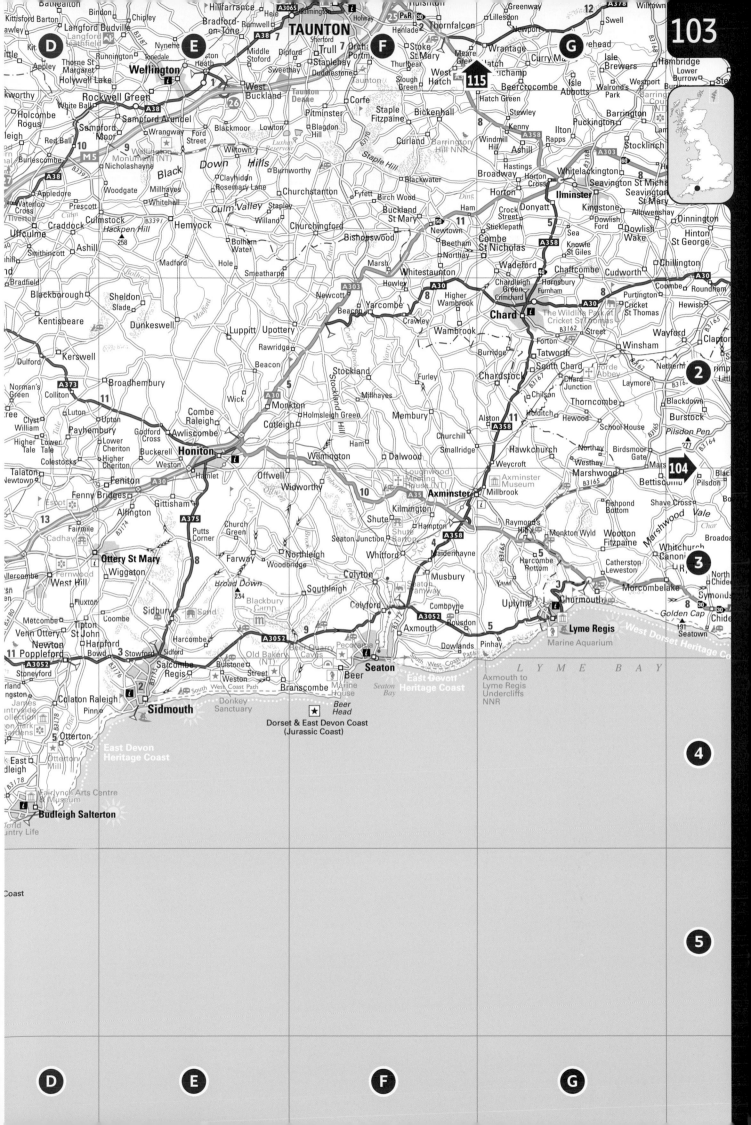

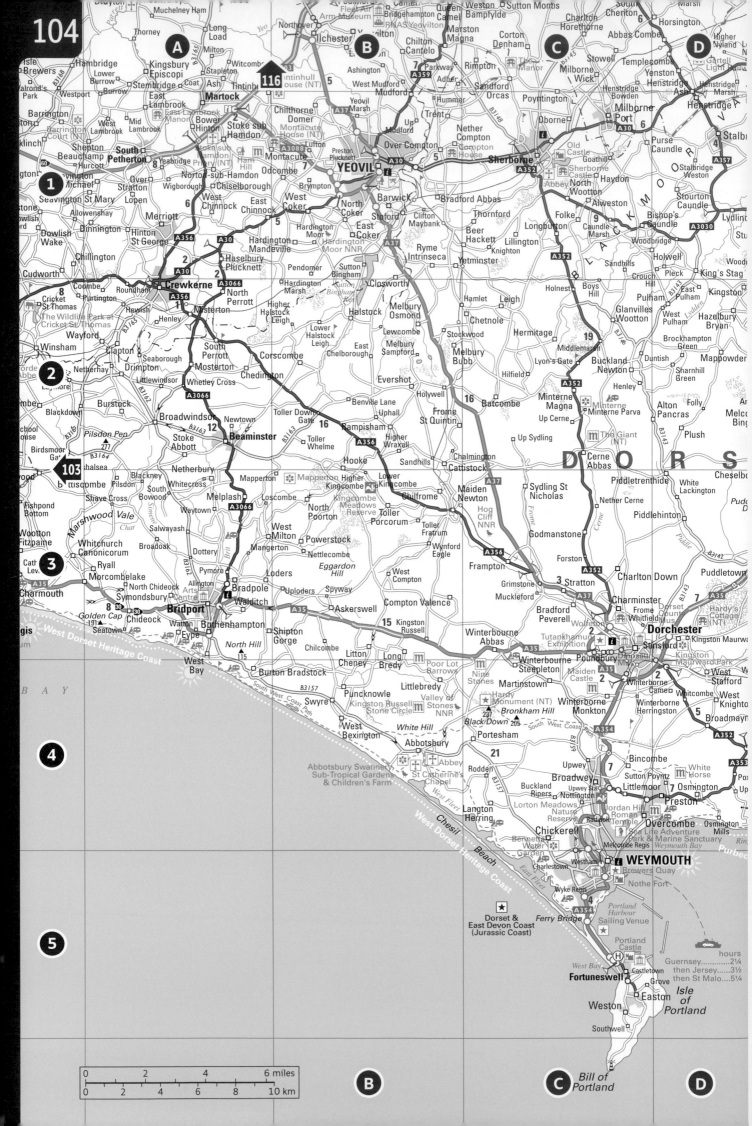

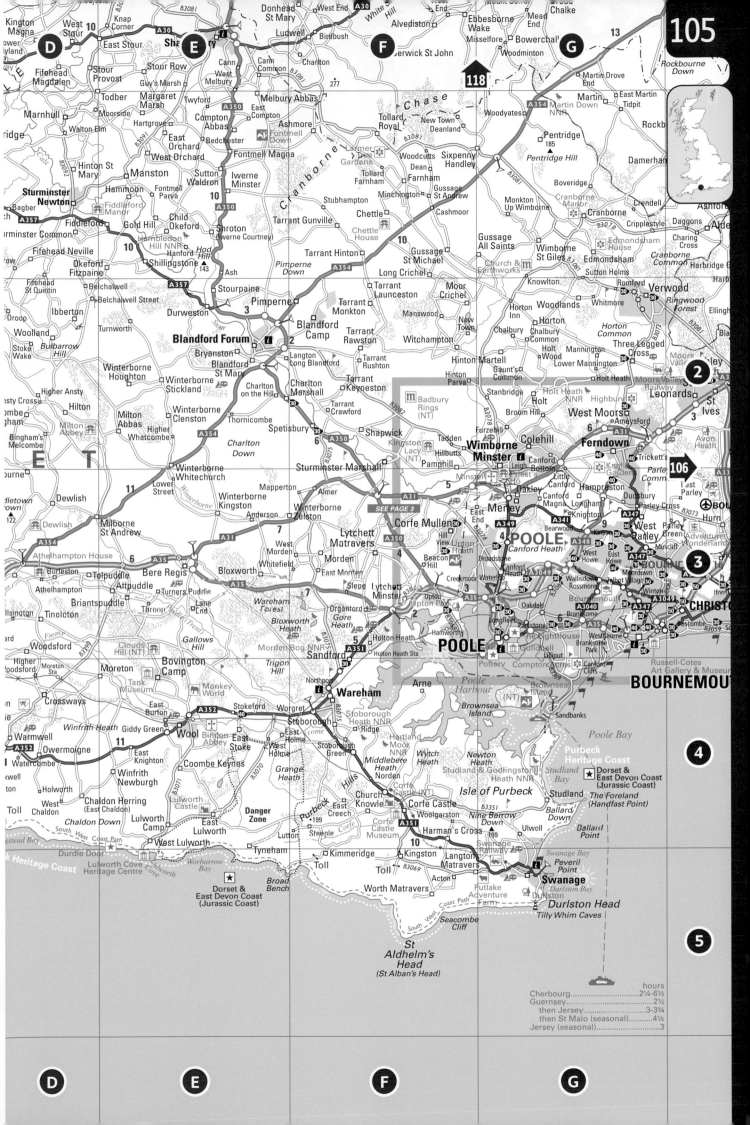

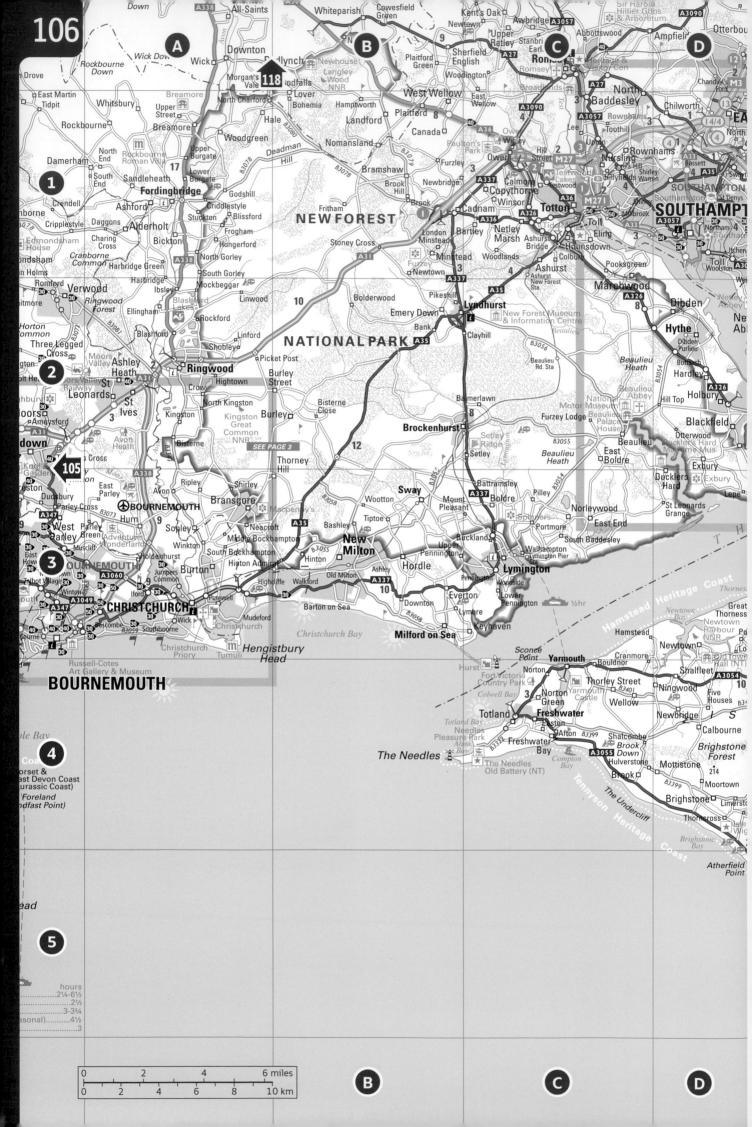

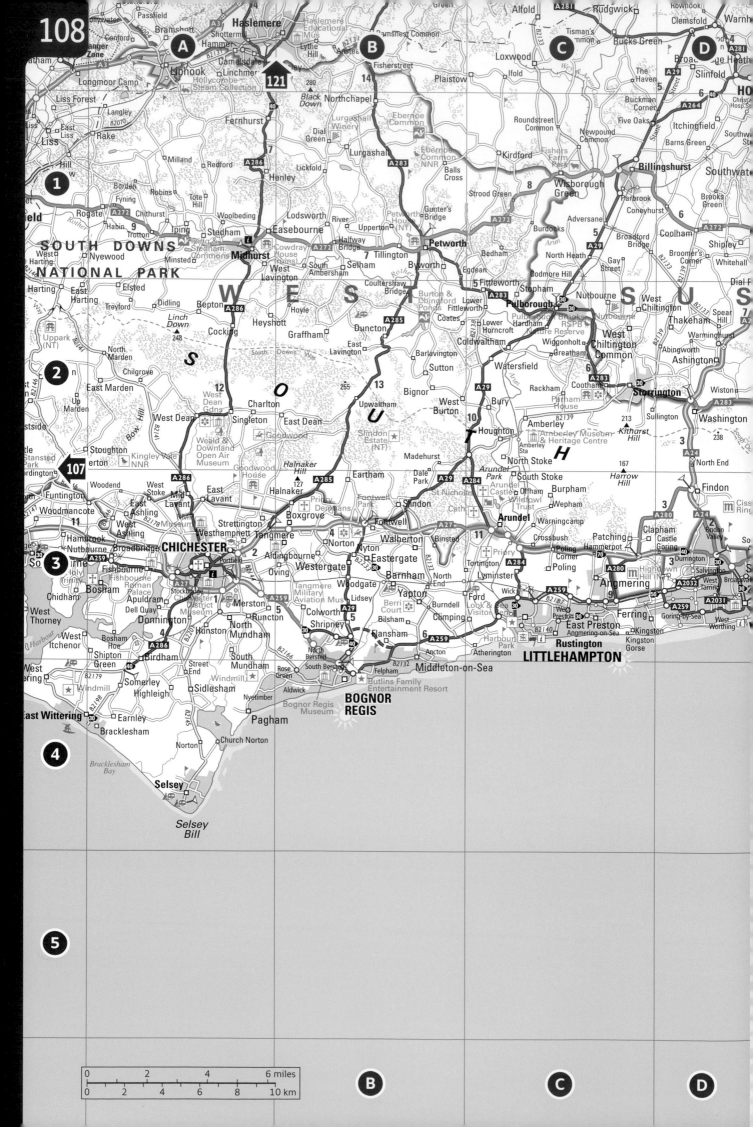

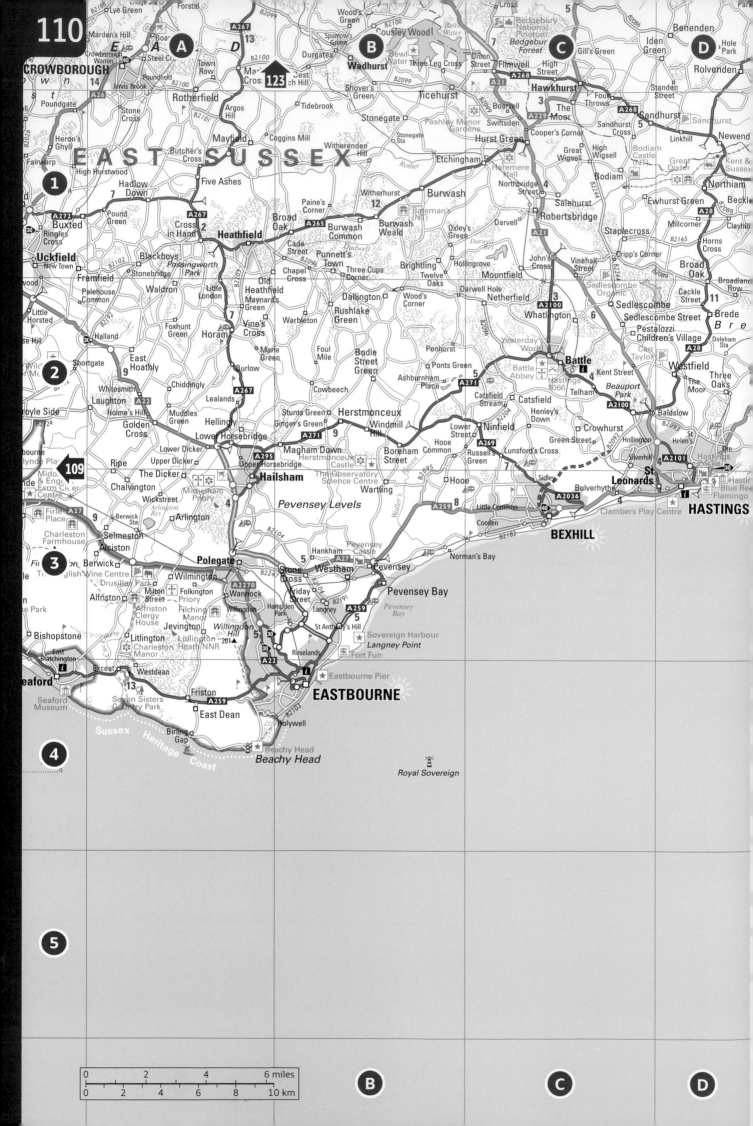

Channel Tunnel terminal maps

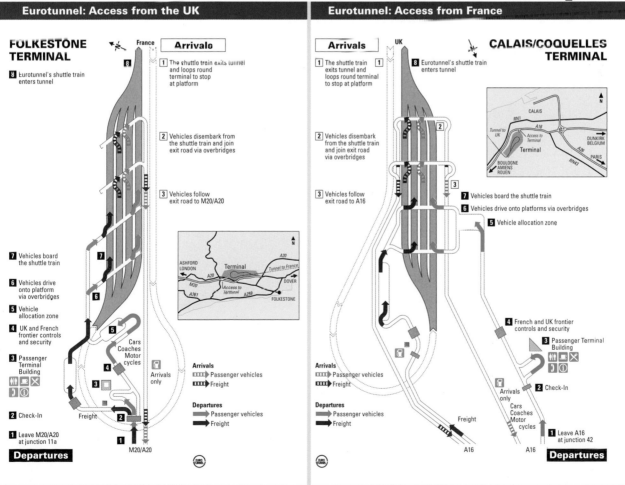

Eurotunnel: Access from the UK

FOLKESTONE TERMINAL

8 Eurotunnel's shuttle train enters tunnel

Arrivals

1 The shuttle train exits tunnel and loops round terminal to stop at platform

2 Vehicles disembark from the shuttle train and join exit road via overbridges

3 Vehicles follow exit road to M20/A20

7 Vehicles board the shuttle train

6 Vehicles drive onto platform via overbridges

5 Vehicle allocation zone

4 UK and French frontier controls and security

3 Passenger Terminal Building

2 Check-In

1 Leave M20/A20 at junction 11a

Cars Coaches Motor cycles

Arrivals only

Freight

Departures

M20/A20

Arrivals
- Passenger vehicles
- Freight

Departures
- Passenger vehicles
- Freight

Eurotunnel: Access from France

Arrivals

1 The shuttle train exits tunnel and loops round terminal to stop at platform

2 Vehicles disembark from the shuttle train and join exit road via overbridges

3 Vehicles follow exit road to A16

CALAIS/COQUELLES TERMINAL

8 Eurotunnel's shuttle train enters tunnel

CALAIS
RN1
A16
Tunnel to UK
Terminal
Access to Terminal
BOULOGNE AMIENS ROUEN
DUNKIRK BELGIUM
PARIS
RN43
N

7 Vehicles board the shuttle train

6 Vehicles drive onto platforms via overbridges

5 Vehicle allocation zone

4 French and UK frontier controls and security

3 Passenger Terminal Building

2 Check-In

Arrivals only

Cars Coaches Motor cycles

Freight

1 Leave A16 at junction 42

A16   A16

Departures

Arrivals
- Passenger vehicles
- Freight

Departures
- Passenger vehicles
- Freight

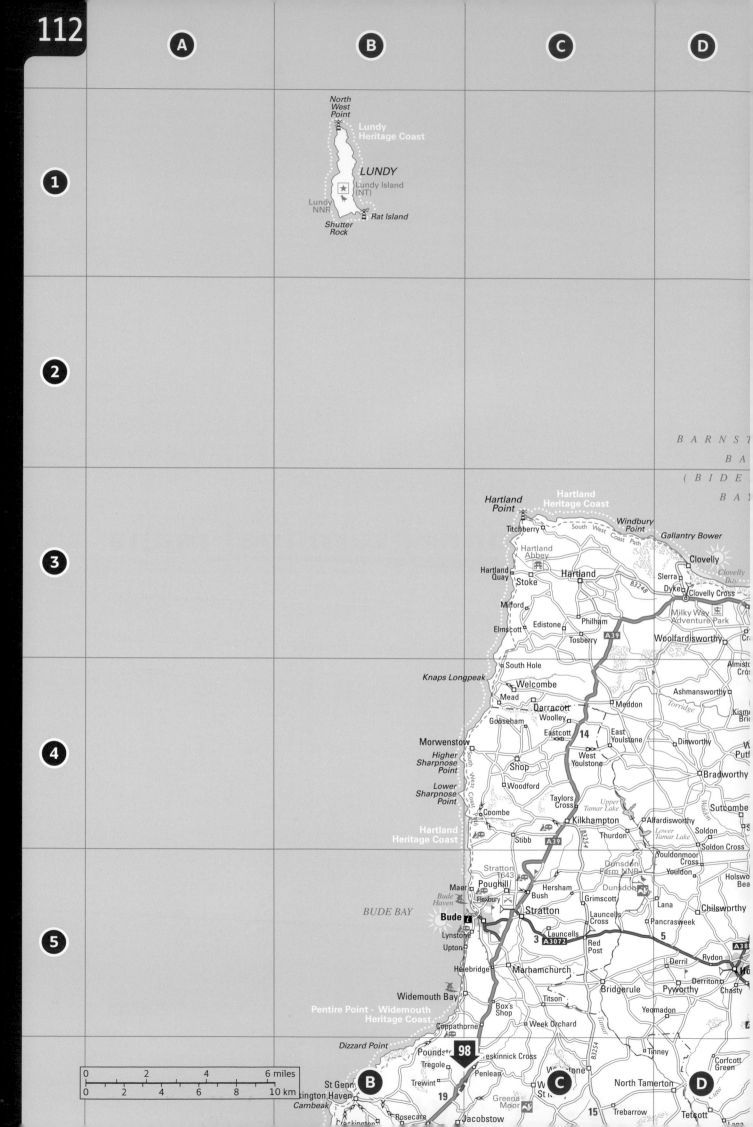

North West Point

Lundy Heritage Coast

LUNDY

Lundy Island (NT)

Lundy NNR

Shutter Rock

Rat Island

BARNST

BA

(BIDE

BAY

Hartland Heritage Coast

Hartland Point

Titchberry

South West Coast Path

Windbury Point

Gallantry Bower

Hartland Abbey

Clovelly

Hartland

Slerra

Clovelly Bay

Hartland Quay

Stoke

B3248

Dyke

Clovelly Cross

Milford

Milky Way Adventure Park

Elmscott

Edistone

Philham

Woolfardisworthy

Cr

Tosberry

A39

Almisto Cross

South Hole

Knaps Longpeak

Welcombe

Ashmansworthy

Kism

Bri

Mead

Torridge

Darracott

Meddon

Woolley

Gooseham

Eastcott

14

East Youlstone

Dinworthy

Morwenstow

West Youlstone

Higher Sharpnose Point

Shop

Bradworthy

South West Coast

Woodford

Upper Tamar Lake

Sutcombe

Lower Sharpnose Point

Taylors Cross

Coombe

Lower Tamar Lake

Kilkhampton

Alfardisworthy

Put

Hartland Heritage Coast

Stibb

A39

B3254

Thurdon

Soldon

Soldon Cross

Youldonmoor Cross

Dunsdon Farm NNR

Youldon

Stratton

1643

Dunsdon

Holsw Bea

Maer

Poughill

Hersham Bush

Grimscott

Lana

Chilsworthy

Bude Haven

Flexbury

Stratton

Launcells Cross

BUDE BAY

Bude

Pancrasweek

Lynstone

3

Launcells

Red Post

5

A38

Upton

A3072

Derril

Rydon

U

Helebridge

Marhamchurch

Derriton

Chasty

Widemouth Bay

Bridgerule

Pyworthy

Pentire Point - Widemouth Heritage Coast

Box's Shop

Titson

Yeomadon

Coppathorne

Week Orchard

Tamar

Tinney

Dizzard Point

Poundst

98

eskinnick Cross

W

Corfcott Green

Tregole

Penlean

North Tamerton

Tetcott

St Genn

Trewint

Greena Moor

Trebarrow

Cambeak

19

St

15

Rosecare

Jacobstow

0   2   4   6 miles

0   2   4   6   8   10 km

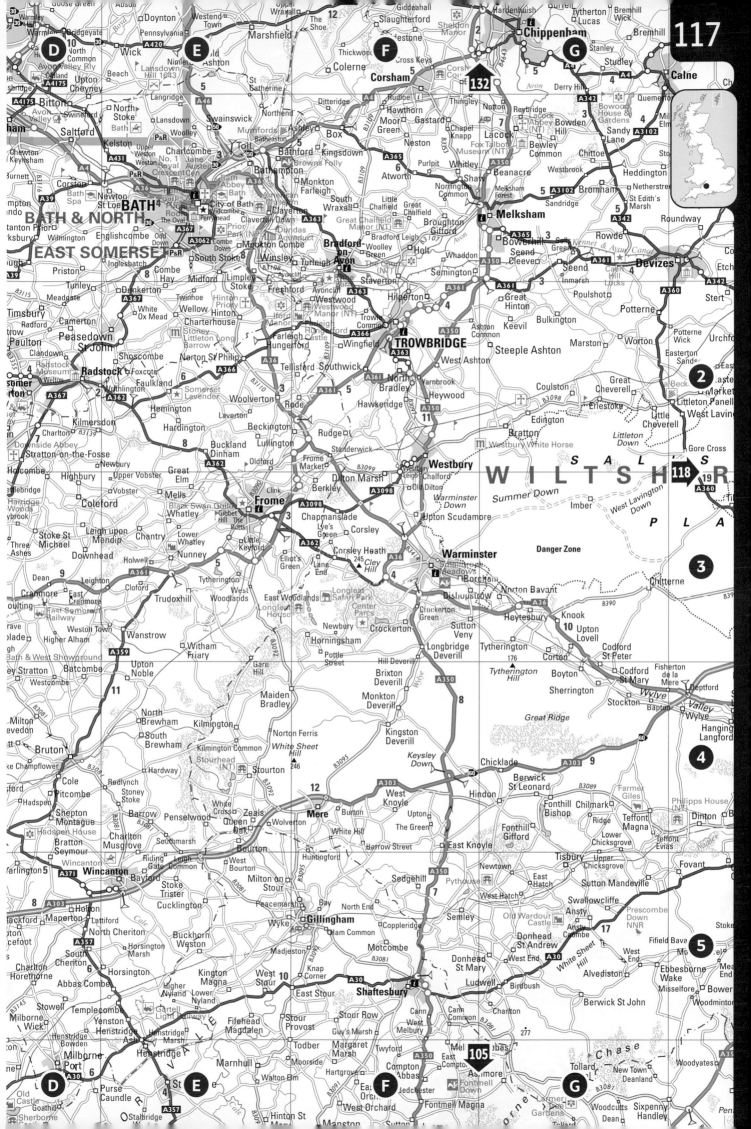

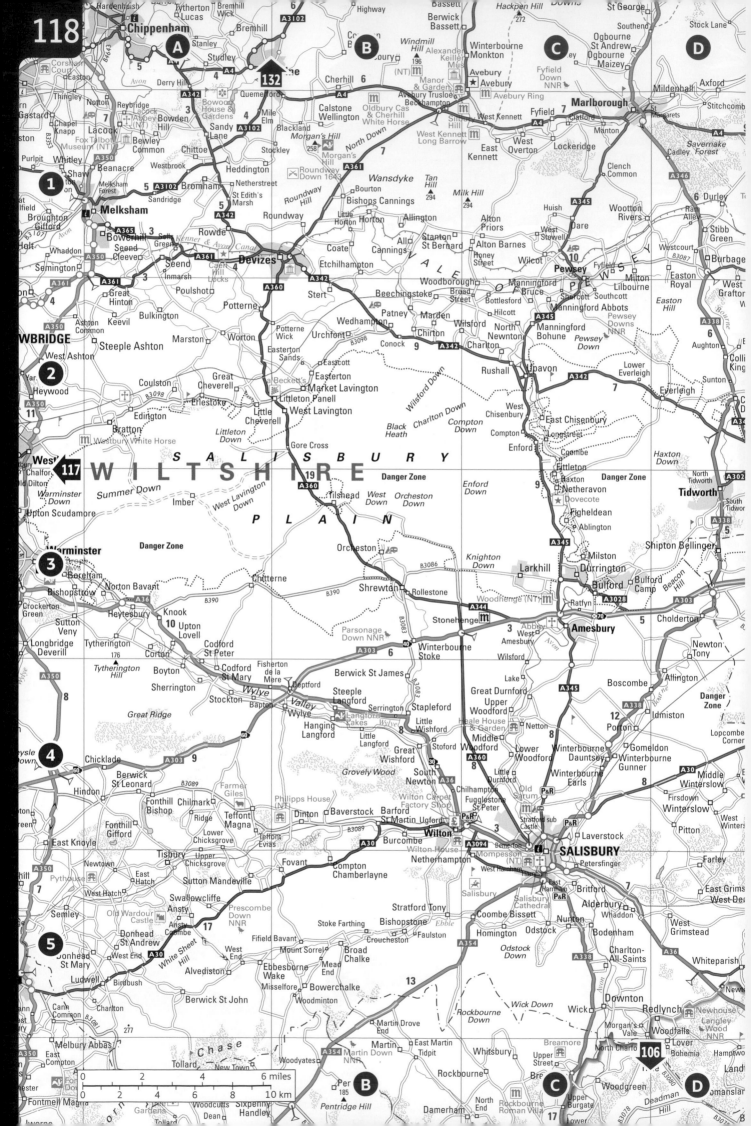

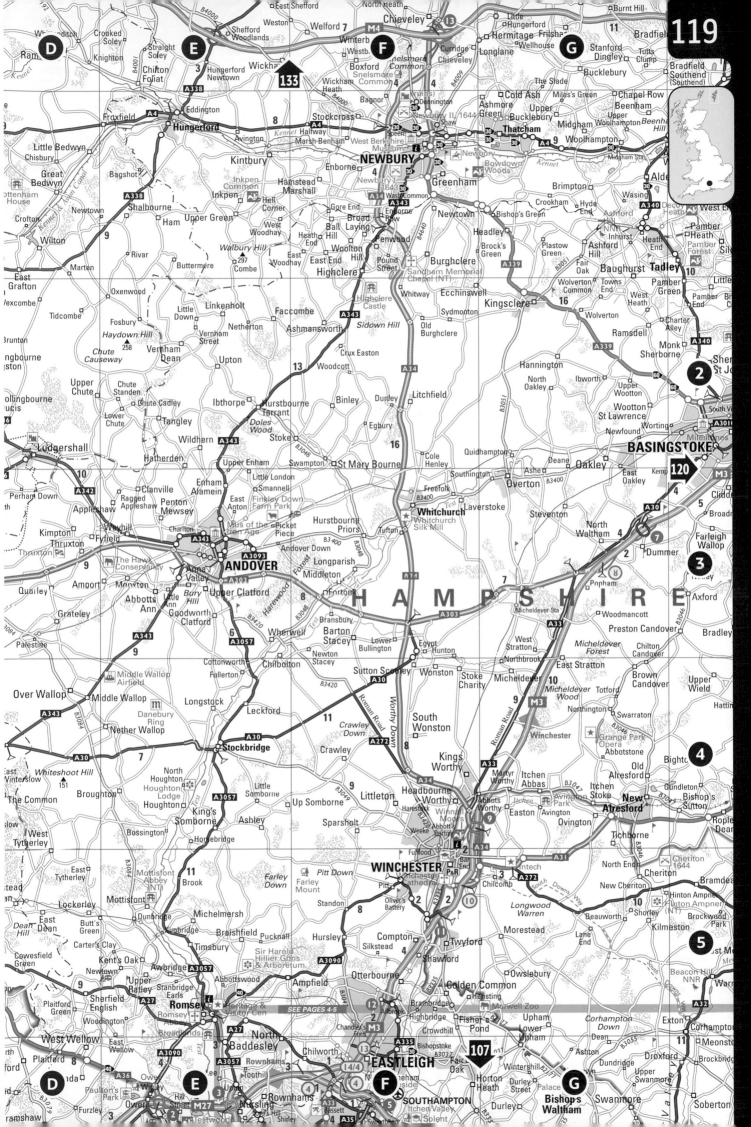

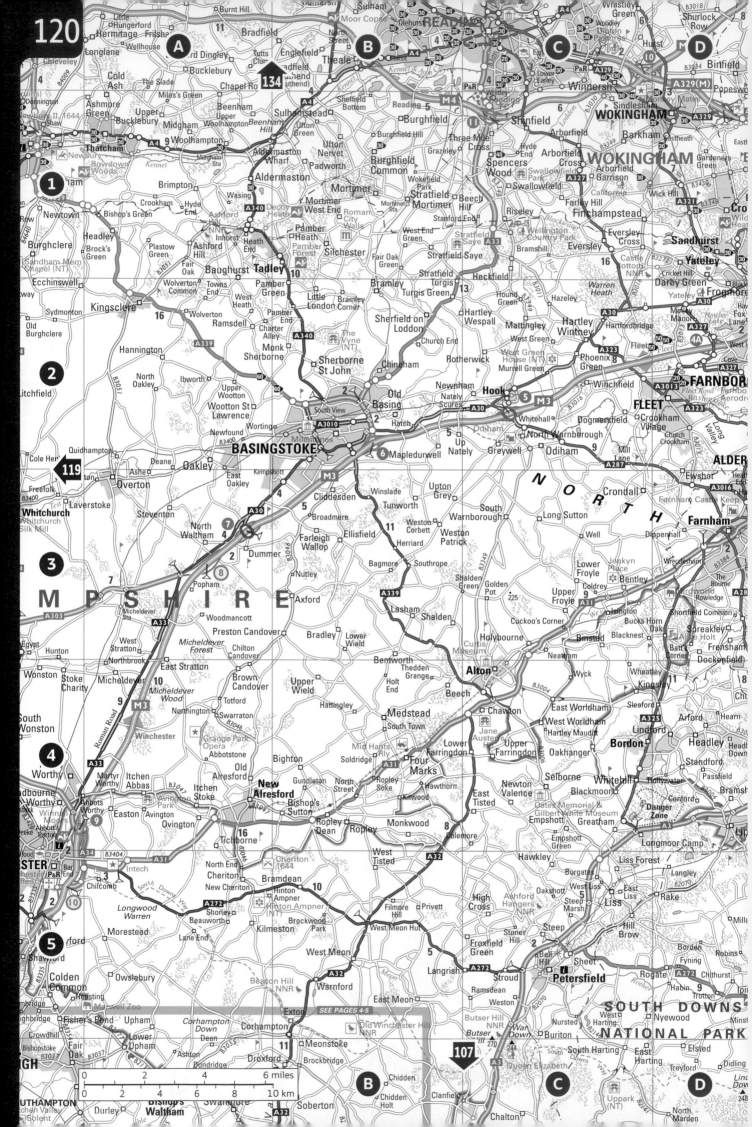

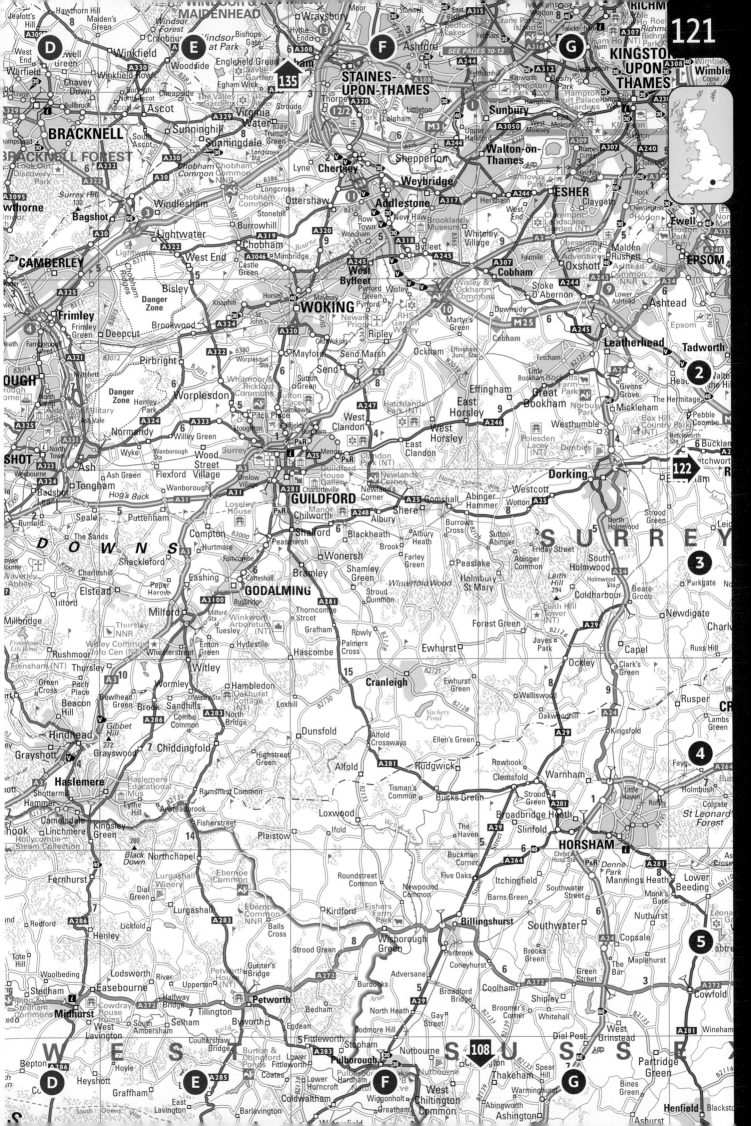

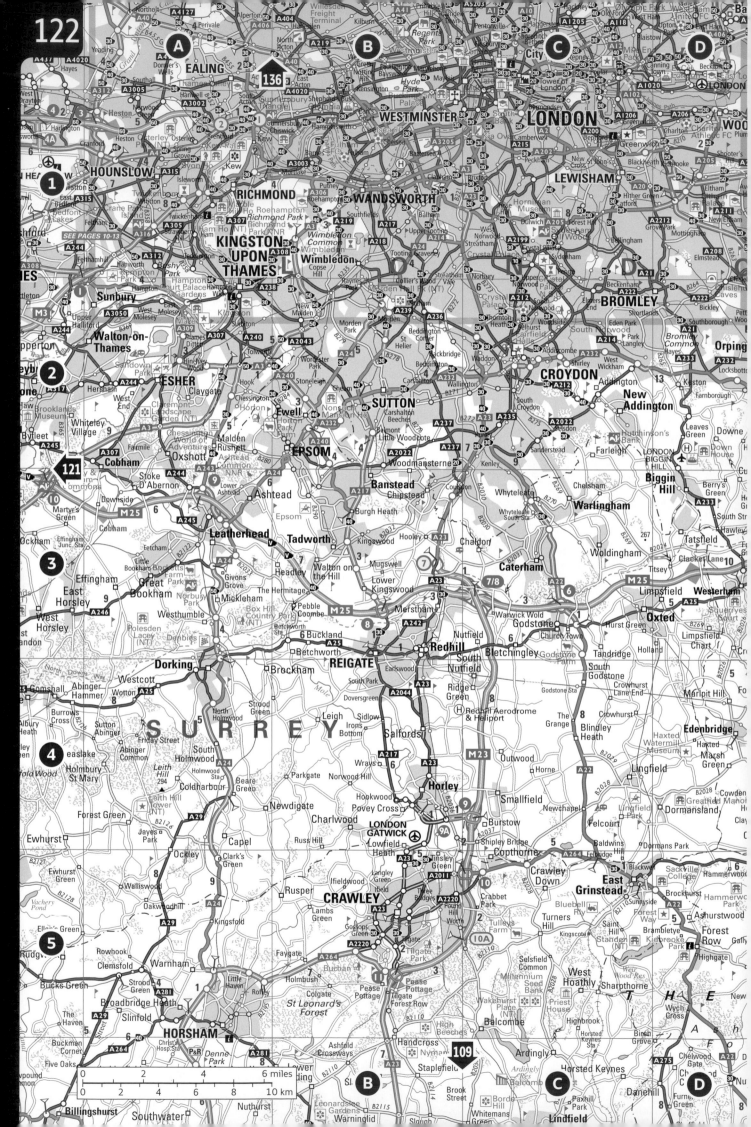

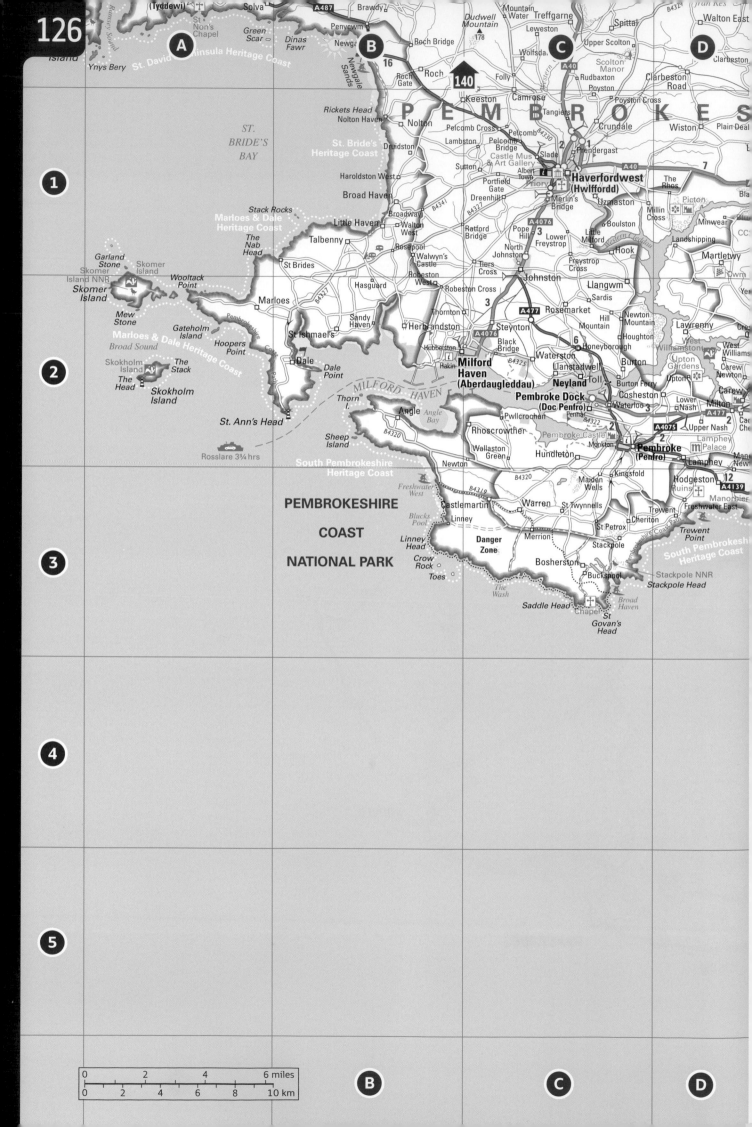

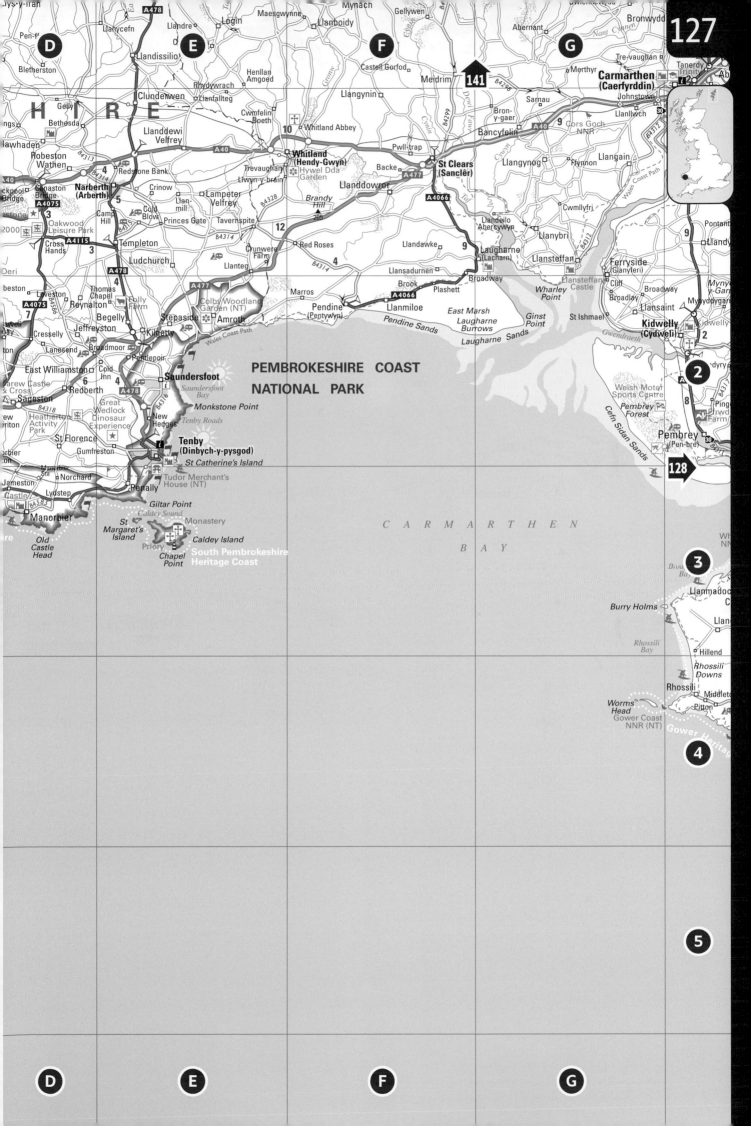

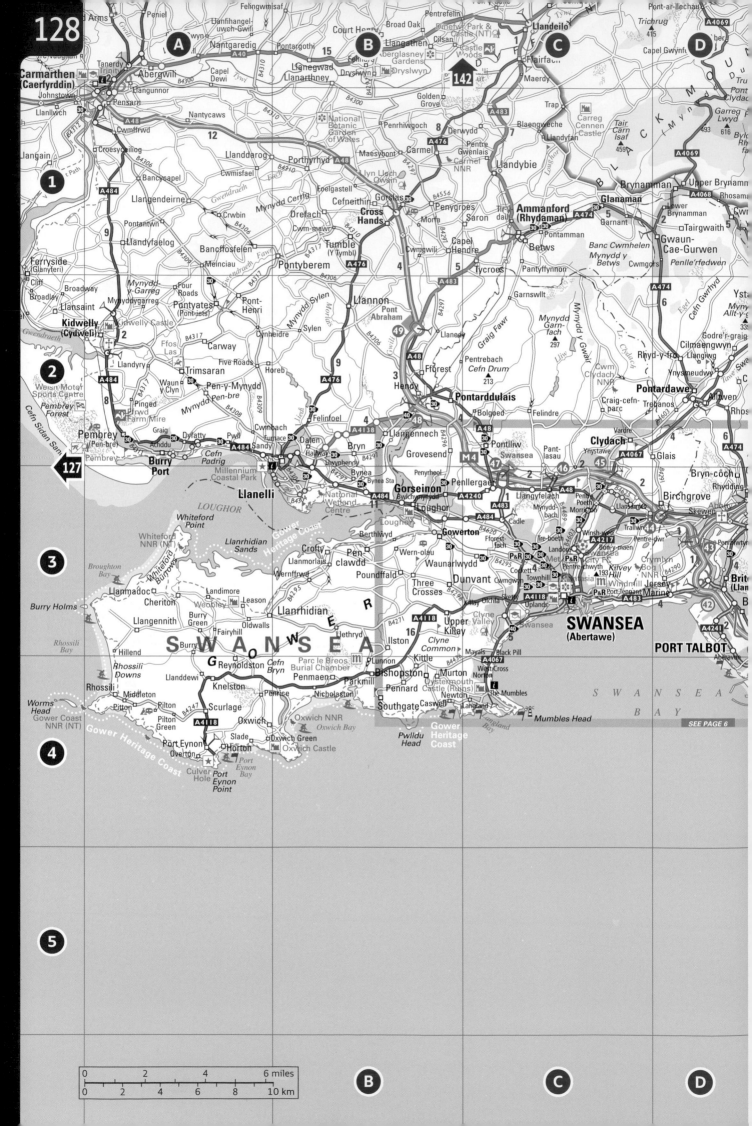

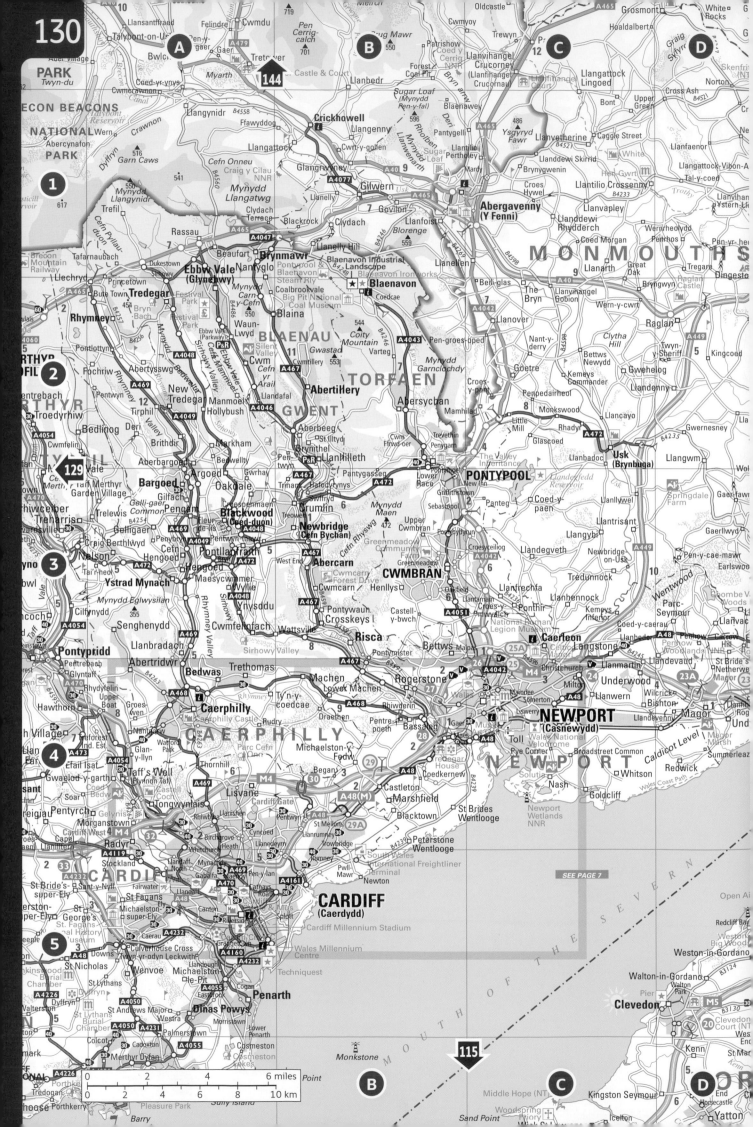

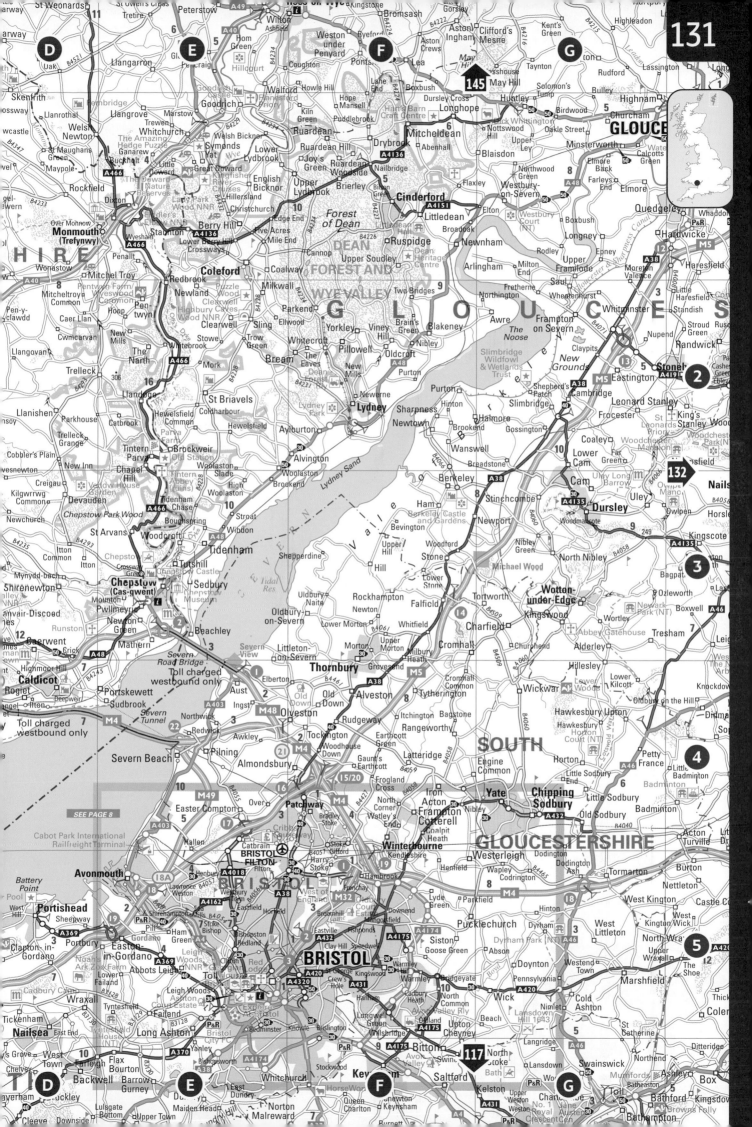

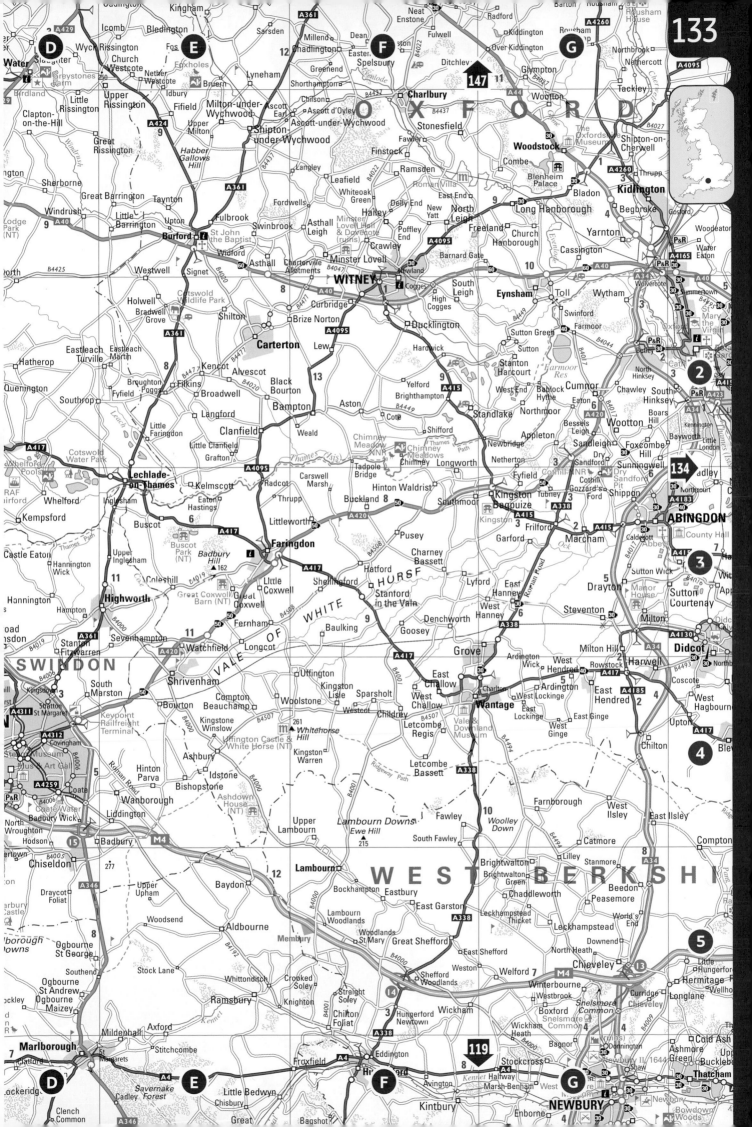

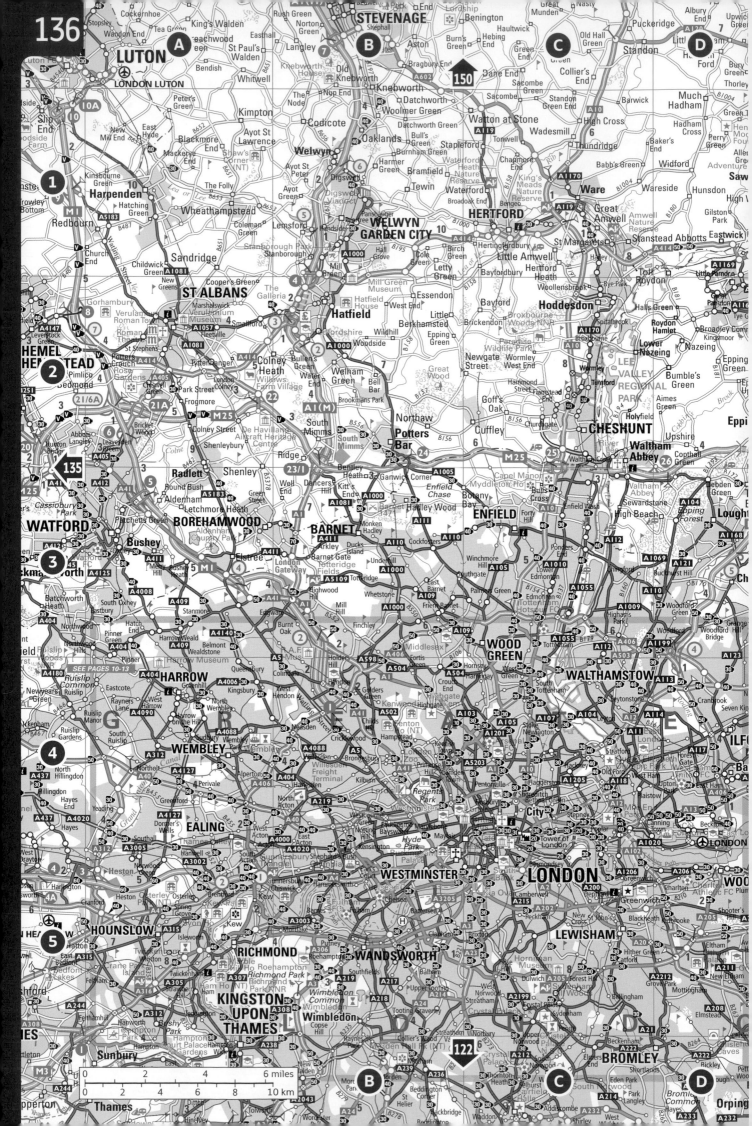

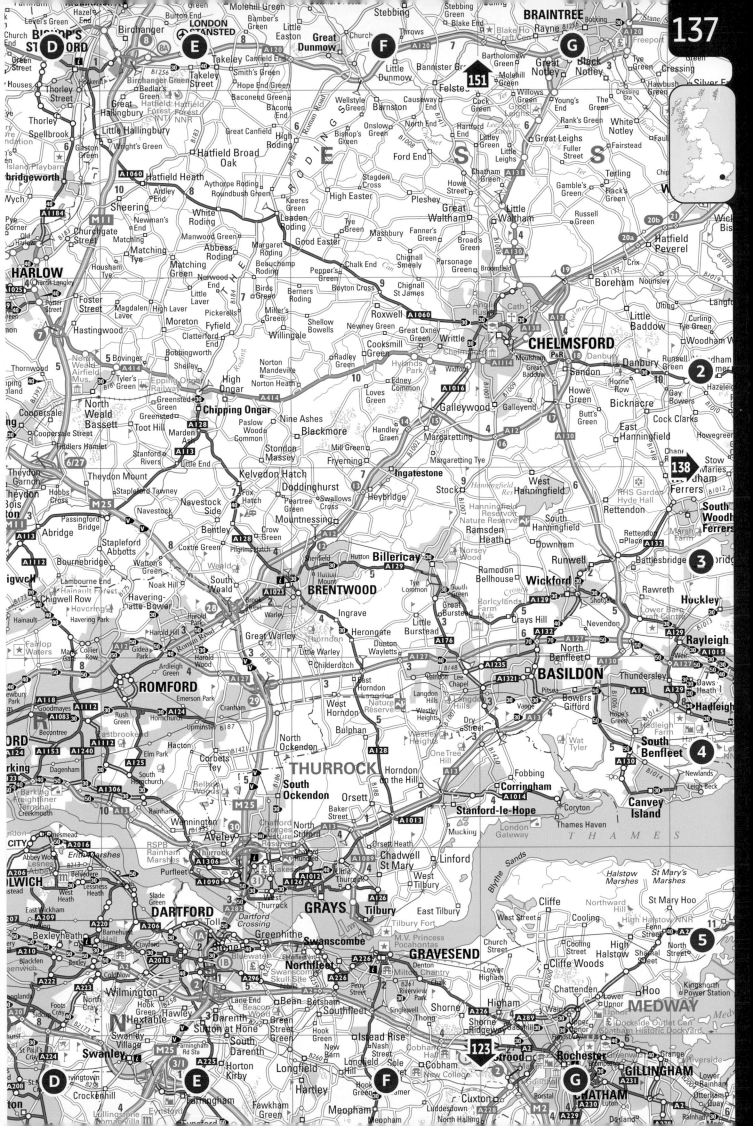

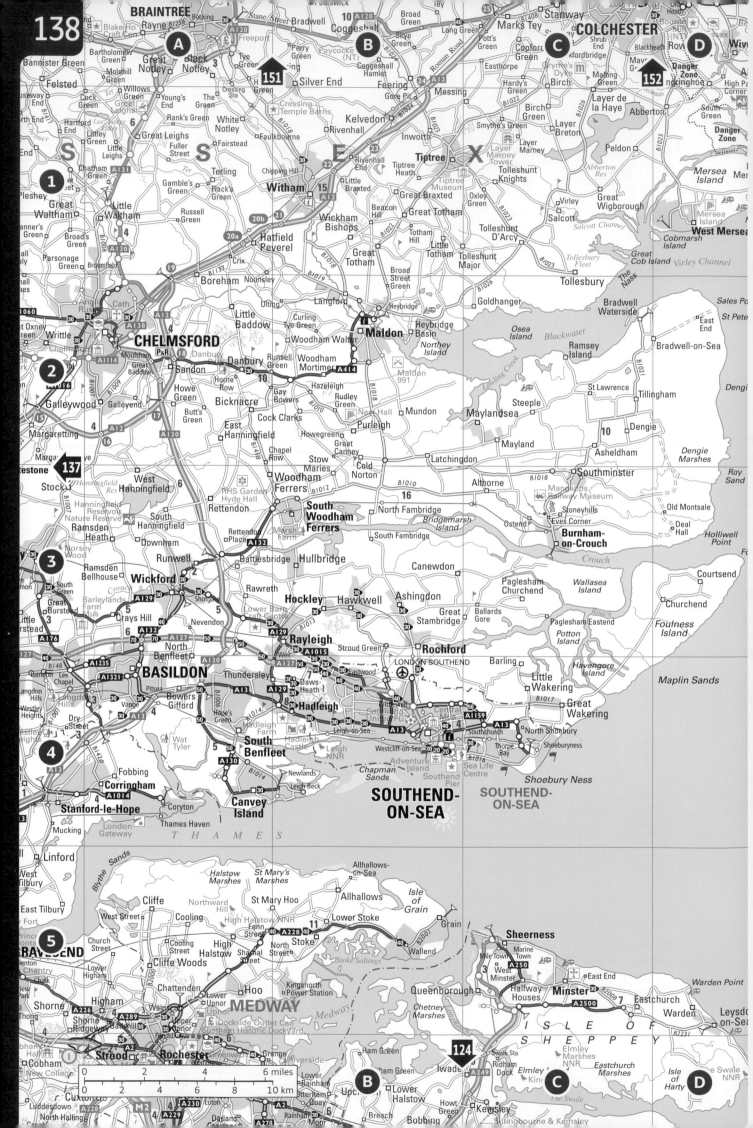

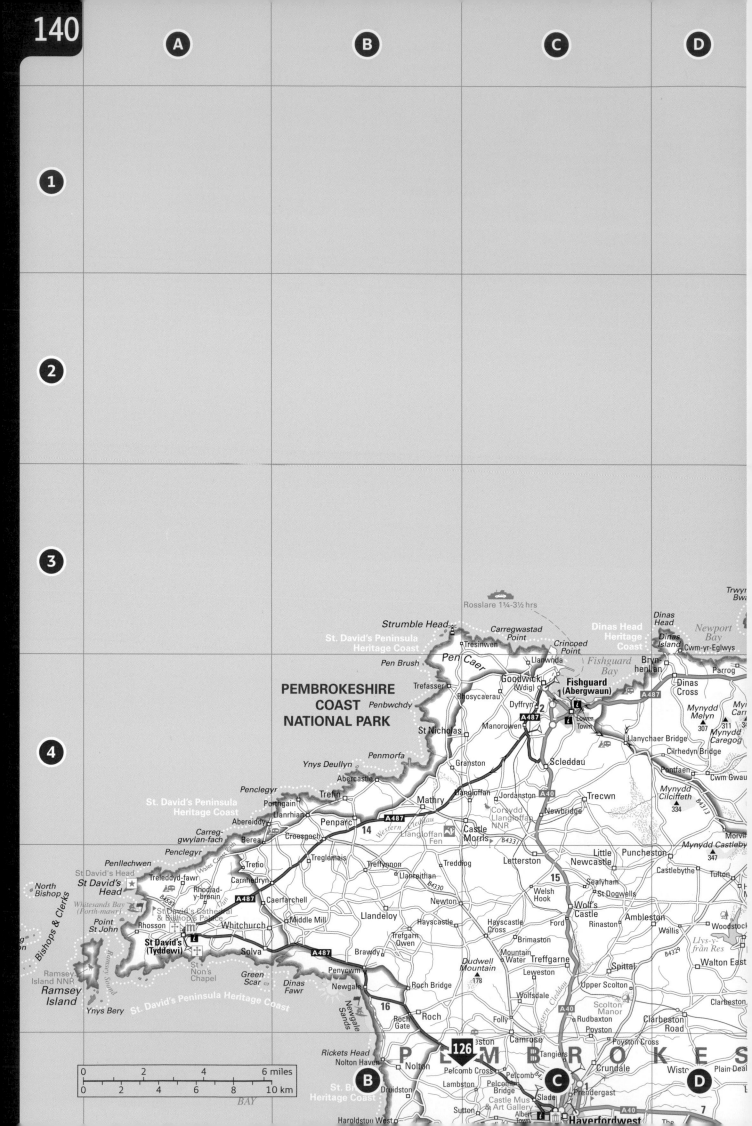

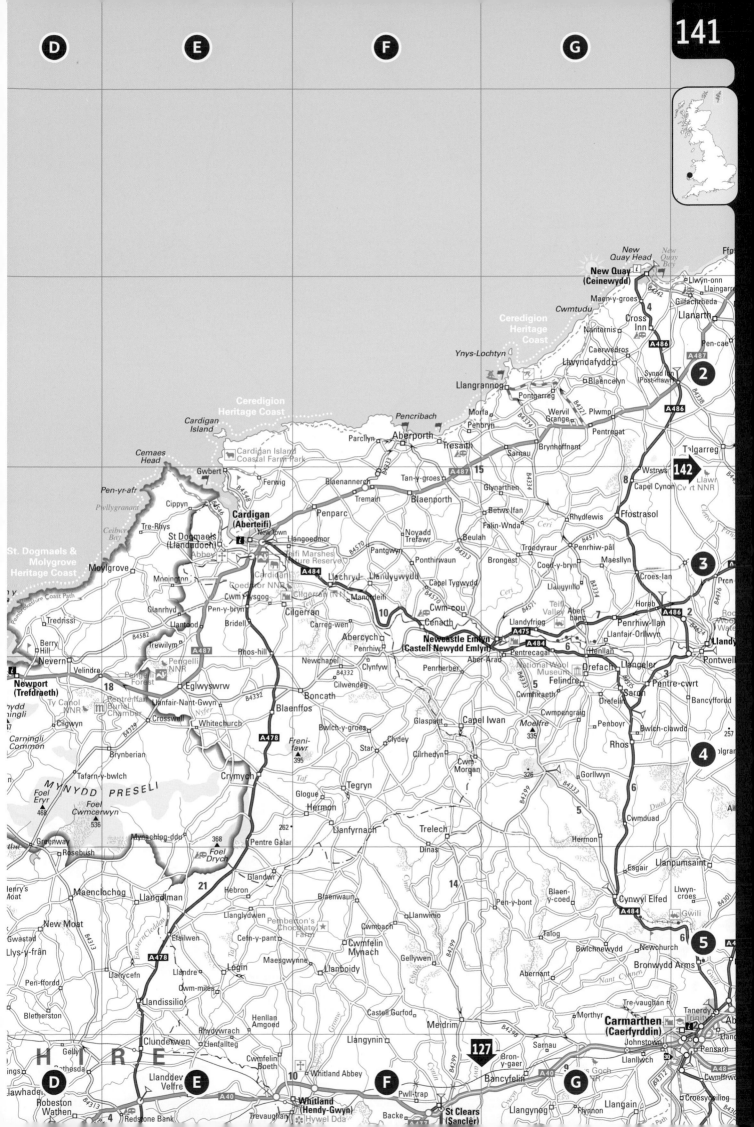

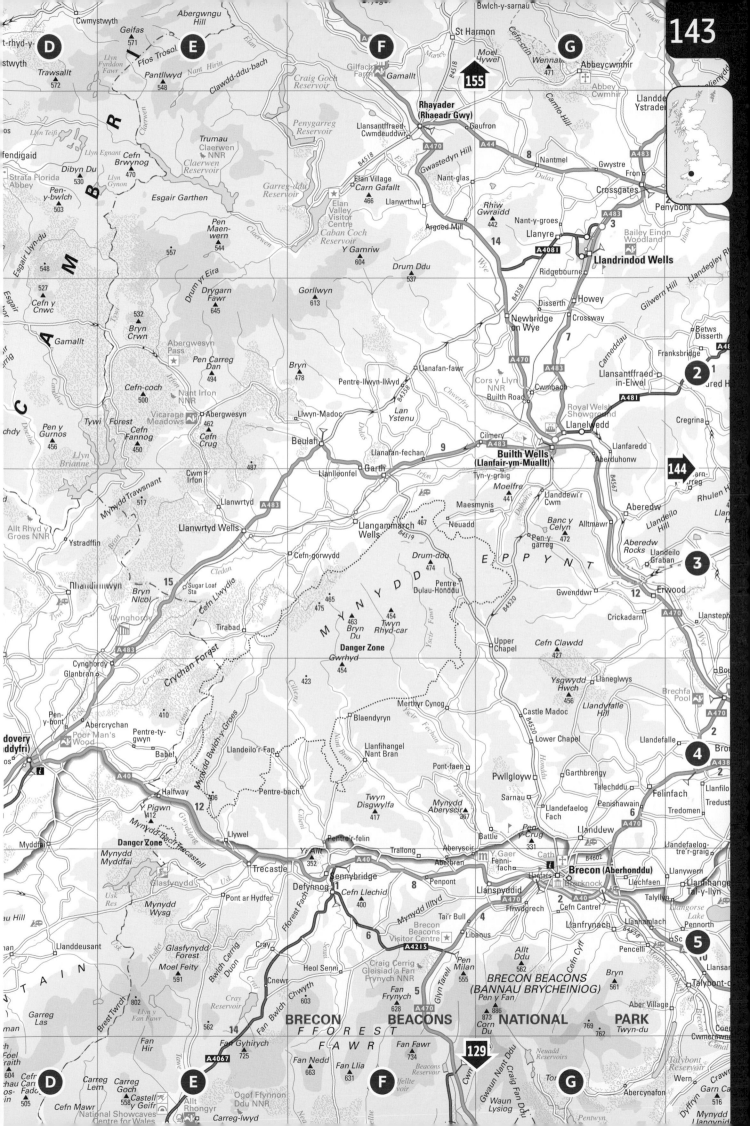

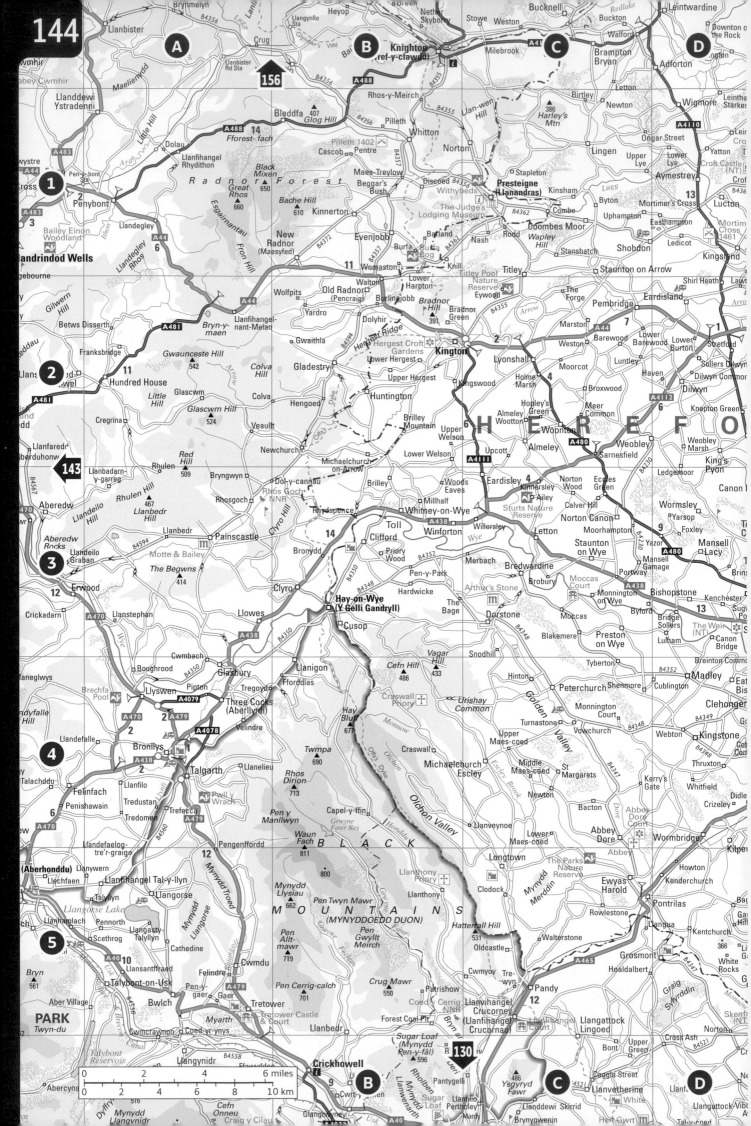

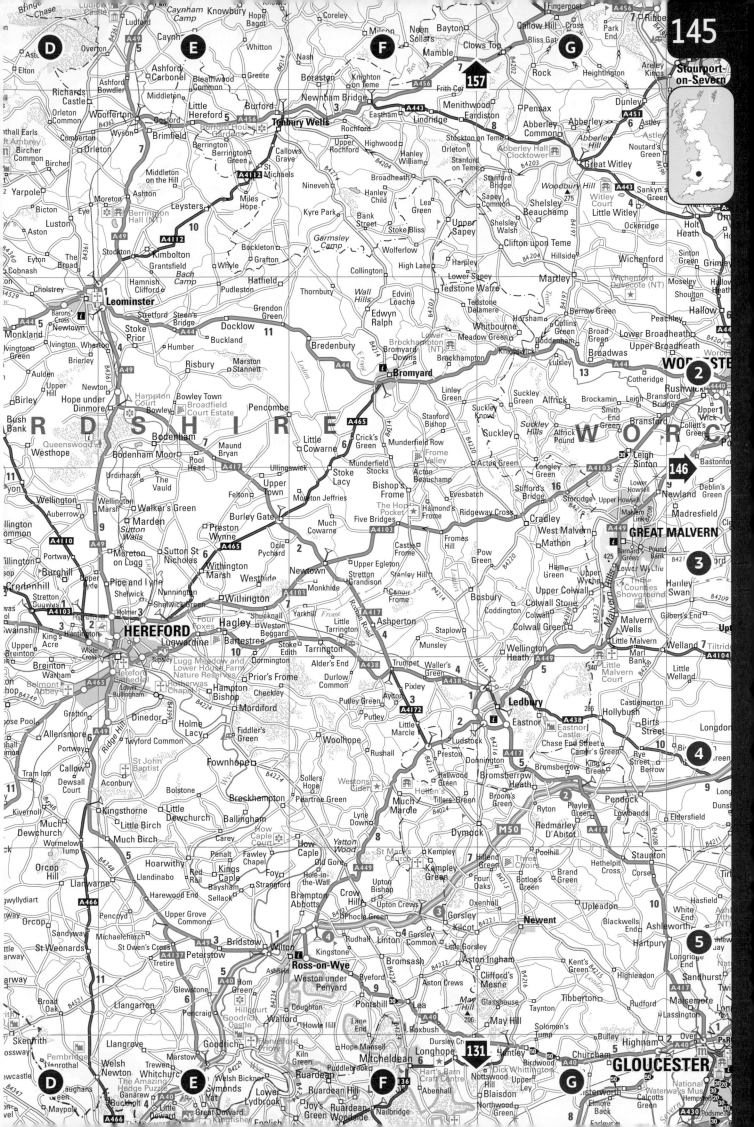

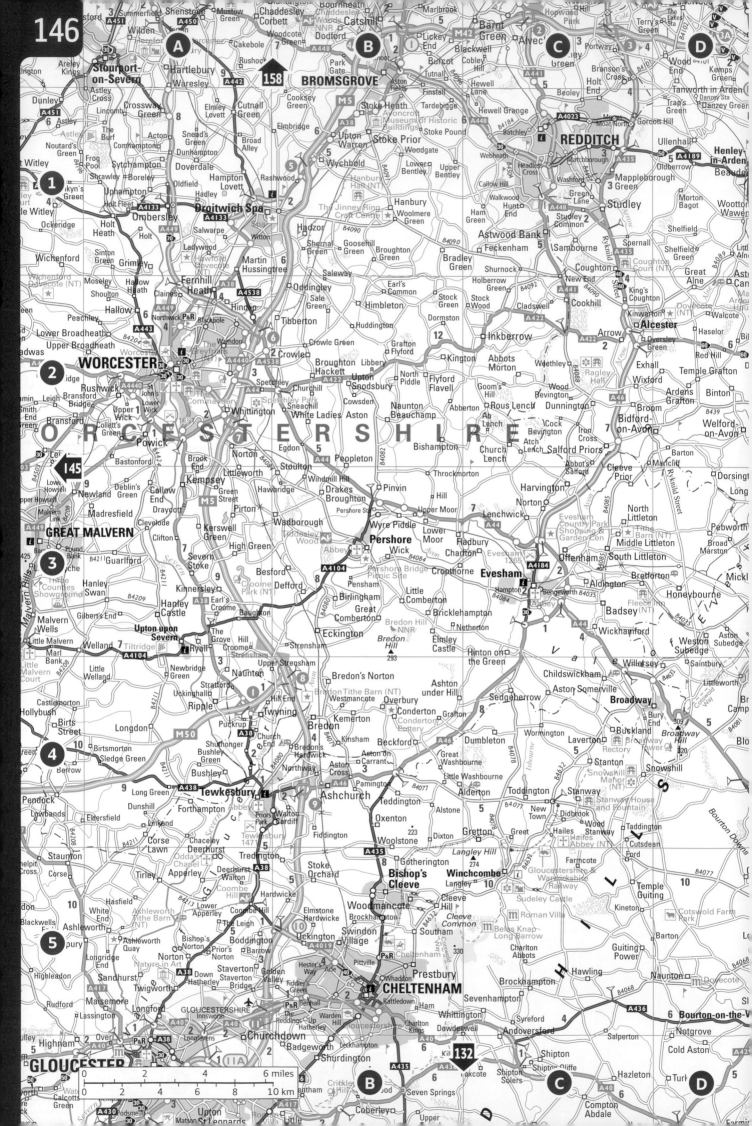

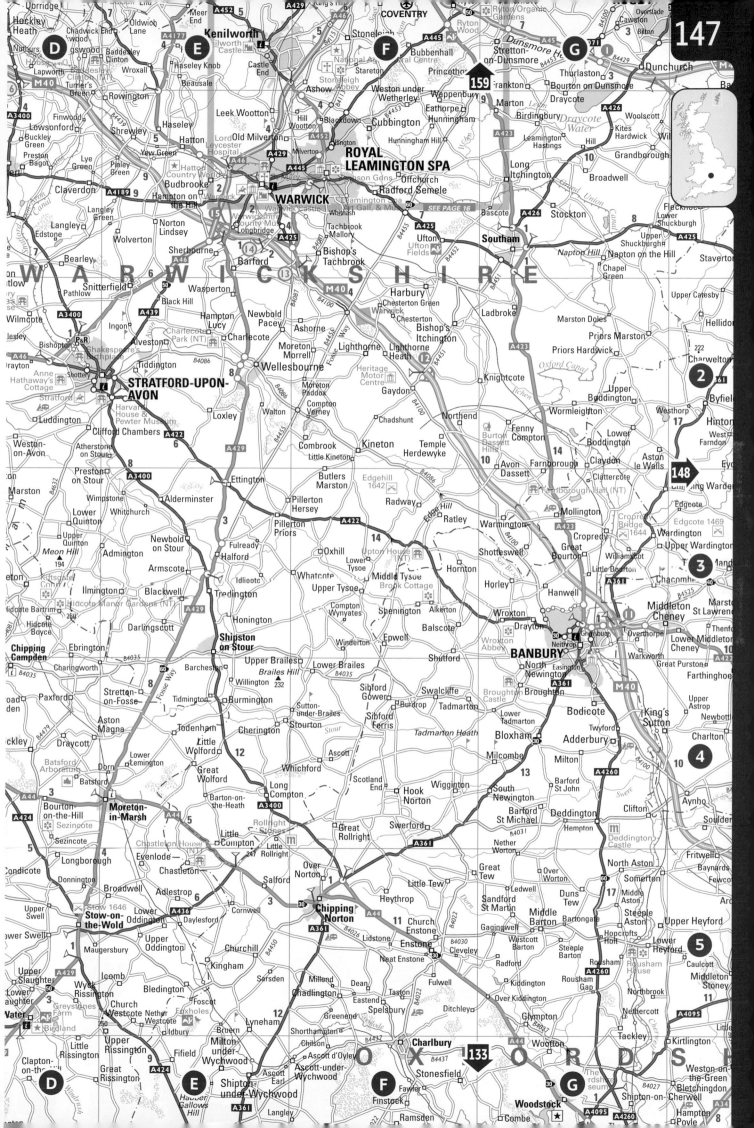

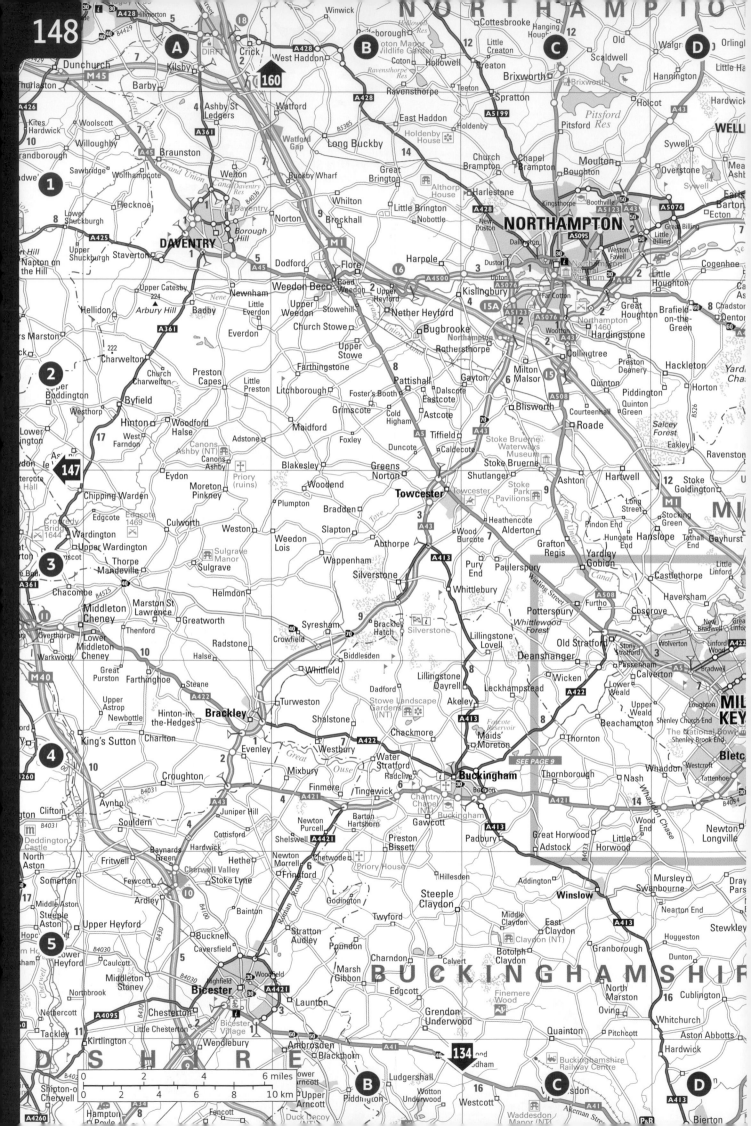

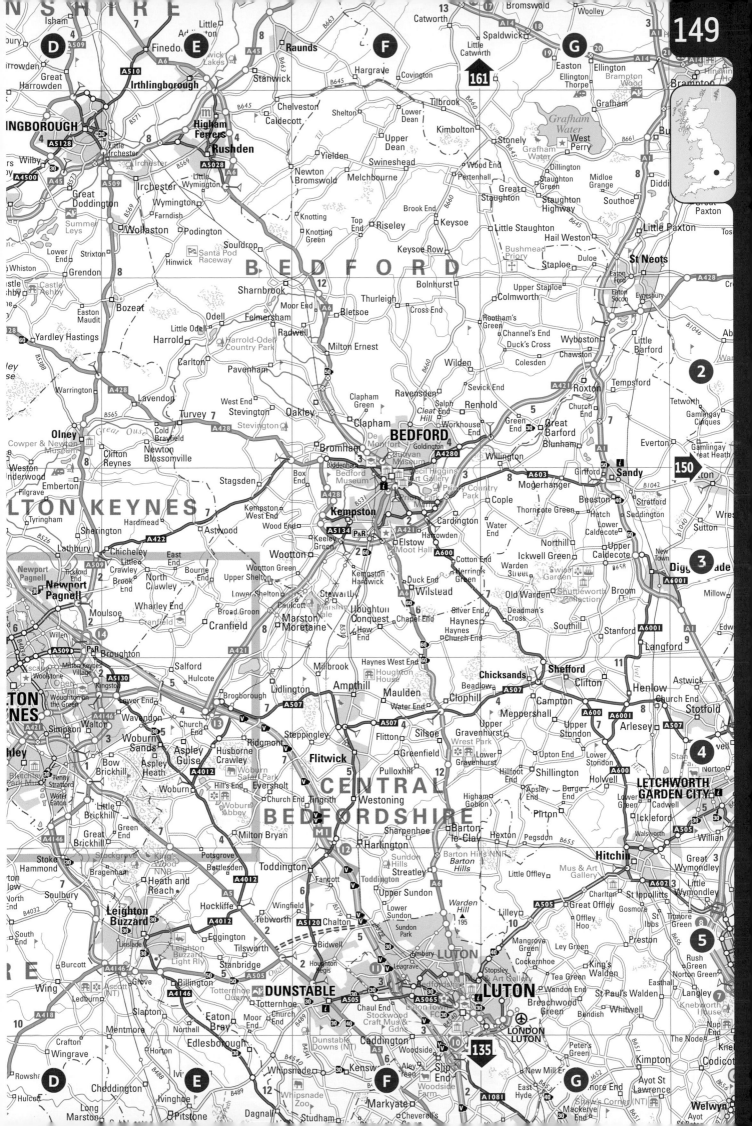

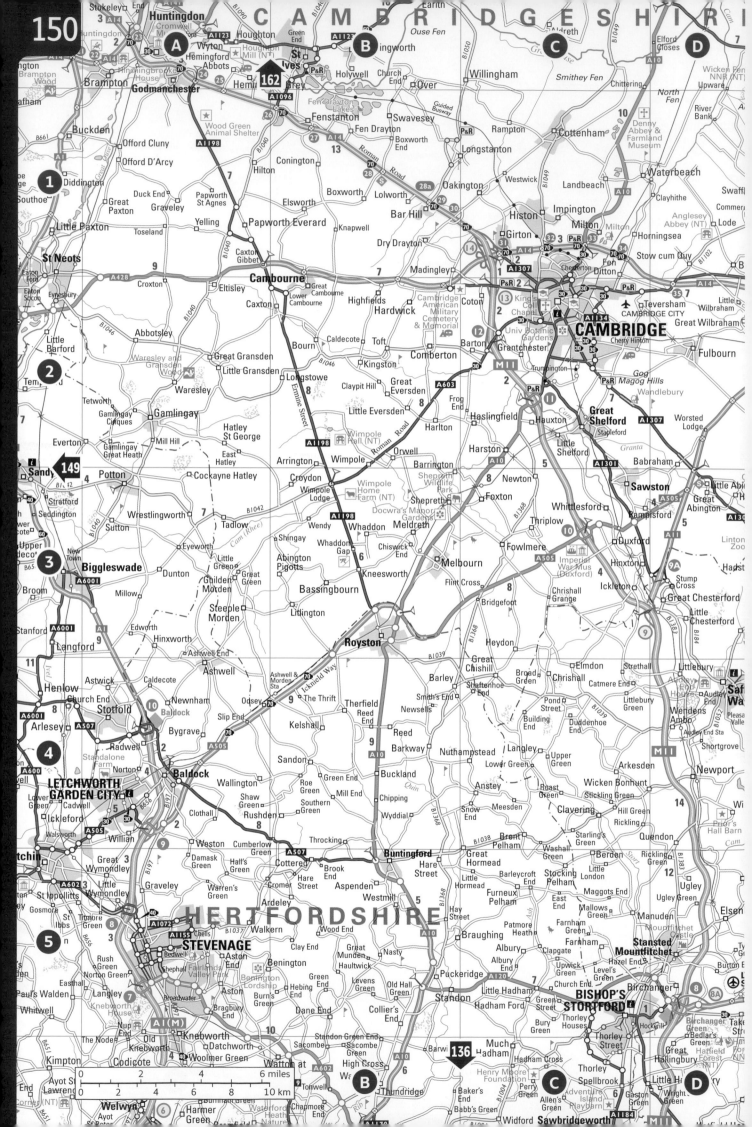

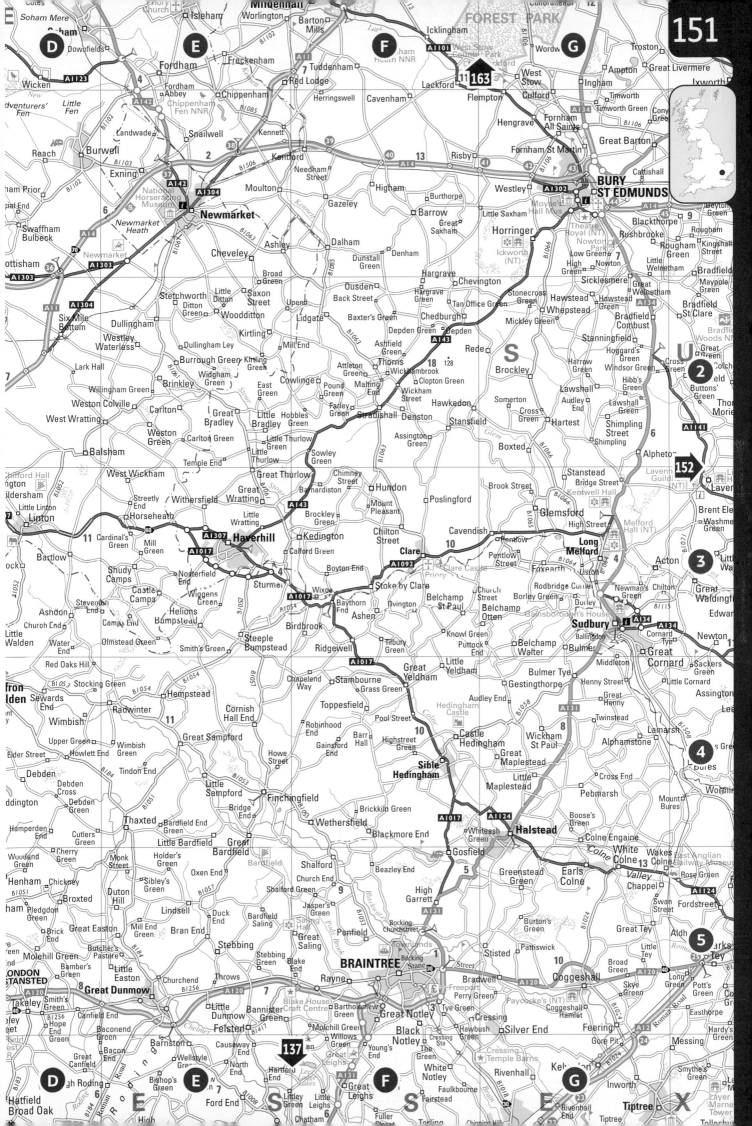

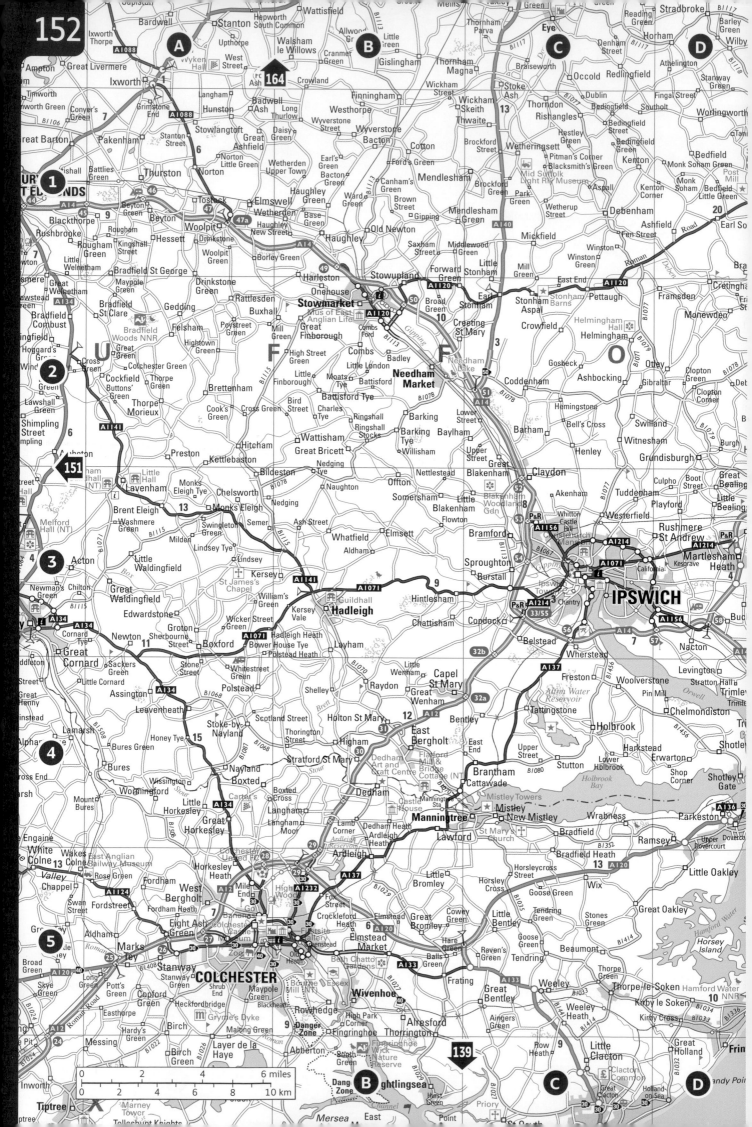

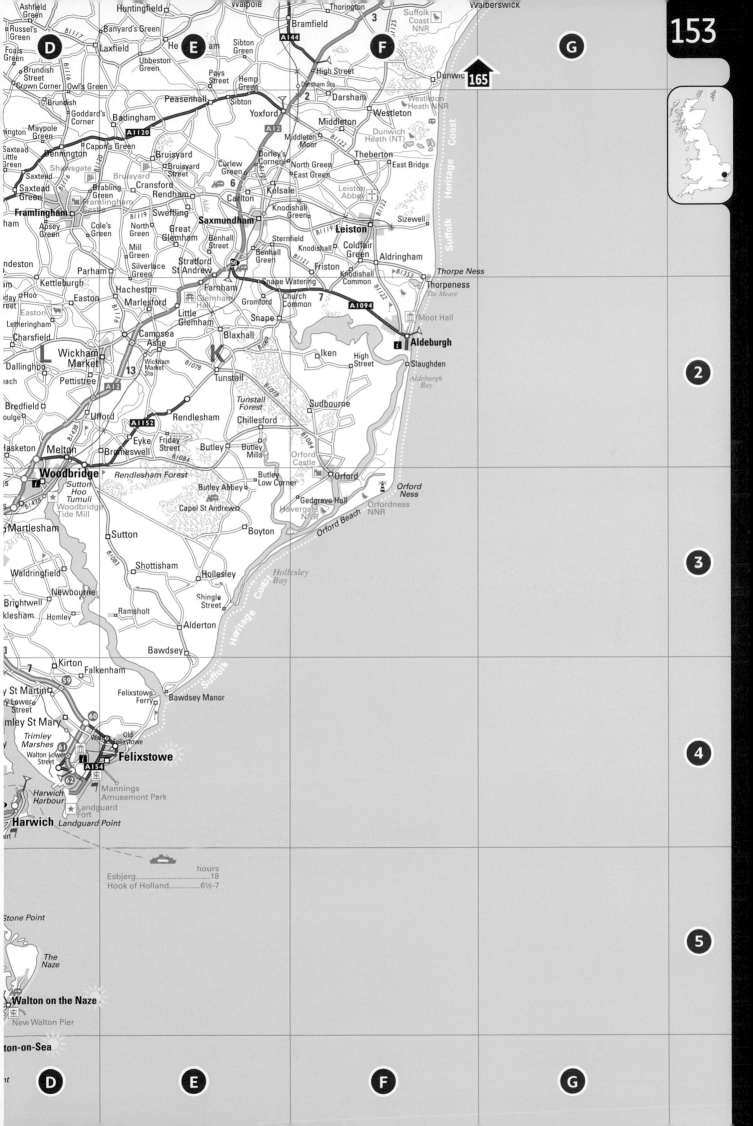

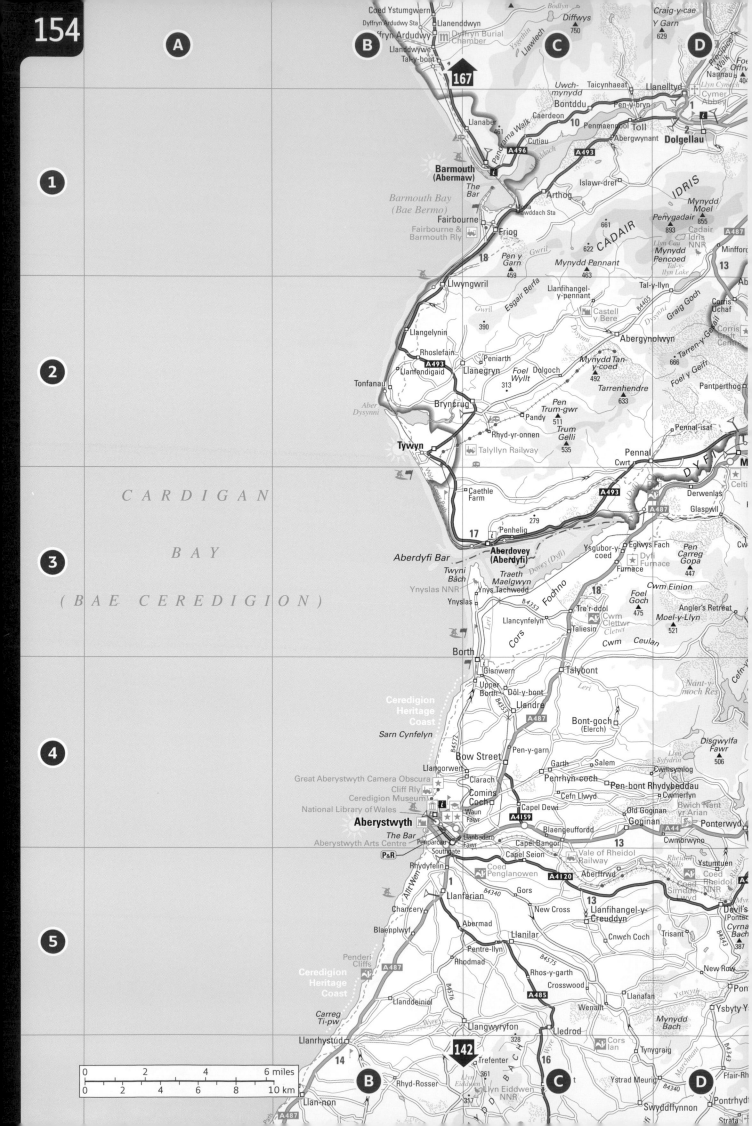

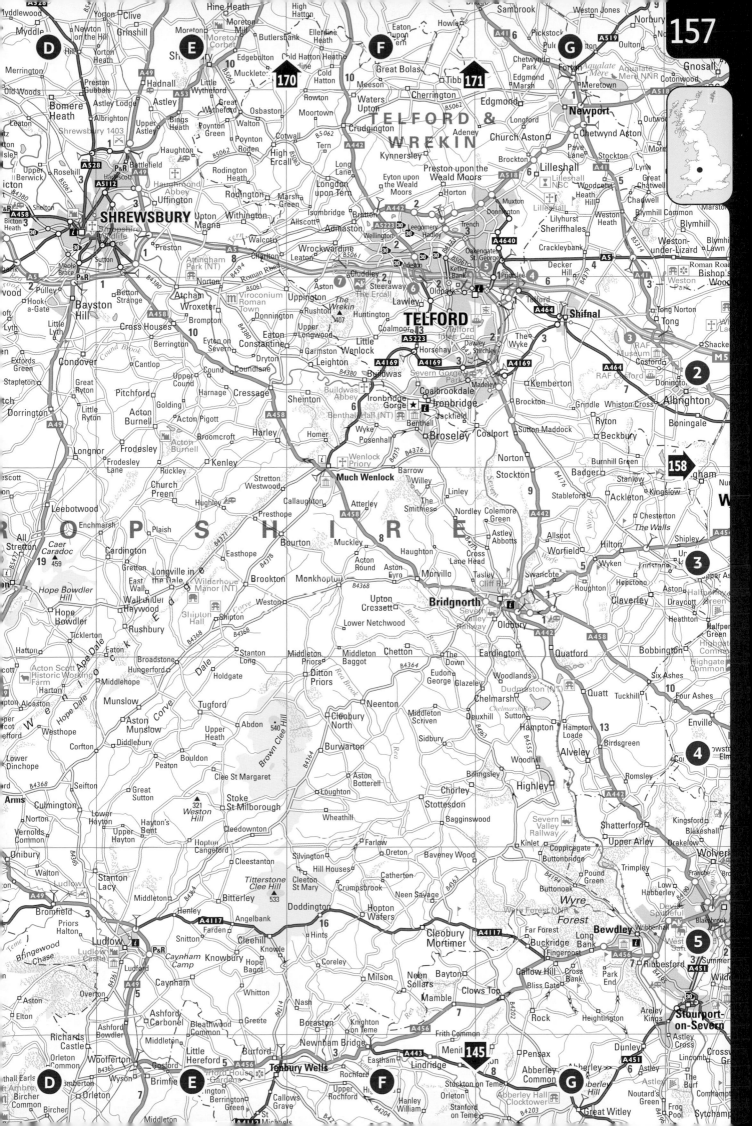

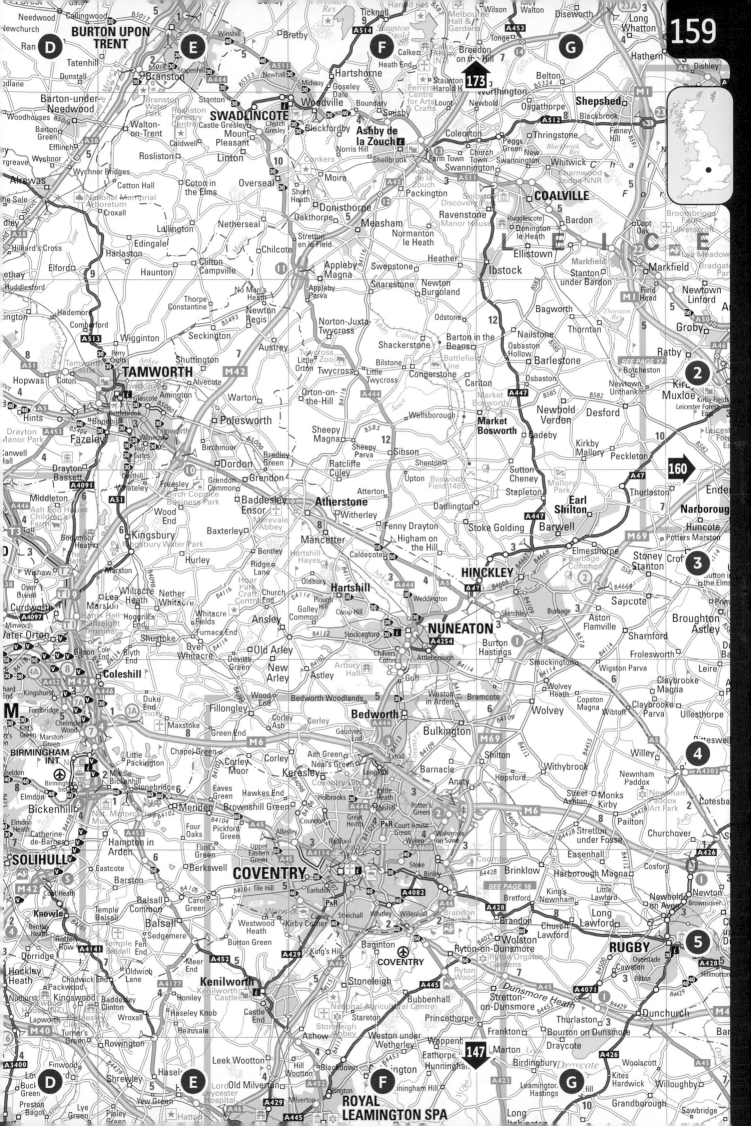

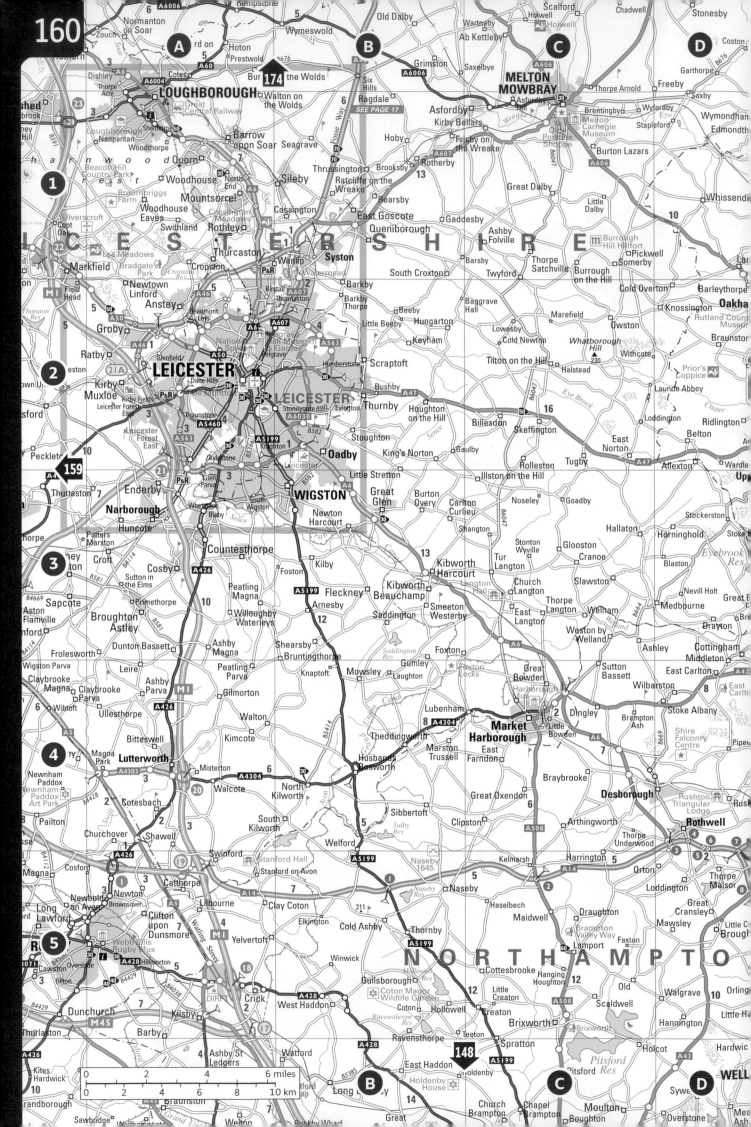

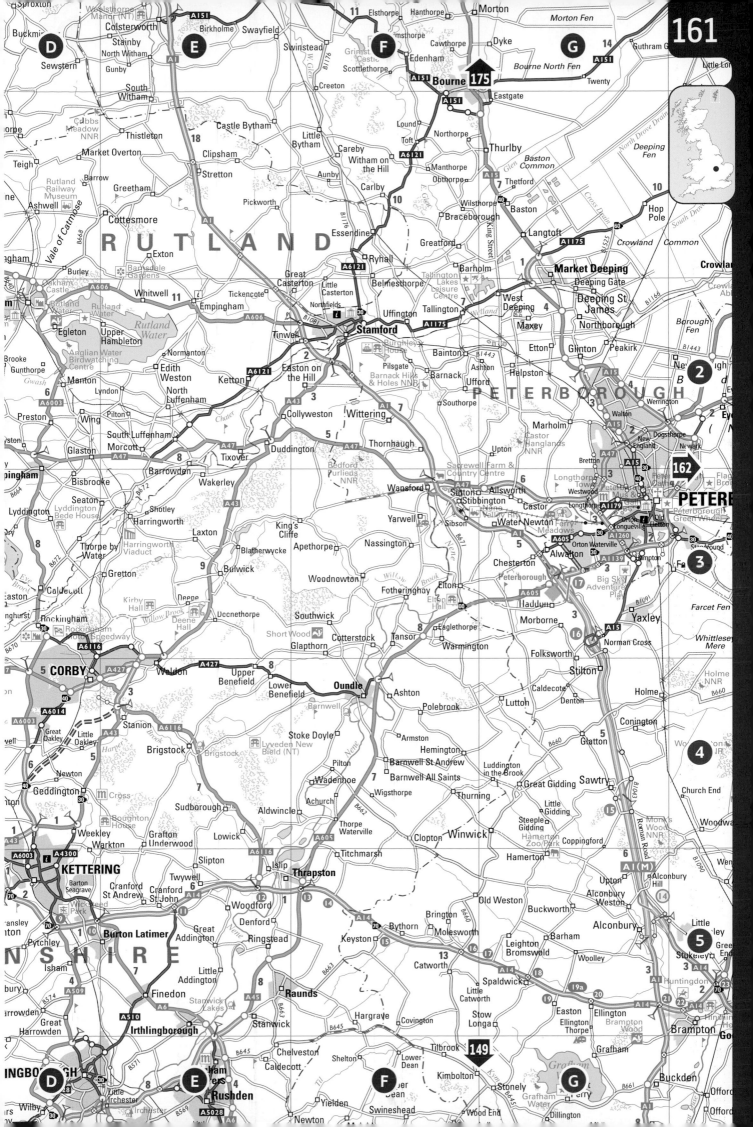

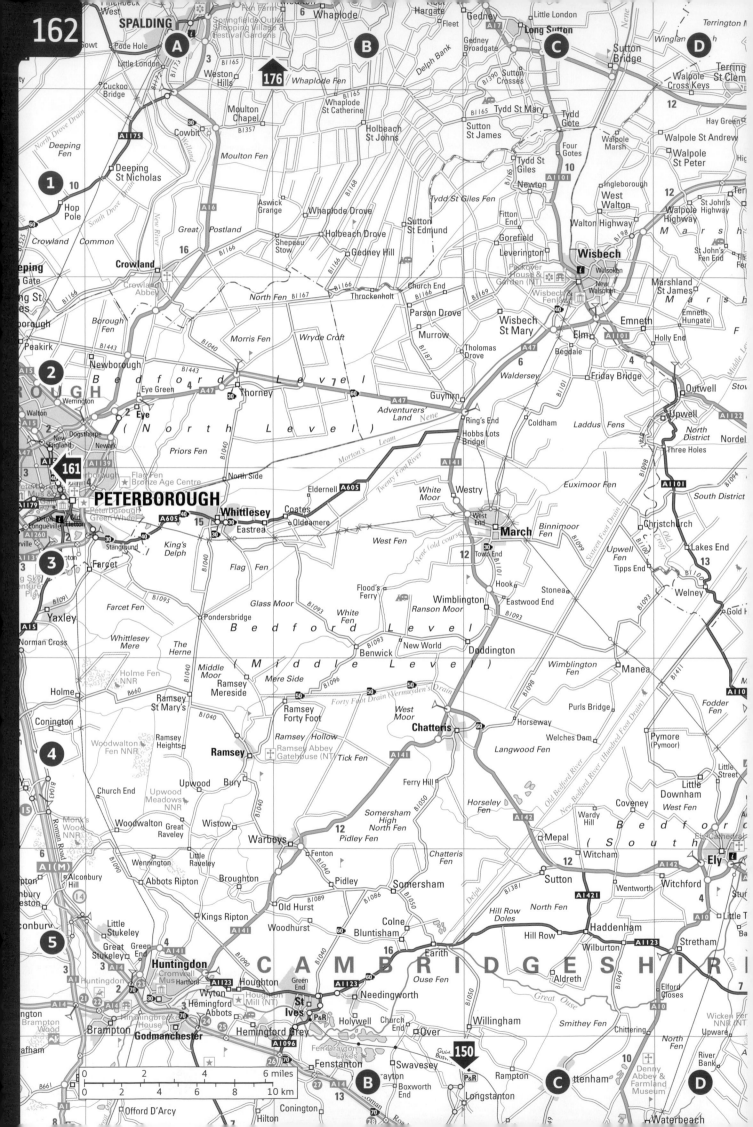

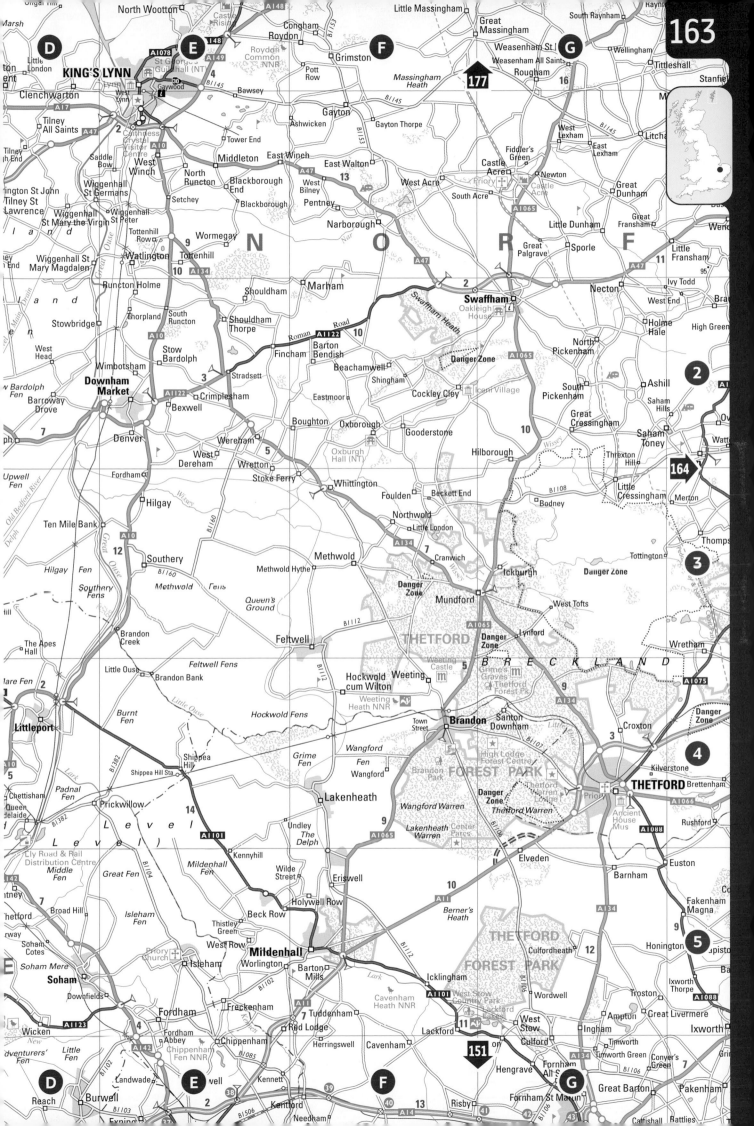

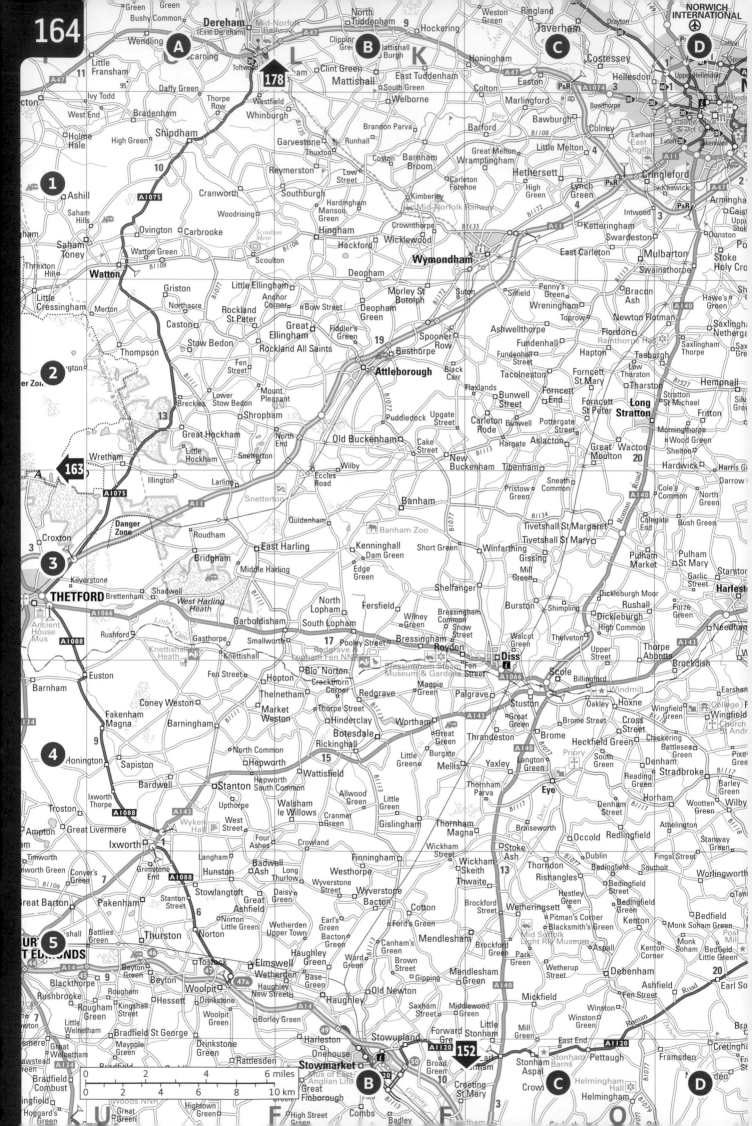

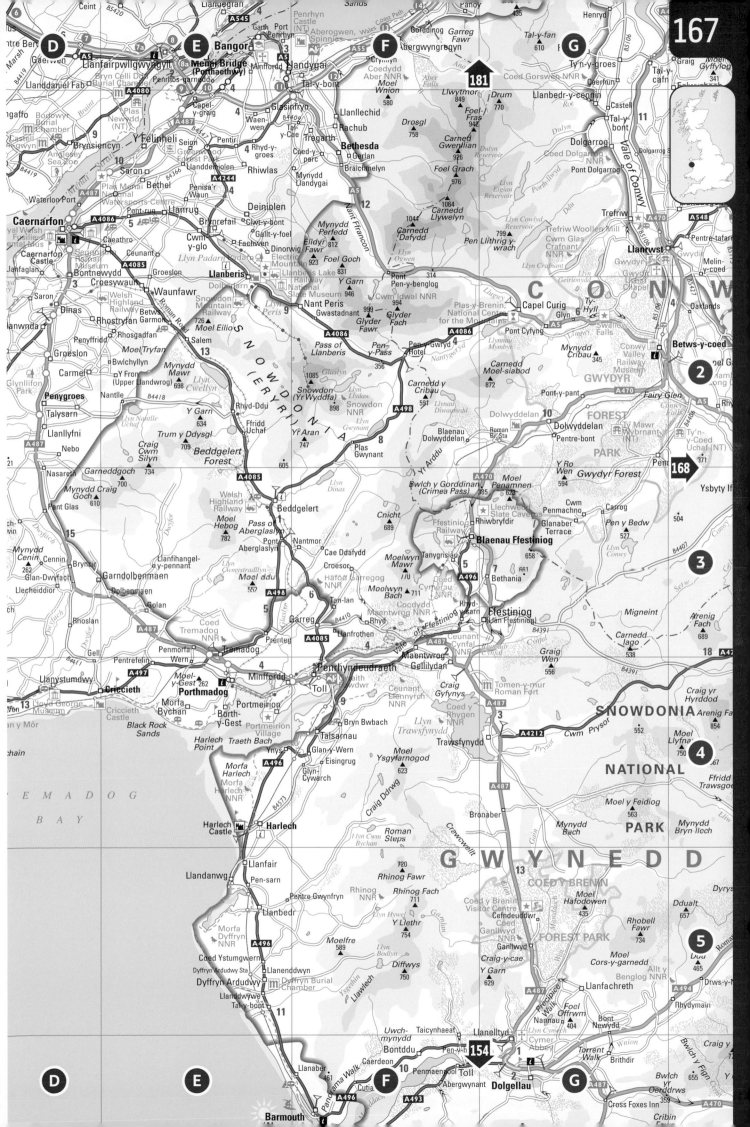

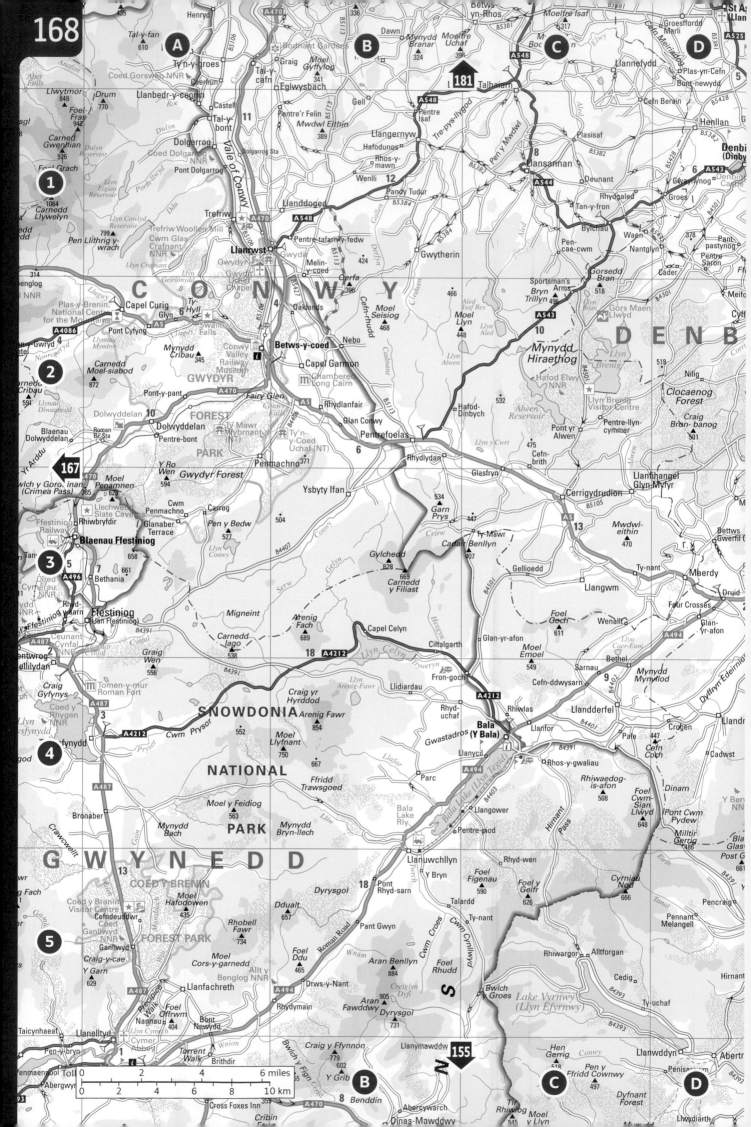

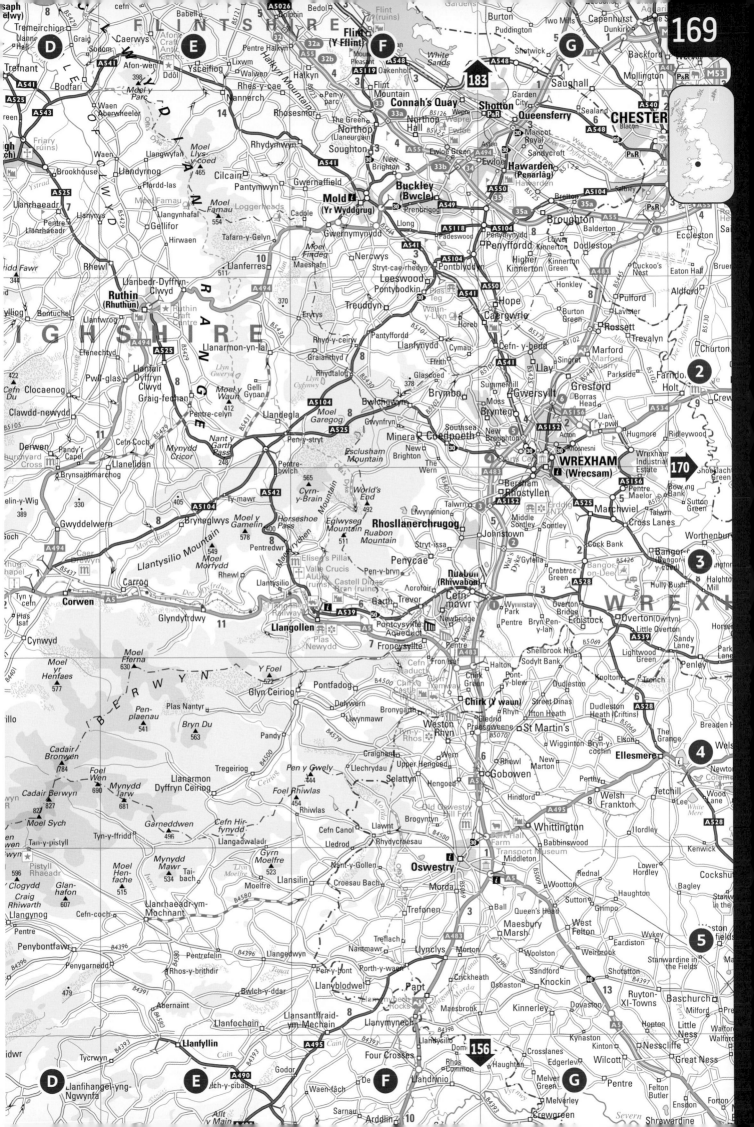

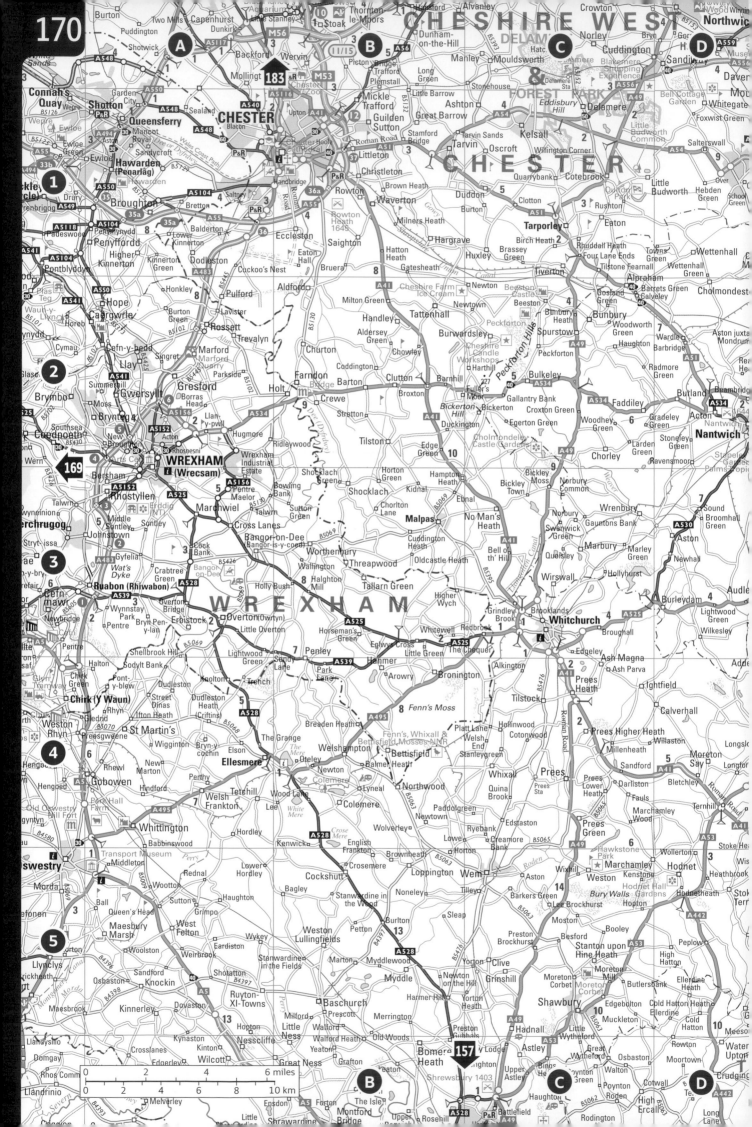

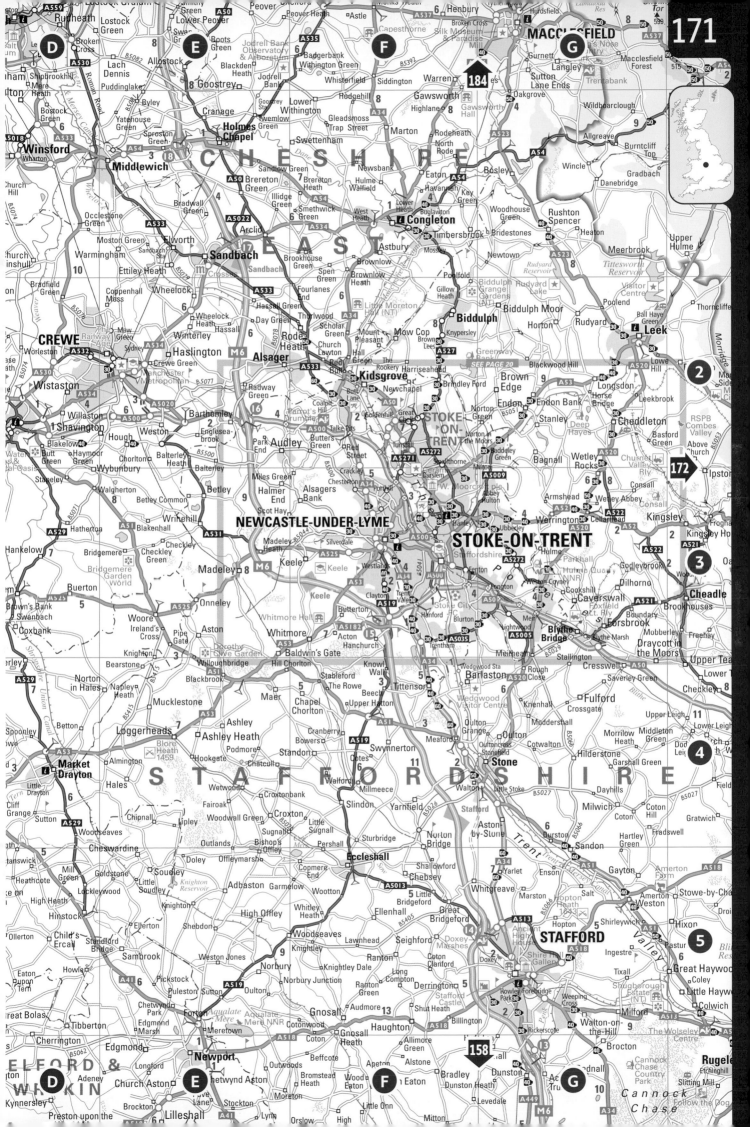

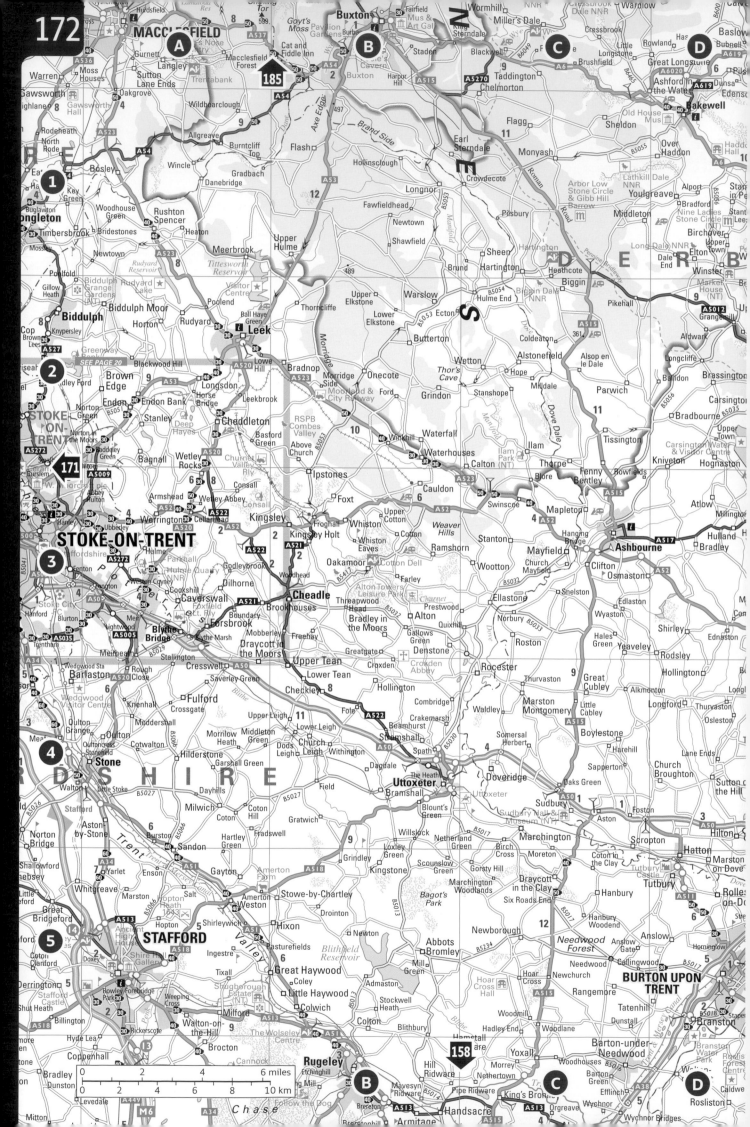

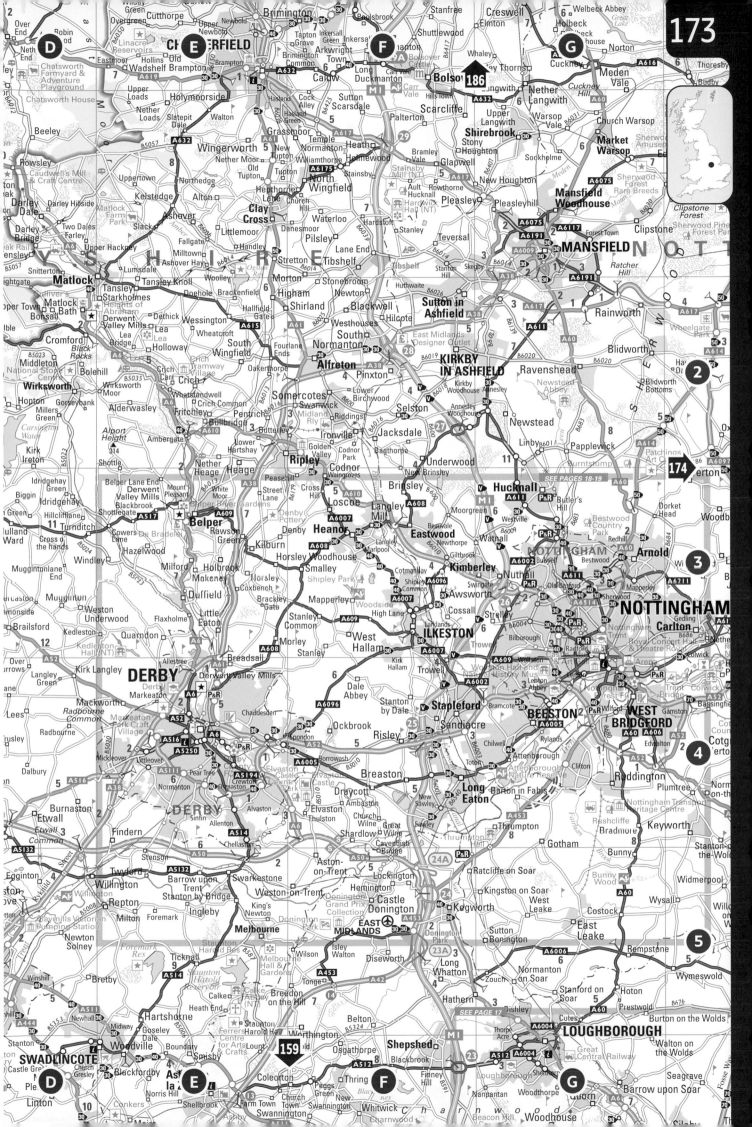

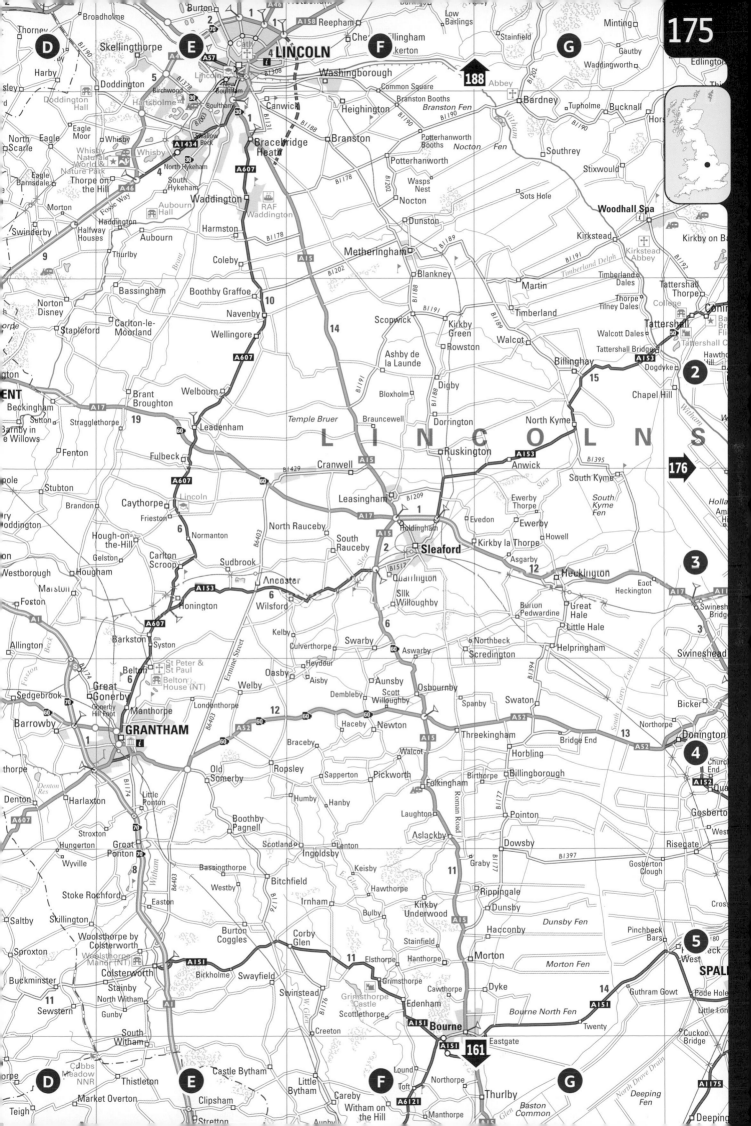

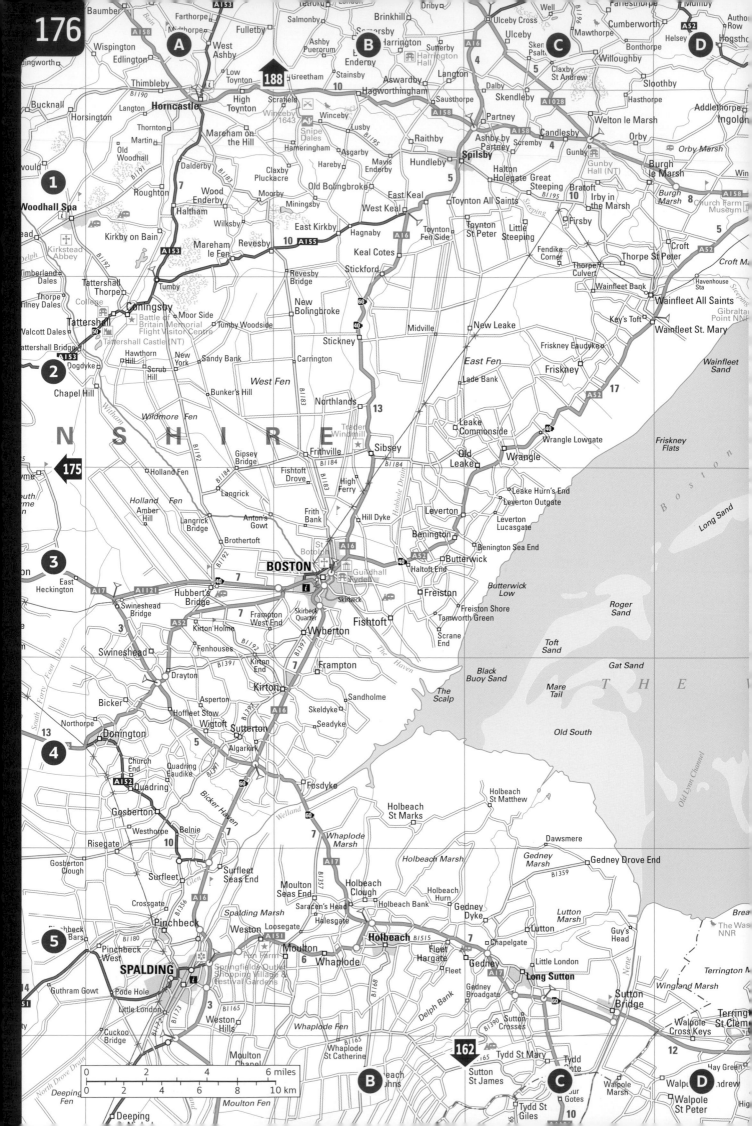

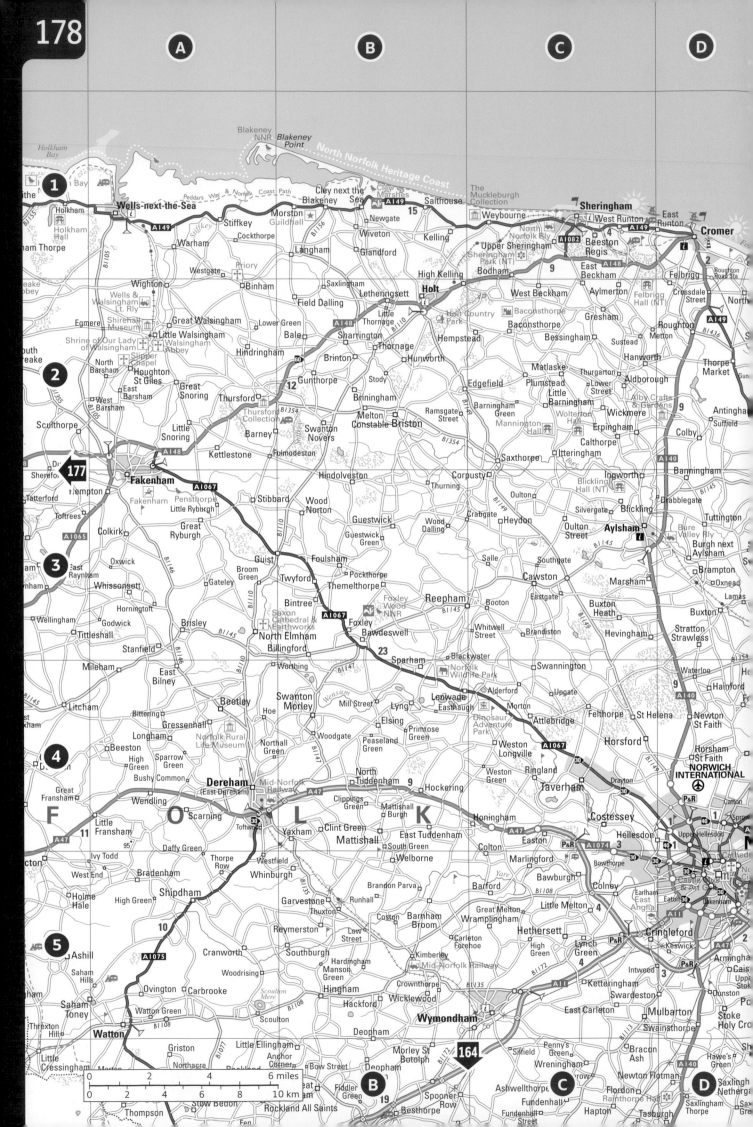

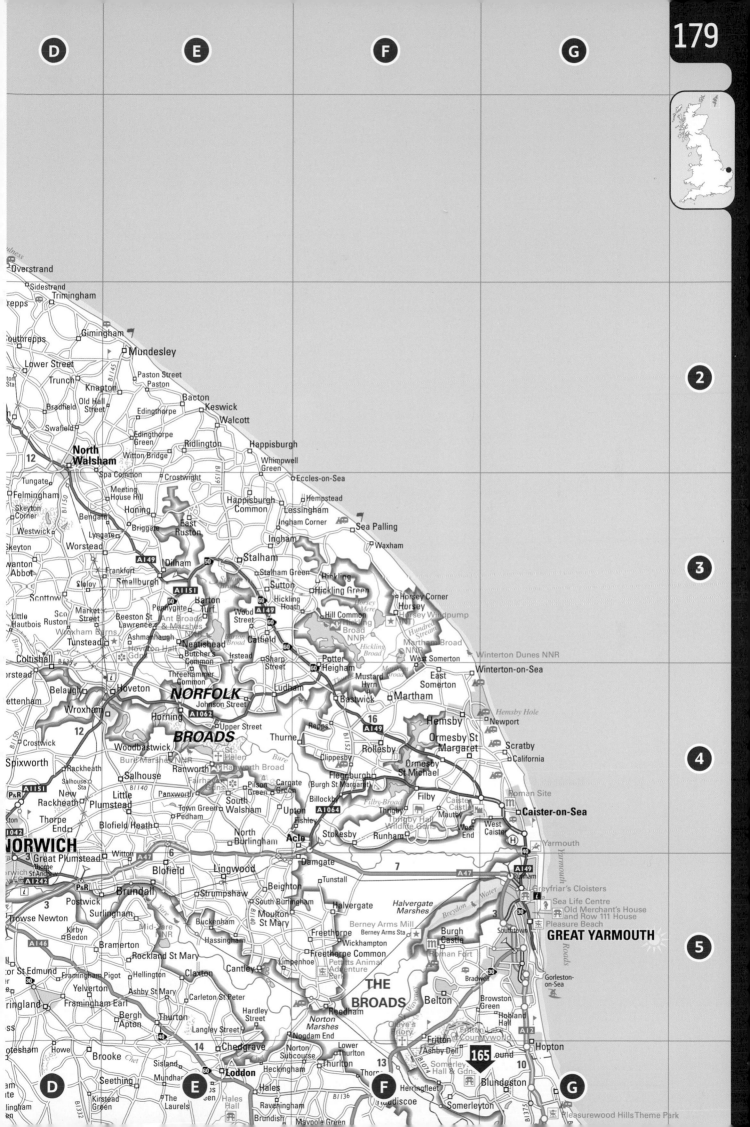

A   B   C   D

1

2

3

The Skerries

Middle Mouse

West Mouse

North Anglesey Heritage Coast

Cemaes Bay

Porth Wen Bay

Bull Bay (Porth Llechog)

Point Lynas

North Anglesey Heritage Coast

Carmel Head

Cemlyn Bay

Llanbadrig

Cemaes

Neuadd

Amlwch

Amlwch Port

Llaneilian

Cemlyn

Tregele

Burwen

Pengorffwysfa

Llanfairynghornwy

Llanfechell

Bodewryd

Pen-y-sarn

Nebo

Ynys Dulas

Mynydd mechell

Rhos-goch

Parys Mountain

A5025

Dulas

Dulas Bay

HOLYHEAD BAY

Llanrhyddlad

Llanfflewyn

Carreglefn

Rhos-y-bol

8

Llaneuddog

Lligwy Bay

Church Bay

Rhyd-wyn

ISLE OF

City Dulas

Capel Lligwy

Llanfaethlu

17

Llanbabo

Gwredog

Capel Parc

Brynrefail

Rhoslligwy

Din Lligwy

Moelfre

Dublin..........................1¾-3¼ hours
Dún Laoghaire (seasonal)...1¾-3¼

A5025

Windmill

Llanddeusant

Elim

Ceidio

Llandyfrydog

Maenaddwyn

Lligwy Burial Chamber

A5108

Marian-glas

Llanallgo

North Stack

Holyhead Mountain 220

Llanfachraeth

Stryd y Facsen

Llantrisant

Llannerch-y-medd

Bachau

Bryn-teg

Tyn-y-gongl

Benllech

Holyhead (Caergybi)

Roman Fort Salt Island

Tregwehelydd Standing Stone

ANGLESEY

Capel Coch

B5110

South Stack

Llaingoch

Pen-llyn

Carmel

ANGLESEY

Cors Goch NNR

Red Wharf (Traeth Coch)

Kingsland

Hut Circles

Penrhos

A5

Llanynghenedl

Llyn Llywenan Burial Chambers

Llechcynfarwy

Cors Erddreiniog NNR

Llanbedrgoch

Standing Stones

Bodedern

B5109

Trefor

Llangwyllog

Tregaian

Llanddyfnan

Pentraeth

Penrhyn Mawr

Holyhead Mountain Heritage Coast

Treaddur

Valley (Y Fali)

Llynfaes

Llyn Frogwy

Cefni Rés

B5109

Myn Llwya

B4545

Wales Coast Path

3

4

Caergeiliog

Bryngwran

A5

Gwalchmai

Bodffordd

Rhosmeirch

Talwrn

Cors Bodeilio NNR

10

B5108

HOLY ISLAND

Four Mile Bridge

Bodior

Llanfihangel-yn-Nhywyn

5

(YNYS MÔN)

Heneglwys

Llangefni

A5025

Rhoscolyn

Tywyn Trewan

Capel Gwyn

A4080

3

A55

6

A5

Rhostrehwfa

Cerrigceinwen

6

Penmynydd

Ceint

B5420

5

Cymyran Bay

Newydd Chamber

Pencarnisiog

Burial Chamber

Llangristiolus

7

Llanfairpwllgwyngyll

8

Rhosneigr

Ty Croes

Pentre Berw

Llanfair-yn-neubwll

Bethel

Capel Mawr

7A

Plas Newydd

Ty Croes Sta

B4422

Gaerwen

A5

Bryn Celli Ddu Burial Chamber

Menai Br (Porthaet)

Barclodiad y Gawres Chambered Cairn

Cefni

Trefdraeth

B4419

Llanddaniel Fab

Bodowyr Burial Chamber

Y Felint

Llangadwaladr

Malltraeth Marsh

Llanfihangel

166

9

Plas Newydd

Aberffraw

10

Malltraeth

Llangaffo

Brynsiencyn

Anglesey Sea Zoo

Greenwo Forest Park

B4421

Sei

Bodorgan

A4080

Dwyran

Aberffraw Bay

0   2   4   6 miles
0 2 4 6 8 10 km

A B C D

1

2

181

3

4

5

Birkenhead to   hours
Belfast................................8
Douglas.....4¼ (Nov-March)
Liverpool to   hours
Douglas......2¾ (March-Oct)
Dublin................................8

L I V E R P O O L

B A Y

West
Hoyle
Bank

East
Hoyle
Bank

Meols
Sta

Mockb

Hoylake

Royal
Liverpool

Manor Road Sta
Hoylake Sta

A553

Hilbre Island

Red
Rocks
Marsh

West
Kirby
Sta

Grange

A540

West Kirby

Frankby

B5139

Caldy

Irb
Hi

B5140

Thurstaston

Dawpool
Bank

D E E

Prestatyn
Sands
Holiday
Centre

Welsh Channel

Talacre

**Point of
Ayr**

Llawndy

Mostyn Bank

Prestatyn

Gronant

Ffrith

Gwespyr

Ffynnongroyw

Pen-y-ffordd

Mostyn Quay

Sky
Tower

A548

A547

Llanasa

Gyrn

Mostyn

Glan-y-don

Rhyl

SeaQuarium

Sun Centre

Meliden
(Gallt Melyd)

B5119

Gwaenysgor

Gop
Hill 8

Trelogan

Llannerch-y-Môr

Kinmel Bay
(Bae Cinmel)

A525

Bodrhyddan
Hall

Tan-yr-
allt

Axton

Whitford
(Chwitffordd)

Holywell Bank

Greenfield Valley

Greenfield
(Maes-Glas)

wyn Bay
(e Colwyn)

A55

22

10

*Abergele
Roads*

23

Llanddulas

Towyn

Pensarn

A548

Morfa
Rhuddlan

Plas
Llwyd

Rhuddlan

Dyserth

Och-
y-foel

Trelawnyd

Hen
Helyg

Maen
Achwyfan

Lloc

3

Basingwerk
Abbey

St Winifred's Holy Well & Chap

Whelston

Wales Coast Path

A55

24

A547

Abergele

23a

Plas-yn-
Rhuddlan

6

Rhuddlan
Cas & Twt Hill

3

Cwm

Marian
Cwm

A5151

Roman

Road

A5026

Gorsedd

Carmel

Pantasaph
Friary

Holywell (Treffynnon)

Bagillt
Bank

Penmaen-
Rhôs

Llysfaen

Rhyd-y-foel

A55

St George

24a

Pengwern

Bodelwyddan

25

27a

A525

28

Rhuallt

29

A55

30

31

Pantasaph

Calcoed

5

A5026

Bagillt

Bedol

Llanelian-
yn-Rh

26

A548

St Asaph
(Llanelwy)

27

Tremeirchion

8

Pen-y-
cefn

Brynford

Dolphin

3

A548

5

Betws-
yn-Rhos

6

Olwen

Moelfre Isaf

B5381

Green

Graig

Caerwys

Babell

F L I N T S H I R E

Flint
(Y Fflint)

Dawn

324

Moelfre Uchaf

317

Mynydd
Bodrochwyn

Llannefydd

Plas-yn-
Cefn

Trefnant

Llannerch
Hall

Sodom

Afon-wen

Ddol

Lixwm

32a

Halkyn

32b

Mount Pleasant

A5119

Oa

Mynydd
Branar

396

Cefn
Berain

A541

Bodfari

VALE OF CLWYD

Moel
y Parc

398

Afonwen
Craft and
Antique
Centre

Ysceifiog

Walwen

Walwen

Rhes-y-cae

Halkyn Mountain

A55

4

Fli
Brig

Pen-y-
parc

Llanfair Talhaiarn

A544

Groesffordd
Marli

B5381

A525

A543

A541

wheeler

168

Nannerch

14

Rhosesmor

B5123

The
Green

rthop

Pentre
Isaf

Tre-pys-llygod

Alel

Cefn
Berain

B5428

A543

Green

Waen

Langwyfan

Moel
Llys-y-coed

Rhydymwyn

Soughton

burgain

A541

rnyw

B5381

B5382

Friary
(ruins)

Denbigh
(Dinbych)

Handyrnog

Llansannan

A543

0   2   4   6 miles

0 2 4 6 8 10 km

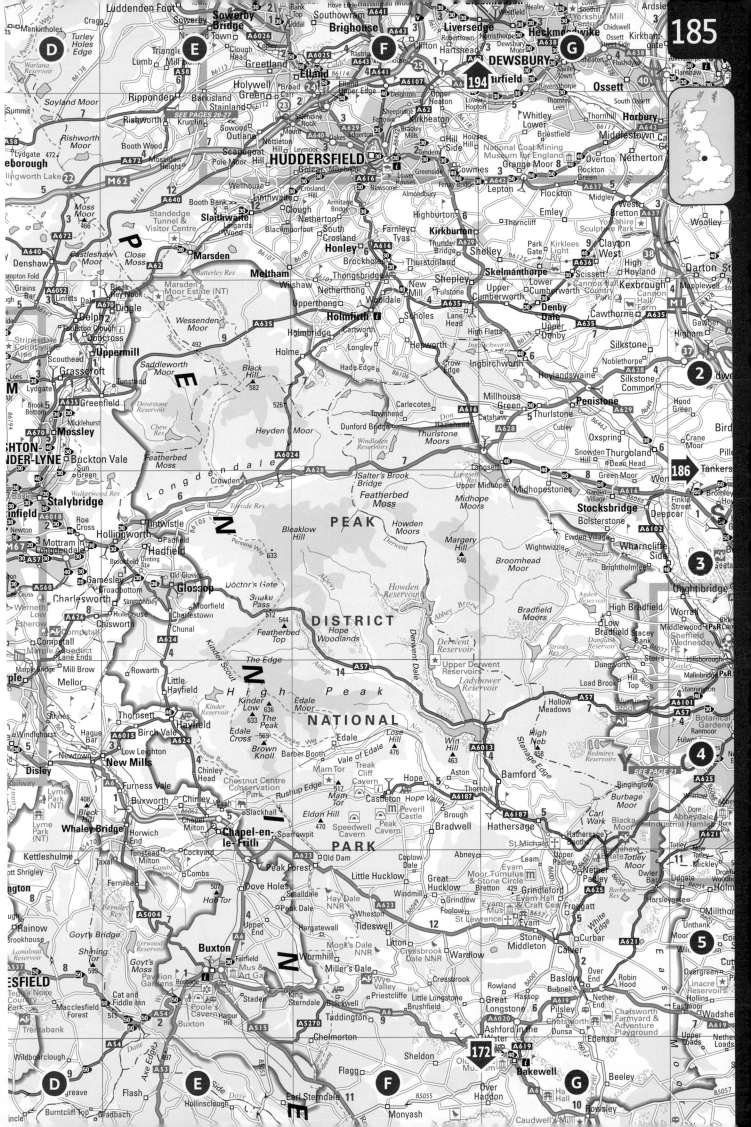

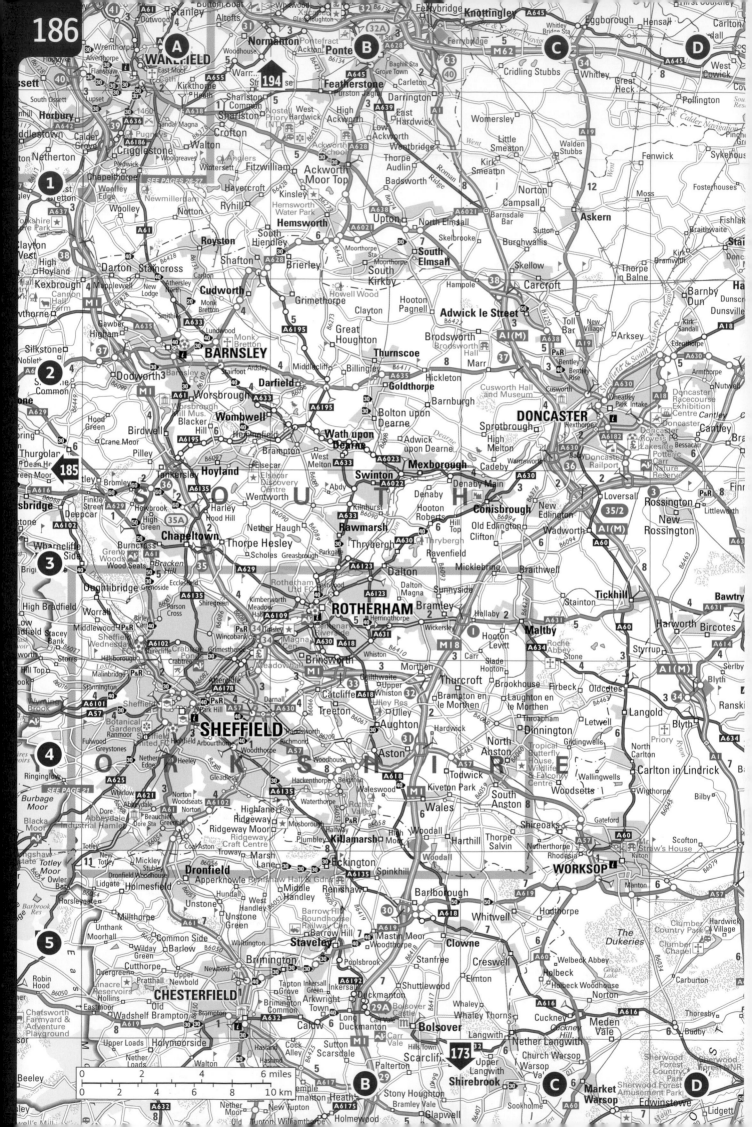

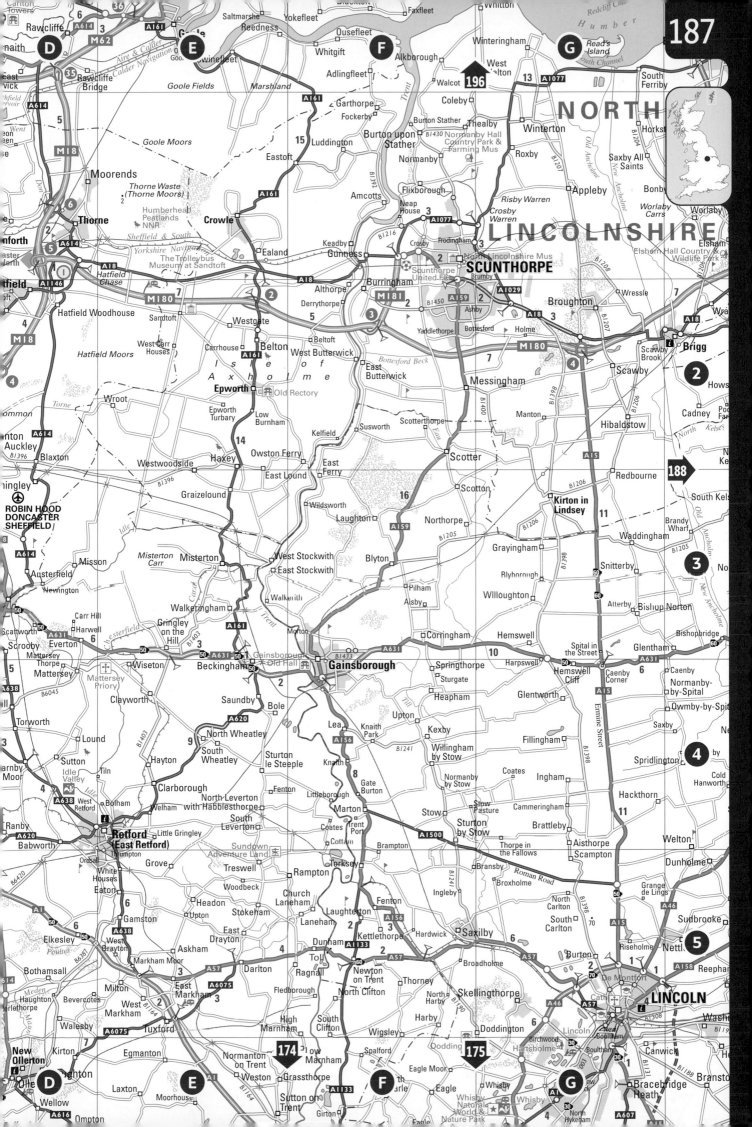

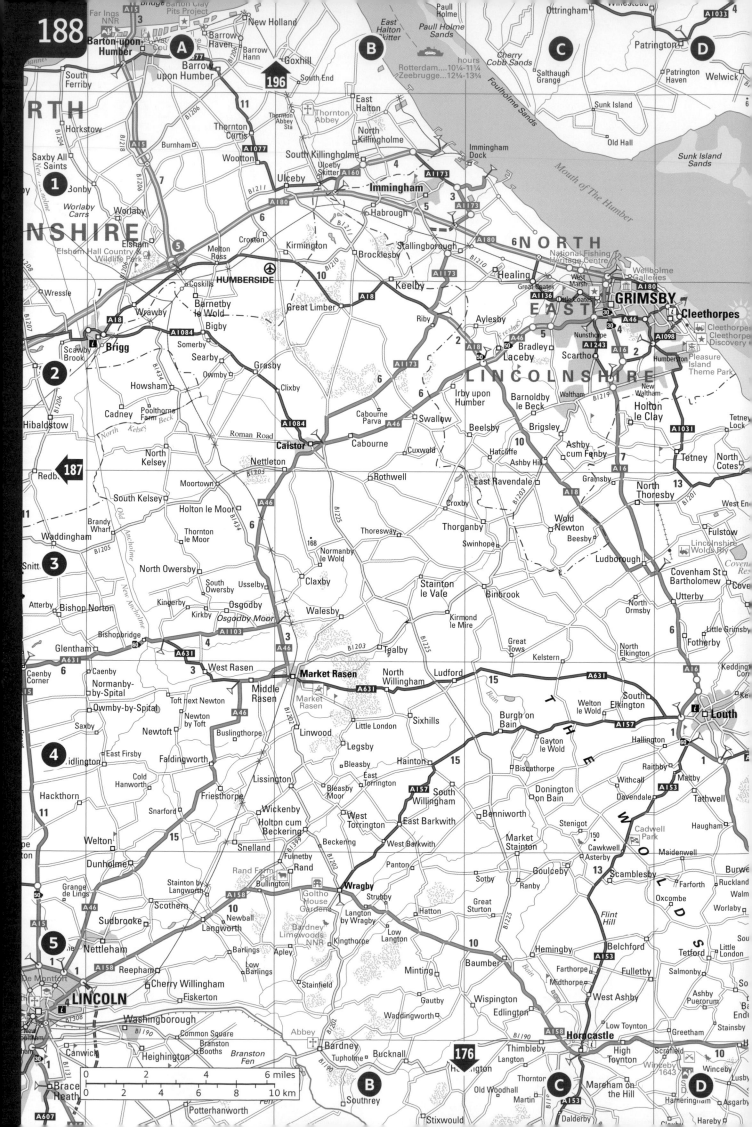

D E F G

Holmpton
Out Newton
197
Weeton
Skeffling Easington
Skeffling Clays
Kilnsea
Spurn Heritage Coast
Kilnsea Clays
Spurn NNR
Spurn Head
Spurn Head

s Coast Light Rly
Centre

2

Marshchapel
Eskham
Wragholme
Donna Nook
Donna Nook
Donna Nook NNR
Grainthorpe Meals
Ludney North Somercotes
Conisholme Church End
Skidbrooke North End
South Somercotes A1031 Saltfleet
liam St Mary South Somercotes Fen Houses
Yarburgh South Somercotes Skidbrooke
Alvingham *Great Eau*
North Cockerington Saltfleetby St Clements
n Saltfleetby All Saints 12 Saltfleetby - Theddlethorpe NNR
South Cockerington Saltfleetby St Peter
ddington Theddlethorpe St Helen
Grimoldby Theddlethorpe All Saints
Stewton B1200 Manby A1031

3

157 Little Carlton Great Carlton Great Eau
Legbourne Mablethorpe
Little Cawthorpe North Reston South Reston Gayton le Marsh Strubby Trusthorpe
11 3 A1104 4
Withern A157 Thorpe A52 Sutton on Sea
Muckton Authorpe Tothill Maltby le Marsh H Beesby Sutton le Marsh Sandilands
Woodthorpe Hagnaby 6 Hannah
Claythorpe Saleby A52
Belleau Aby Markby
8 Greenfield A1104 A1111 Asserby 5
White Pit Swaby Ailby Thoresthorpe The Grange
Ketsby South Thoresby Bilsby Thurlby Huttoft Anderby Creek
th Ormsby Calceby Rigsby Alford Bilsby Field Anderby
mersby Driby Haugh B1449 Farlesthorpe Mumby
Brinkhill Ulceby Cross Well B1196 Cumberworth Authorpe Row
Harrington Sutterby Ulceby Mawthorpe Helsey Hogsthorpe Chapel St Leonards
ag Harrington Hall A16 Skendleby Psalter Bonthorpe
rby Langton 4 Dalby Claxby St Andrew Willoughby
Aswardby Skendleby A1028 Welton le Marsh Sloothby Hasthorpe 10
agworthingham Sausthorpe Partney A52 Addlethorpe Ingoldmells 177
nby 1 A16 Scremby Orby *Ingoldmells Point* Fantasy Island
D Spilsby E by Ashby by Partney Gunby *Orby Marsh* F Butlins Family Entertainment Resort G
Hundleby Halton Gunby Hall (NT) Wintharne Seathorne Skegness Water Leisure Park
A158 A195

4

5

F

Sands

Dalton-in-Furness 5

D **E** Great Urswick
Little Urswick
Bardsea
F 9 Baycliff
Stainton with Adgar
Scales
Hawcoat Newto
G Humphre
Head
Point
Furness
Abbey
Newbarns Furness
Mus
Gleaston
Aldingl
A5087

North Walney NNR
North Scale
Dock Museum
Dendron
Leece
Newbiggin
199

M O R E C A M
Roose
Roosecote
BARROW-IN-FURNESS
B A Y
Cartmel Wharf
Vickerstown
A590
Roosebeck
Tummer
Hill Scar

Biggar
Rampside
Mort
Bank
Yeoman
Wharf

1
Isle of
Walney
Roa Island
Foulney Island
A589 20
Sandylands
B5
Sheep
Island
Piel
Piel Island
Oxcl
3
30
South End
Piel Bar
South
Walney
Piel Bar
Heysham
A68

Hilpsford Point
Heysh
Moss
Middleton
AP

Douglas 3¼-3¾hrs
Sunderland
Bank
Sunderland
2
Sunderland
2
Cockersand
Abbey

Bernard
Wharf
A58

North
Wharf
Pilling Lane
192
22
Rossall
Point
**Knott End-
on-Sea**
Fisher's Row
Pilling
Stake Pool
Fleetwood
Preesall
Scronkey

Freeport
Stalmine
Moor End
Eagland
3
A587
Staynall
Hale Nook
3
A585
Cold
Row
Sower Carr
Bill
Naze
Trunnah
A588
AP
Cleveleys
7
Stanah
Hambleton
Out Rawcliffe
Ra
Thornton
Little
Thornton
Whin Lane End
Larbreck
Toll
Little Bispham
Skippool
Norbreck
30
Carleton
2
Little
Singleton
Little
Eccleston
Copp
Bispham
30
Walbreck
A586
Singleton
Elsw
A584 A587
**Poulton-
le-Fylde**
Thistleton
North Shore
Normoss
B5266
BLACKPOOL
Hardhorn
Newton
A585
Greenhalgh
Wh
BLACKPOOL
30
Clayton
Staining
Esprick
4
30
Great
Marton
Mythop
Weeton
4
dlar
Blackpool Tower
30
Blackpool Zoo
Mereside
Moor
Side
Sea Life Centre
Blackpool
Mereside
4
4
Great
Plumpton
Weshar
South Shore
South Pier
Common
Edge
4
A583
Kir
Little
Plumpton
Westby
50
Wrea Green
Blackpool Pleasure Beach
Squires
Gate
A5230
B5410
Peel
Ballam
Lower
Bryning
50
**BLACKPOOL
INTERNATIONAL**
Higher
Ballam
Moss
Side
Hall Cross
W

St Anne's
Hey Houses
LYTHAM ST ANNE'S
Ansdell
Warton
Fairhaven
Saltcotes
Warton
Bank
Salter's
Bank
Royal Lytham
& St. Anne's
Lytham
A584
10

Ribble
5
Banks Sands
Ribble
Estuary
NNR
West Lancas
Light Rail
5
Hesketh Ba

Hundred End

Banks
Ta
Horse Bank
Crossens
9
183
ry Brow
Marshside
Holmes
Mere
Brow
outhport Pier
Churchtown
SOUTHPORT
D **E** **F** **G**
B5246
P&R
Blowick
Holmeswood
Trans Pennine Trail
P&R

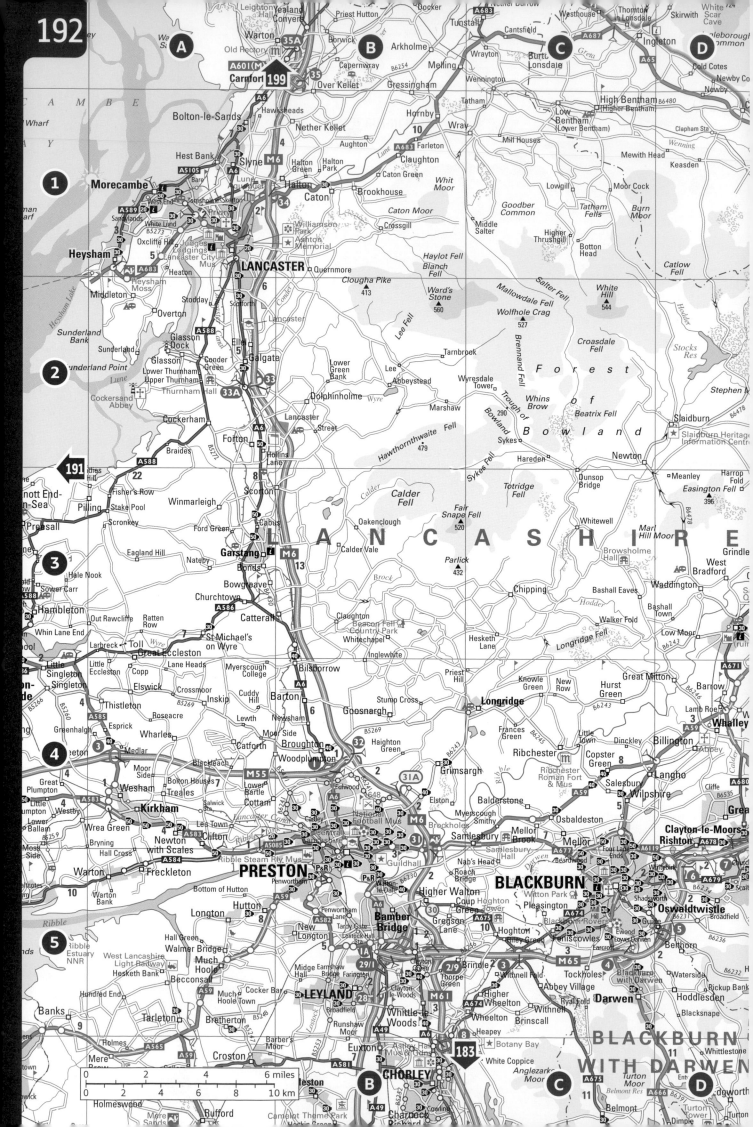

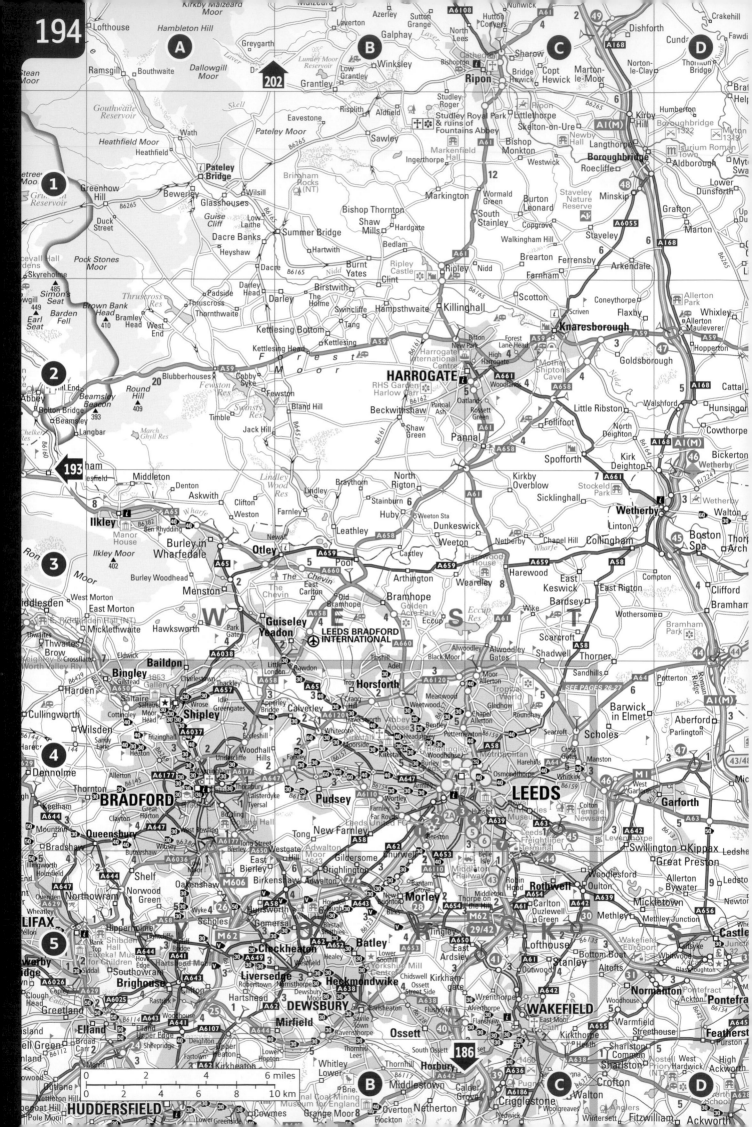

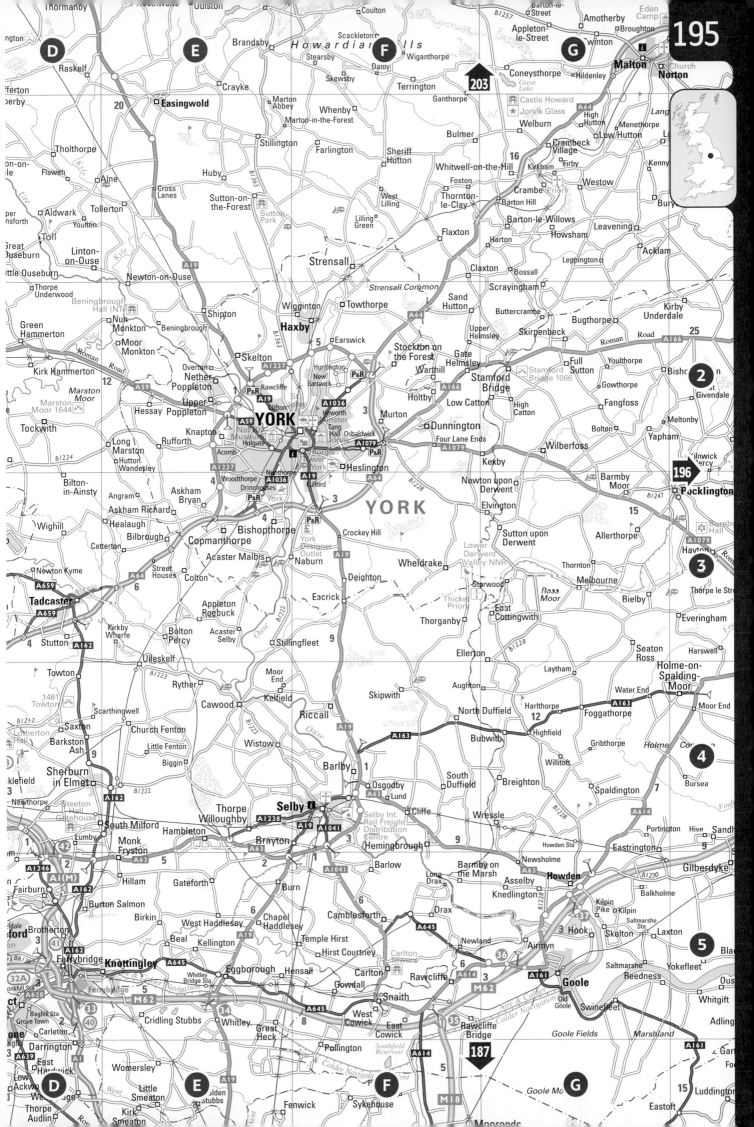

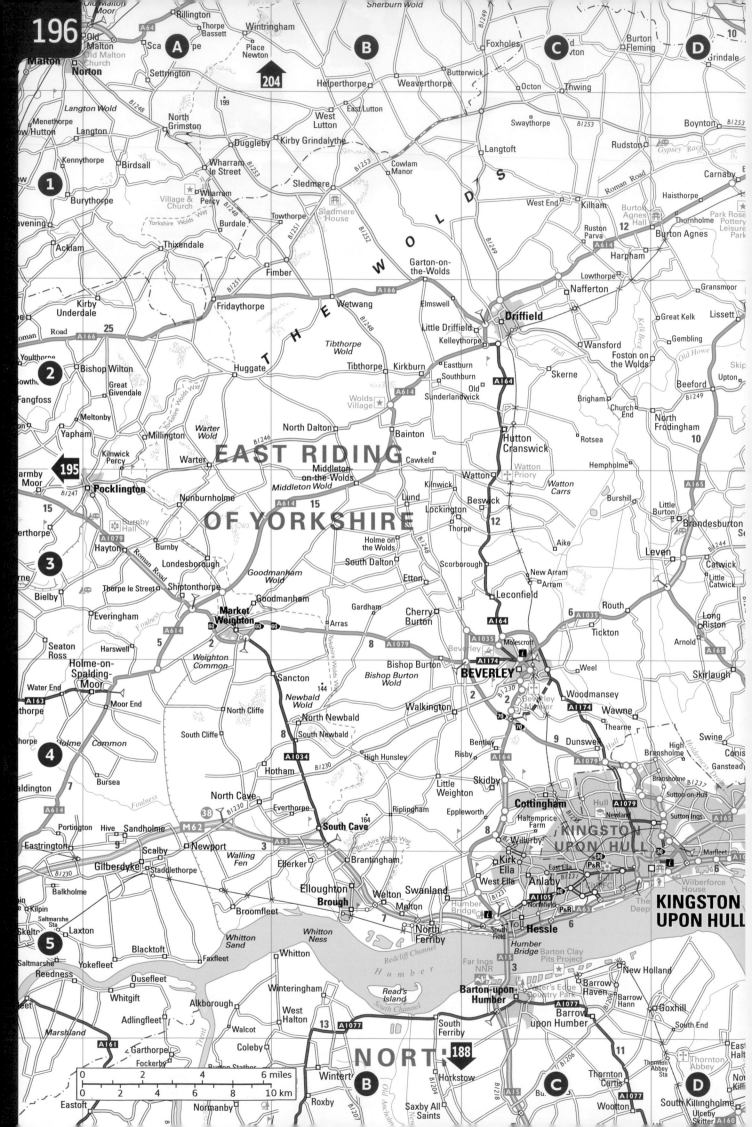

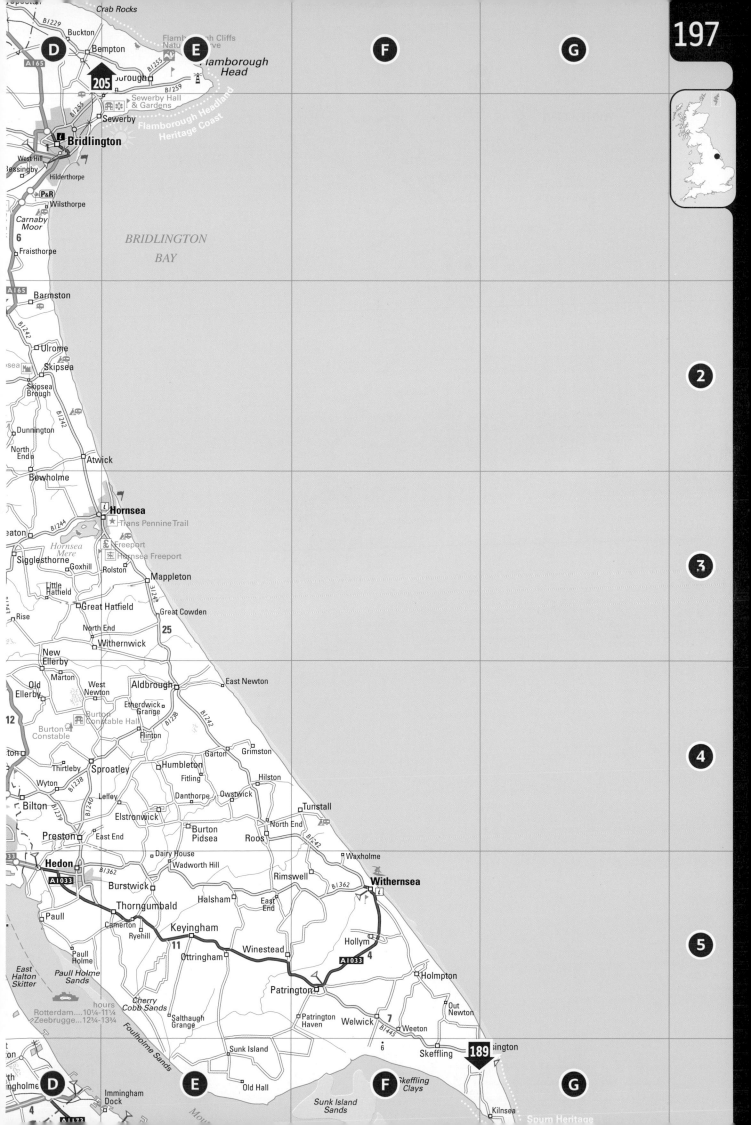

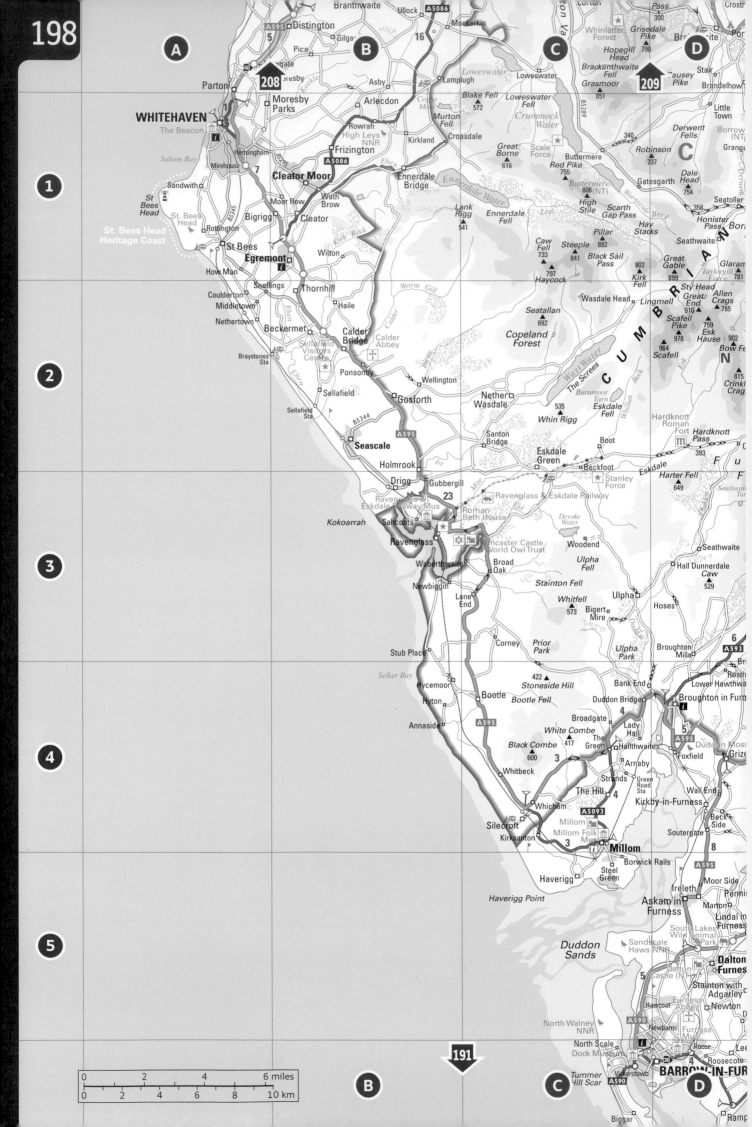

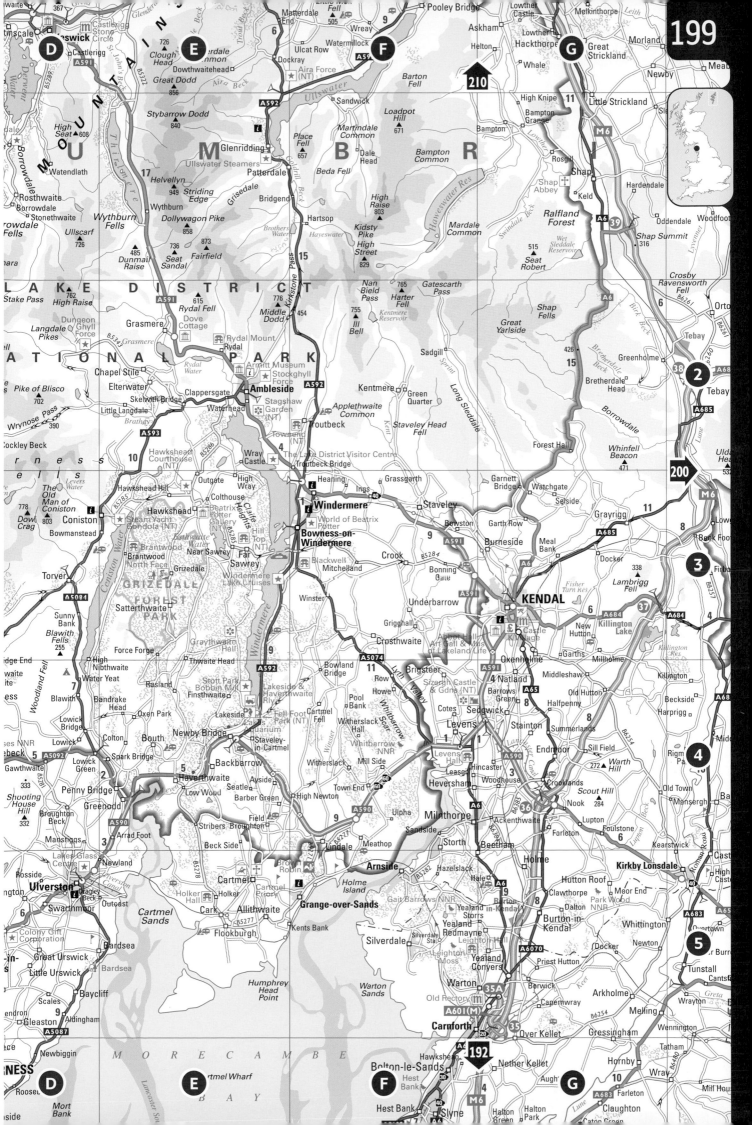

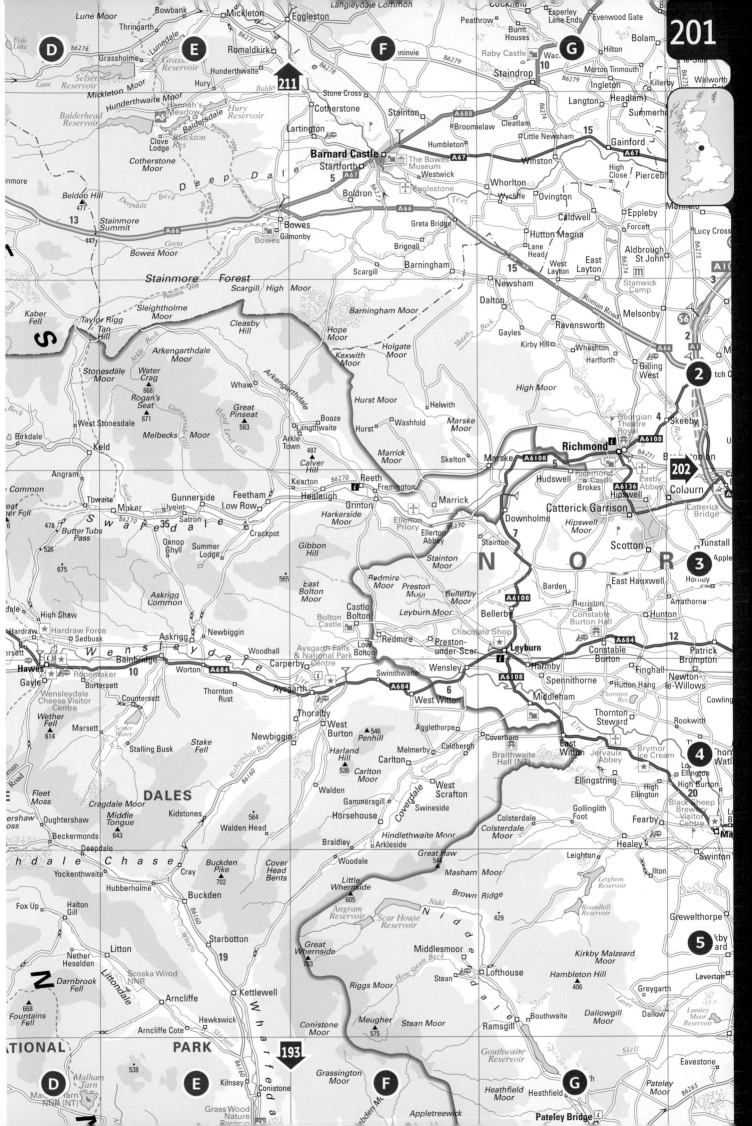

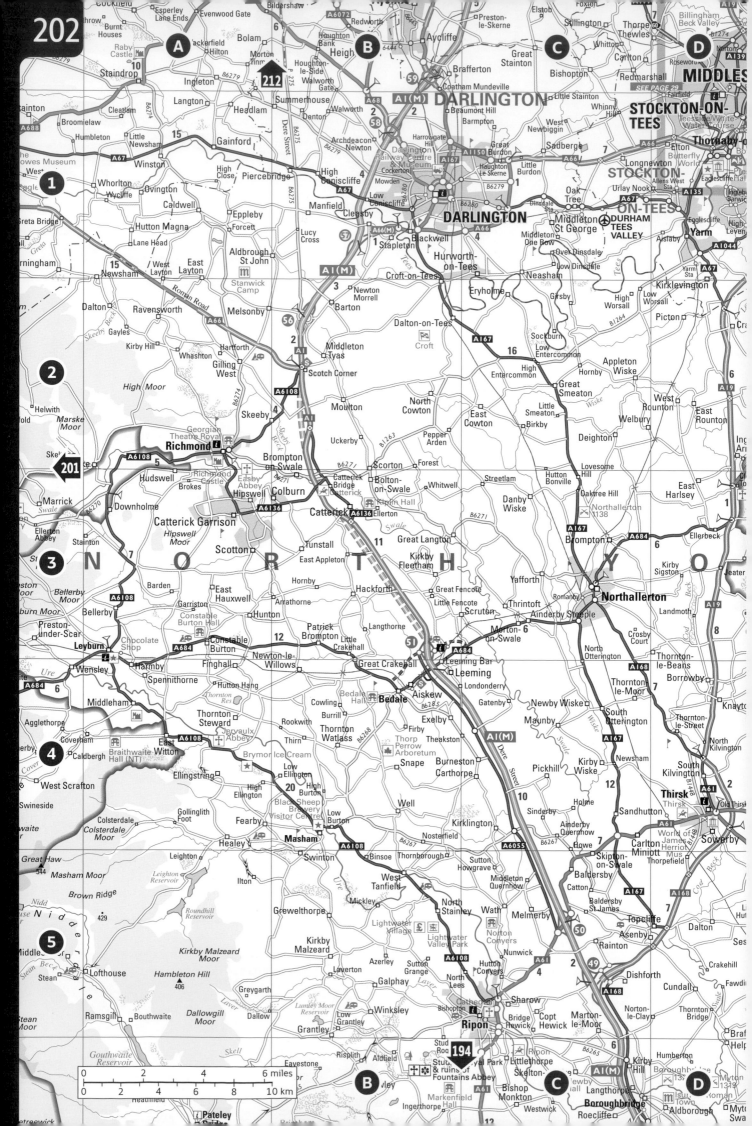

D　　　E　　　F　　　G

197

2

3

4

5

e & Cleveland

int

Ness Rocks
e & Marine Sanctuary
th North Bay
y‿Miniature Railway
🏰 Scarborough Castle
SCARBOROUGH
arborough Art Gall
🏛 *South Bay*
Spa Complex
Black Rocks

P&R
🚉 Osgodby
d⟍ 🚐 *Cayton Bay*
⟍Cayton　**7**
✕Lebberston⟍ 🚐 Gristhorpe
Hertford　　　*The Wyke*
🚉 *Filey Brigg*
A165　　ℹ
⟍Folkton **6** A1039 ⟍ **Filey**
West　Muston
Flotmanby　　　*Filey*
⟍Hunmanby　　　*Bay*

Reighton
Sands
🚐 Reighton
□ Speeton
Crab Rocks
Burton　　B1229
Fleming　　**10**
Wold　　　　□ Buckton
Newton　Grindale　□ Bempton
　　A165　　　*Flamborough Cliffs*
　　　　　　Nature Reserve
Thwing　　　　B1255
　　　　Flamborough□　　🚩
　　　Marton　　　🗼 *Flamborough*
B1253　　　B1255 B1259　*Head*
　　　🎡 🌸 *Sewerby Hall*
Boynton　B1253　　*& Gardens*
　　　□ Sewerby
D　　E　🏰 **Bridlington**　F　　　　　G
udston□　🚐
Gypsey Race⟍
West Hill
B1253　Bessingby
Carnaby

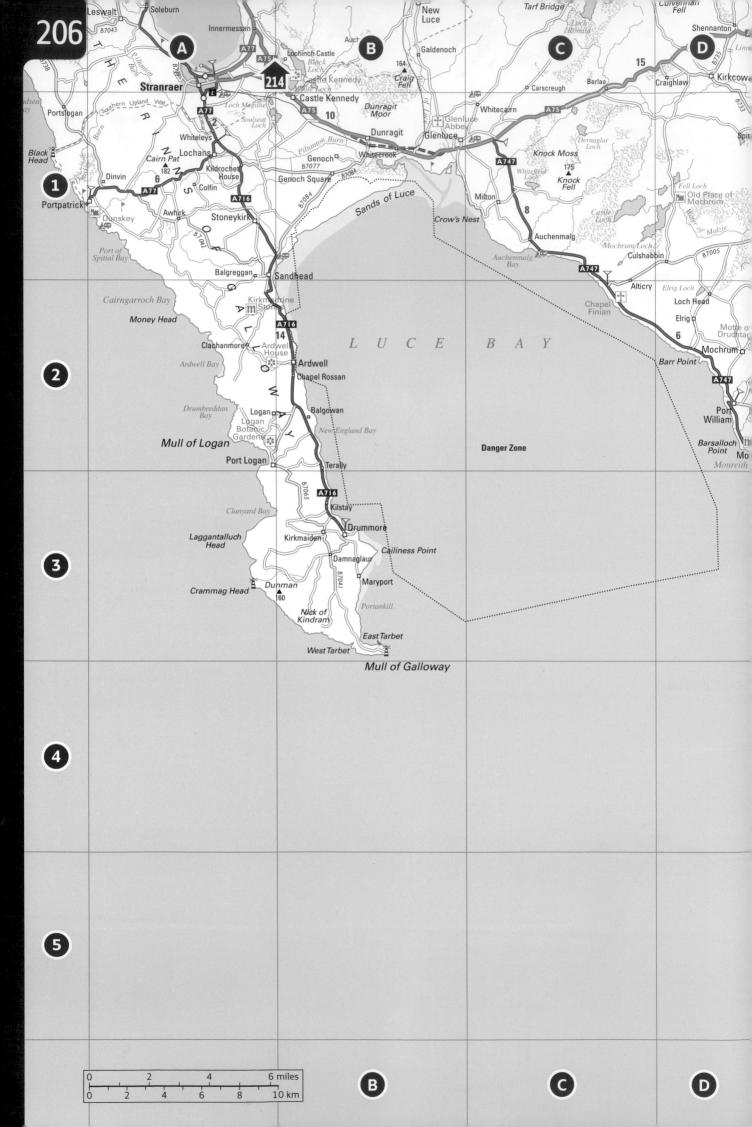

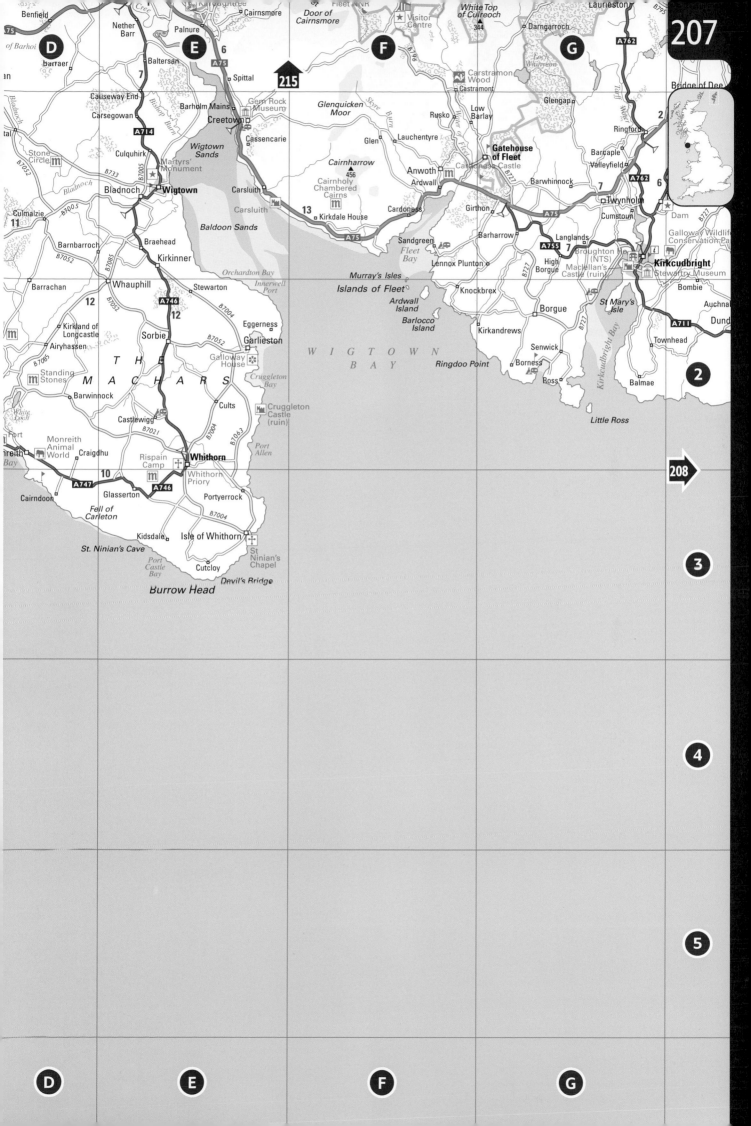

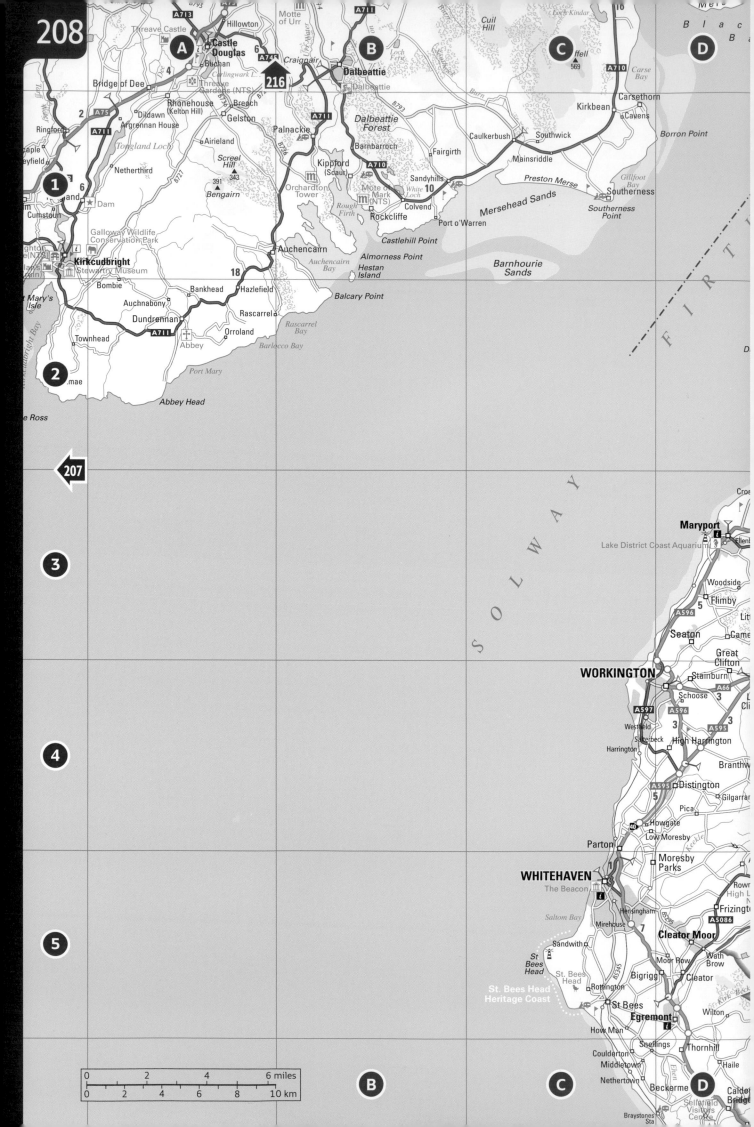

A713
Threave Castle
Hillowton
A711
Motte
of Urr
A711
Loch Kinder
16
Black
Ba
A
Castle
Douglas
B
6
Dalbeattie
C
fell
569
A710
Carse
Bay
D
Buchan
A745
Craignair
Dalbeattie
Carsethorn
Bridge of Dee
4
216
Threave
Gardens (NTS)
Rhonehouse
(Kelton Hill)
Breoch
Dalbeattie
Forest
A710
Kirkbean
Cavens
A75
2
Dildawn
Gelston
A711
Barnbarroch
Caulkerbush
Southwick
Carsethorn
Cavens
Ringford
A711
Argrennan House
Airieland
Palnackie
Kippford
(Scaur)
Fairgirth
Mainsriddle
Borron Point
Tongland Loch
Netherthird
Screel
Hill
Orchardton
Tower
Mote of
Mark
(NTS)
Sandyhills
10
Preston Merse
Gillfoot
Bay
Southerness
1
6
391
343
Bengairn
White
Loch
Colvend
Mersehead Sands
Southerness
Point
Dam
Rockcliffe
Port o'Warren
Cumstoun
Galloway Wildlife
Conservation Park
Auchencairn
Castlehill Point
Barnhourie
Sands
Kirkcudbright
Stewartry Museum
18
Almorness Point
Hestan
Island
Mary's
Isle
Bombie
Bankhead
Hazlefield
Auchencairn
Bay
Auchnabony
Rascarrel
Balcary Point
Dundrennan
Orroland
Rascarrel
Bay
A711
Abbey
Barlocco Bay
Townhead
Port Mary
Ross
mae
2
Abbey Head

207

SOLWAY

Maryport
Lake District Coast Aquarium
Ellenb
Cros
3
Woodside
Flimby
A596
5
Lit
Seaton
Came
Great
Clifton
WORKINGTON
Stainburn
A66
3
Schoose
A597
A596
3
Westfield
3
A595
Salterbeck
High Harrington
Cli
4
Harrington
Branthw
A595
Distington
Gilgarran
5
Pica
40
Howgate
Low Moresby
Parton
Moresby
Parks
Rowr
High L
WHITEHAVEN
1
The Beacon
Hensingham
Frizingt
A5086
Saltom Bay
Mirehouse
7
Cleator Moor
5
Sandwith
St
Bees
Head
Wath
Brow
St. Bees
Head
Rottington
Bigrigg
Moor Row
Cleator
St. Bees Head
Heritage Coast
St Bees
Wilton
Egremont
How Man
Snellings
Thornhill
Coulderton
Middletown
Haile
Nethertown
Beckerme
Braystones
Sta
Sellafield
Visitors
Centre
Cald
Bridge

0   2   4   6 miles
0 2 4 6 8 10 km

B   C   D

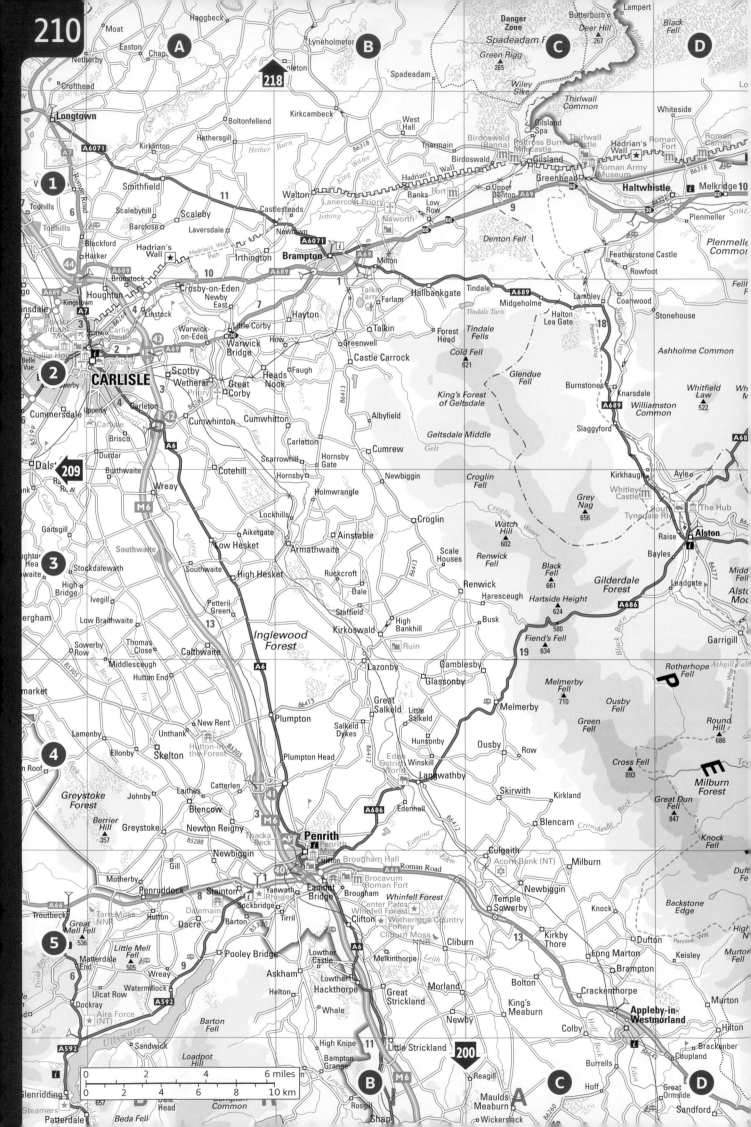

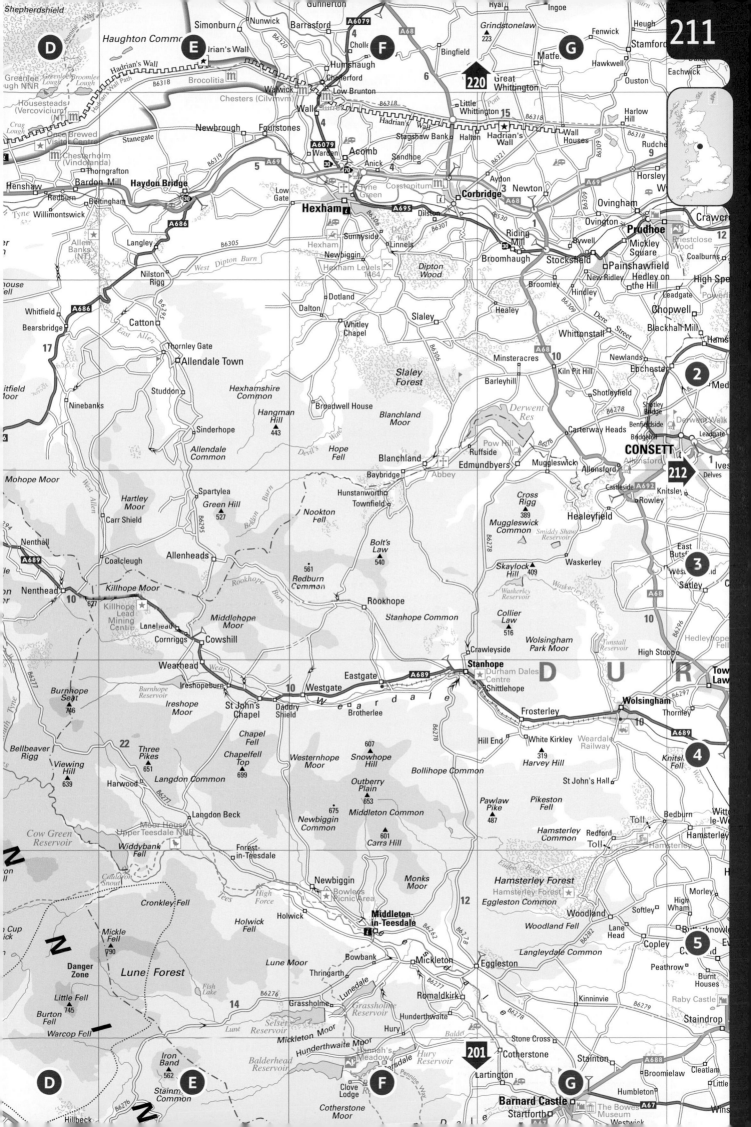

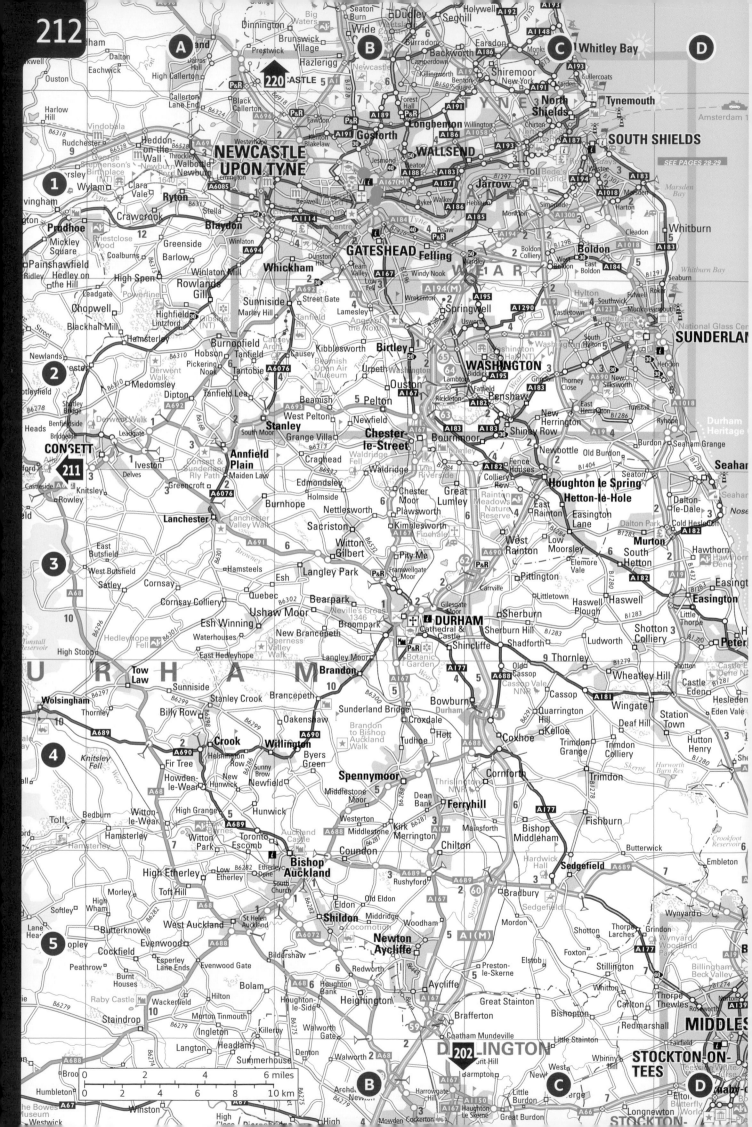

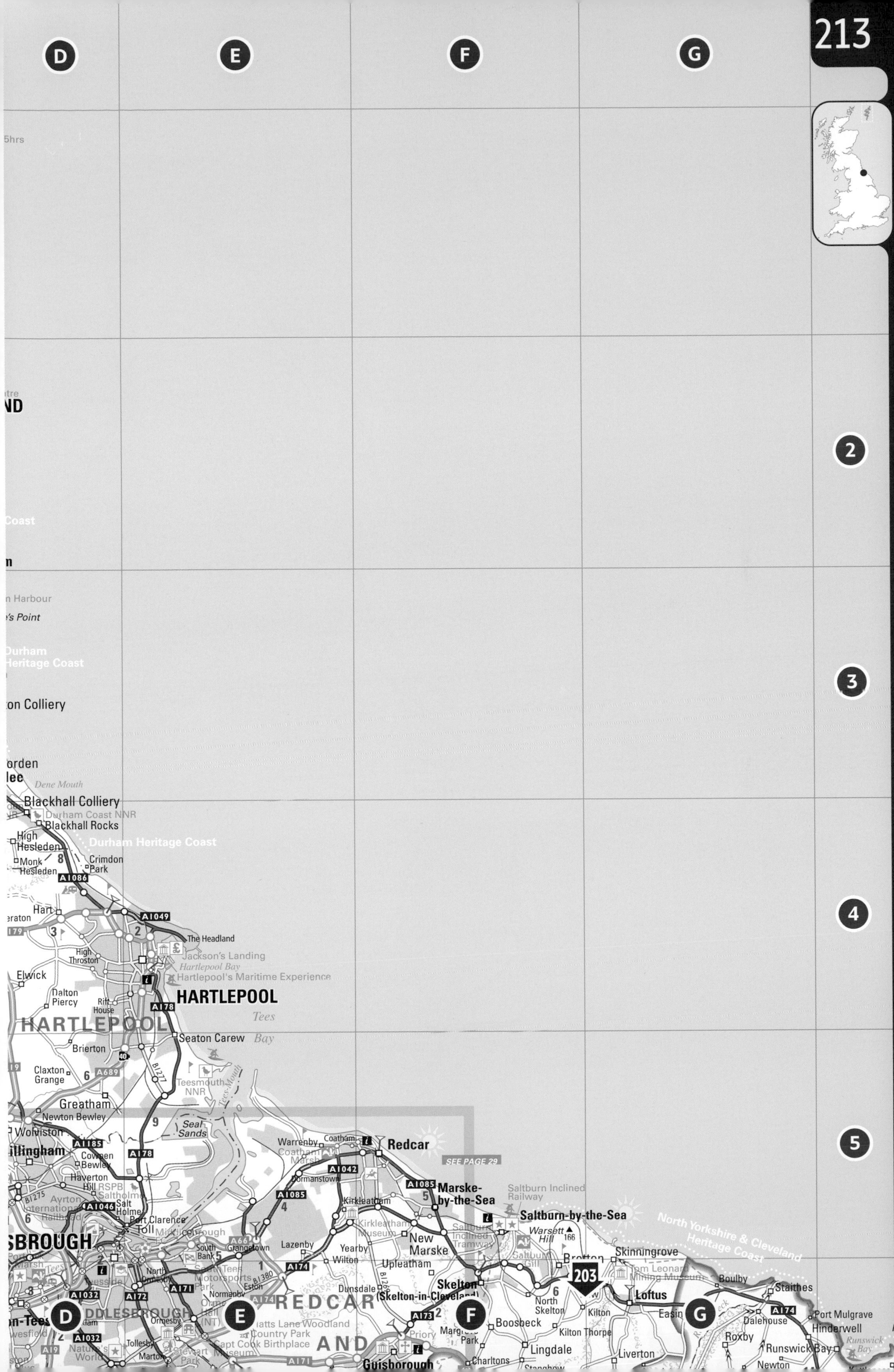

D E F G

2

3

4

5

5hrs

ND

Coast

n

n Harbour

's Point

Durham
Heritage Coast

on Colliery

orden
lee
Dene Mouth
Blackhall Colliery
Durham Coast NNR
Blackhall Rocks
High
Hesleden
8
Monk
Hesleden
Crimdon
Park
A1086

Hart
A1049
eraton
179
3
High
Throston
2
The Headland
Jackson's Landing
Elwick
Hartlepool Bay
Hartlepool's Maritime Experience
Dalton
Piercy
Riff
House
A178
HARTLEPOOL

HARTLEPOOL
Tees
Seaton Carew *Bay*
Brierton
40
Claxton
Grange
6
A689
B1277
Greatham
Teesmouth
NNR
Newton Bewley
9
Wolviston
*Seal
Sands*
A1185
A178
illingham
Cowpen
Bewley
Warrenby Coatham
Coatham
Marsh
Redcar
Haverton
Hill
RSPB
Salt
Holme
A1042
Dormanstown
SEE PAGE 29
Ayrton
International
A1046
Saltholme
A1085
Marske-
by-the-Sea
*Saltburn Inclined
Railway*
6
Port Clarence
Toll
Middlesbrough
A66
Kirkleatham
Kirkleatham
Museum
5
Saltburn-by-the-Sea
BSBROUGH
South
Bank
5
Grangetown
Lazenby
Yearby
New
Marske
Saltburn
Inclined
Tramway
*Warsett
Hill* 166
*North Yorkshire & Cleveland
Heritage Coast*
B1380
A174
Wilton
Upleatham
Saltburn
Gill
Brotton
Skinningrove
Tom Leonard
Mining Museum
A1032
A172
A171
Normanby
Eston
Skelton
(Skelton-in-Cleveland)
203
Loftus
Boulby
Staithes
DDLESBROUGH
dam
Ormesby
(NT)
REDCAR
A173
2
North
Skelton
6
Kilton
Easin
A174
Dalehouse
n-Tees
A1032
Tolleshy
Natures
World
Marton
att's Lane Woodland
Country Park
Capt Cook Birthplace
Museum
AND
Priory
Park
Boosbeck
Kilton Thorpe
Liverton
Roxby
Port Mulgrave
Hinderwell
Runswick Bay
*Runswick
Bay*
Guisborough
Charltons
Lingdale
Stanghow
Newton

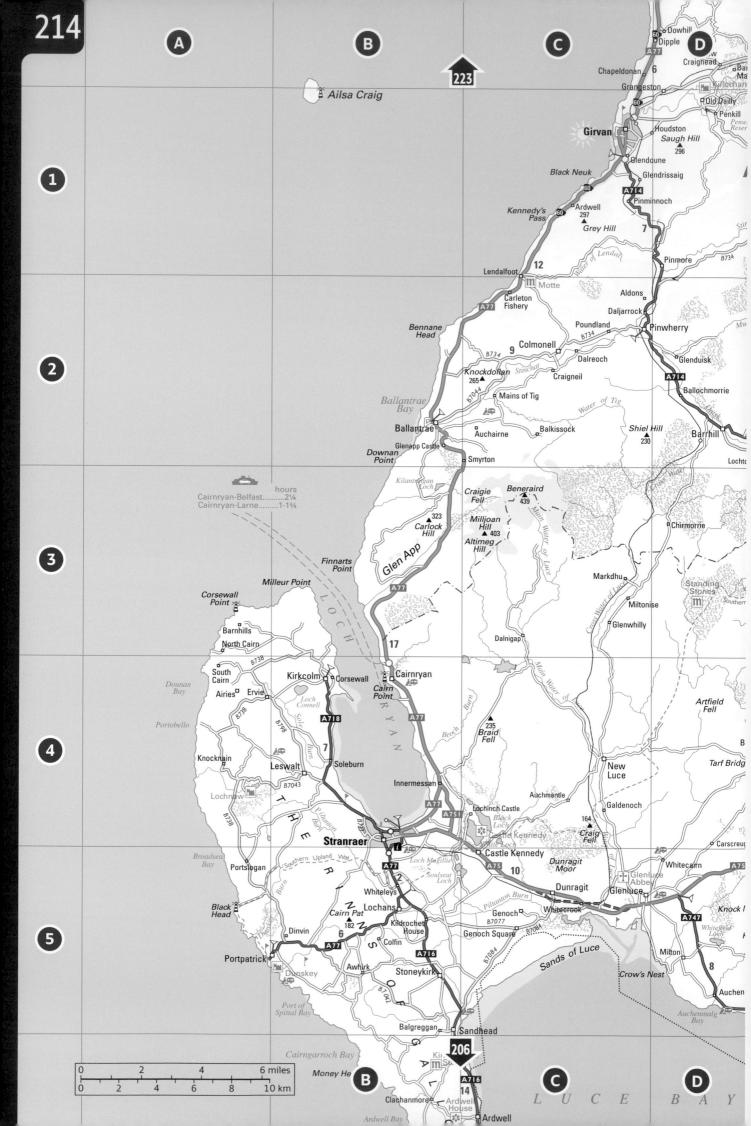

Ailsa Craig

A

B

223

C

D

Dowhill
Dipple
A77
Chapeldonan
Craighead
Grangeston
Old Daily
Penkill

Girvan
Houdston
Saugh Hill
296

1

Black Neuk
Glendoune
Glendrissaig

Kennedy's
Pass
Ardwell
297
Grey Hill
A714
Pinminnoch

7

Pinmore
B734

Lendalfoot
12
Motte
Aldons
Carleton
Fishery
Daljarrock
Poundland
B734
Pinwherry

Bennane
Head
Colmonell
9
Dalreoch
Glenduisk

Knockdolian
265
Stinchar
Craigneil
A714
Ballochmorrie

2

Ballantrae
Bay
Auchairne
Balkissock
Shiel Hill
230
Barrhill

Ballantrae
Mains of Tig
Water of Tig

Glenapp Castle
Downan
Point
Smyrton
Beneraird
439

Kilantringan
Loch
Craigie
Fell
Milljoan
Hill
403
Chirmorrie

hours
Cairnryan-Belfast..........2¼
Cairnryan-Larne.........1-1¾
Carlock
Hill
323
Altimeg
Hill

Finnarts
Point
Glen App
A77
Markdhu
Standing
Stones

3

Milleur Point

Corsewall
Point
Miltonise
Glenwhilly

Barnhills
North Cairn
Dalnigap

South
Cairn
B738
Kirkcolm
Corsewall
Cairnryan
17
Braid
Fell
235
Artfield
Fell

Dounan
Bay
Airies
Ervie
Loch
Connell
A718
Cairn
Point
Beoch
Burn

Portobello
7
Soleburn
New
Luce
Tarf Bridg

4

Knocknain
Leswalt
Innermessan
Auchmantle
Galdenoch

B7043
A77
Lochnaw
A751
Lochinch Castle
164
Craig
Fell

Stranraer
Castle Kennedy
Carscreug

Broadsea
Bay
Portslogan
Southern Upland Way
A77
Loch Magillie
Castle Kennedy
A75
10
Dunragit
Moor
Glenluce
Abbey
Whitecairn
A75

Whiteleys
Soulseat
Loch
Dunragit
Glenluce

Black
Head
Cairn Pat
182
Lochans
Kildrochet
House
Genoch
Whitecrook
A747

Dinvin
6
Colfin
Genoch Square
B7077
Milton

5

Portpatrick
A77
A716
Sands of Luce
8
Auchen

Awhirk
Stoneykirk
Crow's Nest
Auchenmalg
Bay

Dunskey
Port of
Spittal Bay
Balgreggan
Sandhead
206

Cairngarroch Bay

0 2 4 6 miles
0 2 4 6 8 10 km

Money He

B

C

D

L U C E   B A Y

A716
14
Clachanmore
Ardwell
House
Ardwell Bay
Ardwell

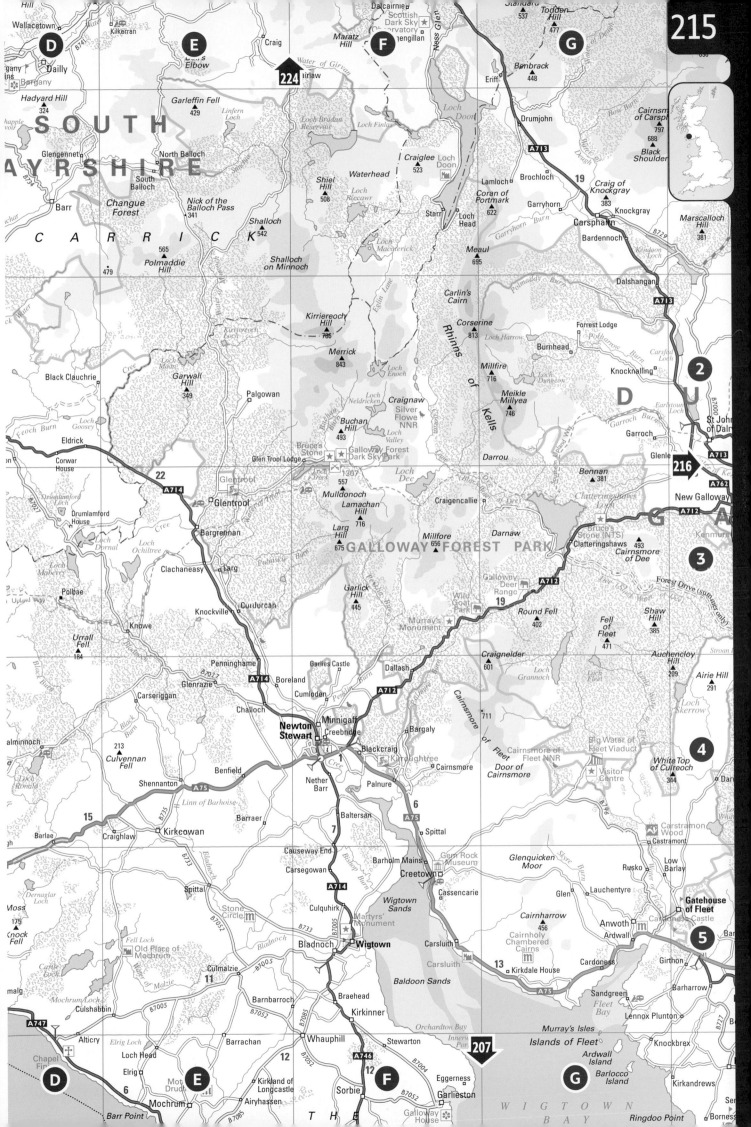

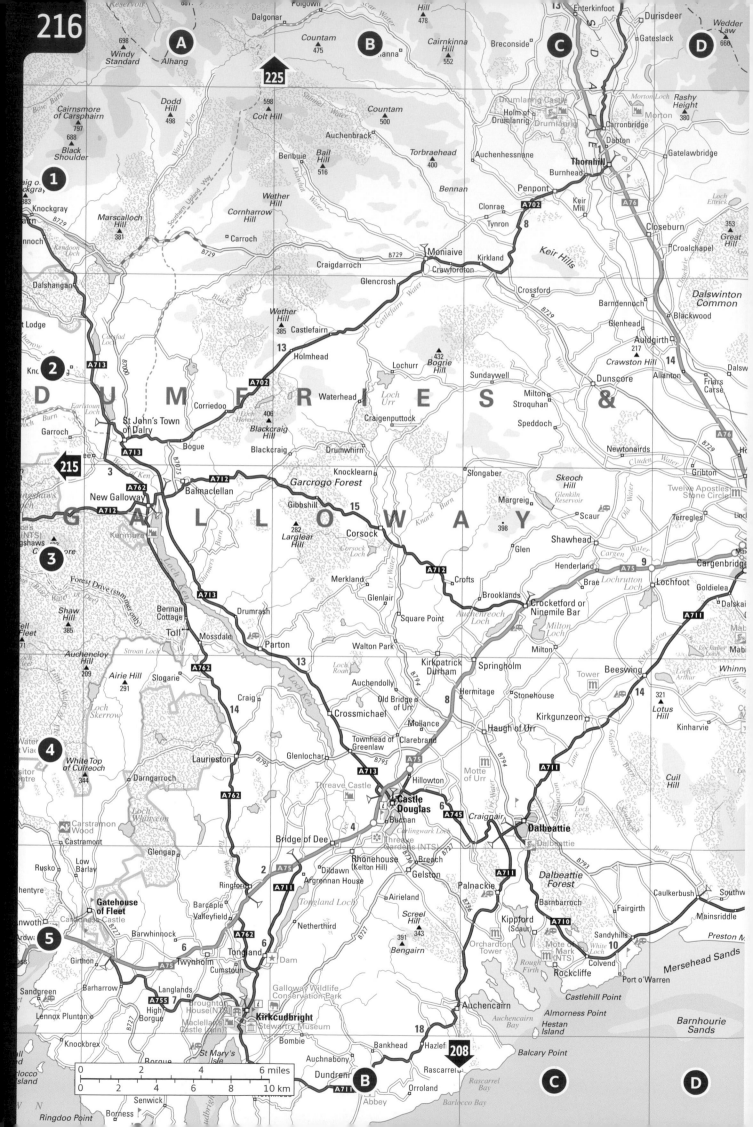

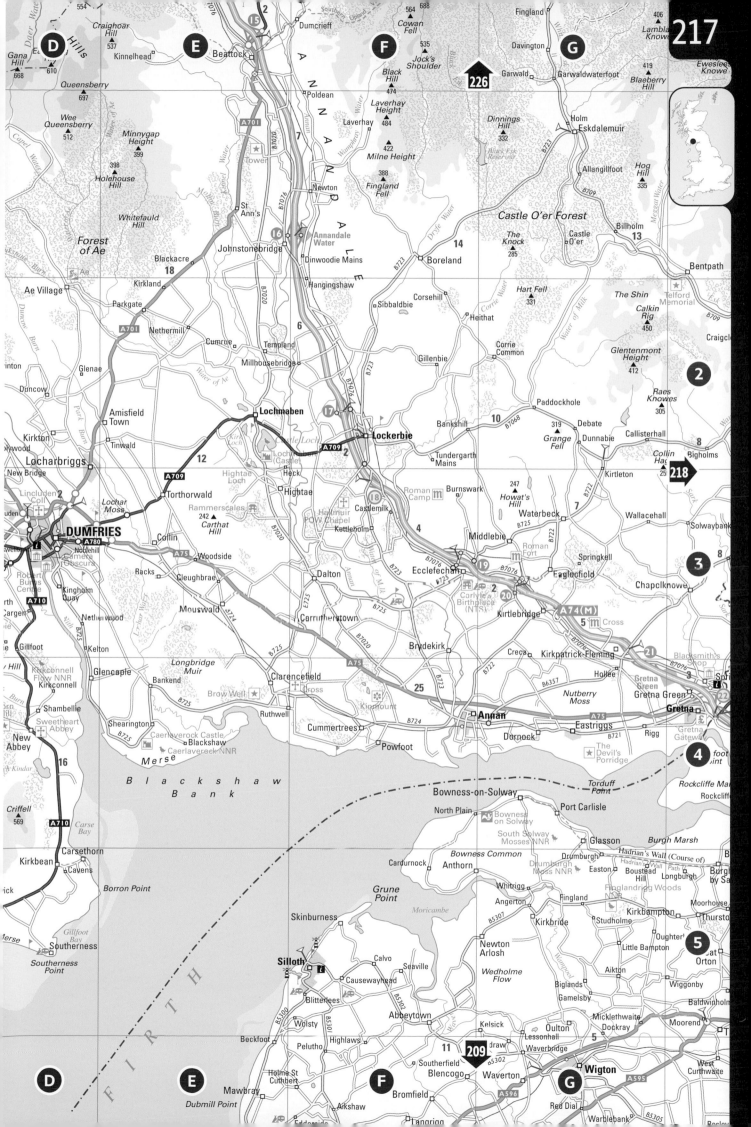

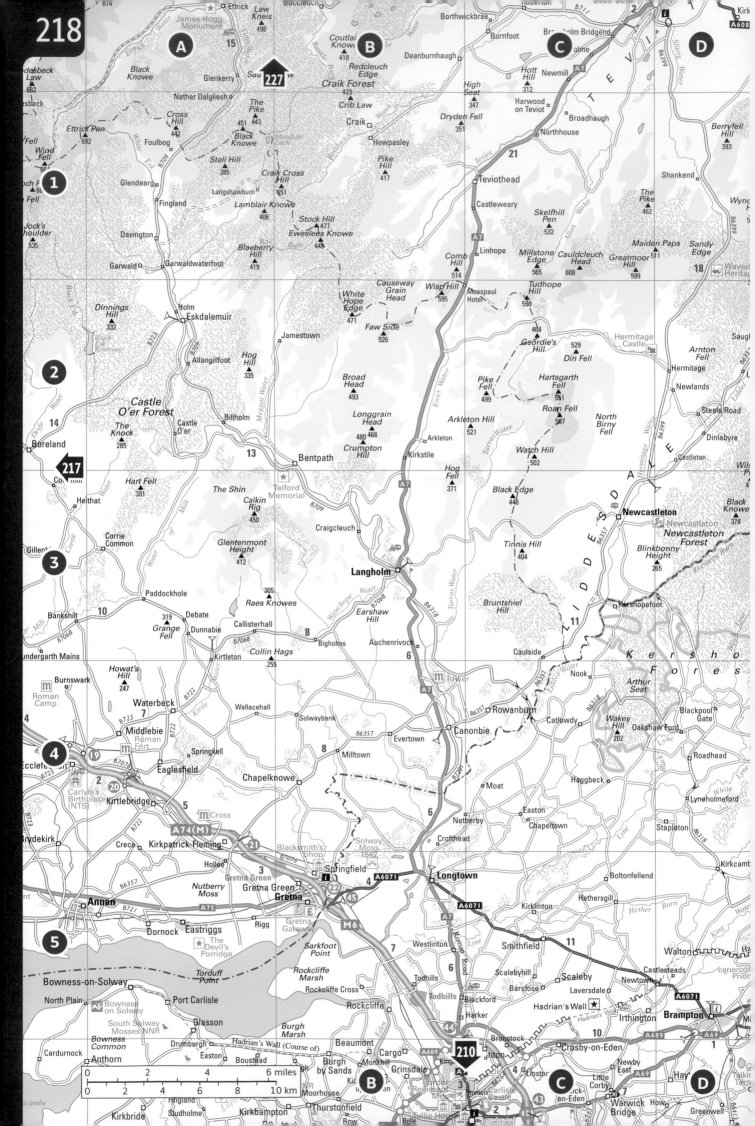

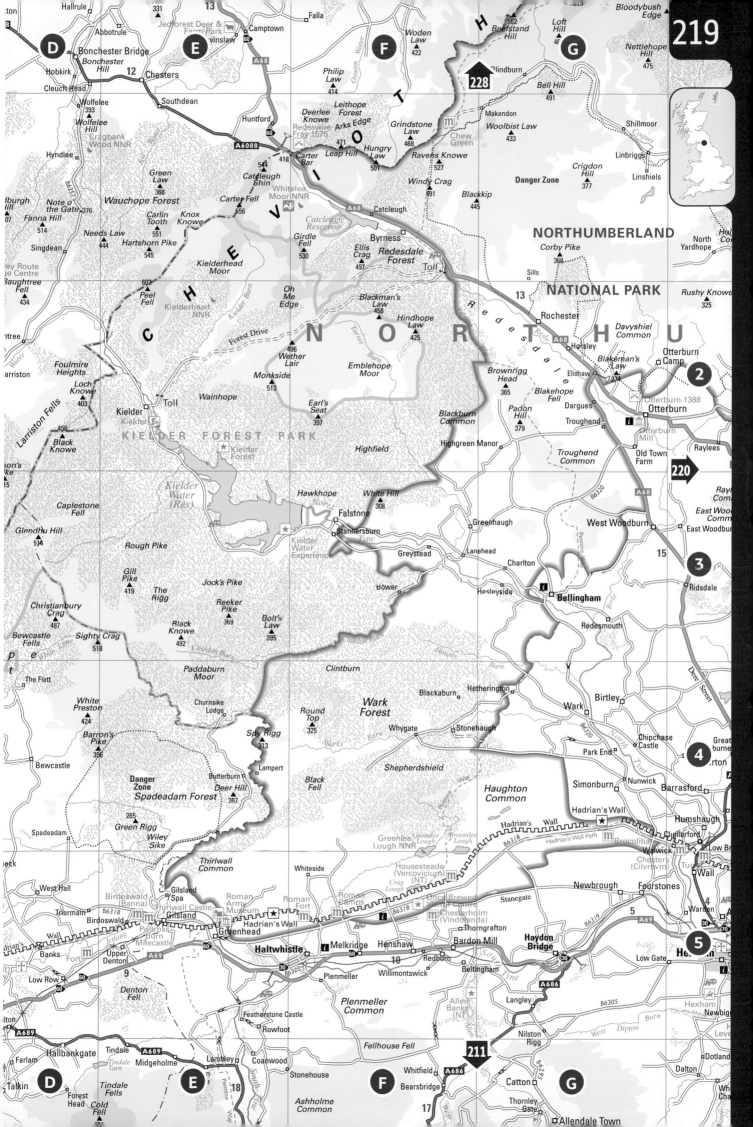

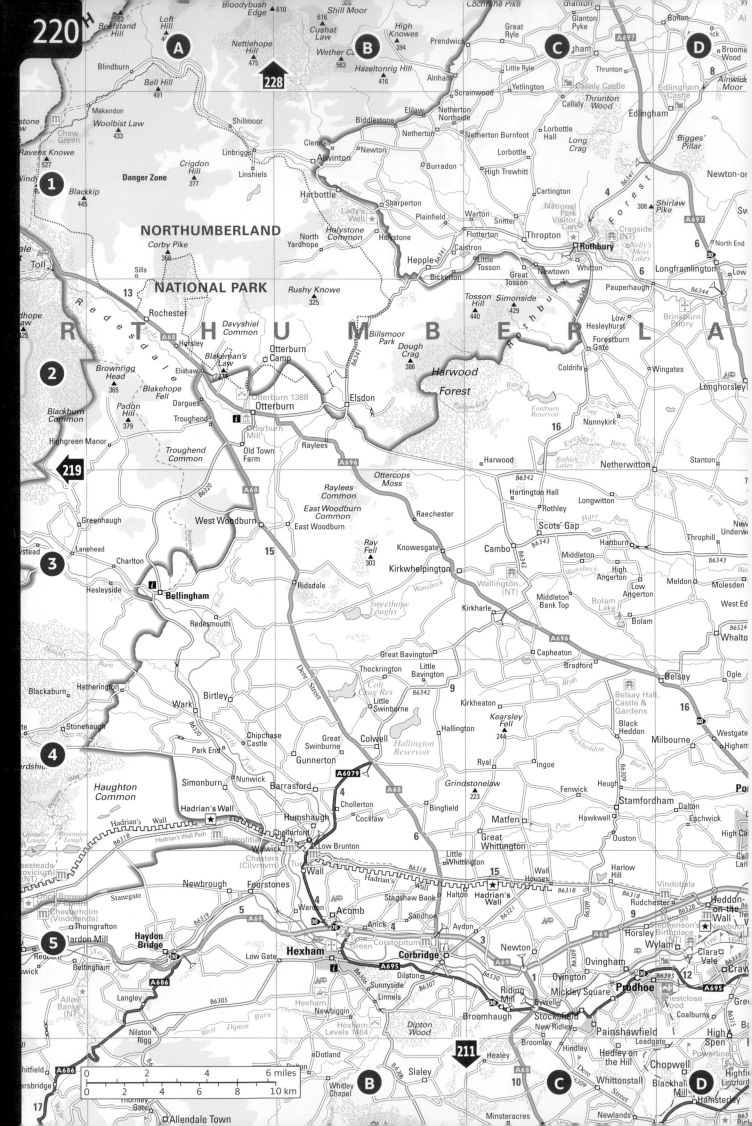

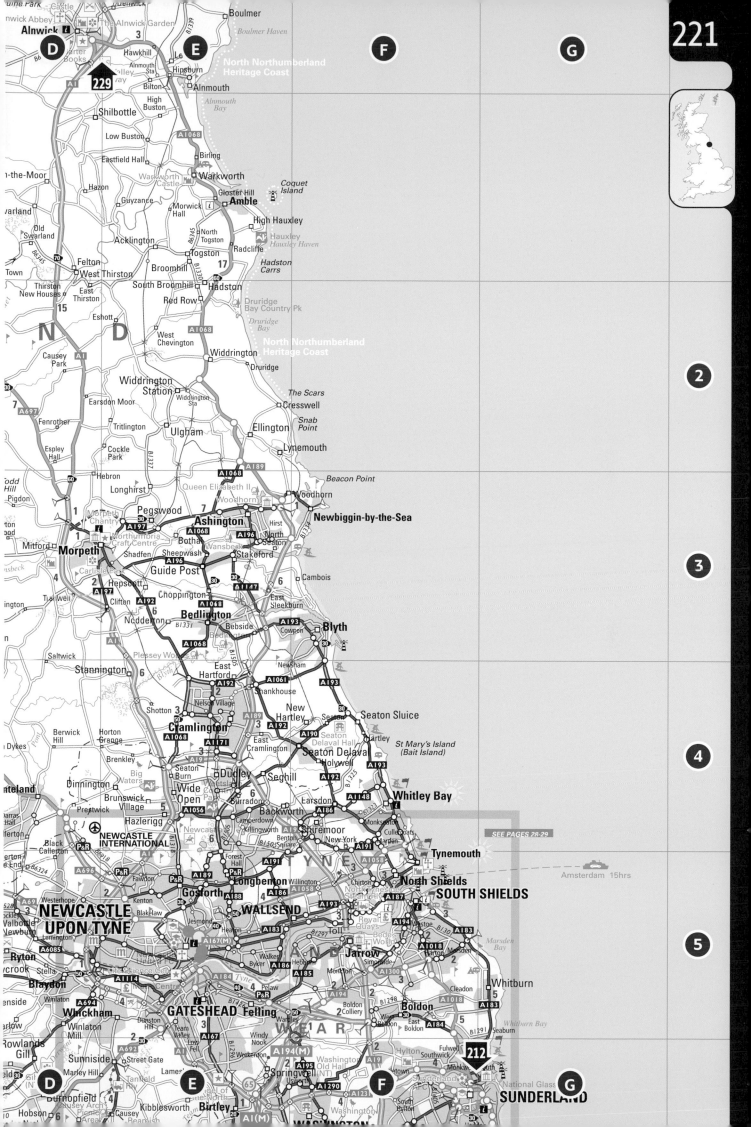

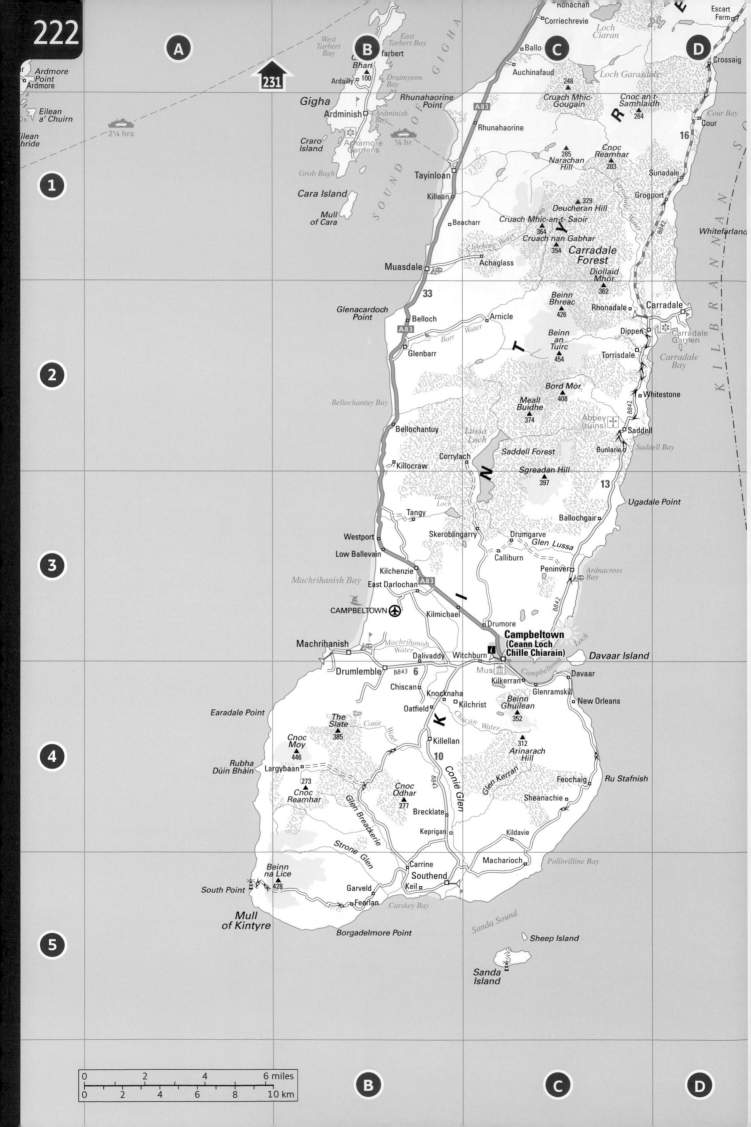

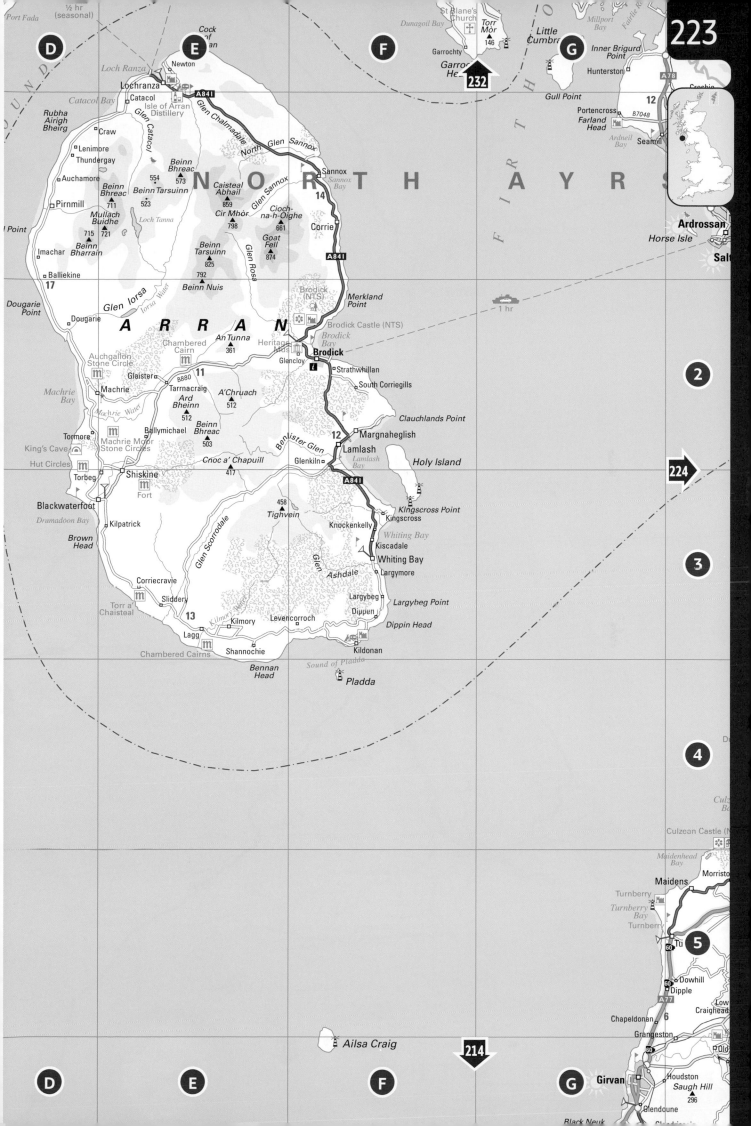

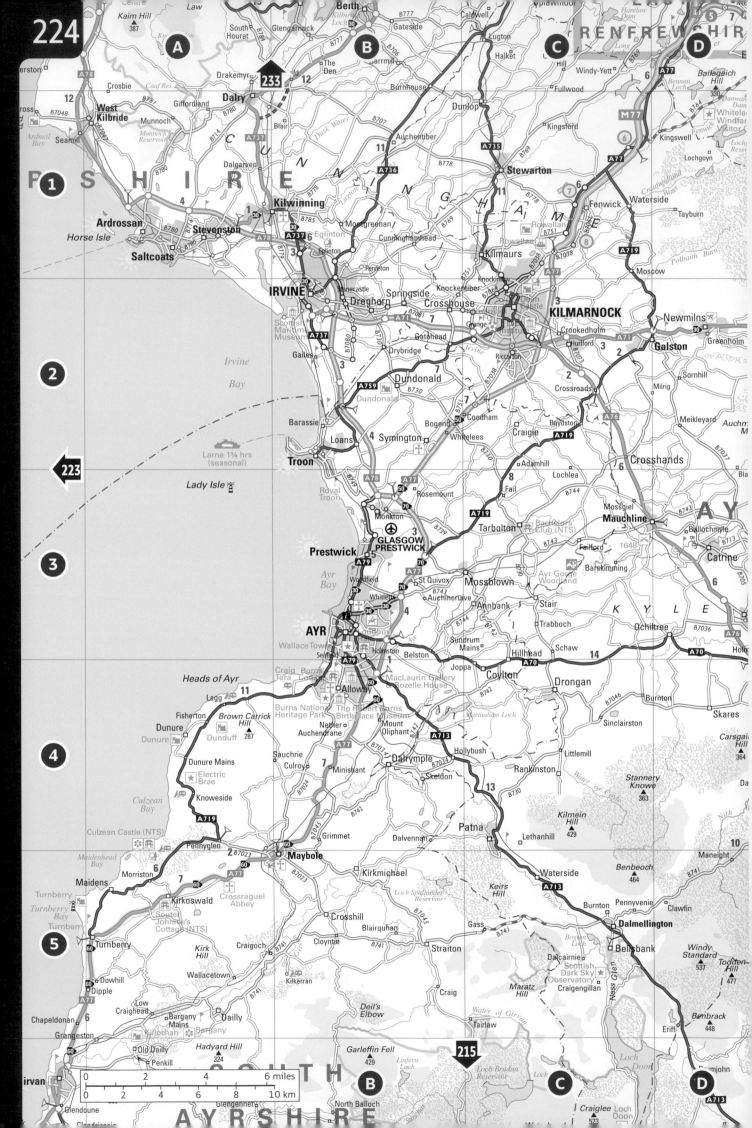

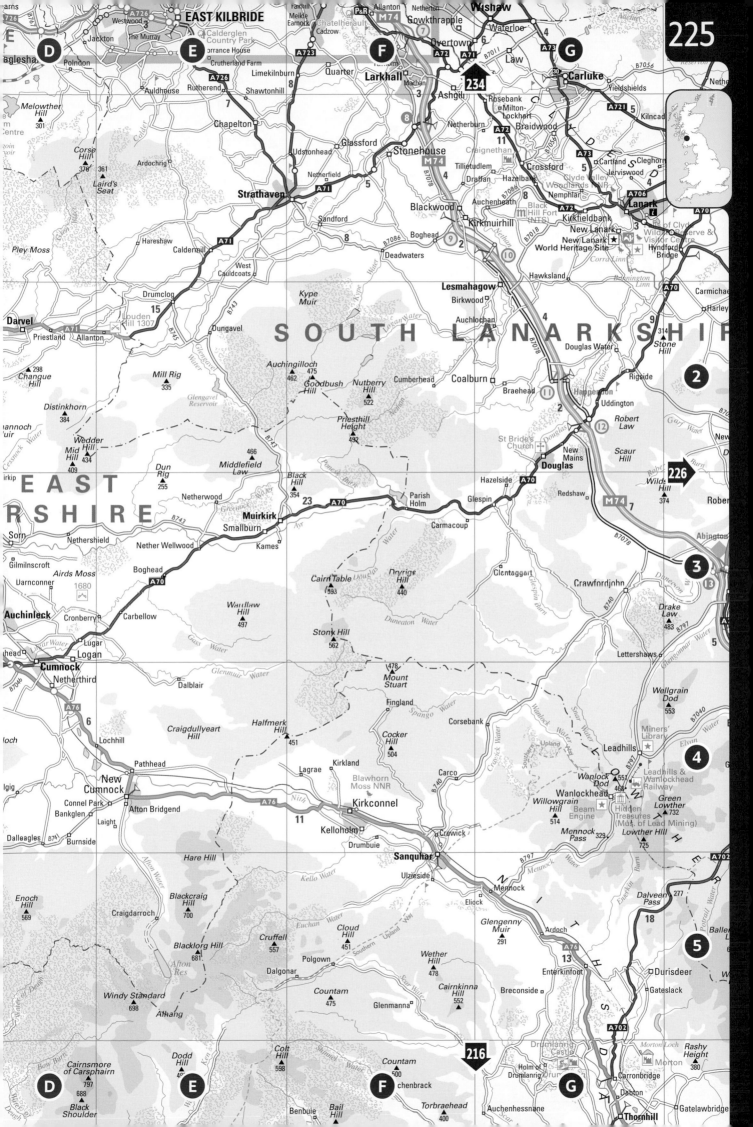

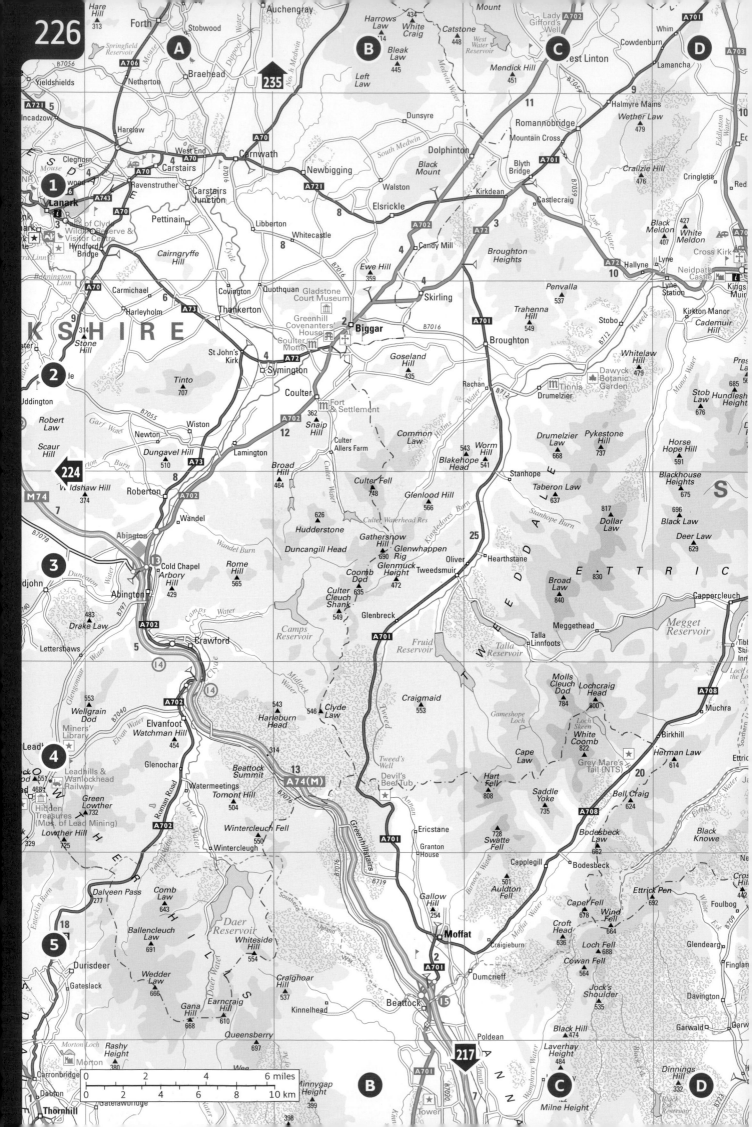

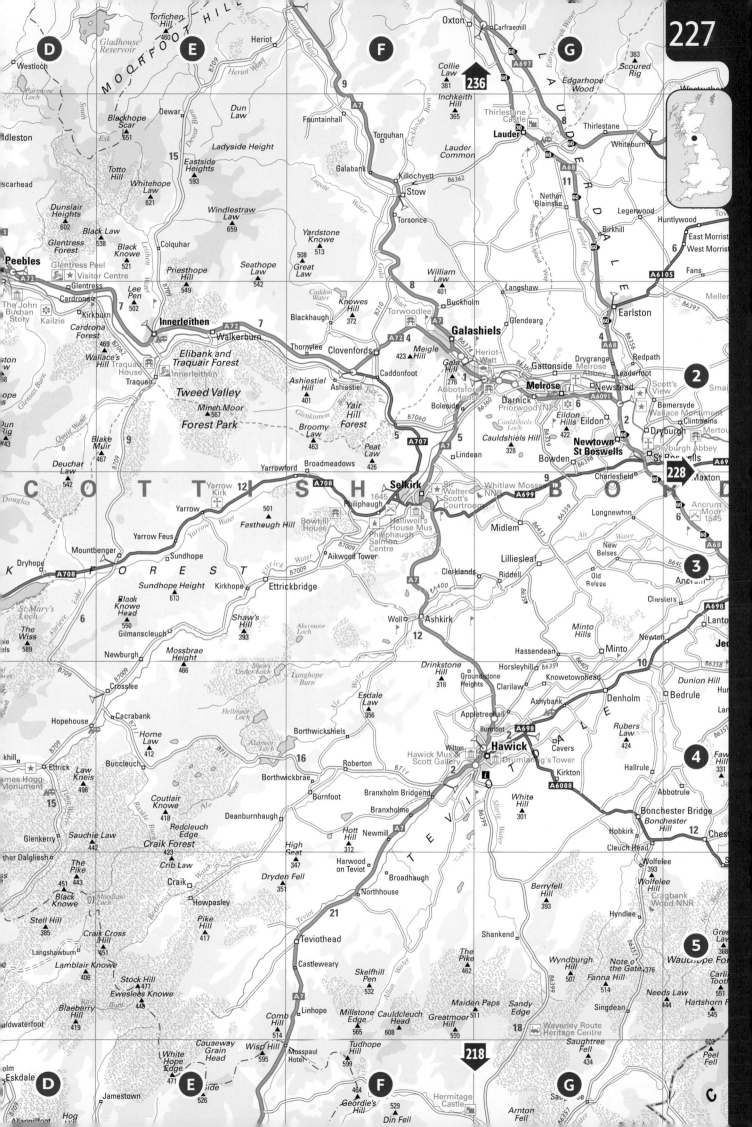

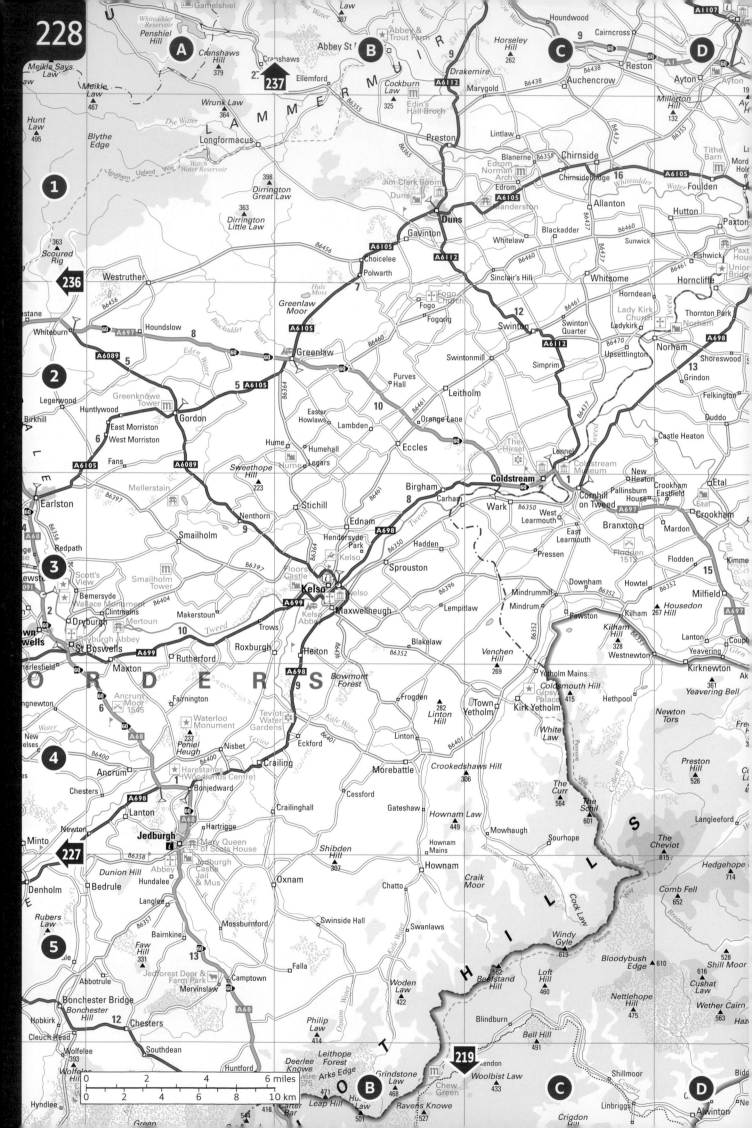

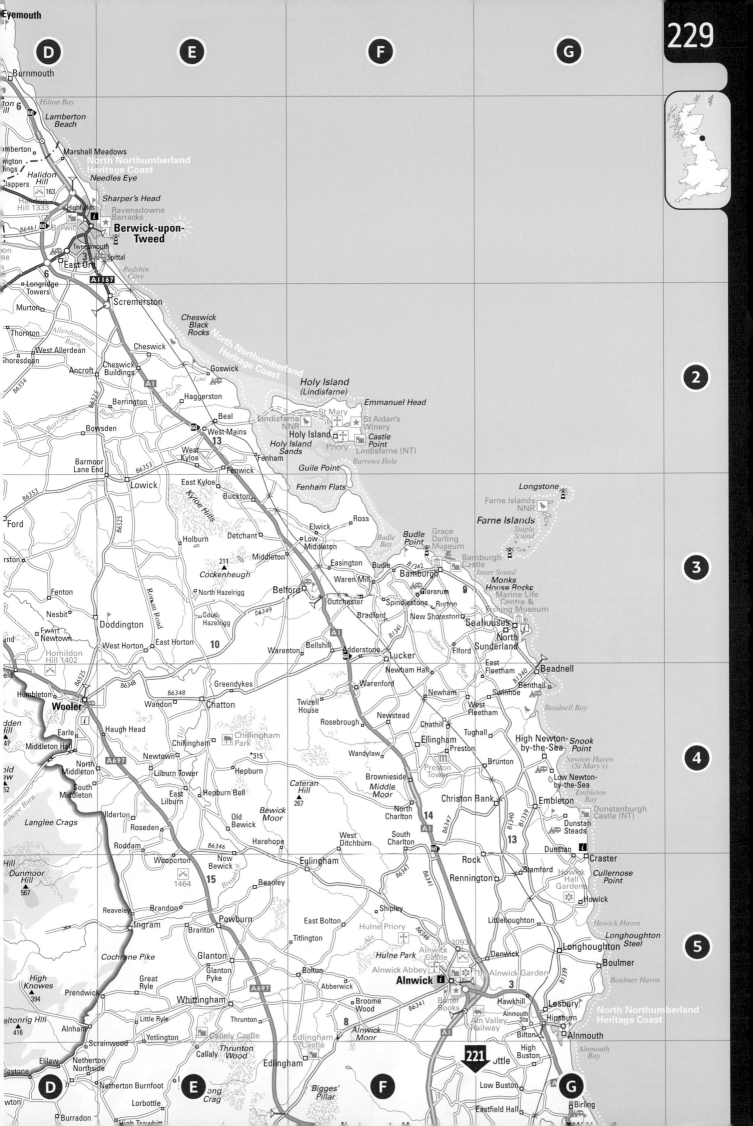

COLONSAY

A   B   C   D

238

1

Port Mòr   Kilchattan
B8086   Scalasaig
Machrins
Loch Staosnaig
Sguide an Leanna   B8085   Baleromindubh
Garvard   Balerominmore   Rubha Dubh

Eilean Mhucaig   Rubha Bàn
Priory   Shian Bay
Dubh Eilean   A
Oronsay   Eilean Ghaoideamal
Eilean nan Ron   Caolas Mòr

Sgeir Mhòr a' Bhrein- phuirt
1¼ hrs (seasonal)   Rubh' an t- Sàilein
Loch Tarbert
Rubh' a' Chrois-aoinidh

Rubh' a' Mhàil
Rubha Bholsa   Glenbatrick
Scrinadle   Beinn Bhreac
Sgarbh Breac   506   439   Beinn Tarsuir
364   416
283   Jura Forest
Margadale Hill   Beinn an Oir   Beinn Shiantaidh
Giurbheinn   785   755
316   Beinn a' Chaolais
Bunnahabhain   734   Paps of Jura
Beinn Bhreac   Ardnahoe   Loch a' Chnuic Bhric   Loch an t-Siob
286   Gleann Asdale
Balulive   Glas Bheinn   Knockro
Keills   561   Feolin   Loch Mile
Loch Finlaggan   Port Askaig   Feolin Ferry
Loch Staoisha   Dubh Bheinn   Keils
530   Craighouse
ISLAY   Ballygrant   8   A846   Sr
Loch Cam   Kilmeny   342   Eilean
Brat Bheinn   Rubha na Tràille
Moin'a'choire   Loch Ballygrant   Crackaig
B8017   Grainel   Esknish   Loch Lossit   A846   Cabrach
B8018   Lyrabus   Ardfin   Sannaig
Craigens   Jura House
Foreland   Blackrock   Islay House   Redhouses   Am Fraoch Eilean   Rubha na Tràille
A847   Bridgend   Cachlaidh Mhòr   Brosdale Island
Coul Point   Machrie   Conisby   Neriby   Laggan   McArthur's Head
Aruadh   Barr   Sgorr nam Faoileann   2 hrs
Rockside   Cattadale   429   Beinn na Caillich
Kilchoman   Bruichladdich   Gartnatra   A846   Cluanach   Glas Bheinn   337
Machir Bay   Bowmore   Cruach   471   Proaig
Kilchiaran   Ronnachmore   Kilennan   Beinn Bhan   Beinn Bheigeir
Port Charlotte   15   Gartbreck   471   491
Kilchiaran Bay   RINNS   Beinn Uraraidh   Rubha Liath
Tormisdale   Gearach   Laggan   454   Ardtalla
Carn   Laggan   Loch Uraraidh
Lossit   OF   Beinn Tart a' Mhill   Dutch   13   Kintour   Claggain Bay
Kelsay   232   A846   B8016   Trudernish
Nerabus   ISLAY   Laggan   Loch Uigeadail
Rubha na Faing   ISLAY   Sgorr Bhogachain   Kintour
Easter Ellister   A847   Glenegedale   Beinn Sholum   Kildalton Church &   Ardmore Point
Portnahaven   Laggan Bay   347   Crosses   Ardmore
Port Wemyss   Machrie   Leorin   Eilean a' Chuirn
Orsay   Kintra   Leorin Lochs
Rinns Point   Rubha Mòr   Eilean Bhride
Maol Buidhe   Cornabus   2¼ hrs
165   Ardbeg
Lower Killeyan   Risabus   Lagavulin   Rubha na Gainmhich
THE   OA   Carnmore   Port Ellen   A846
Mull of Oa   Inerval   Laphroaig   The Ard
Loch Kinnabus   Port Chubaird   Texa
Rubha nan Leacan

Nave Island
Na Peileirean   Ardnave Point
Ardnave
Killinallan Point
Carraig Bhàn   Tayovullin   Gortantaoid Point
Ton Mhòr   Kilnave   Killinallan
Sanaigmore   Ardnave Loch   Rubh' a' Mhàil
Braigo   Leckgruinart   Loch Gruinart
Eilean Mòr   Carnduncan
Rubha Lamanais   Smaull   Aoradh
Ballinaby   Grainel
Saligo Bay   Loch Gorm

0   2   4   6 miles
0   2   4   6   8   10 km

B   C   D

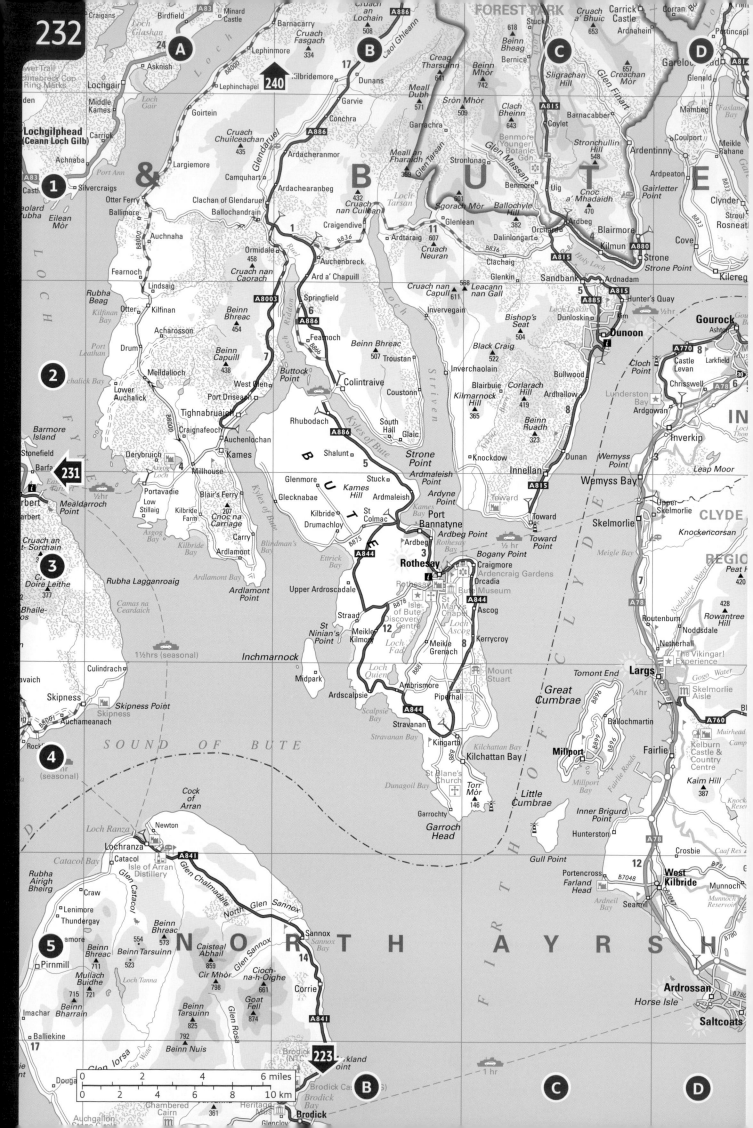

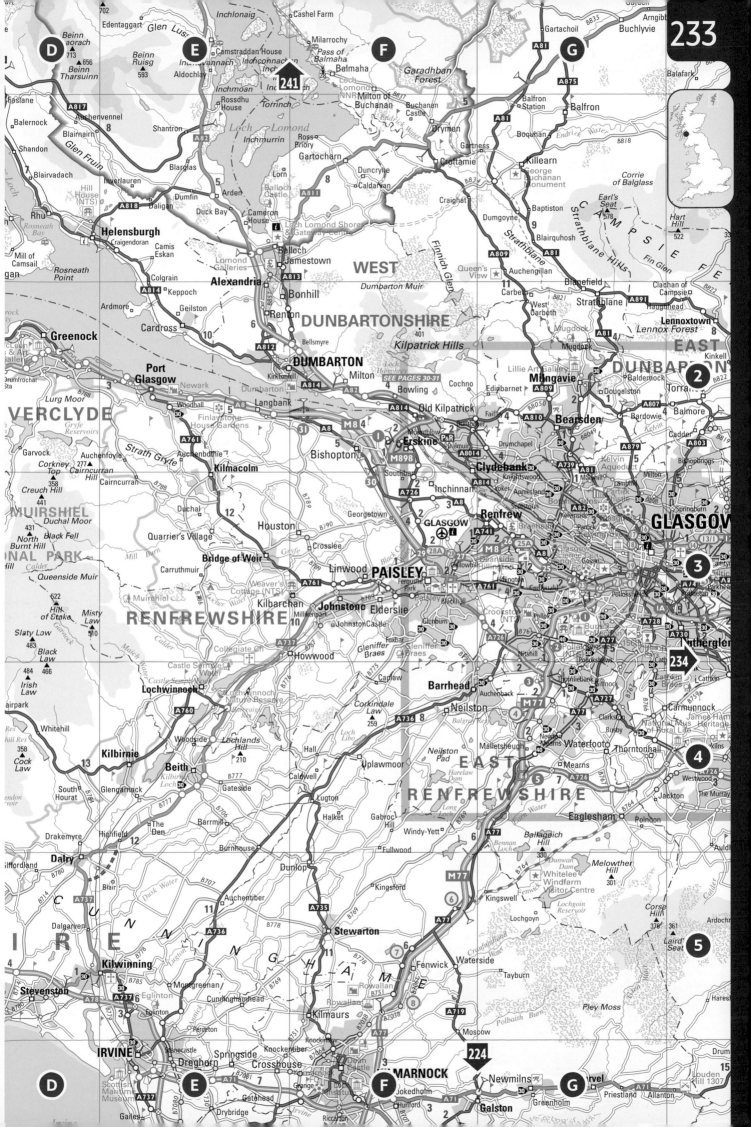

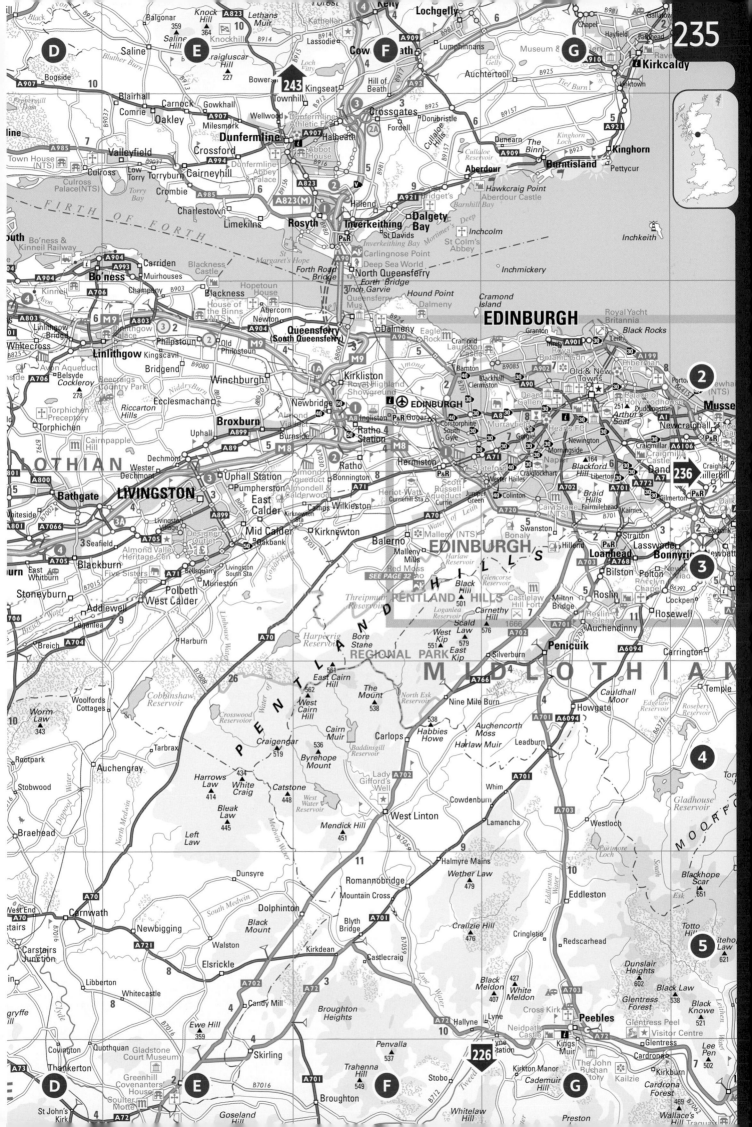

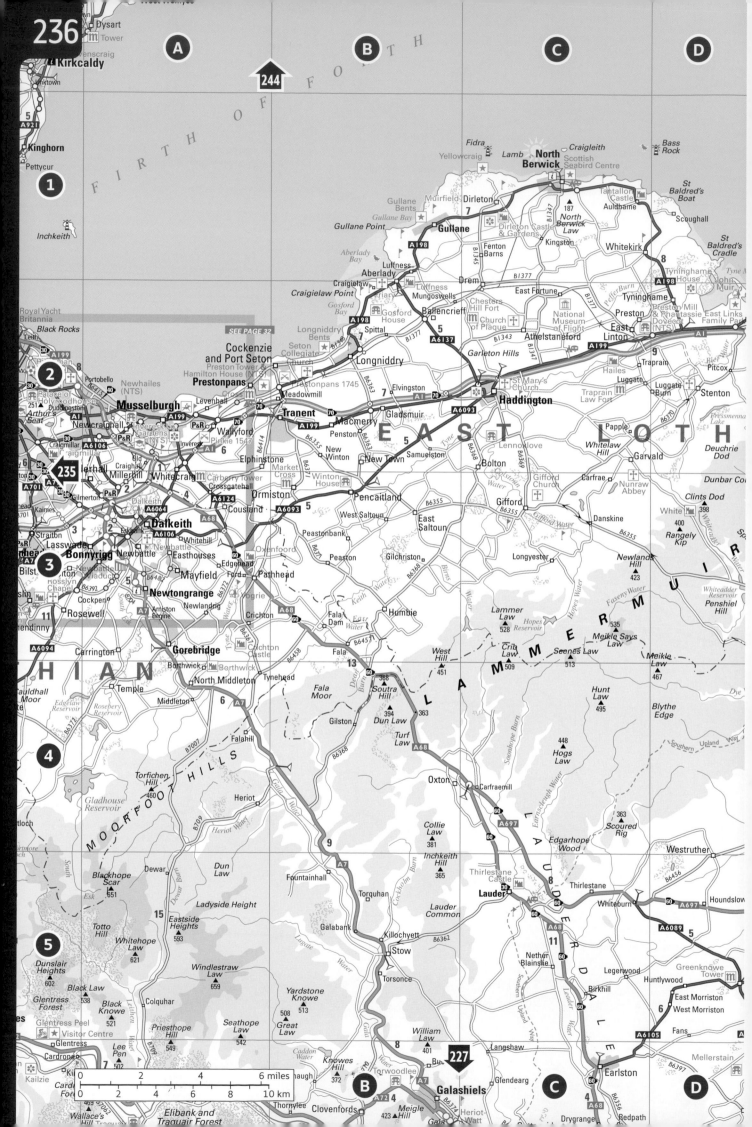

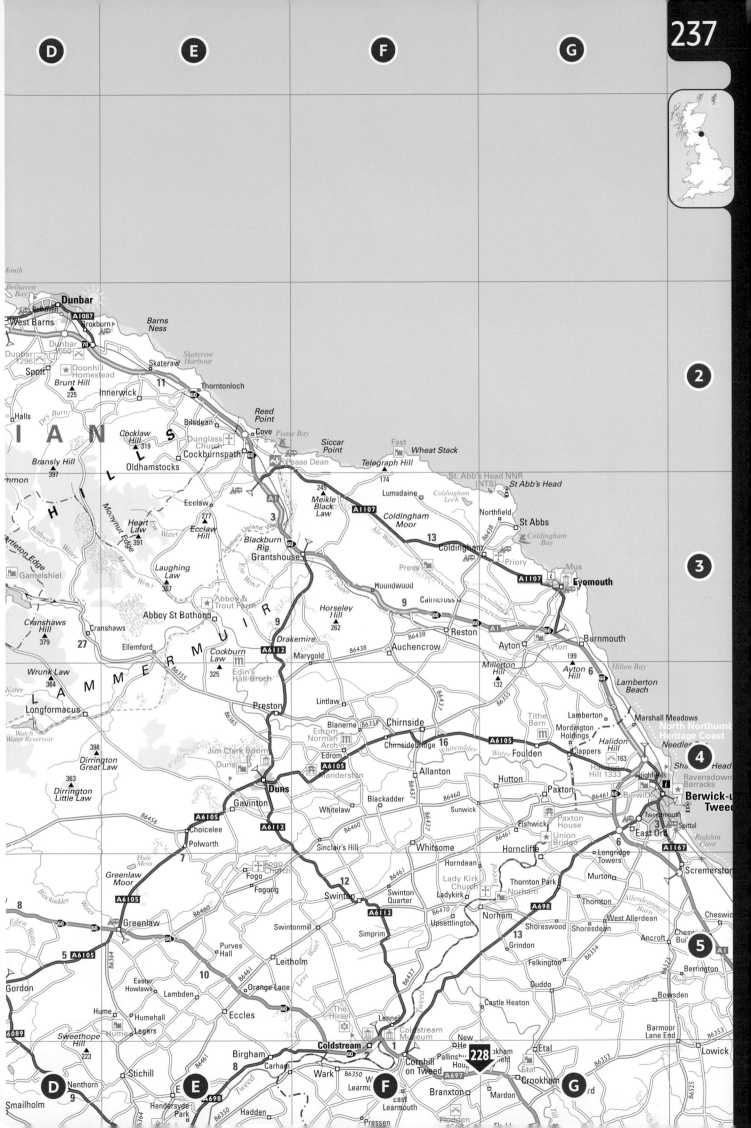

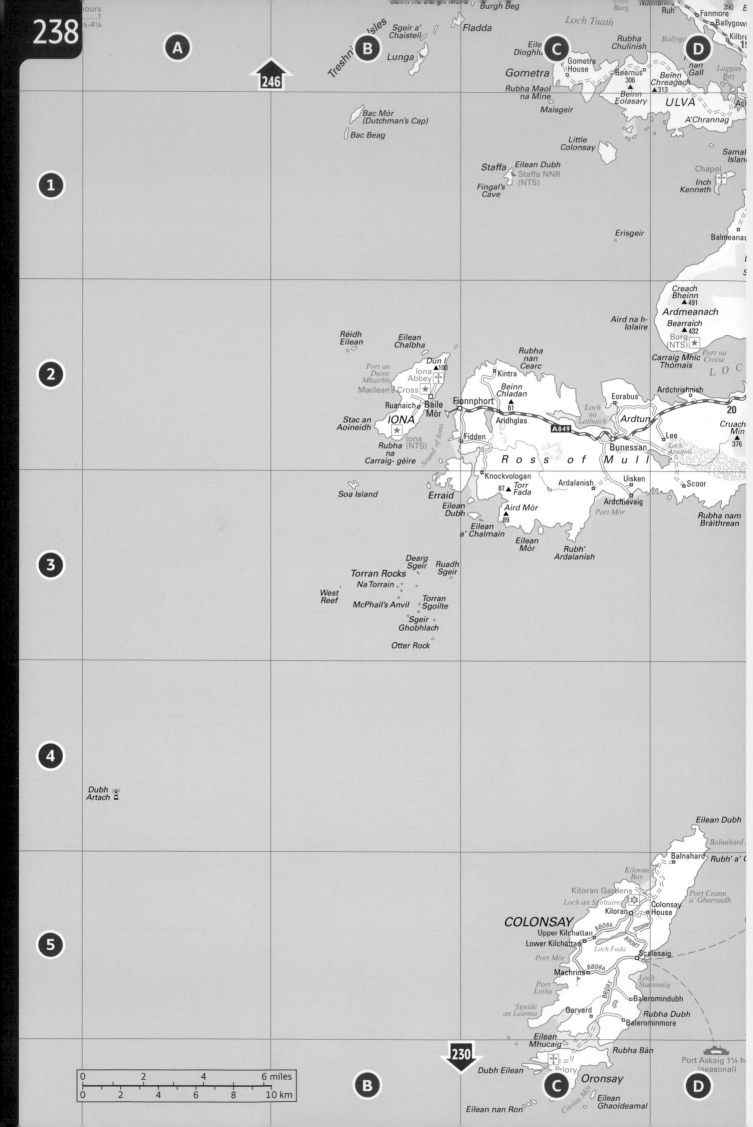

A B C D

1

2

3

4

5

246

230

Treshnish Isles
Sgeir a' Chaisteil
Fladda
Lunga

Eile Dioghlu
Rubha Chulinish
Gometra House
Bearnus 306
Beinn Chreagach
nan Gall
Fanmore
Ballygown
390

Gometra
Rubha Maol na Mine
Beinn Eolasary
Beinn 313
ULVA
A'Chrannag

Bac Mòr (Dutchman's Cap)
Bac Beag

Maisgeir
Little Colonsay

Samal Island

Staffa
Eilean Dubh
Staffa NNR (NTS)
Fingal's Cave

Chapel
Inch Kenneth

Erisgeir

Balmeanac

Creach Bheinn 491
Ardmeanach
Aird na h-Iolaire
Bearraich 432
Burg (NTS)
Carraig Mhic Thòmais
Port na Croise
LOC

Réidh Eilean
Eilean Chalbha
Dùn I 100
Iona Abbey
Maclean's Cross
Rubha nan Cearc
Kintra
Beinn Chladan 81
Eorabus
Ardchrishnish
Ardtun
20

Port an Duine Mhairbh
Ruanaich
Baile Mòr
IONA
Fionnphort
Aridhglas
A849
Loch na Lathaich
Lee
Cruach Min 376

Stac an Aoineidh
Iona (NTS)
Rubha na Carraig-gèire
Fidden
Sound of Iona
Bunessan
Loch Assapol

Soa Island
Erraid
Eilean Dubh
Knockvologan
Torr Fada 87
Ardalanish
Uisken
Scoor

Ross of Mull
Aird Mòr 89
Ardchiavaig
Port Mòr
Rubha nam Bràithrean

Eilean a' Chalmain
Eilean Mòr
Rubh' Ardalanish

Dearg Sgeir
Ruadh Sgeir
Torran Rocks
Na Torrain
West Reef
McPhail's Anvil
Torran Sgoilte
Sgeir Ghobhlach
Otter Rock

Dubh Artach

Eilean Dubh
Balnahard
Balnahard
Rubh' a'
Kiloran Bay
Port Ceann a' Gharraidh

Kiloran Gardens
Loch an Sgoltaire
Kiloran
Colonsay House
COLONSAY
Upper Kilchattan
Lower Kilchattan
B8086
B8087
Loch Fada
Scalasaig
Port Mòr
Machrins
B8086
Loch Staosnaig
Port Lotha
B8085
Balfomindubh
Sguide an Leanna
Garvard
Rubha Dubh
Balerominmore
Port Askaig 1¼ (seasonal)
Eilean Mhucaig
Rubha Bàn
Dubh Eilean
Priory
Oronsay
Caolas Mòr
Eilean Ghaoideamal
Eilean nan Ron

0 2 4 6 miles
0 2 4 6 8 10 km

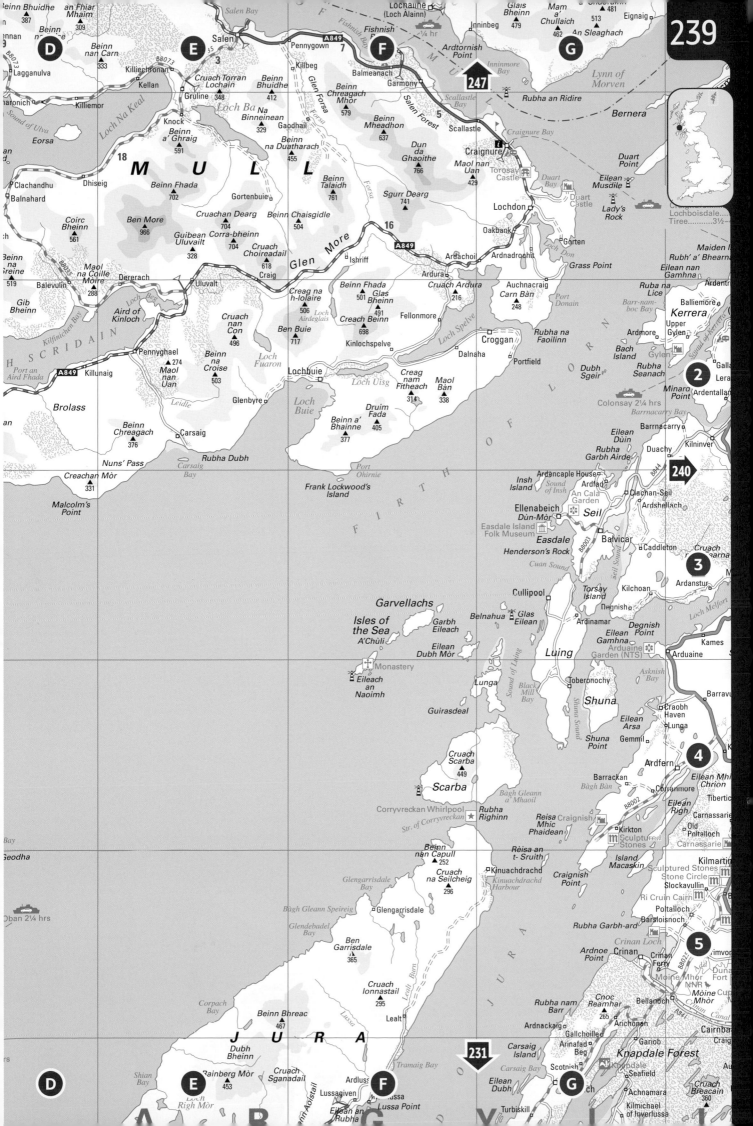

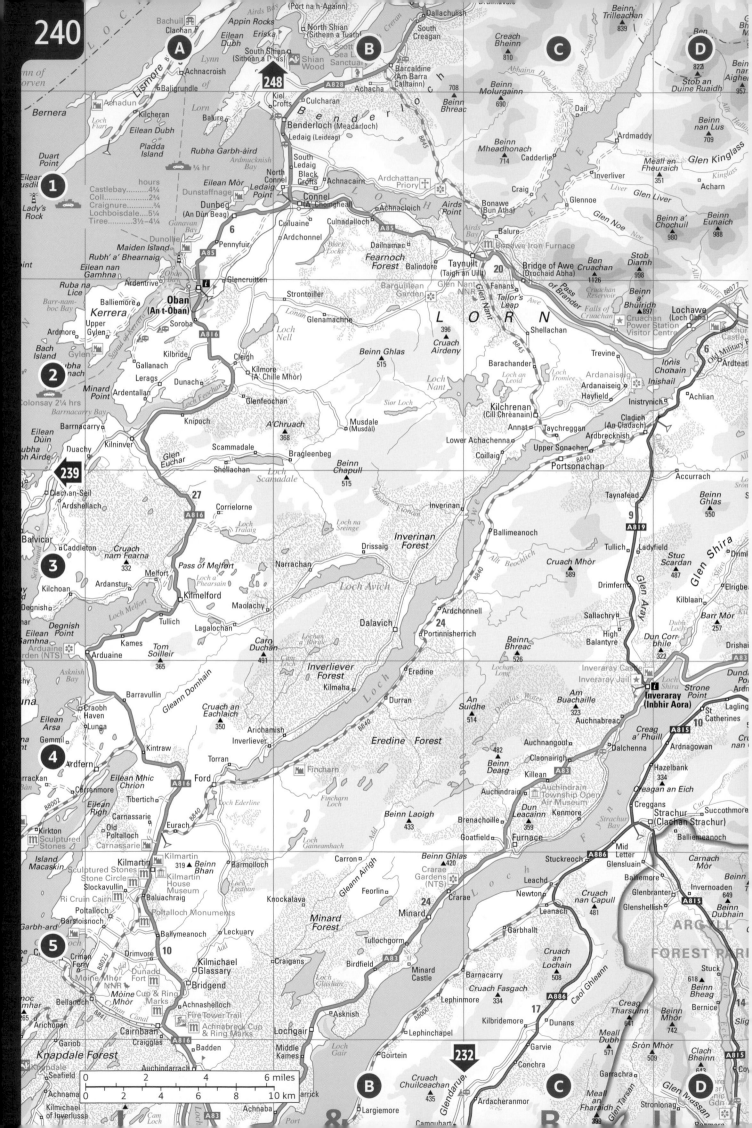

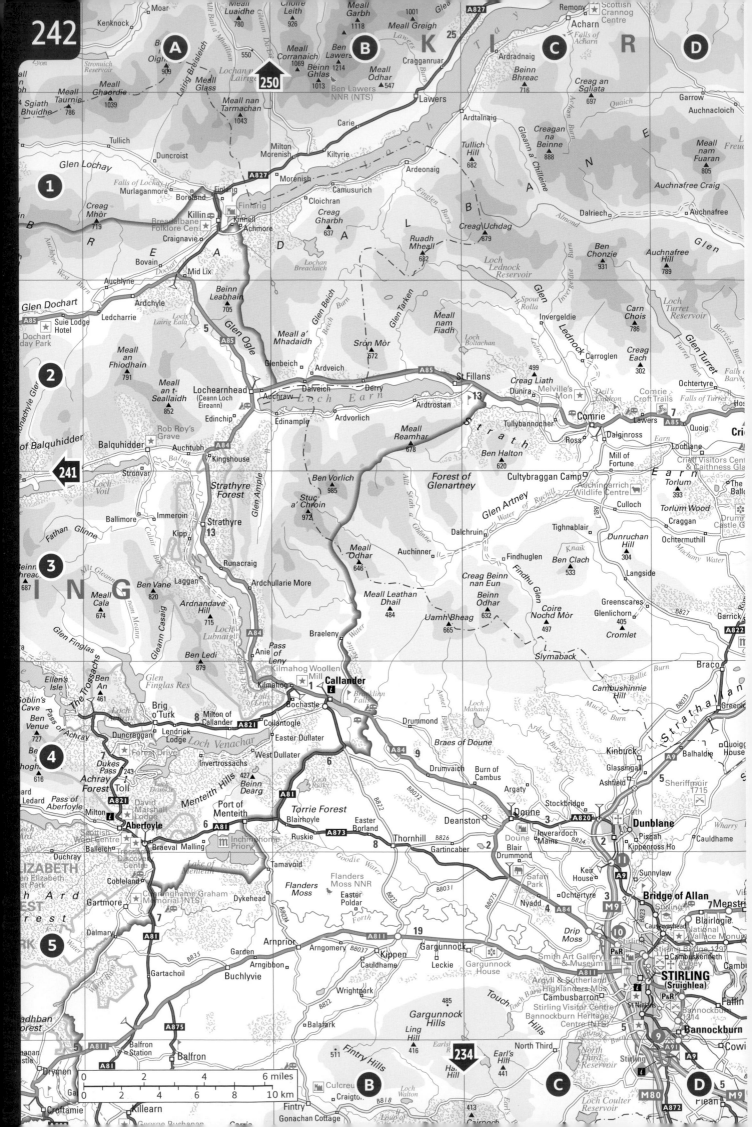

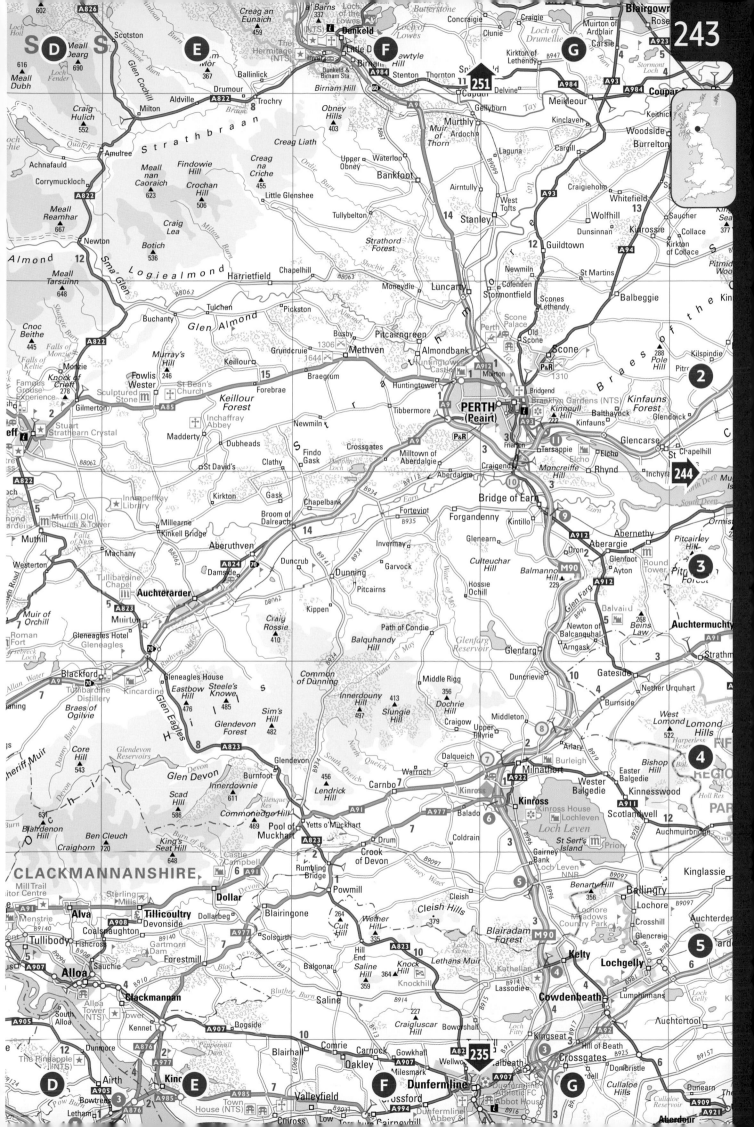

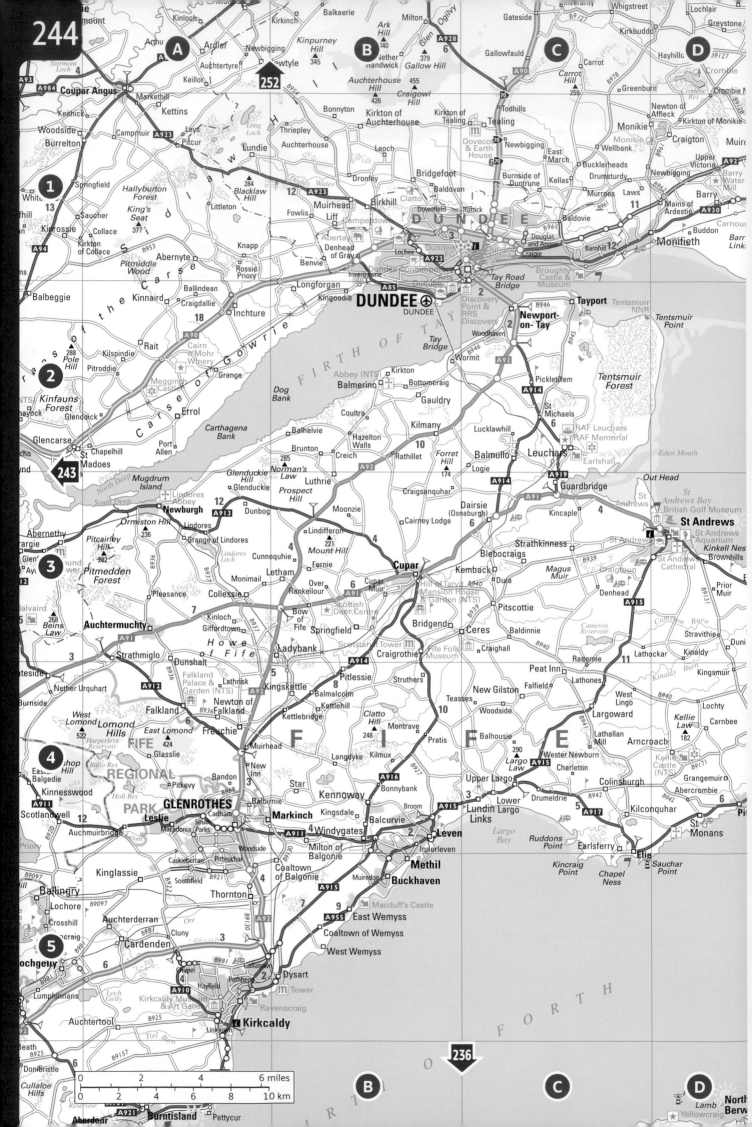

Redford
A933
Marywell
Meg's
Craig
A92
St Vigeans
Denhead of
birlot
Carlingheugh
Bay
Carmyll
D
E
Guy
B9127
The Deil's Heid
Arbirlot
Bonnyton
Arbroath Abbey
Easter
Knox
A92
Elliot
Arbroath
6
Salmond's Muir
drum
East Haven
2
Panbride
Carnoustie

Buddon Ness

F
G
253

2
☀ Bell Rock
(Inchcape)

Buddo Ness
Babbet Ness
3
Boarhills
10
A917
Cambo
Kingsbarns
Estate
no
Cambo
Ness
North
Carr
Tullybothy Craigs
Wormiston
Craighead
B940
Fife Ness
Airdrie
B9171
Crail
4
Spalefield
4
West Ness
A917
Innergellie
B9131
Kilrenny
Cellardyke
i
Anstruther
Scottish Fisheries Museum
ttenweem

North Ness
5
Isle of May NNR
Isle of May
Chapel
South Ness

237

Craig
D
☀ Bass Rock
E
F
G
vick
Scottish
Seabird
Centre

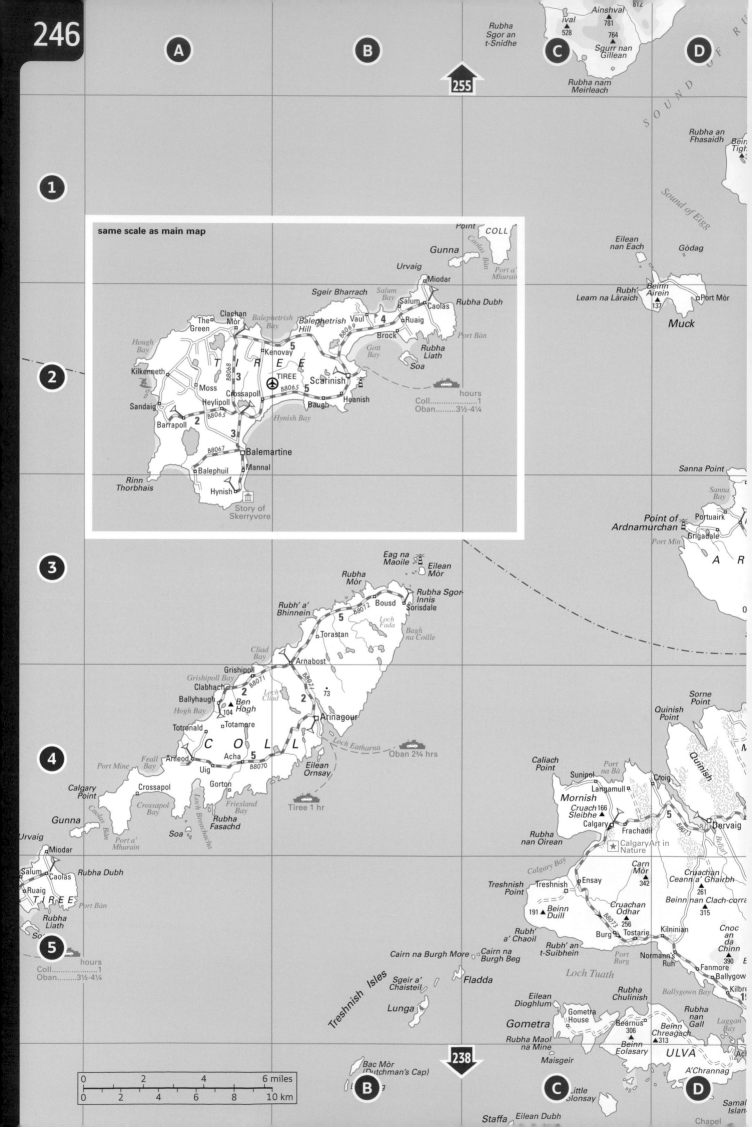

A B C D

1

2

3

4

5

255
238

Rubha
Sgor an
t-Snidhe

ival
528

Ainshval
781

812

Sgurr nan
Gillean

764

Rubha nam
Meirleach

Rubha an
Fhasaidh

Beinn
Tigh

Eilean
nan Each

Gòdag

Rubh'
Leam na Làraich

Beinn
Airein
137

Port Mòr

Muck

same scale as main map

Point
COLL

Gunna

Caolas Bàn

Port a'
Mhurai

Urvaig

Sgeir Bharrach

Salum
Bay

Miodar

Salum

Caolas

Rubha Dubh

Clachan
Mòr

Balephetrish
Bay

Balephetrish
Hill

Vaul

B8069

4

Ruaig

Port Bàn

The
Green

Hough
Bay

Kenovay

5

Brock

Gott
Bay

Rubha
Liath

T I R E E

TIREE

B8068

3

B8065

Scarinish

Soa

Kilkenneth

Moss

Crossapoll

Baugh

Heanish

Sandaig

Heylipoll

2

B8065

2

Barrapoll

3

hours
Coll.....................1
Oban.........3½-4¼

Hynish Bay

B8067

Balemartine

Balephuil

Mannal

Rinn
Thorbhais

Hynish

Story of
Skerryvore

Sanna Point

Sanna
Bay

Point of
Ardnamurchan

Portuairk

Grigadale

Port Min

A R

Eag na
Maoile

Eilean
Mòr

Rubha
Mòr

Rubha Sgor-
Innis

Rubh' a'
Bhinnein

5

B8072

Bousd

Sorisdale

Loch
Fada

Bagh
na Coille

Torastan

Cliad
Bay

Arnabost

Grishipoll

Grishipoll Bay

B8071

2

Loch
Cliad

B8071

73

Clabhach

Ballyhaugh

Ben
Hogh

2

Hogh Bay

104

Totamore

Arinagour

Totronald

C O L L

Loch Eatharna

Oban 2¾ hrs

Feall
Bay

Arileod

Acha

5

Eilean
Ornsay

Quinish
Point

Sorne
Point

Port Mine

Uig

Gorton

B8070

Calgary
Point

Tiree 1 hr

Caliach
Point

Port
na Bà

Croig

Quinish

Gunna

Caolas Bàn

Crossapol

Crossapol
Bay

Loch Breachacha

Rubha
Fasachd

Friesland
Bay

Sunipol

Langamull

Urvaig

Soa

Port a'
Mhurain

Mornish

Cruach
Sleibhe

166

Calgary

Frachadi

5

B8073

Dervaig

Miodar

Calgary Art in
Nature

Bellart

Salum

Caolas

Rubha Dubh

Rubha
nan Oirean

Calgary Bay

Carn
Mòr
342

Cruachan
Ceann a' Ghairbh

261

Ruaig

T I R E E

Port Bàn

Treshnish
Point

Treshnish

Ensay

Beinn
Duill

Cruachan
Odhar

Beinn nan Clach-corra
315

Rubha
Liath

191

256

Kilninian

So

5

hours
Coll.....................1
Oban.........3½-4¼

Cairn na Burgh More

Cairn na
Burgh Beg

Rubh'
a' Chaoil

Rubh' an
t-Suibhein

B8073

Burg

Tostarie

Port
Burg

Cnoc
an
da
Chinn
390

Normann's
Ruh

Fanmore

Ballygow

Treshnish Isles

Sgeir a'
Chaisteil

Fladda

Loch Tuath

Kilbre

Lunga

Eilean
Dioghlum

Gometra
House

Rubha
Chulinish

Ballygown Bay

Rubha
nan
Gall

Laggan
Bay

Gometra

Bèarnus
306

Beinn
Chreagach
313

ULVA

Ac

Rubha Maol
na Mine

Beinn
Eolasary

A'Chrannag

Bac Mòr
(Dutchman's Cap)

Maisgeir

Little
olonsay

Samal
Islan

Chapel

Staffa

Eilean
Dubh

0   2   4   6 miles
0   2   4   6   8   10 km

B C D

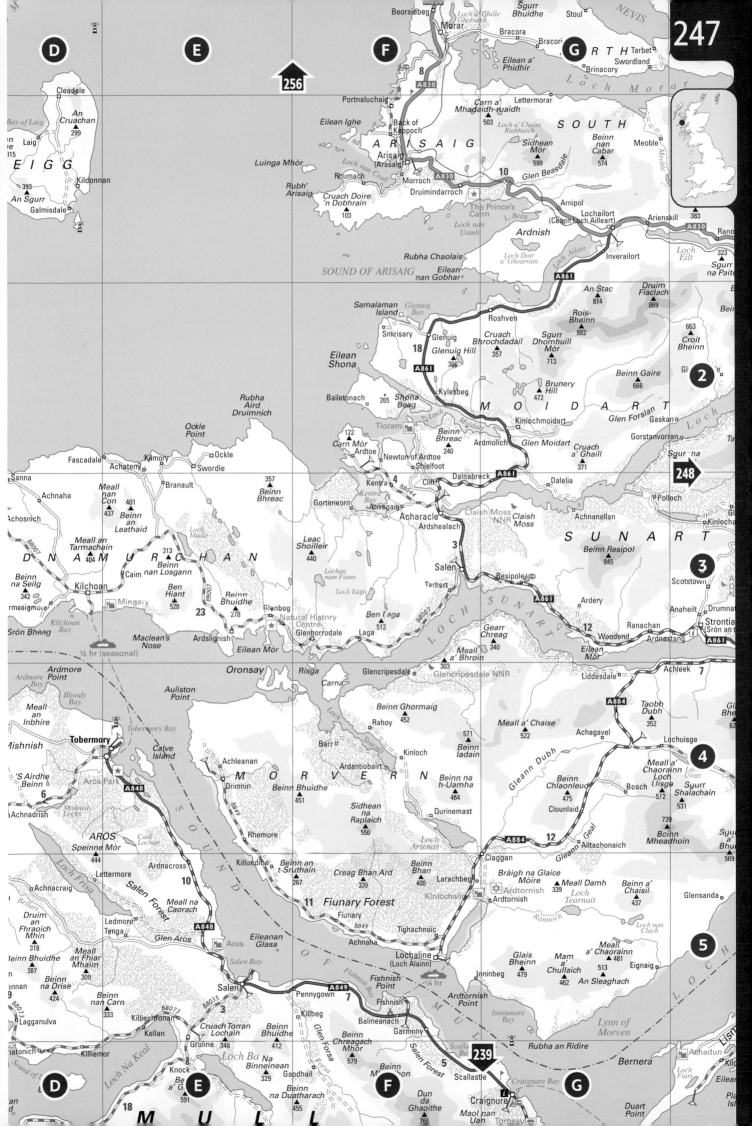

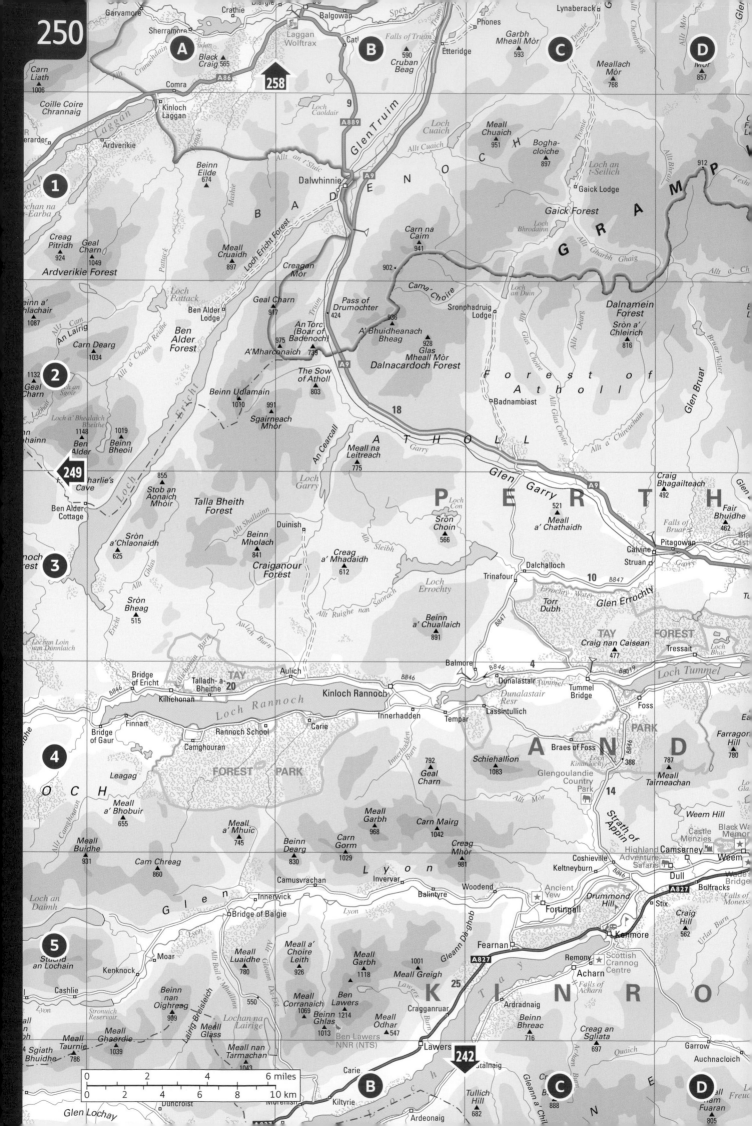

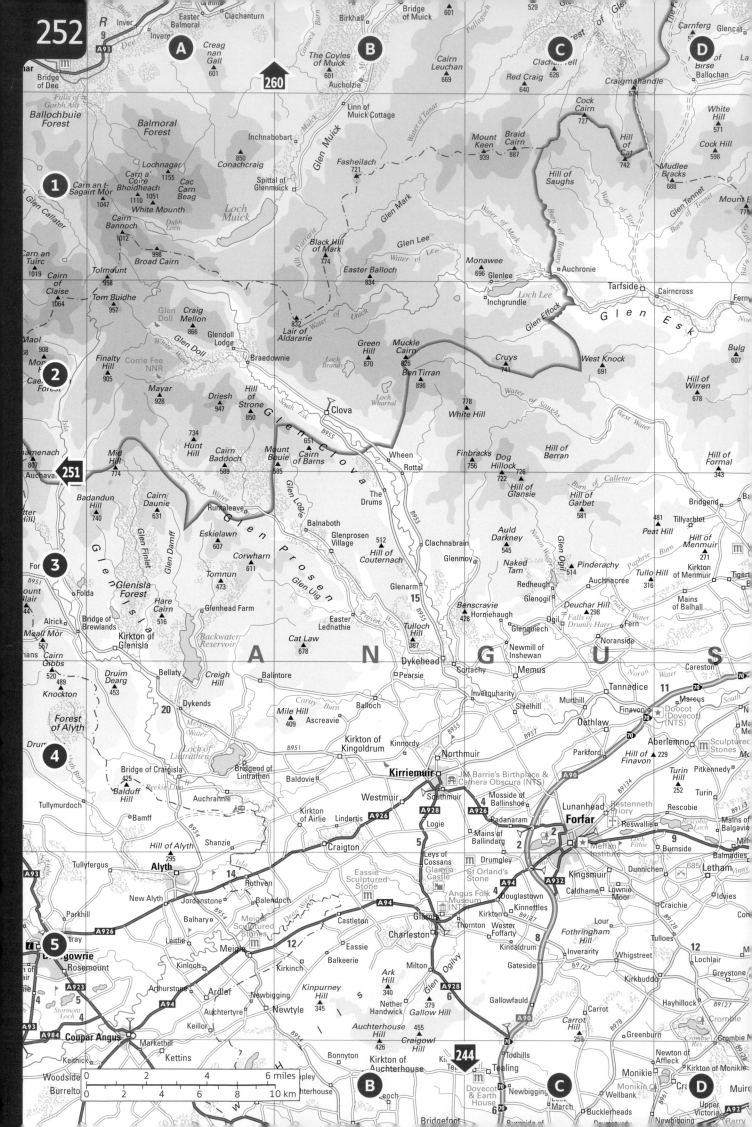

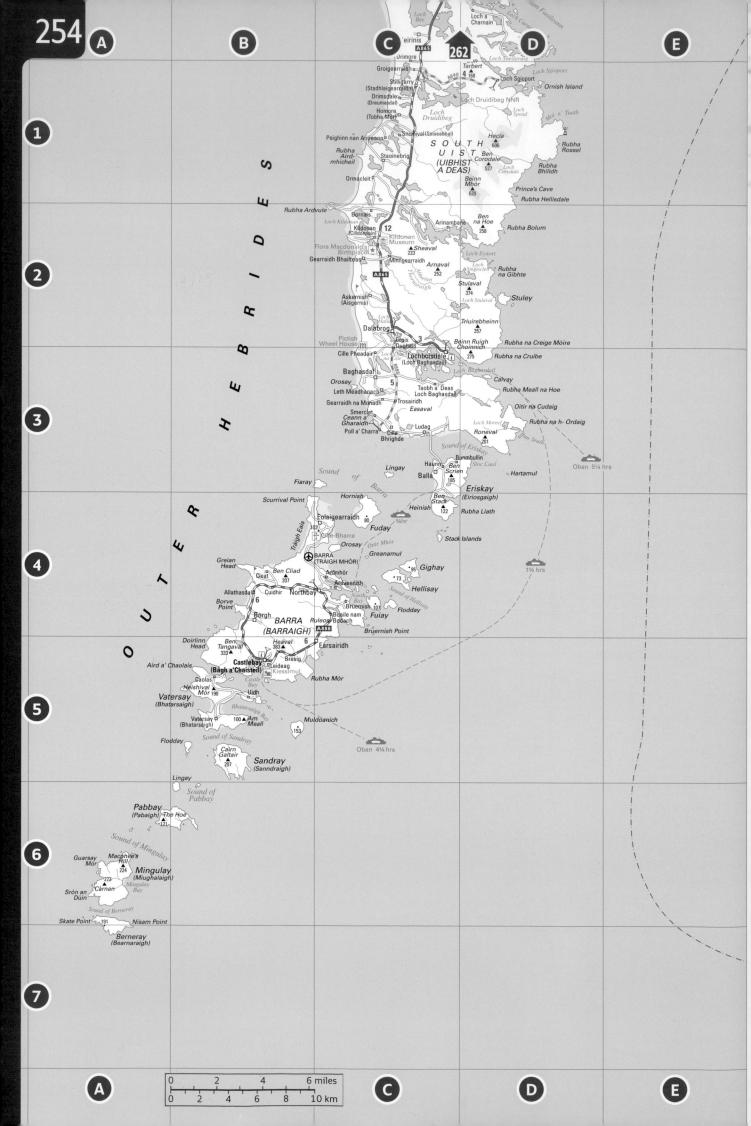

 262

OUTER HEBRIDES

SOUTH UIST (UIBHIST A DEAS)

eirinis
Drimore
Groigearraidh
Tarbert
168
Stilligarry (Stadhlaigearraidh)
Loch Sgioport
Drimsdale (Dreumasdal)
Ornish Island
Homore (Tobha Mòr)
Loch Druidibeg
Loch Druidibeg NNR
Loch Spotal
Mol a' Tuath
Peighinn nan Aoireann
Hecla 606
Rubha Rossel
Rubha Airdmhicheil
Snishival (Sniseabhal)
Ben Corodale
Ormacleit
Staoinebrig
Loch Corodale
Rubha Bhilidh
Beinn Mhòr 620
Prince's Cave
Rubha Hellisdale

Rubha Ardvule
Bornais
Loch Kildonan
Ben na Hoe 258
Rubha Bolum
Kildonan (Cilldonnain)
12
Kildonan Museum
Flora Macdonald's Birthplace
Sheaval 223
Gearraidh Bhailteas
Minngearraidh
Arnaval 252
Rubha na Gibhte
A865
Loch Snigisclett
Abhainn Thorraraigh
Stulaval 374
Loch Eynort
Rubha na Gibhte
Askernish (Aisgernis)
Loch Stulaval
Stuley
Triuirebheinn 357
Dalabrog
Crois Dughaill
Beinn Ruigh Choinnich
Rubha na Creige Mòire
Cille Pheadair
Lochboisdale (Loch Baghasdail)
275
Rubha na Cruibe
Baghasdal
Loch Baghasdail
Calvay
Orosay
Taobh a' Deas Loch Baghasdail
Rubha Meall na Hoe
Leth Meadhanach
Trosairidh
Oitir na Cudaig
Gearraidh na Monadh
Easaval
Smerclet
Ludag
Rubha na h-Ordaig
Ceann a' Gharaidh
Roneval 201
Poll a' Charra
Cille Bhrighde
Sound of Eriskay
Bun Sruth
Bunmhullin
Oban 5¼ hrs
Lingay
Haunn
Ben Scrien 185
Sloc Caol
Hartamul
Balla
Eriskay (Eiriosgaigh)
Fiaray
Ben Stack 122
Rubha Liath
Scurrival Point
Hornish
Heinish
Eolaigearraidh
80
Stack Islands
102
Cille-Bharra
Fuday
¼hr
Orosay
Oitir Mhòr
Greanamul
BARRA (TRÀIGH MHÒR)
Greian Head
Ben Cliad 207
Ardmhòr
95 Gighay
Cleat
Ardveenish
73
Hellisay
1¼ hrs
Allathasdal
Cuidhir
Northbay
North Bay
Sound of Hellisay
Borve Point
6
Bruernish 107
Floddday
Borgh
BARRA (BARRAIGH)
Buaile nam Bodach
Fuiay
Ruleos
A888
Doirlinn Head
Ben Tangaval 333
Heaval 383
6
Earsairidh
Brevig
Bruernish Point
Aird a' Chaolais
Castlebay (Bàgh a'Chaisteil)
Leideag
Kiessimul
Rubha Mòr
Caolas
Heishival Mòr 190
Castle Bay
Uidh
Vatersay (Bhatarsaigh)
Am Meall
Vatersay (Bhatarsaigh)
100
Bhatarsaigh Bay
Muldoanich
Floddday
153
Oban 4¾ hrs
Cairn Galtair 207
Sandray (Sanndraigh)
Lingay
Sound of Sandray
Sound of Pabbay
Pabbay (Pabaigh)
The Hoe 171
Sound of Mingulay
Guarsay Mòr
Macphee's Hill 224
Mingulay (Miughalaigh)
Sròn an Dùin
273
Càrnan
Mingulay Bay
Skate Point
191
Nisam Point
Sound of Berneray
Berneray (Bearnaraigh)

0 2 4 6 miles
0 2 4 6 8 10 km

F G H J K

SKYE
(AN T-EILEAN SGITHEANACH)

Ramasaig
Hoe Rape
The Hoe 233
Lorgill
Ben Connan 244
Beinn na Boineid 371
Healabhal Bheag (Macleod's Table South) 488
Orbost
Harlosh
Glen Ose
Loch Ose
Beinn na Cloiche 232
Am Maol 212
The Prince's

Ben Idrigill 340
Harlosh Point
Loch Bracadale
Tarner Island
Ullinish
Struan
Coillore
Ben Duagrich 304
Mugeary
Strocbheinn 400

An Dubh Sgeir
MacLeod's Maidens
Idrigill Point
Wiay
Oronsay
Rubha nan Clach
Portnalong
Fernilea
Loch Harport
Ardtreck Point
Beinn Totaig
Roineval 439
Meall an Fhuarain 291
Beinn na

Arnaval 369
Carbost
Drynoch
Brocbheinn

Talisker
Talisker Bay
Stockval 416
Gleann Oraid
Merkadale
Glen Drynoch
A863

Biod Mòr 383
Glen Eynort
Beinn Bhreac 370
Beinn Sligachan

Beinn Bhreac 445
Eynort
Grula
Fairy Pools
Cuillin Hills
Am Basteir 935
Sgurr nan Gillean 965

Minginish
Loch Eynort
Beinn a' Bhraghad 461
Beinn Staic 411
Sgurr Thuilm 879
Bruach na Frithe 958
Sgurr a' Mhadaidh 918
Sgurr a' Ghreadaidh 973
Harta Corrie

An Cruachan 435
965
Sgurr na Banachdich
Sgurr Dearg (Inaccessible Pinnacle) 986
Sgurr Mhic Choinnich 948
Loch Coruisk

Glenbrittle
Sgurr Alasdair 993
Sgurr Dubh Mòr 944
Gars- bheinn

Rubha Thearna Sgurr
Bualintur
Beinn an Eòin 312
Culnamean
Sgurr nan Eag 924
895
Sgurr na Stri 497

Loch Brittle
Ceann na Beinne 225

Rubh' an Dùnain
Soay Sound
Beinn Bhreac 141

Leac nam Faoileann
Soay
Camas nan Gall
Molchlach

C U I L L I N   S O U N D

I N N E R   H E B R I D E S

S E A   O F   T H E
H E B R I D E S

CANNA
Camas Tharbernish
Carn a'Ghaill 210
Compass Hill 140
A'Chill

Garrisdale Point
Canna (NTS)
Sròn Ruail
Tarbert Bay
Sanday
Canna Harbour

Humla

Rubha Shamhnan Insir
Kilmory
Rubha na Roinne

278
Sgaorishal
Mullach Mòr 304

Bloodstone Hill 388
Kinloch
Kinloch

A'Bhrideanach
Orval 571
Rùm NNR
Bagh na h-Uamha

Garbh Sgeir
Oigh- sgeir
Sgor Reidh
R U M
(RHUM)
591
Barkeval

Harris
An Dornabac 263
Hallival 723
Askival 812

Rubha Sgor an t-Snidhe
ival 528
Ainshval 781
764
Sgurr nan Gillean

Rubha nam Meirleach
Sound of Rum

Cleadale
An Cruachan 299
Bay of Laig
Rubha an Fhasaidh
Beinn Tighe 315
Laig
EIGG
393
An Sgurr
Galmisdale

Eilean nan Each
Gòdag
Sound of Eigg

Rubh Airein 137
Leam na Làraich
Port Mòr
Muck

Sanna Point
Fascadale
Sanna Bay
Sanna
Achnaha

F G H J K
Ardnamurchan
Portuairk
Grigadale
Meall an

263
246
256

2
3
4
5
6
7

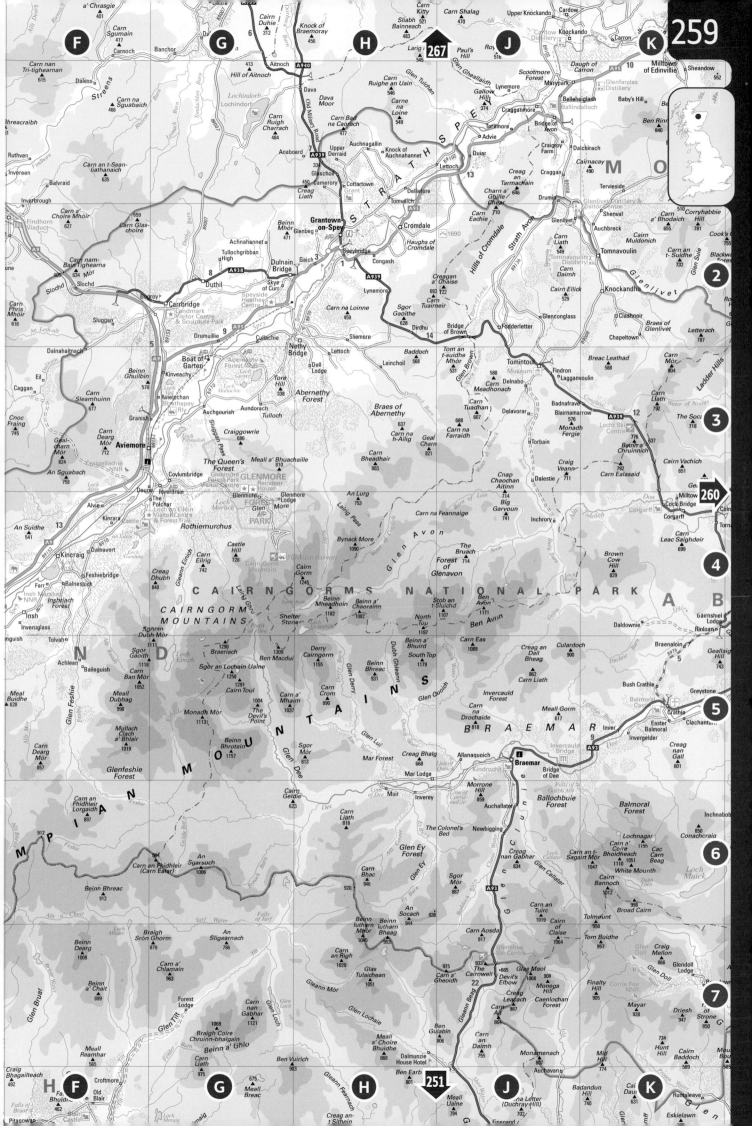

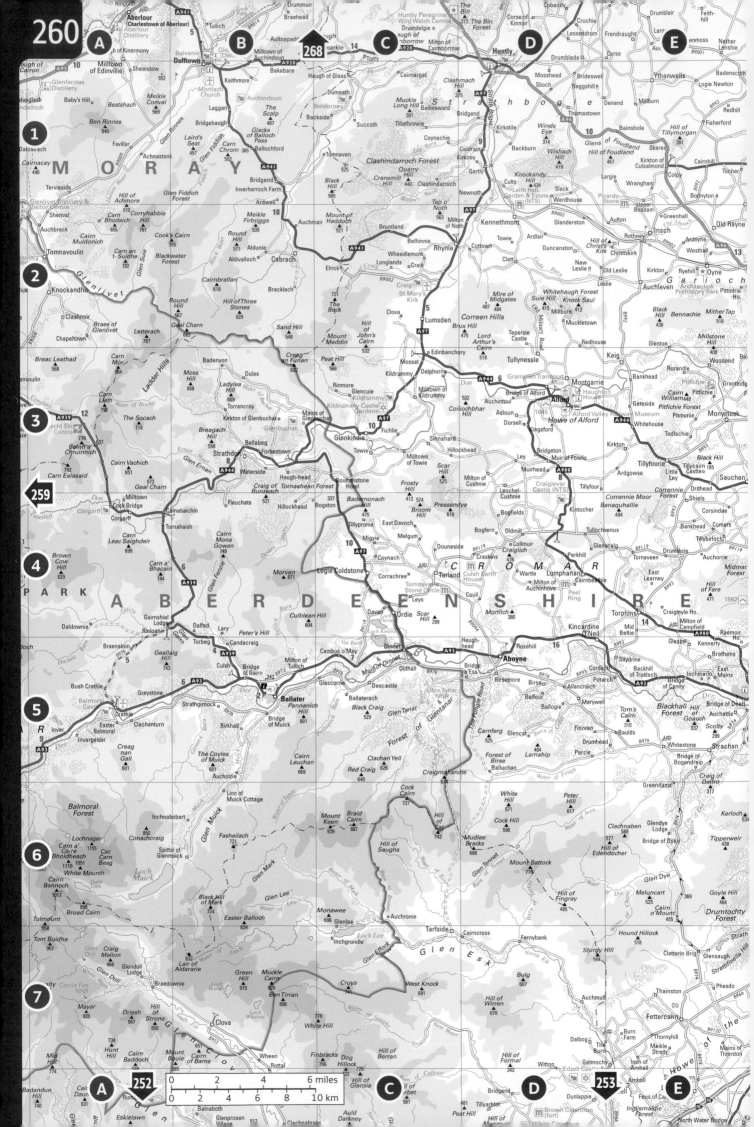

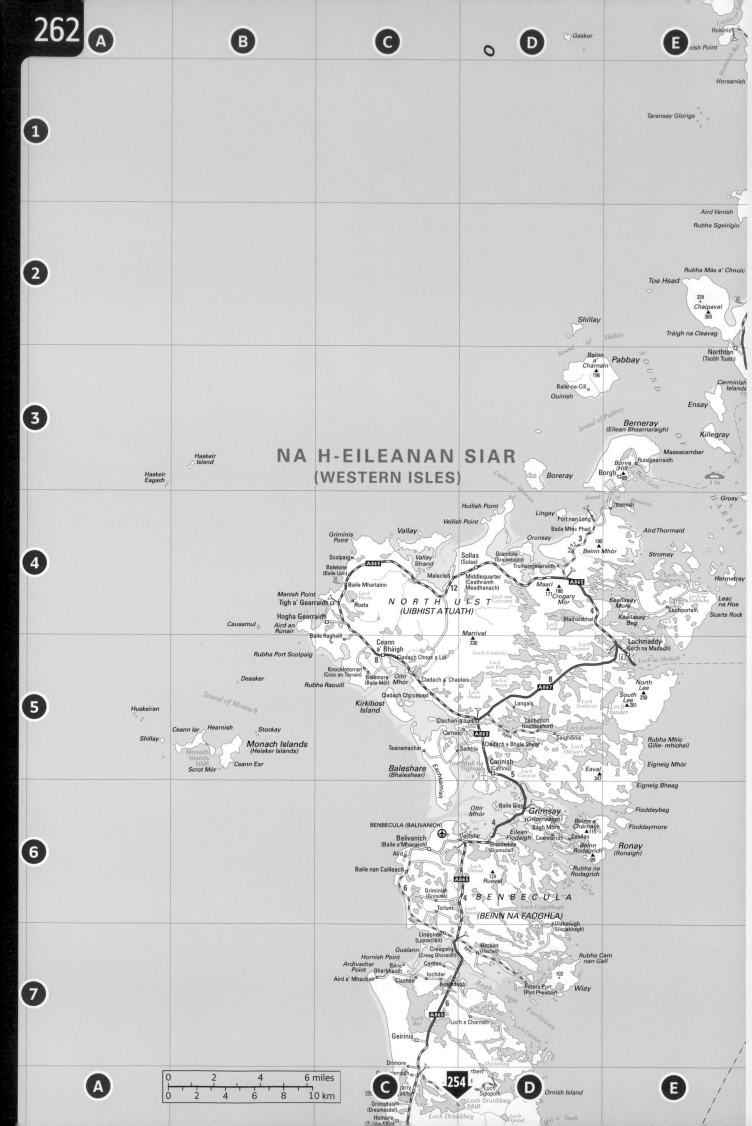

NA H-EILEANAN SIAR
(WESTERN ISLES)

NORTH UIST
(UIBHIST A TUATH)

BENBECULA
(BEINN NA FAOGHLA)

BENBECULA (BALIVANICH)

Gasker

Huisinis
nish Point

Horsanish

Taransay Glorigs

Aird Vanish
Rubha Sgeirigin

Rubha Màs a' Chnuic

Toe Head

Chaipaval
339
365

Tràigh na Cleavag

Northton
(Taobh Tuath)

Shillay

Beinn
a' Chàrnain
196

Pabbay

Carminish
Islands

Baile-na-Cill

Quinish

Ensay

Killegray

Berneray
(Eilean Bhearnaraigh)

Massacamber

Ruisigearraidh

Boreray

Borgh
Borve
Hill
86

Haskeir
Island

Haskeir
Eagach

Caolas a' Mhòrain

Sound of Berneray

Groay

HARRIS

Otternish

Huilish Point

Lingay
Port nan Long
Baile Mhic Phail

Aird Thormaid

Veilish Point

Oronsay
3

Beinn Mhòr
190

Griminis
Point

Valley

Valley
Strand

Sollas
(Solas)

Granitote
(Greinetobht)

Stromay

Scolpaig
Balelone
(Baile Lìon)

Malacleit

Middlequarter
(Ceathramh
Meadhanach)

Trumaisgearraidh

Hermetray

Maari
180
171

Crogary
Mòr

Keallasay
More

Leac
na Hoe

12

Scarts Rock

Baile Mhartainn

Keallasay
Beg

Lochportain

Manish Point
Tigh a' Gearraidh

Loch
Hosta

Hosta

Blathaisbhal

Hogha Gearraidh

Aird an
Rùnair

Marrival
230

Loch
Fada

Lochmaddy
(Loch na Madadh)

Causamul

Baile Raghaill

Ceann
a' Bhàigh

Cladach Chnoc a Lìn

Loch
Scadavay

Loch
Skealtar

North
Lee
250

Rubha Port Scolpaig

8

Oitir
Mhòr

Cladach a' Chaolais

Loch a'
Bharpa

South
Lee
281

8

Knockintorran
(Cnoc an Torrain)

Deasker

Balemore
(Baile Mòr)

Loch
Hunder

Rubha Raouill

Cladach Chircebost

Loch
Huna

Langais

Loch
Scadavay

Kirkibost
Island

Lochport
(Locheuphort)

Loch Euphairt

Rubha Mhic
Gille- mhicheil

Huskeiran

Clachan-a-Luib

Loch
Obisary

Shillay

Carnach

Cladach a Bhale Shear

Saighdinis

Eigneig Mhòr

Ceann Iar

Hearnish

Stockay

Sound of Monach

Teanamachar

Samhla

Carinish
(Cairinis)

Eaval
347

Eigneig Bheag

Monach Islands
(Heisker Islands)

Monach
Islands
NNR

Scrot Mòr

Ceann Ear

Baleshare
(Bhaleshear)

Eachkamish

Loch
Caravat

Floddaybeg

Baile Glas

Grimsay
(Griomsaigh)

Floddaymore

Oitir
Mhòr

Beinn a'
Chàrnain
115

Bàgh Mòr

Eilean
Flodaigh

Ceannaridh

Ronay
(Ronaigh)

Balivanich
(Baile a'Mhanaich)

Uachdar

Gramisdale
(Gramsdal)

Beinn
Rodagrich
99

Rubha na
Rodagrich

Aird

Baile nan Cailleach

Loch
Olavat

Rueval
124

Griminish
(Griminis)

Torlum

Loch
Olavat

Loch Uisgebhagh

Uiskevagh
(Uisgebhagh)

Linaclate
(Lionacleit)

Hornish Point

Gualann

Creagorry
(Creag Ghoraidh)

Racklet
(Haclait)

Rubha Cam
nan Gall

Ardivachar
Point

Baile
Gharbhaidh

Carnan

Aird a' Mhachair

Clachan

Iochdar

Bualadobh

Peters Port
(Port Pheadair)

102

Wiay

Loch Bee

Loch a Charnain

Geirinis

Loch Carnan

Bàgh nam Faoileann

Drimore

254

Drimsdale
(Dreumasdal)

Loch
Sgioport

Loch Druidibeg
NNR

Ornish Island

Homore

Loch Druidibeg

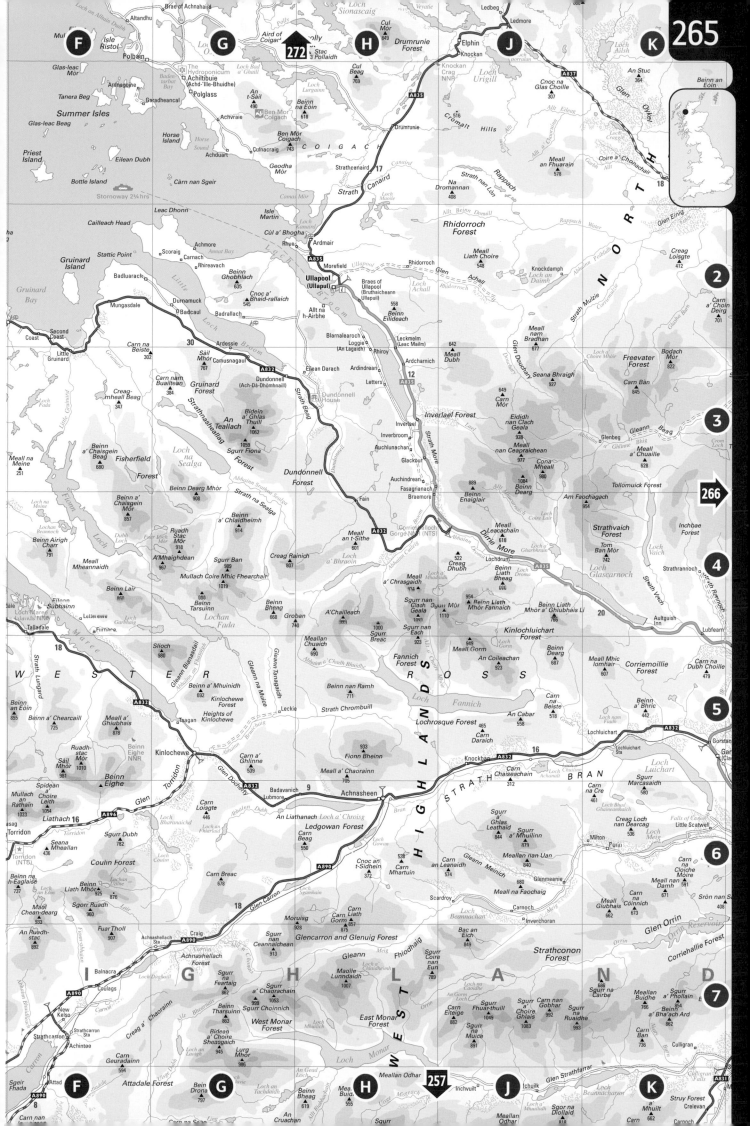

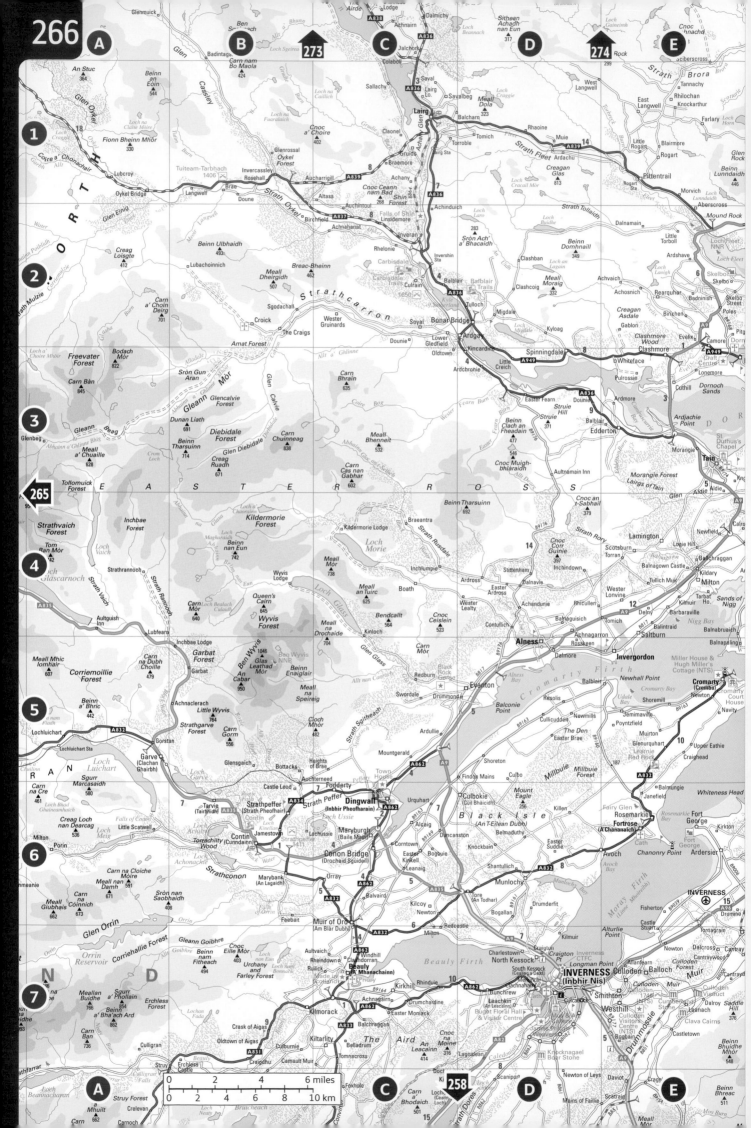

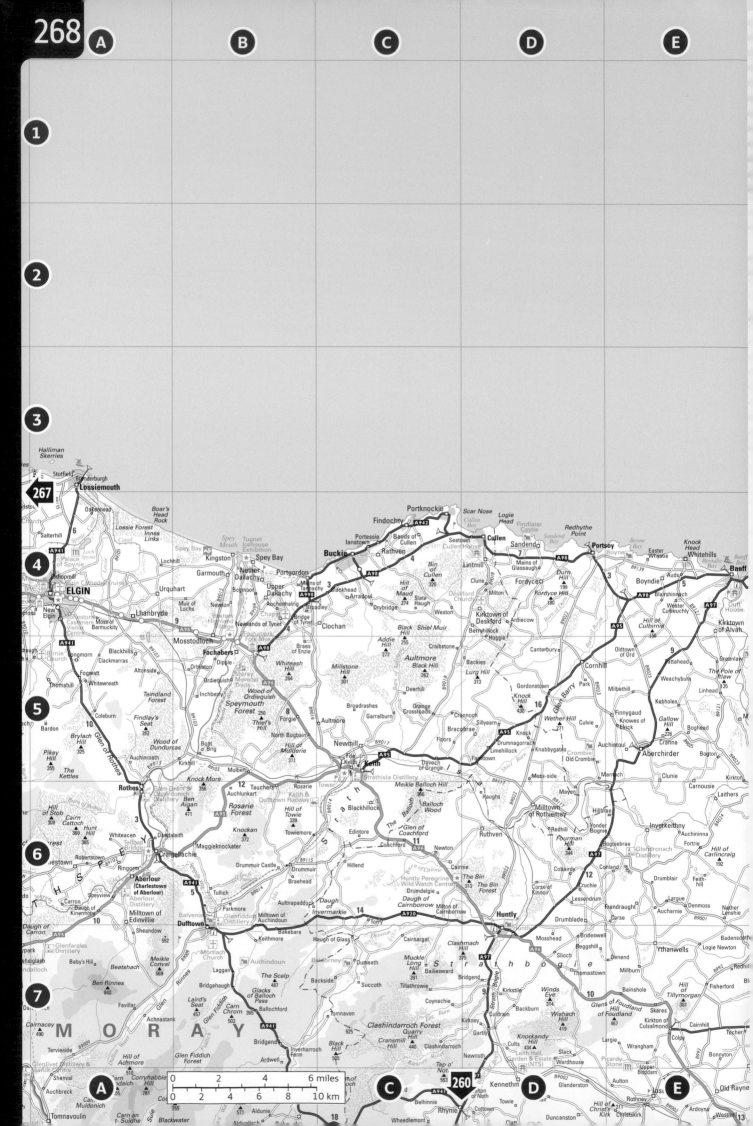

A **B** **C** **D** **E**

1

2

3

OUTER HEBRIDES

Rinn Druim Tallig
Aird Mhòr Bragair
Rubh' an Dùnain
Labost
Fibhig
Shawbost (Siabost)
Siabost Bho Thuath
Siabost Bho Dheas
Pairc
Bagh Dail Beag
Dail Beag
Dail Mòr
Aird Mhòr
20
Gearrannan
Borghastan
Craigeam
Mullach Charlabhaigh
Beinn Bragar 261
Beinn Choinnich 210
Carloway (Carlabhagh)
Loch Carlabhagh
Beinn Rahacleit 248
Creag Mhòr
Cirbhig
Carloway Broch
Little Bernera
Bostadh
Crothair
IS

4

HEBRIDES
Gallan Head
West Loch Roag
East Loch Roag
Pabaidh Mòr
Tobson
Tolastadh a' Chaolais
Great Breacleit
Breascleit
Loch nam Breac
Aird Uig
Bhaltos
Camas Sunig
Vacsay
Bernera
Kirkibost (Circebost)
Geodha Nasavig
Forsnaval 205
Nisa Mhòr
Reef (Riof)
Hacklete (Tacleit)
Barraglom
Aird a' (Gearraidh na h-Aibhne)
Callanish (Calanais)
Calanish Standing Stones
A858
Loch Airigh nan Sloc
Fiavig Bàgh
Miavaig (Miabhaig)
Vuia Mòr
Iarsiadar
Crùlabhig
Eilean Kearstay
Loch an Tairbeart
Cradhlastadh
Uigen
Vuia Beg
Lundale
Timsgearraidh
Cairisiadar
Floday
Geisiadar
Ben Drovinish 185
Linsiadar
Griomarstaidh
5
B8059
Loch Cean Tràlabhig
Camas Uig
Aird Mhòr Mangurstadh
Loch Sgailabhat
Eadar dha Fhadhail
Garrynahine
3
10
Mangurstadh
Suainaval 429
Teahaval 256
Aird Fenish
Ungisiadar
Loch Suainaval
Loch Tungavat
Loch Cleit Steirmeis
Loch Croistean
Einacleit
Aird Breanais
Islibhig
Mealisval 574
Loch Raonasgail
Tahaval 515
16
Scealascro
B8011
Loch Fadagoa
Loch Trealaval
Loch nam Faiceal

5

Breanais
Cracaval 514
Loch Grunavat
Abhainn Giosla
Skeun 265
Giosla
Calltraiseal Bheag
Loch an Fhir Mhaoil
Mealasta
Tamanaisval 467
Loch Dìbadale
Beinn Mheadhonach 241
Kinlochroag (Ceann Lochroag) 228
Beinn Mohal 207
Loch Airigh na h-Airde
Coduinn
226
N A H – E I L E A N A N   S I A R
Mealasta Island
Griomaval
Maghannan
Loch na Craobhaig
Calltraiseal Mhòr
Roineval 281
Balallan (Baile Ailein)
Loch Morsgail
Loch Coirigerod
Sildinis

6

Liongam
Loch Bodavat
Scalaval
Sleiteachal Mhòr 248
Airidh a' Bhruaich
Aird Bheag
Loch Beisval
(WESTERN ISLES)
Kintarvie
Kearstay
Gob na h-Airde Mòire
Aird Mhòr
Morsgail Forest
Aird an Troim
Ceann Loch Shiphoirt
Sgeir Moil Duinn
Beinn a' Bhoth 308
A859
Feirihisval
Sròn Romul 308
Kearnaval 248
Sidhean an Airgid 381
Mòr Mhonadh 326
Scarp
Màs a' Chnoic-chuairtich 386
Mullach na Reidheachd 295
Loch Langavat
Liuthaid 492
Beinn a' Mhuil 378
Beinn Mhuil 370
18
Beinn na h-Uamha 389
Sgianait 425
Rapaire 453
Stulaval 579
Ath Linne
Muaithabhal
Gasker

7

Huisinis
Tirga Mòr 679
Ullaval 659
Aird a' Mhulaidh
Mullach a' Ruisg 424
Seaforth Island
Beannan Mòr 242
Hushinish Point
Husival Mòr 489
Oreval 662
N O R T H   H A R R I S
Beinn Mhòr
Beinn Mhòr 572
Arda Beaga
Leosaval 412
Forest of Harris
Cleiseval 511
Uisgnaval Mòr 729
Mulla-fo-dheas 743
Clisham 799
Clett Ard 328
Maraig (Màraig)
Kenmore
Caiteshal 449
Crionaig 470
Horsanish
Gobhaig
(CEANN A TUATH NA HEARADH)
Rubha Bhuic
Abhainnsuidhe
12
Taransay Glorigs
Soay Beg
Miabhag
Tolmachan
Bun Abhainn Eadarra
A859
Sgaoth Aird 559
Straiaval 389
Toddun 528
Soay Mòr
Rhenigidale (Reinigeadal)
Taransay (Tarasaigh)
Ben Raah 267
WEST LOCH TARBERT
Aird Asaig 3
Taobh Siar
Tarbert (Tairbeart)
Beesdale
Beinn Dhubh 506
Urgha
Uieseval 334
Eilean Mòr na h-Eigheach
Paible
Losgaintir
ann Reamhar
Carragrich
Kyles Scalpay
Caolas Scalpay
Rubha Romagi
Seilebost
A859
Miabhag
Scalpay
Ben Scoravick
Scalnay
Sgeotasaigh
Loch Ceann Dibig
Sgeir na h-Eigheach

263

A **B** 0 2 4 6 miles 0 2 4 6 8 10 km **C** **D** **E**

Butt of Lewis
(Rubha Robhanais)
Port a' Stoth
Cunndal
Teampull Mholuidh
Eoropaidh
Còig Peighinnean
Lionel
Port of Ness (Port Nis)
(Lional)
Bad an Fhithich
Habost
Swainbost
(Tabost)
(Suainebost)
Eorodal
Sgiogarstaigh
Aird Dhail
Meall Geal
South Dell (Dail Bho Dheas)
North
Cross (Cros)
Port Alasdair
Toa Galson
Dell
(Dail Bho
Thuath)
Ness (Niss)
Glen Cross
Gabhsunn Bho Thuath
Cuidhaseadair
Laimhrig
Gabhsunn Bho Dheas
Broch
Airigh
na
Glaice
Melbost Borve
(Mealabost)
Cellar Head
Roinn a' Bhuic
Ben
Dell
Airighean
Beinn nan
Caorach
15
A857
High Borve
Borve
(Borgh)
Airighean
Loch
Breihavat
Loch
Langavat
Siadar Iarach
Steinacleit Cairn
& Standing Stones
Rubha Leathann
Siadar Uarach
Diaval
Baile an Truiseil
A857
Bhaltos
Glen Shader
Loch Mòr
Sandavat
Upper Barvas
Loch Gress
Goile
Chnoic
Loch
Mòr
Bharabhais
Brue
(Bru)
Barvas
(Barabhas)
Blackhouse
Muirneag
248
Tolastadh Úr
A858
Arnol
gar
Glen Bragar
Loch
Casgro
Abhainn Thorraigh
Loch Mòr
Sandavit
Loch an
Tobair
Port Geiraha
Loch Urrahag
Gleann Mòr Bharabhais
Loch Breivat
Abhainn Sgeireach Mòr
Tolastadh
Loch
Sgeireach Mòr
Tolsta Head
Gleann
Bhruthadail
Port nam Bothag
L E   O F   L E W I S
A857
Roishal
Mòr
174
Gleann Tholastaidh
(EILEAN   LEODHAIS)
Abhainn Grinnis
Port Bun a' Ghlinne
Loch na Scaravat
11
12
Gress
(Griais)
Creag Fhraoch
Beinn Mholach
292
Bac
Stacashal
216
Col
Loch nan
Stearnag
Col Uarach
272
Tiumpan
Head
(Rubha an Tiumpain)
Loch Mòr
an Stairr
Breibhig
Col
Sands
Rubha Bhataisgeir
Portnaguran
(Port nan Giùran)
Portvoller
Reinn
nan
Surrag
200
New Valley
Newmarket
Tunga
Aird Thunga
Sròn
Ruadh
LOCH A' TUATH
(Broad Bay)
Flesherin
Aird
Rubha Deas
Loch Vatandip
Laxdale
(Lacasdal)
Siulaisiadar
Elshal
Boinn a'
Bhuna
149
Stornoway
(Steornabhagh)
Melbost Sands
East
Roinish
Garrabost
Seisiadar
Eye
Peninsula
(An Rubha)
Rubha na Greine
Achadh Mòr
Loch Orasay
Maryband
Steinis
Lews Castle
Melbost Pt
Melbost
A866
Aiginis
10
Rubha na Bearnaigh
Loch Thota
Brideln
A859
4
Arnish
Pt
Sandwick
(Sanndwig)
Holm
(Tolm)
Columba's
Church
Knock
Upper Bayble (Pabail Uarach)
6
Arnish Moor
Rubh' a'
Bhàigh Uaine
Drabghult
Banks
Guershil
Lower
Bayble
(Pabail Iarach)
Leurbost
(Liurbost)
Grimshader
(Griomsiadar)
Ceann na
Circ
Bagh Phabail
8897
Loch
Nisreaval
Loch Grimsiadar
Ullapool 2¾ hrs
Crosbost
Ranish
(Ranais)
Raerinish Point
Loch
Fada
Tabhaigh Mhòr
12
Keose
(Ceos)
Eilean
Chaluim Chille
T H E
Lacasaigh
Cromore
Orasaigh
A859
Cearsiadar
Cabharstadh
Torraigh
M I N C H
Gearraidh
Bhaird
Tabost
88060
13
Marbhig
Malasgair
172
Calbost
Rubha Iosal
Glen Ouirn
Grabhair
Loch
Shanndabhat
Tom an
Fhuadain
Loch Odhàirn
Kebock Head
Eisgean
Orasaigh
Leumrabhagh
Gob na Milaid
Srianach
Corlabhadh
298
Eilean
Iubhard
r   k
Uisenis
371
Mulhagery
Mol Truisg
Gob Rubh' Uisenis
S O U N D   O F   S H I A N T
Rubha Bhrollum
Rubh' a' Bhaird
Garbh
Eilean
161
Eil
Eilean an Tighe

Shiant Islands

2
3
4
5
6
7

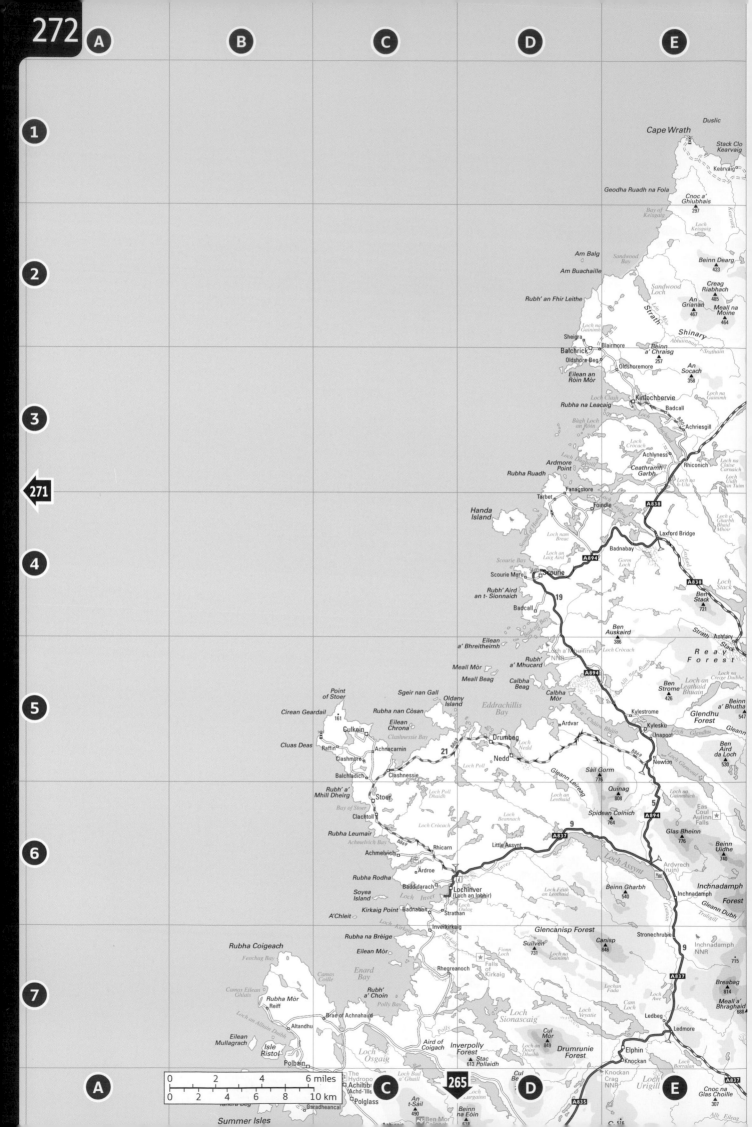

A　B　C　D　E

1

Cape Wrath
Duslic
Stack Clo
Kearvaig
Kearvaig
Geodha Ruadh na Fola
Cnoc a'
Ghiubhais
297
Loch
Keisgaig

2
Am Balg
Sandwood
Bay
Beinn Dearg
423
Am Buachaille
Loch na
Gainimh
Creag
Riabhach
485
Rubh' an Fhir Leithe
An
Grianan
457
Meall na
Moine
464
Sheigra
Blairmore
Balchrick
Beinn
a' Chraisg
257

3
Oldshore Beg
Oldshoremore
An
Socach
358
Kinlochbervie
Eilean an
Ròin Mòr
Rubha na Leacaig
Badcall
Achriesgill
Loch na
Gainimh
Ardmore
Point
Achlyness
Rhiconich
Loch na
Claise
Carnaich
Rubha Ruadh
Ceathramh
Garbh
Loch
Dubh
a' Tuim

271

Fanagmore
Tarbet
Foindle
A838
Loch a'
Gharbh
Bhaid
Mhòir
Handa
Island
Laxford Bridge

4
Loch nam
Breac
Badnabay
A894
Loch
Stack
Scourie More
Scourie
Gorm
Loch
Loch an
Laig Aird
Loch
Stack
Ben
Stack
721
Scourie Bay
Rubh' Aird
an t- Sionnaich
19
Badcall
Ben
Auskaird
386
Strath
Achfary

5
Eilean
a' Bhreitheimh
Loch a' Mhuilinn
NNR
Reay
Forest
Meall Mòr
Rubh'
a' Mhucard
Loch Cròcach
A894
Ben
Strome
426
Loch na
Leathaid
Bhuain
Meall Beag
Calbha
Beag
Calbha
Mòr
Beinn
a' Bhutha
547
Point
of Stoer
Sgeir nan Gall
Kylestrome
Glendhu
Forest
Cirean Geardail
Rubha nan Còsan
Oldany
Island
Eddrachillis
Bay
Kylesku
Culkein
161
Eilean
Chrona
Ardvar
Unapool
Ben
Aird
da Loch
530
Cluas Deas
Clashnessie Bay
Drumbeg
Loch
Nedd
Raffin
Achnacarnin
21
Gleann Leireag
Sàil Gorm
776
Newton
Clashmore
Nedd
Clashnessie
Loch Poll
Balchladich
Rubh' a'
Mhill Dheirg
Stoer
Loch Poll
Dhaidh
Sàil Gorm
776
5
A894
Eas
Coul
Aulinn
Falls

6
Bay of Stoer
Clachtoll
Loch Cròcach
Loch
Beannach
Quinag
808
Loch na
Gainmhich
Spidean Coinich
764
Glas Bheinn
776
Rubha Leumair
Achmelvich Bay
Rhicarn
Little Assynt
9
A837
Loch Assynt
Ardvreck
(ruin)
Beinn
Uidhe
740
Achmelvich
Inver
Beinn Gharbh
540
Inchnadamph
Ardroe
Loch Fèith
an Leothaid
Inchnadamph
Forest
Rubha Rodha
Baddidarach
Lochinver
(Loch an Inbhir)
Gleann Dubh
Soyea
Island
Badnaban
Strathan
Glencanisp Forest
Traligill
Kirkaig Point
Loch
Druing
A'Chleit
Inverkirkaig
Stronechrubie
Suilven
731
Canisp
846
9
Inchnadamph
NNR

7
Rubha na Brèige
Eilean Mòr
Rhegreanoch
Falls
of
Kirkaig
Loch an
Gainmh
715
Rubha Coigeach
Feochag Bay
Enard
Bay
Rubh'
a' Choin
Loch
Sionascaig
Loch
Veatie
Breabag
814
Camas
Coille
Polly Bay
Cam
Loch
Loch
Awe
Ledbeg
Meall a'
Bhraghaid
688
Camas Eilean
Ghlais
Altandhu
Brae of Achnahaird
Aird of
Coigach
Cul Mòr
849
Ledmore
Eilean
Mullagrach
Rubha Mòr
Reiff
Inverpolly
Forest
Drumrunie
Forest
Elphin
Isle
Ristol
Stac
613 Pollaidh
Knockan
Polbain
Loch
Osgaig
Cul
Beg
Knockan
Crag
NNR
Loch
Borralan
Loch
Urigill

A
0　　2　　4　　6 miles
0　2　4　6　8　10 km
C
The
Hydropo
Achiltibu
Achd'-Ille
Polglass
265
Loch Bad
a' Ghaill
An
t-Sàil
490
D
Cul
Be
A835
E
Cnoc na
Glas Choille
307
Summer Isles
Tanera Beg
Garadheancal
An
Beinn
na Eòin
618
Ben Mor
A837

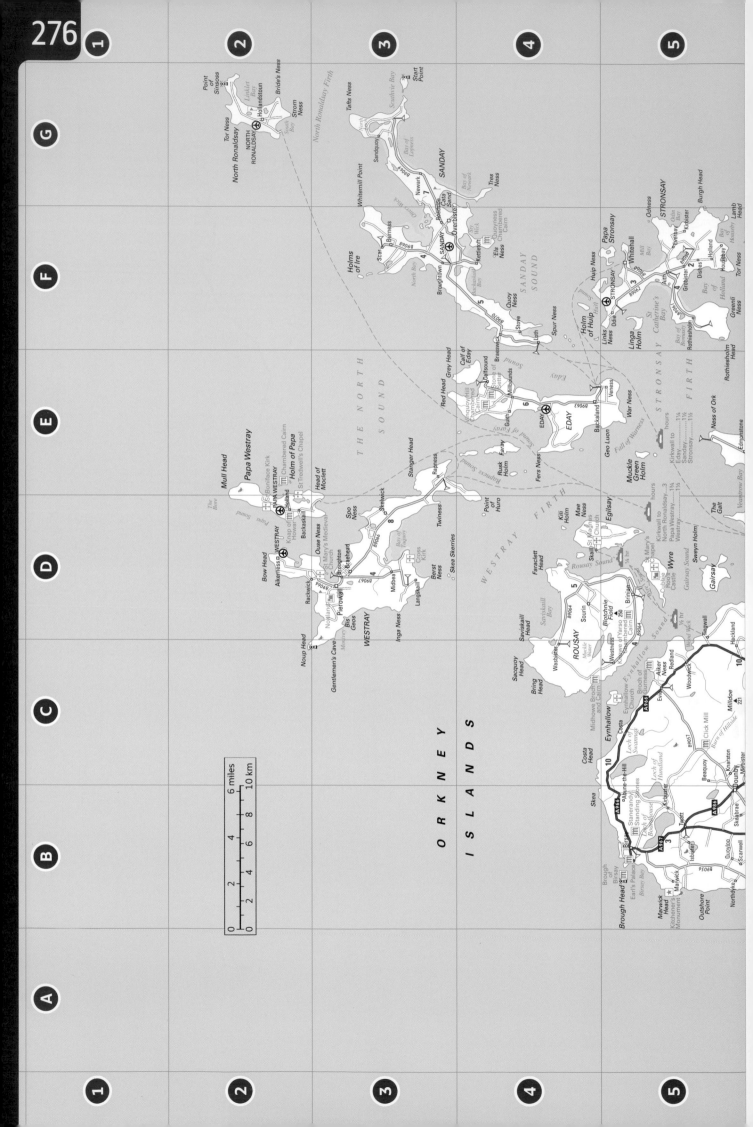

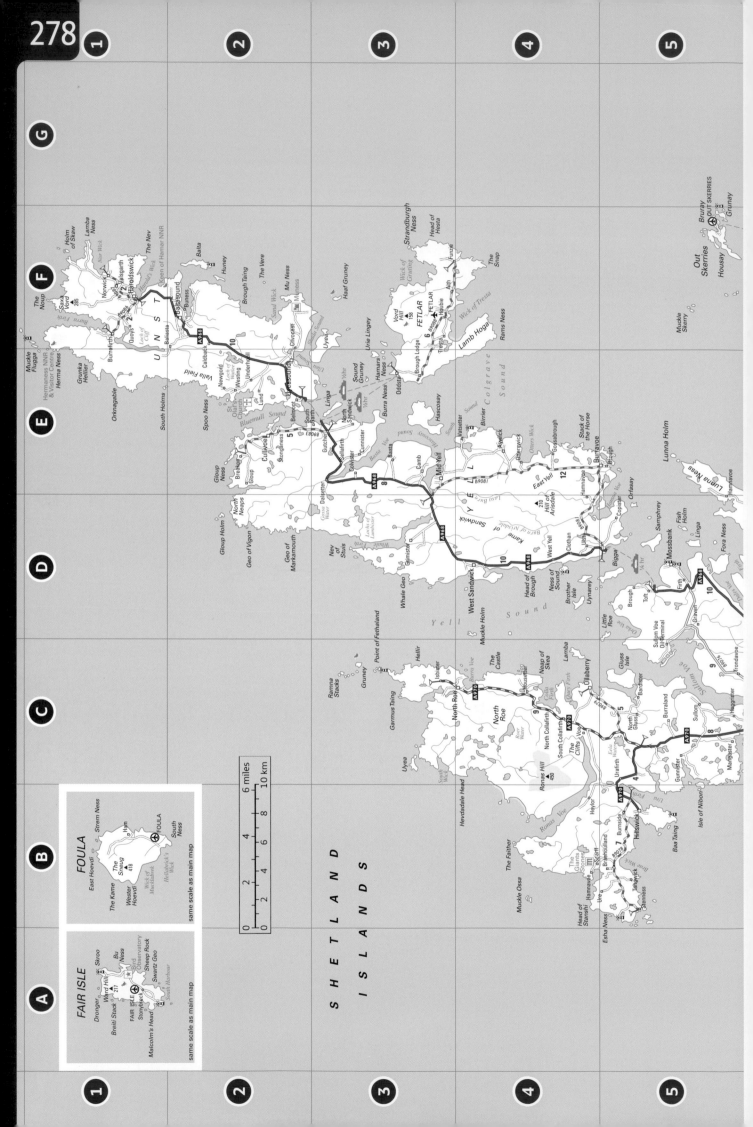

FOULA

East Hoevdi
Strem Ness
The Kame
The Sneug 418
Ham
FOULA
South Ness
Wester Hoevdi
Hellabrick's Wick
Wick of Mucklaberg

same scale as main map

FAIR ISLE

Dronger
Skroo
Ward Hill 217
Bu Ness
Breili Stack
Bird Observatory
Sheep Rock
FAIR ISLE
Stonybreck
Swartz Geo
Malcolm's Head
South Harbour

same scale as main map

SHETLAND ISLANDS

6 miles
10 km
0 2 4 6 8
0 2 4 6 8 10

UNST

The Noup
Saxa Vord 285
Holm of Skaw
Lamba Ness
Norwick
Valsgarth
The Nev
Nor Wick
Muness
Haroldswick
Baltasound
Balta
Muckle Flugga
Hermaness NNR & Visitor Centre
Herma Ness
Grunka Hellier
Burrafirth
Quoys
Loch of Cliff
Baliasta
Buness
Huney
The Vere
Mu Ness
Sand Wick
Brough Taing
Orknagable
South Holms
A968
Caldback
Clivocast
Uyea
Mal Ness
Spoo Ness
Valla Field
Westing
Newgord
Lund
St Olaf's Church
Uyeasound
10
Belmont
South Barth
North Sandwick
Gunnister
Burra Ness
Blue mull Sound
Sound Gruney
Haaf Gruney
Wick of Gratting
Strandburgh Ness
Head of Hesta
Gloup Ness
Breckon
Gloup
Cullivoe
Stonganess
A968
B9083
Gutcher
Sellafirth
Cunnister
Linga
Yhhr
Sound Gruney
Hamars Ness
Oddsta
Brough Lodge
FETLAR
Vord Hill 158
Funzie
The Snap
Aith
Houbie
Tresta
Wick of Tresta
Lamb Hoga
Rams Ness
6

Gloup Holm
Geo of Vigon
North Neaps
Geo of Markamouth
Ness of Stuis
Whale Geo
Dalsetter
A968 8
Basta Voe
Basta
Camb
Mid Yell
Watsetter
Birrier
Hascosay
Otters wick
Aywick
Colgrave Sound
Stack of the Horse
Burravoe
Lunna Holm

Y E L L
Sandwick
Kame of Flouravoug
Burn of Arisdale
Hill of Arisdale 210
West Yell
Ulsta
Clothan
Gossabrough
East Yell
12
Hamnavoe
Brough
Orfasay
Copister
B9081

10
A968
West Sandwick
Head of Brough
Ness of Sound
Brother Isle
Uynarey
Bigga
Samphrey
Fish Holm
Linga
Fora Ness
Hampivae
Lunna Ness

Yell Sound
Muckle Holm
Little Roe
Brough
Toft
Mossbank
¼ hr
Firth
Graven
Sullom Voe Oil Terminal
A968
10
Gluss Isle
Bardister
Burraland
Garth
Sullom
Gunnister
Mondovoe
Isle of Nibon
Orka Voe
Sullom Voe
9
Hogan

Point of Fethaland
Ramna Stacks
Gruney
Garmus Taing
Hellir
Isbister
Burra Voe
The Castle
Neap of Skea
Lamba
Ollaberry
North Glussa
North Roe
North Rob
North Collafirth
The Clifts
A970
9
South Collafirth
Sullom
A970
5
B9079
Burraland

Uyea
South Wick
Hevdadale Head
Uyea
Ronas Hill 450
River Water
Eela Water
A970 4
Urafirth
Heylor
Ronas Voe
Mavis Grind
Gunnister

The Faither
The Giants Stones
Hamarsta
Scarf
Urafirth
Heylor
Braehoulland
A970
Burnside
Hillswick
Hillswick
7
B9078
Ure
Tangwick
Stenness
Brae Wick
Esha Ness
Head of Stanshi
Muckle Ossa
Head of Stanshi

Bruray
OUT SKERRIES
Out Skerries
Housay
Grunay
Muckle Skerry

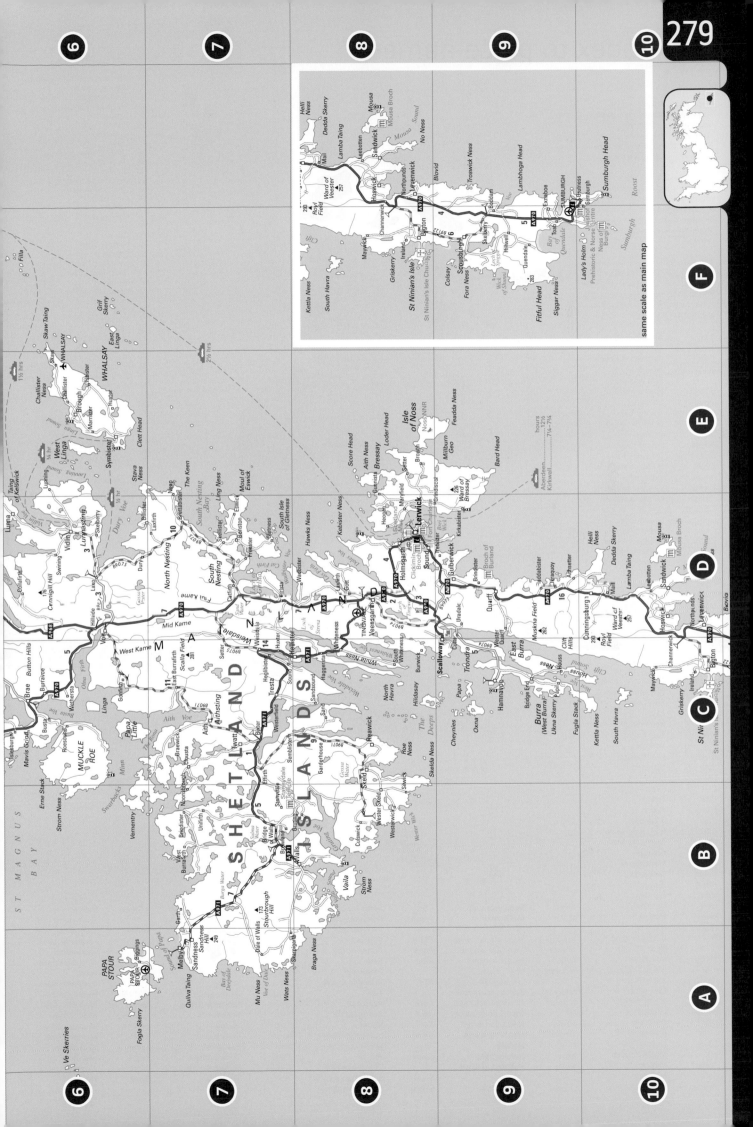

Place and place of interest names are followed by a **page number** and a grid reference in black type. The feature can be found on the map somewhere within the grid square shown.

Where two or more places have the same name the abbreviated *county* or *unitary authority* names are shown to distinguish between them. A list of these abbreviated names appears below.

The top 1000 most visited places of interest are shown within the index in blue type. Their postcode information is supplied after the county names to aid integration with satnav systems.

A&B	Argyll & Bute
Aber	Aberdeenshire
B&H	Brighton & Hove
B&NESom	Bath & North East Somerset
B'burn	Blackburn with Darwen
B'pool	Blackpool
BGwent	Blaenau Gwent
Bed	Bedford
Bourne	Bournemouth
BrackF	Bracknell Forest
Bucks	Buckinghamshire
Caerp	Caerphilly
Cambs	Cambridgeshire
Carmar	Carmarthenshire
CenBeds	Central Bedfordshire
Cere	Ceredigion
Chanl	Channel Islands
ChesE	Cheshire East
ChesW&C	Cheshire West & Chester
Corn	Cornwall
Cumb	Cumbria
D&G	Dumfries & Galloway
Darl	Darlington
Denb	Denbighshire
Derbys	Derbyshire
Dur	Durham
EAyr	East Ayrshire
EDun	East Dunbartonshire
ELoth	East Lothian
ERenf	East Renfrewshire
ERid	East Riding of Yorkshire
ESuss	East Sussex
Edin	Edinburgh
ESiar	Eilean Siar (Western Isles)
Falk	Falkirk
Flints	Flintshire
Glas	Glasgow
Glos	Gloucestershire
GtLon	Greater London
GtMan	Greater Manchester
Gwyn	Gwynedd
Hants	Hampshire
Hart	Hartlepool
Here	Herefordshire
Herts	Hertfordshire
High	Highland
Hull	Kingston upon Hull
Invcly	Inverclyde
IoA	Isle of Anglesey
IoM	Isle of Man
IoS	Isles of Scilly
IoW	Isle of Wight
Lancs	Lancashire
Leic	Leicester
Leics	Leicestershire
Lincs	Lincolnshire
MK	Milton Keynes
MTyd	Merthyr Tydfil
Med	Medway
Mersey	Merseyside

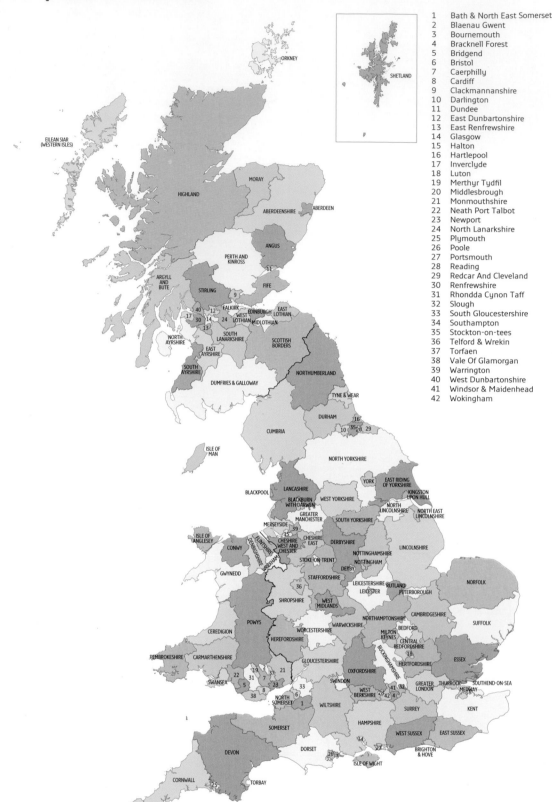

1	Bath & North East Somerset
2	Blaenau Gwent
3	Bournemouth
4	Bracknell Forest
5	Bridgend
6	Bristol
7	Caerphilly
8	Cardiff
9	Clackmannanshire
10	Darlington
11	Dundee
12	East Dunbartonshire
13	East Renfrewshire
14	Glasgow
15	Halton
16	Hartlepool
17	Inverclyde
18	Luton
19	Merthyr Tydfil
20	Middlesbrough
21	Monmouthshire
22	Neath Port Talbot
23	Newport
24	North Lanarkshire
25	Plymouth
26	Poole
27	Portsmouth
28	Reading
29	Redcar And Cleveland
30	Renfrewshire
31	Rhondda Cynon Taff
32	Slough
33	South Gloucestershire
34	Southampton
35	Stockton-on-tees
36	Telford & Wrekin
37	Torfaen
38	Vale Of Glamorgan
39	Warrington
40	West Dunbartonshire
41	Windsor & Maidenhead
42	Wokingham

Middl	Middlesbrough
Midlo	Midlothian
Mon	Monmouthshire
N'hants	Northamptonshire
N'umb	Northumberland
NAyr	North Ayrshire
NELincs	North East Lincolnshire
NLan	North Lanarkshire
NLincs	North Lincolnshire
NPT	Neath Port Talbot
NSom	North Somerset
NYorks	North Yorkshire
Norf	Norfolk
Nott	Nottingham
Notts	Nottinghamshire
Ork	Orkney
Oxon	Oxfordshire

P&K	Perth & Kinross
Pembs	Pembrokeshire
Peter	Peterborough
Plym	Plymouth
Ports	Portsmouth
R&C	Redcar & Cleveland
RCT	Rhondda Cynon Taff
Read	Reading
Renf	Renfrewshire
Rut	Rutland
S'end	Southend-on-Sea
SAyr	South Ayrshire
SGlos	South Gloucestershire
SLan	South Lanarkshire
SYorks	South Yorkshire

ScBord	Scottish Borders
Shet	Shetland
Shrop	Shropshire
Slo	Slough
Som	Somerset
Soton	Southampton
Staffs	Staffordshire
Stir	Stirling
Stock	Stockton-on-Tees
Stoke	Stoke-on-Trent
Suff	Suffolk
Surr	Surrey
Swan	Swansea
Swin	Swindon
T&W	Tyne & Wear
Tel&W	Telford & Wrekin
Thur	Thurrock

VGlam	Vale of Glamorgan
W&M	Windsor & Maidenhead
W'ham	Wokingham
WBerks	West Berkshire
WDun	West Dunbartonshire
WLoth	West Lothian
WMid	West Midlands
WSuss	West Sussex
WYorks	West Yorkshire
Warks	Warwickshire
Warr	Warrington
Wilts	Wiltshire
Worcs	Worcestershire
Wrex	Wrexham

A

1853 Gallery *WYorks* BD18 3LA 26 C1

Ab Kettleby 174 C5
Ab Lench 146 C2
Abbas Combe 117 E5
Abberley 145 G1
Abberley Common 145 G1
Abberton *Essex* 138 D1
Abberton *Worcs* 146 B2
Abberwick 229 F5
Abbess Roding 137 E1
Abbey Dore 144 C4
Abbey Hulton 171 G3
Abbey St. Bathans 237 E3
Abbey Village 192 C5
Abbey Wood 137 D5
Abbeycwmhir 155 G5
Abbeydale 186 A4
Abbeystead 192 B2
Abbeytown 209 E1
Abbotrule 228 A5
Abbots Bickington 113 D4
Abbots Bromley 172 B5
Abbots Langley 135 F2
Abbots Leigh 131 E5
Abbots Morton 146 C2
Abbots Ripton 162 A5
Abbots Worthy 119 F4
Abbotsbury 104 B4
Abbotsbury Swannery, Subtropical Gardens & Children's Farm *Dorset* DT3 4JG 104 B4
Abbotsfield Farm 183 G3
Abbotsham 113 E3
Abbotskerswell 101 E1
Abbotsley 150 A2
Abbotstone 119 G4
Abbotts Ann 119 E3
Abbott's Barton 119 F4
Abbottswood 119 E5
Abdon 157 E4
Abdy 186 B3
Abenhall 131 F1
Aber 142 A3
Aber Village 144 A5
Aberaeron 142 A1
Aberaman 129 G2
Aberangell 155 E2
Aber-Arad 141 G3
Aberarder 249 G1
Aberarder House 258 D2
Aberargie 243 G2
Aberarth 142 A1
Aberavon 129 D3
Aber-banc 141 G3
Aberbargoed 130 A2
Aberbeeg 130 B2
Aberbowlan 142 C4
Aberbran 143 F5
Abercanaid 129 G2
Abercarn 130 B3
Abercastle 140 B4
Abercegir 155 E2
Aberchalder 257 K4
Aberchirder 268 E5
Abercorn 235 E2
Abercraf 129 E1
Abercregan 129 E3
Abercrombie 244 D4
Abercrychan 143 D4
Abercwmboi 129 G2
Abercych 141 F3
Abercynafon 129 G1
Abercynon 129 G3
Abercywarch 155 E1
Aberdalgie 243 F2
Aberdare 129 F2
Aberdaron 166 A5
Aberdeen (Obar Dheathain) 261 H4
Aberdeen Airport 261 G3
Aberdeen Art Gallery AB10 1FQ 63 Aberdeen
Aberdeen Exhibition & Conference Centre *Aberdeen* AB23 8BL 261 H3
Aberdesach 166 D2
Aberdour 235 F1
Aberdovey (Aberdyfi) 154 C3
Aberduhonw 143 G2
Aberdulais 129 D3
Aberedw 143 G3
Abereiddy 140 A4
Abererch 166 C4
Aberfan 129 G2
Aberfeldy 251 D5
Aberffraw 166 C1
Aberffrwd 154 C5
Aberford 194 D4
Aberfoyle 242 A4
Abergavenny (Y Fenni) 130 B1
Abergele 182 A5
Aber-Giâr 142 A5
Abergorlech 142 B4
Abergwesyn 143 E2
Abergwili 142 A5
Abergwydol 155 D2
Abergwynant 154 C1
Abergwynfi 129 E3
Abergwyngregyn 181 E5
Abergynolwyn 154 C2
Aberhafesp 155 G3
Aberhosan 155 E3
Aberkenfig 129 E4
Aberlady 236 B1
Aberlemno 252 D4
Aberllefenni 155 D2
Aber-llia 129 F1
Aberlour (Charlestown of Aberlour) 267 K7
Abermad 154 B5
Abermeurig 142 B2
Abermule (Aber-miwl) 156 A3
Abernaint 169 E5
Abernant *Carmar* 141 G5
Aber-nant *RCT* 129 G2
Abernethy 243 G3
Abernyte 244 A1
Aberporth 141 F2
Abersky 258 C2
Abersoch 166 C5
Abersychan 130 B2
Aberthin 129 G5
Abertillery 130 B2
Abertridwr *Caerp* 130 A4
Abertridwr *Powys* 155 G1
Abertysswg 130 A2
Aberuthven 243 E3
Aberyscir 143 F5
Aberystwyth 154 B4
Aberystwyth Arts Centre *Cere* SY23 3DE 154 B4
Abhainnsuidhe 270 C7
Abingdon 133 G3
Abinger Common 121 G3
Abinger Hammer 121 F3
Abington 226 A3
Abington Pigotts 150 B3
Abingworth 108 D2
Ablington *Glos* 132 D2
Ablington *Wilts* 118 C3
Abney 185 F5
Above Church 172 B2
Aboyne 260 E5
Abram 184 A2
Abriachan (Obar Itheachan) 258 C1
Abridge 137 D3
Abronhill 234 B2
Abson 131 G5
Abthorpe 148 B3
Abune-the-Hill 276 B5
Aby 189 E5
Acaster Malbis 195 E3
Acaster Selby 195 E3
Accrington 193 D5
Accurrach 240 D2
Acha 246 A4
Achadacaie 231 G3
Achadh Mòr 271 F4
Achadh-chaorrunn 231 F4
Achadunan 241 E3
Achagavel 247 G4
Achaglass 231 F5
Achahoish 231 F2
Achalader 251 G5
Achamore 231 D2
Achandunie 266 D4
Achany 266 C1
Achaphubuil 248 C2
Acharacle 247 F3
Achargary 274 C3
Acharn *A&B* 240 D1
Acharn *P&K* 250 C5
Acharonich 239 E1
Acharosson 232 A2
Achateny 247 E2
Achath 261 F3
Achavanich 275 G4
Achddu 128 A2
Achduart 265 G1
Achentoul 274 D5
Achfary 272 E5
Achgarve 264 E2
Achiemore *High* 273 F2
Achiemore *High* 274 D3
Achies 275 G3
A Chill 255 H4
Achiltibuie (Achd-'Ille-Bhuidhe) 265 G1
Achina 274 C2
Achindown 267 F7
Achinduich 266 C2
Achingills 275 G2
Achintee 265 F7
Achintee House (Achadh an t-Suidhe) 248 D2
Achintraid 256 E1
Achlean 259 F5
Achleanan 247 E4
Achleek 247 G4
Achlian 240 D2
Achlyness 272 E3
Achmelvich 272 D6
Achmony 258 C1
Achmore *High* 256 E1
Achmore *High* 265 G2
Achmore *Stir* 242 A1
Achnaba 232 A1
Achnabat 258 C1
Achnabourin 274 C3
Achnacairn 240 B1
Achnacarnin 272 C5
Achnacarry 249 D1
Achnaclerach 266 B5
Achnacloich *A&B* 240 B1
Achnacloich *High* 256 B4
Achnaclyth 275 F5
Achnacraig 247 D5
Achnacroish 248 A5
Achnadrish 246 D4
Achnafalnich 241 E2
Achnafauld 243 D1
Achnagarin 266 C7
Achnagarron 266 D4
Achnaha *High* 247 F5
Achnaha *High* 247 D3
Achnahanat 266 C2
Achnahannet 259 G2
Achnairn 273 H7
Achnalea 248 A3
Achnamara 231 F1
Achnanellan 247 G3
Achnasaul 249 D1
Achnasheen 265 H6
Achnashelloch 240 A5
Achnastank 267 K1
Achorn 275 G5
Achosnich *High* 266 E2
Achosnich *High* 246 D3
Achreamie 275 F2
Achriabhach 248 D3
Achriesgill 272 E3
Achtoty 273 J2
Achurch 161 F4
Achuvoldrach 273 H3
Achvaich 266 E2
Achvarasdal 274 E2
Achvlair 248 B4
Achvraie 265 G1
Ackenthwaite 199 G4
Ackergill 275 J3
Acklam *Middl* 203 D1
Acklam *NYorks* 195 G1
Ackleton 157 G3

Acklington 221 E1
Ackton 194 D5
Ackworth Moor Top 186 B1
Acle 179 F4
Acock's Green 158 D4
Acol 125 F2
Acomb *N'umb* 211 F1
Acomb *York* 195 E2
Aconbury 145 E4
Acre 193 D5
Acrefair 169 F3
Acrise Place 125 D4
Acton *ChesE* 170 D2
Acton *Dorset* 105 F5
Acton *GtLon* 136 A4
Acton *Shrop* 156 C4
Acton *Staffs* 171 F3
Acton *Suff* 151 G3
Acton *Worcs* 146 A1
Acton *Wrex* 170 A2
Acton Beauchamp 145 F2
Acton Bridge 183 G5
Acton Burnell 157 E2
Acton Green 145 F2
Acton Pigott 157 E2
Acton Round 157 F3
Acton Scott 157 D4
Acton Trussell 158 B1
Acton Turville 132 A4
Adamhill 224 C2
Adbaston 171 E5
Adber 116 C4
Adderbury 147 G4
Adderley 171 D4
Adderstone 229 F3
Addiewell 235 E3
Addingham 193 G3
Addington *Bucks* 148 C5
Addington *GtLon* 122 C2
Addington *Kent* 123 F3
Addiscombe 122 C2
Addlestone 121 F1
Addlethorpe 176 D1
Adel 194 B4
Aden Country Park *Aber* AB42 5FQ 269 H6
Adeney 157 G1
Adeyfield 135 F2
Adfa 155 G2
Adforton 156 D5
Adisham 125 E3
Adlestrop 147 E5
Adlingfleet 196 A5
Adlingham 193 G3
Adlington *ChesE* 184 D4
Adlington *Lancs* 183 E1
Admaston *Staffs* 172 B5
Admaston *Tel&W* 157 F1
Admington 147 E3
Adsborough 115 F5
Adscombe 115 E4
Adstock 148 C4
Adstone 148 A2
Adventure Island *S'end* SS1 1EE 138 C4
Adventure Wonderland *Dorset* BH23 6BA 3 D2
Adversane 121 F5
Advie 259 J1
Adwalton 194 B5
Adwell 134 B3
Adwick le Street 186 C2
Adwick upon Dearne 186 B2
Adziel 269 H5
Ae Village 217 D3
Afan Argoed Country Park *NPT* SA13 3HG 129 E3
Affetside 184 B1
Affleck 261 G2
Affpuddle 105 E3
Afon Wen 166 D4
Afon-wen 182 C5
Afonwen Craft & Antique Centre *Flints* CH7 5UB 182 C5
Africa Alive! *Suff* NR33 7TF 165 G3
Afton 106 C4
Afton Bridgend 225 E4
Agglethorpe 201 F4
Aigburth 183 E4
Aiginis 271 G4
Aike 196 C3
Aikerness 276 D2
Aikers 277 D8
Aikshaw 209 E2
Aikton 209 F1
Aikwood Tower 227 F3
Ailby 189 E5
Ailey 144 C3
Ailsworth 161 G3
Aimes Green 136 D2
Aimster 275 G2
Ainderby Quernhow 202 C4
Ainderby Steeple 202 C3
Aingers Green 152 C5
Ainsdale 183 E1
Ainsdale-on-Sea 183 E1
Ainstable 210 B3
Ainsworth 184 B1
Ainthorpe 203 G2
Aintree 183 E3
Aird *ESiar* 262 C6
Aird *ESiar* 271 H4
Aird a' Mhachair 262 C7
Aird a' Mhulaidh 270 D6
Aird Asaig 270 D7
Aird Dhail 271 G1
Aird Leimhe 263 G3
Aird Mhige 263 G2
Aird Mhighe 263 F3
Aird of Sleat 256 B4
Aird Thunga 271 G4
Aird Uig 270 C4
Airdrie *Fife* 245 G3
Airdrie *NLan* 234 B3
Aire View 193 F3
Airidh a' Bhruaich 270 E6
Airieland 216 B5
Airies 214 A4
Airigh-drishaig 256 D1
Airmyn 195 G5
Airntully 243 F1
Airor 256 C4
Airth 234 C1
Airton 193 F2

Airyhassen 207 D2
Aisby *Lincs* 187 F3
Aisby *Lincs* 175 F4
Aisgill 200 C3
Aish *Devon* 100 C1
Aish *Devon* 101 E2
Aisholt 115 E4
Aiskew 202 B4
Aislaby *NYorks* 204 B3
Aislaby *NYorks* 203 G4
Aislaby *Stock* 202 D1
Aisthorpe 187 G4
Aith *Ork* 277 B6
Aith *Ork* 276 F5
Aith *Shet* 279 C7
Aith *Shet* 278 F3
Aithsetter 279 D9
Aitnoch 259 G1
Akeld 229 D4
Akeley 148 C4
Akenham 152 C3
Albaston 99 E3
Albecq 101 E5
Alberbury 156 C1
Albert Park TS1 3LB 78 Middlesbrough
Albert Town 126 C1
Albourne 109 E2
Albourne Green 109 E2
Albrighton *Shrop* 158 A2
Albrighton *Shrop* 157 D1
Alburgh 165 D3
Albury *Herts* 150 C5
Albury *Oxon* 134 B3
Albury *Surr* 121 F3
Albury End 150 C5
Albury Heath 121 F3
Albyfield 210 B2
Alcaig 266 C6
Alcaston 157 D4
Alcester 146 C2
Alciston 110 A3
Alcombe 114 C3
Alconbury 161 G5
Alconbury Hill 161 G5
Alconbury Weston 161 G5
Aldborough *Norf* 178 C2
Aldborough *NYorks* 194 D1
Aldbourne 133 E5
Aldbrough 197 E4
Aldbrough St. John 202 B1
Aldbury 135 F2
Aldclune 251 E3
Aldeburgh 153 F2
Aldeby 165 F2
Aldenham 136 A3
Aldenham Country Park *Herts* WD6 3AT 136 A3
Alderbury 118 C5
Alderford 178 C4
Alderholt 106 A1
Alderley 131 G3
Alderley Edge 184 C5
Aldermaston 119 G1
Aldermaston Wharf 120 B1
Alderminster 147 E3
Alderney 101 G4
Alderney Airport 101 F4
Alder's End 145 F4
Aldersey Green 170 B2
Aldershot 121 D2
Alderton *Glos* 146 B4
Alderton *N'hants* 148 C3
Alderton *Shrop* 157 D1
Alderton *Suff* 153 E4
Alderton *Wilts* 132 A4
Alderwasley 173 E2
Aldfield 194 B1
Aldford 170 B2
Aldham *Essex* 152 A5
Aldham *Suff* 152 B3
Aldie *Aber* 269 J6
Aldie *High* 266 E3
Aldingbourne 108 B3
Aldingham 199 D5
Aldington *Kent* 124 C5
Aldington *Worcs* 146 C3
Aldivalloch 260 B2
Aldochlay 241 F5
Aldons 214 C2
Aldous's Corner 165 E3
Aldreth 162 C5
Aldridge 158 C2
Aldringham 153 F1
Aldsworth *Glos* 133 D2
Aldsworth *WSuss* 107 G2
Aldunie 260 B2
Aldville 243 E1
Aldwark *Derbys* 172 D2
Aldwark *NYorks* 195 D1
Aldwick 108 B4
Aldwincle 161 F4
Aldworth 134 A5
Aldwark 176 D1
Alexandra Palace *GtLon* N22 7AY 12 A1
Alexandria 233 E2
Aley 115 E4
Aley Green 135 F1
Alfardisworthy 112 C4
Alfington 103 E3
Alfold 121 F4
Alfold Crossways 121 F4
Alford *Aber* 260 D3
Alford *Lincs* 189 E5
Alford *Som* 116 D4
Alfreton 173 F2
Alfrick 145 G2
Alfrick Pound 145 G2
Alfriston 110 A3
Algarkirk 176 A4
Alhampton 116 D4
Alkborough 196 A5
Alkerton 147 F3
Alkham 125 E4
Alkington 170 C4
Alkmonton 172 C4
All Cannings 118 B1
All Saints South Elmham 165 E3
All Stretton 157 D3
Allaleigh 101 E2
Allanaquoich 259 J5
Allancreich 260 D5
Allanfearn 266 E7
Allangillfoot 218 A2
Allanton *D&G* 216 C3
Allanton *EAyr* 225 E2
Allanton *NLan* 234 C4

Allanton *ScBord* 237 F4
Allanton *SLan* 234 B4
Allardice 253 G2
Allathasdal 254 B4
Allbrook 119 F5
Allendale Town 211 E2
Allenheads 211 E3
Allen's Green 137 D1
Allensford 211 G2
Allensford Country Park *Dur* DH8 9BA 211 G2
Allensmore 145 D4
Allenton 173 E4
Aller 116 B5
Allerby 209 D3
Allercombe 102 D3
Allerford *Devon* 99 E2
Allerford *Som* 114 C3
Allerston 204 B4
Allerthorpe 195 G3
Allerton *Mersey* 183 F4
Allerton *WYorks* 194 A4
Allerton Bywater 194 D5
Allerton Mauleverer 194 D2
Allesley 159 E4
Allestree 173 E4
Allet Common 96 B5
Allexton 160 D2
Allgreave 171 G1
Allhallows 124 A1
Allhallows-on-Sea 124 A1
Alligin Shuas 264 E6
Allimore Green 158 A1
Allington *Dorset* 104 A3
Allington *Lincs* 175 D3
Allington *Wilts* 118 B1
Allington *Wilts* 132 A5
Allithwaite 199 E5
Allnabad 273 G4
Alloa 243 D5
Allonby 209 D2
Allostock 184 B5
Alloway 224 B4
Allowenshay 103 G1
Allscot 157 G3
Allscott 157 F1
Allt na h-Airbhe 265 H2
Alltachonaich 247 G4
Alltbeithe 257 G2
Alltforgan 168 C5
Alltmawr 143 G3
Alltnacaillich 273 G4
Allt-nan-sùugh 257 F1
Alltsigh 258 B3
Alltwalis 142 A4
Alltwen 128 D2
Alltyblaca 142 B3
Allwood Green 164 B4
Almeley 144 C3
Almeley Wootton 144 C2
Almer 105 E3
Almington 171 E4
Almiston Cross 113 D3
Almondbank 243 F2
Almondbury 185 F1
Almondell & Calderwood Country Park *WLoth* EH52 5PE 235 E3
Almondsbury 131 F4
Alne 195 D1
Alness 266 D5
Alnham 229 D5
Alnmouth 229 G5
Alnwick 229 F5
Alnwick Garden, The *N'umb* NE66 1YU 229 F5
Alperton 136 A4
Alphamstone 151 G4
Alpheton 151 G2
Alphington 102 C3
Alport 172 D1
Alpraham 170 C2
Alresford 152 B5
Alrewas 159 D1
Alrick 251 G3
Alsager 171 E2
Alsagers Bank 171 F3
Alsop en le Dale 172 C2
Alston *Cumb* 210 D3
Alston *Devon* 103 G2
Alston Sutton 116 B2
Alstone *Glos* 146 B4
Alstone *Som* 116 A3
Alstone *Staffs* 158 A1
Alstonefield 172 C2
Alswear 114 A5
Alt 184 D2
Altandhu 272 B7
Altanduin 274 D6
Altarnun 97 G1
Altass 266 C1
Altens 261 H4
Alterwall 275 H2
Altham 193 D4
Althorne 138 C3
Althorp House *N'hants* NN7 4HQ 148 C2
Althorpe 187 F2
Alticry 215 D5
Altnafeadh 249 E4
Altnaharra 273 H5
Altofts 194 C5
Alton *Derbys* 173 E1
Alton *Hants* 120 C4
Alton *Staffs* 172 B3
Alton Barnes 118 C1
Alton Pancras 104 D2
Alton Priors 118 C1
Alton Towers Leisure Park *Staffs* ST10 4DB 172 B3
Alton Water Reservoir *Suff* IP9 2RY 152 C4
Altonside 267 K6
Altrincham 184 B4
Altura 257 J5
Alva 243 D5
Alvanley 183 F5
Alvaston 173 E4
Alvechurch 158 C5
Alvecote 159 E2
Alvediston 118 A5
Aveley 157 G4
Alverdiscott 113 F4
Alverstoke 107 F3
Alverstone 107 E4
Alverthorpe 194 C5
Alverton 174 C3

Alves 267 J5
Alvescot 133 E2
Alveston *SGlos* 131 F4
Alveston *Warks* 147 E2
Alvie 259 F4
Alvingham 189 D3
Alvington 131 F2
Alwalton 161 G3
Alweston 104 C1
Alwington 113 E3
Alwinton 220 B1
Alwoodley 194 C3
Alwoodley Gates 194 C3
Alyth 252 A5
Amalebra 94 B3
Ambaston 173 F4
Amber Hill 176 A3
Ambergate 173 E2
Amberley *Glos* 132 A2
Amberley *WSuss* 108 C2
Amble 221 E1
Amblecote 158 A4
Ambleside 199 E3
Ambleston 140 D5
Ambrismore 232 B4
Ambrosden 134 B1
Amcotts 187 F1
Amersham 135 E3
Amerton 173 E1
Amerton Farm *Staffs* ST18 0LA 171 G5
Amesbury 118 C3
Ameysford 105 G2
Amington 159 E2
Amisfield Town 217 E2
Amlwch 180 C3
Amlwch Port 180 C3
Ammanford (Rhydaman) 128 C1
Amotherby 203 G5
Ampfield 119 E5
Ampleforth 203 E5
Ampleforth College 203 E5
Ampney Crucis 132 C2
Ampney St. Mary 132 C2
Ampney St. Peter 132 C2
Amport 119 E3
Ampthill 149 F4
Ampton 163 G5
Amroth 127 E2
Amulree 243 D1
Anaboard 259 H1
Anaheilt 248 A3
Ancaster 175 E3
Anchor 156 A4
Anchor Corner 164 B2
Ancroft 237 G5
Ancrum 228 A4
Ancton 108 B3
Anderby 189 F5
Anderby Creek 189 F5
Andersea 116 A4
Andersfield 115 F4
Anderson 105 E3
Anderton 184 A5
Anderton Boat Lift *ChesW&C* CW9 6FW 184 A5
Andover 119 E3
Andover Down 119 E3
Andoversford 132 C1
Andreas 190 C2
Anelog 166 A5
Anfield 183 E3
Angarrack 94 C3
Angarrick 95 E3
Angelbank 157 E5
Angerton 209 F1
Angle 126 B2
Anglers Country Park *WYorks* WF4 2EB 186 A1
Angler's Retreat 154 D3
Anglesey (Ynys Môn) 180 B4
Anglesey Abbey *Cambs* CB25 9EJ 150 D1
Angmering 108 C3
Angmering-on-Sea 108 C3
Angram *NYorks* 195 E3
Angram *NYorks* 201 D3
Anick 211 F1
Anie 242 A3
Animal World & Butterfly House *GtMan* BL1 5UG 184 A1
Ankerville 267 F4
Anlaby 196 C5
Anmer 177 F5
Anmore 107 F1
Anna Valley 119 E3
Annan 217 F4
Annaside 198 B4
Annat *A&B* 240 D2
Annat *High* 264 E6
Annbank 224 C3
Anne Hathaway's Cottage *Warks* CV37 9HH 147 D2
Annesley 173 F2
Annesley Woodhouse 173 F2
Annfield Plain 212 A2
Anniesland 233 G3
Annscroft 157 D2
Ansdell 191 G5
Ansford 116 D4
Ansley 159 E3
Anslow 172 D5
Anslow Gate 172 C5
Anstey *Herts* 150 C4
Anstey *Leics* 160 A2
Anstruther 245 E4
Ansty *Warks* 159 F4
Ansty *Wilts* 118 A5
Ansty *WSuss* 109 E1
Ansty Coombe 118 A5
Ansty Cross 105 D2
Anthill Common 107 F1
Anthorn 209 E1
Antingham 179 D2
Anton's Gowt 176 A3
Antony 99 D5
Antrobus 184 A5
Anvil Corner 113 D5
Anvil Green 124 D4
Anwick 175 G2

Anwoth 215 G5
Aonach Mòr Mountain Gondola & Nevis Range Ski Centre *High* PH33 6SW 249 D2
Aoradh 230 A3
Apethorpe 161 F3
Apeton 158 A1
Apley 188 B5
Apperknowle 186 A5
Apperley 146 A5
Apperley Bridge 194 A4
Appersett 201 D3
Appin (An Apainn) 248 B5
Appin House 248 B5
Appleby 187 G1
Appleby Magna 159 F1
Appleby Parva 159 F2
Appleby-in-Westmorland 210 C5
Applecross 264 D7
Appledore *Devon* 113 E2
Appledore *Devon* 103 D1
Appledore *Kent* 111 E1
Appledore Heath 124 B5
Appleford 134 A3
Appleshaw 119 E3
Applethwaite 209 E4
Appleton *Halton* 183 G4
Appleton *Oxon* 133 G2
Appleton Roebuck 195 E3
Appleton Thorn 184 A4
Appleton Wiske 202 D2
Appleton-le-Moors 203 G4
Appleton-le-Street 203 G5
Appletreehall 227 G4
Appletreewick 193 G1
Appley 115 D5
Appley Bridge 183 G2
Apse Heath 107 E4
Apsey Green 153 D1
Apsley 135 F2
Apsley End 149 G4
Apuldram 108 A3
Arbeia Roman Fort & Museum *T&W* NE33 2BB 28 E1
Arbirlot 253 D5
Arborfield 120 C1
Arborfield Cross 120 C1
Arborfield Garrison 120 C1
Arbourthorne 186 A4
Arbroath 253 E5
Arbuthnott 253 F2
Archdeacon Newton 202 B1
Archiestown 267 K7
Arclid 171 E1
Ard a' Chapuill 232 B1
Ardacheranbeg 232 B1
Ardacheranmor 232 B1
Ardachoil 239 G1
Ardachu 266 D1
Ardailly 231 E4
Ardalanish 238 C3
Ardanaiseig 240 C2
Ardaneaskan 256 E1
Ardanstur 240 A3
Ardantiobairt 247 F4
Ardarroch 264 E7
Ardbeg *A&B* 232 B3
Ardbeg *A&B* 230 C5
Ardbeg *A&B* 232 C1
Ardblair 258 C1
Ardbrecknish 240 C2
Ardcharnich 265 H3
Ardchiavaig 238 C3
Ardchonnel 240 B1
Ardchonnell 240 B3
Ardchrishnish 238 D2
Ardchronie 266 D3
Ardchuilk 257 J1
Ardchullarie More 242 A3
Ardchyle 242 A2
Arddlin 156 B1
Ardechive 257 H5
Ardeley 150 B5
Ardelve 256 E2
Arden 233 E1
Ardencaple House 239 G3
Ardens Grafton 146 D2
Ardentallan 240 A2
Ardentinny 232 C1
Ardeonaig 242 B1
Ardersier 266 E6
Ardery 247 G3
Ardessie 265 G3
Ardfad 239 G3
Ardfern 240 A4
Ardfin 230 C3
Ardgartan 241 E4
Ardgay 266 D2
Ardgenavan 241 D3
Ardgour (Corran) 248 C3
Ardgowan 232 D2
Ardgowse 260 E3
Ardgye 267 J5
Ardhallow 232 C2
Ardheslaig 264 D6
Ardiecow 268 D4
Ardinamar 239 G3
Ardindrean 265 H3
Ardingly 109 F1
Ardington 133 G4
Ardington Wick 133 G4
Ardintoul 256 E2
Ardkinglas House 241 D3
Ardlair 260 D2
Ardlamont 232 A3
Ardleigh 152 B5
Ardleigh Green 137 E4
Ardleigh Heath 152 B4
Ardleish 241 F3
Ardler 252 A5
Ardley 148 A5
Ardley End 137 E1
Ardlui (Àird Laoigh) 241 F3
Ardlussa 231 E1
Ardmaddy 240 C1
Ardmair 265 H2
Ardmaleish 232 B3
Ardmay 241 E4
Ardmenish 231 D2
Ardmhòr 254 C4
Ardminish 231 E5
Ardmolich 247 G2

Ardmore *A&B* 230 C4
Ardmore *A&B* 239 G2
Ardmore *A&B* 233 E2
Ardmore *High* 266 E3
Ardnackaig 239 G5
Ardnacross 247 E5
Ardnadam 232 C1
Ardnadrochit 239 G1
Ardnagoine 265 F1
Ardnagowan 240 D4
Ardnahein 241 D5
Ardnahoe 230 C2
Ardnarff 256 E1
Ardnave 230 A2
Ardno 241 D4
Ardo 261 G1
Ardoch *D&G* 225 G5
Ardoch *Moray* 267 J6
Ardoch *P&K* 243 F2
Ardochrig 234 A5
Ardoyne 260 E2
Ardpatrick 231 F3
Ardpeaton 232 D1
Ardradnaig 250 C5
Ardrishaig 231 G1
Ardroe 272 C6
Ardross 266 D4
Ardscalpsie 232 B4
Ardshave 266 E2
Ardshealach 247 F3
Ardshellach 239 G3
Ardsley 186 A2
Ardslignish 247 E3
Ardtalla 230 C4
Ardtaraig 232 B1
Ardteatle 240 D2
Ardtoe 247 F2
Ardtornish 247 G5
Ardtrostan 242 B2
Ardtur 248 B5
Arduaine 240 A3
Ardullie 266 C5
Ardura 239 F1
Ardvar 272 D5
Ardvasar 256 C4
Ardveenish 254 C4
Ardveich 242 B2
Ardverikie 250 A1
Ardvorlich *A&B* 241 F3
Ardvorlich *P&K* 242 B2
Ardwall 215 G5
Ardwell *D&G* 206 B2
Ardwell *Moray* 260 B1
Ardwell *SAyr* 214 C1
Ardwick 184 C3
Areley Kings 158 A5
Arford 120 D4
Argaty 242 C4
Argoed 130 A3
Argoed Mill 143 F1
Argos Hill 110 A3
Argrennan House 216 B5
Arguli & Sutherland
  Highlanders Museum
  Stir FK8 1EH 242 C5
Arichamish 240 B4
Arichastlich 241 E1
Arichonan 239 G5
Aridhglas 238 C2
Arienskill 247 G1
Arileod 246 A4
Arinacrinachd 264 D6
Arinafad Beg 231 F1
Arinagour 246 B4
Arinambane 254 C2
Arisaig (Àrasaig) 247 F1
Arivegaig 247 F3
Arkendale 194 C1
Arkesden 150 C4
Arkholme 199 G5
Arkle Town 201 F2
Arkleby 209 E3
Arkleside 201 F4
Arkleton 218 B2
Arkley 136 B3
Arksey 186 C5
Arkwright Town 186 B5
Arlary 243 G4
Arle 146 B5
Arlecdon 208 D5
Arlesey 149 G4
Arleston 157 F1
Arley 184 A4
Arlingham 131 G1
Arlington *Devon* 113 G1
Arlington *ESuss* 110 A3
Arlington *Glos* 132 D2
Arlington Beccott 113 G1
Armadale *High* 239 J2
Armadale *High* 256 C4
Armadale *WLoth*
  234 D2
Armathwaite 210 B3
Arminghall 179 D5
Armitage 158 C1
Armitage Bridge 185 F1
Armley 194 B4
Armscote 147 E3
Armshead 171 G3
Armston 161 F4
Armthorpe 186 D2
Arnabost 246 B3
Arnaby 198 C4
Arncliffe 201 E5
Arncliffe Cote 201 E5
Arncroach 244 D4
Arne 105 F4
Arnesby 160 B3
Arngask 243 G3
Arngibbon 242 B5
Arngomery 242 B5
Arnhall 253 E3
Arnicle 222 C2
Arnipol 247 G1
Arnisdale
  (Arnasdal) 256 E3
Arnish 264 B7
Arniston Engine 236 A3
Arnol 271 F3
Arnold *ERid* 196 D3
Arnold *Notts* 173 G3
Arnolfini Gallery
  BS1 4QA 66 Bristol
Arnprior 242 B5
Arnside 199 F5

Aros Experience *High*
  IV51 9EU 263 K7
Arowry 170 B4
Arrad Foot 199 E4
Arradoul 268 C4
Arram 196 C3
Arras 196 B3
Arrat 253 E4
Arrathorne 202 B3
Arreton 107 E4
Arrington 150 B2
Arrivain 241 E1
Arrochar 241 F4
Arrow 146 C2
Arscaig 273 H7
Arscott 156 D2
Arthington 194 B3
Arthingworth 160 C4
Arthog 154 C1
Arthrath 261 H1
Arthurstone 252 A5
Artrochie 261 J1
Aruadh 230 A3
Arundel 108 C3
Arundel Castle *WSuss*
  BN18 9AB 108 C3
Arundel Cathedral (R.C.)
  WSuss
  BN18 9AY 108 C3
Aryhoulan 248 C3
Asby 209 D4
Ascog 232 C3
Ascot 121 E1
Ascott 147 F4
Ascott d'Oyley 133 F1
Ascott Earl 133 E1
Ascott-under-
  Wychwood 133 F1
Ascreavie 252 B4
Asenby 202 D5
Asfordby 160 C1
Asfordby Hill 160 C1
Asgarby *Lincs* 176 B1
Asgarby *Lincs* 175 G3
Ash *Dorset* 105 E1
Ash *Kent* 125 E3
Ash *Kent* 123 F2
Ash *Som* 116 B5
Ash *Surr* 121 D2
Ash Barton 113 F5
Ash Bullayne 102 A2
Ash Green *Surr* 121 E3
Ash Green *Warks* 159 F4
Ash Magna 170 C4
Ash Mill 114 A5
Ash Parva 170 C4
Ash Priors 115 E5
Ash Street 152 B3
Ash Thomas 102 D1
Ash Vale 121 D2
Ashampstead 134 A5
Ashbocking 152 C2
Ashbourne 172 C3
Ashbrittle 115 D5
Ashburnham Place 110 B2
Ashburton 101 D1
Ashbury *Devon* 99 F1
Ashbury *Oxon* 133 E4
Ashby 187 F2
Ashby by Partney 176 C1
Ashby cum Fenby 188 C2
Ashby de la Launde 175 F2
Ashby de la Zouch 159 F1
Ashby Dell 165 F2
Ashby Folville 160 C1
Ashby Hill 188 C2
Ashby Magna 160 A3
Ashby Parva 160 A4
Ashby Puerorum 188 D5
Ashby St. Ledgers 148 A1
Ashby St. Mary 179 E5
Ashchurch 146 B4
Ashcombe *Devon* 102 C5
Ashcombe *NSom* 116 A1
Ashcott 116 B4
Ashdon 151 D3
Ashe 119 G3
Asheldham 138 C2
Ashen 151 F3
Ashenden 124 A5
Ashendon 134 C1
Ashens 231 G2
Ashfield *A&B* 231 F1
Ashfield *Here* 145 E5
Ashfield *Stir* 242 C4
Ashfield *Suff* 152 D1
Ashfield Green *Suff* 165 D4
Ashfield Green *Suff* 151 F2
Ashfold Crossways 109 E1
Ashford *Devon* 100 C3
Ashford *Devon* 113 F2
Ashford *Hants* 106 A1
Ashford *Kent* 124 C4
Ashford *Surr* 135 F5
Ashford Bowdler 157 E5
Ashford Carbonel 157 E5
Ashford Hill 119 G1
Ashford in the
  Water 185 F5
Ashgill 234 B4
Ashiestiel 227 F2
Ashill *Devon* 103 D1
Ashill *Norf* 163 G2
Ashill *Som* 103 G1
Ashingdon 138 B3
Ashington *N'umb* 221 E3
Ashington *Som* 116 C5
Ashington
  WSuss 108 D2
Ashkirk 227 F3
Ashlett 107 D2
Ashleworth 146 A5
Ashleworth Quay 146 A5
Ashley *Cambs* 151 E1
Ashley *ChesE* 184 B4
Ashley *Devon* 113 G4
Ashley *Glos* 132 B3
Ashley *Hants* 119 E4
Ashley *Hants* 106 B3
Ashley *Kent* 125 F4
Ashley *N'hants* 160 C3
Ashley *Staffs* 171 E4
Ashley *Wilts* 117 F1
Ashley Down 131 E5
Ashley Green 135 E2
Ashley Heath
  Dorset 106 A2

Ashley Heath
  Staffs 171 E4
Ashmanhaugh 179 E3
Ashmansworth 119 F2
Ashmansworthy 112 D4
Ashmolean Museum
  Oxon OX1 2PH
  80 Oxford
Ashmore *Dorset* 105 F1
Ashmore *P&K* 251 G4
Ashmore Green 119 G1
Ashorne 147 F2
Ashover 173 E1
Ashover Hay 173 E1
Ashow 159 F5
Ashperton 145 F3
Ashprington 101 E2
Ashreigney 113 G4
Ashstead 121 G2
Ashton *ChesW&C* 170 C1
Ashton *Corn* 94 D4
Ashton *Corn* 99 D4
Ashton *Hants* 107 E1
Ashton *Here* 145 E1
Ashton *Invcly* 232 D2
Ashton *N'hants* 161 F4
Ashton *N'hants* 148 C3
Ashton *Peter* 161 G2
Ashton Common 117 F2
Ashton Court Estate
  NSom BS41 9JN 8 B3
Ashton Keynes 132 C3
Ashton under Hill 146 B4
Ashton upon
  Mersey 184 B3
Ashton-in-
  Makerfield 183 G3
Ashton-under-Lyne 184 D3
Ashurst *Hants* 106 C1
Ashurst *Kent* 123 E5
Ashurst *WSuss* 109 D2
Ashurst Bridge 106 C1
Ashurstwood 122 D5
Ashwater 99 E1
Ashwell *Herts* 150 A4
Ashwell *Rut* 161 D1
Ashwell End 150 A3
Ashwellthorpe 164 C2
Ashwick 116 D3
Ashwicken 163 F1
Ashybank 227 G4
Askam in Furness 198 D5
Askern 186 C1
Askernish
  (Aisgernis) 254 C2
Askerswell 104 B3
Askett 134 D2
Askham *Cumb* 210 B5
Askham *Notts* 187 E5
Askham Bryan 195 E3
Askham Richard 195 E3
Asknish 240 B5
Askrigg 201 E3
Askwith 194 A3
Aslackby 175 F4
Aslacton 164 C2
Aslockton 174 C3
Asloun 260 D3
Aspall 152 C1
Aspatria 209 E2
Aspenden 150 B5
Asperton 176 A4
Aspley Guise 149 E4
Aspley Heath 149 E4
Aspull 184 A2
Asselby 195 G5
Asserby 189 E5
Assington 152 A4
Assington Green 151 F2
Astbury 171 F1
Astcote 148 B2
Asterby 188 C5
Asterley 156 C2
Asterton 156 D3
Asthall 133 E1
Asthall Leigh 133 F1
Astle 184 C5
Astley *GtMan* 184 B2
Astley *Shrop* 157 E1
Astley *Warks* 159 F4
Astley *Worcs* 145 G1
Astley Abbotts 157 G3
Astley Bridge 184 B1
Astley Cross 146 A1
Astley Green 184 B3
Astley Lodge 157 E1
Aston *ChesE* 170 D3
Aston *ChesW&C* 183 G5
Aston *Derbys* 185 E4
Aston *Derbys* 172 C4
Aston *Flints* 170 A1
Aston *Here* 157 D5
Aston *Here* 145 D1
Aston *Here* 156 A5
Aston *Oxon* 133 F2
Aston *Shrop* 170 C5
Aston *Shrop* 158 A3
Aston *Staffs* 171 E3
Aston *SYorks* 186 B4
Aston *Tel&W* 157 F2
Aston *W'ham* 134 C4
Aston *WMid* 158 C4
Aston Abbotts 148 D5
Aston Botterell 157 F4
Aston Cantlow 146 D2
Aston Clinton 135 D1
Aston Crews 145 F5
Aston Cross 146 B4
Aston End 150 A5
Aston Eyre 157 F3
Aston Fields 146 B1
Aston Flamville 159 G3
Aston Heath 183 G5
Aston Ingham 145 F5
Aston juxta
  Mondrum 171 D2
Aston le Walls 147 G2
Aston Magna 147 D4
Aston Munslow 157 E4
Aston on Carrant 146 B4
Aston on Clun 156 C4
Aston Pigott 156 C2
Aston Rogers 156 C2
Aston Rowant 134 C3
Aston Sandford 134 C2
Aston Somerville 146 C4

Aston Subedge 146 D3
Aston Tirrold 134 A4
Aston Upthorpe 134 A4
Aston-by-Stone 171 G4
Aston-on-Trent 173 F5
Astwick 150 A4
Astwood 149 E3
Astwood Bank 146 C1
Aswarby 175 F3
Aswardby 189 D5
Aswick Grange 162 B1
Atch Lench 146 C2
Atcham 157 E2
Ath Linne 270 D6
Athelhampton 105 D3
Athelington 164 D4
Athelney 116 A5
Athelstaneford 236 C2
Atherington *Devon* 113 F3
Atherington *WSuss* 108 C3
Athersley North 186 A2
Atherstone 159 F3
Atherstone on Stour 147 E2
Atherton 184 A2
Atlow 172 D3
Attadale 257 F1
Attenborough 173 G4
Atterby 187 G3
Attercliffe 186 A4
Atterley 157 F3
Atterton 159 F3
Attingham Park
  Shrop SY4 4TP 157 E1
Attleborough *Norf*
  164 B2
Attleborough
  Warks 159 F3
Attlebridge 178 C4
Attleton Green 151 F2
Atwick 197 D2
Atworth 117 F1
Auberrow 145 D3
Aubourn 175 E1
Auch 241 F1
Auchairne 214 C2
Auchallater 251 G1
Auchameanach 231 G4
Auchamore 231 G5
Auchamore 268 E6
Aucharnie 260 E1
Aucharrigill 266 B6
Auchattie 260 E5
Auchavan 251 G3
Auchbraad 231 G1
Auchbreck 259 K2
Auchenback 233 G4
Auchenblae 253 F2
Auchenbothie 233 E2
Auchenbrack 216 B1
Auchenbreck 232 B1
Auchencairn 237 F3
Auchendinny 235 G3
Auchendolly 216 B4
Auchenfoyle 233 E2
Auchengillan 233 G1
Auchengray 235 D4
Auchenhalrig 268 B4
Auchenheath 234 C5
Auchenhessnane 216 C1
Auchenlochan 232 A2
Auchenmalg 214 D5
Auchenrivock 218 B3
Auchentiber 233 E5
Auchenvennel 233 D1
Auchessan 241 G2
Auchgourish 259 G3
Auchinafaud 231 F4
Auchincruive 224 B3
Auchindarrach 231 G1
Auchindarroch 248 C4
Auchindrain 240 C4
Auchindrean 265 H3
Auchininna 268 E6
Auchinleck 224 D3
Auchinloch 234 A2
Auchinner 242 B3
Auchinroath 267 K6
Auchintoul *Aber* 260 D3
Auchintoul *Aber* 260 E5
Auchintoul *High* 266 C7
Auchiries 261 J1
Auchleven 260 E2
Auchlochan 225 G2
Auchlunachan 265 H3
Auchlunies 261 G5
Auchlunkart 268 B6
Auchlyne 242 A2
Auchmacoy 261 H1
Auchmair 260 B2
Auchmantle 214 C4
Auchmithie 253 E5
Auchmuirbridge 244 A4
Auchmull 253 D2
Auchnabony 208 A2
Auchnabreac 240 C4
Auchnacloich 242 D1
Auchnacraig 239 G1
Auchnacree 252 C3
Auchnafree 242 D1
Auchnagallin 259 H1
Auchnagatt 269 H6
Auchnaha 232 A1
Auchnangoul 240 C4
Aucholzie 260 B5
Auchorrie 260 E4
Auchrannie 252 A4
Auchraw 242 A2
Auchreoch 241 F2
Auchronie 252 C1
Auchterarder 243 E3
Auchterderran 244 E4
Auchterhouse 244 B1
Auchtermuchty 244 A3
Auchtertool 244 A5
Auchterarder 243 E3
Auchterderran 244 A5
Auchtertyre *Angus* 252 A5
Auchtertyre (Uachdar Thire)
  High 256 E2
Auchtertyre (Uachdar Thire)
  High 256 E2
Auchtertyre *Moray* 267 J6
Auchtertyre *Stir* 241 F2
Auchtubh 242 A2
Auckengill 275 J2
Auckley 186 D2
Audenshaw 184 D3
Audlem 171 D3
Audley 171 E2
Audley End *Essex* 150 D4

Audley End *Essex* 151 G4
Audley End *Suff* 151 G2
Audmore 171 F4
Auds 268 E4
Aughton *ERid* 195 G4
Aughton *Lancs* 183 E2
Aughton *Lancs* 192 B1
Aughton *SYorks* 186 B4
Aughton *Wilts* 118 C2
Aughton Park 183 F2
Auldearn 267 G6
Aulden 145 D2
Auldgirth 216 D2
Auldhame 236 C1
Auldhouse 234 A4
Aulich 250 B3
Ault a'chruinn 257 F2
Ault Hucknall 173 F1
Aultanrynie 273 F5
Aultbea
  (An t-Allt Beithe) 264 E3
Aultgrishan 264 D3
Aultguish Inn 265 K4
Aultibea 275 F6
Aultiphurst 274 D2
Aultmore 268 C5
Aultnagoire 258 C2
Aultnamain Inn 266 D3
Aultnapaddock 268 B6
Aulton 260 E2
Aultvaich 266 C7
Aultvoulin 256 D4
Aunby 161 F2
Aundorach 259 G3
Aunsby 175 F4
Aust 131 E4
Austendike 176 A5
Austerfield 187 D3
Austrey 159 E2
Austwick 193 D1
Authorpe 189 E4
Authorpe Row 189 F5
Avebury 132 D5
Avebury Trusloe 118 B1
Aveley 137 E4
Avening 132 A3
Averham 174 C2
Avery Hill 136 D5
Aveton Gifford 100 C3
Avielochan 259 G3
Aviemore 259 F3
Avington *Hants* 119 G4
Avington *WBerks* 119 E1
Avoch 266 D6
Avon 106 A3
Avon Dassett 147 G2
Avon Heath Country Park
  Dorset BH24 2DA 3 E1
Avon Valley Railway *SGlos*
  BS30 6HD 8 E4
Avonbridge 234 D2
Avoncliff 117 F2
Avonmouth 131 E5
Avonwick 100 D2
Awbridge 119 E5
Awhirk 214 B5
Awkley 131 E4
Awliscombe 103 E2
Awre 131 G2
Awsworth 173 F3
Axbridge 116 B2
Axford *Hants* 120 B3
Axford *Wilts* 133 E5
Axminster 103 F3
Axmouth 103 F3
Axton 182 C4
Axtown 100 B1
Aycliffe 212 B5
Aydon 211 G1
Aylburton 131 F2
Ayle 211 E3
Aylesbeare 102 D3
Aylesbury 134 D1
Aylesby 188 C2
Aylesford 123 G3
Aylesham 125 E4
Aylestone 160 A2
Aylmerton 178 C2
Aylsham 178 C3
Aylton 145 F4
Aymestrey 144 D1
Aynho 148 A4
Ayot Green 136 B1
Ayot St. Lawrence 136 A1
Ayot St. Peter 136 B1
Ayr 224 B3
Aysgarth 201 F4
Ayshford 102 D1
Ayside 199 E4
Ayston 161 D2
Aythorpe Roding 137 E1
Ayton *P&K* 243 G3
Ayton *ScBord* 237 F3
Aywick 278 E4
Azerley 202 B5

B

Babbacombe 101 F1
Babbacombe Model Village
  Torbay TQ1 3LA 101 F1
Babbinswood 170 A4
Babb's Green 136 C1
Babcary 116 C5
Babel 143 F3
Babell 182 C5
Babeny 99 G3
Bablock Hythe 133 G2
Babraham 150 D2
Babworth 187 D4
Baby's Hill 259 K1
Bac 271 G3
Bachau 180 C4
Back of Keppoch 247 F1
Back Street 151 F2
Backaland 276 D2
Backaskaill 276 D2
Backbarrow 199 E4
Backburn 260 D1
Backe 127 F1
Backfolds 269 J5
Backford 183 F5
Backhill 261 F1

Backhill of
  Clackriach 269 H6
Backhill of Trustach 260 E5
Backies *High* 267 F1
Backies *Moray* 268 D5
Backlass 275 H3
Backside 260 C1
Backwell 116 B1
Backworth 221 E4
Bacon End 137 E1
Baconend Green 137 E1
Baconsthorpe 178 C2
Bacton *Here* 144 C4
Bacton *Norf* 179 E2
Bacton *Suff* 152 B1
Bacton Green 152 B1
Bacup 193 E5
Badachro 264 D3
Badanloch Lodge 274 C5
Badavanich 265 H6
Badbea 275 F7
Badbury 133 D4
Badbury Wick 133 D4
Badby 148 A2
Badcall *High* 272 D3
Badcall *High* 272 E3
Badcaul 265 G2
Baddeley Green 171 G2
Badden 231 G2
Baddesley Clinton 159 D5
Baddesley Clinton *Warks*
  B93 0DQ 14 A3
Baddesley Ensor 159 E3
Baddidarach 272 C6
Badenscoth 261 F1
Badenyon 260 B3
Badgall 97 G1
Badger 157 G3
Badgerbank 184 C5
Badgers Mount 123 D2
Badgeworth 132 B1
Badgworth 116 A2
Badicaul 256 D2
Badingham 153 E1
Badintagairt 273 G7
Badlesmere 124 C3
Badley 152 B2
Badlipster 275 H4
Badluarach 265 F2
Badminton 132 A4
Badnaban 272 C6
Badnabay 272 E4
Badnafrave 259 K3
Badnagie 275 G5
Badnambiar 250 C2
Badninish 266 E2
Badrallach 265 G2
Badsey 146 C3
Badshot Lea 121 D3
Badsworth 186 B1
Badwell Ash 152 A1
Badworthy 100 C1
Badyo 251 E2
Bag Enderby 189 D5
Bagber 105 D1
Bagby 203 D4
Bagendon 132 C2
Baggeridge Country Park
  Staffs DY3 4HB 14 A2
Bagginswood 157 F4
Baggrave Hall 160 B2
Baggrow 209 E2
Bagh Mhartainn 262 C4
Bagh Mòr 238 B2
Bagh nan Caileach 262 C6
Baghasdal 254 C3
Bagillt 182 D5
Baginton 159 F5
Baglan 128 C3
Bagley *Shrop* 170 B5
Bagley *Som* 116 B3
Bagmore 120 B3
Bagnor 119 F1
Bagnall 171 G2
Bagpath *Surr* 121 E3
Bagpath *Glos* 132 A3
Bagshot *Surr* 121 E1
Bagshot *Wilts* 119 E1
Bagstone 131 F4
Bagthorpe *Norf* 177 F4
Bagthorpe *Notts* 173 F2
Baguley 184 C4
Bagworth 159 G2
Bagwyllydiart 144 D5
Baildon 194 A4
Baile an Truiseil 271 F2
Baile Boidheach 231 F2
Baile Gharbhaidh 262 C7
Baile Glas 262 D6
Baile Mhartainn 262 C4
Baile Mhic Phail 262 D4
Baile Mòr 238 B2
Baile nan Cailleach 262 C6
Baile Raghaill 262 C5
Bailebeag 258 C3
Baileguish 259 F5
Baile-na-Cille 262 D3
Bailetonach 247 F2
Bailiesward 260 C1
Bailiff Bridge 194 A5
Baillieston 234 A3
Bainbridge 201 E3
Bainsford 234 C1
Bainshole 260 E1
Bainton *ERid* 196 B2
Bainton *Oxon* 148 A5
Bainton *Peter* 161 F2
Bairnkine 228 A5
Baker Street 137 F4
Baker's End 136 C1
Bakewell 172 D1
Bala (Y Bala) 168 C4
Balachuirn 264 B7
Balado 243 F4
Balafark 242 B5
Balaldie 267 F4
Balallan
  (Baile Ailein) 270 E5
Balavil 258 E4
Balbeg *High* 258 B1
Balbeg *High* 258 B2
Balbeggie 243 G2
Balbirnie 244 A4
Balbithan 261 F3
Balblair *High* 266 C7
Balblair *High* 266 E3
Balby 186 C2
Balchladich 272 C5
Balchraggan *High* 266 C7
Balchraggan *High* 258 C1
Balchrick 272 D3
Balcombe 122 C5
Balcurvie 244 B4
Baldernock 233 G2
Baldersby 202 C5
Baldersby
  St. James 202 C5
Balderstone
  GtMan 184 D1
Balderstone *Lancs* 192 C4
Balderton
  ChesW&C 170 A1
Balderton *Notts* 174 D2
Baldhu 96 B5
Baldinnie 244 C3
Baldon Row 134 A2
Baldovan 244 B5
Baldovie *Angus* 252 B4
Baldovie *Dundee* 244 C1
Baldrine 190 C3
Baldslow 110 C2
Baldwin 190 B3
Baldwinholme 209 G1
Baldwin's Gate 171 E3
Baldwins Hill 122 C5
Bale 178 B2
Balelone
  (Baile Lìon) 262 C4
Balemartine 246 A2
Balemore
  (Baile Mòr) 262 C5
Balendoch 252 A5
Balephuil 246 A2
Balerno 235 F3
Balernock 233 D1
Baleromindubh 238 C5
Balerominmore 238 C5
Baleshare
  (Bhaleshear) 262 C5
Balevulin 239 D2
Balfield 252 D3
Balfour *Aber* 260 D5
Balfour *Ork* 277 D6
Balfron 233 G1
Balfron Station 233 G1
Balgonar 243 F5
Balgove 261 G1
Balgowan *D&G* 206 B2
Balgowan *High* 258 D5
Balgown 263 J5
Balgreen 269 F5
Balgy 264 E6
Balhaldie 242 D4
Balhalgardy 261 F2
Balham 136 B5
Balhary 252 A5
Balhelvie 244 B3
Balhousie 244 C4
Baliasta 278 F2
Baligill 274 D2
Baligrundle 248 A5
Balindore 240 B1
Balintore *Angus* 252 A4
Balintore *High* 267 F4
Balintraid 266 E4
Balintyre 250 B5
Balivanich (Baile
  a'Mhanaich) 262 C6
Balkeerie 252 B5
Balkholme 195 G5
Balkissock 214 C2
Ball 170 A5
Ball Haye Green 171 G2
Ball Hill 119 F1
Balla 254 C3
Ballabeg 190 A4
Ballacannell 190 C3
Ballacarnane Beg 190 A3
Ballachulish (Baile a'
  Chaolais) 248 C4
Balladoole 190 A4
Ballafesson 190 A4
Ballagyr 190 A3
Ballajora 190 C2
Ballakilpheric 190 A4
Ballamodha 190 A4
Ballantrae 214 B2
Ballards Gore 138 C3
Ballasalla *IoM* 190 B3
Ballasalla *IoM* 190 B2
Ballater 260 B5
Ballaterach 260 C5
Ballaugh 190 B2
Ballaveare 190 B4
Ballchraggan 266 D3
Ballechin 251 E4
Balleich 242 A4
Ballencrieff 236 B2
Ballidon 172 D2
Balliekine 231 G5
Balliemeanoch 240 D4
Balliemore *A&B* 240 D5
Balliemore *A&B* 240 A4
Ballig 190 A3
Ballimeanoch 240 C3
Ballimore *A&B* 232 A1
Ballimore *Stir* 242 A3
Ballinaby 230 A3
Ballindean 244 A2
Ballingdon 151 G3
Ballinger Common 135 E2
Ballingham 145 E4
Ballingry 243 G5
Ballinlick 251 E5
Ballinluig *P&K* 251 E4
Ballinluig *P&K* 251 F4
Ballintuim 251 G4
Balloch *Angus* 252 B4
Balloch *High* 266 E7
Balloch *NLan* 234 B2
Balloch *WDun* 233 E1
Ballochan 260 D5
Ballochandrain 232 A1
Ballochford 260 B1
Ballochgair 222 C3
Ballochmartin 232 C5
Ballochmorrie 214 C2
Ballochmyle 224 D3
Ballochroy 231 F4
Ballogie 260 D5
Balls Cross 121 E5
Balls Green *Essex* 152 B5

Ball's Green *Glos* 132 A3
Balls Hill 158 B3
Ballyaurgan 231 F2
Ballygown 246 C5
Ballygrant 230 B3
Ballyhaugh 246 A4
Ballymeanoch 240 A5
Ballymichael 223 E2
Balmacara
(Baile Mac Ara) 256 E2
Balmaclellan 216 A3
Balmacneil 251 E4
Balmadies 253 D5
Balmae 207 G2
Balmaha 241 G5
Balmalcolm 244 B4
Balmaqueen 263 G4
Balmeanach *A&B* 247 F5
Balmeanach *A&B* 238 D1
Balmedie 261 H3
Balmedie Country Park
Aber AB23 8XG 261 H3
Balmer Heath 170 B4
Balmerino 244 B3
Balmerlawn 106 C2
Balminnoch 215 D4
Balmore *EDun* 234 A2
Balmore *High* 267 F7
Balmore *High* 257 K1
Balmore *High* 263 H7
Balmore *P&K* 250 C4
Balmullo 244 C2
Balmungie 266 E6
Balmyle 251 F4
Balnaboth 252 B3
Balnabruaich 266 E4
Balnacra 265 F7
Balnafoich 258 D1
Balnagall 267 F3
Balnagown Castle 266 E4
Balnaguard 251 E4
Balnaguisich 266 D4
Balnain 258 B1
Balnakeil 273 F2
Balnaknock 263 K5
Balnapaling 266 E5
Balnespick 259 F4
Balquhidder 242 A2
Balsall 159 E5
Balsall Common 159 E5
Balsall Heath 158 C4
Balscote 147 F3
Balsham 151 D2
Baltasound 278 F2
Balterley 171 E2
Balterley Heath 171 E2
Baltersan 215 F4
Balthangie 269 G5
Balthayock 243 G2
Baltonsborough 116 C4
Baluachraig 240 A5
Balulive 230 C3
Balure *A&B* 240 C1
Balure *A&B* 240 A1
Balvaird 266 C6
Balvicar 239 G3
Balvraid *High* 256 E3
Balvraid *High* 259 F1
Bamber Bridge 192 B5
Bamber's Green 151 D5
Bamburgh 229 F3
Bamburgh Castle *N'umb*
NE69 7DF 229 F3
Bamff 252 A4
Bamford *Derbys* 185 G4
Bamford *GtMan* 184 C1
Bampton *Cumb* 199 G1
Bampton *Devon* 114 C5
Bampton *Oxon* 133 F2
Bampton Grange 199 G1
Banavie
(Banbhaidh) 248 D2
Banbury 147 G3
Banbury Museum *Oxon*
OX16 2PQ 147 G3
Bancffosfelen 128 A1
Banchor 267 G7
Banchory 261 F5
Banchory Devenick 261 H4
Bancycapel 128 A1
Bancyfelin 127 G1
Bancyffordd 142 A4
Bandon 244 A4
Bandrake Head 199 E4
Banff 268 E4
Bangor 181 D5
Bangor on Dee (Bangor-
is-y-coed) 170 A3
Bangor's Green 183 E2
Banham 164 B3
Banham Zoo *Norf*
NR16 2HE 164 B3
Bank 106 B2
Bank End 198 C4
Bank Newton 193 F2
Bank Street 145 F1
Bank Top *Lancs* 183 G2
Bank Top *WYorks* 194 A5
Bankend 217 E4
Bankfoot 243 F1
Bankglen 225 D4
Bankhead *Aber* 260 E3
Bankhead *Aber* 260 D5
Bankhead
Aberdeen 261 G3
Bankhead *D&G* 208 A2
Bankland 116 A5
Banknock 234 B2
Banks *Cumb* 210 B1
Banks *Lancs* 191 G5
Bankshill 217 F2
Banningham 178 D3
Bannister Green 151 E5
Bannockburn 242 D5
Bantam Grove 194 B5
Banstead 122 B3
Bantham 100 C3
Banton 234 B2
Banwell 116 A2
Banwen Pyrddin 129 E2
Banyard's Green 165 E4
Bapchild 124 B2
Baptiston 233 G1
Bapton 118 A4

Bar End 119 F5
Bar Hill 150 B1
Barachander 240 C2
Barassie 224 B2
Barbaraville 266 E4
Barber Booth 185 F4
Barber Green 199 E4
Barber's Moor 183 F1
Barbican Arts & Conference
Centre *GtLon*
EC2Y 8DS 45 J1
Barbon 200 B4
Barbridge 170 D2
Barbrook 114 A3
Barby 160 A5
Barcaldine (Am Barra
Calltainn) 248 B5
Barcaple 216 A3
Barcombe 109 G2
Barcombe Cross 109 G2
Barden 202 A3
Barden Park 123 E4
Bardennoch 215 G1
Bardfield End Green 151 E5
Bardfield Saling 151 E5
Bardister 278 C5
Bardney 175 G1
Bardon *Leics* 159 G1
Bardon *Moray* 267 K6
Bardon Mill 211 D1
Bardowie 233 G2
Bardsea 199 E5
Bardsey 194 C3
Bardsey Island
(Ynys Enlli) 166 A5
Bardwell 164 A4
Bare 192 A1
Barewood 144 C2
Barfad 231 G3
Barford *Norf* 178 C5
Barford *Warks* 147 E1
Barford St. John 147 G4
Barford St. Martin 118 B4
Barford St. Michael 147 G4
Barfrestone 125 E3
Bargaly 215 F4
Bargany Mains 224 A5
Bargeddie 234 A3
Bargoed 130 A3
Bargrennan 215 E3
Barham *Cambs* 161 G5
Barham *Kent* 125 E3
Barham *Suff* 152 C2
Barharrow 216 A5
Barholm 161 F1
Barholm Mains 215 F5
Barkby 160 B2
Barkby Thorpe 160 B2
Barkers Green 170 C5
Barkestone-le-Vale 174 C4
Barkham 120 C1
Barking *GtLon* 136 D4
Barking *Suff* 152 B2
Barking Tye 152 B2
Barkisland 193 G5
Barkston 175 E3
Barkston Ash 195 D4
Barkway 150 B4
Barlae 215 D4
Barland 144 B1
Barlaston 171 F4
Barlavington 108 B2
Barlborough 186 B5
Barley *Herts* 150 B4
Barley *Lancs* 193 E3
Barley Green 164 D4
Barleycroft End 150 C5
Barleyhill 211 G2
Barleythorpe 160 D2
Barling 138 C4
Barlings 188 A5
Barlow *Derbys* 186 A5
Barlow *NYorks* 195 F5
Barlow *T&W* 212 A1
Barmby Moor 195 G3
Barmby on the
Marsh 195 F5
Barmer 177 G4
Barmolloch 240 A5
Barmoor Lane End 229 E3
Barmouth
(Abermaw) 154 C1
Barmpton 202 C1
Barmston 197 D2
Barnaby Green 165 F4
Barnacabber 232 C1
Barnack 161 F2
Barnacle 159 F4
Barnamuc 248 C5
Barnard Castle 201 F1
Barnard Gate 133 G1
Barnardiston 151 F3
Barnard's Green 145 G3
Barnbarroch *D&G* 215 E5
Barnbarroch *D&G* 216 C5
Barnburgh 186 B2
Barnby 165 F3
Barnby Dun 186 D2
Barnby in
the Willows 175 D2
Barnby Moor 187 D4
Barndennoch 216 C2
Barne Barton 100 A2
Barnehurst 137 E5
Barnes 136 B5
Barnes Street 123 F4
Barnet 136 B3
Barnet Gate 136 B3
Barnetby le Wold 188 A2
Barney 178 A2
Barnham *Suff* 163 G5
Barnham *WSuss* 108 B3
Barnham Broom 178 B5
Barnhead 253 E4
Barnhill *ChesW&C* 170 B2
Barnhill *Dundee* 244 C1
Barnhill *Moray* 267 J6
Barnhills 214 A3
Barningham *Dur* 201 F1
Barningham *Suff* 164 A4
Barningham Green 178 C2
Barnoldby le Beck 188 C2
Barnoldswick 193 E3

Barns Green 121 G5
Barnsdale Bar 186 C1
Barnsley *Glos* 132 C2
Barnsley *SYorks* 186 A2
Barnsole 125 E3
Barnstaple 113 F2
Barnston *Essex* 137 F1
Barnston *Mersey* 183 D4
Barnstone 174 C4
Barnt Green 158 C5
Barnton *ChesW&C* 184 A5
Barnton *Edin* 235 F2
Barnwell All Saints 161 F4
Barnwell Country Park
N'hants
PE8 5PB 161 F4
Barnwell St. Andrew 161 F4
Barnwood 132 A1
Barons' Cross 145 D2
Barr *A&B* 230 B3
Barr *High* 247 F4
Barr *SAyr* 215 E1
Barr *Som* 115 E5
Barr Hall 151 F4
Barra (Barraigh) 254 B4
Airport 254 B4
Barrachan 207 D2
Barrackan 239 G4
Barraer 215 E4
Barraglom 270 D4
Barrahormid 231 F1
Barran 241 E2
Barrapoll 246 A2
Barrasford 220 B4
Barravullin 240 A4
Barrets Green 170 C2
Barrhead 233 F4
Barrhill 214 D2
Barrington *Cambs* 150 B3
Barrington *Som* 103 G1
Barripper 94 D3
Barrisdale 256 E4
Barrmill 233 E4
Barrnacarry 240 A2
Barrock 275 H1
Barrow *Glos* 146 A5
Barrow *Lancs* 192 D4
Barrow *Rut* 161 D1
Barrow *Shrop* 157 F2
Barrow *Som* 116 C3
Barrow *Suff* 151 F1
Barrow Gurney 116 C1
Barrow Hann 196 C5
Barrow Haven 196 C5
Barrow Hill 186 B5
Barrow Nook 183 F2
Barrow Street 117 F4
Barrow upon
Humber 196 C5
Barrow upon Soar 160 A1
Barrow upon Trent 173 E5
Barroway Drove 163 D2
Barrowby 175 D4
Barrowcliff 204 D4
Barrowden 161 E2
Barrowford 193 E4
Barrow-in-Furness 191 F1
Barrows Green 199 G4
Barry *Angus* 244 D1
Barry *VGlam* 115 E1
Barry Island Pleasure
Park *VGlam*
CF62 5TR 115 E1
Barsby 160 B1
Barsham 165 E3
Barskimming 224 C3
Barsloisnoch 240 A5
Barston 159 E5
Barter Books,
Alnwick *N'umb*
NE66 2NP 229 F5
Bartestree 145 E3
Barthol Chapel 261 G1
Bartholomew Green 151 F5
Bartholmey 171 E2
Bartley 106 C1
Bartley Green 158 C4
Bartlow 151 D3
Barton *Cambs* 150 C2
Barton *ChesW&C* 170 B2
Barton *Cumb* 210 A3
Barton *Glos* 146 C5
Barton *Lancs* 192 B4
Barton *Lancs* 183 E2
Barton *NYorks* 202 B2
Barton *Oxon* 134 A2
Barton *Torbay* 101 F1
Barton *Warks* 146 D2
Barton Bendish 163 F2
Barton End 132 A3
Barton Green 159 D1
Barton Hartshorn 148 B4
Barton Hill 195 G1
Barton in Fabis 173 G4
Barton in the Beans 159 F2
Barton Mills 163 F5
Barton on Sea 106 B3
Barton St. David 116 C4
Barton Seagrave 161 D5
Barton Stacey 119 F3
Barton Town 113 G1
Barton Turf 179 E3
Bartongate 147 G5
Barton-le-Clay 149 F4
Barton-le-Street 203 G5
Barton-le-Willows 195 G1
Barton-on-
the-Heath 147 E4
Barton-under-
Needwood 159 D1
Barton-upon-
Humber 196 C5
Barvas
(Barabhas) 271 F2
Barway 162 D5
Barwell 159 G3
Barwhinnock 216 A5
Barwick *Herts* 136 C1
Barwick *Som* 104 B3
Barwick in Elmet 194 C4
Barwinnock 207 D2
Baschurch 170 B5
Bascote 147 G1
Base Green 152 B1
Basford Green 171 G2

Bashall Eaves 192 C3
Bashall Town 192 C3
Bashley 106 B3
Basildon *Essex* 137 G4
Basildon *WBerks* 134 B5
Basingstoke 120 B2
Baslow 185 G5
Bason Bridge 116 A3
Bassaleg 130 B4
Bassenthwaite 209 F3
Basset's Cross 113 G5
Bassett 106 D1
Bassingbourn 150 B3
Bassingfield 174 B4
Bassingham 175 E1
Bassingthorpe 175 E5
Basta 278 E3
Baston 161 G1
Bastonford 146 A2
Bastwick 179 F4
Batavaime 241 G1
Batch 116 A2
Batchley 146 C1
Batchworth 135 F3
Batchworth Heath 135 F3
Batcombe
Dorset 104 C2
Batcombe *Som* 117 D4
Bate Heath 184 A5
Bath 117 E1
Bath Abbey *B&NESom*
BA1 1LT 63 Bath
Bathampton 117 E1
Bathealton 115 D5
Batheaston 117 E1
Bathford 117 E1
Bathgate 235 D3
Bathley 174 C2
Bathpool *Corn* 97 G2
Bathpool *Som* 115 F5
Bathway 116 C2
Batley 194 B5
Batsford 147 D4
Batson 100 D4
Battersby 203 E2
Battersea 136 B5
Battersea Cats & Dogs
Home *GtLon*
SW8 4AA 13 A5
Battersea Park Children's
Zoo *GtLon*
SW11 4NJ 13 A5
Battisborough
Cross 100 C3
Battisford 152 B2
Battisford Tye 152 B2
Battle *ESuss* 110 C2
Battle *Powys* 143 G4
Battle Abbey *ESuss*
TN33 0AD 110 C2
Battledown 146 B5
Battlefield 157 E1
Battlesbridge 137 G3
Battlesden 149 E5
Battlesea Green 164 D4
Battleton 114 C5
Battlies Green 152 A1
Battleton 114 C5
Battramsley 106 C3
Batt's Corner 120 D3
Bauds of Cullen 268 C4
Baugh 246 B2
Baughton 146 A3
Baughurst 119 G1
Baulds 260 E5
Baulking 133 F3
Baumber 188 C5
Baunton 132 C2
Baveney Wood 157 F5
Baverstock 118 B4
Bawburgh 178 C5
Bawdeswell 178 B3
Bawdrip 116 A4
Bawdsey 153 E3
Bawdsey Manor 153 E4
Bawsey 163 E1
Bawtry 187 D3
Baxenden 193 D5
Baxterley 159 E3
Baxter's Green 151 F2
Baxters Highland
Village *Moray*
IV32 7LD 268 B4
Bay 117 F5
Baybridge 211 F3
Baycliff 199 D5
Baydon 133 E5
Bayford *Herts* 136 C2
Bayford *Som* 117 E5
Bayfordbury 136 C1
Bayham Abbey 123 F5
Bayles 210 D3
Baylham 152 C2
Baynards Green 148 A5
Baysham 145 E5
Bayston Hill 157 D2
Bayswater 136 B4
Baythorn End 151 F3
Bayton 157 F5
Bayworth 134 A2
Beach 131 G5
Beach *SGlos* 131 G5
Beachampton 148 C4
Beachamwell 163 F2
Beacharr 231 E5
Beachley 131 E3
Beacon *Devon* 103 E2
Beacon *Devon* 103 E2
Beacon Fell Country
Park *Lancs*
PR3 2NL 192 B3
Beacon Hill *Dorset* 105 F3
Beacon Hill *Essex* 138 B1
Beacon Hill *Surr* 121 D4
Beacon Hill Country Park
Leics LE12 8SR 17 A2
Beacon Park,
Up Holland *Lancs*
WN8 7RU 183 G2
Beacon's Bottom 134 C3
Beaconsfield 135 E3
Beacravik 263 G2
Beadlam 203 F4
Beadlow 149 G4
Beadnell 229 G4
Beaford 113 F4
Beal *N'umb* 229 E2
Beal *NYorks* 195 E5
Bealach 248 B4

Beale Park *WBerks*
RG8 9NH 134 B5
Bealsmill 99 D3
Beambridge 170 D2
Beamhurst 172 B4
Beaminster 104 A2
Beamish 212 B2
Beamish, North of England
Open Air Museum
Dur DH9 0RG 29 A1
Beamsley 193 G3
Bean 137 E5
Beanacre 118 A1
Beanley 229 E5
Beaquoy 276 C5
Beardon 99 F3
Beardwood 192 C5
Beare 102 C2
Beare Green 121 G5
Bearley 147 D1
Bearnus 246 C5
Bearpark 212 B3
Bearsbridge 211 E2
Bearsden 233 G2
Bearsted 123 G3
Bearstone 171 E4
Bearwood *Poole* 105 G3
Bearwood *WMid* 158 C4
Beatles Story
Mersey L3 4AD 42 B5
Beattock 226 B5
Beauchamp Roding 137 E1
Beauchief 186 A4
Beaudesert 147 D1
Beaufort 130 A1
Beaulieu 106 C2
Beaulieu: National Motor
Museum, Abbey & Palace
House *Hants*
SO42 7ZN 4 A5
Beauly (A' Mhanachainn)
266 C7
Beaumaris (Biwmares)
181 E5
Beaumont *Chanl* 100 C5
Beaumont *Cumb* 209 G1
Beaumont *Essex* 152 C5
Beaumont Hill 202 B1
Beaumont Leys 160 A2
Beausale 159 E5
Beauvale 173 F3
Beauworth 119 G5
Beazley End 151 F5
Bebington 183 E4
Bebside 221 E4
Beccles 165 F3
Beccles Heliport 165 F3
Becconsall 192 A5
Beck Foot 200 B3
Beck Hole 204 B2
Beck Row 163 E5
Beck Side *Cumb* 198 D4
Beck Side *Cumb* 199 E4
Beckbury 157 G2
Beckenham 122 C2
Beckering 188 B4
Beckermonds 201 D4
Beckett End 163 F3
Beckfoot *Cumb* 198 C2
Beckfoot *Cumb* 209 D2
Beckford 146 B4
Beckhampton 118 B1
Beckingham *Lincs* 175 D2
Beckingham *Notts* 187 E4
Beckington 117 F2
Beckley *ESuss* 111 D1
Beckley *Oxon* 134 A1
Beck's Green 165 E3
Beckside 200 B4
Beckton 136 D4
Beckwithshaw 194 B2
Becontree 137 D4
Bedale 202 B4
Bedburn 211 G4
Bedchester 105 E1
Beddau 129 G4
Beddgelert 167 E3
Beddingham 109 G3
Beddington 122 B2
Beddington Corner 122 B2
Bedfield 152 D1
Bedfield Little
Green 152 D1
Bedford 149 F3
Bedgebury Cross 123 G5
Bedgrove 134 D1
Bedham 121 F5
Bedhampton 107 G2
Bedingfield 152 C1
Bedingfield Green 152 C1
Bedingham Green 165 D2
Bedlam *Lancs* 193 D5
Bedlam *NYorks* 194 B1
Bedlar's Green 150 D5
Bedlington 221 E4
Bedlinog 129 G2
Bedminster 131 E5
Bedmond 135 F2
Bednall 158 B1
Bedol 182 D5
Bedrule 228 A5
Bedstone 156 C5
Bedwas 130 A4
Bedwell 150 A5
Bedwellty 130 A2
Bedworth 159 F4
Bedworth
Woodlands 159 F4
Beeby 160 B2
Beech *Hants* 120 B4
Beech *Staffs* 171 F4
Beech Hill 120 B1
Beechingstoke 118 B2
Beechwood 183 G4
Beecraigs Country
Park *WLoth*
EH49 6PL 235 D2
Beedon 133 G5
Beeford 196 D2
Beeley 173 F1
Beelsby 188 C2
Beenham 119 G1

Beeny 98 B1
Beer 103 F4
Beer Hackett 104 C1
Beercrocombe 116 A5
Beesands 101 E4
Beesby *Lincs* 189 E4
Beesby *NELincs* 188 C3
Beeson 101 E3
Beeston *CenBeds* 149 G3
Beeston *ChesW&C* 170 C2
Beeston *Norf* 178 A4
Beeston *Notts* 173 G4
Beeston *WYorks* 194 B4
Beeston Regis 178 C1
Beeston
St. Lawrence 179 E3
Beeswing 216 C4
Beetham *Cumb* 199 F5
Beetham *Som* 103 F1
Beetley 178 A4
Beffcote 158 A1
Began 130 B4
Begbroke 133 G1
Begdale 162 C2
Begelly 127 E2
Beggar's Bush 144 B1
Beggearn Huish 114 D4
Beguildy (Bugeildy) 156 A5
Beighton *Norf* 179 E5
Beighton *SYorks* 186 B4
Beili-glas 130 C1
Beith 233 E4
Bekesbourne 125 D3
Belaugh 179 D4
Belbroughton 158 B5
Belchalwell 105 D2
Belchalwell Street 105 D2
Belchamp Otten 151 G3
Belchamp St. Paul 151 F3
Belchamp Walter 151 G3
Belchford 188 C5
Belfield 184 D1
Belford 229 F3
Belgrave 160 A2
Belhaven 237 D2
Belhelvie 261 H3
Belhinnie 260 C2
Bell Bar 136 B2
Bell Busk 193 F2
Bell End 158 B5
Bell Heath 158 B5
Bell Hill 120 C5
Bell o' th' Hill 170 C3
Bellabeg 260 B3
Belladrum 266 C7
Bellanoch 240 A5
Bellaty 252 A4
Belle Isle 194 B4
Belle Vue 209 G1
Belleau 189 E5
Belleheiglash 259 J1
Bellerby 202 A3
Bellever 99 G3
Belliehill 253 D3
Bellingdon 135 E2
Bellingham *GtLon* 136 C5
Bellingham *N'umb* 220 A3
Belloch 222 B2
Bellochantuy 222 B2
Bell's Cross 152 C2
Bells Yew Green 123 F5
Bellsbank 224 C5
Bellshill *N'umb* 229 F3
Bellshill *NLan* 234 B3
Bellside 234 C4
Bellsmyre 233 F2
Bellsquarry 235 E3
Belluton 116 D1
Belmaduthy 266 D6
Belmesthorpe 161 F1
Belmont *B'burn* 184 A1
Belmont *GtLon* 122 B2
Belmont *GtLon* 136 A3
Belmont *Shet* 278 E2
Belnie 176 A4
Belowda 97 D3
Belper 173 E3
Belper Lane End 173 E3
Belsay 220 D4
Belsford 101 D2
Belsize 135 F2
Belstead 152 C3
Belston 224 B3
Belstone 99 G1
Belstone Corner 99 G1
Belsyde 235 D2
Belthorn 192 D5
Beltingham 211 D1
Beltoft 187 F2
Belton *Leics* 173 F5
Belton *Lincs* 175 E4
Belton *NLincs* 187 E2
Belton *Norf* 179 F5
Belton *Rut* 160 C2
Belton House *Lincs*
NG32 2LS 175 E4
Beltring 123 F4
Belvedere 137 D5
Belvoir 174 D4
Bembridge 107 F4
Bemersyde 227 G2
Bemerton 118 C4
Bempton 205 E5
Ben Alder Cottage 249 G3
Ben Alder Lodge 250 A2
Ben Rhydding 194 A3
Benacre 165 G3
Benbecula (Beinn na
Faoghla) 262 D6
Benbecula (Balivanich)
Airport 262 C6
Benbuie 216 B1
Benderloch
(Meadarloch) 240 B1
Bendish 149 G5
Benenden 124 A5
Benfield 215 E4
Benfieldside 211 G2
Bengate 179 E3
Bengeo 136 C1
Bengeworth 146 C3
Benhall 146 B5
Benhall Green 153 E1

Benhall Street 153 E1
Benholm 253 G3
Beningbrough 195 E2
Benington *Herts* 150 A5
Benington *Lincs* 176 B3
Benington Sea End 176 C3
Benllech 180 D4
Benmore *A&B* 232 C1
Benmore *Stir* 241 G2
Bennacott 98 C1
Bennan Cottage 216 A3
Bennett End 134 C3
Bennetts End 135 F2
Benniworth 188 C4
Benover 123 G4
Benson 134 B3
Benston 279 D7
Benthall *N'umb* 229 G4
Benthall *Shrop* 157 F2
Bentham 132 B1
Benthoul 261 G4
Bentlawnt 156 C2
Bentley *ERid* 196 C4
Bentley *Essex* 137 E3
Bentley *Hants* 120 C3
Bentley *Suff* 152 C3
Bentley *SYorks* 186 C2
Bentley *Warks* 159 E3
Bentley *WMid* 158 B3
Bentley *WYorks* 194 B4
Bentley Heath
Herts 136 B3
Bentley Heath
WMid 159 D5
Bentley Rise 186 C2
Benton 113 G2
Benton Square 221 F4
Bentpath 218 B2
Bentworth 120 B3
Benvie 244 B1
Benville Lane 104 B2
Benwell 212 B1
Benwick 162 B3
Beoley 146 C1
Beoraidbeg 256 C5
Bepton 108 A2
Berden 150 C5
Bere Alston 100 A1
Bere Ferrers 100 A1
Bere Regis 105 E3
Berea 140 A4
Berepper 95 D4
Bergh Apton 179 E5
Berinsfield 134 A3
Berkeley 131 F3
Berkhamsted 135 E2
Berkley 117 F3
Berkswell 159 E5
Bermondsey 136 C5
Bernera 256 E2
Berners Roding 137 F2
Berneray (Eilean
Bhearnaraigh) 262 E3
Bernice 240 D5
Bernisdale 263 K6
Berrick Prior 134 B3
Berrick Salome 134 B3
Berriedale 275 G6
Berriew (Aberriw) 156 A2
Berrington
N'umb 229 E2
Berrington *Shrop* 157 E2
Berrington *Worcs* 145 E1
Berrington Green 145 E1
Berriowbridge 97 G2
Berrow *Som* 115 G3
Berrow *Worcs* 145 G4
Berrow Green 145 G2
Berry Cross 113 E4
Berry Down Cross 113 F1
Berry Hill *Glos* 131 E1
Berry Hill *Pembs* 141 D3
Berry Pomeroy 101 E1
Berryhillock 268 D4
Berrynarbor 113 F1
Berry's Green 122 D3
Bersham 170 A3
Berstane 277 D6
Berthlwyd 128 B3
Berwick 110 A3
Berwick Bassett 132 D5
Berwick Hill 221 D4
Berwick St. James 118 B4
Berwick St. John 118 A5
Berwick St. Leonard 118 A4
Berwick-upon-
Tweed 237 G4
Bescar 183 E1
Bescot 158 C3
Besford *Shrop* 170 C5
Besford *Worcs* 146 B3
Bessacarr 186 D2
Bessels Leigh 133 G2
Besses o' th' Barn 184 C2
Bessingby 197 D1
Bessingham 178 C2
Best Beech Hill 123 F5
Besthorpe *Norf* 164 B2
Besthorpe *Notts* 174 D1
Bestwood 173 G3
Bestwood Country Park
Notts NG6 8UF 19 G1
Beswick *ERid* 196 C3
Beswick *GtMan* 184 C3
Betchworth 122 B3
Bethania *Cere* 142 B1
Bethania *Gwyn* 168 A3
Bethel *Gwyn* 167 E3
Bethel *Gwyn* 168 C4
Bethel *IoA* 180 B5
Bethersden 124 B5
Bethesda *Gwyn* 167 F1
Bethesda *Pembs* 127 D1
Bethlehem 142 C5
Bethnal Green 136 C4
Betley 171 E3
Betley Common 171 E3
Betsham 137 F5
Betteshanger 125 F3
Bettiscombe 103 G3
Bettisfield 170 B4
Betton *Shrop* 156 C2
Betton *Shrop* 171 D4
Betton Strange 157 E2
Bettws Bridgend 129 F4
Bettws Newport 130 B3
Bettws Bledrws 142 B2
Bettws Cedewain 156 A3

Bettws Gwerfil Goch 168 D3
Bettws Newydd 130 C2
Bettws-y-crwyn 156 B4
Bettyhill 274 C2
Betws 128 C1
Betws Disserth 144 A2
Betws Garmon 167 E2
Betws Ifan 141 G3
Betws-y-coed 168 A2
Betws-yn-Rhos 182 A5
Beulah Cere 141 F3
Beulah Powys 143 F2
Bevendean 109 F3
Bevercotes 187 D5
Beverley 196 C4
Beverston 132 A3
Bevington 131 F3
Bewaldeth 209 F3
Bewcastle 219 D4
Bewdley 157 G5
Bewerley 194 A1
Bewholme 197 D2
Bewl Water ESuss TN3 8JH 123 F5
Bewley Common 118 A1
Bexhill 110 C3
Bexley 137 D5
Bexleyheath 137 D5
Bexwell 163 E2
Beyton 152 A1
Beyton Green 152 A1
Bhalamus 270 E7
Bhaltos 270 C4
Biallaid 258 E5
Bibury 132 D2
Bicester 148 A5
Bickenhall 103 F1
Bickenhill 159 D4
Bicker 176 A4
Bickershaw 184 A2
Bickerstaffe 183 F2
Bickerton ChesW&C 170 C2
Bickerton Devon 101 E4
Bickerton N'umb 220 B1
Bickerton NYorks 195 D2
Bickford 158 A1
Bickham 114 C3
Bickham Bridge 100 D2
Bickham House 102 C4
Bickington Devon 113 F2
Bickington Devon 102 A5
Bickleigh Devon 100 B1
Bickleigh Devon 102 C2
Bickleton 113 F2
Bickley 122 D2
Bickley Moss 170 C3
Bickley Town 170 C3
Bicknacre 137 G2
Bicknoller 115 E4
Bicknor 124 A3
Bickton 106 A1
Bicton Here 145 D1
Bicton Shrop 156 D1
Bicton Shrop 156 B4
Bicton Heath 157 D1
Bicton Park Gardens Devon EX9 7BJ 103 D4
Bidborough 123 E4
Biddenden 124 A5
Biddenden Green 124 A4
Biddenham 149 F3
Biddestone 132 A5
Biddick 212 C2
Biddisham 116 A2
Biddlesden 148 B3
Biddlestone 220 B1
Biddulph 171 F2
Biddulph Moor 171 G2
Bideford 113 E3
Bidford-on-Avon 146 D2
Bidlake 99 E2
Bidston 183 D3
Bidwell 149 F5
Bielby 195 G3
Bieldside 261 G4
Bierley IoW 107 E5
Bierley WYorks 194 A4
Bierton 134 D1
Big Pit National Coal Museum Torfaen NP4 9XP 130 B2
Big Sand 264 D4
Big Sheep, The Devon EX39 5AP 113 E3
Big Sky Adventure Play Peter PE2 7BU 161 G3
Bigbury 100 C3
Bigbury-on-Sea 100 C3
Bigby 188 A2
Bigert Mire 198 C3
Biggar Cumb 191 E1
Biggar SLan 226 B2
Biggin Derbys 173 D3
Biggin Derbys 172 C2
Biggin NYorks 195 E4
Biggin Hill 122 D3
Biggin Hill Airport 122 D2
Biggings 279 A6
Biggleswade 149 G3
Bigholms 218 B3
Bighouse 274 D2
Bighton 120 B4
Biglands 209 F1
Bignor 108 B2
Bigrigg 208 D5
Bigton 279 C10
Bilberry 97 E4
Bilborough 173 G3
Bilbrook Som 114 D3
Bilbrook Staffs 158 A2
Bilbrough 195 E3
Bilbster 275 H3
Bilby 186 D4
Bildershaw 212 A5
Bildeston 152 A3
Billericay 137 F3
Billesdon 160 C2
Billesley 146 D2
Billholm 218 A2
Billingborough 175 G4
Billinge 183 G3
Billingford Norf 164 C4
Billingford Norf 178 B3
Billingham 213 D5
Billinghay 175 G2
Billingley 186 B2
Billingshurst 121 F5
Billingsley 157 G4
Billington CenBeds 149 E5
Billington Lancs 192 D4
Billington Staffs 171 F5
Billister 279 D6
Billockby 179 F4
Billy Row 212 A4
Bilsborrow 192 B4
Bilsby 189 E5
Bilsby Field 189 E5
Bilsdean 237 E2
Bilsham 108 B3
Bilsington 124 C5
Bilson Green 131 F1
Bilsthorpe 174 B1
Bilsthorpe Moor 174 B2
Bilston Midlo 235 G3
Bilston WMid 158 B3
Bilstone 159 F2
Bilting 124 C4
Bilton ERid 197 D4
Bilton N'umb 229 G5
Bilton NYorks 194 C2
Bilton Warks 159 G5
Bilton-in-Ainsty 195 D3
Bimbister 277 C6
Binbrook 188 C3
Bincombe 104 C4
Bindal 267 G3
Bindon 115 E5
Binegar 116 D3
Bines Green 109 D2
Binfield 134 D5
Binfield Heath 134 C5
Bingfield 220 B4
Bingham 174 C4
Bingham's Melcombe 105 D2
Bingley 194 A4
Bings Heath 157 E1
Binham 178 A2
Binley Hants 119 F2
Binley WMid 159 F5
Binniehill 234 C2
Binsoe 202 B5
Binstead 107 E3
Binsted Hants 120 C3
Binsted WSuss 108 B3
Binton 146 D2
Bintree 178 B3
Binweston 156 C2
Birch Essex 152 A5
Birch GtMan 184 C2
Birch Cross 172 C4
Birch Green Essex 138 C1
Birch Green Herts 136 B1
Birch Grove 109 G1
Birch Heath 170 C1
Birch Vale 185 E4
Birch Wood 103 F1
Bircham Newton 177 F4
Bircham Tofts 177 F4
Birchanger 150 D5
Bircher 145 D1
Bircher Common 145 D1
Birchfield 266 B2
Birchgrove Cardiff 130 A4
Birchgrove Swan 128 D3
Birchington 125 F2
Birchmoor 159 E2
Birchover 172 D1
Birchwood Lincs 175 E1
Birchwood Warr 184 A3
Bircotes 186 D3
Bird Street 152 B2
Birdbrook 151 F3
Birdbush 118 A5
Birdfield 240 B5
Birdforth 203 D5
Birdham 108 A3
Birdingbury 147 G1
Birdland, Bourton-on-the-Water Glos GL54 2BN 147 D5
Birdlip 132 B1
Birdoswald 210 C1
Birds Green 137 E2
Birdsall 196 A1
Birdsgreen 157 G4
Birdsmoor Gate 103 G2
Birdston 234 A2
Birdwell 186 A2
Birdwood 131 G1
Birdworld, Farnham Hants GU10 4LD 120 D3
Birgham 228 B3
Birichen 266 E2
Birkby Cumb 209 D3
Birkby NYorks 202 C2
Birkdale Mersey 183 E1
Birkdale NYorks 201 D2
Birkenhead 183 E4
Birkenhills 269 F6
Birkenshaw 194 B5
Birkhall 260 B5
Birkhill Angus 244 B1
Birkhill ScBord 236 C5
Birkhill ScBord 226 D4
Birkholme 175 E5
Birkin 195 E5
Birks 194 B5
Birkwood 225 G2
Birley 145 D2
Birley Carr 186 A3
Birling Kent 123 F2
Birling N'umb 221 E1
Birling Gap 110 A4
Birlingham 146 B3
Birmingham 158 C4
Birmingham Botanical Gardens WMid B15 3TR 34 B7
Birmingham City Museum & Art Gallery WMid B3 3DH 35 E4
Birmingham International Airport 159 D4
Birnam 251 F5
Birsay 276 B5
Birse 260 D5
Birsemore 260 D5
Birstall 160 A2
Birstall Smithies 194 B5
Birstwith 194 B2
Birthorpe 175 G4
Birtle 184 C1
Birtley Here 144 C1
Birtley N'umb 220 A4
Birtley T&W 212 B2
Birts Street 145 G4
Birtsmorton 146 A4
Bisbrooke 161 D3
Biscathorpe 188 C4
Bish Mill 114 A5
Bisham 135 D4
Bishampton 146 B2
Bishop Auckland 212 B5
Bishop Burton 196 B3
Bishop Middleham 212 C4
Bishop Monkton 194 C1
Bishop Norton 187 G3
Bishop Sutton 116 C2
Bishop Thornton 194 B1
Bishop Wilton 195 G2
Bishopbridge 188 A3
Bishopbriggs 234 A2
Bishopmill 267 K5
Bishops Cannings 118 B1
Bishop's Castle 156 C4
Bishop's Caundle 104 C1
Bishop's Cleeve 146 B5
Bishop's Frome 145 F3
Bishops Gate 135 E5
Bishop's Green Essex 137 F1
Bishop's Green Hants 119 G1
Bishop's Hull 115 F5
Bishop's Itchington 147 F2
Bishops Lydeard 115 E5
Bishop's Norton 146 A5
Bishops Nympton 114 A5
Bishop's Offley 171 E5
Bishop's Stortford 150 C5
Bishop's Sutton 120 B4
Bishop's Tachbrook 147 F1
Bishop's Tawton 113 F2
Bishop's Waltham 107 E1
Bishop's Wood 158 A2
Bishopsbourne 125 D3
Bishopsteignton 102 C5
Bishopstoke 107 D1
Bishopston Bristol 131 E5
Bishopston Swan 128 B4
Bishopstone Bucks 134 D1
Bishopstone ESuss 109 G3
Bishopstone Here 144 D3
Bishopstone Swin 133 E4
Bishopstone Wilts 118 B5
Bishopstrow 117 F3
Bishopswood 103 F1
Bishopsworth 116 C1
Bishopthorpe 195 E3
Bishopton Darl 212 C5
Bishopton NYorks 202 B5
Bishopton Renf 233 F2
Bishopton Warks 147 D2
Bishton 130 C4
Bisley Glos 132 B2
Bisley Surr 121 E2
Bispham 191 G4
Bispham Green 183 F1
Bissoe 96 B5
Bisterne 106 A2
Bisterne Close 106 B2
Bitchet Green 123 E3
Bitchfield 175 E5
Bittadon 113 F1
Bittaford 100 C2
Bittering 178 A4
Bitterley 157 E5
Bitterne 107 D1
Bitteswell 160 A4
Bitton 117 D1
Bix 134 C4
Bixter 279 C7
Blaby 160 A3
Black Bourton 133 E2
Black Bridge 126 C2
Black Callerton 212 A1
Black Carr 164 B2
Black Clauchrie 215 D2
Black Corries Lodge 249 E4
Black Country Living Museum WMid DY1 4SQ 14 B2
Black Crofts 240 B1
Black Cross 96 D3
Black Dog 102 B2
Black Heddon 220 C4
Black Hill 147 E2
Black Marsh 156 C3
Black Moor 194 B3
Black Mount 249 E5
Black Notley 151 F5
Black Park Country Park Bucks SL3 6DR 135 F4
Black Pill 128 C3
Black Sheep Brewery Visitor Centre NYorks HG4 4EN 202 B4
Black Street 165 G3
Black Swan Guild, Frome Som BA11 1BB 117 E3
Black Torrington 113 E5
Blackaburn 219 F4
Blackacre 217 E1
Blackadder 237 F4
Blackawton 101 E2
Blackborough Devon 103 D2
Blackborough Norf 163 E1
Blackborough End 163 E1
Blackboys 110 A1
Blackbraes Aber 261 G3
Blackbraes Falk 234 D2
Blackbrook Derbys 173 E3
Blackbrook Leics 159 G1
Blackbrook Mersey 183 G3
Blackbrook Staffs 171 E4
Blackburn Aber 261 G3
Blackburn B'burn 192 C5
Blackburn WLoth 235 D3
Blackbushe 120 C2
Blackcastle 267 F6
Blackchambers 261 F3
Blackcraig D&G 215 F4
Blackcraig D&G 216 B2
Blackden Heath 184 B5
Blackdog 261 H3
Blackdown Devon 99 F3
Blackdown Dorset 103 G2
Blackdown Warks 147 F1
Blacker Hill 186 A2
Blackfen 137 D5
Blackfield 106 D2
Blackford Aber 261 F1
Blackford Cumb 218 B5
Blackford P&K 243 D4
Blackford Som 117 D5
Blackford Som 116 B3
Blackford Bridge 184 C2
Blackfordby 159 F1
Blackgang 107 D5
Blackgang Chine IoW PO38 2HN 107 D5
Blackhall Edin 235 G2
Blackhall Renf 233 F3
Blackhall Colliery 213 D4
Blackhall Mill 212 A2
Blackhall Rocks 213 D4
Blackham 123 E5
Blackhaugh 227 F2
Blackheath Essex 152 B5
Blackheath GtLon 136 C5
Blackheath Suff 165 F4
Blackheath Surr 121 F3
Blackheath WMid 158 B4
Blackhill Aber 269 J5
Blackhill Aber 269 J6
Blackhillock 268 C6
Blackhills 267 K6
Blackland 118 B1
Blacklands 114 B4
Blackleach 192 A4
Blackley 184 C2
Blacklunans 251 G3
Blackmill 129 F4
Blackmoor Hants 120 C4
Blackmoor Som 103 E1
Blackmoor Gate 113 G1
Blackmoorfoot 185 E1
Blackmore 137 F2
Blackmore End Essex 151 F4
Blackmore End Herts 136 A1
Blackness Aber 260 E5
Blackness Falk 235 E2
Blackness High 275 H5
Blacknest 120 C3
Blackney 104 A3
Blacko 193 E3
Blackpole 146 A2
Blackpool B'pool 191 G4
Blackpool Devon 101 E3
Blackpool Bridge 127 D1
Blackpool Gate 218 D4
Blackpool International Airport 191 G4
Blackpool Piers B'pool FY4 1BB 191 G4
Blackpool Pleasure Beach B'pool FY4 1PL 191 G4
Blackpool Tower FY1 4BJ 64 Blackpool
Blackpool Zoo B'pool FY3 8PP 191 G4
Blackridge 234 C3
Blackrock A&B 230 B3
Blackrock Mon 130 B1
Blackrod 184 A1
Blackshaw 217 E4
Blackshaw Head 193 F5
Blacksmith's Green 152 C1
Blacksnape 192 D5
Blackstone 109 E2
Blackthorn 134 B1
Blackthorpe 152 A1
Blacktoft 196 A5
Blacktop 261 G4
Blacktown 130 B4
Blackwater Corn 96 B5
Blackwater Hants 120 D2
Blackwater IoW 107 E4
Blackwater Norf 178 B3
Blackwater Som 103 F1
Blackwaterfoot 223 E3
Blackwell Darl 202 B1
Blackwell Derbys 185 F5
Blackwell Derbys 173 F2
Blackwell Warks 147 E3
Blackwell Worcs 158 B5
Blackwell WSuss 122 C5
Blackwells End 145 G5
Blackwood (Coed-duon) Caerp 130 A3
Blackwood D&G 216 D2
Blackwood SLan 234 B5
Blackwood Hill 171 G2
Blacon 170 A1
Bladbean 125 D4
Bladnoch 215 F5
Bladon 133 G1
Blaen Clydach 129 F3
Blaenannerch 141 F3
Blaenau Dolwyddelan 167 F2
Blaenau Ffestiniog 167 F3
Blaenavon 130 B2
Blaenawey 130 B1
Blaencelyn 141 G2
Blaencwm 129 F2
Blaendyryn 143 F4
Blaenffos 141 E4
Blaengarw 129 F3
Blaengeuffordd 154 C4
Blaengweche 128 C1
Blaengwrach 129 E2
Blaengwynfi 129 E3
Blaenllechau 129 G3
Blaenos 143 D4
Blaenpennal 142 C1
Blaenplwyf 154 B5
Blaenporth 141 F3
Blaenrhondda 129 F2
Blaenwaun 141 F5
Blaen-y-coed 141 G5
Blagdon NSom 116 B2
Blagdon Torbay 101 E1
Blagdon Hill 103 F1
Blaguegate 183 F2
Blaich 248 C2
Blaina 130 A2
Blair 233 E5
Blair Atholl 251 D3
Blair Castle P&K PH18 5TL 251 D3
Blair Drummond 242 C5
Blair Drummond Safari & Adventure Park Stir FK9 4UR 242 C5
Blairannaich 241 F4
Blairbuie 232 C2
Blairgowrie 251 G5
Blairhall 235 E1
Blairhoyle 242 B4
Blairhullichan 241 G4
Blairingone 243 E5
Blairkip 224 D2
Blairlogie 242 D5
Blairmore A&B 232 C1
Blairmore High 266 E1
Blairmore High 272 D3
Blairnairn 233 D1
Blairnamarrow 259 K3
Blairpark 232 D4
Blairquhan 224 B5
Blairquhosh 233 G1
Blair's Ferry 232 A3
Blairshinnoch 268 E4
Blairuskinmore 241 G4
Blairvadach 233 D1
Blairydryne 261 F5
Blairythan Cottage 261 H2
Blaisdon 131 G1
Blake End 151 F5
Blake House Craft Centre Essex CM77 6RA 151 F5
Blakebrook 158 A5
Blakedown 158 A5
Blakelaw ScBord 228 B3
Blakelaw T&W 212 B1
Blakeley 158 A3
Blakelow 171 D2
Blakemere 144 C3
Blakemere Shopping Experience ChesW&C CW8 2EB 183 G5
Blakeney Glos 131 F2
Blakeney Norf 178 B1
Blakenhall ChesE 171 E3
Blakenhall WMid 158 B3
Blakeshall 158 A4
Blakesley 148 B2
Blanchland 211 F2
Bland Hill 194 B2
Blandford Camp 105 F2
Blandford Forum 105 E2
Blandford St. Mary 105 E2
Blanefield 233 G2
Blanerne 237 F4
Blankney 175 F1
Blantyre 234 A4
Blar a' Chaorainn 248 D3
Blargie 258 D5
Blarglas 233 E1
Blarmachfoldach 248 C3
Blarnalearoch 265 H2
Blashford 106 A2
Blaston 160 D3
Blathaisbhal 262 D4
Blatherwycke 161 E3
Blawith 199 D4
Blaxhall 153 E2
Blaxton 187 D2
Blaydon 212 A1
Bleadney 116 B3
Bleadon 116 A2
Bleak Hey Nook 185 E2
Blean 124 D2
Bleasby Lincs 188 B4
Bleasby Notts 174 C3
Bleasby Moor 188 B4
Bleatarn 200 C1
Bleathwood Common 145 E1
Blebocraigs 244 C3
Bleddfa 144 B1
Bledington 147 E5
Bledlow 134 C2
Bledlow Ridge 134 C3
Blencarn 210 C4
Blencogo 209 E2
Blencow 210 A4
Blendworth 107 G1
Blenheim Palace Oxon OX20 1PX 133 G1
Blennerhasset 209 E2
Blervie Castle 267 H6
Bletchingdon 134 A1
Bletchingley 122 C3
Bletchley MK 149 D4
Bletchley Shrop 170 D4
Bletherston 141 D5
Bletsoe 149 F2
Blewbury 134 A4
Blickling 178 C3
Blickling Hall Norf NR11 6NF 178 C3
Blidworth 173 G2
Blidworth Bottoms 173 G2
Blindburn Aber 261 H1
Blindburn N'umb 228 C5
Blindcrake 209 E3
Blindley Heath 122 C4
Blisland 97 E2
Bliss Gate 157 G5
Blissford 106 A1
Blisworth 148 C2
Blithbury 172 B5
Blitterlees 209 E1
Blo' Norton 164 B4
Blockley 147 D4
Blofield 179 E5
Blofield Heath 179 E4
Blore 172 C3
Blossomfield 158 D5
Blount's Green 172 B4
Blowick 183 E1
Bloxham 147 G4
Bloxholm 175 F2
Bloxwich 158 B2
Bloxworth 105 E3
Blubberhouses 194 A2
Blue Anchor Corn 96 D4
Blue Anchor Som 114 D3
Blue Bell Hill 123 G2
Blue Planet Aquarium, Ellesmere Port ChesW&C CH65 9LF 183 F5
Blue Reef Aquarium ESuss TN34 3DW 75 Hastings
Blue Reef Aquarium, Newquay Corn TR7 1DU 96 C3
Blue Reef Aquarium, Southsea Ports PO5 3PB 5 G6
Blue Reef Aquarium, Tynemouth T&W NE30 4JF 28 E1
Bluebell Railway WSuss TN22 3QL 109 F1
Bluewater 137 E5
Blundellsands 183 E3
Blundeston 165 G2
Blunham 149 G2
Blunsdon St. Andrew 132 D4
Bluntington 158 A5
Bluntisham 162 B5
Blunts 98 D4
Blurton 171 F3
Blyborough 187 G3
Blyford 165 F4
Blymhill 158 A1
Blymhill Common 157 G1
Blymhill Lawn 158 A1
Blyth N'umb 221 F3
Blyth Notts 186 D4
Blyth Bridge 235 F5
Blyth End 159 E3
Blythburgh 165 F4
Blythe Bridge 171 G3
Blythe Marsh 171 G3
Blyton 187 F3
Boarhills 245 D3
Boarhunt 107 F2
Boars Hill 133 G2
Boarsgreave 193 E5
Boarshead 123 E5
Boarstall 134 B1
Boarzell 110 C1
Boasley Cross 99 F1
Boat o' Brig 268 B5
Boat of Garten 259 G3
Boath 266 C4
Bobbing 124 A2
Bobbington 158 A3
Bobbingworth 137 E2
Bocaddon 97 F4
Bochastle 242 B4
Bocketts Farm Park Surr KT22 9BS 121 G2
Bockhampton 133 F5
Bocking 151 F5
Bocking Churchstreet 151 F5
Bockleton 145 E1
Boconnoc 97 F3
Boddam Aber 269 K6
Boddam Shet 279 F9
Bodden 116 D3
Boddington 146 A5
Bodedern 180 B4
Bodelwyddan 182 B5
Bodenham Here 145 E2
Bodenham Wilts 118 C5
Bodenham Moor 145 E2
Bodesbeck 226 C5
Bodewryd 180 C3
Bodfari 182 B5
Bodffordd 180 C5
Bodfuan 166 C4
Bodham 178 C1
Bodiam 110 C1
Bodiam Castle ESuss TN32 5UA 110 C1
Bodicote 147 G4
Bodieve 97 D2
Bodinnick 97 F4
Bodior 180 A5
Bodle Street Green 110 B2
Bodleian Library Oxon OX1 3BG 80 Oxford
Bodmin 97 E3
Bodnant Garden Conwy LL28 5RE 181 G5
Bodney 163 G3
Bodorgan 166 C1
Bodrane 97 G3
Bodsham Green 124 D4
Bodwen 97 E3
Bodymoor Heath 159 D3
Bogallan 266 D6
Bogbain 266 E7
Bogbrae 261 J1
Bogbuie 266 C6
Bogend 224 B2
Bogfern 260 D4
Bogfields 260 D4
Bogfold 269 G5
Boghead Aber 268 E5
Boghead EAyr 225 E3
Boghead SLan 234 B5
Boghole Farm 267 G6
Bogmoor 268 B4
Bogniebrae 268 D6
Bognor Regis 108 B4
Bograxie 261 F3
Bogroy 259 G2
Bogside 243 E5
Bogston 260 B4
Bogton 268 E5
Bogue 216 A2
Bohemia 106 B1
Bohenie 249 E1
Bohetherick 100 A1
Bohortha 95 F3
Bohuntine 249 E1
Boirseam 263 F3
Bojewyan 94 A3
Bokiddick 97 E3
Bolam Dur 212 A5
Bolam N'umb 220 C3
Bolam Lake Country Park N'umb NE20 0HE 220 C3
Bolberry 100 C4
Bold Heath 183 G4
Bolderwood 106 B2
Boldon 212 C1
Boldon Colliery 212 C1
Boldre 106 C3
Boldron 201 F1
Bole 187 E4
Bolehill 173 D2
Boleigh 94 B4
Bolenowe 95 D3
Boleside 227 F2
Bolfracks 250 D5
Bolgoed 128 C2
Bolham Devon 102 C1
Bolham Notts 187 E4
Bolham Water 103 E1
Bolingey 96 B4
Bollington 184 D5
Bolney 109 E1
Bolnhurst 149 F2
Bolshan 253 E4
Bolsover 186 B5
Bolsterstone 185 G3
Bolstone 145 E4
Boltby 203 D4
Bolter End 134 C3
Bolton Cumb 210 C5
Bolton ELoth 236 C2
Bolton ERid 195 G2
Bolton GtMan 184 B2
Bolton N'umb 229 F5
Bolton Abbey 193 G2
Bolton Abbey Estate NYorks BD23 6EX 193 G2
Bolton Bridge 193 G2
Bolton by Bowland 193 D3
Bolton Houses 192 A4
Bolton Low Houses 209 F2
Bolton Museum & Art Gallery GtMan BL1 1SE 184 B2
Bolton Percy 195 E3
Bolton Priory NYorks BD23 6EX 193 G2
Bolton upon Dearne 186 B2
Bolton Wood Lane 209 F2
Boltonfellend 210 A1
Boltongate 209 F2
Bolton-le-Sands 192 A1
Bolton-on-Swale 202 B3
Bolventor 97 F2
Bombie 208 A2
Bomere Heath 157 D1
Bonar Bridge 266 D2
Bonawe (Bun Atha) 240 C1
Bonby 188 A1
Boncath 141 F4
Bonchester Bridge 227 G4
Bonchurch 107 E5
Bondleigh 113 G5
Bonds 192 A3
Bonehill 159 D2
Bo'ness 235 D1
Bonhill 233 E2
Boningale 158 A2
Bonjedward 228 A4
Bonkle 234 C4
Bonning Gate 199 F3
Bonnington Edin 235 F3
Bonnington Kent 124 C5
Bonnybank 244 B4
Bonnybridge 234 C1
Bonnykelly 269 G5
Bonnyrigg 236 A3
Bonnyton Aber 260 E1
Bonnyton Angus 245 D1
Bonnyton Angus 253 E4
Bonnyton Angus 244 B1
Bonsall 173 D2
Bont 130 C1
Bont Dolgadfan 155 E2
Bont Newydd 168 A5
Bontddu 154 C1
Bont-goch (Elerch) 154 C4
Bonthorpe 189 E5
Bont-newydd Conwy 182 B5
Bontnewydd Gwyn 167 D1
Bontuchel 169 D2
Bonvilston 129 G5
Bon-y-maen 128 C3
Boode 113 F2
Boohay 101 F2
Booker 134 D3
Booley 170 C5
Boor 264 E3
Boorley Green 107 E1
Boosbeck 203 F1
Boose's Green 151 G4
Boot 198 C2
Boot Street 152 D3
Booth 193 G5
Booth Bank 185 E1
Booth Green 184 D4
Booth Wood 185 E1
Boothby Graffoe 175 E2
Boothby Pagnell 175 E4
Boothstown 184 B2
Boothville 148 C1
Bootle Cumb 198 C4
Bootle Mersey 183 E3
Booton 178 C3
Boots Green 184 B5
Booze 201 F2
Boquhan 233 G1
Boraston 157 F5
Bordeaux 101 F4
Borden Kent 124 A2
Borden WSuss 120 D5
Bordley 193 F1
Bordon 120 C4
Boreham Essex 137 G2
Boreham Wilts 117 F3
Boreham Street 110 B2
Borehamwood 136 A3
Boreland D&G 217 F1
Boreland D&G 215 E4
Boreland Stir 242 A1
Boreley 146 A1
Boreraig 263 G6
Borgh ESiar 262 E3
Borgh ESiar 254 B4
Borghastan 270 D3
Borgie 273 J3
Borgue D&G 207 G2
Borgue High 275 G6
Borley 151 G3
Borley Green Essex 151 G3
Borley Green Suff 152 A1
Bornais 254 C2
Borness 207 G2
Borniskeitaig 263 J4
Borough Green 123 F3
Boroughbridge 194 C1
Borras Head 170 A2
Borrowash 173 F4

Borrowby *NYorks* **203** G1
Borrowby *NYorks* **202** D4
Borrowdale **209** F5
Borrowfield **261** G5
Borth **154** C4
Borthwick **236** A4
Borthwickbrae **227** F4
Borthwickshiels **227** F4
Borth-y-Gest **167** E4
Borve *High* **263** K7
Borve (Borgh)
ESiar **271** G2
Borwick **199** G5
Borwick Rails **198** C5
Bosavern **94** A3
Bosbury **145** F3
Boscarne **97** E3
Boscastle **98** A1
Boscastle Pottery *Corn*
PL35 OHE **98** B1
Boscombe *Bourne* **106** A3
Boscombe *Wilts* **118** D4
Bosham **108** A3
Bosham Hoe **108** A3
Bosherston **126** C3
Bosley **171** G1
Bossall **195** G1
Bossiney **97** E1
Bossingham **125** D4
Bossington *Hants* **119** E4
Bossington *Som* **114** B3
Bostadh **270** D4
Bostock Green **171** D1
Boston **176** B3
Boston Spa **194** D3
Boswarthan **94** B3
Boswinger **97** D5
Bosworth Battlefield
Country Park *Leics*
CV13 0AD **159** G2
Botallack **94** A3
Botanic Garden
Oxon OX1 4AZ
80 Oxford
Botany Bay **136** C3
Botany Bay *Lancs*
PR6 9AF **184** A1
Botcheston **159** G2
Botesdale **164** B4
Bothal **221** E3
Bothamsall **187** D5
Bothel **209** E3
Bothenhampton **104** A3
Bothwell **234** B4
Botley *Bucks* **135** E2
Botley *Hants* **107** E1
Botley *Oxon* **133** G2
Botloe's Green **145** G5
Botolph Claydon **148** C5
Botolphs **109** D3
Botolph's Bridge **124** D5
Bottacks **266** B5
Bottesford *Leics* **174** D4
Bottesford *NLincs* **187** F2
Bottisham **150** D1
Bottlesford **118** C2
Bottom Boat **194** C5
Bottom of Hutton **192** A4
Bottom o'th'Moor **184** A1
Bottomcraig **244** B2
Bottoms **193** F5
Botton Head **192** C1
Botusfleming **100** A1
Botwnnog **166** B4
Bough Beech **123** D4
Boughrood **144** A4
Boughspring **131** E3
Boughton *N'hants* **148** C1
Boughton *Norf* **163** F2
Boughton *Notts* **174** B1
Boughton Aluph **124** C4
Boughton Lees **124** C4
Boughton Malherbe **124** A4
Boughton
Monchelsea **123** G3
Boughton Street **124** C3
Boulby **203** G1
Bouldnor **106** C4
Bouldon **157** E4
Boulge **153** D2
Boulmer **229** G5
Boulston **126** C1
Boultenstone Hotel **260** C3
Boultham **175** E1
Boundary *Derbys* **159** F1
Boundary *Staffs* **171** G3
Bourn **150** B2
Bourne **175** F5
Bourne End *Bucks* **135** D4
Bourne End
CenBeds **149** E3
Bourne End *Herts* **135** F2
Bournebridge **137** E3
Bournemouth **105** G3
Bournemouth
Airport **106** A3
Bournemouth International
Centre BH2 5BH
64
Bournemouth
Bournheath **158** B5
Bournmoor **212** C2
Bournville **158** C4
Bourton *Bucks* **148** C4
Bourton *Dorset* **117** E4
Bourton *NSom* **116** A1
Bourton *Oxon* **133** E4
Bourton *Shrop* **157** E3
Bourton *Wilts* **118** B1
Bourton on
Dunsmore **159** G5
Bourton-on-the-Hill **147** D4
Bourton-on-
the-Water **147** D5
Bousd **246** B3
Boustead Hill **209** F1
Bouth **199** E4
Bouthwaite **202** A5
Bovain **242** A1
Boveney **135** E5
Boveridge **105** G1
Boverton **114** C1
Bovey Tracey **102** B5
Bovingdon **135** F2
Bovinger **137** E2
Bovington Camp **105** E4
Bow *Cumb* **209** G1
Bow *Devon* **102** A2

Bow *Devon* **101** E2
Bow *Ork* **277** C8
Bow Brickhill **149** E4
Bow of Fife **244** B3
Bow Street *Cere* **154** C4
Bow Street *Norf* **164** B2
Bowbank **211** F5
Bowburn **212** C4
Bowcombe **107** D4
Bowd **103** E3
Bowden *Devon* **101** E3
Bowden *ScBord* **227** G2
Bowden Hill **118** A1
Bowdon **184** B4
Bower **219** F3
Bower Hinton **104** A1
Bower House Tye **152** A3
Bowerchalke **118** B5
Bowerhill **118** A1
Bowermadden **275** H2
Bowers **171** F4
Bowers Gifford **137** G4
Bowershall **243** F5
Bowertower **275** H2
Bowes **201** E1
Bowgreave **192** A3
Bowithick **97** F1
Bowker's Green **183** F2
Bowland Bridge **199** F4
Bowley **145** E2
Bowley Town **145** E2
Bowlhead Green **121** E4
Bowling *WDun* **233** F2
Bowling *WYorks* **194** A4
Bowling Bank **170** A3
Bowlish **116** D3
Bowmanstead **199** E3
Bowmore **230** B3
Bowness-on-
Solway **218** A5
Bowness-on-
Windermere **199** F3
Bowood House &
Gardens *Wilts*
SN11 0LZ **118** A1
Bowscale **200** G3
Bowsden **237** G5
Bowside Lodge **274** D2
Bowston **199** F3
Bowthorpe **178** C5
Bowtrees **234** D1
Box *Glos* **132** A2
Box *Wilts* **117** F1
Box End **149** F3
Boxbush *Glos* **131** G1
Boxbush *Glos* **145** F5
Boxford *Suff* **152** A3
Boxford *WBerks* **133** G5
Boxgrove **108** B3
Boxley **123** G3
Boxmoor **135** F2
Box's Shop **112** C5
Boxted *Essex* **152** A4
Boxted *Suff* **151** G2
Boxted Cross **152** A4
Boxwell **132** A3
Boxworth **150** B1
Boxworth End **150** B1
Boyden Gate **125** E2
Boydston **224** C2
Boylestone **172** C4
Boyndie **268** E4
Boynton **196** D1
Boys Hill **104** C2
Boysack **253** D5
Boyton *Corn* **98** D1
Boyton *Suff* **153** E3
Boyton *Wilts* **118** A4
Boyton Cross **137** F2
Boyton End **151** F3
Bozeat **149** E2
Braaid **190** B4
Braal Castle **275** G2
Brabling Green **153** D1
Brabourne **124** C4
Brabourne Lees **124** C4
Brabster **275** J2
Bracadale **255** J1
Braceborough **161** F1
Bracebridge Heath **175** E1
Braceby **175** F4
Bracewell **193** E3
Brachla **258** C1
Brackenber **200** C1
Brackenbottom **200** D5
Brackenfield **173** E2
Brackens **269** F5
Bracklach **260** B2
Bracklamore **269** G5
Bracklesham **108** A4
Brackletter (A' Bhreac-
Leitir) **249** D1
Brackley *A&B* **231** G1
Brackley *High* **267** F6
Brackley *N'hants* **148** A4
Brackley Gate **173** E3
Brackley Hatch **148** B3
Bracknell **121** D1
Braco **242** D4
Bracobrae **268** D5
Bracon Ash **164** C2
Bracora **256** D5
Bracorina **256** D5
Bradbourne **172** D2
Bradbury **212** C5
Bradda **190** A4
Bradden **148** B3
Braddock **97** F3
Bradenham *Bucks* **134** D3
Bradenham *Norf* **178** A5
Bradenstoke **132** C5
Bradfield *Devon* **103** D2
Bradfield *Essex* **152** C4
Bradfield *Norf* **179** D2
Bradfield *WBerks* **134** B5
Bradfield Combust **151** G2
Bradfield Green **171** D2
Bradfield Heath **152** C5
Bradfield St. Clare **152** A2
Bradfield St. George **152** A1
Bradfield Southend
(Southend) **134** A5
Bradford *Corn* **97** F2
Bradford *Derbys* **172** D1
Bradford *Devon* **113** D5
Bradford *N'umb* **229** F3
Bradford *N'umb* **220** C4

Bradford *WYorks* **194** A4
Bradford Abbas **104** B1
Bradford Cathedral
Church of St. Peter
WYorks BD1 4EH
65 Bradford
Bradford Leigh **117** F1
Bradford Peverell **104** C3
Bradford-on-Avon **117** F1
Bradford-on-Tone **115** E5
Bradgate Park *Leics*
LE6 0HE **17** B3
Bradiford **113** F2
Brading **107** F4
Bradley *ChesW&C* **183** G5
Bradley *Derbys* **172** D3
Bradley *Hants* **120** B3
Bradley *NELincs* **188** C2
Bradley (Low Bradley)
NYorks **193** G3
Bradley *Staffs* **158** A1
Bradley *WMid* **158** B3
Bradley Fold **184** B2
Bradley Green
Warks **159** E2
Bradley Green
Worcs **146** B1
Bradley in the
Moors **172** B3
Bradley Mills **185** F1
Bradley Stoke **131** F4
Bradmore *Notts* **173** G4
Bradmore *WMid* **158** A3
Bradney **116** A4
Bradninch **102** D2
Bradnop **172** B2
Bradnor Green **144** B2
Bradpole **104** A3
Bradshaw *GtMan* **184** B1
Bradshaw *WYorks* **193** G4
Bradstone **99** D2
Bradwall Green **171** E1
Bradwell *Derbys* **185** F4
Bradwell *Devon* **113** E1
Bradwell *Essex* **151** G5
Bradwell *MK* **148** D4
Bradwell *Norf* **179** G5
Bradwell Grove **133** E2
Bradwell Waterside **138** C2
Bradwell-on-Sea **138** D2
Bradworthy **112** D4
Brae *D&G* **216** C3
Brae *High* **266** B1
Brae *Shet* **279** C6
Brae of Achnahaird **272** C7
Braeantra **266** C4
Braedownie **252** A2
Braefoot **269** F6
Braegrum **243** F2
Braehead *D&G* **215** F5
Braehead *Glas* **233** G3
Braehead *Moray* **268** B6
Braehead *Ork* **277** E7
Braehead *SLan* **225** G2
Braehead *SLan* **235** D4
Braehead of Lunan **253** E4
Braeleny **242** B3
Braemar **259** J5
Braemore *High* **266** C1
Braemore *High* **275** F5
Braemore *High* **265** H4
Braeswick **276** F4
Braeval **242** A4
Braewick **279** C7
Brafferton *Darl* **212** B5
Brafferton *NYorks* **202** D5
Brafield-on-the-
Green **148** D2
Bragar **270** E3
Bragbury End **150** A5
Bragenham **149** E5
Bragleenbeg **240** B2
Braichmelyn **167** F1
Braides **192** A2
Braidley **201** F4
Braidwood **234** C5
Braigo **230** A3
Brailsford **173** D3
Brain's Green **131** F2
Braintree **151** F4
Braiseworth **164** C4
Braishfield **119** E5
Braithwaite *Cumb* **209** F4
Braithwaite
SYorks **186** D1
Braithwaite
WYorks **193** G3
Braithwell **186** C3
Bramber **109** D2
Brambletye **122** D5
Brambridge **119** F5
Bramcote *Notts* **173** F4
Bramcote *Warks* **159** G4
Bramdean **120** B5
Bramerton **179** D5
Bramfield *Herts* **136** B1
Bramfield *Suff* **165** E4
Bramford **152** C3
Bramhall **184** C4
Bramham **194** D3
Bramhope **194** B3
Bramley *Hants* **120** B2
Bramley *Surr* **121** F3
Bramley *SYorks* **186** B3
Bramley Corner **120** B2
Bramley Head **194** A2
Bramley Vale **173** F1
Bramling **125** E3
Brampford Speke **102** C3
Brampton *Cambs* **162** A5
Brampton *Cumb* **210** C5
Brampton *Cumb* **210** C5
Brampton *Derbys* **186** A5
Brampton *Lincs* **187** F5
Brampton *Norf* **178** D3
Brampton *Suff* **165** F3
Brampton *SYorks* **186** B2
Brampton Abbotts **145** F5
Brampton Ash **160** C4
Brampton Bryan **156** C5

Brampton en le
Morthen **186** B4
Brampton Street **165** F3
Brampton Valley Way
Country Park *N'hants*
NN6 9DG **160** C5
Bramshall **172** B4
Bramshaw **106** B1
Bramshill **120** C1
Bramshott **120** D4
Bramwell **116** B5
Bran End **151** E5
Branault **247** E3
Brancaster **177** F3
Brancaster Staithe **177** F3
Brancepeth **212** B4
Branchill **267** H6
Brand Green **145** G5
Brandelhow **209** F4
Branderburgh **267** K4
Brandesburton **196** D3
Brandeston **153** D1
Brandis Corner **113** E5
Brandiston **178** C3
Brandlingill **209** E4
Brandon *Dur* **212** B4
Brandon *Lincs* **175** E3
Brandon *N'umb* **229** E5
Brandon *Suff* **163** F4
Brandon *Warks* **159** G5
Brandon Bank **163** E4
Brandon Creek **163** E3
Brandon Park *Suff*
IP27 0SU **163** F4
Brandon Parva **178** B5
Brandsby **203** E5
Brandy Wharf **188** A3
Brane **94** B4
Branksome **105** G3
Branksome Park **105** G3
Bransbury **119** F3
Bransby **187** F5
Branscombe **103** E4
Bransford **145** G2
Bransford Bridge **146** A2
Bransgore **106** A3
Bransholme **196** D4
Branson's Cross **158** C5
Branston *Leics* **174** D5
Branston *Lincs* **175** F1
Branston *Staffs* **172** D5
Branston Booths **175** F1
Branston Water Park *Staffs*
DE14 3EZ **172** D5
Brant Broughton **175** E2
Brantham **152** C4
Branthwaite *Cumb* **209** F3
Branthwaite *Cumb* **209** D4
Brantingham **196** B5
Branton *N'umb* **229** E5
Branton *SYorks* **186** D2
Brantwood **199** E3
Branxholm
Bridgend **227** F4
Branxholme **227** F4
Branxton **228** C3
Brassey Green **170** C1
Brassington **172** D2
Brasted **123** D3
Brasted Chart **123** D3
Brathens **260** E5
Bratoft **176** C1
Brattleby **187** G4
Bratton *Som* **114** C3
Bratton *Tel&W* **157** F1
Bratton *Wilts* **118** A3
Bratton Clovelly **99** E1
Bratton Fleming **113** G2
Bratton Seymour **117** D5
Braughing **150** B5
Brauncewell **175** F2
Braunston *N'hants* **148** A1
Braunstone **160** D2
Braunton **113** E2
Brawby **203** G5
Brawdy **140** B5
Brawith **203** E2
Brawl **274** D2
Brawlbin **275** F3
Bray **135** E5
Bray Shop **98** D3
Bray Wick **135** D5
Braybrooke **160** C4
Braydon Side **132** C4
Brayford **113** G2
Brayshaw **193** D2
Braythorn **194** B3
Brayton **195** F4
Braywoodside **135** D5
Brazacott **98** C1
Brea **96** A5
Breach *Kent* **125** D4
Breach *Kent* **124** A2
Breachwood Green **149** G5
Breacleit **270** D4
Breaden Heath **170** B4
Breadsall **173** E4
Breadstone **131** G2
Breage **94** D4
Breakon **278** E2
Breamore **106** A1
Brean **115** F2
Breanais **270** B5
Brearton **194** C1
Breascleit **270** E4
Breaston **173** F4
Brechfa **142** B4
Brechin **253** E3
Breck of Cruan **277** C6
Breckles **164** A2
Brecon
(Aberhonddu) **143** G5
Brecon Beacons Visitor
Centre *Powys*
LD3 8ER **143** F5
Breconside **225** G4
Bredbury **184** D3
Brede **110** D2
Bredenbury **145** F2
Bredfield **153** D2
Bredgar **124** A2
Bredhurst **123** G2
Bredon **146** B4

Bredon's Hardwick **146** B4
Bredon's Norton **146** B4
Bredwardine **144** C3
Breedon on the Hill **173** F5
Breibhig **271** G4
Breich **235** D3
Breightmet **184** B2
Breighton **195** G4
Breinton **145** D4
Breinton Common **145** D4
Bremhill **132** B5
Bremhill Wick **132** B5
Brenachoille **240** C4
Brenchley **123** F4
Brendon *Devon* **114** A3
Brendon *Devon* **113** D4
Brendon *Devon* **113** D5
Brenkley **221** E4
Brent Eleigh **152** A3
Brent Knoll **116** A2
Brent Pelham **150** C4
Brentford **136** A5
Brentingby **160** C1
Brentwood **137** E3
Brenzett **111** F1
Brenzett Green **111** F1
Breoch **216** B5
Brereton **158** C1
Brereton Green **171** E1
Brereton Heath **171** F1
Breretonhill **158** C1
Bressay **279** E8
Bressingham **164** B3
Bressingham
Common **164** B3
Bressingham Steam
Museum & Gardens
Norf IP22 2AA **164** B3
Bretby **173** D5
Bretford **159** G5
Bretforton **146** C3
Bretherdale Head **199** G2
Bretherton **192** A5
Brettabister **279** D7
Brettenham *Norf* **164** A3
Brettenham *Suff* **152** A2
Bretton *Derbys* **185** F5
Bretton *Flints* **170** A1
Bretton *Peter* **161** G2
Brevig **254** B5
Brewood **158** A2
Briach **267** H6
Briantspuddle **105** E3
Brick End **151** D5
Brickendon **136** C2
Bricket Wood **136** A2
Brickfields Horse Country
IoW PO33 3TH **107** E3
Brickkiln Green **151** F4
Bricklehampton **146** B3
Bride **190** C1
Bridekirk **209** E3
Bridell **141** E3
Bridestowe **99** F2
Brideswell **260** D1
Bridford **102** B4
Bridge *Corn* **96** A5
Bridge *Kent* **125** D3
Bridge End *Cumb* **198** D4
Bridge End *Devon* **100** D3
Bridge End *Essex* **151** E4
Bridge End *Lincs* **175** G4
Bridge End *Shet* **279** C9
Bridge Hewick **202** C5
Bridge o'Ess **260** D5
Bridge of Alford **260** D3
Bridge of Allan **242** C5
Bridge of Avon **259** J1
Bridge of Awe
(Drochaid Abha) **240** C1
Bridge of Balgie **250** A5
Bridge of
Bogendreip **260** E5
Bridge of
Brewlands **251** G3
Bridge of Brown **259** J2
Bridge of Cally **251** G4
Bridge of Canny **260** E5
Bridge of Craigisla **252** A4
Bridge of Dee *Aber* **259** J5
Bridge of Dee *D&G* **216** B4
Bridge of Don **261** H4
Bridge of Dun **253** E4
Bridge of Dye **253** E1
Bridge of Earn **243** G3
Bridge of Ericht **250** A4
Bridge of Feugh **260** E5
Bridge of Forss **275** F2
Bridge of Gairn **260** B5
Bridge of Gaur **250** A4
Bridge of Muchalls **261** G5
Bridge of Muick **260** B5
Bridge of Orchy (Drochaid
Urchaidh) **241** E1
Bridge of Tynet **268** B4
Bridge of Walls **279** B7
Bridge of Weir **233** E3
Bridge Reeve **113** G4
Bridge Sollers **144** D3
Bridge Street **151** G3
Bridge Trafford **183** F5
Bridgefoot *Angus* **244** B1
Bridgefoot *Cambs* **150** C3
Bridgefoot *Cumb* **209** D4
Bridgehampton **116** C5
Bridgehaugh **260** B1
Bridgehill **211** G2
Bridgemary **107** E2
Bridgemere **171** E3
Bridgend *A&B* **230** B3
Bridgend *A&B* **240** A5
Bridgend *Aber* **260** D1
Bridgend *Aber* **269** F6
Bridgend *Angus* **252** D3
Bridgend (Pen-y-bont ar
Ogwr) *Bridgend* **129** F5
Bridgend *Corn* **97** F4
Bridgend *Cumb* **199** F1
Bridgend *Fife* **244** B3
Bridgend *Moray* **260** B1
Bridgend *P&K* **243** G2
Bridgend *WLoth* **235** E2
Bridgend of
Lintrathen **252** A4
Bridgerule **112** C5
Bridges **156** C3

Bridgeton *Aber* **260** D3
Bridgeton *Glas* **234** A3
Bridgetown *Corn* **98** D2
Bridgetown *Som* **114** C4
Bridgewater Hall,
Manchester *GtMan*
M2 3WS **46** E5
Bridgeyate **131** F5
Bridgham **164** A3
Bridgnorth **157** G3
Bridgnorth Cliff
Railway *Shrop*
WV16 4AH **157** G3
Bridgtown **158** B2
Bridgwater **115** F4
Bridlington **197** D1
Bridport **104** A3
Bridstow **145** E5
Brierfield **193** E4
Brierley *Glos* **131** F1
Brierley *Here* **145** D2
Brierley *SYorks* **186** B1
Brierley Hill **158** B4
Brierton **213** D5
Briestfield **185** G1
Brig o'Turk **242** A4
Brigg **188** A2
Briggate **179** E3
Briggswath **204** B2
Brigham *Cumb* **209** D3
Brigham *ERid* **196** C2
Brighouse **194** A5
Brighstone **106** D4
Brightgate **173** D2
Brighthampton **133** F2
Brightholmlee **185** G3
Brightling **110** B1
Brightlingsea **139** D1
Brighton *B&H* **109** F3
Brighton *Corn* **96** D4
Brighton Centre, The
B&H BN1 2GR
65 Brighton
Brighton Museum &
Art Gallery *B&H*
BN1 1EE **65** Brighton
Brighton Pier *B&H*
BN2 1TW **65** Brighton
Brightons **234** D2
Brightwalton **133** G5
Brightwalton Green **133** G5
Brightwell **152** D3
Brightwell Baldwin **134** B3
Brightwell
Upperton **134** B3
Brightwell-cum-
Sotwell **134** A3
Brignall **201** F1
Brigsley **188** C2
Brigsteer **199** F4
Brigstock **161** E4
Brill *Bucks* **134** B1
Brill *Corn* **95** E4
Brilley **144** B3
Brilley Mountain **144** B2
Brimaston **140** C5
Brimfield **145** E1
Brimington **186** B5
Brimington
Common **186** B5
Brimley **102** B5
Brimpsfield **132** B1
Brimpton **119** G1
Brims **277** B9
Brimscombe **132** A2
Brimstage **183** E4
Brinacory **256** D5
Brindham **116** C3
Brindister *Shet* **279** D9
Brindister *Shet* **279** B7
Brindle **192** B5
Brindley Ford **171** F2
Brineton **158** A1
Bringhurst **160** D3
Brington **161** F5
Brinian **276** D5
Briningham **178** B2
Brinkhill **189** D5
Brinkley *Cambs* **151** E2
Brinkley *Notts* **174** C2
Brinklow **159** G5
Brinkworth **132** C4
Brinmore **258** D2
Brinscall **192** C5
Brinsea **116** B1
Brinsley **173** F3
Brinsop **144** D3
Brinsworth **186** B3
Brinton **178** B2
Brisco **210** A2
Brisley **178** A3
Brislington **131** F5
Brissenden Green **124** B5
Bristol **131** E5
Bristol Cathedral
BS1 5TJ **66** Bristol
Bristol City Museum &
Art Gallery *Bristol*
BS8 1RL **8** B3
Bristol Filton
Airport **131** E4
Bristol International
Airport **131** D5
Bristol Zoo *Bristol*
BS8 3HA **8** B3
Briston **178** B2
Britain At War Experience
GtLon SE1 2TF **12** C4
Britannia **193** E5
Britford **118** C5
Brithdir *Caerp* **130** A2
Brithdir *Gwyn* **155** D1
Brithem Bottom **102** D1
British Empire &
Commonwealth Museum
BS1 6QH **66** Bristol
British Library
(St. Pancras) *GtLon*
NW1 2DB **12** B4
British Museum *GtLon*
WC1B 3DG **44** E2
Briton Ferry
(Llansawel) **128** D3
Britwell **135** E4
Britwell Salome **134** B3
Brixham **101** F2
Brixton *Devon* **100** B2
Brixton *GtLon* **136** C5

Brixton Deverill **117** F4
Brixworth **160** C5
Brixworth Country Park
N'hants
NN6 9DG **160** C5
Brize Norton **133** E2
Broad Alley **146** A1
Broad Blunsdon **133** D3
Broad Campden **147** D4
Broad Carr **185** E1
Broad Chalke **118** B5
Broad Ford **123** G5
Broad Green
Cambs **151** E2
Broad Green
CenBeds **149** E3
Broad Green *Essex* **151** G5
Broad Green *Essex* **150** C4
Broad Green
Mersey **183** F3
Broad Green *Suff* **152** B2
Broad Green *Worcs* **145** G2
Broad Haven **126** B1
Broad Hill **163** D5
Broad Hinton **132** D5
Broad Laying **119** F1
Broad Marston **146** D3
Broad Oak *Carmar* **142** B5
Broad Oak *Cumb* **198** C3
Broad Oak *ESuss* **110** B1
Broad Oak *Here* **145** D5
Broad Road **165** D3
Broad Street *ESuss* **111** D2
Broad Street *Kent* **124** B5
Broad Street *Kent* **124** D5
Broad Street *Wilts* **118** C1
Broad Street Green **138** B2
Broad Town **132** C5
Broadbottom **185** D3
Broadbridge **108** A3
Broadbridge Heath **121** G4
Broadclyst **102** C3
Broadfield *Lancs* **192** D5
Broadfield *Lancs* **192** B5
Broadford (An t-Ath
Leathann) **256** C2
Broadford Airport **256** C2
Broadford Bridge **121** F5
Broadgate **198** C4
Broadhaugh **227** F5
Broadhaven **275** J3
Broadheath *GtMan* **184** B4
Broadheath *Worcs* **145** F1
Broadhembury **103** E2
Broadhempston **101** E1
Broadholme **187** F5
Broadland Row **110** D2
Broadlay **127** G2
Broadley *Lancs* **184** C1
Broadley *Moray* **268** B4
Broadmayne **104** D4
Broadmeadows **227** F2
Broadmere **120** B3
Broadmoor **127** D2
Broadnymett **102** A2
Broadoak *Dorset* **104** A3
Broadoak *Glos* **131** F1
Broadoak End **136** C1
Broadrashes **268** C5
Broad's Green **137** F1
Broadsea **269** H4
Broadstairs **125** F2
Broadstone *Poole* **105** G3
Broadstone *Shrop* **157** E4
Broadstreet
Common **130** C4
Broadwas **145** G2
Broadwater *Herts* **150** A5
Broadwater *WSuss* **108** D3
Broadwater Down **123** E4
Broadwaters **158** A5
Broadway *Carmar* **127** G2
Broadway *Carmar* **127** F1
Broadway *Pembs* **126** B1
Broadway *Som* **103** G1
Broadway *Suff* **165** E4
Broadwell *Glos* **147** E5
Broadwell *Oxon* **133** E2
Broadwell *Warks* **147** G1
Broadwell House **211** F2
Broadwey **104** C4
Broadwindsor **104** A2
Broadwood Kelly **113** G5
Broadwoodwidger **99** E2
Brobury **144** C3
Brocastle **129** F5
Brochel **264** B7
Brochloch **215** G1
Brock **246** B2
Brockamin **145** G2
Brockbridge **107** F1
Brockdish **164** D4
Brockenhurst **106** B2
Brockford Green **152** C1
Brockford Street **152** C1
Brockhall **148** B1
Brockham **121** G3
Brockhampton
Glos **146** C5
Brockhampton
Glos **146** B5
Brockhampton
Here **145** E4
Brockhampton
Here **145** F2
Brockhampton
Green **104** D2
Brockholes **185** F1
Brockhurst *Hants* **107** E2
Brockhurst *WSuss* **122** D5
Brocklebank **209** G2
Brocklesby **188** B1
Brockley *NSom* **116** B1
Brockley *Suff* **151** G2
Brockley Green **151** F3
Brock's Green **119** F1
Brockton *Shrop* **157** E3
Brockton *Shrop* **157** G2
Brockton *Shrop* **156** C2
Brockton *Tel&W* **157** G1
Brockweir **131** E2
Brockwood Park **120** B5
Brockworth **132** A1

Brocton 158 B1
Brodick 223 F2
Brodsworth 186 C2
Brogborough 149 E4
Brogyntyn 169 F4
Broken Cross
  ChesE 184 C1
Broken Cross
  ChesW&C 184 A5
Brokenborough 132 B4
Brokes 202 A3
Bromborough 183 E4
Brome 164 C4
Brome Street 164 C4
Bromeswell 153 E2
Bromfield Cumb 209 E2
Bromfield Shrop 157 D5
Bromham Bed 149 F2
Bromham Wilts 118 A1
Bromley GtLon 147 G2
Bromley SYorks 186 A3
Bromley Cross 184 B1
Bromley Green 124 B5
Brompton
  Med 123 G2
Brompton NYorks 202 C3
Brompton NYorks 204 C4
Brompton Shrop 157 E2
Brompton on Swale 202 B3
Brompton Ralph 115 D4
Brompton Regis 114 C4
Bromsash 145 F5
Bromsberrow 145 G4
Bromsberrow
  Heath 145 G4
Bromsgrove 158 B5
Bromstead Heath 158 A1
Bromyard 145 F2
Bromyard Downs 145 F2
Bronaber 168 A4
Brondesbury 136 B4
Brongest 141 G3
Bronington 170 B4
Bronllys 144 A4
Bronnant 142 C1
Bronte Weaving Shed
  WYorks
  BD22 8EP 193 G4
Bronwydd Arms 142 A5
Bronydd 144 B3
Bron-y-gaer 127 G1
Bronygarth 169 F4
Brook Carmar 127 F2
Brook Hants 106 B1
Brook Hants 119 E5
Brook IoW 106 C4
Brook Kent 124 C4
Brook Surr 121 E4
Brook Surr 121 F3
Brook Bottom 185 D2
Brook End Bed 149 F1
Brook End Herts 150 B5
Brook End MK 149 F4
Brook End Worcs 146 A3
Brook Hill 106 B1
Brook Street Essex 137 E3
Brook Street Kent 124 C5
Brook Street Suff 151 G3
Brook Street WSuss 109 F1
Brooke Norf 165 D2
Brooke Rut 160 D2
Brookend Glos 131 E3
Brookend Glos 131 F2
Brookfield 185 E3
Brookhampton 134 B3
Brookhouse ChesE 184 D5
Brookhouse Denb 169 D1
Brookhouse Lancs 192 B1
Brookhouse SYorks 186 C4
Brookhouse Green 171 F1
Brookhouses 171 G3
Brookland 111 E1
Brooklands D&G 216 C3
Brooklands Shrop 170 C4
Brooklands Museum Surr
  KT13 0QN 121 F1
Brookmans Park 136 C1
Brooks 156 A3
Brooks Green 121 G5
Brooksby 160 B1
Brookside Miniature
  Railway ChesE
  SK12 1BZ 25 G6
Brookthorpe 132 A1
Brookwood 121 E2
Broom CenBeds 149 G3
Broom Fife 244 B4
Broom Warks 146 C2
Broom Green 178 B4
Broom Hill Dorset 105 G2
Broom Hill Worcs 158 B5
Broom of Dalreach 243 F3
Broomcroft 157 E2
Broome Norf 165 E2
Broome Shrop 156 D4
Broome Worcs 158 B5
Broome Wood 229 F5
Broomedge 184 B4
Broomer's Corner 121 G5
Broomfield Aber 261 H1
Broomfield Essex 137 G1
Broomfield Kent 125 D2
Broomfield Kent 124 A3
Broomfield Som 115 F4
Broomfleet 196 A5
Broomhall Green 170 D3
Broomhaugh 211 G1
Broomhead 269 H4
Broomhill Bristol 131 F5
Broomhill N'umb 221 E1
Broomielaw 201 F1
Broomley 211 G1
Broompark 212 B3
Broom's Green 145 G4
Brora 267 G1
Broseley 157 F2
Brotherlee 211 F4
Brotherton 195 D5
Brotton 203 F1
Broubster 275 F2
Brough Cumb 200 C1
Brough Derbys 185 F4
Brough ERid 196 B5
Brough High 275 H1
Brough Notts 174 D2
Brough Ork 277 C6
Brough Shet 279 E8

Brough Shet 278 B1
Brough Shet 279 E6
Brough Shet 278 E5
Brough Lodge 278 E3
Brough Sowerby 200 C1
Broughall 170 C3
Brougham 210 B5
Brougham Hall Cumb
  CA10 2DE 210 B5
Broughton Bucks 135 E1
Broughton Cambs 162 A5
Broughton Flints 170 A1
Broughton Hants 119 E4
Broughton Lancs 192 B4
Broughton MK 149 D3
Broughton N'hants 160 D5
Broughton NLincs 187 G2
Broughton NYorks 203 G5
Broughton NYorks 193 F2
Broughton Ork 276 D3
Broughton Oxon 147 G4
Broughton ScBord 226 C2
Broughton VGlam 129 F5
Broughton Astley 160 A3
Broughton Beck 199 D4
Broughton Gifford 117 F1
Broughton Green 146 B1
Broughton Hackett 146 B2
Broughton in
  Furness 198 D4
Broughton Mills 198 D3
Broughton Moor 209 D3
Broughton Poggs 133 E2
Broughtown 276 F3
Broughty Ferry 244 C1
Browland 198 C4
Brown Candover 119 G4
Brown Edge Lancs 183 E1
Brown Edge Staffs 171 G2
Brown Heath 170 B1
Brown Lees 171 F2
Brown Street 152 B1
Brownber 200 C2
Browndown 107 E3
Brownheath 170 B5
Brownhill 269 G6
Brownhills Fife 244 D3
Brownhills WMid 158 C2
Brownieside 229 F4
Brownlow 171 F1
Brownlow Heath 171 F1
Brown's Bank 170 D3
Brownsea Island Dorset
  BH13 7EE 105 G4
Brownshill 132 A2
Brownshill Green 159 F4
Brownsover 160 A5
Brownston 100 C2
Browston Green 179 F5
Broxa 204 C3
Broxbourne 136 C2
Broxburn ELoth 237 D2
Broxburn WLoth 235 E2
Broxholme 187 G5
Broxted 151 E5
Broxton 170 B2
Broxwood 144 C2
Broyle Side 109 G2
Bruachmary 267 F7
Bruan 275 J5
Brue (Brù) 271 F3
Bruera 170 B1
Bruern 147 E5
Bruernish 254 C4
Bruisyard 153 E1
Bruisyard Street 153 E1
Brumby 187 G1
Brund 172 C1
Brundall 179 E4
Brundish Norf 165 E2
Brundish Suff 153 D1
Brundish Street 165 D4
Brunstock 210 A2
Brunswick Village 221 E4
Bruntingthorpe 160 B3
Bruntland 260 C2
Brunton Fife 244 B2
Brunton N'umb 229 F4
Brunton Wilts 118 D2
Brushfield 185 F5
Brushford Devon 113 G5
Brushford Som 114 C5
Bruton 117 D4
Bryanston 105 E2
Bryant's Bottom 135 D3
Brydekirk 217 F3
Brymbo 169 F2
Brymor Ice Cream NYorks
  HG4 4PG 202 A4
Brympton 104 B1
Bryn Caerp 130 C3
Bryn Carmar 128 B2
Bryn ChesW&C 184 A5
Bryn GtMan 183 G2
Bryn NPT 129 D3
Bryn Shrop 156 B4
Bryn Bach Country
  Park BGwent
  NP22 3AY 130 A2
Bryn Bwbach 167 F3
Bryn Gates 183 G2
Bryn Pen-y-lan 170 A3
Brynamman 128 D1
Brynberian 141 E4
Bryncae 129 F4
Bryncethin 129 F4
Bryncir 167 D3
Bryncoch Bridgend 129 F4
Bryn-côch NPT 128 D3
Bryncroes 166 B4
Bryncrug 154 C2
Bryneglwys 169 E3
Brynford 182 C5
Bryngwran 180 B5
Bryngwyn Mon 130 C2
Bryngwyn Powys 144 A3
Bryn-henllan 141 D4
Brynhoffnant 141 G2
Bryning 192 A4
Brynithel 130 B2
Brynmawr BGwent 130 A1
Bryn-mawr Gwyn 166 B4
Brynmelyn 156 A5
Brynmenyn 129 F4
Brynna 129 F4
Brynnau Gwynion 129 F4

Bryn-penarth 156 A2
Brynrefail Gwyn 167 E1
Brynrefail IoA 180 C4
Brynsadler 129 F4
Brynsaithmarchog 169 D2
Brynsiencyn 167 D1
Bryn-teg IoA 180 C4
Brynteg Wrex 170 A2
Bryn-y-cochin 170 A4
Brynygwenin 130 C1
Bryn-y-maen 181 G5
Buaile nam Bodach 254 C4
Bualadubh 262 C7
Bualintur 255 K2
Bualnaluib 264 E2
Bubbenhall 159 F5
Bubnell 185 G5
Bubwith 195 G4
Buccleuch 227 E4
Buchan 216 B4
Buchanan Castle 233 F1
Buchanhaven 269 K6
Buchanty 243 E2
Buchlyvie 242 A5
Buckabank 209 G2
Buckby Wharf 148 B1
Buckden Cambs 149 G1
Buckden NYorks 201 D4
Buckenham 179 E5
Buckerell 103 E2
Buckfast 100 D1
Buckfast Abbey Devon
  TQ11 0EE 100 D1
Buckfastleigh 100 D1
Buckhaven 244 B5
Buckholm 227 F2
Buckholt 131 E1
Buckhorn Weston 117 E5
Buckhurst Hill 136 D3
Buckie 268 C4
Buckies 275 G2
Buckingham 148 B4
Buckingham Palace GtLon
  SW1A 1AA 44 B6
Buckland Bucks 135 E1
Buckland Devon 100 C3
Buckland Glos 146 C4
Buckland Hants 106 C3
Buckland Here 145 E2
Buckland Herts 150 B4
Buckland Kent 125 F4
Buckland Oxon 133 F3
Buckland Surr 122 B3
Buckland Brewer 113 E3
Buckland Common 135 E2
Buckland Dinham 117 E2
Buckland Filleigh 113 E4
Buckland in the
  Moor 102 A5
Buckland
  Monachorum 100 A1
Buckland Newton 104 C2
Buckland Ripers 104 C4
Buckland St. Mary 103 F1
Buckland-tout-
  Saints 101 D3
Bucklebury 134 A5
Bucklerheads 244 C1
Bucklers Hard 106 D3
Bucklesham 152 D3
Buckley (Bwcle) 169 F1
Buckley Green 147 D1
Bucklow Hill 184 B4
Buckman Corner 121 G5
Buckminster 175 D5
Bucknall Lincs 188 A5
Bucknall Stoke 171 G3
Bucknell Oxon 148 A5
Bucknell Shrop 156 C5
Buckridge 157 G5
Buck's Cross 112 D3
Bucks Green 121 F4
Bucks Hill 135 F2
Bucks Horn Oak 120 D3
Buck's Mills 113 D3
Buckspool 126 C3
Buckton ERid 205 E5
Buckton Here 156 C5
Buckton N'umb 229 E3
Buckton Vale 185 E2
Buckworth 161 G5
Budbrooke 147 E1
Budby 186 D5
Buddon 244 D1
Bude 112 C5
Budge's Shop 98 D5
Budlake 102 C2
Budle 229 F3
Budleigh Salterton 103 D4
Budock Water 95 E3
Budworth Heath 184 A5
Buerton 171 D3
Bugbrooke 148 B2
Buglawton 171 F1
Bugle 97 E4
Bugthorpe 195 G2
Building End 150 C4
Buildwas 157 F2
Builth Road 143 G2
Builth Wells (Llanfair-
  ym-Muallt) 143 G2
Bulby 175 F5
Bulcote 174 B3
Buldoo 274 E2
Bulford 118 C3
Bulford Camp 118 C3
Bulkeley 170 C2
Bulkington Warks 159 F4
Bulkington Wilts 118 A2
Bulkworthy 113 D4
Bull Bay
  (Porth Llechog) 180 C3
Bull Green Herts 136 B1
Bullbridge 173 E2
Bullbrook 121 D1
Bullen's Green 136 B2
Bulley 131 G1
Bullington 119 F3
Bullwood 232 C1
Bulmer Essex 151 G3
Bulmer NYorks 195 F1
Bulmer Tye 151 G4
Bulphan 137 F4
Bulstone 103 E4

Bulverhythe 110 C3
Bulwark 269 H6
Bulwell 173 G3
Bulwick 161 E3
Bumble's Green 136 D2
Bun Abhainn
  Eadarra 270 D7
Bun Loyne 257 J4
Bunarkaig 249 D1
Bunbury 170 C2
Bunbury Heath 170 C2
Bunchrew 266 D7
Bundalloch 256 E2
Buness 278 F2
Bunessan 238 C2
Bungay 165 E3
Bunker's Hill 176 A2
Bunlarie 222 C2
Bunloit
  (Bun Leothaid) 258 C2
Bunmhullin 254 C3
Bunnahabhain 230 C3
Bunny 173 G5
Buntait 257 K1
Buntingford 150 B5
Bunwell 164 C2
Bunwell Street 164 C2
Burbage Derbys 185 E5
Burbage Leics 159 G3
Burbage Wilts 118 D1
Burbage Common Leics
  LE10 3DD 159 G3
Burchett's Green 134 D4
Burcombe 118 B4
Burcot Oxon 134 A3
Burcot Worcs 158 B5
Burcott 149 D5
Burdale 196 A1
Burdocks 121 F5
Burdon 212 C2
Burdrop 147 F4
Bure Valley Railway Norf
  NR11 6BW 178 D3
Bures 152 A3
Bures Green 152 A4
Burfa 144 B1
Burford Oxon 133 E1
Burford Shrop 145 E1
Burg 246 C5
Burgate End 149 G4
Burgate 164 B4
Burgates 120 C5
Burge End 149 G4
Burgess Hill 109 F2
Burgh 152 D2
Burgh by Sands 209 G1
Burgh Castle 179 F5
Burgh Heath 122 B3
Burgh le Marsh 176 C1
Burgh next
  Aylsham 178 D3
Burgh on Bain 188 C4
Burgh St. Margaret
  (Fleggburgh) 179 F4
Burgh St. Peter 165 F2
Burghclere 119 F1
Burghead 267 J5
Burghfield 120 B1
Burghfield
  Common 120 B1
Burghfield Hill 120 B1
Burghill 145 D3
Burghwallis 186 C1
Burham 123 G2
Buriton 120 C5
Burland 170 D2
Burlawn 97 D3
Burleigh 121 E1
Burlescombe 103 D1
Burleston 105 D3
Burley Hants 106 B2
Burley Rut 161 D1
Burley WYorks 194 B4
Burley Gate 145 E3
Burley in
  Wharfedale 194 A3
Burley Street 106 B2
Burley Woodhead 194 A3
Burleydam 170 D3
Burlingjobb 144 B2
Burlow 110 A2
Burlton 170 B5
Burmarsh 124 D5
Burmington 147 E4
Burn 195 E5
Burn Farm 253 E2
Burn Naze 191 G3
Burn of Cambus 242 C4
Burnage 184 C3
Burnaston 173 D4
Burnby 196 A3
Burncross 186 A3
Burndell 108 B3
Burnden 184 B2
Burnedge 184 D1
Burneside 199 G3
Burness 276 F3
Burneston 202 C4
Burnett 117 D1
Burnfoot High 274 D6
Burnfoot P&K 243 F4
Burnfoot ScBord 227 G4
Burnfoot ScBord 227 F4
Burnham Bucks 135 E4
Burnham NLincs 188 A1
Burnham Deepdale 177 G3
Burnham Green 136 B1
Burnham Market 177 G3
Burnham Norton 177 G3
Burnham Overy
  Staithe 177 G3
Burnham Overy
  Town 177 G3
Burnham Thorpe 177 G3
Burnham-on-
  Crouch 138 C2
Burnham-on-Sea 116 A3
Burnhaven 269 K6
Burnhead D&G 215 F3
Burnhead D&G 216 C1
Burnhervie 261 F3
Burnhill Green 157 G2
Burnhope 212 A3
Burnhouse 233 E4
Burniston 204 D3
Burnley 193 E4
Burnmouth 237 G3
Burnopfield 212 A2

Burn's Green 150 B5
Burns National Heritage
  Park SAyr
  KA7 4PQ 224 B4
Burnsall 193 G1
Burnside Aber 261 F3
Burnside EAyr 225 D4
Burnside Fife 243 F4
Burnside Shet 278 B5
Burnside WLoth 235 E2
Burnside of
  Duntrune 244 C1
Burnstones 210 C2
Burnswark 217 F3
Burnt Hill 134 A5
Burnt Houses 212 A5
Burnt Oak 136 B3
Burnt Yates 194 B1
Burntcliff Top 171 F1
Burntisland 235 G1
Burnton EAyr 224 C4
Burnton EAyr 224 C5
Burntwood 158 C2
Burntwood Green 158 C2
Burnworthy 103 E1
Burpham Surr 121 F2
Burpham WSuss 108 C3
Burra 279 C9
Burradon N'umb 220 B1
Burradon T&W 221 E4
Burrafirth 278 F1
Burraland 278 C5
Burras 95 D3
Burraton Corn 100 A1
Burraton Corn 100 A2
Burravoe Shet 278 E5
Burravoe Shet 279 C6
Burray 277 D8
Burrells 200 B1
Burrelton 244 A1
Burridge Devon 103 G2
Burridge Hants 107 E1
Burrill 202 B4
Burringham 187 F2
Burrington Devon 113 G4
Burrington Here 156 D5
Burrington NSom 116 B2
Burrough Green 151 E2
Burrough on the
  Hill 160 C1
Burrow Som 114 C3
Burrow Som 104 A1
Burrow Bridge 116 A4
Burrowhill 121 E1
Burrows Cross 121 F3
Burry 128 A3
Burry Green 128 A3
Burry Port 128 A2
Burscough 183 F1
Burscough Bridge 183 F1
Bursea 196 A4
Burshill 196 C3
Bursledon 107 D2
Burslem 171 F3
Burstall 152 C3
Burstock 104 A2
Burston Norf 164 C3
Burston Staffs 171 G4
Burstow 122 C4
Burstwick 197 E5
Burtersett 201 D4
Burthorpe 151 F1
Burthwaite 210 A3
Burtle 116 B3
Burtle Hill 116 A3
Burton ChesW&C 183 E5
Burton ChesW&C 170 C1
Burton Dorset 106 A3
Burton Lincs 187 G5
Burton N'umb 229 F3
Burton Pembs 126 C2
Burton Som 115 F3
Burton Wilts 132 A5
Burton Wilts 117 F3
Burton Agnes 196 D1
Burton Bradstock 104 A4
Burton Coggles 175 E5
Burton End 150 D5
Burton Ferry 126 C2
Burton Fleming 205 D5
Burton Green
  Warks 159 E5
Burton Green Wrex 170 A2
Burton Hastings 159 G4
Burton in Lonsdale 200 B5
Burton Joyce 174 B3
Burton Latimer 161 E5
Burton Lazars 160 C1
Burton Leonard 194 C1
Burton on the
  Wolds 173 G5
Burton Overy 160 B3
Burton Pedwardine 175 G3
Burton Pidsea 197 E5
Burton Salmon 195 D5
Burton Stather 187 F1
Burton upon
  Stather 187 F1
Burton upon Trent 172 D5
Burton-in-Kendal 199 G5
Burton's Green 151 G5
Burwardsley 170 C2
Burwarton 157 F4
Burwash 110 B1
Burwash Common 110 B1
Burwash Weald 110 B1
Burwell Cambs 151 D1
Burwell Lincs 189 D5
Burwen 180 C3
Burwick Ork 277 D9
Burwick Shet 279 C8
Bury Cambs 162 A4
Bury GtMan 184 C1
Bury Som 114 C5
Bury WSuss 108 C3
Bury Green 150 C5
Bury St. Edmunds 151 G1
Buryas Bridge 94 B4
Burythorpe 195 G1
Busbridge 121 E3
Busby ERenf 233 G4
Busby P&K 243 F2

Bush 112 C5
Bush Bank 145 D2
Bush Crathie 259 K5
Bush Green 170 C3
Bushbury 158 B2
Bushby 160 B2
Bushey 136 A3
Bushey Heath 136 A3
Bushey Green 146 A4
Bushley 146 A4
Bushton 132 C5
Bushy Common 178 A4
Business Design Centre,
  Islington GtLon
  N1 0QH 12 B3
Busk 210 C3
Buslingthorpe 188 A4
Bussage 132 A2
Busta 279 C6
Butcher's Common 179 E3
Butcher's Cross 110 A1
Butcher's Pasture 151 E5
Butcombe 116 C1
Bute 232 B3
Bute Town 130 A2
Buthill 267 J5
Butleigh 116 C4
Butleigh Wootton 116 C4
Butler's Cross 134 D2
Butler's Hill 173 G3
Butlers Marston 147 F3
Butlersbank 170 C5
Butley 153 E2
Butley Abbey 153 E3
Butley Low Corner 153 E3
Butley Mills 153 E2
Butley Town 184 D5
Butt Green 171 D2
Butt Lane 171 F2
Butterburn 219 E4
Buttercrambe 195 G2
Butterknowle 212 A5
Butterleigh 102 C2
Butterley 173 F2
Buttermere Cumb 209 E5
Buttermere Wilts 119 E1
Butters Green 171 F2
Buttershaw 194 A4
Butterstone 251 F5
Butterton Staffs 172 B2
Butterton Staffs 171 F3
Butterwick Dur 212 C5
Butterwick Lincs 176 B3
Butterwick NYorks 204 C5
Butterwick NYorks 203 G5
Buttington 156 B2
Buttonbridge 157 G5
Buttonoak 157 G5
Buttons' Green 152 A2
Butts 102 B4
Butt's Green
  Hants 119 D5
Buttsash 106 D2
Buxhall 152 B2
Buxted 109 G1
Buxton Derbys 185 E5
Buxton Norf 178 D3
Buxton Heath 178 C3
Buxworth 185 E4
Bwlch 144 A5
Bwlch-clawdd 141 G4
Bwlch-derwin 167 D3
Bwlchgwyn 169 E5
Bwlch-llan 142 B2
Bwlchnewydd 141 G5
Bwlch-y-cibau 156 A1
Bwlch-y-ddar 169 E5
Bwlchyfadfa 142 A3
Bwlch-y-ffridd 155 G3
Bwlch-y-groes 141 F4
Bwlchyllyn 167 E2
Bwlchymynydd 128 B3
Bwlch-y-sarnau 155 G5
Byers Green 212 B4
Byfield 148 A2
Byfleet 121 F1
Byford 144 C3
Bygrave 150 A4
Byker 221 E4
Byland Abbey 203 E5
Bylane End 97 G4
Bylchau 168 C1
Byley 171 E1
Bynea 128 B3
Byness 219 F1
Bystock 102 D4
Bythorn 161 F5
Byton 144 C1
Bywell 211 G1
Byworth 121 E5

C

Cabharstadh 271 F5
Cabourne 188 B2
Cabourne Parva 188 B2
Cabrach A&B 230 C3
Cabrach Moray 260 B2
Cabus 192 A3
Cackle Street
  ESuss 110 D2
Cackle Street
  ESuss 109 G1
Cacrabank 227 E4
Cadbury 102 C2
Cadbury Barton 113 G4
Cadbury Heath 131 F5
Cadbury World WMid
  B30 1JR 15 E5
Cadder 234 A2
Cadderlie 240 C1
Caddington 135 F1
Caddleton 239 G3
Caddonfoot 227 F2
Cade Street 110 B1
Cadeby Leics 159 G2
Cadeby SYorks 186 C2
Cadeleigh 102 C2
Cader 168 C2
Cadgwith 95 E5
Cadham 244 A4
Cadishead 184 B3
Cadle 128 C3
Cadley Lancs 192 B4
Cadley Wilts 118 D1
Cadmore End 134 C3

Cadnam 106 B1
Cadney 188 A2
Cadole 169 F1
Cadover Bridge 100 B1
Cadoxton 115 E1
Cadoxton-Juxta-
  Neath 129 D3
Cadwell 149 G4
Cadwst 168 D4
Cadzow 234 B1
Cae Ddafydd 167 F3
Caeathro 167 E1
Caehopkin 129 E1
Caen 275 F7
Caenby 188 A4
Caenby Corner 187 G4
Caer Llan 131 D2
Caerau Bridgend 129 E3
Caerau Cardiff 130 A5
Caerdeon 154 C1
Caerfarchell 140 A5
Caergeiliog 180 B5
Caergwrle 170 A2
Caerhun 181 F5
Caer-Lan 129 E1
Caerleon 130 C3
Caernarfon 167 D1
Caernarfon Castle Gwyn
  LL55 2AY 167 D1
Caerphilly 130 A4
Caersws 155 G3
Caerwedros 141 G2
Caerwent 131 D3
Caerwys 182 C5
Caethle Farm 154 C3
Caggan 259 F3
Caggle Street 130 C1
Caim Angus 252 D2
Caim IoA 181 E4
Caio 142 C4
Cairisiadar 270 C4
Cairminis 263 F3
Cairnargat 260 C1
Cairnbaan 240 A5
Cairnbeathie 260 D4
Cairnbrogie 261 D4
Cairnbulg 269 J4
Cairncross Angus 252 D2
Cairncross ScBord 237 F3
Cairncurran 233 E3
Cairndoon 207 D3
Cairndow 241 D4
Cairness 269 K4
Cairney Lodge 244 B3
Cairneyhill 235 E1
Cairngorm Mountain High
  PH22 1RB 259 H4
Cairnhill Aber 261 H2
Cairnhill Aber 260 E1
Cairnie Aber 261 G4
Cairnie Aber 268 C6
Cairnorrie 269 G6
Cairnryan 214 B4
Cairnsmore 215 F4
Caister-on-Sea 179 G4
Caistor 188 B2
Caistor St. Edmund 178 D5
Caistron 220 B1
Caithness Crystal Visitor
  Centre Norf
  PE30 4NE 163 E1
Cake Street 164 B2
Cakebole 158 A5
Calbost 271 G6
Calbourne 106 D4
Calceby 189 E5
Calcoed 182 C5
Calcot 134 B5
Calcott Kent 125 D2
Calcott Shrop 156 D1
Calcotts Green 131 G1
Calcutt 132 D3
Caldarvan 233 F1
Caldback 278 F2
Caldbeck 209 G3
Caldbergh 201 F4
Caldecote Cambs 150 B2
Caldecote Cambs 161 G4
Caldecote Herts 150 A4
Caldecote N'hants 148 B2
Caldecott N'hants 149 E1
Caldecott Oxon 133 G3
Caldecott Rut 161 D3
Calder Bridge 198 B2
Calder Grove 186 A1
Calder Mains 275 F3
Calder Vale 192 B3
Calderbank 234 B3
Calderbrook 184 D1
Caldercruix 234 C3
Calderglen 234 A4
Calderglen Country Park
  SLan G75 0QZ 31 E6
Caldermill 234 A1
Caldey Island 127 E3
Caldhame 252 C5
Caldicot 131 D4
Caldwell Derbys 159 F1
Caldwell ERenf 233 F4
Caldwell NYorks 202 A1
Caldy 182 D4
Calebreck 209 G3
Caledrhydiau 142 A2
Calford Green 151 E3
Calfsound 276 E4
Calgary 246 C4
Califer 267 H6
California Falk 234 D2
California Norf 179 G4
California Suff 152 D3
California Country Park
  W'ham
  RG40 4HT 120 C1
Calke 173 E5
Calke Abbey Derbys
  DE73 7LE 173 E5
Callakille 266 C6
Callaly 220 C1
Callander 242 B4
Callanish (Calanais) 270 E4
Callaughton 157 F3
Callerton Lane End 212 A1
Calliburn 222 C3
Calligarry 256 C4
Callington 99 D4
Callingwood 172 C5
Callisterhall 218 A3

Callow 145 D4
Callow End 146 A3
Callow Hill *Wilts* 132 C4
Callow Hill *Worcs* 157 G5
Callow Hill *Worcs* 146 C1
Callows Grave 145 E1
Calmore 106 C1
Calmsden 132 C2
Calne 132 B5
Calow 186 B5
Calrossie 266 E4
Calshot 107 D2
Calstock 100 A1
Calstone
  Wellington 118 B1
Calthorpe 178 C2
Calthwaite 210 A3
Calton *NYorks* 193 F2
Calton *Staffs* 172 C2
Calveley 170 C2
Calver 185 G5
Calver Hill 144 C3
Calverhall 170 D4
Calverleigh 102 C1
Calverley 194 B4
Calvert 148 B5
Calverton *MK* 148 C4
Calverton *Notts* 174 B3
Calvine 250 C3
Calvo 209 E1
Cam 131 G3
Camasnacroise 248 A4
Camastianavaig 256 B1
Camasunary 256 B3
Camault Muir 266 C7
Camb 278 E2
Camber 111 E2
Camberley 121 D1
Camberwell 136 C5
Camblesforth 195 F5
Cambo 220 C3
Cambois 221 F3
Camborne 95 D3
Cambourne 150 B2
Cambridge *Cambs* 150 C2
Cambridge *Glos* 131 G2
Cambridge American
  Military Cemetery &
  Memorial *Cambs*
  CB23 7PH 150 B2
Cambridge City
  Airport 150 C2
Cambridge University
  Botanic Garden *Cambs*
  CB2 1JF 150 C2
Cambus 243 F5
Cambus o'May 260 C5
Cambusbarron 242 C5
Cambuskenneth 242 D5
Cambuslang 234 C4
Cambusnethan 234 C4
Camden Town 136 B4
Camel Hill 116 C5
Camel Trail *Corn*
  PL27 7AL 97 D2
Cameley 116 D2
Camelford 97 F1
Camelon 234 C1
Camelot Theme Park
  Lancs PR7 5LP 183 G1
Camelsdale 121 D4
Camer 123 F2
Cameron House 233 E1
Camerory 259 H1
Camer's Green 145 G4
Camerton
  B&NESom 117 D2
Camerton *Cumb* 208 D3
Camerton *ERid* 197 E5
Camghouran 250 A4
Camis Eskan 233 E1
Cammachmore 261 H5
Cammeringham 187 G4
Camore 266 E2
Camp Hill *Pembs* 127 E1
Camp Hill *Warks* 159 F3
Campbeltown (Ceann Loch
  Chille Chiarain) 222 C3
Campbeltown
  Airport 222 B3
Camperdown 221 E4
Camperdown Country
  Park *Dundee*
  DD2 4TF 244 B1
Campmuir 244 A1
Camps 235 F3
Camps End 151 E3
Camps Heath 165 G2
Campsall 186 C5
Campsea Ashe 153 E2
Campton 149 G4
Camptown 228 A5
Camquhart 232 A1
Camrose 140 C5
Camserney 250 D5
Camstraddan
  House 241 F5
Camus Croise 256 C3
Camus-luinie 257 F2
Camusnagaul *High* 248 C2
Camusnagaul *High* 265 G3
Camusrory 256 E5
Camusteel 264 D7
Camusterrach 242 D7
Camusurich 242 B1
Camusvrachan 250 B5
Canada 106 B1
Canaston Bridge 127 D1
Candacraig 260 B5
Candlesby 176 C1
Candy Mill 235 E5
Cane End 134 B5
Canewdon 138 B3
Canfield End 151 D5
Canford Bottom 105 G2
Canford Cliffs 105 G4
Canford Heath 105 G3
Canford Magna 105 G3
Canham's Green 152 B1
Canisbay 275 J1
Canley 159 F5
Cann 117 F5
Cann Common 117 F5
Canna 255 H4
Cannard's Grave 116 D3
Cannich (Canaich) 257 K1
Canning Town 136 D4
Cannington 115 F4

Cannock 158 B2
Cannock Wood 158 C1
Cannon Hall Country Park
  SYorks S75 4AT 185 G2
Cannon Hall Farm *SYorks*
  S75 4AT 185 G2
Cannon Hill Park *WMid*
  B13 8RD 15 C4
Cannop 131 F1
Canon Bridge 144 D3
Canon Frome 145 F3
Canon Pyon 145 D3
Canonbie 218 B4
Canons Ashby 148 A2
Canon's Town 94 C3
Canterbury *Aber* 268 D5
Canterbury *Kent* 124 D3
Canterbury Cathedral
  Kent CT1 2EH
  67 Canterbury
Canterbury Tales, The
  Kent CT1 2TG
  67 Canterbury
Cantley *Norf* 179 E5
Cantley *SYorks* 186 D2
Cantlop 157 E2
Canton 130 A5
Cantray 266 E7
Cantraydoune 266 E7
Cantraywood 266 E7
Cantsfield 200 B5
Canvey Island 137 G4
Canwell Hall 158 D2
Canwick 175 E1
Canworthy Water 98 C1
Caol 248 D2
Caolas *A&B* 246 B2
Caolas *ESiar* 254 B5
Caolasnacon 248 D3
Capel *Kent* 123 F4
Capel *Surr* 121 G3
Capel Bangor 154 C4
Capel Betws Lleucu 142 C2
Capel Carmel 166 A5
Capel Celyn 168 B3
Capel Coch 180 C4
Capel Curig 168 A2
Capel Cynon 142 A3
Capel Dewi *Carmar* 142 A5
Capel Dewi *Cere* 154 C4
Capel Dewi *Cere* 142 A3
Capel Garmon 168 B2
Capel Gwyn
  Carmar 142 A5
Capel Gwyn *IoA* 180 B5
Capel Gwynfe 142 D5
Capel Hendre 128 B1
Capel Isaac 142 B5
Capel Iwan 141 F4
Capel le Ferne 125 E5
Capel Llanilltern 129 G4
Capel Mawr 180 C5
Capel Parc 180 C3
Capel St. Andrew 153 E3
Capel St. Mary 152 B4
Capel St. Silin 142 B2
Capel Seion 154 C5
Capel Tygwydd 141 F3
Capeluchaf 166 D2
Capelulo 181 F5
Capel-y-ffin 144 B4
Capel-y-graig 167 E1
Capenhurst 183 E5
Capernwray 199 G3
Capheaton 220 C3
Caplaw 233 F4
Capon's Green 153 D1
Cappercleuch 226 D3
Capplegill 218 B5
Capstone 123 G2
Capton *Devon* 101 E2
Capton *Som* 115 D4
Caputh 251 F5
Car Colston 174 C3
Caradon Town 97 G2
Carbellow 225 E3
Carbeth 233 G2
Carbis Bay 94 C3
Carbost *High* 263 K7
Carbost *High* 255 J1
Carbrain 234 B2
Carbrooke 178 A5
Carburton 186 D5
Carcary 253 F4
Carco 225 F4
Carcroft 186 C1
Cardenden 244 A5
Cardeston 156 C1
Cardew 209 G2
Cardiff
  (Caerdydd) 130 A5
Cardiff Bay Visitor Centre
  Cardiff CF10 4PA 7 C4
Cardiff Castle & Museum
  CF10 3RB 67 Cardiff
Cardiff International
  Airport 115 D1
Cardiff Millennium
  Stadium CF10 1GE
  67 Cardiff
Cardigan (Aberteifi) 141 E3
Cardinal's Green 151 E3
Cardington *Bed* 149 F3
Cardington *Shrop* 157 E3
Cardinham 97 F3
Cardno 269 H4
Cardonald 233 G3
Cardoness 215 G5
Cardow 267 J7
Cardrona 227 D2
Cardross 233 E2
Cardurnock 209 E1
Careby 161 F1
Careston 252 D4
Carew 126 D2
Carew Cheriton 126 D2
Carew Newton 126 D2
Carey 145 E4
Carfin 234 B4
Carfrae 236 C3
Carfraemill 236 C2
Cargate Green 179 E4
Cargen 217 D3
Cargenbridge 217 D3
Cargill 243 G1
Cargo 209 G1
Cargreen 100 A1
Carham 228 B3

Carhampton 114 D3
Carharrack 96 B5
Carie *P&K* 250 B4
Carie *P&K* 242 B1
Carines 96 B4
Carinish (Cairinis) 262 D5
Carisbrooke 107 D4
Carisbrooke Castle &
  Museum *IoW*
  PO30 1XY 107 D4
Cark 199 E5
Carkeel 100 A1
Carland Cross 96 C4
Carlatton 210 B2
Carlby 161 F1
Carlecotes 185 F2
Carleen 94 D4
Carleton *Cumb* 210 A2
Carleton *Cumb* 210 B5
Carleton *Lancs* 191 G3
Carleton *NYorks* 193 F3
Carleton *WYorks* 195 D5
Carleton Fishery 214 C2
Carleton Forehoe 178 B5
Carleton Rode 164 C2
Carleton St. Peter 179 E5
Carlin How 203 G1
Carlincraig 268 E6
Carlisle 210 A2
Carlisle Cathedral
  Cumb CA3 8TZ
  68 Carlisle
Carlisle Park,
  Morpeth *N'umb*
  NE61 1YD 221 D3
Carloggas 96 C3
Carlops 235 F4
Carloway
  (Càrlabhagh) 270 E3
Carlton *Bed* 149 E2
Carlton *Cambs* 151 E2
Carlton *Leics* 159 F2
Carlton *Notts* 174 B3
Carlton *NYorks* 195 E5
Carlton *NYorks* 201 E4
Carlton *NYorks* 203 E1
Carlton *Stock* 212 C5
Carlton *Suff* 153 E1
Carlton *SYorks* 186 A1
Carlton *WYorks* 194 C4
Carlton Colville 165 G2
Carlton Curlieu 160 B3
Carlton Green 151 E2
Carlton Husthwaite 203 D5
Carlton in Lindrick 186 C4
Carlton Miniott 202 C4
Carlton Scroop 175 E3
Carlton-in-
  Cleveland 203 E2
Carlton-le-
  Moorland 175 E2
Carlton-on-Trent 174 D1
Carluke 234 C5
Carlyon Bay 97 E4
Carmacoup 225 F3
Carmarthen
  (Caerfyrddin) 142 A5
Carmel *Carmar* 128 B1
Carmel *Flints* 182 C5
Carmel *Gwyn* 167 D2
Carmel *IoA* 180 B4
Carmichael 226 A2
Carmont 253 G1
Carmunnock 233 G4
Carmyle 234 A3
Carmyllie 253 D5
Carn 230 A4
Carn Brea Village 96 A5
Carn Dearg 264 D4
Carnaby 196 D1
Carnach *High* 257 G2
Carnach *High* 265 G2
Carnach *ESiar* 262 D5
Carnan 262 C7
Carnassarie 240 A4
Carnbee 244 D4
Carnbo 243 F4
Carndu 256 E2
Carnduncan 230 A3
Carnforth 199 F5
Carnhedryn 140 B5
Carnhell Green 94 D3
Carnichal 269 H5
Carnkie *Corn* 95 D3
Carnkie *Corn* 95 E3
Carnmore 230 B5
Carno 155 F3
Carnoch *High* 257 K1
Carnoch *High* 257 J6
Carnoch *High* 267 F7
Carnock 235 E1
Carnon Downs 96 C5
Carnousie 245 D1
Carntyne 234 A3
Carnwath 235 D5
Carnyorth 94 A3
Carol Green 159 E5
Carperby 201 F4
Carr 186 C3
Carr Hill 187 D3
Carr Houses 183 E2
Carr Shield 211 E3
Carr Vale 186 B5
Carradale 222 D2
Carragrich 263 G2
Carrbridge 259 G2
Carrefour Selous 100 C5
Carreglefn 180 B4
Carreg-wen 141 F3
Carrhouse 187 E2
Carrick 232 A1
Carrick Castle 241 D5
Carriden 235 E1
Carrine 222 B5
Carrington *GtMan* 184 B3
Carrington *Lincs* 176 B2
Carrington *Midlo* 236 A3
Carroch 216 A1
Carrol 267 F1
Carron *A&B* 240 B5
Carron *Falk* 234 C1
Carron *Moray* 267 K7
Carron Bridge 234 B1
Carronbridge 216 C1
Carronshore 234 C1

Carrot 252 C5
Carrow Hill 130 D3
Carrutherstown 217 F3
Carrutchie 233 E3
Carrville 212 C3
Carry 232 A3
Carsaig 239 E2
Carscreugh 214 D4
Carse 231 F3
Carse of Ardersier 267 F6
Carsegowan 215 F5
Carseriggan 215 E4
Carsethorn 217 D5
Carsgoe 275 G2
Carshalton 122 B2
Carshalton Beeches 122 B2
Carsie 251 G5
Carsington 173 D2
Carsington Water *Derbys*
  DE6 1ST 172 D2
Carsluith 215 F5
Carsphairn 215 G1
Carstairs 234 D5
Carstairs Junction 235 D5
Carswell Marsh 133 F3
Carter's Clay 119 E5
Carterton 133 F2
Carterway Heads 211 G2
Carthew 97 E4
Carthorpe 202 C4
Cartington 220 C1
Cartland 234 C5
Cartmel 199 E5
Cartmel Fell 199 F4
Cartworth 185 F2
Carway 128 A2
Carwinley 218 B4
Cascades Adventure
  Pool *Devon*
  EX33 1NZ 113 E2
Cascob 144 B1
Cashel Farm 241 G5
Cashes Green 132 A2
Cashlie 249 G5
Cashmoor 105 F1
Caskieberran 244 A4
Cassencarie 215 F5
Cassington 133 G1
Cassop 212 C4
Castell 168 A1
Castell Gorfod 141 F5
Castell Howell 142 A3
Castellau 129 G4
Castell-y-bwch 130 B3
Casterton 200 B5
Castle Acre 163 G1
Castle Ashby 149 D2
Castle Bolton 201 F3
Castle Bromwich 158 D4
Castle Bytham 161 E1
Castle Caereinion 156 A2
Castle Camps 151 E3
Castle Carrock 210 B2
Castle Cary 116 D4
Castle Combe 132 A5
Castle Donington 173 F5
Castle Douglas 216 B4
Castle Drogo *Devon*
  EX6 6PB 102 A4
Castle Eaton 132 D3
Castle Eden 212 D4
Castle Eden Dene National
  Nature Reserve *Dur*
  SR8 1NJ 212 D4
Castle End 116 B3
Castle Frome 145 F3
Castle Gate 94 B3
Castle Goring 108 D3
Castle Green 121 E1
Castle Gresley 159 E1
Castle Heaton 237 G5
Castle Hedingham 151 F4
Castle Hill *Kent* 123 F4
Castle Hill *Suff* 152 C3
Castle Howard *NYorks*
  YO60 7DA 195 G1
Castle Kennedy 214 C5
Castle Leod 266 B6
Castle Levan 232 D2
Castle Madoc 143 G4
Castle Morris 140 C4
Castle O'er 218 A2
Castle Rising 177 E5
Castle Semple Water
  Country Park *Renf*
  PA12 4HJ 233 E4
Castle Stuart 266 E7
Castlebay (Bàgh
  a'Chaisteil) 254 B5
Castlebythe 140 D5
Castlecary 234 B2
Castlecraig *High* 267 F5
Castlecraig *ScBord* 235 H5
Castlefairn 216 B2
Castleford 194 D5
Castlehill *Stir* 242 A5
Castlemartin 126 C3
Castlemilk *D&G* 217 F3
Castlemilk *Glas* 234 A4
Castlemorton 145 G4
Castleside 211 G3
Castlesteads 210 B1
Castlethorpe 148 C3
Castleton *A&B* 231 G1
Castleton *Angus* 252 B5
Castleton *Derbys* 185 F4
Castleton *GtMan* 184 C1
Castleton *Newport* 130 B4
Castleton *NYorks* 203 F2
Castletown *Dorset* 104 C5
Castletown *High* 275 G2
Castletown *High* 266 E7
Castletown *IoM* 190 A5
Castletown *T&W* 212 C2
Castleweary 227 F5
Castlewigg 207 E2
Castley 194 B3
Caston 164 A2
Castor 161 G3
Castramont 215 G4
Caswell 128 B4
Cat & Fiddle Inn 185 E5
Catacol 232 A4
Catbrain 131 E4
Catbrook 131 E2
Catchall 94 B4
Catcleugh 219 F1

Catcliffe 186 B4
Catcott 116 A4
Caterham 122 C3
Catfield 179 E3
Catfirth 279 D7
Catford 136 C5
Catforth 192 A4
Cathays 130 A5
Cathcart 233 G3
Cathedine 144 A5
Catherine-de-
  Barnes 159 D4
Catherington 107 F1
Catherston
  Leweston 103 G3
Cathkin 234 A4
Catisfield 107 E2
Catlodge 258 D5
Catlowdy 218 C4
Catmere End 150 C4
Catmore 133 G4
Caton *Devon* 102 A5
Caton *Lancs* 192 B1
Caton Green 192 B1
Cator Court 99 G3
Catrine 224 D3
Catsfield 110 C5
Catsfield Stream 110 C5
Catshaw 185 G2
Catshill 158 B5
Cattadale 230 B3
Cattal 194 D2
Cattawade 152 B4
Catterall 192 B3
Catterick 202 B3
Catterick Bridge 202 B3
Catterick Garrison 202 A3
Catterlen 210 A4
Catterline 253 G2
Catterton 195 E3
Catthorpe 160 A5
Cattishall 151 G1
Cattistock 104 B2
Catton *N'umb* 211 E2
Catton *Norf* 178 D4
Catton *NYorks* 202 C5
Catton Hall 159 E1
Catwick 196 D3
Catworth 161 F5
Caudle Green 132 B1
Caudwell's Mill & Craft
  Centre *Derbys*
  DE4 2EB 173 D1
Caulcott *CenBeds* 149 F3
Caulcott *Oxon* 148 A5
Cauldcots 253 E5
Cauldhame *Stir* 242 B5
Cauldhame *Stir* 242 B5
Cauldon 172 B3
Caulkerbush 216 D5
Caulside 218 C3
Caundle Marsh 104 C1
Caunsall 158 A4
Caunton 174 C1
Causeway End
  D&G 215 F4
Causeway End
  Essex 137 F1
Causeway End
  Lancs 183 F1
Causewayhead
  Cumb 209 E1
Causewayhead
  Stir 242 D5
Causey 212 B2
Causey Arch Picnic Area
  Dur NE16 5EG 28 A4
Causey Park 221 D2
Causeyend 261 H3
Cautley 200 B3
Cavendish 151 G3
Cavendish Bridge 173 F5
Cavenham 151 F1
Cavens 217 D5
Cavers 227 G4
Caversfield 148 A5
Caversham 134 C5
Caverswall 171 G3
Cawdor 267 F6
Cawkeld 196 B2
Cawkwell 188 C4
Cawood 195 E4
Cawsand 100 A3
Cawston *Norf* 178 C3
Cawston *Warks* 159 G5
Cawthorne 185 G2
Cawthorpe 175 F5
Cawton 203 F5
Caxton 150 B2
Caxton Gibbet 150 A1
Caynham 157 E5
Caythorpe *Lincs* 175 E3
Caythorpe *Notts* 174 B3
Cayton 205 D4
Ceallan 262 D6
Ceann a' Bhàigh
  ESiar 262 C5
Ceann a' Bhàigh
  ESiar 263 F3
Ceann Loch
  Shiphoirt 270 E6
Ceannaridh 262 D6
Cearsiadar 271 F6
Cedig 168 C3
Cefn Berain 168 C1
Cefn Canol 169 F4
Cefn Coch *Denb* 169 D5
Cefn Coch *Powys* 155 G2
Cefn Cribwr 129 E4
Cefn Cross 129 E4
Cefn Einion 156 B4
Cefn Hengoed 130 A3
Cefn Llwyd 154 C4
Cefn Rhigos 129 F2
Cefn-brith 168 C3
Cefn-bryn-brain 128 D1
Cefn-caer-Ferch 166 D3
Cefn-coch 169 E5
Cefn-coed-y-
  cymmer 129 G2
Cefn-ddwysarn 168 C4
Cefndeuddwr 168 A5
Cefneithin 128 B1

Cefn-gorwydd 143 F3
Cefn-gwyn 156 A4
Cefn-mawr 169 F3
Cefnpennar 129 G2
Cefn-y-bedd 170 A2
Cefn-y-pant 141 E5
Ceidio 180 C4
Ceidio Fawr 166 B4
Ceint 180 C5
Cellan 142 C3
Cellardyke 245 D4
Cellarhead 171 G3
Cemaes 180 B3
Cemmaes 155 E2
Cemmaes Road
  (Glantwymyn) 155 E2
Cenarth 141 F3
Cennin 167 D3
Centre for Life
  T&W NE1 4EP
  79 Newcastle upon Tyne
Ceramica *Stoke*
  ST6 3DS 20 C2
Ceres 244 C3
Cerist 155 F3
Cerne Abbas 104 C2
Cerney Wick 132 C3
Cerrigceinwen 180 C5
Cerrigydrudion 168 C3
Cessford 228 B4
Ceunant 167 E1
Chaceley 146 A4
Chacewater 96 B5
Chackmore 148 B4
Chacombe 147 G3
Chad Valley 158 C4
Chadderton 184 D2
Chadderton Fold 184 C2
Chaddesden 173 E4
Chaddesley Corbett 158 A5
Chaddleworth 133 G5
Chadlington 147 F5
Chadshunt 147 F2
Chadstone 149 D2
Chadwell *Leics* 174 C5
Chadwell *Shrop* 157 G1
Chadwell St. Mary 137 F5
Chadwick End 159 E5
Chaffcombe 103 G1
Chafford Hundred 137 F5
Chagford 102 A4
Chailey 109 F2
Chainhurst 123 G4
Chalbury 105 G2
Chalbury Common 105 G2
Chaldon 122 C3
Chaldon Herring (East
  Chaldon) 105 D4
Chale 107 D5
Chale Green 107 D4
Chalfont Common 135 F3
Chalfont St. Giles 135 E3
Chalfont St. Peter 135 F3
Chalford *Glos* 132 A2
Chalford *Wilts* 117 F3
Chalgrove 134 B3
Chalk 137 F5
Chalk End 137 F1
Challaborough 100 C3
Challacombe 113 G1
Challister 279 E6
Challoch 215 E4
Challock 124 C3
Chalmington 104 B2
Chalton *CenBeds* 149 F3
Chalton *Hants* 107 G1
Chalvey 135 E5
Chalvington 110 A3
Champany 235 E1
Chancery 154 B5
Chandler's Cross 135 F3
Chandler's Ford 119 E5
Channel Islands 100 A5
Channel's End 149 G2
Channerwick 279 D10
Chantry *Som* 117 E3
Chantry *Suff* 152 C3
Chapel 244 A5
Chapel Allerton
  Som 116 B2
Chapel Allerton
  WYorks 194 C4
Chapel Amble 97 D2
Chapel Brampton 148 C1
Chapel Chorlton 171 F4
Chapel Cleeve 114 D3
Chapel Cross 110 B1
Chapel End 149 F3
Chapel Green
  Warks 159 E4
Chapel Green
  Warks 147 G1
Chapel Haddlesey 195 E5
Chapel Hill *Aber* 261 J1
Chapel Hill *Lincs* 176 A2
Chapel Hill *Mon* 131 E2
Chapel Hill *NYorks* 194 C3
Chapel Knapp 117 F1
Chapel Lawn 156 C5
Chapel Leigh 115 E5
Chapel Milton 185 E4
Chapel of Garioch 261 F2
Chapel Rossan 206 B2
Chapel Row *Essex* 137 G2
Chapel Row
  WBerks 119 G1
Chapel St. Leonards 189 F5
Chapel Stile 199 E2
Chapel Town 96 C4
Chapelbank 243 F3
Chapeldonan 223 G5
Chapelend Way 151 F4
Chapel-en-le-Frith 185 E4
Chapelgate 176 C5
Chapelhall 234 B3
Chapelhill *High* 267 F5
Chapelhill *P&K* 244 A2
Chapelhill *P&K* 243 F1
Chapelknowe 218 B4
Chapel-le-Dale 200 C5
Chapelthorpe 186 A1
Chapelton *Aber* 253 G1
Chapelton *Angus* 253 E5
Chapelton *Devon* 113 F3
Chapelton *SLan* 234 A5
Chapeltown *B'burn* 184 B1
Chapeltown *Cumb* 218 C4
Chapeltown *Moray* 259 K2

Chapeltown *SYorks* 186 A3
Chapmans Well 99 D1
Chapmanslade 117 F3
Chapmore End 136 C1
Chappel 151 G5
Charaton 98 D4
Chard 103 G2
Chard Junction 103 G2
Chardleigh Green 103 G1
Chardstock 103 G2
Charfield 131 G3
Charing 124 B4
Charing Cross 106 A1
Charing Heath 124 B4
Charingworth 147 D4
Charlbury 133 F1
Charlcombe 117 E1
Charlecote 147 E2
Charles 113 G2
Charles Tye 152 B2
Charlesfield 227 G3
Charleshill 121 D3
Charleston 252 B5
Charlestown
  Aberdeen 261 H4
Charlestown *Corn* 97 E4
Charlestown
  Derbys 185 E3
Charlestown
  Dorset 104 C5
Charlestown *Fife* 235 E1
Charlestown
  GtMan 184 C2
Charlestown *High* 264 E4
Charlestown *High* 266 D7
Charlestown
  WYorks 194 A4
Charlestown
  WYorks 193 F5
Charlestown of Aberlour
  (Aberlour) 267 K7
Charlesworth 185 E3
Charleton 244 C4
Charlinch 115 F4
Charlotteville 121 F3
Charlton *GtLon* 136 D5
Charlton *Hants* 119 E3
Charlton *Herts* 149 G5
Charlton *N'hants* 148 A4
Charlton *N'umb* 220 B1
Charlton *Oxon* 133 G4
Charlton *Som* 117 D2
Charlton *Som* 116 D3
Charlton *Som* 115 F5
Charlton *Tel&W* 157 E1
Charlton *Wilts* 118 A5
Charlton *Wilts* 132 B4
Charlton *Wilts* 118 C2
Charlton *Worcs* 146 C3
Charlton *WSuss* 108 A2
Charlton Abbots 146 C5
Charlton Adam 116 C5
Charlton Down 104 C3
Charlton
  Horethorne 117 D5
Charlton Kings 146 B5
Charlton Mackrell 116 C5
Charlton Marshall 105 E2
Charlton Musgrove 117 E5
Charlton on the Hill 105 E2
Charlton All Saints 118 C5
Charlton-on-
  Otmoor 134 A1
Charltons 203 F1
Charlwood 122 B4
Charminster 104 C3
Charmouth 103 G3
Charndon 148 B5
Charney Bassett 133 F3
Charnock Richard 183 G1
Charsfield 153 D2
Chart Corner 123 G4
Chart Sutton 124 A4
Charter Alley 119 G2
Charterhouse 116 B2
Charterville
  Allotments 133 F2
Chartham 124 D3
Chartham Hatch 124 D3
Chartridge 135 E2
Chartwell
  Kent TN16 1PS 123 D3
Charvil 134 C5
Charwelton 148 A2
Chase End Street 145 G4
Chase Terrace 158 C2
Chasetown 158 C2
Chastleton 147 E5
Chasty 112 D5
Chatburn 193 D3
Chatcull 171 E4
Chatham 123 G2
Chatham Green 137 G1
Chatham Historic
  Dockyard *Med*
  ME4 4TZ 123 G2
Chathill 229 F4
Chatsworth Farmyard &
  Adventure Playground
  Derbys
  DE45 1PP 185 G5
Chatsworth House *Derbys*
  DE45 1PP 185 G5
Chattenden 137 G5
Chatteris 162 B4
Chattisham 152 B3
Chatto 228 B5
Chatton 229 E4
Chaul End 149 F5
Chavey Down 121 D1
Chawleigh 102 A1
Chawley 133 G2
Chawston 149 G2
Chawton 120 C4
Chazey Heath 134 B5
Cheadle *GtMan* 184 C4
Cheadle *Staffs* 172 B3
Cheadle Heath 184 C4
Cheadle Hulme 184 C4
Cheam 122 B2
Cheapside 121 E1
Chearsley 134 C1
Chebsey 171 F5
Checkendon 134 B4

Checkley *ChesE* 171 E3
Checkley *Here* 145 E4
Checkley *Staffs* 172 B4
Checkley Green 171 E3
Chedburgh 151 F2
Cheddar 116 B2
Cheddar Caves & Gorge
 Som BS27 3QF 116 B2
Cheddington 135 E1
Cheddleton 171 G2
Chedglow 132 B3
Chedgrave 165 E2
Chedington 104 A2
Chediston 165 E4
Chediston Green 165 E4
Chedworth 132 C1
Chedzoy 116 A4
Cheesden 184 C1
Cheeseman's Green 124 C5
Cheetham Hill 184 C2
Cheglinch 113 E1
Cheldon 102 A1
Chelford 184 C5
Chellaston 173 E4
Chells 150 A5
Chelmarsh 157 G4
Chelmondiston 152 D4
Chelmorton 172 C1
Chelmsford 137 G2
Chelmsford Cathedral
 Essex CM1 1TY 137 G2
Chelmsley Wood 159 D4
Chelsea 136 B5
Chelsfield 123 D2
Chelsham 122 C3
Chelston Heath 115 E5
Chelsworth 152 A3
Cheltenham 146 B5
Chelveston 149 E1
Chelvey 116 B1
Chelwood 116 D1
Chelwood Common 109 G1
Chelwood Gate 109 G1
Chelworth 132 B3
Cheney Longville 156 D4
Chenies 135 F3
Chepstow
 (Cas-gwent) 131 E3
Cherhill 132 C5
Cherington *Glos* 132 B3
Cherington *Warks* 147 E4
Cheriton *Devon* 114 A3
Cheriton *Hants* 119 G5
Cheriton *Kent* 125 D5
Cheriton *Pembs* 127 D3
Cheriton *Swan* 128 A3
Cheriton Bishop 102 A3
Cheriton Cross 102 A3
Cheriton Fitzpaine 102 B2
Cherrington 171 D5
Cherry Burton 196 B3
Cherry Green 151 D5
Cherry Hinton 150 C2
Cherry Willingham 188 A5
Chertsey 121 F1
Cheselbourne 105 D3
Chesham 135 F2
Chesham Bois 135 E2
Cheshire Farm Ice Cream,
 Tattenhall *ChesW&C*
 CH3 9NE 170 B2
Cheshunt 136 C2
Cheslyn Hay 158 B2
Chessington 121 G1
Chessington World of
 Adventures *GtLon*
 KT9 2NE 121 G1
Chestall 158 C1
Chester 170 B1
Chester Cathedral
 ChesW&C CH1 2HU
 69 Chester
Chester Moor 212 B3
Chester Zoo *ChesW&C*
 CH2 1LH 183 F5
Chesterblade 117 D3
Chesterfield
 Derbys 186 A5
Chesterfield *Staffs* 158 D2
Chester-le-Street 212 B2
Chesters *ScBord* 228 A5
Chesters *ScBord* 228 A5
Chesterton *Cambs* 150 C1
Chesterton *Cambs* 161 G3
Chesterton *Oxon* 148 A5
Chesterton *Shrop* 157 G3
Chesterton *Staffs* 171 F3
Chesterton *Warks* 147 F2
Chesterton Green 147 F2
Chestfield 124 D2
Cheston 100 C2
Cheswardine 171 E5
Cheswick 229 E2
Cheswick Buildings 229 E2
Cheswick Green 158 D5
Chetnole 104 C2
Chettiscombe 102 C1
Chettisham 162 D4
Chettle 105 F1
Chetton 157 F3
Chetwode 148 B5
Chetwynd Aston 157 G1
Chetwynd Park 171 E5
Cheveley 151 E1
Chevening 123 D3
Cheverell's Green 135 F1
Chevin Forest Park *WYorks*
 LS21 3JL 194 B3
Chevington 151 F2
Chevithorne 102 C1
Chew Magna 116 C1
Chew Moor 184 A2
Chew Stoke 116 C1
Chewton
 Keynsham 116 D1
Chewton Mendip 116 C2
Chicacott 99 G1
Chicheley 149 E3
Chichester 108 A3
Chichester Cathedral *WSuss*
 PO19 1PX 108 A3
Chickerell 104 C4
Chickering 164 D4
Chicklade 118 A4
Chickney 151 D5
Chicksands 149 G4
Chidden 107 F1

Chidden Holt 107 F1
Chiddingfold 121 E4
Chiddingly 110 A2
Chiddingstone 123 D4
Chiddingstone
 Causeway 123 E4
Chiddingstone
 Hoath 123 D4
Chideock 104 A3
Chidham 107 G2
Chidswell 194 B5
Chieveley 133 G5
Chignall St. James 137 F2
Chignall Smealy 137 F1
Chigwell 136 D3
Chigwell Row 137 D3
Chilbolton 119 E3
Chilcomb 119 G5
Chilcombe 104 B3
Chilcompton 117 D2
Chilcote 159 E1
Child Okeford 105 E1
Childer Thornton 183 E5
Childerditch 137 F4
Childrey 133 F4
Child's Ercall 171 D5
Childs Hill 136 B4
Childswickham 146 C4
Childwall 183 F4
Childwick Green 136 A1
Chilfrome 104 B3
Chilgrove 108 A2
Chilham 124 C3
Chilhampton 118 B4
Chilla 113 E1
Chillaton 99 E2
Chillenden 125 E3
Chillerton 107 D4
Chillesford 153 E2
Chilley 101 D2
Chillingham 229 E4
Chillington *Devon* 101 D3
Chillington *Som* 103 G1
Chilmark 118 A4
Chilson *Oxon* 133 F1
Chilson *Som* 103 G2
Chilsworthy *Corn* 99 E3
Chilsworthy *Devon* 112 D5
Chilthorne Domer 104 B1
Chilton *Bucks* 134 B1
Chilton *Devon* 102 B3
Chilton *Dur* 212 B5
Chilton *Oxon* 133 G4
Chilton *Suff* 151 G3
Chilton Candover 119 G4
Chilton Cantelo 116 C5
Chilton Foliat 133 F5
Chilton Polden 116 A4
Chilton Street 151 F3
Chilton Trinity 115 F4
Chilvers Coton 159 F3
Chilwell 173 G4
Chilworth *Hants* 106 D1
Chilworth *Surr* 121 F3
Chimney 133 F2
Chimney Street 151 F3
Chineham 120 B2
Chingford 136 C3
Chinley 185 E4
Chinley Head 185 E4
Chinnor 134 C2
Chipchase Castle 220 A4
Chipley 115 E5
Chipnall 171 E4
Chippenham
 Cambs 151 E1
Chippenham *Wilts* 132 B5
Chipperfield 135 F2
Chipping *Herts* 150 B4
Chipping *Lancs* 192 C3
Chipping Campden 147 D4
Chipping Hill 138 B1
Chipping Norton 147 F5
Chipping Ongar 137 E2
Chipping Sodbury 131 G4
Chipping Warden 147 G3
Chipstable 114 C5
Chipstead *Kent* 123 D3
Chipstead *Surr* 122 B3
Chirbury 156 B3
Chirk (Y Waun) 169 F4
Chirk Green 169 F4
Chirmorrie 214 D3
Chirnside 237 F4
Chirnsidebridge 237 F4
Chirton *T&W* 212 C1
Chirton *Wilts* 118 B2
Chisbury 119 D1
Chiscan 222 B4
Chiselborough 104 A1
Chiseldon 133 D5
Chiserley 193 G5
Chislehampton 134 A3
Chislehurst 136 D5
Chislet 125 E2
Chiswell Green 136 A2
Chiswick 136 B5
Chiswick End 150 B3
Chisworth 185 D3
Chithurst 120 D5
Chittering 162 C5
Chitterne 118 A3
Chittlehamholt 113 G3
Chittlehampton 113 G3
Chittoe 118 A1
Chivelstone 101 D4
Chivenor 113 F2
Chobham 121 E1
Choicelee 237 E4
Cholderton 118 D3
Cholesbury 135 E2
Chollerford 220 B4
Chollerton 220 B4
Cholmondeston 170 D2
Cholsey 134 A4
Cholstrey 145 D2
Cholwell
 B&NESom 116 D2
Cholwell *Devon* 99 E3
Chop Gate 203 E3
Choppington 221 E3
Chopwell 212 A2
Chorley *ChesE* 170 C2
Chorley *Lancs* 183 G1
Chorley *Shrop* 157 F4
Chorley *Staffs* 158 C1
Chorleywood 135 F3
Chorlton 171 E2

Chorlton Lane 170 B3
Chorlton-cum-
 Hardy 184 C3
Chowley 170 B2
Chrishall 150 C4
Chrishall Grange 150 C3
Chrisswell 232 B2
Christ Church *Oxon*
 OX1 1DP 80 Oxford
Christchurch
 Cambs 162 C3
Christchurch
 Dorset 106 A3
Christchurch
 Newport 130 C4
Christian Malford 132 B5
Christmas Common 134 C3
Christon 116 A2
Christon Bank 229 G4
Christow 102 B4
Christskirk 260 E2
Chryston 234 A2
Chudleigh 102 B5
Chudleigh Knighton 102 B5
Chulmleigh 113 G4
Chunal 185 E3
Church 192 D5
Church Aston 157 G1
Church Brampton 148 C1
Church Brough 200 C1
Church Broughton 172 D4
Church Charwelton 148 A2
Church Common 153 E2
Church Crookham 120 D2
Church Eaton 158 A1
Church End *CenBeds* 162 B2
Church End *CenBeds* 162 B5
Church End *CenBeds* 162 A4
Church End
 CenBeds 149 G4
Church End
 CenBeds 149 E5
Church End
 CenBeds 149 G2
Church End
 CenBeds 149 E4
Church End
 CenBeds 149 G4
Church End *ERid* 196 C2
Church End *Essex* 151 D3
Church End *Essex* 151 F5
Church End *Glos* 146 B5
Church End *Hants* 120 B2
Church End *Herts* 136 A1
Church End *Herts* 150 C5
Church End *Lincs* 176 B4
Church End *Lincs* 189 E3
Church End *Warks* 159 E3
Church End *Wilts* 132 C5
Church Enstone 147 F5
Church Fenton 195 E4
Church Green 103 E3
Church Gresley 159 E1
Church
 Hanborough 133 G1
Church Hill
 ChesW&C 170 D1
Church Hill *Derbys* 173 F1
Church Houses 203 F3
Church Knowle 105 F4
Church Laneham 187 F5
Church Langley 137 D2
Church Langton 160 C3
Church Lawford 159 G5
Church Lawton 171 F2
Church Leigh 172 B4
Church Lench 146 C2
Church Mayfield 172 C3
Church Minshull 171 D1
Church Norton 108 A4
Church of St. Mary-
 in-Castro *Kent*
 CT16 1HU 70 Dover
Church Preen 157 E3
Church Pulverbatch 156 D2
Church Stoke 156 B3
Church Stowe 148 B2
Church Street
 Essex 151 F3
Church Street *Kent* 137 G5
Church Stretton 157 D3
Church Town *Leics* 159 F1
Church Town *Surr* 122 C3
Church Village 129 G4
Church Warsop 173 G1
Church Westcote 147 E5
Church Wilne 173 F4
Churcham 131 G1
Churchdown 132 A1
Churchend *Essex* 138 D3
Churchend *Essex* 151 E5
Churchend *SGlos* 131 G3
Churchfield 158 C3
Churchgate 136 C2
Churchgate Street 137 D1
Churchill *Devon* 113 F1
Churchill *Devon* 103 F1
Churchill *NSom* 116 B2
Churchill *Oxon* 147 E5
Churchill *Worcs* 146 B2
Churchill *Worcs* 158 A5
Churchill Museum &
 Cabinet War Rooms
 GtLon SW1A 2AQ 44 D5
Churchingford 103 F1
Churchover 160 A4
Churchstanton 103 E1
Churchstow 100 D3
Churchtown *Devon* 113 G1
Churchtown *IoM* 190 C2
Churchtown *Lancs* 192 A3
Churchtown
 Mersey 183 E1
Churnsike Lodge 219 E4
Churston Ferrers 101 F2
Churt 121 D4
Churton 170 B2
Churwell 194 B5
Chute Cadley 119 D2
Chute Standen 119 E2
Chwilog 166 D4
Chyandour 94 B3
Chysauster 94 B3
Cilan Uchaf 166 B5
Cilcain 169 E1
Cilcennin 142 B1

Cilcewydd 156 B2
Cilfrew 129 D2
Cilfynydd 129 G3
Cilgerran 141 E3
Cilgwyn *Carmar* 142 D4
Cilgwyn *Pembs* 141 D4
Ciliau Aeron 142 B2
Cille Bhrighde 254 C3
Cille Pheadair 254 C3
Cilmaengwyn 128 D2
Cilmery 143 G2
Cilrhedyn 141 F4
Cilrhedyn Bridge 140 D4
Cilsan 142 B5
Ciltalgarth 168 B3
Cilwendeg 141 F4
Cilybebyll 128 D2
Cilycwm 143 D3
Cimla 129 D3
Cinderford 131 F1
Cippenham 135 E4
Cippyn 141 E3
Cirbhig 270 D3
Cirencester 132 C2
City *GtLon* 136 C4
City *VGlam* 129 F5
City Airport 136 D4
City Dulas 180 C4
Clabhach 246 A4
Clachaig 232 C1
Clachan *A&B* 241 D3
Clachan *A&B* 248 A5
Clachan *A&B* 231 F4
Clachan *High* 256 B1
Clachan *ESiar* 262 C7
Clachan Mòr 246 A2
Clachan of
 Campsie 234 A2
Clachan of
 Glendaruel 232 A1
Clachandhu 239 D1
Clachaneasy 215 E3
Clachanmore 206 A2
Clachan-Seil 239 G3
Clachanturn 259 K5
Clachbreck 231 F2
Clachnabrain 252 B3
Clachnaharry 266 D7
Clachtoll 272 C6
Clackmannan 243 E5
Clackmarras 267 K6
Clacton Pier *Essex*
 CO15 1QX 139 E1
Clacton-on-Sea 139 E1
Cladach a Bhale
 Shear 262 D5
Cladach a' Chaolais 262 C5
Cladach Chirebost 262 C5
Cladach Chnoc a
 Lin 262 C5
Cladich
 (An Cladach) 240 C2
Claggan (An Claigeann)
 High 248 D2
Claggan *High* 247 G5
Claigan 263 H6
Claines 146 A2
Clandown 117 D2
Clanfield *Hants* 107 G1
Clanfield *Oxon* 133 E2
Clannaborough
 Barton 102 A2
Clanville 119 E3
Claonaig 231 G4
Claonairigh 240 C4
Claonel 266 C1
Clapgate 150 C5
Clapham *Bed* 149 F2
Clapham *Devon* 102 B4
Clapham *GtLon* 136 B5
Clapham *NYorks* 192 D1
Clapham *WSuss* 108 C3
Clapham Green 149 F2
Clapham Hill 124 D2
Clappers 237 G4
Clappersgate 199 E2
Clapton *Som* 104 A2
Clapton *Som* 116 D2
Clapton-in-
 Gordano 131 D5
Clapton-on-the-Hill 133 D1
Clapworthy 113 G3
Clara Vale 212 A1
Clarach 154 C4
Clarbeston 141 D5
Clarbeston Road 140 D5
Clarborough 187 E4
Clardon 275 G2
Clare 151 F3
Clare Castle Country Park
 Suff CO10 8NJ 151 F3
Clarebrand 216 B4
Claremont Landscape
 Garden *Surr*
 KT10 9JG 121 G1
Clarencefield 217 E4
Clarilaw 227 G4
Clark's Green 121 G4
Clarkston 233 G4
Clashban 266 D2
Clashcoig 266 D2
Clashdorran 266 C7
Clashgour 249 E5
Clashindarroch 260 D1
Clashmore *High* 266 E3
Clashmore *High* 272 C5
Clashnessie 272 C5
Clashnoir 259 K2
Clatford 118 C1
Clathy 243 F2
Clatt 260 D2
Clatter 155 G3
Clattercote 147 G3
Clatterford 107 D4
Clatterford End 137 E2
Clatterin Brig 253 E2
Clatworthy 115 D4
Claughton *Lancs* 192 B1
Claughton *Lancs* 192 B3

Clavelshay 115 F4
Claverdon 147 D1
Claverham 116 B1
Clavering 150 C4
Claverley 157 G3
Claverton 117 E1
Claverton Down 117 E1
Clawdd-côch 129 G5
Clawdd-newydd 169 D2
Clawfin 224 D5
Clawthorpe 199 G5
Clawton 99 D1
Claxby 188 B3
Claxby Pluckacre 176 B1
Claxby St. Andrew 189 E5
Claxton *Norf* 179 E5
Claxton *NYorks* 195 F1
Claxton Grange 213 D5
Clay Coton 160 A5
Clay Cross 173 E1
Clay End 150 B5
Clay Hill 131 F5
Clay of Allan 267 F4
Claybokie 259 J4
Claybrooke Magna 159 G4
Claybrooke Parva 159 G4
Claydene 123 D4
Claydon *Oxon* 147 G2
Claydon *Suff* 152 C3
Claygate *Kent* 123 G5
Claygate *Surr* 121 G1
Claygate Cross 123 F3
Clayhanger *Devon* 114 D5
Clayhanger *WMid* 158 C2
Clayhidon 103 E1
Clayhill *ESuss* 110 D1
Clayhill *Hants* 106 C3
Clayhithe 150 D1
Clayock 275 G3
Claypits 131 G2
Claypole 174 D3
Claythorpe 189 E5
Clayton *Staffs* 171 F3
Clayton *SYorks* 186 B2
Clayton *WSuss* 109 E2
Clayton *WYorks* 194 A4
Clayton Green 192 B5
Clayton-le-Moors 192 D4
Clayton-le-Woods 192 B5
Clayworth 187 E4
Cleadale 247 D1
Cleadon 212 C1
Clearbrook 100 B2
Clearwell 131 E2
Cleasby 202 B1
Cleat *Ork* 277 D9
Cleat *ESiar* 254 B4
Cleatlam 202 A1
Cleatop 193 E1
Cleator 208 D5
Cleator Moor 208 D5
Cleckheaton 194 A5
Clee St. Margaret 157 E4
Cleedownton 157 E4
Cleehill 157 E5
Cleestanton 157 E5
Cleethorpes 188 D2
Cleethorpes Discovery
 Centre *NELincs*
 DN35 0AG 188 D2
Cleeton St. Mary 157 F5
Cleeve *NSom* 116 B1
Cleeve *Oxon* 134 B4
Cleeve Hill 146 B5
Cleeve Prior 146 C3
Cleghorn 234 C5
Clehonger 145 D4
Cleigh 240 A2
Cleish 243 F5
Cleland 234 B4
Clement's End 135 F1
Clemsfold 121 G4
Clench Common 118 C1
Clenchwarton 177 D5
Clennell 220 B1
Clent 158 B5
Clent Hills
 Worcs DY9 9JR 14 B5
Cleobury Mortimer 157 F5
Cleobury North 157 F4
Clephanton 267 F6
Clerklands 227 G3
Clermiston 235 F2
Clestrain 277 C7
Cleuch Head 227 G4
Cleughbrae 217 E3
Clevancy 132 C5
Clevedon 130 D5
Cleveland Tontine
 Inn 202 D3
Cleveley 147 F5
Cleveleys 191 G3
Clevelode 146 A3
Cleverton 132 B4
Clewer 116 B2
Clewer Green 135 E5
Clewer Village 135 E5
Cley next the Sea 178 B1
Cliburn 210 B5
Cliddesden 120 B3
Cliff *Carmar* 127 G2
Cliff *High* 247 F5
Cliff Grange 170 D4
Cliffe *Lancs* 192 D4
Cliffe *Med* 137 G5
Cliffe *NYorks* 195 F4
Cliffe Woods 137 G5
Clifford *Here* 144 B3
Clifford *WYorks* 194 D3
Clifford Chambers 147 D2
Clifford's Mesne 145 F5
Clifford's Tower
 YO1 9SA 90 York
Cliffs End 125 F2
Clifton *Bristol* 131 E5
Clifton *CenBeds* 149 G4
Clifton *Cumb* 210 B5
Clifton *Derbys* 172 C3
Clifton *Devon* 113 F1
Clifton *Lancs* 192 A4
Clifton *N'umb* 221 E3
Clifton *Nott* 173 G4
Clifton *NYorks* 194 A3
Clifton *Oxon* 147 G4
Clifton *Stir* 241 F1

Clifton *SYorks* 186 C3
Clifton *Worcs* 146 A3
Clifton *WYorks* 194 A5
Clifton *York* 195 E2
Clifton Campville 159 E1
Clifton Hampden 134 A3
Clifton Maybank 104 B1
Clifton Park Museum
 SYorks S65 2AA 21 D1
Clifton Reynes 149 E2
Clifton upon
 Dunsmore 160 A5
Clifton upon Teme 145 G1
Cliftonville 125 F1
Climping 108 C3
Climpy 234 D4
Clink 117 E3
Clint 194 B2
Clint Green 178 B4
Clinterty 261 G3
Clintmains 228 A3
Clippesby 179 F4
Clippings Green 178 B4
Clipsham 161 E1
Clipston *N'hants* 160 B4
Clipston *Notts* 174 B4
Clipstone 173 G1
Clitheroe 192 D3
Clive 170 C5
Clivocast 278 F2
Clixby 188 B2
Clocaenog 169 D2
Clochan 268 C4
Clochtow 261 J1
Clock Face 183 G3
Clockhill 269 G6
Cloddach 267 J6
Cloddiau 156 A2
Clodock 144 C5
Cloford 117 E3
Clola 269 J6
Clola 269 J6
Clonrae 216 C1
Clophill 149 F4
Clopton 161 F4
Clopton Corner 152 D2
Clopton Green *Suff* 151 F2
Clopton Green *Suff* 152 D2
Close Clark 190 A4
Closeburn 216 C1
Closworth 104 B1
Clothall 150 A4
Clothan 278 D4
Clotton 170 C1
Clough *Cumb* 200 C3
Clough *GtMan* 184 D1
Clough *GtMan* 184 D1
Clough *WYorks* 185 E1
Clough Foot 193 F5
Clough Head 193 G5
Cloughfold 193 E5
Cloughton 204 D3
Cloughton
 Newlands 204 D3
Clounlaid 247 G4
Clousta 279 C7
Clouston 277 C6
Clova *Aber* 260 D1
Clova *Angus* 252 B2
Clove Lodge 201 E1
Clovelly 112 D3
Clovelly Cross 112 D3
Clovelly Village *Devon*
 EX39 5TA 112 D3
Clovenfords 227 F2
Clovenstone 261 F3
Cloves 267 J5
Clovullin 248 C3
Clow Bridge 193 E5
Clowne 186 B5
Clows Top 157 G5
Cloyntie 224 B5
Cluanach 230 B4
Clubworthy 98 C1
Cluddley 157 F1
Cluer (Cliuthar) 263 G2
Clumber Country Park
 Notts S80 3AZ 186 D5
Clun 156 B4
Clunas 267 F7
Clunbury 156 C4
Clunderwen 127 E1
Clune *High* 258 E2
Clune *Moray* 268 D4
Clunes 249 E1
Clungunford 156 C5
Clunie *Aber* 268 E5
Clunie *P&K* 251 G5
Clunton 156 C4
Cluny 244 A5
Clutton *B&NESom* 116 D2
Clutton *ChesW&C* 170 B2
Clwt-y-bont 167 E1
Clwydyfagwyr 129 G2
Clydach *Mon* 130 B1
Clydach *Swan* 128 D2
Clydach Terrace 130 A1
Clydach Vale 129 F3
Clydebank 233 F2
Clydey 141 F4
Clyffe Pypard 132 C5
Clynder 232 D1
Clyne 129 F2
Clynelish 267 F1
Clynfyw 141 F4
Clynnog-fawr 166 D2
Clyro 144 B3
Clyst Honiton 102 C3
Clyst Hydon 102 D2
Clyst St. George 102 C4
Clyst St. Lawrence 102 D2
Clyst St. Mary 102 C4
Clyst William 103 D2
Cnewr 143 E5
Cnoc 271 G4
Cnwch Coch 154 C5
Coachford 268 C6
Coad's Green 97 G2
Coal Aston 186 A5
Coalbrookdale 157 F2
Coalbrookvale 130 A2
Coalburn 225 G2
Coalburns 212 A1
Coalcleugh 211 E3
Coaley 131 G2
Coalmoor 157 F2

Coalpit Heath 131 F4
Coalpit Hill 171 F2
Coalport 157 G2
Coalsnaughton 243 E5
Coaltown of
 Balgonie 244 B5
Coaltown of
 Wemyss 244 B5
Coalville 159 G1
Coalway 131 E1
Coanwood 210 C2
Coast 265 F2
Coat 116 B5
Coatbridge 234 B3
Coate *Swin* 133 D4
Coate *Wilts* 118 B1
Coates *Cambs* 162 B3
Coates *Glos* 132 B2
Coates *Lincs* 187 G4
Coates *Notts* 187 F4
Coates *WSuss* 108 B2
Coatham 213 E4
Coatham
 Mundeville 212 B5
Cobairdy 268 D6
Cobbaton 113 G3
Cobbler's Plain 131 D2
Cobby Syke 194 A2
Cobden 102 D3
Coberley 132 B1
Cobhall Common 145 D4
Cobham *Kent* 123 F3
Cobham *Surr* 121 G1
Cobleland 242 A5
Cobley Hill 158 C5
Cobnash 145 D1
Coburty 269 H4
Cochno 233 F2
Cock Alley 173 F1
Cock Bank 170 A3
Cock Bevington 146 C2
Cock Bridge 259 K4
Cock Clarks 138 B2
Cock Green 137 G1
Cock Marling 111 D2
Cockayne 203 F3
Cockayne Hatley 150 A3
Cockburnspath 237 E3
Cockenzie & Port
 Seton 236 B2
Cocker Bar 192 B5
Cockerham 192 A2
Cockermouth 209 E3
Cockernhoe 149 G5
Cockerton 202 B2
Cockett 128 C3
Cockfield *Dur* 212 A5
Cockfield *Suff* 152 A2
Cockfosters 136 B3
Cocking 108 A2
Cockington 101 E1
Cockington Country
 Park *Torbay*
 TQ2 6XA 101 E1
Cocklake 116 B3
Cocklaw 220 B4
Cockle Park 221 E2
Cockleford 132 B1
Cockley Beck 198 D2
Cockley Cley 163 F2
Cockpen 236 A3
Cockpole Green 134 C4
Cockshutt 170 B5
Cockthorpe 178 A1
Cockwood *Devon* 102 C4
Cockwood *Som* 115 F3
Cockyard 185 E4
Codda 97 F2
Coddenham 152 C2
Coddington
 ChesW&C 170 B2
Coddington *Here* 145 G3
Coddington *Notts* 174 D2
Codford St. Mary 118 A4
Codford St. Peter 118 A4
Codicote 136 B1
Codmore Hill 108 C2
Codnor 173 F3
Codnor Park 173 F2
Codrington 131 G5
Codsall 158 A2
Codsall Wood 158 A2
Coed Morgan 130 C1
Coed Ystumgwern 167 E5
Coedcae 130 B2
Coedely 129 G4
Coedkernew 130 B4
Coedpoeth 169 F2
Coedway 156 C1
Coed-y-bryn 141 G3
Coed-y-caerau 130 C3
Coed-y-paen 130 C3
Coed-y-parc 167 F1
Coed-yr-ynys 144 A5
Coelbren 129 E1
Coffinswell 101 E1
Cofton 102 C4
Cofton Hackett 158 C5
Cogan 130 A5
Cogenhoe 148 D1
Cogges 133 F2
Coggeshall 151 G5
Coggeshall Hamlet 151 G5
Coggins Mill 110 A1
Cóig Peighinnean 271 H1
Coilantogh 242 A4
Coileitir 248 D5
Coilessan 241 E4
Coillaig 240 C2
Coille Mhorgil 257 G4
Coille-righ 257 F2
Coillore 255 J1
Coity 129 F4
Col 271 G4
Col Uarach 271 G4
Colaboll 273 H7
Colan 96 C3
Colaton Raleigh 103 D4
Colbost 263 H7
Colburn 202 B3
Colbury 106 C1
Colby *Cumb* 210 C5
Colby *IoM* 190 A4
Colby *Norf* 178 D2
Colchester 152 A5
Colchester Castle Museum
 Essex CO1 1TJ 152 A5
Colchester Green 152 A2

Colchester Zoo Essex CO3 0SL 152 A5
Colcot 115 E1
Cold Ash 119 G1
Cold Ashby 160 B5
Cold Ashton 131 G5
Cold Aston 132 D1
Cold Blow 127 E1
Cold Brayfield 149 E2
Cold Chapel 226 A3
Cold Cotes 200 C5
Cold Hanworth 188 A4
Cold Harbour 134 B4
Cold Hatton 170 D5
Cold Hatton Heath 170 D5
Cold Hesledon 212 D3
Cold Higham 148 B2
Cold Inn 127 E2
Cold Kirby 203 E4
Cold Newton 160 C2
Cold Northcott 97 G1
Cold Norton 138 B2
Cold Overton 160 D2
Cold Row 191 G3
Coldbackie 273 J2
Coldblow 137 E5
Coldean 109 F3
Coldeast 102 B5
Coldeaton 172 C2
Colden Common 119 F5
Coldfair Green 153 F1
Coldham 162 C2
Coldharbour Glos 131 E2
Coldharbour Surr 121 G3
Coldingham 237 G3
Coldrain 243 F4
Coldred 125 E4
Coldrey 120 C3
Coldridge 113 G5
Coldrife 220 C2
Coldstream 228 C3
Coldvreath 97 D4
Coldwaltham 108 C2
Coldwells 269 K6
Cole 117 D4
Cole End 159 D4
Cole Green 136 B1
Cole Henley 119 F2
Colebatch 156 C4
Colebrook 102 D2
Colebrooke 102 A2
Coleburn 267 K6
Coleby Lincs 175 E1
Coleby NLincs 187 F1
Coleford Devon 102 A2
Coleford Glos 131 E1
Coleford Som 117 D3
Colegate End 164 C3
Colehill 105 G2
Coleman Green 136 A1
Coleman's Hatch 122 D5
Colemere 170 B4
Colemore 120 C4
Colemore Green 157 G3
Colenden 243 G2
Coleorton 159 G1
Colerne 132 A5
Cole's Common 164 D3
Cole's Cross 101 D3
Cole's Green 153 D1
Colesbourne 132 C1
Colesden 149 G2
Coleshill Bucks 135 E3
Coleshill Oxon 133 E3
Coleshill Warks 159 E4
Colestocks 103 D2
Coley B&NESom 116 C2
Coley Staffs 172 B3
Colfin 214 B5
Colgate 122 B5
Colgrain 233 E2
Colindale 136 B4
Colinsburgh 244 C4
Colinton 235 G3
Colintraive 232 B2
Colkirk 178 A3
Coll 246 A4
Collace 244 A1
Collafirth 279 D6
Collamoor Head 98 B1
Collaton St. Mary 101 E1
Collessie 244 A3
Colleton Mills 113 G4
Collett's Green 146 A2
Collier Row 137 E3
Collier Street 123 G4
Collier's End 150 B5
Collier's Wood 136 B5
Colliery Row 212 C3
Collieston 261 J2
Collin 217 E3
Collingbourne Ducis 118 D2
Collingbourne Kingston 118 D2
Collingham Notts 174 D1
Collingham WYorks 194 C3
Collington 145 F1
Collingtree 148 C2
Collins End 134 B5
Collins Green Warr 183 G3
Collins Green Worcs 145 G2
Colliston 253 E5
Colliton 103 D2
Collmuir 260 D4
Collycroft 159 F4
Collyhurst 184 C2
Collynie 261 G1
Collyweston 161 E2
Colmonell 214 C2
Colmworth 149 G2
Coln Rogers 132 C2
Coln St. Aldwyns 132 D2
Coln St. Dennis 132 C1
Colnabaichin 259 K4
Colnbrook 135 F5
Colne Cambs 162 B5
Colne Lancs 193 E4
Colne Engaine 151 G4
Colney 178 C5
Colney Heath 136 B2
Colney Street 136 A2
Colonsay 238 C5
Colonsay House 238 C5
Colony Gift Corporation Cumb LA12 0LD 199 D5
Colpy 260 E1
Colquhar 236 A5
Colsterdale 202 A4
Colsterworth 175 E5
Colston Bassett 174 C4
Colston Hall BS1 5AR 66 Bristol
Coltfield 267 J5
Colthouse 199 E3
Coltishall 179 D4
Coltness 234 C4
Colton Cumb 199 E4
Colton Norf 178 C5
Colton NYorks 195 E3
Colton Staffs 172 B5
Colton WYorks 194 C4
Colva 144 B2
Colvend 216 C5
Colvister 278 E3
Colwall 145 G3
Colwall Green 145 G3
Colwall Stone 145 G3
Colwell 220 B4
Colwich 172 B5
Colwick 174 B3
Colwinston 129 F5
Colworth 108 B3
Colwyn Bay (Bae Colwyn) 181 G5
Colyford 103 F3
Colyton 103 F3
Combe Here 144 C1
Combe Oxon 133 G1
Combe Som 116 B5
Combe WBerks 119 E1
Combe Common 121 E4
Combe Cross 102 A5
Combe Down 117 E1
Combe Florey 115 E4
Combe Hay 117 E2
Combe Martin 113 F1
Combe Martin Wildlife & Dinosaur Park Devon EX34 0NG 113 G1
Combe Pafford 101 F1
Combe Raleigh 103 E2
Combe St. Nicholas 103 G1
Combeinteignhead 102 B5
Comberbach 184 A5
Comberford 159 D2
Comberton Cambs 150 B2
Comberton Here 145 D1
Combpyne 103 F3
Combridge 172 B4
Combrook 147 F2
Combs Derbys 185 E5
Combs Suff 152 B2
Combs Ford 152 B2
Combwich 115 F3
Comer 241 F4
Comers 260 E4
Comhampton 146 A1
Comins Coch 154 C4
Commercial End 151 D1
Commins Coch 155 E2
Common Edge 191 G4
Common Moor 97 G2
Common Platt 132 D4
Common Side 186 A5
Common Square 188 A5
Commondale 203 F1
Commonside 172 D3
Compstall 185 D3
Compton Devon 101 E1
Compton Hants 119 F5
Compton Plym 100 A2
Compton Staffs 158 A4
Compton Surr 121 E3
Compton WBerks 134 A5
Compton Wilts 118 C2
Compton WSuss 107 G1
Compton WYorks 194 D3
Compton Abbas 105 E1
Compton Abdale 132 C1
Compton Bassett 132 C5
Compton Beauchamp 133 E4
Compton Bishop 116 A2
Compton Chamberlayne 118 B5
Compton Dando 116 D1
Compton Dundon 116 B4
Compton Martin 116 C2
Compton Pauncefoot 116 D5
Compton Valence 104 B3
Compton Verney 147 F2
Compton Wynyates 147 F3
Comra 258 C5
Comrie Fife 235 E1
Comrie P&K 242 C2
Conchra A&B 232 B1
Conchra High 256 E2
Concraigie 251 G5
Conder Green 192 A2
Conderton 146 B4
Condicote 146 D5
Condorrat 234 B2
Condover 157 D2
Coney Weston 164 A4
Coneyhurst 121 G5
Coneysthorpe 203 G5
Coneythorpe 194 C2
Conford 120 D4
Congash 259 H2
Congdon's Shop 97 G2
Congerstone 159 F2
Congham 177 F5
Congleton 171 F1
Congresbury 116 B1
Congreve 158 B1
Conicavel 267 G6
Coningsby 176 A2
Conington Cambs 161 G4
Conington Cambs 150 B1
Conisbrough 186 C3
Conisby 230 A3
Conisholme 189 E3
Coniston Cumb 199 E3
Coniston ERid 197 D4
Coniston Cold 193 F2
Conistone 193 F1
Conkers, Swadlincote Leics DE12 6GA 159 F1
Conland 268 E6
Connah's Quay 169 F1
Connel (A' Choingheal) 240 B1
Connel Park 225 E4
Connor Downs 94 C3
Conock 118 B2
Conon Bridge (Drochaid Sgùideil) 266 C6
Cononish 241 F2
Cononley 193 F3
Cononsyth 253 D5
Consall 171 G3
Consett 212 A2
Constable Burton 202 A3
Constantine 95 E4
Constantine Bay 96 C2
Contin (Cunndainn) 266 B6
Contlaw 261 G4
Contullich 266 D4
Conwy 181 F5
Conwy Castle Conwy LL32 8LD 181 F5
Conyer 124 B2
Conyer's Green 151 G1
Cooden 110 C3
Coodham 224 C2
Cooil 190 B4
Cookbury 113 E5
Cookbury Wick 113 D5
Cookham 135 D4
Cookham Dean 135 D4
Cookham Rise 135 D4
Cookhill 146 C2
Cookley Suff 165 E4
Cookley Worcs 158 A4
Cookley Green Oxon 134 B3
Cookley Green Suff 165 E4
Cookney 261 G5
Cook's Green 152 A2
Cooksbridge 109 F2
Cooksey Green 146 B1
Cookshill 171 G3
Cooksmill Green 137 F2
Cookston 261 H1
Coolham 121 G5
Cooling 137 G5
Cooling Street 137 G5
Coombe Corn 97 D4
Coombe Corn 112 C4
Coombe Corn 96 A5
Coombe Corn 96 C5
Coombe Devon 101 D3
Coombe Devon 102 B4
Coombe Devon 103 E3
Coombe Som 115 F5
Coombe Som 104 A2
Coombe Wilts 118 C2
Coombe Bissett 118 C5
Coombe Country Park Warks CV3 2AB 16 D3
Coombe End 114 D5
Coombe Hill 146 A5
Coombe Keynes 105 E4
Coombes 109 D3
Coombes Moor 144 C1
Cooper's Corner ESuss 110 C1
Cooper's Corner Kent 123 D4
Cooper's Green 136 A2
Coopersale 137 D2
Coopersale Street 137 D2
Cootham 108 C2
Cop Street 125 E3
Copdock 152 C3
Copford Green 152 A5
Copgrove 194 C1
Copister 278 D5
Cople 149 G3
Copley Dur 211 G5
Copley WYorks 193 G5
Coplow Dale 185 F5
Copmanthorpe 195 E3
Copmere End 171 F5
Copp 192 A4
Coppathorne 112 C5
Coppenhall 158 B1
Coppenhall Moss 171 E2
Copperhouse 94 C3
Coppicegate 157 G4
Coppingford 161 G4
Coppleridge 117 F5
Copplestone 102 A2
Coppull 183 G1
Coppull Moor 183 G1
Copsale 121 G5
Copse Hill 122 B2
Copster Green 192 C4
Copston Magna 159 G4
Copt Heath 159 D5
Copt Hewick 202 C5
Copt Oak 159 G1
Copthall Green 136 D2
Copthorne 122 C5
Copy Lake 113 G4
Copythorne 106 C1
Coralhill 269 J4
Corbets Tey 137 E4
Corbiegoe 275 J4
Corbridge 211 F1
Corby 161 D4
Corby Glen 175 F5
Cordach 260 E5
Cordorcan 215 E3
Coreley 157 F5
Corfcott Green 98 D1
Corfe 103 F1
Corfe Castle 105 F4
Corfe Castle Dorset BH20 5EZ 105 F4
Corfe Mullen 105 F3
Corfton 157 D4
Corgarff 259 K4
Corhampton 120 B5
Corley 159 F4
Corley Ash 159 E4
Corley Moor 159 E4
Corn Exchange Cambs CB2 3QB 66 Cambridge
Cornabus 230 B5
Cornard Tye 152 A3
Corndon 99 G2
Corney 198 C3
Cornforth 212 C4
Cornhill 268 D5
Cornhill on Tweed 228 C3
Cornholme 193 F5
Cornish Gold & Treasure Park Corn TR16 4HN 96 A5
Cornish Hall End 151 E4
Cornquoy 277 E7
Cornriggs 211 E3
Cornsay 212 A3
Cornsay Colliery 212 A3
Corntown High 266 C6
Corntown VGlam 129 F5
Cornwell 147 E5
Cornwood 100 C2
Cornworthy 101 E2
Corpach (A' Chorpaich) 248 D2
Corpusty 178 C3
Corrachree 260 C4
Corran A&B 241 E5
Corran High 256 E4
Corran (Ardgour) High 248 C3
Corranbuie 231 G3
Corranmore 239 G4
Corrany 190 C3
Corribeg 248 B2
Corrie 232 B5
Corrie Common 218 A3
Corriechrevie 231 F4
Corriecravie 223 E3
Corriedoo 216 A2
Corriekinloch 273 F6
Corrielorne 240 A3
Corrievorrie 258 E2
Corrimony 257 K1
Corringham Lincs 187 F3
Corringham Thur 137 G4
Corris 155 D2
Corris Uchaf 154 D2
Corrlarach 248 B2
Corrour Shooting Lodge 249 G3
Corrow 241 D4
Corry 256 C2
Corrychurrachan 248 C3
Corrylach 222 C2
Corrymuckloch 243 D1
Corsback 275 H2
Corscombe 104 B2
Corse Aber 268 E6
Corse Glos 145 G5
Corse Lawn 146 A4
Corse of Kinnoir 268 D6
Corsebank 225 G4
Corsegight 269 G5
Corsehill 217 F2
Corsewall 214 B4
Corsham 132 A5
Corsindae 260 E4
Corsley 117 F3
Corsley Heath 117 F3
Corsock 216 B3
Corston B&NESom 117 D1
Corston Wilts 132 B4
Corstorphine 235 F2
Cortachy 252 B4
Corton Suff 165 G2
Corton Wilts 118 A3
Corton Denham 116 D5
Corwar House 215 D2
Corwen 169 D3
Coryton Devon 99 E2
Coryton Thur 137 G4
Cosby 160 A3
Coscote 134 A4
Coseley 158 B3
Cosford Shrop 157 G2
Cosford Warks 160 A5
Cosgrove 148 C3
Cosham 107 F2
Cosheston 126 D2
Coshieville 250 C5
Coskills 188 A2
Cosmeston 115 E1
Cosmeston Lakes Country Park VGlam CF64 5UY 115 E1
Cossall 173 F3
Cossington Leics 160 B1
Cossington Som 116 A3
Costa 276 C5
Costessey 178 C4
Costock 173 G5
Coston Leics 174 D5
Coston Norf 178 B5
Cote Oxon 133 F2
Cote Som 116 A3
Cotebrook 170 C1
Cotehill 210 A2
Cotes Cumb 199 F4
Cotes Leics 173 G5
Cotes Staffs 171 F4
Cotesbach 160 A4
Cotford St. Luke 115 E5
Cotgrave 174 B4
Cothall 261 G3
Cotham 174 C3
Cothelstone 115 E4
Cotheridge 145 G2
Cotherstone 201 F1
Cothill 133 G3
Cotleigh 103 F2
Cotmanhay 173 F3
Coton Cambs 150 C2
Coton N'hants 160 B5
Coton Staffs 171 G4
Coton Staffs 159 D2
Coton Staffs 171 F5
Coton Clanford 171 F5
Coton Hill 171 G4
Coton in the Clay 172 C5
Coton in the Elms 159 E1
Cotonwood Shrop 170 C4
Cotonwood Staffs 171 F5
Cotswold Water Park Glos GL7 6DF 132 C3
Cotswold Wildlife Park Oxon OX18 4JP 133 E2
Cott 101 D1
Cottam Lancs 192 A4
Cottam Notts 187 F4
Cottartown 259 H1
Cottenham 150 C1
Cotterdale 200 D3
Cottered 150 B5
Cotteridge 158 C5
Cotterstock 161 F3
Cottesbrooke 160 C5
Cottesmore 161 E1
Cottingham ERid 196 C4
Cottingham N'hants 160 D3
Cottingley 194 A4
Cottisford 148 A4
Cotton Staffs 172 B3
Cotton Suff 152 B1
Cotton End 149 F3
Cottonworth 119 E4
Cottown Aber 260 D2
Cottown Aber 269 G6
Cottown Aber 261 F3
Cotts 100 A1
Cottwood 113 G4
Cotwall 157 F1
Cotwalton 171 G4
Couch's Mill 97 F4
Coughton Here 145 E5
Coughton Warks 146 C1
Cougie 257 J2
Coulaghailtro 231 F3
Coulags 265 F7
Coulby Newham 203 E1
Coulderton 198 A2
Coull 260 D4
Coulport 232 D1
Coulsdon 122 B3
Coulston 118 A2
Coulter 226 B2
Coultershaw Bridge 108 B2
Coultings 115 F3
Coulton 203 F5
Coultra 244 B2
Cound 157 E2
Coundlane 157 E2
Coundon Dur 212 B5
Coundon WMid 159 F4
Countersett 201 E4
Countess Wear 102 C3
Countesthorpe 160 A3
Countisbury 114 A3
Coup Green 192 B5
Coupar Angus 252 A5
Coupland Cumb 200 C1
Coupland N'umb 228 D3
Cour 231 G5
Court Colman 129 E4
Court Henry 142 B5
Court House Green 159 F4
Court-at-Street 124 C5
Courtauld Institute of Art Gallery GtLon WC2R 0RN 45 F3
Courteenhall 148 C2
Courtsend 138 D3
Courtway 115 F4
Cousland 236 A3
Cousley Wood 123 F5
Coustonn 232 B2
Cove A&B 232 D1
Cove Devon 102 C1
Cove Hants 120 D2
Cove High 264 E2
Cove ScBord 237 E2
Cove Bay 261 H4
Cove Bottom 165 F3
Covehithe 165 G3
Coven 158 B2
Coveney 162 C4
Covenham St. Bartholomew 188 D3
Covenham St. Mary 188 D3
Coventry 159 F5
Coventry Airport 159 F5
Coventry Cathedral WMid CV1 5AB 69 Coventry
Coventry Transport Museum WMid CV1 1JD 69 Coventry
Coverack 95 F5
Coverham 202 A4
Covesea 267 J4
Covingham 133 D4
Covington Cambs 161 F5
Covington SLan 226 A2
Cowan Bridge 200 B5
Cowbeech 110 B2
Cowbit 162 A1
Cowbridge Som 114 C3
Cowbridge VGlam 129 F5
Cowden 123 D4
Cowden Pound 123 D4
Cowdenbeath 243 G5
Cowdenburn 235 G4
Cowers Lane 173 E3
Cowes 107 D3
Cowesby 203 D4
Cowesfield Green 119 D5
Cowey Green 152 B5
Cowfold 109 E1
Cowgill 200 C4
Cowie Aber 253 G1
Cowie Stir 234 C1
Cowlam Manor 196 B1
Cowley Devon 102 C3
Cowley Glos 132 B1
Cowley GtLon 135 F4
Cowley Oxon 134 A2
Cowling Lancs 183 G1
Cowling NYorks 193 F3
Cowling NYorks 202 B4
Cowlinge 151 F2
Cowmes 185 F1
Cowpe 193 E5
Cowpen 221 E3
Cowpen Bewley 213 D5
Cowplain 107 F1
Cowsden 146 B2
Cowshill 211 E3
Cowthorpe 194 D2
Cox Common 165 E3
Coxbank 171 D3
Coxbench 173 E3
Coxbridge 116 C4
Coxford 177 G5
Coxheath 123 G3
Coxhoe 212 C4
Coxley 116 C3
Coxley Wick 116 C3
Coxpark 99 E3
Coxtie Green 137 E3
Coxwold 203 E5
Coychurch 129 F5
Coylet 232 C1
Coylton 224 C4
Coylumbridge 259 G3
Coynach 260 C4
Coynachie 260 C1
Coytrahen 129 E4
Crabbet Park 122 C5
Crabgate 178 B3
Crabtree Plym 100 B2
Crabtree SYorks 186 A4
Crabtree WSuss 109 E1
Crabtree Green 170 A3
Crackaig 230 D3
Crackenthorpe 210 C5
Crackington 98 B1
Crackington Haven 98 B1
Crackley 171 F2
Crackleybank 157 G1
Crackpot 201 E3
Crackthorn Corner 164 B4
Cracoe 193 F1
Craddock 103 D1
Cradhlastadh 270 C4
Cradley Here 145 G3
Cradley WMid 158 B4
Cradley Heath 158 B4
Crafthole 99 D5
Crafton 135 D1
Cragg 193 G5
Cragg Hill 194 B4
Craggan Moray 259 J1
Craggan P&K 242 D3
Cragganmore 259 J1
Cragganruar 250 B5
Craggie High 258 E1
Craggie High 274 D7
Craghead 212 B2
Cragside N'umb NE65 7PX 220 C1
Craibstone Aberdeen 261 G3
Craibstone Moray 268 C5
Craichie 252 D5
Craig A&B 240 C1
Craig A&B 239 E1
Craig D&G 216 A4
Craig High 264 D5
Craig High 265 G7
Craig SAyr 224 B5
Craig Berthlŵyd 129 G3
Craigans 240 A5
Craigbeg 249 G1
Craig-cefn-parc 128 C2
Craigcleuch 218 B3
Craigculter 269 H5
Craigdallie 244 A2
Craigdam 261 G1
Craigdarroch D&G 216 B1
Craigdarroch EAyr 225 E5
Craigdhu D&G 207 D2
Craigdhu High 266 B7
Craigearn 261 F3
Craigellachie 267 K7
Craigellie 269 J4
Craigencallie 215 G3
Craigend Moray 267 J6
Craigend P&K 243 G2
Craigendive 232 B1
Craigendoran 233 E1
Craigengillan 224 C5
Craigenputtock 216 B2
Craigens 230 A3
Craigglas 240 A5
Craighall 244 C3
Craighat 233 F1
Craighead Fife 245 E3
Craighead High 266 E5
Craighlaw 215 E4
Craighouse 230 D3
Craigie Aber 261 H3
Craigie Dundee 244 C1
Craigie P&K 251 G5
Craigie SAyr 224 C2
Craigie Brae 261 G1
Craigieburn 226 C5
Craigieholm 243 G1
Craigielaw 236 B2
Craiglockhart 235 G2
Craiglug 261 G5
Craigmaud 269 G5
Craigmillar 235 G2
Craigmore 232 C3
Craigmyle House 260 E4
Craignafeoch 232 A2
Craignant 169 F4
Craignavie 242 A1
Craigneil 214 C2
Craigneuk 234 B4
Craignure 239 G1
Craigo 253 E3
Craigoch 224 A5
Craigow 243 F4
Craigrothie 244 B3
Craigroy 267 J6
Craigroy Farm 259 J1
Craigruie 241 G2
Craigsanquhar 244 B3
Craigton Aberdeen 261 G4
Craigton Angus 244 D1
Craigton Angus 252 B4
Craigton High 266 D7
Craigton Stir 234 A1
Craigtown 274 D3
Craig-y-nos 129 E1
Craik Aber 260 C2
Craik ScBord 227 E5
Crail 245 E4
Crailing 228 A4
Crailinghall 228 A4
Crakehill 202 D5
Crakemarsh 172 B4
Crambe 195 G1
Crambeck Village 195 G1
Cramlington 221 E4
Cramond 235 F2
Cranage 171 E1
Cranberry 171 F4
Cranborne 105 G1
Cranbourne 135 E5
Cranbrook GtLon 136 D4
Cranbrook Kent 123 G5
Cranbrook Common 123 G5
Crane Moor 186 A2
Cranfield 149 E3
Cranford Devon 112 D3
Cranford GtLon 136 A5
Cranford St. Andrew 161 E5
Cranford St. John 161 E5
Cranham Glos 132 A1
Cranham GtLon 137 E4
Crank 183 G3
Cranleigh 121 F4
Cranmer Green 164 B4
Cranmore IoW 106 C4
Cranmore Som 117 D3
Cranna 268 E5
Crannoch 268 C5
Cranoe 160 C3
Cransford 153 E1
Cranshaws 237 D3
Cranstal 190 C1
Crantock 96 B3
Cranwell 175 F3
Cranwich 163 F3
Cranworth 178 A5
Craobh Haven 239 G4
Crapstone 100 B1
Crarae 240 B5
Crask Inn 273 H6
Crask of Aigas 266 B7
Craskins 260 D4
Craster 229 G5
Craswall 144 B4
Crateford 158 B2
Cratfield 165 E4
Crathes 261 F5
Crathie Aber 259 K5
Crathie High 258 C5
Crathorne 202 D2
Craven Arms 156 D4
Craw 231 G5
Crawcrook 212 A1
Crawford Lancs 183 F2
Crawford SLan 226 A3
Crawfordjohn 225 G3
Crawfordton 216 B1
Crawick 225 F4
Crawley Devon 103 F2
Crawley Hants 119 F4
Crawley Oxon 133 F1
Crawley WSuss 122 B5
Crawley Down 122 C5
Crawleyside 211 F3
Crawshawbooth 193 E5
Crawton 253 G2
Crawyn 190 B2
Cray NYorks 201 E5
Cray P&K 251 G3
Cray Powys 143 E5
Crayford 137 E5
Crayke 203 E5
Crays Hill 137 G3
Cray's Pond 134 B4
Crazies Hill 134 C4
Creacombe 102 B1
Creagan 248 B5
Creagbheitheachain 248 B3
Creagorry (Creag Ghoraidh) 262 C7
Crealy Adventure Park Devon EX5 1DR 102 C3
Creamore Bank 170 C4
Creaton 160 C5
Creca 218 A4
Credenhill 145 D3
Crediton 102 B2
Creebridge 215 F4
Creech Heathfield 115 F5
Creech St. Michael 115 F5
Creed 96 D5
Creedy Park 102 B2
Creekmoor 105 F3
Creekmouth 137 D4
Creeting St. Mary 152 B2
Creeton 175 F5
Creetown 215 F5
Creggans 240 C4
Cregneash 190 A5
Cregrina 144 A2
Creich 244 B2
Creigau 131 D3
Creigiau 129 G4
Crelevan 257 K1
Crelly 95 D3
Cremyll 100 A2
Crendell 105 G1
Cressage 157 E2
Cressbrook 185 F5
Cresselly 127 D2
Cressing 151 F5
Cresswell N'umb 221 E2
Cresswell Staffs 171 G4
Cresswell Quay 127 D2
Creswell 186 C5
Cretingham 152 D2
Cretshengan 231 F3
Crewe ChesE 171 E2
Crewe ChesW&C 170 B2
Crewe Green 171 E2
Crewgreen 156 C1
Crewkerne 104 A2
Crew's Hole 131 F5
Crewton 173 E4
Crianlarich (A' Chrìon-Làraich) 241 F2
Cribbs Causeway 131 E4
Cribyn 142 B2
Criccieth 167 D4
Crich 173 E2
Crich Carr 173 E2
Crich Common 173 E2
Crich Tramway Village Derbys DE4 5DP 173 E2
Crichie 269 H6
Crichton 236 A3
Crick Mon 131 D3
Crick N'hants 160 A5
Crickadarn 143 G3
Cricket Hill 120 D1
Cricket St. Thomas 103 G2
Crickham 116 B3
Crickheath 169 F5
Crickhowell 130 B1
Cricklade 132 D3
Cricklewood 136 B4
Crickley Hill Country Park Glos GL4 8JY 132 B1
Crick's Green 145 F2
Criddlestyle 106 A1
Cridling Stubbs 195 E5
Crieff 243 D2
Crieff Visitor Centre & Caithness Glass P&K PH7 4HQ 243 D2
Criftins (Dudleston Heath) 170 A4
Criggan 97 E3
Criggion 156 B1
Crigglestone 186 A1

Crimble **184** C1
Crimchard **103** G2
Crimdon Park **213** D4
Crimond **269** J5
Crimonmogate **269** J5
Crimplesham **163** E2
Crinan **239** G5
Crinan Ferry **239** G5
Cringleford **178** C5
Cringletie **235** E2
Crinow **127** E1
Cripplestyle **105** G1
Cripp's Corner **110** C1
Crix **137** G1
Crizeley **144** B4
Croalchapel **216** D1
Croasdale **209** D5
Crock Street **103** G1
Crockenhill **123** E2
Crocker End **134** C4
Crockerhill **107** E2
Crockernwell **102** A3
Crockerton **117** F3
Crockerton Green **117** F3
Crocketford
(Ninemile Bar) **216** C3
Crockey Hill **195** F3
Crockham Hill **122** D3
Crockhurst Street **123** F4
Crockleford Heath **152** B5
Croes Hywel **130** C1
Croesau Bach **169** F5
Croeserw **129** E3
Croesgoch **140** B4
Croes-lan **141** G3
Croesor **167** F3
Croespenmaen **130** A3
Croesyceiliog
Carmar **128** A1
Croesyceiliog
Torfaen **130** C3
Croes-y-mwyalch **130** C3
Croes-y-pant **130** C2
Croesywaun **167** E2
Croford **115** E5
Croft Here **145** D1
Croft Leics **160** A3
Croft Lincs **176** D1
Croft Warr **184** A3
Croftamie **233** F1
Crofthead **218** B4
Croftmore **251** D2
Crofton Wilts **119** D1
Crofton WYorks **186** A1
Croft-on-Tees **202** B2
Crofts **216** B3
Crofts of Benachielt **275** G5
Crofts of Buinach **267** J6
Crofts of Haddo **261** G1
Crofty **128** B3
Crogen **168** D4
Croggan **239** G2
Croglin **210** B3
Croick High **266** B2
Croick High **274** D3
Croig **246** D4
Crois Dughaill **254** C3
Croit e Caley **190** A4
Cromarty (Cromba) **266** E5
Crombie **235** E1
Crombie Country Park
Angus DD5 3QL **252** D5
Crombie Mill **244** D3
Cromblet **261** F1
Cromdale **259** H2
Cromer Herts **150** A5
Cromer Norf **178** D1
Cromford **173** D2
Cromhall **131** F3
Cromhall Common **131** F4
Cromore **271** G5
Crompton Fold **185** D1
Cromwell **174** C1
Cronberry **225** E3
Crondall **120** C3
Cronk-y-Voddy **190** B3
Cronton **183** F4
Crook Cumb **199** F3
Crook Dur **212** A4
Crook of Devon **243** F4
Crooked Soley **133** F5
Crookedholm **224** C2
Crookham N'umb **228** D3
Crookham WBerks **119** D1
Crookham Eastfield **228** D3
Crookham Village **120** C2
Crooklands **199** G4
Cropredy **147** G3
Cropston **160** A1
Cropthorne **146** B3
Cropton **203** G4
Cropwell Bishop **174** B4
Cropwell Butler **174** B4
Crosbie **232** B3
Crosbost **271** F5
Crosby Cumb **209** D3
Crosby IoM **190** B4
Crosby Mersey **183** E3
Crosby NLincs **187** F1
Crosby Court **202** C3
Crosby Garrett **200** C2
Crosby
Ravensworth **200** B1
Crosby Villa **209** D3
Crosby-on-Eden **210** A2
Croscombe **116** C3
Crosemere **170** B5
Crosland Hill **185** F1
Cross Som **116** B2
Cross (Cros) ESiar **271** H1
Cross Ash **130** D1
Cross Bank **157** G5
Cross End Bed **149** F2
Cross End Essex **151** G4
Cross Foxes Inn **155** D1
Cross Gates **194** C4
Cross Green Devon **99** D2
Cross Green Staffs **158** B2
Cross Green Suff **152** A2
Cross Green Suff **151** G2
Cross Green Suff **151** G2
Cross Hands
Carmar **128** B1
Cross Hands
Pembs **127** D1
Cross Hill **173** F3
Cross Hills **193** G3
Cross Houses **157** E2

Cross in Hand **110** A1
Cross Inn Cere **141** G2
Cross Inn Cere **142** B1
Cross Inn RCT **129** G4
Cross Keys **132** A5
Cross Lane **107** E3
Cross Lane Head **157** G3
Cross Lanes Corn **96** B5
Cross Lanes Corn **95** D4
Cross Lanes NYorks **195** D3
Cross Lanes Wrex **170** A3
Cross of Jackston **261** F1
Cross o'th'hands **173** D3
Cross Street **164** C4
Crossaig **231** G4
Crossapol **246** A2
Crossapol **246** A2
Cross-at-Hand **123** G4
Crossbush **108** C3
Crosscanonby **209** D3
Crossdale Street **178** D2
Crossens **183** E1
Crossflatts **194** A3
Crossford D&G **216** C2
Crossford Fife **235** E1
Crossford SLan **234** C3
Crossgate Lincs **176** A5
Crossgate Staffs **171** G4
Crossgatehall **236** A3
Crossgates Fife **235** F1
Crossgates NYorks **204** D4
Crossgates P&K **243** G1
Crossgates Powys **143** G1
Crossgill **192** B1
Crosshands Fife **243** G2
Crosshill Fife **243** G2
Crosshill SAyr **224** B5
Crosshouse **224** B2
Crosskeys **130** B3
Crosskirk **275** F1
Crosslanes **156** C1
Crosslee Renf **233** F3
Crosslee ScBord **227** E4
Crossmichael **216** B4
Crossmoor **192** A4
Crossroads Aber **261** F5
Crossroads EAyr **224** C2
Crossway Mon **130** D1
Crossway Powys **143** G2
Crossway Green
Mon **131** E3
Crossway Green
Worcs **146** A1
Crossways Dorset **105** D4
Crossways Glos **131** E1
Crosswell **141** E4
Crosthwaite **199** F3
Croston **183** F1
Crostwick **179** D4
Crostwight **179** E3
Crothair **270** D4
Crouch **123** F3
Crouch End **136** B4
Crouch Hill **104** D1
Croucheston **118** B5
Croughton **148** A4
Crovie **269** G4
Crow **106** A2
Crow Edge **185** F2
Crow Green **137** E3
Crow Hill **145** F5
Crowan **94** D3
Crowborough **123** E5
Crowborough
Warren **123** E5
Crowcombe **115** E4
Crowdecote **172** C1
Crowden **185** E3
Crowdhill **119** F5
Crowell **134** C3
Crowfield N'hants **148** B3
Crowfield Suff **152** C2
Crowhurst ESuss **110** C2
Crowhurst Surr **122** C4
Crowhurst Lane End **122** C4
Crowland Lincs **162** A3
Crowland Suff **164** B4
Crowlas **94** C3
Crowle NLincs **187** E1
Crowle Worcs **146** B2
Crowle Green **146** B2
Crowmarsh Gifford **134** B4
Crown Corner **165** D4
Crownhill **100** A2
Crownthorpe **178** B5
Crowntown **94** D3
Crow's Nest **97** G3
Crows-an-wra **94** A4
Crowsnest **156** C2
Crowthorne **120** D1
Crowton **183** G5
Croxall **159** E1
Croxby **188** B3
Croxdale **212** B4
Croxden **172** B4
Croxley Green **135** F3
Croxteth Country Park
Mersey L12 0HB **22** C2
Croxteth Hall Mersey
L12 0HB **22** C2
Croxton Cambs **150** A2
Croxton NLincs **188** A1
Croxton Norf **163** G4
Croxton Staffs **171** E4
Croxton Green **170** C2
Croxton Kerrial **174** D5
Croxtonbank **171** E4
Croy High **266** E7
Croy NLan **234** B2
Croyde **113** E2
Croyde Bay **113** E2
Croydon Cambs **150** B3
Croydon GtLon **122** C2
Cruach **230** B4
Cruchie **268** D6
Cruckmeole **156** D2
Cruckton **156** D1
Cruden Bay **261** J1
Crudgington **157** F1
Crudwell **132** B3
Crug **156** A5
Crugmeer **96** D2
Crugybar **142** C4
Crùlabhig **270** D4
Crumlin **130** B3
Crumpsall **184** C2
Crumpsbrook **157** F5
Crundale Kent **124** C4

Crundale Pembs **126** C1
Crunwere Farm **127** E1
Crutherland Farm **234** A4
Cruwys Morchard **102** B1
Crux Easton **119** F2
Crwbin **128** A1
Cryers Hill **135** D3
Crymlyn **181** E5
Crymych **141** E4
Crynant **129** D2
Crystal Palace **136** C5
Crystal Palace Park
GtLon SE20 8DT **13** C7
Cuaig **264** D6
Cubbington **147** F1
Cubert **96** B4
Cubley **185** G2
Cublington Bucks **148** D5
Cublington Here **144** D4
Cuckfield **109** F1
Cucklington **117** E5
Cuckney **186** C5
Cuckold's Green **165** F3
Cuckoo Bridge **176** A5
Cuckoo's Corner **120** C3
Cuckoo's Nest **170** A1
Cuddesdon **134** A2
Cuddington
ChesW&C **183** G5
Cuddington Bucks **134** C1
Cuddington Heath **170** B3
Cuddy Hill **192** A4
Cudham **122** D3
Cudliptown **99** F3
Cudworth Som **103** G1
Cudworth SYorks **186** A2
Cuerdley Cross **183** G4
Cuffley **136** C2
Cuidhaseadair **271** H2
Cuidhir **254** B4
Cuidrach **263** J6
Cuilmuich **241** D5
Cuil-uaine **240** B1
Culag **241** D5
Culbo **266** D5
Culbokie
(Cùil Bhàicidh) **266** D6
Culbone **114** B3
Culburnie **266** B7
Culcabock **266** D7
Culcharry **267** F6
Culcheth **184** A3
Culdrain **260** D1
Culduie **264** D7
Culford **163** G5
Culfordheath **163** G5
Culgaith **210** C5
Culgower **274** E7
Culham **134** A3
Culindrach **232** A4
Culkein **272** C5
Culkerton **132** B3
Cullachie **259** G2
Cullen **268** D4
Cullercoats **221** F4
Cullicudden **266** D5
Culligran **265** K7
Cullingworth **193** G4
Cullipool **239** G3
Cullivoe **278** E2
Culloch **242** C3
Culloden **266** E7
Cullompton **102** D2
Culmaily **267** F2
Culmalzie **215** E5
Culmington **157** D4
Culmstock **103** E1
Culnacraig **265** G1
Culnadalloch **240** B1
Culnaknock **264** B5
Culnamean **255** K2
Culpho **152** D3
Culquhirk **215** F5
Culrain **266** C2
Culross **235** D1
Culroy **224** B4
Culsh **260** B5
Culshabbin **215** E5
Culswick **279** B8
Culter Allers Farm **226** B2
Cultercullen **261** H2
Cults Aber **260** D1
Cults Aberdeen **261** G4
Cults D&G **207** E2
Cultybraggan
Camp **242** C3
Culverhouse Cross **130** A5
Culverstone Green **123** F2
Culverthorpe **175** F3
Culvie **268** D5
Culworth **148** A3
Culzean Castle & Country
Park SAyr
KA19 8LE **224** A4
Cumberhead **225** F2
Cumberlow Green **150** B4
Cumbernauld **234** B2
Cumberworth **189** F5
Cuminestown **269** G6
Cumloden **215** F4
Cummersdale **209** G1
Cummertrees **217** F4
Cummingstown **267** J5
Cumnock **225** D3
Cumnor **133** G2
Cumrew **210** B2
Cumrue **217** E2
Cumstoun **216** A5
Cumwhinton **210** A2
Cumwhitton **210** B2
Cundall **202** D5
Cunninghamhead **233** E5
Cunningsburgh **279** D10
Cunnister **278** E3
Cunnoquhie **244** B3
Cupar **244** B3
Cupar Muir **244** B3
Curbar **185** G5
Curborough **158** D1
Curbridge Hants **107** E1
Curbridge Oxon **133** F2
Curdridge **107** E1
Curdworth **159** D3
Curland **103** F1

Curlew Green **153** E1
Curling Tye Green **138** B2
Curload **116** A5
Curridge **133** G5
Currie **235** F3
Curry Mallet **116** A5
Curry Rivel **116** A5
Curteis' Corner **124** A5
Curtisden Green **123** G4
Curtisknowle **100** D2
Cury **95** D4
Cusgarne **96** B5
Cushnie **269** F4
Cushuish **115** E4
Cusop **144** B3
Cusworth **186** C2
Cutcombe **114** C4
Cutgate **184** C1
Cuthill **266** E3
Cutiau **154** C1
Cutlers Green **151** D4
Cutnall Green **146** A1
Cutsdean **146** D4
Cutsyke **194** D5
Cutthorpe **186** A5
Cutts **279** D9
Cuxham **134** B3
Cuxton **123** G2
Cuxwold **188** B2
Cwm BGwent **130** A2
Cwm Denb **182** B5
Cwm Ffrwd-oer **130** B2
Cwm Gwaun **140** D4
Cwm Head **156** D4
Cwm Irfon **143** E3
Cwm Penmachno **168** A3
Cwm Plysgog **141** E3
Cwmafan **129** E4
Cwmaman **129** G3
Cwmann **142** B3
Cwmbach Carmar **141** F5
Cwmbach Carmar **128** A2
Cwmbach Powys **144** A4
Cwmbach Powys **143** G3
Cwmbach RCT **129** G2
Cwmbelan **155** F4
Cwmbrân **130** B3
Cwmbrwyno **154** D4
Cwmcarn **130** B3
Cwmcarvan **131** D2
Cwm-Cewydd **155** E1
Cwm-cou **141** F3
Cwmcrawnon **130** A1
Cwmdare **129** F2
Cwmdu Carmar **142** C4
Cwmdu Powys **144** A4
Cwmduad **141** G4
Cwmerfyn **154** D4
Cwmfelin **129** G2
Cwmfelin Boeth **127** E1
Cwmfelin Mynach **141** F5
Cwmfelinfach **130** A3
Cwmffrwd **128** A1
Cwmgiedd **129** D1
Cwmgors **128** D1
Cwmgwili **128** B1
Cwmgwrach **129** E2
Cwmgwyn **128** C3
Cwmhiraeth **141** G4
Cwmifor **142** C5
Cwmisfael **128** A1
Cwm-Llinau **155** E2
Cwmllyfri **127** G1
Cwmllynfell **128** D1
Cwm-mawr **128** B1
Cwm-miles **141** E5
Cwm-Morgan **141** F4
Cwm-parc **129** F3
Cwmpengraig **141** G4
Cwmpennar **129** G2
Cwmsychbant **142** A3
Cwmsymlog **154** C4
Cwmtillery **130** B2
Cwm-twrch Isaf **129** D1
Cwm-twrch Uchaf **129** D1
Cwm-y-glo **167** E1
Cwmyoy **144** C5
Cwm-yr-Eglwys **140** D3
Cwmyrhaiadr **155** D3
Cwmystwyth **155** D5
Cwrt **154** C2
Cwrt-newydd **142** A3
Cwrt-y-cadno **142** C3
Cwrt-y-gollen **130** B1
Cyffylliog **169** D2
Cyfronydd **156** A2
Cymau **169** F2
Cymmer NPT **129** E3
Cymmer RCT **129** G3
Cyncoed **130** A4
Cynghordy **143** E4
Cynheidre **128** A2
Cynwyd **169** D3
Cynwyl Elfed **141** G5

D

Dabton **216** C1
Daccombe **101** F1
Dacre Cumb **210** A5
Dacre NYorks **194** A1
Dacre Banks **194** A1
Daddry Shield **211** E4
Dadford **148** B4
Dadlington **159** G3
Dafen **128** B2
Daffy Green **178** A5
Dagdale **172** B4
Dagenham **137** D4
Daggons **106** A1
Daglingworth **132** B2
Dagnall **135** E1
Dail **240** C1
Dail Beag **270** E3
Dail Mòr **270** E3
Dailly **224** B5
Dainton **101** E1
Dairsie (Osnaburgh) **244** C3
Dairy House **197** E3
Daisy Bank **158** C3
Daisy Green **152** B1
Dalabrog **254** C2
Dalavich **240** B3
Dalballoch **258** D5
Dalbeattie **216** C4
Dalblair **225** E4

Dalbog **253** D2
Dalbreck **274** C7
Dalbury **173** D4
Dalby IoM **190** A4
Dalby Lincs **176** C1
Dalby NYorks **203** F5
Dalby Forest Drive NYorks
YO18 7LT **204** B4
Dalcairnie **224** C5
Dalchalloch **250** D3
Dalchalm **267** G1
Dalchirach **259** J1
Dalchork **273** H7
Dalchreichart **257** J3
Dalchruin **242** C3
Dalcross **266** E7
Dalderby **176** A1
Daldownie **259** K4
Dale Cumb **210** B2
Dale GtMan **185** D2
Dale Pembs **126** B2
Dale Abbey **173** F4
Dale End Derbys **172** D1
Dale End NYorks **193** F3
Dale Head **199** F1
Dale of Walls **279** A7
Dale Park **108** B2
Dalehouse **203** G1
Dalelia **247** G3
Dalestie **259** J3
Dalfad **260** B4
Dalfoot **260** E7
Dalganachan **275** F4
Dalgarven **233** D5
Dalgety Bay **235** F1
Dalgig **225** D4
Dalginross **242** C2
Dalgonar **225** F5
Dalguise **251** E2
Dalhalvaig **274** D3
Dalham **151** F1
Daligan **233** E1
Dalinlongart **232** C1
Dalivaddy **222** B3
Daljarrock **214** C2
Dalkeith **236** A3
Dallas **267** J6
Dallaschyle **267** F7
Dallash **215** F4
Dalleagles **225** D4
Dallinghoo **153** D2
Dallington ESuss **110** B2
Dallington N'hants **148** C1
Dallow **202** A5
Dalmadilly **261** F3
Dalmally
(Dail Mhàilidh) **241** D2
Dalmarnock **251** F5
Dalmary **242** A5
Dalmellington **224** C5
Dalmeny **235** F2
Dalmichy **273** H7
Dalmigavie **258** E4
Dalmore **266** D5
Dalmuir **233** F2
Dalmunzie House
Hotel **251** F5
Dalnabreck **247** G3
Dalnacarn **251** F3
Dalnaglar Castle **251** G3
Dalnaha **239** F2
Dalnahaitnach **259** F3
Dalnamain **266** E2
Dalnatrat
(Dail na Tràghad) **248** B4
Dalnavert **259** F4
Dalnavie **266** D4
Dalness **249** D4
Dalnessie **273** J7
Dalnigap **214** C3
Dalqueich **243** F4
Dalreoch **214** C2
Dalriech **242** C1
Dalroy **266** E7
Dalrulzian **251** F4
Dalry **233** D5
Dalrymple **224** B4
Dalscote **148** B2
Dalserf **234** B5
Dalserf **278** B3
Dalshangan **215** G2
Dalskairth **216** D3
Dalston **209** G1
Dalswinton **216** D2
Daltomach **258** E2
Dalton Cumb **199** G5
Dalton D&G **217** E3
Dalton Lancs **183** F2
Dalton N'umb **220** D4
Dalton N'umb **211** F2
Dalton NYorks **202** D5
Dalton NYorks **202** A2
Dalton SYorks **186** B3
Dalton Magna **186** B3
Dalton Piercy **213** D3
Dalton-in-Furness **198** D5
Dalton-le-Dale **212** D4
Dalton-on-Tees **202** B2
Daltote **231** F1
Daltra **267** G7
Dalveich **242** B2
Dalvennan **224** B4
Dalvourn **258** D1
Dalwhinnie **250** B1
Dalwood **103** F2
Dam Green **164** B3
Damerham **106** A1
Damgate **179** F5
Damnaglaur **206** B3
Damside **235** E2
Danaway **124** A2
Danbury **137** G2
Danby **203** G2
Danby Wiske **202** C3
Dancers Hill **136** B3
Dandaleith **267** K7
Danderhall **236** A3
Dane Bank **184** D3
Dane End **150** B5
Dane Hills **160** A2
Danebridge **171** G1
Danehill **109** G1
Danemoor **173** F1
Danesmoor **173** F1
Danestone **261** H3

Daniel's Water **124** B4
Danskine **236** C3
Danthorpe **197** E4
Danzey Green **146** D1
Darby End **158** B4
Darby Green **120** D1
Darenth **137** E5
Daresbury **183** G4
Darfield **186** B2
Dargate **124** C2
Dargues **220** A2
Darite **97** G3
Darland **123** G2
Darlaston **158** B3
Darley **194** B2
Darley Bridge **173** D1
Darley Dale **173** D1
Darley Head **194** A2
Darley Hillside **173** D1
Darlingscott **147** E3
Darlington **202** B2
Darliston **170** C4
Darlton **187** E5
Darnabo **269** F6
Darnall **186** A4
Darnconner **225** D3
Darnford **261** F5
Darngarroch **216** A4
Darnick **227** G2
Darowen **155** E2
Darra **269** F6
Darracott **112** C4
Darras Hall **221** D4
Darrington **186** B1
Darrow Green **165** D3
Darsham **153** F1
Dartfield **269** J5
Dartford **137** E5
Dartington **101** D1
Dartington Cider Press
Centre Devon
TQ9 6TQ **101** D1
Dartington Crystal Ltd.
Devon
EX38 7AN **113** E4
Dartmeet **99** G3
Dartmouth **101** E2
Darton **186** A1
Darvel **225** D2
Darwell Hole **110** B2
Darwen **192** C5
Datchet **135** E5
Datchworth **136** B1
Datchworth Green **136** B1
Daubhill **184** A2
Daugh of
Kinermony **267** K7
Dauntsey **132** B4
Dauntsey Green **132** B4
Dauntsey Lock **132** B4
Dava **259** H1
Davaar **222** C4
Davan **260** C4
Davenham **184** A5
Davenport Green **184** C4
Daventry **148** A1
Daventry Country Park
N'hants
NN11 2JB **148** A1
David Marshall Lodge
Stir FK8 3SX **242** A4
Davidson's Mains **235** F2
Davidstow **97** F1
Davington **226** D5
Daviot Aber **261** F2
Daviot High **258** E1
Davoch of Grange **268** C5
Davyhulme **184** B3
Dawley **157** F2
Dawlish **102** C5
Dawn **181** G5
Daws Heath **138** B4
Daw's House **98** D2
Dawsmere **176** B2
Day Green **171** E2
Dayhills **171** G4
Dayhouse Bank **158** B5
Daylesford **147** E5
Ddôl **182** C5
Deadman's Cross **149** G3
Deadwaters **234** B5
Deaf Hill **212** C4
Deal **125** F3
Deal Hall **139** E3
Dean Cumb **209** D4
Dean Devon **100** D1
Dean Dorset **105** F1
Dean Hants **107** E1
Dean Oxon **147** F5
Dean Som **117** D3
Dean Bank **212** B4
Dean Cross **113** F1
Dean Castle & Country
Park EAyr
KA3 1XB **224** C2
Dean Gallery Edin
EH4 3DS **36** B4
Dean Head **185** G3
Dean Prior **100** D1
Dean Row **184** C4
Dean Street **123** G3
Deanburnhaugh **227** E4
Deane GtMan **184** A2
Deane Hants **119** G2
Deanland **105** F1
Deanlane End **107** G1
Deans **235** E3
Deans Bottom **124** A2
Deanscales **209** D4
Deansgreen **184** A4
Deanshanger **148** C4
Deanston **242** C4
Dearham **209** D3
Debach **152** D2
Debate **218** A3
Debden Essex **151** D4
Debden Green
Essex **151** D4
Debden Green
Essex **136** D3
Debenham **152** C1
Deblin's Green **146** A3
Dechmont **235** E2
Decker Hill **157** G1
Deddington **147** G4
Dedham **152** B4
Dedham Heath **152** B4
Dedworth **135** E5

Deecastle **260** C5
Deene **161** E3
Deenethorpe **161** E3
Deep, The HU1 4DP
76 Kingston upon Hull
Deep Sea World, North
Queensferry Fife
KY11 1JR **235** F1
Deepcar **185** G3
Deepcut **121** E2
Deepdale Cumb **200** C4
Deepdale NYorks **201** D5
Deeping Gate **161** G2
Deeping St. James **161** G2
Deeping
St. Nicholas **162** A1
Deepweir **131** D4
Deerhill **268** C5
Deerhurst **146** A5
Deerhurst Walton **146** A5
Deerness Valley Walk
Dur DH7 7RJ **212** A3
Deerton Street **124** B2
Defford **146** B3
Defynnog **143** F5
Deganwy **181** F5
Degnish **239** G3
Deighton NYorks **202** C2
Deighton WYorks **185** F1
Deighton York **195** F3
Deiniolen **167** E1
Delabole **97** E1
Delamere **170** C1
Delavorar **259** J3
Delfrigs **261** H2
Dell Lodge **259** H3
Dell Quay **108** A3
Delliefure **259** H1
Delly End **133** F2
Delnabo **259** J3
Delny **266** E4
Delph **185** D2
Delphorrie **260** C3
Delves **212** A3
Delvine **251** G5
Dembleby **175** F4
Denaby **186** B3
Denaby Main **186** B3
Denbies Wine Estate
Surr RH5 6AA **121** G2
Denbigh (Dinbych) **168** D1
Denbury **101** E1
Denby **173** E3
Denby Dale **185** G2
Denby Pottery Derbys
DE5 8NX **18** C1
Denchworth **133** F3
Dendron **198** D5
Denend **260** E1
Denford **161** E5
Dengie **138** C2
Denham Bucks **135** F4
Denham Suff **165** E5
Denham Suff **151** F1
Denham Green **135** F4
Denham Street **164** C4
Denhead Aber **261** H5
Denhead Aber **269** J5
Denhead Fife **244** C3
Denhead of
Arbirlot **253** D5
Denhead of Gray **244** B1
Denholm **227** G4
Denholme **193** G4
Denholme Clough **193** G4
Denio **166** C4
Denmead **107** F1
Denmill **261** G3
Denmoss **268** E6
Dennington **153** D1
Denny **234** C1
Dennyloanhead **234** C1
Denshaw **185** D1
Denside **261** G5
Densole **125** E4
Denston **151** F2
Denstone **172** B3
Dent **200** C4
Denton Cambs **161** G4
Denton Darl **202** B1
Denton ESuss **109** G3
Denton GtMan **184** D3
Denton Kent **125** E4
Denton Kent **137** F5
Denton Lincs **175** D4
Denton N'hants **148** D2
Denton Norf **165** D3
Denton NYorks **194** A3
Denton Oxon **134** A2
Denton's Green **183** F3
Denver **163** E2
Denville **107** E2
Denwick **229** G5
Deopham **178** B5
Deopham Green **164** B3
Depden **151** F2
Depden Green **151** F2
Deptford GtLon **136** C5
Deptford Wilts **118** B4
Derby **173** E4
Derby City Museum & Art
Gallery DE1 1BS
70 Derby
Derbyhaven **190** A5
Dereham
(East Dereham) **178** A4
Dererach **239** E2
Deri **130** A2
Derril **112** D5
Derringstone **125** E4
Derrington **171** F5
Derriton **112** D5
Derry **242** B2
Derry Hill **132** B5
Derrythorpe **187** F2
Dersingham **177** E4
Dervaig **246** D4
Derwen **169** D2
Derwenlas **154** D3
Derwent Walk Country Park
Dur NE16 3BN **28** A3
Derwydd **128** C1
Derybruich **232** A2
Desborough **160** D4
Desford **159** G2
Detchant **229** E3
Dethick **173** E2
Detling **123** G3

D

Deuddwr 156 B1
Deunant 168 C1
Deuxhill 157 F4
Devauden 131 D3
Devil's Bridge (Pontarfynach) 154 D5
Devitts Green 159 E3
Devizes 118 B1
Devon Guild of Craftsmen *Devon* TQ13 9AF 102 B5
Devonport 100 A2
Devonside 243 E5
Devoran 95 E3
Dewar 236 A5
Dewlish 105 D3
Dewsall Court 145 D4
Dewsbury 194 B5
Dewsbury Moor 194 B5
Dhiseig 239 D1
Dhoon 190 C3
Dhoor 190 C2
Dhowin 190 C1
Dhuhallow 258 C2
Dial Green 121 E5
Dial Post 109 D2
Dibden 106 D2
Dibden Hill 135 E3
Dibden Purlieu 106 D2
Dick Institute *EAyr* KA1 3BU 224 C2
Dickleburgh 164 C3
Dickleburgh Moor 164 C3
Didbrook 146 C4
Didcot 134 A3
Diddington 149 G1
Diddlebury 157 E4
Didley 145 D4
Didling 108 A2
Didmarton 132 A4
Didsbury 184 C3
Didworthy 100 C1
Digby 175 F2
Digg 263 K5
Diggle 185 E2
Digmoor 183 F2
Digswell 136 B1
Dihewyd 142 A2
Dildawn 216 B5
Dilham 179 E3
Dilhorne 171 G3
Dillington 149 G1
Dilston 211 F1
Dilton Marsh 117 F3
Dilwyn 144 D2
Dilwyn Common 144 D2
Dimple 184 B1
Dinas *Carmar* 141 F4
Dinas *Gwyn* 167 D2
Dinas *Gwyn* 166 B4
Dinas Cross 140 D4
Dinas Dinlle 166 D2
Dinas Mawddwy 155 E1
Dinckley 192 C4
Dinder 116 B3
Dinedor 145 E4
Dingestow 131 D3
Dingley 160 C4
Dingwall (Inbhir Pheofharain) 266 C6
Dinlabyre 218 D2
Dinnet 260 C5
Dinnington *Som* 104 A1
Dinnington *SYorks* 186 C4
Dinnington *Shrop* 157 E2
Dinnington *T&W* 221 E4
Dinorwig 167 F1
Dinosaur Adventure Park *Norf* NR9 5JW 178 C4
Dinosaur Museum, Dorchester *Dorset* DT1 1EW 104 C3
Dinton *Bucks* 134 C1
Dinton *Wilts* 118 B4
Dinton Pastures Country Park *W'ham* RG10 0TH 134 C5
Dinvin 214 B5
Dinwoodie Mains 217 F1
Dinworthy 112 D4
Dipford 115 F5
Dippen *A&B* 222 C2
Dippen *NAyr* 223 F3
Dippenhall 120 D3
Dipple *Moray* 268 B5
Dipple *SAyr* 224 A5
Diptford 100 D2
Dipton 212 A2
Dirdhu 259 H2
Dirleton 236 C1
Discoed 144 B1
Discovery Museum *T&W* NE1 4JA 79 Newcastle upon Tyne
Diseworth 173 F5
Dishes 276 D5
Dishforth 202 C5
Dishley 173 G5
Disley 185 D4
Diss 164 C3
Disserth 143 G2
Distington 208 D4
Ditcheat 116 D4
Ditchingham 165 E2
Ditchley 147 F5
Ditchling 109 F2
Ditteridge 117 F1
Dittisham 101 E2
Ditton *Halton* 183 F4
Ditton *Kent* 123 G3
Ditton Green 151 E2
Ditton Priors 157 F4
Dixton *Glos* 146 B4
Dixton *Mon* 131 E1
Dobcross 185 D2
Dobwalls 97 G3
Doccombe 102 A4
Dochgarroch 258 D1
Dock Museum, Barrow-in-Furness *Cumb* LA14 2PW 191 E1
Dockenfield 120 D3
Docker *Cumb* 199 G3
Docker *Lancs* 199 G5
Docking 177 F4
Docklow 145 E2
Dockray *Cumb* 209 G4
Dockray *Cumb* 209 F1

Dodbrooke 100 D3
Doddenham 145 G2
Doddinghurst 137 E3
Doddington *Cambs* 162 C2
Doddington *Kent* 124 B3
Doddington *Lincs* 187 G5
Doddington *N'umb* 229 D3
Doddington *Shrop* 157 F5
Doddiscombsleigh 102 B4
Doddycross 98 D4
Dodford *N'hants* 148 B1
Dodford *Worcs* 158 B5
Dodington *SGlos* 131 G4
Dodington *Som* 115 E3
Dodington Ash 131 G5
Dodleston 170 A1
Dods Leigh 172 B4
Dodscott 113 F4
Dodworth 186 A2
Doehole 173 E2
Doffcocker 184 A1
Dog Village 102 C3
Dogdyke 176 A2
Dogmersfield 120 C2
Dogsthorpe 162 A2
Dol Fawr 155 E2
Dolanog 155 G1
Dolau *Powys* 144 A1
Dolau *RCT* 129 G4
Dolbenmaen 167 E3
Doley 171 F3
Dolfach 155 F5
Dolfor 156 A4
Dolgarrog 142 D4
Dolgarrog 168 A1
Dolgellau 154 D1
Dolgoch 154 C2
Dolgran 142 A4
Doll 267 F1
Dollar 243 E5
Dollarbeg 243 E5
Dolphin 182 C5
Dolphinholme 192 B2
Dolphinton 235 F5
Dolton 113 F4
Dolwen *Conwy* 181 G5
Dolwen *Powys* 155 F2
Dolwyddelan 168 A2
Dôl-y-bont 154 C4
Dôl-y-cannau 144 A3
Dolyhir 144 B2
Dolwyern 169 F4
Domgay 156 B1
Doncaster 186 C2
Doncaster Racecourse Exhibition Centre *SYorks* DN2 6BB 186 D2
Donhead St. Andrew 118 A5
Donhead St. Mary 118 A5
Donibristle 235 F1
Doniford 115 D3
Donington *Lincs* 176 A4
Donington *Shrop* 158 A2
Donington le Heath 159 G1
Donington *N'hants* 149 G1
Donington on Bain 188 C4
Donisthorpe 159 F2
Donkey Sanctuary, Salcombe Regis *Devon* EX10 0NU 103 D4
Donna Nook 189 E3
Donnington *Glos* 147 D5
Donnington *Here* 145 G4
Donnington *Shrop* 157 E2
Donnington *Tel&W* 157 G1
Donnington *WBerks* 119 F1
Donnington *WSuss* 108 A3
Donyatt 103 G1
Dorchester *Dorset* 104 C3
Dorchester Abbey *Oxon* OX10 7HH 134 A3
Dordon 159 E2
Dore 186 A4
Dores (Duras) 258 C1
Dorket Head 173 G3
Dorking 121 G3
Dorley's Corner 153 E1
Dormans Park 122 C4
Dormansland 122 C4
Dormanstown 213 E5
Dormer's Wells 136 A4
Dormington 145 E3
Dormston 146 B2
Dorn 147 E4
Dorney 135 E5
Dorney Reach 135 E5
Dornie (An Dòrnaidh) 256 E2
Dornoch 266 E3
Dornock 218 A5
Dorrery 275 F3
Dorridge 159 D5
Dorrington *Lincs* 175 F2
Dorrington *Shrop* 157 D2
Dorsell 260 D3
Dorsington 146 D3
Dorstone 144 C3
Dorton 134 B1
Dorusduain 257 F2
Dosthill 159 E5
Dotland 211 F2
Dottery 104 A3
Doublebois 97 F3
Dougalston 233 G2
Dougarie 223 D2
Doughton 132 A3
Douglas *IoM* 190 B4
Douglas *SLan* 225 G2
Douglas & Angus 244 C1
Douglas Water 225 G2
Douglastown 252 C5
Doulting 116 D3
Dounby 276 B5
Doune *A&B* 241 E5
Doune *A&B* 241 F3
Doune *High* 259 F3
Doune *High* 266 B1
Doune *Stir* 242 C4
Dounepark 269 F4
Douneside 260 C4
Dounie *High* 266 D3
Dounie *High* 266 C5
Dounreay 274 E2
Dousland 100 B1
Dovaston 170 A5
Dove Holes 185 E5

Dovenby 209 D3
Dovendale 188 D4
Dover 125 F4
Dover Castle *Kent* CT16 1HU 70 Dover
Dovercourt 152 D4
Doverdale 146 A1
Doveridge 172 C4
Doversgreen 122 B4
Dowally 251 F5
Dowdeswell 146 C5
Dowhill 224 A5
Dowland 113 F4
Dowlands 103 F3
Dowlish Ford 103 G1
Dowlish Wake 103 G1
Down Ampney 132 D3
Down End 116 A3
Down Hatherley 146 A5
Down St. Mary 102 A2
Down Thomas 100 B3
Downderry 98 D5
Downe 122 D2
Downend *IoW* 107 E4
Downend *SGlos* 131 F5
Downend *WBerks* 133 G5
Downfield 244 B1
Downfields 99 D3
Downgate 99 D3
Downham *Essex* 137 G3
Downham *Lancs* 193 D3
Downham *N'umb* 228 C3
Downham Market 163 E2
Downhead *Corn* 97 G1
Downhead *Som* 117 D3
Downhead *Som* 116 C1
Downholland Cross 183 E2
Downholme 202 A3
Downies 261 H5
Downley 135 D3
Downs 116 B1
Downside *NSom* 116 B1
Downside *Som* 116 B1
Downside *Som* 116 D2
Downside *Surr* 121 G2
Downton *Devon* 99 F2
Downton *Devon* 101 E2
Downton *Hants* 106 B3
Downton *Wilts* 118 C5
Downton on the Rock 156 D5
Dowsby 175 G5
Dowthwaitehead 209 G4
Doxey 171 G5
Doynton 131 G5
Drabblegate 178 D3
Draethen 130 A4
Draffan 234 B5
Dragley Beck 199 D5
Drakeland Corner 100 B2
Drakelow 158 A4
Drakemyre 233 D4
Drakes Broughton 146 B3
Drakes Cross 158 C5
Draughton *N'hants* 160 C5
Draughton *NYorks* 193 G2
Drax 195 F5
Draycot Foliat 133 D5
Draycote 147 G1
Draycott *Derbys* 173 F4
Draycott *Glos* 147 D5
Draycott *Shrop* 158 A3
Draycott *Som* 116 B2
Draycott *Worcs* 146 A3
Draycott in the Clay 172 C5
Draycott in the Moors 171 G4
Drayford 102 A1
Draynes 97 G3
Drayton *Leics* 160 D3
Drayton *Lincs* 176 A4
Drayton *Norf* 178 C4
Drayton *Oxon* 147 G3
Drayton *Oxon* 133 G3
Drayton *Ports* 107 F2
Drayton *Som* 116 B5
Drayton *Warks* 147 D2
Drayton *Worcs* 158 B5
Drayton Bassett 159 D2
Drayton Beauchamp 135 E2
Drayton Manor Park *Staffs* B78 3TW 159 D2
Drayton Parslow 148 D5
Drayton St. Leonard 134 A3
Drebley 193 G2
Dreemskerry 190 C2
Dreenhill 126 C1
Drefach *Carmar* 141 G4
Drefach *Carmar* 128 B1
Dre-fach *Cere* 142 B3
Drefelin 141 G4
Dreghorn 224 B2
Drem 269 H6
Drewsteignton 102 A3
Driby 189 D5
Driffield *ERid* 196 C2
Driffield *Glos* 132 C3
Drigg 198 B3
Drighlington 194 B5
Drimfern 240 C3
Drimlee 240 D3
Drimnin 247 E4
Drimore 262 C7
Drimpton 104 A2
Drimsdale (Dreumasdal) 254 C1
Drimsynie 241 D4
Drimvore 240 A5
Drinan 256 B3
Dringhouses 195 E2
Drinisiader 263 G2
Drinkstone 152 A1
Drinkstone Green 152 A1
Drishaig 241 D3
Drissaig 240 B3
Drointon 172 B5
Droitwich Spa 146 A1
Dron 243 G3
Dronfield 186 A5
Dronfield Woodhouse 186 A5
Drongan 224 C4
Dronley 244 B1
Droop 105 D2

Dropmore 135 E4
Droxford 107 F1
Droylsden 184 D3
Druid 168 C2
Druidston 126 B1
Druimarbin 248 C2
Druimavuic 248 C5
Druimdrishaig 231 F2
Druimindarroch 247 F1
Druimkinnerras 258 B1
Drum *A&B* 232 A2
Drum *P&K* 243 F4
Drumachloy 232 B3
Drumbeg 272 D5
Drumblade 268 D6
Drumblair 268 D6
Drumbuie *D&G* 225 F4
Drumbuie *High* 266 E6
Drumburgh 209 F1
Drumchapel 233 G2
Drumchardine 266 C7
Drumchork 264 E3
Drumclog 225 D2
Drumdelgie 268 C6
Drumderfit 266 D6
Drumeldrie 244 C4
Drumelzier 226 C2
Drumfearn 256 C3
Drumfern 248 B2
Drumgarve 222 C3
Drumgley 252 C4
Drumguish 258 C5
Drumhead *Aber* 260 E5
Drumin 259 J1
Drumine 266 E6
Drumjohn 215 G1
Drumlamford House 215 D3
Drumlasie 260 E4
Drumlemble 222 B4
Drumlithie 253 F1
Drummond *High* 266 D5
Drummond *Stir* 242 B4
Drummore 206 B3
Drummuir 268 B6
Drumnadrochit (Druim na Drochaid) 258 C2
Drumnagorrach 268 D5
Drumoak 261 F5
Drumore 222 C3
Drumour 243 E1
Drumpellier Country Park *NLan* ML5 1RX 31 G3
Drumrash 216 A3
Drumrunie 265 H1
Drums 261 H2
Drumsturdy 244 C1
Drumuie 263 K7
Drumuillie 259 G2
Drumvaich 242 B4
Drumwhindle 261 H1
Drumwhirn 216 B3
Drunkendub 253 E5
Druridge 221 E2
Druridge Bay Country Park *N'umb* NE61 5BX 221 E2
Drury 169 F1
Drusillas Park *ESuss* BN26 5QS 110 A3
Dry Doddington 174 D3
Dry Drayton 150 B1
Dry Harbour 264 C6
Dry Sandford 133 G2
Dry Street 137 F4
Drybeck 200 B1
Drybridge *Moray* 268 C4
Drybridge *NAyr* 224 B2
Drybrook 131 F1
Dryburgh 227 G2
Dryhope 226 D3
Drymen 233 F1
Drymuir 269 H6
Drynoch 255 K1
Dryslwyn 142 B5
Dryton 157 E2
Duachy 240 A2
Dubford 269 F4
Dubhchladach 231 G3
Dubheads 243 E2
Dublin 152 C1
Duchal 233 E3
Duchally 273 F7
Duchray 241 G4
Duck Bay 233 E1
Duck End *Bed* 149 F3
Duck End *Cambs* 150 A1
Duck End *Essex* 151 G5
Duck Street 194 A1
Duckington 170 B2
Ducklington 133 F2
Duckmanton 186 B5
Duck's Cross 149 G2
Ducks Island 136 B3
Duddenhoe End 150 C4
Duddingston 235 G2
Duddington 161 E2
Duddlestone 115 F5
Duddleswell 109 G1
Duddo 237 G5
Duddon 170 C1
Duddon Bridge 198 C4
Dudleston 170 A4
Dudleston Heath 170 A4
Dudley *T&W* 221 E4
Dudley *WMid* 158 B3
Dudley Port 158 B3
Dudley Zoo & Castle *WMid* DY1 4QB 14 B3
Dudlow's Green 184 A4
Dudsbury 105 G2
Duffield 173 E3
Duffryn 129 G5
Dufftown 260 B1
Duffus 267 J5
Dufton 210 C5
Duggleby 196 A1
Duiar 259 J1
Duible 274 E6
Duiletter 241 D2
Duinish 250 B3
Duirinish 256 D1

Duisdealmor 256 D3
Duisky 248 C2
Duke End 159 E4
Dukestown 130 A1
Dukinfield 184 D3
Dulas 180 C4
Dulax 260 B3
Dulcote 116 C3
Dulford 103 D2
Dull 250 D5
Dullatur 234 B2
Dullingham 151 E2
Dullingham Ley 151 E2
Dulnain Bridge 259 G2
Duloe *Bed* 149 G1
Duloe *Corn* 97 G4
Dulsie 267 G7
Dulverton 114 C5
Dulwich 136 C5
Dulwich Picture Gallery *GtLon* SE21 7AD 13 C7
Dumbarton 233 E2
Dumbleton 146 C4
Dumcrieff 226 C5
Dumeath 260 C1
Dumfin 233 E1
Dumfries 217 D3
Dumgoyne 233 G1
Dummer 119 G3
Dun 253 E4
Dunach 240 A2
Dunalastair 250 C4
Dunan *A&B* 232 C2
Dunan *High* 256 B2
Dunans 240 C5
Dunball 116 A3
Dunbar 237 D2
Dunbeath 275 G5
Dunbeg (An Dùn Beag) 240 A1
Dunblane 242 C4
Dunbog 244 A3
Dunbridge 119 E5
Duncanston *Aber* 260 D2
Duncanston *High* 266 C6
Dunchideock 102 B4
Dunchurch 159 G5
Duncote 148 B2
Duncow 217 D2
Duncraggan 242 A4
Duncrievie 243 G4
Duncroist 242 A1
Duncrub 243 F3
Duncryne 233 F1
Duncton 108 B2
Dundee 244 C1
Dundee Contemporary Arts DD1 4DY 71 Dundee
Dundon 116 B4
Dundon Hayes 116 B4
Dundonald 224 B2
Dundonnell (Ach-Dà-Dhòmhnaill) 265 G3
Dundraw 209 F2
Dundreggan (Dul Dreagain) 257 K3
Dundrennan 208 A2
Dundridge 107 E1
Dundry 116 C1
Dunearn 235 G1
Dunecht 261 F4
Dunfermline 235 F1
Dunfield 132 D3
Dunford Bridge 185 F2
Dungate 124 B3
Dungavel 225 D2
Dungworth 185 G3
Dunham 148 C1
Dunham Massey Hall, Park & Gardens *GtMan* WA14 4SJ 24 C6
Dunham Town 184 B4
Dunham Woodhouses 184 B4
Dunham-on-the-Hill 183 F5
Dunhampton 146 A1
Dunholme 188 A5
Dunino 244 D3
Dunipace 234 C1
Dunira 242 C2
Dunkeld 251 F5
Dunkerton 117 E2
Dunkeswell 103 E2
Dunkeswick 194 C3
Dunkirk *ChesW&C* 183 E5
Dunkirk *Kent* 124 C3
Dunk's Green 123 F3
Dunlappie 253 D3
Dunley *Hants* 119 F2
Dunley *Worcs* 145 G1
Dunlop 233 F5
Dunloskin 232 C1
Dunmere 97 E3
Dunmore *A&B* 231 F3
Dunmore *Falk* 234 C1
Dunn 275 G3
Dunn Street 123 G2
Dunnabie 218 A3
Dunnet 275 H1
Dunnichen 252 D5
Dunning 243 F3
Dunnington *ERid* 197 D2
Dunnington *Warks* 146 C2
Dunnington *York* 195 F2
Dunnockshaw 193 E5
Dunoon 232 C2
Dunragit 214 C5
Dunrostan 231 F1
Duns 237 E4
Duns Tew 147 G5
Dunsa 185 G5
Dunsby 175 G5
Dunscore 216 C2
Dunscroft 187 D2
Dunsdale 203 F1
Dunsden Green 134 C5
Dunsfold 121 F4
Dunsford 102 B4
Dunshalt 244 A3
Dunshill 146 A4
Dunsill 173 F1
Dunsinnan 243 G1
Dunsland Cross 113 E5
Dunsley *NYorks* 204 B1
Dunsley *Staffs* 158 A4
Dunsmore 135 D2
Dunsop Bridge 192 C2

Dunstable 149 F5
Dunstable Downs *CenBeds* LU6 2GY 149 F5
Dunstall 172 C5
Dunstall Green 151 F5
Dunstan 229 G4
Dunstan Steads 229 G4
Dunster 114 C3
Dunster Castle & Gardens *Som* TA24 6SL 114 C3
Dunston *Lincs* 175 F1
Dunston *Norf* 178 D5
Dunston *Staffs* 158 B1
Dunston Heath 158 B1
Dunston Hill 212 B1
Dunstone *Devon* 102 A3
Dunstone *Devon* 100 B2
Dunsville 187 D2
Dunswell 196 C4
Dunsyre 235 E5
Dunterton 99 D3
Duntisbourne Abbots 132 B2
Duntisbourne Leer 132 B2
Duntisbourne Rouse 132 B2
Duntish 104 C2
Duntocher 233 F2
Dunton *Bucks* 148 D5
Dunton *CenBeds* 150 A3
Dunton *Norf* 177 G4
Dunton Bassett 160 A3
Dunton Green 123 E3
Dunton Wayletts 137 F3
Duntulm 263 K4
Dunure 224 A4
Dunure Mains 224 A4
Dunvant 128 B3
Dunvegan 263 H7
Dunvegan Castle *High* IV55 8WF 263 H7
Dunwich 165 F4
Dura 244 C3
Durdar 210 A2
Durgan 95 E4
Durgates 123 F5
Durham 212 B3
Durham Cathedral *Dur* DH1 3EH 71 Durham
Durham Dales Centre *Dur* DL13 2FJ 211 G3
Durham Tees Valley Airport 202 C1
Durinemast 247 F4
Durisdeer 225 G5
Durleigh 115 F4
Durley *Hants* 107 E1
Durley *Wilts* 118 D1
Durley Street 107 E1
Durlow Common 145 F4
Durnamuck 265 G2
Durness 273 G2
Durno 261 F2
Duror 248 B4
Durran *A&B* 240 B4
Durran *High* 275 G2
Durrants 107 G2
Durrington *Wilts* 118 C3
Durrington *WSuss* 108 D3
Dursley 131 G3
Dursley Cross 131 F1
Durston 115 F5
Durweston 105 E2
Dury 279 D6
Duston 148 C1
Duthie Park & David Welch Winter Gardens Aberdeen AB11 7TH 261 H4
Duthil 259 G2
Dutlas 156 B5
Duton Hill 151 E5
Dutson 98 D2
Dutton 183 G5
Duxford 150 C3
Dwygyfylchi 181 F5
Dwyran 166 D1
Dyce 261 G3
Dyfatty 128 A2
Dyffryn *Bridgend* 129 E3
Dyffryn *Pembs* 140 C4
Dyffryn *VGlam* 129 G5
Dyffryn Ardudwy 167 E5
Dyffryn Castell 155 D4
Dyffryn Ceidrych 142 D5
Dyffryn Cellwen 129 E1
Dyke *Devon* 112 C3
Dyke *Lincs* 175 G5
Dyke *Moray* 267 G6
Dykehead *Angus* 252 B3
Dykehead *NLan* 234 C4
Dykehead *Stir* 242 A4
Dykelands 253 F3
Dykends 252 A4
Dykeside 269 F6
Dylan Thomas Centre SA1 1RR 86 Swansea
Dylife 155 E3
Dymchurch 111 G1
Dymock 145 G4
Dyrham 131 G5
Dyrham Park *SGlos* SN14 8ER 8 F2
Dysart 244 B5
Dyserth 182 B5

E

Eachwick 220 D4
Eadar dha Fhadhail 270 C4
Eagland Hill 192 A3
Eagle 175 D1
Eagle Moor 175 D1
Eaglescliffe 202 D1
Eaglesfield *Cumb* 209 D4
Eaglesfield *D&G* 218 A4
Eaglesham 233 G4
Eaglethorpe 161 F3
Eagley 184 B1
Eairy 190 A4
Eakley 148 D2
Eakring 174 B1
Ealand 187 E1
Ealing 136 A4
Eamont Bridge 210 B5
Earby 193 F3

Earcroft 192 C5
Eardington 157 G3
Eardisland 144 D2
Eardisley 144 C3
Eardiston *Shrop* 170 A5
Eardiston *Worcs* 145 F1
Earith 162 B5
Earl Shilton 159 G3
Earl Soham 152 D1
Earl Sterndale 172 B1
Earl Stonham 152 C2
Earle 229 D4
Earlestown 183 G3
Earley 134 C5
Earlham 178 C5
Earlish 263 J5
Earls Barton 149 D1
Earls Colne 151 G5
Earl's Common 146 B2
Earl's Court 136 B5
Earls Court Exhibition Centre *GtLon* SW5 9TA 11 E5
Earl's Croome 146 A3
Earl's Green 152 B1
Earlsdon 159 F5
Earlsferry 244 C4
Earlsford 261 G1
Earlsheaton 194 B5
Earlston 227 G2
Earlswood *Mon* 131 D3
Earlswood *Surr* 122 B4
Earlswood *Warks* 158 D5
Earnley 108 A3
Earnshaw Bridge 192 B5
Earsairidh 254 C5
Earsdon 221 F4
Earsdon Moor 221 D2
Earsham 165 E3
Earsham Street 164 D4
Earswick 195 F2
Eartham 108 B3
Earthcott Green 131 F4
Easby 203 E2
Easdale 239 G3
Easebourne 121 D5
Easenhall 159 G5
Eashing 121 E3
Easington *Bucks* 134 B1
Easington *Dur* 212 D3
Easington *ERid* 189 D1
Easington *N'umb* 229 F3
Easington *Oxon* 147 G4
Easington *Oxon* 134 B3
Easington *R&C* 203 G1
Easington Colliery 212 D3
Easington Lane 212 C2
Easingwold 195 E1
Easole Street 125 E3
Eassie 252 B5
East Aberthaw 114 D1
East Allington 101 D3
East Anstey 114 B5
East Anton 119 E3
East Appleton 202 B3
East Ardsley 194 C5
East Ashey 107 E4
East Ashling 108 A3
East Auchronie 261 G4
East Ayton 204 C4
East Barkwith 188 B4
East Barnby 204 B1
East Barnet 136 B3
East Barsham 178 A2
East Beckham 178 C2
East Bedfont 135 F5
East Bergholt 152 B4
East Bierley 194 A5
East Bilney 178 A4
East Blatchington 109 G4
East Boldon 212 C1
East Boldre 106 C2
East Bolton 229 F5
East Bower 116 A4
East Brent 116 A2
East Bridge 153 F1
East Bridgford 174 B3
East Brora 267 G1
East Buckland 113 G2
East Budleigh 103 D4
East Burnham 135 E4
East Burra 279 C9
East Burrafirth 279 C6
East Butsfield 212 A3
East Butterleigh 102 C2
East Butterwick 187 F2
East Cairnbeg 253 F2
East Calder 235 E3
East Carleton 178 C5
East Carlton *N'hants* 160 D4
East Carlton *WYorks* 194 B3
East Carlton Countryside Park *N'hants* LE16 8YF 160 D4
East Chaldon (Chaldon Herring) 105 D4
East Challow 133 F4
East Charleton 101 D3
East Chelborough 104 B2
East Chiltington 109 F2
East Chinnock 104 A1
East Chisenbury 118 C2
East Claydon 148 C5
East Clyne 267 G1
East Clyth 275 H5
East Coker 104 B1
East Compton *Dorset* 105 E1
East Compton *Som* 116 D3
East Coombe 102 B2
East Cornworthy 101 E2
East Cottingwith 195 G3
East Cowes 107 E3
East Cowick 195 F5
East Cowton 202 C2
East Cramlington 221 E4
East Cranmore 117 D3
East Creech 105 F4
East Croachy 258 D2
East Darlochan 222 C3
East Davoch 260 C4

East Dean *ESuss* 110 A4
East Dean *Hants* 119 D5
East Dean *WSuss* 108 B2
East Dereham
(Dereham) 178 A4
East Down 113 F1
East Drayton 187 E5
East Dundry 116 C1
East Ella 196 C5
East End *ERid* 197 D4
East End *ERid* 197 E5
East End *Essex* 138 D2
East End *Hants* 119 F1
East End *Hants* 106 C3
East End *Herts* 150 C5
East End *Kent* 124 A5
East End *Kent* 124 B1
East End *MK* 149 E4
East End *NSom* 131 D5
East End *Oxon* 133 F3
East End *Poole* 105 F3
East End *Som* 116 C2
East End *Suff* 152 C4
East End *Suff* 152 C2
East Farleigh 123 G3
East Farndon 160 C4
East Ferry 187 F3
East Firsby 188 A4
East Fleetham 229 G4
East Fortune 236 C2
East Garston 133 F5
East Ginge 133 G4
East Goscote 160 B1
East Grafton 119 D1
East Green *Suff* 153 F1
East Green *Suff* 151 F2
East Grimstead 118 D5
East Grinstead 122 C5
East Guldeford 111 E1
East Haddon 148 B1
East Hagbourne 134 A4
East Halton 188 B1
East Ham 136 D4
East Hanney 133 G3
East Hanningfield 137 G2
East Hardwick 186 B1
East Harling 164 A3
East Harlsey 202 D3
East Harnham 118 C5
East Harptree 116 C2
East Hartford 221 E4
East Harting 107 G1
East Hatch 118 A5
East Hatley 150 A4
East Hauxwell 202 A3
East Haven 245 D1
East Heckington 175 G3
East Hedleyhope 212 A3
East Helmsdale 275 F7
East Hendred 133 G4
East Herrington 212 C2
East Heslerton 204 C5
East Hewish 116 B1
East Hoathly 110 A2
East Holme 105 E4
East Horndon 137 F4
East Horrington 116 C3
East Horsley 121 F2
East Horton 229 E3
East Howe 105 G3
East Huntspill 116 A3
East Hyde 136 A1
East Ilsley 133 G4
East Keal 176 B1
East Kennett 118 C1
East Keswick 194 C3
East Kilbride 234 A4
East Kimber 99 E1
East Kirkby 176 B1
East Knapton 204 B5
East Knighton 105 E4
East Knowstone 114 B5
East Knoyle 117 F4
East Kyloe 229 E3
East Lambrook 104 A1
East Lancashire Railway
Lancs BL9 0EY 193 E5
East Langdon 125 F4
East Langton 160 C3
East Langwell 266 E1
East Lavant 108 A3
East Lavington 108 B2
East Layton 202 A1
East Leake 173 G5
East Learney 260 E4
East Leigh *Devon* 102 A2
East Leigh *Devon* 102 A1
East Leigh *Devon* 101 D2
East Leigh *Devon* 100 C2
East Lexham 163 G1
East Lilburn 229 E4
East Linton 236 C2
East Liss 120 C5
East Lockinge 133 G4
East Looe 97 G4
East Lound 187 E2
East Lulworth 105 E4
East Lutton 196 B1
East Lydford 116 C4
East Lyn 114 A3
East Lyng 116 A3
East Mains 260 E5
East Malling 123 G3
East Malling Heath 123 F3
East March 141 C1
East Marden 108 A2
East Markham 187 E5
East Martin 105 G1
East Marton 193 F2
East Meon 120 B5
East Mere 102 C1
East Mersea 139 D1
East Mey 275 J1
East Midlands
Airport 173 F5
East Molesey 121 G1
East Moor 194 C3
East Morden 105 F3
East Morriston 236 D5
East Morton 194 A3
East Ness 203 F5
East Newton 197 E4
East Norton 160 C2
East Oakley 119 G2
East Ogwell 102 B5
East Orchard 105 E1
East Ord 237 G4

East Panson 99 D1
East Parley 106 A3
East Peckham 123 F4
East Pennard 116 C4
East Point Pavilion,
Lowestoft *Suff*
NR33 0AP 165 G2
East Portlemouth 100 D4
East Prawle 101 D4
East Preston 108 C3
East Pulham 104 D2
East Putford 113 D4
East Quantoxhead 115 E3
East Rainton 212 C3
East Ravendale 188 C3
East Raynham 177 G5
East Retford
(Retford) 187 E4
East Rigton 194 C3
East Rolstone 116 A1
East Rounton 202 D2
East Row 204 B3
East Rudham 177 G5
East Runton 178 D1
East Ruston 179 E3
East Saltoun 236 B3
East Shefford 133 F5
East Sleekburn 221 E3
East Somerton 179 F4
East Stockwith 187 F5
East Stoke *Dorset* 105 E4
East Stoke *Notts* 174 C3
East Stour 117 F5
East Stourmouth 125 E2
East Stratton 119 G3
East Street 116 C4
East Studdal 125 F4
East Suisnish 256 B1
East Taphouse 97 F3
East Thirston 221 D2
East Tilbury 137 F5
East Tisted 120 C4
East Torrington 188 B4
East Town 116 D3
East Tuddenham 178 B4
East Tytherley 119 D5
East Tytherton 132 B5
East Village 132 B2
East Wall 157 E3
East Walton 163 F1
East Wellow 119 E5
East Wemyss 244 B5
East Whitburn 235 D3
East Wickham 137 D5
East Williamston 127 D2
East Winch 163 E1
East Winterslow 119 D4
East Wittering 107 G3
East Witton 202 A4
East Woodburn 220 B3
East Woodhay 119 F1
East Woodlands 117 E3
East Worldham 120 C4
East Worlington 102 A1
East Youlstone 112 C4
Eastacott 113 G3
Eastbourne 110 B4
Eastbourne Pier
ESuss BN21 3EL
72 Eastbourne
Eastbrook 130 A5
Eastburn *ERid* 196 B2
Eastburn *WYorks* 193 G3
Eastbury *Herts* 136 A3
Eastbury *WBerks* 133 F5
Eastby 193 G2
Eastchurch 124 B1
Eastcombe *Glos* 132 A2
Eastcombe *Som* 115 E4
Eastcote *GtLon* 136 A4
Eastcote *N'hants* 148 B2
Eastcote *WMid* 159 D5
Eastcott *Corn* 112 C4
Eastcott *Wilts* 118 B2
Eastcourt 132 B3
Eastdown 101 E3
Eastend 147 F5
Easter Ardross 266 D4
Easter Balgedie 243 G4
Easter Balmoral 259 K5
Easter Boleskine 258 C2
Easter Borland 242 B4
Easter Brae 266 D5
Easter Buckieburn 234 B1
Easter Compton 131 E4
Easter Drummond 258 B3
Easter Dullater 242 B4
Easter Fearn 266 D3
Easter Galcantray 267 F7
Easter Howlaws 237 E5
Easter Kinkell 266 C6
Easter Knox 233 F2
Easter Lednathie 252 B3
Easter Moniack 266 C7
Easter Ord 261 G4
Easter Poldar 242 B5
Easter Skeld (Skeld) 279 C8
Easter Suddie 266 D6
Easter Tulloch 253 F2
Easter Whyntie 268 E4
Eastergate 108 B3
Easterhouse 234 A3
Easterton 118 B2
Easterton Sands 118 B2
Eastertown 116 A2
Eastfield *Bristol* 131 E5
Eastfield *NLan* 235 D3
Eastfield *NYorks* 204 D4
Eastfield Hall 221 E1
Eastgate *Dur* 211 F4
Eastgate *Lincs* 161 G1
Eastgate *Norf* 178 C3
Easthall 150 A5
Eastham *Mersey* 183 E4
Eastham *Worcs* 145 F1
Easthampstead 121 D1
Easthaugh 178 B4
Eastheath 120 D1
Easthope 157 E3
Easthorpe *Essex* 152 A5
Easthorpe *Leics* 174 D4
Easthorpe *Notts* 174 C2
Easthouses 236 A3
Eastington *Devon* 102 A2
Eastington *Glos* 132 D1
Eastington *Glos* 131 G2

Eastleach Martin 133 E2
Eastleach Turville 133 E2
Eastleigh *Devon* 113 E3
Eastleigh *Hants* 106 D1
Eastling 124 B3
Eastmoor *Derbys* 186 A5
Eastmoor *Norf* 163 F2
Eastoft 181 F1
Eastoke 107 G3
Easton *Cambs* 161 G5
Easton *Cumb* 218 C4
Easton *Cumb* 209 F1
Easton *Devon* 102 A4
Easton *Dorset* 104 C5
Easton *Hants* 119 G4
Easton *IoW* 106 C4
Easton *Lincs* 175 E5
Easton *Norf* 178 C4
Easton *Som* 116 C3
Easton *Suff* 153 D2
Easton *Wilts* 132 A5
Easton Grey 132 A4
Easton Maudit 149 D2
Easton on the Hill 161 F2
Easton Royal 118 D1
Easton-in-Gordano 131 E5
Eastrea 162 A3
Eastriggs 218 A5
Eastrington 195 G4
Eastry 126 F3
Eastside 277 D8
East-the-Water 113 E3
Eastville 131 F5
Eastwell 174 C5
Eastwick 136 C3
Eastwood *Notts* 173 F3
Eastwood *S'end* 138 B4
Eastwood *SYorks* 186 B3
Eastwood
WYorks 193 F5
Eastwood End 162 C3
Eathorpe 147 E1
Eaton *ChesE* 171 F1
Eaton *ChesW&C* 170 C1
Eaton *Leics* 174 C5
Eaton *Norf* 178 D5
Eaton *Norf* 177 E4
Eaton *Notts* 187 E5
Eaton *Oxon* 133 G2
Eaton *Shrop* 157 E3
Eaton *Shrop* 156 C4
Eaton Bishop 144 D4
Eaton Bray 149 E5
Eaton Constantine 157 F2
Eaton Ford 149 G2
Eaton Hall 170 B1
Eaton Hastings 133 E3
Eaton Socon 149 G2
Eaton upon Tern 171 D5
Eaves Green 159 E4
Eavestone 194 B1
Ebberston 204 B4
Ebbesborne Wake 118 A5
Ebbw Vale
(Glynebwy) 130 A2
Ebchester 212 A2
Ebdon 116 A1
Ebley 132 A2
Ebnal 170 B3
Ebost 256 J1
Ebrington 147 D3
Ebsworthy Town 99 F1
Ecchinswell 119 F2
Ecclaw 237 E3
Ecclefechan 217 F3
Eccles *GtMan* 184 B1
Eccles *Kent* 123 G2
Eccles *ScBord* 237 E5
Eccles Green 144 C3
Eccles Road 164 B2
Ecclesfield 186 A3
Ecclesgreig 253 F3
Eccleshall 171 F5
Eccleshill 194 A4
Ecclesmachan 235 E2
Eccles-on-Sea 179 F3
Eccleston
ChesW&C 170 B1
Eccleston *Lancs* 183 G1
Eccleston *Mersey* 183 F3
Eccup 194 B3
Echt 261 F4
Eckford 228 B4
Eckington *Derbys* 186 B5
Eckington *Worcs* 146 B3
Ecton *N'hants* 148 D1
Ecton *Staffs* 172 B2
Edale 185 F4
Eday 276 E4
Eday Airfield 276 E4
Edburton 109 E2
Edderside 209 E2
Edderton 266 E3
Eddington 119 E1
Eddleston 235 G5
Eden Camp *NYorks*
YO17 6RT 204 B5
Eden Park 122 C2
Eden Project *Corn*
PL24 2SG 97 E4
Eden Vale 212 D4
Edenbridge 122 D4
Edendonich 241 D2
Edenfield 184 B1
Edenhall 210 B4
Edenham 175 F5
Edensor 185 G5
Edentaggart 241 F5
Edenthorpe 186 D2
Edern 166 B4
EDF Energy London Eye
GtLon SE1 7PB 45 F5
Edgarley 116 C4
Edgbaston 158 C4
Edgcote 148 A3
Edgcott *Bucks* 148 B5
Edgcott *Som* 114 B4
Edgcumbe 95 E3
Edge *Glos* 132 A2
Edge *Shrop* 156 C2
Edge End 131 E1
Edge Green
ChesW&C 170 B2
Edge Green *GtMan* 183 G3
Edge Green *Norf* 164 B3
Edgebolton 170 C5

Edgefield 178 B2
Edgehead 236 A3
Edgeley 170 C3
Edgerley 156 C1
Edgerton 185 F1
Edgeworth 132 B2
Edginswell 101 E1
Edgmond 157 G1
Edgmond Marsh 171 E5
Edgton 156 C4
Edgware 136 B3
Edgworth 184 B1
Edinample 242 B2
Edinbanchory 260 C3
Edinbane 263 J6
Edinbarnet 233 G2
Edinburgh 235 G2
Edinburgh Airport 235 F2
Edinburgh Castle *Edin*
EH1 2NG 37 E4
Edinburgh Zoo *Edin*
EH12 6TS 32 B2
Edinchip 242 A2
Edingale 159 E1
Edingley 174 B2
Edingthorpe 179 E2
Edingthorpe Green 179 E2
Edington *Som* 116 A4
Edington *Wilts* 118 A2
Edintore 268 C6
Edinvale 267 J6
Edistone 112 C4
Edith Weston 161 E2
Edithmead 116 A3
Edlaston 172 C3
Edlesborough 135 E1
Edlingham 220 D1
Edlington 188 C5
Edmondsham 105 G1
Edmondsley 212 B3
Edmondstown 129 G3
Edmondthorpe 160 D1
Edmonstone 276 E5
Edmonton *Corn* 97 D2
Edmonton *GtLon* 136 C3
Edmundbyers 211 G2
Ednam 228 B3
Ednaston 172 D3
Edney Common 137 F2
Edra 241 G3
Edradynate 251 D4
Edrom 237 F4
Edstaston 170 C4
Edstone 147 D1
Edvin Loach 145 F2
Edwalton 173 G4
Edwardstone 152 A3
Edwardsville 129 G3
Edwinsford 142 C4
Edwinstowe 174 B1
Edworth 150 A3
Edwyn Ralph 145 F2
Edzell 253 E3
Efail Isaf 129 G4
Efail-fâch 129 D3
Efailnewydd 166 C4
Efailwen 141 E5
Efenechtyd 169 E2
Effingham 121 F2
Effirth 279 C7
Efflinch 159 D1
Efford 102 B2
Egbury 119 F2
Egdean 121 E5
Egdon 146 B2
Egerton *GtMan* 184 B1
Egerton *Kent* 124 B4
Egerton Forstal 124 A4
Egerton Green 170 C2
Egg Buckland 100 A2
Eggborough 195 E5
Eggerness 207 E2
Eggesford Barton 113 G4
Eggington 149 E5
Egginton 173 D5
Egglescliffe 202 D1
Eggleston 211 F5
Egham 135 F5
Egham Wick 135 E5
Egilsay 276 D5
Egleton 161 D2
Eglingham 229 F5
Eglinton 233 E1
Egloshayle 97 E2
Egloskerry 97 G1
Eglwys Cross 170 B3
Eglwys Fach 154 C3
Eglwys Nunydd 129 D4
Eglwysbach 181 G5
Eglwys-Brewis 114 D1
Eglwyswrw 141 E4
Egmanton 174 C1
Egmere 178 A2
Egmanton 174 C1
Egmere 178 A2
Egremont 208 D5
Egton 204 B2
Egton Bridge 204 B2
Egypt 119 F3
Eigg 247 D1
Eight Ash Green 152 A5
Eignaig 247 F4
Eil 259 F3
Eilanreach 256 C3
Eildon 227 G3
Eilean Darach 265 H3
Eilean Donan Castle *High*
IV40 8DX 256 C3
Eilean Shona 247 F2
Einacleit 270 D5
Eisgean 271 F6
Eisingrug 167 F2
Eisteddfa Gurig 155 D4
Elan Valley Visitor Centre
Powys LD6 5HP 143 F1
Elan Village 143 F1
Elberton 131 F4
Elborough 116 A2
Elburton 100 B2
Elcho 243 G2
Elcombe 132 D4
Elder Street 151 E4
Eldernell 162 B3
Eldersfield 145 G4
Eldersie 233 F3
Eldon 212 B5
Eldrick 215 D2
Eldroth 193 D1
Eldwick 194 A3
Elemore Vale 212 C3

Elford *N'umb* 229 F3
Elford *Staffs* 159 D1
Elford Closes 162 D5
Elgin 267 K5
Elgol 256 B3
Elham 125 D4
Elie 244 C4
Elilaw 220 B1
Elim 180 B4
Eling *Hants* 106 C1
Eling *WBerks* 134 A5
Eling Tide Mill *Hants*
SO40 9HF 4 A3
Eliock 225 G5
Elishader 263 K5
Elishaw 220 A2
Elkesley 187 D5
Elkington 160 B5
Elkstone 132 B2
Elland 194 A5
Elland Upper Edge 194 A5
Ellary 231 F2
Ellastone 172 C3
Ellemford 237 E3
Ellenabeich 239 G3
Ellenborough 208 D3
Ellenhall 171 F5
Ellen's Green 121 F4
Ellerbeck 202 D3
Ellerby 203 E5
Ellerdine 170 D5
Ellerdine Heath 170 D5
Elleric (Eileirig) 248 C5
Ellerker 196 B5
Ellerton *ERid* 195 G3
Ellerton *NYorks* 202 B3
Ellerton *Shrop* 171 E5
Ellerton Abbey 201 F3
Ellesborough 134 D2
Ellesmere 170 A4
Ellesmere Park 184 B3
Ellesmere Port 183 E5
Ellingham *Hants* 106 A2
Ellingham *N'umb* 229 F4
Ellingham *Norf* 165 E2
Ellingstring 202 A4
Ellington *Cambs* 161 G5
Ellington *N'umb* 221 E2
Ellington Thorpe 161 G5
Elliot 245 E1
Elliot's Green 117 E3
Ellisfield 120 B3
Ellistown 159 G1
Ellon 261 H1
Ellonby 210 A4
Ellough 165 F3
Ellough Moor 165 F3
Elloughton 196 B5
Ellwood 131 E2
Elm 162 C2
Elm Park 137 E4
Elmbridge 146 B1
Elmdon *Essex* 150 C4
Elmdon *WMid* 159 D4
Elmdon Heath 159 D4
Elmers End 122 C2
Elmer's Green 183 F2
Elmesthorpe 159 G3
Elmhurst 158 D1
Elmley Castle 146 B3
Elmley Lovett 146 A1
Elmore 131 G1
Elmore Back 131 G1
Elmscott 112 C3
Elmsett 152 B3
Elmstead *Essex* 152 B5
Elmstead *GtLon* 136 D5
Elmstead Market 152 B5
Elmstone 125 E2
Elmstone
Hardwicke 146 B5
Elmswell *ERid* 196 B2
Elmswell *Suff* 152 A1
Elmton 186 C5
Elphin 272 E7
Elphinstone 236 A2
Elrick *Aber* 261 G4
Elrick *Moray* 260 C2
Elrig 206 D2
Elrigbeag 240 D3
Elsdon 220 B2
Elsecar 186 A3
Elsenham 150 D5
Elsfield 134 A1
Elsham 188 A1
Elsing 178 B4
Elslack 193 F3
Elson *Hants* 107 F2
Elson *Shrop* 170 A4
Elsrickle 235 G5
Elstead 108 A2
Elsted 108 A2
Elsthorpe 175 F5
Elstob 212 C5
Elston *Lancs* 192 B4
Elston *Notts* 174 C3
Elstone 113 G4
Elstow 149 F3
Elstree 136 A3
Elstronwick 197 E4
Elswick 192 A4
Elsworth 150 B1
Elterwater 199 E2
Eltham 136 D5
Eltisley 150 A2
Elton *ChesW&C* 183 F5
Elton *Derbys* 172 D1
Elton *Glos* 131 G1
Elton *GtMan* 184 B1
Elton *Here* 157 D5
Elton *Notts* 174 C4
Elton *Stock* 202 D1
Elton Green 183 F5
Elvanfoot 226 A4
Elvaston 173 F4
Elveden 163 G5
Elvingston 236 B2
Elvington *Kent* 125 E3
Elvington *York* 195 G3
Elwick *Hart* 213 D4
Elwick *N'umb* 229 F3

Elworth 171 E1
Elworthy 115 D4
Ely *Cambs* 162 D5
Ely *Cardiff* 130 A5
Emberton 149 D3
Emberton Country Park
MK MK46 5FJ 149 D2
Embleton *Cumb* 209 E3
Embleton *Hart* 212 D5
Embleton *N'umb* 229 G4
Embo 267 F2
Embo Street 267 F2
Emborough 116 D2
Embsay 193 G2
Embsay Steam Railway
NYorks
BD23 6AF 193 G2
Emerson Park 137 E4
Emery Down 106 B2
Emley 185 G1
Emmington 134 C2
Emneth 162 C2
Emneth Hungate 162 D2
Empingham 161 E2
Empshott 120 C4
Empshott Green 120 C4
Emsworth 107 G2
Enborne 119 F1
Enborne Row 119 F1
Enchmarsh 157 E3
Enderby 160 A3
Endmoor 199 G4
Endon 171 G2
Endon Bank 171 G2
Enfield 136 C3
Enfield Wash 136 C3
Enford 118 C2
Engine Common 131 F4
Englefield 134 B5
Englefield Green 135 E5
Englesea-brook 171 E2
English Bicknor 131 E1
English Frankton 170 B5
Englishcombe 117 E1
Enham Alamein 119 E3
Enmore 115 F4
Enmore
Bridge 209 D5
Enniscaven 97 D2
Ennochdhu 251 F3
Ensay 246 C5
Ensdon 156 D1
Ensis 157 F3
Enson 171 G5
Enstone 147 F5
Enterkinfoot 225 G5
Enterpen 203 D2
Enton Green 121 E3
Epney 131 G1
Epperstone 174 B3
Epping 137 D2
Epping Green
Essex 136 D2
Epping Green
Herts 136 B2
Epping Upland 136 D2
Eppleby 202 A1
Eppleworth 196 C4
Epsom 122 B2
Epwell 147 F4
Epworth 187 E2
Epworth Turbary 187 E2
Erbistock 170 A3
Erbusaig 256 D2
Erchless Castle 266 B7
Erdington 158 D3
Eredine 240 B4
Eriboll 273 G3
Ericstane 226 B4
Eridge Green 123 E5
Eriff 224 D5
Erines 231 G2
Eriswell 163 F5
Erith 137 E5
Erlestoke 118 A2
Ermington 100 C2
Ernesettle 100 A1
Erpingham 178 C2
Erringden Grange 193 F5
Errogie (Earagaidh) 258 C2
Errol 244 A2
Errollston 261 J1
Erskine 233 F2
Ervie 214 A4
Erwarton 152 D4
Erwood 143 G3
Eryholme 202 C2
Eryrys 169 F2
Escart 231 G3
Escart Farm 231 G4
Escomb 212 A5
Escrick 195 F3
Esgair 141 G5
Esgairgeiliog 155 D2
Esgyryn 181 G5
Esh 212 A3
Esh Winning 212 A3
Esher 121 G1
Eshott 221 E2
Eshton 193 F2
Eskadale 258 B1
Eskbank 236 A3
Eskdale Green 198 C2
Eskdalemuir 218 A2
Eskham 189 D3
Esknish 230 B3
Esperley Lane Ends 212 A5
Espley Hall 221 D2
Esprick 192 A4
Essendine 161 F1
Essendon 136 B2
Essich 258 D1
Essington 158 B2
Esslemont 261 H2
Eston 203 E1
Eswick 279 D7
Etal 228 D3
Etchilhampton 118 B1
Etchingham 110 C1
Etchingham *Kent* 125 D5

Etchinghill *Staffs* 158 C1
Etherdwick Grange 197 E4
Etherley Dene 212 A5
Etherow Country Park
GtMan SK6 5JQ 25 H5
Ethie Mains 253 E5
Eton 135 E5
Eton Wick 135 E5
Etteridge 258 D5
Ettiley Heath 171 E1
Ettington 147 E3
Etton *ERid* 196 B3
Etton *Peter* 161 G2
Ettrick 227 D4
Ettrickbridge 227 E3
Ettrickhill 227 D4
Etwall 173 D4
Eudon George 157 F4
Eurach 240 A4
Eureka! Museum for
Children *WYorks*
HX1 2NE 26 B4
Euston 163 G5
Euxton 183 G1
Evanstown 129 F4
Evanton 266 D5
Evedon 175 F3
Evelix 266 E2
Evenjobb 144 B1
Evenley 148 A4
Evenlode 147 E5
Evenwood 212 A5
Evenwood Gate 212 A5
Everbay 276 F5
Evercreech 116 D4
Everdon 148 A2
Everingham 196 A3
Everleigh 118 D2
Everley *High* 275 J2
Everley *NYorks* 204 C4
Eversholt 149 E4
Evershot 104 C2
Eversley 120 C1
Eversley Cross 120 C1
Everthorpe 196 B4
Everton *CenBeds* 150 A2
Everton *Hants* 106 B3
Everton *Mersey* 183 E3
Everton *Notts* 187 D3
Evertown 218 B4
Eves Corner 138 C3
Evesbatch 145 F3
Evesham 146 C3
Evesham Country Park
Shopping & Garden
Centre *Worcs*
WR11 4TP 146 C3
Evie 276 C5
Evington 160 B2
Ewart Newtown 229 D3
Ewden Village 185 G3
Ewell 122 B2
Ewell Minnis 125 E4
Ewelme 134 B3
Ewen 132 C3
Ewenny 129 F5
Ewerby 175 G3
Ewerby Thorpe 175 G3
Ewhurst 121 F3
Ewhurst Green
ESuss 110 C1
Ewhurst Green *Surr* 121 F4
Ewloe 170 A1
Ewloe Green 169 F1
Ewood 192 C5
Ewood Bridge 193 D5
Eworthy 99 E1
Ewshot 120 D3
Ewyas Harold 144 C5
Exbourne 113 G5
Exbury 106 D2
Exbury Gardens *Hants*
SO45 1AZ 4 B6
Exceat 110 A4
Exebridge 114 C4
Exelby 202 B4
Exeter 102 C3
Exeter Cathedral *Devon*
EX1 1HS 72 Exeter
Exeter International
Airport 102 C3
Exford 114 B4
Exfords Green 157 D2
Exhall *Warks* 146 D2
Exhall *Warks* 159 F4
Exlade Street 134 B4
Exminster 102 C4
Exmouth 102 D4
Exnaboe 279 F9
Exning 151 E1
Explore-At-Bristol
BS1 5DB 66 Bristol
Exton *Devon* 102 D4
Exton *Hants* 120 B5
Exton *Rut* 161 E1
Exton *Som* 114 C4
Exwick 102 C3
Eyam 185 G5
Eydon 148 A3
Eye *Here* 145 D1
Eye *Peter* 162 A2
Eye *Suff* 164 C4
Eye Green 162 A2
Eyemouth 237 G3
Eyeworth 150 A3
Eyhorne Street 124 A3
Eyke 153 E2
Eynesbury 149 G2
Eynort 255 J2
Eynsford 123 E2
Eynsham 133 G2
Eype 104 A3
Eyre 263 K6
Eythorne 125 E4
Eyton *Here* 145 D1
Eyton *Shrop* 156 C4
Eyton on Severn 157 E2
Eyton upon the Weald
Moors 157 F1
Eywood 144 C2

F

Faccombe 119 E2
Faceby 203 D2
Fachwen 167 E1
Facit 184 C1
Faddiley 170 C2
Fadmoor 203 F4

Faebait 266 B6
Faifley 233 G2
Fail 224 C3
Failand 131 E5
Failsworth 184 C2
Fain 265 H4
Fair Isle 278 A1
Fair Isle Airstrip 278 A1
Fair Oak Devon 102 D1
Fair Oak Hants 107 D1
Fair Oak Hants 119 G1
Fair Oak Green 120 B1
Fairbourne 154 C1
Fairburn 195 D5
Fairfield Derbys 185 E5
Fairfield GtMan 184 D3
Fairfield Kent 111 E1
Fairfield Mersey 183 D4
Fairfield Stock 202 D1
Fairfield Worcs 158 B5
Fairfield Halls, Croydon
  GtLon CR9 1DG 122 C2
Fairford 132 D2
Fairgirth 216 C5
Fairhaven 191 G5
Fairhill 234 B4
Fairholm 234 B4
Fairlands Valley Park Herts
  SG2 0BL 150 A5
Fairley 261 G4
Fairlie 232 D4
Fairlight 111 D2
Fairlight Cove 111 D2
Fairmile Devon 103 D3
Fairmile Surr 121 G1
Fairmilehead 235 G3
Fairnington 228 A4
Fairoak 171 E4
Fairseat 123 F2
Fairstead 137 G1
Fairwarp 109 G1
Fairwater 130 A5
Fairy Cross 113 E3
Fairyhill 128 A3
Fakenham 178 A3
Fakenham Magna 164 A4
Fala 236 B3
Fala Dam 236 B3
Falahill 236 A4
Faldingworth 188 A4
Falfield Fife 244 C4
Falfield SGlos 131 F3
Falin-Wnda 141 G3
Falkenham 153 D4
Falkirk 234 C2
Falkirk Wheel Falk
  FK1 4RS 234 C1
Falkland 244 A4
Falla 228 B5
Fallgate 173 E1
Fallin 242 D5
Falmer 109 F3
Falmouth 95 F3
Falsgrave 204 D4
Falstone 219 F3
Famous Grouse Experience,
  Glenturret Distillery
  P&K PH7 4HA 243 D2
Fanagmore 272 D4
Fanans 240 C2
Fancott 149 F5
Fangdale Beck 203 E3
Fangfoss 195 G2
Fankerton 234 B1
Fanmore 246 D5
Fanner's Green 137 F1
Fans 236 D5
Fantasy Island Lincs
  PE25 1RH 177 D1
Far Cotton 148 C2
Far Forest 157 G5
Far Gearstones 200 C4
Far Green 131 G2
Far Moor 183 G2
Far Oakridge 132 B2
Far Royds 194 B4
Far Sawrey 199 E3
Farcet 162 A3
Farden 157 E5
Fareham 107 E2
Farewell 158 D1
Farforth 188 D5
Faringdon 133 E3
Farington 192 B5
Farlam 210 B2
Farlary 266 E1
Farleigh NSom 116 C1
Farleigh Surr 122 C2
Farleigh Hungerford 117 F2
Farleigh Wallop 120 B3
Farlesthorpe 189 E5
Farleton Cumb 199 G4
Farleton Lancs 192 B1
Farley Derbys 173 D1
Farley Shrop 156 C2
Farley Staffs 172 B3
Farley Wilts 118 D5
Farley Green Suff 151 F2
Farley Green Surr 121 F3
Farley Hill 120 C1
Farleys End 131 G1
Farlington 195 F1
Farlow 157 F4
Farm Town 159 F1
Farmborough 117 D1
Farmcote 146 C4
Farmington 132 D1
Farmoor 133 G2
Farmtown 268 D5
Farnborough
  GtLon 122 D2
Farnborough
  Hants 121 D2
Farnborough
  Works 147 G3
Farnborough
  WBerks 133 G4
Farnborough Street 121 D2
Farncombe 121 E3
Farndish 149 E1
Farndon ChesW&C 170 B2
Farndon Notts 174 C2
Farnell 253 E4
Farnham Dorset 105 F1
Farnham Essex 150 C4
Farnham NYorks 194 C1

Farnham Suff 153 E1
Farnham Surr 120 D3
Farnham Common 135 E4
Farnham Green 150 C5
Farnham Royal 135 E4
Farningham 123 E2
Farnley NYorks 194 B3
Farnley WYorks 194 B4
Farnsfield 174 B2
Farnworth GtMan 184 B2
Farnworth
  Halton 183 G4
Farr High 274 C2
Farr High 258 D1
Farr High 259 F4
Farraline 258 C2
Farrington 102 D3
Farrington
  Gurney 116 D2
Farsley 194 B4
Farthing Corner 124 A2
Farthing Green 124 A4
Farthinghoe 148 A4
Farthingstone 148 B2
Farthorpe 188 C5
Fartown 185 F1
Farway 103 E3
Fasag 264 E6
Fasagrianach 265 H3
Fascadale 247 E2
Fashion Museum
  B&NESom
  BA1 2QH 63 Bath
Faslane 232 D1
Fasnacloich 248 C5
Fasnakyle 257 K2
Fassfern 248 C1
Fatfield 212 C2
Fattahead 268 E5
Faugh 210 B2
Fauldhouse 234 D3
Faulkbourne 137 G1
Faulkland 117 E2
Fauls 170 C4
Faulston 118 B5
Faversham 124 C2
Favillar 259 K1
Fawdington 202 D5
Fawdon 212 B1
Fawfieldhead 172 B1
Fawkham Green 123 E2
Fawler 133 F1
Fawley Bucks 134 C4
Fawley Hants 107 D2
Fawley WBerks 133 F4
Fawley Chapel 145 E5
Fawsyde 253 G2
Faxfleet 196 A5
Faxton 160 C5
Faygate 122 B5
Fazeley 159 E2
Fearby 202 A4
Fearn 267 H4
Fearnan 250 C4
Fearnbeg 264 D6
Fearnhead 184 A3
Fearnmore 264 D5
Featherstone
  Staffs 158 B2
Featherstone
  WYorks 194 D5
Featherstone Castle 210 C1
Feckenham 146 C1
Feering 151 G5
Feetham 201 E3
Feizor 193 D1
Felbridge 122 C5
Felbrigg 178 D2
Felcourt 122 C4
Felden 135 F2
Felhampton 156 D4
Felindre Carmar 142 D5
Felindre Carmar 142 B5
Felindre Carmar 141 G4
Felindre Carmar 142 C4
Felindre Powys 156 A4
Felindre Powys 144 A5
Felindre Swan 128 C2
Felinfach Cere 142 B2
Felinfach Powys 143 G4
Felinfoel 128 B2
Felingwmisaf 142 B5
Felingwmuchaf 142 B5
Felixkirk 203 D4
Felixstowe 153 E4
Felixstowe Ferry 153 E4
Felkington 237 G5
Felldownhead 99 D2
Felling 212 B1
Fellonmore 239 F2
Felmersham 149 E2
Felmingham 179 D3
Felpham 108 B4
Felsham 152 A2
Felsted 151 E5
Feltham 136 A5
Felthamhill 136 A5
Felthorpe 178 C4
Felton Here 145 E3
Felton N'umb 221 D1
Felton NSom 116 C1
Felton Butler 156 C1
Feltwell 163 F3
Fen Ditton 150 C1
Fen Drayton 150 B1
Fen End 159 E5
Fen Street Norf 164 A2
Fen Street Norf 164 A4
Fen Street Suff 152 C1
Fenay Bridge 185 F1
Fence 193 E4
Fence Houses 212 C2
Fencott 134 A1
Fendike Corner 176 C1
Fendaan 107 D1
Fenham 229 E2
Fenhouses 176 A3
Feniscowles 192 C5
Feniton 103 E3
Fenn Street 137 G5
Fenni-fach 143 G5

Fenny Bentley 172 C2
Fenny Bridges 103 E3
Fenny Compton 147 G2
Fenny Drayton 159 F3
Fenny Stratford 149 D4
Fenrother 221 D2
Fenstanton 150 B1
Fenton Cambs 162 B5
Fenton Lincs 187 F5
Fenton Lincs 175 D2
Fenton N'umb 229 D3
Fenton Notts 187 E4
Fenton Stoke 171 F3
Fenton Barns 236 C1
Fenwick EAyr 233 F5
Fenwick N'umb 220 C4
Fenwick N'umb 229 E2
Fenwick SYorks 186 C1
Feochaig 222 C4
Feock 95 F3
Feolin 230 C3
Feolin Ferry 230 C3
Feorlan 222 B5
Feorlin 240 B5
Ferens Art Gallery
  HU1 3RA
  76 Kingston upon Hull
Ferguslie Park 233 F3
Feriniquarrie 263 G6
Fern 252 C2
Ferndale 129 F3
Ferndown 105 G2
Ferness 267 G7
Fernham 133 E3
Fernhill Heath 146 A2
Fernhurst 121 D5
Fernie 244 B3
Fernilea 255 J1
Fernilee 185 E5
Fernybank 252 D2
Ferrensby 194 C1
Ferrers Centre for Arts &
  Crafts Leics
  LE65 1RU 173 E5
Ferrindonald 256 C4
Ferring 108 C3
Ferry Hill 162 B4
Ferrybridge 195 D5
Ferryden 253 F4
Ferryhill 212 B4
Ferryside
  (Glanyferi) 127 G1
Fersfield 164 B3
Fersit 249 F1
Ferwig 141 E3
Feshiebridge 259 F4
Festival Park BGwent
  NP23 8FP 130 A2
Fetcham 121 F2
Fetlar 278 F3
Fetlar Airport 278 F3
Fetterangus 269 H5
Fettercairn 253 E2
Fetternear House 261 F3
Feus of Caldhame 253 E3
Fewcott 148 A5
Fewston 194 A2
Ffairfach 142 C5
Ffair-Rhos 142 D1
Ffaldybrenin 142 C2
Ffarmers 142 C3
Ffawyddog 130 B1
Ffestiniog
  (Llan Ffestiniog) 168 A3
Ffestiniog Railway Gwyn
  LL49 9NF 167 F3
Ffordd-las Denb 169 E1
Fforddlas Powys 144 B4
Fforest 128 B2
Fforest-fach 128 C3
Ffostrasol 141 G3
Ffos-y-ffin 142 A1
Ffridd Uchaf 167 E2
Ffrith Denb 182 B4
Ffrith Flints 169 F2
Ffrwdgrech 143 G5
Ffynnon 127 G1
Ffynnongroyw 182 C4
Fibhig 270 E3
Fichlie 260 C3
Fidden 238 C2
Fiddington Glos 146 B4
Fiddington Som 115 F3
Fiddleford 105 E1
Fiddler's Green
  Glos 146 B5
Fiddler's Green
  Here 145 E4
Fiddler's Green
  Norf 163 G3
Fiddler's Green
  Norf 164 B2
Fiddlers Hamlet 137 D2
Field 172 B4
Field Broughton 199 E4
Field Dalling 178 B2
Field Head 159 G2
Fife Keith 268 B5
Fifehead Magdalen 117 E5
Fifehead Neville 105 D1
Fifehead
  St. Quintin 105 D1
Fifield Oxon 133 E1
Fifield W&M 135 E5
Fifield Bavant 118 B5
Figheldean 118 C3
Filby 179 F4
Filey 205 E4
Filgrave 149 D3
Filham 100 C2
Filkins 133 E2
Filleigh Devon 113 G3
Filleigh Devon 102 A1
Fillingham 187 G4
Fillongley 159 F4
Filmore Hill 120 B5
Filton 131 F5
Fimber 196 A1
Finavon 252 C4
Fincham 163 E2
Finchampstead 120 C1
Finchdean 107 G2
Finchingfield 151 E4
Finchley 136 B3
Findern 173 E5
Findhorn 267 H5
Findhorn Bridge 259 F2
Findhuglen 242 C3

Findo Gask 243 F2
Findochty 268 C4
Findon Aber 261 H5
Findon WSuss 108 D3
Findon Mains 266 D5
Findon Valley 108 D3
Findrassie 267 J5
Finedon 161 E5
Fingal Street 164 D4
Fingask 261 F2
Fingerpost 157 G5
Fingest 134 C3
Finghall 202 A4
Fingland Cumb 209 F1
Fingland D&G 226 D5
Fingland D&G 225 D3
Finglesham 125 F3
Fingringhoe 152 B5
Finkle Street 186 A3
Finlarig 242 A1
Finmere 148 B4
Finnart A&B 241 E5
Finnart P&K 250 A4
Finney Hill 159 G1
Finningham 152 B1
Finningley 187 D3
Finnygaud 268 E5
Finsbay
  (Fionnsbhagh) 263 F3
Finsbury 136 C4
Finstall 158 B5
Finsthwaite 199 E4
Finstock 133 F1
Finstown 277 C6
Fintry Aber 269 F5
Fintry Stir 234 A1
Finwood 147 D1
Finzean 260 D5
Fionnphort 238 B2
Fir Tree 212 A4
Firbank 200 B3
Firbeck 186 C4
Firby NYorks 202 B4
Firby NYorks 195 G1
Firgrove 184 D1
Firs Lane 184 A2
Firsby 176 C1
Firsdown 118 D4
Firth 278 D5
Fishbourne IoW 107 E3
Fishbourne WSuss 108 A3
Fishburn 212 C4
Fishcross 243 E5
Fisherford 260 E1
Fishers Farm Park WSuss
  RH14 0EG 121 F5
Fisher's Pond 119 F5
Fisher's Row 192 A3
Fishersgate 109 E3
Fisherstreet 121 E4
Fisherton High 266 E6
Fisherton SAyr 224 A4
Fisherton de la
  Mere 118 A4
Fishguard
  (Abergwaun) 140 C4
Fishlake 187 D1
Fishleigh Barton 113 F3
Fishley 179 F4
Fishnish 247 F5
Fishpond Bottom 103 G3
Fishponds 131 F5
Fishpool Glos 145 G4
Fishtoft 176 B3
Fishtoft Drove 176 B3
Fishtown of Usan 253 F4
Fishwick 237 G4
Fiskerton Lincs 188 A5
Fiskerton Notts 174 C2
Fitling 197 E4
Fittleton 118 C3
Fittleworth 108 C2
Fitton End 162 C1
Fitz 156 D1
Fitzhead 115 E5
Fitzroy 115 E5
Fitzwilliam 186 B1
Fitzwilliam Museum
  Cambs CB2 1RB
  66 Cambridge
Fiunary 247 F5
Five Acres 131 E1
Five Ash Down 109 G1
Five Ashes 110 A1
Five Bridges 145 F3
Five Houses 106 D4
Five Lanes 130 D3
Five Oak Green 123 F4
Five Oaks Chanl 100 C5
Five Oaks WSuss 121 F5
Five Roads 128 A2
Five Turnings 156 B5
Five Wents 124 A3
Fivehead 116 B5
Fivelanes 97 G1
Flack's Green 137 G1
Flackwell Heath 135 D4
Fladbury 146 B3
Fladdabister 279 D9
Flagg 172 C1
Flambards Experience, The
  Corn TR13 0QA 95 D4
Flamborough 205 F5
Flamingo Land Theme
  Park NYorks
  YO17 6UX 203 G4
Flamingo Park,
  Hastings ESuss
  TN34 3AR 110 D3
Flamstead 135 F1
Flamstead End
  136 C2
Flansham 108 B3
Flanshaw 194 C5
Flasby 193 F2
Flash 172 B1
Flashader 263 J6
Flask Inn 204 C2
Flatts Lane Woodland
  Country Park R&C
  TS6 0NN 29 D4
Flaunden 135 F2
Flawborough 174 C3
Flawith 195 D1
Flax Bourton 116 C1
Flax Moss 193 D5

Flaxby 194 C2
Flaxholme 173 E3
Flaxlands 164 C2
Flaxley 131 F1
Flaxpool 115 E4
Flaxton 195 F1
Fleckney 160 B3
Flecknoe 148 A1
Fledborough 187 F5
Fleet Hants 120 D2
Fleet Hants 107 G2
Fleet Lincs 176 B4
Fleet Air Arm Museum
  Som BA22 8HT 116 C5
Fleet Hargate 176 B4
Fleetville 136 A2
Fleetwood 191 G3
Fleggburgh (Burgh St.
  Margaret) 179 F4
Flemingston 129 G5
Flemington 234 A4
Flempton 151 G1
Fleoideabhagh 263 F3
Flesherin 271 H4
Fletchersbridge 97 F3
Fletchertown 209 F2
Fletching 109 G1
Fleur-de-lis 130 A3
Flexbury 112 C5
Flexford 121 E2
Flimby 208 D3
Flimwell 123 G5
Flint (Y Fflint) 182 D5
Flint Cross 150 C3
Flint Mountain 182 D5
Flintham 174 C3
Flinton 197 E4
Flint's Green 159 E4
Flishinghurst 123 G5
Flitcham 177 F5
Flitholme 200 C1
Flitton 149 F4
Flitwick 149 F4
Flixborough 187 F1
Flixton GtMan 184 B3
Flixton NYorks 204 D5
Flixton Suff 165 E3
Flockton 185 G1
Flockton Green 185 G1
Flodden 228 D3
Flodigarry 263 K4
Flood's Ferry 162 B3
Flookburgh 199 E5
Floors 268 C5
Flordon 164 C2
Flore 148 B1
Flotta 277 C8
Flotterton 220 C1
Flowton 152 B3
Flushing Aber 269 J6
Flushing Corn 95 F3
Flushing Corn 95 E4
Fluxton 103 D3
Flyford Flavell 146 B2
Foals Green 165 D4
Fobbing 137 G4
Fochabers 268 B5
Fochriw 130 A2
Fockerby 187 F1
Fodderletter 259 J2
Fodderty 266 C6
Foddington 116 C5
Foel 155 F1
Foelgastell 128 B1
Foggathorpe 195 G4
Fogo 237 E5
Fogorig 237 E5
Fogwatt 267 K6
Foindle 272 D4
Folda 251 G3
Fole 172 B4
Foleshill 159 F4
Folke 104 C1
Folkestone 125 E5
Folkingham 175 F4
Folkington 110 A3
Folksworth 161 G4
Folkton 205 D5
Folla Rule 261 F1
Follifoot 194 C2
Folly Dorset 104 D2
Folly Pembs 140 C5
Folly Farm, Begelly Pembs
  SA68 0XA 127 E2
Folly Gate 99 F1
Fonmon 115 D2
Fonthill Bishop 118 A4
Fonthill Gifford 118 A4
Fontmell Magna 105 E1
Fontmell Parva 105 E1
Fontwell 108 B3
Font-y-gary 115 D1
Foolow 185 F5
Footherley 158 D2
Foots Cray 137 D5
Forbestown 260 B3
Force Forge 199 E3
Force Green 122 D3
Forcett 202 A1
Forches Cross 102 A2
Ford A&B 240 A4
Ford Bucks 134 C2
Ford Devon 100 C3
Ford Devon 101 D3
Ford Devon 113 E2
Ford Glos 146 C5
Ford Mersey 183 E3
Ford Midlo 236 A3
Ford N'umb 229 D3
Ford Pembs 140 C5
Ford Plym 100 A2
Ford Shrop 156 D1
Ford Som 115 D5
Ford Staffs 172 B2
Ford Wilts 132 A5
Ford WSuss 108 B3
Ford End 137 F1
Ford Green 192 A3
Ford Heath 156 D1
Ford Street 103 E1
Forda 99 F1
Fordbridge 159 D4
Fordcombe 123 E4
Fordell 235 F1
Forden (Fforddun) 156 B2

Fordgate 116 A4
Fordham Cambs 163 E5
Fordham Essex 152 A5
Fordham Norf 163 E3
Fordham Abbey 151 E1
Fordham Heath 152 A5
Fordhouses 158 B2
Fordingbridge 106 A1
Fordon 205 D5
Fordoun 253 F2
Ford's Green 152 B1
Fordstreet 152 A5
Fordwells 133 F1
Fordwich 125 D3
Fordyce 268 D4
Forebrae 243 E2
Forebridge 171 G5
Foredale 193 E1
Foreland 230 A3
Foremark 173 E5
Foremark Reservoir Derbys
  DE65 6EG 173 E5
Forest 202 B2
Forest Coal Pit 144 B5
Forest Gate 136 D4
Forest Green 121 G3
Forest Hall Cumb 199 G2
Forest Hall T&W 212 B1
Forest Head 210 B2
Forest Hill GtLon 136 C5
Forest Hill Oxon 134 A2
Forest Lane Head 194 C2
Forest Lodge (Taigh na
  Frithe) A&B 249 E5
Forest Lodge P&K 251 E2
Forest Row 122 D5
Forest Side 107 D4
Forest Town 173 G1
Forestburn Gate 220 C2
Forest-in-Teesdale 211 E5
Forestmill 243 E5
Forestside 107 G1
Forfar 252 C4
Forfar Loch Country Park
  Angus DD8 1BT 252 C4
Forgandenny 243 F3
Forge 155 D3
Forgie 268 B5
Forhill 158 C5
Formby 183 D2
Forncett End 164 C2
Forncett St. Mary 164 C2
Forncett St. Peter 164 C2
Forneth 251 F4
Fornham All Saints 151 G1
Fornham St. Martin 151 G1
Fornighty 267 G6
Forres 267 H6
Forrest 234 C3
Forrest Lodge 215 G2
Forsbrook 171 G3
Forse 275 H5
Forsie 275 F2
Forsinain 274 E4
Forsinard 274 D4
Forston 104 C3
Fort Augustus (Cille
  Chuimein) 257 K4
Fort William
  (An Gearasdan) 248 D2
Forteviot 243 F3
Forth 234 D4
Forthampton 146 A4
Fortingall 250 C4
Fortis Green 136 B4
Forton Hants 119 F3
Forton Lancs 192 A2
Forton Shrop 156 D1
Forton Som 103 G2
Forton Staffs 171 E5
Fortrie 268 E6
Fortrose
  (A'Chananaich) 266 E6
Fortuneswell 104 C5
Forty Green 135 E3
Forty Hill 136 C3
Forward Green 152 B2
Fosbury 119 E2
Foscot 147 E5
Fosdyke 176 B4
Foss 250 C4
Foss Cross 132 C2
Fossdale 201 D3
Fossebridge 132 C1
Foster Street 137 D2
Fosterhouses 186 D1
Foster's Booth 148 B2
Foston Derbys 172 C4
Foston Leics 160 B3
Foston Lincs 175 D3
Foston NYorks 195 F1
Foston on the
  Wolds 196 D2
Fotherby 188 D3
Fotheringhay 161 F3
Foubister 277 E7
Foul Mile 110 B2
Foula 278 A6
Foula Airstrip 278 A6
Foulbog 226 D5
Foulden Norf 163 F3
Foulden ScBord 237 G4
Foulridge 193 E3
Foulsham 178 B3
Foulstone 199 G4
Foulzie 269 F4
Fountainhall 236 B5
Four Ashes Staffs 158 B2
Four Ashes Staffs 158 A4
Four Ashes Suff 164 A4
Four Crosses
  Denb 168 D2
Four Crosses
  Powys 156 B1
Four Crosses
  Powys 155 G2
Four Crosses
  Staffs 158 B2
Four Elms 123 D4
Four Forks 115 F4
Four Gotes 162 C1
Four Lane Ends
  B'burn 192 C5

Four Lane Ends
  ChesW&C 170 C1
Four Lane Ends
  York 195 F2
Four Lanes 95 D3
Four Marks 120 B4
Four Mile Bridge 180 A5
Four Oaks ESuss 111 D1
Four Oaks Glos 145 F5
Four Oaks WMid 159 E4
Four Oaks WMid 158 D3
Four Oaks Park 158 D3
Four Roads 128 A2
Four Throws 110 C1
Fourlane Ends 173 E2
Fourlanes End 171 F2
Fourpenny 267 F2
Fourstones 211 E1
Fovant 118 B5
Foveran House 261 H3
Fowey 97 F4
Fowlis 244 B1
Fowlis Wester 243 E2
Fowlmere 150 C3
Fownhope 145 E4
Fox Hatch 137 E3
Fox Lane 121 D2
Fox Street 152 B5
Fox Up 201 D5
Foxbar 233 F3
Foxcombe Hill 133 G2
Foxcote Glos 132 C1
Foxcote Som 117 E2
Foxdale 190 A4
Foxearth 151 G3
Foxfield 198 D4
Foxham 132 B5
Foxhole Corn 97 D4
Foxhole High 258 C4
Foxholes 204 D5
Foxhunt Green 110 A2
Foxley Here 144 D3
Foxley N'hants 148 B2
Foxley Norf 178 B3
Foxley Wilts 132 A4
Foxt 172 B3
Foxton Cambs 150 C3
Foxton Dur 212 C5
Foxton Leics 160 B3
Foxton Locks Leics
  LE16 7RA 160 B4
Foxwist Green 170 D1
Foy 145 E5
Foyers (Foithir) 258 B2
Frachadil 246 C4
Fraddam 94 C3
Fraddon 96 D4
Fradley 159 D1
Fradswell 171 G4
Fraisthorpe 197 D1
Framfield 109 G1
Framingham Earl 179 D5
Framingham Pigot 179 D5
Framlingham 153 D1
Frampton Dorset 104 C3
Frampton Lincs 176 B4
Frampton Cotterell 131 F4
Frampton Mansell 132 B2
Frampton on
  Severn 131 G2
Frampton West
  End 176 A3
Framsden 152 C2
Framwellgate Moor 212 B3
France Lynch 132 B2
Frances Green 192 C4
Franche 158 A5
Frandley 184 A5
Frankby 182 D4
Frankfort 179 D3
Frankley 158 B4
Franksbridge 144 A2
Frankton 159 F5
Frant 123 E5
Fraserburgh 269 H4
Frating 152 B5
Fratton 107 F2
Freasley 159 E3
Freathy 99 D5
Freckenham 163 E5
Freckleton 192 A5
Freeby 174 D5
Freefolk 119 F3
Freehay 172 B3
Freeland 133 G1
Freester 279 D7
Freethorpe 179 F5
Freethorpe
  Common 179 F5
Freiston 176 B3
Freiston Shore 176 B3
Fremington Devon 113 F2
Fremington NYorks 201 F3
French Brothers Cruises
  W&M SL4 5JH 135 E5
Frenchay 131 F5
Frenchbeer 99 G2
Frendraught 268 E6
Frenich 241 G4
Frensham 120 D3
Fresgoe 274 F2
Freshbrook 132 D4
Freshfield 183 D2
Freshford 117 E2
Freshwater 106 C4
Freshwater Bay 106 C4
Freshwater East 126 D3
Fressingfield 165 D4
Freston 152 C4
Freswick 275 J2
Fretherne 131 G2
Frettenham 178 D4
Freuchie 244 A4
Freystrop Cross 126 C1
Friars, The, Aylesford Kent
  ME20 7BX 123 G2
Friars Carse 216 D2
Friar's Gate 123 D5
Friarton 243 G2
Friday Bridge 162 C2
Friday Street ESuss 110 B3
Friday Street Suff 153 E1
Friday Street Suff 153 E2
Friday Street Surr 121 G3
Fridaythorpe 196 A2
Friern Barnet 136 B3
Friesthorpe 188 A4
Frieston 175 E3

293

Frieth 134 C3
Frilford 133 G3
Frilsham 134 A5
Frimley 121 D2
Frimley Green 121 D2
Frindsbury 123 G2
Fring 177 F4
Fringford 148 B5
Friningham 124 A3
Frinsted 124 A3
Frinton-on-Sea 139 F1
Friockheim 253 D5
Friog 154 C1
Frisby on the
  Wreake 160 B1
Friskney 176 C2
Friskney
  Eaudyke 176 C2
Friston ESuss 110 A4
Friston Suff 153 F1
Fritchley 173 E2
Frith 124 B3
Frith Bank 176 B3
Frith Common 145 F1
Fritham 106 B1
Frithelstock 113 E4
Frithelstock
  Stone 113 E4
Frithville 176 B2
Frittenden 124 A4
Frittiscombe 101 E3
Fritton Norf 164 D2
Fritton Norf 179 F5
Fritwell 148 A5
Frizinghall 194 A4
Frizington 208 D5
Frocester 131 G2
Frochas 156 B2
Frodesley 157 E2
Frodesley Lane 157 E2
Frodingham 187 F1
Frodsham 183 G5
Frog End 150 C2
Frog Pool 145 G1
Frogden 228 B4
Froggatt 185 G5
Froghall 172 B3
Frogham 106 A1
Frogland Cross 131 F4
Frogmore Devon 101 D3
Frogmore Hants 120 D2
Frogmore Herts 136 A2
Frogwell 98 D4
Frolesworth 160 A3
Frome 117 E3
Frome Market 117 F2
Frome St. Quintin 104 B2
Frome Whitfield 104 C3
Fromes Hill 145 F3
Fron Gwyn 166 C4
Fron Powys 156 B2
Fron Powys 143 G1
Fron Powys 156 A3
Fron Isaf 169 F4
Froncysyllte 169 F3
Fron-goch 168 C4
Frostenden 165 F3
Frosterley 211 G4
Froxfield 119 E1
Froxfield Green 120 C5
Fryerning 137 F2
Fuggleston
  St. Peter 118 C4
Fulbeck 175 E2
Fulbourn 150 D2
Fulbrook 133 E1
Fulflood 119 F5
Fulford Som 115 F5
Fulford Staffs 171 G4
Fulford York 195 F3
Fulham 136 B5
Fulking 109 E2
Full Sutton 195 G2
Fullaford 113 G2
Fuller Street 137 G1
Fuller's Moor 170 B2
Fullerton 119 E4
Fulletby 188 C5
Fullwood 233 F4
Fulmer 135 F4
Fulmodeston 178 A2
Fulnetby 188 B5
Fulready 147 E3
Fulstone 185 F2
Fulstow 188 D3
Fulwell Oxon 147 F5
Fulwell T&W 212 C2
Fulwood Lancs 192 B4
Fulwood SYorks 186 A4
Fun Farm, Spalding Lincs
  PE12 6JU 176 A5
Fundenhall 164 C2
Fundenhall
  Street 164 C2
Funtington 108 A3
Funtley 107 E2
Funzie 278 F3
Furley 103 F2
Furnace A&B 240 C4
Furnace Carmar 128 B2
Furnace Cere 154 C3
Furnace High 265 F4
Furner's Green 109 G1
Furness Vale 185 E4
Furneux Pelham 150 C5
Furnham 103 G2
Further Quarter 124 A5
Furtho 148 C3
Furze Green 164 D3
Furze Platt 135 D4
Furzehill Devon 114 A3
Furzehill Dorset 105 G2
Furzeley Corner 107 F1
Furzey Lodge 106 C2
Furzley 106 B2
Fyfett 103 F1
Fyfield Essex 137 E2
Fyfield Glos 133 E2
Fyfield Hants 119 D3
Fyfield Oxon 133 G3
Fyfield Wilts 118 C1
Fyfield Wilts 118 C1
Fylingthorpe 204 C2
Fyning 120 D5
Fyvie 261 F1

G
Gabalfa 130 A5
Gabhsunn Bho
  Dheas 271 G2
Gabhsunn Bho
  Thuath 271 G2
Gablon 266 E2
Gabroc Hill 233 F4
Gaddesby 160 B1
Gaddesden Row 135 F1
Gadebridge 135 F2
Gadshill 137 G5
Gaer Newport 130 B4
Gaer Powys 144 A5
Gaer-fawr 130 D3
Gaerllwyd 130 D3
Gaerwen 180 C5
Gagingwell 147 G5
Gaich High 259 H2
Gaich High 258 D1
Gaick Lodge 250 C1
Gailes 224 B3
Gailey 158 B1
Gainford 202 A1
Gainsborough 187 F3
Gainsford End 151 F4
Gairloch
  (Geàrrloch) 264 D4
Gairlochy (Geàrr
  Lòchaidh) 249 D1
Gairney Bank 243 G5
Gairnshiel Lodge 259 K4
Gaitsgill 209 G2
Galabank 236 B5
Galashiels 227 F2
Galdenoch 214 C4
Gale 184 D1
Galgate 192 A2
Galhampton 116 D5
Gallanach 240 A2
Gallantry Bank 170 C2
Gallatown 244 A5
Gallchoille 239 G5
Gallery 253 E3
Gallery of Modern Art,
  Glasgow Glas
  G1 3AH 39 F4
Galley Common 159 F3
Galleyend 137 G2
Galleywood 137 G2
Gallowfauld 252 C5
Gallowhill 233 F3
Gallows Green 172 B3
Gallowstree
  Common 134 B4
Gallowstree Elm 158 A4
Galltair 256 E2
Gallt-y-foel 167 E1
Gallypot Street 123 D5
Galmington 115 F5
Galmisdale 247 D1
Galmpton Devon 100 C3
Galmpton Torbay 101 E2
Galmpton
  Warborough 101 E2
Galphay 202 B5
Galston 224 C2
Galtrigill 263 G6
Gamble's Green 137 G1
Gamblesby 210 C4
Gamesley 185 E3
Gamlingay 150 A2
Gamlingay Cinques 150 A2
Gamlingay Great
  Heath 150 A2
Gammaton 113 E3
Gammaton Moor 113 E3
Gammersgill 201 F4
Gamrie 269 F4
Gamston Notts 187 E5
Gamston Notts 174 B4
Ganarew 131 E1
Gang 98 D4
Ganllwyd 168 A5
Gannochy 253 E2
Ganstead 197 D4
Ganthorpe 203 F5
Ganton 204 C5
Ganwick Corner 136 B3
Gaodhail 239 F1
Gappah 102 B5
Gara Bridge 100 D2
Garabal 241 F3
Garadheancal 265 F1
Garbat 266 B5
Garbhallt 240 C5
Garboldisham 164 B3
Garden 242 A5
Garden City 170 A1
Garden Village 185 G3
Gardeners Green 120 D1
Gardenstown 269 F4
Garderhouse 279 C8
Gardham 196 B3
Gare Hill 117 E3
Garelochhead 241 E5
Garford 133 G3
Garforth 194 D4
Gargrave 193 F2
Gargunnock 242 C5
Gariob 231 F3
Garlic Street 164 D3
Garlies Castle 215 F3
Garlieston 207 E2
Garlinge Green 124 D3
Garlogie 261 F4
Garmelow 171 F5
Garmond 269 G5
Garmony 247 F5
Garmouth 268 B4
Garmston 157 F2
Garnant 128 C1
Garndolbenmaen 167 D3
Garneddwen 155 D2
Garnett Bridge 199 G3
Garnfadryn 166 B4
Garnswllt 128 C2
Garrabost 271 H4
Garrachra 232 B1
Garralburn 268 C5
Garras 95 E4
Garreg 167 F3
Garreg Bank 156 B1
Garrett's Green 159 D4
Garrigill 210 D3

Garriston 202 A3
Garroch 215 G2
Garrochty 232 B4
Garros 263 K5
Garryhorn 215 G1
Garrynahine (Gearraidh na
  h-Aibhne) 270 E4
Garsdale 200 C4
Garsdale Head 200 C3
Garsdon 132 B4
Garshall Green 171 G4
Garsington 134 A2
Garstang 192 A3
Garston 183 F4
Garswood 183 G3
Gartachoil 242 A5
Gartally 258 B1
Gartavaich 231 G4
Gartbreck 230 A4
Gartcosh 234 A3
Garth Bridgend 129 E3
Garth Cere 154 C4
Garth Gwyn 181 D5
Garth IoM 190 B4
Garth Powys 143 F3
Garth Shet 279 B7
Garth Wrex 169 F3
Garth Row 199 G3
Garthbrengy 143 G4
Garthdee 261 H4
Gartheli 142 B2
Garthmyl 156 A3
Garthynty 142 D3
Garthorpe Leics 174 D5
Garthorpe NLincs 187 F1
Garths 199 G3
Garthynty 142 D3
Gartincaber 242 B4
Gartly 260 D1
Gartmore 242 A5
Gartnagrenach 231 F4
Gartnatra 230 B3
Gartness 233 G1
Gartocharn 233 F1
Garton 197 E4
Garton-on-the-
  Wolds 196 B1
Gartymore 275 F7
Garvald 236 C2
Garvamore 258 C5
Garvan 248 B2
Garvard 238 C5
Garve (Clachan
  Ghairbh) 265 K5
Garveld 222 B5
Garvestone 178 B5
Garvie 232 B1
Garvock Aber 253 F2
Garvock Invcly 233 D2
Garwald 226 D5
Garwaldwaterfoot 226 D5
Garway 145 D5
Garway Hill 144 D5
Gask Aber 269 J6
Gask Aber 269 F6
Gask P&K 243 E3
Gaskan 248 A2
Gass 224 C5
Gastard 117 F1
Gasthorpe 164 A3
Gaston Green 137 E1
Gatcombe 107 D4
Gate Burton 187 F4
Gate Helmsley 195 F2
Gate House 231 D2
Gateacre 183 F4
Gateford 186 C4
Gateforth 195 E5
Gatehead 224 B2
Gatehouse 251 D5
Gatehouse of Fleet 216 A5
Gateley 178 A3
Gatenby 202 C4
Gatesgarth 209 E5
Gateshaw 228 B4
Gateshead 212 B1
Gatesheath 170 B1
Gateside Aber 260 E3
Gateside Angus 252 C5
Gateside Fife 243 G4
Gateside NAyr 233 E4
Gateslack 225 G5
Gathurst 183 G2
Gatley 184 C4
Gattonside 227 G2
Gatwick Airport 122 B4
Gaufron 143 F1
Gaulby 160 B2
Gauldry 244 B2
Gauntons Bank 170 C3
Gaunt's Common 105 G2
Gaunt's Earthcott 131 F4
Gautby 188 B5
Gavinton 237 E4
Gawber 186 A2
Gawcott 148 B4
Gawsworth 184 C5
Gawthrop 200 B4
Gawthwaite 199 D4
Gay Bowers 137 G2
Gay Street 121 F5
Gaydon 147 F2
Gayhurst 148 D3
Gayle 201 D4
Gayles 202 A2
Gayton Mersey 183 D4
Gayton N'hants 148 C2
Gayton Norf 163 F1
Gayton Staffs 171 G5
Gayton le Marsh 189 E4
Gayton le Wold 188 C4
Gayton Thorpe 163 F1
Gaywood 177 E5
Gazeley 151 F1
Geanies House 267 F4
Gearach 230 A4
Gearnsary 274 D5
Gearradh 248 B3
Gearraidh Bhailteas 254 C2
Gearraidh Bhaird 271 F5
Gearraidh na
  Monadh 254 C3
Geary 232 B2
Geary 263 H5
Gedding 152 A2
Geddington 161 D4

Gedgrave Hall 153 F3
Gedintailor 256 B1
Gedling 174 B3
Gedney 176 C5
Gedney Broadgate 176 C5
Gedney Drove End 176 C5
Gedney Dyke 176 C5
Gee Cross 185 D3
Geilston 233 E2
Geirinis 262 C7
Geisiadar 270 D4
Geldeston 165 E2
Gell Conwy 168 B3
Gell Gwyn 167 D3
Gelli 129 F3
Gelli Aur Country
  Park Carmar
  SA32 8LR 142 C5
Gelli Gynan 169 E2
Gellideg 129 G2
Gellifor 169 E1
Gelligaer 130 A3
Gellilydan 167 F3
Gellioedd 168 C3
Gelly 127 D1
Gellyburn 243 F1
Gellywen 141 F5
Gelston D&G 216 B5
Gelston Lincs 175 E3
Gembling 196 D2
Gemmil 239 G4
Genoch 214 C5
Genoch Square 214 C5
Gentleshaw 158 C1
Geocrab 263 G2
George Green 135 F4
George Nympton 114 A5
Georgeham 113 E2
Georgetown 233 F3
Gerlan 167 E1
Germansweek 99 E1
Germoe 94 C4
Gerrans 95 F3
Gerrards Cross 135 F4
Gerston 275 G3
Gestingthorpe 151 G4
Geufordd 156 B1
Geuffron 155 F4
Gibbet Hill 117 E3
Gibbshill 216 B3
Gibraltar Lincs 177 D2
Gibraltar Suff 152 D2
Gibraltar Point National
  Nature Reserve Lincs
  PE24 4SU 177 D2
Gibside T&W
  NE16 6BG 212 A2
Giddeahall 132 A5
Giddy Green 105 E4
Gidea Park 137 E4
Gidleigh 99 G2
Giffnock 233 G4
Gifford 236 C3
Giffordland 233 D5
Giffordtown 244 A3
Giggleswick 193 E1
Gigha 231 E5
Gilberdyke 196 A5
Gilbert's End 146 A3
Gilchriston 236 B3
Gilcrux 209 E3
Gildersome 194 B5
Gildingwells 186 C4
Gileston 114 D1
Gilfach 130 A3
Gilfach Goch 129 F4
Gilfachrheda 142 A2
Gilgarran 208 D4
Gill 210 A5
Gillamoor 203 F4
Gillen 263 H5
Gillenbie 217 F2
Gillfoot 217 D3
Gilling East 203 F5
Gilling West 202 A2
Gillingham Dorset 117 E5
Gillingham Med 123 G2
Gillingham Norf 165 F2
Gillivoan 275 G5
Gillock 275 H3
Gillow Heath 171 F2
Gills 275 J1
Gill's Green 123 G5
Gilmanscleuch 227 E3
Gilmerton Edin 235 G3
Gilmerton P&K 243 D2
Gilmilnscroft 225 D3
Gilmonby 201 E1
Gilmorton 160 A4
Gilsland 210 C1
Gilsland Spa 210 C1
Gilson 159 D3
Gilstead 194 A4
Gilston 236 B4
Gilston Park 136 D1
Giltbrook 173 F3
Gilwern 130 B1
Gimingham 179 D2
Gin Pit 184 A2
Ginclough 185 D5
Ginger's Green 110 B3
Gipsey Bridge 176 A3
Girlsta 279 D7
Girsby 202 C2
Girtford 149 G3
Girthon 216 A5
Girton Cambs 150 C1
Girton Notts 174 D1
Girvan 214 C1
Gisburn 193 E3
Gisburn Cotes 193 E3
Gisleham 165 G3
Gislingham 164 B4
Gissing 164 C3
Gittisham 103 E3
Givons Grove 121 G2
Glackour 265 H3
Gladestry 144 B2
Gladsmuir 236 B2
Glaic 232 B2
Glais 128 D2
Glaisdale 203 G2
Glaister 223 E2
Glame 264 B7

Glamis 252 B5
Glamis Castle Angus
  DD8 1QJ 252 B5
Glan Conwy 168 B2
Glanaber Terrace 168 A3
Glanaman 128 C1
Glan-Denys 142 B2
Glanderston 260 D2
Glandford 178 B1
Glandwr 141 E5
Glan-Duar 142 B3
Glandy Cross 141 E5
Glan-Dwyfach 167 D3
Glangrwyney 130 B1
Glanllynfi 129 E3
Glanmule 156 A3
Glan-rhyd NPT 129 D2
Glanrhyd Pembs 141 E3
Glanton 229 E5
Glanton Pyke 229 E5
Glanvilles Wootton 104 C2
Glanwern 154 C4
Glanwydden 181 G4
Glan-y-don 182 C5
Glan-y-llyn 130 A4
Glan-y-nant 155 F4
Glan-yr-afon
  Gwyn 168 C3
Glan-yr-afon
  Gwyn 168 D3
Glan-yr-afon IoA 181 E4
Glan-y-Wern 167 F4
Glapthorn 161 F3
Glapwell 173 F1
Glasahoile 241 G4
Glasbury 144 A4
Glaschoil 259 H1
Glascoed Mon 130 C2
Glascoed Wrex 169 F2
Glascorrie 260 C5
Glascote 159 E2
Glascwm 144 A2
Glasdrum 248 C5
Glasfryn 168 C2
Glasgow (Glaschu) 233 G3
Glasgow Airport 233 F3
Glasgow Botanic
  Garden Glas
  G12 0UE 30 C1
Glasgow Prestwick
  Airport 224 B3
Glasgow Royal Concert Hall
  Glas G2 3NY 39 F3
Glasgow Science Centre
  Glas G51 1EA 38 A4
Glashmore 261 F4
Glasinfryn 167 E1
Glasnacardoch 256 C5
Glasnakille 256 B3
Glaspant 141 F4
Glaspwll 154 D3
Glass Studio, Eastbourne
  Pier ESuss
  BN21 3EL 110 B4
Glassburn 257 K1
Glassel 260 E5
Glassenbury 123 G5
Glasserton 207 E3
Glassford 234 B5
Glasshouse 145 G5
Glasshouses 194 A1
Glassingall 242 C4
Glasslie 244 A4
Glasson Cumb 218 A5
Glasson Lancs 192 A2
Glasson Dock 192 A2
Glassonby 210 B4
Glasterlaw 253 D4
Glaston 161 D2
Glastonbury 116 B4
Glastonbury Abbey Som
  BA6 9EL 116 C4
Glatton 161 G3
Glazebrook 184 A3
Glazebury 184 A3
Glazeley 157 G4
Gleadless 186 A4
Gleadsmoss 171 F1
Gleann Tholastaidh 271 H3
Gleaston 199 D5
Glecknabae 232 B3
Gledhow 194 C4
Gledrid 169 F4
Glemsford 151 G3
Glen Cambs 162 D3
Glen D&G 215 G5
Glen Auldyn 190 C2
Glen Mona 190 C2
Glen Parva 160 A3
Glen Trool Lodge 215 F2
Glen Village 234 C2
Glen Vine 190 B4
Glenae 217 D2
Glenaladale 248 A2
Glenald 241 E5
Glenamachrie 240 B2
Glenapp Castle 214 B2
Glenarm 252 B3
Glenbarr 222 B2
Glenbatrick 230 D2
Glenbeg High 265 K3
Glenbeg High 259 H2
Glenbeg High 247 E3
Glenbeich 242 B2
Glenbervie Aber 253 F1
Glenbervie Falk 234 C1
Glenboig 234 B3
Glenborrodale 247 F3
Glenbranter 240 D5
Glenbreck 226 B3
Glenbrittle 255 K2
Glenburn 233 F3
Glenbyre 239 E2
Glencaird 215 F3
Glencaple 217 D4
Glencarse 243 G2
Glencat 260 D5
Glenceitlein 248 D5
Glenclocy 223 D2
Glencoe
  (A' Chàrnaich) 248 D4
Glencoe Visitor Centre
  High PH49 4LA 248 D4
Glenconglass 259 J2
Glencraig 243 G5
Glencripesdale 247 F4
Glencrosh 216 B2
Glencruitten 240 A2
Glencuie 260 C3

Glendearg D&G 226 D5
Glendearg ScBord 227 G2
Glendessary 257 F5
Glendevon 243 E4
Glendoebeg 258 B4
Glendoick 244 A2
Glendoll Lodge 252 A2
Glendoune 214 C1
Glendrissaig 214 C1
Glendye Lodge 253 E1
Gleneagles Hotel 243 E4
Gleneagles House 243 E4
Glenearn 243 G3
Glenegedale 230 B4
Glenelg
  (Gleann Eilg) 256 E3
Glenfarg 243 G3
Glenfeochan 240 A2
Glenfield 160 A2
Glenfinnan (Gleann
  Fhionnainn) 248 B1
Glenfoot 243 G3
Glengalmadale 248 A4
Glengap 216 A5
Glengarnock 233 E4
Glengarrisdale 239 F5
Glengennet 215 D1
Glengolly 275 G2
Glengorm Castle 246 D4
Glengrasco 263 K7
Glengyle 241 F3
Glenhead 216 C2
Glenhead Farm 252 A3
Glenhurich 248 A3
Glenkerry 227 D4
Glenkiln 223 E2
Glenkin 232 C1
Glenkindie 260 C3
Glenlair 216 B3
Glenlatterach 267 K6
Glenlean 232 B1
Glenlee Angus 252 C2
Glenlee D&G 216 A2
Glenlichorn 242 C3
Glenlivet J2
Glenlochar 216 B4
Glenlochsie 251 G3
Glenluce 214 C5
Glenmallan 241 E5
Glenmanna 225 F5
Glenmavis 234 B3
Glenmaye 190 A4
Glenmeanie 265 J6
Glenmore A&B 232 B3
Glenmore High 263 K7
Glenmore High 247 E4
Glenmore Forest Park
  Visitor Centre High
  PH22 1QY 259 G4
Glenmore Lodge 259 G4
Glenmoy 252 C3
Glenmuick 273 F7
Glennoe 240 C1
Glenochar 226 A4
Glenogil 252 C3
Glenprosen
  Village 252 B3
Glenquiech 252 C3
Glenramskill 222 C4
Glenrazie 215 E4
Glenridding 209 G5
Glenrisdell 231 G4
Glenrossal 266 B1
Glenrothes 244 A4
Glensanda 248 A5
Glensaugh 253 E2
Glensgaich 266 B5
Glenshalg 260 D4
Glenshellish 240 D5
Glensluain 240 C5
Glentaggart 225 G3
Glentham 188 A3
Glenton 260 E2
Glentress ScBord
  EH45 8NB 235 G5
Glentrool 215 E3
Glentruan 190 C1
Glentworth 187 G3
Glenuachdarach 263 K6
Glenuig 247 F2
Glenure 248 C5
Glenurquhart 266 E5
Glenwhilly 214 C3
Glespin 225 G3
Gletness 279 D7
Glewstone 145 E5
Glinton 161 G2
Glogue 141 F4
Glooston 160 C3
Glororum 229 F3
Glossop 185 E3
Gloster Hill 221 E1
Gloucester 132 A1
Gloucester Cathedral
  Glos GL1 2LR
  73 Gloucester
Gloucester Historic
  Docks Glos GL1 2ER
  73 Gloucester
Gloucestershire
  Airport 146 A5
Gloucestershire &
  Warwickshire Railway
  Glos GL54 5DT 146 B5
Gloup 278 E2
Gloweth 96 B5
Glusburn 193 G3
Glympton 147 G5
Glyn 168 B2
Glyn Ceiriog 169 F4
Glynarthen 141 G3
Glyncoch 129 G3
Glyncorrwg 129 E3
Glyn-Cywarch 167 F4
Glynde 109 G3
Glyndebourne 109 G2
Glyndyfrdwy 169 E3
Glynneath
  (Glyn-Nedd) 129 E2
Glynogwr 129 F4
Glyntaff 129 G4
Gnosall 171 F5
Gnosall Heath 171 F5
Go Bananas, Colchester
  Essex CO1 1BX 152 A5

Goadby 160 C3
Goadby Marwood 174 C5
Goatacre 132 C5
Goatfield 240 C4
Goathill 104 C1
Goathland 204 B2
Goathurst 115 F4
Gobernuisgeach 274 C5
Gobhaig 270 C6
Gobowen 170 A4
Godalming 121 E3
Goddard's Corner 153 D1
Goddards Green 109 E1
Godden Green 123 E3
Goddington 123 D2
Godford Cross 103 E3
Godington 148 B5
Godleybrook 171 G3
Godmanchester 162 A5
Godmanstone 104 C3
Godmersham 124 C3
Godney 116 B3
Godolphin Cross 94 D3
Godor 156 B1
Godre'r-graig 129 D2
Godshill Hants 106 A1
Godshill IoW 107 E4
Godstone 122 C3
Godstone Farm Surr
  RH9 8LX 122 C3
Godwick 178 A3
Goetre 130 C2
Goff's Oak 136 C2
Gogar 235 F2
Gogarth 181 F4
Goginan 154 C4
Goirtean a'
  Chladaich 248 C2
Goirtein 232 A1
Golan 167 E3
Golant 97 F4
Golberdon 98 D3
Golborne 184 A3
Golcar 185 F1
Gold Hill Cambs 162 D3
Gold Hill Dorset 105 E1
Goldcliff 130 C4
Golden Acre Park
  WYorks
  LS16 8BQ 194 B3
Golden Cross 110 A2
Golden Green 123 F4
Golden Grove 128 B1
Golden Pot 120 C3
Golden Valley
  Derbys 173 F3
Golden Valley Glos 146 B5
Goldenhill 171 F2
Golders Green 136 B4
Goldhanger 138 C2
Goldielea 216 D3
Golding 157 E2
Goldington 149 F2
Goldsborough
  NYorks 204 B1
Goldsborough
  NYorks 194 C3
Goldsithney 94 C3
Goldstone 171 E5
Goldthorn Park 158 B3
Goldthorpe 186 B2
Goldworthy 113 D3
Goleulong 2000 Lightship,
  Cardiff Cardiff
  CF10 4PA 7 C4
Golford 123 G5
Gollanfield 267 F6
Gollinglith Foot 202 A4
Golspie 267 F2
Golval 274 D2
Gomeldon 118 C4
Gomersal 194 B5
Gometra 246 C5
Gometra House 246 C5
Gomshall 121 G3
Gonachan Cottage 234 A1
Gonalston 174 B3
Gonerby Hill Foot 175 E4
Gonfirth 279 C6
Good Easter 137 F1
Gooderstone 163 F2
Goodleigh 113 G2
Goodmanham 196 A3
Goodmayes 137 D4
Goodnestone Kent 125 E3
Goodnestone Kent 124 C2
Goodrich 131 E1
Goodrington 101 E2
Goodshaw 193 E4
Goodshaw Fold 193 E4
Goodwick (Wdig) 140 C4
Goodworth Clatford 119 E3
Goodyers End 159 F4
Goom's Hill 146 C2
Goonbell 96 B5
Goonhavern 96 B4
Goonvrea 96 B5
Goose Green Essex 152 C5
Goose Green Essex 152 C5
Goose Green
  GtMan 183 G2
Goose Green Kent 123 F3
Goose Green SGlos 131 F5
Goose Pool 145 D4
Gooseham 112 C4
Goosehill Green 146 B1
Goosewell 100 B2
Goosey 133 F3
Goosnargh 192 B4
Goostrey 184 B5
Gorcott Hill 146 C1
Gorddinog 181 E5
Gordon 236 D5
Gordonbush 267 F1
Gordonstoun 267 J5
Gordonstown Aber 268 D5
Gordonstown Aber 261 F1
Gore Cross 118 B2
Gore End 119 F1
Gore Pit 138 B1
Gore Street 125 E2
Gorebridge 236 A3
Gorefield 162 C1
Gorey 100 D5
Gorgie 233 G2
Gorgie City Farm Edin
  EH11 2LA 36 B7

Goring **134** B4
Goring Heath **134** B5
Goring-by-Sea **108** D3
Gorleston-on-Sea **179** G5
Gorllwyn **141** G4
Gornalwood **158** B3
Gorrachie **269** F5
Gorran Churchtown **97** D5
Gorran Haven **97** E5
Gors **154** C5
Gorsedd **182** C5
Gorseinon **128** B3
Gorseness **277** D6
Gorseybank **173** D2
Gorsgoch **142** A2
Gorslas **128** B1
Gorsley **145** F5
Gorsley Common **145** F5
Gorstage **184** A5
Gorstan **265** K5
Gorstanvorran **248** A2
Gorsty Hill **172** C5
Gorten **239** G1
Gortenbuie **239** E1
Gorteneorn **247** F3
Gorton *A&B* **246** A4
Gorton *GtMan* **184** C3
Gosbeck **152** C2
Gosberton **176** A4
Gosberton Clough **175** G5
Goseley Dale **173** E5
Gosfield **151** F5
Gosford *Here* **145** E1
Gosford *Oxon* **134** A1
Gosforth *Cumb* **198** B2
Gosforth *T&W* **212** B1
Gosland Green **170** C2
Gosmore **149** G5
Gospel End **158** A3
Gosport **107** F3
Gossabrough **278** E4
Gossington **131** G2
Gossops Green **122** B5
Goswick **229** E2
Gotham **173** G4
Gotherington **146** B5
Gothers **97** D4
Gott **279** D8
Gotton **115** F5
Goudhurst **123** G5
Goulceby **188** C5
Gourdas **269** F6
Gourdon **253** G2
Gourock **232** D2
Govan **233** G3
Goverton **174** C2
Goveton **101** D3
Govilon **130** B1
Gowanhill **269** J4
Gowdall **195** F5
Gowerton **128** B3
Gowkhall **235** E1
Gowkthrapple **234** B4
Gowthorpe **195** G2
Goxhill *ERid* **197** D3
Goxhill *NLincs* **196** D5
Goytre **129** D4
Gozzard's Ford **133** G3
Grabhair **271** F6
Graby **175** F5
Gradbach **171** G1
Grade **95** E5
Gradeley Green **170** C2
Graffham **108** B2
Grafham *Cambs* **149** G1
Grafham *Surr* **121** F3
Grafham Water *Cambs* PE28 0BH **149** G1
Grafton *Here* **145** D4
Grafton *NYorks* **194** D1
Grafton *Oxon* **133** E2
Grafton *Shrop* **156** D1
Grafton *Worcs* **145** E1
Grafton *Worcs* **146** B4
Grafton Flyford **146** B2
Grafton Regis **148** C3
Grafton Underwood **161** E4
Grafty Green **124** A4
Graianrhyd **169** F2
Graig *Carmar* **128** A2
Graig *Conwy* **181** G5
Graig *Denb* **182** B5
Graig-fechan **169** E2
Grain **124** A1
Grainel **230** A3
Grainhow **269** G6
Grains Bar **185** D2
Grainsby **188** C3
Grainthorpe **189** D3
Graizelound **187** E3
Gramisdale (Gramsdal) **262** D6
Grampound **96** D5
Grampound Road **96** D4
Granborough **148** C5
Granby **174** C4
Grand Pier, Teignmouth *Devon* TQ14 8BB **102** C5
Grandborough **147** G1
Grandes Rocques **101** F4
Grandtully **251** E4
Grange *Cumb* **209** F5
Grange *EAyr* **224** C2
Grange *High* **257** K1
Grange *Med* **123** G2
Grange *Mersey* **182** D4
Grange *P&K* **244** A2
Grange Crossroads **268** C5
Grange de Lings **187** G5
Grange Hall **267** H5
Grange Hill **136** D3
Grange Moor **185** G1
Grange of Lindores **244** A3
Grange Villa **212** B2
Grangemill **172** D2
Grangemouth **234** D1
Grangemuir **244** D4
Grange-over-Sands **199** F5
Grangeston **214** D1
Grangetown *Cardiff* **130** A5
Grangetown *R&C* **213** E5
Granish **259** G3
Gransmoor **196** D2
Granston **140** B4
Grantchester **150** C2
Grantham **175** E4
Grantley **202** B5
Grantlodge **261** F3
Granton **235** G2
Granton House **226** B5
Grantown-on-Spey **259** H2
Grantsfield **145** E1
Grantshouse **237** F3
Grappenhall **184** A4
Grasby **188** A2
Grasmere **199** E2
Grass Green **151** F4
Grasscroft **185** D2
Grassendale **183** E4
Grassgarth **199** F3
Grassholme **211** F5
Grassington **193** G1
Grassmoor **173** F1
Grassthorpe **174** C1
Grateley **119** D3
Gratwich **172** B4
Gravel Hill **135** F3
Graveley *Cambs* **150** A1
Graveley *Herts* **150** A5
Gravelly Hill **158** D3
Gravels **156** C2
Graven **278** D5
Graveney **124** C2
Gravesend **137** F5
Grayingham **187** G3
Grayrigg **199** G3
Grays **137** F5
Grayshott **121** D4
Grayswood **121** E4
Grazeley **120** B1
Greasbrough **186** B3
Greasby **183** D4
Great Aberystwyth Camera Obscura *Cere* SY23 2DN **154** B4
Great Abington **150** D3
Great Addington **161** E5
Great Alne **146** D2
Great Altcar **183** E2
Great Amwell **136** C1
Great Asby **200** B1
Great Ashfield **152** A1
Great Ayton **203** E1
Great Baddow **137** G2
Great Bardfield **151** E4
Great Barford **149** G2
Great Barr **158** C3
Great Barrington **133** E1
Great Barrow **170** B1
Great Barton **151** G1
Great Barugh **203** G5
Great Bavington **220** B3
Great Bealings **152** D3
Great Bedwyn **119** D1
Great Bentley **152** C5
Great Bernera **270** D4
Great Billing **148** D1
Great Bircham **177** F4
Great Blakenham **152** C2
Great Bolas **170** D5
Great Bookham **121** G2
Great Bourton **147** G3
Great Bowden **160** C4
Great Bradley **151** E2
Great Braxted **138** B1
Great Bricett **152** B2
Great Brickhill **143** E4
Great Bridgeford **171** F5
Great Brington **148** B1
Great Bromley **152** B5
Great Broughton *Cumb* **209** D3
Great Broughton *NYorks* **203** E2
Great Buckland **123** F2
Great Budworth **184** A5
Great Burdon **202** C1
Great Burstead **137** F3
Great Busby **203** E2
Great Cambourne **150** B2
Great Canfield **137** E1
Great Canney **138** B2
Great Carlton **189** E4
Great Casterton **161** F2
Great Chalfield **117** F1
Great Chart **124** B4
Great Chatwell **157** G1
Great Chell **171** F2
Great Chesterford **150** D3
Great Cheverell **118** A2
Great Chishill **150** C4
Great Clacton **139** E1
Great Clifton **208** D4
Great Coates **188** C2
Great Comberton **146** B3
Great Corby **210** A2
Great Cornard **151** G3
Great Cowden **197** E3
Great Coxwell **133** E3
Great Crakehall **202** B4
Great Cransley **160** D5
Great Cressingham **163** G2
Great Crosby **183** E2
Great Crosthwaite **209** F4
Great Cubley **172** C4
Great Cumbrae **232** C4
Great Dalby **160** C1
Great Doddington **149** D1
Great Doward **131** E1
Great Dunham **163** G1
Great Dunmow **151** E5
Great Durnford **118** C4
Great Easton *Essex* **151** E5
Great Easton *Leics* **160** D3
Great Eccleston **192** A3
Great Edstone **203** G4
Great Ellingham **164** B2
Great Elm **117** E3
Great Eversden **150** B2
Great Fencote **202** B3
Great Finborough **152** B2
Great Fransham **163** G1
Great Gaddesden **135** F1
Great Gidding **161** G4
Great Givendale **196** A2
Great Glemham **153** E1
Great Glen **160** B3
Great Gonerby **175** D4
Great Gransden **150** A2
Great Green *Cambs* **150** A3
Great Green *Norf* **165** D3
Great Green *Suff* **152** A2
Great Green *Suff* **164** C4
Great Green *Suff* **164** B4
Great Habton **203** G5
Great Hale **175** G3
Great Hall *Hants* SO23 8UJ **89** Winchester
Great Hallingbury **137** E1
Great Hampden **134** D2
Great Harrowden **161** D5
Great Harwood **192** D4
Great Haseley **134** B2
Great Hatfield **197** D3
Great Haywood **172** B5
Great Heath **159** F4
Great Heck **195** E5
Great Henny **151** G4
Great Hinton **118** A2
Great Hockham **164** A2
Great Holland **139** F1
Great Horkesley **152** A4
Great Hormead **150** C4
Great Horton **194** A4
Great Horwood **148** C4
Great Houghton *N'hants* **148** C2
Great Houghton *SYorks* **186** B2
Great Hucklow **185** F5
Great Kelk **196** D2
Great Kimble **134** D2
Great Kingshill **135** D3
Great Langton **202** B3
Great Leighs **137** G1
Great Limber **188** B2
Great Linford **148** D3
Great Livermere **163** G5
Great Longstone **185** G5
Great Lumley **212** B3
Great Lyth **157** D2
Great Malvern **145** G3
Great Maplestead **151** G4
Great Marton **191** G4
Great Massingham **177** F5
Great Melton **178** C5
Great Milton **134** B2
Great Missenden **135** D2
Great Mitton **192** D4
Great Mongeham **125** F3
Great Moulton **164** C2
Great Munden **150** B5
Great Musgrave **200** C1
Great Ness **156** D1
Great Notley **151** F5
Great Nurcot **114** C4
Great Oak **130** C2
Great Oakley *Essex* **152** C5
Great Oakley *N'hants* **161** D4
Great Offley **149** G5
Great Orme Tramway *Conwy* LL30 2HG **181** F4
Great Ormside **200** C1
Great Orton **209** G1
Great Ouseburn **194** D1
Great Oxendon **160** C4
Great Oxney Green **137** F2
Great Palgrave **163** G1
Great Parndon **136** D2
Great Paxton **150** A1
Great Plumpton **191** G4
Great Plumstead **179** E5
Great Ponton **175** E4
Great Potheridge **113** F4
Great Preston **194** C5
Great Purston **148** A4
Great Raveley **162** A4
Great Rissington **133** D1
Great Rollright **147** F4
Great Ryburgh **178** A3
Great Ryle **229** E5
Great Ryton **157** D2
Great St. Mary's Church *Cambs* CB2 3PQ **66** Cambridge
Great Saling **151** F5
Great Salkeld **210** B4
Great Sampford **151** E4
Great Sankey **183** G4
Great Saredon **158** B2
Great Saxham **151** F1
Great Shefford **133** F5
Great Shelford **150** C2
Great Smeaton **202** C2
Great Snoring **178** A2
Great Somerford **132** B4
Great Stainton **212** C5
Great Stambridge **138** C3
Great Staughton **149** G1
Great Steeping **176** C1
Great Stonar **125** F3
Great Strickland **210** B5
Great Stukeley **162** A5
Great Sturton **188** C5
Great Sutton *ChesW&C* **183** E5
Great Sutton *Shrop* **157** E4
Great Swinburne **220** B4
Great Tew **147** F5
Great Tey **151** G5
Great Thorness **107** D3
Great Thurlow **151** E3
Great Torr **100** C3
Great Torrington **113** E4
Great Tosson **220** C1
Great Totham *Essex* **138** B1
Great Totham *Essex* **138** B1
Great Tows **188** C3
Great Urswick **199** D5
Great Wakering **138** C4
Great Waldingfield **152** A3
Great Walsingham **178** A2
Great Waltham **137** F1
Great Warley **137** E3
Great Washbourne **146** B4
Great Weeke **102** A4
Great Welnetham **151** G2
Great Wenham **152** B4
Great Whittington **220** C4
Great Wigborough **138** C1
Great Wigsell **110** C1
Great Wilbraham **150** D2
Great Wilne **173** F4
Great Wishford **118** B4
Great Witcombe **132** B1
Great Witley **145** G1
Great Wolford **147** E4
Great Wratting **151** E3
Great Wymondley **150** A5
Great Wyrley **158** B2
Great Wytheford **157** E1
Great Yarmouth **179** G5
Great Yeldham **151** F4
Greatford **161** F1
Greatgate **172** B3
Greatham *Hants* **120** C4
Greatham *Hart* **213** D5
Greatham *WSuss* **108** C2
Greatness **123** E3
Greatstone-on-Sea **111** F1
Greatworth **148** A3
Green **169** D1
Green Cross **121** D4
Green End *Bed* **149** G2
Green End *Bucks* **149** E4
Green End *Cambs* **162** A5
Green End *Cambs* **162** B5
Green End *Herts* **150** B5
Green End *Herts* **150** B4
Green End *Warks* **159** E4
Green Hammerton **195** D2
Green Hill **132** C4
Green Lane **146** C1
Green Moor **185** G3
Green Ore **116** C2
Green Quarter **199** F2
Green Street *ESuss* **110** C2
Green Street *Herts* **136** A3
Green Street *Herts* **150** C5
Green Street *Worcs* **146** A3
Green Street *WSuss* **121** G5
Green Street Green *GtLon* **123** D2
Green Street Green *Kent* **137** E5
Green Tye **136** D1
Greenburn **252** C5
Greencroft **212** A3
Greendams **253** E1
Greendykes **229** E4
Greenend **147** F5
Greenfaulds **234** B2
Greenfield *CenBeds* **149** F4
Greenfield (Maes-Glas) *Flints* **182** C5
Greenfield *GtMan* **185** E2
Greenfield *High* **257** J4
Greenfield *Lincs* **189** E5
Greenfield *Oxon* **134** C3
Greenford **136** A4
Greengairs **234** B2
Greengates **194** A4
Greengill **209** E3
Greenhalgh **192** A4
Greenhall **260** E2
Greenham **119** F1
Greenhaugh **219** F3
Greenhead **210** C1
Greenheads **261** J1
Greenheys **184** B2
Greenhill *GtLon* **136** A4
Greenhill *High* **267** G1
Greenhill *SYorks* **186** A4
Greenhithe **137** E5
Greenholm **224** D2
Greenholme **199** G2
Greenhow Hill **194** A1
Greenigo **277** D7
Greenland **275** H2
Greenlands **134** C4
Greenlaw *Aber* **268** E5
Greenlaw *ScBord* **237** E5
Greenloaning **242** D4
Greenmeadow **130** B3
Greenmoor Hill **134** B4
Greenmount **184** B1
Greenmyre **261** G1
Greenock **233** D2
Greenodd **199** E4
Greens Norton **148** B3
Greenscares **242** C3
Greenside *T&W* **212** A1
Greenside *WYorks* **185** F1
Greenstead **152** B5
Greenstead Green **151** G5
Greensted **137** E2
Greensted Green **137** E2
Greenway *Pembs* **141** D4
Greenway *Som* **116** A5
Greenwell **210** B2
Greenwich **136** C5
Greenwood Forest Park, Y Felinheli *Gwyn* LL56 4QN **167** E1
Greet **146** C4
Greete **157** E5
Greetham *Lincs* **188** D5
Greetham *Rut* **161** E1
Greetland **193** G5
Gregson Lane **192** B5
Greinton **116** B4
Grenaby **190** A4
Grendon *N'hants* **149** D1
Grendon *Warks* **159** E3
Grendon Common **159** E3
Grendon Green **145** E2
Grendon Underwood **148** B5
Grenitote (Greinetobht) **262** D4
Grenofen **99** E3
Grenoside **186** A3
Greosabhagh **263** G2
Gresford **170** A2
Gresham **178** C2
Greshornish **263** J6
Gress (Griais) **271** G3
Gressenhall **178** A4
Gressingham **192** B1
Greta Bridge **201** F1
Gretna **218** B5
Gretna Green **218** B5
Gretton *Glos* **146** C4
Gretton *N'hants* **161** E3
Gretton *Shrop* **157** E3
Grewelthorpe **202** B5
Greygarth **202** A5
Greylake **116** A4
Greys Green **134** C4
Greysouthen **209** D4
Greystead **219** F3
Greystoke **210** A4
Greystone *Aber* **259** K5
Greystone *Angus* **252** D5
Greystone *Lancs* **193** E3
Greystones **186** A4
Greywell **120** C2
Gribthorpe **195** G4
Gribton **216** D2
Griff **159** F4
Griffithstown **130** B3
Grigadale **246** D3
Grigghall **199** F3
Grimeford Village **184** A1
Grimesthorpe **186** A3
Grimethorpe **186** B2
Griminish (Griminis) **262** C6
Grimister **278** D3
Grimley **146** A1
Grimmet **224** B4
Grimness **277** D8
Grimoldby **189** D4
Grimpo **170** A5
Grimsargh **192** B4
Grimsay (Griomsaigh) **262** D6
Grimsbury **147** G3
Grimsby **188** C2
Grimscote **148** B2
Grimscott **112** C5
Grimshader (Griomsiadar) **271** G5
Grimsthorpe **175** F5
Grimston *ERid* **197** E4
Grimston *Leics* **174** B5
Grimston *Norf* **177** F5
Grimstone **104** C3
Grimstone End **152** A1
Grindale **205** E5
Grindiscol **279** D9
Grindle **157** G2
Grindleford **185** G5
Grindleton **193** D3
Grindley **172** B5
Grindley Brook **170** C3
Grindlow **185** F5
Grindon *N'umb* **237** G5
Grindon *Staffs* **172** B2
Grindon *Stock* **212** C5
Grindon *T&W* **212** C2
Gringley on the Hill **187** E3
Grinsdale **209** G1
Grinshill **170** C5
Grinton **201** F3
Griomarstaidh **270** E4
Grisdale **200** C3
Grishipoll **246** A4
Gristhorpe **205** D4
Griston **164** A2
Gritley **277** E7
Grittenham **132** C4
Grittleton **132** A5
Grizebeck **198** D4
Grizedale **199** E3
Grizedale Forest Park *Cumb* LA22 0QJ **199** E3
Grobister **276** F5
Groby **160** A2
Groes **168** D1
Groes-faen **129** G4
Groesffordd **166** B4
Groesffordd Marli **182** B5
Groeslon *Gwyn* **167** D2
Groeslon *Gwyn* **167** E1
Groes-lwyd **156** B1
Groes-wen **130** A4
Grogport **231** G5
Groigearraidh **254** C1
Gromford **153** E2
Gronant **182** B4
Groombridge **123** E5
Groombridge Place Gardens *Kent* TN3 9QG **123** E5
Grosmont *Mon* **144** D5
Grosmont *NYorks* **204** B2
Grotaig **258** B2
Groton **152** A3
Groundistone Heights **227** F4
Grouville **100** C5
Grove *Bucks* **149** E5
Grove *Dorset* **104** C5
Grove *Kent* **125** E2
Grove *Notts* **187** E5
Grove *Oxon* **133** G3
Grove End **124** A2
Grove Green **123** G3
Grove Park **136** D5
Grove Town **195** D5
Grovehill **135** F2
Grovesend *SGlos* **131** F4
Grovesend *Swan* **128** B2
Gruids **266** C1
Grula **255** J2
Gruline **247** E5
Grumbla **94** B4
Grundcruie **243** F2
Grundisburgh **152** D2
Gruting **279** B8
Grutness **279** G10
Gualachulain **248** D5
Guardbridge **244** C3
Guarlford **146** A3
Guay **251** F5
Gubbergill **198** B3
Gubblecote **135** E1
Guernsey **101** F5
Guernsey Airport **101** E5
Guestling Green **111** D2
Guestling Thorn **111** D2
Guestwick **178** B3
Guestwick Green **178** B3
Guide **192** D5
Guide Post **221** E3
Guilden Down **156** C4
Guilden Morden **150** A3
Guilden Sutton **170** B1
Guildford **121** E3
Guildford House Gallery *Surr* GU1 3AJ **74** Guildford
Guildtown **243** G1
Guilsborough **160** B5
Guilsfield (Cegidfa) **156** B1
Guilthwaite **186** B4
Guisborough **203** F1
Guiseley **194** A3
Guist **178** B3
Guith **276** E4
Guiting Power **146** C5
Gulberwick **279** D9
Gullane **236** B1
Gullane Bents *ELoth* EH31 2AZ **236** B1
Gulval **94** B3
Gulworthy **99** E3
Gumfreston **127** E2
Gumley **160** B3
Gunby *Lincs* **175** E5
Gunby *Lincs* **176** C1
Gundleton **120** B4
Gunn **113** G2
Gunnersbury **136** A5
Gunnerside **201** E3
Gunnerton **220** B4
Gunness **187** F1
Gunnislake **99** E3
Gunnista **279** E8
Gunnister **278** C5
Gunstone **158** A2
Gunter's Bridge **121** E5
Gunthorpe *Norf* **178** B2
Gunthorpe *Notts* **174** B3
Gunthorpe *Rut* **161** D2
Gunville **107** D4
Gunwalloe **95** D4
Gupworthy **114** C4
Gurnard **107** D3
Gurnett **184** D5
Gurney Slade **116** D3
Gurnos *MTyd* **129** G2
Gurnos *Powys* **129** D2
Gushmere **124** C3
Gussage All Saints **105** G1
Gussage St. Andrew **105** F1
Gussage St. Michael **105** F1
Guston **125** F4
Gutcher **278** E3
Guthram Gowt **175** G5
Guthrie **253** D4
Guyhirn **162** B2
Guynd **253** D5
Guy's Head **176** C5
Guy's Marsh **117** F5
Guyzance **221** E1
Gwaelod-y-garth **130** A4
Gwaenysgor **182** B4
Gwaithla **144** B2
Gwalchmai **180** B5
Gwastad **140** D5
Gwastadnant **167** F2
Gwaun-Cae-Gurwen **128** D1
Gwaynynog **168** D1
Gwbert **141** E3
Gweek **95** E4
Gwehelog **130** C2
Gwenddwr **143** G3
Gwendreath **95** E5
Gwennap **96** B5
Gwenter **95** E5
Gwernaffield **169** F1
Gwernesney **130** D2
Gwernogle **142** B4
Gwernymynydd **169** F1
Gwern-y-Steeple **129** G5
Gwersyllt **170** A2
Gwespyr **182** C4
Gwinear **94** C3
Gwithian **94** C2
Gwredog **180** C4
Gwrhay **130** A3
Gwyddelwern **169** D3
Gwyddgrug **142** A4
Gwynfryn **169** F2
Gwystre **143** G1
Gwytherin **168** B1
Gyfelia **170** A3
Gyre **277** C7
Gyrn Goch **166** D3

H

H.M.S. Belfast *GtLon* SE1 2JH **12** C4
H.M.S. Victory PO1 3PX **82** Portsmouth
H.M.S. Warrior PO1 3QX **82** Portsmouth
Habberley **156** C2
Habin **120** D5
Habrough **188** B1
Haccombe **102** B5
Hacconby **175** G5
Haceby **175** F4
Hacheston **153** E2
Hackbridge **122** B2
Hackenthorpe **186** B4
Hackford **178** B5
Hackforth **202** B3
Hackland **276** C5
Hacklet (Haclait) **262** D7
Hacklete (Tacleit) **270** D4
Hackleton **148** D2
Hacklinge **125** F3
Hackness *NYorks* **204** C3
Hackness *Ork* **277** C8
Hackney **136** C4
Hackthorn **187** G4
Hackthorpe **210** B5
Hacton **137** E4
Hadden **228** B3
Haddenham *Bucks* **134** C2
Haddenham *Cambs* **162** C5
Haddington *ELoth* **236** C2
Haddington *Lincs* **175** E1
Haddiscoe **165** F2
Haddo Country Park *Aber* AB41 7EQ **261** G1
Haddon **161** G3
Hade Edge **185** F2
Hademore **159** D2
Hadfield **185** E3
Hadham Cross **136** D1
Hadham Ford **150** C5
Hadleigh *Essex* **138** B4
Hadleigh *Suff* **152** B3
Hadleigh Castle Country Park *Essex* SS7 2PP **138** B4
Hadleigh Farm *Essex* SS7 2AP **138** B4
Hadleigh Heath **152** A3
Hadley *Tel&W* **157** F1
Hadley *Worcs* **146** A1
Hadley End **172** C5
Hadley Wood **136** B3
Hadlow **123** F4
Hadlow Down **110** A1
Hadnall **170** C5
Hadspen **117** D4
Hadstock **151** D3
Hadston **221** E2
Hadzor **146** B1
Haffenden Quarter **124** A4
Hafod Bridge **142** C4
Hafod-Dinbych **168** B2
Hafodunos **168** B1
Hafodyrynys **130** B3
Haggate **193** E4
Haggbeck **218** C4
Haggersta **279** C8
Haggerston *GtLon* **136** C4
Haggerston *N'umb* **229** E2
Haggrister **278** C5
Haggs **234** B2
Hagley *Here* **145** E3
Hagley *Worcs* **158** B4
Hagnaby *Lincs* **176** B1
Hagnaby *Lincs* **189** E5
Hague Bar **185** D4
Hagworthingham **176** B1
Haigh **184** A2
Haigh Hall Country Park *GtMan* WN2 1PE **183** G2
Haighton Green **192** B4
Hail Weston **149** G1
Haile **198** B2
Hailes **146** C4
Hailey *Herts* **136** C1
Hailey *Oxon* **134** B4
Hailey *Oxon* **133** F1
Hailsham **110** A3
Haimer **275** G2
Hainault **137** D3
Hainault Forest Country Park *Essex* IG7 4QN **137** D3
Haine **125** F2
Hainford **178** D4
Hainton **188** B4
Haisthorpe **196** D1
Hakin **126** B2
Halam **174** B2
Halbeath **235** F1
Halberton **102** D1
Halcro **275** H2
Hale *Cumb* **199** G5
Hale *GtMan* **184** B4
Hale *Halton* **183** F4
Hale *Hants* **106** A1
Hale *Surr* **120** D3
Hale Bank **183** F4
Hale Barns **184** B4
Hale Nook **191** G3
Hale Street **123** F4
Hales *Norf* **165** E2
Hales *Staffs* **171** E4
Hales Green **172** C3
Hales Place **124** D3
Halesgate **176** B5
Halesowen **158** B4
Halesworth **165** E4
Halewood **183** F4
Half Way Inn **102** D3
Halford *Devon* **102** B5
Halford *Shrop* **156** D4
Halford *Warks* **147** E3
Halfpenny **199** G4
Halfpenny Green **158** A3
Halfway *Carmar* **142** C4
Halfway *Carmar* **128** B2
Halfway *Powys* **143** E4
Halfway *SYorks* **186** B4
Halfway *WBerks* **119** F1
Halfway Bridge **121** E5
Halfway House **156** C1
Halfway Houses *Kent* **124** B1
Halfway Houses *Lincs* **175** D1
Halghton Mill **170** B3
Halifax **193** G5
Halistra **263** H6
Halket **233** F4
Halkirk **275** G3
Halkyn **182** D5
Hall **233** F4
Hall Cross **192** A5
Hall Dunnerdale **198** D3
Hall Green *ChesE* **171** F2
Hall Green *Lancs* **192** A5
Hall Green *WMid* **158** D4
Hall Grove **136** B1
Hall of the Forest **156** B4
Halland **110** A2
Hallaton **160** C3
Hallatrow **116** D2
Hallbankgate **210** B2
Hallen **131** E4
Hallfield Gate **173** E2
Hallglen **234** C2
Hallin **263** H6
Halling **123** G2
Hallington *Lincs* **188** D4
Hallington *N'umb* **220** B4
Halliwell **184** A1
Halloughton **174** B2
Hallow **146** A2
Hallow Heath **146** A2
Hallrule **227** G4
Halls **237** D2
Halls Green *Essex* **136** D2
Hall's Green *Herts* **150** A5
Hallsands **101** E4
Hallthwaites **198** C4
Hallwood Green **145** F4
Hallworthy **97** F1
Hallyne **235** F5
Halmer End **171** E3
Halmond's Frome **145** F3
Halmore **131** F2
Halmyre Mains **235** F5
Halnaker **108** B3
Halsall **183** E1
Halse *N'hants* **148** A3
Halse *Som* **115** E5
Halsetown **94** C3
Halsham **197** E5
Halsinger **113** F2
Halstead *Essex* **151** G4
Halstead *Kent* **123** D2
Halstead *Leics* **160** C2

Halstock 104 B2
Halsway 115 E4
Haltemprice Farm 196 C4
Haltham 176 A1
Haltoft End 176 B3
Halton *Bucks* 135 D1
Halton *Halton* 183 G4
Halton *Lancs* 192 B1
Halton *N'umb* 211 F1
Halton *Wrex* 170 A4
Halton East 193 G2
Halton Gill 201 D5
Halton Holegate 176 C1
Halton Lea Gate 210 C2
Halton Park 192 B1
Halton West 193 E2
Haltwhistle 210 D1
Halvergate 179 F5
Halwell 101 D2
Halwill 99 E1
Halwill Junction 99 E1
Ham *Devon* 103 F2
Ham *Glos* 131 F3
Ham *Glos* 146 B5
Ham *GtLon* 136 A5
Ham *High* 275 H1
Ham *Kent* 125 F3
Ham *Plym* 100 A2
Ham *Shet* 278 B1
Ham *Som* 115 F5
Ham *Som* 103 F1
Ham *Wilts* 119 E1
Ham Common 117 F5
Ham Green *Here* 145 G3
Ham Green *Kent* 124 A2
Ham Green *Kent* 111 D1
Ham Green *NSom* 131 E5
Ham Green *Worcs* 146 C1
Ham Hill 123 F2
Ham Hill Country Park
   Som TA14 6RW 104 A1
Ham Street 116 C4
Hambleden 134 C4
Hambledon *Hants* 107 F1
Hambledon *Surr* 121 E4
Hamble-le-Rice 107 D2
Hambleton *Lancs* 191 G3
Hambleton *NYorks* 195 E4
Hambridge 116 A5
Hambrook *SGlos* 131 F5
Hambrook *WSuss* 107 G2
Hameringham 176 B1
Hamerton 161 G5
Hamilton 234 B4
Hamlet *Devon* 103 E3
Hamlet *Dorset* 104 B2
Hammer 121 D4
Hammersmith 136 B5
Hammersmith Apollo
   GtLon W6 9QH 11 E3
Hammerwich 158 C2
Hammerwood 122 D5
Hammond Street 136 C2
Hammoon 105 E1
Hamnavoe *Shet* 279 C9
Hamnavoe *Shet* 278 D4
Hamnavoe *Shet* 278 B4
Hamnavoe *Shet* 278 D5
Hamnish Clifford 145 E2
Hamp 115 F4
Hampden Park 110 B3
Hampden Park Stadium
   Glas G42 9BA 30 D4
Hamperden End 151 D4
Hampnett 132 D1
Hampole 186 C2
Hampreston 105 G3
Hampstead 136 B4
Hampstead
   Norreys 134 A5
Hampsthwaite 194 B2
Hampton *Devon* 103 F3
Hampton *GtLon* 121 G1
Hampton *Kent* 125 D2
Hampton *Peter* 161 G3
Hampton *Shrop* 146 B5
Hampton *Swin* 133 D3
Hampton *Worcs* 146 C3
Hampton Bishop 145 E4
Hampton Court Palace &
   Garden *GtLon*
   KT8 9AU 11 B8
Hampton Fields 132 A3
Hampton Heath 170 B3
Hampton in Arden 159 E4
Hampton Loade 157 G4
Hampton Lovett 146 A1
Hampton Lucy 147 E2
Hampton on the
   Hill 147 E2
Hampton Poyle 134 A1
Hampton Wick 121 G1
Hamptworth 106 B1
Hamsey 109 G2
Hamstall Ridware 158 D1
Hamstead 106 C2
Hamstead Marshall 119 F1
Hamsteels 182 A1
Hamsterley *Dur* 212 A4
Hamsterley *Dur* 212 A2
Hamsterley Forest *Dur*
   DL13 3NL 211 G5
Hamstreet 124 C5
Hamworthy 105 F3
Hanbury *Staffs* 172 C5
Hanbury *Worcs* 146 B1
Hanbury Woodend 172 C5
Hanby 175 F4
Hanchurch 171 F3
Handa Island 272 D4
Handale 203 G1
Handbridge 170 B1
Handcross 122 B5
Handforth 184 C4
Handley *ChesW&C* 170 B2
Handley *Derbys* 173 E1
Handley Green 137 F2
Handsacre 158 C1
Handside 136 B1
Handsworth *SYorks* 186 B4
Handsworth *WMid* 158 C3
Handwoodbank 156 D1
Handy Cross 135 D3
Hanging Bridge 172 C3
Hanging Houghton 160 C5
Hanging Langford 118 B4
Hanginghaw 217 F2
Hanham 131 F5
Hankelow 171 D5
Hankerton 132 B3
Hanley 171 F3
Hanley Castle 146 A3
Hanley Child 145 F1
Hanley Swan 146 A3
Hanley William 145 F1
Hanlith 193 F1
Hanmer 170 B4
Hannah 189 E5
Hannington
   Hants 119 G2
Hannington
   N'hants 160 D5
Hannington *Swin* 133 D3
Hannington Wick 133 D3
Hanslope 148 D3
Hanthorpe 175 F5
Hanwell *GtLon* 136 A4
Hanwell *Oxon* 147 G3
Hanwood 156 D2
Hanworth *GtLon* 136 A5
Hanworth *Norf* 178 C2
Happisburgh 179 E2
Happisburgh
   Common 179 E3
Hapsford 183 F5
Hapton *Lancs* 193 D4
Hapton *Norf* 164 C2
Harberton 101 D2
Harbertonford 101 D2
Harborne 158 C4
Harborough Magna 159 G5
Harbost (Tabost) 271 H1
Harbottle 220 B1
Harbour Park Amusements,
   Littlehampton *WSuss*
   BN17 5LL 108 C3
Harbourneford 100 D1
Harbridge 106 A1
Harbridge Green 106 A1
Harburn 235 E3
Harbury 147 F2
Harby *Leics* 174 C4
Harby *Notts* 187 F5
Harcombe 103 E3
Harcombe Bottom 103 G3
Harden *WMid* 158 C2
Harden *WYorks* 193 G4
Hardendale 199 G1
Hardenhuish 132 B5
Hardgate *Aber* 261 F4
Hardgate *NYorks* 194 B1
Hardham 108 C2
Hardhorn 191 G4
Hardingham 178 B5
Hardingstone 148 C2
Hardington 117 E2
Hardington
   Mandeville 104 B1
Hardington Marsh 104 B2
Hardington Moor 104 B1
Hardley 106 D2
Hardley Street 179 E5
Hardmead 149 E3
Hardraw 201 D3
Hardstoft 173 F1
Hardway *Hants* 107 F3
Hardway *Som* 117 E4
Hardwick *Bucks* 134 D1
Hardwick *Cambs* 150 B2
Hardwick *Lincs* 187 F5
Hardwick *N'hants* 149 D1
Hardwick *Norf* 164 D3
Hardwick *Oxon* 133 F3
Hardwick *Oxon* 148 A5
Hardwick *SYorks* 186 B4
Hardwick *WMid* 158 C3
Hardwick Hall *Derbys*
   S44 5QJ 173 F1
Hardwick Hall Country Park,
   Sedgefield *Dur*
   TS21 2EH 212 C5
Hardwick Village 186 D5
Hardwicke *Glos* 146 B5
Hardwicke *Glos* 131 G1
Hardwicke *Here* 144 B3
Hardy's Green 152 A5
Hare Green 152 B5
Hare Hatch 134 D5
Hare Street *Herts* 150 B5
Hare Street *Herts* 150 B5
Hareby 176 B1
Harecroft 193 G4
Hareden 192 C2
Harefield 135 F3
Harehill 172 C4
Harehills 194 C4
Harehope 229 E4
Harelaw 234 D5
Hareplain 124 A5
Harescombe 132 A1
Haresceugh 210 C3
Haresfield 132 A1
Hareshaw *NLan* 234 C3
Hareshaw *SLan* 234 A5
Harestock 119 F4
Harewood 194 C3
Harewood End 145 E5
Harewood House *WYorks*
   LS17 9LG 194 C3
Harford *Devon* 100 C2
Harford *Devon* 102 B3
Hargate 164 C2
Hargatewall 185 F5
Hargrave *ChesW&C* 170 B1
Hargrave *N'hants* 161 F5
Hargrave *Suff* 151 F2
Hargrave Green 151 F2
Harker 218 B5
Harkstead 152 D4
Harlaston 159 E1
Harlaxton 175 D4
Harle Syke 193 E4
Harlech 167 E4
Harlech Castle *Gwyn*
   LL46 2YH 167 E4
Harlequin 174 B4
Harlescott 157 E1
Harlesden 136 B4
Harleston *Devon* 101 D3
Harleston *Norf* 164 D3
Harleston *Suff* 152 B1
Harlestone 148 C1
Harley *Shrop* 157 E2
Harley *SYorks* 186 A3
Harleyholm 226 A2
Harlington
   CenBeds 149 F4
Harlington *GtLon* 135 F5
Harlosh 263 H7
Harlow 136 D2
Harlow Hill 211 G1
Harlthorpe 195 G4
Harlton 150 B2
Harlyn 96 C2
Harman's Cross 105 F4
Harmby 202 A4
Harmer Green 136 B1
Harmer Hill 170 B5
Harmondsworth 135 F5
Harmston 175 E1
Harnage 157 E2
Harnham 118 C5
Harnhill 132 C2
Harold Hill 137 E3
Harold Park 137 E3
Harold Wood 137 E3
Haroldston West 126 B1
Haroldswick 278 F1
Harome 203 F4
Harpenden 136 A1
Harpford 103 D3
Harpham 196 C1
Harpley *Norf* 177 F5
Harpley *Worcs* 145 F1
Harpole 148 B1
Harpsdale 275 G3
Harpsden 134 C4
Harpswell 187 G4
Harpur Hill 185 F5
Harpurhey 184 C2
Harracott 113 F3
Harrapool 256 C2
Harrietfield 243 E2
Harrietsham 124 A3
Harringay 136 C4
Harrington *Cumb* 208 C4
Harrington *Lincs* 189 D5
Harrington *N'hants* 160 C5
Harringworth 161 E3
Harris 255 J5
Harris Green 164 D2
Harris Museum & Art
   Gallery, Preston *Lancs*
   PR1 2PP 192 B5
Harriseahead 171 F2
Harriston 209 E2
Harrogate 194 C2
Harrogate International
   Centre *NYorks* HG1 5LA
   74 Harrogate
Harrold-Odell Country Park
   Bed MK43 7DS 149 E2
Harrop Fold 192 D3
Harrow *GtLon* 136 A4
Harrow *High* 275 H1
Harrow Green 151 G2
Harrow Museum *GtLon*
   HA2 6PX 10 B1
Harrow on the Hill 136 A4
Harrow Weald 136 A3
Harrowbarrow 99 E3
Harrowden 149 F3
Harrowgate Hill 202 B1
Harry Stoke 131 F5
Harston *Cambs* 150 C2
Harston *Leics* 174 D4
Harswell 196 A3
Hart 213 D4
Hartburn 220 C3
Hartest 151 G2
Hartfield *ESuss* 123 D5
Hartfield *High* 264 D7
Hartford *Cambs* 162 A5
Hartford
   ChesW&C 184 A5
Hartford *Som* 114 C5
Hartford End 137 F1
Hartfordbridge 120 C2
Hartforth 202 A2
Hartgrove 105 E1
Harthill *ChesW&C* 170 C2
Harthill *NLan* 234 D3
Harthill *SYorks* 186 B4
Hartington 172 C1
Hartington Hall 220 C3
Hartland 112 C3
Hartland Quay 112 C3
Hartlebury 158 A5
Hartlepool 213 E4
Hartlepool's Maritime
   Experience *Hart*
   TS24 0XZ 213 E4
Hartley *Cumb* 200 C2
Hartley *Kent* 123 F2
Hartley *Kent* 123 G5
Hartley *N'umb* 221 F4
Hartley Green 171 G5
Hartley Mauditt 120 C4
Hartley Wespall 120 B2
Hartley Wintney 120 C2
Hartlington 193 G1
Hartlip 124 A2
Hartoft End 203 G3
Harton *NYorks* 195 G1
Harton *Shrop* 157 D4
Harton *T&W* 212 C1
Hartpury 146 A5
Hartridge 228 A4
Hartshead 194 A5
Hartshill 159 F3
Hartshorne 173 E5
Hartsop 199 F1
Hartwell *Bucks* 134 C1
Hartwell *ESuss* 123 D5
Hartwell *N'hants* 148 C2
Hartwith 194 B1
Hartwood 184 D1
Harvel 123 F2
Harvington *Worcs* 146 C3
Harvington *Worcs* 158 A5
Harwell *Notts* 187 D3
Harwell *Oxon* 133 G4
Harwich 152 D5
Harwood *Dur* 211 E4
Harwood *GtMan* 184 B1
Harwood *N'umb* 220 C2
Harwood Dale 204 C3
Harwood on
   Teviot 227 F5
Harworth 186 D3
Hasbury 158 B4
Hascombe 121 F3
Haselbech 160 C5
Haselbury
   Plucknett 104 A1
Haseley 147 E1
Haseley Knob 159 E5
Haselor 146 D2
Hasfield 146 A5
Hasguard 126 B2
Haskayne 183 E2
Hasketon 153 D2
Hasland 173 E1
Hasland Green 173 E1
Haslemere 121 E4
Haslingden 193 D5
Haslingden Grane 193 D5
Haslingfield 150 C2
Haslington 171 E2
Hassall 171 E2
Hassall Green 171 E2
Hassall Street 124 C4
Hassendean 227 G3
Hassingham 179 E5
Hassocks 109 F2
Hassop 185 G5
Haster 275 J3
Hasthorpe 176 C1
Hastigrow 275 H2
Hastingleigh 124 C4
Hastings *ESuss* 110 D3
Hastings *Som* 103 G1
Hastings Fishermen's
   Museum *ESuss*
   TN34 3DW 75 Hastings
Hastingwood 137 D2
Hastoe 135 E2
Haswell 212 C3
Haswell Plough 212 C3
Hatch *CenBeds* 149 G3
Hatch *Hants* 120 B2
Hatch Beauchamp 116 A5
Hatch End 136 A3
Hatch Green 103 G1
Hatching Green 136 A1
Hatchmere 183 G5
Hatcliffe 188 C2
Hatfield *Here* 145 E2
Hatfield *Herts* 136 B2
Hatfield *SYorks* 187 D2
Hatfield Broad Oak 137 E1
Hatfield Heath 137 E1
Hatfield House *Herts*
   AL9 5NF 136 B2
Hatfield Peverel 137 G1
Hatfield
   Woodhouse 187 D2
Hatford 133 F3
Hatherden 119 E2
Hatherleigh 113 F5
Hathern 173 F5
Hatherop 133 D2
Hathersage 185 G4
Hathersage Booths 185 G4
Hathershaw 184 D2
Hatherton *ChesE* 171 D3
Hatherton *Staffs* 158 B1
Hatley St. George 150 A2
Hatt 99 D4
Hattingley 120 B4
Hatton *Aber* 261 J1
Hatton *Derbys* 172 D5
Hatton *GtLon* 136 A5
Hatton *Lincs* 188 B5
Hatton *Shrop* 157 D3
Hatton *Warks* 147 E1
Hatton *Warr* 183 G4
Hatton Castle 269 F6
Hatton Country World
   Warks
   CV35 8XA 147 E1
Hatton Heath 170 B1
Hatton of Fintray 261 G3
Hattoncrook 261 G2
Haugh 189 E5
Haugh Head 229 E4
Haugh of Glass 260 C1
Haugh of Urr 216 C4
Haugham 188 D4
Haughead 234 A4
Haughley 152 B1
Haughley Green 152 B1
Haughley New
   Street 152 B1
Haughs 268 D6
Haughton *ChesE* 170 C2
Haughton *Notts* 187 D5
Haughton *Powys* 156 C1
Haughton *Shrop* 157 F3
Haughton *Shrop* 157 E1
Haughton *Shrop* 170 A3
Haughton *Staffs* 171 F5
Haughton Green 184 D3
Haughton
   Le Skerne 202 C1
Haultwick 150 B5
Haunn 254 B3
Haunton 159 E1
Hauxton 150 C2
Havannah 171 F1
Havant 107 G2
Haven 145 D2
Haven Side 197 E5
Havenstreet 107 E3
Haverfordwest
   (Hwlffordd) 126 C1
Haverhill 151 E3
Haverigg 198 C5
Havering Park 137 D3
Havering-atte-
   Bower 137 E3
Haversham 148 D3
Haverthwaite 199 E4
Haverton Hill 213 D5
Haviker Street 123 G4
Havyat 116 C4
Hawarden
   (Penarlâg) 170 A1
Hawbridge 146 B3
Hawbush Green 151 F5
Hawcoat 198 D5
Hawes 201 D4
Hawe's Green 164 D2
Hawick 227 G4
Hawkchurch 103 G2
Hawkedon 151 F2
Hawkenbury *Kent* 123 E5
Hawkenbury *Kent* 124 A4
Hawkeridge 117 F2
Hawkerland 103 D4
Hawkes End 159 E4
Hawkesbury 131 G4
Hawkesbury
   Upton 131 G4
Hawkhill 229 G5
Hawkhurst 123 G5
Hawkinge 125 E4
Hawkley 120 C5
Hawkridge 114 B4
Hawkshead 199 E3
Hawkshead Hill 199 E3
Hawksheads 192 A1
Hawkswick 201 E5
Hawksworth
   Notts 174 C3
Hawksworth
   WYorks 194 A3
Hawksworth
   WYorks 194 B4
Hawkwell *Essex* 138 B3
Hawkwell *N'umb* 220 C4
Hawley *Hants* 121 D2
Hawley *Kent* 137 E5
Hawley's Corner 122 D3
Hawling 146 C5
Hawnby 203 E4
Haworth 193 G4
Hawstead 151 G2
Hawstead Green 151 G2
Hawthorn *Dur* 212 D3
Hawthorn *Hants* 120 B5
Hawthorn *RCT* 129 G4
Hawthorn *Wilts* 117 F1
Hawthorn Hill
   BrackF 135 D5
Hawthorn Hill
   Lincs 176 A2
Hawthorpe 175 F5
Hawton 174 C2
Haxby 195 F2
Haxey 187 E2
Haxted 122 D4
Haxton 118 C3
Hay *Green* 162 D1
Hay Mills 158 D4
Hay Street 150 B5
Haydock 183 G3
Haydon *Dorset* 104 C1
Haydon *Swin* 133 D4
Haydon Bridge 211 F1
Haydon Wick 132 D4
Hayes *GtLon* 135 F4
Hayes *GtLon* 122 D2
Hayes End 135 F4
Hayfield *A&B* 240 C2
Hayfield *Derbys* 185 E4
Hayfield *Fife* 244 A5
Hayfield *High* 275 G2
Haygrove 115 F4
Hayhillock 252 D5
Hayle 94 C3
Hayling Island 107 G2
Haymoor Green 171 D2
Hayne 102 C1
Haynes 149 G3
Haynes Church End 149 F3
Haynes West End 149 F3
Hay-on-Wye (Y Gelli
   Gandryll) 144 B3
Hayscastle 140 B5
Hayscastle Cross 140 C5
Hayton *Cumb* 210 B2
Hayton *Cumb* 209 E2
Hayton *ERid* 196 A3
Hayton *Notts* 187 E4
Hayton's Bent 157 E4
Haytor Vale 102 A5
Haytown 113 D4
Hayward Gallery
   GtLon SE1 8XZ 45 F4
Haywards Heath 109 F1
Haywood Oaks 174 B2
Hazel End 150 C5
Hazel Grove 184 D4
Hazel Street 123 G5
Hazelbank *A&B* 240 C4
Hazelbank *SLan* 234 C5
Hazelbury Bryan 104 D2
Hazeleigh 138 B2
Hazeley 120 C2
Hazelhurst 184 D2
Hazelside 225 G3
Hazelslack 199 F5
Hazelslade 158 C1
Hazelton Walls 244 B3
Hazelwood *Derbys* 173 E3
Hazelwood *GtLon* 122 D2
Hazlefield 208 A2
Hazlehead
   Aberdeen 261 G4
Hazlehead *SYorks* 185 F2
Hazlemere 135 D3
Hazlerigg 221 E4
Hazleton 132 C1
Hazon 221 D1
Heacham 177 E4
Head Bridge 113 G4
Headbourne
   Worthy 119 F4
Headcorn 124 A4
Headingley 194 B4
Headington 134 A2
Headlam 202 A1
Headless Cross 146 C1
Headley *Hants* 120 D4
Headley *Hants* 119 G1
Headley *Surr* 122 B3
Headley Down 120 D4
Headley Heath 158 C5
Headon 187 E5
Heads Nook 210 A2
Heady Hill 184 C1
Heage 173 E2
Healabhal 256 B2
Heald Green 184 C4
Heale *Devon* 113 G1
Heale *Som* 116 A5
Healey *Lancs* 184 C1
Healey *N'umb* 211 G2
Healey *NYorks* 202 A4
Healey *WYorks* 194 B5
Healeyfield 211 G3
Healey's Cornish Cyder Farm
   Corn TR4 9LW 96 B4
Healing 188 C2
Heamoor 94 B3
Heaning 199 F3
Heanish 246 B2
Heanor 173 F3
Heanton
   Punchardon 113 F2
Heanton Satchville 113 F4
Heap Bridge 184 C1
Heapey 192 C5
Heapham 187 F4
Hearn 120 D4
Heart of the Country
   Centre *Staffs*
   WS14 9QR 158 D2
Hearthstane 226 C3
Heasley Mill 114 A4
Heast 256 C3
Heath *Cardiff* 130 A4
Heath *Derbys* 173 F1
Heath *WYorks* 186 A1
Heath & Reach 149 E5
Heath End *Derbys* 173 E5
Heath End *Hants* 119 G1
Heath End *Hants* 119 F1
Heath End *Surr* 120 D3
Heath Hayes 158 C1
Heath Hill 157 G1
Heath House 116 B3
Heath Town 158 B2
Heathbrook 170 D5
Heathcot 261 G4
Heathcote *Derbys* 172 C1
Heathcote *Shrop* 171 D5
Heathencote 148 C3
Heather 159 F1
Heatherton Activity Park
   Pembs
   SA70 8RJ 127 E2
Heathfield *Devon* 102 B5
Heathfield *ESuss* 110 A1
Heathfield *NYorks* 194 A1
Heathfield *Som* 115 E5
Heathrow Airport 135 F5
Heathton 158 A3
Heatley 184 B4
Heaton *Lancs* 192 A1
Heaton *Staffs* 171 G1
Heaton *T&W* 212 B1
Heaton *WYorks* 194 A4
Heaton Moor 184 C3
Heaton Park *GtMan*
   M25 2SW 25 C2
Heaton's Bridge 183 F1
Heaverham 123 E3
Heaviley 184 D4
Heavitree 102 C3
Hebburn 212 C1
Hebden 193 G1
Hebden Bridge 193 F5
Hebden Green 170 D1
Hebing End 150 B5
Hebron *Carmar* 141 E5
Hebron *N'umb* 221 D3
Heck 217 E2
Heckfield 120 C1
Heckfield Green 164 C4
Heckfordbridge 152 A5
Heckingham 165 E2
Heckington 175 G3
Heckmondwike 194 B5
Heddington 118 A1
Heddle 277 C6
Heddon 113 G2
Heddon-on-the-
   Wall 212 A1
Hedenham 165 E2
Hedge End 107 D1
Hedgerley 135 E4
Hedging 116 A5
Hedley on the Hill 211 G2
Hednesford 158 C1
Hedon 197 D5
Hedsor 135 E4
Heeley 186 A4
Heglibister 279 C7
Heighington *Darl* 212 B5
Heighington *Lincs* 175 F1
Heightington 157 G5
Heights of Brae 266 C5
Heilam 273 G3
Heiskar Islands (Monach
   Islands) 262 B5
Heithat 217 F2
Heiton 228 B3
Hele *Devon* 113 F1
Hele *Devon* 102 C2
Hele *Devon* 98 D1
Hele *Devon* 102 A5
Hele *Som* 115 E5
Hele *Torbay* 101 F1
Hele Bridge 113 F5
Hele Lane 102 A1
Helebridge 112 C5
Helensburgh 233 D1
Helford 95 E4
Helhoughton 177 G5
Helions Bumpstead 151 E3
Hell Corner 119 E1
Hellaby 186 C3
Helland *Corn* 97 E2
Helland *Som* 116 A5
Hellandbridge 97 E2
Hellesdon 178 D4
Hellidon 148 A2
Hellifield 193 E2
Hellingly 110 A2
Hellington 179 E5
Hellister 279 C8
Helmdon 148 A3
Helmingham 152 C2
Helmington Row 212 A4
Helmsdale 275 F7
Helmshore 193 D5
Helmsley 203 F4
Helperby 194 D1
Helperthorpe 204 C5
Helpringham 175 G3
Helpston 161 G2
Helsby 183 F5
Helsey 189 F5
Helston 95 D4
Helstone 97 E1
Helton 210 B5
Helwith 201 F2
Helwith Bridge 193 E1
Hem 156 B2
Hemborough Post 101 E2
Hemel Hempstead 135 F2
Hemerdon 100 B2
Hemingbrough 195 F4
Hemingby 188 C5
Hemingfield 186 A2
Hemingford Abbots 162 A5
Hemingford Grey 162 A5
Hemingstone 152 C2
Hemington *Leics* 173 F5
Hemington
   N'hants 161 F4
Hemington *Som* 117 E2
Hemley 153 D3
Hemlington 203 D1
Hemp Green 153 E1
Hempholme 196 C2
Hempnall 164 D2
Hempnall Green 164 D2
Hempriggs 267 J5
Hempriggs House 275 J4
Hempstead *Essex* 151 E4
Hempstead *Med* 123 G2
Hempstead *Norf* 179 F3
Hempstead *Norf* 178 C2
Hempsted 132 A1
Hempton *Norf* 178 A3
Hempton *Oxon* 147 G4
Hemsby 179 F4
Hemswell 187 G3
Hemswell Cliff 187 G4
Hemsworth 186 B1
Hemyock 103 E1
Henbury *Bristol* 131 E5
Henbury *ChesE* 184 C5
Henderland 216 C3
Hendersyde Park 228 B3
Hendham 100 D2
Hendon *GtLon* 136 B4
Hendon *T&W* 212 D2
Hendraburnick 97 F1
Hendre *Bridgend* 129 F4
Hendre *Gwyn* 168 B2
Hendreforgan 129 F4
Hendy 128 B2
Heneglwys 180 C5
Henfield *SGlos* 131 F5
Henfield *WSuss* 109 E2
Henford 99 D1
Hengherst 124 B5
Hengoed *Caerp* 130 A3
Hengoed *Powys* 144 B2
Hengoed *Shrop* 169 F4
Hengrave 151 G1
Henham 150 D5
Heniarth 156 A2
Henlade 115 F5
Henley *Dorset* 104 C2
Henley *Shrop* 157 E5
Henley *Som* 116 B4
Henley *Som* 104 A2
Henley *Suff* 152 C2
Henley *WSuss* 121 D5
Henley Corner 116 B4
Henley Park 121 E2
Henley-in-Arden 147 D1
Henley-on-Thames 134 C4
Henley's Down 110 C2
Henllan *Carmar* 141 G3
Henllan *Denb* 168 D1
Henllan Amgoed 141 E5
Henllys 130 B3
Henlow 149 G4
Hennock 102 B4
Henny Street 151 G4
Henryd 181 F5
Henry's Moat 140 D5
Hensall 195 E5
Henshaw 211 D1
Hensingham 208 C5
Henstead 165 F3
Hensting 119 F5
Henstridge 104 D1
Henstridge Ash 104 D1
Henstridge Bowden 117 D5
Henstridge Marsh 117 E5
Henton *Oxon* 134 C2
Henton *Som* 116 B3
Henwood 97 G2
Heogan 279 D8
Heol Senni 143 F5
Heol-y-Cyw 129 F4
Heolgerrig 129 G2
Hepburn 229 E4
Hepburn Bell 229 E4
Hepple 220 B1
Hepscott 221 E3
Hepthorne Lane 173 F1
Heptonstall 193 F5
Hepworth *Suff* 164 A4
Hepworth *WYorks* 185 F2
Hepworth South
   Common 164 A4
Herbrandston 126 B2
Hereford 145 E4
Hereford Cathedral
   Here HR1 2NG
   75 Hereford
Heriot 236 A4
Heritage Motor Centre,
   Gaydon *Warks*
   CV35 0BJ 147 F2
Herm 101 G5
Hermiston 235 F2
Hermitage *D&G* 216 B4
Hermitage *Dorset* 104 C2
Hermitage *ScBord* 218 D2
Hermitage *WBerks* 134 A5
Hermitage *WSuss* 107 G2
Hermitage Green 184 A3
Hermon *Carmar* 141 G4
Hermon *IoA* 166 C1
Hermon *Pembs* 141 F4
Herne 125 D2
Herne Bay 125 D2
Herne Common 125 D2
Herne Pound 123 F3
Herner 113 F3
Hernhill 124 C2
Herodsfoot 97 G3
Herongate 137 F3
Heron's Ghyll 109 G1
Heronsgate 135 F3
Herriard 120 B3
Herringfleet 165 F2
Herringswell 151 F1
Herrington 212 C2
Hersden 125 D2
Hersham *Corn* 112 C5
Hersham *Surr* 121 G1
Herstmonceux 110 B2
Herston 277 D8
Hertford 136 C1
Hertford Heath 136 C1
Hertingfordbury 136 C1
Hesket
   Newmarket 209 G3
Hesketh Bank 192 A5
Hesketh Lane 192 C3
Heskin Green 183 F1
Hesleden 212 D4
Hesleyside 220 A3
Heslington 195 F2
Hessay 195 E2
Hessenford 97 G4
Hessett 152 A1
Hessle *ERid* 196 C5
Hessle *WYorks* 186 B1

Her - Hou

Herringfleet 165 F2
Herring's Green 149 F3
Herringswell 151 F1
Herringthorpe 186 B3
Hersden 125 D2
Hersham Corn 112 C5
Hersham Surr 121 G1
Herstmonceux 110 B2
Herston 277 D8
Hertford 136 C1
Hertford Heath 136 C1
Hertingfordbury 136 C1
Hesket Newmarket 209 G3
Hesketh Bank 192 A5
Hesketh Lane 192 C3
Heskin Green 183 G1
Hesleden 212 D4
Hesleyside 220 A3
Heslington 195 F2
Hessay 195 E2
Hessenford 98 D5
Hessett 152 A1
Hessle 196 C5
Hest Bank 192 A1
Hester's Way 146 B5
Hestley Green 152 C1
Heston 136 A5
Heswall 183 D4
Hethe 148 A5
Hethelpit Cross 145 G5
Hetherington 220 A4
Hethersett 178 C5
Hethersgill 210 A1
Hethpool 228 C4
Hett 212 B4
Hetton 193 F2
Hetton-le-Hole 212 C3
Heugh 220 C4
Heugh-head Aber 260 B3
Heugh-head Aber 260 D5
Heveningham 165 E4
Hever 123 D4
Hever Castle & Gardens Kent TN8 7NG 123 D4
Heversham 199 F4
Hevingham 178 C3
Hewas Water 97 D5
Hewell Grange 146 C1
Hewell Lane 146 C1
Hewelsfield 131 E2
Hewelsfield Common 131 E2
Hewish NSom 116 B1
Hewish Som 104 A2
Hewood 103 G2
Heworth 195 F2
Hewton 99 F1
Hexham 211 F1
Hexham Abbey N'umb NE46 3NB 211 F1
Hextable 137 E5
Hexthorpe 186 C2
Hexton 149 G4
Hexworthy 99 G3
Hey 193 E3
Hey Houses 191 G5
Heybridge Essex 137 F3
Heybridge Essex 138 B2
Heybridge Basin 138 B2
Heybrook Bay 100 A3
Heydon Cambs 150 C3
Heydon Norf 178 C3
Heydour 175 F4
Heylipoll 246 A2
Heylor 278 B4
Heyop 156 B5
Heysham 192 A1
Heyshaw 194 A1
Heyshott 108 A2
Heyside 184 D2
Heytesbury 118 A3
Heythrop 147 F5
Heywood GtMan 184 C1
Heywood Wilts 117 F2
Hibaldstow 187 G2
Hibb's Green 151 G2
Hickleton 186 B2
Hickling Norf 179 F3
Hickling Notts 174 B5
Hickling Green 179 F3
Hickling Heath 179 F3
Hickstead 109 E1
Hidcote Bartrim 147 D3
Hidcote Boyce 147 D3
Hidcote Manor Garden Glos GL55 6LR 147 D3
High Ackworth 186 B1
High Angerton 220 C3
High Balantyre 240 C3
High Bankhill 210 B3
High Beach 136 D3
High Bentham (Higher Bentham) 192 C1
High Bickington 113 F3
High Birkwith 200 C5
High Blantyre 234 A4
High Bonnybridge 234 C2
High Borgue 216 A5
High Borve 271 G2
High Bradfield 185 G3
High Bradley 193 G3
High Bransholme 196 D4
High Bray 113 G2
High Bridge 209 G2
High Brooms 123 E4
High Bullen 113 F3
High Burton 202 B4
High Buston 221 E1
High Callerton 221 D4
High Casterton 200 B5
High Catton 195 G2
High Close 202 A1
High Cogges 133 F2
High Common 164 C3
High Coniscliffe 202 B1
High Crompton 184 D2
High Cross Hants 120 C5
High Cross Herts 136 C1
High Cross WSuss 109 E2
High Easter 137 F1
High Ellington 202 A4
High Entercommon 202 C2
High Ercall 157 E1
High Etherley 212 A5
High Ferry 176 B3
High Flatts 185 G2
High Garrett 151 F5
High Gate 193 F5
High Grange 212 A4
High Green Norf 178 C5
High Green Norf 178 A4
High Green Norf 178 A5
High Green Suff 151 G1
High Green SYorks 186 A3
High Green Worcs 146 A3
High Halden 124 A5
High Halstow 137 G5
High Ham 116 B4
High Harrington 208 D4
High Harrogate 194 C2
High Hatton 170 D5
High Hauxley 221 E1
High Hawsker 204 C2
High Heath Shrop 171 D5
High Heath WMid 158 C2
High Hesket 210 A3
High Hesleden 213 D4
High Hoyland 185 G1
High Hunsley 196 B4
High Hurstwood 109 G1
High Hutton 195 G1
High Ireby 209 F3
High Kelling 178 B2
High Kilburn 203 E5
High Kingthorpe 204 B4
High Knipe 199 G1
High Lane Derbys 173 F3
High Lane GtMan 185 D4
High Lane Worcs 145 F1
High Laver 137 E2
High Legh 184 B4
High Leven 203 D1
High Littleton 116 D2
High Lodge Forest Centre Suff IP27 0AF 163 G4
High Lorton 209 E4
High Marishes 204 B5
High Marnham 187 F5
High Melton 186 C2
High Moor 186 B4
High Moorland Visitor Centre, Princetown Devon PL20 6QF 99 F3
High Newton 199 F4
High Newton-by-the-Sea 229 G4
High Nibthwaite 199 D3
High Offley 171 E5
High Ongar 137 E2
High Onn 158 A1
High Park Corner 152 B5
High Roding 137 F1
High Shaw 201 D3
High Spen 212 A1
High Stoop 212 A3
High Street Corn 97 D4
High Street Kent 123 G5
High Street Suff 153 F2
High Street Suff 165 E3
High Street Suff 165 F4
High Street Suff 151 G3
High Street Green 152 B2
High Throston 213 D4
High Town 158 B1
High Toynton 176 A1
High Trewhitt 220 C1
High Wham 212 A5
High Wigsell 110 C1
High Woods Country Park Essex CO4 5JR 152 B5
High Woolaston 131 E3
High Worsall 202 C2
High Wray 199 E3
High Wych 137 D1
High Wycombe 135 D3
Higham Derbys 173 E2
Higham Kent 137 G5
Higham Lancs 193 E4
Higham Suff 151 F1
Higham Suff 152 B4
Higham SYorks 186 A2
Higham Dykes 220 D4
Higham Ferrers 149 E1
Higham Gobion 149 G4
Higham on the Hill 159 F3
Higham Wood 123 F4
Highampton 113 E5
Highams Park 136 C3
Highbridge Hants 119 F5
Highbridge Som 116 A3
Highbrook 122 C5
Highburton 185 F1
Highbury 117 D3
Highclere 119 F1
Highcliffe 106 B3
Higher Alham 117 D3
Higher Ansty 105 D2
Higher Ashton 102 B4
Higher Ballam 191 G4
Higher Bentham (High Bentham) 192 C1
Higher Blackley 184 C2
Higher Brixham 101 F2
Higher Cheriton 103 E2
Higher Combe 114 C4
Higher Folds 184 A2
Higher Gabwell 101 F1
Higher Green 184 B3
Higher Halstock Leigh 104 B2
Higher Kingcombe 104 B3
Higher Kinnerton 170 A1
Higher Muddiford 113 F2
Higher Nyland 117 E5
Higher Prestacott 99 D1
Higher Standen 193 D3
Higher Tale 103 D2
Higher Thrushgill 192 C1
Higher Town Corn 97 E3
Higher Town IoS 96 B1
Higher Walreddon 99 E3
Higher Walton Lancs 192 B5
Higher Walton Warr 183 G4
Higher Wambrook 103 F2
Higher Whatcombe 105 E2
Higher Wheelton 192 C5
Higher Whiteleigh 98 C1
Higher Whitley 184 A4
Higher Wincham 184 A5
Higher Woodhill 184 B1
Higher Woodsford 105 D4
Higher Wraxall 104 B2
Higher Wych 170 B3
Highfield ERid 195 G4
Highfield NAyr 233 E4
Highfield Oxon 148 A5
Highfield SYorks 186 A4
Highfield T&W 212 A2
Highfields Cambs 150 B2
Highfields N'umb 237 G4
Highgate ESuss 122 D5
Highgate GtLon 136 B4
Highgreen Manor 220 A2
Highlane ChesE 171 F1
Highlane Derbys 186 B4
Highlaws 209 E2
Highleadon 145 G5
Highleigh Devon 114 C5
Highleigh WSuss 108 A4
Highley 157 G4
Highmead 142 B3
Highmoor Cross 134 B4
Highmoor Hill 131 D4
Highnam 131 G1
Highstead 125 E2
Highsted 124 B2
Highstreet 124 C2
Highstreet Green Essex 151 F4
Highstreet Green Surr 121 E4
Hightae 217 E3
Highter's Heath 158 C5
Hightown Hants 106 A2
Hightown Mersey 183 D2
Hightown Green 152 A2
Highway 132 C5
Highweek 102 B5
Highwood 145 F1
Highwood Hill 136 B3
Highworth 133 E3
Hilborough 163 G2
Hilcote 173 F2
Hilcott 118 C2
Hilden Park 123 E4
Hildenborough 123 E4
Hildenley 203 G5
Hildersham 150 D3
Hilderstone 171 G4
Hilderthorpe 197 D1
Hilfield 104 C2
Hilgay 163 E3
Hill SGlos 131 F3
Hill Warks 147 G1
Hill Worcs 146 B3
Hill Brow 120 C5
Hill Chorlton 171 E4
Hill Common 179 F3
Hill Cottages 203 G3
Hill Croome 146 A3
Hill Deverill 117 F3
Hill Dyke 176 B3
Hill End Dur 211 G4
Hill End Fife 243 F5
Hill End Glos 146 A4
Hill End GtLon 135 F3
Hill End NYorks 193 G2
Hill Green 150 C4
Hill Head 107 E2
Hill Houses 157 F5
Hill Mountain 126 C2
Hill of Beath 235 F1
Hill of Fearn 267 F4
Hill Ridware 158 C1
Hill Row 162 C5
Hill Side 185 F1
Hill Street 106 C1
Hill Top Hants 106 D2
Hill Top SYorks 186 B3
Hill Top SYorks 185 G4
Hill View 105 F3
Hill Wootton 147 F1
Hillam 195 E5
Hillbeck 200 C1
Hillberry 190 B4
Hillborough 125 E2
Hillbrae Aber 268 E6
Hillbrae Aber 261 F2
Hillbrae Aber 261 G1
Hillbutts 105 F2
Hillclifflane 173 D3
Hillend Aber 268 C6
Hillend Fife 235 F1
Hillend Midlo 235 G3
Hillend NLan 234 C3
Hillend Swan 128 A3
Hillend Green 145 G5
Hillersland 131 E1
Hillesden 148 B5
Hillesley 131 G4
Hillfarrance 115 E5
Hillfoot End 149 G4
Hillhead Devon 101 F2
Hillhead SAyr 224 C3
Hillhead of Auchentumb 269 H5
Hillhead of Cocklaw 269 J6
Hilliard's Cross 159 D1
Hilliclay 275 G2
Hillingdon 135 F4
Hillington Glas 233 G3
Hillington Norf 177 F5
Hillmorton 160 A5
Hillockhead Aber 260 B4
Hillockhead Aber 260 C3
Hillowton 216 B4
Hillpound 107 E1
Hill's End 149 E4
Hills Town 173 F1
Hillsborough 186 A3
Hillsford Bridge 114 A3
Hillside Aber 261 H5
Hillside Angus 253 F3
Hillside Moray 267 J5
Hillside Shet 279 D6
Hillside Worcs 145 G1
Hillswick 278 B5
Hillway 107 F4
Hillwell 279 F9
Hillyfields 106 C1
Hilmarton 132 C5
Hilperton 117 F2
Hilsea 107 F2
Hilston 197 E4
Hilton Cambs 150 A1
Hilton Cumb 210 D5
Hilton Derbys 172 D4
Hilton Dorset 105 D2
Hilton Dur 212 A5
Hilton High 267 G3
Hilton Shrop 157 G3
Hilton Staffs 158 C2
Hilton Stock 203 D1
Hilton Croft 261 H1
Hilton of Cadboll 267 F4
Hilton of Delnies 267 F6
Himbleton 146 B2
Himley 158 A3
Himley Hall & Park WMid DY3 4DF 14 A2
Hincaster 199 G4
Hinchley Wood 121 G1
Hinckley 159 G3
Hinderclay 164 B4
Hinderton 183 E5
Hinderwell 203 G1
Hindford 170 A4
Hindhead 121 D4
Hindley GtMan 184 A2
Hindley N'umb 211 G2
Hindley Green 184 A2
Hindlip 146 A2
Hindolveston 178 B3
Hindon Som 114 C3
Hindon Wilts 118 A4
Hindringham 178 A2
Hingham 178 B5
Hinksford 158 A4
Hinstock 171 D5
Hintlesham 152 B3
Hinton Glos 131 F2
Hinton Hants 106 B3
Hinton Here 144 C4
Hinton N'hants 148 A2
Hinton SGlos 131 G5
Hinton Shrop 156 D2
Hinton Admiral 106 B3
Hinton Ampner 119 G5
Hinton Blewett 116 C2
Hinton Charterhouse 117 E2
Hinton Martell 105 G2
Hinton on the Green 146 C3
Hinton Parva Dorset 105 F2
Hinton Parva Swin 133 E4
Hinton St. George 104 A1
Hinton St. Mary 105 D1
Hinton Waldrist 133 F3
Hinton-in-the-Hedges 148 A4
Hints Shrop 157 F5
Hints Staffs 159 D2
Hinwick 149 E1
Hinxhill 124 C4
Hinxton 150 C3
Hinxworth 150 A3
Hipperholme 194 A5
Hipsburn 229 G5
Hipswell 202 A3
Hirn 261 F4
Hirnant 169 D5
Hirst 221 E3
Hirst Courtney 195 F5
Hirwaen 169 E1
Hirwaun 129 F2
Hiscott 113 F3
Histon 150 C1
Hitcham Bucks 135 E4
Hitcham Suff 152 A2
Hitchin 149 G5
Hither Green 136 C5
Hittisleigh 102 A3
Hittisleigh Barton 102 A3
Hive 196 A4
Hixon 172 B5
Hoaden 125 E3
Hoaldalbert 144 C5
Hoar Cross 172 C5
Hoar Park Craft Centre Warks CV10 0QU 159 E3
Hoarwithy 145 E5
Hoath 125 E2
Hobarris 156 C5
Hobbister 277 C7
Hobbles Green 151 F2
Hobbs Cross 137 D3
Hobbs Lots Bridge 162 B2
Hobkirk 227 G4
Hobland Hall 179 G5
Hobson 212 A2
Hoby 160 B1
Hockerill 150 C5
Hockering 178 B4
Hockerton 174 C2
Hockley 138 B3
Hockley Heath 159 D5
Hockliffe 149 E5
Hockwold cum Wilton 163 F4
Hockworthy 102 D1
Hoddesdon 136 C2
Hoddlesden 192 D5
Hodgehill 171 F1
Hodgeston 126 D3
Hodnet 170 D5
Hodnetheath 170 D5
Hodsoll Street 123 F2
Hodson 133 D4
Hodthorpe 186 C5
Hoe 178 A4
Hoe Gate 107 F1
Hoff 200 B1
Hoffleet Stow 176 A4
Hoggard's Green 151 G2
Hoggeston 148 D5
Hoggie 268 D5
Hoggrill's End 159 E3
Hogha Gearraidh 262 C4
Hoghton 192 C5
Hognaston 172 D2
Hogsthorpe 189 F5
Holbeach 176 B5
Holbeach Bank 176 B5
Holbeach Clough 176 B5
Holbeach Drove 162 B1
Holbeach Hurn 176 B5
Holbeach St. Johns 162 B1
Holbeach St. Marks 176 B4
Holbeach St. Matthew 176 C4
Holbeck 186 C5
Holbeck Woodhouse 186 C5
Holberrow Green 146 C2
Holbeton 100 C2
Holborough 123 G2
Holbrook Derbys 173 E3
Holbrook Suff 152 C4
Holbrooks 159 F4
Holburn 229 E3
Holbury 106 D2
Holcombe Devon 102 C5
Holcombe GtMan 184 B1
Holcombe Som 117 D3
Holcombe Burnell Barton 102 B3
Holcombe Rogus 103 D1
Holcot 148 C1
Holden 193 D3
Holden Gate 193 E5
Holdenby 148 B1
Holdenhurst 106 A3
Holder's Green 151 E5
Holders Hill 136 B4
Holdgate 157 E4
Holdingham 175 F3
Holditch 103 G2
Hole 103 E1
Hole Park 124 A5
Holehouse 185 E3
Hole-in-the-Wall 145 F5
Holford 115 E3
Holgate 195 E2
Holker 199 E5
Holkham 177 G3
Hollacombe Devon 113 D5
Hollacombe Devon 102 B2
Hollacombe Town 113 G4
Holland Ork 276 D2
Holland Ork 276 F5
Holland Surr 122 D3
Holland Fen 176 A3
Holland-on-Sea 139 E1
Hollandstoun 276 G2
Hollee 218 A5
Hollesley 153 E3
Hollicombe 101 F1
Hollingbourne 124 A3
Hollingbury 109 F3
Hollingrove 110 B1
Hollington Derbys 172 D4
Hollington ESuss 110 C2
Hollington Staffs 172 B4
Hollingworth 185 E3
Hollins 186 A5
Hollins Green 184 A3
Hollins Lane 192 A2
Hollinsclough 172 B1
Hollinwood GtMan 184 D2
Hollinwood Shrop 170 C4
Hollocombe 113 G4
Hollow Meadows 185 G4
Holloway 173 E2
Hollowell 160 B5
Holly Bush 170 B3
Holly End 162 C2
Holly Green 134 C2
Hollybush Caerp 130 A2
Hollybush EAyr 224 B4
Hollybush Worcs 145 G4
Hollyhurst 170 C3
Hollym 197 F5
Hollywater 120 D4
Hollywood 158 C5
Holm D&G 218 A2
Holm (Tolm) ESiar 271 G4
Holm of Drumlanrig 216 C1
Holmbridge 185 F2
Holmbury St. Mary 121 G3
Holmbush 122 B5
Holme Cambs 161 G4
Holme Cumb 199 G5
Holme NLincs 187 G2
Holme Notts 174 D2
Holme NYorks 202 C4
Holme WYorks 185 F2
Holme Chapel 193 E5
Holme Hale 163 G2
Holme Lacy 145 E4
Holme Marsh 144 C2
Holme next the Sea 177 F3
Holme on the Wolds 196 B3
Holme Pierrepont 174 B4
Holme St. Cuthbert 209 E2
Holme-on-Spalding-Moor 196 A4
Holmer 145 E3
Holmer Green 135 E3
Holmes 183 F1
Holmes Chapel 171 E1
Holme's Hill 110 A2
Holmesfield 186 A5
Holmeswood 183 F1
Holmewood 173 F1
Holmfield 193 G5
Holmfirth 185 F2
Holmhead D&G 216 B2
Holmhead EAyr 225 D3
Holmpton 197 F5
Holmrook 198 B2
Holmsgarth 279 D8
Holmside 212 B3
Holmsleigh Green 103 F2
Holmston 224 B3
Holmwrangle 210 B3
Holne 100 D1
Holnest 104 C2
Holnicote 114 C3
Holsworthy 112 D5
Holsworthy Beacon 113 D5
Holt Dorset 105 G2
Holt Norf 178 B2
Holt Wilts 117 F1
Holt Worcs 146 A1
Holt Wrex 170 B2
Holt End Hants 120 B4
Holt End Worcs 146 C1
Holt Fleet 146 A1
Holt Heath Dorset 105 G2
Holt Heath Worcs 146 A1
Holt Wood 105 G2
Holtby 195 F2
Holton Oxon 134 B2
Holton Som 117 D5
Holton Suff 165 F4
Holton cum Beckering 188 B4
Holton Heath 105 F3
Holton le Clay 188 C2
Holton le Moor 188 A3
Holton St. Mary 152 B4
Holtspur 135 E4
Holtye 123 D5
Holtye Common 123 D5
Holway 115 F5
Holwell Dorset 104 C1
Holwell Herts 149 G4
Holwell Leics 174 C5
Holwell Oxon 133 E2
Holwell Som 117 E3
Holwick 211 F5
Holworth 105 D4
Holy Cross 158 B5
Holy Island IoA 180 A5
Holy Island (Lindisfarne) N'umb 229 F2
Holy Trinity Church, Skipton NYorks BD23 1NJ 193 F2
Holy Trinity Church, Stratford-upon-Avon Warks CV37 6BG 85 Stratford-upon-Avon
Holybourne 120 C3
Holyfield 136 C2
Holyhead (Caergybi) 180 A4
Holymoorside 173 E1
Holyport 135 D5
Holystone 220 B1
Holytown 234 B3
Holywell Cambs 162 B5
Holywell Corn 96 B4
Holywell Dorset 104 B2
Holywell ESuss 110 B4
Holywell (Treffynnon) Flints 182 C5
Holywell N'umb 221 F4
Holywell Bay Fun Park Corn TR8 5PW 96 B4
Holywell Green 185 E1
Holywell Lake 115 E5
Holywell Row 163 F5
Holywood 216 D2
Hom Green 145 E5
Homer 157 F2
Homersfield 165 D3
Homington 118 C5
Homore (Tobha Mòr) 254 C1
Honey Hill 124 D2
Honey Street 118 C1
Honey Tye 152 A4
Honeyborough 126 C2
Honeybourne 146 D3
Honeychurch 113 G5
Honicknowle 100 A2
Honiley 159 E5
Honing 179 E3
Honingham 178 C4
Honington Lincs 175 E3
Honington Suff 164 A4
Honington Warks 147 E3
Honiton 103 E2
Honkley 170 A2
Honley 185 F1
Hoo Med 137 G5
Hoo Suff 153 D2
Hoo Green 184 B4
Hoo Meavy 100 B1
Hood Green 186 A2
Hood Hill 186 A3
Hooe ESuss 110 B3
Hooe Plym 100 B2
Hooe Common 110 B2
Hook Cambs 162 C3
Hook ERid 195 G5
Hook GtLon 121 G1
Hook Hants 120 C2
Hook Hants 107 E2
Hook Pembs 126 C1
Hook Wilts 132 C4
Hook Green Kent 123 F5
Hook Green Kent 123 F2
Hook Green Kent 137 F5
Hook Green Kent 137 E5
Hook Norton 147 F4
Hook-a-Gate 157 D2
Hooke 104 B2
Hookgate 171 E4
Hookway 102 B3
Hookwood 122 B4
Hoole 170 B1
Hooley 122 B3
Hoop 131 E2
Hooton 183 E5
Hooton Levitt 186 C3
Hooton Pagnell 186 B2
Hooton Roberts 186 B3
Hop Farm, The Kent TN12 6PY 123 F4
Hop Pocket, The Here WR6 5BT 145 F3
Hop Pole 161 G1
Hopcrofts Holt 147 G5
Hope Derbys 185 F4
Hope Devon 100 C4
Hope Flints 170 A2
Hope Powys 156 B2
Hope Shrop 156 C2
Hope Staffs 172 C2
Hope Bagot 157 E5
Hope Bowdler 157 D3
Hope End Green 151 D5
Hope Mansell 131 F1
Hope under Dinmore 145 E2
Hopehouse 227 D4
Hopeman 267 J5
Hope's Green 137 G4
Hopesay 156 C4
Hopkinstown 129 G3
Hopley's Green 144 C2
Hopperton 194 D2
Hopsford 159 G4
Hopstone 157 G3
Hopton Derbys 173 D2
Hopton Norf 165 G2
Hopton Shrop 170 C5
Hopton Shrop 170 A5
Hopton Staffs 171 G5
Hopton Suff 164 A4
Hopton Cangeford 157 E4
Hopton Castle 156 C5
Hopton Wafers 157 F5
Hoptonheath 156 C5
Hopwas 159 D2
Hopwood 158 C5
Horam 110 A2
Horbling 175 G4
Horbury 185 G1
Horden 212 D3
Horderley 156 D4
Hordle 106 B3
Hordley 170 A4
Horeb Carmar 128 A2
Horeb Cere 141 G3
Horeb Flints 169 F2
Horfield 131 E5
Horham 164 D4
Horkesley Heath 152 A5
Horkstow 187 G1
Horley Oxon 147 G3
Horley Surr 122 B4
Horn Hill 135 F3
Hornblotton 116 C4
Hornblotton Green 116 C4
Hornby Lancs 192 B1
Hornby NYorks 202 B3
Hornby NYorks 202 C2
Horncastle 176 A1
Hornchurch 137 E4
Horncliffe 237 G5
Horndean Hants 107 G1
Horndean ScBord 237 G5
Horndon 99 F2
Horndon on the Hill 137 F4
Horne 122 C4
Horne Row 137 G2
Horner 114 B3
Horniehaugh 252 C3
Horniman Museum GtLon SE23 3PQ 13 C7
Horning 179 E4
Horninghold 160 D3
Horninglow 172 D5
Horningsea 150 C1
Horningsham 117 F3
Horningtoft 178 A3
Horningtops 97 G3
Horns Cross Devon 113 D3
Horns Cross ESuss 110 D1
Horns Green 123 D3
Hornsbury 103 G1
Hornsby 210 B3
Hornsby Gate 210 B2
Hornsea 197 E3
Hornsea Freeport ERid HU18 1UT 197 E3
Hornsey 136 C4
Hornton 147 F3
Horrabridge 100 B1
Horridge 102 A5
Horringer 151 G1
Horrocks Fold 184 B1
Horse Bridge 171 G2
Horsebridge Devon 99 E3
Horsebridge Hants 119 E4
Horsebrook 158 A1
Horsecastle 116 B1
Horsehay 157 F2
Horseheath 151 E3
Horsehouse 201 F4
Horsell 121 E2
Horseman's Green 170 B3
Horsenden 134 C2
Horseshoe Green 123 D4
Horseway 162 C4
Horsey 179 F3
Horsey Corner 179 F3
Horsford 178 C4
Horsforth 194 B4
Horsham Worcs 145 G2
Horsham WSuss 121 G4
Horsham St. Faith 178 D4
Horsington Lincs 175 G1
Horsington Som 117 E5
Horsington Marsh 117 E5
Horsley Derbys 173 E3
Horsley Glos 132 A3
Horsley N'umb 211 G1
Horsley N'umb 220 A2
Horsley Cross 152 C5
Horsley Woodhouse 173 E3
Horsleycross Street 152 C5
Horsleygate 186 A5
Horsleyhill 227 G4
Horsmonden 123 F4
Horspath 134 A2
Horstead 179 D4
Horsted Keynes 109 F1
Horton Bucks 135 E1
Horton Dorset 105 G2
Horton Lancs 193 E2
Horton N'hants 148 D2
Horton SGlos 131 G4
Horton Shrop 170 B5
Horton Som 103 G1
Horton Staffs 171 G2
Horton Swan 128 A4
Horton Tel&W 157 F1
Horton W&M 135 F5
Horton Wilts 118 B1
Horton Cross 103 G1
Horton Grange 221 E4
Horton Green 170 B3
Horton Heath 107 D1
Horton in Ribblesdale 200 D5
Horton Inn 105 G2
Horton Kirby 123 E2
Horton Park Farm Surr KT19 8PT 121 G1
Horton-cum-Studley 134 B1
Horwich 184 A1
Horwich End 185 E4
Horwood 113 F3
Hoscar 183 F1
Hose 174 C5
Hoses 198 D3
Hosh 243 D2
Hosta 262 C4
Hoswick 279 D10
Hotham 196 A4
Hothfield 124 B4
Hoton 173 G5
Houbie 278 F3
Houdston 214 C1
Hough 171 E2
Hough Green 183 F4
Hougham 175 D3
Hough-on-the-Hill 175 E3
Houghton Cambs 162 A5
Houghton Cumb 210 A2
Houghton Devon 100 C3
Houghton Hants 119 E4
Houghton Pembs 126 C2
Houghton WSuss 108 C2

Houghton Bank 212 B5
Houghton Conquest 149 F3
Houghton le Spring 212 C3
Houghton on the
  Hill 160 B2
Houghton Regis 149 F5
Houghton St. Giles 178 A2
Houghton-le-Side 212 B5
Houlsyke 203 G2
Hound 107 D2
Hound Green 120 C2
Houndslow 236 D5
Houndsmoor 115 E5
Houndwood 237 F3
Hounsdown 106 C1
Hounslow 136 A5
House of Marbles & Teign
  Valley Glass Devon
  TQ13 9DS 102 B5
Housebay 276 F5
Househill 267 F6
Houses Hill 185 F1
Housesteads Roman
  Fort N'umb
  NE47 6NN 211 D1
Housham Tye 137 E1
Houss 279 C9
Houston 233 F3
Houstry 275 G5
Houstry of Dunn 275 H3
Houton 277 C7
Hove 109 E3
Hove Edge 194 A5
Hoveringham 174 B3
Hoveton 179 E4
Hovingham 203 F5
How 210 B2
How Caple 145 F4
How End 149 F3
How Green 123 D4
How Man 208 C5
Howbrook 186 A3
Howden 195 G5
Howden Clough 194 B5
Howden-le-Wear 212 A4
Howe Cumb 199 F4
Howe High 275 J2
Howe Norf 165 D2
Howe NYorks 202 C4
Howe Green 138 B2
Howe of Teuchar 269 F6
Howe Street Essex 137 F1
Howe Street Essex 151 E4
Howegreen 138 B2
Howell 175 G2
Howey 143 G2
Howgate Cumb 208 C4
Howgate Midlo 235 G4
Howgill Lancs 193 F2
Howgill NYorks 193 G2
Howick 229 G5
Howle 171 D5
Howle Hill 145 F5
Howlett End 151 D4
Howletts Wild Animal Park
  Kent CT4 5EL 125 D3
Howley 103 F2
Hownam 228 B5
Hownam Mains 228 B4
Howpasley 227 E5
Howsham NLincs 188 A2
Howsham NYorks 195 G1
Howt Green 124 A2
Howtel 228 C3
Howton 144 D5
Howwood 233 F3
Hoxa 277 D8
Hoxne 164 C4
Hoy High 275 H2
Hoy Ork 277 B8
Hoylake 182 D4
Hoyland 186 A2
Hoylandswaine 185 G2
Hoyle 108 B2
Hubberholme 201 E5
Hubberston 126 B2
Hubbert's Bridge 176 A3
Huby NYorks 195 E1
Huby NYorks 194 B3
Hucclecote 132 A1
Hucking 124 A3
Hucknall 173 G3
Huddersfield 185 F1
Huddington 146 B2
Huddlesford 158 D2
Hudnall 135 F1
Hudscott 113 G3
Hudswell 202 A3
Huggate 196 A2
Hugglescote 159 G1
Hugh Town 96 B1
Hughenden Valley 135 D3
Hughley 157 E3
Hugmore 170 A2
Hugus 96 B5
Huish Devon 113 F4
Huish Wilts 118 C1
Huish Champflower 114 D5
Huish Episcopi 116 B5
Huisinis 270 B6
Hulcote 149 E4
Hulcott 135 D1
Hull 196 D5
Hulland 172 D3
Hulland Ward 173 D3
Hullavington 132 A4
Hullbridge 138 B3
Hulme 171 G3
Hulme End 172 C2
Hulme Walfield 171 F1
Hulver Street 165 F4
Hulverstone 106 C4
Humber Devon 102 B5
Humber Here 145 E2
Humber Bridge Country
  Park ERid
  HU13 0LN 196 C5
Humberston 188 D2
Humberston Airport 188 A1
Humberstone 160 B2
Humberton 194 D1
Humbie 236 B3
Humbleton Dur 201 F1
Humbleton ERid 197 E4
Humbleton N'umb 229 D4
Humby 175 F4
Hume 237 E5

Humehall 237 E5
Hummer 104 B1
Humshaugh 220 B4
Huna 275 J1
Huncoat 193 D4
Huncote 160 A3
Hundall 186 A5
Hunderthwaite 211 F5
Hundleby 176 B1
Hundleton 126 C2
Hundon 151 F3
Hundred Acres 107 E1
Hundred End 192 A5
Hundred House 144 A2
Hungarton 160 B2
Hungate End 148 C3
Hungerford Hants 106 A1
Hungerford Shrop 157 E4
Hungerford WBerks 119 E1
Hungerford
  Newtown 133 F5
Hungerton 175 D5
Hunglader 263 J4
Hunmanby 205 D5
Hunningham 147 F1
Hunningham Hill 147 F1
Hunsdon 136 D1
Hunsingore 194 D2
Hunslet 194 C4
Hunsonby 210 B4
Hunspow 275 H1
Hunstanton 177 E3
Hunston Suff 152 A1
Hunston WSuss 108 A3
Hunsworth 194 A5
Hunt End 146 C1
Hunt House 204 B2
Huntercombe End 134 B4
Hunters Forstal 125 D2
Hunter's Inn 113 G1
Hunter's Quay 232 C2
Hunterston 232 C4
Huntford 219 E1
Huntham 116 A5
Huntingdon 162 A5
Huntingfield 165 E4
Huntingford 117 F4
Huntington Here 144 B2
Huntington Here 145 D3
Huntington Staffs 158 B1
Huntington Tel&W 157 F2
Huntington York 195 F2
Huntingtower 243 F2
Huntley 131 G1
Huntly 260 D1
Huntlywood 236 D5
Hunton Hants 119 F4
Hunton Kent 123 G4
Hunton NYorks 202 A3
Hunton Bridge 135 F2
Hunt's Cross 183 F4
Huntscott 114 C3
Huntsham 114 D1
Huntshaw 113 F3
Huntshaw Cross 113 F3
Huntshaw Water 113 F3
Huntspill 116 A3
Huntworth 116 A4
Hunwick 212 A4
Hunworth 178 B2
Hurcott Som 116 C5
Hurcott Som 103 G1
Hurdley 156 B3
Hurdsfield 184 D5
Hurley W&M 134 D4
Hurley Warks 159 E3
Hurley Bottom 134 D4
Hurlford 224 C2
Hurliness 277 B9
Hurlston Green 183 E1
Hurn 106 A3
Hursley 119 F5
Hurst NYorks 201 F2
Hurst W'ham 134 C5
Hurst Green Essex 139 D1
Hurst Green ESuss 110 C1
Hurst Green Lancs 192 C4
Hurst Green Surr 122 C3
Hurst Wickham 109 E2
Hurstbourne Priors 119 F3
Hurstbourne
  Tarrant 119 E2
Hurstpierpoint 109 E2
Hurstwood 193 E4
Hurtmore 121 E3
Hurworth-on-Tees 202 C1
Hury 211 F5
Husabost 263 G6
Husbands
  Bosworth 160 B4
Husborne Crawley 149 E4
Husthwaite 203 E5
Hutcherleigh 101 D2
Huthwaite 173 F2
Huttoft 189 E5
Hutton Cumb 210 A5
Hutton ERid 196 C2
Hutton Lancs 192 A5
Hutton NSom 116 A2
Hutton ScBord 237 G4
Hutton Bonville 202 C2
Hutton Buscel 204 C4
Hutton Conyers 202 C5
Hutton Cranswick 196 C2
Hutton End 210 A4
Hutton Hang 202 A4
Hutton Henry 212 C4
Hutton Magna 202 A1
Hutton Mount 137 F3
Hutton Mulgrave 204 B2
Hutton Roof Cumb 199 G5
Hutton Roof Cumb 209 G3
Hutton Rudby 203 D2
Hutton Sessay 203 D5
Hutton Wandesley 195 E2
Hutton-le-Hole 203 G3
Huxham 102 C3
Huxham Green 116 C4
Huxley 170 C1
Huxter Shet 279 C7
Huxter Shet 279 E6
Huyton 183 F3
Hycemoor 198 B4
Hyde Glos 132 A2
Hyde GtMan 184 D3

Hyde End W'ham 120 C1
Hyde End WBerks 119 G1
Hyde Heath 135 E2
Hyde Lea 158 B1
Hydestile 121 E3
Hylands Park Essex
  CM2 8WQ 137 F2
Hyndford Bridge 234 D5
Hyndlee 227 G5
Hynish 246 A3
Hyssington 156 C3
Hythe Hants 106 D2
Hythe Kent 125 D5
Hythe End 135 F5
Hythie 269 J5
Hyton 198 B4

I

Ianstown 268 C4
Iarsiadar 270 D4
Ibberton 105 D2
Ible 172 D2
Ibsley 106 A2
Ibstock 159 G1
Ibstone 134 C3
Ibthorpe 119 E2
Ibworth 119 G2
Icelton 116 A1
Ickburgh 163 G3
Ickenham 135 F4
Ickford 134 B2
Ickham 125 E3
Ickleford 149 G4
Icklesham 111 D2
Ickleton 150 C3
Icklingham 163 F5
Ickwell Green 149 G3
Icomb 147 E5
Idbury 147 E5
Iddesleigh 113 F5
Ide 102 C3
Ide Hill 123 D3
Ideford 102 B5
Iden 111 E1
Iden Green Kent 123 G5
Iden Green Kent 124 A5
Idle 194 A4
Idless 96 C5
Idlicote 147 E3
Idmiston 118 C4
Idridgehay 173 D3
Idridgehay Green 173 D3
Idrigil 263 J5
Idstone 133 E4
Idvies 252 D5
Iffley 134 A2
Ifield 122 B5
Ifieldwood 122 B5
Ifold 121 F4
Iford Bourne 106 A3
Iford ESuss 109 G3
Ifton 231 D4
Ifton Heath 170 A4
Ightfield 170 C4
Ightham 123 E3
Ightham Mote Kent
  TN15 0NT 123 E3
Iken 165 E2
Ilam 172 C2
Ilchester 116 C5
Ilderton 229 E4
Ilford 136 D4
Ilfracombe 113 F1
Ilketshall
  St. Andrew 165 E3
Ilketshall
  St. Lawrence 165 E3
Ilketshall
  St. Margaret 165 E3
Ilkley 194 A3
Illey 158 B4
Illidge Green 171 E1
Illington 164 A3
Illingworth 193 G5
Illogan 96 A5
Illston on the Hill 160 C3
Ilmer 134 C2
Ilmington 147 E2
Ilminster 103 G1
Ilsington Devon 102 A5
Ilsington Dorset 105 D3
Ilston 128 B3
Ilton NYorks 202 A5
Ilton Som 103 G1
Imachar 231 G5
Imber 118 B3
Immeroin 242 A3
Immingham 188 B1
Immingham Dock 188 C1
Imperial War Museum,
  Duxford Cambs
  CB22 4QR 150 C3
Imperial War Museum,
  London GtLon
  SE1 6HZ 45 G7
Imperial War Museum
  North GtMan
  M17 1TZ 24 D3
Impington 150 C1
Ince 183 F5
Ince Blundell 183 E2
Ince-in-Makerfield 183 G2
Inch Kenneth 238 D1
Inch of Arnhall 253 E2
Inchbae Lodge 266 B5
Inchbare 253 E3
Inchberry 268 B5
Inchbraoch 253 F4
Inchgrundle 252 C2
Inchindown 266 D4
Inchinnan 233 F3
Inchkinloch 273 J4
Inchlaggan 257 H4
Inchlumpie 266 C4
Inchmarlo 260 E5
Inchmarnock 232 B4
Inchnabobart 252 B1
Inchnacardoch
  Hotel 257 K3
Inchnadamph 272 E6
Inchock 253 E5
Inchree 248 C3
Inchrory 259 J4
Inchture 244 A2
Inchvuilt 257 H2
Inchyra 243 G2
Indian Queens 96 D4

Inerval 230 B5
Ingatestone 137 F3
Ingbirchworth 185 G2
Ingerthorpe 194 B1
Ingestre 171 G5
Ingham Lincs 187 G4
Ingham Norf 179 E3
Ingham Suff 163 G5
Ingham Corner 179 E3
Ingleborough 162 C1
Ingleby Derbys 173 E5
Ingleby Lincs 187 F5
Ingleby Arncliffe 202 D2
Ingleby Barwick 202 D1
Ingleby Cross 202 D2
Ingleby Greenhow 203 E2
Inglesbatch 117 E1
Inglesham 133 E3
Ingleton Dur 212 A5
Ingleton NYorks 200 B5
Inglewhite 192 B4
Ingliston 235 F2
Ingmire Hall 200 B3
Ingoe 220 C4
Ingoldisthorpe 177 E4
Ingoldmells 177 D1
Ingoldsby 175 F4
Ingon 147 E2
Ingram 229 E5
Ingrave 137 F3
Ingrow 193 G4
Ings 199 F3
Ingst 131 E4
Ingworth 178 C3
Inhurst 119 G1
Inistrynich 240 D2
Injebreck 190 B3
Inkberrow 146 C2
Inkersall 186 B5
Inkersall Green 186 B5
Inkhorn 261 H1
Inkpen 119 E1
Inkstack 275 H1
Inmarsh 118 A1
Innellan 232 C3
Innergellie 245 D4
Innerhadden 250 B4
Innerleithen 227 E2
Innerleven 244 B4
Innermessan 214 B4
Innerwick ELoth 237 E2
Innerwick P&K 250 A5
Inninbeg 247 F3
Innsworth 146 A5
Insch 260 E2
Insh 259 F4
Inshore 273 F2
Inskip 192 A4
Instow 113 E2
Intake 186 C2
Inver A&B 248 B5
Inver Aber 259 K5
Inver High 267 F3
Inver High 275 G5
Inver P&K 251 F5
Inver Mallie 247 G1
Inverailort 247 F4
Inveraldie 244 C1
Inverallochy 269 J4
Inveran A&B 238 A6
Inveran High 266 C2
Inveraray
  (Inbhir Aora) 240 C2
Inverardoch Mains 242 C4
Inverardran 242 A2
Inverarish 256 B1
Inverarity 252 C5
Inverarnan
  (Inbhir Àirnein) 241 F3
Inverasdale 264 E3
Inverbeg 241 F5
Inverbervie 253 G2
Inverboyndie 268 D4
Inverbroom 265 H3
Inverbrough 259 F2
Invercassley 266 B1
Invercharnan 248 D5
Inverchaolain 232 B2
Invercharnan 248 D5
Invercharroch 265 J6
Invercreran 248 C5
Inverdruie 259 G3
Inverebrie 261 H1
Invereen 258 E1
Inveresk 236 A2
In_
Inverey 251 F1
Inverfarigaig 258 C2
Invergarry
  (Inbhir Garadh) 257 K4
Invergelder 259 K5
Invergeldie 242 C2
Invergloy 249 E1
Invergordon 266 D5
Invergowrie 244 B1
Inverguseran 256 D4
Inverharroch Farm 260 B1
Inverherive 241 F2
Inverhope 273 G2
Inverie 256 D4
Inverinan 240 B3
Inverinate 257 F2
Inverkeilor 253 E5
Inverkeithing 235 F1
Inverkeithny 268 E6
Inverkip 232 D2
Inverkirkaig 272 C7
Inverlael 265 H3
Inverlauren 233 E1
Inverliever 240 A4
Inverliver 240 C1
Inverlochlarig 241 G3
Inverlochy 241 E2
Inverlussa 231 E1
Invermay 243 F3
Invermoriston (Inbhir
  Moireasdan) 258 B3
Invernaver 274 C2
Inverneil 231 G1
Inverness
  (Inbhir Nis) 266 D7
Inverness Airport 266 E6

Invernettie 269 K6
Invernoaden 240 D5
Inveroran Hotel (Inbhir
  Orain) 249 E5
Inverquharity 252 C4
Inverquhomery 269 J6
Inverroy 249 E1
Inversanda 248 B4
Invershiel 257 F3
Invershore 275 H5
Inversnaid Hotel 241 F4
Invertrossachs 242 A4
Inverugie 269 K6
Inveruglas (Inbhir
  Dhubhghlais) 241 F4
Inveruglass 259 F4
Inverurie 261 F2
Invervar 250 B5
Invervegain 232 B2
Invery House 260 E5
Inverythan 269 F6
Inworth 138 B1
Iochdar 262 C7
Iona 238 B2
Iping 121 D5
Ipplepen 101 E1
Ipsden 134 B4
Ipstones 172 B3
Ipswich 152 C3
Irby 183 D4
Irby Hill 183 D4
Irby in the Marsh 176 C1
Irby upon Humber 188 B2
Irchester 149 E1
Ireby Cumb 209 F3
Ireby Lancs 200 B5
Ireland Ork 277 C7
Ireland's Cross 171 E3
Ireleth 199 D5
Ireshopeburn 211 E4
Irlam 184 B3
Irnham 175 F5
Iron Acton 131 F4
Iron Cross 146 C2
Ironbridge 157 F2
Ironbridge Gorge Tel&W
  TF8 7DQ 157 F2
Irons Bottom 122 B4
Ironside 269 G5
Ironville 173 F2
Irstead 179 E3
Irthington 210 A1
Irthlingborough 161 E5
Irton 204 D4
Irvine 224 B2
Isauld 274 E2
Isbister Ork 277 C6
Isbister Ork 276 B5
Isbister Shet 279 E6
Isbister Shet 278 C3
Isfield 109 G2
Isham 161 D5
Ishriff 239 F1
Isington 120 C3
Island of Stroma 275 J1
Islawr-dref 154 C1
Islay 230 A3
Islay Airport 230 B4
Islay House 230 B3
Isle Abbotts 116 A5
Isle Brewers 116 A5
Isle of Bute Discovery Centre
  A&B PA20 0AH 232 B3
Isle of Lewis (Eilean
  Leodhais) 271 F3
Isle of Man 190 B3
Isle of Man Airport 190 A5
Isle of May 245 E5
Isle of Noss 279 E8
Isle of Sheppey 124 B1
Isle of Walney 191 E1
Isle of Whithorn 207 E3
Isle of Wight 107 D4
Isle of Wight Pearl IoW
  PO30 4DD 106 D4
Isle of Wight (Sandown)
  Airport 107 E4
Isle of Wight Zoo IoW
  PO36 8QB 107 F4
Isleham 163 E5
Isleornsay (Eilean
  Iarmain) 256 C3
Isles of Scilly
  (Scilly Isles) 96 B1
Islesburgh 279 C6
Isleworth 136 A5
Isley Walton 173 F5
Islibhig 270 B5
Islip N'hants 161 E5
Islip Oxon 134 A1
Isombridge 157 F1
Istead Rise 123 F2
Itchen 106 D1
Itchen Abbas 119 G4
Itchen Stoke 119 G4
Itchen Valley Country Park
  Hants SO30 3HQ 4 C2
Itchingfield 121 G5
Itchington 131 F4
Itteringham 178 C2
Itton Devon 99 G1
Itton Mon 131 D3
Itton Common 131 D3
Ivegill 210 A3
Ivelet 201 E3
Iver 135 F4
Iver Heath 135 F4
Iveston 212 A2
Ivetsey Bank 158 A1
Ivinghoe 135 E1
Ivinghoe Aston 135 E1
Ivington 145 D2
Ivington Green 145 D2
Ivy Hatch 123 E3
Ivy Todd 163 G2
Ivybridge 100 C2
Ivychurch 111 F1
Iwade 124 B2
Iwerne Courtney
  (Shroton) 105 E1
Iwerne Minster 105 E1
Ixworth 164 A4
Ixworth Thorpe 164 A4

J

Jack Hill 194 A2
Jackfield 157 F2
Jacksdale 173 F2
Jackstown 261 F1
Jackton 233 G4
Jacobstow 98 B1
Jacobstowe 113 F5
Jacobswell 121 E2
James Hamilton
  Heritage Park SLan
  G74 5LB 31 E5
Jameston 127 D3
Jamestown D&G 218 B2
Jamestown High 266 B6
Jamestown WDun 233 E1
Janefield 266 E6
Janetstown High 275 F2
Janetstown High 275 J3
Jarrow 212 C1
Jarvis Brook 123 E5
Jasper's Green 151 F4
Jawcraig 234 C2
Jayes Park 121 G3
Jaywick 139 E1
Jealott's Hill 135 D5
Jeater Houses 202 D3
Jedburgh 228 A4
Jeffreyston 127 D2
Jemimaville 266 E5
Jephson Gardens Warks
  CV32 4ER 16 B6
Jericho 184 C1
Jersay 234 C3
Jersey 100 C5
Jersey Airport 100 B5
Jersey Marine 128 D3
Jerviswood 234 C5
Jesmond 212 B1
Jevington 110 A3
Jinney Ring Craft Centre,
  The Worcs
  B60 4BU 146 B1
Jockey End 135 F1
Jodrell Bank 184 B5
Jodrell Bank Observatory &
  Arboretum ChesE
  SK11 9DL 184 B5
John Muir Country Park
  ELoth
  EH42 1UW 236 D2
John o' Groats 275 J1
Johnby 210 A4
John's Cross 110 C1
Johnshaven 253 F3
Johnson Street 179 E4
Johnston 126 C1
Johnston Mains 253 F2
Johnstone 233 F3
Johnstone Castle 233 F3
Johnstonebridge 217 E1
Johnstown Carmar 127 G1
Johnstown Wrex 170 A3
Joppa 224 C4
Jordans 135 E3
Jordanston 140 C4
Jordanstone 252 A5
Jorvik YO1 9WT 90 York
Jorvik Glass NYorks
  YO60 7DA 195 G1
Joy's Green 131 F1
Jumpers Common 106 A3
Juniper Green 235 F3
Juniper Hill 148 A4
Jura 231 D1
Jura House 230 C3
Jurby East 190 B2
Jurby West 190 B2

K

Kaber 200 C1
Kaimes 235 G3
Kames A&B 232 A2
Kames A&B 240 A3
Kames EAyr 225 E3
Kathellan Fife
  KY4 0JR 243 G5
Kea 96 C5
Keadby 187 F1
Keal Cotes 176 B1
Kearsley 184 B2
Kearstwick 200 B5
Kearton 201 F3
Kearvaig 272 E1
Keasden 192 D1
Kebholes 268 E5
Keckwick 183 G4
Keddington 188 D4
Keddington Corner 189 D4
Kedington 151 F3
Kedleston 173 E3
Keelby 188 B1
Keele 171 F3
Keeley Green 149 F3
Keelham 193 G4
Keenthorne 115 F4
Keeres Green 137 E1
Keeston 126 B1
Keevil 118 A2
Kegworth 173 F5
Kehelland 96 A5
Keig 260 E3
Keighley 193 G3
Keighley & Worth Valley
  Railway WYorks
  BD22 8NJ 193 G3
Keil A&B 222 B5
Keil High 248 B3
Keilhill 269 F5
Keillmore 231 E1
Keillor 252 A5
Keillour 243 E2
Keills 230 C3
Keils 230 C3
Keinton Mandeville 116 C4
Keir House 242 C5
Keir Mill 216 C1
Keisby 175 F5
Keisley 210 D5
Keiss 275 J2
Keith 268 C5

Keithick 244 A1
Keithmore 260 B1
Keithock 253 F2
Kelbrook 193 F3
Kelby 175 F3
Keld Cumb 199 G1
Keld NYorks 201 D2
Keldholme 203 G4
Keldy Castle 203 G3
Kelfield NLincs 187 F2
Kelfield NYorks 195 E4
Kelham 174 C2
Kella 190 B2
Kellacott 99 E2
Kellan 247 E5
Kellas Angus 244 C1
Kellas Moray 267 J6
Kellaton 101 D4
Kellaways 132 B5
Kelleth 200 B1
Kelleythorpe 196 C2
Kelling 178 B1
Kellington 195 E5
Kelloe 212 C4
Kelloholm 225 F4
Kelly Corn 97 E2
Kelly Devon 99 D2
Kelly Bray 99 D3
Kelmarsh 160 C5
Kelmscott 133 E3
Kelsale 153 E1
Kelsall 170 C1
Kelsay 230 A4
Kelshall 150 B4
Kelsick 209 E1
Kelso 228 B3
Kelstedge 173 E1
Kelstern 188 C3
Kelston 117 E1
Keltneyburn 250 C5
Kelton 217 D3
Kelton Hill
  (Rhonehouse) 216 B5
Kelty 243 G5
Kelvedon 138 B1
Kelvedon Hatch 137 E3
Kelvingrove Art Gallery &
  Museum Glas
  G3 8AG 38 B2
Kelvinside 233 G3
Kelynack 94 A4
Kemacott 113 G1
Kemback 244 C3
Kemberton 157 G2
Kemble 132 B3
Kemerton 146 B4
Kemeys
  Commander 130 C2
Kemeys Inferior 130 C3
Kemnay 261 F3
Kemp Town 109 F3
Kempe's Corner 124 C4
Kempley 145 F5
Kempley Green 145 F5
Kemps Green 158 D5
Kempsey 146 A3
Kempsford 133 D3
Kempshott 119 G3
Kempston 149 F3
Kempston Hardwick 149 F3
Kempston West End 149 E3
Kempton 156 C4
Kemsing 123 E3
Kemsley 124 B2
Kenardington 124 B5
Kenchester 144 D3
Kencot 133 E2
Kendal 199 G3
Kenderchurch 144 D5
Kendleshire 131 F5
Kenfig 129 D4
Kenfig Hill 129 E4
Kenidjack 94 A3
Kenilworth 159 E5
Kenilworth Castle Warks
  CV8 1NE 16 A4
Kenknock P&K 250 A5
Kenknock Stir 241 G1
Kenley GtLon 122 C2
Kenley Shrop 157 E2
Kenmore A&B 240 C4
Kenmore High 264 D6
Kenmore P&K 250 C5
Kenmore ESiar 270 E7
Kenn Devon 102 C4
Kenn NSom 116 B1
Kennacley 263 G2
Kennacraig 231 G3
Kennards House 97 G1
Kennavay 263 H2
Kenneggy Downs 94 C4
Kennerleigh 102 B2
Kennerty 260 E5
Kennet 243 E5
Kennethmont 260 D2
Kennett 151 E1
Kennford 102 C4
Kenninghall 164 B3
Kennington Kent 124 C4
Kennington Oxon 134 A2
Kennoway 244 B4
Kenny 103 G1
Kennyhill 163 E5
Kennythorpe 195 G1
Kenovay 246 A2
Kensaleyre 263 K6
Kensington 136 B4
Kensington Palace GtLon
  W8 4PX 10 E4
Kenstone 170 C5
Kensworth 135 F1
Kent & East Sussex Railway
  Kent TN30 6HE 124 A5
Kent International
  Airport 125 F2
Kent Street ESuss 110 C2
Kent Street Kent 123 F3
Kentallen (Ceann an t-
  Sàilein) 248 C4
Kentchurch 144 D5
Kentford 151 F1
Kentisbeare 103 D2
Kentisbury 113 G1
Kentisbury Ford 113 G1
Kentish Town 136 B4
Kentmere 199 F2
Kenton Devon 102 C4
Kenton Suff 152 C1

Kenton *T&W* 212 B1
Kenton Corner 152 D1
Kentra 247 F3
Kents Bank 199 E5
Kent's Oak 119 E5
Kenwick 170 B4
Kenwood House *GtLon*
NW3 7JR 10 F2
Kenwyn 96 C5
Kenyon 184 A3
Keoldale 273 F2
Keose (Ceòs) 271 F5
Keppanach 248 C3
Keppoch *A&B* 233 E2
Keppoch *High* 256 E2
Keprigan 222 B4
Kepwick 203 D3
Keresley 159 F4
Kernborough 101 D3
Kerrera *A&B* 240 A2
Kerridge 184 D5
Kerris 94 B4
Kerry (Ceri) 156 A3
Kerrycroy 232 C3
Kerry's Gate 144 C4
Kerrysdale 264 E4
Kersall 174 C1
Kersey 152 B3
Kersey Vale 152 B3
Kershopefoot 218 C3
Kerswell 103 D2
Kerswell Green 146 A3
Kerthen Wood 94 C3
Kesgrave 152 D3
Kessingland 165 G3
Kessingland Beach 165 G3
Kestle 97 D5
Kestle Mill 96 C4
Keston 123 D2
Keswick *Cumb* 209 F4
Keswick *Norf* 178 D5
Keswick *Norf* 179 E2
Ketley Bank 157 F1
Ketsby 189 D5
Kettering 161 D5
Ketteringham 178 C5
Kettins 244 A1
Kettle Corner 123 G3
Kettlebaston 152 A2
Kettlebridge 244 B4
Kettlebrook 159 E2
Kettleburgh 153 D1
Kettlehill 244 B4
Kettleholm 217 F3
Kettleness 204 B1
Kettleshulme 185 D5
Kettlesing 194 B2
Kettlesing Bottom 194 B2
Kettlesing Head 194 B2
Kettlestone 178 A4
Kettlethorpe 187 F5
Kettletoft 276 F4
Kettlewell 201 E5
Ketton 161 E2
Kevingtown 123 D2
Kew 136 A5
Kewstoke 116 A1
Kexbrough 186 A2
Kexby *Lincs* 187 F4
Kexby *York* 195 G2
Key Green 171 F1
Keyham 160 B2
Keyhaven 106 C3
Keyingham 197 E5
Keymer 109 F2
Keynsham 117 D1
Key's Toft 176 C2
Keysoe 149 F1
Keysoe Row 149 F1
Keyston 161 F5
Keyworth 174 B4
Kibblesworth 212 B2
Kibworth
Beauchamp 160 B3
Kibworth Harcourt 160 B3
Kidbrooke 136 D5
Kiddemore Green 158 A2
Kidderminster 158 A5
Kiddington 147 G5
Kidlington 133 G1
Kidmore End 134 B5
Kidnal 170 B3
Kidsdale 207 E3
Kidsgrove 171 F2
Kidstones 201 E4
Kidwelly (Cydweli) 128 A2
Kiel Crofts 240 A1
Kielder 219 E2
Kielder Forest *N'umb*
NE48 1ER 219 E2
Kielder Water *N'umb*
NE48 1BX 219 F3
Kilbarchan 233 F3
Kilbeg 256 C4
Kilberry 231 F3
Kilbirnie 233 E4
Kilblaan 240 D3
Kilbraur 274 D7
Kilbrennan 246 D5
Kilbride *A&B* 240 A2
Kilbride *A&B* 232 B3
Kilbride *High* 256 B3
Kilbride Farm 232 A3
Kilbridemore 240 C5
Kilburn *Derbys* 173 E3
Kilburn *GtLon* 136 B4
Kilburn *NYorks* 203 E5
Kilby 160 B3
Kilchattan Bay 232 C4
Kilchenzie 222 B3
Kilcheran 240 A1
Kilchiaran 230 A3
Kilchoan *A&B* 239 G3
Kilchoan *High* 247 E2
Kilchoman 230 A3
Kilchrenan
(Cill Chrèanain) 240 C2
Kilchrist 222 B4
Kilcoy 266 C6
Kilcreggan 232 D1
Kildale 203 F2
Kildavie 222 C4
Kildermorie Lodge 266 C4
Kildonan *NAyr* 223 F3

Kildonan (Cilldonnain)
ESiar 254 C2
Kildonan Lodge 274 E6
Kildonnan 247 D1
Kildrochet House 214 B5
Kildrummy 260 C3
Kildwick 193 G3
Kilfinan 232 A2
Kilfinnan 257 J5
Kilgetty 127 E2
Kilgwrrwg Common 131 D3
Kilham *ERid* 196 C1
Kilham *N'umb* 228 C3
Kilkenneth 246 A2
Kilkenny 132 C1
Kilkerran *A&B* 222 C4
Kilkerran *SAyr* 224 B5
Kilkhampton 112 C4
Killamarsh 186 B4
Killay 128 C3
Killbeg 247 F5
Killean *A&B* 231 E5
Killean *A&B* 240 C4
Killearn 233 G1
Killellan 222 B4
Killen 266 D6
Killerby 212 A5
Killerton 102 C2
Killerton *Devon*
EX5 3LE 102 C2
Killichonan 250 A4
Killiechonate 249 E1
Killiechronan 247 E5
Killiecrankie 251 E4
Killiehuntly 258 E5
Killilan 257 F3
Killimster 275 J3
Killin *High* 267 F1
Killin *Stir* 242 A1
Killinallan 230 B2
Killinghall 194 B2
Killington *Cumb* 200 B4
Killington *Devon* 113 G1
Killingworth 221 E4
Killochyett 236 B5
Killocrae 232 B3
Killundine 247 F5
Kilmacolm 233 E3
Kilmaha 239 E5
Kilmahog 242 B4
Kilmalieu 248 A4
Kilmaluag 263 K4
Kilmany 244 B2
Kilmarie 256 B3
Kilmarnock 224 C2
Kilmartin 240 A5
Kilmaurs 233 F5
Kilmelford 240 A3
Kilmeny 230 B3
Kilmersdon 117 D2
Kilmeston 119 G5
Kilmichael
Glassary 240 A5
Kilmichael of
Inverlussa 231 F1
Kilmington *Devon* 103 F3
Kilmington *Wilts* 117 E4
Kilmington
Common 117 E4
Kilmorack 266 B7
Kilmore (A' Chille Mhòr)
A&B 240 A2
Kilmory *A&B* 231 F1
Kilmory *A&B* 231 F2
Kilmory *High* 255 J4
Kilmory *High* 247 E2
Kilmory *NAyr* 223 E3
Kilmote 274 E7
Kilmuir *High* 263 H7
Kilmuir *High* 266 D7
Kilmuir *High* 266 E4
Kilmuir *High* 263 J4
Kilmun 232 C1
Kilmux 244 B4
Kiln Green *Here* 131 F1
Kiln Green *W'ham* 134 D5
Kiln Pit Hill 211 G2
Kilnave 230 A2
Kilncadzow 234 C5
Kilndown 123 G5
Kilnhurst 186 B3
Kilninian 246 D5
Kilninver 240 A2
Kilnsea 189 E1
Kilnsey 193 F1
Kilnwick 196 B3
Kilnwick Percy 196 A2
Kiloran 238 C5
Kilpatrick 223 E3
Kilpeck 144 D4
Kilphedir 274 E7
Kilpin 195 G5
Kilpin Pike 195 G5
Kilrenny 245 D4
Kilsby 160 A5
Kilspindie 244 A2
Kilstay 206 B3
Kilsyth 234 B2
Kiltarlity 266 C7
Kilton *Notts* 186 C5
Kilton *R&C* 203 F1
Kilton *Som* 115 E4
Kilton Thorpe 203 F1
Kiltyrie 242 B1
Kilvaxter 263 J5
Kilve 115 E3
Kilverstone 163 G4
Kilvington 174 D3
Kilwinning 233 E5
Kimberley *Norf* 178 B5
Kimberley *Notts* 173 G3
Kimberworth 186 B3
Kimble Wick 134 D2
Kimblesworth 212 B3
Kimbolton *Cambs* 149 F1
Kimbolton *Here* 145 E1
Kimbridge 119 E5
Kimcote 160 A4
Kimmeridge 105 F5
Kimmerston 229 D3
Kimpton *Hants* 119 D3
Kimpton *Herts* 136 A1
Kinaldy 244 C4
Kinblethmont 253 E5

Kinbrace 274 D5
Kinbreack 257 G5
Kinbuck 242 C4
Kincaldrum 252 C5
Kincaple 244 C3
Kincardine *Fife* 234 D1
Kincardine *High* 266 D3
Kincardine O'Neil 260 D5
Kinclaven 243 G1
Kincorth 261 H4
Kincraig *Aber* 261 H2
Kincraig *High* 259 F4
Kincraigie 251 E5
Kindallachan 251 E4
Kindrogan Field
Centre 251 F3
Kinellar 261 G3
Kineton *Glos* 146 C5
Kineton *Warks* 147 F2
Kineton Green 158 D4
Kinfauns 243 G2
King Sterndale 185 E5
Kingarth 232 B4
Kingcoed 130 D2
Kingerby 188 A3
Kingham 147 E5
Kingholm Quay 217 D3
Kinghorn 235 G1
Kinglassie 244 A5
Kingoodie 244 B2
King's Acre 145 D3
King's Bank 111 D1
King's Bromley 158 D1
Kings Caple 145 E5
King's Cliffe 161 F3
King's Coughton 146 C2
King's Green 145 G4
King's Heath 158 C4
Kings Hill *Kent* 123 F3
King's Hill *Warks* 159 F5
King's Hill *WMid* 158 B3
Kings Langley 135 F2
King's Lynn 177 E5
King's Meaburn 210 C5
King's Mills 101 E5
King's Moss 183 G2
Kings Muir 227 D2
King's Newnham 159 G5
King's Newton 173 E5
King's Norton *Leics* 160 B2
King's Norton
WMid 158 C5
Kings Nympton 113 G4
King's Pyon 144 D2
Kings Ripton 162 A5
King's Somborne 119 E4
King's Stag 104 D1
King's Stanley 132 A2
King's Sutton 147 G4
King's Tamerton 100 A2
King's Walden 149 G5
Kings Worthy 119 F4
Kingsand 100 A2
Kingsbarns 245 D3
Kingsbridge *Devon* 100 D3
Kingsbridge *Som* 114 C4
Kingsburgh 263 J6
Kingsbury *GtLon* 136 B4
Kingsbury *Warks* 159 F3
Kingsbury Episcopi 116 B5
Kingsbury Water Park
Warks B76 0DY 159 E3
Kingscavil 235 E2
Kingsclere 119 G2
Kingscote 132 A3
Kingscott 113 F4
Kingscross 223 F3
Kingsdale 244 B4
Kingsdon 116 C5
Kingsdown *Kent* 125 F4
Kingsdown *Swin* 133 D4
Kingsdown *Wilts* 117 F1
Kingseat 243 G5
Kingsey 134 C2
Kingsfold *Pembs* 126 C3
Kingsfold *WSuss* 121 G4
Kingsford *Aber* 269 F6
Kingsford *Aber* 260 D3
Kingsford
Aberdeen 261 G4
Kingsford *EAyr* 233 F5
Kingsford *Worcs* 158 A4
Kingsgate 125 F1
Kingshall Street 152 A1
Kingsheanton 113 F2
Kingshouse 242 A2
Kingshouse Hotel 249 E4
Kingshurst 159 D4
Kingskerswell 101 E1
Kingskettle 244 B4
Kingsland *Here* 144 D1
Kingsland *IoA* 180 A4
Kingsley *ChesW&C* 183 G5
Kingsley *Hants* 120 C4
Kingsley *Staffs* 172 B3
Kingsley Green 121 D4
Kingsley Holt 172 B3
Kingslow 157 G3
Kingsmoor 136 D2
Kingsmuir *Angus* 252 C5
Kingsmuir *Fife* 244 D4
Kingsnorth 124 C5
Kingsnorth Power
Station 124 A1
Kingstanding 158 C3
Kingsteignton 102 B5
Kingsteps 267 G6
Kingsthorpe 148 C1
Kingston *Cambs* 150 B2
Kingston *Corn* 99 D3
Kingston *Devon* 100 C3
Kingston *Devon* 103 D4
Kingston *Dorset* 105 E4
Kingston *Dorset* 105 F5
Kingston *ELoth* 236 C1
Kingston *GtMan* 184 D3
Kingston *Hants* 106 A2
Kingston *IoW* 107 D4
Kingston *Kent* 125 D3
Kingston *MK* 149 E4
Kingston *Moray* 268 B4
Kingston *WSuss* 108 C3
Kingston Bagpuize 133 G3
Kingston Blount 134 C3

Kingston by Sea 109 E3
Kingston Deverill 117 F4
Kingston Gorse 108 C3
Kingston Lacy *Dorset*
BH21 4EA 3 A1
Kingston Lisle 133 F4
Kingston Maurward 104 D3
Kingston near
Lewes 109 F3
Kingston on Soar 173 G5
Kingston Russell 104 B3
Kingston St. Mary 115 F5
Kingston Seymour 116 B1
Kingston Stert 134 C2
Kingston upon Hull 196 D5
Kingston upon
Thames 121 G1
Kingston upon
Thames 121 G1
Kingston Warren 133 F4
Kingstone *Here* 145 D4
Kingstone *Here* 145 F5
Kingstone *Som* 103 G1
Kingstone *Staffs* 172 B5
Kingstone Winslow 133 E4
Kingstown 209 G1
Kingswear 101 E2
Kingswell 233 G5
Kingswells 261 G4
Kingswinford 158 A4
Kingswood *Bucks* 134 B1
Kingswood *Glos* 131 G3
Kingswood *Here* 144 B2
Kingswood *Kent* 124 A3
Kingswood *Powys* 156 B2
Kingswood *SGlos* 131 F5
Kingswood *Som* 115 E4
Kingswood *Surr* 122 B3
Kingswood *Warks* 159 D5
Kingthorpe 188 B5
Kington *Here* 144 B2
Kington *Worcs* 146 B2
Kington Langley 132 B5
Kington Magna 117 E5
Kington St. Michael 132 B5
Kingussie 258 E4
Kingweston 116 C4
Kinharrachie 261 H1
Kinharvie 216 D4
Kinkell 234 B2
Kinkell Bridge 243 E3
Kinknockie 269 J6
Kinlet 157 G4
Kinloch *Fife* 244 A3
Kinloch *High* 273 F5
Kinloch *High* 247 F4
Kinloch *High* 255 K5
Kinloch *High* 266 D2
Kinloch *P&K* 252 A5
Kinloch *P&K* 251 G5
Kinloch Hourn (Ceann Loch
Shubhairne) 257 F4
Kinloch Laggan 250 A1
Kinloch Rannoch 250 B4
Kinlochan 248 A3
Kinlochard 241 G4
Kinlocharkaig 257 F5
Kinlochbeoraid 248 A1
Kinlochbervie 272 E3
Kinlocheil 248 B2
Kinlochetive 248 D5
Kinlochewe 265 G5
Kinlochlaich 248 B5
Kinlochleven (Ceann Loch
Liobhann) 249 D3
Kinlochmoidart 247 G2
Kinlochmorar 256 E5
Kinlochmore 249 D3
Kinlochroag (Ceann
Lochroag) 270 D5
Kinloid 256 C1
Kinloss 267 H5
Kinmel Bay
(Bae Cinmel) 182 A4
Kinmuck 261 G3
Kinnaber 253 E4
Kinnadie 269 H6
Kinnaird 244 A2
Kinneff 253 G2
Kinnelhead 226 B5
Kinnell *Angus* 253 E4
Kinnell *Stir* 242 A1
Kinnerley 170 A5
Kinnersley *Here* 144 C3
Kinnersley *Worcs* 146 A3
Kinnerton 144 B1
Kinnerton Green 170 A1
Kinnesswood 243 G4
Kinnettles 252 C5
Kinninvie 211 G5
Kinnordy 252 B4
Kinoulton 174 B4
Kinrara 259 F4
Kinross 243 G4
Kinrossie 243 G1
Kinsbourne Green 136 A1
Kinsham *Here* 144 C1
Kinsham *Worcs* 146 B4
Kinsley 186 B1
Kinson 105 G3
Kintarvie 270 E6
Kintbury 119 E1
Kintessack 267 G5
Kintillo 243 G3
Kintocher 260 D4
Kinton *Here* 156 D5
Kinton *Shrop* 156 C1
Kintore 261 F3
Kintour 230 C4
Kintra *A&B* 230 B5
Kintra *A&B* 238 C3
Kintradwell 267 G1
Kintraw 240 A4
Kinuachdrachd 239 G5
Kinveachy 259 G3
Kinver 158 A4
Kinwarton 146 D2
Kiplaw Croft 261 J1
Kipp 242 A1
Kippen *P&K* 243 F3
Kippen *Stir* 242 B5
Kippenross House 242 C4
Kippford (Scaur) 216 C5
Kipping's Cross 123 F4
Kippington 123 E3
Kirbister *Ork* 277 C7
Kirbister *Ork* 276 F5
Kirbuster 276 B5
Kirby Bedon 179 D5

Kirby Bellars 160 C1
Kirby Cane 165 E2
Kirby Corner 159 E5
Kirby Cross 152 D5
Kirby Fields 160 A2
Kirby Green 165 E2
Kirby Grindalythe 196 B1
Kirby Hill *NYorks* 202 A2
Kirby Hill *NYorks* 194 C1
Kirby Knowle 203 D4
Kirby le Soken 152 D5
Kirby Misperton 203 G5
Kirby Muxloe 160 A2
Kirby Row 165 E2
Kirby Sigston 202 D3
Kirby Underdale 196 A2
Kirby Wiske 202 D4
Kirdford 121 F5
Kirk 275 H3
Kirk Bramwith 186 D1
Kirk Deighton 194 C2
Kirk Ella 196 C5
Kirk Hallam 173 F3
Kirk Hammerton 195 D2
Kirk Ireton 173 D2
Kirk Langley 173 D4
Kirk Merrington 212 B4
Kirk Michael 190 B2
Kirk of Shotts 234 C3
Kirk Sandall 186 D2
Kirk Smeaton 186 C1
Kirk Yetholm 228 C4
Kirkabister 279 D9
Kirkandrews 207 G2
Kirkandrews-upon-
Eden 209 G1
Kirkbampton 209 G1
Kirkbean 217 D5
Kirkbride 209 F1
Kirkbuddo 252 D5
Kirkburn *ERid* 196 B3
Kirkburn *ScBord* 227 D2
Kirkburton 185 F1
Kirkby *Lincs* 188 A3
Kirkby *Mersey* 183 F3
Kirkby *NYorks* 203 E2
Kirkby Fleetham 202 B3
Kirkby Green 175 F2
Kirkby in Ashfield 173 F2
Kirkby la Thorpe 175 F3
Kirkby Lonsdale 200 B5
Kirkby Malham 193 E1
Kirkby Mallory 159 G2
Kirkby Malzeard 202 B5
Kirkby on Bain 176 A1
Kirkby Overblow 194 C3
Kirkby Stephen 200 C2
Kirkby Thore 210 C5
Kirkby Underwood 175 F5
Kirkby Wharfe 195 E3
Kirkby Woodhouse 173 F2
Kirkby-in-Furness 198 D4
Kirkbymoorside 203 F4
Kirkcaldy 244 A5
Kirkcambeck 210 B1
Kirkcolm 214 B4
Kirkconnel 225 F4
Kirkconnell 217 D4
Kirkcowan 215 E4
Kirkcudbright 216 A5
Kirkdale House 215 G5
Kirkdean 235 F5
Kirkfieldbank 234 C5
Kirkgunzeon 216 C4
Kirkham *Lancs* 192 A4
Kirkham *NYorks* 195 G1
Kirkhamgate 194 C5
Kirkharle 220 C3
Kirkhaugh 210 C2
Kirkheaton *N'umb* 220 C4
Kirkheaton *WYorks* 185 F1
Kirkhill *Angus* 253 E3
Kirkhill *High* 266 C7
Kirkhill *Moray* 268 B5
Kirkhope 227 E3
Kirkibost (Circebost)
ESiar 270 D4
Kirkinch 252 B5
Kirkinner 215 F5
Kirkintilloch 234 A2
Kirkland *Cumb* 210 C4
Kirkland *Cumb* 209 D5
Kirkland *D&G* 216 C1
Kirkland *D&G* 217 E2
Kirkland of
Longcastle 207 D2
Kirkleatham 213 E5
Kirklevington 202 D1
Kirkley 165 G2
Kirklington *Notts* 174 B2
Kirklington *NYorks* 202 C4
Kirklinton 210 A1
Kirkliston 235 F2
Kirkmaiden 206 B3
Kirkmichael *P&K* 251 F3
Kirkmichael *SAyr* 224 B5
Kirkmuirhill 234 B5
Kirknewton *N'umb* 228 D3
Kirknewton *WLoth* 235 F3
Kirkney 260 D1
Kirkoswald *Cumb* 210 B3
Kirkoswald *SAyr* 224 A5
Kirkpatrick Durham 216 B3
Kirkpatrick-Fleming 218 A4
Kirksanton 198 C4
Kirkstall 175 G1
Kirkstile *Aber* 260 D1
Kirkstile *D&G* 218 B2
Kirkstyle 275 J1
Kirkton *A&B* 239 G4
Kirkton *Aber* 260 D2
Kirkton *Aber* 268 E5
Kirkton *Aber* 261 F3
Kirkton *Angus* 252 C5
Kirkton *D&G* 217 D2
Kirkton *Fife* 244 B2
Kirkton *High* 258 D1
Kirkton *High* 266 E2
Kirkton *High* 274 D7
Kirkton *High* 256 E2
Kirkton *ScBord* 227 G4
Kirkton Manor 226 D2

Kirkton of Airlie 252 B4
Kirkton of
Auchterhouse 244 A1
Kirkton of Barevan 267 F7
Kirkton of Bourtie 261 G2
Kirkton of Collace 243 G1
Kirkton of Craig 253 F4
Kirkton of
Culsalmond 260 E1
Kirkton of Durris 261 F5
Kirkton of
Glenbuchat 260 B3
Kirkton of Glenisla 252 A4
Kirkton of
Kingoldrum 252 B4
Kirkton of Lethendy 251 G5
Kirkton of Logie
Buchan 261 H2
Kirkton of
Maryculter 261 G5
Kirkton of Menmuir 252 D3
Kirkton of Monikie 244 D1
Kirkton of Rayne 260 E1
Kirkton of Skene 261 G4
Kirkton of Tealing 244 C1
Kirktonhill *Aber* 253 E3
Kirktonhill *WDun* 233 E2
Kirktown 269 J5
Kirktown of
Auchterless 269 F6
Kirktown of
Deskford 268 D4
Kirktown of
Fetteresso 253 G1
Kirktown of Slains 261 J2
Kirkwall 277 D6
Kirkwall Airport 277 D7
Kirkwhelpington 220 B3
Kirmington 188 B1
Kirmond le Mire 188 B3
Kirn 232 C2
Kirriemuir 252 B4
Kirstead Green 165 D2
Kirtlebridge 218 A4
Kirtleton 218 A3
Kirtling 151 E2
Kirtling Green 151 E2
Kirtlington 134 A1
Kirtomy 274 C2
Kirton *Lincs* 176 B4
Kirton *Notts* 174 B1
Kirton *Suff* 153 D4
Kirton End 176 A3
Kirton Holme 176 A3
Kirton in Lindsey 187 G3
Kiscadale 223 F3
Kislingbury 148 B2
Kismeldon Bridge 113 D4
Kit Hill Country Park
Corn PL17 8AX 99 D3
Kites Hardwick 147 G1
Kitley 100 B2
Kittisford 115 D5
Kittisford Barton 115 D5
Kittle 128 B4
Kitt's End 136 B3
Kitt's Green 159 D4
Kitwood 120 B4
Kivernoll 145 D4
Kiveton Park 186 B4
Kilbreck 273 H5
Knabbygates 268 D5
Knaith 187 F4
Knaith Park 187 F4
Knap Corner 117 F5
Knaphill 121 F2
Knaplock 114 B4
Knapp *P&K* 244 A1
Knapp *Som* 116 A5
Knapthorpe 174 C2
Knaptoft 160 B4
Knapton *Norf* 179 E2
Knapton *York* 195 E2
Knapton Green 144 D2
Knapwell 150 B1
Knaresborough 194 C2
Knarsdale 210 C2
Knarston 276 C5
Knaven 269 G6
Knayton 202 D3
Knebworth 150 A5
Knebworth House *Herts*
SG3 6PY 150 A5
Knedlington 195 G5
Kneesall 174 C1
Kneesworth 150 B3
Kneeton 174 C3
Knelston 128 A4
Knenhall 171 G4
Knettishall 164 A3
Knettishall Heath Country
Park *Suff*
IP22 2TQ 164 A3
Knightacott 113 G2
Knightcote 147 G2
Knightley 171 F5
Knightley Dale 171 F5
Knighton *Devon* 100 B3
Knighton *Dorset* 104 C1
Knighton *Leic* 160 A2
Knighton *Poole* 105 G3
Knighton *Som* 115 E3
Knighton *Staffs* 171 E3
Knighton *Staffs* 171 E4
Knighton *Wilts* 133 E5
Knighton on Teme 157 F5
Knightswood 233 G3
Knightwick 145 G2
Knill 144 B1
Knipoch 240 A2
Knipton 174 D4
Knitsley 212 A3
Kniveton 172 C2
Knock *A&B* 239 G1
Knock *Cumb* 210 C5
Knock *D&G* 217 D2
Knock *High* 256 C4
Knock *Moray* 268 D5
Knock of
Auchnahannet 259 H1
Knockalava 240 B5
Knockally 275 G6
Knockan 272 E1
Knockandhu 259 K2
Knockando 267 J7

Knockarthur 266 E2
Knockbain 266 D6
Knockban 265 J5
Knockbreck 266 E3
Knockbrex 207 F2
Knockdamph 265 J2
Knockdee 275 G2
Knockdow 232 C2
Knockenkelly 223 F3
Knockentiber 224 B2
Knockfin 257 K2
Knockgray 215 G1
Knockholt 123 D3
Knockholt Pound 123 D3
Knockin 170 A5
Knockinlaw 224 C2
Knockintorran (Cnoc an
Torrain) 262 C5
Knocklearn 216 B3
Knockmill 123 E2
Knocknaha 222 B4
Knocknain 214 A4
Knocknalling 215 G2
Knockrome 231 D2
Knocksharry 190 A3
Knockville 215 E3
Knockvologan 238 C3
Knodishall 153 F1
Knodishall
Common 153 F1
Knodishall Green 153 F1
Knole 116 B5
Knolls Green 184 C5
Knolton 170 A4
Knook 118 A3
Knossington 160 D2
Knott End-on-Sea 191 G3
Knotting 149 F1
Knotting Green 149 F1
Knottingley 195 E5
Knotts 193 D2
Knotty Green 135 E3
Knowbury 157 E5
Knowe 215 E3
Knowes of Elrick 268 E5
Knowesgate 220 B3
Knoweside 224 A4
Knowetownhead 227 G4
Knowhead 269 H5
Knowl Green 151 F3
Knowl Hill 134 C5
Knowl Wall 171 F4
Knowle *Bristol* 131 F5
Knowle *Devon* 100 B3
Knowle *Devon* 113 E2
Knowle *Devon* 103 D4
Knowle *Shrop* 157 E5
Knowle *Som* 114 C3
Knowle *WMid* 159 D5
Knowle Cross 102 D3
Knowle Green 192 C4
Knowle Hall 116 A3
Knowle St. Giles 103 G1
Knowlton *Dorset* 105 G1
Knowlton *Kent* 125 E3
Knowsley 183 F3
Knowsley Safari Park
Mersey L34 4AN 23 E2
Knowstone 114 B5
Knox Bridge 123 G4
Knucklas (Cnwclas) 156 B5
Knutsford 184 B5
Knypersley 171 F2
Krumlin 185 E1
Kuggar 95 E5
Kyle of Lochalsh (Caol
Loch Aillse) 256 D2
Kyleakin
(Caol Acain) 256 D2
Kylerhea
(Ceol Reatha) 256 D2
Kyles Scalpay (Caolas
Scalpaigh) 263 H2
Kylesbeg 247 F2
Kylesknoydart 256 E5
Kylesku 272 E5
Kylesmorar 256 E5
Kylestrome 272 E5
Kyloag 266 D2
Kynaston 170 A5
Kynnersley 157 F2
Kyre Park 145 F1

L

Labost 270 E3
Lacasaigh 271 F5
Lace Market Centre
NG1 1HF 80 Nottingham
Laceby 188 C2
Lacey Green 134 D2
Lach Dennis 184 B5
Lackford 163 F5
Lacklee
(Leac a' Li) 263 G2
Lacock 118 A1
Ladbroke 147 G2
Laddingford 123 F4
Lade Bank 176 B2
Ladies Hill 192 A3
Ladock 96 C4
Lady Hall 198 C4
Lady Lever Art Gallery
Mersey
CH62 5EQ 22 B4
Ladybank 244 B3
Ladycross 98 D2
Ladyfield 240 C4
Ladykirk 237 F5
Ladysford 269 H4
Ladywood 146 A1
Laga 247 F3
Lagalochan 240 A3
Lagavulin 230 C5
Lagg *A&B* 231 D2
Lagg *NAyr* 223 E3
Lagg *SAyr* 224 B5
Laggan *A&B* 230 A4
Laggan (An Lagan)
High 257 J3
Laggan *High* 258 D5
Laggan *Moray* 260 B1
Laggan *Stir* 242 A3
Lagganulva 247 D5
Lagganvoulin 259 J3
Laglingarten 240 D4
Lagnalean 266 D7
Lagrae 225 F4

Laguna 243 G1
Laid 273 G3
Laide 265 F2
Laig 247 D1
Laight 225 E4
Lainchoil 259 H3
Laindon 137 F4
Laing Art Gallery T&W
NE1 8AG
79 Newcastle upon Tyne
Lair 251 G3
Lairg 266 C1
Lairgmor 248 D3
Laisterdyke 194 A4
Laithers 248 E6
Laithes 210 A4
Lake *Devon* 113 F2
Lake *Devon* 100 B1
Lake *IoW* 107 E4
Lake *Wilts* 118 C4
Lake District Visitor Centre
at Brockhole Cumb
LA23 1LJ 199 E2
Lakenham 178 D5
Lakenheath 163 F4
Lakes Aquarium Cumb
LA12 8AS 199 E4
Lakes End 162 D3
Lakes Glass Centre,
Ulverston Cumb
LA12 7LY 199 D5
Lakeside *Cumb* 199 E4
Lakeside *Thur* 137 E5
Lakeside & Haverthwaite
Railway Cumb
LA12 8AL 199 E4
Laleham 121 F1
Laleston 129 E5
Lamancha 235 G4
Lamarsh 151 G4
Lamas 178 D3
Lamb Corner 152 B4
Lamb Roe 192 D4
Lambden 237 E5
Lamberhurst 123 F5
Lamberhurst
Quarter 123 F5
Lamberton 237 G4
Lambfell Moor 190 A3
Lambley *N'umb* 210 C2
Lambley *Notts* 174 B3
Lambourn 133 F5
Lambourn
Woodlands 133 F5
Lambourne End 137 D3
Lambs Green 122 B5
Lambston 126 C1
Lambton 212 B2
Lamellion 97 G3
Lamerton 99 E3
Lamesley 212 B2
Lamington *High* 266 E4
Lamington *SLan* 226 A2
Lamlash 223 F2
Lamloch 215 G1
Lamonby 210 A4
Lamorna 94 B4
Lamorran 96 C5
Lampert 219 E4
Lampeter (Llanbedr Pont
Steffan) 142 B3
Lampeter Velfrey 127 E1
Lamphey 126 C2
Lamplugh 209 D4
Lamport 160 C2
Lamyatt 117 E4
Lana *Devon* 98 D1
Lana *Devon* 112 D5
Lanark 234 C1
Lanarth 95 E4
Lancaster 192 A1
Lancaster Leisure Park
Lancs LA1 3LA 192 A1
Lancaster Priory Lancs
LA1 1YZ 192 A1
Lanchester 212 A3
Lancing 109 D3
Landbeach 150 C1
Landcross 113 E3
Landerberry 261 F4
Landewednack 95 E5
Landford 106 B1
Landhallow 275 G5
Landican 183 D4
Landimore 128 A3
Landkey 113 F2
Landmoth 202 D3
Landore 128 C3
Landrake 99 D4
Land's End Corn
TR19 7AA 94 A4
Land's End Airport 94 A4
Landscove 101 D1
Landshipping 126 D1
Landulph 100 A1
Landwade 151 E1
Landywood 158 B2
Lane Bottom 193 E4
Lane End *Bucks* 134 D3
Lane End *Cumb* 198 C3
Lane End *Derbys* 173 F1
Lane End *Dorset* 105 E3
Lane End *Hants* 119 G5
Lane End *Here* 131 F1
Lane End *Kent* 137 E5
Lane End *Wilts* 117 F3
Lane Ends *Derbys* 172 D4
Lane Ends *GtMan* 185 D3
Lane Ends *Lancs* 193 D4
Lane Ends *NYorks* 193 F3
Lane Green 158 A2
Lane Head *Dur* 202 A1
Lane Head *Dur* 211 G5
Lane Head *GtMan* 184 A3
Lane Head *WYorks* 185 F2
Lane Heads 192 A4
Laneham 187 F5
Lanehead *Dur* 211 E3
Lanehead *N'umb* 219 F3
Lanesend 127 D2
Lanesfield 158 B3
Laneshawbridge 193 F3
Langais 262 D5
Langamull 246 C4

Langar 174 C4
Langbank 233 E2
Langbar 193 G2
Langbaurgh 203 E1
Langcliffe 193 E1
Langdale End 204 C3
Langdon *Corn* 98 C1
Langdon *Corn* 98 D2
Langdon Beck 211 E4
Langdon Hills 137 F4
Langdon Hills Country Park
Essex SS17 9NH 137 F4
Langdon House 102 C3
Langdyke 244 B4
Langford *CenBeds* 149 G3
Langford *Essex* 138 B2
Langford *Notts* 174 D2
Langford *Oxon* 133 E2
Langford Budville 115 E5
Langham *Essex* 152 B4
Langham *Norf* 178 B1
Langham *Rut* 160 D1
Langham *Suff* 152 A3
Langham Moor 152 B4
Langho 192 C4
Langholm 218 B3
Langland 128 C4
Langlands 216 A5
Langlee 228 A5
Langleeford 228 D4
Langley *ChesE* 184 D5
Langley *Derbys* 173 F3
Langley *Essex* 150 C4
Langley *Glos* 146 C5
Langley *GtMan* 184 C2
Langley *Hants* 106 D2
Langley *Herts* 150 A5
Langley *Kent* 123 G3
Langley *N'umb* 211 E1
Langley *Oxon* 133 F1
Langley *Som* 115 D5
Langley *Warks* 147 D1
Langley *WSuss* 122 B5
Langley Burrell 132 B5
Langley Corner 135 F4
Langley Green
Derbys 173 D4
Langley Green
Warks 147 E1
Langley Green
WSuss 122 B5
Langley Heath 124 A3
Langley Marsh 115 D5
Langley Mill 173 F3
Langley Moor 212 B3
Langley Park 212 B3
Langley Park Bucks
SL3 6DW 135 F4
Langley Street 179 E5
Langney 110 B3
Langold 186 C4
Langore 97 G1
Langport 116 B5
Langrick 176 A3
Langrick Bridge 176 A3
Langridge
B&NESom 117 E1
Langridge *Devon* 113 F3
Langridgeford 113 F3
Langrigg 209 E2
Langrish 120 C5
Langsett 185 G2
Langshaw 227 G2
Langshawburn 227 D5
Langside *Glas* 233 G3
Langside *P&K* 242 C3
Langskaill 276 D3
Langstone *Hants* 107 G2
Langstone
Newport 130 C3
Langthorne 202 B3
Langthorpe 194 C1
Langthwaite 201 F3
Langtoft *ERid* 196 C1
Langtoft *Lincs* 161 G1
Langton *Dur* 202 A1
Langton *Lincs* 189 D5
Langton *Lincs* 176 A1
Langton *NYorks* 195 G5
Langton by Wragby 188 B5
Langton Green *Kent* 123 E5
Langton Green *Suff* 164 C3
Langton Herring 104 C4
Langton Long
Blandford 105 E2
Langton Matravers 105 F5
Langtree 113 E4
Langtree Week 113 E4
Langwathby 210 B4
Langwell 266 B1
Langwell House 275 G6
Langwith 186 C5
Langworth 188 A5
Lanhydrock Corn
PL30 5AD 97 E3
Lanivet 97 E3
Lank 97 E2
Lanlivery 97 F4
Lanner 96 B5
Lanoy 97 G2
Lanreath 97 F4
Lansallos 97 F4
Lansdown 117 E1
Lanteglos 97 E1
Lanteglos Highway 97 F4
Lanton *N'umb* 228 D3
Lanton *ScBord* 228 A4
Lanvean 96 C3
Lapford 102 A2
Laphroaig 230 B5
Lapley 158 A1
Lapworth 159 D5
Larach na Gaibhre 231 F2
Larachbeg 247 F5
Larbert 234 C1
Larbreck 192 A4
Larden Green 170 C2
Larg 215 E3
Largie 260 E1
Largiemore 232 A1
Largoward 244 C4
Largs 232 D3
Largue 268 E6
Largybaan 222 B4
Largybeg 223 F3
Largymore 223 F3
Lark Hall 151 D2

Larkfield 232 D2
Larkhall 234 B4
Larkhill 118 C3
Larklands 173 F3
Larling 164 A3
Larriston 218 D2
Lary 260 B4
Lasborough 132 A3
Lasham 120 B3
Lashbrook 113 E5
Lashenden 124 A4
Lassington 145 G5
Lassintullich 250 C4
Lasswade 236 A3
Lastingham 203 G3
Latchford 184 A5
Latchingdon 138 B2
Latchley 99 E3
Lately Common 184 A3
Lathallan Mill 244 C4
Lathbury 149 D3
Latheron 275 G5
Latheronwheel 275 G5
Lathockar 244 C3
Lathones 244 C4
Lathrisk 244 A4
Latimer 135 F3
Latteridge 131 F4
Lattiford 117 D5
Latton 132 C3
Lauchentyre 215 G5
Lauchintilly 261 F3
Lauder 236 C5
Laugharne
(Lacharn) 127 G1
Laughterton 187 F5
Laughton *ESuss* 110 A2
Laughton *Leics* 160 B4
Laughton *Lincs* 175 F4
Laughton *Lincs* 187 F3
Laughton en le
Morthen 186 C4
Launcells 112 C5
Launcells Cross 112 C5
Launceston 99 D2
Laund Abbey 160 C2
Launton 148 B5
Laurencekirk 253 F2
Laurieston *D&G* 216 A4
Laurieston *Falk* 234 D2
Lavendon 149 E2
Lavenham 152 A3
Laverhay 217 F1
Lavernock 115 E1
Laversdale 210 A1
Laverstock 118 C4
Laverstoke 119 F3
Laverton *Glos* 146 C4
Laverton *NYorks* 202 B5
Laverton *Som* 117 E2
Lavister 170 A2
Law 234 C4
Lawers *P&K* 242 C2
Lawers *P&K* 242 B1
Lawford *Essex* 152 B4
Lawford *Som* 115 E4
Lawhitton 99 D2
Lawkland 193 D1
Lawkland Green 193 D1
Lawley 157 F2
Lawnhead 171 F4
Lawrence Weston 131 E5
Lawrenny 126 D2
Laws 244 C1
Lawshall 151 G2
Lawshall Green 151 G2
Lawton 144 D2
Laxdale (Lacasdal) 271 G4
Laxey 190 C3
Laxfield 165 D4
Laxfirth *Shet* 279 D7
Laxfirth *Shet* 279 D8
Laxford Bridge 272 E4
Laxo 278 D6
Laxton *ERid* 195 G5
Laxton *N'hants* 161 E3
Laxton *Notts* 174 C1
Laycock 193 G3
Layer Breton 138 C1
Layer de la Haye 138 C1
Layer Marney 138 C1
Layham 152 B3
Laymore 103 G2
Layter's Green 135 E3
Laytham 195 G4
Layton 191 G4
Lazenby 213 E5
Lazonby 210 B4
Lea *Derbys* 173 E2
Lea *Here* 145 F5
Lea *Lincs* 187 F4
Lea *Shrop* 156 C4
Lea *Shrop* 156 D2
Lea *Wilts* 132 B4
Lea Bridge 173 F2
Lea Green 145 F1
Lea Marston 159 E3
Lea Town 192 A4
Lea Yeat 200 C4
Leachd 240 C5
Leachkin
(An Leacainn) 266 D7
Leadburn 235 G4
Leadendale 173 E2
Leaden Roding 137 E1
Leadenham 175 E2
Leaderfoot 227 G2
Leadgate *Cumb* 210 D3
Leadgate *Dur* 212 A2
Leadgate *N'umb* 212 A2
Leadhills 225 G4
Leadingcross Green 124 A3
Leafield 133 F1
Leagrave 149 F5
Leake Commonside 176 B2
Leake Hurn's End 176 C3
Lealands 110 A2
Lealholm 203 G2
Lealt *A&B* 239 F5
Lealt *High* 264 B5
Leam 185 G5
Leamington
Hastings 147 G1
Leamington Spa 147 F1
Leamington Spa Art Gallery
& Museum Warks
CV32 4AA 16 B6
Leamside 212 C3

Leamoor Common 156 D4
Leanach *A&B* 240 C5
Leanach *High* 266 E7
Leanaig 266 C6
Leanoch 267 J6
Leargybreck 230 D2
Leasgill 199 F4
Leasingham 175 F3
Leask 261 J1
Leason 128 A3
Leasowe 183 D3
Leat 98 D2
Leatherhead 121 G2
Leathley 194 B3
Leaton *Shrop* 157 D1
Leaton *Tel&W* 157 F1
Leaveland 124 B3
Leavenheath 152 A4
Leavening 195 G1
Leaves Green 122 D2
Leavesden Green 136 A2
Lebberston 205 D4
Lechlade-on-
Thames 133 E3
Leck 200 B5
Leckford 119 E4
Leckfurin 274 C3
Leckgruinart 230 A3
Leckhampstead
Bucks 148 C4
Leckhampstead
WBerks 133 G5
Leckhampstead
Thicket 133 G5
Leckhampton 132 B1
Leckie *High* 265 G5
Leckie *Stir* 242 B5
Leckmelm
(Leac Mailm) 265 H3
Leckroy 257 K5
Leckuary 240 A5
Leckwith 130 A5
Leconfield 196 C3
Ledaig (Leideag) 240 B1
Ledard 241 G4
Ledbeg 272 E7
Ledburn 149 D5
Ledbury 145 G4
Ledcharrie 242 A2
Ledgemoor 144 D2
Ledicot 144 D1
Ledmore *A&B* 247 D5
Ledmore *High* 272 E7
Lednagullin 274 D2
Ledsham *ChesW&C* 183 E5
Ledsham *WYorks* 195 D5
Ledston 194 D5
Ledstone 100 D3
Ledwell 147 F5
Lee *A&B* 238 D2
Lee *Devon* 113 E1
Lee *Hants* 106 C1
Lee *Lancs* 192 B2
Lee *Shrop* 170 B4
Lee Brockhurst 170 C5
Lee Chapel 137 F4
Lee Clump 135 E2
Lee Mill Bridge 100 B2
Lee Moor 100 B1
Lee Valley Park Essex
EN9 1XQ 136 C2
Leebotten 279 D10
Leebotwood 157 D3
Leece 191 F1
Leeds *Kent* 124 A3
Leeds *WYorks* 194 B4
Leeds Art Gallery WYorks
LS1 3AA 40 M3
Leeds Bradford International
Airport 194 B3
Leeds Castle & Gardens
Kent ME17 1PL 124 A3
Leedstown 94 D3
Leegomery 157 F1
Leek 171 G2
Leek Wootton 147 E1
Leekbrook 171 G2
Leeming *NYorks* 202 B4
Leeming *WYorks* 193 G4
Leeming Bar 202 B4
Lee-on-the-Solent 107 E2
Lees *Derbys* 173 D4
Lees *GtMan* 185 D2
Leeswood 169 F2
Leftwich 184 A5
Legars 237 E5
Legbourne 189 D4
Legerwood 236 C5
Legoland Windsor W&M
SL4 4AY 135 E5
Legsby 188 B4
Leicester 160 A2
Leicester Forest
East 160 A2
Leideag 254 B5
Leigh *Dorset* 104 C2
Leigh *Dorset* 105 G3
Leigh *GtMan* 184 A2
Leigh *Kent* 123 E4
Leigh *Shrop* 156 C2
Leigh *Surr* 122 B4
Leigh *Wilts* 132 C3
Leigh *Worcs* 145 G2
Leigh Beck 138 B4
Leigh Common 117 E5
Leigh Delamere 132 A5
Leigh Green 124 B5
Leigh Park 107 G2
Leigh Sinton 145 G2
Leigh upon
Mendip 117 D3
Leigh Woods 131 E5
Leigham 100 B2
Leighland Chapel 114 D4
Leigh-on-Sea 138 B4
Leighterton 132 A3
Leighton *NYorks* 202 A5
Leighton (Tre'r Llai)
Powys 156 B2
Leighton *Shrop* 157 F2
Leighton *Som* 117 E3
Leighton
Bromswold 161 G5
Leighton Buzzard 149 E5
Leinthall Earls 144 D1
Leinthall Starkes 144 D1
Leintwardine 156 D5
Leire 160 A4

Leirinmore 273 G2
Leiston 153 F1
Leitfie 252 A5
Leith 235 G2
Leitholm 237 E5
Lelant 94 C3
Lelley 197 E4
Lemington 212 A1
Lemnas 269 G4
Lempitlaw 228 B3
Lemreway 271 G6
Lemsford 136 B1
Lenchwick 146 C3
Lendalfoot 214 C1
Lendrick Lodge 242 A4
Lenham 124 A3
Lenham Heath 124 B4
Lenie 258 C2
Lennel 237 F5
Lennox Plunton 216 A5
Lennoxtown 234 A2
Lent Rise 135 E4
Lenton *Lincs* 175 F4
Lenton *Nott* 173 G4
Lenton Abbey 173 G4
Lenwade 178 B4
Lenzie 234 A2
Leoch 244 B1
Leochel-Cushnie 260 D3
Leominster 145 D2
Leonard Stanley 132 A2
Leorin 230 B5
Lepe 106 D3
Lephin 263 G7
Lephinchapel 240 B5
Lephinmore 240 B5
Leppington 195 G1
Lepton 185 G1
Lerags 240 A2
Lerryn 97 F4
Lerwick 279 D8
Lesbury 229 G5
Leschangie 261 F3
Leslie *Aber* 260 D2
Leslie *Fife* 244 A4
Lesmahagow 225 G2
Lesnewth 98 B1
Lessendrum 268 D6
Lessingham 179 E3
Lessness Heath 137 D5
Lessonhall 209 F1
Leswalt 214 B4
Letchmore Heath 136 A3
Letchworth Garden
City 150 A4
Letcombe Bassett 133 F4
Letcombe Regis 133 F4
Leth Meadhanach 254 C3
Letham *Angus* 252 D5
Letham *Falk* 234 C1
Letham *Fife* 244 B3
Lethanhill 224 C4
Lethenty 269 G6
Letheringham 153 D2
Letheringsett 178 B2
Lettaford 102 A4
Letter Finlay 257 J5
Letterewe 265 F4
Letterfearn
(Leitir Fheàrna) 256 E2
Lettermorar 247 G1
Lettermore *A&B* 247 D5
Lettermore *High* 273 J4
Letters 265 H3
Lettershaws 225 G3
Letterston 140 C5
Lettoch *High* 259 H3
Lettoch *High* 259 J1
Letton *Here* 156 C5
Letton *Here* 144 C3
Letty Green 136 B1
Letwell 186 C4
Leuchars 244 C2
Leumrabhagh 271 F6
Leurbost (Liurbost) 271 F5
Leusdon 102 A5
Levalsa Meor 97 E5
Level's Green 150 C5
Leven *ERid* 196 D3
Leven *Fife* 244 B4
Levencorroch 223 F3
Levenhall 236 A2
Levens 199 F4
Levens Green 150 B5
Levenshulme 184 C3
Levenwick 279 D10
Leverburgh
(An T-Òb) 263 F3
Leverington 162 C1
Leverstock Green 135 F2
Leverton 176 B3
Leverton Lucasgate 176 C3
Leverton Outgate 176 C3
Levington 152 D4
Levisham 204 B3
Levishie 258 B3
Lew 133 F2
Lewannick 97 G1
Lewcombe 104 C2
Lewdown 99 E2
Lewes 109 G3
Leweston 140 C5
Lewisham 136 C5
Lewiston
(Blàr na Maigh) 258 C2
Lewistown 129 F3
Lewknor 134 C3
Leworthy 113 G2
Lewson Street 124 B2
Lewth 192 A4
Lewtrenchard 99 E2
Ley *Aber* 260 D3
Ley *Corn* 97 F3
Ley Green 149 G5
Leybourne 123 F3
Leyburn 202 A3
Leyland 192 B5
Leylodge 261 F3
Leymoor 185 F1
Leys *Aber* 269 J5
Leys *Aber* 260 D3
Leys *P&K* 244 A1
Leys of Cossans 252 B5
Leysdown-on-Sea 124 C1
Leysmill 253 E5
Leysters 145 E1
Leyton 136 C4
Leytonstone 136 C4

Lezant 98 D3
Lezerea 95 D3
Lhanbryde 267 K5
Liatrie 257 J7
Libanus 143 F5
Libberton 235 D5
Liberton 235 G3
Liceasto 263 G2
Lichfield 158 D2
Lichfield Cathedral Staffs
WS13 7LD 158 D2
Lickey 158 B5
Lickey End 158 B5
Lickey Hills Country Park
Worcs B45 8ER 14 C6
Lickfold 121 E5
Liddaton Green 99 E2
Liddel 277 D9
Liddesdale 247 G4
Liddington 133 E4
Lidgate *Derbys* 186 A5
Lidgate *Suff* 151 F2
Lidgett 174 B1
Lidlington 149 E4
Lidsey 108 A3
Lidsing 123 G2
Lidstone 147 F5
Lienassie 257 F2
Lieurary 275 F2
Liff 244 B1
Lifton 99 D2
Liftondown 99 D2
Lightcliffe 194 A5
Lighthorne 147 F2
Lighthorne Heath 147 F2
Lighthouse, The, Glasgow
Glas G1 3NU 39 F4
Lighthouse, The - Poole's
Centre for the Arts
Poole BH15 1UG 3 B4
Lightwater 121 E1
Lightwater Valley Park
NYorks
HG4 3HT 202 B5
Lightwood 171 G3
Lightwood Green
ChesE 170 D3
Lightwood Green
Wrex 170 A3
Lilbourne 160 A5
Lilburn Tower 229 E4
Lillesdon 116 A5
Lilleshall 157 G1
Lilley *Herts* 149 G5
Lilley *WBerks* 133 G5
Lilliesleaf 227 G3
Lilling Green 195 F1
Lillingstone Dayrell 148 C4
Lillingstone Lovell 148 C3
Lillington *Dorset* 104 C1
Lillington *Warks* 147 F1
Lilliput 105 G4
Lilly 133 F7
Lilstock 115 E3
Lilyhurst 157 G1
Limbury 149 G5
Lime Side 184 D2
Limefield 184 C1
Limehillock 268 D5
Limehurst 184 D2
Limekilnburn 234 B4
Limekilns 235 E1
Limerigg 234 C2
Limerstone 106 D4
Limington 116 C5
Limpenhoe 179 E5
Limpley Stoke 117 E1
Limpsfield 122 D3
Limpsfield Chart 122 D3
Linaclate
(Lionacleit) 262 C7
Linacre Reservoirs Derbys
S42 7JW 186 A5
Linbriggs 220 A1
Linby 173 G2
Linchmere 121 D4
Lincluden 217 D3
Lincoln 187 F5
Lincoln Castle Lincs
LN1 3AA 77 Lincoln
Lincoln Cathedral Lincs
LN2 1PL 77 Lincoln
Lincomb 146 A1
Lincombe *Devon* 100 D3
Lincombe *Devon* 100 D3
Lindal in Furness 199 D5
Lindale 199 F4
Lindean 227 F2
Lindertis 252 B4
Lindfield 109 F1
Lindford 120 D3
Lindifferon 244 B3
Lindisfarne
(Holy Island) 229 F2
Lindley 194 B3
Lindores 244 A3
Lindow End 184 C5
Lindridge 145 F1
Lindsaig 232 A2
Lindsell 151 E5
Lindsey 152 A3
Lindsey Tye 152 A3
Linfitts 185 D2
Linford *Hants* 106 A2
Linford *Thur* 137 F5
Linford Wood 148 D3
Lingague 190 A4
Lingards Wood 185 E1
Lingdale 203 F1
Lingen 144 C1
Lingfield 122 C4
Lingley Green 183 G4
Lingwood 179 E5
Linhead 268 E5
Linhope 227 F5
Linicro 263 J5
Linkend 146 A4
Linkenholt 119 E2
Linkhill 110 D1
Linkinhorne 98 D3
Linklater 277 D9
Linksness *Ork* 277 B7
Linksness *Ork* 277 E6
Linktown 244 A5
Linley *Shrop* 156 C3
Linley *Shrop* 157 F3
Linley Green 145 F2

Linlithgow 235 E2
Linlithgow Bridge 235 D2
Linn of Muick
Cottage 252 B1
Linnels 211 F1
Linney 126 B3
Linshiels 220 A1
Linsiadar 270 E4
Linslade 149 E5
Linstead Parva 165 E4
Linstock 210 A2
Linthwaite 185 F1
Lintlaw 237 F4
Lintmill 268 D4
Linton *Cambs* 151 D3
Linton *Derbys* 159 E1
Linton *Here* 145 F5
Linton *Kent* 123 G3
Linton *NYorks* 193 F1
Linton *ScBord* 228 B4
Linton *WYorks* 194 C3
Linton-on-Ouse 195 D1
Lintzford 212 A2
Linwood *Hants* 106 A2
Linwood *Lincs* 188 B4
Linwood *Renf* 233 F3
Lionel (Lional) 271 H1
Liphook 120 D4
Liscard 183 E3
Liscombe 114 B4
Liskeard 97 G3
L'Islet 97 F4
Lismore 240 A1
Liss 120 D5
Liss Forest 120 C5
Lissett 196 D2
Lissington 188 B4
Liston 151 G3
Lisvane 130 A4
Liswerry 130 C4
Litcham 163 G1
Litchborough 148 B2
Litchfield 119 F2
Litherland 183 E3
Litlington *Cambs* 150 B3
Litlington *ESuss* 110 A3
Little Abington 150 D3
Little Addington 161 E5
Little Alne 146 D1
Little Altcar 183 E2
Little Amwell 136 C1
Little Ann 119 E3
Little Asby 200 B2
Little Aston 158 C3
Little Atherfield 107 D5
Little Ayton 203 E1
Little Baddow 137 G2
Little Badminton 132 A4
Little Ballinluig 251 E4
Little Bampton 209 F1
Little Bardfield 151 E4
Little Barford 149 G2
Little Barningham 178 C2
Little Barrington 133 E1
Little Barrow 170 B1
Little Barugh 203 G5
Little Bavington 220 B4
Little Bealings 152 D3
Little Bedwyn 119 D1
Little Beeby 160 B2
Little Bentley 152 C5
Little Berkhamsted 136 B2
Little Billing 148 D1
Little Birch 145 E4
Little Bispham 191 G3
Little Blakenham 152 C3
Little Bloxwich 158 C2
Little Bollington 184 B4
Little Bookham 121 G2
Little Bourton 147 G3
Little Bowden 160 C4
Little Bradley 151 E2
Little Brampton 156 C4
Little Braxted 138 B1
Little Brechin 253 D3
Little Brickhill 149 E4
Little Bridgeford 171 F5
Little Brington 148 B1
Little Bromley 152 B5
Little Broughton 209 D3
Little Budworth 170 C1
Little Burdon 202 C1
Little Burstead 137 F3
Little Burton 196 D3
Little Bytham 161 F1
Little Canford 105 G3
Little Carlton *Lincs* 189 D4
Little Carlton *Notts* 174 C2
Little Casterton 161 F1
Little Catwick 196 D3
Little Catworth 161 F5
Little Cawthorpe 189 D4
Little Chalfield 117 F1
Little Chalfont 135 E3
Little Chart 124 B4
Little Chesterford 150 D3
Little Chesterton 148 A5
Little Cheverell 118 A2
Little Clacton 139 E1
Little Clanfield 133 E2
Little Clifton 209 D4
Little Coates 188 C3
Little Comberton 146 B3
Little Common 110 C3
Little Compton 147 E4
Little Corby 210 A2
Little Cornard 151 G4
Little Cowarne 145 F2
Little Coxwell 133 E3
Little Crakehall 202 B3
Little Cransley 160 D5
Little Crawley 149 E3
Little Creich 266 D3
Little Cressingham 163 G3
Little Crosby 183 E2
Little Crosthwaite 209 F4
Little Cubley 172 C4
Little Dalby 160 C1
Little Dens 269 J6
Little Dewchurch 145 E4
Little Ditton 151 E2
Little Doward 131 E1
Little Down 119 E2
Little Downham 162 D4

Little Drayton **171** D4
Little Driffield **196** C2
Little Dunham **163** G1
Little Dunkeld **251** F5
Little Dunmow **151** E5
Little Durnford **118** C4
Little Easton **151** E5
Little Eaton **173** E3
Little Eccleston **192** A4
Little Ellingham **164** B2
Little End **137** E2
Little Everdon **148** A2
Little Eversden **150** B2
Little Faringdon **133** E2
Little Fencote **202** B3
Little Fenton **195** E4
Little Finborough **152** B2
Little Fransham **178** A4
Little Gaddesden **135** E1
Little Garway **144** D5
Little Gidding **161** G4
Little Glemham **153** E2
Little Glenshee **243** E1
Little Gorsley **145** F5
Little Gransden **150** A2
Little Green *Cambs* **150** A3
Little Green *Notts* **174** C3
Little Green *Suff* **164** B4
Little Green *Suff* **164** B4
Little Green *Wrex* **170** B3
Little Grimsby **188** D3
Little Gringley **187** E4
Little Gruinard **265** F3
Little Habton **203** G5
Little Hadham **136** D1
Little Hale **175** G3
Little Hallingbury **137** D1
Little Hampden **135** D2
Little Haresfield **132** A2
Little Harrowden **161** D5
Little Haseley **134** B2
Little Hatfield **197** D3
Little Hautbois **179** D3
Little Haven
    Pembs **126** B1
Little Haven *WSuss* **121** G4
Little Hay **158** D2
Little Hayfield **185** E4
Little Haywood **172** B5
Little Heath **159** F4
Little Hereford **145** E1
Little Hockham **164** A2
Little Horkesley **152** A4
Little Hormead **150** C5
Little Horsted **109** G2
Little Horton **118** B1
Little Horwood **148** C4
Little Houghton **148** D2
Little Hucklow **185** F5
Little Hulton **184** B4
Little Hungerford **134** A5
Little Hutton **203** D5
Little Irchester **149** E1
Little Keyford **117** F3
Little Kimble **134** D2
Little Kineton **147** F2
Little Kingshill **135** D3
Little Langdale **199** E2
Little Langford **118** B4
Little Laver **137** E2
Little Lawford **159** G5
Little Leigh **184** A5
Little Leighs **137** G1
Little Lever **184** B2
Little Ley **260** E3
Little Linford **148** D3
Little Linton **151** D3
Little London
    Bucks **134** B1
Little London
    Essex **150** C5
Little London
    ESuss **110** A2
Little London
    Hants **119** E3
Little London
    Hants **120** B2
Little London *IoM* **190** B3
Little London *Lincs* **176** C5
Little London *Lincs* **188** D5
Little London *Lincs* **188** B4
Little London *Norf* **177** D5
Little London *Norf* **163** F3
Little London *Oxon* **134** A2
Little London
    Powys **155** G4
Little London *Suff* **152** B2
Little London
    WYorks **194** B4
Little Longstone **185** F5
Little Lyth **157** D2
Little Malvern **145** G3
Little Maplestead **151** G4
Little Marcle **145** F4
Little Marland **113** F4
Little Marlow **135** D4
Little Marsden **193** E4
Little Massingham **177** F5
Little Melton **178** C4
Little Milford **126** C1
Little Mill **130** C2
Little Milton **134** B2
Little Missenden **135** E3
Little Musgrave **200** C1
Little Ness **156** D1
Little Neston **183** D5
Little Newcastle **140** C5
Little Newsham **202** A1
Little Oakley *Essex* **152** D5
Little Oakley
    N'hants **161** D4
Little Offley **149** G5
Little Onn **158** A1
Little Orton *Cumb* **209** G1
Little Orton *Leics* **159** F2
Little Ouse **163** D4
Little Ouseburn **194** D1
Little Overton **170** A3
Little Packington **159** E4
Little Parndon **136** D1
Little Paxton **149** G1
Little Petherick **96** D2
Little Plumpton **191** G4
Little Plumstead **179** E4
Little Ponton **175** E4
Little Posbrook **107** E2

Little Potheridge **113** F4
Little Preston **148** A2
Little Raveley **162** A4
Little Ribston **194** C2
Little Rissington **133** D1
Little Rogart **266** E1
Little Rollright **147** E4
Little Ryburgh **178** A3
Little Ryle **229** E5
Little Ryton **157** D2
Little Salkeld **210** B4
Little Sampford **151** E5
Little Saxham **151** G1
Little Scatwell **265** K6
Little Shelford **150** C2
Little Shrawardine **156** C1
Little Silver **102** C3
Little Singleton **191** G4
Little Smeaton
    NYorks **186** C1
Little Smeaton
    NYorks **202** C2
Little Snoring **178** A2
Little Sodbury **131** G4
Little Sodbury End **131** G4
Little Somborne **119** E4
Little Somerford **132** B4
Little Soudley **171** E5
Little Stainforth **193** E1
Little Stainton **202** C1
Little Stanney **183** F5
Little Staughton **149** G1
Little Steeping **176** C1
Little Stoke **171** G4
Little Stonham **152** C2
Little Street **162** D4
Little Stretton *Leics* **160** B2
Little Stretton
    Shrop **156** D3
Little Strickland **199** G1
Little Stukeley **162** A5
Little Sugnall **171** F4
Little Sutton **183** E5
Little Swinburne **220** B4
Little Tarrington **145** F3
Little Tew **147** F5
Little Tey **151** G5
Little Thetford **162** D5
Little Thornage **178** B2
Little Thornton **191** G3
Little Thorpe **212** D3
Little Thurlow **151** E2
Little Thurlow
    Green **151** E2
Little Thurrock **137** F5
Little Torboll **266** E2
Little Torrington **113** E4
Little Tosson **220** C1
Little Totham **138** B1
Little Town *Cumb* **209** F5
Little Town *Lancs* **192** C4
Little Town *Warr* **184** A3
Little Twycross **159** F2
Little Urswick **199** D5
Little Wakering **138** C4
Little Walden **150** D3
Little Waldingfield **152** A3
Little Walsingham **178** A2
Little Waltham **137** G1
Little Warley **137** F3
Little Washbourne **146** B4
Little Weighton **196** B4
Little Welland **146** A4
Little Welnetham **151** G1
Little Wenham **152** B4
Little Wenlock **157** F2
Little Whittington **211** F1
Little Wilbraham **150** D2
Little Wishford **118** B4
Little Witcombe **132** B1
Little Witley **145** G1
Little Wittenham **134** A4
Little Wittingham
    Green **165** D4
Little Wolford **147** E4
Little Woodcote **122** B4
Little Wratting **151** E3
Little Wymington **149** E1
Little Wymondley **150** A5
Little Wyrley **158** C2
Little Wytheford **157** E1
Little Yeldham **151** F4
Littlebeck **204** B2
Littleborough
    Devon **102** B1
Littleborough
    GtMan **184** D1
Littleborough
    Notts **187** F4
Littlebourne **125** E3
Littlebredy **104** B4
Littlebury **150** D4
Littlebury Green **150** C4
Littledean **131** F1
Littleferry **267** F2
Littleham *Devon* **113** E3
Littleham *Devon* **102** D4
Littlehampton **108** C3
Littlehempston **101** E1
Littlehoughton **229** G5
Littlemill *EAyr* **224** C4
Littlemill *High* **267** G6
Littlemoor *Derbys* **173** E1
Littlemoor *Dorset* **104** C4
Littlemore **134** A2
Littlemoss **184** D3
Littleover **173** E4
Littleport **163** D4
Littlestone-on-Sea **111** F1
Littlethorpe **194** C1
Littleton *ChesW&C* **170** B1
Littleton *Hants* **119** F4
Littleton *P&K* **244** A1
Littleton *Som* **116** B4
Littleton *Surr* **121** F1
Littleton Drew **132** A4
Littleton Panell **118** B2
Littletown *Dur* **212** C3
Littletown *IoW* **107** E3
Littlewick Green **134** D5
Littleworth *Glos* **146** D4
Littleworth *Oxon* **133** F3
Littleworth *Staffs* **158** C1
Littleworth *SYorks* **186** D3

Littleworth *Worcs* **146** A3
Littley Green **137** F1
Litton *Derbys* **185** F5
Litton *NYorks* **201** E5
Litton *Som* **116** C2
Litton Cheney **104** B3
Liverpool **183** E3
Liverpool Cathedral
    Mersey L1 7AZ **42** E6
Liverpool John Lennon
    Airport **183** F4
Liverpool Metropolitan
    Cathedral (RC) *Mersey*
    L3 5TQ **43** E4
Liversedge **194** B5
Liverton *Devon* **102** B5
Liverton *R&C* **203** G1
Liverton Street **124** A4
Living Coasts, Torquay
    Torbay TQ1 2BG **101** F1
Livingston **235** E3
Livingston Village **235** E3
Lixwm **182** C5
Lizard **95** E5
Llaingarreglwyd **142** A2
Llaingoch **180** A4
Llaithddu **155** G4
Llampha **129** F5
Llan **155** E2
Llanaber **154** C1
Llanaelhaearn **166** C3
Llanaeron **142** A1
Llanafan **154** C5
Llanafan-fawr **143** E1
Llanafan-fechan **143** F2
Llanallgo **180** C4
Llanarmon **166** D4
Llanarmon-yn-Ial **169** E2
Llanarmon Dyffryn
    Ceiriog **169** E4
Llanarth *Cere* **142** A2
Llanarth *Mon* **130** C1
Llanarthney **142** B5
Llanasa **182** C4
Llanbabo **180** B4
Llanbadarn Fawr **154** B4
Llanbadarn Fynydd **155** G5
Llanbadarn-y-
    garreg **144** A3
Llanbadoc **130** C2
Llanbadrig **180** B3
Llanbeder **130** C3
Llanbedr *Gwyn* **167** E5
Llanbedr *Powys* **144** B5
Llanbedr *Powys* **144** A3
Llanbedr-Dyffryn-
    Clwyd **169** E2
Llanbedrgoch **180** D4
Llanbedrog **166** C4
Llanbedr-y-cennin **168** A1
Llanberis **167** E2
Llanbethery **114** D1
Llanbister **156** A5
Llanblethian **129** F5
Llanboidy **141** F5
Llanbradach **130** A3
Llanbryn-mair **155** E2
Llancadle **114** D1
Llancarfan **129** G5
Llancayo **130** C2
Llancynfelyn **154** C3
Llandafal **130** A2
Llandaff **130** A5
Llandaff North **130** A5
Llandanwg **107** E5
Llandawke **127** F1
Llanddaniel Fab **180** C5
Llanddarog **128** A1
Llanddeiniol **154** B5
Llanddeiniolen **167** E1
Llandderfel **168** C4
Llanddeusant
    Carmar **143** D5
Llanddeusant *IoA* **180** B4
Llanddew **143** G4
Llanddewi **128** A4
Llanddewi
    Rhydderch **130** C1
Llanddewi
    Skirrid **130** C1
Llanddewi Velfrey **127** E1
Llanddewi
    Ystradenni **144** A1
Llanddoged **168** B1
Llanddona **181** D5
Llanddowror **127** F1
Llanddulas **182** A5
Llanddwywe **167** E5
Llanddyfnan **180** C5
Llandefaelog Fach **143** G4
Llandefaelog-
    tre'r-graig **144** A5
Llandefalle **144** A4
Llandegfan **181** D5
Llandegla **169** E2
Llandegley **144** A1
Llandegveth **130** C3
Llandegwning **166** B4
Llandeilo **142** C5
Llandeilo
    Abercywyn **127** G1
Llandeilo Graban **143** G3
Llandeilo'r-Fan **143** E4
Llandeloy **140** B5
Llandenny **130** D2
Llandevaud **130** D4
Llandevenny **130** D4
Llandinabo **145** E5
Llandinam **155** G4
Llandissilio **141** E5
Llandogo **131** E2
Llandough *VGlam* **130** A5
Llandough *VGlam* **129** F5
Llandovery
    (Llanymddyfri) **143** D4
Llandow **129** F5
Llandre *Carmar* **142** C3
Llandre *Carmar* **141** E5
Llandre *Cere* **154** C4
Llandrillo **168** D4
Llandrindod Wells **143** G1
Llandrinio **156** B1
Llandudno **181** F4
Llandudno Junction **181** F5

Llandwrog **167** D2
Llandybie **128** C1
Llandyfaelog **128** A1
Llandyfan **128** C1
Llandyfriog **141** G3
Llandyfrydog **180** C4
Llandygai **181** D5
Llandygwydd **141** F3
Llandyrnog **169** E1
Llandyry **128** A2
Llandysilio **156** B1
Llandyssil **156** A2
Llandysul **142** A3
Llanedeyrn **130** B4
Llanedy **128** B2
Llaneglwys **143** G4
Llanegryn **154** C2
Llanegwad **128** B1
Llaneilian **180** C3
Llanelian-yn-Rhos **181** G5
Llanelidan **169** E2
Llanelieu **144** A4
Llanellen **130** C1
Llanelli **128** B2
Llanelli Millennium Coastal
    Park *Carmar*
    SA15 2LF **128** A3
Llanelltyd **154** D1
Llanelly **130** B1
Llanelly Hill **130** B1
Llanelwedd **143** G2
Llanenddwyn **167** E5
Llanengan **166** B5
Llanerfyl **155** G2
Llaneuddog **180** C4
Llanfachraeth **180** B4
Llanfachreth **168** A5
Llanfaelog **180** B5
Llanfaelrhys **166** B5
Llanfaenor **130** C1
Llan-faes *IoA* **181** E5
Llanfaes *Powys* **143** G5
Llanfaethlu **180** B4
Llanfaglan **167** D1
Llanfair **167** E5
Llanfair Caereinion **156** A2
Llanfair Clydogau **142** C2
Llanfair Dyffryn
    Clwyd **169** E2
Llanfair Talhaiarn **182** A5
Llanfair Waterdine **156** B5
Llanfairfechan **181** E5
Llanfair-Nant-Gwyn **141** E4
Llanfair-Orllwyn **141** G3
Llanfairpwllgwyngyll
    180 D5
Llanfairynghornwy **180** B3
Llanfair-yn-neubwll **180** B5
Llanfallteg **127** E1
Llanfaredd **143** G2
Llanfarian **154** B5
Llanfechain **156** A1
Llanfechell **180** B3
Llanfendigaid **154** B2
Llanferres **169** E1
Llanfflewyn **180** B4
Llanfigael **180** B4
Llanfihangel Glyn
    Myfur **168** C3
Llanfihangel Nant
    Bran **143** F4
Llanfihangel
    Rhydithon **144** A1
Llanfihangel Rogiet **130** D4
Llanfihangel
    Tal-y-llyn **144** A5
Llanfihangel-
    ar-arth **142** A3
Llanfihangel-nant-
    Melan **144** A1
Llanfihangel-uwch-
    Gwili **142** A5
Llanfihangel-y-
    Creuddyn **154** C5
Llanfihangel-yng-
    Ngwynfa **155** G1
Llanfihangel-yn-
    Nhywyn **180** B5
Llanfihangel-y-pennant
    Gwyn **167** E3
Llanfihangel-y-pennant
    Gwyn **154** C2
Llanfilo **144** A4
Llanfoist **130** B1
Llanfor **168** C4
Llanfrechfa **130** C3
Llanfrothen **167** F3
Llanfrynach **130** A5
Llanfwrog *Denb* **169** E2
Llanfwrog *IoA* **180** B4
Llanfyllin **156** A1
Llanfynydd *Carmar* **142** B5
Llanfynydd *Flints* **169** F2
Llanfyrnach **141** F4
Llangadfan **155** G1
Llangadog **142** D5
Llangadwaladr *IoA* **166** C1
Llangadwaladr
    Powys **169** E4
Llangaffo **166** D1
Llangain **127** G1
Llangammarch
    Wells **143** F3
Llangan **129** F5
Llangarron **145** E5
Llangasty-Talyllyn **144** A5
Llangathen **142** B5
Llangattock **130** B1
Llangattock
    Lingoed **130** C1
Llangattock-Vibon-
    Avel **131** D1
Llangedwyn **169** E5
Llangefni **180** C5
Llangeinor **129** F4
Llangeitho **142** C2
Llangeler **141** G4
Llangelynin **154** B2
Llangendeirne **128** A2
Llangennech **128** B2
Llangennith **128** A3
Llangenny **130** B1
Llangernyw **168** B1
Llangian **166** B5
Llangiwg **128** D2
Llangloffan **140** C4
Llanglydwen **141** E5
Llangoed **181** E5

Llangoedmor **141** E3
Llangollen **169** E3
Llangollen Railway *Denb*
    LL20 8SN **169** F3
Llangolman **141** E5
Llangorse **144** A5
Llangorwen **154** C4
Llangovan **131** D2
Llangower **168** C4
Llangrannog **141** G2
Llangristiolus **180** C5
Llangrove **131** E1
Llangua **144** C5
Llangunllo **156** B5
Llangunnor **142** A5
Llangurig **155** F5
Llangwm *Conwy* **168** C3
Llangwm *Mon* **130** D2
Llangwm *Pembs* **126** C2
Llangwnnadl **166** B4
    Bridge **140** C4
Llangwyfan **169** E1
Llangwyllog **180** C5
Llangwyryfon **154** C5
Llangybi *Cere* **142** C2
Llangybi *Gwyn* **166** D3
Llangybi *Mon* **130** C3
Llangyfelach **128** C3
Llangynhafal **169** E1
Llangynidr **130** A1
Llangyniew **156** A2
Llangynin **127** F1
Llangynllo **141** G3
Llangynog *Carmar* **127** G2
Llangynog *Powys* **169** D5
Llangynwyd **129** E4
Llanhamlach **143** G5
Llanharan **129** G4
Llanharry **129** G4
Llanhennock **130** C3
Llanhilleth **130** B2
Llanidloes **155** F4
Llaniestyn **166** B4
Llanigon **144** B4
Llanilar **154** C5
Llanilid **129** F4
Llanishen *Cardiff* **130** A4
Llanishen *Mon* **131** D2
Llanllawddog **142** A5
Llanllechid **167** F1
Llanlleonfel **143** F2
Llanllugan **155** G2
Llanllwch **127** G1
Llanllwchaiarn **156** A3
Llanllwni **142** A3
Llanllyfni **167** D2
Llanllywel **130** C3
Llanmadoc **128** A3
Llanmaes **114** C1
Llanmartin **130** C4
Llanmerewig **156** A3
Llanmihangel **129** F5
Llan-mill **127** E1
Llanmiloe **127** F2
Llanmorlais **128** B3
Llannefydd **182** A5
Llannerch-y-medd **180** C4
Llannerch-y-Môr **182** C5
Llannon *Carmar* **128** B2
Llan-non *Cere* **142** B1
Llannor **166** C4
Llanover **130** C2
Llanpumsaint **142** A5
Llanreithan **140** B5
Llanrhaeadr **169** D1
Llanrhaeadr-ym-
    Mochnant **169** E5
Llanrhian **140** B4
Llanrhidian **128** A3
Llanrhyddlad **180** B4
Llanrhystud **142** B1
Llanrothal **131** D1
Llanrug **167** E1
Llanrumney **130** B4
Llanrwst **168** A1
Llansadurnen **127** F1
Llansadwrn *Carmar* **142** C4
Llansadwrn *IoA* **181** D5
Llansaint **127** G2
Llansamlet **128** C3
Llansanffraid **142** B1
Llansanffraid Glan
    Conwy **181** G5
Llansannan **168** C1
Llansannor **129** F5
Llansantffraed **144** A5
Llansantffraed-
    Cwmdeuddwr **143** F1
Llansantffraed-in-
    Elwel **143** G2
Llansantffraid-ym-
    Mechain **169** F5
Llansawel **142** C4
Llansilin **169** F5
Llansoy **130** D2
Llanspyddid **143** G5
Llanstadwell **126** C2
Llansteffan **127** G1
Llanstephan **144** A3
Llantarnam **130** C3
Llanteg **127** E1
Llanthony **144** B5
Llantilio Crossenny **130** C1
Llantilio Pertholey **130** C1
Llantood **141** E3
Llantrisant *IoA* **180** B4
Llantrisant *Mon* **130** C3
Llantrisant *RCT* **129** G4
Llantrithyd **129** G5
Llantwit Fardre **129** G4
Llantwit Major **114** C1
Llantysilio **169** E3
Llanuwchllyn **168** B5
Llanvaches **130** D3
Llanvair-Discoed **130** D3
Llanvapley **130** C1
Llanvetherine **130** C1
Llanveynoe **144** C4
Llanvihangel Crucorney
    (Llanfihangel Crucornau)
    144 C5
Llanvihangel
    Gobion **130** C2
Llanvihangel-Ystern-
    Llewern **130** D1
Llanvihangel **129** D1
Llanwarne **145** E5
Llanwddyn **155** G1

Llanwenog **142** A3
Llanwern **130** C4
Llanwinio **141** F5
Llanwnda *Gwyn* **167** D2
Llanwnda *Pembs* **140** C4
Llanwnnen **142** B3
Llanwnog **155** G3
Llanwonno **129** G3
Llanwrda **142** D4
Llanwrin **155** D2
Llanwrthwl **143** F1
Llanwrtyd **143** E3
Llanwrtyd Wells **143** E3
Llanwyddelan **155** G2
Llanyblodwel **169** F5
Llanybri **127** G1
Llanybydder **142** B3
Llanycefn **141** E5
Llanychaer
    Bridge **140** C4
Llanycil **168** C4
Llanycrwys **142** C3
Llanymawddwy **155** E1
Llanymynech **169** F5
Llanynghenedl **180** B4
Llanynys **169** E1
Llan-y-pwll **170** A2
Llanyre **143** G1
Llanystumdwy **167** D4
Llanywern **144** A5
Llawhaden **127** D1
Llawndy **182** C4
Llawnt **169** F4
Llawr-y-dref **166** B5
Llawryglyn **155** F3
Llay **170** A2
Llechcynfarwy **180** B4
Llecheiddior **167** D3
Llechfaen **143** G5
Llechryd *Caerp* **130** A2
Llechryd *Cere* **141** F3
Llechrydau **169** F4
Llechwedd Slate Caverns
    Gwyn LL41 3NB **168** A3
Lledrod *Cere* **154** C5
Lledrod *Powys* **169** F5
Llethryd **128** B3
Llidiad-Nenog **142** B4
Llidiardau **168** B4
Llithfaen **166** C3
Lloc **182** C5
Llong **169** F1
Llowes **144** A3
Lloyney **156** B5
Llundain-fach **142** B2
Llwydcoed **129** F3
Llwydiarth **155** G1
Llwyn **156** B4
Llwyncelyn **142** A2
Llwyn-croes **142** A5
Llwyndafydd **141** G2
Llwynderw **156** B2
Llwyndyrys **166** C3
Llwyneinion **169** F3
Llwyngwril **154** B2
Llwynhendy **128** B3
Llwyn-Madoc **143** F2
Llwynmawr **169** F4
Llwyn-onn *Cere* **142** A2
Llwyn-onn *MTyd* **129** G1
Llwyn-y-brain
    Carmar **127** E1
Llwyn-y-brain
    Carmar **143** D1
Llwyn-y-groes **142** B2
Llwynypia **129** F3
Llyn Brenig *Conwy*
    LL21 9TT **168** C2
Llyn Llech Owain Country
    Park *Carmar*
    SA14 7NF **128** B1
Llynclys **169** F5
Llynfaes **180** C5
Llysfaen **181** G5
Llyswen **144** A4
Llysworney **129** F5
Llys-y-frân **140** D5
Llywel **143** E4
Load Brook **185** G4
Loandhu **267** F4
Loanhead *Aber* **261** H1
Loanhead *Midlo* **235** G3
Loans **224** B2
Lobb **113** E2
Lobhillcross **99** E2
Loch a Charnain **262** D7
Loch an Eilein Visitor Centre
    & Forest Trail *High*
    PH22 1QT **259** F4
Loch Choire Lodge **273** J5
Loch Eil Outward
    Bound **248** C2
Loch Head *D&G* **206** D2
Loch Head *D&G* **215** F1
Loch Lomond Shores &
    Gateway Centre *WDun*
    G83 8QL **233** E1
Loch Ness Exhibition Centre
    High IV63 6TU **258** C2
Loch Sgioport **254** D1
Loch a' Charnain **262** D7
Lochailort (Ceann Loch
    Ailleart) **247** G1
Lochaline
    (Loch Àlainn) **247** F5
Lochans **214** B5
Locharbriggs **217** D2
Lochawe
    (Loch Obha) **240** D2
Lochboisdale (Loch
    Baghasdail) **254** C3
Lochbuie **239** F2
Lochcarron
    (Loch Carrann) **264** E7
Lochdhu Hotel **275** F4
Lochdon **239** G1
Lochdrum **265** J4
Lochearnhead (Ceann Loch
    Èireann) **242** A2
Lochee **244** B4
Lochend *High* **275** I12
Lochend (Ceann Loch)
    High **258** C1

Lochgilphead (Ceann Loch
    Gilb) **231** G1
Lochgoilhead **241** E4
Lochgoyn **233** G3
Lochhill *EAyr* **225** D4
Lochhill *Moray* **267** K5
Lochinch Castle **214** C4
Lochinver
    (Loch an Inbhir) **272** C6
Lochlair **252** D5
Lochlane **242** D2
Lochlea **224** C2
Lochluichart **265** K5
Lochmaben **217** E2
Lochmaddy (Loch na
    Madadh) **262** E5
Lochore **243** G5
Lochore Meadows Country
    Park *Fife*
    KY5 8BA **243** G5
Lochportain **262** E4
Lochranza **232** A4
Lochside *Aber* **253** F3
Lochside *High* **273** G3
Lochside *High* **274** D5
Lochside *High* **275** H2
Lochslin **267** F3
Lochton **215** D2
Lochty **244** D4
Lochuisge **247** G3
Lochurr **216** B2
Lochussie **266** B6
Lochwinnoch **233** E4
Lockengate **97** E3
Lockerbie **217** F2
Lockeridge **118** C1
Lockerley **119** D5
Lockhills **210** B3
Locking **116** A2
Lockington *ERid* **196** B3
Lockington *Leics* **173** F5
Lockleywood **171** D5
Locks Heath **107** E2
Locksbottom **122** D2
Locksgreen **106** D3
Lockton **204** B3
Locomotion: The National
    Railway Museum at
    Shildon *Dur*
    DL4 1PQ **212** B5
Loddington
    Leics **160** C2
Loddington
    N'hants **160** D5
Loddiswell **100** D3
Loddon **165** E2
Lode **150** D1
Loders **104** A3
Lodsworth **121** E5
Lofthouse *NYorks* **202** A5
Lofthouse *WYorks* **194** C5
Loftus **203** G1
Logan *D&G* **206** A2
Logan *EAyr* **225** D3
Loganlea **235** E3
Loggerheads **171** E4
Loggerheads Country Park
    Denb CH7 5LH **169** E1
Loggie
    (An Lagaidh) **265** H2
Logie *Angus* **253** E3
Logie *Angus* **252** B4
Logie *Fife* **244** C2
Logie *Moray* **267** H6
Logie Coldstone **260** C4
Logie Hill **266** C4
Logie Newton **260** E1
Logie Pert **253** E3
Logierait **251** E4
Login **141** E5
Lolworth **150** B1
Lonbain **264** C6
Londesborough **196** A3
London **136** C4
London Apprentice **97** E5
London Aquarium *GtLon*
    SE1 7PD **45** E4
London Ashford
    Airport **111** F1
London Beach **124** A5
London Biggin Hill
    Airport **122** D2
London City
    Airport **136** D4
London Colney **136** A3
London Gatwick
    Airport **122** B4
London Heathrow
    Airport **135** F5
London Luton
    Airport **149** G5
London Minstead **106** B1
London Southend
    Airport **138** B4
London Stansted
    Airport **150** D5
London Transport Museum
    GtLon WC2E 7BB **45** E3
London Wetland Centre
    GtLon SW13 9WT **11** E6
Londonderry **202** B4
Londonthorpe **175** E4
Londubh **264** E3
Lonemore **266** E3
Long Ashton **131** E5
Long Bank **157** G5
Long Bennington **174** D3
Long Bredy **104** B3
Long Buckby **148** B1
Long Clawson **174** C5
Long Compton
    Staffs **171** F5
Long Compton
    Warks **147** E4
Long Crendon **134** B2
Long Crichel **105** F1
Long Dean **132** A5
Long Downs **95** E3
Long Drax **195** F5
Long Duckmanton **186** B5
Long Eaton **173** F4
Long Gill **193** D2
Long Green
    ChesW&C **183** E5
Long Green *Essex* **152** A5
Long Green *Worcs* **146** A4
Long Hanborough **133** G1
Long Itchington **147** G1

Lon - Mar

Long Lane 157 F1
Long Lawford 159 G5
Long Load 116 B5
Long Marston Herts 135 D1
Long Marston NYorks 195 E2
Long Marston Warks 147 D3
Long Marton 210 C5
Long Meadowend 156 D4
Long Melford 151 G3
Long Newnton 132 B3
Long Preston 193 E2
Long Riston 196 D3
Long Stratton 164 C2
Long Street 148 C3
Long Sutton Hants 120 C3
Long Sutton Lincs 176 C5
Long Sutton Som 116 B5
Long Thurlow 152 B1
Long Whatton 173 F5
Long Wittenham 134 A3
Longbenton 212 B1
Longborough 147 D5
Longbridge Plym 100 B2
Longbridge Warks 147 E1
Longbridge WMid 158 C5
Longbridge Deverill 117 F3
Longburgh 209 G1
Longburton 104 C1
Longcliffe 172 D2
Longcombe 101 E2
Longcot 133 E3
Longcroft 234 B2
Longcross Devon 99 E3
Longcross Surr 121 E1
Longden 156 D2
Longdon Staffs 158 C1
Longdon Worcs 146 A4
Longdon Green 158 C1
Longdon upon Tern 157 F1
Longdown 102 B3
Longdrum 261 H3
Longfield 123 F2
Longfield Hill 123 F2
Longfleet 105 G3
Longford Derbys 172 D4
Longford Glos 146 A5
Longford GtLon 135 F5
Longford Shrop 170 D4
Longford Tel&W 157 G1
Longford WMid 159 F4
Longforgan 244 B2
Longformacus 237 D4
Longframlington 220 D1
Longham Dorset 105 G3
Longham Norf 178 A4
Longhill 269 H5
Longhirst 221 E3
Longhope Glos 131 F1
Longhope Ork 277 C8
Longhorsley 220 D2
Longhoughton 229 G5
Longlands Aber 260 C2
Longlands Cumb 209 F3
Longlands GtLon 136 D5
Longlane Derbys 173 D4
Longlane WBerks 133 G5
Longleat House Wilts BA12 7NW 117 F3
Longleat Safari Park Wilts BA12 7NW 117 F3
Longlevens 132 A1
Longley 185 F2
Longley Green 145 G2
Longmanhill 269 F4
Longmoor Camp 120 C4
Longmorn 267 K6
Longnewton ScBord 227 G3
Longnewton Stock 202 C1
Longney 131 G1
Longniddry 236 B2
Longniddry Bents ELoth EH32 0PX 236 B2
Longnor Shrop 157 D2
Longnor Staffs 172 B1
Longparish 119 F3
Longridge Lancs 192 C4
Longridge Staffs 158 B1
Longridge WLoth 235 D3
Longridge End 146 A5
Longridge Towers 237 G4
Longriggend 234 C2
Longrock 94 C3
Longsdon 171 G2
Longshaw 183 G2
Longside 269 J6
Longslow 171 D4
Longsowerby 209 G1
Longstanton 150 C1
Longstock 119 E4
Longstone 94 C3
Longstowe 150 B2
Longstreet 118 C2
Longthorpe 161 G3
Longton Lancs 192 A5
Longton Stoke 171 G3
Longtown Cumb 218 B5
Longtown Here 144 C5
Longville in the Dale 157 E3
Longwell Green 131 F5
Longwick 134 C2
Longwitton 220 C3
Longworth 133 F3
Longyester 236 C3
Lonmay 269 J5
Lonmore 263 H7
Looe 97 G4
Look Out Discovery Park, Bracknell BrackF RG12 7QW 121 D1
Loose 123 G3
Loosebeare 102 A2
Loosegate 176 B5
Loosley Row 134 D2
Lopcombe Corner 119 D4
Lopen 104 A1
Loppington 170 B5
Lorbottle 220 C1
Lorbottle Hall 220 C1
Lordington 107 G2
Lord's Cricket Ground & Museum GtLon NW8 8QN 10 F4
Lord's Hill 106 C1
Lorgill 263 G7
Lorn 233 E1
Lornty 251 G5
Loscoe 173 F3
Loscombe 104 A3
Losgaintir 263 F2
Lossiemouth 267 K4
Lossit 230 A4
Lost Gardens of Heligan Corn PL26 6EN 97 D5
Lostock Gralam 184 A5
Lostock Green 184 A5
Lostock Junction 184 A2
Lostwithiel 97 F4
Loth 276 F4
Lothbeg 274 E7
Lothersdale 193 F3
Lotherton Hall Estate WYorks LS25 3EB 195 D4
Lothmore 274 E7
Loudwater 135 E3
Loughborough 160 A1
Loughor 128 B3
Loughton Essex 136 D3
Loughton MK 148 D4
Loughton Shrop 157 F4
Louis Tussaud's Waxworks FY1 5AA 64 Blackpool
Lound Lincs 161 F1
Lound Notts 187 D4
Lound Suff 165 G2
Lount 159 F1
Lour 252 C5
Louth 188 D4
Love Clough 193 E5
Lovedean 107 F1
Lover 106 B1
Loversall 186 C3
Loves Green 137 F2
Lovesome Hill 202 C3
Loveston 127 D2
Lovington 116 C4
Low Ackworth 186 B1
Low Angerton 220 C3
Low Ballevain 222 B3
Low Barlay 215 G5
Low Barlings 188 A5
Low Bentham (Lower Bentham) 192 C1
Low Bolton 201 F3
Low Bradfield 185 G3
Low Bradley (Bradley) 193 G3
Low Braithwaite 210 A3
Low Brunton 220 B4
Low Burnham 187 E2
Low Burton 202 B4
Low Buston 221 E1
Low Catton 195 G2
Low Coniscliffe 202 B1
Low Craighead 224 A5
Low Dinsdale 202 C1
Low Ellington 202 B4
Low Entercommon 202 C2
Low Etherley 212 A5
Low Fell 212 B2
Low Gate 211 F1
Low Grantley 202 B5
Low Green 151 G1
Low Habberley 158 A5
Low Ham 116 B5
Low Hawsker 204 C2
Low Haygarth 200 B3
Low Hesket 210 A3
Low Hesleyhurst 220 C2
Low Hutton 195 G1
Low Kingthorpe 204 B4
Low Laithe 194 A1
Low Langton 188 B5
Low Leighton 185 E4
Low Lorton 209 E4
Low Marishes 204 B5
Low Marnham 174 D1
Low Middleton 229 F3
Low Mill 203 F3
Low Moor Lancs 192 D3
Low Moor WYorks 194 A5
Low Moorsley 212 C3
Low Moresby 208 C4
Low Newton-by-the-Sea 229 G4
Low Row Cumb 210 B1
Low Row NYorks 201 E3
Low Stillaig 232 A3
Low Street 178 B5
Low Tharston 164 C2
Low Torry 235 E1
Low Town 220 D1
Low Toynton 188 C5
Low Wood 199 E4
Low Worsall 202 C2
Lowbands 145 G4
Lowdham 174 B3
Lowe 170 C4
Lowe Hill 171 G2
Lower Achachenna 240 C2
Lower Aisholt 115 F4
Lower Apperley 146 A5
Lower Arncott 134 B1
Lower Ashtead 121 G2
Lower Ashton 102 B4
Lower Assendon 134 C4
Lower Auchalick 232 A2
Lower Ballam 191 G4
Lower Barewood 144 C2
Lower Bartle 192 A4
Lower Bayble (Pabail Iarach) 271 H4
Lower Beeding 109 E1
Lower Benefield 161 E4
Lower Bentham (Low Bentham) 192 C1
Lower Bentley 146 B1
Lower Berry Hill 131 E1
Lower Birchwood 173 F2
Lower Boddington 147 G2
Lower Boscaswell 94 A3
Lower Bourne 120 D3
Lower Brailes 147 F4
Lower Breakish 256 C2
Lower Bredbury 184 D3
Lower Broadheath 146 A2
Lower Brynamman 128 D1
Lower Bullingham 145 E4
Lower Bullington 119 F3
Lower Burgate 106 A1
Lower Burrow 116 B5
Lower Burton 144 D2
Lower Caldecote 149 G3
Lower Cam 131 G2
Lower Cambourne 150 B2
Lower Camster 275 H4
Lower Chapel 143 G4
Lower Cheriton 103 E2
Lower Chicksgrove 118 A4
Lower Chute 119 E2
Lower Clent 158 B4
Lower Creedy 102 B2
Lower Cumberworth 185 G2
Lower Darwen 192 C5
Lower Dean 149 F1
Lower Diabaig 264 D5
Lower Dicker 110 A2
Lower Dinchope 157 D4
Lower Down 156 C4
Lower Drift 94 B4
Lower Dunsforth 194 D1
Lower Earley 134 C5
Lower Edmonton 136 C3
Lower Elkstone 172 B2
Lower End Bucks 134 B2
Lower End MK 149 E4
Lower End N'hants 149 D1
Lower Everleigh 118 C2
Lower Eythorne 125 E4
Lower Failand 131 E5
Lower Farringdon 120 C4
Lower Fittleworth 108 C2
Lower Foxdale 190 A4
Lower Freystrop 126 C1
Lower Froyle 120 C3
Lower Gabwell 101 F1
Lower Gledfield 266 C2
Lower Godney 116 B3
Lower Gravenhurst 149 G4
Lower Green Essex 150 C4
Lower Green Herts 149 G4
Lower Green Kent 123 F4
Lower Green Norf 178 A2
Lower Green Staffs 158 B2
Lower Green Bank 192 B2
Lower Halstock Leigh 104 B2
Lower Halstow 124 A2
Lower Hardres 124 D3
Lower Harpton 144 B1
Lower Hartshay 173 E2
Lower Hartwell 134 C1
Lower Hawthwaite 198 D4
Lower Haysden 123 E4
Lower Hayton 157 E4
Lower Heath 171 F1
Lower Hergest 144 B2
Lower Heyford 147 G5
Lower Higham 137 G5
Lower Holbrook 152 C4
Lower Hopton 185 G1
Lower Hordley 170 A5
Lower Horncroft 108 C2
Lower Horsebridge 110 A2
Lower Houses 185 F1
Lower Howsell 145 G3
Lower Kersal 184 C2
Lower Kilchattan 238 C5
Lower Kilcott 131 G4
Lower Killeyan 230 A5
Lower Kingcombe 104 B3
Lower Kingswood 122 B3
Lower Kinnerton 170 A1
Lower Langford 116 B1
Lower Largo 244 C4
Lower Leigh 172 B4
Lower Lemington 147 E4
Lower Lovacott 113 F3
Lower Loxhore 113 G2
Lower Lydbrook 131 E1
Lower Lye 144 D1
Lower Machen 130 B4
Lower Maes-coed 144 C4
Lower Mannington 105 G2
Lower Middleton Cheney 148 A3
Lower Milton 116 C3
Lower Moor 146 B3
Lower Morton 131 F3
Lower Nash 126 D2
Lower Nazeing 136 C2
Lower Netchwood 157 F3
Lower Nyland 117 E5
Lower Oddington 147 E5
Lower Ollach 256 B1
Lower Penarth 130 A5
Lower Penn 158 A3
Lower Pennington 106 C3
Lower Peover 184 B5
Lower Pollicott 134 C1
Lower Quinton 147 D3
Lower Race 130 B2
Lower Rainham 124 A2
Lower Roadwater 114 D4
Lower Sapey 145 F1
Lower Seagry 132 B4
Lower Shelton 149 E3
Lower Shiplake 134 C5
Lower Shuckburgh 147 G1
Lower Slaughter 147 D5
Lower Soothill 194 B5
Lower Stanton St. Quintin 132 B4
Lower Stoke 124 A1
Lower Stondon 149 G4
Lower Stone 131 F3
Lower Stonnall 158 C2
Lower Stow Bedon 164 A2
Lower Street Dorset 105 E3
Lower Street ESuss 110 C2
Lower Street Norf 179 D2
Lower Street Norf 178 C2
Lower Street Suff 152 C2
Lower Stretton 184 A4
Lower Sundon 149 F5
Lower Swanwick 107 D2
Lower Swell 147 D5
Lower Tadmarton 147 G4
Lower Tale 103 D2
Lower Tean 172 B4
Lower Thurlton 165 F2
Lower Thurnham 192 A2
Lower Town Corn 95 D4
Lower Town Devon 102 A5
Lower Town IoS 96 B1
Lower Town Pembs 140 C4
Lower Trebullett 98 D3
Lower Tysoe 147 F3
Lower Upcott 102 B4
Lower Upham 107 E1
Lower Upnor 137 G5
Lower Vexford 115 E4
Lower Wallop 156 C2
Lower Walton 184 A4
Lower Waterhay 132 C3
Lower Weald 148 C4
Lower Wear 102 C4
Lower Weare 116 B2
Lower Welson 144 B2
Lower Whatley 117 E3
Lower Whitley 184 A5
Lower Wick 146 A2
Lower Wield 120 B3
Lower Winchendon (Nether Winchendon) 134 C1
Lower Withington 171 F1
Lower Woodend 134 D4
Lower Woodford 118 C4
Lower Wyche 145 G3
Lowerhouse 193 E4
Lowertown 277 D8
Lowesby 160 C2
Lowestoft 165 G2
Loweswater 209 E4
Lowfield Heath 122 B4
Lowgill Cumb 200 B3
Lowgill Lancs 192 C1
Lowick Cumb 199 D4
Lowick N'hants 161 E4
Lowick N'umb 229 E3
Lowick Bridge 199 D4
Lowick Green 199 D4
Lownie Moor 252 C5
Lowry, The GtMan M50 3AZ 24 D3
Lowsonford 147 D1
Lowther 210 B5
Lowther Castle 210 B5
Lowthorpe 196 C1
Lowton Devon 113 G5
Lowton GtMan 184 A3
Lowton Som 103 E1
Lowton Common 184 A3
Loxbeare 102 C1
Loxhill 121 F4
Loxhore 113 G2
Loxley 147 E2
Loxley Green 172 B4
Loxton 116 A2
Loxwood 121 F4
Lubachoinnich 266 B2
Lubcroy 265 K1
Lubenham 160 C4
Lubfearn 265 K4
Lubmore 265 G6
Lubreoch 249 G5
Luccombe 114 C3
Luccombe Village 107 E4
Lucker 229 F3
Luckett 99 D3
Luckington 132 A4
Lucklawhill 244 C2
Luckwell Bridge 114 C4
Lucton 144 D1
Lucy Cross 202 B1
Ludag 254 C3
Ludborough 188 C3
Ludbrook 100 C2
Ludchurch 127 E1
Luddenden 193 G5
Luddenden Foot 193 G5
Luddenham Court 124 B2
Luddesdown 123 F2
Luddington NLincs 187 F1
Luddington Warks 147 D2
Luddington in the Brook 161 G4
Ludford Lincs 188 B4
Ludford Shrop 157 E5
Ludgershall Bucks 134 B1
Ludgershall Wilts 119 D2
Ludgvan 94 C3
Ludham 179 E4
Ludlow 157 E5
Ludney 189 D3
Ludstock 145 F4
Ludstone 158 A3
Ludwell 118 A5
Ludworth 212 C3
Luffincott 98 D1
Luffness 236 B1
Lufton 104 B1
Lugar 225 D3
Luggate 236 C2
Luggate Burn 236 D2
Luggiebank 234 B2
Lugton 233 F4
Lugwardine 145 E3
Luib 256 B2
Luibeilt 249 E3
Luing 239 G3
Lulham 144 D3
Lullington Derbys 159 E1
Lullington Som 117 E2
Lulsgate Bottom 116 C1
Lulsley 145 G2
Lulworth Camp 105 E4
Lulworth Cove & Heritage Centre Dorset BH20 5RQ 105 E5
Lumb Lancs 193 E5
Lumb WYorks 193 G5
Lumbutts 193 F5
Lumby 195 D4
Lumphanan 260 D4
Lumphinnans 243 G5
Lumsdaine 237 F3
Lumsdale 173 E1
Lumsden 260 C2
Lunan 253 E4
Lunanhead 252 C4
Luncarty 243 F2
Lund ERid 196 B3
Lund NYorks 195 F4
Lund Shet 278 E2
Lundale 270 D4
Lundavra 248 C3
Lunderston Bay Invcly PA16 0DN 232 D2
Lunderton 269 K6
Lundie Angus 244 A1
Lundie High 257 H3
Lundin Links 244 C4
Lundwood 186 A2
Lundy 112 B1
Lunga 240 A4
Lunna 279 D6
Lunning 279 E6
Lunnon 128 B4
Lunsford's Cross 110 C2
Lunt 183 E2
Luntley 144 C2
Luppitt 103 E2
Lupset 186 A1
Lupton 199 G4
Lurgashall 121 E5
Lurignich 248 B4
Lusby 176 B1
Luss 241 F5
Lussagiven 231 E1
Lusta 263 H6
Lustleigh 102 A4
Luston 145 D1
Luthermuir 253 E3
Luthrie 244 B3
Luton Devon 103 D2
Luton Devon 102 C5
Luton Luton 149 F5
Luton Med 123 G2
Luton Airport 149 G5
Lutterworth 160 A4
Lutton Devon 100 B2
Lutton Dorset 105 F4
Lutton Lincs 176 C5
Lutton N'hants 161 G4
Luxborough 114 C4
Luxulyan 97 E4
Lybster High 275 F2
Lybster High 275 H5
Lydacott 113 E5
Lydbury North 156 C4
Lydcott 113 G2
Lydd 111 F1
Lydden 125 E4
Lyddington 161 D3
Lydd-on-Sea 111 F1
Lyde Green 131 F5
Lydeard St. Lawrence 115 E4
Lydford 99 F2
Lydford-on-Fosse 116 C4
Lydgate GtMan 185 D1
Lydgate GtMan 185 D2
Lydgate WYorks 193 F5
Lydham 156 C3
Lydiard Millicent 132 C4
Lydiard Tregoze 132 D4
Lydiate 183 E2
Lydlinch 104 D1
Lydney 131 F2
Lydstep 127 D3
Lye 158 B4
Lye Cross 116 B1
Lye Green Bucks 135 E2
Lye Green ESuss 123 E5
Lye Green Warks 147 D1
Lye's Green 117 F3
Lyford 133 F3
Lymbridge Green 124 D4
Lyme Regis 103 G3
Lymekilns 234 A4
Lyminge 125 D4
Lymington 106 C3
Lyminster 108 C3
Lymm 184 A4
Lymore 106 B3
Lympne 124 D5
Lympsham 116 A2
Lympstone 102 C4
Lynaberack 258 E5
Lynch 114 B3
Lynch Green 178 C5
Lynchat 258 E4
Lyndale House 263 J6
Lyndhurst 106 B2
Lyndon 161 E2
Lyne Aber 261 F4
Lyne ScBord 235 G5
Lyne Surr 121 F1
Lyne Down 145 F4
Lyne of Gorthleck 258 C2
Lyne of Skene 261 F3
Lyne Station 235 G5
Lyneal 170 B4
Lynegar 275 H3
Lyneham Oxon 147 E5
Lyneham Wilts 132 C5
Lyneholmeford 218 D4
Lynemore High 259 H2
Lynemore Moray 259 J1
Lynemouth 221 E2
Lyness 277 C8
Lynford 163 G3
Lyng 178 B4
Lyngate 179 E3
Lynmouth 114 A3
Lynn 157 G1
Lynsted 124 B2
Lynstone 112 C5
Lynton 114 A3
Lynton & Lynmouth Cliff Railway Devon EX35 6EP 114 A3
Lyon's Gate 104 C2
Lyonshall 144 C2
Lyrabus 230 A3
Lytchett Matravers 105 F3
Lytchett Minster 105 F3
Lyth 275 H2
Lytham 191 G5
Lytham St. Anne's 191 G5
Lythe 204 B1
Lythe Hill 121 E4
Lythes 277 D9
Lythmore 275 F2

M

M.V. Princess Pocahontas Kent DA11 0BS 137 F5
Mabe Burnthouse 95 E3
Mabie 217 D3
Mablethorpe 189 F4
Macclesfield 184 D5
Macclesfield Forest 185 D5
Macduff 269 F4
Macedonia 244 A4
Machan 234 B4
Machany 243 D3
Macharioch 222 C5
Machen 130 B4
Machrie A&B 230 A3
Machrie A&B 230 B5
Machrie NAyr 223 D2
Machrihanish 222 B3
Machrins 238 C5
Machynlleth 154 D2
McInroy's Point 232 D2
Mackerye End 136 A1
Mackworth 173 E4
Macmerry 236 B2
Macterry 269 F6
Madame Tussauds GtLon NW1 5LR 12 A4
Madderty 243 E2
Maddiston 234 D2
Madehurst 108 B2
Madeley Staffs 171 E3
Madeley Tel&W 157 G2
Madeley Heath 171 E3
Maders 98 D3
Madford 103 E1
Madingley 150 B1
Madjeston 117 F5
Madley 144 D4
Madresfield 146 A3
Madron 94 B3
Maenaddwyn 180 C4
Maenclochog 141 D5
Maendy Cardiff 130 A5
Maendy VGlam 129 G5
Maenporth 95 E4
Maentwrog 167 F3
Maen-y-groes 141 G2
Maer Corn 112 C5
Maer Staffs 171 E4
Maerdy Carmar 142 C5
Maerdy Carmar 142 C5
Maerdy Conwy 168 D3
Maerdy RCT 129 F3
Maesbrook 169 F5
Maesbury Marsh 170 A5
Maes-glas 130 B4
Maesgwynne 141 F5
Maeshafn 169 F1
Maesllyn 141 G3
Maesmynis 143 G3
Maesteg 129 E3
Maes-Treylow 144 B1
Maesybont 128 B1
Maesycrugiau 142 A3
Maesycwmmer 130 A3
Magdalen Laver 137 E2
Maggieknockater 268 B6
Maggots End 150 C5
Magham Down 110 B2
Maghull 183 E2
Magna Centre, Rotherham SYorks S60 1DX 21 C1
Magna Park 160 A4
Magor 130 D4
Magpie Green 164 B4
Maiden Bradley 117 E4
Maiden Head 116 C1
Maiden Law 212 A3
Maiden Newton 104 B3
Maiden Wells 126 C3
Maidencombe 101 F1
Maidenhayne 103 F3
Maidenhead 135 D4
Maidens 224 A5
Maiden's Green 135 D5
Maidensgrove 134 C4
Maidenwell Corn 97 F2
Maidenwell Lincs 188 D5
Maidford 148 B2
Maids' Moreton 148 C4
Maidstone 123 G3
Maidwell 160 C5
Mail 279 D10
Maindee 130 C4
Mainland Ork 277 B6
Mainland Shet 279 C7
Mains of Ardestie 244 D1
Mains of Balgavies 252 D4
Mains of Balhall 252 D3
Mains of Ballindarg 252 C4
Mains of Burgie 267 H6
Mains of Culsh 269 G6
Mains of Dillavaird 253 F1
Mains of Drum 261 G4
Mains of Dudwick 261 H1
Mains of Faillie 258 E1
Mains of Fedderate 269 G6
Mains of Glack 261 F2
Mains of Glassaugh 268 D4
Mains of Glenbuchat 260 B3
Mains of Linton 261 F3
Mains of Melgund 252 D4
Mains of Pitfour 269 H6
Mains of Pittrichie 261 G2
Mains of Sluie 267 H6
Mains of Tannachy 268 B4
Mains of Thornton 253 E2
Mains of Tig 214 C2
Mains of Watten 275 H3
Mainsforth 212 C4
Mainsriddle 216 D5
Mainstone 156 B4
Maisemore 146 A5
Major's Green 158 D5
Makendon 220 A1
Makeney 173 E3
Makerstoun 228 A3
Malacleit 262 C4
Malborough 100 D4
Malden Rushett 121 G1
Maldon 138 B2
Malham 193 F1
Maligar 263 K5
Malinbridge 186 A4
Mallaig (Malaig) 256 C5
Mallaigmore 256 C5
Mallaigvaig 256 C5
Malleny Mills 235 F3
Malletsheugh 233 G4
Malling 242 A4
Mallows Green 150 C5
Malltraeth 166 D1
Mallwyd 155 E1
Malmesbury 132 B4
Malmsmead 114 A3
Malpas ChesW&C 170 B3
Malpas Corn 96 C5
Malpas Newport 130 C3
Maltby Lincs 188 D4
Maltby Stock 203 D1
Maltby SYorks 186 C3
Maltby le Marsh 189 E4
Malting End 151 F2
Malting Green 138 C1
Maltman's Hill 124 A4
Malton 203 G5
Malvern Link 145 G3
Malvern Wells 145 G3
Mambeg 232 D1
Mamble 157 F5
Mamhead 102 C4
Mamhilad 130 C2
Manaccan 95 E4
Manadon 100 A2
Manafon 156 A2
Manaton 102 A4
Manby 189 D4
Mancetter 159 F3
Manchester 184 C3
Manchester Airport 184 C4
Manchester Apollo GtMan M12 6AP 47 H6
Manchester Art Gallery GtMan M2 3JL 47 E4
Manchester Central GtMan M2 3GX 46 D5
Manchester Craft & Design Centre GtMan M4 5JD 47 F3
Manchester Museum GtMan M13 9PL 47 F7
Manchester United Museum & Stadium Tour Centre GtMan M16 0RA 24 D3
Mancot Royal 170 A1
Mandally (Manndalaidh) 257 J4
Manea 162 C4
Maneight 224 D5
Manfield 202 B1
Mangaster 278 C5
Mangerton 104 A3
Mangotsfield 131 F5
Mangrove Green 149 G5
Mangurstadh 270 C4
Manish (Manais) 263 G3
Mankinholes 193 F5
Manley 183 G5
Manmoel 130 A2
Mannal 246 A2
Manningford Abbots 118 C2
Manningford Bohune 118 C2
Manningford Bruce 118 C2
Manningham 194 A4
Mannings Amusement Park Suff IP11 2DW 153 D4
Mannings Heath 109 E1
Mannington 105 G2
Manningtree 152 C4
Mannofield 261 H4
Manor Farm Country Park Hants SO30 2ER 4 D3
Manor Park 135 E4
Manorbier 127 D3
Manorbier Newton 126 D2
Manordeifi 141 F3
Manordeilo 142 C5
Manorowen 140 C4
Mansell Gamage 144 C3
Mansell Lacy 144 D3
Mansergh 200 B4
Mansfield 173 G1
Mansfield Woodhouse 173 G1
Manson Green 178 B5
Mansriggs 199 D4
Manston Dorset 105 E1
Manston Kent 125 F2
Manston WYorks 194 C4
Manswood 105 F2
Manthorpe Lincs 161 F1
Manthorpe Lincs 175 E4
Manton NLincs 187 G2
Manton Notts 186 C5
Manton Rut 161 D2
Manton Wilts 118 C1
Manuden 150 C5
Manwood Green 137 E1
Maolachy 240 A3
Maperton 117 D5
Maple Cross 135 F3
Maplebeck 174 C1
Mapledurham 134 B5
Mapledurwell 120 B2
Maplehurst 121 G5
Maplescombe 123 E2
Mapleton 172 C3
Mapperley Derbys 173 F3
Mapperley Notts 173 G3
Mapperton Dorset 104 B3
Mapperton Dorset 105 F3
Mappleborough Green 146 C1
Mappleton 197 E3
Mapplewell 186 A2
Mappowder 104 D2
Mar Lodge 259 H5
Maraig (Maaruig) 270 E7
Marazion 94 C3
Marbhig 271 G6
Marbury 170 C3
Marbury Country Park ChesW&C CW9 6AT 184 A5
March 162 C3
Marcham 133 G3
Marchamley 170 C5
Marchamley Wood 170 C4
Marchington 172 C4
Marchington Woodlands 172 C5
Marchwiel 170 A3
Marchwood 106 C1
Marcross 114 C1
Marcus 252 D4
Marden Here 145 E3
Marden Kent 123 G4
Marden T&W 221 F4
Marden Wilts 118 B2
Marden Ash 137 E2
Marden Beech 123 G4
Marden Thorn 123 G4
Marden's Hill 123 D5
Mardon 228 D3
Mardy 130 C1
Mare Green 116 A5
Marefield 160 C2
Mareham le Fen 176 A1
Mareham on the Hill 176 A1

Maresfield 109 G1
Marfleet 196 D4
Marford 170 A2
Margam 129 D4
Margam Country Park
NPT SA13 2TJ 129 E4
Margaret Marsh 105 E1
Margaret Roding 137 E1
Margaretting 137 F2
Margaretting Tye 137 F2
Margate 125 F1
Margnaheglish 223 F2
Margreig 216 C3
Margrove Park 203 F1
Marham 163 F2
Marhamchurch 112 C5
Marholm 161 G2
Marian Cwm 182 B5
Mariandyrus 181 E4
Marian-glas 180 D4
Mariansleigh 114 A5
Marine Town 124 B1
Marishader 263 K5
Maristow House 100 A1
Mark 116 A3
Mark Causeway 116 A3
Mark Cross 123 E5
Markbeech 123 D4
Markby 189 E5
Markdhu 214 C3
Markeaton 173 E4
Markeaton Park Craft Village
Derby DE22 3BG 18 A3
Market Bosworth 159 G2
Market Bosworth Country
Park Leics
CV13 0LP 159 G2
Market Deeping 161 G1
Market Drayton 171 D4
Market Harborough 160 C4
Market Lavington 118 B2
Market Overton 161 D1
Market Rasen 188 B4
Market Stainton 188 C5
Market Street 179 D3
Market Warsop 173 G1
Market Weighton 196 A3
Market Weston 164 A4
Markethill 244 B5
Markfield 159 G1
Markham 130 A2
Markham Moor 187 E5
Markinch 244 A4
Markington 194 B1
Marks Gate 137 D3
Marksbury 117 D1
Markyate 135 F1
Markwell 99 D5
Marland 184 C1
Marlborough 118 C1
Marlbrook 158 B5
Marlcliff 146 C2
Marldon 101 E1
Marle Green 110 A2
Marlesford 153 E2
Marley Green 170 C3
Marley Hill 212 B2
Marlingford 178 C5
Marloes 126 A2
Marlow Bucks 135 D4
Marlow Here 156 D5
Marlpit Hill 122 D4
Marlpool 173 F3
Marnhull 105 D1
Marnoch 268 D5
Marple 185 D4
Marple Bridge 185 D4
Marr 186 C2
Marrel 275 F7
Marrick 201 F3
Marrister 279 E6
Marros 127 F2
Marsden T&W 212 C1
Marsden WYorks 185 E1
Marsett 201 E4
Marsh 103 F1
Marsh Baldon 134 A3
Marsh Benham 119 F1
Marsh Farm Country Park
Essex CM3 5WP 138 B3
Marsh Gibbon 148 B5
Marsh Green
Devon 102 D3
Marsh Green
GtMan 183 G2
Marsh Green
Kent 122 D4
Marsh Green
Tel&W 157 F1
Marsh Lane 186 B5
Marsh Street 114 C3
Marshall Meadows 237 G4
Marshalsea 103 G2
Marsham 178 C3
Marshaw 192 D2
Marshborough 125 F3
Marshbrook 156 D4
Marshchapel 189 D3
Marshfield
Newport 130 B4
Marshfield SGlos 131 G5
Marshgate 98 B1
Marshland
St. James 162 D2
Marshside 183 E1
Marshwood 103 G3
Marske 202 A2
Marske-by-the-Sea 213 F5
Marsland Green 184 A3
Marston ChesW&C 184 A5
Marston Here 144 C2
Marston Lincs 175 D3
Marston Oxon 134 A2
Marston Staffs 171 G5
Marston Staffs 158 A1
Marston Warks 159 E4
Marston Wilts 118 A2
Marston Doles 147 G2
Marston Green 159 D4
Marston Magna 116 C5
Marston Meysey 132 C3
Marston
Montgomery 172 C4
Marston Moretaine 149 E3
Marston on Dove 172 D5

Marston
St. Lawrence 148 A3
Marston Stannett 145 E2
Marston Trussell 160 B4
Marston Vale Millennium
Country Park CenBeds
MK43 0PR 149 F3
Marstow 131 E1
Marsworth 135 E1
Marten 119 D1
Martham 179 F4
Martin Hants 105 G1
Martin Lincs 175 G2
Martin Lincs 176 A1
Martin Drove End 118 B5
Martin Hussingtree 146 A1
Martin Mere
L40 OTA 183 F1
Martinhoe 113 G1
Martinscroft 184 A4
Martinstown 104 C4
Martlesham 152 D3
Martlesham Heath 152 D3
Martletwy 126 D1
Martley 145 G1
Martock 104 A1
Marton ChesE 171 F1
Marton Cumb 198 D5
Marton ERid 197 D4
Marton ERid 197 D4
Marton Lincs 187 F4
Marton Middl 203 E1
Marton NYorks 194 D1
Marton NYorks 203 G4
Marton Shrop 156 B2
Marton Shrop 170 B5
Marton Warks 147 G1
Marton Abbey 195 E1
Marton-in-the-
Forest 195 E1
Marton-le-Moor 202 C5
Martyr Worthy 119 G4
Martyr's Green 121 F2
Marwell Zoo Hants
SO21 1JH 4 D1
Marwick 276 B5
Marwood 113 F2
Mary Rose PO1 3LX
82 Portsmouth
Mary Tavy 99 F3
Marybank (An Lagaidh)
High 266 B6
Marybank ESiar 271 G4
Maryburgh
(Baile Mairi) 266 C6
Maryfield Corn 100 A2
Maryfield Shet 279 D8
Marygold 237 F4
Maryhill Aber 269 G6
Maryhill Glas 233 G3
Marykirk 253 E3
Marylebone GtLon 136 B4
Marylebone
GtMan 183 G2
Marypark 259 J1
Maryport Cumb 208 D3
Maryport D&G 206 B3
Marystow 99 E2
Maryton 253 E4
Marywell Aber 261 H5
Marywell Aber 260 D5
Marywell Angus 253 E5
Masham 202 B4
Mashbury 137 F1
Masongill 200 B5
Mastin Moor 186 B5
Mastrick 261 H4
Matchborough 146 C1
Matching 137 E1
Matching Green 137 E1
Matching Tye 137 E1
Matfen 220 C4
Matfield 123 F4
Mathern 131 E3
Mathon 145 G3
Mathry 140 B4
Matlaske 178 C2
Matlock 173 E1
Matlock Bank 173 E1
Matlock Bath 173 D2
Matson 132 A1
Matterdale End 209 G4
Mattersey 187 D4
Mattersey Thorpe 187 D4
Mattingley 120 C2
Mattishall 178 B4
Mattishall Burgh 178 B4
Mauchline 224 C3
Maud 269 H6
Maufant 100 C5
Maugersbury 147 D5
Maughold 190 C2
Mauld 257 K1
Maulden 149 F3
Maulds Meaburn 200 B1
Maunby 202 C4
Maund Bryan 145 E2
Maundown 115 D5
Mautby 179 F4
Mavesyn Ridware 158 C1
Mavis Enderby 176 B1
Maw Green 171 E2
Mawbray 209 D2
Mawdesley 183 F1
Mawdlam 129 E4
Mawgan 95 E4
Mawgan Porth 96 C3
Mawla 96 B5
Mawnan 95 E4
Mawnan Smith 95 E4
Mawsley 160 D5
Mawthorpe 189 E5
Maxey 161 G2
Maxstoke 159 E4
Maxted Street 124 D4
Maxton Kent 125 E4
Maxton ScBord 228 A3
Maxwellheugh 228 B3
Maxworthy 98 C1
May Hill 145 G5
Mayals 128 C3
Maybole 224 B5
Maybury 121 F2
Mayen 268 D6
Mayfair 136 B4
Mayfield ESuss 110 A1

Mayfield Midlo 236 A3
Mayfield Staffs 172 C3
Mayford 121 E2
Mayland 138 C2
Maylandsea 138 C2
Maynard's Green 110 A2
Maypole IoS 96 B1
Maypole Kent 125 D2
Maypole Mon 131 D1
Maypole Green
Essex 152 A5
Maypole Green
Norf 165 F2
Maypole Green
Suff 153 D1
Maypole Green
Suff 152 A5
May's Green NSom 116 A1
Mays Green Oxon 134 C4
Maywick 279 C10
Mead 112 C4
Mead End 118 B5
Meadgate 117 D2
Meadle 134 D2
Meadow Green 145 G2
Meadowhall 186 A3
Meadowmill 236 B2
Meadowtown 156 C2
Meadwell 99 E2
Meaford 171 F4
Meal Bank 199 G3
Mealabost 271 G4
Mealasta 270 B5
Meals 189 E3
Mealsgate 209 F2
Meanley 192 D3
Meanwood 194 B4
Mearbeck 193 E1
Meare 116 B3
Meare Green 115 F5
Mearns 233 G4
Mears Ashby 148 D1
Measham 159 F1
Meath Green 122 B4
Meathop 199 F4
Meavy 100 B1
Medbourne 160 D3
Meddon 112 C4
Meden Vale 173 G1
Medlar 192 A4
Medmenham 134 D4
Medomsley 212 A2
Medstead 120 B4
Meer Common 144 C2
Meer End 159 E5
Meerbrook 171 G1
Meesden 150 C4
Meeson 171 D5
Meeth 113 F5
Meeting House Hill 179 E3
Meggethead 226 C3
Meifod Denb 168 D2
Meifod Powys 156 A1
Meigle 252 A5
Meikle Earnock 234 B4
Meikle Grenach 232 B3
Meikle Kilmory 232 B3
Meikle Rahane 232 D1
Meikle Strath 253 E2
Meikle Tarty 261 H2
Meikle Wartle 261 F1
Meikleour 243 G1
Meikleyard 224 D3
Meinciau 128 A1
Meir 171 G3
Meir Heath 171 G3
Melbost 271 G4
Melbost Borve
(Mealabost) 271 G2
Melbourn 150 B3
Melbourne Derbys 173 E5
Melbourne ERid 195 G3
Melbury 113 D4
Melbury Abbas 105 E1
Melbury Bubb 104 B2
Melbury Osmond 104 B2
Melbury Sampford 104 B2
Melby 279 A7
Melchbourne 149 F1
Melcombe
Bingham 105 D2
Melcombe Regis 104 C4
Meldon Devon 99 F1
Meldon N'umb 220 D3
Meldreth 150 B3
Meledor 96 D4
Melfort 240 A3
Melgarve 258 B5
Melgum 260 C4
Meliden
(Gallt Melyd) 182 B4
Melincourt 129 E2
Melin-y-coed 168 B1
Melin-y-ddol 155 G2
Melin-y-grug 155 G2
Melin-y-Wig 168 D3
Melkinthorpe 210 B5
Melkridge 210 D1
Melksham 118 A1
Melksham Forest 118 A1
Melldalloch 232 A1
Melling Lancs 199 G5
Melling Mersey 183 E2
Melling Mount 183 F2
Mellis 164 C4
Mellon Charles 264 E2
Mellon Udrigle 264 E2
Mellor GtMan 185 D4
Mellor Lancs 192 C4
Mellor Brook 192 C4
Mells 117 E3
Melmerby Cumb 210 C4
Melmerby NYorks 202 C5
Melmerby NYorks 202 C5
Melplash 104 A3
Melrose Aber 269 F4
Melrose ScBord 227 G2
Melsetter 277 B9
Melsonby 202 A2
Meltham 185 E1
Melton ERid 196 B5
Melton Suff 153 D2
Melton
Constable 178 B2
Melton Mowbray 160 C1
Melton Ross 188 A1
Meltonby 195 G2
Melvaig 264 D3
Melverley 156 C1

Melverley Green 156 C1
Melvich 274 D2
Membury 103 F2
Memsie 269 H4
Memus 252 C4
Menabilly 97 E4
Menai Bridge
(Porthaethwy) 181 D5
Mendham 165 D3
Mendlesham 152 C1
Mendlesham Green 152 B1
Menethorpe 195 G1
Menheniot 97 G3
Menie House 261 H2
Menithwood 145 G1
Mennock 225 G5
Menston 194 B3
Menstrie 242 D5
Mentmore 135 E1
Meoble 247 G1
Meole Brace 157 D1
Meols 182 D3
Meon 107 E2
Meonstoke 107 F1
Meopham 123 F2
Meopham Green 123 F2
Mepal 162 C4
Meppershall 149 G4
Merbach 144 C3
Mercaston 173 D3
Mere ChesE 184 B4
Mere Wilts 117 F4
Mere Brow 183 F1
Mere Green 158 D3
Mere Heath 184 A5
Mereclough 193 E4
Mereside 191 G4
Meretown 171 E5
Merewurth 123 F3
Mergie 253 F1
Meriden 159 E4
Merkadale 255 J1
Merkinch 266 D7
Merkland 216 B3
Merley 105 G3
Merlin's Bridge 126 C1
Merridge 115 F4
Merrington 170 B5
Merrion 126 C3
Merriott 104 A1
Merrivale 99 F3
Merrow 121 F2
Merry Hill Herts 136 A3
Merry Hill WMid 158 B4
Merry Hill WMid 158 A3
Merrymeet 97 G3
Mersea Island 138 D1
Mersey Ferries Mersey
CH44 6QY 42 A4
Merseyside Maritime
Museum Mersey
L3 4AQ 42 B5
Mersham 124 C5
Merstham 122 B3
Merston 108 A3
Merstone 107 E4
Merther 96 C5
Merthyr 141 G5
Merthyr Cynog 143 F4
Merthyr Dyfan 115 E1
Merthyr Mawr 129 E5
Merthyr Tydfil 129 G2
Merthyr Vale 129 G3
Merton Devon 113 F4
Merton GtLon 136 B5
Merton Norf 164 A2
Merton Oxon 134 A1
Mervinslaw 228 A5
Meshaw 102 A1
Messing 138 C1
Messingham 187 F2
Metcombe 103 D3
Metfield 165 D3
Metherell 100 A1
Metheringham 175 F1
Methil 244 B5
Methlem 166 A4
Methley 194 C5
Methley Junction 194 C5
Methlick 261 G1
Methven 243 F2
Methwold 163 F3
Methwold Hythe 163 F3
MetroCentre 212 B1
Mettingham 165 E3
Metton 178 C2
Mevagissey 97 E5
Mewith Head 192 D1
Mexborough 186 B3
Mey 275 H1
Meysey Hampton 132 D2
Miabhag ESiar 263 G2
Miabhag ESiar 270 C7
Mial 264 D4
Miavaig (Miabhaig) 270 C4
Michaelchurch 145 E5
Michaelchurch
Escley 144 C4
Michaelchurch-on-
Arrow 144 B2
Michaelston-le-Pit 130 A5
Michaelston-super-
Ely 130 A5
Michaelston-y-
Fedw 130 B4
Michaelstow 97 E2
Michelcombe 100 C1
Micheldever 119 G4
Michelmersh 119 E5
Mickfield 152 C1
Mickle Trafford 170 B1
Micklebring 186 C3
Mickleby 204 B1
Micklefield 194 D4
Micklefield Green 135 F3
Mickleham 121 G2
Micklehurst 185 D2
Mickleover 173 E4
Micklethwaite
Cumb 209 F1
Micklethwaite
WYorks 193 G3
Mickleton Dur 211 F5
Mickleton Glos 147 D3
Mickletown 194 C5
Mickley Derbys 186 A5
Mickley NYorks 202 B5
Mickley Green 151 G2
Mickley Square 211 G1

Mid Ardlaw 269 H4
Mid Beltie 260 E4
Mid Calder 235 E3
Mid Clyth 275 H5
Mid Hants Railway
Hants SO24 9JG 120 B4
Mid Lambrook 104 A1
Mid Lavant 108 A3
Mid Lix 242 A1
Mid Mossdale 200 D3
Mid Yell 278 E3
Midbea 276 D3
Middle Assendon 134 C4
Middle Aston 147 G5
Middle Barton 147 G5
Middle Bickenhill 159 E4
Middle
Bockhampton 106 A3
Middle Claydon 148 C5
Middle Drift 97 F3
Middle Drums 253 D4
Middle
Duntisbourne 132 B2
Middle Handley 186 B5
Middle Harling 164 A3
Middle Kames 232 A1
Middle Littleton 146 C3
Middle Maes-coed 144 C4
Middle Marwood 113 F2
Middle Mill 140 B5
Middle Quarter 124 A5
Middle Rasen 188 A4
Middle Rigg 243 F4
Middle Salter 192 C1
Middle Sontley 170 A3
Middle Stoford 115 E5
Middle Taphouse 97 F3
Middle Town 96 B1
Middle Tysoe 147 F3
Middle Wallop 119 D4
Middle Winterslow 118 D4
Middle Woodford 118 C4
Middlebie 218 A4
Middlecliff 186 B2
Middlecott 113 E5
Middleham 202 A4
Middlehill Aber 269 G6
Middlehill Corn 97 G3
Middlehope 157 E4
Middlemarsh 104 C2
Middlemoor 99 E3
Middlesbrough 213 D5
Middlesceugh 210 A3
Middleshaw 199 G4
Middlesmoor 201 F5
Middlestone 212 B4
Middlestone Moor 212 B4
Middlestown 185 G1
Middlethorpe 195 E2
Middleton Aber 261 G3
Middleton Angus 253 D5
Middleton Cumb 200 B4
Middleton Derbys 173 D2
Middleton Derbys 172 D1
Middleton Essex 151 G3
Middleton GtMan 184 C2
Middleton Hants 119 F3
Middleton Here 145 E1
Middleton Lancs 192 A1
Middleton Midlo 236 A4
Middleton N'hants 160 D4
Middleton N'umb 220 C3
Middleton N'umb 229 E3
Middleton Norf 163 E1
Middleton NYorks 203 G4
Middleton P&K 243 E1
Middleton P&K 251 G5
Middleton Shrop 156 B3
Middleton Shrop 157 E5
Middleton Shrop 170 A5
Middleton Suff 153 E1
Middleton Swan 128 A4
Middleton Warks 159 D3
Middleton WYorks 194 A3
Middleton WYorks 194 C5
Middleton Baggot 157 F3
Middleton Bank Top 220 C3
Middleton Cheney 147 G3
Middleton Green 171 G4
Middleton Hall 229 D4
Middleton Moor 153 F1
Middleton of
Potterton 261 H3
Middleton on the
Hill 145 E1
Middleton One Row 202 C1
Middleton Park 261 H3
Middleton Priors 157 F3
Middleton
Quernhow 202 C5
Middleton
St. George 202 C1
Middleton Scriven 157 F4
Middleton Stoney 148 A5
Middleton Tyas 202 B2
Middleton-in-
Teesdale 211 F5
Middleton-on-
Leven 203 D1
Middleton-on-Sea 108 B3
Middleton-on-the-
Wolds 196 B3
Middletown Cumb 198 A2
Middletown Powys 156 C1
Middlewich 171 E1
Middlewood ChesE 185 D4
Middlewood SYorks 186 A3
Middlewood Green 152 B1
Middlezoy 116 A4
Middridge 212 B5
Midfield 273 H2
Midford 117 E1
Midge Hall 192 B5
Midgeholme 210 C2
Midgham 119 G1
Midgley WYorks 193 G5
Midgley WYorks 185 G1
Midhopestones 185 G3
Midhurst 121 D5
Midland Railway Centre
Derbys DE5 3QZ 173 F2
Midlem 227 G3
Midloe Grange 149 G1
Midpark 232 B4
Midsomer Norton 117 D2
Midthorpe 188 C5

Midtown High 273 H2
Midtown High 264 E3
Midtown of Barras 253 G1
Midville 176 B2
Midway 173 E5
Migdale 266 D2
Migvie 260 C4
Milarrochy 241 G5
Milber 102 B5
Milborne Port 104 C1
Milborne St. Andrew 105 D3
Milborne Wick 117 D5
Milbourne
N'umb 220 D4
Milburn 210 C5
Milbury Heath 131 F3
Milcombe 147 G4
Milden 152 A3
Mildenhall Suff 163 F5
Mildenhall Wilts 118 D1
Mile Elm 118 A1
Mile End Essex 152 A5
Mile End Glos 131 E1
Mile End Park GtLon
E3 4HL 12 D1
Mile Oak 123 F4
Mile Town 124 B1
Milebrook 156 C5
Milebush 123 G4
Mileham 178 A4
Miles Green 171 F3
Miles Hope 145 E1
Milesmark 235 E1
Mile's Green 119 G1
Milfield 228 D3
Milford Derbys 173 E3
Milford Devon 112 C3
Milford Shrop 170 B5
Milford Staffs 171 G5
Milford Surr 121 E3
Milford Haven
(Aberdaugleddau)
126 B2
Milford on Sea 106 B3
Milkwall 131 E2
Milky Way Adventure
Park Devon
EX39 5RY 112 D3
Mill Bank 193 G5
Mill Brow 185 D4
Mill End Bucks 134 C4
Mill End Cambs 151 E2
Mill End Herts 150 B4
Mill End Herts 150 B5
Mill Green Cambs 151 E3
Mill Green Essex 137 F2
Mill Green Herts 136 B2
Mill Green Norf 164 C3
Mill Green Shrop 171 D5
Mill Green Staffs 172 B5
Mill Green Suff 152 E1
Mill Green Suff 152 C2
Mill Green WMid 158 C2
Mill Hill Cambs 150 A2
Mill Hill GtLon 136 B3
Mill Houses 192 C1
Mill Lane 120 C2
Mill of Camsail 233 D1
Mill of Elrick 269 H6
Mill of Fortune 242 C2
Mill of Kingoodie 261 G2
Mill of Monquich 261 G5
Mill of Uras 253 G1
Mill Side 199 F4
Mill Street Kent 123 F3
Mill Street Norf 178 B4
Milland 120 D5
Millbank 269 J6
Millbeck 209 F4
Millbounds 276 E4
Millbreck 269 J6
Millbridge 120 D3
Millbrook CenBeds 149 F4
Millbrook Corn 100 A2
Millbrook Devon 103 G3
Millbrook Soton 106 C1
Millburn Aber 260 E1
Millburn Aber 260 E1
Millcombe 101 E3
Millcorner 110 D1
Milldale 172 C2
Millden 261 H3
Milldens 252 D4
Millearne 243 E3
Millend 147 F5
Millenheath 170 C4
Millennium Seed Bank,
Wakehurst Place WSuss
RH17 6TN 122 C5
Millerhill 236 A3
Miller's Dale 185 F5
Miller's Green
Derbys 173 D2
Miller's Green
Essex 137 E2
Millgate 193 E5
Millhalf 144 B3
Millhayes Devon 103 E1
Millhayes Devon 103 F2
Millholme 199 G3
Millhouse A&B 232 A2
Millhouse Cumb 209 G3
Millhouse Green 185 G2
Millhousebridge 217 F2
Millikenpark 233 F3
Millin Cross 126 C1
Millington 196 A2
Millington Green 173 D3
Millmeece 171 F4
Millness 257 K1
Millom 198 C4
Millow 150 A3
Millpool 97 F2
Millport 232 C4
Millthorpe 186 A5
Millthrop 200 B3
Milltimber 261 G4
Milltown Aber 259 K4
Milltown Corn 97 F4
Milltown D&G 218 B4
Milltown Derbys 173 E1
Milltown Devon 113 F2

Milltown High 267 G7
Milltown of
Aberdalgie 243 F2
Milltown of
Auchindoun 260 B1
Milltown of
Craigston 269 F5
Milltown of
Edinvillie 267 K7
Milltown of
Kildrummy 260 C3
Milltown of
Rothiemay 268 D6
Milltown of Towie 260 C3
Milnathort 243 G4
Milners Heath 170 B1
Milngavie 233 G2
Milnrow 184 D1
Milnsbridge 185 F1
Milnthorpe 199 F4
Milovaig 263 G6
Milrig 224 D2
Milson 157 F5
Milstead 124 B3
Milston 118 C3
Milton Angus 252 B5
Milton Cambs 150 C1
Milton Cumb 210 B1
Milton D&G 216 C2
Milton D&G 216 A3
Milton D&G 214 D5
Milton Derbys 173 E5
Milton High 255 K6
Milton High 266 E4
Milton High 267 G6
Milton High 266 C7
Milton High 264 D7
Milton High 275 J3
Milton (Baile a' Mhuilinn)
High 258 B1
Milton Moray 268 D4
Milton Newport 130 C4
Milton Notts 187 E5
Milton NSom 116 A1
Milton Oxon 147 G4
Milton Oxon 133 G3
Milton P&K 243 E1
Milton Pembs 126 D2
Milton Ports 107 F3
Milton Som 116 B5
Milton Stir 242 A4
Milton Stoke 171 G2
Milton WDun 233 F2
Milton Abbas 105 D2
Milton Abbot 99 E3
Milton Bridge 235 G3
Milton Bryan 149 E4
Milton Clevedon 117 D4
Milton Combe 100 A1
Milton Country Park Cambs
CB24 6AZ 150 C1
Milton Damerel 113 D4
Milton End 131 D1
Milton Ernest 149 F2
Milton Green 170 B2
Milton Hill 133 G3
Milton Keynes 149 D4
Milton Keynes
Village 149 D4
Milton Lilbourne 118 C1
Milton Malsor 148 C2
Milton Morenish 242 D1
Milton of
Auchinhove 260 D4
Milton of Balgonie 244 B4
Milton of Buchanan 241 G5
Milton of
Cairnborrow 268 C6
Milton of Callander 242 A4
Milton of Campfield 260 E4
Milton of Campsie 234 A2
Milton of Coldwells 261 H1
Milton of Cullerlie 261 F4
Milton of Cushnie 260 D3
Milton of Dalcapon 251 E4
Milton of
Inveramsay 261 F2
Milton of Noth 260 D2
Milton of Tullich 260 B5
Milton on Stour 117 E5
Milton Regis 124 A2
Milton Street 110 A3
Miltonduff 267 J5
Miltonhill 267 H5
Miltonise 214 C3
Milton-Lockhart 234 C5
Milton-under-
Wychwood 133 E1
Milverton Som 115 E5
Milverton Warks 147 F1
Milwich 171 G4
Mimbridge 121 E1
Minack Theatre Corn
TR19 6JU 94 A4
Minard 240 B5
Minard Castle 240 B5
Minchington 105 F1
Minchinhampton 132 A2
Mindrum 228 C3
Mindrummill 228 C3
Minehead 114 C3
Minera 169 F2
Minety 132 C3
Minety Lower Moor 132 C3
Minffordd Gwyn 154 D1
Minffordd Gwyn 167 E4
Minffordd Gwyn 181 D5
Miningsby 176 B1
Minions 97 G2
Minishant 224 B4
Minley Manor 120 D2
Minllyn 155 E1
Minnes 261 H2
Minngearraidh 254 C2
Minnigaff 215 F4
Minnonie 269 F4
Minskip 194 C1
Minstead 106 B1
Minsted 121 D5
Minster Kent 124 D1
Minster Kent 125 F2
Minster Lovell 133 F1
Minsteracres 211 G2
Minsterley 156 C2
Minsterworth 131 G1
Minterne Magna 104 C2
Minterne Parva 104 C2
Minting 188 B5

Mintlaw 269 J6
Minto 227 G3
Minton 156 D3
Minwear 126 D1
Minworth 159 D3
Miodar 246 B1
Mirbister 277 C6
Mirehouse 208 C5
Mireland 275 J2
Mirfield 194 B5
Miserden 132 B2
Miskin RCT 129 G4
Miskin RCT 129 G3
Misselfore 118 B5
Misson 187 D3
Misterton Leics 160 A4
Misterton Notts 187 E3
Misterton Som 104 A2
Mistley 152 C4
Mitcham 122 B2
Mitchel Troy 131 D1
Mitcheldean 131 F1
Mitchell 96 C4
Mitchelland 199 F3
Mitcheltroy
  Common 131 D2
Mitford 221 D3
Mithian 96 B4
Mitton 158 A1
Mixbury 148 B4
Mixenden 193 G5
Moar 250 A5
Moat 218 C4
Moats Tye 152 B2
Mobberley ChesE 184 B5
Mobberley Staffs 172 B3
Moccas 144 C3
Mochdre Conwy 181 G5
Mochdre Powys 155 G4
Mochrum 206 D2
Mockbeggar Hants 106 A2
Mockbeggar Kent 123 G4
Mockerkin 209 D4
Modbury 100 C2
Moddershall 171 G4
Modern Art Oxford Oxon
  OX1 1BP 80 Oxford
Modsarie 273 J2
Moel Famau Country Park
  Denb LL15 1US 169 E1
Moelfre IoA 180 D4
Moelfre Powys 169 E5
Moffat 226 B5
Mogerhanger 149 G3
Moin'a'choire 230 B3
Moine House 273 H3
Moira 159 F1
Molash 124 C3
Mol-chlach 255 K3
Mold (Yr Wyddgrug) 169 F1
Molehill Green
  Essex 151 D5
Molehill Green
  Essex 151 F5
Molescroft 196 C3
Molesden 220 D3
Molesworth 161 F5
Mollance 216 B4
Molland 114 B5
Mollington
  ChesW&C 183 E5
Mollington Oxon 147 G3
Mollinsburn 234 A2
Monach Islands (Heisker
  Islands) 262 B5
Monachty 142 B1
Monachyle 241 G3
Monewden 152 D2
Moneydie 243 F2
Moneyrow Green 135 D5
Moniaive 216 B3
Monifieth 244 D1
Monikie 244 D1
Monikie Country Park
  Angus DD5 3QN 244 C1
Monimail 244 A3
Monington 141 E3
Monk Bretton 186 A2
Monk Fryston 195 E5
Monk Hesleden 213 D4
Monk Sherborne 120 B2
Monk Soham 152 D1
Monk Soham
  Green 152 D1
Monk Street 151 E4
Monken Hadley 136 B3
Monkey Mates W'ham
  RG41 1JA 134 C5
Monkey World, Wareham
  Dorset
  BH20 6HH 105 E4
Monkhide 145 F3
Monkhill 209 G1
Monkhopton 157 F3
Monkland 144 D2
Monkleigh 113 E3
Monknash 129 F5
Monkokehampton 113 F5
Monks Eleigh 152 A3
Monks Eleigh Tye 152 A3
Monk's Gate 109 E1
Monks' Heath 184 C5
Monk's Hill 124 A4
Monks Kirby 159 G4
Monks Risborough 134 D2
Monkscross 99 D3
Monkseaton 221 F4
Monkshill 269 F6
Monksilver 115 D4
Monkstadt 263 J5
Monkswood 130 C2
Monkton Devon 103 E2
Monkton Kent 125 E2
Monkton Pembs 126 C2
Monkton SAyr 224 B3
Monkton T&W 212 C1
Monkton VGlam 129 F5
Monkton Combe 117 E1
Monkton Deverill 117 F4
Monkton Farleigh 117 E1
Monkton Heathfield 115 F5
Monkton Up
  Wimborne 105 G1
Monkton Wyld 103 G3
Monkwearmouth 212 C2
Monkwood 120 B4

Monmouth
  (Trefynwy) 131 E1
Monnington Court 144 C4
Monnington on
  Wye 144 C3
Monreith 207 D2
Montacute 104 B1
Montacute House Som
  TA15 6XP 104 B1
Monteach 269 G6
Montford 156 C1
Montford Bridge 156 D1
Montgarrie 260 D3
Montgomery
  (Trefaldwyn) 156 B3
Montgreenan 233 E5
Montpellier Gallery Warks
  CV37 6EP
  85 Stratford-upon-Avon
Montrave 244 B4
Montrose 253 F4
Monxton 119 E3
Monyash 172 C1
Monymusk 260 E3
Monzie 243 D2
Moodiesburn 234 A2
Moons Moat North 146 C1
Moonzie 244 B3
Moor Allerton 194 C4
Moor Cock 192 C1
Moor Crichel 105 F2
Moor End Bed 149 F2
Moor End CenBeds 149 E5
Moor End Cumb 199 G5
Moor End ERid 196 B5
Moor End Lancs 191 G3
Moor End NYorks 195 E4
Moor End WYorks 193 G5
Moor Green Wilts 117 F1
Moor Green WMid 158 C4
Moor Head 194 B4
Moor Monkton 195 E2
Moor Row 208 D5
Moor Side Cumb 198 D5
Moor Side Lancs 192 A4
Moor Side Lancs 192 A4
Moor Side Lincs 176 A2
Moor Street 124 A2
Moorby 176 A1
Moorcot 144 C2
Moordown 105 G3
Moore 183 G4
Moorend 209 G1
Moorends 187 D1
Moorfield 185 E3
Moorgreen 173 F3
Moorhall 186 A5
Moorhampton 144 C3
Moorhouse Cumb 209 G1
Moorhouse Notts 174 C1
Moorland (Northmoor
  Green) 116 A4
Moorlinch 116 A4
Moors Centre, Danby
  NYorks
  YO21 2NB 203 G2
Moors Valley Country Park
  Dorset
  BH24 2ET 106 A2
Moors Valley Railway
  Dorset
  BH24 2ET 105 G2
Moorsholm 203 F1
Moorside Dorset 105 D1
Moorside GtMan 185 D2
Moorside WYorks 194 B4
Moorthorpe 186 B1
Moortown IoW 106 D4
Moortown Lincs 188 A3
Moortown Tel&W 157 F1
Morangie 266 E3
Morar 256 C5
Morborne 161 G3
Morchard Bishop 102 A2
Morcombelake 104 A3
Morcott 161 E2
Morda 169 F5
Morden Dorset 105 F3
Morden GtLon 122 B2
Morden Hall Park GtLon
  SM4 5JD 11 F8
Morden Park 122 B2
Mordiford 145 E4
Mordington
  Holdings 237 G4
Mordon 212 C5
More 156 C3
Morebath 114 C5
Morebattle 228 B4
Morecambe 192 A1
Morefield 265 H2
Moreleigh 101 D3
Morenish 242 B1
Moresby Parks 208 C5
Morestead 119 G5
Moreton Dorset 105 E4
Moreton Essex 137 E2
Moreton Here 145 E1
Moreton Mersey 183 D4
Moreton Oxon 134 B3
Moreton Staffs 172 C4
Moreton Staffs 157 G1
Moreton Corbet 170 C5
Moreton Jeffries 145 F3
Moreton Mill 170 C5
Moreton Morrell 147 F2
Moreton on Lugg 145 E3
Moreton Paddox 147 F2
Moreton Pinkney 148 A3
Moreton Say 170 B3
Moreton Valence 131 G2
Moretonhampstead 102 A4
Moreton-in-Marsh 147 D4
Morfa Carmar 128 B1
Morfa Cere 141 G2
Morfa Bychan 167 E4
Morfa Glas 129 E2
Morfa Nefyn 166 B3
Morgan's Vale 118 C5
Morganstown 130 A4
Mork 131 E2
Morland 210 B5
Morley Derbys 173 E3
Morley Dur 212 A5
Morley WYorks 194 B5
Morley Green 184 C4
Morley St. Botolph 164 B2
Mornick 98 D3

Morningside Edin 235 G2
Morningside NLan 234 C4
Morningthorpe 164 D2
Morpeth 221 E3
Morphie 253 F3
Morrey 158 D1
Morridge Side 172 B2
Morrilow Heath 171 G4
Morriston SAyr 224 A5
Morriston Swan 128 C3
Morristown 130 A5
Morroch 247 F1
Morston 178 B1
Mortehoe 113 E1
Morthen 186 B4
Mortimer 120 B1
Mortimer West End 120 B1
Mortimer's Cross 144 D1
Mortlake 136 B5
Morton Derbys 173 F1
Morton Lincs 175 F5
Morton Lincs 187 F3
Morton Lincs 175 D1
Morton Notts 174 C2
Morton SGlos 131 F3
Morton Shrop 169 F5
Morton Bagot 146 D1
Morton on the Hill 178 C4
Morton Tinmouth 212 A5
Morton-on-Swale 202 C3
Morvah 94 B3
Morval 97 G4
Morvich (A'Mhormhaich)
  High 257 F2
Morvich High 266 E1
Morvil 140 D4
Morville 157 F3
Morwellham 100 A1
Morwellham Quay Museum
  Devon PL19 8JL 99 E3
Morwenstow 112 C4
Morwick Hall 221 E1
Mosborough 186 B4
Moscow 233 F5
Mosedale 209 G3
Moseley Height 185 E1
Moseley WMid 158 B3
Moseley Worcs 146 A2
Moses Gate 184 B2
Moss A&B 246 A2
Moss SYorks 186 C1
Moss Bank 183 G3
Moss Houses 184 C5
Moss Nook 184 C4
Moss of Barmuckity 267 K5
Moss Side GtMan 184 C3
Moss Side Lancs 191 G4
Moss Side Mersey 183 E2
Mossat 260 C2
Mossbank 278 D5
Mossblown 224 C3
Mossburnford 228 A5
Mossdale 216 A3
Mossend 234 B3
Mosser 209 E4
Mossgiel 224 C3
Mosshead 260 D1
Mosside of
  Ballinshoe 252 C4
Mossley ChesE 171 F1
Mossley GtMan 185 D2
Mossley Hill 183 E4
Mosspaul Hotel 218 B2
Moss-side High 267 F6
Moss-side Moray 268 D5
Mosstodloch 268 B4
Mosston 252 D5
Mossy Lea 183 G1
Mosterton 104 A2
Moston GtMan 184 C2
Moston Shrop 170 C5
Moston Green 171 E1
Mostyn 182 C4
Motcombe 117 F5
Mothecombe 100 C3
Mother Shipton's Cave
  NYorks
  HG5 8DD 194 C2
Motherby 210 A5
Motherwell 234 B4
Mottingham 136 D5
Mottisfont 119 E5
Mottisfont Abbey Hants
  SO51 0LP 119 E5
Mottistone 106 D4
Mottram in
  Longdendale 185 D3
Mottram
  St. Andrew 184 C5
Mouldsworth 183 G5
Moulin 251 E4
Moulsecoomb 109 F3
Moulsford 134 A4
Moulsham 137 G2
Moulsoe 149 E3
Moulton ChesW&C 171 D1
Moulton Lincs 176 B5
Moulton N'hants 148 C1
Moulton NYorks 202 B2
Moulton Suff 151 E1
Moulton VGlam 129 G5
Moulton Chapel 162 A2
Moulton St. Mary 179 F5
Moulton Seas End 176 B5
Mounie Castle 261 F2
Mount Corn 96 B4
Mount Corn 97 F3
Mount High 267 G7
Mount Kent 125 D4
Mount WYorks 185 F1
Mount Ambrose 96 B5
Mount Bures 152 A4
Mount Charles 97 E4
Mount Edgcumbe Country
  Park Corn
  PL10 1HZ 99 E3
Mount Hawke 96 B5
Mount Manisty 183 E5
Mount Oliphant 224 B4
Mount Pleasant
  ChesE 171 F2
Mount Pleasant
  Derbys 173 E3
Mount Pleasant
  Derbys 159 E1
Mount Pleasant
  ESuss 109 G2

Mount Pleasant
  Flints 182 D5
Mount Pleasant
  GtLon 135 F3
Mount Pleasant
  Hants 106 C3
Mount Pleasant
  Norf 164 A2
Mount Pleasant
  Suff 151 F3
Mount Sorrel 118 B5
Mount Tabor 193 G5
Mountain 193 G4
Mountain Ash
  (Aberpennar) 129 G3
Mountain Cross 235 F5
Mountain Water 140 C5
Mountbenger 227 E3
Mountblairy 268 E5
Mountblow 257 A2
Mountfield 110 C1
Mountgerald 266 C5
Mountjoy 96 C3
Mountnessing 137 F3
Mounton 131 E3
Mountsorrel 160 A1
Mousa 279 D10
Mousehole 94 B4
Mouswald 217 E3
Mow Cop 171 F2
Mowden 202 B1
Mowhaugh 228 C4
Mowsley 160 B4
Mowtie 253 G1
Moxley 158 B3
Moy High 249 D1
Moy High 249 G1
Moy High 258 E1
Moy House 267 H6
Moylgrove 141 E3
Muasdale 231 E5
Much Birch 145 E4
Much Cowarne 145 F3
Much Dewchurch 145 D4
Much Hadham 136 C1
Much Hoole 192 A5
Much Hoole Town 192 A5
Much Marcle 145 F4
Much Wenlock 157 F2
Muchalls 261 H5
Muchelney 116 A5
Muchelney Ham 116 B5
Muchlarnick 97 G4
Muchra 226 D4
Muchrachd 257 J1
Muck 246 D2
Mucking 137 F4
Muckle Roe 279 C6
Muckleford 104 C3
Mucklestone 171 E4
Muckleton 170 C5
Muckletown 260 D2
Muckley 157 F3
Muckley Corner 158 C2
Muckton 189 D4
Mudale 273 H5
Muddiford 113 F2
Muddles Green 110 A2
Muddleswood 109 E2
Mudeford 106 A3
Mudford 104 B1
Mudgley 116 B3
Mugdock 233 G2
Mugdock Country Park
  Stir G62 8EL 30 C1
Mugeary 255 K1
Mugginton 173 D3
Muggintonlane
  End 173 D3
Muggleswick 211 G3
Mugswell 122 B3
Muie 266 D1
Muir 251 F1
Muir of Fowlis 260 D3
Muir of Lochs 268 B4
Muir of Ord
  (Am Blàr Dubh) 266 C6
Muirden 269 F5
Muirdrum 245 D1
Muiredge 244 B5
Muirhead Aber 260 D3
Muirhead Angus 244 B1
Muirhead Fife 244 A4
Muirhead Moray 267 H5
Muirhead NLan 234 A3
Muirhouses 235 E1
Muirkirk 225 E3
Muirmill 234 B1
Muirtack Aber 261 H1
Muirtack Aber 269 G6
Muirton High 266 E5
Muirton P&K 243 E3
Muirton P&K 243 G2
Muirton of Ardblair 251 G5
Muirton of Ballochy 253 E3
Muirtown 267 G6
Muiryfold 269 F5
Muker 201 E3
Mulbarton 178 C5
Mulben 268 B5
Mulhagery 271 F7
Mull 239 E1
Mullach
  Chàrlabhaigh 270 E3
Mullacott Cross 113 F1
Mullion 95 D5
Mullion Cove 95 D5
Mumby 189 F5
Munderfield Row 145 F2
Munderfield Stocks 145 F2
Mundesley 179 E2
Mundford 163 G3
Mundham 165 E2
Mundon 138 B2
Mundurno 261 H3
Munerigie 257 J4
Mungasdale 265 F2
Mungoswells 236 B2
Mungrisdale 209 G3
Munlochy 266 D6
Munnoch 232 D5
Munsley 145 F3
Munslow 157 E4
Murchington 99 G2

Murdostoun 234 C4
Murieston 235 E3
Murkle 275 G2
Murlaganmore 242 A1
Murlaggan High 257 G2
Murlaggan High 249 F1
Murra 277 B7
Murrell Green 120 C2
Murroes 244 C1
Murrow 162 B2
Mursley 148 D5
Murston 124 B2
Murthill 252 C4
Murthly 243 F1
Murton Cumb 210 D5
Murton Dur 212 C3
Murton N'umb 237 G5
Murton Swan 128 B4
Murton York 195 F2
Musbury 103 F3
Muscliff 105 G3
Musdale (Musdàl) 240 B2
Museum in Docklands
  GtLon E14 4AL 12 D4
Museum of Childhood,
  Edinburgh Edin
  EH1 1TG 37 G4
Museum of Childhood,
  London GtLon
  E2 9PA 12 C4
Museum of Flight ELoth
  EH39 5LF 236 C2
Museum of Garden History,
  London GtLon
  SE1 7LB 45 F7
Museum of London GtLon
  EC2Y 5HN 45 J2
Museum of Science &
  Industry, Manchester
  GtMan M3 4FP 46 C4
Museum of Transport,
  Glasgow Glas
  G3 8DP 38 C2
Musselburgh 236 A2
Mustard Hyrn 179 F4
Mustard Shop Norf
  NR2 1NQ 79 Norwich
Muston Leics 174 D4
Muston NYorks 205 E5
Mustow Green 158 A5
Mutford 165 F3
Muthill 243 D3
Mutley 100 A2
Mutterton 102 D2
Muxton 157 G1
Mybster 275 G3
Myddfai 143 E4
Myddle 170 B5
Myddlewood 170 B5
Mydroilyn 142 A2
Myerscough
  College 192 A4
Myerscough Smithy 192 C4
Mylor 95 F3
Mylor Bridge 95 F3
Mynachdy 130 A5
Mynachlog-ddu 141 E4
Myndtown 156 C4
Mynydd Llandygai 167 F1
Mynydd Mechell 180 B4
Mynydd-bach Mon 131 D3
Mynydd-bach
  Swan 128 C3
Mynyddgarreg 128 A2
Mynytho 166 C4
Myrebird 261 F5
Myrelandhorn 275 H3
Myrtle Hill 143 D4
Mytchett 121 D2
Mytholm 193 G5
Mytholmroyd 193 G5
Mythop 191 G4
Myton-on-Swale 194 D1
Mytton 156 D1

N

Naast 264 E3
Nab's Head 192 C5
Na-Buirgh 263 F2
Naburn 195 E3
Nackington 125 D3
Nacton 152 D3
Nadderwater 102 B3
Nafferton 196 C2
Nailbridge 131 F1
Nailsbourne 115 F5
Nailsea 131 D5
Nailstone 159 G2
Nailsworth 132 A3
Nairn 267 F6
Nancegollan 94 D3
Nancekuke 96 A5
Nancledra 94 B3
Nannau 167 F2
Nannerch 169 E1
Nanpantan 160 A1
Nanpean 97 D4
Nanquidno 94 A4
Nant Peris 167 F2
Nant-ddu 129 G1
Nanternis 141 G2
Nantgaredig 142 A5
Nantgarw 130 A4
Nant-glas 143 G1
Nantglyn 168 D1
Nantgwyn 155 F5
Nantlle 167 E2
Nantmawr 169 F5
Nantmel 143 G1
Nantmor 167 F2
Nantwich 170 D2
Nantycaws 128 A1
Nant-y-derry 130 C2
Nant-y-dugoed 155 F1
Nantyffyllon 129 E3
Nantyglo 130 A1
Nant-y-Gollen 169 F5
Nant-y-groes 143 G1
Nant-y-moel 129 F3
Nant-y-Pandy 181 E5
Naphill 135 D3
Napley Heath 171 E4
Nappa 193 E3
Napton on the Hill 147 G1
Narberth (Arberth) 127 E1
Narborough Leics 160 A3
Narborough Norf 163 F1
Narkurs 98 D5
Narrachan 240 B3

Nasareth 167 D3
Naseby 160 B5
Nash Bucks 148 C4
Nash Here 144 C1
Nash Newport 130 C4
Nash Shrop 157 F5
Nash VGlam 129 F5
Nash Street 123 F2
Nassington 161 F3
Nasty 150 B5
Nateby Cumb 200 C2
Nateby Lancs 192 A3
Nately Scures 120 C2
National Agricultural Centre,
  Stoneleigh Warks
  CV8 2LZ 16 B5
National Army Museum
  GtLon
  SW3 4HT 13 A5
National Botanic Garden
  of Wales Carmar
  SA32 8HG 128 B1
National Coal Mining
  Museum for England
  WYorks
  WF4 4RH 27 F6
National Exhibition Centre
  WMid B40 1NT 15 H4
National Fishing Heritage
  Centre, Grimsby NELincs
  DN31 1UZ 188 C2
National Gallery GtLon
  WC2N 5DN 44 D4
National Gallery of Scotland
  Edin EH2 2EL 37 F4
National Indoor Arena,
  Birmingham
  WMid B1 2AA 34 D4
National Marine Aquarium
  PL4 0LF 81 Plymouth
National Maritime Museum
  Cornwall Corn
  TR11 3QY 95 F3
National Maritime Museum,
  Greenwich GtLon
  SE10 9NF 13 D5
National Media Museum
  WYorks BD1 1NQ
  65 Bradford
National Memorial
  Arboretum, Alrewas
  Staffs
  DE13 7AR 159 D3
National Motorcycle
  Museum, Solihull WMid
  B92 0EJ 159 E4
National Museum Cardiff
  CF10 3NP
  67 Cardiff
National Museum of
  Scotland Edin
  EH1 1JF 37 G5
National Portrait Gallery
  GtLon
  WC2H 0HE 44 D4
National Railway Museum
  YO26 4XJ 90 York
National Sea Life Centre,
  Birmingham
  WMid B1 2JB 34 D4
National Seal Sanctuary
  Corn TR12 6UG 95 E4
National Slate Museum,
  Llanberis Gwyn
  LL55 4TY 167 E2
National Space Centre,
  Leicester Leic
  LE4 5NS 17 C4
National Wallace Monument
  Stir FK9 5LF 242 D5
National War Museum,
  Edinburgh Edin
  EH1 2NG 37 F4
National Waterfront
  Museum SA1 3RD
  86 Swansea
National Wildflower Centre,
  Liverpool Mersey
  L16 3NA 22 D4
Natland 199 G4
Natural History Museum
  at Tring Herts
  HP23 6AP 135 E1
Natural History Museum,
  London GtLon
  SW7 5BD 11 F5
Natureland Seal
  Sanctuary Lincs
  PE25 1DB 177 D1
Naughton 152 B3
Naunton Glos 146 D5
Naunton Worcs 146 A4
Naunton
  Beauchamp 146 B2
Navenby 175 E2
Navestock 137 E3
Navestock Side 137 E3
Navidale 275 F4
Navity 266 E5
Nawton 203 F4
Nayland 152 A4
Nazeing 136 D2
Neacroft 106 A3
Neal's Green 159 F4
Neap 279 E7
Neap House 187 F1
Near Sawrey 199 E3
Nearton End 148 D5
Neasden 136 B4
Neasham 202 C1
Neat Enstone 147 F5
Neath
  (Castell-nedd) 129 D3
Neatham 120 C3
Neatishead 179 E3
Nebo Cere 142 B1
Nebo Conwy 168 B2
Nebo Gwyn 167 D2
Nebo IoA 180 C3
Necton 163 G2
Nedd 272 D5
Nedderton 221 E3
Nedging 152 A3
Nedging Tye 152 B3
Needham 164 D3
Needham Lake Suff
  IP6 8NU 152 B2
Needham Market 152 B2

Needham Street 151 F1
Needingworth 162 B5
Needles Pleasure Park IoW
  PO39 0JD 106 C4
Needwood 172 C5
Neen Savage 157 F5
Neen Sollars 157 F5
Neenton 157 F4
Nefyn 166 C3
Neighbourne 116 D3
Neilston 233 F4
Neithrop 147 G3
Nelson Caerp 130 A3
Nelson Lancs 193 E4
Nelson Village 221 E4
Nemphlar 234 C5
Nempnett
  Thrubwell 116 C1
Nenthall 211 D3
Nenthead 211 D3
Nenthorn 228 A3
Neopardy 102 A3
Nerabus 230 B3
Nercwys 169 F1
Neriby 230 B3
Nerston 234 A4
Nesbit 229 D3
Nesfield 193 G3
Ness 183 E5
Ness Botanic Gardens
  ChesW&C
  CH64 4AY 183 E5
Ness of Tenston 277 B6
Nesscliffe 156 C1
Neston ChesW&C 183 D5
Neston Wilts 117 F1
Nether
  Auchendrane 224 B4
Nether Barr 215 F4
Nether Blainslie 236 C5
Nether Broughton 174 B5
Nether Burrow 200 B5
Nether Cerne 104 C3
Nether Compton 104 B1
Nether Crimond 261 G2
Nether Dalgliesh 227 D5
Nether Dallachy 268 B4
Nether Edge 186 A4
Nether End 185 G5
Nether Exe 102 C2
Nether Glasslaw 269 G5
Nether Handwick 252 B5
Nether Haugh 186 B3
Nether Heage 173 E2
Nether Heselden 201 D5
Nether Heyford 148 B2
Nether Kellet 192 B1
Nether Kinmundy 269 J6
Nether Langwith 186 C5
Nether Lenshie 268 E6
Nether Loads 173 E1
Nether Moor 173 E1
Nether Padley 185 G5
Nether Pitforthie 253 G2
Nether Poppleton 195 E2
Nether Silton 203 D3
Nether Skyborry 156 B5
Nether Stowey 115 E4
Nether Urquhart 243 G4
Nether Wallop 119 E4
Nether Wasdale 198 C2
Nether Welburn 225 E3
Nether Welton 209 G2
Nether Westcote 147 E5
Nether Whitacre 159 E3
Nether Winchendon (Lower
  Winchendon) 134 C1
Nether Worton 147 G5
Netheravon 118 C3
Netherbrae 269 F5
Netherbrough 277 C6
Netherburn 234 C5
Netherbury 104 A3
Netherby Cumb 218 B4
Netherby NYorks 194 C3
Nethercott 147 E5
Netherfield ESuss 110 C2
Netherfield Notts 174 B3
Netherfield SLan 234 B5
Netherhall 232 D3
Netherhampton 118 C5
Netherhay 104 A2
Netherland Green 172 C4
Netherley 261 G5
Nethermill 217 E2
Nethermuir 269 H6
Netherseal 159 E1
Nethershield 225 D3
Netherstreet 118 A1
Netherthird D&G 216 B5
Netherthird EAyr 225 D4
Netherthong 185 F2
Netherthorpe 186 C4
Netherton Angus 252 D4
Netherton
  ChesW&C 183 F5
Netherton Devon 102 B5
Netherton Hants 119 E2
Netherton Mersey 183 E2
Netherton N'umb 220 B1
Netherton NLan 234 B4
Netherton Oxon 133 G2
Netherton P&K 251 G4
Netherton SLan 234 D4
Netherton WMid 158 B4
Netherton Worcs 146 B3
Netherton WYorks 185 F1
Netherton
  Burnfoot 220 B1
Netherton
  Northside 220 B1
Nethertown Cumb 198 A2
Nethertown Ork 275 J1
Nethertown Staffs 158 D1
Netherwitton 220 D2
Netherwood D&G 217 D3
Netherwood EAyr 225 E3
Nethy Bridge 259 H2
Netley Abbey 107 D2
Netley Marsh 106 C1
Nettlebed 134 B4
Nettlebridge 116 D3
Nettlecombe
  Dorset 104 B3
Nettlecombe IoW 107 E5
Nettlecombe Som 115 D4

Nettleden **135** F1
Nettleham **188** A5
Nettlestead *Kent* **123** F3
Nettlestead *Suff* **152** B3
Nettlestead Green **123** F3
Nettlestone **107** F3
Nettlesworth **212** B3
Nettleton *Lincs* **188** B2
Nettleton *Wilts* **132** A5
Nettleton Hill **185** E1
Netton *Devon* **100** B3
Netton *Wilts* **118** C4
Neuadd *Cere* **142** A2
Neuadd *IoA* **180** B3
Neuadd *Powys* **143** F3
Nevendon **137** G3
Nevern **141** D4
Nevill Holt **160** D3
New Abbey **217** D4
New Aberdour **269** G4
New Addington **122** C2
New Alresford **119** G4
New Alyth **252** A5
New Arley **159** E3
New Arram **196** C3
New Ash Green **123** F2
New Balderton **174** D2
New Barn **123** F2
New Belses **227** G3
New Bewick **229** E4
New Bolingbroke **176** B2
New Boultham **187** G5
New Bradwell **148** D3
New Brancepeth **212** B3
New Bridge *D&G* **216** D3
New Bridge
Devon **102** A5
New Brighton
Flints **169** F1
New Brighton
Hants **107** G2
New Brighton
Mersey **183** E3
New Brighton
Wrex **169** F2
New Brighton
WYorks **194** B5
New Brinsley **173** F2
New Broughton **170** A2
New Buckenham **164** B2
New Byth **269** G5
New Cheriton **119** G5
New Cross *Cere* **154** C5
New Cross *GtLon* **136** C5
New Cumnock **225** E4
New Deer **269** G6
New Duston **148** C1
New Earswick **195** F2
New Edlington **186** C3
New Elgin **267** K5
New Ellerby **197** D4
New Eltham **136** D5
New End **146** C1
New England **161** G2
New Farnley **194** B4
New Ferry **183** E4
New Galloway **216** A3
New Gilston **244** C4
New Greens **136** A2
New Grimsby **96** A1
New Hartley **221** F4
New Haw **121** F1
New Heaton **220** C3
New Hedges **127** E2
New Herrington **212** C2
New Hinksey **134** A2
New Holland **196** C5
New Houghton
Derbys **173** G1
New Houghton
Norf **177** F5
New Houses **200** D5
New Hunwick **212** A4
New Hutton **199** G3
New Hythe **123** G3
New Inn *Carmar* **142** A4
New Inn *Fife* **244** A4
New Inn *Mon* **131** D2
New Inn *Torfaen* **130** B3
New Invention
Shrop **156** B5
New Invention
WMid **158** B2
New Kelso **265** F7
New Lanark **234** C5
New Lanark World Heritage
Site *SLan*
ML11 9DB **234** C5
New Lane **183** F1
New Lane End **184** A3
New Leake **176** C2
New Leeds **269** H5
New Leslie **260** D2
New Lodge **186** A2
New Longton **192** B5
New Luce **214** C4
New Mains **225** G2
New Mains of Ury **253** G1
New Malden **122** B2
New Marske **213** F5
New Marton **170** A4
New Mill *Corn* **94** B3
New Mill *Herts* **135** E1
New Mill *WYorks* **185** F2
New Mill End **136** A1
New Mills *Corn* **96** C4
New Mills *Derbys* **185** E4
New Mills *Glos* **131** F2
New Mills *Mon* **131** E2
New Mills (Y Felin Newydd)
Powys **155** G2
New Milton **106** B3
New Mistley **152** C4
New Moat **141** D5
New Ollerton **174** B1
New Orleans **222** C4
New Oscott **158** C3
New Palace &
Adventureland, New
Brighton *Mersey*
CH45 2JX **22** A2
New Park *Corn* **97** F1
New Park *NYorks* **194** B2
New Pitsligo **269** G5
New Polzeath **96** D2
New Quay
(Ceinewydd) **141** G1
New Rackheath **179** D4
New Radnor
(Maesyfed) **144** B1
New Rent **210** A4
New Ridley **211** G1
New Road Side **193** F3
New Romney **111** F1
New Rossington **186** D3
New Row *Cere* **154** D5
New Row *Lancs* **192** C4
New Sawley **173** F4
New Shoreston **229** F3
New Silksworth **212** C2
New Stevenston **234** B4
New Swannington **159** G1
New Totley **186** A5
New Town *CenBeds* **149** G3
New Town *Cere* **141** E3
New Town *Dorset* **105** F1
New Town *Dorset* **105** F2
New Town *ELoth* **236** B2
New Town *ESuss* **109** G1
New Town *Glos* **146** C4
New Tredegar **130** A2
New Tupton **173** E1
New Ulva **231** F1
New Valley **271** G4
New Village **186** C2
New Walk Museum & Art
Gallery LE1 7EA
77 Leicester
New Walsoken **162** C2
New Waltham **188** C2
New Walton Pier *Essex*
CO14 8ES **153** D5
New Winton **236** B2
New World **162** B3
New Yatt **133** F1
New York *Lincs* **176** A2
New York *T&W* **221** F4
Newall **194** B3
Newark *Ork* **276** G3
Newark *Peter* **162** A2
Newark Castle, Newark-on-
Trent *Notts*
NG24 1BG **174** C2
Newark-on-Trent **174** D2
Newarthill **234** B4
Newball **188** A5
Newbarn **125** D5
Newbarns **198** D5
Newbattle **236** A3
Newbiggin *Cumb* **210** A5
Newbiggin *Cumb* **210** C5
Newbiggin *Cumb* **210** B3
Newbiggin *Cumb* **191** F1
Newbiggin *Cumb* **198** B3
Newbiggin *Dur* **211** F5
Newbiggin *N'umb* **211** F1
Newbiggin *NYorks* **201** F4
Newbiggin *NYorks* **201** E3
Newbiggin-by-the-
Sea **221** F3
Newbigging *Aber* **261** G5
Newbigging *Aber* **251** G1
Newbigging *Angus* **244** C1
Newbigging *Angus* **244** C1
Newbigging *Angus* **252** A5
Newbigging *SLan* **235** E5
Newbiggin-on-Lune **200** C2
Newbold *Derbys* **186** A5
Newbold *Leics* **159** G1
Newbold on Avon **159** G5
Newbold on Stour **147** E4
Newbold Pacey **147** E2
Newbold Verdon **159** G2
Newborough
(Niwbwrch) *IoA* **166** D1
Newborough *Peter* **162** A2
Newborough *Staffs* **172** C5
Newbottle *N'hants* **148** A4
Newbottle *T&W* **212** C2
Newbourne **153** D3
Newbridge (Cefn Bychan)
Caerp **130** B3
Newbridge *Corn* **94** B3
Newbridge *Corn* **98** D4
Newbridge *Edin* **235** F2
Newbridge *ESuss* **123** D5
Newbridge *Hants* **106** B1
Newbridge *IoW* **106** D4
Newbridge *NYorks* **204** B4
Newbridge *Oxon* **133** G2
Newbridge *Pembs* **140** C4
Newbridge *Wrex* **169** F3
Newbridge Green **146** A4
Newbridge on Wye **143** G2
Newbridge-on-Usk **130** C3
Newbrough **211** E1
Newbuildings **102** A2
Newburgh *Aber* **269** H5
Newburgh *Aber* **261** H2
Newburgh *Fife* **244** A3
Newburgh *Lancs* **183** F1
Newburgh *ScBord* **227** E3
Newburn **212** A1
Newbury *Som* **117** D2
Newbury *WBerks* **119** F1
Newbury *Wilts* **117** F3
Newbury Park **136** D4
Newby *Cumb* **210** B5
Newby *Lancs* **193** E3
Newby *NYorks* **203** E1
Newby *NYorks* **192** D1
Newby *NYorks* **204** D4
Newby Bridge **199** E4
Newby Cote **200** C5
Newby Cross **209** G1
Newby East **210** A2
Newby Hall *NYorks*
HG4 5AE **194** C1
Newby West **209** G1
Newby Wiske **202** C4
Newcastle
Bridgend **129** E5
Newcastle *Mon* **130** D1
Newcastle *Shrop* **156** B4
Newcastle Emlyn (Castell
Newydd Emlyn) **141** G3
Newcastle International
Airport **221** D4
Newcastle upon
Tyne **212** B1
Newcastleton **218** C3
Newcastle-under-
Lyme **171** F3
Newchapel *Pembs* **141** F4
Newchapel *Staffs* **171** F2
Newchapel *Surr* **122** C4
Newchurch *Carmar* **141** G5
Newchurch *IoW* **107** E4
Newchurch *Kent* **124** C5
Newchurch *Lancs* **193** E5
Newchurch *Lancs* **193** E4
Newchurch *Mon* **131** D3
Newchurch *Powys* **144** B2
Newchurch *Staffs* **172** C5
Newcott **103** F2
Newcraighall **236** A2
Newdigate **121** G3
Newell Green **135** D5
Newenden **110** D1
Newent **145** G5
Newerne **131** F2
Newfield *Dur* **212** B4
Newfield *Dur* **212** B2
Newfield *High* **266** E4
Newfound **119** G2
Newgale **140** B5
Newgate **178** B1
Newgate Street **136** C2
Newgord **278** E2
Newhall *ChesE* **170** D3
Newhall *Derbys* **173** D5
Newham **229** F4
Newham Hall **229** F4
Newhaven **109** G3
Newhey **184** D1
Newholm **204** B1
Newhouse **234** B3
Newick **109** G1
Newingreen **124** D5
Newington *Edin* **235** G2
Newington *Kent* **125** D5
Newington *Kent* **124** A2
Newington *Notts* **187** D3
Newington *Oxon* **134** B3
Newington
Bagpath **132** A3
Newland *Cumb* **199** E5
Newland *Glos* **131** E2
Newland *Hull* **196** C4
Newland *NYorks* **195** F5
Newland *Oxon* **133** F1
Newland *Worcs* **145** G3
Newlandrig **236** A3
Newlands *Cumb* **209** G3
Newlands *Essex* **138** B4
Newlands *N'umb* **211** G2
Newlands *ScBord* **218** D2
Newland's Corner **121** F3
Newlands of Geise **275** F2
Newlands of Tynet **268** B4
Newlyn **94** B4
Newmachar **261** G3
Newmains **234** C4
Newman's End **137** E1
Newman's Green **151** G3
Newmarket *Suff* **151** E1
Newmarket *ESiar* **271** G4
Newmill *Aber* **253** F1
Newmill *Aber* **269** G6
Newmill *Aber* **261** G2
Newmill *Moray* **268** C5
Newmill *ScBord* **227** F4
Newmill of
Inshewan **252** C3
Newmillerdam **186** A1
Newmillerdam Country Park
WYorks WF2 6QP **27** H6
Newmills **266** D5
Newmiln *P&K* **243** G1
Newmiln *P&K* **243** F2
Newmilns **224** D2
Newney Green **137** F2
Newnham *Glos* **131** F1
Newnham *Hants* **120** C2
Newnham *Herts* **150** A4
Newnham *Kent* **124** B3
Newnham *N'hants* **148** A2
Newnham Bridge **145** F1
Newnham Paddox **159** G4
Newnoth **260** D1
Newport *Corn* **98** D2
Newport *Devon* **113** F2
Newport *ERid* **196** A4
Newport *Essex* **150** D4
Newport *Glos* **131** F3
Newport *High* **275** G6
Newport *IoW* **107** E4
Newport (Casnewydd)
Newport **130** C4
Newport *Norf* **179** G4
Newport (Trefdraeth)
Pembs **141** D4
Newport *Som* **116** A5
Newport *Tel&W* **157** G1
Newport Pagnell **149** D3
Newport-on-Tay **244** C2
Newpound
Common **121** F5
Newquay **96** C3
Newquay Cornwall
International Airport **96** C3
Newquay Zoo *Corn*
TR7 2LZ **96** C3
Newsbank **171** F1
Newseat **261** F1
Newsells **150** B4
Newsham *Lancs* **192** B4
Newsham *N'umb* **221** E4
Newsham *NYorks* **202** A1
Newsham *NYorks* **202** C4
Newsholme *ERid* **195** G5
Newsholme *Lancs* **193** E2
Newsome **185** F1
Newstead *N'umb* **229** F4
Newstead *Notts* **173** G2
Newstead *ScBord* **227** G2
Newstead Abbey *Notts*
NG15 8NA **173** G2
Newthorpe *Notts* **173** F3
Newthorpe *NYorks* **195** D4
Newtoft **188** A4
Newton *A&B* **240** C5
Newton *Aber* **268** C6
Newton *Aber* **269** J6
Newton *Bridgend* **129** E5
Newton *Cambs* **162** C1
Newton *Cambs* **150** C3
Newton *Cardiff* **130** B5
Newton *ChesW&C* **170** C2
Newton *ChesW&C* **183** G5
Newton *Cumb* **198** D5
Newton *D&G* **217** F1
Newton *Derbys* **173** F2
Newton *GtMan* **185** D3
Newton *Here* **144** C1
Newton *Here* **145** E2
Newton *Here* **144** C4
Newton *High* **275** J3
Newton *High* **266** E7
Newton *High* **275** H3
Newton *High* **272** E5
Newton *High* **266** C6
Newton *High* **266** E5
Newton *Lancs* **192** C2
Newton *Lancs* **199** G5
Newton *Lancs* **191** G4
Newton *Lincs* **175** F4
Newton *Moray* **268** B4
Newton *N'hants* **161** D4
Newton *N'umb* **211** G1
Newton *N'umb* **220** B1
Newton *NAyr* **232** A4
Newton *Norf* **163** G1
Newton *Notts* **174** B3
Newton *P&K* **243** D1
Newton *Pembs* **140** B5
Newton *Pembs* **126** C2
Newton *ScBord* **228** A4
Newton *SGlos* **131** F3
Newton *Shrop* **170** B4
Newton *SLan* **226** A2
Newton *Som* **115** E4
Newton *Staffs* **172** B5
Newton *Suff* **152** A3
Newton *Swan* **128** C4
Newton *Warks* **160** A5
Newton *Wilts* **118** D5
Newton *WLoth* **235** E2
Newton *WYorks* **194** D5
Newton Abbot **102** B5
Newton Arlosh **209** F1
Newton Aycliffe **212** B5
Newton Bewley **213** D5
Newton
Blossomville **149** E2
Newton Bromswold **149** E1
Newton Burgoland **159** F2
Newton by Toft **188** A4
Newton Ferrers **100** B3
Newton Flotman **164** D2
Newton Green **131** E3
Newton Harcourt **160** B3
Newton Kyme **195** D3
Newton Longville **148** D4
Newton Mearns **233** G4
Newton Morrell
NYorks **202** B2
Newton Morrell
Oxon **148** B5
Newton Mountain **126** C2
Newton Mulgrave **203** G1
Newton of Affleck **244** C1
Newton of Ardtoe **247** F2
Newton of
Balcanquhal **243** G3
Newton of Dalvey **267** H6
Newton of Falkland **244** A4
Newton of Leys **258** D1
Newton on the Hill **170** B5
Newton on Trent **187** F5
Newton Poppleford **103** D4
Newton Purcell **148** B4
Newton Regis **159** E2
Newton Reigny **210** A4
Newton St. Cyres **102** B3
Newton St. Faith **178** D4
Newton St. Loe **117** E1
Newton St. Petrock **113** E4
Newton Solney **173** D5
Newton Stacey **119** F3
Newton Stewart **215** F4
Newton Tony **118** D3
Newton Tracey **113** F3
Newton under
Roseberry **203** E1
Newton
Underwood **221** D3
Newton upon
Derwent **195** G3
Newton Valence **120** C4
Newton with
Scales **192** A4
Newtonairds **216** C2
Newtongrange **236** A3
Newtonhill **261** H5
Newton-le-Willows
Mersey **183** G3
Newton-le-Willows
NYorks **202** B4
Newtonmill **253** E3
Newtonmore (Baile Ùr
an t-Slèibh) **258** E5
Newton-on-Ouse **195** E2
Newton-on-
Rawcliffe **204** B3
Newton-on-the-
Moor **221** D1
Newtown *Bucks* **135** E2
Newtown
ChesW&C **170** C2
Newtown *Corn* **97** G2
Newtown *Corn* **94** C4
Newtown *Cumb* **210** B1
Newtown *Derbys* **185** D4
Newtown *Devon* **114** A5
Newtown *Devon* **103** D3
Newtown *Dorset* **104** A2
Newtown *Glos* **131** F2
Newtown *GtMan* **183** G2
Newtown *GtMan* **184** B2
Newtown *Hants* **107** F1
Newtown *Hants* **119** F1
Newtown *Hants* **106** B1
Newtown *Hants* **119** E5
Newtown *Hants* **107** E1
Newtown *Here* **145** F3
Newtown *Here* **145** D2
Newtown *High* **257** K4
Newtown *IoM* **190** B4
Newtown *IoW* **106** D3
Newtown *N'umb* **220** C1
Newtown *N'umb* **229** E4
Newtown *Oxon* **134** C4
Newtown (Y Drenewydd)
Powys **156** A3
Newtown *RCT* **129** G3
Newtown *Shrop* **170** B4
Newtown *Som* **115** F4
Newtown *Som* **103** F1
Newtown *Staffs* **171** G1
Newtown *Staffs* **172** B1
Newtown *Staffs* **158** B2
Newtown *Wilts* **118** A5
Newtown *Wilts* **119** E1
Newtown Linford **160** A2
Newtown
St. Boswells **227** G2
Newtown Unthank **159** G2
Newtown-in-Saint-
Martin **95** E4
Newtyle **252** A5
Newyears Green **135** F4
Neyland **126** C2
Nibley *Glos* **131** F2
Nibley *SGlos* **131** F4
Nibley Green **131** G3
Nicholashayne **103** E1
Nicholaston **128** B4
Nidd **194** C1
Nigg *Aberdeen* **261** H4
Nigg *High* **267** F4
Nightcott **114** B5
Nilig **168** D2
Nilston Rigg **211** E1
Nimlet **131** G5
Nine Ashes **137** E2
Nine Elms **132** D4
Nine Mile Burn **235** F4
Ninebanks **211** D2
Ninemile Bar
(Crocketford) **216** C3
Nineveh **145** F1
Ninfield **110** C2
Ningwood **106** D4
Nisbet **228** A4
Niton **107** E5
Nitshill **233** G3
Nizels **123** E3
No Man's Heath
ChesW&C **170** C3
No Man's Heath
Warks **159** E2
No Man's Land **97** G4
Noah's Ark **123** E3
Noak Hill **137** E3
Noblehill **217** D3
Noblethorpe **185** G2
Nobottle **148** B1
Nocton **175** F1
Noddsdale **232** D3
Nogdam End **179** E5
Noke **134** A1
Nolton **126** B1
Nolton Haven **126** B1
Nomansland
Devon **102** B1
Nomansland *Wilts* **106** B1
Noneley **170** B5
Nonington **125** E3
Nook *Cumb* **218** C4
Nook *Cumb* **199** G4
Noonsbrough **279** B7
Noranside **252** C3
Norbreck **191** G3
Norbury *ChesE* **170** C3
Norbury *Derbys* **172** C3
Norbury *GtLon* **136** C5
Norbury *Shrop* **156** C3
Norbury *Staffs* **171** E5
Norbury Common **170** C3
Norbury Junction **171** E5
Norchard **127** D3
Norcott Brook **184** A4
Nordelph **163** D2
Norden *Dorset* **105** F4
Norden *GtMan* **184** C1
Nordley **157** F3
Norfolk Lavender, Heacham
Norf PE31 7JE **177** E4
Norham **237** G5
Norland Town **193** G5
Norley **183** G5
Norleywood **106** C3
Norlington **109** G2
Norman Cross **161** G3
Normanby *NLincs* **187** F1
Normanby *NYorks* **203** G4
Normanby *R&C* **203** E1
Normanby by Stow **187** F4
Normanby Hall Country
Park *NLincs*
DN15 9HU **187** F1
Normanby le Wold **188** B3
Normanby-by-
Spital **188** A4
Normandy **121** E2
Normann's Ruh **246** D5
Norman's Bay **110** B3
Norman's Green **103** D2
Normanston **165** G2
Normanton *Derby* **173** E4
Normanton *Leics* **174** D3
Normanton *Lincs* **175** E3
Normanton *Notts* **174** C2
Normanton *Rut* **161** E2
Normanton
WYorks **194** C5
Normanton le
Heath **159** F1
Normanton on Soar **173** G5
Normanton on
Trent **174** C1
Normanton-on-the-
Wolds **174** B4
Normoss **191** G4
Norrington
Common **117** F1
Norris Green **100** A1
Norris Hill **159** F1
Norristhorpe **194** B5
North Acton **136** B4
North Anston **186** C4
North Ascot **121** E1
North Aston **147** G5
North Baddesley **106** C1
North Ballachulish
(Baile a' Chaolais a
Tuath) **248** C3
North Balloch **215** E1
North Barrow **116** D5
North Barsham **178** A2
North Bay Miniature
Railway *NYorks*
YO12 6PF **204** D3
North Benfleet **137** G4
North Bersted **108** B3
North Berwick **236** C1
North Boarhunt **107** F1
North Bogbain **268** B5
North Bovey **102** A4
North Bradley **117** F2
North Brentor **99** E2
North Brewham **117** E4
North Bridge **121** E4
North Buckland **113** E1
North Burlingham **179** E4
North Cadbury **116** D5
North Cairn **214** A3
North Camp **121** D2
North Carlton
Lincs **187** G5
North Carlton
Notts **186** C4
North Cave **196** A4
North Cerney **132** C2
North Chailey **109** F1
North Charford **106** A1
North Charlton **229** F4
North Cheriton **117** D5
North Chideock **104** A3
North Cliffe **196** A4
North Clifton **187** F5
North Cockerington **189** D3
North Coker **104** B1
North Collafirth **278** C4
North Common
SGlos **131** F5
North Common
Suff **164** A4
North Commonty **269** G6
North Connel **240** B1
North Coombe **102** B2
North Cornelly **129** E4
North Corner **131** F4
North Cotes **188** D2
North Cove **165** F3
North Cowton **202** B2
North Crawley **149** E3
North Cray **137** D5
North Creake **177** G4
North Curry **116** A5
North Dallens **248** B5
North Dalton **196** B2
North Dawn **277** D7
North Deighton **194** C2
North Dell (Dail Bho
Thuath) **271** G1
North Duffield **195** F4
North Elkington **188** C3
North Elmham **178** A3
North Elmsall **186** B1
North End *Bucks* **148** D5
North End *Dorset* **117** F5
North End *ERid* **197** D2
North End *ERid* **197** D3
North End *ERid* **197** E4
North End *Essex* **137** F1
North End *Hants* **119** G5
North End *Hants* **106** A1
North End *Leics* **160** A1
North End *N'umb* **220** D1
North End *Norf* **164** B2
North End *NSom* **116** B1
North End *Ports* **107** F2
North End *WSuss* **108** D2
North End *WSuss* **108** B3
North Erradale **264** D3
North Essie **269** J5
North Fambridge **138** B3
North Ferriby **196** B5
North Frodingham **196** D2
North Gluss **278** C5
North Gorley **106** A1
North Green *Norf* **164** D3
North Green *Suff* **165** E4
North Green *Suff* **153** E1
North Green *Suff* **153** E1
North Grimston **196** A1
North Halling **123** G2
North Harby **187** F5
North Hayling **107** G2
North Hazelrigg **229** E3
North Heasley **114** A4
North Heath
WBerks **133** G5
North Heath
WSuss **121** F5
North Hill **97** G2
North Hillingdon **135** F4
North Hinksey **133** G2
North Holmwood **121** G3
North Houghton **119** E4
North Huish **100** D2
North Hykeham **175** E1
North Johnston **126** C1
North Kelsey **188** A2
North Kessock **266** D7
North Killingholme **188** B1
North Kilvington **202** D4
North Kilworth **160** B4
North Kingston **106** A2
North Kyme **175** G2
North Lancing **109** D3
North Lee **134** D2
North Lees **202** C5
North Leigh **133** F1
North Leverton with
Habblesthorpe **187** E4
North Littleton **146** C3
North Lopham **164** B3
North Luffenham **161** E2
North Marden **108** A2
North Marston **148** C5
North Middleton
Midlo **236** A4
North Middleton
N'umb **229** E4
North Millbrex **269** G6
North Molton **114** A5
North Moreton **134** A4
North Mundham **108** A3
North Muskham **174** C2
North Newbald **196** B4
North Newington **147** G4
North Newnton **118** C2
North Newton **115** F4
North Nibley **131** G3
North Norfolk Railway
Norf NR26 8RA **178** C1
North Oakley **119** G2
North Ockendon **137** E4
North Ormesby **203** E1
North Ormsby **188** C3
North Otterington **202** C4
North Owersby **188** A3
North Perrott **104** A2
North Petherton **115** F4
North Petherwin **97** G1
North Pickenham **163** G2
North Piddle **146** B2
North Plain **217** F4
North Pool **101** D3
North Poorton **104** B3
North Quarme **114** C4
North Queensferry **235** F1
North Radworthy **114** A4
North Rauceby **175** F3
North Reston **189** D4
North Riding Forest Park
NYorks
YO18 7LT **204** B3
North Rigton **194** B3
North Rode **171** F1
North Roe **278** C4
North Ronaldsay **276** G2
North Ronaldsay
Airfield **276** G2
North Runcton **163** E1
North Sandwick **278** E3
North Scale **191** E1
North Scarle **175** D1
North Seaton **221** E3
North Shian (Sithean a
Tuath) **248** B5
North Shields **212** C1
North Shoebury **138** C4
North Side **162** A3
North Skelton **203** F1
North Somercotes **189** E3
North Stainley **202** B5
North Stainmore **200** D1
North Stifford **137** F4
North Stoke
B&NESom **117** E1
North Stoke *Oxon* **134** B4
North Stoke *WSuss* **108** C2
North Stoneham **106** D1
North Street *Hants* **120** B4
North Street *Kent* **124** C3
North Street *Med* **124** A1
North Street
WBerks **134** B5
North Sunderland **229** G3
North Tamerton **98** D1
North Tarbothill **261** H3
North Tawton **113** G5
North Third **234** B1
North Thoresby **188** C3
North Tidworth **118** D3
North Togston **221** E1
North Town *Devon* **113** F5
North Town *Hants* **121** D2
North Town *W&M* **135** D4
North Tuddenham **178** B4
North Uist (Uibhist a
Tuath) **262** D4
North Walsham **179** D2
North Waltham **119** G3
North
Warnborough **120** C2
North Water Bridge **253** E3
North Watten **275** H3
North Weald
Bassett **137** D2
North Wembley **136** A4
North Wheatley **187** E4
North Whilborough **101** E1
North Wick **116** C1
North Widcombe **116** C2
North Willingham **188** B4
North Wingfield **173** F1
North Witham **175** E5
North Wootton
Dorset **104** C1
North Wootton
Norf **177** E5
North Wootton
Som **116** C3
North Wraxall **132** A5
North Wroughton **132** D4
North Yardhope **220** B1
North Yorkshire Moors
Railway *NYorks*
YO18 7AJ **204** B4
Northacre **164** A2
Northall **149** E5
Northall Green **178** A4
Northallerton **202** C3
Northam *Devon* **113** E3
Northam *Soton* **106** D1
Northam Burrows Country
Park *Devon*
EX39 1XR **113** E2
Northampton **148** C1
Northaw **136** B2
Northay *Devon* **103** G2
Northay *Som* **103** F1
Northbay **254** C4
Northbeck **175** F3
Northborough **161** G2
Northbourne *Kent* **125** F3
Northbourne *Oxon* **134** A4
Northbridge Street **110** C1
Northbrook *Hants* **119** G4
Northbrook *Oxon* **147** G5
Northburnhill **269** G6
Northchapel **121** E5
Northchurch **135** E2
Northcote Manor **113** G4
Northcott **98** D1
Northcourt **134** A3
Northdyke **276** B5
Northedge **173** E1
Northend
B&NESom **117** E1
Northend *Bucks* **134** C3
Northend *Warks* **147** F2
Northfield *Aber* **269** G4
Northfield
Aberdeen **261** H4
Northfield *High* **275** J4
Northfield *Hull* **196** C5
Northfield *ScBord* **237** G3
Northfield *Som* **115** F4
Northfield *WMid* **158** C5
Northfields **161** F2
Northfleet **137** F5
Northhouse **227** F5
Northiam **110** D1
Northill **149** G3
Northington *Glos* **131** G2
Northington
Hants **119** G4
Northlands **176** B2
Northleach **132** D1
Northleigh *Devon* **103** E3

Northleigh *Devon* 113 G2
Northlew 99 F1
Northmoor 133 G2
Northmoor Green
(Moorland) 116 A4
Northmuir 252 B4
Northney 107 G2
Northolt 136 A4
Northop
(Llaneurgain) 169 F1
Northop Hall 169 F1
Northorpe *Lincs* 176 A4
Northorpe *Lincs* 187 F3
Northorpe *Lincs* 161 F1
Northover *Som* 116 C5
Northover *Som* 116 B4
Northowram 194 A5
Northport 105 F4
Northpunds 279 D10
Northrepps 178 D2
Northton
(Taobh Tuath) 262 E3
Northtown 277 D8
Northumbria Craft Centre,
Morpeth *N'umb*
NE61 1PD 221 E3
Northway *Glos* 146 B4
Northway *Som* 115 E5
Northwich 184 A5
Northwick *SGlos* 131 E4
Northwick *Som* 116 A1
Northwick *Worcs* 146 A2
Northwold 163 F3
Northwood *GtLon* 135 F3
Northwood *IoW* 107 D3
Northwood *Kent* 125 F2
Northwood *Mersey* 183 F3
Northwood *Shrop* 170 B4
Northwood Green 131 G1
Northwood Hills 136 A3
Norton *Glos* 146 A5
Norton *Halton* 183 G4
Norton *IoW* 106 C4
Norton *Mon* 144 D5
Norton *N'hants* 148 B1
Norton *Notts* 186 C5
Norton *NSom* 116 A1
Norton *NYorks* 203 G5
Norton *Powys* 144 C1
Norton *Shrop* 157 E2
Norton *Shrop* 157 G2
Norton *Shrop* 157 D4
Norton *Stock* 212 D5
Norton *Suff* 152 A1
Norton *Swan* 128 C4
Norton *SYorks* 186 C1
Norton *SYorks* 186 A4
Norton *VGlam* 129 E5
Norton *Wilts* 132 A4
Norton *Worcs* 146 A2
Norton *Worcs* 146 C3
Norton *WSuss* 108 B3
Norton *WSuss* 108 A4
Norton Bavant 118 A3
Norton Bridge 171 F4
Norton Canes 158 C2
Norton Canon 144 C3
Norton Disney 175 D2
Norton Ferris 117 E4
Norton Fitzwarren 115 E5
Norton Green
Herts 150 A5
Norton Green *IoW* 106 C4
Norton Green
Stoke 171 G2
Norton Hawkfield 116 C1
Norton Heath 137 F2
Norton in Hales 171 E4
Norton in the
Moors 171 F2
Norton Lindsey 147 E1
Norton Little Green 152 A1
Norton Malreward 116 D1
Norton Mandeville 137 E2
Norton St. Philip 117 E2
Norton Subcourse 165 F2
Norton Wood 144 C3
Norton Woodseats 186 A4
Norton-Juxta-
Twycross 159 F2
Norton-le-Clay 202 D5
Norton-sub-
Hamdon 104 A1
Norwell 174 C1
Norwell Woodhouse 174 C1
Norwich 178 D5
Norwich Castle Museum &
Art Gallery *Norf*
NR1 3JU 79 Norwich
Norwich Cathedral *Norf*
NR1 4DH 79 Norwich
Norwich International
Airport 178 D4
Norwick 278 F1
Norwood End 137 E2
Norwood Green
GtLon 136 A5
Norwood Green
WYorks 194 A5
Norwood Hill 122 B4
Norwood Park 116 C4
Noseley 160 C3
Noss Mayo 100 B3
Nosterfield 202 B4
Nosterfield End 151 E3
Nostie 256 E2
Notgrove 146 D5
Nottage 129 E5
Notting Hill 136 B4
Nottingham *High* 275 H5
Nottingham *Nott* 173 G3
Nottingham Castle Museum
& Art Gallery NG1 6EL
80 Nottingham
Nottington 104 C4
Notton *Wilts* 118 A1
Notton *WYorks* 186 A1
Nottswood Hill 131 G1
Nounsley 137 G1
Noutard's Green 145 G1
Nowton 151 G1
Nowton Park *Suff*
IP29 5LU 151 G1
Nox 156 D1
Noyadd Trefawr 141 F3
Nuffield 134 B4

Nun Monkton 195 E2
Nunburnholme 196 A3
Nuneaton 159 F3
Nuneham
Courtenay 134 A3
Nunney 117 E3
Nunnington *Here* 145 E3
Nunnington
NYorks 203 F5
Nunnington Park 115 D5
Nunnykirk 220 C2
Nunsthorpe 188 C2
Nunthorpe *Middl* 203 E1
Nunthorpe *York* 195 E2
Nunton 118 C5
Nunwick *N'umb* 220 A4
Nunwick *NYorks* 202 C5
Nup End 134 B1
Nupend 131 G2
Nursted 120 C5
Nurton 158 A3
Nutbourne *WSuss* 108 C2
Nutbourne *WSuss* 107 G2
Nutfield 122 C3
Nuthall 173 G3
Nuthampstead 150 C4
Nuthurst *Warks* 159 D5
Nuthurst *WSuss* 121 G5
Nutley *ESuss* 109 G1
Nutley *Hants* 120 B3
Nutwell 186 D2
Nyadd 242 C5
Nybster 275 J2
Nyetimber 108 A4
Nyewood 120 C5
Nymans *WSuss*
RH17 6EB 109 E1
Nymet Rowland 102 A2
Nymet Tracey 102 A2
Nympsfield 132 A2
Nynehead 115 E5
Nythe 116 B4
Nyton 108 B3

O

O2, The *GtLon*
SE10 0BB 13 E5
Oad Street 124 A2
Oadby 160 B2
Oak Cross 99 F1
Oak Tree 202 C1
Oakamoor 172 B3
Oakbank *A&B* 239 G1
Oakbank *WLoth* 235 E3
Oakdale *Caerp* 130 A3
Oakdale *Poole* 105 G3
Oake 115 E5
Oaken 158 A2
Oakenclough 192 B3
Oakengates 157 G1
Oakenhead 267 K5
Oakenholt 183 G5
Oakenshaw *Dur* 212 B4
Oakenshaw
WYorks 194 A5
Oakerthorpe 173 E2
Oakes 185 F1
Oakfield *IoW* 107 E3
Oakford *Cere* 142 A2
Oakford *Devon* 114 C5
Oakfordbridge 114 C5
Oakgrove 171 G1
Oakham 161 D2
Oakhanger 120 C4
Oakhill 116 D3
Oakington 150 C1
Oaklands *Conwy* 168 B2
Oaklands *Herts* 136 B1
Oakle Street 131 G1
Oakley *Bed* 149 F2
Oakley *Bucks* 134 B1
Oakley *Fife* 235 E1
Oakley *Hants* 119 G3
Oakley *Oxon* 134 B2
Oakley *Poole* 105 G3
Oakley *Suff* 164 C4
Oakley Green 135 E5
Oakley Park 155 F4
Oakridge Lynch 132 B2
Oaks 156 D2
Oaks Green 172 C4
Oaksey 132 B3
Oakshaw Ford 218 D4
Oakshott 120 C5
Oakthorpe 159 F1
Oaktree Hill 202 C3
Oakwell Hall & Country Park
WYorks
WF17 9LG 27 E4
Oakwood Leisure Park
Pembs
SA67 8DE 127 D1
Oakwoodhill 121 G4
Oakworth 193 G4
Oare *Kent* 124 C2
Oare *Som* 114 B3
Oare *Wilts* 118 C1
Oasby 175 F4
Oatfield 222 B4
Oath 116 A5
Oathlaw 252 C4
Oatlands 194 C2
Oban
(An t-Òban) 240 A2
Obley 156 C5
Oborne 104 C1
Obthorpe 161 F1
Occlestone Green 171 D1
Occold 164 C4
Occumster 275 H5
Oceanarium BH2 5AA
64 Bournemouth
Ochiltree 224 D3
Ochr-y-foel 182 B5
Ochtermuthill 242 D3
Ochtertyre *P&K* 242 D2
Ochtertyre *Stir* 242 C5
Ockbrook 173 F4
Ockeridge 145 G1
Ockham 121 F2
Ockle 247 E2
Ockley 121 G4
Ocle Pychard 145 E3
Octon 204 D5
Odcombe 104 B1
Odd Down 117 E1

Oddendale 200 B1
Oddingley 146 B2
Oddington 134 A1
Odds Farm Park *Bucks*
HP10 0LX 135 E4
Oddsta 278 E3
Odell 149 E2
Odham 113 E5
Odiham 120 C2
Odsey 150 A4
Odstock 118 C5
Odstone 159 F2
Offchurch 147 F1
Offenham 146 C3
Offerton 184 D4
Offham *ESuss* 109 F2
Offham *Kent* 123 F3
Offham *WSuss* 108 C3
Offley Hoo 149 G5
Offleymarsh 171 E5
Offord Cluny 150 A1
Offord D'Arcy 150 A1
Offton 152 B3
Offwell 103 E3
Ogbourne Maizey 133 D5
Ogbourne
St. Andrew 133 D5
Ogbourne
St. George 133 D5
Ogden Water *WYorks*
HX2 8YA 26 A3
Ogil 252 C3
Ogle 220 D4
Oglet 183 F4
Ogmore 129 E5
Ogmore Vale 129 F3
Ogmore-by-Sea 129 E5
Ogston Reservoir *Derbys*
DE55 6EL 173 E1
Oil Terminal 277 C8
Okeford Fitzpaine 105 E1
Okehampton 99 F1
Okehampton Camp 99 F1
Okraquoy 279 D9
Olchard 102 B5
Olchfa 128 C3
Old 160 C5
Old Aberdeen 261 H4
Old Alresford 119 G4
Old Arley 159 E3
Old Basford 173 G3
Old Basing 120 B2
Old Belses 227 G3
Old Bewick 229 F4
Old Blacksmith's Shop,
Gretna Green *D&G*
DG16 5DY 218 B5
Old Blair 251 E3
Old Bolingbroke 176 B1
Old Bramhope 194 B3
Old Brampton 186 A5
Old Bridge of Urr 216 B4
Old Buckenham 164 B2
Old Burdon 212 C2
Old Burghclere 119 F2
Old Byland 203 E4
Old Cassop 212 C4
Old Church Stoke 156 B3
Old Cleeve 114 D3
Old Clipstone 174 B1
Old Colwyn 181 G5
Old Craig 261 H2
Old Craighall 236 A2
Old Crombie 268 D5
Old Dailly 214 D1
Old Dalby 174 B5
Old Dam 185 F5
Old Deer 269 H6
Old Dilton 117 F3
Old Down *SGlos* 131 F4
Old Down *Som* 116 D2
Old Edlington 186 C3
Old Eldon 212 B5
Old Ellerby 197 D4
Old Felixstowe 153 E4
Old Fletton 161 G3
Old Ford 136 C4
Old Glossop 185 E3
Old Goginan 154 C4
Old Goole 195 G5
Old Gore 145 F5
Old Grimsby 96 A1
Old Hall 188 C1
Old Hall Green 150 B5
Old Hall Street 179 E2
Old Harlow 137 D1
Old Heath 152 B5
Old Heathfield 110 A1
Old Hill 158 B4
Old Hurst 162 B5
Old Hutton 199 G4
Old Kea 96 C5
Old Kilpatrick 233 F2
Old Kinnernie 261 F4
Old Knebworth 150 A5
Old Leake 176 B1
Old Leslie 260 D2
Old Malton 204 B5
Old Milton 106 B3
Old Milverton 147 E1
Old Montsale 138 D3
Old Netley 107 D1
Old Newton 152 B1
Old Philpstoun 235 E2
Old Poltalloch 240 A4
Old Radnor
(Pencraig) 144 B2
Old Rayne 260 E2
Old Romney 111 F1
Old Royal Naval College,
Greenwich *GtLon*
SE10 9LW 13 E5
Old Scone 243 G2
Old Shields 234 C2
Old Sodbury 131 G4
Old Somerby 175 E4
Old Station, The, Tintern
Parva *Mon*
NP16 7NX 131 E2
Old Stratford 148 C3
Old Sunderlandwick 196 C2
Old Swarland 221 D1
Old Swinford 158 B4
Old Thirsk 202 D4
Old Town *Cumb* 199 G4
Old Town *IoS* 96 B1

Old Town Farm 220 A2
Old Tupton 173 E1
Old Warden 149 G3
Old Weston 161 F5
Old Windsor 135 E5
Old Wives Lees 124 C3
Old Woking 121 F2
Old Woodhall 176 A1
Old Woods 170 B5
Oldberrow 146 D1
Oldborough 102 A2
Oldbury *Kent* 123 E3
Oldbury *Shrop* 157 G3
Oldbury *WMid* 158 B4
Oldbury Court Estate
Bristol BS16 2JH 8 D2
Oldbury Naite 131 F3
Oldbury on the Hill 132 A4
Oldbury-on-Severn 131 F3
Oldcastle *Mon* 144 D4
Oldcastle Heath 170 B3
Oldcotes 186 C5
Oldcroft 131 F2
Oldeamere 162 B3
Oldfield 146 A1
Oldford 117 E2
Oldhall *Aber* 260 C5
Oldhall *High* 275 H3
Oldham 184 D2
Oldham Edge 184 D2
Oldhamstocks 237 E2
Oldland 131 F5
Oldmeldrum 261 G2
Oldmill 260 D4
Oldpark 157 F2
Oldridge 102 B3
Oldshore Beg 272 D3
Oldshoremore 272 E3
Oldstead 203 E4
Oldtown 266 C3
Oldtown of Aigas 266 B7
Oldtown of Ord 268 E5
Oldwalls 128 A3
Oldways End 114 B5
Oldwhat 269 G5
Oldwich Lane 159 E5
Olgrinmore 275 G3
Oliver 226 C3
Oliver's Battery 119 F5
Ollaberry 278 C4
Ollerton *ChesE* 184 B5
Ollerton *Notts* 174 B1
Ollerton *Shrop* 170 D5
Olmstead Green 151 E3
Olney 149 D2
Olrig House 275 G2
Olton 158 D4
Olveston 131 F4
Ombersley 146 A1
Ompton 174 B1
Onchan 190 B4
Onecote 172 B2
Onehouse 152 B2
Ongar Hill 177 D5
Ongar Street 144 C1
Onibury 157 D5
Onich
(Omhanaich) 248 C3
Onllwyn 129 E1
Onneley 171 E3
Onslow Green 137 F1
Onslow Village 121 E3
Opinan *High* 264 E2
Opinan *High* 264 D4
Orange Lane 237 E5
Orasaigh 271 F6
Orbliston 268 B5
Orbost 263 H7
Orby 176 C1
Orcadia 232 C3
Orchard 232 C1
Orchard Portman 115 F5
Orcheston 118 B3
Orcop 145 D5
Orcop Hill 145 D5
Ord 256 C3
Ordhead 260 E3
Ordie 260 C4
Ordiequish 268 B5
Ordsall 187 D5
Ore 110 D2
Oreham Common 109 E2
Oreston 100 B2
Oreton 157 F5
Orford *Suff* 153 F3
Orford *Warr* 184 A3
Organford 105 F3
Orgreave 158 D1
Orleton *Here* 145 D1
Orleton *Worcs* 145 F1
Orleton Common 145 D1
Orlingbury 161 D5
Ormacleit 254 C1
Ormesby 203 E1
Ormesby
St. Margaret 179 F4
Ormesby
St. Michael 179 F4
Ormidale 232 B1
Ormiscaig 264 E2
Ormiston 236 B3
Ormlie 275 G2
Ormsaigmore 247 D3
Ormsary 231 F2
Ormskirk 183 F2
Oronsay 230 B1
Orphir 277 C7
Orpington 123 D2
Orrell *GtMan* 183 G2
Orrell *Mersey* 183 E3
Orrisdale 190 B2
Orrok House 261 H3
Orroland 208 A2
Orsett 137 F4
Orsett Heath 137 F4
Orslow 158 A1
Orston 174 C3
Orton *Cumb* 200 B2
Orton *N'hants* 160 D5
Orton Longueville 161 G3

Orton Rigg 209 G1
Orton Waterville 161 G3
Orton-on-the-Hill 159 F2
Orwell 150 B2
Osbaldeston 192 C4
Osbaldwick 195 F2
Osbaston *Leics* 159 G2
Osbaston *Shrop* 170 A5
Osbaston *Tel&W* 157 E1
Osbaston Hollow 159 G2
Osborne 107 E3
Osborne House *IoW*
PO32 6JX 107 E3
Osbournby 175 F4
Oscroft 170 C1
Ose 263 J7
Osgathorpe 159 G1
Osgodby *Lincs* 188 A3
Osgodby *NYorks* 195 F4
Osgodby *NYorks* 205 D4
Oskaig 256 B1
Osleston 172 D4
Osmaston *Derbys* 173 E4
Osmaston *Derbys* 172 C3
Osmington 104 D4
Osmington Mills 104 D4
Osmondthorpe 194 C4
Osmotherley 203 D3
Osnaburgh (Dairsie) 244 C3
Ospringe 124 C2
Ossett 194 B5
Ossett Street Side 194 B5
Ossington 174 C1
Ostend 138 C2
Osterley 136 A5
Osterley Park & House
GtLon TW7 4RB 11 B5
Oswaldkirk 203 F5
Oswaldtwistle 192 D5
Oswestry 169 F5
Oteley 170 B4
Otford 123 E3
Otham 123 G3
Otherton 158 B1
Othery 116 A4
Otley *Suff* 152 D2
Otley *WYorks* 194 B3
Otter 232 A2
Otter Ferry 232 A1
Otterbourne 119 F5
Otterburn *N'umb* 220 A2
Otterburn *NYorks* 193 E2
Otterburn Camp 220 A2
Otterham 98 B1
Otterham Quay 124 A2
Otterhampton 115 F3
Otternish 262 E4
Ottershaw 121 F1
Otterswick 278 E4
Otterton 103 E4
Otterton Mill *Devon*
EX9 7HG 103 E4
Otterwood 106 D2
Ottery St. Mary 103 D3
Ottinge 125 D4
Ottringham 197 E5
Oughterby 209 F1
Oughtershaw 201 E3
Oughterside 209 E2
Oughtibridge 186 A3
Oulston 203 E5
Oulton *Cumb* 209 F1
Oulton *Norf* 178 C3
Oulton *Staffs* 171 G4
Oulton *Staffs* 171 E5
Oulton *Suff* 165 G2
Oulton *WYorks* 194 C4
Oulton Broad 165 G2
Oulton Grange 171 G4
Oulton Street 178 C3
Oultoncross 171 G4
Oundle 161 F4
Our Dynamic Earth *Edin*
EH8 8AS 37 J4
Ousby 210 C4
Ousdale 275 F6
Ousden 151 F2
Ousefleet 196 A5
Ouston *Dur* 212 B2
Ouston *N'umb* 220 C4
Out Newton 197 F5
Out Rawcliffe 192 A3
Out Skerries
Airstrip 278 F5
Outcast 199 E5
Outchester 229 F3
Outertown 277 B7
Outgate 199 E3
Outhgill 200 C2
Outlands 171 E5
Outlane 185 E1
Outwell 162 D2
Outwood *Surr* 122 C4
Outwood *WYorks* 194 C5
Outwoods 157 G1
Ouzlewell Green 194 C5
Ovenden 193 G5
Over *Cambs* 162 B5
Over *ChesW&C* 170 D1
Over *Glos* 132 A1
Over *SGlos* 131 E4
Over Burrows 173 D4
Over Compton 104 B1
Over Dinsdale 202 C1
Over End 185 G5
Over Green 159 D3
Over Haddon 172 D1
Over Hulton 184 A2
Over Kellet 192 B1
Over Kiddington 147 G5
Over Monnow 131 D1
Over Norton 147 F5
Over Peover 184 B5
Over Rankeilour 244 B3
Over Silton 203 D3
Over Stowey 115 E4
Over Stratton 104 A1
Over Tabley 184 B4
Over Wallop 119 D4
Over Whitacre 159 E3
Over Worton 147 G5
Overbister 276 F3
Overbrae 269 G5
Overbury 146 B4
Overcombe 104 C4

Overgreen 186 A5
Overleigh 116 B4
Overpool 183 E5
Overscaig Hotel 273 G6
Overseal 159 E1
Overslade 159 G5
Oversland 124 C3
Overstone 148 D1
Overstrand 178 D1
Overthorpe 147 G3
Overton *Aber* 261 F3
Overton *Aberdeen* 261 G3
Overton *ChesW&C* 183 G5
Overton *Hants* 119 G3
Overton *Lancs* 192 A2
Overton *NYorks* 195 E2
Overton *Shrop* 157 E5
Overton *Swan* 128 A4
Overton (Owrtyn)
Wrex 170 A3
Overton Bridge 170 A3
Overtown *Lancs* 200 B5
Overtown *NLan* 234 C4
Overtown *Swin* 133 D5
Overy 134 A3
Oving *Bucks* 148 C5
Oving *WSuss* 108 B3
Ovingdean 109 F3
Ovingham 211 G1
Ovington *Dur* 202 A1
Ovington *Essex* 151 F3
Ovington *Hants* 119 G4
Ovington *N'umb* 211 G1
Ovington *Norf* 178 A5
Ower *Hants* 106 C1
Ower *Hants* 107 D2
Owermoigne 105 D4
Owler Bar 185 G5
Owlpen 131 G3
Owl's Green 153 D1
Owlswick 134 C2
Owmby 188 A2
Owmby-by-Spital 188 A4
Owslebury 119 G5
Owston 160 C2
Owston Ferry 187 F2
Owstwick 197 E4
Owthorpe 174 B4
Oxborough 163 F2
Oxcombe 188 D5
Oxen End 151 E5
Oxen Park 199 E4
Oxencombe 102 B4
Oxenhall 145 G5
Oxenholme 199 G3
Oxenhope 193 G4
Oxenpill 116 B3
Oxenton 146 B4
Oxenwood 119 E2
Oxford 134 A2
Oxford Cathedral *Oxon*
OX1 1AB 80 Oxford
Oxford Story *Oxon*
OX1 3AJ 80 Oxford
Oxford University Museum
of Natural History
Oxon OX1 3PW
80 Oxford
Oxhey 136 A3
Oxhill 147 F3
Oxley 158 B2
Oxley Green 138 C1
Oxley's Green 110 B1
Oxnam 228 B5
Oxnead 178 D3
Oxnop Ghyll 201 E3
Oxshott 121 G1
Oxspring 185 G2
Oxted 122 C3
Oxton *Mersey* 183 E4
Oxton *Notts* 174 B3
Oxton *ScBord* 236 B4
Oxwich 128 A4
Oxwich Green 128 A4
Oxwick 178 A3
Oykel Bridge 265 K1
Oyne 260 E2
Ozleworth 131 G3

P

Pabbay 262 D3
Packington 159 F1
Packwood 159 D5
Padanaram 252 C4
Padarn Country Park
Gwyn
LL55 4TY 167 E1
Padbury 148 C4
Paddington 136 B4
Paddlesworth 125 D4
Paddock 124 C3
Paddock Wood 123 F4
Paddockhaugh 267 K6
Paddockhole 218 A3
Paddolgreen 170 C4
Padeswood 169 F1
Padfield 185 E3
Padiham 193 D4
Padside 194 A2
Padstow 96 D2
Padworth 120 B1
Paganhill 132 A2
Pagham 108 A4
Paglesham
Churchend 138 C3
Paglesham
Eastend 138 C3
Paible 263 F2
Paignton 101 E1
Paignton & Dartmouth
Steam Railway
Torbay
TQ4 6AF 101 E2
Paignton Pier
Torbay
TQ4 6BW 101 E1
Paignton Zoo
Torbay
TQ4 7EU 101 E2
Pailton 159 G4
Paine's Corner 110 B1
Painscastle 144 A3
Painshawfield 211 G1
Painswick 132 A2
Pairc 270 E3

Paisley 233 F3
Pakefield 165 G2
Pakenham 152 A1
Palace of Holyroodhouse
Edin EH8 8DX 37 J4
Palacerigg Country Park
NLan G67 3HU 234 B2
Pale 168 C4
Palehouse
Common 109 G2
Palestine 119 D3
Paley Street 135 D5
Palgowan 215 E3
Palgrave 164 C4
Pallinsburn House 228 C3
Palmarsh 124 D5
Palmers Cross 121 F3
Palmers Green 136 C3
Palmerscross 267 K5
Palmerstown 130 A5
Palnackie 216 C5
Palnure 215 F4
Palterton 173 F1
Pamber End 120 B2
Pamber Green 120 B2
Pamber Heath 120 B1
Pamington 146 B4
Pamphill 105 F2
Pampisford 150 C3
Pan 277 C8
Panborough 116 B3
Panbride 245 D1
Pancrasweek 112 C5
Pancross 114 C7
Pandy *Gwyn* 154 C2
Pandy *Mon* 144 C5
Pandy *Powys* 155 F2
Pandy *Wrex* 169 E4
Pandy Tudur 168 B1
Pandy'r Capel 169 D2
Panfield 151 F5
Pangbourne 134 B5
Pannal 194 C2
Pannal Ash 194 B2
Panshanger 136 B1
Pant 169 F5
Pant Glas 167 D3
Pant Gwyn 168 B5
Pant Mawr 155 E4
Pantasaph 182 C5
Panteg 130 C3
Pantglas 155 D3
Pantgwyn *Carmar* 142 B5
Pantgwyn *Cere* 141 F3
Pant-lasau 128 C2
Panton 188 B5
Pant-pastynog 168 D1
Pantperthog 154 D2
Pant-y-dwr 155 F5
Pantyffordd 169 F2
Pant-y-ffridd 156 A2
Pantyffynnon 128 C1
Pantygasseg 130 B3
Pantygelli 130 C1
Pantymwyn 169 E1
Panxworth 179 E4
Papa Stour 279 A6
Papa Stour Airstrip 279 A6
Papa Westray 276 D2
Papa Westray
Airfield 276 D2
Papcastle 209 E3
Papil 279 C9
Papple 236 C2
Papplewick 173 G2
Papworth Everard 150 A1
Papworth St. Agnes 150 A1
Par 97 E4
Paradise Park, Newhaven
ESuss BN9 0DH 109 G3
Paradise Wildlife Park,
Broxbourne *Herts*
EN10 7QA 136 C2
Parbold 183 F1
Parbrook *Som* 116 C4
Parbrook *WSuss* 121 F5
Parc 168 B2
Parcllyn 141 F2
Parc-seymour 130 D3
Parc-y-rhôs 142 B3
Pardshaw 209 D4
Parham 153 E1
Parish Holm 225 F3
Park 268 D5
Park Corner *ESuss* 123 E5
Park Corner *Oxon* 134 B4
Park End *N'umb* 220 A4
Park End *Staffs* 171 E2
Park End *Worcs* 157 G5
Park Gate *Hants* 107 D2
Park Gate *Worcs* 158 B5
Park Gate *WYorks* 194 A3
Park Gate *WYorks* 185 G1
Park Green 152 C1
Park Hill 186 A4
Park Lane 170 B4
Park Langley 122 C2
Park Rose Pottery & Leisure
Park *ERid*
YO15 3QF 196 D1
Park Street 136 A2
Parkend *Cumb* 209 G3
Parkend *Glos* 131 F2
Parker's Green 123 F4
Parkeston 152 D4
Parkfield *Corn* 98 D4
Parkfield *SGlos* 131 F5
Parkfield *WMid* 158 B3
Parkford 252 C4
Parkgate *ChesW&C* 183 D5
Parkgate *D&G* 217 E2
Parkgate *Kent* 124 A5
Parkgate *Surr* 122 B4
Parkgate *SYorks* 186 B3
Parkham 113 D3
Parkham Ash 113 D3
Parkhead 234 A2
Parkhill *Angus* 253 E5
Parkhill *P&K* 251 G5
Parkhouse 131 D2
Parkhurst 107 D3
Parkmill 128 B4
Parkmore 268 B6
Parkneuk 253 F2
Parkside 170 A2
Parkstone 105 G3

Parkway **116** C5
Parley Cross **105** G3
Parley Green **106** A3
Parlington **194** D4
Parracombe **113** E1
Parrog **140** D4
Parson Cross **186** A3
Parson Drove **162** B2
Parsonby **209** E3
Partick **233** F3
Partington **184** B3
Partney **176** C1
Parton Cumb **208** C4
Parton D&G **216** A3
Partridge Green **109** D2
Parwich **172** C2
Paslow Wood
  Common **137** E2
Passenham **148** C4
Passfield **120** D4
Passingford Bridge **137** E3
Paston **179** E2
Paston Street **179** E2
Pasturefields **171** G5
Patchacott **99** E1
Patcham **109** F3
Patchetts Green **136** A3
Patching **108** C3
Patchole **113** G1
Patchway **131** F4
Pateley Bridge **194** A1
Path of Condie **243** F3
Pathe **116** A4
Pathfinder Village **102** B3
Pathhead Aber **253** F3
Pathhead EAyr **225** E4
Pathhead Fife **244** A5
Pathhead Midlo **236** A3
Pathlow **147** D2
Patmore Heath **150** C5
Patna **224** C4
Patney **118** B2
Patrick **190** A3
Patrick Brompton **202** B3
Patrington **197** F5
Patrington Haven **197** F5
Patrishow **144** B3
Patrixbourne **125** D3
Patterdale **209** G5
Pattingham **158** A3
Pattishall **148** B2
Pattiswick **151** G5
Paul **94** B4
Paulerspury **148** C3
Paull **197** D5
Paull Holme **197** D5
Paul's Green **94** D3
Paulton **117** D2
Pauntonley **157** G1
Pavenham **149** E2
Pavilion Gardens, Buxton
  Derbys
  SK17 6XN **185** E5
Pawlett **116** A3
Pawston **228** C3
Paxford **147** D4
Paxhill Park **109** F1
Paxton **237** G4
Payden Street **124** B3
Payhembury **103** D2
Paythorne **193** E2
Peacehaven **109** G3
Peacemarsh **117** F5
Peachley **146** A2
Peak Dale **185** E5
Peak Forest **185** F5
Peakirk **161** G2
Pean Hill **124** D2
Pear Tree **173** E4
Pearsie **252** B4
Pearson's Green **123** F4
Peartree **136** B1
Peartree Green
  Essex **137** E3
Peartree Green
  Here **145** F4
Pease Pottage **122** B5
Peasedown
  St. John **117** E2
Peasehill **173** F3
Peaseland Green **178** B4
Peasemore **133** G5
Peasenhall **153** E1
Peaslake **121** F3
Peasley Cross **183** G3
Peasmarsh
  ESuss **111** D1
Peasmarsh Surr **121** E3
Peaston **236** B3
Peastonbank **236** B3
Peathill **269** H4
Peatling Magna **160** A3
Peatling Parva **160** A4
Peaton **157** E4
Pebble Coombe **122** B3
Pebmarsh **151** G4
Pebworth **146** D3
Pecket Well **193** F5
Peckforton **170** C2
Peckham **136** C5
Peckleton **159** G2
Pedham **179** E4
Pedmore **158** B4
Pedwell **116** B4
Peebles **235** G5
Peel IoM **190** A3
Peel Lancs **191** G4
Peening Quarter **111** D1
Peggs Green **159** G1
Pegsdon **149** G4
Pegswood **221** E3
Pegwell **125** F2
Peighinn nan
  Aoireann **254** C1
Peinchorran **256** B1
Peinlich **263** K6
Pelaw **212** B1
Pelcomb **126** C1
Pelcomb Bridge **126** C1
Pelcomb Cross **126** C1
Peldon **138** C1
Pellon **193** G5

Pelsall **158** C2
Pelton **212** B2
Pelutho **209** E2
Pelynt **97** G4
Pemberton **183** G2
Pembrey (Pen-bre) **128** A2
Pembrey Country Park
  Carmar
  SA16 0EJ **128** A2
Pembridge **144** C2
Pembroke (Penfro) **126** C2
Pembroke Dock
  (Doc Penfro) **126** C2
Pembury **123** F4
Pen-bont
  Rhydybeddau **154** C4
Penboyr **141** G4
Penbryn **141** F2
Pencader **142** A4
Pen-cae **142** A3
Pen-cae-cwm **168** C1
Pencaenewydd **166** D3
Pencaitland **236** B3
Pencarnisiog **180** B5
Pencarreg **142** B3
Pencarrow **97** F1
Pencelli **143** G5
Pen-clawdd **128** B3
Pencoed **129** F4
Pencombe **145** E2
Pencoyd **145** E5
Pendeen **94** A3
Penderyn **129** F2
Pendine
  (Pentywyn) **127** F2
Pendlebury **184** B2
Pendleton **193** D4
Pendock **145** G4
Pendoggett **97** E2
Pendomer **104** B1
Pendoylan **129** G5
Penegoes **155** D2
Penelewey **96** C5
Pen-ffordd **141** D5
Pengam **130** A3
Penge **136** C5
Pengenffordd **144** A5
Pengorffwysfa **180** C3
Pengover Green **97** G3
Pen-groes-oped **130** C2
Pengwern **182** B5
Penhale **95** D5
Penhallow **96** B4
Penhalvean **95** E3
Penhill **154** C3
Penhill **133** D4
Penhow **130** D3
Penhurst **110** B2
Peniarth **154** C2
Penicuik **235** G3
Penifiler **263** K7
Peninver **222** C3
Penisa'r Waun **167** E1
Penisarcwm **155** G1
Penishawain **143** G4
Penistone **185** G2
Penjerrick **95** E3
Penketh **183** G4
Penkill **214** D1
Penkridge **158** B1
Penlean **98** C1
Penley **170** B4
Penllech **166** B4
Penllergaer **128** C3
Pen-llyn IoA **180** B4
Penllyn VGlam **129** F5
Pen-lôn **166** D1
Penmachno **168** A2
Penmaen **128** B4
Penmaenan **181** F5
Penmaenmawr **181** F5
Penmaenpool (Llyn
  Penmaen) **154** C1
Penmaen-Rhôs **181** G5
Penmark **115** D5
Penmon **181** E4
Penmorfa **167** E3
Penmynydd **180** D5
Penn Bucks **135** E3
Penn WMid **158** A3
Penn Street **135** E3
Pennal **154** C2
Pennal-isaf **154** D2
Pennan **269** G4
Pennance **96** B5
Pennant Cere **142** B1
Pennant Powys **155** D3
Pennant Melangell **168** D5
Pennar **126** C2
Pennard **128** B4
Pennerley **156** C3
Pennington Cumb **199** D5
Pennington Hants **106** C3
Pennington Flash Country
  Park GtMan
  WN7 3PA **184** A3
Pennington Green **184** A2
Pennorth **144** A5
Pennsylvania **131** G5
Penny Bridge **199** E4
Pennycross **100** A2
Pennyfuir **240** A1
Pennygate **179** E3
Pennyghael **239** E2
Pennyglen **224** A4
Pennygown **247** F5
Pennymoor **102** B1
Pennywick **97** E4
Penwood **119** F1
Penwortham **192** B5
Penwortham Lane **192** B5
Penwyllt **129** E1
Pen-y-banc **142** C5
Pen-y-bont
  Carmar **143** D4
Pen-y-bont
  Carmar **142** A5
Pen-y-bont Powys **155** G1
Pen-y-bont Powys **169** F5

Penpont D&G **216** C1
Penpont Powys **143** F5
Penprysg **129** F4
Penquit **100** C2
Penrherber **141** F4
Penrhiw **141** F3
Penrhiwceiber **129** G3
Penrhiwgoch **128** B1
Penrhiw-llan **141** G3
Penrhiw-pâl **141** G3
Penrhiwtyn **128** D3
Penrhos Gwyn **166** C4
Penrhos IoA **180** A4
Penrhos Mon **130** D1
Penrhos Powys **129** E1
Penrhos-garnedd **181** D5
Penrhyn Bay
  (Bae Penrhyn) **181** G4
Penrhyn Castle Gwyn
  LL57 4HN **181** E4
Penrhyn-coch **154** C4
Penrhyndeudraeth **167** F4
Penrhyn-side **181** G4
Penrhys **129** G3
Penrice **128** A4
Penrith **210** B5
Penrose Corn **96** C2
Penrose Corn **97** G1
Penruddock **210** A5
Penryn **95** E3
Pensarn Carmar **128** A1
Pensarn Conwy **182** A5
Pen-sarn Gwyn **167** E5
Pen-sarn Gwyn **166** D3
Pensax **145** G1
Pensby **183** D4
Penselwood **117** E4
Pensford **116** D1
Pensham **146** B3
Penshaw **212** C2
Penshurst **123** E4
Pensilva **97** G3
Pensnett **158** B4
Penston **236** B2
Pentewan **97** E5
Pentir **167** E1
Pentire **96** D2
Pentireglaze **96** D2
Pentlepoir **127** E2
Pentlow **151** G3
Pentlow Street **151** G3
Pentney **163** F1
Penton Mewsey **119** E3
Pentonville **136** C4
Pentraeth **180** D5
Pentre Powys **169** D5
Pentre Powys **155** G4
Pentre Powys **144** B1
Pentre Powys **156** B3
Pentre Powys **156** A4
Pentre RCT **129** F3
Pentre Shrop **156** C5
Pentre Shrop **156** C5
Pentre Wrex **169** F3
Pentre Wrex **170** A3
Pentre Berw **180** C5
Pentrebach Caerp **130** A2
Pentre-bach Cere **142** B3
Pentrebach MTyd **129** G2
Pentre-bach Powys **143** F4
Pentrebach RCT **129** G4
Pentrebach Swan **128** B2
Pentre-bont **168** A2
Pentre-bwlch **169** E3
Pentrecagal **141** G3
Pentre-celyn
  Denb **169** E2
Pentre-celyn
  Powys **155** E2
Pentre-chwyth **128** C3
Pentreclwydau **129** E2
Pentre-cwrt **141** G4
Pentre-Dolau-
  Honddu **143** F3
Pentredwr Denb **169** E3
Pentre-dwr Swan **128** C3
Pentrefelin Carmar **142** C5
Pentre-felin Cere **142** C3
Pentrefelin Conwy **181** E5
Pentrefelin Gwyn **167** E4
Pentrefelin Powys **169** E5
Pentrefoelas **168** B2
Pentregat **141** G2
Pentre-Gwenlais **128** C1
Pentreheyling **156** B3
Pentre-llwyn-
  llŵyd **143** F2
Pentre llyn **154** C4
Pentre-llyn-
  cymmer **168** C2
Pentre-piod **168** B4
Pentre-poeth **130** B4
Pentre'r beirdd **156** A1
Pentre'r-felin **168** B1
Pentre'r-felin **143** F4
Pentre-tafarn-y-
  fedw **168** B1
Pentre-ty-gwyn **143** E4
Pentrich **173** E2
Pentridge **105** G1
Pentwyn Caerp **130** A2
Pen-twyn Caerp **130** B1
Pentwyn Cardiff **130** B4
Pentwyn Mon **131** E2
Pentwyn-mawr **130** A3
Pentyrch **130** A4
Penuwch **142** B1
Penwithick **97** E4
Penwood **119** F1

Penybont Powys **144** A1
Penybontfawr **169** D5
Penybryn Caerp **130** A3
Pen-y-bryn Gwyn **154** C1
Pen-y-bryn Wrex **169** F3
Pen-y-bryn Pembs **141** E3
Penycae Wrex **169** F3
Pen-y-cae Powys **129** E1
Pen-y-cae-mawr **130** D3
Pen-y-cefn **182** C5
Pen-y-clawdd **130** D2
Pen-y-coedcae **129** G4
Penycwm **140** B5
Pen-y-Darren **129** G2
Pen-y-fai **129** E4
Penyffordd Flints **170** A1
Pen-y-ffordd Flints **182** C4
Penyffridd **167** E2
Pen-y-gaer **144** B5
Pen-y-garn Carmar **142** B4
Pen-y-garn Cere **154** C4
Penygarnedd **169** E5
Pen-y-garreg **143** D2
Pen-y-Graig Gwyn **166** B4
Penygraig RCT **129** F3
Penygroes Carmar **128** B1
Penygroes Gwyn **167** D2
Pen-y-Gwryd Hotel **167** F2
Pen-y-lan **145** D3
Pen-y-Mynydd
  Carmar **128** A2
Penymynydd
  Flints **170** A1
Pen-y-parc **169** F1
Pen-y-Park **144** B3
Pen-yr-englyn **129** F3
Pen-yr-heol Mon **130** C1
Penyrheol Swan **128** B3
Pen-y-sarn **180** C3
Pen-y-stryt **169** E2
Penywaun **129** F2
Penzance **94** B3
Penzance Heliport **94** B3
People's Palace & Winter
  Gardens Glas
  G40 1AT **39** H6
Peopleton **146** B2
Peover Heath **184** B5
Peper Harow **121** D3
Peplow **170** D5
Pepper Arden **202** B2
Pepper's Green **137** F1
Perceton **233** E5
Percie **260** D5
Percyhorner **269** H4
Perham Down **119** D3
Periton **114** C3
Perivale **136** A4
Perkhill **260** D4
Perkins Beach **156** C2
Perkin's Village **102** D3
Perran Downs **94** C3
Perranarworthal **95** E3
Perranporth **96** B4
Perranuthnoe **94** C4
Perranzabuloe **96** B4
Perrott's Brook **132** C2
Perry Barr **158** C3
Perry Crofts **159** E2
Perry Green
  Essex **151** G5
Perry Green Herts **136** D1
Perry Green Wilts **132** B4
Perry Street **137** F5
Perrymead **117** E1
Pershall **171** F5
Pershore **146** B3
Persie House **251** G4
Pert **253** E2
Pertenhall **149** F1
Perth (Peairt) **243** G2
Perthcelyn **129** G3
Perthy **170** A4
Perton **158** A3
Pestalozzi Children's
  Village **110** C2
Peter Tavy **99** F3
Peterborough **161** G3
Peterburn **264** D3
Peterchurch **144** C4
Peterculter **261** G4
Peterhead **269** K6
Peterlee **212** D3
Peter's Green **136** A1
Peters Marland **113** E4
Peters Port
  (Port Pheadair) **262** D7
Petersfield **120** C5
Petersfinger **118** C5
Peterstone
  Wentlooge **130** B4
Peterston-super-
  Ely **129** G5
Peterstow **145** E5
Petham **124** D3
Petrockstowe **113** F5
Pett **111** D2
Pettaugh **152** C2
Petteril Green **210** A3
Pettinain **235** D5
Pettistree **153** D2
Petton Devon **114** D5
Petton Shrop **170** B5
Petts Wood **122** D5
Petty **261** F1
Petty France **131** G4
Pettycur **235** F1
Pettymuick **261** H2
Petworth **121** E5
Pevensey **110** B3
Pevensey Bay **110** B3
Peverell **100** A2
Pewsey **118** C1
Pheasant's Hill **134** C4
Phesdo **253** E1
Philham **112** C3
Philharmonic Hall, Liverpool
  Mersey L1 9BP **43** E5
Philiphaugh **227** F3
Phillack **94** C3
Philleigh **95** F3
Philpstoun **235** E2
Phocle Green **145** F5
Phoenix Green **120** C2
Phones **258** E5
Phorp **267** H6

Pitney **116** B5
Pitroddie **244** A2
Pitscottie **244** C3
Pitsea **137** G4
Pitsford **148** C1
Pitsford Hill **115** D4
Pitstone **135** E4
Pitt Devon **102** D1
Pitt Hants **119** F5
Pitt Rivers Museum Oxon
  OX1 3PP **80** Oxford
Pittendreich **267** J5
Pittentrail **266** E1
Pittenweem **244** D4
Pittington **212** C3
Pitton Swan **128** A4
Pitton Wilts **118** D4
Pittulie **269** H4
Pittville **146** B5
Pity Me **212** B3
Pityme **96** D2
Pixey Green **164** D4
Pixley **145** F4
Place Newton **204** B5
Plaidy **269** F5
Plain Dealings **127** D1
Plainfield **220** B1
Plains **234** B2
Plainsfield **115** E4
Plaish **157** E3
Plaistow GtLon **136** C4
Plaistow WSuss **121** F4
Plaitford **106** B1
Plaitford Green **119** D5
Plas **142** A5
Plas Gwynant **167** F2
Plas Isaf **169** D3
Plas Llwyd **182** A5
Plas Llwyngwern **155** D2
Plas Llysyn **155** F3
Plas Nantyr **169** E4
Plashett **127** E2
Plasisaf **168** C1
Plas-rhiw-Saeson **155** F2
Plastow Green **119** G1
Plas-yn-Cefn **182** B5
Platt **123** F3
Platt Bridge **184** A2
Platt Lane **170** C4
Platt's Heath **124** A3
Plawsworth **212** B3
Plaxtol **123** F3
Play Hatch **134** C5
Playden **111** E1
Playford **152** D3
Playing Place **96** C5
Playley Green **145** G4
Plealey **156** D2
Plean **234** C1
Pleasance **244** A3
Pleasant Valley **150** C4
Pleasington **192** C5
Pleasley **173** G1
Pleasure Beach, Great
  Yarmouth Norf
  NR30 3EH **179** G5
Pleasure Island Theme Park
  NELincs
  DN35 0PL **188** D2
Pleasurewood Hills Theme
  Park Suff
  NR32 5DZ **165** G2
Pleck Dorset **104** C1
Pleck WMid **158** B3
Pledgdon Green **151** D5
Pledwick **186** A1
Plemstall **183** F5
Plenmeller **210** D1
Pleshey **137** F1
Plessey Woods Country
  Park N'umb
  NE22 6AN **221** E3
Plockton (Am Ploc) **256** E1
Plocrapol **263** G2
Plomer's Hill **135** D3
Plot Gate **116** C4
Plough Hill **159** F3
Plowden **156** C4
Ploxgreen **156** C2
Pluckley **124** B4
Pluckley Thorne **124** B4
Plucks Gutter **125** E2
Plumbland **209** E3
Plumbley **186** B4
Plumley **184** B5
Plumpton Cumb **210** A4
Plumpton ESuss **109** F2
Plumpton Green **109** F2
Plumpton N'hants **148** B3
Plumpton Head **210** B4
Plumstead GtLon **137** D5
Plumstead Norf **178** C2
Plumtree **174** B4
Plungar **174** C4
Plush **104** D2
Plusha **97** G1
Plushabridge **98** D3
Plwmp **141** G2
Plym Bridge **100** B2
Plymouth **100** A2
Plymouth City
  Airport **100** B1
Plymouth Pavilions
  PL1 3LF **81** Plymouth
Plympton **100** B2
Plymstock **100** B2
Plymtree **103** D2
Pockley **203** F4
Pocklington **196** A3
Pockthorpe **178** B3
Pocombe Bridge **102** B3
Podimore **116** C5
Podington **149** E1
Podmore **171** E4
Podsmead **132** A1
Poffley End **133** F1
Point Clear **139** D1
Pointon **175** G4
Polanach **248** B4
Polapit Tamar **98** D2
Polbae **215** D3
Polbain **272** B7
Polbathic **98** D5
Polbeth **235** E3

Poldean **217** F1
Pole Moor **185** E1
Polebrook **161** F4
Polegate **110** A3
Poles **266** E2
Polesden Lacey Surr
  RH5 6BD **121** G2
Polesworth **159** E2
Polglass **265** G1
Polgooth **97** D4
Polgown **225** F5
Poling **108** C3
Poling Corner **108** C3
Polkemmet Country Park
  WLoth
  EH47 0AD **234** D3
Polkerris **97** E4
Poll a' Charra **254** C3
Polla **273** F3
Pollardras **94** D3
Polldubh **248** D3
Pollie **274** C7
Pollington **186** D1
Polloch **247** G2
Pollok **233** G3
Pollokshaws **233** G3
Pollokshields **233** G3
Polmassick **97** D5
Polmont **234** D2
Polnoon **233** G4
Polperro **97** G4
Polruan **97** F4
Polsham **116** C3
Polstead **152** A4
Polstead Heath **152** A3
Poltalloch **240** A5
Poltimore **102** C3
Polton **235** G3
Polwarth **237** E4
Polyphant **97** G1
Polzeath **96** D2
Pomphlett **100** B2
Pond Street **150** C4
Ponders End **136** C3
Pondersbridge **162** A3
Ponsanooth **95** E3
Ponsonby **198** B2
Ponsongath **95** E5
Ponsworthy **102** A5
Pont Aber **142** D5
Pont Aberglaslyn **167** E3
Pont ar Hydfer **143** E5
Pont Crugnant **155** E3
Pont Cyfyng **168** A2
Pont Dolgarrog **168** A1
Pont Pen-y-benglog **167** F1
Pont Rhyd-sarn **168** C3
Pont Rhyd-y-cyff **129** E4
Pont Walby **129** E2
Pont yr Alwen **168** C2
Pontamman **128** C1
Pontantwn **128** A1
Pontardawe **128** D2
Pontarddulais **128** B2
Pontargothi **142** B5
Pont-ar-llechau **142** D5
Pontarsais **142** A5
Pontblyddyn **169** F1
Pontbren Llwyd **129** F2
Pontefract **195** D5
Ponteland **221** D4
Ponterwyd **154** D4
Pontesbury **156** C2
Pontesbury Hill **156** C2
Pontestord **156** D2
Pontfadog **169** F4
Pontfaen Pembs **140** D4
Pont-faen Powys **143** F4
Pontgarreg **141** G2
Pont-Henri **128** A2
Ponthir **130** C3
Ponthirwaun **141** F3
Pontllanfraith **130** A3
Pontllie **128** C2
Pontllyfni **166** D2
Pontlottyn **130** A2
Pontneddfechan **129** F2
Pontrhydfendigaid **142** D1
Pontrhydyfen **129** D3
Pont-rhyd-y-groes **154** D5
Pontrhydyrun **130** B3
Pontrilas **144** C5
Pontrobert **156** A1
Ponts Green **110** B2
Pontshill **145** F5
Pont-siân **142** A3
Pontsticill **129** G1
Pontwelly **142** A4
Pontyates
  (Pont-iets) **128** A2
Pontyberem **128** B1
Pont-y-blew **170** A4
Pontybodkin **169** F2
Pontyclun **129** F4
Pontycymer **129** F3
Pontygwaith **129** G3
Pontymister **130** B3
Pontymoel **130** B2
Pont-y-pant **168** A2
Pontypool **130** B2
Pontypridd **129** G3
Pont-y-rhyl **129** F4
Pontywaun **130** B3
Pooksgreen **106** C1
Pool Corn **96** A5
Pool WYorks **194** B3
Pool Bank **199** F4
Pool Green **158** C2
Pool Head **145** E2
Pool of Muckhart **243** F4
Pool Quay **156** B1
Pool Street **151** F4
Poole **105** G3
Poole Keynes **132** B3
Poole Pottery Poole
  BH15 1HJ **3** B4
Poolend **171** G2
Poolewe **264** E3
Pooley Bridge **210** A5
Pooley Street **164** B3
Poolfold **171** F2
Poolhill **145** G5
Poolsbrook **186** B5
Poolthorne Farm **188** A2
Pope Hill **126** C1
Popeswood **120** D1
Popham **119** G3

Poplar 136 C4
Porchfield 106 D3
Porin 265 K6
Poringland 179 D5
Porkellis 95 D3
Porlock 114 B3
Porlock Weir 114 B3
Port Allen 244 A2
Port Appin (Port na
    h-Apainn) 248 B5
Port Askaig 230 C3
Port Bannatyne 232 B3
Port Carlisle 218 A5
Port Charlotte 230 A4
Port Clarence 213 E5
Port Driseach 232 A2
Port e Vullen 190 C2
Port Ellen 230 A5
Port Elphinstone 261 F3
Port Erin 190 A5
Port Erroll 261 J1
Port Eynon 128 A4
Port Gaverne 97 E1
Port Glasgow 233 E2
Port Henderson 264 D4
Port Isaac 97 D1
Port Logan 206 A2
Port Lympne Wild Animal
    Park Kent
    CT21 4PD 124 D5
Port Mòr 246 D2
Port Mulgrave 203 G1
Port na Craig 251 E4
Port nan Long 262 D4
Port of Menteith 242 A4
Port of Ness
    (Port Nis) 271 H1
Port o'Warren 216 C5
Port Penrhyn 181 D5
Port Quin 97 D1
Port Ramsay 248 A5
Port St. Mary 190 A5
Port Solent 107 F2
Port Sunlight 183 E4
Port Talbot 129 D4
Port Tennant 128 C3
Port Wemyss 230 A4
Port William 206 D2
Portachoillan 231 F4
Portavadie 232 A3
Portbury 131 E5
Portchester 107 F2
Portencross 232 C5
Portesham 104 C4
Portessie 268 C4
Portfield A&B 239 G2
Portfield WSuss 108 A3
Portfield Gate 126 C1
Portgate 99 E2
Portgordon 268 B4
Portgower 275 F7
Porth Corn 96 C3
Porth RCT 129 G3
Porth Colmon 166 A4
Porth Navas 95 F4
Porthallow Corn 95 E4
Porthallow Corn 97 G4
Porthcawl 129 E5
Porthcothan 96 C2
Porthcurno 94 A4
Porthgain 140 B4
Porthill 171 F3
Porthkerry 115 D1
Porthkerry Country Park
    VGlam
    CF62 3BY 115 D1
Porthleven 94 D4
Porthmadog 167 E4
Porthmeor 94 B3
Portholland 95 F5
Porthoustock 95 F4
Porthpean 97 E4
Porthtowan 96 A5
Porthyrhyd
    Carmar 142 D4
Porthyrhyd
    Carmar 128 B1
Porth-y-waen 169 F5
Portincaple 241 E5
Portington 195 G4
Portinnisherrich 240 B3
Portinscale 209 F4
Portishead 131 D5
Portknockie 268 C4
Portland Basin Museum
    GtMan
    OL7 0QA 25 H3
Portlethen 261 H5
Portlethen Village 261 H5
Portloe 95 F5
Portlooe 97 G4
Portmahomack 267 G3
Portmeirion 167 E4
Portmeirion Village Gwyn
    LL48 6ET 167 E4
Portmellon 97 E5
Portmore 106 C3
Port-na-Con 273 G2
Portnacroish
    (Port na Croise) 248 B5
Portnaguran (Port nan
    Giùran) 271 H4
Portnahaven 230 A4
Portnalong 255 J1
Portnaluchaig 247 F1
Portobello 236 A2
Porton 118 C4
Portpatrick 214 B5
Portreath 96 A5
Portree (Port Righ) 263 K7
Portscatho 95 F3
Portsea 107 F2
Portskerra 274 C2
Portskewett 131 E4
Portslade 109 E3
Portslade-by-Sea 109 E3
Portslogan 214 A5
Portsmouth 107 F3
Portsmouth Guildhall
    PO1 2AB
    82 Portsmouth
Portsmouth Historic
    Dockyard PO1 3LJ
    82 Portsmouth
Portsonachan 240 C2
Portsoy 268 D4
Portuairk 246 D3
Portvoller 271 H4

Portway Here 144 C3
Portway Here 145 D3
Portway Here 145 D4
Portway Worcs 158 C5
Portwrinkle 99 D5
Portyerrock 207 E3
Posenhall 157 F2
Poslingford 151 F3
Postbridge 99 G3
Postcombe 134 C3
Postling 124 D5
Postwick 179 D5
Potarch 260 E5
Potsgrove 149 E5
Pott Row 177 F5
Pott Shrigley 184 D5
Potten End 135 F2
Potter Brompton 204 C5
Potter Heigham 179 F4
Potter Street 137 D2
Pottergate Street 164 C2
Potterhanworth 175 F1
Potterhanworth
    Booths 175 F1
Potteries Museum & Art
    Gallery ST1 3DW
    85 Stoke-on-Trent
Potterne 118 A2
Potterne Wick 118 B2
Potternewton 194 C4
Potters Bar 136 B2
Potters Crouch 136 A2
Potter's Green 159 F4
Potters Marston 159 G3
Pottle Street 117 F3
Potto 203 D2
Potton 150 A3
Pott's Green 152 A5
Poughill Corn 112 C5
Poughill Devon 102 B2
Poulshot 118 A2
Poulton 132 D2
Poulton-le-Fylde 191 G4
Pound Bank 145 G3
Pound Green ESuss 110 A1
Pound Green Suff 151 F2
Pound Green
    Worcs 157 G5
Pound Hill 122 B5
Pound Street 119 F1
Poundbury 104 C3
Poundffald 128 B3
Poundfield 123 E5
Poundgate 109 G1
Poundland 214 C2
Poundon 148 B5
Poundsbridge 123 E4
Poundsgate 102 A5
Poundstock 98 C1
Povey Cross 122 B4
Pow Green 145 G3
Powburn 229 E5
Powderham 102 C4
Powderham Castle Devon
    EX6 8JQ 102 C4
Powerstock 104 B3
Powfoot 217 F4
Powick 146 A2
Powis Castle & Garden
    Powys
    SY21 8RG 156 B2
Powler's Piece 113 D4
Powmill 243 F5
Poxwell 104 D4
Poyle 135 F5
Poynings 109 E2
Poyntington 117 D5
Poynton ChesE 184 D4
Poynton Tel&W 157 E1
Poynton Green 157 E1
Poyntzfield 266 D5
Poys Street 165 E4
Poyston 126 C1
Poyston Cross 126 C1
Poystreet Green 152 A2
Praa Sands 94 C4
Pratis 244 B4
Pratt's Bottom 123 D2
Praze-an-Beeble 94 D3
Predannack Wollas 95 D5
Prees 170 C4
Prees Green 170 C4
Prees Heath 170 C4
Prees Higher Heath 170 C4
Prees Lower Heath 170 C4
Preesall 191 G3
Preesgweene 169 F4
Prenbrigog 169 F1
Prendergast 126 C1
Prendwick 229 E5
Pren-gwyn 142 A3
Prenteg 167 E3
Prenton 183 E4
Prescot 183 F3
Prescott Devon 103 D1
Prescott Shrop 170 B5
Presley 267 H6
Pressen 228 C3
Prestatyn 182 B4
Prestbury ChesE 184 D5
Prestbury Glos 146 B5
Presteigne
    (Llanandras) 144 C1
Presthope 157 E3
Prestleigh 116 D3
Prestolee 184 B2
Preston B&H 109 F3
Preston Devon 102 B5
Preston Dorset 104 D4
Preston ELoth 236 C2
Preston ERid 197 D4
Preston Glos 145 F4
Preston Glos 132 C2
Preston Herts 149 G5
Preston Kent 124 C2
Preston Kent 125 E2
Preston Lancs 185 E2
Preston N'umb 229 F4
Preston Rut 161 D2
Preston ScBord 237 E4
Preston Shrop 157 E1
Preston Som 115 D4
Preston Torbay 101 E1
Preston Wilts 132 C5

Preston Bagot 147 D1
Preston Bissett 148 B4
Preston Bowyer 115 E5
Preston Brockhurst 170 C5
Preston Brook 183 G4
Preston Candover 120 B3
Preston Capes 148 A2
Preston Deanery 148 C2
Preston Gubbals 157 D1
Preston Guildhall Lancs
    PR1 1HT 192 B5
Preston on Stour 147 E3
Preston on the Hill 183 G4
Preston on Wye 144 C3
Preston Plucknett 104 B1
Preston upon the Weald
    Moors 157 F1
Preston Wynne 145 E3
Preston-le-Skerne 212 C5
Prestonpans 236 A2
Preston-under-Scar 201 F3
Prestwich 184 C2
Prestwick N'umb 221 E5
Prestwick SAyr 224 B3
Prestwold 173 G5
Prestwood Bucks 135 D2
Prestwood Staffs 172 C3
Price Town 129 F3
Prickly Ball Farm &
    Hedgehog Hospital
    Devon
    TQ12 6BZ 101 E1
Prickwillow 163 D4
Priddy 116 C2
Priest Hill 192 C4
Priest Hutton 199 G5
Priest Weston 156 B3
Priestcliffe 185 F5
Priestland 225 D2
Priestwood 123 F2
Primethorpe 160 A3
Primrose Green 178 B4
Primrose Hill 136 B4
Princes End 158 B3
Princes Gate 127 E1
Princes Risborough 134 D2
Princethorpe 159 G5
Princetown Caerp 130 A1
Princetown Devon 99 F3
Prior Muir 244 D3
Prior's Frome 145 E4
Priors Halton 157 D5
Priors Hardwick 147 G2
Priors Marston 147 G2
Prior's Norton 146 A5
Priors Park 146 A4
Priorslee 157 G1
Priory Country Park Bed
    MK41 9SH 149 F2
Priory Wood 144 B3
Priston 117 E2
Pristow Green 164 C3
Prittlewell 138 B4
Privett 120 B5
Prixford 113 F2
Proaig 230 C4
Probus 96 C4
Protstonhill 269 G4
Prudhoe 211 G1
Prussia Cove 94 C4
Pubil 249 G5
Publow 116 D1
Puckeridge 150 B5
Puckington 103 G1
Pucklechurch 131 F5
Pucknall 119 E5
Puckrup 146 A4
Puddinglake 171 E1
Puddington
    ChesW&C 183 E5
Puddington
    Devon 102 B1
Puddlebrook 131 F1
Puddledock 164 B2
Puddletown 105 D3
Pudleston 145 E2
Pudsey 194 B4
Pugneys Country Park
    WYorks
    WF2 7EQ 27 G6
Pulborough 108 C2
Pulborough Brooks RSPB
    Nature Reserve WSuss
    RH20 2EL 108 C2
Puldagon 275 J4
Puleston 171 E5
Pulford 170 A2
Pulham 104 D2
Pulham Market 164 C3
Pulham St. Mary 164 D3
Pulley 157 D2
Pulloxhill 149 F4
Pulrossie 266 E3
Pulverbatch 156 D2
Pumpherston 235 E3
Pumsaint 142 C3
Puncheston 140 D5
Puncknowle 104 B4
Punnett's Town 110 B1
Purbrook 107 F2
Purewell 106 A3
Purfleet 137 E5
Puriton 116 A3
Purleigh 138 B2
Purley 122 C2
Purley on Thames 134 B5
Purlogue 156 B5
Purlpit 117 F1
Purls Bridge 162 C4
Purse Caundle 104 C1
Purslow 156 C4
Purston Jaglin 186 B1
Purtington 103 G2
Purton Glos 131 F2
Purton Glos 131 F2
Purton Wilts 132 C4
Purton Stoke 132 C3
Purves Hall 237 E5
Pury End 148 C3
Pusey 133 F3
Putley 145 F4
Putley Green 145 F4
Putney 136 B5
Putsborough 113 E1
Puttenham Herts 135 D1
Puttenham Surr 121 E3

Puttock End 151 G3
Putts Corner 103 E3
Puxton 116 B1
Pwll 128 A2
Pwllcrochan 126 C2
Pwlldefaid 166 A5
Pwll-glas 169 E2
Pwllgloyw 143 G4
Pwlli 166 C1
Pwll-Mawr 130 B5
Pwllmeyric 131 E3
Pwll-trap 127 F1
Pwll-y-glaw 129 D3
Pye Corner Herts 137 D1
Pye Corner Kent 124 A4
Pye Corner
    Newport 130 C4
Pye Green 158 B1
Pyecombe 109 E2
Pyle Bridgend 129 E4
Pyle IoW 107 D5
Pyleigh 115 E4
Pylle 116 D4
Pymore (Pymore) 162 C4
Pymore (Pymoor)
    Cambs 162 C4
Pymore Dorset 104 A3
Pyrford 121 F2
Pyrford Green 121 F2
Pyrton 134 B3
Pytchley 161 D5
Pyworthy 112 D5

Q

Quabbs 156 B4
Quadring 176 A4
Quadring Eaudike 176 A4
Quainton 148 B5
Quarff 279 D9
Quarley 119 D3
Quarndon 173 E3
Quarr Hill 107 E3
Quarrier's Village 233 E3
Quarrington 175 F3
Quarrington Hill 212 C4
Quarry Bank 158 B2
Quarry Bank Mill & Styal
    Estate ChesE
    SK9 4LA 184 C4
Quarrybank 170 C1
Quarrywood 267 J5
Quarter 234 B4
Quatford 157 G3
Quatt 157 G4
Quebec 212 A3
Quedgeley 132 A1
Queen Adelaide 163 D4
Queen Camel 116 C5
Queen Charlton 116 D1
Queen Dart 102 B1
Queen Elizabeth Country
    Park, Petersfield Hants
    PO8 0QE 107 G1
Queen Elizabeth Forest Park
    Stir FK8 3SX 241 G4
Queen Elizabeth Hall
    GtLon SE1 8XX 45 F4
Queen Elizabeth II
    Conference Centre GtLon
    SW1P 3EE 44 D6
Queen Elizabeth II Country
    Park, Ashington N'umb
    NE63 9YF 221 E3
Queen Oak 117 E4
Queen Street 123 F4
Queenborough 124 B1
Queen's Bower 107 E4
Queen's Gallery,
    Buckingham Palace
    GtLon SW1A 1AA 44 B6
Queen's Hall, Edinburgh
    Edin EH8 9JG 37 H6
Queen's Head 170 A5
Queen's View Centre P&K
    PH16 5NR 251 E2
Queensbury
    GtLon 136 A4
Queensbury
    WYorks 194 A4
Queensferry (South
    Queensferry)
    Edin 235 E2
Queensferry Flints 170 A1
Queenswood Country Park
    Here HR6 0PY 145 D2
Queenzieburn 234 A2
Quemerford 118 B1
Quendale 279 F9
Quendon 150 D4
Queniborough 160 B1
Quenington 132 D2
Quernmore 192 B1
Queslett 158 C3
Quethiock 98 D4
Quick's Green 134 A5
Quidenham 164 B3
Quidhampton 119 G2
Quidinish
    (Cuidhtinis) 263 F3
Quilquox 261 H1
Quina Brook 170 C4
Quindry 277 D8
Quine's Hill 190 B4
Quinhill 231 F4
Quinton N'hants 148 C2
Quinton WMid 158 C4
Quinton Green 148 C2
Quintrell Downs 96 C3
Quixhill 172 C3
Quoditch 99 E1
Quoig 242 D2
Quoigs 242 D2
Quoisley 170 C3
Quorn (Quorndon) 160 A1
Quorndon (Quorn) 160 A1
Quothquan 226 A2
Quoyloo 276 B5
Quoys 278 E1
Quoys of Reiss 275 J3

R

R.A.F. Museum, Cosford
    Shrop
    TF11 8UP 157 G2
R.A.F. Museum, Hendon
    GtLon
    NW9 5LL 10 D1

R.H.S. Garden Harlow Carr
    NYorks
    HG3 1QB 194 B2
R.H.S. Garden Hyde Hall
    Essex
    CM3 8ET 137 G3
R.H.S. Garden Rosemoor
    Devon EX38 8PH 113 F4
R.H.S. Garden Wisley Surr
    GU23 6QB 121 F2
Raasay 264 B7
Raby 183 E5
Rachan 226 C2
Rachub 167 E1
Rackenford 102 B1
Rackham 108 C2
Rackheath 179 D4
Racks 217 E3
Rackwick Ork 277 B8
Rackwick Ork 276 D3
Radbourne 173 E4
Radcliffe GtMan 184 B2
Radcliffe N'umb 221 E1
Radcliffe on Trent 174 B4
Radclive 148 B4
Radcot 133 E3
Raddington 114 D5
Radernie 244 C4
Radford B&NESom 117 D2
Radford Oxon 147 G5
Radford WMid 159 F4
Radipole 104 C4
Radlett 136 A2
Radley 134 A3
Radley Green 137 F2
Radmore Green 170 C2
Radnage 134 C3
Radstock 117 D2
Radstone 148 A3
Radway 147 F3
Radway Green 171 E2
Radwell Bed 149 F2
Radwell Herts 150 A4
Radwinter 151 E3
Radyr 130 A4
Raechester 220 C3
Raemoir House 260 E5
Raffin 272 C5
Rafford 267 H6
Ragdale 160 B1
Ragged Appleshaw 119 E3
Raglan 130 D2
Ragnall 187 F5
Rahoy 247 F4
Rainford 183 F2
Rainham GtLon 137 E4
Rainham Med 124 A2
Rainhill 183 F3
Rainhill Stoops 183 G3
Rainow 184 D5
Rainsough 184 B2
Rainton 202 C5
Rainworth 173 G2
Raisbeck 200 B2
Raise 210 D3
Rait 244 A2
Raithby Lincs 176 B1
Raithby Lincs 188 D4
Rake 120 D5
Raleigh's Cross 114 D4
Ram 142 B3
Ram Alley 118 D1
Ram Lane 124 B4
Ramasaig 263 G7
Rame Corn 95 E3
Rame Corn 100 A3
Rampisham 104 B2
Rampside 191 F1
Rampton Cambs 150 C1
Rampton Notts 187 F5
Ramsbottom 184 B1
Ramsbury 133 E5
Ramscraigs 275 G6
Ramsdean 120 C5
Ramsdell 119 G2
Ramsden 133 F1
Ramsden Bellhouse 137 G3
Ramsden Heath 137 G3
Ramsey Cambs 162 A4
Ramsey Essex 152 D4
Ramsey IoM 190 C2
Ramsey Forty Foot 162 B4
Ramsey Heights 162 A4
Ramsey Island
    Essex 138 C2
Ramsey Island
    Pembs 140 A5
Ramsey Mereside 162 A4
Ramsey St. Mary's 162 A4
Ramsgate 125 F2
Ramsgate Street 178 B2
Ramsgill 202 A5
Ramsholt 153 E3
Ramshorn 172 B3
Ramsnest Common 121 E4
Ranachan 247 G3
Ranby Lincs 188 C5
Ranby Notts 187 D4
Rand 188 B5
Rand Farm Park Lincs
    LN8 5NJ 188 B5
Randwick 132 A2
Rangemore 172 C5
Rangeworthy 131 F4
Ranish (Ranais) 271 G5
Rankinston 224 C4
Rank's Green 137 G1
Ranmoor 186 A4
Rannoch School 250 A4
Ranochan 248 A1
Ranscombe 114 C3
Ranskill 187 D4
Ranton 171 F5
Ranton Green 171 F5
Ranworth 179 E4
Rapness 276 E3
Rapps 180 B3
Rascarrel 208 A2
Rashwood 146 B1
Raskelf 203 D5
Rassau 130 A1
Rastrick 194 A5
Ratagan 257 F3
Ratby 160 A2

Ratcliffe Culey 159 F3
Ratcliffe on Soar 173 F5
Ratcliffe on the
    Wreake 160 B1
Ratford Bridge 126 B1
Ratfyn 118 C3
Rathen 269 H4
Rathillet 244 B2
Rathliesbeag 249 E1
Rathmell 193 E1
Ratho 235 E1
Ratho Station 235 F2
Rathven 268 C4
Ratley 147 F3
Ratling 125 E3
Ratlinghope 156 D3
Ratsloe 102 C3
Rattar 275 H1
Ratten Row Cumb 209 G2
Ratten Row Lancs 192 A3
Rattery 100 D1
Rattlesden 152 A2
Rattray 251 G5
Raughton Head 209 G2
Raunds 161 E5
Ravenfield 186 B3
Ravenglass 198 B3
Ravenglass & Eskdale
    Railway Cumb
    CA18 1SW 198 C3
Raveningham 165 E2
Raven's Green 152 C5
Ravenscar 204 C2
Ravensdale 190 B2
Ravensden 149 F2
Ravenshaw 193 F3
Ravenshayes 102 C2
Ravenshead 173 G2
Ravensmoor 170 D2
Ravensthorpe
    N'hants 160 B5
Ravensthorpe
    WYorks 194 B5
Ravenstone Leics 159 G1
Ravenstone MK 149 D2
Ravenstonedale 200 C2
Ravenstruther 234 D5
Ravensworth 202 A2
Raw 204 C2
Rawcliffe ERid 195 E5
Rawcliffe York 195 E2
Rawcliffe Bridge 195 F5
Rawdon 194 B4
Rawmarsh 186 B3
Rawnsley 158 C1
Rawreth 138 A3
Rawridge 103 F2
Rawson Green 173 E3
Rawtenstall 193 E5
Rawyards 234 B3
Raxton 261 G1
Raydon 152 B4
Raylees 220 B2
Rayleigh 138 B3
Raymond's Hill 103 G3
Rayne 151 F5
Rayners Lane 136 A4
Raynes Park 122 B2
Reach 151 D1
Read 193 D4
Reading 134 C5
Reading Green 164 C4
Reading Street 124 B5
Reagill 200 B1
Real Mary King's Close, The
    Edin EH1 1PG 37 F4
Rearquhar 266 E2
Rearsby 160 B1
Rease Heath 170 D2
Reaster 275 H2
Reaveley 229 E5
Reawick 279 C8
Reay 274 D2
Reculver 125 E2
Red Ball 103 D1
Red Bull 171 F2
Red Dial 209 F2
Red Hill Hants 107 G1
Red Hill Warks 146 D2
Red Lodge 163 E5
Red Lumb 184 C1
Red Oaks Hill 151 D4
Red Point 264 D5
Red Post Corn 112 C5
Red Post Devon 101 E1
Red Rail 145 E5
Red Rock 183 G2
Red Roses 127 F1
Red Row 221 E2
Red Street 171 F2
Red Wharf Bay
    (Traeth Coch) 180 D4
Redberth 127 D2
Redbourn 136 A1
Redbourne 187 G3
Redbrook Glos 131 E1
Redbrook Wrex 170 C3
Redbrook Street 124 B5
Redburn High 266 C5
Redburn High 267 G6
Redburn N'umb 211 D1
Redcar 213 F5
Redcastle Angus 253 E4
Redcastle High 266 C7
Redcliff Bay 130 D5
Redcloak 253 G1
Reddingmuirhead 234 D2
Reddish 184 C3
Redditch 146 C1
Rede 151 G2
Redenhall 165 D3
Redesmouth 220 A3
Redford Aber 253 F2
Redford Angus 253 D5
Redford Dur 211 G4
Redford WSuss 121 D5
Redgrave 164 B4
Redheugh 252 D4
Redhill Aber 260 E1
Redhill Aber 261 F3
Redhill Moray 268 D6
Redhill Notts 173 G3
Redhill NSom 116 B1
Redhill Surr 122 B3
Redhill Aerodrome &
    Heliport 122 B4
Redhouse A&B 231 G3
Redhouse Aber 260 D2

Redhouses 230 B3
Redisham 165 F3
Redland Bristol 131 E5
Redland Ork 276 C5
Redlingfield 164 C4
Redlynch Som 117 E5
Redlynch Wilts 118 D5
Redmarley D'Abitot 145 G4
Redmarshall 212 C5
Redmile 174 C4
Redmire 201 F3
Redmoor 97 E3
Rednal 170 A5
Redpath 227 G2
Redruth 96 A5
Redscarhead 235 G5
Redshaw 225 G3
Redstone Bank 127 E1
Redwick Newport 130 D4
Redwick SGlos 131 E4
Redworth 212 B5
Reed 150 B4
Reed End 150 B4
Reedham 179 F5
Reedley 193 E4
Reedness 195 G5
Reef (Riof) 270 D4
Reepham Lincs 188 A5
Reepham Norf 178 B3
Reeth 201 F3
Regaby 190 C2
Regil 116 C1
Regoul 267 G7
Reiff 272 B7
Reigate 122 B3
Reighton 205 E5
Reisgill 275 H5
Reiss 275 J3
Rejerrah 96 C3
Releath 95 D3
Relubbus 94 C3
Relugas 267 G7
Remenham 134 C4
Remenham Hill 134 C4
Remony 250 C5
Rempstone 173 G5
Rendcomb 132 C1
Rendham 153 E1
Rendlesham 153 E2
Renfrew 233 G2
Renhold 149 F2
Renishaw 186 B5
Rennington 229 G5
Renton 233 E2
Renwick 210 B3
Repps 179 F4
Repton 173 E5
Rescobie 252 D4
Rescorla 97 E4
Resipole 247 G3
Resolis 266 D5
Resolven 129 E2
Resourie 248 A2
Respryn 97 F3
Reston 237 F3
Restormel 97 F3
Reswallie 252 D4
Reterth 96 C3
Retew 96 C4
Retford
    (East Retford) 187 E4
Rettendon 137 G3
Rettendon Place 137 G3
Retyn 96 C4
Revesby 176 A1
Revesby Bridge 176 B1
Rew 102 A5
Rew Street 107 D3
Rewe Devon 102 C3
Rewe Devon 102 B3
Reybridge 118 A1
Reydon 165 F4
Reydon Smear 165 G4
Reymerston 178 B5
Reynalton 127 D2
Reynoldston 128 A4
Rezare 99 D3
Rhadyr 130 C2
Rhandirmwyn 143 D3
Rhaoine 266 D1
Rhayader
    (Rhaeadr Gwy) 143 F1
Rhedyn 166 B4
Rheged - the Village in the
    Hill Cumb
    CA11 0DQ 210 A5
Rhegreanoch 272 C7
Rheindown 266 C7
Rhelonie 266 C2
Rhemore 247 E4
Rhenigidale
    (Reinigeadal) 270 E7
Rheola 129 E2
Rhes-y-cae 169 E1
Rhewl Denb 169 E3
Rhewl Denb 169 E1
Rhewl Shrop 170 A4
Rhian 273 H7
Rhicarn 272 C6
Rhiconich 272 E3
Rhicullen 266 D4
Rhidorroch 265 H2
Rhifail 274 C3
Rhigos 129 F2
Rhilochan 266 E1
Rhinduie 266 C7
Rhireavach 265 G3
Rhiroy 265 H3
Rhiston 156 B3
Rhiw 166 B5
Rhiwargor 168 C5
Rhiwbina 130 A4
Rhiwbryfdir 167 F3
Rhiwderin 130 B4
Rhiwinder 129 G4
Rhiwlas Gwyn 167 E1
Rhiwlas Gwyn 168 C4
Rhiwlas Powys 169 F4
Rhode 115 F4
Rhodes Minnis 124 D4
Rhodesia 186 C5
Rhodiad-y-brenin 140 A5
Rhodmad 154 B3
Rhonadale 222 C2
Rhonehouse
    (Kelton Hill) 216 B5
Rhoose 115 D1
Rhos Carmar 141 G4

Rhos *NPT* **128** D2
Rhos Common **156** B1
Rhoscolyn **180** A5
Rhoscrowther **126** C2
Rhosesmor **169** F1
Rhos-fawr **166** C4
Rhosgadfan **167** E2
Rhosgoch *IoA* **180** C4
Rhosgoch *Powys* **144** A3
Rhos-hill **141** E3
Rhoshirwaun **166** A5
Rhoslan **167** D3
Rhoslefain **154** B2
Rhosllanerchrugog **169** F3
Rhoslligwy **180** C4
Rhosmaen **142** C5
Rhosmeirch **180** C5
Rhosneigr **180** B5
Rhosnesni **170** A2
Rhôs-on-Sea **181** G4
Rhossili **128** A4
Rhosson **140** A5
Rhostrehwfa **180** C5
Rhostryfan **167** D2
Rhostyllen **170** A3
Rhos-y-bol **180** C4
Rhos-y-brithdir **169** E5
Rhoscaerau **140** C4
Rhos-y-garth **154** C5
Rhos-y-gwaliau **168** C4
Rhos-y-llan **166** B4
Rhos-y-mawn **168** B1
Rhos-y-Meirch **144** B1
Rhu **233** D1
Rhuallt **182** B5
Rhubodach **232** B2
Rhuddall Heath **170** C1
Rhuddlan **182** B5
Rhue **265** H2
Rhulen **144** A3
Rhunahaorine **231** F5
Rhyd *Gwyn* **167** F3
Rhyd *Powys* **155** F2
Rhydargaeau **142** A5
Rhydcymerau **142** B4
Rhyd-Ddu **167** E2
Rhydding **128** D3
Rhydgaled **168** C1
Rhydlanfair **168** B2
Rhydlewis **141** G3
Rhydlios **166** A4
Rhydlydan *Conwy* **168** B2
Rhydlydan *Powys* **155** G3
Rhydolion **166** B5
Rhydowen **142** A3
Rhyd-Rosser **142** B1
Rhydspence **144** B3
Rhydtalog **169** F2
Rhyd-uchaf **168** B4
Rhyd-wen **168** C5
Rhyd-wyn **180** B4
Rhyd-y-ceirw **169** F2
Rhyd-y-clafdy **166** C4
Rhydcroesau **169** F4
Rhydyfelin *Cere* **154** B5
Rhydyfelin *RCT* **129** G4
Rhyd-y-foel **182** A5
Rhyd-y-fro **128** D2
Rhyd-y-groes **167** E1
Rhydymain **168** B5
Rhydymwyn **169** E1
Rhyd-yr-onnen **154** C2
Rhyd-y-sarn **167** F3
Rhydywrach **127** E1
Rhyl **102** B4
Rhyl Sun Centre *Denb*
  LL18 3AQ **182** B4
Rhymney **130** A2
Rhyn **170** A4
Rhynd **243** G2
Rhynie *Aber* **260** C2
Rhynie *High* **267** F4
Ribbesford **157** G5
Ribchester **192** C4
Ribigill **273** H3
Riby **188** B2
Riccall **195** F4
Riccarton **224** C2
Richards Castle **145** D1
Richings Park **135** F5
Richmond *GtLon* **136** A5
Richmond *NYorks* **202** A2
Richmond *SYorks* **186** B4
Rich's Holford **115** E4
Rickarton **253** G1
Rickerscote **171** G5
Rickford **116** B2
Rickinghall **164** B4
Rickleton **212** B2
Rickling **150** C4
Rickling Green **150** D5
Rickmansworth **135** F3
Riddell **227** G3
Riddings **173** F2
Riddlecombe **113** G4
Riddlesden **193** G3
Ridge *Dorset* **105** F4
Ridge *Herts* **136** B2
Ridge *Wilts* **118** A4
Ridge Green **122** C4
Ridge Lane **159** E3
Ridgebourne **143** G3
Ridgeway **186** B4
Ridgeway Cross **145** G3
Ridgeway Moor **186** B4
Ridgewell **151** F2
Ridgewood **109** G1
Ridgmont **149** E4
Ridham Dock **124** B2
Riding Gate **117** E5
Riding Mill **211** G1
Ridley **123** F2
Ridleywood **170** A2
Ridlington *Norf* **179** E2
Ridlington *Rut* **160** D2
Ridsdale **220** B3
Riechip **251** F5
Rievaulx **203** E4
Rift House **213** D4
Rigg *D&G* **218** A5
Rigg *High* **264** B6
Riggend **234** B3
Rigifa **275** J1
Rigmaden Park **200** B4
Rigsby **189** E5
Rigside **225** G2

Riley Green **192** C5
Rileyhill **158** D1
Rilla Mill **97** G2
Rillaton **97** G2
Rillington **204** B5
Rimington **193** E3
Rimpton **116** D5
Rimswell **197** F5
Rinaston **140** C5
Ring o' Bells **183** F1
Ringford **216** A5
Ringinglow **185** G4
Ringland **178** C4
Ringles Cross **109** G1
Ringmer **109** G2
Ringmore *Devon* **100** C3
Ringmore *Devon* **102** C5
Ringorm **267** K7
Ring's End **162** B1
Ringsfield **165** F3
Ringsfield Corner **165** F3
Ringshall *Herts* **135** E1
Ringshall *Suff* **152** B2
Ringshall Stocks **152** B2
Ringstead *N'hants* **161** E5
Ringstead *Norf* **177** F3
Ringwood **106** A2
Ringwould **125** F4
Rinloan **259** K4
Rinmore **260** C3
Rinnigill **277** C8
Rinsey **94** C4
Ripe **110** A3
Ripley *Derbys* **173** E2
Ripley *Hants* **106** A3
Ripley *NYorks* **194** B1
Ripley *Surr* **121** F2
Riplingham **196** B4
Ripon **202** B5
Rippingale **175** G5
Ripple *Kent* **125** F4
Ripple *Worcs* **146** A4
Ripponden **185** E1
Risabus **230** B5
Risbury **145** E2
Risby *ERid* **196** C4
Risby *Suff* **151** F1
Risca **130** B3
Rise **197** D3
Riseden **123** G5
Risegate **176** A5
Riseholme **187** G5
Riseley *Bed* **149** F1
Riseley *W'ham* **120** C1
Rishangles **152** C1
Rishton **192** D4
Rishworth **185** E1
Risinghurst **134** A2
Risley *Derbys* **173** F4
Risley *Warr* **184** A3
Risplith **194** B1
Rispond **273** G2
Rivar **119** E1
Rivenhall **138** B1
Rivenhall End **138** B1
River *Kent* **125** E4
River *WSuss* **121** E5
River Bank **150** D1
River Bridge **116** A3
Riverford Bridge **101** D1
Riverhead **123** E3
Riverside **130** A5
Riverside Country Park *Med*
  ME7 2XH **124** A2
Riverside Museum &
  Tall Ship Glenlee
  Glas G3 8RS **30** C3
Riverton **113** G2
Riverview Park **137** F5
Riviera International Centre
  Torbay TQ2 5LZ
  87 Torquay
Rivington **184** A1
Roa Island **191** F1
Roach Bridge **192** B5
Road Green **165** D2
Road Weedon **148** B2
Roade **148** C2
Roadhead **218** D4
Roadside *High* **275** G2
Roadside *Ork* **276** F3
Roadside of Kinneff **253** G2
Roadwater **114** D4
Roag **263** H7
Roast Green **150** C4
Roath **130** A5
Robert Burns Birthplace
  Museum *SAyr*
  KA7 4PQ **224** B4
Roberton *ScBord* **227** F4
Roberton *SLan* **226** A3
Robertsbridge **110** C1
Robertstown
  Moray **267** K7
Robertstown *RCT* **129** G2
Roberttown **194** A5
Robeston Cross **126** B2
Robeston Wathen **127** D1
Robeston West **126** B2
Robin Hill Countryside
  Adventure Park *IoW*
  PO30 2NU **107** E4
Robin Hood
  Derbys **185** G5
Robin Hood *Lancs* **183** G1
Robin Hood *WYorks* **194** C5
Robin Hood Doncaster
  Sheffield Airport **187** D3
Robin Hood's Bay **204** C2
Robinhood End **151** F2
Robins **120** D5
Robinswood Hill Country
  Park *Glos*
  GL4 6SX **132** A1
Roborough *Devon* **113** F4
Roborough *Plym* **100** B1
Roby **183** F3
Roby Mill **183** G2
Rocester **172** C4
Roch **140** B5
Roch Bridge **140** B5
Roch Gate **140** B5
Rochdale **184** C1
Roche **97** D3
Rochester *Med* **123** G2

Rochester *N'umb* **220** A2
Rochester Cathedral *Med*
  ME1 1SX **123** G2
Rochford *Essex* **138** B3
Rochford *Worcs* **145** F1
Rock *Corn* **96** D2
Rock *N'umb* **229** G5
Rock *Worcs* **157** G5
Rock Ferry **183** E4
Rockbeare **102** D3
Rockbourne **106** A1
Rockcliffe *Cumb* **218** B5
Rockcliffe *D&G* **216** C5
Rockcliffe Cross **218** B5
Rockfield *A&B* **231** G4
Rockfield *High* **267** G3
Rockfield *Mon* **131** D1
Rockford **106** A2
Rockhampton **131** F3
Rockhead **97** E1
Rockingham **161** D3
Rockland All Saints **164** A2
Rockland St. Mary **179** E5
Rockland St. Peter **164** A2
Rockley **133** D5
Rockside **230** A3
Rockwell End **134** C4
Rockwell Green **103** E1
Rodborough **132** A2
Rodbourne **132** B4
Rodbridge Corner **151** G3
Rodd **144** C1
Roddam **229** E4
Rodden **104** C4
Rode **117** F2
Rode Heath **171** F2
Rodeheath **171** F1
Rodel (Roghadal) **263** F3
Roden **157** E1
Rodhuish **114** D4
Rodington **157** E1
Rodington Heath **157** E1
Rodley **131** G1
Rodmarton **132** B3
Rodmell **109** G3
Rodmersham **124** B2
Rodmersham Green **124** B2
Rodney Stoke **116** B2
Rodsley **172** D3
Rodway **115** F3
Roe Cross **185** D3
Roe Green **150** B4
Roecliffe **194** C1
Roehampton **136** B5
Roesound **279** C6
Roffey **121** G4
Rogart **266** E1
Rogate **120** D5
Rogerstone **130** B4
Roget **131** D1
Rokemarsh **134** B3
Roker **212** D2
Rollesby **179** F4
Rolleston *Leics* **160** C2
Rolleston *Notts* **174** C2
Rolleston **118** B3
Rolleston-on-Dove **172** D5
Rolston **197** E3
Rolstone **116** A1
Rolvenden **124** A5
Rolvenden Layne **124** A5
Romaldkirk **211** F5
Romanby **202** C3
Roman Baths & Pump Room
  B&NESom BA1 1LZ
  63 Bath
Romanby **202** C3
Romannobridge **235** F5
Romansleigh **114** A5
Romesdal **263** K6
Romford *Dorset* **105** G2
Romford *GtLon* **137** E4
Romiley **184** D3
Romney, Hythe &
  Dymchurch Railway
  Kent TN28 8PL **124** D3
Romney Street **123** E2
Romsey **119** E5
Romsley *Shrop* **158** A4
Romsley *Worcs* **158** B5
Rona **264** C6
Ronachan **231** F4
Ronague **190** A4
Ronnachmore **230** B4
Rood End **158** C4
Rookhope **211** F3
Rookley **107** E4
Rookley Green **107** E4
Rooks Bridge **116** A2
Rook's Nest **115** D4
Rookwith **202** B4
Roos **197** E4
Roose **191** F1
Roosebeck **191** F1
Roosecote **191** F1
Rootham's Green **149** F2
Rootpark **235** D4
Ropley **120** B4
Ropley Dean **120** B4
Ropley Soke **120** B4
Ropsley **175** E4
Rora **269** J5
Rorandle **260** E3
Rorrington **156** C2
Rosarie **268** B6
Rose **96** B4
Rose Ash **114** A5
Rose Green *Essex* **152** A5
Rose Green *WSuss* **108** B4
Rose Hill **109** G2
Roseacre *Kent* **123** G3
Roseacre *Lancs* **192** A4
Rosebank **234** C5
Rosebrough **229** F4
Rosebush **141** D5
Rosecare **98** B1
Rosecliston **96** C4
Rosedale Abbey **203** G3
Roseden **229** E4
Rosehall **266** B1
Rosehearty **269** H4
Rosehill *Aber* **260** D5
Rosehill *Shrop* **157** D1
Roseisle **267** J5
Roselands **110** B3
Rosemarket **126** C2
Rosemarkie **266** E6
Rosemary Lane **103** E1
Rosemount *P&K* **251** G5

Rosemount *SAyr* **224** B3
Rosenannon **97** D3
Rosenithon **95** F4
Rosepool **126** B1
Rosevean **97** E4
Roseville **158** B3
Roseworth **212** D5
Roseworthy **94** D4
Rosgill **199** E3
Roshven **247** G2
Roskhill **263** H7
Roskorwell **95** E4
Rosley **209** G2
Roslin **235** G3
Rosliston **159** E1
Rosliston Forestry Centre
  Derbys
  DE12 8JX **159** E1
Rosneath **233** D1
Ross *D&G* **207** G2
Ross *N'umb* **229** F3
Ross *P&K* **242** C2
Rossett **170** A2
Rossett Green **194** C2
Rosside **199** D5
Rossie Farm School **253** E4
Rossie Ochill **243** F3
Rossie Priory **244** A1
Rossington **186** D3
Rossmore **105** G3
Ross-on-Wye **145** F5
Roster **275** H5
Rostherne **184** B4
Rosthwaite *Cumb* **209** F5
Rosthwaite *Cumb* **198** D4
Roston **172** C3
Rosudgeon **94** C4
Rosyth **235** F1
Rothbury **220** C1
Rotherby **160** B1
Rotherfield **123** E5
Rotherfield Greys **134** C4
Rotherfield Peppard **134** C4
Rotherham **186** B3
Rothersthorpe **148** C2
Rotherwick **120** C2
Rothes **267** K7
Rothesay **232** B3
Rothiebrisbane **261** F1
Rothiemurchus *High*
  PH22 1QH **259** G4
Rothienorman **261** F1
Rothiesholm **276** F5
Rothley *Leics* **160** A1
Rothley *N'umb* **220** C3
Rothney **260** E2
Rothwell *Lincs* **188** B3
Rothwell *N'hants* **160** D4
Rothwell *WYorks* **194** C5
Rotsea **196** C2
Rottal **252** B3
Rotten Row *Bucks* **134** C4
Rotten Row *WMid* **159** D5
Rottingdean **109** F3
Rottington **208** C5
Roud **107** E4
Rough Close **171** G4
Rough Common **124** D3
Rougham *Norf* **177** G5
Rougham *Suff* **152** A1
Roughburn **249** F1
Roughlee **193** E3
Roughley **158** D3
Roughton *Lincs* **176** A1
Roughton *Norf* **178** D2
Roughton *Shrop* **157** G3
Round Bush **136** A3
Roundbush Green **137** E1
Roundham **104** A2
Roundhay **194** C4
Roundstreet
  Common **121** F5
Roundway **118** B1
Rous Lench **146** C2
Rousay **276** D4
Rousdon **103** F3
Rousham **147** G5
Rousham Gap **147** G5
Routenburn **232** C3
Routh **196** C3
Rout's Green **134** C3
Row *Corn* **97** E2
Row *Cumb* **199** F4
Row *Cumb* **210** C4
Row Heath **139** E1
Row Town **121** F1
Rowanburn **218** C4
Rowardennan
  Lodge **241** F5
Rowarth **185** E4
Rowbarton **115** F5
Rowberrow **116** B2
Rowchoish **241** F4
Rowde **118** A1
Rowden **99** G1
Rowen **181** F5
Rowfields **172** C3
Rowfoot **210** C1
Rowhedge **152** B5
Rowhook **121** G4
Rowington **147** E1
Rowland **185** G5
Rowland's Castle **107** G1
Rowlands Gill **212** A2
Rowledge **120** D3
Rowlestone **144** C5
Rowley *Devon* **102** A3
Rowley *Dur* **211** G3
Rowley *Shrop* **156** C2
Rowley Park **171** G5
Rowley Regis **158** B4
Rowly **121** F3
Rowner **107** E2
Rowney Green **158** C5
Rownhams **106** C1
Rowrah **209** D5
Rowsham **134** D1
Rowsley **173** D1
Rowstock **133** G4

Rowston **175** F2
Rowthorne **173** F1
Rowton
  ChesW&C **170** B1
Rowton *Shrop* **156** C1
Rowton *Tel&W* **157** F1
Roxburgh **228** B3
Roxby *NLincs* **187** G1
Roxby *NYorks* **203** G5
Roxton **149** G2
Roxwell **137** F2
Royal Academy of Arts
  GtLon W1J 0BD **44** C4
Royal Albert Hall *GtLon*
  SW7 2AP **11** F5
Royal Albert Memorial
  Museum & Art Gallery
  Devon EX4 3RX
  72 Exeter
Royal Armouries Museum,
  Leeds *WYorks*
  LS10 1LT **41** G5
Royal Artillery Barracks
  GtLon SE18 5DP **13** F5
Royal Bath & West
  Showground *Som*
  BA4 6QN **116** D4
Royal Botanic Garden,
  Edinburgh *Edin*
  EH3 5LR **36** D1
Royal Botanic Gardens,
  Kew *GtLon*
  TW9 3AB **11** C6
Royal British Legion
  Village **123** G3
Royal Cornwall Museum
  Corn TR1 2SJ **96** C5
Royal Festival Hall *GtLon*
  SE1 8XX **45** F5
Royal Highland Showground
  Edin EH28 8NB **32** A2
Royal Horticultural Halls
  GtLon SW1P 2PB **44** D7
Royal Hospital Chelsea
  GtLon SW3 4SR **13** A5
Royal Leamington
  Spa **147** F1
Royal Mews, Buckingham
  Palace *GtLon*
  SW1W 0QH **44** B6
Royal Naval Museum
  PO1 3NH
  82 Portsmouth
Royal Oak **183** F2
Royal Observatory
  Greenwich *GtLon*
  SE10 8XJ **13** F5
Royal Opera House *GtLon*
  WC2E 9DD **45** E3
Royal Pavilion *B&H*
  BN1 1EE **65** Brighton
Royal Scots Regimental
  Museum, The *Edin*
  EH1 2YT **37** E5
Royal Scottish Academy
  Edin EH2 2EL **37** F4
Royal Tunbridge
  Wells **123** E5
Royal Victoria Country Park
  Hants SO31 5GA
Royal Welch Fusiliers
  Regimental Museum
  Gwyn
  LL55 2AY **167** D1
Royal Wootton
  Bassett **132** C4
Royal Yacht Britannia
  Edin EH6 6JJ **32** C1
Roybridge (Drochaid
  Ruaidh) **249** E1
Roydon *Essex* **136** D1
Roydon *Norf* **164** B3
Roydon *Norf* **177** F5
Roydon Hamlet **136** D2
Royston *Herts* **150** B3
Royston *SYorks* **186** A1
Royton **184** D2
Rozel **100** C5
Ruabon (Rhiwabon) **170** A3
Ruaig **246** B2
Ruan Lanihorne **96** C5
Ruan Major **95** D5
Ruan Minor **95** E5
Ruanaich **238** B2
Ruardean **131** F1
Ruardean Hill **131** F1
Ruardean Woodside **131** F1
Rubery **158** B5
Ruckcroft **210** B3
Ruckinge **124** C5
Rucklers Lane **135** F2
Ruckley **157** E2
Rudbaxton **140** C5
Rudby **203** D2
Ruddington **173** G4
Ruddlemoor **97** E4
Rudford **145** G5
Rudge **117** F2
Rudgeway **131** F4
Rudgwick **121** F4
Rudhall **145** F5
Rudheath **184** A5
Rudley Green **138** B2
Rudloe **117** F1
Rudry **130** A4
Rudston **196** C1
Rudyard **171** G2
Rudyard Lake *Staffs*
  ST13 8RT **171** G2
Rufford **183** F1
Rufford Country Park *Notts*
  NG22 9DF **174** B1
Rufforth **195** E2
Ruffside **211** F2
Rugby **160** A5
Rugby Football Union,
  Twickenham *GtLon*
  TW1 1DZ **11** B6
Rugeley **158** C1
Ruilick **266** C7
Ruishton **115** F5
Ruisgarry **262** E3
Ruisigearraidh **262** E3
Ruislip **135** F4
Ruislip Gardens **135** F4

Ruislip Manor **136** A4
Rum **255** J5
Rumbling Bridge **243** F5
Rumburgh **165** E3
Rumford **96** C2
Rumleigh **100** A1
Rumney **130** B5
Rumwell **115** E5
Runacraig **242** A3
Runcorn **183** G4
Runcton **108** A3
Runcton Holme **163** E2
Runfold **121** D3
Runhall **178** B5
Runham *Norf* **179** G4
Runham *Norf* **179** G5
Runnington **115** E5
Runsell Green **137** G2
Runshaw Moor **183** G1
Runswick Bay **204** B1
Runtaleave **252** A3
Runwell **137** G3
Ruscombe *Glos* **132** A2
Ruscombe
  W'ham **134** C5
Rush Green
  GtLon **137** E4
Rush Green *Herts* **150** A5
Rushall *Here* **145** F4
Rushall *Norf* **164** C3
Rushall *Wilts* **118** C2
Rushall *WMid* **158** C2
Rushbrooke **151** G1
Rushbury **157** E3
Rushden *Herts* **150** B4
Rushden *N'hants* **149** E1
Rushford *Devon* **99** E3
Rushford *Norf* **164** A3
Rushgreen **184** A4
Rushlake Green **110** B2
Rushmere **165** F3
Rushmere
  St. Andrew **152** D3
Rushmoor *High* **121** D3
Rushock **158** A5
Rusholme **184** C3
Rushton *ChesW&C* **170** C1
Rushton *N'hants* **160** D4
Rushton *Shrop* **157** F2
Rushton Spencer **171** G1
Rushwick **146** A2
Rushy Green **109** G2
Rushyford **212** B5
Ruskie **242** A4
Ruskington **175** F2
Rusko **215** G5
Rusland **199** E4
Rusper **122** B5
Ruspidge **131** F1
Russ Hill **122** B4
Russel **264** F7
Russell Green **137** G1
Russell's Green **110** C2
Russell's Water **134** C3
Russel's Green **165** D4
Rusthall **123** E5
Rustington **108** C3
Ruston **204** B4
Ruston Parva **196** C1
Ruswarp **204** B2
Rutherford **228** A3
Rutherglen **234** A3
Ruthernbridge **97** E3
Ruthers of Howe **275** J2
Ruthin (Rhuthun)
  Denb **169** E1
Ruthin *VGlam* **129** F5
Ruthrieston **261** H4
Ruthven *Aber* **268** D6
Ruthven *Angus* **252** A5
Ruthven *High* **259** F3
Ruthven *High* **258** E5
Ruthvoes **96** D3
Ruthwaite **209** F3
Ruthwell **217** E4
Rutland Water *Rut*
  LE15 8QL **161** D2
Ruyton-XI-Towns **170** A5
Ryal **220** C4
Ryal Fold **192** C5
Ryall *Dorset* **104** A3
Ryall *Worcs* **146** A3
Ryarsh **123** F3
Rydal **199** E2
Ryde **107** E3
Rydon **112** D5
Rye **111** E1
Rye Foreign **111** D1
Rye Harbour **111** E2
Rye Park **136** C2
Rye Street **145** G4
Ryebank **170** C4
Ryeford **145** F5
Ryehill *Aber* **260** E2
Ryehill *ERid* **197** E5
Ryhall **161** F1
Ryhill **186** A1
Ryhope **212** D2
Rylands **173** G4
Rylstone **193** F2
Ryme Intrinseca **104** B1
Ryther **195** E4
Ryton *Glos* **145** G4
Ryton *NYorks* **203** G5
Ryton *Shrop* **157** G2
Ryton *T&W* **212** A1
Ryton-on-
  Dunsmore **159** F5

S

S.S. Great Britain *Bristol*
  BS1 6TY **8** B3
Saasaig **256** C4
Sabden **193** D4
Sabden Fold **193** E4
Sackers Green **152** A4
Sacombe **136** C1
Sacombe Green **136** C1
Sacriston **212** B3
Sadberge **202** C1
Saddell **222** A1
Saddington **160** B3
Saddle Bow **163** E1
Sadgill **199** F2
Saffron Walden **150** D4
Sageston **127** D2

Saham Hills **178** A5
Saham Toney **163** G2
Saighdinis **262** D5
Saighton **170** B1
St. Abbs **237** G3
St. Agnes **96** B4
St. Aidan's Winery *N'umb*
  TD15 2RX **229** F2
St. Albans **136** A2
St. Albans Cathedral *Herts*
  AL1 1BY **136** A2
St. Allen **96** C4
St. Andrews **244** C3
St. Andrew's & Blackfriars
  Halls *Norf* NR3 1AU
  79 Norwich
St. Andrews Major **130** A5
St. Anne **101** G4
St. Anne's **191** G5
St. Ann's **217** E1
St. Ann's Chapel
  Corn **99** E3
St. Ann's Chapel
  Devon **100** C3
St. Anthony **95** F3
St. Anthony-in-
  Meneage **95** E4
St. Anthony's Hill **110** B3
St. Arvans **131** E3
St. Asaph
  (Llanelwy) **182** B5
St. Athan **114** D1
St. Aubin **100** C5
St. Audries **115** E3
St. Austell **97** E4
St. Bees **208** C5
St. Blazey **97** E4
St. Blazey Gate **97** E4
St. Boswells **227** G2
St. Botolph's Church, Boston
  Lincs PE21 6NP **176** B3
St. Brelade **100** B5
St. Breock **97** D2
St. Breward **97** E2
St. Briavels **131** E2
St. Brides **126** B1
St. Brides Major **129** E5
St. Bride's
  Netherwent **130** D4
St. Brides
  Wentlooge **130** B4
St. Bride's-super-
  Ely **129** G5
St. Budeaux **100** A2
St. Buryan **94** B4
St. Catherine **117** E1
St. Catherines **240** D4
St. Clears (Sanclêr) **127** E1
St. Cleer **97** G3
St. Clement *Chanl* **100** C5
St. Clement *Corn* **96** C5
St. Clether **97** G1
St. Colmac **232** B3
St. Columb Major **96** D3
St. Columb Minor **96** C3
St. Columb Road **96** D4
St. Combs **269** J4
St. Cross South
  Elmham **165** D3
St. Cyrus **253** F3
St. Davids *Fife* **235** F1
St. David's P&K **243** E2
St. David's (Tyddewi)
  Pembs **140** A5
St. David's Hall *CF10 1AH*
  67 Cardiff
St. Day **96** B5
St. Decumans **115** D3
St. Dennis **97** D4
St. Denys **106** D1
St. Dogmaels
  (Llandudoch) **141** E3
St. Dogwells **140** C5
St. Dominick **100** A1
St. Donats **114** C1
St. Edith's Marsh **118** A1
St. Endellion **97** D2
St. Enoder **96** C4
St. Erme **96** C5
St. Erney **99** D5
St. Erth **94** C3
St. Erth Praze **94** C3
St. Ervan **96** C2
St. Eval **96** C3
St. Ewe **97** D5
St. Fagans **130** A5
St. Fagans National History
  Museum *Cardiff*
  CF5 6XB **7** A4
St. Fergus **269** J5
St. Fillans **242** B2
St. Florence **127** D2
St. Gennys **98** B1
St. George *Bristol* **131** F5
St. George *Conwy* **182** A5
St. George's *Tel&W* **157** G1
St. George's
  VGlam **129** G5
St. George's Hall, Liverpool
  Mersey L1 1JJ **42** D3
St. Germans **99** D5
St. Giles' Cathedral,
  Edinburgh *Edin*
  EH1 1RE **37** F4
St. Giles in the
  Wood **113** F4
St. Giles on the
  Heath **99** D1
St. Harmon **155** F5
St. Helen Auckland **212** A5
St. Helena **164** C4
St. Helen's *ESuss* **110** D2
St. Helens *IoW* **107** F4
St. Helens *Mersey* **183** G3
St. Helier *Chanl* **100** C5
St. Helier *GtLon* **122** B2
St. Hilary *Corn* **94** C3
St. Hilary *VGlam* **129** G5
St. Hill **122** C5
St. Ibbs **149** G5
St. Illtyd **130** B2
St. Ippollitts **149** G5
St. Ishmael **127** G2
St. Ishmael's **126** B2
St. Issey **96** D2
St. Ive **98** D4
St. Ives *Cambs* **162** B5

St. Ives *Corn* **94** C2
St. Ives *Dorset* **106** A2
St. James South
  Elmham **165** E3
St. John *Chanl* **100** C4
St. John *Corn* **100** D1
St. John the Baptist Church,
  Cirencester *Glos*
  GL7 2NX **132** C2
St. John's *GtLon* **136** C5
St. John's *IoM* **190** A3
St. John's *Surr* **121** E3
St. John's *Worcs* **146** A2
St. John's Chapel
  Devon **113** F3
St. John's Chapel
  Dur **211** E4
St. John's Fen End **162** D1
St. John's Hall **211** E4
St. John's Highway **162** D1
St. John's Kirk **226** A2
St. John's Town of
  Dalry **216** D4
St. Judes **190** B2
St. Just **94** A3
St. Just in Roseland **95** F3
St. Katherines **261** F1
St. Keverne **95** E4
St. Kew **97** E2
St. Kew Highway **97** E2
St. Keyne **97** G3
St. Lawrence *Corn* **97** E3
St. Lawrence *Essex* **138** C2
St. Lawrence *IoW* **107** E5
St. Lawrence's Church,
  Eyam *Derbys*
  S32 5QH **185** G5
St. Leonards
  Bucks **135** E2
St. Leonards
  Dorset **106** A2
St. Leonards
  ESuss **110** D3
St. Leonards
  Grange **106** D3
St. Leonard's Street **123** F3
St. Levan **94** A4
St. Lythans **130** A5
St. Mabyn **97** E2
St. Madoes **243** G2
St. Margaret South
  Elmham **165** E3
St. Margarets
  Here **144** C4
St. Margarets
  Herts **136** C4
St. Margarets
  Wilts **118** D1
St. Margaret's at
  Cliffe **125** F4
St. Margaret's Hope **277** D8
St. Mark's **190** A4
St. Martin *Chanl* **101** F5
St. Martin *Chanl* **100** C5
St. Martin *Corn* **97** G4
St. Martin *Corn* **95** E4
St. Martin-in-the-Fields
  Church *GtLon*
  WC2N 4JH **44** E4
St. Martin's *IoS* **96** B1
St. Martins *P&K* **243** G1
St. Martin's *Shrop* **170** A4
St. Mary **100** C5
St. Mary Bourne **119** F2
St. Mary Church **129** G5
St. Mary Cray **123** D2
St. Mary Hill **129** F5
St. Mary Hoo **137** G5
St. Mary in the
  Marsh **111** F1
St. Mary Magdalene Chapel,
  Sandringham *Norf*
  PE35 6EH **177** E5
St. Mary the Virgin Church,
  Holy Island *N'umb*
  TD15 2RX **229** F2
St. Mary the Virgin Church,
  Oxford *Oxon*
  OX1 4AH **134** A2
St. Mary the Virgin Church,
  Rye *ESuss*
  TN31 7HE **111** E2
St. Marychurch **101** F1
St. Mary's *IoS* **96** B1
St. Mary's *Ork* **277** D7
St. Mary's Airport **96** B1
St. Mary's Bay **111** F1
St. Mary's Church, Whitby
  NYorks
  YO22 4JT **204** C1
St. Mary's Grove **116** B1
St. Maughans
  Green **131** D1
St. Mawes **95** F3
St. Mawgan **96** C3
St. Mellion **99** D4
St. Mellons **130** B4
St. Merryn **96** C2
St. Mewan **97** D4
St. Michael Caerhays **97** D5
St. Michael Church **116** A4
St. Michael Penkevil **96** C5
St. Michael South
  Elmham **165** E3
St. Michaels *Fife* **244** C2
St. Michaels *Kent* **124** A5
St. Michaels *Worcs* **145** E1
St. Michael's Church,
  Hathersage *Derbys*
  S32 1AJ **185** G4
St. Michael's Mount *Corn*
  TR17 0HT **94** C3
St. Michael's on
  Wyre **192** A3
St. Mildred's Church,
  Whippingham *IoW*
  PO32 6LP **107** E3
St. Minver **97** D2
St. Monans **244** D4
St. Mungo Museum of
  Religious Life & Art
  Glas G4 0RH **39** H3
St. Mungo's Cathedral,
  Glasgow *Glas*
  G4 0QZ **39** J3
St. Neot **97** F3
St. Neots **149** G1
St. Newlyn East **96** C4

St. Nicholas *Pembs* **140** C4
St. Nicholas *VGlam* **129** G5
St. Nicholas at
  Wade **125** E2
St. Ninians **242** C5
St. Osyth **139** E1
St. Ouen **100** B5
St. Owen's Cross **145** E5
St. Paul's Cathedral,
  London *GtLon*
  EC4M 8AD **45** J3
St. Paul's Cray **123** D2
St. Paul's Walden **149** G5
St. Peter **100** C5
St. Peter Port **101** F5
St. Peter's **125** F2
St. Petrox **126** C3
St. Pinnock **97** G3
St. Quivox **224** B3
St. Ruan **95** E5
St. Sampson **101** F4
St. Saviour *Chanl* **101** E5
St. Saviour *Chanl* **100** C5
St. Stephen **96** D4
St. Stephens *Corn* **100** A2
St. Stephens *Corn* **98** D2
St. Stephens *Herts* **136** A2
St. Teath **97** E1
St. Thomas **102** C3
St. Tudy **97** E2
St. Twynnells **126** C3
St. Veep **97** F4
St. Vigeans **253** E5
St. Wenn **97** D4
St. Weonards **145** D5
St. Winnow **97** F4
St. Winwaloe's Church,
  Gunwalloe *Corn*
  TR12 7QE **95** D4
Saintbury **146** B4
Salachail **248** C4
Salcombe **100** D4
Salcombe Regis **103** E4
Salcott **138** C1
Sale **184** B3
Sale Green **146** B2
Saleby **189** E5
Salehurst **110** C3
Salem *Carmar* **142** C5
Salem *Cere* **154** C4
Salem *Gwyn* **167** E2
Salen *A&B* **247** E5
Salen *High* **247** F3
Salendine Nook **185** F1
Salesbury **192** C4
Saleway **146** B2
Salford *CenBeds* **149** E4
Salford *GtMan* **184** C1
Salford *Oxon* **147** E5
Salford Priors **146** C2
Salfords **122** B4
Salhouse **179** E4
Saline **243** F5
Salisbury **118** C5
Salisbury Cathedral
  Wilts SP1 2EF
  83 Salisbury
Salkeld Dykes **210** B4
Sallachan **248** B3
Sallachy **240** C3
Sallachy *High* **266** C1
Sallachy *High* **257** F1
Salle **178** C3
Salmonby **188** D5
Salmond's Muir **245** D1
Salperton **146** C5
Salph End **149** F2
Salsburgh **234** C3
Salt **171** G5
Salt Hill **135** E4
Salt Holme **213** D5
Saltaire **194** A4
Saltash **100** A2
Saltburn **266** C3
Saltburn-by-the-
  Sea **213** F5
Saltburn's Inclined
  Tramway *R&C*
  TS12 1DP **213** F5
Saltby **175** D5
Saltcoats *Cumb* **198** B3
Saltcoats *NAyr* **232** D5
Saltcotes **191** G5
Saltdean **109** F3
Salterbeck **208** C4
Salterforth **193** E3
Saltergate **204** B3
Salterhill **267** K5
Salterswall **170** D1
Saltfleet **189** E3
Saltfleetby All
  Saints **189** E3
Saltfleetby
  St. Clements **189** E3
Saltfleetby St. Peter **189** E4
Saltford **117** D1
Salthaugh Grange **197** E5
Salthouse **178** B1
Saltley **158** C4
Saltmarshe **195** G5
Saltness **277** B8
Saltney **170** A1
Salton **203** G4
Saltrens **113** E3
Saltwell Park, Gateshead
  T&W NE9 5AX **28** B3
Saltwick **221** D4
Saltwood **125** D5
Salum **246** B2
Salvington **108** D3
Salwarpe **146** A1
Salwayash **104** A3
Sambourne **146** C1
Sambrook **171** E5
Samhla **262** C5
Samlesbury **192** C4
Sampford Arundel **103** E1
Sampford Brett **115** D3
Sampford
  Courtenay **113** G5
Sampford Moor **103** E1
Sampford Peverell **102** D1
Sampford Spiney **99** F3
Samuelston **236** B2
Sanaigmore **230** A2

Sancreed **94** B4
Sancton **196** B4
Sand *Shet* **279** C8
Sand *Som* **116** B3
Sand Hutton **195** F2
Sandaig *A&B* **246** A2
Sandaig *High* **256** D4
Sandaig *High* **256** D3
Sandal Magna **186** A1
Sandbach **171** E1
Sandbank **232** C1
Sandbanks **105** G4
Sandend **268** D4
Sanderstead **122** C2
Sandford *Cumb* **200** C1
Sandford *Devon* **102** B2
Sandford *Dorset* **105** F4
Sandford *IoW* **107** E4
Sandford *NSom* **116** B2
Sandford *Shrop* **170** C4
Sandford *Shrop* **170** A5
Sandford *SLan* **234** B5
Sandford Orcas **116** D5
Sandford St. Martin **147** G5
Sandfordhill **269** K6
Sandford-on-
  Thames **134** A2
Sandgarth **277** E6
Sandgate **125** E5
Sandgreen **215** G5
Sandhaven **269** H4
Sandhead **206** B2
Sandhills *Dorset* **104** C1
Sandhills *Dorset* **104** B2
Sandhills *Surr* **121** E4
Sandhills *WYorks* **194** C4
Sandhoe **211** F1
Sandholme *ERid* **196** A4
Sandholme *Lincs* **176** B4
Sandhurst *BrackF* **120** D1
Sandhurst *Glos* **146** A5
Sandhurst *Kent* **110** C1
Sandhurst Cross **110** C1
Sandhutton **202** C4
Sandiacre **173** F4
Sandilands **189** F4
Sandiway **184** A5
Sandleheath **106** A1
Sandleigh **133** G2
Sandling **123** G3
Sandlow Green **171** E1
Sandness **279** A7
Sandon *Essex* **137** G2
Sandon *Herts* **150** B4
Sandon *Staffs* **171** G5
Sandown **107** F4
Sandplace **97** G4
Sandquoy **276** E2
Sandridge *Devon* **101** E2
Sandridge *Herts* **136** A1
Sandridge *Wilts* **118** A1
Sandringham **177** E5
Sandrocks **109** F1
Sandsend **204** B1
Sandside **199** F4
Sandside House **274** E2
Sandsound **279** C8
Sandtoft **187** E2
Sanduck **102** A4
Sandway **124** A3
Sandwell **158** C4
Sandwell Park Farm *WMid*
  B71 4BG **14** D2
Sandwell Valley Country
  Park *WMid*
  B71 4BG **14** D2
Sandwich **125** F3
Sandwick *Cumb* **199** F1
Sandwick *Shet* **279** D10
Sandwick (Sanndabhaig)
  ESiar **271** G4
Sandwith **208** C5
Sandy *Carmar* **128** A2
Sandy *CenBeds* **149** G3
Sandy Bank **176** A2
Sandy Haven **126** B2
Sandy Lane *Wilts* **118** A1
Sandy Lane *Wrex* **170** B3
Sandy Lane
  WYorks **194** A4
Sandy Way **107** D4
Sandycroft **170** A1
Sandygate *Devon* **102** B5
Sandygate *IoM* **190** B2
Sandyhills **216** C5
Sandylands **192** A3
Sandypark **102** A4
Sandyway **145** D5
Sangobeg **273** G2
Sankyn's Green **145** G1
Sanna **247** D3
Sannaig **230** D3
Sannox **232** B5
Sanquhar **225** F5
Santon Bridge **198** C2
Santon Downham **163** G4
Sant-y-Nyll **129** G5
Sapcote **159** G3
Sapey Common **145** G1
Sapiston **164** A4
Sapperton *Derbys* **172** C4
Sapperton *Glos* **132** B2
Sapperton *Lincs* **175** F3
Saracen's Head **176** B5
Sarclet **275** J4
Sardis **126** C2
Sarisbury **107** E2
Sark **101** G5
Sarn *Bridgend* **129** F4
Sarn *Powys* **156** B3
Sarn Bach **166** C5
Sarn Meyllteyrn **166** B4
Sarnau *Carmar* **127** G1
Sarnau *Cere* **141** G2
Sarnau *Gwyn* **168** C4
Sarnau *Powys* **156** B1
Sarnau *Powys* **143** G4
Sarnesfield **144** C2
Saron *Carmar* **128** C1
Saron *Carmar* **141** G4
Saron *Gwyn* **167** E1
Saron *Gwyn* **167** D2
Sarratt **135** F3
Sarre **125** E2
Sarsden **147** E5
Sarsgrum **273** F2

Sartfield **190** B2
Sartfield **190** B2
Satley **212** A3
Satron **201** E3
Satterleigh **113** G3
Satterthwaite **199** E3
Sauchen **260** E3
Saucher **243** G1
Sauchie **243** G1
Sauchieburn **253** E3
Sauchrie **224** B4
Saughall **183** E5
Saughall Massie **183** D4
Saughtree **219** D2
Saul **131** G2
Saundby **187** E4
Saundersfoot **127** E2
Saunderton **134** C2
Saunton **113** E2
Sausthorpe **176** B1
Saval **266** C1
Savalbeg **266** C1
Saverley Green **171** G4
Savile Town **194** B5
Sawbridge **148** A1
Sawbridgeworth **137** D1
Sawdon **204** C4
Sawley *Derbys* **173** F4
Sawley *Lancs* **193** D3
Sawley *NYorks* **194** B1
Sawston **150** C3
Sawtry **161** G4
Saxby *Leics* **160** D1
Saxby *Lincs* **188** A4
Saxby All Saints **187** G1
Saxelbe **174** B5
Saxham Street **152** B1
Saxilby **187** F5
Saxlingham **178** B2
Saxlingham Green **164** D2
Saxlingham
  Nethergate **164** D2
Saxlingham Thorpe **164** D2
Saxmundham **153** E1
Saxon Street **151** E2
Saxondale **174** B4
Saxtead **153** D1
Saxtead Green **153** D1
Saxtead Little
  Green **153** D1
Saxthorpe **178** C2
Saxton **195** D4
Sayers Common **109** E2
Scackleton **203** F5
Scadabhagh **263** G2
Scaftworth **187** D3
Scagglethorpe **204** B5
Scaitcliffe **193** D5
Scalasaig **238** C5
Scalby *ERid* **196** A5
Scalby *NYorks* **204** D3
Scaldwell **160** C5
Scale Houses **210** B3
Scaleby **210** A1
Scalebyhill **210** A1
Scales *Cumb* **209** G4
Scales *Cumb* **199** D5
Scalford **174** C5
Scaling **203** G1
Scallasaig **256** D3
Scallastle **239** G1
Scalloway **279** C9
Scalpay (Eilean
  Scalpaigh) **263** H2
Scamblesby **188** C5
Scammadale **240** A2
Scamodale **248** A2
Scampston **204** B5
Scampton **187** G5
Scaniport **258** D1
Scapa **277** D7
Scapegoat Hill **185** E1
Scar **277** F3
Scarborough **204** D4
Scarcewater **96** D4
Scarcliffe **173** F1
Scarcroft **194** C3
Scardroy **265** J6
Scarff **278** B4
Scarfskerry **275** H1
Scargill **201** F1
Scarinish **246** B2
Scarisbrick **183** E1
Scarning **178** A4
Scarrington **174** C3
Scarrowhill **210** B2
Scarth Hill **183** F2
Scarthingwell **195** D4
Scartho **188** C2
Scarwell **276** B5
Scatraig **258** E1
Scaur (Kippford)
  D&G **216** C5
Scaur *D&G* **216** A2
Scawby **187** G2
Scawby Brook **187** G2
Scawton **203** E4
Scayne's Hill **109** F1
Scealascro **270** D5
Scethrog **144** A5
Scholar Green **171** F2
Scholes *SYorks* **186** A3
Scholes *WYorks* **194** C4
Scholes *WYorks* **185** F2
Scholes *WYorks* **194** A5
School Green **170** D1
School House **103** G2
Schoose **208** B4
Sciberscross **266** E1
Science Museum *GtLon*
  SW7 2DD **11** F5
Scilly Isles
  (Isles of Scilly) **96** B1
Scissett **185** G1
Scleddau **140** C4
Sco Ruston **179** D3
Scofton **186** D4
Scole **164** C4
Scolpaig **262** C4
Scone **243** G2
Scones Lethendy **243** G2
Sconser **256** B1
Scoor **238** D3
Scopwick **175** F2

Scoraig **265** G2
Scorborough **196** C3
Scorrier **96** B5
Scorriton **100** D1
Scorton *Lancs* **192** B3
Scorton *NYorks* **202** B3
Scot Hay **171** F3
Scotby **210** A2
Scotch Corner **202** B2
Scotch Whisky Heritage
  Centre *Edin*
  EH1 2NE **37** F4
Scotforth **192** A2
Scothern **188** A5
Scotland **175** F4
Scotland End **147** F4
Scotland Street **152** A4
Scotland Street School
  Museum of Education
  Glas G5 8QB **38** C6
Scotlandwell **243** G4
Scotnish **231** F1
Scots' Gap **220** C3
Scotsburn **266** E4
Scotston *Aber* **253** F2
Scotston *P&K* **251** E5
Scotstoun **233** G3
Scotstown **248** A3
Scott Willoughby **175** F4
Scotter **187** F2
Scotterthorpe **187** F2
Scottlethorpe **175** F5
Scotton *Lincs* **187** F3
Scotton *NYorks* **202** A3
Scotton *NYorks* **194** C2
Scottow **179** D3
Scoughall **236** D1
Scoulton **178** A5
Scounslow Green **172** B5
Scourie **272** D4
Scourie More **272** D4
Scousburgh **279** F9
Scouthead **185** D2
Scrabster **275** G1
Scrafield **176** B1
Scrainwood **220** B1
Scrane End **176** B3
Scraptoft **160** B2
Scratby **179** G4
Scrayingham **195** G2
Scredington **175** F3
Scremby **176** C1
Scremerston **229** E2
Screveton **174** C3
Scriven **194** C2
Scronkey **192** A3
Scrooby **187** D3
Scropton **172** C4
Scrub Hill **176** A2
Scruton **202** C3
Sculcoates **196** C4
Sculthorpe **177** G4
Scunthorpe **187** F1
Scurlage **128** A4
Sea **103** G1
Sea Life Centre, Blackpool
  FY1 5AA
  64 Blackpool
Sea Life Centre, Brighton
  B&H BN2 1TB
  65 Brighton
Sea Life Centre, Great
  Yarmouth *Norf*
  NR30 3AH **179** G5
Sea Life Sanctuary,
  Hunstanton *Norf*
  PE36 5BH **177** E5
Sea Mills **131** E5
Sea Palling **179** F3
Seabank **248** B5
Seaborough **104** A2
Seaburn **212** D1
Seacombe **183** E3
Seacroft *Lincs* **177** D1
Seacroft *WYorks* **194** C4
Seadyke **176** B4
Seafield *A&B* **231** F1
Seafield *SAyr* **224** B3
Seafield *WLoth* **235** E3
Seaford **109** G4
Seaforth **183** E3
Seagrave **160** B1
Seagry Heath **132** B4
Seaham **212** D3
Seaham Grange **212** D2
Seahouses **229** G3
Seal **123** E3
Sealand **170** A1
Seale **121** D3
Sea-Life Adventure,
  Southend-on-Sea *S'end*
  SS1 2ER **138** B4
Sealyham **140** C5
Seamer *NYorks* **203** D1
Seamer *NYorks* **204** D4
Seamill **232** C5
SeaQuarium, Rhyl *Denb*
  LL18 3AF **182** B4
Searby **188** A2
Seasalter **124** C2
Seascale **198** B2
Seathorne **177** D1
Seathwaite *Cumb* **209** F5
Seathwaite *Cumb* **198** D3
Seatle **199** E4
Seaton *Corn* **98** D5
Seaton *Cumb* **208** D3
Seaton *Devon* **103** F3
Seaton *Dur* **212** D4
Seaton *ERid* **197** D3

Seaton *N'umb* **221** F4
Seaton *Rut* **161** E3
Seaton Burn **221** E4
Seaton Carew **213** E5
Seaton Delaval **221** F4
Seaton Junction **103** F3
Seaton Ross **195** G3
Seaton Sluice **221** F4
Seaton Tramway *Devon*
  EX12 2NQ **103** F3
Seatown *Aber* **269** J5
Seatown *Dorset* **104** A3
Seatown *Moray* **268** D4
Seave Green **203** E2
Seaview **107** F3
Seaville **209** E1
Seavington
  St. Mary **104** A1
Seavington
  St. Michael **104** A1
Seawick **139** E1
Sebastopol **130** B3
Seberham **209** G2
Seckington **159** E2
Second Coast **265** F2
Sedbury **200** B3
Sedbury **131** E3
Sedbusk **201** D3
Seddington **149** G3
Sedgeberrow **146** C4
Sedgebrook **175** D4
Sedgefield **212** C5
Sedgeford **177** F4
Sedgehill **117** F5
Sedgemere **159** E5
Sedgley **158** B3
Sedgwick **199** G4
Sedlescombe **110** C2
Sedlescombe
  Street **110** C2
Seend **118** A1
Seend Cleeve **118** A1
Seer Green **135** E3
Seething **165** E2
Sefton **183** E2
Seghill **221** E4
Seifton **157** D4
Seighford **171** F5
Seil **239** G3
Seilebost **263** F2
Seion **167** E1
Seisdon **158** A3
Seisiadar **271** H4
Seized! Revenue &
  Customs Uncovered
  Mersey L3 4AQ
  42 B5
Selattyn **169** F4
Selborne **120** C4
Selby **195** F4
Selham **121** E5
Selhurst **122** C2
Selkirk **227** F3
Sellack **145** E5
Sellafield **198** B2
Sellafield Visitors Centre
  Cumb
  CA20 1PG **198** B2
Sellafirth **278** E3
Sellindge **124** D5
Selling **124** C3
Sells Green **118** A1
Selly Oak **158** C4
Selmeston **110** A3
Selsdon **122** C2
Selsey **108** A4
Selsfield Common **122** C5
Selside *Cumb* **199** G3
Selside *NYorks* **200** C5
Selsley **132** A2
Selstead **125** E4
Selston **173** F2
Selworthy **114** C3
Semblister **279** C7
Semer **152** A3
Semington **117** F1
Semley **117** F5
Send **121** F2
Send Marsh **121** F2
Senghenydd **130** A3
Sennen **94** A4
Sennen Cove **94** A4
Sennybridge **143** F5
Senwick **207** G2
Sequer's Bridge **100** C2
Serlby **186** D4
Serpentine Gallery *GtLon*
  W2 3XA **11** F5
Serrington **118** B4
Sessay **203** D5
Setchey **163** E1
Setley **106** C2
Setter *Shet* **279** E8
Setter *Shet* **279** C7
Settiscarth **277** C6
Settle **193** E1
Settrington **204** B5
Seven Ash **115** E4
Seven Bridges **132** D3
Seven Kings **137** D4
Seven Sisters **129** E2
Seven Springs **132** B1
Sevenhampton
  Glos **146** C5
Sevenhampton
  Swin **133** E3
Sevenoaks **123** E3
Sevenoaks Weald **123** E3
Severn Beach **131** E4
Severn Stoke **146** A3
Severn Valley Railway
  Shrop
  DY12 1BG **157** G4
Sevick End **149** F2
Sevington **124** C4
Sewards End **151** D4
Sewardstone **136** C3
Sewerby **197** D1
Sewerby Hall & Gardens
  ERid
  YO15 1EA **197** E1
Seworgan **95** E3
Sewstern **175** D5
Seymour Villas **113** E1
Sezincote **147** D4
Sgarasta Mhòr **263** F2
Sgiogarstaigh **271** H1
Sgodachail **266** B2

Shabbington **134** B2
Shackerley **158** A2
Shackerstone **159** F2
Shackleford **121** E3
Shadfen **221** E3
Shadforth **212** C3
Shadingfield **165** F3
Shadoxhurst **124** B5
Shadsworth **192** D5
Shadwell *Norf* **164** A3
Shadwell *WYorks* **194** C3
Shaftenhoe End **150** C4
Shaftesbury **117** F5
Shafton **186** A1
Shakespeare's Birthplace
  Warks CV37 6QW
  85 Stratford-upon-Avon
Shakespeare's Globe Theatre
  GtLon SE1 9DT **45** J4
Shalbourne **119** E1
Shalcombe **106** C4
Shalden **120** B3
Shalden Green **120** C3
Shaldon **102** C5
Shalfleet **106** D4
Shalford *Essex* **151** F5
Shalford *Surr* **121** F3
Shalford Green **151** F5
Shallowford *Devon* **114** A3
Shallowford *Staffs* **171** F5
Shalmsford Street **124** C3
Shalmstry **275** G2
Shalstone **148** B4
Shalunt **232** B2
Shambellie **217** D4
Shamley Green **121** F3
Shandon **233** D1
Shandwick **267** F4
Shangton **160** C3
Shankend **227** G5
Shankhouse **221** E4
Shanklin **107** E4
Shanklin Chine *IoW*
  PO37 6BW **107** E4
Shannochie **223** E3
Shantron **233** E1
Shantullich **266** D6
Shanzie **252** A4
Shap **199** G1
Shapinsay **277** E6
Shapwick *Dorset* **105** F2
Shapwick *Som* **116** B4
Sharcott **118** C2
Shard End **159** D4
Shardlow **173** F4
Shareshill **158** B2
Sharlston **186** A1
Sharlston Common **186** A1
Sharnal Street **137** G5
Sharnbrook **149** E2
Sharneyford **193** E5
Sharnford **159** G3
Sharnhill Green **104** D2
Sharow **202** C5
Sharp Street **179** E3
Sharpenhoe **149** F4
Sharperton **220** B1
Sharpham House **101** E2
Sharpness **131** F2
Sharpthorne **122** C5
Sharrington **178** B2
Shatterford **157** G4
Shatterling **125** E3
Shaugh Prior **100** B1
Shave Cross **104** A3
Shavington **171** E2
Shaw *GtMan* **184** D2
Shaw *Swin* **132** D4
Shaw *WBerks* **119** F1
Shaw *Wilts* **117** F1
Shaw Green *Herts* **150** A4
Shaw Green
  NYorks **194** B2
Shaw Mills **194** B1
Shaw Side **184** D2
Shawbost
  (Siabost) **270** E3
Shawbury **170** C5
Shawell **160** A4
Shawfield *GtMan* **184** C1
Shawfield *Staffs* **172** B1
Shawford **119** F5
Shawforth **193** E5
Shawhead **216** C3
Shawtonhill **234** A5
Sheanachie **222** C4
Sheandow **259** K1
Shearington **217** E4
Shearsby **160** B3
Shebbear **113** E5
Shebdon **171** E4
Shebster **275** F2
Shedfield **107** E1
Sheen **172** C1
Sheepridge **185** F1
Sheepscombe **132** A1
Sheepstor **100** B1
Sheepwash *Devon* **113** E5
Sheepwash *N'umb* **221** E3
Sheepway **131** D5
Sheepy Magna **159** F2
Sheepy Parva **159** F2
Sheering **137** E1
Sheerness **124** B1
Sheet **120** C5
Sheffield **186** A4
Sheffield Botanic Gardens
  SYorks S10 2LN **21** B3
Sheffield Bottom **120** B1
Sheffield Green **109** G1
Sheffield Park Garden
  ESuss
  TN22 3QX **109** G1
Shefford **149** G4
Shefford Woodlands **133** F5
Sheigra **272** D2
Sheinton **157** F2
Shelderton **156** D5
Sheldon *Derbys* **172** C1
Sheldon *Devon* **103** E2
Sheldon *WMid* **158** D4
Sheldwich **124** C3
Sheldwich Lees **124** C3
Shelf *Bridgend* **129** F4
Shelf *WYorks* **194** A5
Shelfanger **164** C3
Shelfield *Warks* **146** D1
Shelfield *WMid* **158** C2

Shelfield Green **146** D1
Shelford **174** B3
Shellachan *A&B* **240** A2
Shellachan *A&B* **240** C2
Shellbrook **159** F1
Shellbrook Hill **170** A3
Shelley *Essex* **137** E2
Shelley *Suff* **152** B4
Shelley *WYorks* **185** G1
Shellingford **133** F3
Shellow Bowells **137** F2
Shelsley
　Beauchamp **145** G1
Shelsley Walsh **145** G1
Shelswell **148** B4
Shelthorpe **160** A1
Shelton *Bed* **149** F1
Shelton *Norf* **164** D2
Shelton *Notts* **174** C3
Shelton *Shrop* **157** D1
Shelve **156** C3
Shelwick **145** E3
Shelwick Green **145** E3
Shenfield **137** F3
Shenington **147** F3
Shenley **136** A2
Shenley Brook End **148** D4
Shenley Church End **148** D4
Shenleybury **136** A2
Shenmore **144** C4
Shennanton **215** E4
Shenstone *Staffs* **158** D2
Shenstone *Worcs* **158** A5
Shenstone
　Woodend **158** D2
Shenton **159** F2
Shenval **259** K2
Shepeau Stow **162** B1
Shephall **150** A5
Shepherd's Bush **136** B5
Shepherd's Green **134** C5
Shepherd's Patch **131** G2
Shepherdswell
　(Sibertswold) **125** E4
Shepley **185** F2
Sheppardstown **275** H5
Shepperdine **131** F3
Shepperton **121** F1
Shepreth **150** B3
Shepreth Wildlife Park
　Cambs SG8 6PZ **150** B3
Shepshed **159** G1
Shepton
　Beauchamp **104** A1
Shepton Mallet **116** D3
Shepton Montague **117** D4
Shepway **123** G3
Sheraton **212** D4
Sherborne *Dorset* **104** C1
Sherborne *Glos* **133** E1
Sherborne St. John **120** B2
Sherbourne **147** E1
Sherbourne Street **152** A3
Sherburn *Dur* **212** C3
Sherburn *NYorks* **204** C5
Sherburn Hill **212** C3
Sherburn in Elmet **195** D4
Shere **121** F3
Shereford **177** G5
Sherfield English **119** D5
Sherfield on
　oddon **120** B2
Sherford *Devon* **101** D3
Sherford *Som* **115** F5
Sheriff Hutton **195** F1
Sheriffhales **157** G1
Sheringham **178** C1
Sheringham Park Norf
　NR26 8TL **178** C1
Sherington **149** D3
Shernal Green **146** B1
Shernborne **177** F4
Sherramore **258** C5
Sherrington **118** A4
Sherston **132** A4
Sherwood **173** G3
Sherwood Forest Country
　Park Notts
　NG21 9HN **174** B1
Sherwood Forest Fun Park
　Notts
　NG21 9QA **174** B1
Sherwood Green **181** E5
Sherwood Pines Forest
　Park Notts
　NG21 9JL **174** B1
Shetland Islands **279** B7
Shevington **183** G1
Shevington Moor **183** G1
Sheviock **99** D5
Shide **107** E4
Shiel Bridge
　(Drochaid Sheile) **257** F3
Shieldaig *High* **264** E6
Shieldaig *High* **264** E4
Shieldhill **234** C2
Shielfoot **247** F2
Shielhill **252** C4
Shiels **260** E4
Shifford **133** F2
Shifnal **157** G2
Shilbottle **221** D1
Shildon **212** B5
Shillingford
　Devon **114** C5
Shillingford *Oxon* **134** A3
Shillingford Abbot **102** C4
Shillingford
　St. George **102** C4
Shillingstone **105** E1
Shillington **149** G4
Shillmoor **220** A1
Shilstone **113** F5
Shilton *Oxon* **133** E2
Shilton *Warks* **159** G4
Shimpling *Norf* **164** C3
Shimpling *Suff* **151** G2
Shimpling Street **151** G2
Shincliffe **212** B3
Shiney Row **212** C2
Shinfield **120** C1
Shingay **150** B3
Shingham **163** F2
Shingle Street **153** E3
Shinness Lodge **273** H7
Shipbourne **123** E3
Shipbrookhill **184** A5
Shipdham **178** A5

Shipham **116** B2
Shiphay **101** E1
Shiplake **134** C5
Shiplake Row **134** C5
Shipley *N'umb* **229** F5
Shipley *Derbys* **173** F3
Shipley *Shrop* **158** A3
Shipley *WSuss* **121** G5
Shipley *WYorks* **194** A4
Shipley Bridge
　Devon **100** C1
Shipley Bridge *Surr* **122** C4
Shipley Common **173** F3
Shipley Country Park
　Derbys DE75 7GX **18** D2
Shipmeadow **165** E2
Shippea Hill **163** E4
Shippon **133** G3
Shipston on Stour **147** E3
Shipton *Glos* **132** D1
Shipton *NYorks* **195** E2
Shipton *Shrop* **157** D3
Shipton Bellinger **118** D3
Shipton Gorge **104** A3
Shipton Green **108** A3
Shipton Moyne **132** A4
Shipton Oliffe **132** C1
Shipton Solers **132** C1
Shipton-on-
　Cherwell **133** G1
Shiptonthorpe **196** A3
Shipton-under-
　Wychwood **133** E1
Shira **241** D3
Shirburn **134** B3
Shirdley Hill **183** E1
Shire Hall Gallery, Stafford
　Staffs ST16 2LD **171** G3
Shire Oak **158** C2
Shirebrook **173** G1
Shirecliffe **186** A3
Shiregreen **186** A3
Shirehampton **131** E5
Shiremoor **221** E4
Shirenewton **131** D3
Shireoaks **186** C4
Shirl Heath **144** D2
Shirland **173** E2
Shirley *Derbys* **172** D3
Shirley *GtLon* **122** C2
Shirley *Hants* **106** A3
Shirley *Soton* **106** D1
Shirley *WMid* **158** D5
Shirley Heath **158** D5
Shirley Warren **106** C1
Shirleywich **171** G3
Shirrell Heath **107** E1
Shirwell **113** F2
Shirwell Cross **113** F2
Shiskine **223** E3
Shittlehope **211** G4
Shobdon **144** C1
Shobley **106** A2
Shobrooke **102** B2
Shocklach **170** B3
Shocklach Green **170** B3
Shoeburyness **138** C4
Sholden **125** F3
Sholing **107** D1
Shoot Hill **156** D1
Shooter's Hill **136** D5
Shop *Corn* **96** C2
Shop *Corn* **112** C4
Shop Corner **152** D4
Shoppnoller **115** E4
Shore **184** D1
Shoreditch **136** C4
Shoreham **123** E2
Shoreham Airport **109** D3
Shoreham-by-Sea **109** E3
Shoremill **266** E3
Shoresdean **237** G5
Shoreswood **237** G5
Shoreton **266** D5
Shorley **119** G5
Shorncote **132** C3
Shorne **137** F5
Shorne Ridgeway **137** F5
Short Cross **156** B2
Short Green **164** B3
Short Heath *Derbys* **159** F1
Short Heath *WMid* **158** C3
Shortacombe **99** F2
Shortbridge **109** G1
Shortfield Common **120** D3
Shortgate **109** G2
Shortgrove **150** D4
Shorthampton **147** F5
Shortlands **122** C2
Shortlanesend **96** C5
Shorton **101** E1
Shorwell **107** D4
Shoscombe **117** E2
Shotatton **170** A5
Shotesham **164** D2
Shotgate **137** G3
Shotley *N'hants* **161** E3
Shotley *Suff* **152** D4
Shotley Bridge **211** G2
Shotley Gate **152** D4
Shotleyfield **211** G2
Shottenden **124** C3
Shottermill **121** D4
Shottery **147** D2
Shotteswell **147** G3
Shottisham **153** E3
Shottle **173** E2
Shottlegate **173** E2
Shotton *Dur* **212** D4
Shotton *Dur* **212** D3
Shotton *Flints* **170** A1
Shotton *N'umb* **221** E4
Shotton Colliery **212** C3
Shotts **234** C3
Shotwick **183** E5
Shouldham **163** E2
Shouldham Thorpe **163** E2
Shoulton **146** A2
Shover's Green **123** F5
Shrawardine **156** C1
Shrawley **146** A1
Shreding Green **135** F4
Shrewley **147** E1
Shrewsbury **157** D1
Shrewton **118** B3
Shri Venkateswara (Balaji)
　Temple of the United
　Kingdom WMid
　B69 3DU **14** C3

Shrine of Our Lady of
　Walsingham (Anglican)
　Norf NR22 6EF **178** A2
Shripney **108** B3
Shrivenham **133** E4
Shropham **164** A2
Shroton (Iwerne
　Courtney) **105** E1
Shrub End **152** A5
Shucknall **145** E3
Shudy Camps **151** E3
Shurdington **132** B1
Shurlock Row **134** D5
Shurnock **146** C1
Shurrery **275** F3
Shurrery Lodge **275** F3
Shurton **115** F3
Shustoke **159** E3
Shut Heath **171** F5
Shute *Devon* **103** F3
Shute *Devon* **102** B2
Shutford **147** F3
Shuthonger **146** A4
Shutlanger **148** C3
Shutt Green **158** A2
Shuttington **159** E2
Shuttlewood **186** B5
Shuttleworth **184** B1
Siabost Bho Dheas **270** E3
Siabost Bho Thuath **270** E3
Siadar Iarach **271** F2
Siadar Uarach **271** F2
Sibbaldbie **217** F2
Sibbertoft **160** B4
Sibdon Carwood **156** D4
Sibertswold
　(Shepherdswell) **125** E4
Sibford Ferris **147** F4
Sibford Gower **147** F4
Sible Hedingham **151** F4
Sibley's Green **151** E5
Sibsey **176** B2
Sibson *Cambs* **161** F3
Sibson *Leics* **159** F2
Sibster **275** J3
Sibthorpe **174** C3
Sibton **153** E1
Sibton Green **165** E4
Sicklesmere **151** G1
Sicklinghall **194** C3
Sidbury *Devon* **103** E3
Sidbury *Shrop* **157** F4
Sidcot **116** B2
Sidcup **137** D5
Siddal **194** A5
Siddington *ChesE* **184** C5
Siddington *Glos* **132** C3
Sidemoor **158** B5
Sidestrand **179** D2
Sidford **103** E3
Sidlesham **108** A4
Sidley **110** C3
Sidlow **122** B4
Sidmouth **103** E4
Sigford **102** A5
Sigglesthorne **197** D3
Sigingstone **129** F5
Signet **133** E1
Silchester **120** B1
Sildinis **270** E6
Sileby **160** B1
Silecroft **190** C4
Silfield **164** C2
Silian **142** B1
Silk Willoughby **175** F3
Silksted **119** F5
Silkstone **185** G2
Silkstone Common **185** G2
Sill Field **199** G4
Silloth **209** E1
Sills **220** A1
Sillyearn **268** D5
Silpho **204** C3
Silsden **193** G3
Silsoe **149** F4
Silver End *CenBeds* **149** G3
Silver End *Essex* **151** G5
Silver Green **165** D2
Silver Street *Kent* **124** A2
Silver Street *Som* **116** C4
Silverburn **235** G3
Silvercraigs **231** G1
Silverdale *Lancs* **199** F5
Silverdale *Staffs* **171** F3
Silvergate **178** C3
Silverhill **110** C2
Silverlace Green **153** E2
Silverley's Green **165** D4
Silvermoss **261** G1
Silverstone **148** B3
Silverton **102** C2
Silvington **157** F5
Silwick **279** B8
Simister **184** C2
Simmondley **185** E3
Simonburn **220** A4
Simonsbath **114** A4
Simonside **212** C1
Simonstone
　Bridgend **129** F4
Simonstone
　Lancs **193** D4
Simprim **237** F5
Simpson **149** D4
Sinclair's Hill **237** F4
Sinclairston **224** C4
Sinderby **202** C4
Sinderhope **211** E2
Sindlesham **120** C1
Sinfin **173** E4
Singdean **227** G5
Singleton *Lancs* **191** G4
Singleton *WSuss* **108** A2
Singlewell **137** F5
Singret **170** A2
Sinkhurst Green **124** A4
Sinnahard **260** C3
Sinnington **203** G4
Sinton Green **146** A1
Sipson **135** F5
Sirhowy **130** A1
Sirhowy Valley Country
　Park Caerp
　NP11 7BD **130** A3
Sisland **165** E2
Sissinghurst **123** G5

Sissinghurst Castle Garden
　Kent TN17 2AB **124** A5
Siston **131** G5
Sithney **94** D4
Sittingbourne **124** B2
Siulaisiadar **271** H4
Sisland *Lincs* **175** F3
Sleagill **199** G3
Sledge Green **146** A4
Sledmere **196** B1
Sleights **204** B2
Slepe **105** F3
Slerra **112** D3
Slickly **275** H2
Sliddery **223** E3
Sliemore **259** H2
Sligachan **255** K2
Slimbridge **131** G2
Slimbridge Wildfowl &
　Wetlands Trust Glos
　GL2 7BT **131** G2
Slindon *Staffs* **171** F4
Slindon *WSuss* **108** B3
Slinfold **121** G5
Sling **131** E1
Slingsby **203** F5
Slioch **260** D1
Slip End *CenBeds* **135** F1
Slip End *Herts* **150** A4
Slipper Chapel, Houghton
　St. Giles Norf
　NR22 6AL **178** A2
Slipton **161** E5
Slitting Mill **158** C1
Slochd **259** F2
Slockavullin **240** A5
Slogarie **216** A4
Sloley **179** D3
Slongaber **216** C3
Sloothby **189** E5
Slough **135** E4
Slough Green
　Som **115** F5
Slough Green
　WSuss **109** E1
Sluggan **259** F2
Slyne **192** A1
Smailholm **228** A3
Small Dole **109** E2
Small Hythe **124** A5
Smallbridge **184** D1
Smallbrook **102** B3
Smallburgh **179** E3
Smallburn *Aber* **269** J6
Smallburn *EAyr* **225** E3
Smalldale **185** E5
Smalley **173** F3
Smallfield **122** C4
Smallford **136** A2
Smallridge **103** F2
Smallthorne **171** F2
Smallworth **164** B3
Smannell **119** E3
Smardale **200** C2
Smarden **124** A4
Smaull **230** A3
Smeatharpe **103** E1
Smeeth **124** C5
Smeeton
　Westerby **160** B3
Smercleit **254** C3
Smerral **275** G5
Smestow **158** A3
Smethwick **158** C4
Smethwick Green **171** F1
Sminsary **247** G5
Smisby **159** F1
Smith End Green **145** G2
Smithfield **210** A1
Smithies **186** A2
Smithincott **103** D1
Smith's End **150** B4
Smith's Green
　Essex **151** D5
Smith's Green
　Essex **151** E4
Smithstown **264** D4
Smithton **266** E7
Smithy Green **184** B5
Smockington **159** G4
Smugglers Adventure
　ESuss TN34 3HY
　75 Hastings
Smyrton **214** C2
Smythe's Green **138** C1
Snailbeach **156** C2
Snailwell **151** E1
Snainton **204** C4
Snaith **195** G5
Snape *NYorks* **202** B4
Snape *Suff* **153** E2
Snape Green **183** E1
Snape Watering **153** E2
Snarestone **159** F2
Snarford **188** A4
Snargate **111** E1
Snave **111** E1
Sneachill **146** B2
Snead **156** C3
Snead's Green **146** A1
Sneaton **204** B2
Sneatonthorpe **204** C2
Snelland **188** A4
Snellings **198** A2
Snelston **172** C3
Snetterton **164** A2
Snettisham **177** E4
Snipeshill **124** B2
Snishival
　(Sniseabhal) **254** C1
Snitter **220** C1
Snitterby **187** G3
Snitterfield **147** E2
Snitterton **173** D1
Snittlegarth **209** F3
Snitton **157** E5
Snodhill **144** C3
Snodland **123** G2
Snow End **150** C4
Snow Street **164** B3
Snowden Hill **185** G2
Snowdon Mountain Railway
　Gwyn
　LL55 4TY **167** E2
Snowshill **146** C4
Snowshill Manor Glos
　WR12 7JU **146** C4

Slaugham **109** E1
Slaughden **153** E2
Slaughterford **132** A5
Slawston **160** C3
Sleaford *Hants* **120** D4
Sleaford *Lincs* **175** F3
Soar *Cardiff* **129** G4
Soar *Carmar* **142** C5
Soar *Devon* **100** D4
Soay **255** K3
Soberton **107** F1
Soberton Heath **107** F1
Sockbridge **210** B5
Sockburn **202** C2
Sodom **182** B5
Sodylt Bank **170** A4
Softley **211** G5
Soham **163** D5
Soham Cotes **163** D5
Solas (Solas) **262** D4
Soldon **112** D4
Soldon Cross **112** D4
Soldridge **120** B4
Solihull **159** D5
Solihull Lodge **158** C5
Sollas (Solas) **262** D4
Sollers Dilwyn **144** D2
Sollers Hope **145** F4
Sollom **183** F1
Solomon's Tump **131** G1
Solsgirth **243** E5
Solva **140** A5
Solwaybank **218** B4
Somerby *Leics* **160** C1
Somerby *Lincs* **188** A3
Somercotes **173** F2
Somerford **158** B2
Somerford Keynes **132** C3
Somerley **106** A3
Somerleyton **165** F2
Somersal Herbert **172** C4
Somersby **189** D5
Somerset House GtLon
　WC2R 1LA **45** F3
Somersham
　Cambs **162** B5
Somersham *Suff* **152** B3
Somerton *Newport* **130** C4
Somerton *Oxon* **147** G5
Somerton *Som* **116** B5
Somerton *Suff* **151** G2
Sompting **109** D3
Sompting Abbotts **109** D3
Sonning **134** C5
Sonning Common **134** C4
Sonning Eye **134** C5
Sontley **170** A3
Sookholme **173** G1
Sopley **106** A3
Sopworth **132** A4
Sorbie **207** E2
Sordale **275** G2
Sorisdale **246** B3
Sorn **225** D3
Sornhill **224** D2
Soroba **240** A2
Sortat **275** H2
Sotby **188** C5
Sots Hole **175** G1
Sotterley **165** F3
Soudley **171** E5
Soughton **169** F1
Soulbury **149** D5
Soulby **200** C1
Souldern **148** B4
Souldrop **149** E1
Sound *ChesE* **170** D3
Sound *Shet* **279** D8
Sound *Shet* **279** C7
Sourhope **228** C4
Sourin **276** D4
Sourton **99** F1
Soutergate **198** D4
South Acre **163** G1
South Acton **136** A5
South Alkham **125** E4
South Allington **101** D4
South Alloa **243** D5
South Ambersham **121** E5
South Anston **186** C4
South Ascot **121** E1
South Baddesley **106** C3
South Ballachulish (Baile a'
　Chaolais a Deas) **248** C4
South Balloch **215** E1
South Bank **213** E5
South Barrow **116** D5
South Bellsdyke **234** D1
South Benfleet **137** G4
South Bersted **108** B3
South Blackbog **261** F1
South
　Bockhampton **106** A3
South Bowood **104** A3
South Brentor **99** E2
South Brent **100** C1
South Brewham **117** E4
South Broomhill **221** E2
South Burlingham **179** E5
South Cadbury **116** D5
South Cairn **214** A4
South Carlton **187** G5
South Cave **196** B4
South Cerney **132** C3
South Chard **103** G2
South Charlton **229** F4
South Cheriton **117** D5
South Church **212** B5
South Cliffe **196** A4
South Clifton **187** F5
South Cockerington **189** D4
South Collafirth **278** C4
South Common **109** F2
South Cornelly **129** E4
South Corriegills **223** F2
South Cove **165** F3
South Creagan **248** B5
South Creake **177** G4
South Crosland **185** F1
South Croxton **160** B1
South Croydon **122** C2
South Dalton **196** B3
South Darenth **137** E5
South Dell
　(Dail Bho Dheas) **271** G1
South Duffield **195** F4
South Elkington **188** C4
South Elmsall **186** B1
South End *Bucks* **149** D5
South End *Cumb* **191** F1
South End *Hants* **106** A1
South End *NLincs* **196** D5

South Erradale **264** D4
South Fambridge **138** B3
South Fawley **133** F4
South Ferriby **196** B5
South Field **196** C5
South Flobbets **261** F1
South Garth **278** E3
South Godstone **122** C4
South Gorley **106** A1
South Green *Essex* **137** F3
South Green *Essex* **138** D1
South Green *Norf* **178** B4
South Green *Suff* **164** C4
South Gyle **235** F2
South Hall **232** B2
South Hanningfield **137** G3
South Harefield **135** F4
South Harting **107** G1
South Hayling **107** G3
South Hazelrigg **229** E3
South Heath **135** E2
South Heighton **109** G3
South Hetton **212** C3
South Hiendley **186** A1
South Hill **98** D3
South Hinksey **134** A2
South Hole **112** C4
South Holme **203** F5
South Holmwood **121** G3
South Hornchurch **137** E4
South Hourat **233** D4
South Huish **100** C3
South Hykeham **175** E1
South Hylton **212** C2
South Kelsey **188** A3
South Kessock (Ceasag a
　Deas) **266** D7
South Killingholme **188** B1
South Kilvington **202** D4
South Kilworth **160** B4
South Kirkby **186** B1
South Kirkton **261** F4
South Knighton **102** B5
South Kyme **175** G3
South Lakes Wild Animal
　Park Cumb
　LA15 8JR **198** D5
South Lancing **109** D3
South Ledaig **240** B1
South Leigh **133** F2
South Leverton **187** E4
South Littleton **146** C3
South Lopham **164** B3
South Luffenham **161** E2
South Malling **109** G2
South Marston **133** D4
South Middleton **229** D4
South Milford **195** D4
South Milton **100** C3
South Mimms **136** B2
South Molton **114** A5
South Moor **212** A2
South Moreton **134** A4
South Mundham **108** A3
South Muskham **174** C2
South Newbald **196** B4
South Newington **147** G4
South Newton **118** B4
South Normanton **173** F2
South Norwood **122** C2
South Nutfield **122** C4
South Ockendon **137** E4
South Ormsby **189** D5
South Ossett **185** G1
South Otterington **202** C4
South Owersby **188** A3
South Oxhey **136** A3
South Park **122** B4
South Parks **244** A4
South Perrott **104** A2
South Petherton **104** A1
South Petherwin **98** D2
South Pickenham **163** G2
South Pool **100** D3
South Queensferry
　(Queensferry) **235** F2
South Radworthy **114** A4
South Rauceby **175** F3
South Raynham **177** G5
South Redbriggs **269** F6
South Reston **189** E4
South Ronaldsay **277** D9
South Ruislip **136** A4
South Runcton **163** E2
South Scarle **174** D1
South Shian
　(Sithean a Deas) **248** B5
South Shields **212** C1
South Shields Museum &
　Art Gallery T&W
　NE33 2JA **28** E2
South Somercotes **189** E3
South Somercotes Fen
　Houses **189** E3
South Stainley **194** C1
South Stoke
　B&NESom **117** E1
South Stoke *Oxon* **134** B4
South Stoke *WSuss* **108** C3
South Street
　GtLon **122** D3
South Street *Kent* **123** F2
South Street *Kent* **124** D3
South Street *Kent* **124** A2
South Street *ESuss* **109** F2
South Tawton **99** G1
South Thoresby **189** E5
South Tidworth **118** D3
South Town **136** C4
South Town *Devon* **102** C4
South Town *Hants* **120** B4
South Uist
　(Uibhist a Deas) **254** C1
South Upper
　Barrack **269** H6
South View **120** B2
South Walsham **179** E4
South
　Warnborough **120** C3
South Weald **137** F3
South Weston **134** C3
South Wheatley
　Corn **98** C1
South Wheatley
　Notts **187** E4
South Whiteness **279** C8
South Wigston **160** A3
South Willingham **188** B4

311

South Wingfield 173 E2
South Witham 161 E1
South Wonston 119 F4
South Woodham
  Ferrers 138 B3
South Wootton 177 E5
South Wraxall 117 F1
South Yardle 158 D4
South Zeal 99 G1
Southall 136 A4
Southam Glos 146 B5
Southam Warks 147 G1
Southampton 106 D1
Southampton
  Airport 107 D1
Southbar 233 F3
Southborough
  GtLon 122 D2
Southborough Kent 123 E4
Southbourne
  Bourne 106 A3
Southbourne
  WSuss 107 G2
Southbrook 102 D3
Southburgh 178 B5
Southburn 196 B2
Southchurch 138 C4
Southcott Devon 99 F1
Southcott Wilts 118 C2
Southcourt 134 C1
Southdean 219 E1
Southdene 183 F3
Southease 109 G3
Southend A&B 222 B5
Southend Aber 269 F6
Southend Bucks 134 C4
Southend (Bradfield
  Southend)
  WBerks 134 A5
Southend Wilts 133 D5
Southend Airport 138 B4
Southend Pier S'end
  SS1 1EE 138 B4
Southerfield 209 E2
Southerly 99 F2
Southern Green 150 B4
Southerndown 129 E5
Southerness 217 G1
Southery 163 E3
Southfield 244 A5
Southfields 136 B5
Southfleet 137 F5
Southoe Cere 154 B4
Southolt 152 C1
Southorpe 161 F2
Southowram 194 A5
Southport 183 E1
Southport Pier Mersey
  PR8 1QX 183 E1
Southrepps 179 D2
Southrey 175 G1
Southrop 133 D2
Southrope 120 B3
Southsea Ports 107 F3
Southsea Wrex 169 F2
Southtown Norf 179 G5
Southtown Ork 277 D8
Southwaite Cumb 200 C2
Southwaite Cumb 210 A3
Southwark Cathedral GtLon
  SE1 9DA 12 B4
Southwater 121 G5
Southwater Street 121 G5
Southway 116 C3
Southwell Dorset 104 C5
Southwell Notts 174 B2
Southwell Minster Notts
  NG25 0HD 174 C2
Southwick D&G 216 D5
Southwick Hants 107 F2
Southwick N'hants 161 F3
Southwick Som 116 A3
Southwick T&W 212 C2
Southwick Wilts 117 F2
Southwick WSuss 109 E3
Southwold 165 G4
Southwood 116 C4
Sowden 102 C4
Sower Carr 191 G3
Sowerby NYorks 202 D4
Sowerby WYorks 193 G5
Sowerby Bridge 193 G5
Sowerby Row 209 G2
Sowerhill 114 B5
Sowley Green 151 F2
Sowood 185 G1
Sowton 102 C3
Soyal 266 C2
Spa Common 179 D2
Spa Complex NYorks
  YO11 2HD
  83 Scarborough
Spadeadam 219 D4
Spalding 176 A5
Spaldington 195 G4
Spaldwick 161 G5
Spalefield 245 D4
Spalford 174 D1
Spanby 175 F4
Sparham 178 B4
Spark Bridge 199 E4
Sparkford 116 D5
Sparkhill 158 C4
Sparkwell 100 B2
Sparrow Green 178 A4
Sparrowpit 185 E4
Sparrow's Green 123 F5
Sparsholt Hants 119 F4
Sparsholt Oxon 133 F4
Spartylea 211 E3
Spaxton 115 F4
Spaunton 203 G4
Spean Bridge (Drochaid an
  Aonachain) 249 E1

Spean Bridge Woollen Mill
  High PH34 4EP 249 E1
Spear Hill 108 D2
Speddoch 216 C2
Speedwell 131 F5
Speen Bucks 134 D2
Speen WBerks 119 F1
Speeton 205 E5
Speke 183 F4
Speldhurst 123 E4
Spellbrook 137 E1
Spelsbury 147 F5
Spen Green 171 F1
Spencers Wood 120 C1
Spennithorne 202 A4
Spennymoor 212 B4
Spernall 146 C1
Spetchley 146 A2
Spetisbury 105 F2
Spexhall 165 E3
Spey Bay 268 B4
Speyview 267 K7
Spilsby 176 B1
Spindlestone 229 F3
Spinkhill 186 B5
Spinnaker Tower PO1 3TN
  82 Portsmouth
Spinningdale 266 D3
Spirthill 132 B5
Spital High 275 G3
Spital W&M 135 E5
Spital in the Street 187 G3
Spitalbrook 136 C2
Spitfire & Hurricane
  Memorial, R.A.F. Manston
  Kent CT12 5DF 125 F2
Spithurst 109 G2
Spittal D&G 215 F4
Spittal D&G 215 F4
Spittal ELoth 236 B2
Spittal N'umb 229 F3
Spittal Pembs 140 C5
Spittal of
  Glenmuick 252 B1
Spittal of Glenshee 251 G3
Spittalfield 251 G5
Spixworth 178 D4
Splayne's Green 109 G1
Splott 130 B5
Spofforth 194 C2
Spondon 173 F4
Spooner Row 164 B2
Spoonley 171 D4
Sporle 163 G1
Sportsman's Arms 168 C2
Spott 237 D2
Spratton 160 C5
Spreakley 120 D3
Spreyton 99 G1
Spriddlestone 100 B2
Spridlington 188 A4
Spring Grove 136 A5
Spring Vale 234 A3
Springburn 234 A3
Springfield A&B 242 B2
Springfield D&G 218 B5
Springfield Fife 244 B3
Springfield Moray 267 H6
Springfield P&K 243 E2
Springfield WMid 158 C4
Springhill Staffs 158 B3
Springhill Staffs 158 B3
Springholm 216 C4
Springkell 218 A4
Springleys 261 F1
Springside 224 B2
Springthorpe 187 F4
Springwell 212 B2
Sproatley 197 D4
Sproston Green 171 E1
Sprotbrough 186 C2
Sproughton 152 C3
Sprouston 228 B3
Sprowston 178 D4
Sproxton Leics 175 D5
Sproxton NYorks 203 F4
Sprytown 99 E2
Spurlands End 135 D3
Spurstow 170 C2
Spyway 104 B3
Square Point 216 B3
Squires Gate 191 F4
Sröndoire 231 G2
Sronphadruig
  Lodge 250 C2
Stableford Shrop 157 G3
Stableford Staffs 171 F4
Stacey Bank 185 G3
Stackhouse 193 E1
Stackpole 126 C3
Stacksteads 193 E5
Staddiscombe 100 B2
Staddlethorpe 196 A5
Staden 185 E5
Stadhampton 134 B3
Staffield 210 B3
Staffin 263 K5
Stafford 171 G5
Stagden Cross 137 F1
Stagsden 149 E3
Stagshaw Bank 211 F1
Stain 275 J2
Stainburn Cumb 208 D4
Stainburn NYorks 194 B3
Stainby 175 E5
Staincross 186 A1
Staindrop 212 A5
Staines-upon-Thames
  135 F5
Stainfield Lincs 175 F5
Stainfield Lincs 188 B5
Stainforth NYorks 193 E1
Stainforth SYorks 186 D1
Staining 191 G4
Stainland 185 E1
Stainsacre 204 C2
Stainsby Derbys 173 F1
Stainsby Lincs 188 D5
Stainton Cumb 199 G4
Stainton Cumb 210 A5
Stainton Dur 201 F1
Stainton Middl 203 D1
Stainton NYorks 202 A3
Stainton SYorks 186 C3
Stainton by
  Langworth 188 A5
Stainton le Vale 188 B3

Stainton with
  Adgarley 198 D5
Staintondale 204 C3
Stair Cumb 209 F4
Stair EAyr 224 C3
Stairfoot 186 A2
Staithes 203 G1
Stake Pool 192 A3
Stakeford 221 E3
Stakes 107 F2
Stalbridge 104 D1
Stalbridge Weston 104 D1
Stalham 179 E3
Stalham Green 179 E3
Stalisfield Green 124 B3
Stalling Busk 201 E4
Stallingborough 188 B1
Stallington 171 G4
Stalmine 191 G3
Stalybridge 185 D3
Stambourne 151 F4
Stamford Lincs 161 F2
Stamford N'umb 229 G5
Stamford Bridge
  ChesW&C 170 B1
Stamford Bridge
  ERid 195 G2
Stamfordham 220 C4
Stanah 191 G3
Stanborough 136 B1
Stanborough Park Herts
  AL8 6XF 136 B1
Stanbridge
  CenBeds 149 E5
Stanbridge
  Dorset 105 G2
Stanbridge Earls 119 E5
Stanbury 193 G4
Stand 234 B3
Standalone Farm,
  Letchworth Garden City
  Herts SG6 4JN 150 A4
Standburn 234 B2
Standeford 158 B2
Standen 124 A5
Standen Street 124 A5
Standerwick 117 F2
Standford 120 D4
Standford Bridge 171 E5
Standish Glos 132 A2
Standish GtMan 183 G1
Standlake 133 F2
Standon Hants 119 F5
Standon Herts 150 B5
Standon Staffs 171 F4
Standon Green End
  136 C1
Stane 234 C1
Stanecastle 224 B2
Stanfield 178 A3
Stanford CenBeds 149 G3
Stanford Kent 124 D5
Stanford Shrop 156 C1
Stanford Bishop 145 F2
Stanford Bridge 145 G1
Stanford Dingley 134 A5
Stanford End 120 C1
Stanford in the Vale 133 F3
Stanford on Avon 160 A5
Stanford on Soar 173 G5
Stanford on Teme 145 G1
Stanford Rivers 137 E2
Stanford-le-Hope 137 F4
Stanfree 186 B5
Stanghow 203 F1
Stanground 162 A3
Stanhoe 177 G4
Stanhope Dur 211 F4
Stanhope ScBord 226 C3
Stanion 161 E4
Stanklyn 158 A5
Stanley Derbys 173 F3
Stanley Dur 212 A2
Stanley Notts 173 F1
Stanley P&K 243 G1
Stanley Staffs 171 G2
Stanley Wilts 132 B5
Stanley WYorks 194 C5
Stanley Common 173 F3
Stanley Crook 212 A4
Stanley Gate 183 F2
Stanley Hill 145 F3
Stanleygreen 170 C4
Stanlow ChesW&C 183 F5
Stanlow Shrop 157 G5
Stanmer 109 F2
Stanmore GtLon 136 A3
Stanmore WBerks 133 G5
Stannersburn 219 F3
Stanningfield 151 G2
Stannington
  N'umb 221 E4
Stannington
  SYorks 186 A4
Stansbatch 144 C1
Stansfield 151 F2
Stanshope 172 C2
Stanstead 151 G3
Stanstead Abbotts 136 C1
Stansted 123 F2
Stansted Airport 150 D5
Stansted
  Mountfitchet 150 D5
Stanton Derbys 159 E1
Stanton Glos 146 C4
Stanton N'umb 220 D2
Stanton Staffs 172 C3
Stanton Suff 164 A5
Stanton by Bridge 173 E5
Stanton by Dale 173 F4
Stanton Drew 116 C1
Stanton Fitzwarren 133 D3
Stanton Harcourt 133 G2
Stanton Hill 173 F1
Stanton in Peak 172 D1
Stanton Lacy 157 D5
Stanton Lees 173 D1
Stanton Long 157 E3
Stanton Prior 117 D1
Stanton St. Bernard 118 B1
Stanton St. John 134 A2
Stanton St. Quintin 132 B5
Stanton Street 152 A1
Stanton under
  Bardon 159 G1

Stanton upon Hine
  Heath 170 C5
Stanton Wick 116 D1
Stanton-on-the-
  Wolds 174 B4
Stanwardine in the
  Fields 170 B5
Stanwardine in the
  Wood 170 B5
Stanway Essex 152 A5
Stanway Glos 146 C4
Stanway Green
  Essex 152 A5
Stanway Green
  Suff 164 D4
Stanwell 135 F5
Stanwell Moor 135 F5
Stanwick 161 E5
Stanwix 210 A2
Stanydale 279 B7
Staoinebrig 254 C1
Stapeley 171 D3
Stapeley Water Gardens
  ChesE CW5 7LH 171 D2
Stapenhill 173 D5
Staple Kent 125 E3
Staple Som 115 F4
Staple Cross 114 D5
Staple Fitzpaine 103 F1
Staplecross 110 C5
Staplefield 109 E1
Stapleford Cambs 150 C2
Stapleford Herts 136 C1
Stapleford Leics 160 D1
Stapleford Lincs 175 D2
Stapleford Notts 173 F4
Stapleford Wilts 118 B4
Stapleford Abbotts 137 D3
Stapleford Tawney 137 E3
Staplegrove 115 F5
Staplehay 115 F5
Staplehurst 123 G4
Staplers 107 E4
Staplestreet 124 C2
Stapleton Cumb 218 D4
Stapleton Here 144 C1
Stapleton Leics 159 E3
Stapleton NYorks 202 B1
Stapleton Shrop 157 D2
Stapleton Som 116 B5
Stapley 103 E1
Staploe 149 G1
Staplow 145 F3
Star Fife 244 B4
Star Pembs 141 F4
Star Som 116 B2
Starbotton 201 E5
Starcross 102 C4
Stareton 159 F5
Starkholmes 173 E2
Starling 184 B1
Starling's Green 150 C4
Starr 215 F1
Starston 164 D3
Startforth 201 F1
Startley 132 B4
Statham 184 A4
Stathern 174 C4
Station Town 212 D4
Staughton Green 149 G1
Staughton
  Highway 149 G1
Staughton
  Highway 149 G1
Staunton Glos 131 G5
Staunton Glos 145 G5
Staunton Harold
  Hall 173 E5
Staunton Harold Reservoir
  Derbys
  DE73 8DN 173 E5
Staunton in the Vale 174 D3
Staunton on Arrow 144 C1
Staunton on Wye 144 C3
Staveley Cumb 199 F3
Staveley Derbys 186 B5
Staveley NYorks 194 C1
Staveley-in-Cartmel 199 E4
Staverton Devon 101 D1
Staverton Glos 146 A5
Staverton N'hants 148 A1
Staverton Wilts 117 F1
Staverton Bridge 146 A5
Stawell 116 A4
Stawley 115 D5
Staxigoe 275 J3
Staxton 204 B5
Staylittle
  (Penfordd-las) 155 E3
Staynall 191 G3
Staythorpe 174 C2
Stean 201 F5
Steane 148 A4
Stearsby 203 F5
Steart 115 F3
Stebbing 151 E5
Stebbing Green 151 E5
Stechford 158 D4
Stedham 108 B2
Steel Cross 123 E5
Steel Green 198 C5
Steele Road 218 D2
Steen's Bridge 145 E2
Steep 120 C5
Steep Marsh 120 C5
Steeple Dorset 105 F4
Steeple Essex 138 C2
Steeple Ashton 118 A2
Steeple Aston 147 G5
Steeple Barton 147 G5
Steeple Bumpstead 151 E3
Steeple Claydon 148 B5
Steeple Gidding 161 G4
Steeple Langford 118 B4
Steeple Morden 150 A3
Steeraway 157 F2
Steeton 193 G3
Stein 263 H6
Steinmanhill 269 F6
Stella 212 A1
Stelling Minnis 124 D4
Stembridge 116 B5
Stemster High 275 G2
Stemster High 275 G3
Stemster House 275 G2
Stenalees 97 E4
Stenhill 103 D1
Stenhousemuir 234 C1

Stenigot 188 C4
Stenness 278 B5
Stenscholl 263 K5
Stenson 173 E5
Stenton ELoth 236 D2
Stenton P&K 251 F5
Stepaside Pembs 127 E2
Stepaside Powys 155 G4
Stepney 136 C4
Steppingley 149 F4
Stepps 234 A3
Sternfield 153 E1
Sterridge 113 F1
Stert 118 B2
Stetchworth 151 E2
Stevenage 150 A5
Stevenston 233 D5
Steventon Hants 119 G3
Steventon Oxon 133 G3
Steventon End 151 E2
Stevington 149 E2
Stewartby 149 F3
Stewarton D&G 207 E2
Stewarton EAyr 233 F5
Stewkley 149 D5
Stewton 189 D4
Steynton 126 C2
Stibb 112 C4
Stibb Cross 113 E4
Stibb Green 118 D1
Stibbard 178 A3
Stibbington 161 F3
Stichill 228 B3
Sticker 97 D4
Stickford 176 B1
Sticklepath Devon 99 G1
Sticklepath Som 103 G1
Stickling Green 150 C4
Stickney 176 B2
Stiff Street 124 A2
Stiffkey 178 A1
Stifford's Bridge 145 G3
Stileway 116 B3
Stilligarry
  (Stadhlaigearraidh) 254 C1
Stillingfleet 195 E3
Stillington NYorks 195 E1
Stillington Stock 212 C5
Stilton 161 G4
Stinchcombe 131 G3
Stinsford 104 D3
Stirchley Tel&W 157 G2
Stirchley WMid 158 C4
Stirkoke House 275 J3
Stirling Aber 269 K6
Stirling (Sruighlea)
  Stir 242 C5
Stirling Castle Stir
  FK8 1EJ 242 C5
Stirling Visitor Centre Stir
  FK8 1EH 242 C5
Stirton 193 F2
Stisted 151 F5
Stitchcombe 118 D1
Stithians 95 E3
Stittenham 266 D4
Stivichall 159 F5
Stix 250 C5
Stixwould 175 G1
Stoak 183 F5
Stobo 226 C2
Stoborough 105 F4
Stoborough Green 105 F4
Stobwood 235 D4
Stock 137 F3
Stock Green 146 B2
Stock Lane 133 E5
Stock Wood 146 C2
Stockbridge Hants 119 E4
Stockbridge Stir 242 C4
Stockbridge WSuss 108 A3
Stockbury 124 A2
Stockcross 119 F1
Stockdale 95 E3
Stockdalewath 209 G2
Stockerston 160 D3
Stockgrove Country Park
  CenBeds
  LU7 0BA 149 E5
Stocking Green Essex
  151 E4
Stocking Green MK 148 D3
Stocking Pelham 150 C5
Stockingford 159 F3
Stockinish (Stocinis) 263 G2
Stockland Cardiff 130 A5
Stockland Devon 103 F2
Stockland Bristol 115 F3
Stockleigh English 102 B2
Stockleigh Pomeroy 102 B2
Stockley 118 B1
Stocklinch 103 G1
Stockport 184 C3
Stocksbridge 185 G3
Stocksfield 211 G1
Stockton Here 145 E1
Stockton Norf 165 E2
Stockton Shrop 157 G3
Stockton Shrop 156 B2
Stockton Tel&W 157 G1
Stockton Warks 147 G1
Stockton Wilts 118 A4
Stockton Heath 184 A4
Stockton on Teme 145 G1
Stockton on the
  Forest 195 F2
Stockton-on-Tees 202 D1
Stockwell 132 B1
Stockwell Heath 172 B5
Stockwood Bristol 116 D1
Stockwood Dorset 104 B2
Stodday 192 A2
Stodmarsh 125 E2
Stody 178 B2
Stoer 272 C6
Stoford Som 104 B1
Stoford Wilts 118 B4
Stogumber 115 E4
Stogursey 115 F3
Stoke Devon 112 C3
Stoke Hants 119 F2
Stoke Hants 107 G2
Stoke Med 124 A1

Stoke Plym 100 A2
Stoke WMid 159 F5
Stoke Abbott 104 A2
Stoke Albany 160 D4
Stoke Ash 164 C4
Stoke Bardolph 174 B3
Stoke Bishop 131 E5
Stoke Bliss 145 F1
Stoke Bruerne 148 C2
Stoke by Clare 151 F3
Stoke Canon 102 C3
Stoke Charity 119 F4
Stoke Climsland 99 D3
Stoke D'Abernon 121 G2
Stoke Doyle 161 F4
Stoke Dry 161 D3
Stoke Edith 145 F3
Stoke Farthing 118 B5
Stoke Ferry 163 F2
Stoke Fleming 101 E3
Stoke Gabriel 101 E2
Stoke Gifford 131 F5
Stoke Golding 159 F3
Stoke Goldington 148 D3
Stoke Green 135 E4
Stoke Hammond 149 D5
Stoke Heath Shrop 171 D5
Stoke Heath Worcs 146 B1
Stoke Holy Cross 178 D5
Stoke Lacy 145 F3
Stoke Lyne 148 A5
Stoke Mandeville 134 D1
Stoke Newington 136 C4
Stoke on Tern 170 D5
Stoke on Trent 171 G3
Stoke Orchard 146 B5
Stoke Pero 114 B3
Stoke Poges 135 E4
Stoke Pound 146 B1
Stoke Prior Here 145 E2
Stoke Prior Worcs 146 B1
Stoke Rivers 113 G2
Stoke Rochford 175 E5
Stoke Row 134 B4
Stoke St. Gregory 116 A5
Stoke St. Mary 115 F5
Stoke St. Michael 117 D3
Stoke St.
  Milborough 157 E4
Stoke sub Hamdon 104 A1
Stoke Talmage 134 B3
Stoke Trister 117 E5
Stoke Villice 116 C1
Stoke Wake 105 D2
Stoke-by-Nayland 152 A4
Stokeford 105 E4
Stokeham 187 E5
Stokeinteignhead 102 C5
Stokenchurch 134 C3
Stokenham 101 E3
Stoke-on-Trent 171 G3
Stokesay 156 D4
Stokesby 179 F4
Stokesley 203 E2
Stolford 115 F3
Ston Easton 116 D2
Stonar Cut 125 F2
Stondon Massey 137 E2
Stone Bucks 134 C1
Stone Glos 131 F3
Stone Kent 137 E5
Stone Kent 111 E1
Stone Som 116 C4
Stone Staffs 171 G4
Stone SYorks 186 C4
Stone Worcs 158 A5
Stone Allerton 116 B2
Stone Cross Dur 201 F1
Stone Cross ESuss 110 B3
Stone Cross ESuss 110 A1
Stone Cross Kent 125 F4
Stone Cross Kent 123 E5
Stone House 200 C4
Stone Street Kent 123 E3
Stone Street Suff 165 E3
Stone Street Suff 152 A4
Stonea 162 C3
Stonebridge ESuss 110 A1
Stonebridge NSom 116 A2
Stonebridge Warks 159 E4
Stonebroom 173 F2
Stonecross Green 151 G2
Stonefield A&B 231 G2
Stonefield Staffs 171 G4
Stonegate ESuss 110 B1
Stonegate NYorks 203 G2
Stonegrave 203 F5
Stonehaugh 219 F4
Stonehaven 253 G1
Stonehenge Wilts
  SP4 7DE 118 C3
Stonehill 121 E1
Stonehouse
  ChesW&C 183 G5
Stonehouse D&G 216 C4
Stonehouse Glos 132 A2
Stonehouse N'umb 210 D2
Stonehouse Plym 100 A2
Stonehouse SLan 234 B5
Stoneleigh Surr 122 B2
Stoneleigh Warks 159 F5
Stoneley Green 170 D2
Stonely 149 G1
Stoner Hill 120 C5
Stones 193 F5
Stones Green 152 C5
Stonesby 174 D5
Stonesfield 133 F1
Stonestreet Green 124 C5
Stonethwaite 209 F5
Stoney Cross 106 A2
Stoney Middleton 185 G5
Stoney Stanton 159 G3
Stoney Stoke 117 E4
Stoney Stretton 156 C2
Stoneyburn 235 D3
Stoneyford 103 D4
Stoneygate 160 B2
Stoneyhills 138 C3
Stoneykirk 214 B5
Stoneywood 261 G3
Stonganess 278 E2
Stonham Barns Suff
  IP14 6AT 152 C2
Stonnall 158 C2
Stonor 134 C4
Stonton Wyville 160 C3

Stony Houghton 173 F1
Stony Stratford 148 C3
Stonybreck 278 A1
Stoodleigh Devon 102 C1
Stoodleigh Devon 113 G2
Stopham 108 C2
Stopsley 149 G5
Stoptide 96 C2
Storeton 183 E4
Stormontfield 243 G2
Stornoway
  (Steornabhagh) 271 G4
Stornoway Airport 271 G4
Storridge 145 G3
Storrington 108 C2
Storrs 185 C2
Storth 199 F4
Storwood 195 G3
Storybook Glen Aber
  AB12 5FT 261 G5
Stotfield 267 K4
Stotfold 150 A4
Stottesdon 157 F4
Stoughton Leics 160 B2
Stoughton Surr 121 E2
Stoughton WSuss 107 G1
Stoughton Cross 116 B3
Stoul 256 C5
Stoulton 146 B3
Stour Provost 117 E5
Stour Row 117 F5
Stourbridge 158 A4
Stourhead Wilts
  BA12 6QD 117 E4
Stourpaine 105 E2
Stourport-on-Severn
  158 A5
Stourton Staffs 158 A4
Stourton Warks 147 E4
Stourton Wilts 117 E4
Stourton Caundle 104 D1
Stove 276 F4
Stoven 165 F3
Stow Lincs 187 F4
Stow ScBord 236 B5
Stow Bardolph 163 E2
Stow Bedon 164 A2
Stow cum Quy 150 D1
Stow Longa 161 G5
Stow Maries 138 B3
Stow Pasture 187 F4
Stowbridge 163 D2
Stowe Glos 131 E2
Stowe Shrop 156 C5
Stowe Staffs 158 D1
Stowe Landscape Gardens
  Bucks
  MK18 5DQ 148 B4
Stowe-by-Chartley 172 B5
Stowehill 148 B2
Stowell Glos 132 C1
Stowell Som 117 D5
Stowey 116 C2
Stowford Devon 99 E2
Stowford Devon 113 G2
Stowford Devon 103 E4
Stowlangtoft 152 A1
Stowmarket 152 B2
Stow-on-the-Wold 147 D5
Stowting 124 D4
Stowupland 152 B2
Straad 232 B3
Stracathro 253 E3
Strachan 260 E5
Strachur (Clachan
  Strachur) 240 C4
Stradbroke 164 D4
Stradishall 151 F2
Stradsett 163 E2
Stragglethorpe 175 E2
Straight Soley 133 F5
Straiton Edin 235 G3
Straiton SAyr 224 B5
Straloch Aber 261 G2
Straloch P&K 251 F3
Stramshall 172 B4
Strands 198 C4
Strang 190 B4
Strangford 145 E4
Strannda 263 F3
Stranraer 214 B4
Strata Florida 142 D1
Stratfield Mortimer 120 B1
Stratfield Saye 120 B1
Stratfield Turgis 120 B2
Stratford CenBeds 149 G3
Stratford Glos 146 A4
Stratford GtLon 136 C4
Stratford St. Andrew 153 E2
Stratford St. Mary 152 B4
Stratford sub Castle 118 C4
Stratford Tony 118 B5
Stratford-upon-Avon 147 E2
Stratford-upon-Avon
  Butterfly Farm
  Warks CV37 7LS
  85 Stratford-upon-Avon
Strath 275 H3
Strathan High 272 C6
Strathan High 257 F5
Strathaven 234 B5
Strathblane 233 G2
Strathcanaird 265 H1
Strathclyde Country Park
  NLan ML1 3ED 31 G5
Strathdon 260 B3
Strathgirnock 260 B5
Strathkinness 244 C3
Strathmiglo 244 A3
Strathpeffer (Strath
  Pheofhair) 266 B6
Strathrannoch 265 K4
Strathtay 251 E4
Strathwhillan 223 F2
Strathy 242 A3
Strathyre 242 A3
Stratton Corn 112 C5
Stratton Dorset 104 C3
Stratton Glos 132 C2
Stratton Audley 148 B5
Stratton Hall 152 C4
Stratton St.
  Margaret 133 D4
Stratton St. Michael 164 D2
Stratton Strawless 178 D3
Stratton-on-the-Fosse
  117 D2

Stravanan 232 B4
Stravithie 244 D3
Strawberry Hill 136 A5
Stream 115 D4
Streat 109 F2
Streatham 136 B5
Streatham Vale 136 B5
Streatley CenBeds 149 F5
Streatley WBerks 134 A4
Street Lancs 192 B2
Street NYorks 203 G2
Street Som 116 B4
Street Som 103 G2
Street Ashton 159 G4
Street Dinas 170 A4
Street End 108 A4
Street Gate 212 B2
Street Houses 195 E3
Street Lane 173 E3
Street on the Fosse 116 D4
Streethay 158 D1
Streethouse 194 C5
Streetly 158 D3
Streetly End 151 E3
Strefford 156 D4
Strelley 173 G3
Strensall 195 F1
Strensham 146 B3
Stretcholt 115 F3
Strete 101 E3
Stretford GtMan 184 B3
Stretford Here 144 D2
Stretford Here 145 E2
Strethall 150 C4
Stretham 162 D5
Strettington 108 A3
Stretton ChesW&C 170 B2
Stretton Derbys 173 E1
Stretton Rut 161 E1
Stretton Staffs 158 A1
Stretton Staffs 173 G1
Stretton Warr 184 A4
Stretton en le Field 159 F1
Stretton Grandison 145 F3
Stretton Heath 156 C1
Stretton Sugwas 145 D3
Stretton under
  Fosse 159 G4
Stretton Westwood 157 E3
Stretton-on-
  Dunsmore 159 G5
Stretton-on-Fosse 147 E4
Stribers 199 E4
Strichen 269 H5
Strines 185 D4
Strinesdale Countryside
  Area GtMan
  OL4 2JJ 25 H1
Stringston 115 E3
Strixton 149 E1
Stroat 131 E3
Stromeferry 256 E1
Stromemore 256 E1
Stromness 277 B7
Stronaba 249 E1
Stronachlachar 241 G3
Strone A&B 232 C1
Strone High 258 C2
Strone High 248 D1
Strone Stir 241 G3
Stronechrubie 272 E7
Stronlonag 232 C1
Stronmilchan (Sròn nam
  Mialchon) 241 D2
Stronsay 276 F5
Stronsay Airfield 276 F5
Strontian (Sròn an
  t-Sìthein) 248 A3
Stronvar 242 A2
Strood 123 G2
Strood Green Surr 122 B4
Strood Green
  WSuss 121 F5
Strood Green
  WSuss 121 G4
Stroquhan 216 C2
Stroud Glos 132 A2
Stroud Hants 120 C5
Stroud Common 121 F3
Stroud Green Essex 138 B3
Stroud Green Glos 132 A2
Stroude 121 F1
Stroul 232 D1
Stroxton 175 E4
Struan High 255 J1
Struan P&K 250 C3
Strubby Lincs 189 E4
Strubby Lincs 188 B5
Strumpshaw 179 E5
Struthers 244 B4
Struy 258 B1
Stryd y Facsen 180 B4
Stryt-cae-rhedyn 169 F1
Stryt-issa 169 F1
Stuart & Waterford Crystal
  Factory Shop, Crieff P&K
  PH7 4HQ 243 D2
Stuart Line Cruises, Exmouth
  Devon EX8 1EJ 102 D4
Stuartfield 269 H6
Stub Place 198 B3
Stubber's Green 158 C2
Stubbington 107 E2
Stubbins 184 B1
Stubbs Green 165 E2
Stubhampton 105 F1
Stubley 186 A5
Stubshaw Cross 183 G2
Stubton 175 D3
Stuck A&B 232 B3
Stuck A&B 240 D5
Stuckbeg 241 E5
Stuckgowan 241 F4
Stuckindroin 241 F3
Stuckreoch 240 C5
Stuckton 106 A1
Stud Green 135 D5
Studdon 211 E2
Studfold 200 D5
Studham 135 F1
Studholme 209 F1
Studland 105 G4
Studland & Godlington
  Heath NNR Dorset
  BH19 3AX 105 G4
Studley Warks 146 C1
Studley Wilts 132 B5
Studley Common 146 C1
Studley Green 134 C3
Studley Roger 202 B5
Studley Royal Park & ruins of
  Fountains Abbey NYorks
  HG4 3DY 194 B1
Stuggadhoo 190 B4
Stump Cross Essex 150 D3
Stump Cross Lancs 192 B4
Stuntney 163 E3
Stunts Green 110 B2
Sturbridge 171 F4
Sturgate 187 F4
Sturminster 151 E3
Sturminster
  Common 105 D1
Sturminster
  Marshall 105 F2
Sturminster
  Newton 105 D1
Sturry 125 D2
Sturton by Stow 187 F4
Sturton le Steeple 187 E4
Stuston 164 C4
Stutton NYorks 195 D3
Stutton Suff 152 C3
Styal 184 C4
Stynie 268 D4
Styrrup 186 D3
Suardail 271 G4
Succoth A&B 241 E4
Succoth Aber 260 C1
Succothmore 240 D4
Suckley 145 G2
Suckley Green 145 G2
Suckley Knowl 145 G2
Sudborough 161 E4
Sudbourne 153 F2
Sudbrook Lincs 175 E3
Sudbrook Mon 131 E4
Sudbrooke 188 A5
Sudbury Derbys 172 C4
Sudbury GtLon 136 A4
Sudbury Suff 151 G3
Sudbury Hall Derbys
  DE6 5HT 172 C4
Sudden 184 C1
Sudgrove 132 B2
Suffield Norf 178 D2
Suffield NYorks 204 C3
Sugarloaf 124 B5
Sugnall 171 E4
Sugwas Pool 145 D3
Suie Lodge Hotel 241 G2
Suisnish 256 B3
Sulby IoM 190 B2
Sulby IoM 190 B2
Sulgrave 148 A3
Sulham 134 B5
Sulhamstead 120 B1
Sullington 108 C2
Sullom 278 C5
Sullom Voe Oil
  Terminal 278 C5
Sully 141 F5
Sumburgh 279 F10
Sumburgh Airport 279 F9
Summer Bridge 194 B1
Summer Isles 265 F1
Summer Lodge 201 E3
Summercourt 96 C4
Summerfield Norf 177 F4
Summerfield Worcs 158 A5
Summerhill 170 A2
Summerhouse 202 B1
Summerlands 199 G4
Summerleaze 130 D4
Summertown 134 A2
Summit 184 D1
Sun Green 185 D3
Sunadale 231 G5
Sunbiggin 200 B2
Sunbury 121 E1
Sundaywell 216 C2
Sunderland Cumb 209 E3
Sunderland Lancs 192 A3
Sunderland T&W 212 C2
Sunderland Bridge 212 B4
Sunderland Museum &
  Winter Gardens
  T&W SR1 1PP
  86 Sunderland
Sundhope 227 E3
Sundon Park 149 F5
Sundown Adventure Land
  Notts
  DN22 0HX 187 E5
Sundridge 123 D3
Sundrum Mains 224 C3
Sunhill 132 D2
Sunipol 246 C4
Sunk Island 188 C1
Sunningdale 121 E1
Sunninghill 121 E1
Sunningwell 133 G2
Sunniside Dur 212 A4
Sunniside T&W 212 B2
Sunny Bank 199 E3
Sunny Brow 212 A4
Sunnylaw 242 C5
Sunnyside Aber 261 G5
Sunnyside N'umb 211 F3
Sunnyside SYorks 186 B3
Sunnyside WSuss 122 C5
Sunton 118 D2
Sunwick 237 F4
Surbiton 121 G1
Surfleet 176 A3
Surfleet Seas End 176 A5
Surlingham 179 E5
Sustead 178 C2
Susworth 187 F2
Sutcombe 112 D4
Sutcombemill 112 D4
Suton 164 B2
Sutterby 189 D5
Sutterton 176 A4
Sutton Cambs 162 C5
Sutton CenBeds 150 A3
Sutton Devon 102 A2
Sutton Devon 100 D3
Sutton GtLon 122 B2
Sutton Kent 125 F4
Sutton Lincs 175 D2
Sutton Norf 179 E3
Sutton Notts 174 C4
Sutton Notts 187 D4
Sutton Oxon 133 G2
Sutton Pembs 126 C1
Sutton Peter 161 F3
Sutton Shrop 157 G4
Sutton Shrop 171 D4
Sutton Shrop 157 E1
Sutton Shrop 170 A5
Sutton Staffs 171 E5
Sutton Suff 153 E3
Sutton SYorks 186 C1
Sutton WSuss 108 B2
Sutton Abinger 121 G3
Sutton at Hone 137 E5
Sutton Bank National Park
  Centre NYorks
  YO7 2EH 203 E4
Sutton Bassett 160 C4
Sutton Benger 132 B5
Sutton Bingham 104 B1
Sutton Bonington 173 G5
Sutton Bridge 176 C5
Sutton Cheney 159 F2
Sutton Coldfield 158 D3
Sutton Courtenay 134 A3
Sutton Crosses 176 C5
Sutton Grange 202 B5
Sutton Green Oxon 133 G2
Sutton Green Surr 121 F2
Sutton Green Wrex 170 B3
Sutton Holms 105 G2
Sutton Howgrave 202 C5
Sutton in Ashfield 173 F2
Sutton in the Elms 160 A3
Sutton Ings 196 C4
Sutton Lane Ends 184 D5
Sutton le Marsh 189 F4
Sutton Leach 183 G3
Sutton Maddock 157 G2
Sutton Mallet 116 A4
Sutton Mandeville 118 A5
Sutton Montis 116 D5
Sutton on Sea 189 F4
Sutton on the Hill 172 D4
Sutton on Trent 174 C1
Sutton Poyntz 104 D4
Sutton St. Edmund 162 B1
Sutton St. James 162 C1
Sutton St. Nicholas 145 E3
Sutton Scarsdale 173 F1
Sutton Scotney 119 F4
Sutton upon Derwent
  195 G3
Sutton Valence 124 A4
Sutton Veny 117 F3
Sutton Waldron 105 E1
Sutton Weaver 183 G5
Sutton Wick
  B&NESom 116 C2
Sutton Wick Oxon 133 G3
Sutton-in-Craven 193 G3
Sutton-on-Hull 196 D4
Sutton-on-the-Forest
  195 E1
Sutton-under-Brailes
  147 F4
Sutton-under-
  Whitestonecliffe 203 D4
Swaby 189 D5
Swadlincote 159 F1
Swaffham 163 G2
Swaffham Bulbeck 151 E1
Swaffham Prior 151 D1
Swafield 179 D2
Swainbost
  (Suaineabost) 271 H1
Swainby 203 D2
Swainshill 145 D3
Swainsthorpe 178 D5
Swainswick 117 E1
Swalcliffe 147 F4
Swalecliffe 124 D2
Swallow 188 B2
Swallow Beck 175 E1
Swallow Falls Conwy
  LL24 0DW 168 A2
Swallowcliffe 118 A5
Swallowfield 120 C1
Swallows Cross 137 F3
Swampton 119 F2
Swan Green
  ChesW&C 184 B5
Swan Green Suff 165 D4
Swan Street 151 G5
Swanage 105 G5
Swanage Railway Dorset
  BH19 1HB 105 G5
Swanbach 171 D3
Swanbourne 148 D5
Swanbridge 115 E1
Swancote 157 G3
Swanland 196 B5
Swanlaws 228 B5
Swanley 123 E2
Swanley Village 123 E2
Swanmore Hants 107 E1
Swanmore IoW 107 E3
Swannington Leics 159 G1
Swannington Norf 178 C4
Swanscombe 137 F5
Swansea
  (Abertawe) 128 C3
Swansea Museum SA1 1SN
  86 Swansea
Swanston 235 G3
Swanton Abbot 179 D3
Swanton Morley 178 B4
Swanton Novers 178 B3
Swanton Street 124 A3
Swanwick Derbys 173 F2
Swanwick Hants 107 E2
Swanwick Green 170 C3
Swarby 175 F3
Swardeston 178 D5
Swarkestone 173 E5
Swarland 221 D1
Swarraton 119 G4
Swarthmoor 199 D5
Swaton 175 G4
Swavesey 150 B1
Sway 106 B3
Swayfield 175 E5
Swaythling 106 D1
Swaythorpe 196 C1
Sweetham 102 B3
Sweetholme 200 B1
Sweets 97 E1
Sweetshouse 97 E3
Sweffling 153 E1

Swell 116 A5
Swepstone 159 F1
Swerford 147 F4
Swettenham 171 F1
Swffryd 130 B3
Swift's Green 124 A4
Swiftsden 110 C3
Swilland 152 C2
Swillington 194 C4
Swimbridge 113 G3
Swimbridge Newland
  113 F2
Swinbrook 133 E1
Swincliffe 194 B2
Swincombe 113 G1
Swinden 193 E2
Swinderby 175 D1
Swindon Staffs 158 A3
Swindon Swin 133 E4
Swindon Village 146 B5
Swine 196 C4
Swinefleet 195 G5
Swineford 117 D1
Swineshead Bed 149 F1
Swineshead Lincs 176 A3
Swineshead Bridge 176 A3
Swineside 201 F4
Swiney 275 H5
Swinford Leics 160 A5
Swinford Oxon 133 G2
Swingate 173 G2
Swingfield Minnis 125 E4
Swingleton Green 152 A3
Swinhoe 229 G4
Swinhope 188 C3
Swining 279 D6
Swinithwaite 201 F4
Swinscoe 172 C3
Swinside Hall 228 B5
Swinstead 175 F5
Swinton GtMan 184 B2
Swinton NYorks 203 G5
Swinton NYorks 202 B5
Swinton ScBord 237 F5
Swinton SYorks 186 B3
Swinton Quarter 237 F5
Swintonmill 237 F5
Swithland 160 A1
Swordale 266 C5
Swordland 256 D5
Swordle 247 E2
Swordly 274 C2
Sworton Heath 184 A4
Swydffynnon 142 C1
Swyncombe 134 B3
Swynnerton 171 F4
Swyre 104 B4
Sychnant 155 F5
Syde 132 B2
Sydenham GtLon 136 C5
Sydenham Oxon 134 C2
Sydenham Damerel 99 E3
Syderstone 177 F4
Sydling St. Nicholas 104 C3
Sydmonton 119 F2
Sydney 171 E2
Syerston 174 C3
Sykehouse 186 D1
Sykes 192 C2
Sylen 128 B2
Symbister 279 E6
Symington SAyr 224 D2
Symington SLan 225 G2
Symonds Yat 131 E1
Symondsbury 104 A3
Synod Inn
  (Post-mawr) 142 A2
Syre 273 J4
Syreford 146 C5
Syresham 148 A3
Syston Leics 160 B1
Syston Lincs 175 E3
Sytchampton 146 A1
Sywell 148 D1
Sywell Country Park N'hants
  NN6 0QX 148 D1

T

Taagan 265 G5
Tableyhill 184 B5
Tabost 271 F6
Tachbrook Mallory 147 F1
Tacher 275 G4
Tackley 147 G5
Tacolneston 164 C2
Tadcaster 195 D3
Tadden 105 F2
Taddington Derbys 185 F5
Taddington Glos 146 C4
Taddiport 113 E4
Tadley 120 B1
Tadlow 150 A3
Tadmarton 147 F4
Tadpole Bridge 133 G2
Tadworth 122 B3
Tafarnaubach 130 A1
Tafarn-y-bwlch 141 D4
Tafarn-y-Gelyn 169 E1
Taff Merthyr Garden
  Village 130 A3
Taff's Well
  (Ffynnon Taf) 130 A4
Tafolwern 155 F2
Taibach NPT 129 D4
Tai-bach Powys 169 G5
Taicynhaeaf 154 C1
Tai'n Lôn 166 D3
Tai'r Bull 143 F5
Tairgwaith 128 D1
Tai'r-heol 130 A3
Tai'r-ysgol 128 C3
Takeley 151 D5
Takeley Street 150 D5
Talachddu 143 G4
Talacre 182 C4
Talardd 168 B5
Talaton 103 D3
Talbenny 126 B1
Talbot Green 129 G4
Talbot Village 105 G3
Talerddig 155 F2
Talgarreg 142 A2
Talgarth 144 A4
Taliesin 154 C3
Talisker 255 J1

Talke Pits 171 F2
Talkin 210 B2
Talkin Tarn Country Park
  Cumb CA8 1HN 210 B2
Talla Linnfoots 226 C3
Talladale 265 F4
Talladh-a-Bheithe 250 A4
Talland 97 G4
Tallarn Green 170 B3
Tallentire 209 E3
Talley (Talyllychau) 142 C4
Tallington 161 F2
Talmine 273 H2
Talog 141 G5
Talsarn 142 B2
Talsarnau 167 F4
Talskiddy 96 D3
Talwrn IoA 180 C5
Talwrn Wrex 169 F1
Talwrn Wrex 170 A3
Talybont Cere 154 C4
Tal-y-bont Conwy 168 A1
Tal-y-bont Gwyn 167 E5
Tal-y-bont Gwyn 181 E5
Talybont-on-Usk 144 A5
Tal-y-Cae 167 F1
Tal-y-cafn 181 F5
Tal-y-coed 130 D1
Talygarn 129 G4
Talyllyn Powys 144 A5
Tal-y-llyn Gwyn 154 D2
Talysarn 167 E2
Tal-y-wern 155 E2
Tamavoid 242 A5
Tamerton Foliot 100 A1
Tamworth 159 E2
Tamworth Green 176 B3
Tan Office Green 151 F2
Tandem 185 F1
Tandridge 122 C3
Tanerdy 142 A5
Tanfield 212 A2
Tanfield Lea 212 A2
Tang 194 B2
Tang Hall 195 F2
Tangiers 126 C1
Tanglandford 261 G1
Tangley 119 E2
Tangmere 108 B3
Tangwick 278 B5
Tangy 222 C3
Tank Museum, Bovington
  Dorset
  BH20 6JG 105 E4
Tankerness 277 E7
Tankersley 186 A2
Tankerton 124 D2
Tan-lan 167 F3
Tannach 275 J4
Tannachie 253 F1
Tannadice 252 C4
Tannington 152 D1
Tannochside 234 A3
Tansley 173 E2
Tansley Knoll 173 E2
Tansor 161 F3
Tantobie 212 A2
Tanton 203 E1
Tanworth in Arden 158 D5
Tan-y-fron 168 C1
Tan-y-graig 166 C4
Tanygrisiau 167 F3
Tan-y-groes 141 F3
Tan-y-pistyll 169 D5
Tan-yr-allt 182 B4
Taobh a' Deas Loch
  Baghasdail 254 C3
Taobh Siar 270 D7
Tapeley 113 E3
Taplow 135 E4
Tapton Grove 186 B5
Taransay
  (Tarasaigh) 270 C7
Taraphocain 248 C5
Tarbat House 266 E4
Tarbert A&B 231 G3
Tarbert A&B 231 E4
Tarbert A&B 231 E3
Tarbert High 247 F3
Tarbert (Tairbeart)
  ESiar 270 D7
Tarbet A&B 231 F1
Tarbet (An Tairbeart)
  A&B 241 F4
Tarbet High 256 D5
Tarbet High 272 D4
Tarbock Green 183 F4
Tarbolton 224 C3
Tarbrax 235 E4
Tardebigge 146 B1
Tardy Gate 192 B5
Tarfside 252 C2
Tarland 260 C4
Tarleton 192 A5
Tarlscough 183 F1
Tarlton 132 B3
Tarnbrook 192 B2
Tarnock 116 A2
Tarporley 170 C1
Tarr 115 E4
Tarrant Crawford 105 F2
Tarrant Gunville 105 F1
Tarrant Hinton 105 F1
Tarrant Keyneston 105 F2
Tarrant
  Launceston 105 F2
Tarrant Monkton 105 F2
Tarrant Rawston 105 F2
Tarrant Rushton 105 F2
Tarring Neville 109 G3
Tarrington 145 F3
Tarscabhaig 256 B4
Tarsappie 243 G2
Tarskavaig 256 B4
Tarves 261 G1
Tarvie P&K 251 F3
Tarvie (Tairbhidh)
  High 266 B6
Tarvin 170 B1
Tarvin Sands 170 B1
Tasburgh 164 D2
Tasley 157 F3
Tassley 173 G5
Taston 147 F5
Taston 147 F5
Tate Britain GtLon
  SW1P 4RG 13 B5
Tate Liverpool
  Mersey L3 4BB 42 B5

Tate Modern GtLon
  SE1 9TG 45 H4
Tate St. Ives Corn
  TR26 1TG 94 C2
Tatenhill 172 D5
Tathall End 148 D3
Tatham 192 C1
Tathwell 188 D4
Tatsfield 122 D3
Tattenhall 170 B2
Tattenhoe 148 D4
Tatterford 177 G5
Tattersett 177 G4
Tattershall 176 A2
Tattershall Bridge 175 G2
Tattershall Thorpe 176 A2
Tattingstone 152 C3
Tatton Park ChesE
  WA16 6QN 184 B4
Tatworth 103 G2
Tauchers 268 B6
Taunton 115 F5
Tavelty 261 F3
Taverham 178 C4
Taverspite 127 E1
Tavistock 99 E3
Taw Bridge 113 G5
Taw Green 99 G5
Tawstock 113 F3
Taxal 185 E5
Tayburn 233 G5
Taychreggan 240 C2
Tayinloan 231 E5
Taylors Cross 112 C4
Taynafead 240 C3
Taynish 231 F1
Taynton Glos 145 G5
Taynton Oxon 133 E1
Taynuilt
  (Taigh an Uillt) 240 C1
Tayock 253 E4
Tayovullin 230 A2
Tayport 244 C2
Tayvallich 231 F1
Tea Green 149 G5
Tealby 188 B3
Tealing 244 C1
Team Valley 212 B1
Teanamachar 262 C5
Teangue 256 C4
Teasses 244 C4
Tebay 200 B3
Tebworth 149 E5
Technquest, Cardiff Cardiff
  CF10 5BW 7 B4
Tedburn St. Mary 102 B3
Teddington Glos 146 B4
Teddington GtLon 136 A5
Tedstone Delamere 145 F2
Tedstone Wafre 145 F2
Teeton 160 B5
Teffont Evias 118 A4
Teffont Magna 118 A4
Tegryn 141 F4
Teigh 161 D1
Teign Village 102 B4
Teigncombe 102 B5
Teigngrace 102 B5
Teignmouth 102 C5
Telford 157 G2
Telford Wonderland Tel&W
  TF3 4AY 157 G2
Telham 110 C2
Tellisford 117 F2
Telscombe 109 G3
Telscombe Cliffs 109 G3
Tempar 250 B4
Templand 217 E2
Temple Corn 97 F2
Temple Midlo 236 A4
Temple Balsall 159 E5
Temple Bar 142 B2
Temple Cloud 116 D2
Temple End 151 E2
Temple Ewell 125 E4
Temple Grafton 146 C2
Temple Guiting 146 C5
Temple Herdewyke 147 F2
Temple Hirst 195 F5
Temple Newsam WYorks
  LS15 0AE 27 H2
Temple Normanton 173 F1
Temple Sowerby 210 C5
Templecombe 117 E5
Templeton Devon 102 B1
Templeton Pembs 127 E1
Templeton Bridge 102 B1
Templewood 253 E3
Tempsford 149 G2
Ten Mile Bank 163 E3
Tenbury Wells 145 E1
Tenby (Dinbych-y-
  pysgod) 127 E2
Tendring 152 C5
Tendring Green 152 C5
Tenga 247 E5
Tenston 277 C6
Ten 157 F1
Terregles 216 D3
Terriers 135 D3
Terrington 203 F5
Terrington
  St. Clement 177 D5
Terrington
  St. John 162 D1
Terry's Green 158 D5
Tervieside 259 K1
Teston 123 G3
Testwood 106 C1
Tetbury 132 A3
Tetbury Upton 132 A3
Tetchill 170 A4
Tetcott 98 C1
Tetford 188 D5
Tetney 188 D5
Tetney Lock 188 D2
Tetsworth 134 B2
Tettenhall 158 A2
Tettenhall Wood 158 A3
Tetworth 150 A2
Teuchan 261 J1
Teversal 173 F1
Teversham 150 C2

Teviot Water Gardens
  ScBord
  TD5 8LE 228 B4
Teviothead 227 F5
Tewel 253 G1
Tewin 136 B1
Tewkesbury 146 A4
Tewkesbury Abbey Glos
  GL20 5RZ 146 A4
Teynham 124 B2
Thackley 194 A4
Thainston 253 E2
Thainstone 261 F3
Thakeham 108 D2
Thame 134 C2
Thames Ditton 121 G1
Thames Haven 137 G4
Thamesmead 137 D4
Thanington 124 D3
Thankerton 226 A2
Tharston 164 C2
Thatcham 119 G1
Thatto Heath 183 G3
Thaxted 151 E4
The Apes Hall 163 D3
The Bage 144 B3
The Balloch 242 D3
The Banking 261 F1
The Bar 121 G5
The Birks 261 F4
The Bog 156 C3
The Bourne 120 D3
The Bratch 158 A3
The Broad 145 D1
The Bryn 130 C2
The Burf 146 A1
The Burn 253 D2
The Butts 117 E3
The Camp 132 B2
The Chequer 170 B3
The City Bucks 134 C3
The City Suff 165 E3
The Common Wilts 118 D4
The Common Wilts 132 C4
The Craigs 266 C2
The Cronk 190 B2
The Delves 158 C3
The Den 233 E4
The Dicker 110 A3
The Down 157 F3
The Drums 252 B3
The Eaves 131 F2
The Flatt 219 D4
The Folly 136 A1
The Forge 144 C2
The Forstal ESuss 123 E5
The Forstal Kent 124 C5
The Grange Lincs 189 F5
The Grange Shrop 170 A4
The Grange Surr 122 C4
The Green A&B 246 A2
The Green Cumb 198 C4
The Green Essex 137 G1
The Green Flints 169 F1
The Green Wilts 117 F4
The Grove 146 A3
The Haven 121 F4
The Headland 213 E4
The Heath 172 B4
The Herberts 129 F5
The Hermitage 122 B3
The Hill 198 C4
The Holme 194 B2
The Howe 190 A5
The Isle 157 D1
The Laurels 165 E2
The Leacon 124 B5
The Lee 135 E2
The Leigh 146 A5
The Lhen 190 B1
The Lodge 241 D5
The Marsh 156 C3
The Moor ESuss 110 D2
The Moor Kent 110 C1
The Mumbles 128 C4
The Murray 234 A4
The Mythe 146 A4
The Narth 131 E2
The Neuk 261 F5
The Node 136 B1
The Oval 117 E1
The Polchar 259 G4
The Quarter 124 A4
The Reddings 146 B5
The Rhos 126 D1
The Rookery 171 F2
The Rowe 171 F4
The Sale 159 D1
The Sands 121 D3
The Shoe 132 A5
The Slade 134 A5
The Smithies 157 F3
The Stocks 111 E1
The Swillett 135 F3
The Thrift 150 B4
The Vauld 145 E3
The Wern 169 F2
The Wyke 157 G2
Theakston 202 C4
Thealby 187 F1
Theale Som 116 B3
Theale WBerks 134 B5
Thearne 196 C4
Theberton 153 F1
Thedden Grange 120 B4
Theddingworth 160 B4
Theddlethorpe
  All Saints 189 E4
Theddlethorpe
  St. Helen 189 E4
Thelbridge Barton 102 A1
Thelbridge Cross 102 A1
Thelnetham 164 B4
Thelveton 164 C3
Thelwall 184 A4
Themelthorpe 178 B3
Thenford 148 A3
Therfield 150 B4
Thermae Bath Spa
  B&NESom
  BA1 1SJ 63 Bath
Thetford Lincs 161 G1
Thetford Norf 163 G4
Thetford Forest Park Norf
  IP27 0TJ 163 G4
Thethwaite 209 G2
Theydon Bois 136 D3
Theydon Garnon 137 D3

Theydon Mount 137 D3
Thickwood 132 A5
Thimbleby Lincs 176 A1
Thimbleby NYorks 202 D3
Thingley 117 F1
Thirkleby 203 D5
Thirlby 203 D4
Thirlestane 236 C5
Thirn 202 B4
Thirsk 202 D4
Thirston New
  Houses 221 D2
Thirtleby 197 D4
Thistleton Lancs 192 A4
Thistleton Rut 161 E1
Thistley Green 163 E5
Thixendale 196 A1
Thockrington 220 B4
Tholomas Drove 162 B2
Tholthorpe 195 D3
Thomas Chapel 127 E2
Thomas Close 210 A3
Thomastown 260 D1
Thomshill 267 K6
Thong 137 F5
Thongsbridge 185 F2
Thoralby 201 E4
Thoresby 186 D5
Thoresthorpe 189 E5
Thoresway 188 B3
Thorganby Lincs 188 C3
Thorganby NYorks 195 F3
Thorgill 203 G3
Thorington 165 F4
Thorington Street 152 B4
Thorley 137 D1
Thorley Houses 150 C5
Thorley Street Herts 137 D1
Thorley Street IoW 106 C4
Thormanby 203 D5
Thornaby-on-Tees 203 D1
Thornage 178 B2
Thornborough
  Bucks 148 C4
Thornborough
  NYorks 202 B5
Thornbury Devon 113 D5
Thornbury Here 145 F2
Thornbury SGlos 131 F3
Thornbury WYorks 194 A4
Thornby 160 B5
Thorncliff 185 G1
Thorncliffe 172 B2
Thorncombe 103 G2
Thorncombe Street 121 F3
Thorncote Green 149 G3
Thorncross 106 D4
Thorndon 152 C1
Thorndon Country Park Essex
  CM13 3RZ 137 F3
Thorndon Cross 99 F1
Thorne 187 D1
Thorne St. Margaret 115 D5
Thorner 194 C1
Thorney Bucks 135 F5
Thorney Notts 187 F5
Thorney Peter 162 A2
Thorney Som 116 B5
Thorney Close 212 C2
Thorney Hill 106 B3
Thornfalcon 115 F5
Thornford 104 C1
Thorngrafton 211 D1
Thorngrove 116 A4
Thorngumbald 197 E5
Thornham 177 F3
Thornham Magna 164 C4
Thornham Parva 164 C4
Thornhaugh 161 F2
Thornhill Cardiff 130 A4
Thornhill Cumb 198 B2
Thornhill Derbys 185 F4
Thornhill Soton 107 D1
Thornhill Stir 242 B4
Thornhill WYorks 185 G1
Thornhill Lees 185 G1
Thornholme 196 B4
Thornicombe 105 E2
Thornley Dur 212 C4
Thornley Dur 212 A4
Thornley Gate 211 E2
Thornliebank 233 G4
Thornroan 261 G1
Thorns 151 F2
Thorns Green 184 B4
Thornsett 185 E4
Thornthwaite Cumb 209 F4
Thornthwaite NYorks 194 A2
Thornton Angus 252 B5
Thornton Bucks 148 C4
Thornton ERid 195 G3
Thornton Fife 244 A5
Thornton Lancs 191 G3
Thornton Leics 159 G2
Thornton Lincs 176 A1
Thornton Mersey 183 E2
Thornton Middl 203 D1
Thornton N'umb 237 G5
Thornton P&K 251 F5
Thornton Pembs 126 C2
Thornton WYorks 194 A4
Thornton Bridge 202 D5
Thornton Curtis 188 A1
Thornton Heath 122 C2
Thornton Hough 183 E4
Thornton in Lonsdale 200 B5
Thornton le Moor 188 A3
Thornton Park 237 G5
Thornton Rust 201 E4
Thornton Steward 202 A4
Thornton Watlass 202 B4
Thornton-in-Craven 193 F3
Thornton-le-Beans 202 D3
Thornton-le-Clay 195 F1
Thornton-le-Dale 204 B4
Thornton-le-Moor 202 C4
Thornton-le-Moors 183 F5
Thornton-le-Street 202 D4
Thorntonloch 237 E2
Thornwood 137 D2
Thornylee 227 F2
Thoroton 174 C3
Thorp Arch 194 D3
Thorpe Derbys 172 C2

Thorpe ERid 196 B3
Thorpe Lincs 189 E4
Thorpe Norf 165 F2
Thorpe Notts 174 C2
Thorpe NYorks 193 G1
Thorpe Surr 121 F1
Thorpe Abbotts 164 C3
Thorpe Acre 173 G5
Thorpe Arnold 174 C5
Thorpe Audlin 186 B1
Thorpe Bassett 204 B5
Thorpe Bay 138 C4
Thorpe by Water 161 D3
Thorpe Constantine 159 E2
Thorpe Culvert 176 C1
Thorpe End 179 D4
Thorpe Green Essex 152 C5
Thorpe Green Lancs 192 B5
Thorpe Green Suff 152 A2
Thorpe Hall 203 E5
Thorpe Hesley 186 A3
Thorpe in Balne 186 C1
Thorpe in the Fallows 187 G4
Thorpe Langton 160 C3
Thorpe Larches 212 C4
Thorpe le Street 196 A3
Thorpe Malsor 160 D5
Thorpe Mandeville 148 A3
Thorpe Market 178 D2
Thorpe Morieux 152 A2
Thorpe on the Hill
  Lincs 175 E1
Thorpe on the Hill
  WYorks 194 C1
Thorpe Park Surr
  KT16 8PN 121 F1
Thorpe Row 178 A5
Thorpe St. Andrew 179 D5
Thorpe St. Peter 176 C1
Thorpe Salvin 186 C4
Thorpe Satchville 160 C1
Thorpe Street 164 B3
Thorpe Thewles 212 D5
Thorpe Tilney Dales 175 G2
Thorpe Underwood
  N'hants 160 C4
Thorpe Underwood
  NYorks 195 D2
Thorpe Waterville 161 F4
Thorpe Willoughby 195 E4
Thorpefield 202 D5
Thorpe-le-Soken 152 C5
Thorpeness 153 F1
Thorpland 163 E2
Thorrington 152 B5
Thorverton 102 C2
Thrandeston 164 C4
Thrapston 161 E5
Threapland 193 F1
Threapwood 170 B3
Threapwood Head 172 B3
Three Ashes 117 D3
Three Bridges 122 B5
Three Burrows 96 B5
Three Chimneys 124 A5
Three Cocks
  (Aberllynfi) 144 A4
Three Counties Showground
  Worcs WR13 6NW 145 G3
Three Crosses 128 B3
Three Cups Corner 110 B1
Three Hammers 97 G1
Three Holes 162 D2
Three Leg Cross 123 F5
Three Legged Cross 105 G2
Three Mile Cross 120 C1
Three Oaks 110 D2
Threehammer
  Common 179 E4
Threekingham 175 F4
Threemilestone 96 B5
Threlkeld 209 G4
Threshfield 193 F1
Threxton Hill 163 G2
Thriepley 244 B1
Thrigby 179 F4
Thringarth 211 F3
Thringstone 159 G1
Thrintoft 202 D3
Thriplow 150 C3
Throapham 186 C4
Throckenholt 162 B2
Throcking 150 B4
Throckley 212 A1
Throckmorton 146 B3
Throop 105 E3
Throphill 220 D3
Thropton 220 C1
Througham 132 B2
Throwleigh 99 G1
Throwley 124 B3
Throws 151 E5
Thrumpton Notts 173 G4
Thrumpton Notts 187 E5
Thrumster 275 J4
Thrunton 229 E5
Thrupp Glos 132 A2
Thrupp Oxon 133 G1
Thrupp Oxon 133 E3
Thruscross 194 A2
Thrushelton 99 E2
Thrussington 160 B1
Thruxton Hants 119 D3
Thruxton Here 144 D4
Thrybergh 186 B3
Thrybergh Country Park
  SYorks S65 4NU 186 B3
Thulston 173 F4
Thunder Bridge 185 F1
Thundergay 231 G5
Thundersley 138 B4
Thunderton 269 J6
Thundridge 136 C1
Thurcaston 160 A1
Thurcroft 186 B4
Thurdon 112 C4
Thurgarton Norf 178 C2
Thurgarton Notts 174 B3
Thurgoland 185 G2
Thurlaston Leics 160 A3
Thurlaston Warks 159 G5
Thurlbear 115 F5
Thurlby Lincs 161 G1
Thurlby Lincs 175 E1
Thurlby Lincs 189 E5

Thurleigh 149 F2
Thurlestone 100 C3
Thurloxton 115 F4
Thurlstone 185 G2
Thurlton 165 F2
Thurlwood 171 F2
Thurmaston 160 B2
Thurnby 160 B2
Thurne 179 F4
Thurnham 124 A3
Thurning N'hants 161 F4
Thurning Norf 178 B3
Thurnscoe 186 B2
Thursby 209 G1
Thursden 193 F4
Thursford 178 A2
Thursford Collection Norf
  NR21 0AS 178 A2
Thursley 121 E4
Thurso (Inbhir
  Theòrsa) 275 G2
Thurstaston 182 D4
Thurston 152 A1
Thurston Clough 185 D2
Thurstonfield 209 G1
Thurstonland 185 F1
Thurton 179 E5
Thurvaston Derbys 172 D4
Thurvaston Derbys 172 C4
Thuster 275 H3
Thuxton 178 B5
Thwaite NYorks 201 D3
Thwaite Suff 152 C1
Thwaite Head 199 E3
Thwaite St. Mary 165 E2
Thwaites 193 G3
Thwaites Brow 193 G3
Thwing 205 D5
Tibbermore 243 F2
Tibberton Glos 145 G5
Tibberton Tel&W 171 D5
Tibberton Worcs 146 B2
Tibbie Shiels Inn 226 D3
Tibenham 164 C2
Tibertich 240 A4
Tibshelf 173 F1
Tibthorpe 196 B2
Ticehurst 123 F5
Tichborne 119 G4
Tickencote 161 E2
Tickenham 131 E5
Tickford End 149 D3
Tickhill 186 C3
Ticklerton 157 D3
Ticknall 173 E5
Tickton 196 C3
Tidbury Green 158 D5
Tidcombe 119 D2
Tiddington Oxon 134 B2
Tiddington Warks 147 E2
Tiddleywink 132 A5
Tidebrook 110 B1
Tideford 98 D5
Tideford Cross 98 D4
Tidenham 131 E3
Tidenham Chase 131 E3
Tideswell 185 F5
Tidmarsh 134 B5
Tidmington 147 E4
Tidpit 105 G1
Tidworth 118 D3
Tiers Cross 126 C1
Tiffield 148 B2
Tifty 269 F6
Tigerton 252 D3
Tigh a' Gearraidh 262 C4
Tighachnoic 247 E4
Tighnablair 242 C3
Tighnabruaich 232 A2
Tighnacomaire 248 B3
Tigley 101 D1
Tilbrook 149 F1
Tilbury 137 F5
Tilbury Green 151 F3
Tile Hill 159 F5
Tilehurst 134 B5
Tilford 121 D3
Tilgate 122 B5
Tilgate Forest Row 122 B5
Tilgate Park WSuss
  RH10 5PQ 122 B5
Tillathrowie 260 C1
Tillers' Green 145 F4
Tillery 261 H2
Tilley 170 C5
Tillicoultry 243 E5
Tillietudlem 225 G1
Tillingham 138 C2
Tillington Here 145 D3
Tillington WSuss 121 E5
Tillington Common 145 D3
Tillyarblet 252 D3
Tillybirloch 260 E4
Tillycairn Castle 260 E3
Tillycorthie 261 H2
Tillydrine 260 E5
Tillyfar 269 G6
Tillyfour 260 D3
Tillyfourie 260 E3
Tillygreig 261 G2
Tillypronie 260 C4
Tilmanstone 125 F3
Tiln 187 E4
Tilney All Saints 163 D1
Tilney Fen End 162 C1
Tilney High End 163 D1
Tilney St. Lawrence 162 D1
Tilshead 118 B3
Tilstock 170 C4
Tilston 170 B2
Tilstone Fearnall 170 C1
Tilsworth 149 E5
Tilton on the Hill 160 C2
Tiltups End 132 A3
Timberland 175 G1
Timberland Dales 175 G1
Timbersbrook 171 F1
Timberscombe 114 C3
Timble 194 A2
Timewell 114 C5
Timperley 184 B4
Timsbury B&NESom 117 D2
Timsbury Hants 119 E5
Timsgearraidh 270 C4
Timworth 151 G1
Timworth Green 151 G1
Tincleton 105 D3
Tindale 210 C2

Tindon End 151 E4
Tingewick 148 B4
Tingley 194 B5
Tingrith 149 F4
Tingwall 276 D5
Tingwall (Lerwick)
  Airport 279 D8
Tinhay 99 D2
Tinney 98 C1
Tinshill 194 B4
Tinsley 186 B3
Tinsley Green 122 B5
Tintagel 97 E1
Tintagel Castle Corn
  PL34 0HE 97 E1
Tintern Parva 131 E2
Tintinhull 104 A1
Tintwistle 185 E3
Tinwald 217 E2
Tinwell 161 F2
Tippacott 114 A3
Tipperty Aber 253 F1
Tipperty Aber 261 H2
Tipps End 162 C3
Tiptoe 106 B3
Tipton 158 B3
Tipton St. John 103 D3
Tiptree 138 C1
Tiptree Heath 138 B1
Tiptree Museum Essex
  CO5 0RF 138 C1
Tirabad 143 E3
Tiree 246 A2
Tiree Airport 249 E1
Tirindrich 249 E1
Tirley 146 A5
Tirphil 130 A2
Tirril 210 B5
Tir-y-dail 128 C1
Tisbury 118 A5
Tisman's Common 121 F4
Tissington 172 C2
Tister 275 H2
Titchberry 112 C3
Titchfield 107 E2
Titchmarsh 161 F5
Titchwell 177 F3
Titchwell Marsh Norf
  PE31 8BB 177 F3
Tithby 174 B4
Titley 144 C1
Titlington 229 F5
Titmore Green 150 A5
Titsey 122 D3
Titson 112 C5
Tittensor 171 F4
Tittesworth Reservoir & Visitor
  Centre Staffs
  ST13 8TQ 171 G2
Tittleshall 177 G5
Tiverton ChesW&C 170 C1
Tiverton Devon 102 C3
Tivetshall
  St. Margaret 164 C3
Tivetshall St. Mary 164 C3
Tivington 114 C3
Tixall 171 G5
Tixover 161 E2
Toab Ork 277 E7
Toab Shet 279 F9
Toadmoor 173 E2
Tobermory 247 E4
Toberonochy 239 G4
Tobson 270 D4
Tocher 260 E1
Tockenham 132 C5
Tockenham Wick 132 C4
Tockholes 192 C5
Tockington 131 F4
Tockwith 195 D2
Todber 117 E5
Toddington CenBeds 149 F5
Toddington Glos 146 C4
Todenham 147 E4
Todhills Angus 244 C1
Todhills Cumb 218 B5
Todlachie 260 E3
Todwick 186 B4
Toft Cambs 150 B2
Toft Lincs 161 F1
Toft Shet 278 D5
Toft Hill 212 A5
Toft Monks 165 F2
Toft next Newton 188 A4
Toftcarl 275 J4
Toftrees 177 G5
Tofts 275 J2
Toftwood 178 A4
Togston 221 E1
Tokavaig 256 C3
Tokers Green 134 B5
Tolastadh 271 H3
Tolastadh a' Chaolais 270 D4
Tolastadh Ur 271 H3
Toll Bar 186 C2
Toll of Birness 261 J1
Tolland 115 E4
Tollard Farnham 105 F1
Tollard Royal 105 F1
Tollcross 234 A3
Toller Down Gate 104 B2
Toller Fratrum 104 B3
Toller Porcorum 104 B3
Toller Whelme 104 B2
Tollerton Notts 174 B4
Tollerton NYorks 195 E1
Tollesbury 138 C1
Tollesby 203 E1
Tolleshunt D'Arcy 138 C1
Tolleshunt Knights 138 C1
Tolleshunt Major 138 C1
Tolmachan 270 C7
Tolpuddle 105 D3
Tolvah 259 F5
Tolworth 121 G1
Tom an Fhuadain 271 F6
Tomatin 259 F2
Tombreck 258 D1
Tomchrasky
  (Tom Chrasgaidh) 257 J3
Tomdoun 257 H4
Tomdow 267 H7
Tomich High 257 K2
Tomich High 266 E4
Tomich High 266 D1
Tomintoul 259 J3
Tomnacross 266 C7
Tomnamoon 267 H6

Tomnaven 260 C1
Tomnavoulin 259 K2
Ton Pentre 129 F3
Tondu 129 E4
Tonedale 115 E5
Tonfanau 154 B2
Tong Kent 124 A4
Tong Shrop 157 G2
Tong WYorks 194 B4
Tong Norton 157 G2
Tong Street 194 A4
Tonge 173 F5
Tongham 121 D3
Tongland 216 A5
Tongue 273 H3
Tongue House 273 H3
Tongwynlais 130 A4
Tonmawr 129 E3
Tonna 129 D3
Tonwell 136 C1
Tonypandy 129 F3
Tonyrefail 129 G4
Toot Baldon 134 A2
Toot Hill 137 E2
Toothill Hants 106 C1
Toothill Swin 132 D4
Tooting Graveney 136 B5
Top End 149 F1
Top of Hebers 184 C2
Topcliffe 202 D5
Topcroft 165 D2
Topcroft Street 165 D2
Toppesfield 151 F4
Toppings 184 B1
Toprow 164 C2
Topsham 102 C4
Topsham Bridge 100 D2
Torastan 246 B3
Torbain 259 J3
Torbeg Aber 260 C5
Torbeg NAyr 223 E3
Torbothie 234 C4
Torbryan 101 E1
Torcastle 248 D2
Torcross 101 E3
Tordarroch 258 D1
Tore (An Todhar) 266 D6
Toredruff 267 J5
Toremore High 259 J1
Toremore High 275 G5
Torfrey 97 F4
Torgyle 257 K3
Torinturk 231 G3
Tormarton 131 G5
Tormisdale 230 A4
Tormore 223 D2
Tornagrain 266 E6
Tornahaish 259 K4
Tornaveen 260 E4
Torness 258 C2
Toronto 212 A4
Torpenhow 209 F3
Torphichen 235 D2
Torphins 260 E4
Torpoint 100 A2
Torquay 101 F1
Torquhan 236 B5
Torr 100 B2
Torran A&B 240 A4
Torran High 266 E4
Torran High 264 B7
Torrance 234 A2
Torrance House 234 A4
Torrancroy 260 B3
Torre Som 114 D3
Torre Torbay 101 F1
Torrich 267 F6
Torridon 264 E6
Torrin 256 B2
Torrisdale A&B 222 C2
Torrisdale High 273 J2
Torrish 274 E7
Torrisholme 192 A1
Torroble 266 C1
Torry Aber 268 C5
Torry Aberdeen 261 H4
Torryburn 235 E1
Torsonce 236 B5
Torterston 269 J6
Torthorwald 217 E3
Tortington 108 B3
Torton 158 A5
Torworth 187 D4
Tosberry 112 C3
Toscaig 256 D1
Toseland 150 A1
Tosside 193 D1
Tostarie 246 C5
Tostock 152 A1
Totaig 263 G6
Totamore 246 A4
Tote 263 K7
Tote Hill 121 D5
Totegan 274 D2
Totford 119 G4
Totham Hill 138 B1
Tothill 189 E4
Totland 106 C4
Totley 186 A5
Totnes 101 E1
Toton 173 G4
Totronald 246 A4
Totscore 263 J5
Tottenham 136 C3
Tottenhill 163 E1
Tottenhill Row 163 E1
Totteridge GtLon 136 B3
Totternhoe 149 E5
Tottington GtMan 184 B1
Tottington Norf 163 G3
Totton 106 C1
Toulston 195 E1
Toulton 115 E4
Toux 269 H5
Tovil 123 G3
Tow Law 212 A4
Towan Cross 96 B5

Toward 232 C3
Towednack 94 B3
Towcester 148 B3
Tower Bridge Exhibition
  GtLon SE1 2UP 12 C4
Tower End 163 E1
Tower of London GtLon
  EC3N 4AB 12 C4
Towersey 134 C2
Towie Aber 269 G4
Towie Aber 260 D2
Towie Aber 260 C3
Towiemore 268 B6
Town End Cambs 162 C3
Town End Cumb 199 F4
Town End Mersey 183 F4
Town Green Lancs 183 F2
Town Green Norf 179 E4
Town of Lowton 184 A3
Town Row 123 E5
Town Street 163 F4
Town Yetholm 228 C4
Towneley Hall Art Gallery &
  Museum Lancs
  BB11 3RQ 193 E4
Townfield 211 F3
Townhead D&G 207 G2
Townhead SYorks 185 F2
Townhead of
  Greenlaw 216 B4
Townhill Fife 235 F1
Townhill Swan 128 C3
Towns End 119 G2
Towns Green 170 D1
Townshend 94 C3
Towthorpe ERid 196 B1
Towthorpe York 195 F2
Towton 195 D4
Towyn 182 A5
Toynton All Saints 176 B1
Toynton Fen Side 176 B1
Toynton St. Peter 176 C1
Toy's Hill 123 D3
Trabboch 224 C3
Traboe 95 E4
Tradespark High 267 F6
Tradespark Ork 277 D7
Trafford Centre 184 B3
Trafford Park 184 B3
Trago Mills, Newton Abbot
  Devon TQ12 6JD 102 B5
Trallong 143 F3
Trallwn 128 C3
Tram Inn 145 D4
Tranent 236 B2
Tranmere 183 E4
Trantlebeg 274 D3
Trantlemore 274 D3
Tranwell 221 D3
Trap 128 C1
Trap Street 171 F1
Traprain 236 C2
Trap's Green 146 D1
Traquair 227 E2
Trawden 193 F4
Trawscoed
  (Crosswood) 154 C5
Trawsfynydd 168 A4
Trealaw 129 G3
Treales 192 A4
Trearddur 180 A5
Treaslane 263 J6
Tre-Aubrey 129 G5
Trebah Garden Corn
  TR11 5JZ 95 E4
Trebanog 129 G3
Trebanos 128 D2
Trebarrow 98 C1
Trebartha 97 G2
Trebarvah 95 E3
Trebarwith 97 E1
Trebeath 97 G1
Trebetherick 96 D2
Trebister 279 D9
Treborough 114 D4
Trebudannon 96 C3
Trebullett 98 D3
Treburley 98 D3
Treburrick 96 C2
Trebyan 97 E3
Trecastle 143 E5
Trecott 113 G5
Trecrogo 98 D2
Trecwn 140 C4
Trecynon 129 F2
Tredaule 97 G1
Tredavoe 94 B4
Treddiog 140 B5
Tredegar 130 A2
Tredington Glos 146 B5
Tredington Warks 147 E3
Tredinnick Corn 96 C3
Tredinnick Corn 97 G4
Tredogan 115 D1
Tredomen 144 A4
Tredrissi 141 D3
Tredunnock 130 C3
Tredustan 144 A4
Tredworth 132 A1
Treen Corn 94 A4
Treen Corn 94 B3
Treesmill 97 E4
Treeton 186 B4
Trefasser 140 B4
Trefdraeth 180 C5
Trefecca 144 A4
Trefechan 129 G2
Trefeglwys 155 F3
Trefenter 142 C1
Treffgarne 140 C5
Treffynnon 140 B5
Trefgarn Owen 140 B5
Trefil 130 A1
Trefilan 142 B2
Trefin 140 B4
Treflach 169 F5
Trefnanney 156 B1
Trefnant 182 B5
Trefonen 169 F5
Trefor Gwyn 166 C3
Trefor IoA 180 B4
Treforest 129 G4
Treforest Industrial
  Estate 130 A4
Trefriw 181 G1
Tregadillett 97 G1
Tregaian 180 C5

Tregare 130 D1
Tregarland 97 G4
Tregarne 95 E4
Tregaron 142 C2
Tregarth 167 F1
Tregaswith 96 C3
Tregavethan 96 B5
Tregear 96 C4
Tregeare 97 G1
Tregeiriog 169 E4
Tregele 180 B3
Tregidden 95 E4
Tregiskey 97 E5
Treglemais 140 B5
Tregolds 96 C2
Tregole 98 B1
Tregonetha 97 D3
Tregony 96 D5
Tregoodwell 97 F1
Tregoss 97 D3
Tregowris 95 E4
Tregoyd 144 A4
Tregrehan Mills 97 E4
Tre-groes 142 A3
Treguff 129 G5
Tregullon 97 E3
Tregunnon 97 G1
Tregurrian 96 C3
Tregynon 155 G3
Trehafod 129 G3
Trehan 100 A2
Treharris 129 G3
Treherbert 129 F3
Tre-hill 129 G5
Trekenner 98 D3
Treknow 97 E1
Trelan 95 E5
Trelash 98 B1
Trelassick 96 C4
Trelawnyd 182 B5
Trelech 141 F4
Treleddyd-fawr 140 A5
Trelewis 130 A3
Treligga 97 E1
Trelights 97 D2
Trelill 97 E2
Trelissick 95 F3
Trelissick Corn
  TR3 6QL 95 F3
Trelleck 131 E2
Trelleck Grange 131 D2
Trelogan 182 C4
Trelowla 97 G4
Trelystan 156 B2
Tremadog 166 E3
Tremail 97 F1
Tremain 141 F3
Tremaine 97 G1
Tremar 97 G3
Trematon 99 D5
Tremeirchion 182 B5
Tremethick Cross 94 B3
Tremore 97 D3
Trenance Corn 96 C3
Trenance Corn 96 D2
Trenarren 97 E5
Trench Tel&W 157 F1
Trench Wrex 170 A4
Trencreek 96 C3
Trenear 95 D3
Treneglos 97 G1
Trenewan 97 F4
Trengune 98 B1
Trent 104 B1
Trent Port 187 F4
Trent Vale 171 F3
Trentham 171 F3
Trentishoe 113 G1
Trenwheal 94 D3
Treoes 129 F5
Treorchy 129 F3
Treowen 130 B3
Trequite 97 E2
Tre'r-ddol 154 C3
Trerhyngyll 129 G5
Tre-Rhys 141 E3
Trerulefoot 98 D5
Tresaith 141 F2
Tresco 96 A1
Trescott 158 A3
Trescowe 94 C3
Tresean 96 B4
Tresham 131 G3
Treshnish 246 C5
Tresillian 96 C5
Tresinney 97 F1
Tresinwen 140 B3
Treskinnick Cross 98 C1
Treslea 97 F3
Tresmeer 97 G1
Tresowes Green 94 D4
Tresparrett 98 B1
Tresparrett Posts 98 B1
Tressait 250 C4
Tresta Shet 278 F3
Tresta Shet 279 C7
Treswell 187 E5
Trethewey 94 A4
Trethomas 130 A4
Trethurgy 97 E4
Tretio 140 A5
Tretire 145 E5
Tretower 144 A5
Treuddyn 169 F2
Trevadlock 97 G2
Trevalga 98 A1
Trevalyn 170 A2
Trevanson 96 D2
Trevarnon 94 C3
Trevarrack 94 B3
Trevarren 96 C3
Trevarrian 96 C3
Trevarrick 97 D5
Tre-vaughan Carmar 141 G5
Trevaughan Carmar 127 E1
Treveighan 97 E2
Trevellas 96 B4
Treverva 95 E3
Trevescan 94 A4
Trevethin 130 B2
Trevigro 98 D4
Trevine 240 C2
Treviscoe 96 D4
Trevivian 97 F1
Trevone 96 C2
Trevor 169 F3

Trewalder 97 E1
Trewarmett 97 E1
Trewarthenick 96 D5
Trewassa 97 F1
Trewellard 94 A3
Trewen Corn 98 B1
Trewen Here 131 E1
Trewennack 95 D4
Trewent 126 D3
Trewern 156 B1
Trewethern 97 E2
Trewidland 97 G4
Trewilym 141 E3
Tre-wyn 144 C4
Treyarnon 96 C2
Treyford 108 A2
Trezaise 97 D4
Triangle 193 G5
Trickett's Cross 105 G2
Triermain 210 B1
Trimdon 212 C4
Trimdon Colliery 212 C4
Trimdon Grange 212 C4
Trimingham 179 D2
Trimley Lower Street 153 D4
Trimley St. Martin 153 D4
Trimley St. Mary 153 D4
Trimpley 157 G5
Trimsaran 128 A2
Trimstone 113 E1
Trinafour 250 C3
Trinant 130 B3
Tring 135 E1
Trinity Angus 253 E3
Trinity Chanl 100 C5
Trinity Edin 235 G2
Trisant 154 D5
Triscombe Som 114 C4
Triscombe Som 115 E4
Trislaig 248 C2
Trispen 96 C4
Tritlington 221 E2
Trochry 243 D4
Troedyraur 141 G3
Troedyrhiw 129 G2
Trofarth 181 G5
Trondavoe 278 C5
Troon Corn 95 D4
Troon SAyr 224 B2
Tropical Butterfly House,
   Wildlife & Falconry Centre
   SYorks S25 4EQ 21 F3
Tropical World, Roundhay
   WYorks LS8 2ER 27 G1
Trosairidh 254 C3
Troston 163 G5
Troswell 98 C1
Trottick 244 C1
Trottiscliffe 123 F2
Trotton 120 D5
Trough Gate 193 E5
Troughend 220 A2
Troustan 232 B2
Troutbeck Cumb 199 F2
Troutbeck Cumb 209 G4
Troutbeck Bridge 199 F2
Trow Green 131 E2
Troway 186 A5
Trowbridge Cardiff 130 B4
Trowbridge Wilts 117 F2
Trowell 173 F4
Trowle Common 117 F2
Trowley Bottom 135 F1
Trows 228 A3
Trowse Newton 178 D5
Troy 194 B4
Trudernish 230 C4
Trudoxhill 117 E3
Trull 115 F5
Trumaisgearraidh 262 D4
Trumpan 263 H5
Trumpet 145 F4
Trumpington 150 C2
Trumps Green 121 E1
Trunch 179 D2
Trunnah 191 G3
Truro 96 C5
Truro Cathedral Corn
   TR1 2AF 96 C5
Truscott 98 C1
Trusham 102 B4
Trusley 173 D4
Trusthorpe 189 F4
Truthan 96 C4
Trysull 158 A3
Tubney 133 G3
Tuckenhay 101 E2
Tuckhill 157 G4
Tuckingmill 96 A5
Tuddenham Suff 152 C3
Tuddenham Suff 163 F5
Tudeley 123 F4
Tudeley Hale 123 F4
Tudhoe 212 B4
Tudweiliog 166 B4
Tuesley 121 E3
Tuffley 132 A1
Tufton Hants 119 F3
Tufton Pembs 140 D5
Tugby 160 C2
Tugford 157 E4
Tughall 229 G4
Tulchan 243 E2
Tulleys Farm WSuss
   RH10 4PE 122 C5
Tullibardine Distillery P&K
   PH4 1QG 243 E4
Tullibody 243 D5
Tullich A&B 240 C4
Tullich A&B 240 A3
Tullich High 267 F4
Tullich High 258 D2
Tullich Moray 268 B6
Tullich Muir 266 E4
Tullie House Museum & Art
   Gallery Cumb CA3 8TP
   68 Carlisle
Tulliemet 251 E4
Tulloch Aber 261 G1

Tulloch High 266 D2
Tulloch Moray 267 H6
Tullochgorm 240 B5
Tullochgribban High 259 G2
Tullochvenus 260 D4
Tulloes 252 D5
Tullybannocher 242 C2
Tullybelton 243 F1
Tullyfergus 252 A5
Tullymurdoch 251 G4
Tulse Hill 136 C5
Tumble (Y Tymbl) 128 B1
Tumby 176 A2
Tumby Woodside 176 A2
Tummel Bridge 250 C4
Tunbridge Wells 123 E5
Tundergarth Mains 217 F2
Tunga 271 G4
Tungate 179 D3
Tunley 117 D2
Tunstall ERid 197 F4
Tunstall Kent 124 A2
Tunstall Lancs 200 B5
Tunstall Norf 179 F5
Tunstall NYorks 202 B3
Tunstall Stoke 171 F2
Tunstall Suff 153 E2
Tunstall T&W 212 C2
Tunstead GtMan 185 E2
Tunstead Norf 179 E3
Tunstead Milton 185 E4
Tunworth 120 B3
Tupholme 175 G1
Tupsley 145 E4
Tupton 173 E1
Tur Langton 160 C3
Turbiskill 231 F1
Turclossie 269 G5
Turgis Green 120 B2
Turin 252 D4
Turkdean 132 D1
Turleigh 117 F1
Turn 184 C1
Turnastone 144 C4
Turnberry 224 A5
Turnchapel 100 A2
Turnditch 173 D3
Turner's Green 147 D1
Turners Hill 122 C5
Turners Puddle 105 E3
Turnford 136 C2
Turnworth 105 E2
Turret Bridge 257 K5
Turriff 269 F6
Turton Bottoms 184 B1
Turvey 149 G2
Turville 134 C3
Turville Heath 134 C3
Turweston 148 B4
Tutankhamun Exhibition,
   Dorchester Dorset
   DT1 1UW 104 C3
Tutbury 172 D5
Tutbury Castle Staffs DE13
   9JF 172 D5
Tutnall 158 B5
Tutshill 131 E3
Tuttington 178 D3
Tutts Clump 134 A5
Tutwell 99 D3
Tuxford 187 E5
Twatt Ork 276 B5
Twatt Shet 279 C7
Twechar 234 B2
Tweedmouth 237 G4
Tweedsmuir 226 B3
Twelve Oaks 110 B1
Twelveheads 96 B5
Twemlow Green 171 E1
Twenty 175 G2
Twickenham 136 A5
Twineham 109 E1
Twineham Green 109 E1
Twinhoe 117 E2
Twinstead 151 G4
Twiss Green 184 A3
Twiston 193 E3
Twitchen Devon 114 A4
Twitchen Shrop 156 C5
Twitton 123 E3
Twizell House 229 F4
Two Bridges Devon 99 G3
Two Bridges Glos 131 F2
Two Dales 173 D1
Two Gates 159 F2
Two Mills 183 E5
Twycross 159 F2
Twycross Zoo Leics
   CV9 3PX 159 F2
Twyford Bucks 148 B5
Twyford Derbys 173 E5
Twyford Dorset 105 E1
Twyford Hants 119 F5
Twyford Leics 160 C1
Twyford Norf 178 B3
Twyford Oxon 147 G4
Twyford W'ham 134 C5
Twyford Common 145 E4
Twyn Shôn-Ifan 130 A3
Twynholm 216 A5
Twyning 146 A4
Twynllanan 143 D5
Twyn-yr-odyn 130 A5
Twyn-y-Sheriff 130 D2
Twywell 161 E5
Ty Croes 180 B5
Tyberton 144 C4
Tycroes 128 C1
Tycrwyn 156 A1
Tydd Gote 162 C1
Tydd St. Giles 162 C1
Tydd St. Mary 162 C1
Tye Common 137 F3
Tye Green Essex 151 E4
Tye Green Essex 150 D3
Tye Green Essex 137 E1
Tye Green Essex 136 D2
Tyersal 194 A4
Ty-hen 166 A4
Tyldesley 184 A2
Tyle-garw 129 G4
Tyler Hill 124 D2
Tylers Green Bucks 135 E3
Tyler's Green Essex 137 E2
Tylorstown 129 G3
Tylwch 155 F5

Ty-Mawr Conwy 168 C3
Ty-mawr Denb 169 E3
Ty-nant Conwy 168 C3
Ty-nant Gwyn 168 C5
Tyndrum
   (Taigh an Droma) 241 F1
Tyne Green Country Park
   N'umb NE46 3RY 211 F3
Tyneham 105 E4
Tynehead 236 A4
Tynemouth 212 C1
Tynewydd 129 F3
Tyninghame 236 D2
Tynron 216 C1
Tyntesfield 131 E5
Tyn-y-cefn 169 D3
Ty'n-y-coedcae 130 A4
Tyn-y-ffridd 169 E4
Ty'n-y-garn 129 E4
Tyn-y-gongl 180 D4
Tynygraig Cere 142 C1
Tyn-y-graig
   Powys 143 G3
Ty'n-y-groes 181 F5
Tyringham 149 D3
Tyseley 158 C4
Tythegston 129 E5
Tytherington ChesE 184 D5
Tytherington SGlos 131 F4
Tytherington Som 117 E3
Tytherington Wilts 118 A3
Tytherleigh 103 G2
Tytherton Lucas 132 B5
Tyttenhanger 136 B3
Ty-uchaf 168 C5
Tywardreath 97 E4
Tywardreath Highway 97 E4
Tywyn 154 B2

U

Uachdar 262 D6
Uags 256 D1
Ubberley 171 G3
Ubbeston Green 165 E4
Ubley 116 C2
Uckerby 202 B2
Uckfield 109 G1
Uckinghall 146 A4
Uckington 146 B5
Uddingston 234 A3
Uddington 225 G2
Udimore 111 D2
Udley 116 B1
Udny Green 261 G2
Udny Station 261 H2
Udston 234 B4
Udstonhead 234 B5
Uffcott 132 D5
Uffculme 103 D1
Uffington Lincs 161 G2
Uffington Oxon 133 F4
Uffington Shrop 157 E1
Ufford Peter 161 F2
Ufford Suff 153 D2
Ufton 147 F1
Ufton Green 120 B1
Ufton Nervet 120 B1
Ugborough 100 C2
Ugford 118 B4
Uggeshall 165 F3
Ugglebarnby 204 B2
Ugley 150 D5
Ugley Green 150 D5
Ugthorpe 203 G1
Uidh 254 B5
Uig A&B 246 A4
Uig A&B 232 C1
Uig (Uige) High 263 J5
Uig High 263 G6
Uigen 270 C4
Uiginish 263 H7
Uigshader 263 K7
Uisken 238 C3
Uiskevagh
   (Uisgebhagh) 262 D6
Ulbster 275 J4
Ulcat Row 210 A5
Ulceby Lincs 189 E5
Ulceby NLincs 188 B1
Ulceby Cross 189 E5
Ulceby Skitter 188 B1
Ulcombe 124 A4
Uldale 209 F3
Uldale House 200 C3
Uley 131 G2
Ulgham 221 E2
Ullapool (Ullapul) 265 H2
Ullenhall 146 D1
Ullenwood 132 B1
Ulleskelf 195 E4
Ullesthorpe 160 A4
Ulley 186 B4
Ulley Reservoir Country Park
   SYorks S26 3XL 21 E2
Ullingswick 145 E3
Ullinish 255 J1
Ullock 209 D4
Ullswater Steamers Cumb
   CA11 0US 209 G5
Ulpha Cumb 198 C3
Ulpha Cumb 199 F4
Ulrome 197 D2
Ulsta 278 D4
Ulting 138 B2
Ulva 238 D1
Ulverston 199 D5
Ulwell 105 G4
Ulzieside 225 F5
Umberleigh 113 G3
Unapool 272 E5
Underbarrow 199 F3
Undercliffe 194 A4
Underhill 136 B3
Underhoull 278 E2
Underling Green 123 G4
Underriver 123 E3
Underwood Newport 130 C4
Underwood Notts 173 F2
Underwood Plym 100 B2
Undley 163 E4
Undy 130 D4
Ungisiadar 270 D5
Unifirth 279 B7
Union Croft 261 G5
Union Mills 190 B4
Union Street 123 G5

University of Glasgow Visitor
   Centre Glas
   G12 8QQ 38 B1
Unst 278 F1
Unst Airport 278 F2
Unstone 186 A5
Unstone Green 186 A5
Unsworth 184 C2
Unthank Cumb 210 A4
Unthank Derbys 186 A5
Up Cerne 104 C2
Up Exe 102 C2
Up Hatherley 146 B5
Up Holland 183 G2
Up Marden 107 G1
Up Mudford 104 B1
Up Nately 120 B2
Up Somborne 119 E4
Up Sydling 104 C2
Upavon 118 C2
Upchurch 124 A2
Upcott Devon 99 E1
Upcott Devon 113 F2
Upcott Here 144 C2
Upcott Som 114 C5
Upend 151 E2
Upgate 178 C4
Upgate Street Norf 164 B2
Upgate Street Norf 165 D2
Uphall Dorset 104 B2
Uphall WLoth 235 E2
Uphall Station 235 E3
Upham Devon 102 B2
Upham Hants 119 F5
Uphampton Here 144 C1
Uphampton Worcs 146 A1
Uphempston 101 E1
Uphill 116 A2
Uplands Glos 132 A2
Uplands Swan 128 C3
Uplawmoor 233 F4
Upleadon 145 G5
Upleatham 203 F1
Uplees 124 C2
Uploders 104 B3
Uplowman 102 D1
Uplyme 103 G3
Upminster 137 E4
Upottery 103 E2
Upper Affcot 156 D4
Upper Ardroscadale 232 B3
Upper Arley 157 G4
Upper Arncott 134 A1
Upper Astley 157 E1
Upper Aston 158 A3
Upper Astrop 148 A4
Upper Barvas 271 F2
Upper Basildon 134 B5
Upper Bayble
   (Pabail Uarach) 271 H4
Upper Beeding 109 D2
Upper Benefield 161 E4
Upper Bentley 146 B1
Upper Berwick 157 D1
Upper Bighouse 274 D3
Upper Boat 130 A4
Upper Boddam 260 E1
Upper Boddington 147 G2
Upper Borth 154 C4
Upper Boyndlie 269 H4
Upper Brailes 147 F4
Upper Breakish 256 C2
Upper Breinton 145 D3
Upper Broadheath 146 A2
Upper Broughton 174 B5
Upper Brynamman 128 D1
Upper Buckenhill 145 E4
Upper Burgate 106 A1
Upper Burnhaugh 261 G5
Upper Caldecote 149 G3
Upper Camster 275 H4
Upper Canada 116 A2
Upper Catesby 148 A2
Upper Catshill 158 B5
Upper Chapel 143 G3
Upper Cheddon 115 F5
Upper Chicksgrove 118 A4
Upper Chute 119 D2
Upper Clatford 119 E3
Upper Coberley 132 B1
Upper Colwall 145 G3
Upper Cotton 172 B3
Upper Cound 157 E2
Upper Cumberworth 185 G2
Upper Cwmbran 130 B3
Upper Dallachy 268 B4
Upper Dean 149 F1
Upper Denby 185 G2
Upper Denton 210 C1
Upper Derraid 259 H1
Upper Diabaig 264 D5
Upper Dicker 110 A2
Upper Dovercourt 152 D4
Upper Dunsforth 195 D2
Upper Dunsley 135 E1
Upper Eastern Green 159 E4
Upper Eathie 266 E5
Upper Egleton 145 F3
Upper Elkstone 172 B2
Upper End 185 E5
Upper Enham 119 E3
Upper Farringdon 120 B4
Upper Framilode 131 G1
Upper Froyle 120 B4
Upper Gills 275 J1
Upper Glendessarry 257 F3
Upper Godney 116 B3
Upper Gornal 158 B3
Upper Gravenhurst 149 G4
Upper Green Essex 150 C4
Upper Green Mon 130 C1
Upper Green WBerks 119 E1
Upper Grove Common 145 E5
Upper Gylen 240 A2
Upper Hackney 173 D1
Upper Halliford 121 F1
Upper Halling 123 F2
Upper Hambleton 161 E2
Upper Hardres Court 125 D3
Upper Hartfield 123 D5
Upper Hatton 171 F4
Upper Hawkhillock 261 J1
Upper Hayesden 123 E4
Upper Hayton 157 E4

Upper Heath 157 E4
Upper Heaton 185 F1
Upper Hellesdon 178 D4
Upper Helmsley 195 F2
Upper Hengoed 169 F4
Upper Hergest 144 B2
Upper Heyford
   N'hants 148 B2
Upper Heyford Oxon 147 G5
Upper Hill Here 145 D2
Upper Hill SGlos 131 F3
Upper Horsebridge 110 A2
Upper Howsell 145 G3
Upper Hulme 172 B1
Upper Inglesham 133 E3
Upper Kilchattan 238 C5
Upper Killay 128 B3
Upper Knockando 267 J7
Upper Lambourn 133 F4
Upper Langford 116 B2
Upper Langwith 173 G1
Upper Largo 244 C4
Upper Leigh 172 B4
Upper Ley 131 G1
Upper Loads 173 E1
Upper Lochton 260 E5
Upper London 988 C1
Upper Longwood 157 F2
Upper Ludstone 158 A3
Upper Lybster 275 H5
Upper Lydbrook 131 F1
Upper Lyde 145 D3
Upper Lye 144 C1
Upper Maes-coed 144 C4
Upper Midhope 185 G3
Upper Milovaig 263 G7
Upper Milton 133 E1
Upper Minety 132 C3
Upper Moor 146 B3
Upper Morton 131 F3
Upper Muirskie 261 G5
Upper Nash 126 D2
Upper Newbold 186 A5
Upper North Dean 135 D3
Upper Norwood 136 C5
Upper Obney 243 F1
Upper Oddington 147 E5
Upper Ollach 256 D1
Upper Padley 185 G5
Upper Pennington 106 C3
Upper Pollicott 134 C1
Upper Poppleton 195 E2
Upper Quinton 147 D3
Upper Ratley 119 E5
Upper Ridinghill 269 J5
Upper Rissington 147 E5
Upper Rochford 145 F1
Upper Sanday 277 E7
Upper Sapey 145 F1
Upper Scolton 140 C5
Upper Seagry 132 B4
Upper Shelton 149 E3
Upper Sheringham 178 C1
Upper Shuckburgh 147 G1
Upper Siddington 132 C3
Upper Skelmorlie 232 D3
Upper Slaughter 147 D5
Upper Sonachan 240 C2
Upper Soudley 131 F1
Upper Staploe 149 G2
Upper Stoke 179 D5
Upper Stondon 149 G4
Upper Stowe 148 B2
Upper Street Hants 106 A1
Upper Street Norf 179 E4
Upper Street Norf 164 C4
Upper Street Suff 152 C4
Upper Street Suff 152 C3
Upper Strensham 146 B4
Upper Sundon 149 F5
Upper Swanmore 107 E1
Upper Swell 147 D5
Upper Tean 172 B4
Upper Thurnham 192 A2
Upper Tillyrie 243 G4
Upper Tooting 136 B5
Upper Town Derbys 172 D1
Upper Town Derbys 172 D2
Upper Town Derbys 172 D2
Upper Town Here 145 E3
Upper Town NSom 116 C1
Upper Tysoe 147 F3
Upper Upham 133 E5
Upper Upnor 137 G5
Upper Victoria 244 D1
Upper Vobster 117 E3
Upper Wardington 147 G3
Upper Waterhay 132 C3
Upper Weald 148 D4
Upper Weedon 148 B2
Upper Welson 144 B2
Upper Weston 117 E1
Upper Whiston 186 B4
Upper Wick 146 A2
Upper Wield 120 B4
Upper Winchendon (Over
   Winchendon) 134 C1
Upper Witton 158 C3
Upper Woodford 118 C4
Upper Woolhampton 119 G1
Upper Wootton 119 G2
Upper Wraxall 132 A5
Upper Wyche 145 G3
Upperby 210 A2
Uppermill 185 D2
Upperthong 185 F2
Upperton 121 E5
Uppertown Derbys 173 E1
Uppertown Ork 275 J1
Uppingham 161 D2
Uppington 157 E2
Upsall 203 D4
Upsettlington 237 F5
Upshire 136 C2
Upstreet 125 E2
Upthorpe 164 A4
Upton Bucks 134 C1
Upton Cambs 161 G5
Upton ChesW&C 170 B1
Upton Corn 97 G3
Upton Corn 112 C5
Upton Devon 103 D3
Upton Devon 100 D3
Upton Dorset 105 F3
Upton Dorset 104 D4
Upton ERid 196 D2
Upton Hants 119 E2
Upton Hants 106 C1

Upton Leics 159 F3
Upton Lincs 187 F4
Upton Mersey 183 D4
Upton N'hants 148 C1
Upton Norf 179 E4
Upton Notts 187 E5
Upton Notts 174 C2
Upton Oxon 134 A4
Upton Oxon 133 E1
Upton Pembs 126 D2
Upton Peter 161 G2
Upton Slo 135 E5
Upton Som 114 C5
Upton Som 116 B5
Upton Wilts 117 F4
Upton WYorks 186 B1
Upton Bishop 145 F5
Upton Cheyney 117 D1
Upton Country Park Poole
   BH17 7BJ 3 A3
Upton Cressett 157 F3
Upton Crews 145 F5
Upton Cross 97 G2
Upton End 149 G4
Upton Grey 120 B3
Upton Hellions 102 B2
Upton Lovell 118 A3
Upton Magna 157 E1
Upton Noble 117 E4
Upton Park 136 D4
Upton Pyne 102 C3
Upton St. Leonards 132 A1
Upton Scudamore 117 F3
Upton Snodsbury 146 B2
Upton upon Severn 146 A3
Upton Warren 146 B1
Upwaltham 108 B2
Upware 162 D5
Upwell 162 D2
Upwey 104 C4
Upwick Green 150 C5
Upwood 162 A4
Uradale 279 D9
Urafirth 278 C5
Urchany 267 F7
Urchfont 118 B2
Urdimarsh 145 E3
Ure 278 B5
Urgha 263 G2
Urlay Nook 202 D2
Urmston 184 B3
Urpeth 212 B2
Urquhart High 266 C6
Urquhart Moray 267 K5
Urquhart Castle High
   IV63 6XJ 258 C2
Urra 203 E2
Urray 266 C6
Ushaw Moor 212 B3
Usk (Brynbuga) 130 C2
Usselby 188 A3
Usworth 212 C2
Utley 193 G3
Uton 102 B3
Utterby 188 D3
Uttoxeter 172 B4
Uwchmynydd 166 A3
Uxbridge 135 F4
Uyeasound 278 E2
Uzmaston 126 C1

V

Valley (Y Fali) 180 A5
Valley Truckle 97 F1
Valleyfield D&G 216 A5
Valleyfield Fife 235 E1
Valsgarth 278 F1
Vange 137 G4
Vardre 128 C2
Varteg 130 B2
Vatersay
   (Bhatarsaigh) 254 B5
Vatsetter 278 E4
Vatten 263 H7
Vaul 246 B2
Vaynor 129 G1
Vaynor Park 156 A2
Veaullt 144 A2
Veensgarth 279 D8
Velindre Pembs 141 D4
Velindre Powys 144 A4
Vellow 115 D4
Veness 276 D5
Venn 100 D3
Venn Ottery 103 D3
Venngreen 113 D4
Vennington 156 C2
Venny Tedburn 102 B3
Venterdon 99 D3
Ventnor 107 E5
Ventnor Botanic Gardens IoW
   PO38 1UL 107 E5
Venton 100 B1
Venue Cymru, Llandudno
   Conwy LL30 1BB 181 F4
Vernham Dean 119 E2
Vernham Street 119 E2
Vernolds Common 157 D4
Verwood 105 G2
Veryan 95 G3
Veryan Green 96 D5
Vickerstown 191 E3
Victoria 97 D3
Victoria & Albert Museum
   GtLon SW7 2RL 11 A3
Victoria Art Gallery B&NESom
   BA2 4AT 63 Bath
Vidlin 279 D6
Viewfield 275 F2
Viewpark 234 B3
Vigo 158 C2
Vigo Village 123 F2
Villavin 113 F4
Vinehall Street 110 C1
Vine's Cross 110 A2
Viney Hill 131 F1
Virginia Water 121 E1
Virginstow 99 D1
Virley 138 C1
Vobster 117 E3
Voe Shet 279 D6
Voe Shet 278 C4
Vogrie Country Park Midlo
   EH23 4NU 32 F4

Voirrey Embroidery Mersey
   CH63 6JA 22 A5
Volks Electric Railway B&H
   BN2 1EN 109 F3
Vowchurch 144 C4
Voy 277 B6
Vron Gate 156 C2

W

W.R. Outhwaite & Son
   Ropemakers NYorks
   DL8 3NT 201 D4
Waberthwaite 198 C3
Wackerfield 212 A5
Wacton 164 C3
Wadbister 279 D8
Wadborough 146 B3
Waddesdon 134 C1
Waddesdon Manor Bucks
   HP18 0JH 134 C1
Waddeton 101 E2
Waddicar 183 E3
Waddingham 187 G3
Waddington Lancs 192 D3
Waddington Lincs 175 E1
Waddingworth 188 B5
Waddon Devon 102 B5
Waddon GtLon 122 C2
Wadebridge 97 D2
Wadeford 103 G2
Wadenhoe 161 F4
Wadesmill 136 C1
Wadhurst 123 F5
Wadshelf 186 A5
Wadworth 186 C2
Wadworth Hill 197 E5
Waen Denb 169 D1
Waen Denb 168 C1
Waen Aberwheeler 169 D1
Waen-fâch 156 B1
Waen-wen 167 E1
Wag 275 F6
Wainfleet All Saints 176 C2
Wainfleet Bank 176 C2
Wainfleet St. Mary 176 C2
Wainford 165 E2
Waingroves 173 F3
Wainhouse Corner 98 B1
Wainscott 137 G5
Wainstalls 193 G5
Waitby 200 C2
Wakefield 194 C5
Wakehurst Place WSuss
   RH17 6TN 122 C5
Wakerley 161 E3
Wakes Colne 151 G5
Walberton 108 B3
Walbottle 212 A1
Walcot Lincs 175 F4
Walcot Lincs 175 G2
Walcot NLincs 196 A5
Walcot Shrop 156 C4
Walcot Tel&W 157 E1
Walcot Green 164 C2
Walcote Leics 160 A4
Walcote Warks 146 D2
Walcott 179 E2
Walcott Dales 175 G2
Walden 201 F4
Walden Head 201 E4
Walden Stubbs 186 C1
Walderslade 123 G2
Walderton 107 G1
Walditch 104 A3
Waldley 172 C4
Waldridge 212 B3
Waldringfield 153 D3
Waldron 110 A2
Wales 186 B4
Wales Millennium Centre,
   Cardiff Cardiff
   CF10 5AL 130 A5
Walesby Lincs 188 B3
Walesby Notts 187 D5
Waleswood 186 B4
Walford Here 156 C5
Walford Here 145 E5
Walford Shrop 170 B5
Walford Staffs 171 F4
Walford Heath 156 D1
Walgherton 171 D3
Walgrave 160 D5
Walhampton 106 C3
Walk Mill 193 E4
Walkden 184 B2
Walker 212 B1
Walker Art Gallery, Liverpool
   Mersey L3 8EL 42 D3
Walker Fold 192 C3
Walkerburn 227 E2
Walkeringham 187 E3
Walkerith 187 E3
Walkern 150 A5
Walker's Green 145 E3
Walkford 106 B3
Walkhampton 100 B1
Walkingham Hill 194 C1
Walkington 196 B4
Walkwood 146 C1
Wall Corn 94 D3
Wall N'umb 211 F1
Wall Staffs 158 D2
Wall End 198 D4
Wall Heath 158 A4
Wall Houses 211 G1
Wall under Heywood 157 E3
Wallace Collection, London
   GtLon W1U 3BN 44 A2
Wallacehall 218 A4
Wallacetown 224 A5
Wallasey 183 D3
Wallaston Green 126 C2
Wallend 124 A1
Waller's Green 145 F4
Wallingford 134 B4
Wallington GtLon 122 B2
Wallington Hants 107 E2
Wallington Herts 150 A4
Wallington Wrex 170 C3
Wallingwells 186 C4
Wallis 140 D4
Wallisdown 105 G3
Walliswood 121 G4
Walls 279 B8
Wallsend 212 B1
Wallyford 236 A2
Walmer 125 F3

Wal - Wes

Walmer Bridge 192 A5
Walmersley 184 C1
Walmley 158 D3
Walmsgate 189 D5
Walpole 165 E4
Walpole Cross Keys 162 D1
Walpole Highway 162 D1
Walpole Marsh 162 C1
Walpole St. Andrew 162 D1
Walpole St. Peter 162 D1
Walrond's Park 116 A5
Walrow 116 A3
Walsall 158 C4
Walsall Arboretum Illuminations WMid WS1 2AB 14 D1
Walsall Wood 158 C2
Walsden 193 F5
Walsgrave on Sowe 159 F4
Walsham le Willows 164 B4
Walshford 194 D2
Walsoken 162 C1
Walston 235 E5
Walsworth 149 G4
Walter's Ash 134 D3
Walterston 129 G5
Walterstone 144 C5
Waltham Kent 124 D4
Waltham NELincs 188 C2
Waltham Abbey 136 C2
Waltham Chase 107 E1
Waltham Cross 136 C2
Waltham on the Wolds 174 C5
Waltham St. Lawrence 134 D5
Walthamstow 136 C4
Walton Bucks 134 D1
Walton Cumb 210 B1
Walton Derbys 173 E1
Walton Leics 160 A4
Walton Mersey 183 E3
Walton MK 149 D4
Walton Peter 161 G2
Walton Powys 144 B2
Walton Shrop 157 D5
Walton Som 116 B4
Walton Staffs 171 F4
Walton Suff 153 E4
Walton Tel&W 157 E1
Walton Warks 147 E2
Walton WYorks 186 A1
Walton WYorks 194 D3
Walton Cardiff 146 B4
Walton East 140 D5
Walton Elm 105 D1
Walton Hall Gardens Warr WA4 6SN 23 H4
Walton Highway 162 C1
Walton Lower Street 153 D4
Walton on the Hill 122 B3
Walton on the Naze 153 D5
Walton on the Wolds 160 A1
Walton Park D&G 216 B3
Walton Park NSom 130 D5
Walton West 126 B1
Walton-in-Gordano 130 D5
Walton-le-Dale 192 B5
Walton-on-Thames 121 G1
Walton-on-the-Hill 171 G5
Walton-on-Trent 159 E1
Walwen Flints 182 C5
Walwen Flints 182 D5
Walwick 220 B4
Walworth 202 B1
Walworth Gate 212 B5
Walwyn's Castle 126 B1
Wambrook 103 F2
Wanborough Surr 121 E3
Wanborough Swin 133 E4
Wandel 226 A3
Wandon 229 E4
Wandon End 149 G5
Wandsworth 136 B5
Wandylaw 229 F4
Wangford Suff 165 F4
Wangford Suff 163 F4
Wanlip 160 A1
Wanlockhead 225 G4
Wannock 110 A3
Wansbeck Riverside Park N'umb NE63 8TX 221 E3
Wansford ERid 196 C2
Wansford Peter 161 F3
Wanshurst Green 123 G4
Wanstrow 117 E3
Wanswell 131 F2
Wantage 133 F4
Wapley 131 G5
Wappenbury 147 F1
Wappenham 148 B3
Warblebank 209 F2
Warbleton 110 B2
Warblington 107 G2
Warborough 134 A3
Warboys 162 B4
Warbreck 191 G4
Warbstow 98 C1
Warburton 184 A4
Warcop 200 C1
Ward End 158 D4
Ward Green 152 B1
Warden Kent 124 C1
Warden N'umb 211 F1
Warden Hill 146 B5
Warden Street 149 G3
Wardhouse 260 D1
Wardington 147 G3
Wardle ChesE 170 D2
Wardle GtMan 184 D1
Wardley GtMan 184 B2
Wardley Rut 160 D2
Wardley T&W 212 C1
Wardlow 185 F5
Wardsend 184 D4
Wardy Hill 162 C4
Ware Herts 136 C1
Ware Kent 125 E2
Wareham 105 F4
Warehorne 124 B5
Waren Mill 229 F3
Warenford 229 F4
Warenton 229 F3
Wareside 136 C1
Waresley Cambs 150 A2
Waresley Worcs 158 A5
Warfield 135 D5
Wargrave Mersey 183 G3
Wargrave W'ham 134 C5
Warham Here 145 D4
Warham Norf 178 A1
Wark N'umb 220 A4
Wark N'umb 228 C3
Warkleigh 113 G3
Warkton 161 D5
Warkworth N'hants 147 G3
Warkworth N'umb 221 E1
Warland 193 F5
Warleggan 97 F3
Warley Essex 137 E3
Warley WMid 158 C4
Warley Town 193 G5
Warlingham 122 C3
Warmfield 194 C5
Warmingham 171 E1
Warminghurst 108 D2
Warmington N'hants 161 F3
Warmington Warks 147 G3
Warminster 117 F3
Warmlake 124 A4
Warmley 131 F5
Warmley Hill 131 F5
Warmsworth 186 C2
Warmwell 105 D4
Warndon 146 A2
Warners End 135 F2
Warnford 120 B5
Warnham 121 G4
Warningcamp 108 C3
Warninglid 109 E1
Warren ChesE 184 C5
Warren Pembs 126 C3
Warren House 99 G2
Warren Row 134 D4
Warren Street 124 B3
Warrenby 213 E5
Warren's Green 150 A5
Warrington MK 149 D2
Warrington Warr 184 A4
Warroch 243 F4
Warsash 107 D2
Warslow 172 B2
Warsop Vale 173 G1
Warter 196 A2
Warthill 195 F2
Wartle 260 D4
Wartling 110 B3
Wartnaby 174 C5
Warton Lancs 199 G5
Warton Lancs 192 A5
Warton N'umb 220 C1
Warton Warks 159 E2
Warton Bank 192 A5
Warwick 147 E1
Warwick Bridge 210 A2
Warwick Castle Warks CV34 4QU 16 A6
Warwick Wold 122 C3
Warwick-on-Eden 210 A2
Wasbister 276 C4
Wasdale Head 198 C2
Waseley Hills Country Park Worcs B45 9AT 14 C6
Wash 185 E4
Wash Common 119 F1
Washall Green 150 C4
Washaway 97 E3
Washbourne 101 D2
Washbrook 116 B3
Washfield 102 C1
Washfold 201 F2
Washford Som 114 D3
Washford Warks 146 C1
Washford Pyne 102 B1
Washingborough 188 A5
Washington T&W 212 C2
Washington WSuss 108 D2
Washmere Green 152 A3
Wasing 119 G1
Waskerley 211 G3
Wasperton 147 E2
Wasps Nest 175 F1
Wass 203 E5
Wat Tyler Country Park Essex SS16 4UH 137 G4
Watchet 115 D3
Watchfield Oxon 133 E3
Watchfield Som 116 A3
Watchgate 199 G3
Watcombe 101 F1
Watendlath 209 F5
Water 193 E5
Water Eaton MK 149 D4
Water Eaton Oxon 134 A1
Water End Bed 149 G3
Water End CenBeds 149 F4
Water End ERid 195 G4
Water End Essex 151 D3
Water End Herts 136 B2
Water End Herts 135 F1
Water Newton 161 G3
Water Orton 159 D3
Water Stratford 148 B4
Water Yeat 199 D4
Waterbeach 150 C1
Waterbeck 218 A4
Watercombe 105 D4
Waterend 134 C3
Waterfall 172 B2
Waterfoot ERenf 233 G4
Waterfoot Lancs 193 E5
Waterford 136 C1
Watergate 97 F1
Waterhead Cumb 199 E2
Waterhead D&G 216 B2
Waterheath 165 F2
Waterhill of Bruxie 269 H6
Waterhouses Dur 212 A3
Waterhouses Staffs 172 B2
Wateringbury 123 F3
Waterlane 132 B2
Waterloo Aber 261 J1
Waterloo Derbys 173 F1
Waterloo GtMan 184 D2
Waterloo High 256 C2
Waterloo Mersey 183 E3
Waterloo NLan 234 C4
Waterloo Norf 178 D4
Waterloo P&K 243 F1
Waterloo Pembs 126 C2
Waterloo Poole 105 G3
Waterloo Cross 103 D1
Waterloo Port 167 D1
Waterlooville 107 F1
Watermead Country Park Leics LE7 4PF 17 C3
Watermeetings 226 A4
Watermillock 210 A5
Watermouth Castle Devon EX34 9SL 113 F1
Waterperry 134 B2
Waterperry Oxon OX33 1JZ 134 B2
Waterrow 115 D5
Waters Upton 157 F1
Watersfield 108 C2
Watershed Mill Visitor Centre, Settle NYorks BD24 9LR 193 E1
Watersheddings 184 D2
Waterside Aber 260 B3
Waterside Aber 261 J2
Waterside B'burn 192 D5
Waterside Bucks 135 E2
Waterside EAyr 224 C5
Waterside EAyr 233 F5
Waterside EDun 234 A2
Watersmeet House Devon EX35 6NT 114 A3
Waterstock 134 B2
Waterston 126 C2
Waterthorpe 186 B4
Waterworld, Hanley ST1 5PU 85 Stoke-on-Trent
Watford Herts 136 A3
Watford N'hants 148 B1
Watford Park 130 A4
Wath NYorks 202 C5
Wath NYorks 194 A1
Wath Brow 208 D5
Wath upon Dearne 186 B2
Watley's End 131 F4
Watlington Norf 163 E1
Watlington Oxon 134 B3
Watnall 173 G3
Watten 275 H3
Wattisfield 164 B4
Wattisham 152 B2
Watton Dorset 104 A3
Watton ERid 196 C3
Watton Norf 178 A5
Watton at Stone 136 C1
Watton Green 178 A5
Watton's Green 137 E3
Wattston 234 B3
Wattstown 129 G3
Wattsville 130 B3
Waughtonhill 269 H5
Waun Fawr 154 C4
Waun y Clyn 128 A2
Waunarlwydd 128 C3
Waunclunda 142 C4
Waunfawr 167 E2
Waun-Lwyd 130 A2
Wavendon 149 E4
Waverbridge 209 F2
Waverton ChesW&C 170 B1
Waverton Cumb 209 F2
Wavertree 183 E4
Wawne 196 C4
Waxham 179 F3
Waxholme 197 F5
Way Gill 193 F1
Way Village 102 B1
Way Wick 116 A1
Wayford 104 A2
Waytown 104 A3
Weachyburn 268 E5
Weacombe 115 E3
Weald 133 F2
Weald & Downland Open Air Museum WSuss PO18 0EU 108 A2
Weald Country Park Essex CM14 5QS 137 E3
Wealdstone 136 A3
Weardley 194 B3
Weare 116 B2
Weare Giffard 113 E3
Wearhead 211 E4
Wearne 116 B5
Weasenham All Saints 177 G5
Weasenham St. Peter 177 G5
Weathercote 200 C5
Weatheroak Hill 158 C5
Weaverham 184 A5
Weaverthorpe 204 C5
Webheath 146 C1
Webton 144 D4
Wedderlairs 261 G1
Weddington 159 F3
Wedhampton 118 B2
Wedmore 116 B3
Wednesbury 158 B3
Wednesfield 158 B3
Weedon 134 D1
Weedon Bec 148 B2
Weedon Lois 148 B3
Weeford 158 D2
Week Devon 102 A1
Week Devon 101 D1
Week Som 114 C4
Week Orchard 112 C5
Week St. Mary 98 C1
Weeke 119 F4
Weekley 161 D4
Weel 196 C4
Weeley 152 C5
Weeley Heath 152 C5
Weem 250 D4
Weeping Cross 171 G5
Weethley 146 C2
Weeting 163 F4
Weeton ERid 197 F5
Weeton Lancs 191 G4
Weeton NYorks 194 B3
Weetwood 194 B4
Weir Essex 138 B4
Weir Lancs 193 E5
Weir Quay 100 A1
Weirbrook 170 A5
Weisdale 279 C7
Welbeck Abbey 186 C5
Welborne 178 B5
Welbourn 175 E2
Welburn NYorks 195 G1
Welburn NYorks 203 F4
Welbury 202 C2
Welby 175 E4
Welches Dam 162 C4
Welcombe 112 C4
Weldon 161 E4
Welford N'hants 160 B4
Welford WBerks 133 G5
Welford-on-Avon 146 D2
Welham Leics 160 C3
Welham Notts 187 E4
Welham Green 136 B2
Well Hants 120 C3
Well Lincs 189 E5
Well NYorks 202 B4
Well End Bucks 135 D4
Well End Herts 136 B3
Well Hill 123 D2
Well Street 123 F3
Well Town 102 C2
Welland 145 G3
Wellbank 244 C1
Wellesbourne 147 E2
Wellhill 267 G5
Wellhouse WBerks 134 A5
Wellhouse WYorks 185 E1
Welling 137 D5
Wellingborough 149 D1
Wellingham 177 G5
Wellingore 175 E2
Wellington Cumb 198 B2
Wellington Here 145 D3
Wellington Som 115 E5
Wellington Tel&W 157 F1
Wellington Heath 145 G3
Wellington Marsh 145 D3
Wellow B&NESom 117 E2
Wellow IoW 106 C4
Wellow Notts 174 B1
Wells 116 C3
Wells Cathedral Som BA5 2UE 116 C3
Wells Green 158 D4
Wellsborough 159 F2
Wells-next-the-Sea 178 A1
Wellstyle Green 137 F1
Wellwood 235 E1
Welney 162 D3
Welsh Bicknor 131 E1
Welsh End 170 C4
Welsh Frankton 170 A4
Welsh Hook 140 C5
Welsh Mountain Zoo Conwy LL28 5UY 181 G5
Welsh Newton 131 D1
Welsh St. Donats 129 G5
Welshampton 170 B4
Welshpool (Y Trallwng) 156 B2
Welton B&NESom 117 D2
Welton Cumb 209 G2
Welton ERid 196 B5
Welton Lincs 188 A4
Welton N'hants 148 A1
Welton le Marsh 176 C1
Welton le Wold 188 C4
Welwick 197 F5
Welwyn 136 B1
Welwyn Garden City 136 B1
Wem 170 C5
Wembdon 115 F4
Wembley 136 A4
Wembley GtLon HA9 0WS 10 C3
Wembley Park 136 A4
Wembury 100 B3
Wembworthy 113 G4
Wemyss Bay 232 C3
Wenallt Cere 154 C5
Wenallt Gwyn 168 C3
Wendens Ambo 150 D4
Wendlebury 134 A1
Wendling 178 A4
Wendover 135 D2
Wendover Dean 135 D2
Wendron 95 D3
Wendy 150 B3
Wenfordbridge 97 E2
Wenhaston 165 F4
Wenlli 168 B1
Wennington Cambs 162 A5
Wennington GtLon 137 E4
Wennington Lancs 200 B5
Wensley Derbys 173 D1
Wensley NYorks 201 F4
Wensleydale Cheese Visitor Centre, Hawes NYorks DL8 3RN 201 D4
Wentbridge 186 B1
Wentnor 156 C3
Wentworth Cambs 162 C5
Wentworth SYorks 186 A3
Wenvoe 130 A5
Weobley 144 C2
Weobley Marsh 144 D2
Weoley Castle 158 C4
Wepham 108 C3
Wepre 169 F1
Wepre Country Park Flints CH5 4HL 169 F1
Wereham 163 E2
Wergs 158 A2
Wern Gwyn 167 E4
Wern Powys 156 B1
Wern Powys 130 A1
Wern Shrop 169 F4
Wernffrwd 128 B3
Wern-olau 128 B3
Wernrheolydd 130 C1
Wern-y-cwrt 130 C2
Werrington Corn 98 D2
Werrington Peter 161 G2
Werrington Staffs 171 G3
Wervil Grange 141 G2
Wervin 183 F5
Wesham 192 A4
Wessington 173 E2
West Aberthaw 114 D1
West Acre 163 F1
West Acton 136 A4
West Allerdean 237 G5
West Alvington 100 D3
West Amesbury 118 C3
West Anstey 114 B5
West Ashby 188 C5
West Ashford 113 F2
West Ashling 108 A3
West Ashton 117 F2
West Auckland 212 A5
West Ayton 204 C4
West Bagborough 115 E4
West Barkwith 188 B4
West Barnby 204 B1
West Barns 237 D2
West Barsham 178 A2
West Bay 104 A3
West Beckham 178 C2
West Benhar 234 C3
West Bergholt 152 A5
West Bexington 104 B4
West Bilney 163 F1
West Blatchington 109 E3
West Boldon 212 C1
West Bourton 117 E5
West Bowling 194 A4
West Brabourne 124 C4
West Bradford 192 D3
West Bradley 116 C4
West Bretton 185 G1
West Bridgford 173 G4
West Bromwich 158 C3
West Buckland Devon 113 G2
West Buckland Som 115 E5
West Burrafirth 279 B7
West Burton NYorks 201 F4
West Burton WSuss 108 B2
West Butsfield 211 G3
West Butterwick 187 F2
West Byfleet 121 F1
West Cairncake 269 G6
West Caister 179 G4
West Calder 235 E3
West Camel 116 C5
West Carbeth 233 G2
West Carr Houses 187 E2
West Cauldcoats 234 A5
West Chaldon 105 D4
West Challow 133 F4
West Charleton 101 D3
West Chevington 221 E2
West Chiltington 108 C2
West Chiltington Common 108 C2
West Chinnock 104 A1
West Chisenbury 118 C2
West Clandon 121 F2
West Cliffe 125 F4
West Clyne 267 F1
West Coker 104 B1
West Compton Dorset 104 B3
West Compton Som 116 C3
West Cowick 195 F5
West Cross 128 C4
West Crudwell 132 B3
West Curry 98 C1
West Curthwaite 209 G2
West Dean Wilts 119 D5
West Dean WSuss 108 A2
West Deeping 161 G2
West Derby 183 E3
West Dereham 163 E2
West Ditchburn 229 F4
West Down 113 F1
West Drayton GtLon 135 F5
West Drayton Notts 187 E5
West Dullater 242 A4
West Dunnet 275 H1
West Edington 221 D3
West Ella 196 C5
West End Bed 149 E2
West End BrackF 135 D5
West End Caerp 130 B3
West End Cambs 162 C3
West End ERid 196 C1
West End Hants 107 D1
West End Herts 136 B2
West End Kent 125 D2
West End Lancs 192 A1
West End Lincs 189 D3
West End Norf 179 F4
West End Norf 178 A5
West End NSom 116 B1
West End NYorks 194 A2
West End Oxon 133 G2
West End Oxon 134 A4
West End SLan 235 D5
West End Suff 165 F3
West End Surr 121 G1
West End Surr 121 E1
West End Wilts 132 B5
West End Wilts 118 A5
West End Wilts 118 A5
West End Green 120 B1
West Farleigh 123 G3
West Farndon 148 A2
West Felton 170 A5
West Firle 109 G3
West Fleetham 229 F4
West Flotmanby 205 D5
West Garforth 194 C4
West Ginge 133 G4
West Glen 232 A2
West Grafton 118 D1
West Green GtLon 136 C4
West Green Hants 120 C2
West Grimstead 118 D5
West Grinstead 121 G5
West Haddlesey 195 E5
West Haddon 160 B5
West Hagbourne 134 A4
West Hagley 158 B4
West Hall 210 B1
West Hallam 173 F3
West Halton 196 B5
West Ham 136 C4
West Handley 186 A5
West Hanney 133 G3
West Hanningfield 137 G3
West Hardwick 186 B1
West Harnham 118 C5
West Harptree 116 C2
West Harrow 136 A4
West Harting 120 C5
West Hatch Som 115 F5
West Hatch Wilts 118 A5
West Head 163 D2
West Heath ChesE 171 F1
West Heath GtLon 137 D5
West Heath Hants 121 D2
West Heath Hants 119 G2
West Heath WMid 158 C5
West Helmsdale 275 F7
West Hendon 136 B4
West Hendred 133 G4
West Heslerton 204 C5
West Hewish 116 A1
West Hill Devon 103 D3
West Hill ERid 197 D1
West Hill NSom 131 D5
West Hoathly 122 C5
West Holme 105 E4
West Horndon 137 F4
West Horrington 116 C3
West Horsley 121 F2
West Horton 229 E3
West Hougham 125 E5
West Howe 105 G3
West Howetown 114 C4
West Huntspill 116 A3
West Hyde 135 F3
West Hythe 124 D5
West Ilsley 133 G4
West Itchenor 107 G2
West Keal 176 B1
West Kennett 118 C1
West Kilbride 232 D5
West Kingsdown 123 E2
West Kington 132 A5
West Kington Wick 132 A5
West Kirby 182 D4
West Knapton 204 B5
West Knighton 104 D4
West Knoyle 117 F4
West Kyloe 229 E2
West Lambrook 104 A1
West Langdon 125 F4
West Langwell 266 D1
West Lavington Wilts 118 B2
West Lavington WSuss 121 D5
West Layton 202 A2
West Leake 173 G5
West Learmouth 228 C3
West Lees 203 D2
West Leigh Devon 113 G5
West Leigh Devon 101 D2
West Leigh Som 115 E4
West Leith 135 E1
West Lexham 163 G1
West Lilling 195 F1
West Lingo 244 C4
West Linton 235 F4
West Liss 120 C5
West Littleton 131 G5
West Lockinge 133 G4
West Looe 97 G4
West Lulworth 105 E4
West Lutton 196 B1
West Lydford 116 C4
West Lyn 114 A3
West Lyng 116 A5
West Lynn 163 E1
West Mains 229 E2
West Malling 123 F3
West Malvern 145 G3
West Marden 107 G1
West Markham 187 E5
West Marsh 188 C2
West Marton 193 E2
West Melbury 117 F5
West Melton 186 B2
West Meon 120 B5
West Meon Hut 120 B5
West Mersea 138 D1
West Midland Safari Park & Leisure Park Worcs DY12 1LF 158 A5
West Milton 104 A3
West Minster 124 B1
West Molesey 121 G1
West Monkton 115 F5
West Moors 105 G2
West Morden 105 F3
West Morriston 236 D5
West Morton 193 G3
West Mostard 200 C3
West Mudford 116 C5
West Muir 253 D3
West Ness 203 F5
West Newbiggin 202 C1
West Newton ERid 197 D4
West Newton Norf 177 E5
West Norwood 136 C5
West Ogwell 101 E1
West Orchard 105 E1
West Overton 118 C1
West Panson 98 D1
West Park Aber 261 F5
West Park Mersey 183 G3
West Parley 105 G3
West Peckham 123 F3
West Pelton 212 B2
West Pennard 116 C4
West Pentire 96 B3
West Perry 149 G1
West Porlock 114 B3
West Prawle 101 D4
West Preston 108 C3
West Pulham 104 D2
West Putford 113 D4
West Quantoxhead 115 E3
West Raddon 102 B2
West Rainton 212 C3
West Rasen 188 A4
West Raynham 177 G5
West Retford 187 D4
West Rounton 202 D2
West Row 163 E5
West Rudham 177 G5
West Runton 178 C1
West Saltoun 236 B3
West Sandford 102 B2
West Sandwick 278 D4
West Scrafton 201 F4
West Shepton 116 D3
West Shinness Lodge 273 H7
West Somerset Railway Som TA24 5BG 115 E4
West Somerton 179 F4
West Stafford 104 D4
West Stockwith 187 E3
West Stoke 108 A3
West Stonesdale 201 D2
West Stoughton 116 B3
West Stour 117 E5
West Stourmouth 125 E2
West Stow 163 G5
West Stow Country Park Suff IP28 6HG 163 F5
West Stowell 118 C1
West Stratton 119 G3
West Street Kent 124 B3
West Street Med 137 G5
West Street Suff 164 A4
West Tanfield 202 B5
West Taphouse 97 F3
West Tarbert 231 G3
West Tarring 108 D3
West Thirston 221 D1
West Thorney 107 G2
West Thurrock 137 E5
West Tilbury 137 F5
West Tisted 120 B5
West Tofts Norf 163 G3
West Tofts P&K 243 G1
West Torrington 188 B4
West Town B&NESom 116 C1
West Town Hants 107 G3
West Town NSom 116 B1
West Town Som 116 C4
West Tytherley 119 D5
West Walton 162 C1
West Wellow 106 B1
West Wembury 100 B3
West Wemyss 244 B5
West Wick 116 A1
West Wickham Cambs 151 E3
West Wickham GtLon 122 C2
West Williamston 126 D2
West Winch 163 E1
West Winterslow 118 D4
West Wittering 107 G3
West Witton 201 F4
West Woodburn 220 A3
West Woodhay 119 E1
West Woodlands 117 E3
West Worldham 120 C4
West Worlington 102 A1
West Worthing 108 D3
West Wratting 151 E2
West Wycombe 134 D3
West Yatton 132 A5
West Yell 278 D4
West Youlstone 112 C4
Westbere 125 D2
Westborough 174 D3
Westbourne Bourne 105 G3
Westbourne WSuss 107 G2
Westbourne Green 136 B4
Westbrook Kent 125 F1
Westbrook WBerks 133 G5
Westbrook Wilts 118 A1
Westbury Bucks 148 B4
Westbury Shrop 156 C2
Westbury Wilts 117 F2
Westbury Leigh 117 F2
Westbury on Trym 131 E5
Westbury-on-Severn 131 G1
Westbury-sub-Mendip 116 C3
Westby Lancs 191 G4
Westby Lincs 175 E5
Westcliff-on-Sea 138 B4
Westcombe 117 D4
Westcot 133 F4
Westcott Bucks 134 C1
Westcott Devon 102 D2
Westcott Surr 121 G3
Westcott Barton 147 G5
Westcourt 118 D1
Westcroft 148 D4
Westdean 110 A4
Westdowns 97 E1
Westend Town 131 G5
Wester Aberchalder 258 C2
Wester Badentyre 269 F5
Wester Balgedie 243 G4
Wester Culbeuchly 268 E4
Wester Dechmont 235 E2
Wester Fintray 261 G3
Wester Foffarty 252 C5
Wester Greenskares 269 F4
Wester Gruinards 266 C2
Wester Hailes 235 G3
Wester Lealty 266 D4
Wester Lonvine 266 E4
Wester Newburn 244 C4
Wester Ord 261 G4
Wester Quarff 279 D9
Wester Skeld 279 B8
Westerdale High 275 G3
Westerdale NYorks 203 F2
Westerfield Shet 279 C7
Westerfield Suff 152 C3
Westergate 108 B3
Westerham 122 D3
Westerhope 212 A1
Westerleigh 131 F5
Westerloch 275 J3
Westerton Aber 261 F5
Westerton Angus 253 E4
Westerton Dur 212 B4
Westerton P&K 243 D3
Westerwick 279 B8
Westfield Cumb 208 C4
Westfield ESuss 110 D2
Westfield High 275 F2
Westfield NLan 234 B2
Westfield Norf 178 A5
Westfield WLoth 234 D2
Westfield WYorks 194 B5
Westfield Sole 123 G2
Westgate Dur 211 F4
Westgate N'umb 220 D4
Westgate NLincs 187 E2
Westgate Norf 178 A1
Westgate Hill 194 B5
Westgate on Sea 125 F1
Westhall Aber 260 E2
Westhall Suff 165 F3
Westham Dorset 104 C5
Westham ESuss 110 B3
Westham Som 116 B3
Westhampnett 108 A3
Westhay Devon 103 G2
Westhay Som 116 B3
Westhead 183 F2
Westhide 145 E3
Westhill Aber 261 G4
Westhill High 266 E7
Westhope Here 145 D2
Westhope Shrop 157 D4
Westhorp 148 A2
Westhorpe Lincs 176 A4
Westhorpe Notts 174 B2
Westhorpe Suff 152 B1
Westhoughton 184 A2
Westhouse 200 B5
Westhouses 173 F2
Westhumble 121 G2
Westing 278 E2
Westlake 100 C2
Westlands 171 F3
Westlea 132 D4
Westleigh Devon 113 E3

Westleigh *Devon* 103 D1
Westleigh *GtMan* 184 A2
Westleton 153 F1
Westley *Shrop* 156 C2
Westley *Suff* 151 E2
Westley Heights 137 F4
Westley Waterless 151 E2
Westlington 134 C1
Westloch 235 G4
Westmancote 146 B4
Westmarsh 125 E2
Westmeston 109 F2
Westmill 150 B5
Westminster 136 B5
Westminster Abbey *GtLon*
SW1P 3PA 44 E6
Westminster Abbey - Chapter
House & Pyx Chamber
GtLon SW1P 3PA 44 E6
Westminster Cathedral
GtLon SW1P 2QW 44 C7
Westmuir 252 B4
Westness 276 C5
Westnewton *Cumb* 209 E2
Westnewton
N'umb 228 D3
Westoe 212 C4
Weston *B&NESom* 117 E1
Weston *ChesE* 171 E2
Weston *Devon* 103 E4
Weston *Devon* 103 E2
Weston *Dorset* 104 C5
Weston *Halton* 183 G4
Weston *Hants* 120 C5
Weston *Here* 145 E4
Weston *Herts* 150 A4
Weston *Lincs* 176 A5
Weston *Moray* 268 C4
Weston *N'hants* 148 A3
Weston *Notts* 174 C1
Weston *NYorks* 194 A3
Weston *Shrop* 170 C5
Weston *Shrop* 157 E3
Weston *Shrop* 156 C5
Weston *Soton* 107 D1
Weston *Staffs* 171 G5
Weston *WBerks* 133 G5
Weston Bampfylde 116 D5
Weston Beggard 145 E3
Weston by Welland 160 C3
Weston Colville 151 E2
Weston Corbett 120 B3
Weston Coyney 171 G3
Weston Favell 148 C1
Weston Green
Cambs 151 E2
Weston Green *Norf* 178 C4
Weston Heath 157 G1
Weston Hills 176 A5
Weston in Arden 159 F4
Weston Jones 171 E5
Weston Longville 178 C4
Weston Lullingfields 170 B5
Weston Park *Staffs*
TF11 8LE 158 A1
Weston Patrick 120 B3
Weston Point 183 F4
Weston Rhyn 169 F4
Weston Subedge 146 D3
Weston Town 117 F3
Weston Turville 135 D1
Weston under
Penyard 145 F5
Weston under
Wetherley 147 F1
Weston Underwood
Derbys 173 D3
Weston Underwood
MK 149 D2
Westonbirt 132 A4
Westonbirt - The National
Arboretum *Glos*
GL8 8QS 132 A4
Westoning 149 F4
Weston-in-Gordano 131 D5
Weston-on-Avon 147 D2
Weston-on-the-Green 134 A1
Weston-on-Trent 173 F2
Weston-super-Mare 116 A1
Weston-under-Lizard 158 A1
Westonzoyland 116 A4
Westow 195 G1
Westpoint Arena, Clyst St.
Mary *Devon*
EX5 1DJ 102 C3
Westport *A&B* 222 B3
Westport *Som* 116 A5
Westra 130 A5
Westray 276 D3
Westray Airfield 276 D2
Westridge Green 134 A5
Westrigg 234 D3
Westruther 236 D5
Westry 162 B3
Westside 261 G5
Westvale 183 F3
Westville 173 G3
Westward 209 F2
Westward Ho! 113 E3
Westwell *Kent* 124 B4
Westwell *Oxon* 133 E2
Westwell Leacon 124 B4
Westwick *Cambs* 150 C1
Westwick *Dur* 201 E4
Westwick *Norf* 179 D3
Westwick *NYorks* 194 C1
Westwood *Devon* 102 D3
Westwood *Peter* 161 G3
Westwood *SLan* 234 A4
Westwood *Wilts* 117 F2
Westwood Heath 159 E5
Westwoodside 187 F3
Wetham Green 124 A2
Wetheral 210 A2
Wetherby 194 D3
Wetherden 152 B1
Wetherden Upper
Town 152 B1
Wetheringsett 152 C1
Wethersfield 151 F4
Wetherup Street 152 C1
Wetley Abbey 171 G3
Wetley Rocks 171 G3
Wettenhall 170 D1
Wettenhall Green 170 D1
Wetton 172 C2

Wetwang 196 B2
Wexcombe 119 D2
Wexham Street 135 E4
Weybourne *Norf* 178 C1
Weybourne *Surr* 121 D3
Weybread 164 D3
Weybread Street 165 D4
Weybridge 121 F1
Weycroft 103 G2
Weydale 275 G2
Weyhill 119 E3
Weymouth 104 C5
Weymouth Sea Life Adventure
Park & Marine Sanctuary
Dorset DT4 7SX 104 C4
Whaddon *Bucks* 148 D4
Whaddon *Cambs* 150 B3
Whaddon *Glos* 132 A1
Whaddon *Glos* 146 B5
Whaddon *Wilts* 117 F1
Whaddon *Wilts* 118 C2
Whaddon Gap 150 B3
Whale 210 B5
Whaley 186 C5
Whaley Bridge 185 E4
Whaley Thorns 186 C5
Whaligoe 275 J4
Whalley 192 D4
Whalsay 279 E6
Whalsay Airport 279 E6
Whalton 202 A2
Wham 193 D1
Whaplode 176 B5
Whaplode Drove 162 B1
Whaplode
St. Catherine 162 B1
Wharfe 193 D1
Wharles 192 A4
Wharley End 149 E3
Wharncliffe Side 185 G3
Wharram le Street 196 A1
Wharram Percy 196 A1
Wharton
ChesW&C 171 D1
Wharton *Here* 145 E2
Whashton 202 A2
Whatcote 147 F3
Whateley 159 E3
Whatfield 152 B3
Whatley 117 E3
Whatlington 110 C2
Whatsole Street 124 D4
Whatstandwell 173 E2
Whatton 174 C4
Whauphill 207 E2
Whaw 201 E2
Wheatacre 165 F2
Wheatcroft 173 E2
Wheatenhurst 131 G2
Wheathampstead 136 A1
Wheathill *Shrop* 157 F4
Wheathill *Som* 116 D4
Wheatley *Hants* 120 C4
Wheatley *Oxon* 134 B2
Wheatley *WYorks* 193 G5
Wheatley Hill 212 C4
Wheatley Lane 193 E4
Wheatley Park 186 C2
Wheaton Aston 158 A1
Wheddon Cross 114 C4
Wheedlemont 260 C2
Wheelerstreet 121 E3
Wheelock 171 E1
Wheelock Heath 171 E1
Wheelton 192 C5
Wheen 252 B2
Wheldale 195 D5
Wheldrake 195 F3
Whelford 133 D3
Whelley 183 G2
Whelpley Hill 135 E2
Whelpo 209 G3
Whelston 182 D5
Whenby 195 F1
Whepstead 151 G2
Wherstead 152 C3
Wherwell 119 E3
Wheston 185 F5
Whetley Cross 104 A2
Whetsted 123 F4
Whetstone *GtLon* 136 B3
Whetstone *Leics* 160 A3
Whicham 198 C4
Whichford 147 F4
Whickham 212 B1
Whiddon 113 E5
Whiddon Down 99 G1
Whifflet 234 B3
Whigstreet 252 C5
Whilton 148 B1
Whim 235 G4
Whimble 112 D5
Whimple 102 D3
Whimpwell Green 179 E3
Whin Lane End 191 G3
Whinburgh 178 B5
Whinlatter Forest *Cumb*
CA12 5TW 209 E4
Whinny Hill 202 C1
Whinnyfold 261 J1
Whippingham 107 E3
Whipsnade 135 F1
Whipsnade Zoo *CenBeds*
LU6 2LF 135 F1
Whipton 102 C3
Whirlow 186 A4
Whisby 175 E1
Whissendine 160 D1
Whissonsett 178 A3
Whisterfield 184 C5
Whistley Green 134 C5
Whiston *Mersey* 183 F3
Whiston *N'hants* 148 D1
Whiston *Staffs* 172 B3
Whiston *Staffs* 158 A1
Whiston *SYorks* 186 B3
Whiston Cross 157 G2
Whiston Eaves 172 B3
Whitacre Fields 159 E3
Whitacre Heath 159 E3
Whitbeck 198 C4
Whitbourne 145 G2
Whitburn *T&W* 212 D1
Whitburn *WLoth* 234 D3
Whitby *ChesW&C* 183 E5
Whitby *NYorks* 204 B1

Whitby Abbey *NYorks*
YO22 4JT 204 C1
Whitby Lifeboat Museum
NYorks YO21 3PU 204 C1
Whitbyheath 183 E5
Whitchurch
B&NESom 116 C1
Whitchurch *Bucks* 148 D5
Whitchurch *Cardiff* 130 A4
Whitchurch *Devon* 100 A4
Whitchurch *Hants* 119 F3
Whitchurch *Here* 131 E1
Whitchurch *Pembs* 140 A5
Whitchurch *Shrop* 170 C3
Whitchurch *Warks* 147 E3
Whitchurch
Canonicorum 103 G3
Whitchurch Hill 134 B5
Whitchurch-on-
Thames 134 B5
Whitcombe 104 D4
Whitcott Keysett 156 B4
White Ball 103 D1
White Colne 151 G5
White Coppice 184 A1
White Cross *Corn* 96 C4
White Cross *Devon* 102 D5
White Cross *Here* 145 D3
White Cross *Wilts* 117 E4
White Cube *GtLon*
N1 6PB 12 C4
White End 146 A5
White Hill 117 F4
White Houses 187 E5
White Kirkley 211 G4
White Ladies Aston 146 B2
White Lund 192 A1
White Mill 142 A5
White Moor 173 E3
White Ox Mead 117 E2
White Pit 189 D5
White Post Farm Centre,
Farnsfield *Notts*
NG22 8HL 174 B2
White Rocks 144 D5
White Roding 137 E1
White Waltham 134 D5
Whiteacen 267 K7
Whiteash Green 151 F4
Whitebog 269 H5
Whitebridge *High* 275 H1
Whitebridge (An Drochaid
Bhàn) *High* 258 B3
Whitebrook 131 E1
Whiteburn 236 C5
Whitecairn 214 D5
Whitecairns 261 H3
Whitecastle 235 E5
Whitechapel 183 B3
Whitecote 194 B4
Whitecraig 236 A2
Whitecroft 131 F2
Whitecrook 214 C5
Whitecross *Corn* 94 C3
Whitecross *Corn* 97 D2
Whitecross *Dorset* 104 A3
Whitecross *Falk* 235 D2
Whiteface 266 E3
Whitefield *Aber* 261 F2
Whitefield *Devon* 114 A4
Whitefield *Dorset* 105 F3
Whitefield *GtMan* 184 C2
Whitefield *High* 258 C2
Whitefield *High* 275 H3
Whitefield *P&K* 243 G1
Whiteford 261 F2
Whitegate 170 D1
Whitehall *Devon* 103 E1
Whitehall *Hants* 120 C2
Whitehall *Midlo* 236 A3
Whitehall *NAyr* 233 D4
Whitehills 268 E4
Whitehouse *A&B* 231 G3
Whitehouse *Aber* 260 E3
Whitehouse Common 158 D3
Whitekirk 236 C1
Whitelackington 103 G1
Whitelaw 237 F4
Whiteleen 275 J4
Whitelees 224 B2
Whiteley 107 E2
Whiteley Bank 107 E4
Whiteley Green 184 D5
Whiteley Village 121 F1
Whiteleys 214 B5
Whitemans Green 109 F1
Whitemire 267 G6
Whitemoor 97 D4
Whiteness 279 C8
Whiteoak Green 133 F1
Whiteparish 118 D5
Whiterashes 261 G2
Whiterow 275 J4
Whiteshill 132 A2
Whiteside *N'umb* 210 D1
Whiteside *WLoth* 235 D3
Whitesmith 110 A2
Whitestaunton 103 F1
Whitestone *A&B* 222 C4
Whitestone *Aber* 260 E5
Whitestone *Devon* 102 B3
Whitestreet Green 152 A4
Whitestripe 269 H5
Whiteway 132 B1
Whitewell *Aber* 269 H4
Whitewell *Lancs* 192 C3
Whitewell *Wrex* 170 B3
Whiteworks 99 G3
Whitewreath 267 K6
Whitfield *Here* 144 D4
Whitfield *Kent* 125 F4
Whitfield *N'hants* 148 B4
Whitfield *N'umb* 211 D2
Whitfield *SGlos* 131 F3
Whitford *Devon* 103 F3
Whitford (Chwitffordd)
Flints 182 C5
Whitgift 196 A5

Whitgreave 171 F5
Whithorn 207 E2
Whiting Bay 223 F3
Whitkirk 194 C4
Whitlam 261 G2
Whitland
(Hendy-Gwyn) 127 F1
Whitland Abbey 127 F1
Whitleigh 100 A1
Whitletts 224 B3
Whitley *NYorks* 195 E5
Whitley *Read* 120 C1
Whitley *Wilts* 117 F1
Whitley *WMid* 159 F5
Whitley Bay 221 F4
Whitley Chapel 211 F2
Whitley Heath 171 F5
Whitley Lower 185 G1
Whitley Row 123 D3
Whitlock's End 158 D5
Whitminster 131 G2
Whitmore *Dorset* 105 G2
Whitmore *Staffs* 171 F3
Whitnage 102 D1
Whitnash 147 F1
Whitnell 115 F4
Whitney-on-Wye 144 B3
Whitrigg *Cumb* 209 F1
Whitrigg *Cumb* 209 F3
Whitsbury 106 A1
Whitsome 237 F4
Whitson 130 C4
Whitstable 124 D2
Whitstone 98 C1
Whittingham 229 E5
Whittingslow 156 D4
Whittington *Derbys* 186 C5
Whittington *Glos* 146 C5
Whittington *Lancs* 200 B5
Whittington *Norf* 163 F3
Whittington *Shrop* 170 A4
Whittington *Staffs* 158 A4
Whittington *Staffs* 159 D2
Whittington *Worcs* 146 A2
Whittlebury 148 B3
Whittle-le-Woods 192 B5
Whittlesey 150 C3
Whittlesford 150 C3
Whittlestone Head 184 B1
Whitton *GtLon* 136 A5
Whitton *N'umb* 220 C1
Whitton *NLincs* 196 B5
Whitton *Powys* 144 B1
Whitton *Shrop* 157 E5
Whitton *Stock* 212 C5
Whitton *Suff* 152 C3
Whittonditch 133 E5
Whittonstall 211 G2
Whitway 119 F2
Whitwell *Derbys* 186 C5
Whitwell *Herts* 149 G5
Whitwell *IoW* 107 E5
Whitwell *NYorks* 202 B3
Whitwell *Rut* 161 E2
Whitwell Street 178 C3
Whitwell-on-the-Hill 195 G1
Whitwick 159 G1
Whitwood 194 D5
Whitworth 184 C1
Whitworth Art Gallery,
Manchester *GtMan*
M15 6ER 25 E4
Whixall 170 C4
Whixley 194 D2
Whorlton *Dur* 201 E4
Whorlton *NYorks* 203 D2
Whygate 219 F4
Whyle 145 E1
Whyteleafe 122 C3
Wibdon 131 E3
Wibsey 194 A4
Wibtoft 159 G4
Wichenford 145 G1
Wichling 124 B3
Wick *Bourne* 106 A3
Wick *Devon* 103 E1
Wick (Inbhir Ùige)
High 275 J3
Wick *SGlos* 131 G5
Wick *Som* 115 F3
Wick *Som* 116 C4
Wick *VGlam* 129 F5
Wick *Wilts* 118 C5
Wick *Worcs* 146 B3
Wick Airport 275 J3
Wick Hill *Kent* 124 A4
Wick Hill *W'ham* 120 C1
Wck St. Lawrence 116 A1
Wicken *Cambs* 163 D5
Wicken *N'hants* 148 C4
Wicken Bonhunt 150 C4
Wickenby 188 A4
Wicker Street Green 152 A3
Wickerslack 200 B1
Wickersley 186 B3
Wickford 137 G3
Wickham *Hants* 107 E1
Wickham *W'Berks* 133 F5
Wickham Bishops 138 B1
Wickham Heath 119 F1
Wickham Market 153 E2
Wickham St. Paul 151 G4
Wickham Skeith 152 B1
Wickham Street 151 F2
Wickham Street *Suff* 152 B1
Wickhambreaux 125 E3
Wick'hambrook 151 F2
Wickhamford 146 C3
Wickhampton 179 E5
Wicklewood 178 B5
Wickmere 178 C2
Wicksteed Park *N'hants*
NN15 6NJ 161 D5
Wickstreet 110 A1
Wickwar 131 G4
Widcombe 117 E1
Widdington 150 D4
Widdop 193 F4
Widdrington 221 E2
Widdrington Station 221 E1
Wide Open 221 E4
Widecombe in the
Moor 102 A5
Widegates 97 G4
Widemouth Bay 112 C5
Widewall 277 D8

Widford *Essex* 137 F2
Widford *Herts* 136 D1
Widford *Oxon* 133 E1
Widmer End 135 D3
Widmerpool 174 B5
Widnes 183 G4
Widworthy 103 F3
Wigan 183 G2
Wigan Pier *GtMan*
WN3 4EU 183 G2
Wiganthorpe 203 F5
Wigborough 104 A1
Wiggaton 103 E3
Wiggenhall
St. Germans 163 D1
Wiggenhall St. Mary
Magdalen 163 D1
Wiggenhall St. Mary the
Virgin 163 E1
Wiggenhall St. Peter 163 E1
Wiggens Green 151 E3
Wigginton *Herts* 135 E1
Wigginton *Oxon* 147 F4
Wigginton *Shrop* 170 A4
Wigginton *Staffs* 159 E2
Wigginton *York* 195 E2
Wigglesworth 193 E2
Wiggonby 209 G1
Wiggonholt 108 C2
Wighill 195 D3
Wighton 178 A2
Wightwizzle 185 G3
Wigley 106 C1
Wigmore *Here* 144 D1
Wigmore *Med* 124 A2
Wigsley 187 F5
Wigsthorpe 161 F4
Wigston 160 B2
Wigston Parva 159 G4
Wigthorpe 186 C4
Wigtoft 176 A4
Wigton 209 F2
Wigtown 215 F5
Wike 194 C3
Wilbarston 160 D4
Wilberfoss 195 G2
Wilburton 162 C5
Wilby *N'hants* 149 D1
Wilby *Norf* 164 B2
Wilby *Suff* 165 D4
Wilcot 118 C1
Wilcott 156 C1
Wilcrick 130 C4
Wilday Green 186 A5
Wildboarclough 171 G1
Wilde Street 163 F5
Wilden *Bed* 149 F2
Wilden *Worcs* 158 A5
Wildern 119 E2
Wildhill 136 B2
Wildmoor 158 B5
Wildsworth 187 F3
Wilford 173 G4
Wilkesley 170 D3
Wilkhaven 267 G3
Wilkieston 235 F3
Wilksby 176 A1
Willand *Devon* 102 D1
Willand *Som* 103 E1
Willaston *ChesE* 171 D2
Willaston *ChesW&C* 183 E5
Willaston *Shrop* 170 C3
Willen 149 D3
Willen Lakeside Park *MK*
MK15 9HQ 9 D2
Willenhall *WMid* 158 B3
Willenhall *WMid* 159 F5
Willerby *ERid* 196 C4
Willerby *NYorks* 204 C5
Willersey 146 D4
Willersley 144 C3
Willesborough 124 C4
Willesborough Lees 124 C4
Willesden 136 B4
Willesleigh 113 F2
Willesley 132 A4
Willett 115 E4
Willey *Shrop* 157 F3
Willey *Warks* 159 G4
Willey Green 121 E2
William's Green 152 A3
Williamscot 147 G3
Williamson Park, Lancaster
Lancs LA1 1UX 192 A1
Williamthorpe 173 F1
Willian 150 A4
Willimontswick 211 D1
Willingale 110 D1
Willingham 110 A3
Willingham 162 B5
Willingham by Stow 187 F4
Willingham Green 151 E2
Willington *Bed* 149 F2
Willington *Derbys* 173 D5
Willington *Dur* 212 A4
Willington *Kent* 123 G3
Willington *T&W* 212 C1
Willington *Warks* 147 E4
Willington Corner 170 C1
Willisham 152 B2
Willitoft 195 G4
Williton 115 D3
Willoughbridge 171 E3
Willoughby *Lincs* 189 E5
Willoughby *Warks* 148 A1
Willoughby Waterleys 160 A3
Willoughby-on-the-
Wolds 174 B5
Willoughton 187 G3
Willow Green 184 A5
Willows Farm Village *Herts*
AL2 1BB 136 A2
Willows Green 137 G1
Willsbridge 131 F5
Willslock 172 B4
Willsworthy 99 F2
Willtown 116 A5
Wilmcote 147 D2
Wilmington
B&NESom 117 D1
Wilmington *Devon* 103 F2
Wilmington *ESuss* 110 A3
Wilmington *Kent* 137 E5
Wilmslow 184 C4
Wilnecote 159 E2
Wilney Green 164 B3
Wilpshire 192 C4

Wilsden 193 G4
Wilsford *Lincs* 175 F3
Wilsford *Wilts* 118 C2
Wilsford *Wilts* 118 C2
Wilsham 114 A3
Wilshaw 185 F2
Wilsill 194 A1
Wilsley Green 123 G5
Wilsley Pound 123 G5
Wilson 173 F5
Wilstead 149 F2
Wilsthorpe *ERid* 197 D1
Wilsthorpe *Lincs* 161 F1
Wilstone 135 E1
Wilton *Cumb* 208 D5
Wilton *Here* 145 E5
Wilton *NYorks* 204 B4
Wilton *R&C* 203 F1
Wilton *ScBord* 227 F4
Wilton *Wilts* 119 D1
Wilton *Wilts* 118 B4
Wilton House *Wilts*
SP2 0BJ 108 B4
Wiltown 103 E1
Wimbish 151 D4
Wimbish Green 151 E4
Wimbledon 136 C1
Wimblington 162 C3
Wimborne Minster 105 G2
Wimborne Minster *Dorset*
BH21 1HT 3 B2
Wimborne St. Giles 105 G1
Wimbotsham 163 E2
Wimpole 150 B2
Wimpole Home Farm *Cambs*
SG8 0BW 150 B3
Wimpole Lodge 150 B3
Wimpstone 147 E3
Wincanton 117 E5
Winceby 176 B1
Wincham 184 A5
Winchburgh 235 E2
Winchcombe 146 C5
Winchelsea 111 E2
Winchelsea Beach 111 E2
Winchester 119 F5
Winchester Cathedral
Hants SO23 9LS 89 Winchester
Winchet Hill 123 G4
Winchfield 120 C2
Winchmore Hill
Bucks 135 E3
Winchmore Hill
GtLon 136 C3
Wincle 171 G1
Wincobank 186 A3
Windermere 199 F3
Windermere Lake Cruises
Cumb LA12 8AS 199 E3
Winderton 147 F3
Windhill 266 C7
Windle Hill 183 E5
Windlehurst 185 D4
Windlesham 121 E1
Windley 173 E3
Windmill *Corn* 97 D1
Windmill 185 F5
Windmill Hill *ESuss* 110 B2
Windmill Hill *Shrop* 170 C4
Windmill Hill *Worcs* 146 B3
Windrush 133 E1
Windsor 135 E5
Windsor Castle *W&M*
SL4 1NJ 89 Windsor
Windsor Green 151 G2
Windy Nook 212 B1
Windygates 244 B4
Windy-Yett 233 F4
Wineham 109 E1
Winestead 197 E5
Winewall 193 F4
Winfarthing 164 C3
Winford *IoW* 107 E4
Winford *NSom* 116 C1
Winforton 144 B3
Winfrith Newburgh 105 E4
Wing *Bucks* 149 D5
Wing *Rut* 161 D2
Wingate 212 C4
Wingates *GtMan* 184 A2
Wingates *N'umb* 220 C2
Wingerworth 173 E1
Wingfield *CenBeds* 149 F5
Wingfield *Suff* 164 D3
Wingfield *Wilts* 117 F2
Wingfield Green 164 D4
Wingham 125 E3
Wingham Well 125 E3
Wingmore 125 E4
Wingrave 135 D1
Winkburn 174 C2
Winkfield 135 E5
Winkfield Row 135 D5
Winkhill 172 B2
Winkleigh 113 G5
Winksley 202 B5
Winkton 106 A3
Winlaton 212 A1
Winlaton Mill 212 A1
Winless 275 J3
Winmarleigh 192 A3
Winnard's Perch 96 D3
Winnersh 134 C5
Winnington 184 A5
Winscombe 116 B2
Winsford *ChesW&C* 171 D1
Winsford *Som* 114 C4
Winsham *Devon* 113 F2
Winsham *Som* 103 G2
Winshill 173 D5
Winsh-wen 128 C3
Winskill 210 B4
Winslade 120 B3
Winsley 117 F1
Winslow 148 C5
Winson 132 C2
Winsor 106 C1
Winster *Cumb* 199 F3
Winster *Derbys* 172 D1
Winston *Dur* 202 A1
Winston *Suff* 152 C1
Winstone 132 B2
Winswell 113 E4

Winter Gardens FY1 1HW
64 Blackpool
Winter Gardens *NSom*
BS23 1AJ
88 Weston-super-Mare
Winterborne Came 104 D4
Winterborne Clenston 105 E2
Winterborne
Herringston 104 C4
Winterborne
Houghton 105 E2
Winterborne Kingston 105 E3
Winterborne Monkton 104 C4
Winterborne Stickland 105 E2
Winterborne
Whitechurch 105 E2
Winterborne Zelston 105 E3
Winterbourne *SGlos* 131 F4
Winterbourne *WBerks* 133 G5
Winterbourne Abbas 104 C3
Winterbourne Bassett 132 D5
Winterbourne
Dauntsey 118 C4
Winterbourne Earls 118 C4
Winterbourne Gunner 118 C4
Winterbourne
Monkton 132 D5
Winterbourne
Steepleton 104 C4
Winterbourne Stoke 118 B3
Winterbrook 134 B4
Winterburn 193 F2
Wintercleugh 226 A4
Winteringham 196 B5
Winterley 171 E2
Wintersett 186 A1
Wintershill 107 E1
Winterslow 118 D4
Winterton 187 G5
Winterton-on-Sea 179 F4
Winthorpe *Lincs* 177 D1
Winthorpe *Notts* 174 D2
Winton *Bourne* 105 G3
Winton *Cumb* 200 C1
Wintringham 204 B5
Winwick *Cambs* 161 G4
Winwick *N'hants* 160 B5
Winwick *Warr* 184 A3
Wirksworth 173 D2
Wirksworth Moor 173 E2
Wirral Country Park *Mersey*
CH61 0HN 182 D4
Wirswall 170 C3
Wisbech 162 C2
Wisbech St. Mary 162 C2
Wisborough Green 121 F5
Wiseton 187 E4
Wishaw *NLan* 234 B4
Wishaw *Warks* 159 D3
Wisley 121 F2
Wispington 188 C5
Wissett 165 E4
Wissington 152 A4
Wistanstow 156 D4
Wistanswick 171 D5
Wistaston 171 D2
Wiston *Pembs* 126 D1
Wiston *SLan* 226 A2
Wiston *WSuss* 108 D2
Wistow *Cambs* 162 A4
Wistow *Leics* 160 B3
Wistow *NYorks* 195 E4
Wiswell 192 D4
Witcham 162 C5
Witchampton 105 F2
Witchburn 222 C3
Witchford 162 D5
Witcombe 116 B5
Witham 138 B1
Witham Friary 117 E3
Witham on the Hill 161 F1
Withcall 188 C4
Withcote 160 C2
Withdean 109 F3
Witherenden Hill 110 B1
Witherhurst 110 B1
Witheridge 102 B1
Witherley 159 F3
Withern 189 E4
Withernsea 197 F5
Withernwick 197 D3
Withersdale Street 165 D3
Withersfield 151 E3
Witherslack 199 F4
Witherslack Hall 199 F4
Withiel 97 E3
Withiel Florey 114 C5
Withielgoose 97 E3
Withington *Glos* 132 C1
Withington *GtMan* 184 C3
Withington *Here* 145 E3
Withington *Shrop* 157 E1
Withington *Staffs* 172 B4
Withington Green 184 C5
Withington Marsh 145 E3
Withleigh 102 C1
Withnell 192 C5
Withnell Fold 192 C5
Withybrook *Som* 117 D3
Withybrook *Warks* 159 G4
Withycombe 114 D3
Withycombe Raleigh 102 D4
Withyham 123 D5
Withypool 114 B4
Witley 121 E4
Witnesham 152 C2
Witney 133 F2
Wittering 161 F2
Wittersham 111 D1
Witton *Angus* 253 D2
Witton *Norf* 179 E5
Witton *Worcs* 146 A1
Witton Bridge 179 E2
Witton Park 212 A4
Witton-le-Wear 212 A4
Wiveliscombe 115 D5
Wivelsfield 109 F1
Wivelsfield Green 109 F2
Wivenhoe 152 B5
Wiveton 178 B1
Wix 152 C5
Wixford 146 C2
Wixhill 170 C5
Wixoe 151 F3
Woburn 149 E4
Woburn Safari Park *CenBeds*
MK17 9QN 9 F3
Woburn Sands 149 E4

Wokefield Park 120 B1
Woking 121 F2
Wokingham 120 D1
Wolborough 102 B5
Wold Newton ERid 204 D4
Wold Newton NELincs 188 C3
Woldingham 122 C3
Wolds Village, Bainton ERid
  YO25 9EF 196 B2
Wolfelee 227 G5
Wolferlow 145 F1
Wolferton 177 E5
Wolfhampcote 148 A1
Wolfhill 243 G1
Wolfpits 144 B2
Wolf's Castle 140 C5
Wolfsdale 140 C5
Woll 227 F3
Wollaston N'hants 149 E1
Wollaston Shrop 156 C1
Wollaston WMid 158 A4
Wollaton 173 G4
Wollerton 170 D5
Wollescote 158 B4
Wolsingham 211 G4
Wolston 159 G5
Wolsty 209 E1
Wolvercote 134 A2
Wolverhampton 158 B3
Wolverhampton Art Gallery
  WMid WV1 1DU 14 A1
Wolverley Shrop 170 B4
Wolverley Worcs 158 A5
Wolvers Hill 116 A1
Wolverton Hants 119 G2
Wolverton MK 148 D3
Wolverton Warks 147 E1
Wolverton Wilts 117 E4
Wolverton Common 119 G2
Wolvesnewton 131 D3
Wolvey 159 G4
Wolvey Heath 159 G4
Wolviston 213 D5
Womaston 144 B1
Wombleton 203 F4
Wombourne 158 A3
Wombwell 186 A2
Womenswold 125 E3
Womersley 186 C1
Wonastow 131 D1
Wonersh 121 F3
Wonford 102 C3
Wonson 99 G2
Wonston 119 F4
Wooburn 135 E4
Wooburn Green 135 E4
Wood Bevington 146 C2
Wood Burcote 148 B3
Wood Dalling 178 B3
Wood Eaton 158 A1
Wood End Bed 149 E4
Wood End Bed 149 F1
Wood End Bucks 148 C4
Wood End Herts 150 B5
Wood End Warks 159 E3
Wood End Warks 158 D5
Wood End Warks 159 E4
Wood End WMid 158 B2
Wood Enderby 176 A1
Wood Green GtLon 136 C3
Wood Green Norf 164 D2
Wood Green Animal Shelter,
  Godmanchester Cambs
  PE29 2NH 150 A1
Wood Lane 170 B4
Wood Norton 178 B3
Wood Seats 186 A3
Wood Stanway 146 C4
Wood Street 179 E3
Wood Street Village 121 E2
Woodacott 113 D5
Woodale 201 F5
Woodall 186 B4
Woodbastwick 179 E4
Woodbeck 187 E5
Woodborough Notts 174 B3
Woodborough Wilts 118 C2
Woodbridge Devon 103 E3
Woodbridge Dorset 104 D1
Woodbridge Suff 153 D3
Woodbury Devon 102 D4
Woodbury Som 116 C3
Woodbury Salterton 102 D4
Woodchester 132 A2
Woodchurch Kent 124 B5
Woodchurch Mersey 183 D4
Woodcombe 114 C3
Woodcote Oxon 134 B4
Woodcote Tel&W 157 G2
Woodcote Green 158 B5
Woodcott 119 F2
Woodcroft 131 E3
Woodcutts 105 F1
Woodditton 151 E2
Woodeaton 134 A1
Woodend Aber 260 E3
Woodend Cumb 198 C2
Woodend High 258 E2
Woodend High 247 G3
Woodend N'hants 148 B3
Woodend P&K 250 C5
Woodend WSuss 108 A3
Woodend Green 151 D5
Woodfields 118 C5
Woodfield Oxon 148 A5
Woodfield SAyr 224 B3
Woodfoot 200 B1
Woodford Corn 112 C4
Woodford Devon 101 D2
Woodford Glos 131 F3
Woodford GtLon 136 D3
Woodford GtMan 184 D4
Woodford N'hants 161 E5
Woodford Som 115 D4
Woodford Bridge 136 D3
Woodford Green 136 D3
Woodford Halse 148 A2
Woodgate Devon 103 E1
Woodgate Norf 178 B4
Woodgate WMid 158 B4
Woodgate Worcs 146 B1
Woodgate WSuss 108 B3
Woodgreen 106 A1
Woodhall Invcly 233 E2
Woodhall NYorks 201 E3
Woodhall Hills 194 A4
Woodhall Spa 175 G1
Woodham Bucks 134 B1

Woodham Dur 212 B5
Woodham Surr 121 F1
Woodham Ferrers 137 G3
Woodham Mortimer 138 B2
Woodham Walter 138 B2
Woodhaven 244 C4
Woodhead Aber 261 F1
Woodhead Staffs 172 B3
Woodhey 183 E4
Woodhey Green 170 C2
Woodhill Shrop 157 G4
Woodhill Som 116 A5
Woodhorn 221 E3
Woodhouse Cumb 199 G4
Woodhouse Leics 160 A1
Woodhouse SYorks 186 B4
Woodhouse WYorks 194 B4
Woodhouse WYorks 194 C5
Woodhouse WYorks 194 A5
Woodhouse Down 131 F4
Woodhouse Eaves 160 A1
Woodhouse Green 171 G1
Woodhouses GtMan 184 C2
Woodhouses Staffs 159 D1
Woodhouses Staffs 158 C2
Woodhuish 101 F2
Woodhurst 162 B5
Woodingdean 109 F3
Woodington 119 E5
Woodland Devon 101 D1
Woodland Dur 211 G5
Woodland Kent 124 D4
Woodland Head 102 A3
Woodlands Dorset 105 G2
Woodlands Hants 106 C1
Woodlands NYorks 194 C4
Woodlands Shrop 157 G4
Woodlands Som 115 E3
Woodlands Leisure Park,
  Dartmouth Devon
  TQ9 7DQ 101 E2
Woodlands Park 135 D5
Woodlands St. Mary 133 F5
Woodlane 172 C5
Woodleigh 100 D3
Woodlesford 194 C5
Woodley GtMan 184 D3
Woodley W'ham 134 C5
Woodmancote Glos 132 C2
Woodmancote Glos 146 B5
Woodmancote Glos 131 G3
Woodmancote WSuss 109 E2
Woodmancote WSuss 107 G2
Woodmancott 119 G3
Woodmansey 196 C4
Woodmansterne 122 B3
Woodmanton 102 D4
Woodmill 172 C5
Woodminton 118 B5
Woodmoor 156 B2
Woodnesborough 125 F3
Woodnewton 161 F3
Woodperry 134 A1
Woodplumpton 192 B4
Woodrising 178 A5
Woodrow 105 D1
Wood's Corner 110 B2
Woods Eaves 144 B3
Wood's Green 123 F5
Woodseaves Shrop 171 D4
Woodseaves Staffs 171 E5
Woodsend 133 E5
Woodsetts 186 C4
Woodsford 105 D3
Woodside Aberdeen 261 H4
Woodside BrackF 135 E5
Woodside CenBeds 135 F1
Woodside Cumb 208 D3
Woodside D&G 217 E3
Woodside Fife 244 C4
Woodside Fife 244 A4
Woodside GtLon 122 C2
Woodside Hants 106 C3
Woodside Herts 136 B2
Woodside NAyr 233 E4
Woodside P&K 243 G1
Woodside Shrop 156 C4
Woodside WMid 158 B4
Woodside Animal Farm &
  Leisure Park CenBeds
  LU1 4DG 135 F1
Woodside Green 124 B3
Woodstock Oxon 133 G1
Woodstock Pembs 140 D5
Woodthorpe Derbys 186 B5
Woodthorpe Leics 160 A1
Woodthorpe Lincs 189 E4
Woodthorpe SYorks 186 A4
Woodthorpe York 195 E3
Woodton 165 D2
Woodtown 113 E3
Woodvale 183 E1
Woodville 159 F1
Woodwall Green 171 E4
Woodwalton 162 A4
Woodwick 276 C5
Woodworth Green 170 C2
Woodyates 105 G1
Woofferton 145 E1
Wookey 116 C3
Wookey Hole 116 C3
Wookey Hole Caves &
  Papermill Som
  BA5 1BB 116 C3
Wool 105 E4
Woolacombe 113 E1
Woolage Green 125 E4
Woolage Village 125 E3
Woolaston 131 E2
Woolaston Slade 131 E2
Woolavington 116 A3
Woolbeding 121 D5
Woolcotts 114 C4
Wooldale 185 F2
Wooler 229 D4
Woolfardisworthy
  Devon 102 B2
Woolfardisworthy
  Devon 112 D3
Woolfold 184 B1
Woolfords Cottages 235 E4
Woolgarston 105 F4
Woolgreaves 186 A1
Woolhampton 119 G1
Woolhope 145 F4
Woolland 105 D2
Woollard 116 D1
Woollaton 113 E4

Woollensbrook 136 C2
Woolley B&NESom 117 E1
Woolley Cambs 161 G5
Woolley Corn 112 C4
Woolley Derbys 173 E1
Woolley Green W&M 135 D5
Woolley Green Wilts 117 F1
Woolmer Green 136 B1
Woolmere Green 146 B1
Woolmersdon 115 F4
Woolpit 152 A1
Woolpit Green 152 A1
Woolscott 147 G1
Woolsgrove 102 A2
Woolstaston 157 D3
Woolsthorpe 174 D4
Woolsthorpe by
  Colsterworth 175 E5
Woolston Devon 100 D3
Woolston Shrop 170 A5
Woolston Shrop 156 D1
Woolston Soton 106 D1
Woolston Warr 184 A4
Woolston Green 101 D1
Woolstone Glos 146 B4
Woolstone MK 149 D4
Woolstone Oxon 133 E4
Woolton 183 F4
Woolton Hill 119 F1
Woolverstone 152 C4
Woolverton 117 E2
Woolwich 136 D5
Woonton 144 C2
Wooperton 229 E5
Woore 171 E3
Wootten Green 164 D4
Wootton Bed 149 F3
Wootton Hants 106 B3
Wootton IoW 107 E3
Wootton Kent 125 E4
Wootton N'hants 148 C4
Wootton NLincs 188 A1
Wootton Oxon 133 G1
Wootton Oxon 133 G1
Wootton Shrop 157 D5
Wootton Shrop 170 A5
Wootton Staffs 171 F5
Wootton Staffs 172 C3
Wootton Bassett 132 C4
Wootton Bridge 107 E3
Wootton Common 107 E3
Wootton Courtenay 114 C3
Wootton Fitzpaine 103 G3
Wootton Green 149 F3
Wootton Rivers 118 C1
Wootton
  St. Lawrence 119 G2
Wootton Wawen 147 D1
Worcester 146 A2
Worcester Cathedral Worcs
  WR1 2LH 90 Worcester
Worcester Park 122 B2
Worcester Woods Country Park
  Worcs WR5 2LG 146 A2
Wordsley 158 A4
Wordwell 163 G5
Worfield 157 G3
Worgret 105 F4
Work 277 D6
Workhouse End 149 G2
Workington 208 D4
Worksop 186 C5
Worlaby Lincs 188 D5
Worlaby NLincs 188 C4
World Museum Liverpool
  Mersey L3 8EN 42 A3
World of Beatrix Potter
  Attraction Cumb
  LA23 3BX 199 F3
World of James Herriot, Thirsk
  NYorks YO7 1PL 202 D4
World's End Bucks 135 D2
Worlds End Hants 107 F1
World's End WBerks 133 G5
Worlds End WMid 158 D4
Worle 116 A1
Worleston 171 D2
Worlingham 165 F3
Worlington 163 E5
Worlingworth 152 D1
Wormald Green 194 C1
Wormbridge 144 D4
Wormegay 163 E1
Wormelow Tump 145 D4
Wormhill 185 F5
Wormingford 152 A4
Worminghall 134 B2
Wormington 146 C4
Worminster 116 C3
Wormiston 245 E4
Wormit 244 B2
Wormleighton 147 G2
Wormley Herts 136 C2
Wormley Surr 121 E4
Wormley West End 136 C2
Wormshill 124 A3
Wormsley 144 D3
Worplesdon 121 E2
Worrall 186 A3
Worsbrough 186 A2
Worsley 184 B2
Worstead 179 E3
Worsted Lodge 150 D2
Worsthorne 193 E4
Worston 193 D3
Worswell 100 B3
Worth Kent 125 F3
Worth WSuss 122 B5
Worth Matravers 105 F5
Wortham 164 B4
Worthen 156 C2
Worthenbury 170 B3
Worthing Norf 178 A4
Worthing WSuss 108 D3
Worthington 173 F5
Worting 120 B2
Wortley Glos 131 G3
Wortley SYorks 186 A3
Wortley WYorks 194 B4
Worton NYorks 201 E4
Worton Wilts 118 A2
Wortwell 165 D3
Wothersome 194 D3
Wotherton 156 B2
Wotter 100 B1
Wotton 121 G3
Wotton Underwood 134 B1

Woollensbrook 136 C2
Wotton-under-Edge 131 G3
Woughton on the
  Green 149 D4
Wouldham 123 G2
Wrabness 152 C4
Wrae 269 F5
Wrafton 113 E2
Wragby 188 B5
Wragholme 189 D3
Wramplingham 178 C2
Wrangaton 100 C3
Wrangham 260 E1
Wrangle 176 C2
Wrangle Lowgate 176 C2
Wrangway 103 E1
Wrantage 116 A5
Wrawby 188 A2
Wraxall NSom 131 D5
Wraxall Som 116 D4
Wray 192 C1
Wray Castle 199 E2
Wrays 122 B4
Wraysbury 135 F5
Wrayton 200 B5
Wrea Green 191 G4
Wreay Cumb 210 A5
Wreay Cumb 210 A3
Wrecclesham 120 D3
Wrekenton 212 B2
Wrelton 203 G4
Wrenbury 170 C3
Wrench Green 204 C4
Wreningham 164 C2
Wrentham 165 F2
Wrenthorpe 194 C5
Wrentnall 156 D2
Wressle ERid 195 G4
Wressle NLincs 187 G2
Wrestlingworth 150 A3
Wretham 164 A2
Wretton 163 E2
Wrexham (Wrecsam) 170 A3
Wrexham Arts Centre Wrex
  LL11 1AU 170 A2
Wrexham Industrial
  Estate 170 A3
Wribbenhall 157 G5
Wrightington Bar 183 G1
Wrightpark 242 B5
Wright's Green 137 E1
Wrinehill 171 E3
Wrington 116 B1
Writhlington 117 D2
Writtle 137 E2
Wrockwardine 157 F1
Wroot 187 E2
Wrose 194 A4
Wrotham 123 F3
Wrotham Heath 123 F3
Wrotham Hill Park 123 F2
Wrottesley 158 A2
Wroughton 132 D4
Wroxall IoW 107 E5
Wroxall Warks 159 E5
Wroxeter 157 E2
Wroxham 179 E4
Wroxham Barns Norf
  NR12 8QU 179 E4
Wroxton 147 G3
Wstrws 141 G3
Wyaston 172 D3
Wyberton 176 B3
Wyboston 149 G2
Wybunbury 171 D3
Wych Cross 122 D5
Wychbold 146 B1
Wychnor 159 D1
Wychnor Bridges 159 D1
Wyck 120 C4
Wyck Rissington 147 D5
Wycliffe 202 A1
Wycoller 193 F4
Wycoller Country Park
  Lancs BB8 8SY 193 F4
Wycomb 174 C5
Wycombe Marsh 135 D3
Wyddial 150 B4
Wye 124 C4
Wyesham 131 E1
Wyfordby 160 C1
Wyke Devon 102 B2
Wyke Dorset 117 E5
Wyke Shrop 157 F2
Wyke Surr 121 E2
Wyke WYorks 194 A5
Wyke Champflower 117 D4
Wyke Regis 104 C5
Wykeham NYorks 204 C4
Wykeham NYorks 204 B5
Wyken Shrop 157 G3
Wyken WMid 159 F4
Wykey 170 A5
Wylam 212 A1
Wylde Green 158 D3
Wyllie 130 A3
Wylye 118 B4
Wymering 107 F2
Wymeswold 174 B5
Wymington 149 E1
Wymondham Leics 161 D1
Wymondham Norf 178 C5
Wyndham 129 F3
Wynford Eagle 104 B3
Wynnstay Park 170 A3
Wynyard 129 F2
Wynyard Woodland Park
  Stock TS21 3JG 212 C5
Wyre Forest Worcs
  DY14 9XQ 157 G5
Wyre Piddle 146 B3
Wyresdale Tower 192 C2
Wysall 174 B5
Wyson 145 E1
Wythall 158 C5
Wytham 133 G2
Wythburn 209 G5
Wythenshawe 184 C4
Wyton Cambs 162 A5
Wyton ERid 197 D4
Wyverstone 152 B1
Wyverstone Street 152 B1
Wyville 175 D5
Wyvis Lodge 266 B4

X
Xscape Castleford WYorks
  WF10 4DA 194 D5

Y
Y Bryn 168 B5
Y Fan 155 F4
Y Felinheli 167 E1
Y Fôr 166 D2
Y Fron (Upper
  Llandwrog) 167 E2
Yaddlethorpe 187 F2
Yafford 107 D4
Yafforth 202 C3
Yalberton 101 E2
Yalding 123 F4
Yanley 116 C1
Yanwath 210 B5
Yanworth 132 C1
Yapham 195 G2
Yapton 108 B3
Yarburgh 188 D3
Yarcombe 103 F2
Yardley 158 D4
Yardley Gobion 148 C3
Yardley Hastings 149 D2
Yardro 144 B2
Yarford 115 F5
Yarkhill 145 F3
Yarlet 171 G5
Yarley 116 C3
Yarlington 117 D5
Yarm 202 C2
Yarmouth 106 C4
Yarnacott 113 G2
Yarnbrook 117 F2
Yarnfield 171 F4
Yarnscombe 113 F3
Yarnton 133 G1
Yarpole 145 D1
Yarrow ScBord 227 E3
Yarrow Som 116 A3
Yarrow Feus 227 E3
Yarrowford 227 F3
Yarsop 144 D3
Yarwell 161 F3
Yate 131 G4
Yatehouse Green 171 E1
Yateley 120 D1
Yatesbury 132 C5
Yattendon 134 A5
Yatton Here 144 D1
Yatton NSom 116 B1
Yatton Keynell 132 A5
Yaverland 107 F4
Yawl 103 G3
Yaxham 178 B4
Yaxley Cambs 161 G3
Yaxley Suff 164 C4
Yazor 144 D3
Ye Olde Pork Pie Shoppe,
  Melton Mowbray Leics
  LE13 1NW 160 C1
Yeabridge 104 A1
Yeading 136 A4
Yeadon 194 B3
Yealand Conyers 199 G5
Yealand Redmayne 199 G5
Yealand Storrs 199 G5
Yealmbridge 100 B2
Yealmpton 100 B2
Yearby 213 F5
Yearsley 203 E5
Yeaton 156 D1
Yeaveley 172 C3
Yeavering 228 D3
Yedingham 204 B5
Yelford 133 F2
Yell 278 D4
Yelland Devon 113 E2
Yelland Devon 99 F1
Yelling 150 A1
Yelvertoft 160 A5
Yelverton Devon 100 B1
Yelverton Norf 179 D5
Yenston 117 E5
Yeo Mill 114 B5
Yeo Vale 113 E3
Yeoford 102 A3
Yeolmbridge 98 D2
Yeomadon 112 D5
Yeovil 104 B1
Yeovil Country Park Som
  BA20 1QZ 104 B1
Yeovil Marsh 104 B1
Yeovilton 116 C5
Yerbeston 127 D2
Yesnaby 277 B6
Yesterday's World, Battle
  ESuss TN33 0AQ 110 C2
Yetholm Mains 228 C4
Yetlington 229 E5
Yetminster 104 B1
Yettington 103 D4
Yetts o'Muckhart 243 F4
Yew Green 147 E1
Yielden 149 F1
Yieldshields 234 C4
Ynys 167 E4
Ynys Tachwedd 154 C3
Ynysboeth 129 G3
Ynysddu 130 A3
Ynyshir 129 G3
Ynyslas 154 C3
Ynysmaerdy 129 G4
Ynysmeudwy 128 D2
Ynystawe 128 C2
Ynyswen 129 F3
Ynysybwl 129 G3
Yockenthwaite 201 D5
Yockleton 156 C1
Yokefleet 196 A5
Yoker 233 G3
Yonder Bognie 268 E6
York 195 F2
York Castle Museum
  YO1 9SA 90 York
York Dungeon
  YO1 9RD 90 York
York Minster
  YO1 7HH 90 York
Yorkletts 124 C2
Yorkley 131 F2
Yorkshire Museum
  YO1 7FR 90 York
Yorkshire Sculpture Park
  WYorks WF4 4LG 185 G1
Yorton 170 C5
Yorton Heath 170 C5

Youldon 112 D5
Youldonmoor Cross 112 D5
Youlgreave 172 D1
Youlthorpe 195 G2
Youlton 195 D1
Young's End 137 G1
Yoxall 158 D1
Yoxford 153 E1
Ysbyty Cynfyn 155 D5
Ysbyty Ifan 168 B3
Ysbyty Ystwyth 154 D5
Ysceifiog 182 C5
Ysgubor-y-coed 154 C3
Ystalyfera 129 D2
Ystrad 129 F3
Ystrad Aeron 142 B2
Ystrad Meurig 142 D1
Ystrad Mynach 130 A3
Ystradfellte 129 E1
Ystradffin 143 D3
Ystradgynlais 129 D1
Ystradowen Carmar 128 D1
Ystradowen VGlam 129 G5
Ystumtuen 154 D5
Ythanwells 260 E1
Ythsie 261 G1

Z
Zeal Monachorum 102 A2
Zeals 117 E4
Zelah 96 C4
Zennor 94 B3
Zouch 173 G5
ZSL London Zoo GtLon
  NW1 4RY 12 A3

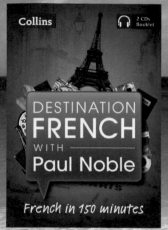
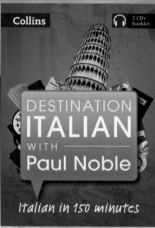